THE OXFORD HANDBOOK OF

ISLAMIC
ARCHAEOLOGY

THE OXFORD HANDBOOK OF

ISLAMIC

ARCHAEOLOGY

Edited by

BETHANY J. WALKER,
TIMOTHY INSOLL,

and

CORISANDE FENWICK

OXFORD
UNIVERSITY PRESS

Oxford University Press is a department of the University of Oxford. It furthers the University's objective of excellence in research, scholarship, and education by publishing worldwide. Oxford is a registered trade mark of Oxford University Press in the UK and certain other countries.

Published in the United States of America by Oxford University Press
198 Madison Avenue, New York, NY 10016, United States of America.

© Oxford University Press 2020

Library of Congress Cataloging-in-Publication Data
Names: Walker, Bethany J., editor. | Fenwick, Corisande, editor. | Insoll, Timothy, editor.
Title: The Oxford handbook of Islamic archaeology / edited by Bethany J. Walker, Corisande Fenwick, and Timothy Insoll.
Description: New York, NY : Oxford University Press, [2020]
Identifiers: LCCN 2020031517 (print) | LCCN 2020031518 (ebook) |
ISBN 9780199987870 (hardback) | ISBN 9780197507872 (epub) |
Subjects: LCSH: Islamic antiquities. | Archaeology—Islamic countries. |
Islamic civilization—Study and teaching. | Cultural
property—Protection—Islamic countries.
Classification: LCC DS56 .O924 2020 (print) | LCC DS56 (ebook) |
DDC 909/.09767—dc23
LC record available at https://lccn.loc.gov/2020031517
LC ebook record available at https://lccn.loc.gov/2020031518

1 3 5 7 9 8 6 4 2

Printed by Sheridan Books, Inc., United States of America

CONTENTS

SECTION III THE ISLAMIC WEST

SECTION IV SUB-SAHARAN AFRICA

SECTION V ASIA

SECTION VI HERITAGE MANAGEMENT AND COMMUNITY DEVELOPMENT

List of Contributors

Alkindi Aljawabra, University College London, UCL Qatar Department, PhD candidate

Jacqueline M Armijo, Associate Professor of the Humanities, Asian University for Women, Chittagong, Bangladesh

Vesna Bikić, Researcher, Institute of Archaeology, Serbian Academy of Sciences and Arts, Belgrade

Svitlana Biliaieva, Researcher, Institute of Archaeology, National Academy of Sciences of Ukraine

José C Carvajal López, Lecturer in Historical Archaeology, Department of Archaeology and Ancient History, University of Leicester

Patrice Cressier, Chargé de recherche, CNRS, Université de Lyon, Centre National de la Recherche Scientifique

Bert de Vries, Professor Emeritus, Department of History, Calvin College

Niculina Dinu, Researcher, Museum of Brăila, "Carol I"

Intisar Soghayroun El Zein, Professor of Archaeology, Department of Archaeology, University of Khartoum

Corisande Fenwick, Associate Professor in Mediterranean Archaeology, Institute of Archaeology, University College London, UK

Abdallah Fili, Professor of Medieval History and Archaeology, Université d'El-Jadida, Morocco

Jeffrey Fleisher, Professor of Anthropology, Rice University

Alison L Gascoigne, Associate Professor in Medieval Archaeology, University of Southampton

Ibolya Gerelyes, Curator Emeritus, Department of Archaeology, Hungarian National Museum, Budapest

Sonia Gutiérrez Lloret, Directora del Instituto Universitario de Investigación en Arqueología y Patrimonio Histórico-INAPH, Universidad de Alicante, Spain

Noël Harris, PhD candidate, Institute of Archaeology, Andrews University

Timothy Insoll, Al-Qasimi Professor of African and Islamic Archaeology in the Institute of Arab and Islamic Studies, University of Exeter

Marek Jankowiak, Associate Professor of Byzantine History, University of Oxford, UK

Rim Lababidi, Researcher, University College London Qatar

Øystein S LaBianca, Professor of Anthropology, Associate Director, Institute of Archaeology, Andrews University

Carlos Magnavita, Frobenius Institute for Research in Cultural Anthropology, Goethe University Frankfurt

Alessandra Molinari, Professor of Medieval Archaeology, Tor Vergata University of Rome, Italy

Stephennie Mulder, Associate Professor of Art History, The University of Texas

Sam Nixon, Curator and Head of Africa Section, Department of Africa, Oceania and the Americas. The British Museum, UK

Alastair Northedge, Professor Emeritus, Université Paris 1, Panthéon-Sorbonne, UFR d'Art et d'Archéologie

Andrew Petersen, Director of Research in Islamic Archaeology, University of Wales Trinity Saint David

Nasser Rabbat, Aga Khan Professor, Director of Aga Khan Program for Islamic Architecture, MIT

Rocco Rante, Research Archeologist, Louvre Museum, Paris

Scott Redford, Nasser D Khalili Professor of Islamic Art and Archaeology, University of London

Trinidad Rico, Assistant Professor and Director of CHAPS, Rutgers University

Maria Elena Ronza, Sela for vocational training and protection of cultural heritage, Jordan

Marie-Odile Rousset, Professor of Archaeology, Université Lyon

Mehrdad Shokoohy, Emeritus Professor of Architecture and Urban Studies, The University of Greenwich

Natalie H Shokoohy, Architectural Historian, Independent Scholar

Pierre Siméon, Research Associate Staatliche Museen zu Berlin-Pergamonmuseum, Department Member

Abubakar S Sule, Senior Lecturer and the Head of the Department of Archaeology at Ahmadu Bello University Zaria, Nigeria

Athanasios Vionis, Lecturer in Byzantine Art and Archaeology, University of Cyprus

Alexander Wain, IAIS, Malaysia, Civilisation, Interfaith, Peace and Security Unit, Faculty Member

Bethany J Walker, Research Professor of Mamluk Studies; Director, Research Unit of Islamic Archaeology, Department of Islamic Studies, University of Bonn

Stephanie Wynne-Jones, Senior Lecturer, Department of Archaeology, University of York,

Filiz Yenişehirlioğlu, Professor of History of Art, Department of Archaeology and History of Art, Koç University

Jelena Živković, PhD candidate, University College London, UCL Qatar Department

SECTION I

....

EDITORS'
INTRODUCTION

....

ALTHOUGH its roots can be traced to the work of Classical, Biblical, and Near Eastern archaeologists and Islamic art historians of the late 19th and early 20th centuries, as an independent academic discipline Islamic archaeology is quite young. The occasional university course in Europe and North America began to be offered in archaeology, history, area studies, and art history departments only gradually from the 1980s, and specialized graduate programs appeared only from the 1990s. The establishment of institutions and research centers dedicated to Islamic archaeology—of which there are only a handful worldwide—is an even later development.

As the archaeological study of Muslim societies, polities, and communities, Islamic archaeology is by default concerned with a relatively recent period of human history, which extends to the Modern era.[1] The "Early Modern era" is generally not covered by the antiquities laws of most modern Muslim countries, relegating their study to the field of ethnography and removing sites of this period from legal protection. This is particularly true in Greater Syria (Bilād al-Shām), which has some of the oldest departments of antiquities in the world and a long history of archaeological study of Islamic societies. The Jordanian Law of Antiquities No. 21[1988], which was amended by Law No. 23 [2004], covers "any movable or immovable object which was made, written, inscribed,

---

[1] This is the definition also adopted by the *Journal of Islamic Archaeology* (https://journals. equinoxpub.com/index.php/JIA).

built, discovered or modified by a human being before the year AD 1750."[2] In Mandate-era Palestine, an "antiquity" was defined as any building or product of human activity dating before 1700. In Israel today, according to its 1978 Antiquities Law, an "antiquity" is defined as "any object, which was made by man before 1700 CE, or any zoological or botanical remains from before the year 1300 CE."[3] These laws are slowly changing, however, reflecting a growing appreciation for the cultural heritage of the later historical periods. For example, Decree Law no. 11 on Tangible Cultural Heritage in Palestine, passed by the Palestinian Authority in June 2018, expands the timeframe of heritage protection to all structures built before 1917 CE and including all material heritage of cultural, economic, or natural value.[4] In Bahrain, the Antiquities laws are even more inclusive: "anything descended from civilizations or left over by previous generations explored or discovered . . . or daily life or public events or anything that is at least 50 years of age that has an artistic or historical value is considered a monument."[5] This Handbook devotes its final section to cultural heritage management, with a particular focus on the later centuries and best practices in cultural heritage management (CHM). Islamic archaeology, as it practiced today in many countries, is committed to safeguarding cultural heritage, including the manmade and natural worlds of the relatively modern periods.

What is essentially "Islamic" in this heritage is loosely defined and regionally specific. "Islamic archaeology" in this sense does not serve the same function as "Biblical" archaeology in the Holy Land. Research has never been directed at illustrating or investigating events, peoples/places, or the societies described in the Qur'an.[6] Nor does it focus solely on religious architecture or artifacts in the same way as "Christian archaeology" has often done in Europe and the Mediterranean. "Islamic" here describes, in a very general sense, a political geography: it is those regions that are under Muslim control in a particular period (the "Islamic world," as it existed at a certain time) or in which Muslims lived, not necessarily under Muslim control. It does not necessarily mean that the majority of the population at that place and time were Muslim or that the culture was dominated by Islamic norms, although that generally tends to be the case. Islamic archaeology is as much concerned with non-Muslim societies under the control of Muslim powers (whatever the institutional configuration). The geographical focus, of course, changes over time, as the center of the Islamic world shifted with the dissolution of old imperial systems and the emergence of new ones.[7]

---

[2] https://www.unodc.org/res/cld/document/law-of-antiquities_html/Law_of_Antiquities-1-_jordan.pdf (accessed August 24, 2018)

[3] http://www.antiquities.org.il/Article_list_eng.aspx?sub_menu=2&section_id=42&Module_id=6 (accessed August 24, 2018)

[4] http://www.unesco.org/new/en/ramallah/about-this-office/single-view/news/joint_statement_the_palestinian_ministry_of_tourism_and_anti/ (accessed August 24, 2018)

[5] Article 2 of Decree Law No. 11. Regarding the Protection of Antiquities, Ministry of Cabinet Affairs and Information, Directorate of Heritage and Museums, State of Bahrain, June 25, 1995.

[6] The recent movement in "Qur'anic archaeology" essentially serves that purpose and has not yet entered the mainstream of world archaeology.

[7] To see the shifting global centers of the Islamic world over time, compare the following maps: 2.1.1, 2.2.1, 2.3.1, 2.5.1, 3.1.1, 3.2.1, 3.3.1, 3.4.1, 3.5.1, 4.1.1, 4.2.1, 4.3.1, 4.4.1, 4.5.1, 5.1.9, 5.2.1, 5.3.1, and 5.4.1.

Some parts of the world entered Dar al-Islam later than others: the earliest known Islamic Kingdoms of Southeast Asia, for example, were established only in the 13th century CE (see Chapter 5.5); by contrast, in Egypt the process began with the Islamic conquests of the 7th century (see Chapter 2.4). The chronological coverage of this volume reflects the diverse regional histories of Islamic conquest, conversion, and trade. It is roughly "medieval-to-modern," beginning with the 7th century CE (the "Islamic conquest" in the Levant) and ending with the 21st century (during which time the making of cultural heritage policy and "community archaeology" gain the greatest significance).

Perhaps more than any other factor, it is geography and language that offer the greatest challenge to assembling a Handbook such as this. Most scholarship in English has focused on the "Arab heartland" and specifically the Levant. Other regions of the pre-modern Islamic world—al-Andalus and the Maghreb, Africa, and Asia—have their own rich histories of scholarship in the field.[8] They are less well known to the Anglophone world, however, because of linguistic issues and limited distribution of local journals and publications. Russian publications on Central Asia are rarely read by or available to scholars outside the region, and ongoing research on China-Indian Ocean trade, Muslim-Buddhist-Hindu relations, and the culturally and religiously hybrid societies of southeast Asia are practically terra incognito due to the scarcity of reports in Western languages. Linguistic issues are not restricted to non-European languages: troublingly, even French, Spanish, and Italian publications on the Western Islamic world are not so familiar to Anglophone scholars. The results of such scholarship, however, open up new lines of inquiry and reveal cultural and socio-economic patterns that provide valuable contrasts with those of the Levant, the traditional heartland of Islamic archaeology. Regionalism is a key characteristic of pre-modern Islamic material culture, and it is certainly a phenomenon with which we must reckon when reconstructing "culture" from the local archaeological record.

This volume is not the first English-language survey of the field. It has been preceded by several important works, the sequence of which tracks the ways that Islamic archaeology has developed institutionally since the 1990s. Several have become required reading for university students (Insoll 1999; Milwright 2010; Rosen-Ayalon 2006) and adopt different methodological approaches: phenomenological, cultural-historical, art historical. Baram and Carroll's conference volume *A Historical Archaeology of the Ottoman Empire: Breaking New Ground* is considered by many to have officially launched Ottoman archaeology. More recent regional studies (Sutton 2000, Zarinebaf et al 2005, and Davies and Davis 2007 on Ottoman Greece; Insoll 2003 on sub-Saharan Africa;

---

[8] For some surveys in English, see Insoll 1999, 2003 (for sub-Saharan Africa); Fenwick 2013, 2019 (for the Maghreb); SPAFA 1984 and Ali 1994 (for southeast Asia); and Priestman 2016 (for East Asia). The *SPAFA Digest*—the journal published by the Southeast Asian Ministers of Education Organization (SAMEO) Regional Center in Archaeology and Fine Arts—provides convenient summaries in English of local archaeological research on the later historical periods and maritime trade. (It is, however, of limited distribution.) Special issues of the *Journal of Islamic Archaeology* deal with the archaeology of African Islam.

Walmsley 2007 on Syria; Walker 2011 on Jordan; Power 2012 on the Red Sea; Avni 2014 on Palestine; Cooper 2014 on the medieval Nile basin; Valor and Gutiérrez 2015 on Spain; Fenwick 2019 on North Africa) consciously combine textual and archaeological methods to differing degrees.

This Handbook is distinguished from these important contributions, however, by its global coverage and inclusion of very contemporary issues, such as engagement with local communities and best practices in CHM. The contributors have the highest reputations today in their geographical areas of expertise, yet represent different stages of the academic career as well as diverse international backgrounds. Because a wide range of languages are represented in this global scholarship, many contributions have been translated into English (namely from French, Spanish, and Italian). Global coverage also means that a range of methods, archaeological traditions, and research priorities are represented in this volume. Even so, the Handbook is not intended to be an encyclopedic compendium but to provide an introduction into the different regional trajectories of Islamic archaeology. Reflections on the many disciplinary roots of Islamic archaeology and its vast geographical and complex chronological scope complete this Foreword.

ISLAMIC ARCHAEOLOGY AND ISLAMIC ART HISTORY: THE SPECIAL RELATIONSHIP

Islamic archaeology has an intimate but fraught relationship with art history. In Europe, Islamic archaeology began as a methodological specialization within Islamic art history, and, until the latter part of the 20th century, most field practitioners were formally trained as art (or architectural) historians. Today, in contrast, Islamic archaeology is far closer to history and anthropology, and there is limited interdisciplinary dialogue with art history, despite their shared focus on material culture. This is not the place to delve into a detailed genealogy of the historiography of Islamic archaeology, which is still to be written (see Rogers 1974; Vernoit 1997 for brief overviews), but a few remarks on the complex legacy of this relationship are necessary.

In the 18th and early 19th centuries, the accounts of explorers, diplomats, and missionaries, as well as a growing Orientalist interest in Arabic languages, spurred European scholarly interest in Islamic art and architecture in Spain, the Middle East, and North Africa (Vernoit 2000). These antiquarian efforts gained momentum with growing European and Russian interest in North Africa, the Middle East, and Central Asia and the imposition of colonial rule; indeed, the earliest excavations of Islamic sites took place in the immediate aftermath of annexation, as was the case, for example, for the Russians at Samarqand and Merv in the 1870s and 1880s and the French at the Qala'a of the Beni Hammad in Algeria in 1898. These and other early excavations at Samarra (Iraq), Madinat al-Zahra (Spain), Fustat (Egypt), and the often-overlooked Ottoman work at Raqqa (Syria) established the focus of Islamic archaeology: the study of monumental urban and palatial architecture (especially palaces, gardens, mosques, fortifications), the analysis of architectural décor (capitals, stucco, woodwork), and the study of high-quality objects (glazed ceramics, metalwork, glass) (Vernoit 1997). Accordingly, archaeologists devoted their energies to early Islamic palatial and urban sites such as Samarra or the desert castles of Jordan, where rich architecture and decorative items (which could then be displayed in museums) were to be located. The emphasis on museum-quality artifacts had many unfortunate tendencies: only whole vessels tended to be recorded (and often kept), and contextual information was rarely recorded. But excavations were not sufficient to meet the rising demands for Islamic artifacts, and many sites were looted to provide artifacts for museums and collectors.

Archaeology's close relationship with art history in this formative period also established the geographic focus of the field: the so-called *central Islamic lands*: the Levant, Egypt, Iraq, Iran (and Anatolia for the Ottoman period) which were the heartlands of the great Islamic empires. Central Asia remained disconnected from mainstream scholarship on Islamic art and architecture, as did India, China, Mongolia, and Africa and even the Islamic West (North Africa and al-Andalus). These regions were regarded as provincial and interpreted through core–periphery models which depicted artistic and architectural production as inferior to or derivative of developments in the heartlands. So powerful were these colonial models that, even today, Islamic art survey books rarely include material from these regions except in passing. Of course, archaeological and art historical research on the Islamic period was not neglected in these "peripheral" regions—each has its own complex scholarly traditions—but the result was a fragmented discipline divided into regional schools of research that rarely communicated with one another.

In the post-World War II period, the continued close relationship of the two disciplines was acknowledged in the first state-of-the-field articles written by Richard Ettinghausen (1951) and Oleg Grabar (1976), both of which were tellingly titled "Islamic Art and Archaeology." Both identified archaeology as pivotal in shaping the research agendas of art historical scholarship, with its focus on the early and middle Islamic periods, architecture and the "Islamic city," and the central Arab lands. Their understanding of what archaeology was, what it could offer (a technique, a method), and its relationship to art history (a supporting, secondary methodology) was quite different from today. For Grabar, for example, archaeology's main function was to catalogue, locate, date, and describe objects, buildings, and construction/manufacturing techniques, rather than to interpret or build theories about past societies. The potentially transformative impact of archaeology on the broader discipline was hindered by a widespread failure to publish the results of these earlier digs (some of which still remain unpublished to this day), a problem that both Ettinghausen and Grabar complained about in their reviews of the field.

In the 1980s, art history distanced itself from archaeology, and Grabar's (1983) essay "Reflections on the Study of Islamic Art" in the inaugural volume of *Muqarnas* dropped archaeology from the name of the field in a reflection of the increasing dominance of art historical approaches as well as a growing frustration with the poor publication record of archaeologists and the appearance of new "abstruse and overly abstract" theoretical models in archaeology (1983: 4). This separation came at a pivotal point for Islamic archaeology. The methodologies and theoretical models of New Archaeology and post-processual archaeology, together with the increasing maturity of medieval European archaeology as a discipline, heavily impacted the practice of archaeology in the Middle East from the 1970s. The spread of open-area excavation techniques, stratigraphic analysis, diachronic field surveys, and the increasing use of radiocarbon dating for chronological precision started to shed light on the later phases of biblical and Classical sites. In Jordan, an important turning point was the work of Jim Sauer in the 1970s in distinguishing Islamic-era ceramics from that of Late Antiquity; his seriation of Islamic pottery at Tall Ḥisbān in many ways laid the foundations for the field in Jordan. Beyond the Middle East, excavations began to rapidly increase, particularly in sub-Saharan Africa, with for example, fieldwork at Kilwa, Manda, and Shanga shedding light on Islamization and Indian Ocean trade in East Africa and work at Gao, Tegdaost, and Timbuktu on trans-Saharan sites (see Insoll 2003 for an overview). With the publication of Insoll's (1999) *The Archaeology of Islam*, it was clear that Islamic archaeology was a field of research distinctly different from, although still overlapping to some degree with and often heavily influenced by, Islamic art history.

No field of research stays the same, nor should it. Many of the circumstances that pushed Insoll to express his concern about the marginalization of the field vis-à-vis Islamic art history are no longer issues today (Insoll 1999: 3–7). Islamic archaeology is now in the mainstream of world archaeology—technologically, conceptually, methodologically. The scale of analysis is now larger and the questions broader. Our view of the Islamic world is being de-centered from Syria-Palestine and Iraq by new work by archaeologists on the edges—in Spain, Central Asia, East Africa, and beyond. Rather than privileging the mosque, *ribat*, or palace, archaeologists now excavate houses, shops, and craft quarters to understand the spaces of everyday life. Excavation now goes beyond establishing architectural phases and floor plans of monuments and extends to understanding their role in the larger built (urban landscapes, settlements) and natural (rural landscapes) setting. This, in turn, has generated interest in rural society, their socialized landscapes, and a wide range of environmental and economic issues. Likewise, the study of the artifact has turned from typo-chronologies to that of the assemblage and its social context in order to understand the household, labor history, and even gender roles (Walker 2010). At the same time, Islamic archaeology is increasingly concerned with its responsibilities to local, living communities, which has resulted in efforts in heritage management, community development, and an expressed commitment to sustainability (agricultural, environmental, social, economic).

These shifts toward the social and economic in the past and present have widened the gap between archaeologists and art historians who rarely talk to one another despite a shared emphasis on material culture. No longer are Islamic archaeologists trained in art history departments, but in archaeology, anthropology, or history departments, and it is far more common for archaeologists to collaborate with historians, cultural heritage specialists, and (less frequently) anthropologists in conferences, publications, and even fieldwork. All the same, in recent years, the "social turn" in the humanities and social sciences has the potential to bring about a renewed convergence between Islamic art and archaeology. Just as many archaeologists have moved away from the typo-chronology of object or monument, so, too, some art historians are moving away from the traditional approaches which privileged the visual and aesthetic properties of objects and buildings in the central Islamic lands before 1800 and toward post-colonial, anthropological, and socio-historical approaches with a greater chronological and geographical scope (e.g., Flood and Necipoğlu 2017). One promising avenue for interdisciplinary dialogue is the move toward considering the materiality of things (whether the art historian's "object," or the archaeologist's "artifact"), which allows one to speak at the same time about a thing as an expression of beauty, a marker of class and ethnicity, symbol of the household, function of political-economic networks, and proof of social and political encounters and exchanges across imaginary borders (for the latter, see Flood 2009).

The museum is becoming a new arena for conflict, with increasingly oppositional stances taken by archaeologists and art historians. Since the 2000s, a number of significant museum collections of Islamic art have been established in Kuwait, Sharjah, Doha, Abu Dhabi, and Toronto, and major museums in Paris, London, New York, Cairo, and Copenhagen (to name a few) have reorganized their galleries (Junod et al. 2013). These new collections have spectacular objects, many with dubious provenances. This new interest in Islamic art has reopened debates about the problematic choices made in collecting and displaying objects from the Islamic world and the close ties between curators, collectors, academics, and the auction houses. Ongoing conflict in the Middle East-North Africa (MENA) region and the corresponding increase in looting, destruction of heritage (for a myriad of reasons), and the boom of illicit objects entering the art and antiquities markets raises a whole host of contentious issues for protection, repatriation, conservation, and reconstruction that archaeologists, art historians, and heritage officials, local and international alike, need to grapple with together rather than in isolation.

ISLAMIC ARCHAEOLOGY AND ISLAMIZATION

The extent to which Islamization has been explored through archaeological evidence differs regionally. Debates over the timing and process of Islamization have driven much archaeological work in the last decade in the Central Lands, and particularly Greater Syria, keeping pace with currents in Islamic history. How to methodologically distinguish between religious conversion and acculturation and the role of demographic change and migration in all of this has been an area of heated debate. Archaeologists are now looking beyond the 7th-century conquests for triggers of meaningful and lasting religious and cultural change, arguing for long-term developments and even different "spurts" in Islamization taking place at different periods in different regions and under quite local conditions. This topic is dealt with extensively in each of the chapters of Section II.

Likewise, archaeological studies of Islamization have been quite comprehensive in many areas of sub-Saharan Africa and South-East Asia (e.g., Lape 2000; Insoll 2017). Here, influential formative studies of religious conversion were developed by historians, anthropologists, and religious studies specialists involving phased conversion (e.g., Trimingham 1968; Fisher 1973, 1985) or tiers of religious beliefs that had to be overcome for Islam (and Christianity) to succeed (e.g., Horton 1971, 1975, 1993). Occasionally, elements of these models can help in archaeological interpretation of conversion and to a lesser extent Islamization, but they are also problematic in being too all-encompassing and universal to explain such diverse and complex phenomena (Insoll 2017: 246). In other parts of the same regions, on the other hand, this topic is rarely a focus of study, if at all, thus reflecting a paucity of research and comparative data as well as different methodological and theoretical approaches and influences (cf. Peacock 2017).

More useful are models which acknowledge local cultural adaptations, staggered chronologies, and gradual religious change, such as that proposed by Eaton (1993) to explain Islamization in Bengal, with its important concepts of "inclusion," "identification," and "displacement," and which could be successfully employed outside of the African and South Asian contexts where it has thus far been used (Insoll 2017: 247; Peacock 2017: 9).

ISLAMIC ARCHAEOLOGY AS "HISTORICAL ARCHAEOLOGY" IN THE MIDDLE EAST

In the Middle East, where textual sources are more readily available, the academic discipline of Islamic archaeology has had an ambivalent relationship with the textual record. Although the later medieval periods, in particular, are richly endowed with texts in Arabic, Persian, Turkish, and Western languages, archaeologists of the Islamic world have been more hesitant to use the written record than their colleagues in other "historical" archaeologies, such as that of the New World and medieval Europe. This is, in part, a legacy of the "New Archaeology" and post-processual movements of the later 20th century, which had the effect in this field of discouraging archaeologists from being overly dependent on the historical record for project design, interpretation, and narrative-building. It was also a reaction against the reliance on Latin and Greek texts that long molded the archaeology of the classical world, Byzantium, and medieval Europe. As Islamic archaeology has gravitated toward anthropological approaches in the Middle East and away from the textual-historical, however, we risk losing valuable information directly relevant to archaeological inquiry, such as land use, social and political structures, and economic life.

Today a balance between the two approaches is being achieved. The academic training of Islamic archaeologists is increasingly retooling scholars for historically savvy research, bringing Islamic archaeology into the mainstream of Middle Eastern studies.

The emphasis on advanced Arabic-language training in Middle East studies programs in North America (or Islamic studies in Germany, for example) for archaeology students reflects this reorientation. Islamic archaeology in Bilād al-Shām, Egypt, the Maghrib, and Andalusia has been radically transformed in recent decades as a result, with multidisciplinary and theory-rich research on urbanism, rural life, farming, natural resource management, and environmental history (Wordworth and McPhillips 2016; Cooper 2014; Cressier 1998; Ennahid 2002; Ettahiri et al. 2013; Walker 2011, 2017; Walker et al. 2017; Éychenne et al. 2018). Advances in the kinds of questions we can ask about the archaeological record in the Middle East and Islamic West have resulted through the analysis of documentary sources such as tax and court registers, *waqfiyyāt* (endowment deeds), *fatwa* manuals, and water and agrarian treatises, which are largely available to us only in manuscript form. These have yielded abundant information on land tenure and use, management of water, daily life in local communities, and relations between these communities and the state. Document-informed archaeology, moreover, has revolutionized the archaeological study of the Ottoman period in Greece and Cyprus and has become a foundation for landscape studies there (Given 2000, Given and Hadjianastasis 2010, and literature discussed earlier). Rather than blindly lead the interpretation of archaeological data, when read as historical documents by historically trained scholars, they enrich the archaeological record.[9] As for the kinds of narrative sources traditionally used by archaeologists for chronological and spatial information—chronicles, geographies, and travelers' accounts—many studies today of individual archaeological sites, monuments, and ceramic assemblages and ceramic exchange continue to make use of them but in a more comprehensive way and with an increasingly critical eye than ever before (François 2013; Milwright 1999, 2008, and 2009; and Cytryn-Silvermann 2010, for example, for Bilād al-Shām).

PROBLEMS OF PERIODIZATION

Chronological terminology and periodization remain a contested arena.[10] This, of course, has always been the archaeologist's dilemma: chronological terminology is either site- or region-specific, which raises challenges for interregional comparison. All the same, periodization is key if we wish to explore difference and diversity across space and time rather than risk falling into the trap of an ahistorical approach. Should we use dynastic periodizations, such as Umayyad, Fatimid, or Mamluk, to frame material culture and sites, as many art historians and historians continue to do? Or should we use broader categories, such as "early," "middle," and "late" Islamic, each with its own starting and ending points in different regions? Is "Islamic" synonymous with

---

[9] For debates on how to combine textual analysis with interpretation of the archaeological record for the Islamic periods, see Talmon-Heller and Cytryn-Silvermann (2015) and Walker (2013, 2015).

[10] See the special issue of *Der Islam* (2014).

"medieval"? Or does the scope of Islamic archaeology include the early modern and contemporary moments?

Part of the problem stems from the fact that the Muslim conquests in the 7th century are often seen as one of the ternary points in global history: in the vision of Henri Pirenne (1939), they meant the end of Mediterranean unity and the classical world and marked a decisive rupture between West (Europe) and East (the Orient) that continues today. This highly negative view of the Muslim conquests is, of course, closely linked to Western colonialism and Orientalism in the 19th and 20th centuries and has been comprehensively overturned by archaeologists, historians, and art historians in the past four decades who have demonstrated both that the Muslim conquests were not catastrophic for daily life and that Islam and early Muslim rule were strongly shaped by earlier Arabian, Byzantine, and Sassanian traditions. Where, then, should we place the formative period of Islam? Is it more productive to consider it within the remit of the late antique world or do the revelations to the Prophet, the journey to Medina, or the Muslim conquests mark the start of a discrete period in its own right?

Recently, some scholars have begun toying with the idea of an "Islamic Late Antiquity" to get around these problems. Peter Brown in *The World of Late Antiquity: AD 150–750* (1971) was the first to integrate Muhammad and the Umayyad dynasty into the reach of late antiquity, a chronological expansion into the 8th century that was matched with a geographic expansion of coverage to include Western Asia and the Arabian Peninsula. The year 750 and the movement of the caliphal capital from Mediterranean Damascus to Baghdad is frequently taken as an end-point for late antiquity, firmly putting the formative period of Islam and the Umayyad caliphate in the world of late antiquity. More recently, however, scholars have been arguing for a much longer late antiquity: Garth Fowden (2014: 18–47), for example, argues that the first millennium is a more effective periodization. There are some benefits of moving away from seeing the Arab conquest as a ternary point in world history, and these resonate particularly well with archaeology. Inspired by Hugh Kennedy's (1985) *Polis to Madina* article, archaeologists have demonstrated that the 7th century does not equate to a rupture in urbanism, the countryside, religion, and technology: the scale and timing of these changes varies at the regional and site levels. Seductive though the notion of a long late antiquity may be, in practice, if not intent, it privileges scholarship on the Mediterranean and the endurance of a Romano-Byzantine heritage. Far more troubling, however, is that it overemphasizes continuity and underplays the dramatic changes brought about by the imposition of Muslim rule on the former Byzantine and Sasanian realms and those regions beyond their borders.

Other scholars employ the term "medieval" as an alternative in reference to the Islamic world. The term "medieval," of course, has been adopted in Europe in reference to the chronological period following the collapse of the western Roman Empire. This period is neither "ancient" nor "modern," but somewhere in between, and it represents an era of cultural co-existence, confrontation, and symbiosis between Muslim and Christian societies. It is also the term most frequently bantered when scholars of pre-modern societies in Europe and in the Middle East meet for conferences. It is the term often adopted in Spain (al-Andalus), Sicily, North Africa, Cyprus, central Europe (the Ottoman's "Rumelia"), and Central Asia but far less frequently in the Middle East. There is no "Middle Ages," however, from a Middle Eastern, Islamic perspective as the chronological and cultural points of reference are uniquely Western. The combined terminology "medieval Islam" is a frequent compromise, referring to Muslim societies in the pre-modern era.

Similar problems of applicability exist in relation to using the term "medieval" in South East Asia or sub-Saharan Africa. In the latter, for example, Islamic archaeology forms part of what is generally referred to as Iron Age archaeology: the period, varying regionally, after which iron was commonly in use (cf. Phillipson 2005: 214–216). This in itself means something quite different from "Iron Age" in European archaeological chronology, which generally refers to the pre-Roman period (e.g., Collis 1984). However, "medieval" is now routinely employed in sub-Saharan African contexts (Insoll 2018) because, though inappropriate to African chronology, it is commonly understood, and as such, in the words of de Moraes Farias (2003: xxiii), has become a "dead metaphor" and thus can be used outside its "original frame of reference."

If these shifts are intended to bring the Islamic world into conversation with developments in Europe and Asia as part of the new emphasis on global history, we still need to grapple with how to break down these very large periods into meaningful chunks of time that can be compared with one another. The traditional solution has been a dynastic periodization which follows the general precepts of Islamic history, beginning with the Umayyad and Abbasid dynasties that governed vast "universal" empires and concluding with regional dynasties, such as the Safavids, the Ottomans, and the Mughals (the modern period tends to be divided along nationalist lines). The Mongol sack of Baghdad in 1258, and with it the collapse of the Abbasid caliphate, is widely agreed to mark both a watershed in Islamic history and in the development of Islamic art and architecture, and it continues to be used as a dividing point, particularly in art historical surveys (e.g., Ettinghausen et al. 2001; Blair and Bloom 1995). Such periodizations sit uneasily with archaeological evidence that rarely, if ever, maps neatly onto dynastic history (people do not begin to cook in different pots because a new caliph or sultan is on the throne) or reveals ruptures in the material record that relate to conquests or regime change. Similarly, they do not allow sufficiently for regional diversity, particularly after the collapse of the Fatimid caliphate, and, as a result, many areas are left out.

Another way out of the quandary is to adopt a periodization that reflects general socio-cultural changes relevant on a regional level. For Islamic historians working in the Middle East and Egypt, the division of time into the Classical Period, Age of the Sultanates, and Age of the Gunpowder Empires are convenient reference points, representing the interplay between political institutions and cultural forms (Hodgson 1975).[11] Even this broad characterization of Islamic political history assumes that political

---

[11] Hodgson's Age of the Sultanates was problematized by a group of historians, archaeologists, and art historians by the French and American institutes in Cairo and Amman in a series of conferences (Walker and Salles 2008; Denoix and Bierman 2012).

institutions are created the same way at the same time in different regions; the institutionalization of sultanates, for example, was not contemporary in the Levant and Egypt. Alternatively, one can adopt a cultural periodization that emerges from the archaeological record itself, such as the Early Islamic (630–1055), Middle Islamic (1055–1500), Late Islamic (1500–1750) scheme proposed by Whitcomb (2000), which has come to be adopted by most archaeologists working on, for instance, Islamic Syria or Bahrain, but not in the Islamic West or Central Asia. Such schema rarely include the Modern period, and, in practice, it remains difficult to incorporate the period 1800–1950 into archaeological narratives: so little archaeology has been conducted on this period outside the Arabian Gulf (see, e.g., Eddisford and Carter 2017). Art historians have grappled far more intensively with this problem than archaeologists in recent years. Flood and Necipoğlu's (2017) *Companion to Islamic Art and Architecture* effectively proposes a new eight-phase chronology for the Islamic world stretching from 650 to the present that may prove useful to archaeologists seeking to make transregional comparisons.[12] Like them, our vision of an "Islamic archaeology" is far more inclusive than exclusive—we include here the material culture of Muslim communities and those living under Muslim rule from the 7th century to the present day. However, we found it more useful to organize the Handbook geographically by region rather than to divide it chronologically into periods: each chapter can thus define the chronology used in its particular region, explain the historiography behind it, and outline the key chronological gaps and holes in archaeological knowledge which differ markedly from region to region.

ORGANIZATION OF THE VOLUME AND FINAL NOTE

Because of its global coverage and because of the issues related to periodization, this Handbook is organized geographically, with sections devoted to the Central Islamic Lands, the Islamic West, sub-Saharan Africa, and Asia. Each section is further subdivided into chapters on specific regions, an organization that best reflects the development of Islamic archaeology in that region and adopts regionally acceptable chronologies. Each section begins with a brief introduction to the region and its general historiography. The contributors were asked to address as much as was relevant to their region from a range of topics: historiography and chronology; survey of main sites; rural and urban landscapes; health, diet, and climate; archaeology of religion; gender; labor; and new

---

[12] They divide their chronology as follows: (I) The Early Caliphates, Umayyads, and the End of Late Antiquity (650–750); (II) Abbasids and the Universal Caliphate (750–900); (III) Fragmentation and the Rival Caliphates (900–1050); (IV) "City States" and the Later Baghdad Caliphate (1050–1250); (V) "Global" Empires and the World System (1250–1450); (VI) Early Modern Empires and Their Neighbors (1450–1700); (VII) Modernity, Empire, Colony, and Nation (1700–1950); (VIII) Islam, Art, and the Contemporary (1950–Present).

(unpublished) research. The volume's final section is rather unique for the Oxford series of archaeology Handbooks because it is dedicated to heritage management and community development, highlighting the very special responsibility of practitioners in the field of Islamic archaeology toward local communities.

The production of this Handbook was a group effort. We (the co-editors) want, first, to thank the contributors for their enormous efforts in producing chapters that reflect not only the state of the field but also visions for the future. We also are indebted to the many individuals who helped with editing at different stages at the University of Bonn: Felicitas Weber, Greg Williams, and Britta Wagner. To our Series Editor, Stefan Vranka, and the entire University of Oxford Press staff we also owe a debt of gratitude.

A final word should be said about spelling and dating formulae. While there has been an effort to standardize to some degree transliteration of Arabic terms and phrases (adopting the guidelines used by the University of Chicago for *Mamluk Studies Review*), for site names local traditions of spelling (reflecting local Arabic dialect) have priority. Diacritics appear only when a technical term in Arabic is used; diacritics are not used for persons, places, and terms that are generally known in Western scholarship by their Arabic names. The authors had the choice to use Gregorian or Hijri calendars, which are differentiated in the texts with CE and H; unless otherwise noted, the date follows the Christian calendar.

References

Ali, Z. 1994. *Islamic Art: Southeast Asia, 830 A.N.–1570 A.D.* (Kuala Lumpur: Dewan Bahasa dan Pustaka).

Avni, G. 2014. *The Byzantine-Islamic Transition in Palestine: An archaeological approach.* Oxford Studies in Byzantium (Oxford: Oxford University Press).

Blair, S. S., and Bloom, J. M. 1995. *The Art and Architecture of Islam 1250–1800* (New Haven: Yale University Press).

Collis, J. 1984. *The European Iron Age* (London: Batsford).

Cooper, J. P. 2014. *The Medieval Nile: Route, Navigation and Landscape in Islamic Egypt* (Cairo: AUC Press).

Cressier, P. 1998. "Urbanisation, arabisation, islamisation au Maroc du Nord: quelques remarques depuis l'archéologie," in J. Aguadé, P. Cressier, and A. Vicente (eds.), *Peuplement et arabisation au Magreb occidental. Dialectologie et histoire* (Madrid: Casa de Velázquez), 27–39.

Cytryn-Silvermann, K. 2010. *The Road Inns (Khāns) of Bilād al-Shām.* BAR International Series 2130 (Oxford: Archaeopress).

Davies, S., and Davis, J. (eds.) 2007. *Between Venice and Istanbul: Colonial Landscape in Early Modern Greece* (Princeton: Hesperia Supplements 40).

de Moraes Farias, P. F. 2003. *Arabic Medieval Inscriptions from the Republic of Mali* (Oxford: Oxford University Press).

Denoix, S., and Bierman, I. (eds.) 2012. *L'exercice du pouvoir à l'âge des sultanats. Production, manifestation, réception.* Annales islamologiques 46 (Kairo: Ifao).

Eaton, R. M. 1993. *The Rise of Islam and the Bengal Frontier, 1204–1760* (Berkeley: University of California Press).

Eddisford, D., and Carter, R. 2017. "The Vernacular Architecture of Doha, Qatar," *Post-Medieval Archaeology*, 51, 1, 81–107.

Ennahid, S. 2002. *Political Economy and Settlement Systems of Medieval Northern Morocco. An Archaeological-Historical Approach*. BAR International Series 1059 (Oxford: Archaeopress).

Ettahiri, A. S., Fili, A., and van Staëvel, J.-P. 2013. "Nouvelles recherches archéologiques sur les origines de l'empire Almohade au Maroc: Les fouilles d'Îgîlîz," *Comptes Rendus de l'Académie des Inscriptions et Belles-Lettres*, 2 (avril–juin), 1109–1142.

Ettinghausen, R. 1951. "Islamic Art and Archeology," in T. Cuyler Young ed., *Near Eastern Culture and Society* (Princeton), 17–47.

Ettinghausen, R., Grabar, O., and Jenkins, M. 2001. *Islamic Art and Architecture 650–1250* (New Haven: Yale University Press).

Éychenne, M., Meier, A., and Vigouroux, E. 2018. *Le waqf de la mosquée des Omeyyades de Damas. Le manuscrit ottoman d'un inventaire mamelouk établi en 816/1413* (Damascus/Beirut: Institut Français du Proche Orient).

Fenwick, C. 2013. "From Africa to Ifrīqiya: Settlement and Society in Early Medieval North Africa (650–800) ", *Al-Masāq*, 25, 1, 9–33.

Fenwick, C. 2019. *Early Islamic North Africa: A New Perspective* (London: Bloomsbury).

Fisher, H. J. 1973. "Conversion Reconsidered: Some Historical Aspects of Religious Conversion in Black Africa," *Africa*, 43, 27–40.

Fisher, H. J. 1985. "The Juggernaut's Apologia: Conversion to Islam in Black Africa," *Africa*, 55, 153–173.

Flood, F. B. 2009. *Objects of Translation: Material Culture and Medieval "Hindu-Muslim" Encounter* (Princeton: Princeton University Press).

Flood, F. B., and Necipoğlu, G. (eds.) 2017. *A Companion to Islamic Art and Architecture* (Oxford: Blackwells).

Fowden, G. 2014. *Before and After Muhammad: The First Millennium Refocused* (Princeton: Princeton University Press).

François, V. 2013. "Objets du quotidien à Damas à l'époque ottomane," *Bulletin d'Etudes Orientales*, 61, 475–506.

Given, M. 2000. "Agriculture, Settlement and Landscape in Ottoman Cyprus," *Levant*, 32, 215–236.

Given, M., and Hadjianastasis, M. 2010. "Landholding and Landscape in Ottoman Cyprus," *Byzantine and Modern Greek Studies*, 34, 38–60.

Grabar, O. 1976. "Islamic Art and Archaeology," in L. Binder (ed.), *The Study of the Middle East: Research in the Humanities and the Social Sciences* (New York: John Wiley and Sons), 229–263.

Grabar, O. 1983. "Reflections on the Study of Islamic Art," *Muqarnas*, 1, 1–14.

Hodgson, M. 1975. *The Venture of Islam*. 3 vols. (Chicago: University of Chicago Press).

Horton, R. 1971. "African Conversion," *Africa*, 41, 85–108.

Horton, R. 1975. "On the Rationality of Conversion," *Africa*, 45, 219–235.

Horton, R. 1993. *Patterns of Thought in Africa and the West: Essays on Magic, Religion* (Cambridge: Cambridge University Press).

Insoll, T. 1999. *The Archaeology of Islam* (Oxford: Blackwell Publishers).

Insoll, T. 2003. *The Archaeology of Islam in Sub-Saharan Africa* (Cambridge: Cambridge University Press).

Insoll, T. 2017. "The Archaeology of Islamisation in Sub-Saharan Africa: A Comparative Study," in A. C. S. Peacock (ed.), *Islamisation: Comparative Perspectives from History* (Edinburgh: Edinburgh University Press), 244–273.

Insoll, T. 2018. "Trans-Saharan Trade and Islam: Great States and Urban Centres in the Medieval West African Sahel," in P. Linehan, J. Nelson, and M. Costambeys (eds.), *The Medieval World* (2nd ed.) (Abingdon: Routledge), 549–567.

Junod, B., Khalil, G., Weber, S., and Wolf, G. *Islamic Art and the Museum: Approaches to Art and Archaeology of the Muslim World in the Twenty-First Century* (London: Saqi Books).

Kennedy, H. 1985. "From Polis to Madina: Urban Change in Late Antique and Early Islamic Syria," *Past and Present*, 106, 1–27.

Lape, P. V. 2000. "Political Dynamics and Religious Change in the late Pre-Colonial Banda Islands, Eastern Indonesia," *World Archaeology*, 32, 138–155.

Milwright, M. 1999. "Pottery in Written Sources of the Ayyubid-Mamluk Period (c.567–923/1171–1517)," *Bulletin of the School of Oriental and African Studies*, 62, 3, 504–518.

Milwright, M. 2008. *The Fortress of the Raven: Karak in the Middle Islamic Period (1100–1650)* (Leiden: Brill).

Milwright, M. 2009. "Written Sources and the Study of Pottery in Ottoman Bilad al-Sham," *Al-Rafidan*, 30, 37–52.

Milwright, M. 2010. *An Introduction to Islamic Archaeology* (Edinburgh: Edinburgh University Press).

Peacock, A. C. S. 2017. "Introduction: Comparative Perspectives on Islamisation," in A. C. S. Peacock (ed.), *Islamisation: Comparative Perspectives from History* (Edinburgh: Edinburgh University Press), 1–18.

Phillipson, D. 2005. *African Archaeology* (Cambridge: Cambridge University Press).

Pirenne, H. 1939. *Mohammed and Charlemagne* (London: Unwin).

Power, T. 2012. *The Red Sea from Byzantium to the Caliphate, AD500–1000* (Cairo: AUC Press).

Priestman, S. P. N. 2016. "The Silk Road or the Sea? Sasanian and Islamic Exports to Japan," *Journal of Islamic Archaeology*, 3, 1, 1–35.

Rogers, J. M. 1974. *From Antiquarianism to Islamic Archaeology* (Cairo: Istituto italiano di cultura per la RAE).

Rosen-Ayalon, M. 2006. *Islamic Art and Archaeology of Palestine* (Walnut Creek, CA: Left Coast Press).

SPAFA (SEAMEO Project in Archaeology and Fine Arts) 1984. *Final Report: Consultative Workshop on Research on Maritime Shipping and Trade Networks in Southeast Asia (I-W7)* (Cisarua, West Java, Indonesia: SPAFA).

Sutton, S. (ed.) 2000. *Contingent Countryside: Settlement, Economy, and Land Use in the Southern Argolid Since 1700* (Stanford: Stanford University Press).

Talmon-Heller, D., and Cytryn-Silverman, K. (eds.) 2015. *Material Evidence and Narrative Sources: Interdisciplinary Studies of the History of the Middle East* (Leiden: Brill).

Trimingham, J. S. 1968. *The Influence of Islam on Africa* (London: Longman).

Valor, M., and Gutiérrez, A. 2015. *The Archaeology of Medieval Spain: 1100–1500* (Sheffield: Equinox).

Vernoit, S. 1997. "The Rise of Islamic Archaeology," *Muqarnas*, 14, 1–10.

Vernoit, S. 2000. *Discovering Islamic Art: Collectors and Collections 1850–1950* (London: I.B. Tauris).

Walker, B. J. 2010. "From Ceramics to Social Theory: Reflections on Mamluk Archaeology Today," *Mamluk Studies Review*, 14, 109–157.

Walker, B. J. 2011. *Jordan in the Late Middle Ages: Transformation of the Mamluk Frontier* (Chicago: Middle East Documentation Center, University of Chicago).

Walker, B. J. 2013. "What Can Archaeology Contribute to the New Mamlukology?: Where Culture Studies and Social Theory Meet," in S. Conermann (ed.), *Ubi sumus? Quo vademus? Mamluk Studies—State of the Art* (Bonn: University of Bonn Press), 311–335.

Walker, B. J. 2015. "On Archives and Archaeology: Reassessing Mamluk Rule from Documentary Sources and Jordanian Fieldwork," in D. Talmon-Heller and K. Cytryn-Silverman (eds.), *Material Evidence and Narrative Sources: Interdisciplinary Studies of the History of the Middle East* (Leiden: Brill), 113–143.

Walker, B. J. 2017. "The Struggle over Water: Evaluating the 'Water Culture' of Syrian Peasants Under Mamluk Rule," in Y. Ben-Bassat (ed.), *Developing Perspectives in Mamluk History* (Leiden-Boston: Brill), 287–310 (chapter 14).

Walker, B. J., Laparidou, S., Hansen, A., and Corbino, C. 2017. "Did the Mamluks Have an Environmental Sense?: Natural Resource Management in Syrian Villages," *Mamluk Studies Review*, 20, 167–245.

Walker, B. J., and Salles, J.-F. (eds.) 2008. *Le pouvoir à l'âge des sultanats dans le Bilâd al-Shâm* (Damascus: Institut Français du Proche Orient).

Walmsley, A. 2007. *Early Islamic Syria: An Archaeological Assessment*. Duckworth Debates in Archaeology (London: Duckworth).

Whitcomb, D. 2000. "Hesban, Amman, and Abbasid Archaeology in Jordan," in L. E. Stager, J. A. Greene, and M. D. Coogan (eds.), *The Archaeology of Jordan and Beyond, Essays in Honor of James A. Sauer* (Winona Lake, IN: Harvard Semitic Museum Publications), 505–515.

Wordworth, P., and McPhillips. S. (eds.) 2016. *Landscapes of the Islamic World: Archaeology, History, and Ethnography* (Philadelphia: University of Pennsylvania Press).

Zarinebaf, F., Bennet, J., and Davis, J. 2005. *A Historical and Economic Geography of Ottoman Greece: The Southwestern Morea in the 18th Century* (Athens: The American Schools of Classical Studies at Athens).

SECTION II

....

CENTRAL
ISLAMIC LANDS

....

BETHANY J. WALKER

THIS volume begins, appropriately, with the central Islamic lands: the "Arab heartland" (Bilād al-Shām, Egypt, Iraq, the Arabian Peninsula), Persia, and the western lands of the Ottoman Empire (Anatolia and Rumelia). The "Central Lands" is a familiar concept in Islamic studies, emphasizing the important legacy of this region for the religious, cultural, and political development of the Islamic world. The region gave birth to Islam as a religion and as a socio-political system, laid the parameters for Islamic law, and formulated the basic templates of "Islamic art" and material culture. Though there were early explorations of medieval Islamic-era sites and monuments in other parts of the world, the earliest systematic, scientific archaeological studies of the Islamic periods, which gave rise to the discipline as it is practiced today, were in the Central Lands. Growing out of the Biblical and ancient Near Eastern archaeologies of the 19th and early 20th centuries, the modern discipline of Islamic archaeology was impacted by the priorities of the pioneers working in the "Holy Land." Islamic archaeology, as a discipline of its own, was born here and, in the past several decades, has developed into a mature field of research. Fieldwork in the region continues to impact the discipline globally in terms of research questions, development of new methods and multidisciplinary approaches, and theoretical and conceptual precision.

The preoccupation with urban sites and urban monuments, first cultivated by the "pioneers," is gradually giving way in this region to a concern with rural societies, land use and landscapes, and regional surveys. As a result, environmental and palaebotanical analyses have become regular and expected components of project design. The "rural turn" has also ensured study of local, small-scale communities and the related topics of social and ethnic identity and identity-making. The focus of a previous generation on the Islamic conquests and their impact on the Late Antique city has developed into more nuanced explorations of the timing and process of Islamization and material expressions of religious and cultural identity. Collaborations with natural scientists, ethnographers, and historians are rapidly transforming the ways that Islamic archaeology in the Central Lands is practiced and the kinds of questions that are being asked.

In spite of forty years of conceptual and scientific progress and sustained interest in the later historical periods, Islamic archaeology here remains hampered by several common challenges. The inability to date coarse wares—and overcome, in the process, the problem of the strong regionalisms in material culture—is one of the greatest hurdles as the field diverges even further from its roots in classical Islamic art history (and its obsession with glazed wares). More excavation of small-scale, rural sites is needed, with proper and timely publication of the results. The complex, and ambivalent, relationship with contemporary written sources has created three camps of archaeologists working in the region: those who embrace a critical reading of Arabic, Turkish, and Persian texts as important sources of data ("historical archaeologists"); those who favor anthropological approaches, casting a distrustful glance to texts and textual approaches as a thing of the past ("anthropological archaeologists"); and those who combine anthropological theory with some degree of textual analysis. The battle over the written word is an important one, particularly in a region so rich in archaeologically relevant primary sources and archives. Finally, as is true for the archaeological work described in other chapters of this volume, while archaeologists working in each country tend to follow one another's scholarship closely and collaborate on many projects, there is less communication across international borders. Islamic archaeology in Europe, for example, is generally unfamiliar territory to those working in the eastern Mediterranean. As reflected in this volume, scientific developments in the Gulf, Africa, and Asia are less known to the "mainstream" represented in the major international conferences on Islamic archaeology in North America and Europe. As the discipline grows, its global reach pushes our current academic networks to their limits. The sections in this volume aim to address this problem.

The following section is organized geographically and historiographically, in a way to best survey developments and present debates in the field. Bilād al-Shām (Greater Syria) is divided into two chapters: Northern and Southern Syria. Scholars of all disciplines readily acknowledge the regionalisms in material culture, exchange networks, and societies that have created distinctive socio-cultural histories for the lands north and south of Damascus. The chapter on Northern Syria geographically covers southeastern Anatolia, southern Iraq, the northern Syrian plain, and the lands south to Damascus. The region of Damascus south to the Gulf of Aqaba and the Mediterranean to the modern Iraqi border is covered in the chapter on Southern Syria. Culturally and historically forming coherent units, Egypt, the lands of modern Iraq, and Persia (modern Iran) constitute individual chapters. The Anatolian Plateau and what is today central and western Turkey is covered in two chapters on Medieval and Ottoman Anatolia, a division that is justified by different historiographies, professional networks, and research questions. The chapter on Arabia and the Gulf presents for the first time a regional picture of the dynamic developments in recent years in the field of Islamic archaeology in the Arabian Peninsula. This section then closes with a co-authored chapter on Ottoman Europe (Rumelia), which surveys the very diverse cultural and historical landscape of the Empire's westernmost lands, critiquing the legacy of the Ottoman period in the historiography of the modern nation states.

CHAPTER 2.1

···

NORTHERN SYRIA

···

MARIE-ODILE ROUSSET

IN this chapter we consider the material sources for reconstructing the history of Northern Syria from the 7th century. It will cover the area limited to the north by the modern border with Turkey, to the east by the Khabur Valley, and to the south by a line from Palmyra to Beirut (Figure 2.1.1). This region, between the Mediterranean coast and Mesopotamia, comprises several large geographical regions. To the north, a large plateau extends as far as the Jazira, with large cereal plains intersected by the valleys of the Euphrates and its tributaries (the Khabur and Balikh). The Limestone Massif is made up of three groups of hills, 550 meters high on average, spreading from Aleppo to Antioch. The western coastal mountains reach more than 3,000 meters in Lebanon and can only be crossed through the region of Homs. They form a significant barrier between the Mediterranean and the marshy areas of the Bekaa, the Ghab, and the Amuq in which the Orontes flows. In the central zone, the steppe is increasingly arid toward the southeast. It is cut by low reliefs which follow a line from Damascus to Dayr al-Zor through Palmyra. It is the domain of nomadic tribes. Depending on the region, the geological situation influences the architectural tradition. Clay bricks, usually sundried and only rarely fired, were the building material of choice throughout the Jazira, the valley of the Euphrates, and the steppe. Masonry construction dominates in the hills and western mountains.

The Islamic conquest of Syria began in 634 CE. Syria (with its capital in Damascus) was the seat of the power of the Umayyad dynasty (660–750) and the architecture of this period is still clearly visible in the present landscape. With the relocation of power to Baghdad (founded in 762), the Abbasids (750–1055) rather concentrated their efforts in the valleys of the Euphrates and its tributaries. Political disturbances during the 10th century divided Syria between Byzantine control to the northwest, the Hamdanids (947–1015) to the north and east, and the Fatimids (969–1076) to the south. This period was followed by incursions by the Seljuqs (1055–1127). The architectural traces and patronage during these periods are less well known than that of the earlier era. From the beginning of the 12th century, the Zenguids (1127–1174) and the Ayyubids (1174–1258) controlled various territories while a number of Crusader states settled west of the

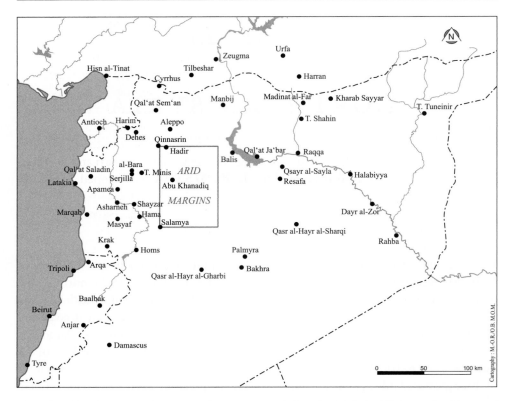

FIGURE 2.1.1 Map of Northern Syria with places mentioned in the text. Courtesy of M.-O. Rousset and O. Barge.

Orontes River basin from 1098. They asserted their power and the unity of the Islamic religion by a strong edilitary activity, especially in the cities. A desire to defend the territory spurred the construction and restoration of fortifications, including fortresses to defend against Crusaders and the reinforcement of city walls. This activity continued into the Mamluk period (1258–1512).

HISTORIOGRAPHY AND CHRONOLOGY

The first studies in the Islamic archaeology of Northern Syria originated in travelers' descriptions of monumental architecture, studies of historical topography, and the recording of inscriptions in the late 18th century. A topic that has attracted much research by orientalists from the mid-19th century is that of Crusader fortifications, with the aim of showing the greatness of this period. From the beginning of the 20th century, the first important inventories were carried out specifically on the Islamic monuments of Syria by F. Sarre and H. Herzfeld (1911–1920) in the Euphrates valley and by M. van Berchem and E. Fatio (1914–1915) for the region west of the steppe.

In 1929–1931, the first earnest excavations of an Islamic site in Syria began at Balis-Meskéné (by G. Salles, E. de Lorey, and L. Cavro). Excavations there consisted of four long trenches across the site and the clearing of a mosque whose stucco decorations are now on display at Damascus museum. The results of this work have remained largely unpublished. The 1930s saw the rise of Islamic archaeology in Syria. It was sometimes incorporated as part of the larger studies on ancient settlements, such as the excavations and research on Hama by the Danish Carlsberg Foundation between 1931 and 1938 (Riis and Poulsen 1957; Ploug et al. 1969; Pentz 1997). Studies also developed on strictly Islamic subjects, such as the Umayyad *qusur* (Seyrig 1931, 1934 on Qasr al-Hayr al-Sharqi and its gardens; Schlumberger 1986 on his excavations at Qasr al-Hayr al-Gharbi in 1936–1938). However, the study of the latter was based mainly on the architectural remains (for example the stucco decoration of the main door has been reconstructed in the archaeological Museum of Damascus), and no attention has been paid to the finds of the excavations. The true founder of Islamic archaeology in Syria was J. Sauvaget (1901–1950). He covered diverse fields of research including architecture (palaces, madrasas, mosques, and caravanserais), town planning (Aleppo, Latakia, and Damascus), Islamic decorative arts (ceramics and metalwork), epigraphy, and the editing and translation of Arabic texts. His work on Aleppo (1941) was one of the first syntheses on an Arab city.

Excavations of the early Islamic palaces of Raqqa began in 1944 (M. Dunand on palace A). They were continued by the Syrian Department of Antiquities between 1950 and 1958 and focused mainly on the architectural plans and decorations (Saliby 2004). Work on Umayyad Resafa in Syria, or 'Anjar in Lebanon since 1953, were unfortunately conducted in the same way (Otto-Dorn 1957; Chehab 1993). The positive contribution of these studies was a better knowledge of early Islamic architecture which allowed K. A. C. Creswell to revise and expand his volume on *Early Muslim Architecture* (1932 and 1940, revised 1969).

Gradually, Islamic archaeology incorporated more rigorous and systematic methods of excavation and documentation of material finds. Archaeological investigation began in Harran's citadel in 1950 (Lloyd and Brice 1951: 97–108; Rice 1952). The excavations of Qasr al-Hayr al-Sharqi, carried out by O. Grabar between 1964 and 1972, were published only a few years later (Grabar et al. 1978). Those of Balis-Meskéné were taken over by L. Golvin, A. Raymond, and J.-L. Paillet from 1969 to 1974 as part of the rescue excavations in anticipation of the flooding of the Euphrates valley upstream of the great al-Thawra dam. Balis was founded in the Byzantine period and occupied until the Mongol invasion of 1260. Excavations there uncovered a domestic quarter with a *suq* and an Ayyubid period mosque. The minaret of the great mosque, dated by an inscription from 1210–1211, was relocated and renovated. An unfinished fortification, dating to the beginning of the Mamluk period, was also excavated along with roughly forty pottery kilns outside the ramparts of the city. Unfortunately, only the numismatics and parts of the domestic quarter have been published to date (Raymond and Paillet 1995). Princeton University, in 1996 and 1998, excavated other houses and an Umayad castle on a hill overlooking the city (Leisten 1999–2000).

Since the late 1980s, Islamic archeology has benefited from an acceptance of other disciplines such as geography and geomorphology. The primary contribution of these disciplines has been the analysis of landscape evolution and regional development. This is the methodology used in the study of rural settlement in the Middle Euphrates Valley during the Islamic period carried out by S. Berthier and B. Geyer from 1987 to 1990 (Berthier 2001). From 1982 until 1994, the German Archaeological Institute conducted rescue excavations under the direction of M. Meinecke in the southeastern section of the palace area of Raqqa (Siegel 2017), which led to a better understanding of the city.

Since 1995, with the evolution of measurement technology, architectural and topographic plans have become increasingly more precise. The first years of the 21st century have seen more systematic use of methods such as photogrammetry applied to the study of buildings, for example at Shayzar, Krac des Chevaliers, and Urfa (Tonghini 2012; Zimmer et al. 2013; Tonghini 2016) or geophysical survey for urban mapping of Kharab Sayyar, excavated since 1998 (Meyer 2008) ans Resafa (Sack et al. 2004). But the whole range of possible studies are not yet completely integrated to excavation projects. Studies of artifacts, such as glass finds (Foy 2000, 2012; Dussart 2017) or archaeobotanical and archaeozoological studies, are still too infrequent to allow for the proper investigation of topics such as diet or agriculture (Loyet 2000; Genequand et al. 2006: 188–200; Genequand et al. 2008: 168–171; Studer et al. 2013; Ramsay and Eger 2015).

Chronological considerations in archaeology rely heavily on ceramic studies. Unfortunately, the recording of excavated pottery finds was not considered important until the late 1970s. In addition, publications concerning Islamic pottery have traditionally been confined to art historical studies of glazed ceramics, which has led to a strong imbalance in the knowledge of this material. As the oldest archaeological works have concentrated on the best preserved buildings, knowledge of the ceramics of each subperiod of the Islamic period is inversely proportional to that of architecture. Numerous excavations at Umayyad *qusur* have hardly provided properly studied and published material. We do have a better knowledge of the pottery of the pre and early Islamic period since the studies of Dehes pottery by D. Orssaud (Sodini et al. 1980: 234–266), Zeugma (Kenrick 2013), Halabiyya (Haidar-Vela 2017), Qsayr al-Sayla (Konrad 2001), and al-Hadir (Rousset 2012: 73–118) where well stratified assemblages have been published. They show both continuity with Byzantine ceramics but also the appearance of new forms in the Umayyad period, such as certain types of amphorae or cooking vessels (Vokaer 2011). Recent advances in research on ceramics have shown that it is no longer possible to link the beginning of the Abbasid period and the appearance of polychrome glazes: Raqqa palaces (Saliby 2004), al-Hadir (Rousset 2012), and Qasr al-Hayr al-Sharqi (Genequand 2012) have provided examples of early Abbasid levels without polychrome glazed pottery. They corroborate the dating of the development, under the influence of Far Eastern imports, of the first polychrome glazed wares from the reign of al-Mu'tasim (833–842). "Classical" Abbasid horizons (9th–10th century) have been excavated and the material has been published at Qasr al-Hayr al-Sharqi (Grabar et al. 1978), Rahba (Rousset 1997), Raqqa (Miglus 1999), and Kharab Sayyar, which has been dated from the second half of the 9th century (Falb 2012; unfortunately the study is only about unglazed wares). Too often, however, their typological classification makes it difficult for the reader to distinguish a chronological evolution of pottery from the stratigraphic study and to determine the archaeological context of the ceramic assemblages.

Until the 1980s, pottery of the 11th century remained unrecognized because no excavations specifically focused on the Fatimid and Seljuk periods in Syria. Indeed, in this region, these periods are hardly represented in terms of monumental architecture. Only sites located in the Euphrates Valley have produced pottery of this period. The study of the material of several sites in the Balikh and Euphrates Valleys, Qal'at Ja'bar (Tonghini 1998), Raqqa/Tall al-Fakhar (Tonghini and Henderson 1998), Tell Shahin (Tonghini 1995), and Rahba (Rousset 2017) highlighted the presence of several production workshops of glazed earthernwares, decorated with *sgraffiato*, slip-painted, or painted in green and brown. They find parallels in the northeastern regions of Iran and may have been strongly influenced by patterns emerging with the arrival of the Seljuqs in Syria. Another characteristic marker is the appearance of the first *stonepaste wares* in Syria at the end of the 11th century. These are white synthetic wares, which were often engraved, underglaze painted, or lustre painted. They were produced, for a century and a half, in different workshops, the oldest being that of Tell Minis (Porter and Watson 1987). Others were highlighted in Beirut (Waksman 2011), Aleppo (Gonnella 1999), and Qal'at Ja'bar (Tonghini 1998). But the most important production center is Raqqa, which would have developed during the reign of Ayyubid Prince al-Malik al-Ashraf Musa between 1201 and 1228 (Jenkins-Madina 2006; see also for a synthesis Mason 2004). The productions of Raqqa are characterized by figural or vegetal designs in black or dark blue under a transparent colorless or turquoise glaze, luster on turquoise or purple glazes, or colored designs under a colorless glaze. Again, glazed pottery was studied more frequently than the entire ceramic assemblage.

Common or domestic wares are known only from a handful of sites in the Euphrates valley: Qal'at Ja'bar (Tonghini 1998), Resafa (Logar 1991, 1992, 1995, 1996; Knötzele 2006), and Rahba (Rousset 1997). A chronology for molded ware has been assessed at Balis (Mulder 2014, to be completed with the stratified assemblages cited earlier). A kind of ware specific to Northern Syria is the cooking *brittle ware*, which was produced from the Roman to the Mamluk period in different workshops (Vokaer 2011). The typical ceramic assemblage of the Mamluk period is well known on the coast and in the middle Orontes Valley, at the sites of Arqa, Masyaf, Apamea, and Shayzar (Hakimian and Salamé-Sarkis 1988; Shaddoud 2015; Vezzoli 2016). At that time, stonepaste had almost disappeared from places outside the main towns, and there is little development in the decorations and shapes of common wares during these centuries. The most numerous in the Orontes River basin but totally absent from the coast, "handmade geometrical painted ware," is known from the late 12th century until the Ottoman period. Finally, it is regrettable that the castles, with phases of construction often dated by inscriptions, did not give rise to more comprehensive excavations producing reliable ceramic typologies.

URBAN AND RURAL LANDSCAPES

The Early Islamic City in North Syria

The research on the urban history of the cities of north Syria at the beginning of the Islamic period is more closely associated to the history of architecture and traditional historical narratives than the archaeological evidence. In the large Classical cities, the Islamic monuments are often the result of refurbishment or are built into the preexisting urban form. For example the great mosque of Aleppo was built in 715 on the square next to the cathedral. Sauvaget's theory, elaborated from the analysis of the modern urban network of the cities of Damascus, Aleppo, and Lattakia (Sauvaget 1934, 1941) was that the Classical city (with its well-known characteristics: orthogonal and geometric plan, wide streets with colonnades, open spaces and public buildings, agora, theaters, and baths) gave way then to an "Islamic" city. This one would have been characterized by the anarchy of the plan, tortuous alleys, the absence of public spaces (having been gradually annexed by private constructions), and the importance of the market (*suq*), closed and covered. A rejection of the idea that there was a decline in urban areas as a result of the Islamic conquest and instead an evolution from the *polis* to the *madina* was developed thanks to Hugh Kennedy (1985), who considered that this process was the fruit of a long evolution, begun well before the Islamic conquest, and was due to a series of political, economic, social, and religious factors beyond just the conquest. Numerous researchers also explained the manufacturing of an "Islamic" city and tried to define its characteristics (e.g., Foss 1997 about Antioch, Apamea, Hama, and Bosra; Wirth 2000: 515–522; van Staëvel 2012).

Yet recent works on the cities of Syria have put in perspective these hypotheses. A. Eger (2013) showed that, in Antioch, the decline of the city was a subjective perception and that the city's urbanism, with minor fluctuations, remained more or less stable until the 12th century. It follows an orthogonal plan, incorporating differences in functionality and accessibility. The orthogonal grid of the Roman city remained in use, with the *cardo* as the main artery for transportation and market, although with shops and houses built on the colonnaded street. The great mosque and the governor's residence also held place along the same axis of the residential expanse. Areas beyond the commercial and industrial quarters were mainly agricultural fields and cemeteries.

At Chalcis/Qinnasrin, no obvious evidence of the foundation of a new town was found; most of the late antique city continued to be occupied, along with the Acropolis, the seat of power, and the *intra muros* city. But the early Islamic agglomeration also extends beyond the walls reconstructed in the middle of the 6th century: in a residential and artisanal suburb attached to the enclosure wall already partially occupied during late antiquity, in the fortress atop the mountain, and also in other neighboring settlements (Rousset 2020). The large hamlet of al-Hadir was just 4 kilometers from Qinnasrin, and the excavations showed that the site was established during immigration to the region during the first decades after the conquest (Rousset 2012). Both sites were largely abandoned after the middle of the 10th century, when the city of Aleppo emerged as the regional center. During the 11th and early 12th centuries, the settlement of Qinnasrin was reduced to its tell and the previous acropolis, and some of the ruins were used as cemeteries.

At Resafa, which was one of the capitals of the caliph Hisham b. 'Abd al-Malik (724–743), the occupation of the city was continuous until the Mongol invasions. Christian and Muslim communities coexisted there: the Umayyad mosque was installed just next to the great basilica (Sack 1996), and the *suq* developed nearby in the porticoes of colonnaded streets (the width of which was again reduced during the medieval period: Westphalen 2000; Sack 2008). The constructions extend well beyond the enclosure wall, particularly to the south. Residential areas, hydraulic structures, and agricultural and industrial installations extend up to 1.5 kilometers from the walled city, with occupied zones shifting from west to east from late antiquity to the 13th century (Sack et al. 2004; Gussone and Müller-Wiener 2012).

At Palmyra, like at Harran, Resafa, Raqqa, Damascus, Aleppo, Homs, Hama, and Baalbak a large mosque was erected in the center of the late antique city, near the Roman *tetrakonia* and the Umayyad *suq*. It testifies to the development and transformation of the city center around the religious and economic poles under the Marwanid caliphs (684–750). The city remained an important and relatively prosperous urban area with significant fortifications through the middle of the 9th century, under the Abbasids (Genequand 2012: 52–67). Settlement then became concentrated in and around the temple of Baal, which was fortified in 1132–1133. At that time, its *cella* was transformed into a mosque (Sauvaget 1931). After 1230, the defense of the city was completed by the building of the fortress which overlooked it from the northwest (Bylinski 1999).

Next to these antique cities, which continued to be occupied and benefited from a new monumental ornamentation ("organic cities"), princely cities were built in the Umayyad period on virgin soil, such as the complexes of 'Anjar (Finster 2003, 2008) and Qasr al-Hayr al-Sharqi (Grabar et al. 1978; Genequand 2012: 95–159). They also exhibit prestigious architecture and the patronage of the Umayyad caliphs in large-scale urban programs. Thus, we cannot speak about decline, nor even about a unique model of evolution of cities after the Muslim conquest but much rather about a variety of situations of development which, besides the previously mentioned factors, seem connected to local contingencies.

New cities were also built in the Abbasid period, as regional centers from which the surrounding areas developed, in the Euphrates and Balikh Valleys (Heidemann 2008). The more famous of these is al-Rafiqa, founded in 772 near the preexisting city of Raqqa Gallinicum, as the military and administrative center of the Abbasid Empire. In a horseshoe-shaped plan of 1,300 meters in width, the city was enclosed by a mudbrick rampart, an advance wall, and a moat (Figure 2.1.2). Three axial entrances lead to the great mosque in the center. An extensive palatial quarter was built to the north of the twin cities, when caliph Harun al-Rashid settled there from 796 to 808. This area included about twenty large-scale complexes, of which several were partly excavated, some of them left

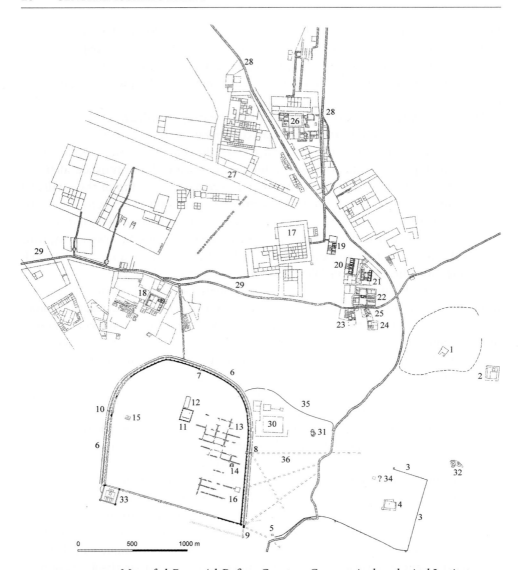

FIGURE 2.1.2 Map of al-Raqqa/al-Rafiqa. Courtesy German Archaeological Institute.

unfinished, others which were in use only intermittently (Daiber and Becker 2004; Siegel 2017). Many other buildings and complexes lay north of al-Rafiqa, like barracks for the soldiers, canals, and a hippodrome. Large-scale industrial activities were located between palatial and urban areas. Workshops for brick, pottery, and glass production have been excavated there (Miglus 1999; Heidemann and Becker 2003; Khalil and Henderson 2011; Heidemann 2006b). Around 815, this area was enclosed by a wall and became an urban entity on its own. Excavations reveal that potters were brought from Iraq to satisfy the needs of the new capital under Harun al-Rashid. They were working in an organized area, with walls demarcating groups of kilns. Industrial production was carried out in Raqqa until the mid-13th century, and the luxurious stonepaste pottery was exported all over the Middle East (Jenkins-Madina 2006). Al-Raqqa and al-Rafiqa together formed the largest urban entity in early Abbasid Syria and northern Mesopotamia: 8 kilometers to the west of the city is the victory monument of Harun al-Rashid, Hiraqla, a 100-square-meter building surrounded by a circular enclosure wall of 500 meters in diameter (Toueir et al. 2004). The size of the inhabited city area became drastically diminished after the reign of Harun al-Rashid, and new structures were built up on top of the suburban area between the two cities. Political instability along with a fire in 944 in part of the city of al-Raqqa resulted in the gradual depopulation of the initial urban settlement at al-Rafiqa. The revival of al-Raqqa in the Zangid and Ayyubid periods is attested by the building of the Qasr al-Banat (Toueir 1985), the restoration of the great mosque (though smaller than the original Abbasid structure), and the construction of the Bab Baghdad main city gate in the southeastern corner of the Abbasid enclosure (Hillenbrand 1985). The citadel of Raqqa was built between 1192 and 1199. Located in the southwest corner of the city, it had a residential rather than military role, linked to the southern quarter of the city to which the Baghdad gate was oriented. This extension, between the inner wall and the outer enclosure, would be the precious garden of the Ayyubid Prince al-Malik al-Ashraf Musa (Heidemann 2006a). Al-Raqqa was depopulated after the Mongol invasions and was dismantled around 1265, at the beginning of the Mamluk period.

At Madinat al-Far, two construction phases are apparent in the urban enclosure. With a square plan of 330 meters in length, it is surrounded by a ditch and pierced by four doors with an almost trapezoid extension extending about 1,000 meters, which was also equipped with a rampart dated to the beginning of the Abbasid period (Haase 2006). Kharab Sayyar, the ancient city of al-Jarud, was founded after the 840s. The city features a square enclosure 650 meters in length and includes an ancient *tell* which was reused as a citadel. Its main settlement phase, corroborated by coins and stucco ornamentation styles, can be dated from the middle until the end of the 9th century. Within the central urban zone, which is not quite orthogonal, are streets and various buildings, including a mosque, *suq*, palatial complexes, a bathhouse with polychrome mural paintings, and large houses with stucco decoration (Würz 2014) and large cisterns. Square structures have also been discovered outside of the city to the north (Meyer 2008; Würz 2018). Rahba Mayadin (excavated from 1976 to 1981) was one of the most important towns of the Middle Euphrates Valley in the medieval period. Like Raqqa, the city was occupied until the mid-13th century. It had been founded at the time of al-Ma'mun (813–833) along the Euphrates River (Rousset 1997 and 2017) and featured a triangular urban layout.

Certain patterns in urban structure appear in northern Syria in the early Islamic period. There does not seem to have been an abrupt discontinuity with the Late Antique world in the Umayyad period, an overall urban "decline." Nor is there a unique model of urban evolution after the Muslim conquest but rather diverse developments which, in addition to the previously discussed factors, seem connected to local contingencies. The new urban centers of the early Abbasid period, furthermore, represent a wide range of forms and functions. The archaeological record thus argues against an essentialist "Islamic city" and instead presents evidence of regional diversity and adaptability to local conditions.

The Settlements of the Umayyad Elites

In the Umayyad period, the caliphs invested in towns, but they also did so in the country-side, with the acquisition and foundation of large farm estates owned by the members of the ruling Umayyad family and the construction of "desert castles," a term generally understood as buildings built primarily (but not exclusively) in steppe-land areas. Over the course of the past century their dating and function have generated lively archaeo-logical debates. Generally accepted for a long time were the original arguments put forth by Herzfeld about their dating (1921). More recently the ideas about their func-tion have been challenged (see a discussion of these debates in Genequand 2012: 1–3; 379–396). These buildings, interpreted from the perspective of later Arabic sources which often painted the Umayyad period in a negative light, were considered for a long time as palaces made for hunting and to enjoy the pleasures of court life far from cities. J. Sauvaget was the first to consider this type of site from an archaeological perspective, showing that the palaces are generally accompanied by other domestic structures and hydraulic and agricultural installations. He confirmed the attribution to this period of some twenty monuments previously considered to be Roman or Byzantine works and proposed to interpret them as expressions of Umayyad sovereignty (Sauvaget 1939, 1967). Their economic role was sometimes questioned (Northedge 1993): they were attributed to a more tribal role, to maintain networks (Grabar et al. 1978: 155–156; Gaube 1979), and some were considered to be caravanserais (Grabar et al. 1978: 29–33) or fortresses (Creswell 1952). Nevertheless, the interpretation of Sauvaget is most widely accepted today.

D. Genequand compiled a systematic inventory of these settlements (around thirty), defined their components, and revised their previous interpretations by taking into account simultaneously the archaeological and historical sources (Genequand 2012). The vast majority of sites consist of a set of various buildings and structures around a main building, typically a palace or a residence with mosques, baths, service buildings, and houses; hydraulic installations, reservoirs, ponds, aqueducts, *qanat*, canals, cisterns, and other hydro-agricultural installations; industrial installations (olive and grape presses, water mills, infrastructure for wool production); and warehouses, stables, and industrial and artisanal installations. Genequand demonstrated the economic function of most of these settlements, which were a source of income for their owners. Other features of these complexes would actually have served a political and diplomatic function as places of contact between the caliphal power and the local elites, in particular the leaders of the powerful tribe of Kalb. But these were aspects developed during the second half of the Umayyad and early Abbasid periods. Recent excavations in al-Bakhra showed the successive transformations of a Late Roman military fort which was turned into a civil establishment. Those of Qasr al-Hayr al-Sharqi established new interpretations for that site, with Genequand arguing that it became a new city (although of reduced size), caliphal or aristocratic, with the intention of being a self-sufficient entity (Genequand 2012: 95–160).

Growth of the rural economy was made possible with the digging of long irrigation canals. In Palmyrena, the arid climate requires the use of such installations to reach profitable outputs and allowed for quasi-autonomous establishments for Umayyad elites (Genequand 2012). The same phenomenon was recently observed in the arid margins of North Syria: impressive buildings, which we interpreted as palatial residences (due to fragments of decorative elements such as polychromatic mosaics, colored glazing, painted plasters, and marble panels) were built in the Umayyad period near the outlet of the irrigation canals set up in the proto-Byzantine period (see later discussion; Rousset 2010). They could be connected with the implementation of land tenure attributed to the Arab elite stemming from the conquest (Genequand and Rousset 2016).

The Evolution of Rural Settlement

Rural farming was not only an aspect of elite complexes. Adjacent to these complexes often subsisted more modest installations, the villages of farmers and breeders. Recent research suggests these activities often continued from the late Roman or Byzantine period into early Islamic times. Nevertheless, as in the case of cities, the idea of a decline of the Syro-Palestinian countryside after the Islamic conquest prevailed for a long time. In the region of the "dead cities" or Limestone Massif of North Syria, west of Aleppo, the late antique villages remained in a very good state of preservation. Thus they were some of the earliest sites to have inventories, records, and interpretations of the archaeological evidence. Settlement, and thus the economy of the campaigns of North Syria, would have relied heavily on the cultivation of olive groves and pastoralism. The settlements of this region were considered to be in a state of crisis or stagnation beginning in the middle of the 6th century (Tate 1992). This moment would have marked the beginning of an agricultural decline, up to the 10th century when military conflicts caused another shift in settlement patterns (a useful synthesis of studies on the Islamic period occupation can be found in Eddé and Sodini 2005).

The incorporation of archaeological methods in the Limestone Massif, at Dehes, led to the revision of these initial hypotheses and showed that this village was prosperous from the 7th to the 10th centuries (Sodini et al. 1980), with around thirty presses working at that time and evidence of technological transformations which increased their production. The great majority of the presses produced wine- or grape juice–based products (Callot 2017). So the culture of the large-scale vineyard was still an important source of income for the inhabitants of the northern Massif in the beginning of the Umayyad period, where the olive tree was just one part of the arboriculture. The abandonment of the presses began during the Abbasid period. The early Islamic presence is also attested in al-Bara, where the archaeological works in the center of the largest late antique establishment of Jabal Zawiya produced a mosque, an Abbasid necropolis, and the transformation of a bathhouse into a *hammam* (Charpentier 2013). Several indications of an early Islamic occupation were also found at Serjilla, notably an unpublished bilingual Syriac/Arabic inscription and a mosque (Tate et al. 2013, vol. 1: 179 and 552–554). Rather than a slow degradation of the rural zones, these studies suggest changes in the types of settlements, with regional variations.

The situation is slightly different in the region of the arid margins of North Syria (east of Hama; see Figure 2.1.3) where sites, most of them built in mudbrick, had never been studied prior to the 1990s (Geyer and Rousset 2011). Geographical and archaeological surveys traced the evolution of the settlement in this region from the earliest human occupation and more specifically from the 5th to the 13th centuries. During the proto-Byzantine period, the region was subject to an overall development, with various sites associated with the specific resources of their local environments (429 sites; Geyer and Rousset 2001 ; Rivoal and Rousset 2019). The most fertile zones (i.e., the basaltic mesa) have been devoted to the cultivation of trees and cereals, especially wheat. Cultivation of wheat on the large central plain was enabled by a system of *qanats*, large hydraulic installations discussed earlier (Rousset 2010). Further east, large pasture lands allowed for herding (Rousset and Duvette 2005). Farms with property enclosures were installed in the eastern wadis, the most convenient place to cultivate barley (Geyer 2000). The pastoralists also benefited from state infrastructure: cisterns, which were essential for survival in such an arid environment (Geyer et al. 2016).

This model of settlement developed in the 7th–8th century with a general decrease in human occupation in the region (149 sites with Umayyad period pottery) and the eventual abandonment of the western agricultural zones. On the other hand, the exploitation of irrigated agricultural zones shifted from a state managed process to one managed by landowning elites, a process also seen in other parts of Bilad al-Sham (Genequand and Rousset 2016). During the Abbasid period, occupation continued to decrease (98 sites) and fundamentally changed in nature. Constructions attributed to this period of time feature new, fortified aspects, such as ditches dig around preexisting buildings (see later discussion). Until the middle of the 10th century and the near-complete abandonment of the region, the nomadic presence shrinks in the same proportion as that of the sedentary population. From the 11th century to the beginning of the 12th, only the caravan stations and fortified strongholds remain settled (10 sites). The populations return in great numbers in the Ayyubid period (230 sites) when agriculture and nomadic herding are once again apparent. It reflects both a certain continuity with earlier settlement patterns but also the development of marginal areas, such as the swampy regions of Amuq

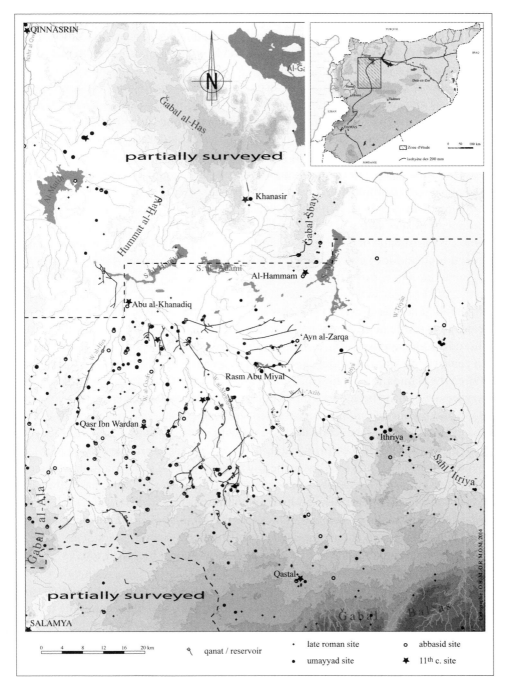

FIGURE 2.1.3 Map of the arid margin area, with late Roman (5th–6th centuries), Umayyad (7th–8th centuries), Abbassid (9th–10th centuries), and 11th-century settlements. With permission from Mission Marges Arides, O. Barge, and M.-O. Rousset.

and Ghab (Eger 2011). In spite of many important surveys in this region, the Orontes basin in the Islamic era still lacks archaeological visibility due to a lack of knowledge of the pottery from the beginning of the period and from the 14th century and due to the poor conservation of sites.

Agricultural development has also been explored in the region north of Raqqa (Bartl 1994) and in the middle Euphrates Valley where huge irrigation channels were built in the Abbasid period, for example the 16 kilometer-long Nahr al-Nil west of Raqqa (Toueir 1990). S. Berthier (2001) analyzed the agricultural development system of the valley of the Euphrates, in the Rahba region, from the irrigation provided by the Nahr Sa'id. This canal, 35 kilometers in length, was dug at the beginning of the Abbasid period and remained in operation until the Mamluk period.

Settlement in Northern Syria immediately before the Crusades is poorly known. Monuments or sites dating to the 11th century are very rare in that area. The best known example is the minaret of the Umayyad mosque of Aleppo, added by the Seljuqid Tutush between 1090 and 1092 and destroyed in 2013. We have previously discussed the case of Qinnasrin, where the settlement was reduced on the Acropolis (Rousset 2013a: 333) and that of its region, with only a dozen caravan station sites identified. In the area of the Balikh Valley, studies of written sources show the fortification of cities in the Seldjuk period as a result of changes in the military balance of power leading up to the Crusades (Heidemann 2005). Altogether, the period from the end of the 10th to the 12th century remains still widely unexplored by archaeology. The geopolitical conflicts between the Hamdanids, Byzantines, and Fatimids; the extensive construction activity associated with the increase in population observed everywhere in the Ayyubid period; and the limited number of surveyed sites from this period make it difficult for archaeological inquiry. The study of medieval settlement patterns of the Syrian coastal region in the 12th and 13th centuries mainly focus on Crusader territories (Major 2016). In the 'Akkar plain area (Bartl 2008), as in the arid margins east of Hama, Mamluk settlement is difficult to evaluate for reasons we have mentioned. In the Orontes River basin, the rural economy was heavily dependent on hydraulic infrastructure for irrigation, such as the *norias* attested since the 5th century and water mills (McPhillips 2016). Mamluk occupation is better known in the major cities or fortifications, such as Damascus, Aleppo, Baalbak, Homs, Hama, Apamea-Qal'at al-Mudiq, and Antioch (Meinecke 1992).

In spite of some recent advances (e.g., the study of the marginal regions), several aspects of rural settlement study still need further investigation. This includes but is not limited to the city–rural relationship, coastal occupation, and settlement in the mountainous regions. These topics have been examined only in rare case studies.

ARCHAEOLOGY OF RELIGION

In Northern Syria, the archaeology of religion from the middle of the 7th century concerns mainly Islam and a single type of building: the mosque. Little is known about the earliest phases of urban mosques that are still in use because restorations and reconstructions make it difficult to evaluate previous phases. This is the case, for example, of the so-called Umayyad mosques of Aleppo (Sauvaget 1941: 75–76; Allen 1983), Hama (Creswell 1959) or Harran (Creswell and Allan 1989: 218–221). Small mosques associated to the Umayyad princely residences are better known (Genequand 2012: 222–223). Several Umayyad congregational mosques have been excavated: at Qasr al-Hayr al-Sharqi (Grabar et al. 1978: 46–51), Resafa (Sack 1996), 'Anjar (Finster 2003: 229–232), and Palmyra (Genequand 2012: 52–66). The irregular layout of the latter is due to the reuse of a Roman building and the need to have the *qibla* wall oriented toward Mecca. They all have a hypostyle prayer hall with three aisles and a courtyard with porticoes. In the cases of Resafa, 'Anjar, and Palmyra, the mosques are situated near the *suq*.

Abbasid mosques in Northern Syria are characterized by their large dimensions and belong to a Mesopotamian tradition, as those of Samarra. The great mosque built in the center of the city of al-Rafiqa in 772 under Caliph al-Mansur measures 112 × 97 meters, and its exterior walls are strengthened by semi-circular buttresses. The prayer hall consisted of three aisles and fifteen naves, with cylindrical piers. Double porticos stand on the three other sides of the courtyard, each with three entrance doors to the mosque (Hagen et al. 2004). The Kharab Sayyar mosque, built in the middle of the 9th century, features a double-aisled prayer hall above cisterns and porticoes on three sides of the courtyard. It is also quite large as it measures about 50 meters in length. It has two entrances, and ablution areas are situated on either side of the eastern entrance (Meyer et al. 2010).

Under Nour al-Din (1146–1174) there was intense architectural activity in the region. Many fortifications were restored, and many buildings were erected or renovated to establish Sunni orthodoxy and for the teaching of the legal and religious sciences. These structures included mosques, madrasas, convents, and mausoleums (Elisseeff 1949–1951). These works are often commemorated by inscriptions, such as the restoration of the great mosque of Raqqa in 1165 (prayer hall façade) or the building of the baked brick minaret of Qal'at Ja'bar. However, very few buildings of this period have been studied archeologically. From the great mosque of Balis only the minaret remains, dated by an inscription to 1210. Apart from this still-unpublished mosque, a district mosque of the first half of the 13th century has been excavated. The first building, 9.25 × 5.50 meters, had two aisles and was then expanded to double its size (Raymond and Paillet 1995: 63–73).

The mosque of Rahba was excavated in the small town at the foot of the citadel (Figure 2.1.4). The original plan, from the beginning of the 13th century, measures 29 × 31 meters and has a rectangular prayer hall with two bays and seven naves, along with a *mihrab* lined with marble plates and a *minbar*. It opens on a courtyard with porticos on three of its sides (west, north, and east) and lateral entrances at their junction with the prayer hall. The minaret occupies the center of the north wall, and a basin is located in the courtyard. In the second half of the 13th century, the mosque was enlarged to the west, increasing its dimensions to 33 × 31 meters (Rousset 1998).

The medieval mosque of Qasr al-Hayr al-Sharqi is located between the two Umayyad enclosures, then connected by walls. It is a Friday mosque, in the central part of the

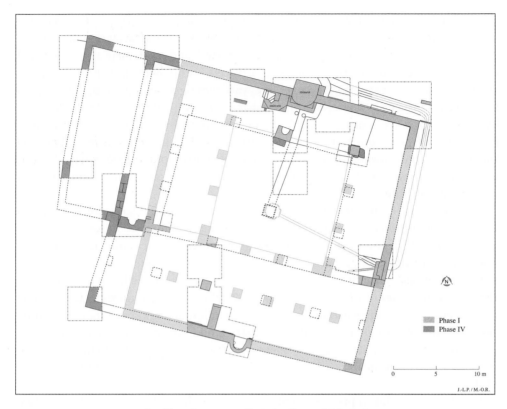

FIGURE 2.1.4 Mosque of Rahba. Courtesy of J.-L. Paillet and M.-O. Rousset.

small fortified town. The building, 21 meters long, has a prayer room with two bays and six naves, with an axial *mihrab* and a *minbar*. A square minaret is located in the northeast corner of the courtyard, and a small necropolis with a collective tomb occupies the eastern part. The building was dated to the second half of the 13th or 14th century (Genequand 2004–2005). There was a reduction of the scale of the Friday mosque between the early Islamic phase (48.5 × 38 meters) and the medieval one, as in al-Bara (Charpentier 2013), Palmyra (42.5 × 26 meters for the Umayyad phase and 20 × 10.5 meters for the medieval mosque dated 1132 inside Baal temple; Wiegand 1932, vol. 2: 83), and Resafa (58 × 41.5 meters for the early Islamic phase mosque and 14 × 8.5 meters for the Ayyubid phase mosque; Sack 1996).

   Excavations of religious buildings other than mosques are very scarce. At Tell Tuneinir on the Khabur, the church of the monastery in Area 9 was built during the caliphate of Harun al-Rashid and remained in use until the Mongol invasions. The mud brick church in Area 3 was also in use until the same time. The site was inhabited by Syriac people, but there was also a small mosque (about 8 × 5 meters) associated with the Ayyubid khan in Area 4, which was decorated with stucco panels (Fuller and Fuller 1994; Fuller and Bastell Fuller 2011).

In the coastal region, the castles of the Crusader period all had at least one religious building. For example at Qal'at Saladin, a Byzantine chapel, a Crusader church, and a Mamluk mosque reflect the religious tendencies of the successive owners of the fortress (Michaudel and Haidar 2010). In cities taken by the Crusaders, the replacement of congregational mosques by cathedrals implies an evident will to show the supremacy of the Christian religion: at Tyre, in Lebanon, only the ablution room of the congregational mosque remained after its destruction by the Crusaders (Rousset 2016b). In the fortifications taken by the Crusaders, the preexisting religious buildings were adapted to the new inhabitants. In the same way as in Marqab during the Mamluk period, the chapel of the Krak des Chevaliers was transformed into a mosque by the addition of a *mihrab* in the eastern wall and by the concealment of mural paintings under monochrome coatings (Zimmer et al. 2013; Mesqui 2018).

For a long time, the funerary archeology of the medieval Middle East has remained synonymous with the study of epigraphic stelea and mausoleums. Rarely are the necropolises excavated; funerary archaeology is still in its infancy. In the medieval Islamic necropolis of Balis, seventy-four graves dated before the destruction of the city by the Mongols in 1260 have been studied (Sakal 2010). They bear witness to burial methods that are typically Muslim: tombs are in vertical pits with lateral chambers along the south side. The bodies rest on the right side, looking south. There are no funeral deposits (precious or rare objects), but there are elements that suggest the use of burial shrouds. Though the position of dorsal decubitus seems to be typical of Christian burials, it is sometimes observed in Muslim cemeteries, especially when the body has shifted from its original position. Three examples of dorsal or ventral decubitus were observed in the Muslim cemetery of the early Mamluk period of Qasr al-Hayr al-Sharqi (out of a total of thirteen skeletons). These were buried in wooden coffins, at least one of which was transportable (Genequand 2004–2005: 279–284). At Qinnasrin, the nine individuals of the small necropolis were obviously Christian, buried on their back in shrouds (Ali et al. 2020).

THE DEFENSE OF THE TERRITORY

Because of its proximity to the Anatolian plateau and its location to the east of the Mediterranean Sea, Northern Syria was one of the regions of contact with the Byzantines and then with the Crusaders. Potential sites for the study of military architecture and the defense of the territory are thus more numerous there than elsewhere and are relevant for our understanding of that region.

Studies of the militarization of the settlements of North Syria from the Abbasid period are relatively new and developed out of several different fields of study. In the Limestone Massif, from the beginning of the 10th century, the agricultural function of villages seems to be superseded by a military function above all (Eddé and Sodini 2005: 467).

However, the vestiges which testify to this are often obliterated by later constructions, and few sites allow for a proper opportunity to investigate these questions. The convent of Qal'at Sem'an, the spiritual Mecca of the Limestone Massif, continued to be occupied, although in a diminished way, up to the 10th–11th century (Sodini and Morrisson 2011). Located not so far from Aleppo on a rocky spur, it was fortified in 966 then in 979/980 and was at the heart of the conflict between the Byzantines and Hamdanids. Its fortifications, contemporaneous to the restoration of the sanctuary and the church, must have had a more symbolic than functional role because they were not able to resist the attacks of 985 and 1017 (Biscop 2006). To the north of the Limestone Massif, the recommencement of the archaeological works at Cyrrhus/Qurus have already produced the discovery of a section of the wall of the citadel dated on the basis of ceramic finds to the beginning of the Islamic period. The wall, stone cut, rests directly on the Hellenistic ashlars (Abdul Massih 2019).

In Cilicia, Asa Eger made a survey of the *thughurs*, early Islamic strongholds known from the texts and well identified on the ground (Eger 2012). He showed that the border must be envisaged as a whole, with a network of villages, and not only as a line of fortresses. The study of these establishments was completed by the excavation of a coastal fortress built in the middle of the 8th century, identified with Hisn al-Tinat (Eger 2010) and the survey of some others in the Amuq Valley (Gerritsen et al. 2008). Recently, the archaeological surveys in the region south of Aleppo led to the fortuitous discovery of two fortifications which may have been connected with the activity of local governors specifically assigned to the defense of the border area with the Byzantines in North Syria: Qinnasrin and Abu al-Khanadiq (Rousset 2020; Rousset 2013). At Qinnasrin, research on the morphology of the town showed that a fortress had been established on the strategic location seated above the region between Aleppo and Salamya. The use of this construction ended with the decline of the city in the 10th century. It then served as a quarry in the medieval period, which led to its almost total disappearance. All that remains is the filling of the interior of the ashlar walls, which were robbed out.

Abu al-Khanadiq was discovered during the "arid margin" survey (Rousset 2013: 80–87). The site is large (1,300 × 800 meters), fenced with a double line of ditches and mudbrick outer walls pierced by four doors. In the inside lays a stone fortress which protected about twenty cisterns, a residence built in mudbrick, and a village which was partially resettled in the Ayyubid period. Massive refuse dumps provide evidence of the temporary establishment of a large camp from the end of the 8th to the beginning of the 9th century. If we keep in mind the residence's strengthening at the same time and the presence of regularly spaced cisterns along routes (Geyer et al. 2016), we can suggest that the entire region was a militarized zone at this time.

At the time of the Crusades, western Syria was occupied by the Latin States (Principality of Antioch, County of Tripoli, and northern part of the Kingdom of Jerusalem). Castles have been analyzed as a testimony to foreign technology and culture, based primarily on an analysis of architectural forms. The main focus of the research was then to determine the respective contribution of the Crusaders and Muslims to the evolution of castle architecture and fighting techniques. The task is difficult since the buildings have been many times occupied, restored, and rebuilt (some since the Byzantine period). But the analysis of the standing remains alone cannot be sufficient to solve the question of the transformation processes of these sites. The typological study of the constitutive elements of the fortifications, coupled with that of the masonry and inscriptions, has, since the 1980s, been supplemented by cleanings and archaeological excavations (Kennedy 2006; Yovitchitch 2011). Those of Qal'at Ja'bar (Tonghini 1998: 25–26) and Rahba citadel (Paillet 1983) are, alas, unpublished. Apart from Marqab (Major 2019) and Masyaf (Hasan 2008), excavated on large tracts, those of Harim (Gelichi 2006), Tell Asharneh (Mason and Dejardine 2006), and Qal'at Saladin (Michaudel and Haidar 2010) are more like soundings.

Though the archeology of fortifications still remains a traditional one, some works and methods have renewed research in this field. At Shayzar, settled from the 10th to the 13th century, the study of cutting techniques and placement of stones and mortars has been essential in establishing a precise chrono-typology of the masonry. Analysis of the materials and building techniques renewed and reinforced the historical and archaeological contributions. J.-C. Bessac (2012) estimated the time necessary to create the different types of bossed facings recorded in Shayzar and emphasized the aesthetic effect desired by the builders. His analysis of the masonry showed the great amount of reuse within the building. His observation of the cut loopholes suggests their prefabrication by a traveling team of specialists and their installation by a much less experienced local team. These conclusions show the value of such a methodological approach, with a practical and economic perspective.

Fortifications are generally divided between urban defenses and castles. But other types exist and appear in the archaeological record, such as towers or fortified caves (Major 2006, 2008). Fortresses associated with city walls are the largest category and show the longest duration of occupation. Some lasted until the Ottoman period in Aleppo, Homs, Hama, Masyaf, Baalbak and Tripoli (Gonnella 2006; King 2002; Pentz 1997; Hasan 2008; Lehmann 2015; Salamé-Sarkis 1960). Recently, several works have concluded that some of the castles were not simply fortifications but real towns, as at Shayzar (Tonghini 2012). Some of the strongholds with a fortress and a lower town have suburbs which expand well beyond the fortified enclosure, as at Marqab, where the nearby town of Valenia (modern-day Banyas) has been reestablished under the protection of the castle in a fortified suburb of about 10 hectares (Major 2019). Recent work at Sayhun has shown the same development on the other side of the ditch, east of the castle (Michaudel and Haidar 2010). In Tilbeshar, there were also two lower towns, not completely covering the entire surface of the Bronze Age walled town (Rousset 2016a).

Conclusion

Due to its position as a crossroads, northern Syria is marked by the amalgamation of the historical and geographical characteristics of its diverse regions through time. Archaeology is uniquely qualified to investigate this melting pot by combining the study of artifacts, architecture, landscapes, and societies in a broad and multidisciplinary approach.

REFERENCES

Abdul Massih, J. 2019. "Développement et urbanisme du secteur méridional de Cyrrhus-Nebi Houri," *Syria*, 95, 397–412.

Ali, R., Rochette, M., and Rousset, M.-O. 2020. "La nécropole médiévale de Qinnasrin," in M.-O. Rousset (ed.), *Chalcis/Qinnasrin. De l'Âge du Bronze à l'époque mamelouke, Qinnasrin II* (Lyons: Maison de l'Orient et de la Méditerranée).

Allen, T. 1983. "Some Pre-Mamluk Portions of the Courtyard Façades of the Great Mosque of Aleppo," *Bulletin d'Etudes Orientales*, 35, 7–12.

Bartl, K. 1994. *Frühislamische Besiedlung im Baliḫ-Tal/Nordsyrien*. Berliner Beiträge zum Vorderen Orient 15 (Berlin: Dietrich Reimer Verlag).

Bartl, K. 2008. "Settlements in Antiquity and the Islamic Periods: The Plain of Akkar and the Middle Orontes region," in K. Bartl and A. Al-Razzaq Moaz (eds.), *Residences, Castles, Settlements: Transformation Processes from Late Antiquity to Early Islam in Bilad al-Sham*. Orient Archäologie 24 (Rahden: M. Leidorf), 517–537.

Berthier, S. (ed.) 2001. *Peuplement rural et aménagements hydroagricoles dans la moyenne vallée de l'Euphrate fin VIIᵉ–XIXᵉ siècle : région de Deir ez Zor—Abu Kemal, Syrie* (Damas: Institut français d'études arabes de Damas).

Bessac, J.-C. 2012. "Observations sur les matériaux et les techniques de construction de la forteresse de Shayzar," in C. Tonghini (ed.), *Shayzar I: The Fortification of the Citadel*. History of Warfare 71 (Leiden, Boston: Brill), 326–389.

Biscop, J.-L. 2006. "The 'Kastron' of Qal'at Sim'an," in H. Kennedy (ed.), *Muslim Military Architecture in Greater Syria: From the Coming of Islam to the Ottoman Period*. History of Warfare 35 (Leiden, Boston: Brill), 75–83.

Bylinski, J. 1999. "Qal'at Shirkuh at Palmyra: A Medieval Fortress Reinterpreted," *Bulletin d'études orientales*, 51, 151–208.

Callot, O. 2017. *Déhès II Les pressoirs*. Bibliothèque Archéologique et Historique 210 (Beyrouth: Presses de l'Ifpo).

Charpentier, G. 2013. "La mosquée du bourg d'El-Bâra en Syrie du Nord," in G. Charpentier and V. Puech (eds.), *Villes et campagnes aux rives de la Méditerranée ancienne. Hommages à Georges Tate*. Topoï, Supplément 12 (Lyons: Maison de l'Orient et de la Méditerranée), 285–309.

Chehab, M. 1993. "On the Identification of 'Anjar ('Ayn al-Jarr) as an Umayyad Foundation," *Muqarnas*, 10, 42–48.

Creswell, K. A. C. 1932 and 1940 (revised 1969). *Early Muslim Architecture* (Cairo: AUC).

Creswell, K. A. C. 1952. "Fortification in Islam Before AD 1250," *Proceedings of the British Academy*, 38, 89–125.

Creswell, K. A. C. 1959. "The Great Mosque of Hama," in R. Ettinghausen (ed.), *Aus der Welt der islamischen Kunst. Festschrift für Ernst Kühnel zum 75. Geburtstag* (Berlin: Gebr. Mann), 48–53.

Creswell, K. A. C., and Allan, J. W. 1989. *A Short Account of Early Muslim Architecture* (Aldershot: Scolar Press).

Daiber, V., and Becker, A. (eds.) 2004. *Raqqa III. Baudenkmäler und Paläste I* (Mainz: Ph. von Zabern).

Dussart, O. 2017. *Qal'at Sem'an. Rapport final. Le verre*. Vol. IV, fasc. 4. Bibliothèque archéologique et historique 208 (Beyrouth: Presses de l'Ifpo).

Eddé, A.-M., and Sodini, J.-P. 2005. "Les villages de Syrie du Nord du VIIe au XIIIe siècle," in J. Lefort, C. Morisson, and J.-P. Sodini (eds.), *Les Villages dans l'Empire byzantin (IVe–XVe siècle)*. Réalités byzantines 11 (Paris: Editions Lethielleux), 465–483.

Eger, A. 2010. "Hisn al-Tinat on the Islamic-Byzantine Frontier: Synthesis and the 2005–2008 Survey and Excavation on the Cilician Plain (Turkey)," *BASOR,* 357, 49–76.

Eger, A. 2011. "The Swamps of Home: Marsh Formation and Settlement in the Early Medieval Near East," *Journal of Near Eastern Studies,* 70, 55–79.

Eger, A. 2012. *The Spaces Between the Teeth: A Gazetteer of Towns on the Islamic-Byzantine Frontier* (Istanbul: Ege Yayinlari).

Eger, A. 2013. "(Re)Mapping Medieval Antioch: Urban Transformations from the Early Islamic to the Middle Byzantine Periods," *Dumbarton Oaks Papers,* 67, 95–134.

Elisséeff, N. 1949–1951. "Les monuments de Nūr ad-Dīn," *Bulletin d'études orientales,* 13, 5–43.

Falb, C. 2012. *Die unverzierte frühislamische Keramik aus Kharab Sayyar, Nordostsyrien.* Ausgrabungen Kharab Sayyar 1. (Wiesbaden: Reichert).

Finster, B. 2003. "Researches in 'Anjar I. Preliminary Report on the Architecture of 'Anjar," *Baal,* 7, 209–244.

Finster, B. 2008. "Anjar: spätantik oder frühislamisch?," in K. Bartl and A. Al-Razzaq Moaz (eds.), *Residences, Castles, Settlements: Transformation Processes from Late Antiquity to Early Islam in Bilad al-Sham.* Orient Archäologie 24 (Rahden: M. Leidorf), 229–242.

Foss, C. 1997. "Syria in Transition, A. D. 550–750: An Archaeological Approach," *Dumbarton Oaks Papers,* 51, 189–269.

Foy, D. 2000. "Un atelier de verrier à Beyrouth au début de la conquête islamique," *Syria,* 77, 239–90.

Foy, D. 2012. "Le verre d'al-Hadir," in M.-O. Rousset (ed.), *Al-Hadir. Etude archéologique d'un hameau de Qinnasrin (Syrie du Nord, VIIe–XIIe siècles).* Travaux de la Maison de l'Orient et de la Méditerranée 59. Recherches archéologiques (Lyon: MOM), 129–138.

Fuller, M., and Bastell Fuller, N. 2011. *Tell Tuneinir Syria, St. Louis Archaeological Expeditions,* accessed at http://users.stlcc.edu/mfuller/tuneinir/.

Fuller, M., and Fuller, N. 1994. "A Medieval Church in Mesopotamia," *Biblical Archaeologist,* 57, 38–45.

Gaube, H. 1979. "Die syrischen Wüstenschlösser. Einige wirtschaftliche und politische Gesichtspunkte zu ihrer Entstehung," *ZDPV,* 95, 182–209.

Gelichi, S. 2006. "The Citadel of Harim," in H. Kennedy (ed.), *Muslim Military Architecture in Greater Syria: From the Coming of Islam to the Ottoman Period.* History of Warfare 35 (Leiden, Boston: Brill), 184–200.

Genequand, D. 2004–2005. "Nouvelles recherches à Qasr al-Hayr al-Sharqi: la mosquée ayyoubide et la nécropole," *Annales Archéologiques Arabes Syriennes,* 47–48, 271–293.

Genequand, D. 2012. *Les établissements des élites omeyyades en Palmyrène et au Proche-Orient.* Bibliothèque archéologique et historique 200 (Beyrouth: Institut français du Proche-Orient).

Genequand, D., Amoroso, H., Haldemann, M., Hull, D., Kühn, M., and Studer, J. 2008. "Rapport préliminaire des travaux de la mission archéologqie syro-suisse à Qasr al-Hayr al-Sharqi en 2007," *Schweizerisch-Liechtensteinische Stiftung für Archäologische Forschungen im Ausland (SLSA/FSLA/SLFA)—Jahresbericht 2007,* 141–178.

Genequand, D., de Reynier, C., and Kühn, M. 2006. "Rapport préliminaire des travaux de la mission archéologique syro-suisse à Qasr al-Hayr al-Sharqi (Syrie) en 2005," *Schweizerisch-Liechtensteinische Stiftung für Archäologische Forschungen im Ausland (SLSA/FSLA/SLFA)—Jahresbericht 2005,* 161–203.

Genequand, D., and Rousset, M.-O. 2016. "Résidences aristocratiques protobyzantines et omeyyades des Marges arides du nord de la Syrie," in M.-O. Rousset, B. Geyer, and P.-L. Gatier (eds.), *Habitat et environnement. Prospections dans les Marges arides de la Syrie du Nord* (Lyons: Travaux de la Maison de l'Orient), 207–265.

Gerritsen, F., de Giorgi, A., Eger, A., Özbal, R., and Vorderstrasse, T. 2008. "Settlement and Landscape Transformations in the Amuq Valley, Hatay. A Long-Term Perspective," *Anatolica*, 34, 241–314.

Geyer, B. 2000. "Des fermes byzantines aux palais omayyades, ou l'ingénieuse mise en valeur des plaines steppiques de Chalcidique," in L. Nordiguian and J.-F. Salles (eds.), *Aux origines de l'archéologie aérienne, A. Poidebard (1878–1955)* (Beyrouth: Presses de l'USJ), 109–122.

Geyer, B., and Rousset, M.-O. 2001. "Les steppes arides de la Syrie du Nord à l'époque byzantine ou 'la ruée vers l'est,'" in B. Geyer (ed.), *Conquête de la steppe et appropriation des terres sur les marges arides du Croissant fertile*. TMO 36 (Lyons: Maison de l'Orient), 111–121.

Geyer, B., and Rousset, M.-O. 2011. "Déterminants géoarchéologiques du peuplement rural dans les Marges arides de Syrie du Nord aux VIIe–IXe siècles," in A. Borrut, M. Debié, A. Papaconstantinou, D. Pieri, and J.-P. Soldine (eds.), *Le Proche-Orient de Justinien Aux Abbassides: Peuplement et Dynamiques Spatiales*. Bibliothèque de l'Antiquité Tardive 19 (Turnhout: Brepols), 77–92.

Geyer, B., Rousset, M.-O., and Besançon, J. 2016. "Les citernes pluviales des steppes syriennes, éléments de la conquête d'une marge aride," in M.-O. Rousset, B. Geyer, and P.-L. Gatier (eds.), *Habitat et environnement. Prospections dans les Marges arides de la Syrie du Nord* (Lyons: Travaux de la Maison de l'Orient), 45–88.

Gonnella, J. 1999. "Eine neue zangidisch-aiyûbidische Keramikgruppe aus Aleppo," *Damaszener Mitteilungen*, 11, 163–177.

Gonnella, J. 2006. "The Citadel of Aleppo: Recent Studies," in H. Kennedy (ed.), *Muslim Military Architecture in Greater Syria: From the Coming of Islam to the Ottoman Period*. History of Warfare 35 (Leiden, Boston: Brill), 165–175.

Grabar, O., Holod, R., Knustad, J., and Trousdale, W. 1978. *City in the Desert: Qasr al-Hayr East* (Cambridge, MA: Harvard University Press).

Gussone, M., and Müller-Wiener, M. 2012. "Resafa-Rusafat Hisham, Syria. 'Long-Term Survival' of an Umayyad Residence: First Results of the Extended Surface Survey," in R. Matthews and J. Curtis (eds.), *Proceedings of the 7th ICAANE. Volume 2* (Wiesbaden: Harrassowitz), 569–584.

Haase, C.-P. 2006. "The Excavations at Madīnat al-Fār/ Ḥiṣn Maslama on the Balikh Road," in H. Kennedy (ed.), *Muslim Military Architecture in Greater Syria: From the Coming of Islam to the Ottoman Period*. History of Warfare 35 (Leiden, Boston: Brill), 54–60.

Hagen, L., al-Hassoun, M., and Meinecke, M. 2004. "Die grosse Moschee von ar-Rāfiqa," in V. Daiber and A. Becker (eds.), *Raqqa III. Baudenkmäler und Paläste I* (Mainz: Ph. von Zabern), 25–39.

Haidar-Vela, N. 2017. "New insights from the 7th century ceramics in Halabiyye-Zenobia, Syria," in D. Dixneuf (ed.), *LRCW 5: Late Roman Coarse Wares, Cooking Wares and Amphorae in the Mediterranean: Archaeology and Archaeometry*, Études Alexandrines 43 (Alexandrie: Centre d'Etudes Alexandrines), 759–777.

Hakimian, S., and Salamé-Sarkis, H. 1988. "Céramiques médiévales trouvées dans une citerne à Tell 'Arqa," *Syria*, 65, 1–61.

Hasan, H. 2008. *The Citadel of Masyaf* (Geneva: Aga Khan Trust for Culture).

Heidemann, S. 2005. "Numayrid Ar-Raqqa Archaeological and Historical Evidence for a 'Dimorphic State' in the Bedouin Dominated Fringes of the Fāṭimid Empire," in U. Vermeulen and J. van Steenbergen (eds.), *Egypt and Syria in the Fatimid, Ayyubid and Mamluk Eras IV* (Leuven: Peeters), 85–110.

Heidemann, S. 2006a. "The Citadel of al-Raqqa and Fortifications in the Middle Euphrates Area," in H. Kennedy (ed.), *Muslim Military Architecture in Greater Syria: From the Coming of Islam to the Ottoman Period*. History of Warfare 35 (Leiden, Boston: Brill), 122–150.

Heidemann, S. 2006b. "The History of the Industrial and Commercial Area of 'Abbāsid Al-Raqqa, called Al-Raqqa Al-Muḥtariqa," *BSOAS*, 69, 32–52.

Heidemann, S. 2008. "Settlement Patterns, Economic Development and Archaeological Coin Finds in Bilad al-Sham: The Case of the Diyar Mudar: The Process of Transformation from the 6th to the 10th Century A.D," in K. Bartl and A. al-Razzaq Moaz (eds.), *Residences, Castles, Settlements : Transformation Processes from Late Antiquity to Early Islam in Bilad al-Sham*. Orient Archäologie 24 (Rahden: M. Leidorf), 493–516.

Heidemann, S., and Becker, A. 2003. *Ar-Raqqa II. Die Islamische Stadt* (Mainz: Ph. von Zabern).

Herzfeld, E. 1921. "Mshatta, Hira und Badiya, die Mittelländer des Islam und ihre Baukunst," *Jahrbuch der Preussischen Kunstsammlungen, 42*,104–146.

Hillenbrand, R. 1985. "Eastern Islamic Influences in Syria: Raqqa and Qal'at Ja'bar in the Later 12th century," in J. Raby (ed.), *The Art of Syria and the Jazira 1100–1250*. Oxford Studies in Islamic Art no. 1 (Oxford: Oxford University Press), 27–48.

Jenkins-Madina, M. 2006. *Raqqa Revisited: Ceramics of Ayyubid Syria* (New York: Metropolitan Museum of Art).

Kennedy, H. 1985. "From *Polis* to *Madina*: Urban Change in Late Antique and Early Islamic Syria," *Past and Present, 106*, 3–27.

Kennedy, H. (ed.) 2006. *Muslim Military Architecture in Greater Syria: From the Coming of Islam to the Ottoman Period*. History of Warfare 35 (Leiden, Boston: Brill).

Kenrick, P.M. 2013. "Pottery Other Than Transport Amphorae," in W. Aylward (ed.), *Excavations at Zeugma: Conducted by Oxford Archaeology* (Los Altos, California: The Packard Humanities Institute), 1–81.

Khalil, I., and Henderson, J. 2011. "An Interim Report on New Evidence for Early Islamic Glass Production at al-Raqqa, Northern Syria," *Journal of Glass Studies, 53*, 237–242.

King, G. R. 2002. "Archaeological Fieldwork at the Citadel of Homs, Syria: 1995–1999," *Levant, 34*, 39–58.

Knötzele, P. 2006. "Die Gefäßkeramik der Stadtgrabung 1997–1999," in F. Bloch, V. Daiber, and P. Knötzele (eds.), *Studien zur spätantiken und islamischen Keramik: Hirbat al-Minya, Baalbek, Resafa*. Orient-Archäologie 18 (Rahden: M. Leidorf), 167–268.

Konrad, M. 2001. *Resafa V. Der spätrömische Limes in Syrien. Archäologische Untersuchungen an den Grenzkastellen von Sura, Tetrapyrgium, Cholle und in Resafa* (Mainz: Ph. von Zabern).

Lehmann, H. 2015. *Baalbek in nachantiker Zeit : Untersuchungen zur Stadtbaugeschichte vom 5. bis zum 20. Jahrhundert*. Orient-Archäologie 35 (Rahden: Leidorf).

Leisten, T. 1999–2000. "II. Balis. Preliminary report on the Campaign 1996 & 1998," *Berytus, 44*, 35–57.

Lloyd, S., and Brice, W. 1951. "Harran," *Anatolian Studies, 1*, 77–111.

Logar, N. 1991. "Katalog der Keramikfunde aus dem Wasserverteiler," *Damaszener Mitteilungen, 5*, 147–168.

Logar, N. 1992. "Die Kleinfunde aus dem Westhofbereich der Großen Basilika von Resafa," *Damaszener Mitteilungen, 6*, 417–477.

Logar, N. 1995. "Die Keramik des mittelalterlichen Wohnkomplexes in Resafa," *Damaszener Mitteilungen*, 8, 269–292.

Logar, N. 1996. "Die Keramik und andere Kleinfunde," in D. Sack (ed.), *Die Große Moschee von Resafa-Rusafat Hisam* (Mainz: Ph. von Zabern), 77–110.

Loyet, M. 2000. "The Potential for Within-Site Variation of Faunal Remains: A Case Study from the Islamic Period Urban Center of Tell Tuneinir, Syria," *BASOR*, 320, 23–48.

Major, B. 2006. "Medieval Cave Fortifications of the Upper Orontes Valley (A Preliminary Report)," in H. Kennedy (ed.), *Muslim Military Architecture in Greater Syria: From the Coming of Islam to the Ottoman Period*. History of Warfare 35 (Leiden, Boston: Brill), 251–268.

Major, B. 2008. "Muslim Towers in the Medieval Syrian Countryside," in K. K. Hulster and J. van Steenbergen (eds.), *Continuity and Change in the Realms of Islam*. Orientalia Lovaniensia Annalecta 171 (Leuven: Peeters), 423–438.

Major, B. 2019. "Constructing a Medieval Fortification in Syria: Margat between 1187 and 1285," in P. W. Edbury, D. Edbury, B. Major (dir.), Bridge of civilizations: the Near East and Europe c. 1100–1300 (Oxford: Archaeopress), 1–22.

Major, B. 2016. *Medieval Rural Settlements in the Syrian Coastal Region (12th and 13th Centuries)* (Oxford: Archaeopress).

Mason, R. 2004. *Shine Like the Sun, Lustre-painted and Associated Pottery from the Medieval Middle East*. Bibliotheca Iranica. Islamic art and architecture series 12 (Costa Mesa: Mazda Publishers).

Mason, R., and Dejardine, É. 2006. "Preliminary Considerations of Tell 'Acharneh in the Medieval Period and Later," in M. Fortin (ed.), *Tell 'Acharneh 1998–2004: rapports préliminaires sur les campagnes de fouilles et saison d'études*. Subartu 18 (Turnhout: Brepols), 215–223.

McPhillips, S. 2016. "Harnessing Hydraulic Power in Ottoman Syria: Water Mills and the Rural Economy of the Upper Orontes Valley," in S. McPhillips and P. Wordsworth (eds.), *Landscapes of the Islamic World. Archaeology, History, and Ethnography* (Philadelphia: University of Pennsylvania Press), 143–166.

Meinecke, M. 1992. *Die mamlukische Architektur in Ägypten und Syrien (648/1250 bis 923/1517)* (Glückstadt: J. J. Agustin GmbH).

Mesqui, J. 2018. *Le Crac des Chevaliers (Syrie): histoire et architecture* (Paris: Académie des inscriptions et belles-lettres).

Meyer, J.-W. 2008. "Die deutsch-syrischen Ausgrabungen in Kharab Sayyar/Nordostsyrien," in K. Bartl and A. al-Razzaq Moaz (eds.), *Residences, Castles, Settlements: Transformation Processes from Late Antiquity to Early Islam in Bilad al-Sham*. Orient Archäologie 24 (Rahden: M. Leidorf), 419–432.

Meyer, J.-W., Mussa, I., and Würz, M. 2010. "Report About the 11th Excavation Campaign 2008 at Kharab Sayyar," *Chronique archéologique en Syrie*, 4, 321–327.

Michaudel, B., and Haidar, J. 2010. "Le château de Saladin (Saône/Sahyun) et son territoire (vallée du Nahr al-Kabîr al-Shamâlî) 2008," *Chronique archéologique en Syrie*, 4, 329–338.

Miglus, P.(ed.) 1999. *Ar-Raqqa I. Die frühislamische Keramik von Tall Aswad* (Mainz: Ph. von Zabern).

Mulder, S. 2014. "A Survey and Typology of Islamic Molded Ware (9th-13th centuries) based on the Discovery of A Potter's Workshop at Medieval Balis, Syria," *Journal of Islamic Archaeology*, 1, 2, 143–192, accessed at https://doi.org/10.1558/jia.v1i2.21864.

Northedge, A. 1993. "Les omeyyades et leurs residences," in Institut du Monde Arabe (ed.), *Syrie, mémoire et civilisation* (Paris: Flammarion), 374–377.

Otto-Dorn, K. 1957. "Grabung im umayyadischen Rusafa," *Ars Orientalis,* 2, 119–133.

Paillet, J.-L. 1983. *Le château de Raḥba, étude d'architecture militaire islamique médiévale* (Unpublished diss., Université de Lyon 2).

Pentz, P. 1997. *Hama: fouilles et recherches de la Fondation Carlsberg 1931–1938. IV. 1, The Medieval Citadel and Its Architecture* (Copenhague: Nationalmuseet).

Ploug, G., Oldenburg, E., Hammershaimb, E., and Riis, P. J. 1969. *Hama: fouilles et recherches de la Fondation Carlsberg, 1931–1938. IV.3, Les petits objets médiévaux sauf les verreries et poteries* (Copenhague: Nationalmuseet).

Porter, V., and Watson, O. 1987. "Tell Minis' Wares," in J. W. Allan and C. Roberts (eds.), *Syria and Iran: Three Studies in Medieval Ceramics.* Oxford Studies in Islamic Art 4 (Oxford: Oxford University Press), 175–191.

Ramsay, J., and Eger, A. A. 2015. "Analysis of Archaeobotanical Material from the Tüpraş Field Project of the Kinet Höyük Excavations, Turkey," *Journal of Islamic Archaeology,* 2, 1, 35–50, accessed at https://doi.org/10.1558/jia.v2i1.26939.

Raymond, A., and Paillet, J.-L. 1995. *Bālis II, Histoire de Bālis et fouilles des îlots I et II* (Damas: IFEAD).

Rice, D. S. 1952. "Medieval Ḥarrān: Studies on Its Topography and Monuments, I," *Anatolian Studies,* 2, 36–84.

Riis, P. J., and Poulsen, V. (eds.) 1957. *Hama: fouilles et recherches de la Fondation Carlsberg 1931–1938. IV. 2, Les verreries et poteries médiévales* (Copenhague: Nationalmuseet).

Rivoal, M. and Rousset, M.-O. 2019. "Les aménagements agricoles dans les Marges arides de Syrie du Nord (5e–10e siècles)," in A. Delattre, M. Legendre and P. Sijpesteijn (eds.), *Authority and Control in the Countryside from Antiquity to Islam in the Mediterranean and Near East (6th–10th Century),* Leiden Studies in Islam and Society 9 (Leiden, Boston: Brill), 210–264.

Rousset, M.-O. 1997. *Contribution à l'étude de la céramique islamique: analyse du matériel archéologique de Rahba-Mayadin (Syrie, Vallée de l'Euphrate)* (PhD diss., Université de Lyon 2), accessed at http://tel.archives-ouvertes.fr/tel-00280710/fr/.

Rousset, M.-O. 1998. "La mosquée de Rahba," *Annales Islamologiques,* 32, 177–217.

Rousset, M.-O. 2010. "Qanats de la steppe syrienne," in P.-L. Gatier, B. Geyer, and M.-O. Rousset (eds.), *Entre nomades et sédentaires. Propections en Syrie du Nord et en Jordanie du Sud.* TMO 55, Conquête de la steppe 3 (Lyons: Maison de l'Orient et de la Méditerranée), 241–270.

Rousset, M.-O. (ed.) 2012. *Al-Hadir. Etude archéologique d'un hameau de Qinnasrin (Syrie du Nord, VIIe–XIIe siècles).* Travaux de la Maison de l'Orient et de la Méditerranée 59 (Lyons: Maison de l'Orient et de la Méditerranée).

Rousset, M.-O. 2013. "Traces of the Banu Salih in the Syrian Steppe? The Fortresses of Qinnasrin and Abu al-Khanadiq," *Levant,* 45, 69–95.

Rousset, M.-O. 2016a. "La forteresse médiévale de Tilbeshar (Tell Bashir, Turbessel)," in B. Perello and A. Tenu (eds.), *Parcours d'Orient. Recueil de textes offert à Christine Kepinski* (Oxford: Archaeopress), 219–228.

Rousset, M.-O. 2016b. "Latrines et espaces d'ablution dans les mosquées du Proche-Orient médiéval: l'enseignement des fouilles de Tyr," *Médiévales,* 70, 105–128.

Rousset, M.-O. 2017. "De l'hypothèse fatimide à l'évidence seldjoukide: des traces matérielles des xie–xiie siècles à Raḥba-Mayādīn (Syrie)," *BEO,* 66: 197–226.

Rousset, M.-O. (ed.) 2020. *Chalcis/Qinnasrin. De l'âge du Bronze à l'époque mamelouke,* Archéologie(s) 5, Qinnasrin II (Lyons: Maison de l'Orient et de la Méditerranée).

Rousset, M.-O., and Duvette, C. 2005. "L'élevage dans la steppe à l'époque byzantine: indices archéologiques," J. Lefort, C. Morisson, and J.-P. Sodini (eds.), *Les Villages dans l'Empire byzantin (IVe–XVe siècle)*. Réalités byzantines 11 (Paris: Editions Lethielleux), 485–494.

Sack, D. 1996. *Die Große Moschee von Resafa-Rusafat Hisam*. Resafa 4 (Mainz: Ph. von Zabern).

Sack, D. 2008. "Resafa – Sergiupolis/Rusafat Hisham – neue Forschungsansätze," in K. Bartl and A. al-Razzaq Moaz (eds.), *Residences, Castles, Settlements: Transformation Processes from Late Antiquity to Early Islam in Bilad al-Sham*. Orient Archäologie 24 (Rahden: M. Leidorf), 31–44.

Sack, D., Becker, H., Stephani, M. and Chouker, F. 2004. "Resafa-Umland. Archäologische Geländebegehungen, geophysikalische Untersuchungen und digitale Geländemodelle zur Prospektion in Resafa-Rusāfat Hišām. Bericht über die Kampagnen 1997-2001," *Damaszener Mitteilungen*, 14, 207–232.

Sakal, F. 2010. "Graves and Grave Goods of the Late Roman and Medieval Cemeteries," in U. Finkbeiner and F. Sakal (eds.), *Emar After the Closure of the Tabqa Dam: The Syrian-German excavations 1996–2002. Volume 1, Late Roman and Medieval Cemeteries and Environmental Studies*. Subartu 25 (Turnhout: Brepols), 3–31.

Salamé-Sarkis, H. 1960. *Contribution à l'histoire de Tripoli et de sa région à l'époque des Croisades. Problèmes d'histoire, d'architecture et de céramique*. Bibliothèque Archéologique et Historique 106 (Paris: Geuthner).

Saliby, N. 2004. "Les fouilles du palais B 1950–1952," "Les fouilles du palais C 1953," and "Les fouilles du palais D 1954 et 1958," in V. Daiber and A. Becker (eds.), *Raqqa III, Baudenkmäler und Paläste I* (Mainz: Ph. von Zabern), 77–130.

Sarre, F., and Herzfeld, E. 1911–1920. *Archäologische Reise im Euphrat und Tigris-Gebiet*. 4 vols. (Berlin: Reimer).

Sauvaget, J. 1931. "Inscriptions arabes du Temple de Bêl à Palmyre," *Syria*, 12, 143–153.

Sauvaget, J. 1934. "Le plan de Laodicée-sur-mer," *Bulletin d'Etudes Orientales*, 4, 81–114.

Sauvaget, J. 1939. "Remarques sur les monuments omeyyades, I: Châteaux de Syrie," *Journal Asiatique*, 231, 1–59.

Sauvaget, J. 1941. *Alep. Essai sur le développement d'une grande ville syrienne, des origines au milieu du XIXe siècle*. Bibliothèque archéologique et historique 36 (Paris: Librairie Orientaliste Geuthner).

Sauvaget, J. 1967. "Châteaux umayyades de Syrie. Contribution à l'étude de la colonisation arabe aux Ier et IIe siècles de l'Hégire," *Revue des Etudes Islamiques*, 35, 1–52.

Schlumberger, D. 1986. *Qasr el-Heir el-Gharbi*. Bibliothèque archéologique et historique 120 (Paris: Librairie Orientaliste Geuthner).

Seyrig, H. 1931. "Antiquités syriennes. 1. Les jardins de Kasr el-Heir," *Syria*, 12, 316–325.

Seyrig, H. 1934. "Antiquités syriennes. Retour aux jardins de Kasr el-Heir," *Syria*, 15, 24–32.

Shaddoud, I., 2015. "Production de poterie chez les Nizarites de Syrie: l'atelier de Massyaf (milieu XIIe-premier tiers du XIVe siècle)," in M. J. Gonçalves, S. Gómez Martínez (ed.), *Actas do X Congresso Internacional A Cerâmica Medieval no Mediterrâneo*. (Silves; Mértola: Câmara Municipal de Silves, Campo Arqueológico de Mértola), 525–533.

Siegel, U. 2017. *Die Residenz des Kalifen Hārūn Ar-Rašīd in Ar-Raqqa/Ar-Rāfiqa (Syrien)*. Raqqa IV (Berlin, Boston: de Gruyter).

Sodini, J.-P., Bavant, B., Bavant, S., Biscop, J.-L., Orssaud, D., Tate, G., Will, E., Morrisson, C., and Poplin, F. 1980. *Déhès (Syrie du nord): campagnes I–III (1976–1978): recherches sur l'habitat rural*. Institut français d'archéologie du Proche-Orient, Hors série 15 (Paris: Geuthner).

Sodini, J.-P., and Morrisson, C. 2011. "Niveaux d'occupation et de fréquentation d'un site de pèlerinage: Saint-Syméon des Byzantins aux califes," in A. Borrut, M. Debié, A. Papaconstantinou, D. Pieri, and J.-P. Sodini (eds.), *Le Proche-Orient de Justinien Aux Abbassides: Peuplement et Dynamiques Spatiales*. Bibliothèque de l'Antiquité Tardive 19 (Turnhout: Brepols), 123–138.

Studer, J., Genequand, D., and Rousset, M.-O. 2013. "Environmental Influence on Animal Exploitation and Meat Consumption During the Early Islamic Period in Syria. A Case Study from Qasr al-Hayr al-Sharqi and al-Hadir," in B. de Cupere, V. Linseele, and S. Hamilton-Dyer (eds.), *Archaeozoology of the Near East X*. Ancient Near Eastern Studies 44 (Leuven: Peeters), 265–282.

Tate, G. 1992. *Les Campagnes de la Syrie du nord du IIe au VIIe siècle: un exemple d'expansion démographique et économique à la fin de l'Antiquité*. Bibliothèque archéologique et historique 133 (Paris: Librairie Orientaliste Geuthner).

Tate, G., Abdulkarim, M., Charpentier, G., Duvette, C., and Piaton, C. 2013. *Sergilla, village d'Apamène. Tome 1. Une architecture de pierre*. Bibliothèque archéologique et historique 203 (Beyrouth: Presses de l'Ifpo).

Tonghini, C. 1995. "A New Islamic Pottery Phase in Syria: Tell Shahin," *Levant*, 27, 197–207.

Tonghini, C. 1998. *Qalat Jabar Pottery: A Study of a Syrian Fortified Site of the Late 11th–14th Centuries*. British Academy Monographs in Archaeology 11 (New York: Oxford University Press).

Tonghini, C. 2012. *Shayzar I: The Fortification of the Citadel*. History of Warfare 71 (Leiden, Boston: Brill).

Tonghini, C. 2016. "Şanliurfa Kalesi: stratigrafik analizlerin ilk sonuçlari," *Arastirma Sonuclari Toplantisi*, 33, 427–442.

Tonghini, C., and Henderson, J. 1998. "An Eleventh-Century Pottery Production Workshop at al-Raqqa. Preliminary Report," *Levant*, 30, 113–127.

Toueir, K. 1985. "Der Qasr al-Banāt in ar-Raqqa. Ausgrabung, Rekonstruktion und Wiederaufbau (1977–1982)," *Damaszener Mitteilungen*, 2, 297–319.

Toueir, K 1990. "Le Nahr el-Nil entre Raqqa et Heraqleh," in B. Geyer (ed.), *Techniques et pratiques hydro-agricoles traditionnelles en domaine irrigué. Actes du Colloque de Damas* (Paris: Geuthner), 217–227.

Toueir, K., Chmelnizkij, D., and Becker, U. 2004. "Hiraqla," in V. Daiber and A. Becker (eds.), *Raqqa III, Baudenkmäler und Paläste I* (Mainz: Ph. von Zabern), 135–156.

van Berchem, M., and Fatio, E. 1914–1915. *Voyage en Syrie*. MIFAO 37 and 38 (Cairo: Ifao).

van Staëvel, J.-P. 2012. "Débats autour de la 'ville musulmane'. Évolution des paysages urbains et de l'économie," in T. Bianquis, P. Guichard, and M. Tillier (eds.), *Les débuts du monde musulman (VIIe–Xe siècle): de Muhammad aux dynasties autonomes*. Nouvelle Clio (Paris: Presses universitaires de France), 531–546.

Vezzoli, V. 2016. *La céramique islamique d'Apamée de Syrie. Histoire de l'occupation du Quartier Nord-Est du XIIe au XIVe siècle*. Fouilles d'Apamée de Syrie 3 (Bruxelles: Académie royale de Belgique).

Vokaer, A. 2011. *La Brittle Ware en Syrie: production et diffusion d'une céramique culinaire de l'époque hellénistique à l'époque omeyyade* (Bruxelles: Académie royale de Belgique).

Waksman, Y. 2011. "Ceramics of the 'Serçe Limanı Type' and Fatimid Pottery Production in Beirut," *Levant*, 43, 201–212.

Westphalen, S. 2000. "Resafa. Bericht über die Ausgrabungen 1997 bis 1999," *Damaszener Mitteilungen*, 12, 325–366.

Wiegand, T. (ed.) 1932. *Palmyra. Ergebnisse der Expeditionen von 1902 und 1917*, 2 vols. (Berlin: H. Keller).

Wirth, E. 2000. *Die orientalische Stadt im islamischen Vorderasien und Nordafrika: städtische Bausubstanz und räumliche Ordnung, Wirtschaftsleben und soziale Organisation* (Mainz: Ph. von Zabern).

Würz, M. 2014. *Architektur und Struktur des nordöstlichen Stadtgebietes von Kharab Sayyar, Nordsyrien*. Ausgrabungen Kharab Sayyar 1 (Wiesbaden: Reichert).

Würz, M. 2018. *Organizing an Urban Way of Life in the Steppe: Water, Agriculture, Townscape and Economy in the Early Islamic Town of Kharab Sayyar*. Ausgrabungen Kharab Sayyar 3 (Wiesbaden: Reichert).

Yovitchitch, C. 2011. *Forteresses du Proche-Orient* (Paris: Presses de l'Université Paris-Sorbonne).

Zimmer, J., Meyer, W., and Boscardin, L. 2013. *Krak des Chevaliers en Syrie: Archéologie du sol et du bâti 2003–2007* (Braubach: Deutsche Burgenvereinigung).

CHAPTER 2.2

··

SOUTHERN SYRIA

··

BETHANY J. WALKER

INTRODUCTION

Geography and Environment

A region that is in many ways a cultural and historical unit, Southern Syria (the southern portion of Bilād al-Shām) includes the city of Damascus (the cultural, economic, and political hub) and those regions south to the Gulf of Aqaba, Gaza, and the Egyptian border and from the Mediterranean in the west to the eastern steppe (*bādiyya*) and Iraqi border (Figure 2.2.1).[1] These are the modern political boundaries of southern Syria, modern Jordan and Israel, and the Palestinian territories. The climate of much of the region can be described as "Mediterranean," with evaporation rates well below that of semi-arid regions; the remainder consists of steppe (the *bādiyya*, the Negev) and desert (southern Jordan).

The natural environment is distinguished by its largely dry-farmed agricultural regime and its fractured landscape. Groundwater—the most reliable source of water in the region—is released through the springs which feed the small-scale, runoff irrigation systems upon which most local agriculture depends. Household cisterns, constructed and maintained locally, capture winter rains and have traditionally been the method of harvesting and storing water. In urban centers like Damascus and Abila, large urban irrigation systems have historically transported water to suburban gardens and fields, and subterranean aqueducts (*qanāt*s) constructed in the Roman, Byzantine, and Early Islamic periods channeled water from springs to the cities (Walker 2017; for the spread

---

[1] While the Syrian territories from Damascus south are included, this chapter will largely concentrate on Palestine and the Transjordan. The Syrian conflict, which began in 2011 in the border town of Darʿaa as a local expression of the Arab Spring protests, has put an end to most fieldwork in this area since then.

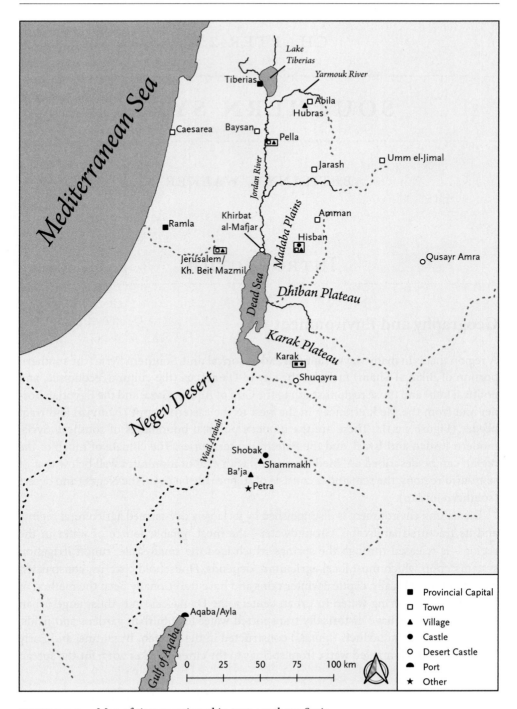

FIGURE 2.2.1 Map of sites mentioned in text, southern Syria.

Courtesy of Luigi Pinchetti, University of Bonn.

of the *qanāt* system in Early Islamic times, see Avni 2019). Water systems—sources, drainage, harvesting methods—could differ significantly from one region to another, as they do now. Because annual rainfall throughout many regions of Syria was, and is, unpredictable, agriculture here was, and continues to be, highly susceptible to drought, with an annual wheat risk in many areas of 50 percent.[2] The region is equally vulnerable to heavy rainfall, which leads to flooding and erosion.[3] Rainfall is highly variable from year to year and from one locality to the next, ranging from below the 200 millimeters needed annual for dry-fed agriculture (the threshold for wheat cultivation) to as high as 700 millimeters annually in mountainous areas. The result is a complex configuration of localized eco-zones, with significant differences in frequency, quantity, and quality of rainfall and in soil quality.

Southern Syria has some of the highest mountains in the Levant (Mount Hermon in the Golan Heights, at 2,236 meters above sea level) and is home to the lowest point on the earth (the Dead Sea, 432.65 meters below sea level). It is the unique landscape of this region—defined by canyons, hills, deserts, and lush highland plateaus, each with their own distinctive soils and water regimes—that is the single most important factor behind these localized eco-zones. The northern Rift Valley occupies the center of the region, creating the Jordan River and the series of wadis that flow into it. Uplift of the Rift Valley has created the series of mountains, and their canyons, that flank it. Tectonic activity in the region controls spring outflow and has left the region highly susceptible to earthquakes, which have, in turn, impacted settlements not only through destruction of the built environment but also by blocking springs and transforming watering and drainage systems. Associated with the movement of tectonic plates is volcanic activity, which has created the basaltic soils and rock formations along fault zones (such as the Wadi Hama in Jordan) and in the Hawran and southern Jordan. Basalt in these areas is used as building material (Umm al-Jamal in northeast Jordan is the best-known example of this) and appears as temper in the clay of locally made pottery (al-Sababha 2018). Soil erosion is marked in regions with the highest hills and deepest valleys, creating a complex mosaic of aeolian, alluvial, and colluvial sediments, reflecting, in Macumber's words, "fine-scale temporal instability" (Macumber 2008: 7). The region as a whole is well suited to agriculture when there is sufficient annual rainfall. The soils include the Mediterranean terra rossa that is common to the Levant and basaltic soils in ancient volcanic regions, which originate from the limestone and basalt source rock units that characterize the geology of southern Syria.

Topographically and ecologically the region is quite diverse, representing a wide range of hydrological and geological environments with varying agricultural potential. The northern Rift Valley (Lake Tiberias; the Jordan Valley, or Ghūr in Arabic; and the Wadi Arabah) is flanked by the heavily dissected mountainous highlands of the north,

[2] Grain harvests in present-day Jordan, for example, fail an average of once of every five years for lack of rainfall (Palmer 1998: 132). Jordan's limited water resources are notorious: its ranking as one of the most water-starved in the world is constantly adjusted by international agencies.

[3] Heavy rainfall events may have had a greater impact on landscape transformation than land use in this period (Lucke et al. 2008, 2012).

which gradually flatten into the central highland plateaus (the central Palestinian highlands to the west; the Madaba Plains and Dhiban and Karak plateaus to the east; and to the northeast the treeless, rock-strewn, volcanic plateau of the Hawran). These descend into lowlands (the Israeli Shephelah, the Petra Valley) before finally forming the coastal plain in the west and the eastern steppe (the *bādiyya* with its basalt and limestone plateaus), and the semi-arid lands and deserts of the south. The imperial administrative structures of the Islamic periods largely reflected these environment zones, and they were serviced economically by a network of local markets and the well-traveled trade routes that connected them.[4]

The distinctive regionalism of Syrian material culture is well known to archaeologists and art historians and is, in part, a cultural by-product of this landscape diversity. The regional differences in ceramic assemblages between northern and southern Jordan in the Early Islamic period, for example, stem from changes in trade routes after the Islamic conquest as well as the dominance of particular production centers (namely Jerash and Ayla/Aqabah) and regionalism in distribution (Watson 1992).

Historiography

Historical Palestine and the Transjordan are among the most heavily studied regions of the world by archaeologists. The region caught the early interest of archaeologists because of its association with the Bible Lands and its concentration of Classical and Late Antique ruins.

Since its founding in 1964, the Archaeological Survey of Israel has recorded as many as 23,000 sites (Avni 2014: 21). There are seventy-six foreign archaeological missions licensed to work in Jordan today, presenting a challenge to the Department of Antiquities in its attempts to monitor all of the sites.[5]

The origins of archaeological investigations of the Islamic periods here can be traced to the explorations by surveyors, scientists, pilgrims, and travelers of various ilk in the later 19th century.[6] The reforms (*Tanzimat*) of the Ottoman government made travel in its Arab lands more secure than it had been for centuries. While the Islamic centuries were never a focus of these investigations, many important Islamic sites were first recorded then. These include the Palestine Exploration Fund surveys of Palestine and Transjordan from 1872 to 1878 (which were concerned mainly with Biblical sites), the Survey of Western Palestine in 1871–1877, and the explorations of Rudolf Brünnow and

---

[4] For a detailed description of these geomorphological subregions, see Bender (1974, for Jordan) and Magness (2003: 75–78 and 130–131, for Israel, with a focus on the Negev).

[5] Address by Dr. Monther Jamhawi, former Director of the Department of Antiquities, to the North American project directors at the Annual Meeting of the American Schools of Oriental Research in November 2014. To address this challenge of site protection and maintenance, the Department issued a moratorium on new excavations in the country, with the exception of those focused on the Islamic periods.

[6] For a survey of early surveys and excavations, see Schick (1998: 80–84), Milwright (2010: 11–20), and Avni (2014: 17–23).

Alfred von Domaszewski in southern Syria and Transjordan in 1897–1898, with their focus on Roman sites, and of Alois Musil in the 1890s and early 1900s.[7] The Brünnow-von Domaszewski and Musil reports provided some of the earliest modern documentation of the so-called Early Islamic "desert castles." Systematic epigraphical study began with Max van Berchem's documentation of Arabic inscriptions in Jerusalem during his visits there in 1888, 1893–1894, and 1914.

Excavations in Palestine relevant to the Islamic periods began in earnest before World War I, with a real growth in archaeological fieldwork across the region by mid-century. The "desert castles" (Khirbet al-Mafjar in the 1930s and 1940s; Khirbet Minya in the 1930s) were an early target of investigation. Nelson Glueck's surveys of the first half of the 20th century and the work of the Archaeological Survey of Israel (which began in 1965) succeeded in documenting the Islamic phases of Biblical and Classical sites that would later become the focus of archaeological excavations. The first major "Islamic" excavation in Palestine was at Beth-Shean in the 1920s, and excavations of other major Early Islamic sites, such as Tiberias, Jarash, Caesarea, Ramla, and Jerusalem, would soon follow. Fieldwork in Syria in the interwar period—most notably Sarre's and Herzfeld's excavations of Raqqa, the Danish project at Hama's citadel, and research at Antioch—was largely concentrated in the north, beyond the limits of this chapter.

Islamic archaeology came of its own after World War II, with a surge in fieldwork in the 1970s and 1980s. Excavations of a wider range of sites made it possible to go beyond the study of monuments to exploration of larger settlements. These included citadels and castles in their larger setting (Amman, from the 1940s; Karak, in the 1980s), tell sites (Dhiban, from 1950; Hisban, from 1968), Classical and Late Antique towns with Islamic occupation (Pella, from 1967; Tiberias, in spurts from 1969; Abila, from 1980; Jarash, from the early 1980s; Beth-Shean, renewed excavations from 1986), and ports (Caesarea, from 1971; Aqaba/Ayla, from 1986). These were foundational years for Islamic archaeology in Greater Syria as they established the first sequences of Islamic pottery in the region (Sauer 1973, for Jordan), identified for the first time ceramic production sites (Gawlikowski 1986; Schaefer and Falkner 1986, the 8th/9th-c. kilns at Jarash), and provided the first publications of Fatimid strata (Northedge 1992, Amman Citadel; Whitcomb 1998, Aqaba/Ayla).

While the "archaeology of Islam" in southern Syria has long been devoted to the cities and "desert castles" of the Early Islamic period, fieldwork since the 1990s has shifted to rural sites and the later historical periods. Today salvage excavations in Israel and regional surveys in Jordan, many of which have been running for years, are rapidly identifying new sites of the Islamic periods, including the ephemeral remains of villages (Walker 2010).[8] Long-term excavations of Decapolis (Abila, Pella, Jerash), Classical (Caesarea), and Late Antique towns (Umm el-Jimal, Madaba, Yoqne'am, Jaffa) are documenting continuity of urban life well beyond the Islamic conquests. Ongoing excavations in

---

[7] A survey of all of the explorations of the period is beyond the scope of this chapter.

[8] Brief reports on IAA salvage excavations are published online in Hebrew and English in Ḥadashot Arkheologiyot (*Excavations and Surveys in Israel*) (http://www.hadashot-esi.org.il/). For a review of and bibliography of published reports on regional surveys in Jordan relevant to the Islamic periods, see Walker (2011: 213, note 310).

Jerusalem (and its hinterland), the Negev, Tiberias, Ramla, and Tall Ḥisban—important for the detailed information they are providing on daily life—will be discussed in detail later. Recent surveys and excavations in the Hawran, while primarily focused on the Roman and Byzantine eras, have identified Islamic sites and Islamic phases at sites of older foundation. The period of 1993–2000 was the "golden age" of Syrian archaeology, during which time large-scale and international excavations of threatened sites were prioritized.[9] During this time the joint French-Syrian archaeological mission at Damascus was established, running under the direction Sophie Berthier until the close of the project in 2006. One of the most important results has been in ceramic chronology: the stratigraphic separation of a long sequence of Islamic glazed wares (François 2008), including those of the elusive 11th and 12th centuries (McPhillips 2012). Epigraphical surveys in the *bādiyya* and Petra Valley are an exciting and relatively recent effort to record the wealth of medieval rock inscriptions in Arabic in the arid lands; these are described later.

Periodization

Changes in material culture do not happen concurrently political developments: objects for daily use do not immediately change or disappear because a new ruler has been installed or the dynastic capital has been transferred to a new locale. While there is no clear consensus on periodization by archaeologists working in southern Syria, for the Islamic periods, the chronological subdivision of the post-conquest era generally reflects the Early-Middle-Late Islamic sequence championed by Whitcomb for Jordan and embraced by many historians working in Greater Syria (Whitcomb 1988; Heidemann 2015). The Early Islamic period generally corresponds to the Umayyad and Abbasid caliphates (roughly 7th–11th centuries CE), the Middle Islamic period to the Ayyubid and Mamluk sultanates (12th–15th), and the Late Islamic to the Ottoman and Mandate eras (16th–early 20th centuries). The Fatimid horizon (11th and 12th centuries) is frequently lost in this system, which reflects the poor visibility of Fatimid ceramics and a general abatement of settlement in this period (as discussed later). Archaeological reports often include a combination of such cultural and dynastic (political) chronologies in order to represent smaller divisions of time. Periodization based on centuries is seldom adopted, though such a system would be more useful in communicating with historians. While this kind of cultural periodization, which is largely based on ceramics, is well suited to Bilād al-Shām, it is irrelevant to other regions of the Islamic world which do not share the same political history. It is an important lesson to learn: no single periodization works for everyone.[10]

---

[9] "Cultural Heritage in Syria in the Current Conflict: Heritage in Syria in Danger," https://hisd.tors. ku.dk/institutions/ (last accessed August 31, 2018)

[10] The observations of the historian Fred Donner are germane to this issue: there is no perfect periodization, and the historian should simply adopt what is best suited to addressing what he or she wants to better understand (Donner 2014).

Urban Spaces

Post-Conquest Urban Transformations

The impact of the Islamic conquests on the region in the 630s CE has generally been evaluated against the backdrop of the structural and functional changes in Late Antique cities (including the Decapolis cities) over the course of the 7th and 8th centuries.[11] Multicampaign excavations of such urban centers as Beth Shean (Baysan), Caesarea, Tiberias, Jarash, Ramla, and Jerusalem—and their assumed "decline" after the conquests— was a major factor in the development of Islamic archaeology in the region. The encroachment of private dwelling, shops, and workshops into the previously public spaces of the *cardo* is often cited as evidence of the economic decline of the Late Antique cities, though the origins of such developments may be sought in the Byzantine period (Kennedy 1985). Nonetheless, the privatization of public spaces and narrowing of main arteries through the cities were gradual developments and ones related more to the changing function of the urban centers (shifting away from religious and administrative hubs to commercial ones) and evidence of economic prosperity than decline (Walmsley 2012). Such changes may also reflect a slow demographic shift.

The processes of Islamization and urban development have thus been studied together as part of the same phenomenon. In this regard, the "shifting paradigms" (Avni 2014) of earlier scholarship, which emphasized ruptures in settlement and economic life during the Late Byzantine–Early Islamic transition, have generally been replaced with an acknowledgment that very little changed with the advent of Muslim rule (Schick 1995; Magness 2003; Walmsley 2012; Avni 2014). A re-dating of pottery from sites excavated years ago, such as Khirbet al-Mafjar, has made it possible to distinguish Umayyad and Abbasid phases of occupation and document with greater clarity post-conquest settlement histories (Whitcomb 1988; see also the later discussion of ceramics). On the basis of such revised ceramic typo-chronologies, it is clear that urban and rural life continued—there was no "decline" or destruction—and Christian institutions thrived. Over the course of Umayyad rule and beyond, in fact, many urban centers experienced growth; new cities were established (Ramla); new, rural settlements appeared (villages such as Yoqneʿam), buttressed by an expansion of a market-based agriculture in environmentally marginal areas (the Negev, ʿArabah, the Maʿān region of southern Jordan, and the Yavneh dune fields of the coastal plain from the 10th century); and the coasts were "militarized" through the construction of a network of ribats, walled settlements, and watch towers (Avni 2014; Taxel 2018; Taxel et al. 2018). Some urban centers did contract (Caesarea, Ṣaffūriyah/Sepphoris, Sīsiyah/Hippos); at others the center of the

---

[11] The Late Antique "polis" is only one urban form of the Early Islamic period. There is a rich literature on the garrisons (*amṣār*) and newly established cities (*madīnah*s), which is beyond the scope of this chapter. For further reading on Ayla-Aqaba, for example, see Whitcomb (1998) and Damgaard (2009) and the literature cited in their bibliographies.

settlement shifted to other parts of town or new neighborhoods were built (Tiberias). The settlement history of the region was far from uniform, and the process of change was quite slow: the transition to Islamic rule impacted local communities in different ways, and contraction and growth was cyclical.

In spite of the regional differences, a few general settlement trends for the period can be identified. A decrease in the volume of international trade and a shift to regional and local exchange was a factor in limited settlement abatement (not abandonment) at some sites in the 7th century. Long identified as a watershed event in the settlement history of the Early Islamic period, the earthquake of 749, while it did damage to urban structures, did not lead to wide-scale abandonment. In fact, careful study of architectural phasing at Tiberias and Jarash has documented the ability of local communities to adjust and reorient their local economies. More than the transfer of the imperial capital from Damascus to Baghdad (which was once identified as the catalyst for settlement and economic decline of southern Syria in the early Abbasid period), it was political instability that led to the contraction of settlement and the abandonment of some sites in the 9th and 10th centuries. Nonetheless, during this time, the number of rural settlements increased, suggesting migration out of urban centers and the development of a rural landscape that would characterize the later historical periods. Widespread abandonment of sites, both urban and rural, was a later phenomenon of the 11th century. The problems of identifying Fatimid-era pottery aside (see later discussion), the decline in agricultural production, abandonment of settlements (particularly pronounced in the region of Lake Tiberias and Golan, the Negev, and the central plains of Transjordan), and hoarding of jewelry, metalwork, and money (at Ramla, Tiberias, and Caesarea) allude to a crisis that spanned the entire region. It is likely that a combination of several factors combined to disrupt settlement: political turmoil (the Abbasid–Fatimid rivalry over Palestine), two major earthquakes (in 1033 and 1068), and years of drought (Ellenblum 2012).

Many of these urban, or urbanizing, centers across the region were reoccupied after a period of abandonment, in the Middle Islamic period. Economic growth, investment in infrastructure, and perhaps also migration (through both natural processes and very deliberate state-led population transfers and forced settlement; Walker 2011) combined to create a new map of settlement under the Mamluk Sultanate. Across the region, the ruins of houses built hundreds of years earlier were repaired, roofs replaced, and water systems put back into use, with wide-scale resettlement in the 13th and 14th centuries (for Tall Ḥisbān in Jordan, see later discussion; for examples from Palestine, see Walker 2010). Church buildings that had not been used for worship since the 8th and 9th centuries were converted to industrial centers and cemeteries (Tiberias, Cytryn-Silverman 2009: 46; Cytryn 2016: 239; Tall Ḥisbān's North Church, Lawlor 1980). As is common for archaeological ruins, some abandoned cities and towns, such as Jarash and Ḥisbān, were reoccupied in the Middle Islamic period. At these sites, neighborhoods were rebuilt as agglomerated housing units dispersed throughout the old urban fabric, and perhaps functioning as farmsteads (northwest quarter of Jarash, Lichtenberger and Raja 2016; the flatlands below the tell at Ḥisbān, Walker et al. 2017a); the ruins of other buildings were converted to garden plots (southwest quarter of Jarash, Rattenborg and Blanke 2017: 329; the tall slopes at Ḥisbān, Walker 2014b).[12]

What do these patterns of abandonment, resettlement, and reuse tell us about the process of Islamization in the region? The phenomenon behind the massive cemetery at Ḥisbān North Church is a matter of debate. The original excavations of 1975, only partially published, recovered some eighty burials (Lawlor 1980). A handful of intact burials in the central nave, supplied with imported sgraffito bowls as burial goods, have led this author to identify at least some of them, on the basis of parallels with 14th-century burial customs in Cyprus, with a community of migrant Orthodox Christians (Walker 2013). Recent excavations of the church, conducted as part of efforts to present the site to the public, have exposed several more cist burials. On the eve of the Crusades, the majority of the population of Palestine remained overwhelmingly Christian (Avni 2014: 14). This may be true, as well, in parts of Transjordan, where Christian burials and pilgrims' graffiti (see later discussion) attest to the survival of sizeable Christian communities well into the Mamluk period (14th century).[13] Avni appropriately refers to the slow cultural changes of the Early Islamic period (the 7th–11th centuries) as a transition "from a Christian majority to a multicultural, dynamic society" (Avni 2014: 9). Two recent excavations of large and well-preserved Late Antique and Early Islamic cities in Palestine and Transjordan—Tiberias and Jarash—reveal important social and cultural changes behind the early stages of Islamization.

Tiberias: Growth and Accommodation

The city of Tiberias on the lake of the same name, which has been subject to excavation since the 1950s, is a perfect example of the demographic growth and religious accommodation that characterized the urban scene in the Early Islamic period. The growth of Tiberias over the course of the Umayyad period can in part be attributed to its replacement of Baysan as the provincial capital of Jund al-Urdunn. Instead of spatial contraction, the city grew beyond the limits of the original walls of the Late Antique period by the 9th century. The ongoing "New Tiberias Excavation Project," launched in 2009 to locate and uncover the city's original congregational mosque, has revealed fascinating patterns of demographic change and intercommunal relations from the Islamic conquest of the city in 635 CE to the 10th century (Cytryn-Silverman 2009, 2010). The Great Mosque, first identified as a Byzantine covered market in the 1950s, is, in fact, a smaller replica of the Great Mosque of Damascus. Its structural history can be reconstructed through a stratigraphically sound series of coin-dated floors: built in the 7th or early 8th

---

[12] Archaeological ruins are often converted to agricultural use, and their associated soils are nitrate-rich and fertile (Walker 2018a). On the extraction of soils from ruins for fertilizer, see Quickel and Williams (2016).

[13] In a similar vein, there is a general consensus today among historians that the conversion of Coptic Christians in Egypt was a very slow and gradual process, accelerated only with the establishment and spread of *madrasa*s (Islamic law schools) in the Ayyubid and Mamluk periods (Leiser 1985).

century, it continued to be used for worship until its structural damage in the 1068 earthquake. Two meters to the north of the mosque stood a five-aisled basilica (one of at least three churches serving the city), which continued to accommodate Christian worship until the late 10th century. Not only did the Muslim urban planners maintain the original Byzantine grid of the city, placing the congregational mosque at the city center, but Muslims and Christians continued to worship in the same neighborhood for more than 200 years. The same was true for Jarash in the same period.

Jarash: Commerce and Industry

The well-preserved Late Roman provincial town of Jarash is one of the most intensively studied cities of the Late Antique and Early Islamic periods in southern Bilād al-Shām. Subject to excavations since 1925, some 25 percent of the 85-hectare site has been investigated archaeologically (Rattenborg and Blanke 2017). Recent fieldwork by international projects in different parts of the city has documented varied patterns of urban renewal, economic diversification, and demographic transformation that parallel those of other urban centers, such as Tiberias. The projects include the Danish-Jordanian Islamic Jarash Project, which conducted excavations focused on the congregational mosque in the center-city from 2002 to 2010 (Simpson 2008; Walmsley et al. 2008; Walmsley 2012: 84–86); the Danish-German Jarash Northwest Quarter Project, launched in 2011 to investigate the highest area of the walled city (Lichtenberger and Raja 2016, 2017; Lichtenberger et al. 2016); the Late Antique Jarash Project, its fieldwork conducted in a residential area to the southwest of the Early Islamic congregational mosque (Blanke et al. 2010; Rattenborg and Blanke 2017: 321ff); and the Jarash Hinterland Survey, which led documentation efforts in an area of rapid development from 2005 to 2010 (Baker and Kennedy 2011). Together, they have identified patterns of settlement, commerce, and industrial activities that parallel those of other Early Islamic towns, such as Tiberias and Pella. There is very little evidence of any occupational (or stratigraphic) break between the Late Byzantine and Early Islamic periods. With the exception of the northwest quarter of town, occupation generally continued through the 9th and, in some cases, to the 10th centuries, with evidence of repairs and repurposing after the 749 earthquake. Many new buildings were constructed on collapse layers. Abatement of urban settlement at Jarash began at the turn of the 10th century, with most parts of town, including the congregational mosque, eventually abandoned. In the Middle Islamic period (12th–14th centuries), some parts of town (the northwest quarter and the vicinity of the ruins of the Temple of Zeus, for example) were resettled in what appear to have been farmsteads; other neighborhoods were converted to industrial use and trash disposal (inside and in the vicinity of the old congregational mosque) or developed as intramural gardens (the southwest quarter).

While many of these patterns were repeated at other urban centers throughout the region, what distinguished Jarash was its extensive commercial development over the course of the Umayyad and Abbasid periods and the transformation of its urban ruins to farmsteads (or "hamlets," Lichtenberger and Raja 2016) in the Mamluk era. In the 7th and 8th centuries, a series of shops in the form of stalls were built along the east wall of the congregational mosque, in what was at the time "open" space "downtown," near the intersection of the *cardo* and *decamanus*. One shop yielded marble slabs inscribed in Arabic, recycled for use as commercial ledgers, with the names of patrons and amounts of money owed or credited to the shopkeeper (Simpson 2008). Although industrial spaces could be found in different quarters of the Late Antique city, their concentration in abandoned public spaces in the 8th century in workshops (ceramic, textile) attests to new modes of organization of production and industrial revival (Bessard 2007, 2013). The reoccupation of ruins in the northwest quarter hundreds of years later alludes to a different kind of process: the "ruralization" of the region in the 13th and 14th centuries. In a pattern repeated throughout Transjordan and Palestine, new domestic structures were either built on top of (or into) ruined structures of the Byzantine and Early Islamic period. In this quarter a large residential, courtyard complex was discovered, bordered by two smaller houses with plastered walls and all framing a central courtyard. One of the smaller houses sits above a cave, in which were installed several olive presses that were in use during this period.[14] Carbon-14 (C14) dates and ceramics suggest dates of occupation for this rural "hamlet" in the 13th–15th centuries.

Crusader and Post-Crusader Castles

The Middle Islamic era (13th–15th centuries CE) has become increasingly associated with the militarization of Islamic society, in the arts (heraldic blazons, monumental designs, and script) and in political and economic institutions (the sultanate, *iqṭaʿāt*). This should not be confused with "militancy"; rather it is more the visible and very public expressions of secular power based on a professional army.

The general investment in fortifications and the infrastructures to support them are very tangible evidence of this process. In Bilād al-Shām, the Fatimid, Crusader, and Mongol threats initially rationalized this concern for defense and control of the imperial frontiers. In the 11th and 12th centuries forts were constructed on both sides of the Jordan River, in the Golan Heights and Lake Tiberias, the highlands of northern Jordan, the Petra Valley, and the highlands south of Wadi Mujīb. A review of what we have learned from the extensive scholarship on the Crusader and Ayyubid-Mamluk castles

---

[14] Natural caves, with which the region is richly provided, were modified for a number of purposes in the Middle Islamic period, including industrial-scale production of olive oil and storage of grains. A cave complex similar to that in Jarash was identified as part of archaeological surveys in the village of Malka near Umm Qeis, where a series of large presses were installed in the cave walls (Walker et al. 2007).

and urban garrisons (Damascus Citadel) is beyond the scope of this chapter.[15] While the castles themselves have been thoroughly studied by architectural historians and archaeologists, the towns that supported them have been largely overlooked as the medieval sites are overlaid by modern settlement. One fortunate exception is the *madīnah* of Ḥisbān in central Jordan, which has been subject to American and joint American-German excavations for five decades.

Ḥisbān Citadel

The archaeological site of Tall Ḥisbān is located in central Jordan on the Madaba Plains, between Amman and Madaba. The site actually consists of two parts: the walled citadel on the summit of the tell and the ruins of the medieval settlement below it. Since the 1970s, the site has belonged to the Jordanian Department of Antiquities and is currently being developed as an archaeological park in conjunction with ongoing excavations.[16] Fifty years of intermittent excavations at the site have uncovered a 14th-century Mamluk garrison (fairly well preserved, with an intact storeroom) and its supporting village (or "town," *madīnah*, as contemporary Arabic sources called it for a short period). In this period, as we know from chronicles, it was a small administrative center—the capital of the rural Balqā District (in the southernmost portion of the Province of Damascus)— and hosted a very modest garrison. There is, however, no reference to the physical citadel in any of the narrative or documentary sources of the period. The defensive capabilities of the castle and the spatial distribution of ceramics and small finds suggest that the Citadel served more domestic and administrative, rather than defensive, functions.

There is little spatial division between the Citadel and the town/village: the houses creep up the slopes of the tell to the Citadel walls. There is, likewise, little to distinguish the ceramic and glass assemblages of the two parts of the site: common handmade geometrically painted ware bowls and jars are found in the Citadel storeroom; glazed bowls (mostly imports) are found in the farmhouses; and large sugar molasses transport/storage jars and enameled and lustred glass lamps, vials, and drinking vessels of Damascene manufacture have been recovered from both contexts. According to recent faunal analysis, the diet of soldiers serving at Ḥisbān was relatively indistinguishable from that of villagers, except for the consumption of game animals and generally better cuts of meat; in fact, there is evidence of sharing of meat and meat distribution between the Citadel and village (see Corbino in Walker et al. 2017c). It would appear, then, that very little separated the consumption patterns of the garrison from that of the civilian settlement.

---

[15] The Jordanian castles have been studied the most thoroughly. For excavation reports on Shobak Castle, see Brown (1988) and Vannini and Nucciotti (2009); for Karak Castle, Brown (1989, 2013); and Milwright (2008) for a summary of fieldwork there and a catalogue of pottery from local surveys. Walmsley (2001) also provides a good overview of literature on the fortifications of Middle Islamic Jordan.

[16] The excavations are under the direction of the author and are part of a larger archaeological and community development initiative, the "Hisban Cultural Heritage Project," led by Øystein LaBianca of Andrews University. For more information, on the CRM and community archaeology efforts of the project, see Chapter 6.1 in this volume LaBianca, Ronza, and Harris.

More surprising are the results of ongoing analysis of the vast complexes of cisterns and subterranean channels at the site, which indicate that the water (and drainage) systems of the Citadel and the village were interconnected, requiring collaboration in their maintenance. The garrison and village, then, appear to have lived in a symbiotic relationship with another.

RURAL SPACES

Early Islamic "Desert Castles"

Exploration of the so-called Early Islamic "desert castles," which are neither located in the desert nor truly castles, is one of the longest chapters in the history of Islamic archaeology in Bilād al-Shām. The term covers a diverse body of palace-like structures and complexes built in the late Umayyad period (most in the early 8th century) and located in the semi-arid regions of Jordan, Israel, and the Palestinian territories and in northeastern Syria. Some thirty-eight monuments have been identified as desert castles, with the highest concentration in northeast Jordan at the border between cultivable land and the eastern steppe (the *bādiyya*). Several—located on hilltops, on lake shores, and close to wadis—may have been positioned for their scenic views (Ben Badhann 2009); others, flanking ancient trade routes, likely served more economic functions. Many are repurposings of Roman or Byzantine forts and fortified complexes. Collectively, they represent an important stage in the development of Islamic architecture and settlement in Umayyad Syria. Functionally, they belong to a larger group of Early Islamic settlements—the caliphal "estates" (*ḍiyāʾ al-khilāfah*)—which included the private villages and land grants (*qataʾiʿ*) that helped to revive the "dead lands" (*mawāt*) on the agricultural periphery (Taxel 2018).

As discussed in Chapter 2.1, debate continues over the ultimate function of these structures. While explorations of the 19th and early 20th centuries focused on the architecture itself, current excavations, which aim at revisiting the chronology of the earlier expeditions, are providing a clearer, though more complex, picture of why they were built and how they changed over time. Important in this regard is recent fieldwork at Qasr al-Hayr al-Sharqi (located in the Syrian steppe, 110 kilometers northeast of Palmyra and covered in the previous chapter) and Khirbet al-Mafjar (on the edge of the fertile lands of Jericho).[17] An inscription in the Large Enclosure at Qasr al-Hayr al-Sharqi referring to a "*madinah*" (city) led Oleg Grabar in the 1970s to identify this single-walled complex, which is only part of the site, as a proto-urban form. Renewed excavations by a

---

[17] Although Qasr al-Hayr al-Sharqi falls outside the geographical coverage of this chapter, recent excavations there shed light on the development of the desert castles of southern Syria.

Swiss-Syrian team under the direction of Denis Genequand have provided evidence for the gradual urbanization of the entire site (Genequand 2012). Suggesting that the site as a whole served both political and economic functions, Genequand emphasizes its palatial aspects, which include a palace proper, congregational mosque, bath, service buildings, non-elite housing, hydro-agricultural and industrial installations, and something akin to suburbs (which developed later to the north of the site). The watermill, warehouses, stables, and oil presses speak to an agricultural complex, much like the "desert castles" in Jordan, with their elaborate water harvesting systems (dams, reservoirs, aqueducts, qanats), agricultural enclosures, and cultivated zones. The majority of the desert castles were organized in this way for agricultural production and redistribution. Joint Palestinian-American excavations at Khirbet al-Mafjar have suggested a similar pattern. Considered an "incipient city" by Whitcomb, the site is endowed with public buildings and the remains of an agricultural estate to the north of the palatial structure, as at Qasr al-Hayr al-Sharqi (Whitcomb 2012–2013; Whitcomb and Taha 2013).

For Genequand, the desert castles were primarily elite residences, built by caliphs and princes in places where they were allotted land grants (s. *qaṭīʿa*). They were purposively developed as agricultural estates in order to diversify economically beyond tax revenues and state salaries (Genequand 2012: 398). Some may have been planned as "settlement magnets" from the start to attract settlement and cultivation in undeveloped, abandoned, or agriculturally marginal areas. Over time they developed into cities, with a full complement of public services and suburbs. In this sense, Khirbet al-Mafjar was a palace-estate (*ḍayʿa*), which became a (short-lived) model of early Islamic settlement. The same has been argued for Shuqayra al-Gharbiyya on the Karak Plateau, which may have served as the summer residence of caliph Hisham, as Khirbet al-Mafjar was his winter residence (Ben Badhann 2009) (Figure 2.2.2).[18] The view from the belvedere of Shuqayra is striking: a broad span of the Wadi al-Hasa and its terraced slopes.

The desert castles continued to be occupied into the Abbasid period and then were abandoned, having lost their original functions in a state apparatus that was decentralized, mobile, and tied to local tribes (Genequand 2012: 398). Many of them, however, were reoccupied for a short period in the Middle Islamic period, a phenomenon that has only been fully appreciated as a result of recent excavations. At Qasr al-Hayr al-Sharqi, the ruins of the Umayyad and Abbasid complexes were reoccupied, and new housing complexes, a mosque, and a cemetery with mausoleum were built in the 12th and 13th centuries (dates confirmed by C14 analysis of the wooden coffins, Genequand 2005). The palace at Khirbet al-Mafjar was reoccupied, as well, circa 1100–1300. There is evidence of Middle Islamic reuse of other desert castles. Italian restorations of the famous frescoes of Qusayr Amra in Jordan have revealed a series of graffiti from various periods; the corpus of Mamluk-period inscriptions is under study by the Department of Antiquities (personal communication, Ahmad Lash). In this case, the ruins of the

---

[18] Ben Badhann originally attributed Shuqayra al-Gharbiyya to the patronage of al-Walid II, the successor of Hisham to the Umayyad caliphate.

FIGURE 2.2.2 Shuqayra al-Gharbiyya, southern Jordan.

Photo by author.

bathhouse were used as a kind of caravanserai, providing overnight shelter for travelers. What these visitors thought the building was originally is not indicated by the content of the graffiti.

Villages

Central Plateaus of Jordan: The Madaba Plains

While current salvage excavations in Israel are revealing the traces of rural settlements at a rapid pace, exposures are limited and architectural plans few. The most extensive information about rural society on the scale of the village is coming from Jordan, where long-term excavations of tell sites have uncovered the remains of complete housing complexes. Few rural sites are as well preserved or as thoroughly explored as that of Tall Ḥisbān, which has become a type site for rural archaeology of the Mamluk period. The citadel, described earlier in this chapter, is perched on the summit of an archaeological tell that overlooks a dense configuration of barrel-vaulted, single-roomed structures— the remains of the Early and Middle Islamic village of Ḥisbān. These multipurpose buildings, which in some cases preserve as many as ten courses of their walls and vault

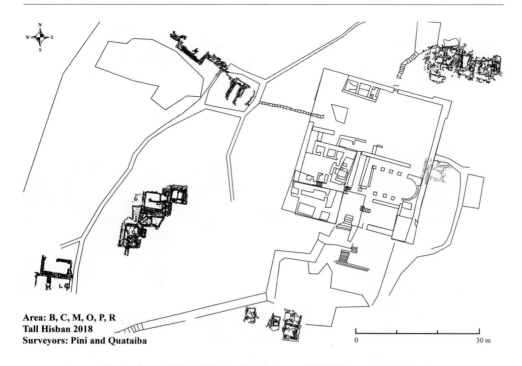

Area: B, C, M, O, P, R
Tall Hisban 2018
Surveyors: Pini and Quataiba

0   30 m

FIGURE 2.2.3 Floor plans of Mamluk-era farmhouses, Tall Ḥisbān, central Jordan.

Courtesy of Nicoló Pini, Research Unit of Islamic Archaeology, University of Bonn.

springers, are built against one another in a row, all facing a common courtyard and shared cistern (Figure 2.2.3). Their walls and floors were plastered in white gypsum; they had windows, benches, indoor plumbing, and lockable (apparently wooden) doors. They belong to a koïne of medieval vernacular architecture of the central highlands of the Transjordan and Palestine that spans the Islamic periods (see Walker 2014b for the Madaba Plains; see Nashef 2000; Nashef and Abd Rabu 2000; Abd Rabu 2000 for Khirbet Birzeit). Though they have been subject to excavation since the last 1970s, the Ḥisbān "farmhouses" have been the focus of archaeological investigations only since 2013. As in many village sites throughout southern Syria, these structures are largely refurbishings and reoccupations of Late Byzantine and Early Islamic domestic ruins, which were at the time hundreds of years old. Few buildings at the site were built anew in the Mamluk era.

It is not clear how large the medieval settlement was, how many people lived there, or where its Muslims residents were buried.[19] No pathways connecting "neighborhoods" have been identified. The house clusters have been interpreted as the housing compounds of extended families, which shared resources, including the traditional family

---

[19] In contrast to the Roman and Byzantine necropoli beyond the tell and the Late Ottoman mass "Bedouin" burials on the summit, the medieval Muslim cemetery has never been identified. The North Church burials, arguably of a Christian population, were discussed earlier.

cistern. Individual houses were added on to the cluster as the family grew. The village of Ḥisbān appears with regular frequency as a "*madīnah*" in contemporary Arabic sources in the 14th century, when the garrison and district governorship were moved to the summit of the tell and the village came to acquire urban amenities. The villagers were known by the *nisbah* "Ḥisbānī," and the local pastoral nomadic tribes were the Banu Mahdi (for a review of textual sources, see Walker 2011). The villagers included peasants, state officials, clerics (with professional ties to Damascus), and businessmen.

There is a disconnect between the vernacular style of the houses and the pottery and glass recovered from them, which include imports (of some expense) from Damascus and Cairo. A hoard of more than sixty silver coins (dirhams) was hidden in a lamp recovered under the bench (*maṣṭabah*) of one house in the 1970s. From a stone outlined pit in another house were recovered complete glazed jars of Damascene manufacture (Walker et al. 2017b). The architecture and small finds together suggest a rural population that was in the process of urbanizing, for a short time, when Hisban had a garrison. Unlike the villages of northern Jordan, Ḥisbān was gradually abandoned over the course of the late 15th and early 16th centuries until it was reoccupied in the Tanzimat era and the center of the settlement shifted south.

The way the village of Ḥisbān developed over time mirrors that of the desert castles: Middle Islamic reoccupation of Early Islamic ruins and a brief period of urbanization. Rural Bilād al-Shām experienced a renaissance in the 14th century due to the stability of the Mamluk Sultanate and state investments in local infrastructure and agriculture. Complex patterns of rural migration, settlement (some through forced population transfers by imperial fiat, Walker 2011, 2014b), and natural demographic growth are expressed in these occupational cycles. These were localized patterns, however, with one region experiencing different degrees (and timing) of growth and abatement from another.

Negev and Petra Valley

The process of sedentarization and the factors behind the expansion of agriculture in the Early Islamic period are central themes in the archaeology of rural settlement in the Negev. They are also at the heart of debates on the impact of the Islamic conquests on settlement in marginal zones. The number of rural settlements and farms in the Negev grew in the 7th and 8th centuries. Debates center on the reasons why: either the decline of towns forced nomads to settle and engage in run-off farming (Avni 1996), or a strong Umayyad state enacted a policy of settlement (Haiman 1995), or, alternatively, under a strong Umayyad state, the circumstances were right for agricultural expansion into marginal zones under individual initiative (Rosen 2007). In fact, the towns of these southern zones prospered in the Early Islamic period, and rural settlements were simply pulled into their orbit. Growth in settlement and agricultural production throughout Palestine and Syria in the mid-6th to mid-7th centuries, in fact, continued unabated after the conquests. The structure of the settlements in this period, however, was quite different from that of other regions. Modular development of single-room housing clusters suggests a process of settlement by a segmented society (Magness 2004).

The settlement history of the Petra Valley in much later historical periods followed a different course. In recent years archaeologists have prioritized the history of post-Nabataean settlement in Petra and the Petra Valley, with careful study of the "medieval" (i.e., Crusader and Middle and Late Islamic-era) strata at Aaron's Tomb (Kouki and Laven 2013), among many other sites as yet unpublished, and new excavation of purely Middle and Late Islamic-era sites, such as Baydā (Sinibaldi and Tuttle 2011) and the large village of Baʿja (Lindner 1999; Bienert et al. 2000).[20] It is now becoming clear that the Petra region was periodically reoccupied in the Fatimid period (Makowski 2020) and continued to be settled long after the Crusader interlude in the region, its villages supported through the revitalization of ancient canals and dams. Unlike those of the central plains, these villages are "invisible" textually, not appearing in written sources of the period in spite of their size. The German excavations of Baʿja in 1999 identified as many as fifty houses and excavated one six-room structure built directly on bedrock. If this structure reflects the occupational history of the rest of the site, then the village of Baʿja was newly settled in the Middle Islamic (Mamluk) period, with a second phase of occupation in the Late Islamic (Ottoman) era. What the sites of this period in the Petra Valley share is an architectural and ceramic tradition distinguished from that of the central plains: stone-built houses, some with multiple rooms and roofed in timber beams and a largely handmade assemblage of handmade pottery with chaff inclusions and poorly oxidized and low-temperature firing (producing a dark core). Incomplete publication has hampered research in this area, but increased coordination among the many missions working there is promising for the future.

Highland Quṣūr and Khirāb

Small hilltop fortifications overlooking terraced fields were a familiar component of the landscape of the central Palestinian highlands in the Late Islamic (Ottoman) period. While the term "qaṣr" carries different meaning by region and period, in Ottoman Palestine it was a stone structure (or walled complex) with a view, which incorporated circular agricultural watch towers (manāṭīr- ʿĀmirī and Riḥāl 2003). Seasonal domestic use meant that such structures were "empty" for much of the year, leading travelers to call them khirāb, or "ruins" (Walker 2020). Such complexes often began as settlement offshoots of larger villages and over time grew into independent villages. Along with agricultural terraces, they transformed the landscapes of the central highlands.

They are also a rapidly disappearing component of Palestinian cultural heritage. Stratigraphic excavations of manṭarah complexes (quṣūr) are rare (Edelstein et al. 1998; Walker 2017). Begun in 2015, German-Israeli excavations of the qaṣr of Khirbet Beit Mazmil, sitting atop the highest hill of Jerusalem's immediate hinterland, have revealed a complex history of occupation and reuse tied to changes in land use and land tenure

---

[20] Baʿja I was first excavated by a German team in 1999. A small American-German team revisited the site in 2017 for survey and small probes in the "Islamic" field.

FIGURE 2.2.4 Late Ottoman *qaṣr* at Khirbet Beit Mazmil, Jerusalem.

Photo by author.

over the later Islamic centuries (Walker and Dolinka 2020). A Late Ottoman *manṭarah* complex, preserved to its roof, both overlays and incorporates the remains of a large Late Mamluk-era (14th and 15th centuries) farmstead that may have served as an amiral estate (Figure 2.2.4). Although today located in a heavily developed urban neighborhood, it was once surrounded by terraced fields and orchards. This single farmstead offers a glimpse into the history of an important settlement form in Late Islamic Palestine.

Habitation Caves

The domestic use of modified caves and shelters is a ubiquitous but less visible form of rural settlement in southern Syria. Over time, rainfall and wind have eroded the calcareous limestone hills of the region, producing caves and cavernous systems that were modified through the centuries by human hands for housing, stables, storage, cisterns, burials, and middens. Caves (*kuhūf*) are listed as amenities of villages in Mamluk-era endowment documents (for grain storage), thus serving an economic role; they continue to be used in many villages in Jordan today to store farm tools and equipment. They also represent an intermediary stage in the sedentarization process, in combination with tents (set up in front of cave entrances) and stone-built houses (erected above them) (Carroll et al. 2005) (Figure 2.2.5). The Christian village of Shammakh on the

FIGURE 2.2.5 Habitational caves and tents at Ḥisbān, 1930s.

Courtesy of Palestine Exploration Fund.

Karak Plateau was a true "cave village" from at least the 19th century until a generation ago, when electricity was installed and a road was laid at some distance away (Noca 1985). In Amman, many caves continued to be used as housing until the 1950s.

In spite of their rich potential for recovering data on diet, animal husbandry, and household life through the Islamic centuries, very few "cave villages" have been systematically studied. One reason for this is the poor preservation of many cavernous interiors, with precariously positioned ceilings and walls and heavy infill. Nonetheless, there has been some attempt to map those located in the hinterland of large excavation sites. At Tall Ḥisbān, the local caves and the cavernous chambers of multiple rooms that honeycomb the tell have been mapped throughout the fifty years of ongoing excavation there, making use of traditional mapping techniques, laser mapping, and 3D modeling. Limited probes placed in the first chamber of the "Abu Nur Cave" of the southern slopes produced a stratified sequence of Middle Islamic surfaces and middens (Walker et al. 2017a).

Agriculture and Landscapes

While climate studies are well developed in southern Syria, archaeobotanical analysis is a relatively new but rapidly growing method of studying changes in landscape, land use, and foodways in the Islamic periods. Refining sampling strategies for microstratigraphic recovery of botanical remains, particularly at the scale of the household, has resulted in fine resolution reconstructions of food processing, use, and disposal. It has also permitted the formulation of new research questions. Archaeobotanical research at Islamic-period sites, particularly in Jordan, includes macrobotanical and microbotanical methods (namely phytolith, starch, and residue analysis) and has centered on themes related to communal decision-making about cropping and watering. These include debates over the merits of Watson's (1983) theory of agricultural innovation, describing in detail cereal production (and differentiating among different kinds of wheats and barleys), identifying different kinds of cooking installations and cooking practices (with an emphasis on *tābūn*s and cooking pots, Ebeling and Rogel 2015; Hansen et al. 2017), documenting changes in cropping over *la longue durée* (and historically accounting for the factors behind those changes, Farahani 2018), and identifying evidence of irrigation and garden agriculture (Laparidou and Rosen 2015). Archaeobotanical data are increasingly being interpreted against a critical reading of contemporary Arabic documents—such as papyri (the Nessana documents), endowment documents (*waqfiyyāt*), agrarian manuals (*filāḥah* texts), tax registers (Ottoman *tapu defter*s), and legal manuals (*fatwa* collections)—which yield important information about communal labor, the types of crops grown and their market value, agricultural installations, "best practices" in farming and water use, the size of agricultural fields, the division of water rights, and methods of land development (Walker in Walker et al. 2017c).

The single most widespread landscape feature in the highlands of southern Syria is the agricultural terrace. Terraces have functions both hydrological (to control water flow and reduce surface runoff) and purely agricultural (to prevent soil erosion and water evaporation, to create agricultural fields on slopes), and they directly reflect the ways local communities made decisions related to land use and local markets. They can technically be used for any kind of cropping (orchards or cereals) and watering regime (dry-farmed or irrigated). There are great regional differences among them in size, form, and structure which reflect local patterns of land tenure, social organization, and technical traditions. The decision to construct agricultural terraces was predominantly an economic one, in part a response to changes in land tenure, such as the privatization of land in the 15th century and the rise of commercial gardening in the 17th and 18th centuries. It was likely not driven by demographic growth.

Like field walls and cisterns, terraces are notoriously difficult to date. Traditional archeological methods—such as coins and pottery recovered from excavated terraces and the association of terrace walls with excavated sites—have failed to satisfactorily date terrace construction, stymying attempts to chronologically trace the development of field systems over time. A breakthrough in dating agricultural terraces was achieved lately with the introduction of the luminescence methods, used with success in Israel and Jordan (for Israel, Davidovich et al. 2012; Avni et al. 2013; Gadot et al. 2016, 2018; for Jordan, Knabb et al. 2016; al-Qudah et al. 2016). Optically stimulated luminescence (OSL) is based on solar resetting (or bleaching) of the luminescence signal (on mainly the ubiquitous quartz and feldspar minerals in the soil) during sediment transport. The technique, in short, dates when soil was placed behind the walls. Though it has been the fulcrum of debate in recent years, when interpreted against the backdrop of formation processes it is the most reliable way today of dating agricultural terraces.

Surveys of the Negev Highlands in the 1980s and subsequent excavations of agricultural terraces and OSL-dating of their soils have provided strong evidence for the intensification of field use in the Early Islamic period until the 10th and 11th centuries (Avni et al. 2013; Avni 2014: 37). "The Formation of Terraced Landscapes in the Judean Highlands Project" of 2014–2017, in which terraces, field walls, and rock piles were likewise excavated and their constituent soils OSL-dated, followed the development of field systems in the Wadis Soreq and Rafaim and Mt. Eitan from 1400 to 1750 (Walker et al. 2020). Archaeological and OSL study of the terraces in the hinterland of Khirbet Beit Mazmil has identified peaks in land development through terracing and the construction of field walls to the 13th–15th and 18th centuries. Such fieldwork ultimately paints a picture of rural renewal through agricultural terracing in Jerusalem's immediate western hinterland from the 15th century. This presents a stark contrast to the central highlands of Transjordan, which experienced a peak in agricultural productivity in the 14th century but dispersal of village communities and abandonment of grain fields thereafter.

MATERIAL CULTURE

The Late Antique-Early Islamic Ceramic Transition

Ceramic "gaps" are produced by dating wares too early or too late in a ceramic sequence. The traditional historical narrative about the Byzantine–Islamic transition in the 7th century in southern Syria—which is one of settlement decline and abandonment—has been reinforced by the inability to accurately date pottery of the 7th–9th centuries CE. Until the 1990s, much pottery we now know to be Abbasid (Early Islamic, late 8th/9th century) in date was attributed to the Umayyad era (Early Islamic, 7th/early 8th century), such as cream ware/"Mafjar Ware" (which continues well beyond the Umayyad era), red-painted ware (associated with the northern and central regions), and channel nozzle lamps. Likewise, some Umayyad wares, which were generally a continuation of Byzantine wares, were misidentified as purely Byzantine in date. These include Jerash bowls, fine '"Byzantine" ware'/Palestinian fine ware, late Roman wares, white jugs with an omphalos base, arched-rim combed basins, lidded casseroles, and white-painted brittleware *zīr*s (Magness 1993; Schick 1998: 90–94; Walmsley 2012 49–59; Avni 2014: 22, 32–33). The result has been the creation of a chronological "gap" of as much as two centuries in which the Abbasid and Fatimid periods disappeared. The ceramic sequences dated in this manner suggested that, after the Islamic conquest, settlements were abandoned.

Since the late 1980s, excavations of large archaeological sites with secure stratigraphy sequences (Jerusalem, Caesarea, Ramla, Pella, Yoqnema, Aqaba/Ayla) and reexamination of pottery from old excavations (Capernaum, Nabratein, Hammat Gader, and

Khirbet Abu Suwwana) have allowed a reevaluation of the settlement map in the Early Islamic period (Avni 2014: 32). Among these, the site of Pella, on the Jordanian side of the upper Jordan Valley, stands out. Its excellent stratigraphy—which includes two earthquake levels (dating to 659–60 and 749 CE)—has made it possible to distinguish nineteen different major wares at the site. On the basis of the typo-chronology established at Pella, it is now clear that the Islamic conquest had a "low cultural impact" (Walmsley 2012: 51). The emergence of new "Islamic" wares is a phenomenon of the 9th century and not earlier.

Handmade Geometrically Painted (HMGP) Ware

Handmade pottery dominates the assemblages of rural sites in southern Syria. Handmade geometrically painted ware (generally referred to HMGP in publication; Figure 2.2.6) is the most characteristic of this pottery and has become the primary chronological marker of the Middle and Late Islamic periods on archaeological surveys. A specialized craft of southern Bilād al-Shām (Johns 1998), HMGP is associated more with the highlands, although it has been recovered in lower quantities in southern Jordan and the Negev. HMGP ware is

FIGURE 2.2.6 Handmade Geometrically Painted Ware, from Mamluk Citadel storeroom at Tall Ḥisbān.

Photo by author.

generally handmade, with large jars mold-formed over sand-filled cloth bags (Franken and Kalsbeek 1975). The finest wares, however, are thrown on a slow wheel. The fabric is highly regional, with the degree and composition of inclusions (grog or chaff) highly variable. The surface is painted in different shades of black, red, and brown in geometric patterns. While appearing in a range of forms (jars and jugs, bowls, incense burners, boxes), HMGP ware was primarily produced as a tableware.

In spite of its wide distribution and recovery in large quantities from excavations, HMGP ware has until now eluded confident dating, thus exacerbating the problems of identifying Ottoman-era occupation during surveys. Stratigraphically associated with late 11th-century levels at Shobak Castle (Brown 1988) and Gharandal in southern Jordan (Walmsley and Grey 2001), it appears to have been produced for several centuries and perhaps as late as the mid-20th century (Walker 2009). There is a general consensus that production of the ware peaked in the 14th century (during the period of Mamluk hegemony), when the form, fabric, and surface decoration were of the best quality and distribution was extensive. Because recovery of HMGP sherds from well-stratified sites has been limited, archaeologists have generally resorted to changes in the painted decorative patterns to chronologically subdivide this 900-year period of production. This method has ultimately failed because decorative patterns seem to vary as much geographically as they do chronologically, and production appears to have been, at least in part, a cottage industry.

Although there has been little progress on dating the ware, Gabrieli et al.'s (2014) petrographic and comparative analysis of HMGP sherds from sites in Israel and Jordan has been the first published attempt to use archaeometry to document production and distribution. The study revealed ways in which production was much more complex than the "locally produced and locally consumed" paradigm assumed by most archaeologists, proposing different but contemporary modes of craft specialization (handmade, mold-made, wheelmade); a congruence of local, regional, *and* intraregional exchange; divergence in production of HMGP and plain handmade wares; and changes in the location of production centers over time.

Much more research on the ware is required before we can properly date Middle and Late Islamic sites. We still do not know to what degree the industry was centralized or decentralized, how production knowledge was transferred from one village another, or how it was marketed. Study of HMGP ware, moreover, promises to shed light on household industry and division of labor if proper methods of microstratigraphic analysis and ceramic quantification are adopted.

Rock Inscriptions

Epigraphical studies in Greater Syria have been dominated by documentation of architectural inscriptions, which are formal, public texts. In the past two decades the documentation of more informal archaeological texts, such as tombstones, graffiti (scratched texts on building blocks), and rock inscriptions (on bare rock in more remote locations) have become a priority (Sharon 1997–2004). The identification and recording of medieval Arabic inscriptions grew out of epigraphical surveys of Greek, Latin,

Nabatean, and Safaitic inscriptions in the deserts of Syria, Transjordan, and the Arabian Peninsula.[21] Graffiti and rock inscriptions served as ego-texts, giving voice to rural peoples and travelers and supplementing the formal written record. There is a growing effort today, particularly in Jordan (Imbert 1996), to record such inscriptions, some of which are comprised of multiple lines and include texts written by pilgrims and caravan drivers offering such information as prices of wheat and locations of watering holes. Many are placed in very visible locations, guiding travelers. Others are graffiti in the pure sense of the word and cover the walls of ancient ruins (such as the "desert castles" of Qusair Amra) and abandoned mosques and churches (al-Bqain et al. 2015; Walker 2014a). These archaeological texts are shedding light on migration, Islamization, and the evolving structure of rural communities.

CONCLUSION

Since the 1980s, fieldwork in southern Syria has generated a large body of literature on, and has helped to articulate the debates that define, the archaeology of Islamic societies in the Levant. Interest in natural resource management, rural society, and migration and Islamization is driving much of today's scholarship and has cultivated ties to the natural sciences and anthropology. The archaeology of the Ottoman centuries is a promising new line of research, one that has advanced through studying vernacular architecture, identifying the traces of pastoral nomadism, and incorporating ethnography into research design. New perspectives on urban development are revealing just how religiously diverse Early Islamic society was and how intercommunal relations may have played out.

One of the greatest challenges to Islamic archaeology in this region today, however, remains ceramic chronology and specifically the continued inability to more precisely date handmade wares. This has particularly impacted the study of the later Islamic periods. The strong regionalisms of Syrian material culture and the longevity of local ceramic and architectural traditions make it all the more critical that archaeological research be conducted in a regionally comparative framework.

REFERENCES

ʿĀmirī, S., and Riḥāl, F. 2003. *Manāṭīr: Quṣūr al-Mazāriʿ fī Filisṭīn* (Ramallah: RIWAQ).

Abd Rabu, O. 2000. "Khirbet Birzeit Research and Excavation Project 1999: The Pottery," *Journal of Palestinian Archaeology*, 1, 2, 7–18 (English) and 13–25 (Arabic).

Avni, G. 1996. *Nomads, Farmers, and Town-Dwellers: Pastoral-Sedentist Interaction in the Negev Highlands* (Jerusalem: Israel Antiquities Authority).

[21] Such studies can be found in the journal *Arabian Archaeology and Epigraphy*, which is now published online (https://onlinelibrary.wiley.com/journal/16000471), and in short reports in *Arabian Epigraphic Notes*.

Avni, G. 2014. *The Byzantine-Islamic Transition in Palestine: An Archaeological Approach* (Oxford: Oxford University Press).

Avni, G. 2019. "Revolution or Evolution?: Agricultural Fields in Early Islamic Palestine," in D. Whitcomb, C. Dagaard, and K. Cytryn-Silverman (eds.), *Recent Advances in Islamic Archaeology: A Conference in Jerusalem* (Chicago: University of Chicago. In print).

Avni, G., Porat, N., and Avni, Y. 2013. "Byzantine-Early Islamic Agricultural Systems in the Negev Highlands: Stages of Development as Interpreted Through OSL Dating," *Journal of Field Archaeology*, 38, 333–347.

Baker, F. M. A., and Kennedy, D. L. 2011. "Jarash Hinterland Survey 2010: An Overview of the Results," *Annual of the Department of Antiquities of Jordan*, 55, 451–466.

Ben Badhann (Naʿimat), Z. 2009. "Shuqayra al-Gharbiyya: an Early Islamic Elite Community in Central Jordan," *al-ʿUsur al-Wusta*, 21, 8–13.

Bender, F. 1974. *Geology of Jordan* (Berlin: Brüder Bornträger).

Bessard, F. 2007. "Foundations of Umayyad Economy: Jerash, a Case Study," *al-'Usur al-Wusta*, 19, 1, 1–10.

Bessard, F. 2013. "The Urban Economy in Southern Inland Greater Syria from the Seventh Century to the End of the Umayyads," in L. Lavan (ed.), *Local Economies? Production and Exchange of Inland Regions in Late Antiquity* (Leiden: Brill), 377–421.

Bienert, H.-D., Lamprichs, R., and Vieweger, D. 2000. "Ba'ja: The Archaeology of a Landscape. 9000 Years of Human Occupation. A Preliminary Report on the 1999 Field Season," *Annual of the Department of Antiquities of Jordan*, 44, 119–148.

Blanke, L., Lorien, P. D., Rattenborg, R. 2010. "Changing Landscapes in Central Jarash: Between Late Antiquity and the Abbasid Period," *Annual of the Department of Antiquities of Jordan*, 54, 311–327.

al-Bqain, F., Corbett, G. J., and Khamis, E. 2015. "An Umayyad Era Mosque and Desert Waystation from Wadi Shīreh, Southern Jordan," *Journal of Islamic Archaeology*, 2, 1, 93–126.

Brown, R. 1988. "Summary Report of the 1986 Excavations: Late Islamic Shobak," *Annual of the Department of Antiquities of Jordan*, 32, 225–245.

Brown, R. 1989. "Excavations in the 14th Century A.D. Mamluk Palace at Kerak," *Annual of the Department of Antiquities of Jordan*, 33, 287–304.

Brown, R. 2013. "The Middle Islamic Palace at Karak: A New Interpretation of the Grand Qaʿa (Reception Hall)," *Annual of the Department of Antiquities of Jordan*, 57, 309–335.

Carroll, L., Fenner, A., and LaBianca, Ø. S. 2005. "The Ottoman Qasr at Hisban: Architecture, Reform, and New Social Relations," *Near Eastern Archaeology*, 69, 3–4, 138–145.

Cytryn, K. 2016. "Tiberias' Places of Worship in Context," in J. Patrich, O. Peleg-Barkat, and E. Ben-Yosef (eds.), *Arise, Walk Through the Land: Studies in the Archaeology and History of the Land of Israel in Memory of Yizhar Hirschfeld on the Tenth Anniversary of His Demise* (Jerusalem: The Israel Exploration Society), 235–248.

Cytryn-Silverman, K. 2009. "The Umayyad Mosque of Tiberias," *Muqarnas*, 26, 37–61.

Cytryn-Silverman, K. 2010. "City Centre of Early Islamic Tiberias (Tabariyya)," *Fondation Max van Berchem Bulletin*, 23, 5–7.

Damgaard, K. 2009. "A Palestinian Red Sea Port on the Egyptian Road to Arabia: Early Islamic Aqaba and Its Many Hinterlands," in L. Blue, J. Cooper, R. Thomas, and J. Whitewright (eds.), *Connected Hinterlands: Proceedings of the Red Sea Project IV Held at the University of Southampton September 2008*. BAR International Series 2052 (Oxford: Archaeopress), 85–97.

Davidovich, U., Porat, N., Gadot, Y., Avni, Y., and Lipschits, O. 2012. "Archaeological Investigations and OSL Dating of Terraces at Ramat Rahel, Israel," *Journal of Field Archaeology*, 37, 3, 192–208.

Donner, F. 2014. "Periodization as a Tool of the Historian with Special Reference to Islamic History," *Der Islam* 91, 1, 20–36.

Ebeling, J., and Rogel, M. 2015. "The *Tabun* and Its Misidentification in the Archaeological Record," *Levant*, 47, 3, 328–349.

Edelstein, G., Milevski, I., and Avrant, S. 1998. *Villages, Terraces, and Stone Mounds: Excavations at Manaḥat, Jerusalem, 1987–1989*. IAA Reports, No. 3 (Jerusalem: Israel Antiquities Authority).

Ellenblum, R. 2012. *The Collapse of the Eastern Mediterranean: Climate Change and the Decline of the East, 950–1072* (Cambridge: Cambridge University Press).

Farahani, A. 2018. "A 2500-Year Historical Ecology of Agricultural Production Under Empire in Dhiban, Jordan," *Journal of Anthropological Archaeology*, 43, 1–32.

François, V. 2008. *Céramiques de la citadelle de Damas. Époques mamlouke et ottomane* (Aix-en-Provence: CNRS-LAMM [CD-ROM]).

Franken, H. J., and Kalsbeek, J. 1975. *Potters of a Medieval Village in the Jordan Valley: Excavations at Tell Deir Alla, a Medieval Tell, Tell Abu Gourdan, Jordan* (Amsterdam and New York: Elsevier).

Gabrieli, R. S., Ben-Shlomo, D., and Walker, B. J. 2014. "Production and Distribution of Geometrical-Painted (HMGP) and Plain Hand-Made Wares of the Mamluk Period: A Case Study from Northern Israel, Jerusalem and Tall Hisban," *Journal of Islamic Archaeology*, 1, 2, 193–229.

Gadot, Y., Davidovich, U., Avni, G., Avni, Y., Piasetzky, M., Faershtein, G., Golan, D., and Porat, N. 2016. "The Formation of a Mediterranean Terraced Landscape: Mount Eitan, Judean Highlands, Israel," *Journal of Archaeological Science: Reports*, 6, 397–417.

Gadot, Y., Elgart-Sharon, Y., Ben-Melech, N., Davidovich, U., Avni, G., Avni, Y., Porat, N. 2018. "OSL Dating of Pre-Terraced and Terraced Landscape: Land Transformation in Jerusalem's Rural Hinterland," *Journal of Archaeological Science: Reports*, 21, 575–583.

Gawlikowski, M. 1986. "A Residential Area by the South Decumanus," in F. Zayadine (ed.), *Jerash Archaeological Project 1981–1983, vol. 1* (Amman: Department of Antiquities), 107–136.

Genequand, D. 2005. "From 'Desert Castle' to Medieval Town: Qasr al-Hayr al-Sharqi (Syria)," *Antiquity*, 79, 350–361.

Genequand, D. 2012. *Les Établissements des élites Omeyyades en Palmyrène et au Proche-Orient* (Beirut: Institut Français du Proche Orient).

Haiman, M. 1995. "Agriculture and Nomad-State Relations in the Byzantine and Early Islamic Periods," *Bulletin of the American Schools of Oriental Research*, 297, 29–53.

Hansen, A. M., Walker, B. J., and Heinrich, F. 2017. " 'Impressions' of the Mamluk Agricultural Economy: Archaeobotanical Evidence from Clay Ovens (ṭābūn) at Tall Hisban, Jordan," *Tijdschrift voor Mediterrane Archeologie*, 56, 58–69.

Heidemann, S. 2015. "How to Measure Economic Growth in the Middle East?: A Framework of Inquiry for the Middle Islamic Period," in D. Talmon-Heller and K. Cytryn-Silverman (eds.), *Material Evidence and Narrative Sources: Interdisciplinary Studies of the History of the Muslim Middle East* (Leiden: Brill), 30–57.

Imbert, F. 1996. *Corpus des inscriptions arabes de Jordanie du Nord* (PhD diss., Aix-Marseille 1).

Johns, J. 1998. "The Rise of Middle Islamic Hand-Made Geometrically-Painted Ware in Bilâd al-Shâm (11th–13th centuries A.D.)," in R.-P. Gayraud (ed.), *Colloque internationale d'archéologie islamique. IFAO, Le Caire, 3–7 février 1993*. Institut français d'archéologie orientale, Textes arabes et études islamiques, vol. 36 (Cairo: Institut français d'archéologie orientale), 65–93.

Kennedy, H. 1985. "From Polis to Madina: Urban Change in Late Antique and Early Islamic Syria," *Past and Present*, 106, 3–27.

Knabb, K. A., Erel,Y., Tirosh, O., Rittenour, T., Laparidou, S., Najjar, M., Levy, T. E. 2016. "Environmental Impacts of Ancient Copper Mining and Metallurgy: Multi-Proxy Investigation of Human-Landscape Dynamics in the Faynan Valley, Southern Jordan," *Journal of Archaeological Science*, 74, 85–101.

Kouki, P., and Laven, M. (eds.) 2013. *Petra, the Mountain of Aaron. Vol. III. The Archaeological Survey* (Helsinki: Societas Scientiarum Fennica).

Laparidou, S., and. Rosen, A. M. 2015. "Intensification of Production in Medieval Islamic Jordan and Its Ecological Impact: Towns of the Anthropocene," *Holocene*, 25, 10, 1685–1697.

Lawlor, J. I. 1980. "The Excavation of the North Church at Hesban, Jordan: A Preliminary Report," *Andrews University Seminar Studies*, 18, 65–76.

Leiser, G. 1985. "The Madrasa and the Islamization of the Middle East: The Case of Egypt," *Journal of the American Research Center in Egypt*, 22, 29–47.

Lichtenberger, A., and Raja, R. 2016. "Jerash in the Middle Islamic Period: Connecting Texts and Archaeology Through New Evidence from the Northwest Quarter," *Zeitschrift des Deutschen Palästina-Vereins*, 132, 63–81.

Lichtenberger, A., and Raja, R. (eds.) 2017. *Gerasa/Jerash: From the Urban Periphery* (Højbjers: Centre for Urban Network Evolutions [UrbNet], Aarhus University).

Lichtenberger, A., and Raja, R. (eds.) 2018. *Middle Islamic Jerash (9th Century–15th Century): Archaeology and History of an Ayyubid-Mamluk Settlement* (Turnhout: Brepol).

Lichtenberger, A., Raja, R., Eger, C., Kalaitzoglou, G., and Højen Sørensen, A. 2016. "A Newly Excavated Private House in Jerash: Reconsidering Aspects of Continuity and Change in Material Culture from Late Antiquity to the Early Islamic Period," *Antiquité Tardive*, 24, 317–359.

Lindner, M. 1999. "Late Islamic Villages in the Greater Petra Region and Medieval 'Hormuz,'" *Annual of the Department of Antiquities of Jordan*, 43, 479–500.

Lucke, B., al-Saad, Z., Schmidt, M., Bäumler, R., Lorenz, S. O., Udluft, P., Heussner, K.-U, and Walker, B. J. 2008. "Soils and Land Use in the Decapolis Region (Northern Jordan): Implications for Landscape Development and the Impact of Climate Change," *Zeitschrift des Deutschen Palästina-Vereins*, 124, 2, 171–188.

Lucke, B., Shunnaq, M., Walker, B. J., Shiyab, A., al-Muheisen, Z., al-Sababha, H., Bäumler, R., and Schmidt, M. 2012. "Questioning Transjordan's Historic Desertification: A Critical Review of the Paradigm of 'Empty Lands,'" *Levant*, 44, 1, 100–126.

Macumber, P. G. 2008. "Evolving Landscape and Environment in Jordan," in R. B. Adams (ed.), *Jordan: An Archaeological Reader* (London/Oakville: Equinox), 7–34.

Magness, J. 1993. *Jerusalem Ceramic Chronology, circa 200–800 CE* (Sheffield: Sheffield Academic Press).

Magness, J. 2003. *The Archaeology of the Early Islamic Settlement in Palestine* (Winona Lake, IN: Eisenbrauns).

Magness, J. 2004. "Khirbet Abu Sawwana and Ein ʿAneva: Two Early Islamic Settlements on Palestine's Desert Periphery," in D. Whitcomb (ed.), *Changing Social Identity with the Spread of Islam* (Chicago: Oriental Institute), 11–24.

Makowski, P. 2020. *Life among the ruins: an archaeological assessment of Khirbat esh-Dharih and the southern Transjordan during the 10th–12th centuries* (Unpublished PhD diss., University of Warsaw).

McPhillips, S. 2012. "Continuity and Innovation in Syrian Artisanal Traditions of the 9th to 13th Centuries: Ceramic Evidence from the Syrian-French Citadel of Damascus Excavations," *Bulletin d'Études Orientales*, 61, 447–473.

Milwright, M. 2008. *The Fortress of the Raven: Karak in the Middle Islamic Period (1100–1650)* (Leiden: Brill).

Milwright, M. 2010. *An Introduction to Islamic Archaeology* (Edinburgh: Edinburgh University Press).

Nashef, K. 2000. "Khirbet Birzeit Research and Excavation Project, 1996," *Journal of Palestinian Archaeology*, 1, 1: 4–27 (English) and 4–57 (Arabic).

Nashef, K., and Abd Rabu, O. 2000. "Khirbet Birzeit Research and Excavation Project 1999: Third Season Excavation," *Journal of Palestinian Archaeology*, 1, 2, 4–12 (Arabic) and 4–6 (English summary).

Noca, L. 1985. *Smakieh: Un village de Jordanie* (École d'architecture de Lyon: Travail Personnel de Troisième Cycle. Lyon).

Northedge, A. 1992. *Studies on Roman and Islamic ʿAmman* (Oxford: Oxford University Press).

Palmer, C. 1998. "'Following the Plough': The Agricultural Environment of Northern Jordan," *Levant*, 30, 1, 129–165.

al-Qudah, K., Abdelal, Q., Hamarneh, C., and Abu-Jaber, N. 2016. "Taming the Torrents: The Hydrological Impacts of Ancient Terracing Practices in Jordan," *Journal of Hydrology*, 542, 913–922.

Quickel, A. T., and Williams, G. 2016. "In Search of Sibākh: Digging Up Egypt from Antiquity to the Present Day," *Journal of Islamic Archaeology*, 3, 1, 89–108.

Rosen, A. 2007. *Civilizing Climate: Social Responses to Climate Change in the Ancient Near East* (New York: Altamira Press).

Rattenborg, R., and Blanke, L. 2017. "Jarash in the Islamic Ages (ca. 700–1200 CE): A Critical Review," *Levant*, 49, 3, 312–332.

al-Sababha, H. 2018. *Pottery and Communal Identity: Archaeometrical Study of Islamic Ceramic Assemblages in Northern Jordan* (Unpublished PhD diss., University of Bonn).

Sauer, J. 1973. *Hesban Pottery 1971* (Berrien Springs, MI: Andrews University Press).

Schaefer, J., and Falkner, R. 1986. "An Umayyad Potters' Complex in the North Theater, Jerash," in F. Zayadine (ed.), *Jerash Archaeological Project 1981–1983, vol. 1* (Amman: Department of Antiquities), 411–459.

Schick, R. 1995. *The Christian Communities of Palestine from Byzantine to Islamic Rule: An Historical and Archaeological Study* (Princeton: Darwin Press).

Schick, R. 1998. "Palestine in the Early Islamic Period: Luxuriant Legacy," *Near Eastern Archaeology*, 61, 2, 74–108.

Sharon, M. 1997–2004. *Corpus Inscriptionum Arabicarum Palaestinae* (Leiden: Brill).

Simpson, I. 2008. "Market Building at Jarash: Commercial Transformation at the Tetrakionion in the 6th to 9th Centuries C.E.," in K. Bartl and A. Moaz (eds.), *Residences, Castles, Settlement: Transformation Processes from Late Antiquity to Early Islam in Bilad al-Sham* (Rahden: Leidorf), 115–124.

Sinibaldi, M., and Tuttle, C. A. 2011. "The Brown University Petra Archaeological Project: 2010 Excavations at Islamic Bayḍā," *Annual of the Department of Antiquities of Jordan*, 55, 431–450.

Taxel, I. 2018. "Early Islamic Palestine: Toward a More Fine-Tuned Recognition of Settlement Patterns and Land Uses in Town and Country," *Journal of Islamic Archaeology*, 5, 2, 153–180.

Taxel, I., Sivan, D., Bookman, R., Roskin, J. 2018. "An Early Islamic Inter-Settlement Agroecosystem in the Coastal Sand of the Yavneh Dunefield, Israel," *Journal of Field Archaeology*, accessed at https://doi.org/10.1080/00934690.2018.1522189).

Vannini, G., and Nucciotti, M. (eds.) 2009. *Da Petra a Shawbak: Archeologia di una Frontiera* (Florence: University of Florence).

Walker, B. J. (ed.) 2009. *Reflections of Empire: Archaeological and Ethnographic Studies on the Pottery of the Ottoman Levant*. Annual of the American Schools of Oriental Research, vol. 64 (Boston: American Schools of Oriental Research).

Walker, B. J. 2010. "From Ceramics to Social Theory: Reflections on Mamluk Archaeology Today," *Mamluk Studies Review*, 14, 109–157.

Walker, B. J. 2011. *Jordan in the Late Middle Ages: Transformation of the Mamluk Frontier* (Chicago: Middle East Documentation Center, University of Chicago).

Walker, B. J. 2013. "Islamization of Central Jordan in the 7th–9th Centuries: Lessons Learned from Tall Hisban," *Jerusalem Studies in Arabic and Islam*, 40, 143–175.

Walker, B. J. 2014a. "Mobility and Migration in Mamluk Syria: The Dynamism of Villagers 'on the Move'," in S. Conermann (ed.), *Everything Is on the Move: The 'Mamluk Empire' as a Node in (Trans-) Regional Networks* (Bonn: Bonn University Press, Mamluk Studies Series), 325–348.

Walker, B. J. 2014b. "Planned Villages and Rural Resilience on the Mamluk Frontier: A Preliminary Report on the 2013 Excavation Season at Tall Hisban," in S. Conermann (ed.), *History and Society during the Mamluk Period (1250–1517)*. Studies of the Annemarie Schimmel Research College I (Bonn: University of Bonn Press), 157–192.

Walker, B. J. 2017. "The Struggle over Water: Evaluating the 'Water Culture' of Syrian Peasants Under Mamluk Rule" (ch. 14), in Y. Ben-Bassat (ed.), *Developing Perspectives in Mamluk History* (Leiden: Brill), 287–310.

Walker, B. J. 2018a. "Settlement Abandonment and Site Formation Processes: Case Studies from Late Islamic Syria," in M. Ritter and M. Guidetti (eds.), *Proceedings of the Tenth International Conference on the Archaeology of the Near East, 2016* (Leipzig: Harrassowitz Verlag), 681–694.

Walker, B. J. 2020. "Khirbah," *Encyclopaedia of Islam*, 3rd revised version (Leiden: Brill. In print, online version: https://referenceworks.brillonline.com/browse/encyclopaedia-of-islam-3).

Walker, B. J., Bates, R., Hudon, J., and LaBianca, Ø. S. 2017a. "Tall Hisban 2013 and 2014 Excavation Seasons: Exploration of the Medieval Village and Long-Term Water Systems," *Annual of the Department of Antiquities of Jordan*, 58, 483–523.

Walker, B. J., Bates, R., Polla, S., Springer, A., Weihe, S. 2017b. "Residue Analysis as Evidence of Activity Areas and Phased Abandonment in a Medieval Jordanian Village," *Journal of Islamic Archaeology*, 4, 2, 217–248.

Walker, B. J., and Dolinka. B. 2020. "Khirbet Beit Mazmil, Investigations of Medieval Jerusalem's Hinterland: Preliminary Report on the 2015 and 2017 Seasons," *Zeitschrift des Deutschen Palästina-Vereins*, 136, 2, in print.

Walker, B. J., Gadot, Y., Elgart-Sharon, E., and Ze'evi, O. 2020. "Agricultural Terracing and Rural Revival in Late Medieval Palestine," in A. Otto, M. Herles, K. Kaniuth, L. Korn, and A. Heidenreich (eds.), *Proceedings of the 11th International Congress on the Archaeology of the Ancient Near East, 03–07 April 2018*, Munich (Wiesbaden: Harrassowitz Verlag), 651–662.

Walker, B. J., Kenney, E., Carroll, L., Holzweg, L., Boulogne, S., Lucke, B. 2007. "The Northern Jordan Project 2006: Village Life in Mamluk and Ottoman Hubras and Sahm: A Preliminary Report," *Annual of the Department of Antiquities of Jordan*, 51, 429–470.

Walker, B. J., Laparidou, S., Hansen, A., Corbino, C. 2017c. "Did the Mamluks Have an Environmental Sense? Natural Resources Management in Syrian Villages," *Mamluk Studies Review*, 20, 167–245.

Walmsley, A. 2001. "Fatimid, Ayyubid and Mamluk Jordan and the Crusader Interlude," in B. Macdonald, R. Adams, and P. Bienkowski (eds.), *The Archaeology of Jordan* (Sheffield: Sheffield Academic Press), 515–560.

Walmsley, A. 2012. *Early Islamic Syria: An Archaeological Assessment* (London: Bristol Classical Press).

Walmsley, A., Blanke, L., Damgaard, K., Mellah, A., McPhillips, S., Roenje, L., Simpson, I., and Bessard, F. 2008. "A Mosque, Shops and Bath in Central Jerash: The 2007 Season of the Islamic Jerash Project," *Annual of the Department of Antiquities of Jordan,* 52, 109–137.

Walmsley, A., and Grey, A. 2001. "An Interim Report on the Pottery from Gharandal (Arindela), Jordan," *Levant,* 33, 139–164.

Watson, A. M. 1983. *Agricultural Innovation in the Early Islamic World: The Diffusion of Crops and Farming Techniques* (Cambridge: Cambridge University Press).

Watson, P. 1992. "Change in Foreign and regional Economic Links with Pella in the Seventh Century A.D.: The Ceramic Evidence," in P. Canivet and J.P. Rey-Coquais (eds.), *La Syrie de Byzance à l'Islam VIIe—VIIIe siècles* (Damascus: Institute Français de Damas), 233–247.

Whitcomb, D. 1988. "Khirbet al-Mafjar Reconsidered: The Ceramic Evidence," *Bulletin of the American Schools of Oriental Research,* 271, 51–79.

Whitcomb, D. 1998. "A Fatimid Residence at Aqaba, Jordan," *Annual of the Department of Antiquities of Jordan,* 32, 207–224.

Whitcomb, D. 2012–2013. "Jericho Mafjar Project," *The Oriental Institute 2012–2013 Annual Report* (University of Chicago), 61–65.

Whitcomb, D., and Taha, H. 2013. "Khirbat al-Mafjar and Its Place in Archeological Heritage of Palestine," *Journal of Eastern Mediterranean Archaeology and Heritage Studies,* 1, 1, 54–65.

FURTHER READING

Ababsa, M. (ed.) 2014. *Atlas of Jordan: History, Territories and Society* (Beirut: Institut Français du Proche Orient).

Avissar, M., and Stern, E. J. 2005. *Pottery of the Crusader, Ayyubid and Mamluk Periods in Israel* (Jerusalem: Israel Antiquities Authority).

McPhillips, S., and Wordsworth, P. D. (eds.) 2016. *Landscapes of the Islamic World: Archaeology, History, and Ethnography* (Philadelphia: University of Pennsylvania Press).

McQuitty, A. 2008. "The Ottoman Period," in R. B. Adams (ed.), *Jordan: An Archaeological Reader* (London/Oakville: Equinox), 539–568.

Sauer, J., and Magness, J. 1997. "Ceramics: Ceramics of the Islamic Period," in *The Oxford Encyclopedia of Archaeology in the Near East* (New York: Oxford University Press), 475–479.

Walker, B. J. 1999. "Militarization to Nomadization: The Middle and Late Islamic Periods," *Near Eastern Archaeology,* 62, 4, 202–232.

Walmsley, A. 2008. "The Middle Islamic and Crusader Periods," in R. B. Adams (ed.), *Jordan: An Archaeological Reader* (London/Oakville: Equinox), 495–537.

Whitcomb, D. 2008. "The Umayyad and Abbasid Periods," in R. B. Adams (ed.), *Jordan: An Archaeological Reader* (London/Oakville: Equinox), 483–493.

IRAQ

ALASTAIR NORTHEDGE

IRAQ is a very different sort of country from those discussed elsewhere in this section, those surrounding the Mediterranean, and the deserts of Arabia (Figure 2.3.1). It is divided into two: the alluvial plain of the south, a desert watered by the Tigris and the Euphrates, and the rolling country of the north. The south is the true al-'Iraq, which extends in the map of Ibn Hawqal in the manuscripts of *Surat al-Ard* as far north as Tikrit. The present state also includes the north, ancient Assyria, a land which frequently receives enough rain for cultivation without irrigation, and is bordered by the mountains of Kurdistan to the east. In medieval times this was divided off into the separate province of al-Jazira.[1]

It is particularly unusual in having begun the Islamic period at the height of its prosperity and wealth and ending up in Ottoman times as a poor frontier territory, its position of prominence taken by Egypt and Iran. Quite why this might have been is naturally a major theme of this chapter and is certainly related to the very unusual nature of the Iraqi environment. Because it is a flat land at the foot of the Iranian plateau, with the Mediterranean states to the west, Iraq has always been a land particularly exposed to foreign invasion and occupation, mainly from Iran. The location of Baghdad itself made it a target, such as at the time of the Mongols.

There has been relatively little work on the Islamic archaeology of Iraq and less synthesis. Part of the reason has been the political difficulties since 1958, which have sometimes impeded and at other times outright prevented fieldwork: Why should Islamic archaeologists go and have a hard time in Iraq when it is easier to work elsewhere? Another significant reason is the lack of evident fine medieval architecture in Iraq because nearly all was built of mudbrick. Only at the beginning of the 20th century did

---

[1] The identity of Iraq as a genuine entity has been often questioned for political reasons. This subject was studied by the author in Northedge (2007). The conclusion was that in ancient times Mesopotamia was divided into two, Assyria and Babylonia, populations who both spoke the same language, Akkadian, in different dialects, which distinguished them from surrounding countries, and Iraq was thus as unified as any state existing today.

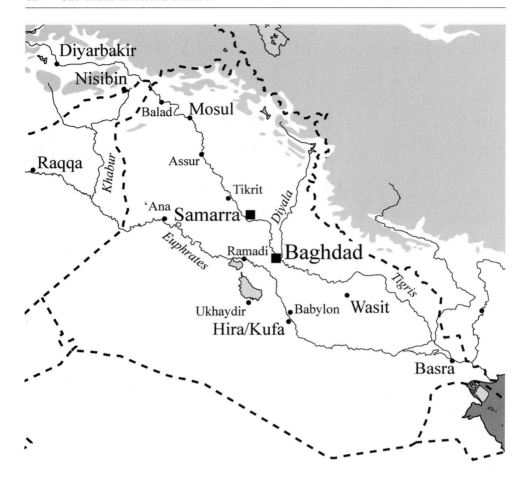

FIGURE 2.3.1 Map of Iraq showing sites.

Sarre and Herzfeld (1911) do studies of the medieval architecture, followed by the German expedition for the excavation of Samarra in 1911–1913.

Even more important was the concentration of Western archaeologists on ancient Mesopotamia. Rich finds were to be made from Assyrian, Babylonian, and Sumerian sites, which could be exported to museums in the West. It was not until the British mandate period, when an Arab nationalist, Sati' al-Husri, formerly Minister of Education, was appointed Director of Antiquities in 1932, that Islamic period excavations were renewed at the classic Islamic sites of Kufa, Wasit, and Samarra from 1936 onward, entirely an Iraqi operation.

The first new elements came from the technique of surface survey, newly introduced to the Middle East by the Americans, notably in the Diyala project. Published in 1965 as *Land Behind Baghdad*, Adams, though primarily a Mesopotamian archaeologist, brought to life the landscape of the Islamic period even if today we may have some doubts about his dating and understanding of Islamic history. This study was followed by surveys of the south, published as *The Uruk Countryside*, of lesser importance for us, and *Heartland of Cities*. Since then we have had the survey of Samarra and a good number of Iraqi excavations, but little synthesis of understanding the settlement processes. A bibliography of Islamic archaeology in Iraq was published by Rousset in 1992.

SOUTHERN IRAQ AND THE IRRIGATION SYSTEM

The Environment

Iraq has quite a severe continental climate, with temperatures varying between 5° C in the winter, and 42° C in the summer. The rainfall is an average of 108 millimeters per annum at Baghdad, ranging up to 134 millimeters in wetter decades, but in any case insufficient for cultivation. Southern Iraq is necessarily a land of irrigation agriculture.

The land is an alluvial plain formed by the Tigris and the Euphrates, the consequence of the alluvium washed down by the rivers from the highlands of Anatolia. The alluvial plain begins just south of Samarra on the Tigris and at Ramadi on the Euphrates, and it stretches more than 600 kilometers, as far as the Gulf. The altitude of the Tigris is 50 meters at Qadisiyya, and it follows that the fall of the Tigris is a gradient of only 1:12,000. The major supplier of water is the Tigris, with the Euphrates in second place, but there are minor additional supplies from the Iranian plateau from the rivers Karun, Diyala, 'Adhaym, and the two Zabs.

The regime of the two rivers is such that when the snows of Anatolia melt, it causes a rush of water and flooding. This occurs in the spring, not the ideal time for irrigating winter wheat, which is sown in January and harvested in May. The floods have largely been stopped now in modern times, first by the construction of a diversion channel to fill Lake Tharthar, northwest of Baghdad, and second by modern dams. Floods, however, were an ever-present threat in medieval times, and Baghdad was frequently flooded (Sousa 1963).

The flat landscape meant that the water moved slowly and tended to deposit its alluvium quickly, although the characteristics of the water from Anatolia are not unusually silty or salty. Major changes of the river courses could occur, provoked usually at the crisis times of the floods but frequently taking centuries to finally confirm. A famous event was the flood at the end of the Sasanian period which diverted the water of the Euphrates into the marshes of southern Iraq with no apparent outlet of the river into the Gulf, as it is depicted in early Islamic maps, although it is probable that the water did find its way out (Le Strange 1895; Nützel 1982). This occurred under Khusraw Parviz in the year 7 or 8 of the hijra (628), although earlier events had occurred under Qubad I a century earlier. The Euphrates channel was not restored until the 9th (15th) century (Nützel 1982). A second event was the diversion of the Tigris channel between Samarra and Baghdad further to the east, culminating in the 7th (13th) century, when the caliph al-Mustansir was obliged to dig new canals and build the bridge at Harba that bears his name (Northedge 2005: 39). A third significant event was the drying out of the course of the Tigris which led directly south from Kut al-Amara and past Wasit. It slowly dried out, and the water was diverted further east into the present channel.

In Islamic times, the Tigris moved east; the Euphrates moved west until it hit the barrier of the higher land of the Iraqi Western Desert. It has been suggested that it was only very slight changes of height, some caused by alluviation on the old course, which could persuade the water to flow otherwise once the break was made in the floods.

Human Development of the Landscape

The southern alluvial plain was first exploited in the Ubaid period (5400–4300 BC), as far as is known. At any rate, significant urban development was based on the advantages of irrigation agriculture. For example, winter wheat will give a product of six times the quantity of seed sown if irrigated, whereas the harvest is only 2–2.5 times in the case of rain-fed dry agriculture in the Middle East. In the second millennium BC, the center of settlement moved further north to the region of Babylon and then in Classical times to the region of Baghdad.

Already in the third millennium BC there are recorded signs of salinity affecting the crops. The problem is not that the Tigris and Euphrates water is exceptionally saline, but evidently the high summer temperatures evaporate water and concentrate its salt. In particular, in the soil, hygrometric processes bring the salt up to the surface and leave a coating of salt on the surface. Many crops, such as wheat, are not salt tolerant, and the phenomenon seriously disrupts agriculture. It is more severe, the more irrigation water is supplied. This problem was notoriously brought to the fore in Islamic times, in the 3rd (9th) century in the revolt of the Zanj slaves around Basra (Popovic 1976). They had been set to work to scrape the salt off the surface of the land (sabkha)—an ineffective solution in practice because more salt will only leach up.

The other aspect which affected settlement was the small-scale changes to elevations caused by alluviation in the flat landscape, which nevertheless led to significant changes in the settlement pattern and major river movements, mentioned earlier. One case is the desert space between the Tigris and the Euphrates, though now largely cultivated, where many of the city-sites of ancient Mesopotamia are located. The Euphrates flowed substantially to the east of its present course. The area was extensively surveyed by Adams in the 1960s and 1970s and was published in 1981 as *Heartland of Cities*. Adams's technique was to locate sites from aerial photographs—which were difficult to obtain at the time—and then collect surface sherds from site visits. Not much work went into identifying remains of actual irrigation canals—it was rather presumed that a canal existed if occupation sites were there. To a certain extent, this was inevitable as the remains of very ancient canals do not preserve well, though Islamic-period canals are often preserved in good condition. Today the work would be easier with availability of satellite imagery. Evidently, the area surveyed was mainly outside the cultivated area and so does not tell us as much about the Islamic period occupation, which is mainly in the areas still occupied today. At any rate the main central group of canals derived from the Euphrates, south of and near Nippur. With the Euphrates flowing at a higher level, all canals flowing between the two rivers took their water from the Euphrates. Cultivation and occupation slowly expanded until it reached a maximum in the Sasanian period. The situation was slightly more complicated in the sense that, after the conquests of Alexander and the foundation of a new capital at Seleucia, and subsequently added to by the Partho-Sasanian city of Ctesiphon, the focus moved further north to the area of Baghdad and, more importantly, to the Tigris basin. That only confirms the efforts made under the Sasanians to expand agriculture as the canal system ran down as far as Ruqbat al-Mada'in, at that time on the edge of the marshes. According to Adams, the apogee was only reached in the 5th and 6th centuries, but in fact his dating material was not so refined, and he was mainly depending on historical sources.

In Abbasid times the system was slowly cut back. Adams gives a date of the Samarra period in the 9th century and earlier, but in fact the ceramic type series he was using has been shown to be inaccurate. Some of the type fossils used to date for the Sasanian period could in fact be Umayyad, and at least one major type fossil of the Samarra period—early sgraffiato ware—was in fact not introduced before the first half of the 10th century. So Adams's dating must be pushed back later by approximately a century.

When a new canal was dug from the same point in Umayyad times (it remained into the Il-Khanid period), it went in a different direction—directly east to the Tigris (Shatt al-Nil), and the formerly rich area was left increasingly to the desert. This suggests that the primary reason for decline was not economic or political, but environmental. Over the centuries, the deposit of alluvium had raised the land surface, and the water would no longer flow easily. In this flat landscape even minor changes in altitude cause canal beds to divert (Gasche and Tanret 1998). Supplementary factors might be the difficulty of cleaning out a canal system stretching for 225 kilometers as well as potential salinization, though no trace of this remains.

The sequence of events in different regions is rarely the same. It cannot be said that what happened in the central plain was repeated elsewhere. The case of the Diyala basin, however, is important for the Islamic period. The Diyala was seen as relatively provincial in Babylonian times, home to the Diyala culture at the end of the third millennium BC. Without doubt the use of water from the Diyala became far more significant with the foundation of Seleucia as the de facto capital, succeeded as it was under the Parthians by Ctesiphon on the east side of the Tigris. There were already canal systems deriving from the Diyala and irrigating the plain south of the Diyala in early times, but a new massive system was dug, according to Adams's *Land Behind Baghdad*, in Parthian times, though it might have been under the early Sasanians. This system drained back into the Tigris at Madharaya (Muqdadiyya) and was named Nahrawan, after the town at its offtake from the Diyala.

In the 6th century, a new feeder was added, leaving the Tigris at Samarra and with two entrances to accommodate low- and high-water conditions. This massive enterprise, with beds varying between 25 and 90 meters wide, was called in part al-Qatul al-Kisrawi (Cut of Khusraw), and its royal character was signaled by a commemorative tower (Burj al-Qa'im) at the southern entrance and a hunting palace at the northern entrance. The system was extended by the early Abbasids—Harun al-Rashid and al-Ma'mun—and stimulated the foundation of Samarra as the second Abbasid capital. The new feeder probably lasted into the 10th century, when, at some stage not precisely defined, the Tigris broke into the extended system and slowly turned part of it into the Tigris bed, culminating in the 7th (13th) century, when it left the previous bed dry, an event which led to the construction of the bridge at Harba in 1232 (Northedge 2005). The lower Nahrawan was cut deliberately in 937, but restored, and it continued to flow until about 1150. That is, it flowed for about six to seven centuries, an impressive duration without major renewal.

There were also the Ishaqi and Dujayl systems on the west side of the Tigris, and the four canals derived from the Euphrates which flowed into the Tigris: Nahr 'Isa, Nahr Sarsar, Nahr al-Malik, and Nahr Kutha. Unfortunately the history of these canals has not been studied in much detail.

The story in the written texts is completely different, particularly the chronicles recounting the decline of Abbasid power in the 10th century. According to Ibn Miskawaih's *The Experiences of the Nations*, the problem was the fecklessness of the politicians of the day, and this explanation has largely been taken up by today's historians. But it is evident that the long-term themes of Iraq's development were invisible to medieval chroniclers. Although we do not know all the details, and there are some disputes about how high late Sasanian revenues really were, it is evident that Sasanian investment in agriculture was considerable. At the time of the conquest, agricultural revenues in Iraq were exceptionally high, and early Abbasid Caliphs up to al-Ma'mun and al-Mu'tasim (Nahr al-Ishaqi) were interested in expanding the cultivated area, following the Sasanian policy. The historical sources talk about administrative irresponsibility and lack of interest leading to the decline of revenues from agriculture from the 9th century onward. But it is obvious that Iraq was a declining asset for caliphal revenues. It was very difficult to maintain such long canals and to prevent alluviation. The rush of new water has been shown to stimulate salinization in other irrigation schemes, such as those of the British in the Punjab in the early 20th century. It is striking that these canals were never substantially renovated to sustain this agricultural production. Although rulers were condemned for not investing in agriculture, projects of such dimensions were probably beyond the feeble financial capacities of the medieval city-states, whose finance depended on the *iqta'* (the allotment of districts to military commanders from which they themselves collected the taxes). But the consequence was the decline of state revenues in Iraq, and it lost its primacy.

THE MAIN CITIES

The Early *Amsar*

With the success of the conquests of Syria in 634–636, and Iraq in 637, the question arose of how to settle the troops in the captured territories—troops who were then to furnish the forces for extending these conquests further. The texts present the issue as the decadence of existing cities and the necessity to maintain contact with the caliph in Medina. In general, it was decided to settle them in new cities, called *misr* (pl. *amsar*). The first two were in Iraq: Basra and Kufa, both founded in 17 (638). Old Basra was located at the modern town of al-Zubayr, west of modern Basra, and much of it remains an open archaeological site, although little excavated. It was divided into five tribal quarters in the early period, and the site of the mosque is known (Al-'Azzawi 1994). Recently the alignment of the wall has been defined, which gives us the area of the city.

Kufa is much better known from the texts (Djait 1986) but since a modern town exists there covering the remains, only the site of the mosque and the governor's palace is known archaeologically. The site was located on the north side of the Lakhmid capital of al-Hira and can be considered a suburb of it, though it quickly replaced al-Hira. In its initial form, there was a central square with a mosque featuring a prayer hall with reused columns from al-Hira. Although Creswell thought there was a ditch around the mosque (Creswell 1969: 24, fig. 14), Antun has argued that the ditch surrounded the central square, separating it from the surrounding cantonments (Antun 2016). Thus the courtyard of the mosque was the central square, which was also used for the main market. There was a residence for the governor separated by a roadway. In 670, Ziyad b. Abi Sufyan rebuilt the mosque in fired brick and the governor's palace (*Qasr al-Imara*, elsewhere more generally *Dar al-Imara*), which was moved adjacent to the *qibla* wall. Although some have objected (Johns 1999: 111), it seems likely that the present remains are those of 670 in their origin. Stylistically, the remains are very archaic. Only the *qibla* wall of the early mosque exists today—a fired brick enclosure with half-round buttresses, 103 meters square (200 cubits)[2]—and the interior is new. Between 1938 and 1956, the Directorate-General of Antiquities excavated the *Qasr al-Imara*, finding a palace with a double enclosure. In the interior enclosure, there is a four-*iwan* plan with a main *iwan* with a vault supported on piers in the Sasanid style, surrounded by apartments, much rebuilt later on. According to the excavators the mosque and palace are bonded, but only in the second phase. Probably what was taken as the first phase was in fact the foundation (Northedge 2017).

According to the texts, the city was unwalled, but the extent of the ancient city can be detected in Corona satellite images from 1968. At the end of the Umayyad period, there were fifteen avenues dividing the tribal quarters (*manahij*). It is unlikely that the

---

[2] The cubit (ar. *dhira'*), though with many variants, is approximately equal to 50 centimeters.

suggestion of Djait—that the plan was orthogonal—is correct. One supposes that, situated adjacent to al-Hira, it followed a similar arrangement but with the addition of the central public area which survives today, borrowed from Medina of the time of the Prophet. The problem of Kufa was that large numbers of tribal contingents immigrated, no doubt seeking paid employment as *muqatila* (fighters) for the further conquests. So one has the image of a large number of small tribal leaders surrounded by the houses of their followers, all paid by the state. No doubt the free spaces found earlier were filled with the mudbrick houses of the followers. The result was quite unstable. There were many revolts, including that of al-Husayn b. 'Ali b. Abi Talib in 680, and the revolts were only suppressed by the brutal Umayyad governor, al-Hajjaj b. Yusuf al-Thaqafi, when he demobilized the Iraqi fighters in the reign of 'Abd al-Malik. Nevertheless the Abbasid conspiracy started there and led to the revolution of 132 (750) that toppled the Umayyad dynastic state. Even then Kufa continued to be important, until the rise of Najaf in the 4th (10th) century with its tomb of the Prophet's son-in-law 'Ali, 11 kilometers to the west.

The third early Islamic city was Wasit, located south of Kut on an earlier branch of the Shatt al-Gharraf, founded by Hajjaj b. Yusuf as the Syrian garrison in Iraq after the demobilization of the Iraqi *muqatila* in 705. The mosque has been excavated, but otherwise only a *madrasa* is to be seen, dating to the 7th (13th) century. The city survived into the 11th (17th) century.

BAGHDAD AND THE ABBASIDS

Once in power, after 750, the Abbasids built a series of new capitals—two called al-Hashimiyya (after their dynastic ancestor) whose locations remain unknown—before Abu Ja'far al-Mansur founded Baghdad in 762–766. Baghdad, formally *Madinat al-Salam*, was laid out in a way that developed from the *amsar*. At the center, on the west bank of the Tigris, was the caliph's circular city, called Madinat Abi Ja'far (known to us as the Round City; Figure 2.3.2). To the south of it lay the market area of al-Karkh. According to the sources, this only became the market area after the merchants were expelled from the Round City (Lassner 1970a: 60–62). However, as is evident from the name, al-Karkh, a Syriac word meaning "fortified city" (*Karkhe*), must have been a small pre-Islamic town, outside which the Round City was built. From the four gates of the Round City, the four Grand Avenues extended into the suburbs (*rabad* pl. *arbad*). The suburbs were divided into four quarters (*arba'*), and each was governed by an associate of al-Mansur. There was a further Grand Avenue (*shari' a'zam*) on the Tigris. From 769 onward, the heir of al-Mansur, al-Mahdi, came back from Rayy in Iran and settled on the east bank of the Tigris in al-Rusafa, in a typical arrangement where the eldest son had his own establishment.

The new element in the plan, apart from the fact that the quarters were no longer divided by tribe, was the Round City. The city was famous for being circular, with the mosque and the caliph's palace placed in the center. The detailed textual description

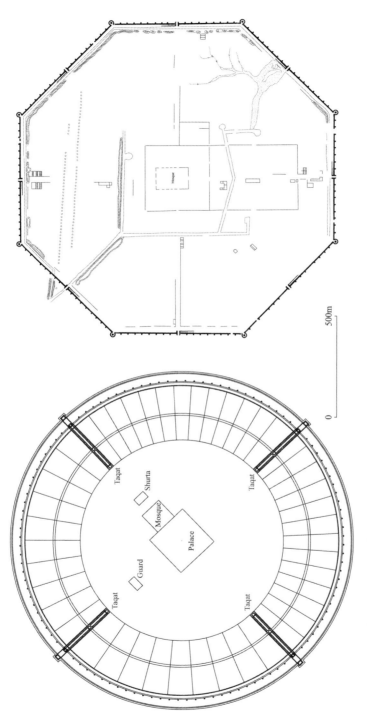

Taqat

Shurta

Taqat

Mosque

Palace

Guard

Taqat

Taqat

Mosque

500m

0

FIGURE 2.3.2 The Round City of Baghdad compared to the Octagon at Qadisiyya (Samarra Archaeological Survey).

found in the *Kitab al-Buldan* of al-Ya'qubi and the topographical introduction of the *Ta'rikh Baghdad* of al-Khatib al-Baghdadi, translated by Lassner (Lassner 1970a), is difficult to confirm as no archaeological trace of it has been discovered. The plan was first reconstructed by Herzfeld and then corrected by Lassner, from the textual sources without much reference to archaeological evidence. However two imitations of the Round City still exist by which one can judge the descriptions of Baghdad: al-Rafiqa: the Abbasid city at Raqqa and the Octagon of Qadisiyya, called al-Mubarak. Al-Rafiqa is not circular, but rather horseshoe-shaped, but it was described as imitating Baghdad (Al-Tabari 1879–1901: III, 276; Al-Baladhuri 1866: 179). Al-Qadisiyya is an octagon, geometrically related to a circle.

The concept of the Round City, if new, was however based on existing ideas, including partly on the plans of the *amsar*. Al-Ya'qubi tells us that the circular plan had never been seen before (Al-Ya'qubi 1982: 242). However, in reality, circular plans are quite frequent in Mesopotamian architecture, and concentric, roughly circular city plans are already known from the Bronze Age at Mari and Tell Chuera in Syria. The closest example is that of the early Sasanian circular city of Ardashir-Khurreh (Firuzabad), southeast of Shiraz in Iran (3rd century CE); it is 1,900 meters in diameter, with double walls and a radial plan (Huff 1969–1970).

In the round city of Baghdad, all as described by al-Ya'qubi (1982: 240), in the center of the *rahba* (courtyard) lay the palace of al-Mansur, whose gate was called Bab al-Dhahab (Golden Gate), 400 cubits a side, and the mosque, 200 cubits square. In a circle around the *rahba* were the following buildings:

> The residences of the younger children of al-Mansur, and his vassals (*mawali*) who are close to him in his service, the *bayt al-mal* (the treasury), the arsenal, the *diwan al-rasa'il* (bureau of correspondence), the *diwan al-kharaj* (the land tax), the *diwan al-khatam* (the seal), the *diwan al-jund* (the army), the *diwan al-hawa'ij* (requirements), the *diwan* of the entourages (*ahsham*), the public kitchen, and the *diwan al-nafaqat* (expenditures).

Then there were four vaulted streets (*taqat*), which led to the gates of Kufa, Basra, Khurasan, and al-Sham (Damascus). These were initially occupied by merchants, providing local markets of the type seen in the cantonments at Samarra. There were also forty-five radial streets (*sikka*), which were "known by [the names of] his *quwwad* and his *mawali*." The great prison, al-Matbaq, was also located in the streets. The expression "*mawali*" normally refers to personal vassals, but may here refer to the servants of the palace, probably also including other officials. It is certain that the *quwwad* were the commanders of the army. In Samarra, these commanders were quartered with their soldiers, with one exception.

The Round City must have been an important military settlement in the time of al-Mansur. Al-Ḥarbiyya, the northwestern suburb outside the Round City, was also an important settlement of the army: according to al-Ya'qubi (1982: 248), it was settled by Central Asians "the people of Balkh, Merv, al-Khuttal, Bukhara, Isbishab, Ishtakhanj, the people of the Kabulshah, the people of Khwarazm." In this last text it is not certain whether al-Ya'qubi is speaking of his own lifetime in the 3rd (9th) century. The names appear to speak of later recruitment than the time of al-Mansur, such as that of the 'Abbasiyya of Harun al-Rashid or the Iranian and Central Asian forces recruited by al-Ma'mun.

One may conclude that the Round City was intended by al-Mansur to accommodate the palace, the mosque, the administration, the servants of the palace, and an important part of the army. Other units of the army were later settled outside the walls. Al-Mansur settled in the Round City all the elements of the state which were important to him, if we compare these details with the detailed state budget of al-Mu'tadid at the end of the 3rd (9th) century, which has survived. This was the new concept in Baghdad: a royal city in which the majority of the functions of the state were assembled under the eyes of the caliph and separated from the public areas of the city by a fortification. The public only entered for prayers in the congregational mosque, which, according to the earlier tradition, was placed next to the palace. The problem of the security of the caliph is much mentioned in the historical sources—that of letting the general public in for prayers in the mosque—and, in the end, it was al-Mansur who left the Round City and settled in a new palace, al-Khuld (Eternity), on the banks of the Tigris, in 159 (774).

Imitating Baghdad

The Abbasid caliph al-Mahdi (r. 158 [775]–169 [785]) built al-Rusafa on the east bank of the Tigris in Baghdad, and, later, Isabadh, both now lost. Harun al-Rashid began the construction of the Octagon at Qadisiyya, under the name of al-Mubarak, to celebrate the new canal, the Qatul Abi al-Jund. But the construction was abandoned in 180 (796), when he moved to Raqqa in Syria, and settled round the earlier imitation of the Round City at al-Rafiqa.

The Octagon of Qadisiyya (al-Mubarak)

The Octagon of Qadisiyya (Figure 2.3.2) is an unfinished, almost regular octagon. Three avenues lead to the central square where the mosque is the central element, placed on the axis of the city. By contrast with the Round City and al-Rafiqa, where the palace is the central element, the mosque is now centrally placed and the palace displaced to the south, a separation that was perpetuated in Samarra and later cites. Nevertheless, the correspondence of the details to those of the Round City is remarkable. Although octagonal and possessing only a single fortification wall, the city was built with mudbricks measuring 1 cubit, a canal was led into the city for the construction, and ramps led up to the top of the walls, probably leading to reception halls over the gates, all as described for Baghdad.

The site appears to be identified with a *qasr* built by Harun al-Rashid called al-Mubarak (the Blessed) (Al-Hamadhani 1987: 143). Al-Ṭabari (1879–1901: III, 1180) however calls it a city and tells us that it was abandoned unfinished on Harun's departure to Raqqa in 180 (796). Evidently it was built first to commemorate the digging of the canal Qatul Abi al-Jund. However it was too large for a simple hunting palace, and Harun must have been intending to settle there permanently, in the way he did later at Raqqa.

The most important point in the comparison of the Round City of Baghdad to Qadisiyya and Raqqa is that the two copies both have similar dimensions: Raqqa is 1,350 meters overall across the grid, and the Octagon is approximately 1,500 meters between the sides. It has been thought that the Round City was larger, about 2,500–2,638 meters in diameter, according to the conclusions of Creswell (1940: 7–8). According to al-Ya'qubi the Round City was 5,000 cubits from one gate to the other, outside the moat. This figure has been presumed by Creswell to be one-quarter of the circumference, but the text could also mean half the circumference. In this latter case, the Round City would have been of similar dimensions to its two imitations, for its overall diameter would have been 1,655 meters, and the largest overall dimension of the Octagon, between the corner towers, is 1,659 meters.

EARLY CASTLES

In fact the early architecture, such as that of Baghdad, can only be judged from the Iraqi equivalents of the Umayyad castles—in particular the two castles of Tulul al-Ukhaydir (Sassano-Umayyad) and Ukhaydir itself (c. 770, built by an uncle of the caliph al-Mansur, 'Isa b. 'Ali, who died in that year). Castles were evidently a feature of late pre-Islamic Arab construction, continuing to the beginning of the Abbasid period, as much in Iraq as in Syria. Tulul al-Ukhaydir, partly excavated by Finster in 1973, is a rectangular structure with an *iwan* and evidence of both Christian and Muslim cults (Finster and Schmidt 1976, 2005). Ukhaydir is a building contemporaneous with Baghdad, with a plan in common with Mshatta in Jordan, but with a double enclosure. There is little decoration, vaulted roofing, and, at Ukhaydir, apartments with facing *iwan*s. These buildings together with Anba' on the Euphrates represent the last elements of the "desert castle" tradition.

SAMARRA

Samarra (Figure 2.3.3) was built as the new seat of the caliphs and as a military base in 221 (836) (Northedge 2005). In many ways, the archaeological interest of Samarra is not only that it is the open site of a major Islamic capital city, but also that it provides the archaeological evidence for one point in the less fully evidenced development of urbanism seen elsewhere.

FIGURE 2.3.3 The site of Samarra (Samarra Archaeological Survey).

A site as well preserved as Samarra has attracted many to work on it, notably Henri Viollet's limited sondages and Ernst Herzfeld's more extensive expedition at the beginning of the 20th century. Most work on Samarra has been from the Iraqis, though I have conducted surface work mainly from air photos and satellite images.

The foundation is to be connected with the recruitment by al-Mu'tasim of the regiment of slave Turks from 200 (816) onward. Fortunately, at Samarra, we have a more or less complete list of the army, which we do not have in Baghdad. The army of Samarra was not limited to Turks, and there were many other units. The so-called *jund* was probably composed of the descendants of the Khurasani army of the early Abbasid period. There were the slave Turks, but also princes from Central Asia taken into the service of the caliph together with their military followings. There were ethnic groups of Khazar and Faraghina (from Farghana in Uzbekistan). On the other side there were Arabs: Maghariba, ex-prisoners from al-Mu'tasim's campaigns in Egypt, and the 12,000 "Arabs, Ṣa'alik and others" who were settled around the Balkuwara palace.

The city of Samarra, laid out on the east bank of the Tigris, can be described as composed of an unwalled agglomeration of a number of units, each one with an orthogonal grid of streets. The central unit was the city of al-Mu'tasim, Surra Man Ra'a ("He who sees it is delighted"), founded in 221 (836). The caliph's palace, which was called the Dar al-Khilafa (House of the Caliphate) but has been generally known as the Jawsaq al-Khaqani (Castle of the Khaqan), was placed at the north end of the city. It was divided into two units: the Dar al-'Amma (House of the Public) and al-Jawsaq al-Khaqani. The Dar al-'Amma corresponds to the *dar al-imara* in other cities (though it is no longer adjacent to the Friday mosque), and al-Jawsaq al-Khaqani was the private residence of the caliph. From the south gate of the Dar al-Khilafa, a main avenue (later called by al-Ya'qubi the Shari' Abi Ahmad) led to the mosque of al-Mu'tasim, the markets. and then farther south. On both sides of the avenue were military cantonments. The expression used by al-Ya'qubi for both military and civil cantonments is "*qati'a*," in the place of "*rabad*" used in Baghdad. The original plan was then built over by the development of the city under later caliphs.

The basic plan of palace, avenue, and grid of streets was copied for the cantonment of the Turks to the north at al-Karkh under Ashnas (*qata'i' al-Karkh*) and to the south for the cantonment of the Soghdians under al-Afshin at al-Matira. The establishment of these large military cantonments separated from Surra Man Ra'a was driven by the desire of al-Mu'tasim to isolate the Turks from mixing with the native population of the city. These military cantonments were based on the model of the suburbs (*rabads*) of Baghdad. The plan of the *qata'i'*, with its palace, avenue, and grid of streets, is very similar to the descriptions by al-Ya'qubi of the principles used in setting out the *rabads* in Baghdad.

The city of Samarra contained elements both of the "created" and "spontaneous" city. That is, the central city was founded in 221 (836) and then continued to develop in a spontaneous way, while new planned quarters were added around the central core. This agglomerative structure recalls the way Baghdad developed and, further back, the tribal quarters of the *amsar* of Kufa and Basra. There was little difference between the military cantonments and the caliphal settlements other than the fact that the military quarters were provided with more houses. The cantonments for the huntsmen at al-Istablat and al-Musharrahat are barely distinguishable from military settlements. In particular the same basic model was used for the city of the caliph (ex. al-Mutawakkiliyya) and the military cantonments. The major military cantonments at al-Karkh and al-Matira were on land allotted by the caliph to a governor who was responsible for a group of military units of the same ethnic origin, each attached to a *qa'id* (officer). The governor was responsible for the construction, and it is for this reason that the cantonments have a unified plan (e.g., the cantonment of the Turks at al-Karkh, although the governor of al-Karkh, Ashnas, did not lead the troops in the field).

One of the most interesting parts of Samarra is the new royal city added to the north by al-Mutawakkil in 245 (859)–247 (861). Founded after al-Mutawakkil's return from Damascus in 244 (858), it was abandoned upon his assassination in December 861. As a consequence, the plan is almost perfectly preserved and has survived in the main until today. The plan matches that of al-Mu'tasim's Surra Man Ra'a: a main palace, al-Ja'fari, linked to an avenue which runs straight for 7 kilometers past the Abu Dulaf mosque and the houses of the elite with their followings. It is the only case where the entire plan is preserved covering 1,100 hectares.

As the world's largest well-preserved archaeological city site, Samarra evidently preserves a wide range of the building types current in the 9th century, though mainly in unexcavated condition—four congregational mosques, four caliphal palaces, 30 other mosques, 23 palaces, 214 residences of more than 2,000 square meters, and more than 18,000 small houses (Northedge and Kennet 2015). Nearly all the architecture was single story, of beaten earth or fired brick. The exception was towers and mounds, intended to give height over the flat landscape. The standard small house was four to seven rooms and a courtyard. The larger residences are based on variants of *T-iwans* (an *iwan* with a transverse portico in front) and courtyards, with numbers of *bayt*s for accommodation. The decoration is in the famous three styles of carved stucco, replaced by marble only in parts of the Dar al-Khilafa, and supplemented by wall paintings only in that palace and two other residences.

Also at Samarra can be found the main evidence for the archaeology of sport—the four great hunting reserves (of which al-Hayr was the most important) and then again four courses for horse racing and thirteen polo *maydan*s, similar to the Safavid *maydan* of Isfahan.

POST-SAMARRAN CITIES

With the abandonment of Samarra between 884 and 892, and the return of the Caliphate to Baghdad, the major cities in Iraq began to change. The open plans of Baghdad and Samarra no longer worked well. Increasing insecurity was due to the increasing revolts of the Arab tribes and heretical movements such as that of the Qaramita—which was in fact much the same thing as the adherents were drawn from the tribes.

In spite of insecurity, many Iraqi cities remained unwalled for centuries. Kufa, for example, never seems to have been walled, and Baghdad underwent a massive contraction in size from the vast early Abbasid city of around 60 square kilometers to a city at the end of the 11th century of about 500 hectares. A similar contraction happened in Samarra, where the maximal dimension of 58 square kilometers under the caliphs declined to about 250 hectares in the 11th century, still unwalled, until it was finally fortified in the 1840s, with an area of 35 hectares.

PROVINCIAL AND PILGRIMAGE CITIES

There are only two provincial cities that have been extensively excavated: Balad (Eski Mosul) on the Tigris north of Mosul and 'Ana on the Euphrates. Balad, a mudbrick enclosure of 94 hectares with a citadel on the banks of the Tigris, was extensively excavated by the Antiquities Organization but little was ever published. The other is 'Ana on the Euphrates, a city located in medieval times on a 900-meter-long island in the river—a situation also replicated at Haditha (Northedge et al. 1988). The origins are known in the cuneiform texts to go back to the Old Babylonian period in the second millennium but became more important in the first millennium as the center of the Assyrian satellite state of Suhu. Occupation of the island continued until sometime in the Ottoman period, when the town moved to the Syrian bank, and the island turned into palm gardens, which preserved a good part of the old street system but also cut away much of the later deposits. The palace, which included an Ottoman phase, and the mosque have been excavated along with stratigraphic sondages illustrating a dense development. The mosque was repeatedly restored from the Umayyad period to the beginning of Ottoman times. However one late provincial town has been excavated: Harba, south of Samarra, which flourished from Il-Khanid times into the 19th century.

A new development was the *pilgrimage city* for the visits to the Shi'a shrines of Najaf and Karbala'. In these cases, the pilgrimage developed from the 4th (10th) century onward, when the tombs were first built under the Shi'i dynasties of the Hamdanids and the Buyids. The same development also occurred at Kadhimiyya outside Baghdad, and in Samarra, around the tombs of the Imams. The tombs were increasingly richly built, and a city notably furnished with markets and hostels in the form of *khans* developed around them, finally being fortified. A particularity of Najaf is the vast cemetery of Wadi al-Salam, which today extends 5 kilometers to the north, to satisfy the desire of the Shi'a faithful to be buried close to Imam 'Ali, the bodies being frequently brought from Iran in caskets of ice. To serve the pilgrims the finest networks of caravanserais were built between Najaf and Karbala and on the road to Samarra.

TRADE AND ARTISANAL PRODUCTION

Abbasid Iraq, together with the Gulf, was the site of major commercial and production development from the 8th century onward. Unfortunately, owing to the limited possibilities for archaeological work in Iraq, the picture cannot be defined as well as might be desired. The emplacement of the Abbasid Caliphate in Iraq was due to the high tax revenues stemming from agriculture, and this led to the creation of a populous, wealthy capital and its market. The capital, Baghdad and later Samarra, had to be fed by grain brought down the Tigris in boats (Kennedy 2011). At the same time we see the beginnings of Far Eastern and Indian maritime trade.[3] There was already an Arab and Persian colony in Canton in the first half of the 8th century. Evidently, what one can see in the archaeological record is mainly the ceramics traded, but a wide range of products may have been imported: for example, the roof timbers in the Samarran palaces were teak from India, imported as keels built into the ships.

The interaction between Iraq and the East is best seen in ceramics. While functional and practical, Mesopotamian potters maintained a glazed ceramics tradition that can be traced back to the second millennium in its origins. The earliest Islamic pottery in Iraq used monochrome glaze, most frequently blue-green, and surface decoration, such as the barbotine of Sasano-Islamic jars or the finger decoration of honeycomb ware. These two are definitely Iraqi productions, though Sasano-Islamic jars are found all around the Indian Ocean. The new element is the import of Chinese white wares and painted stoneware at the end of the 8th century, according to the excavation of the port of Siraf in Iran.

At this time, there was a major change in the production of pottery in Iraq, with the beginnings of what has been called the "Samarra Horizon," the introduction of polychrome glazed wares (Northedge and Kennet 1994). Although there is some scholarly debate on the matter, this was a new idea, and it must have been stimulated by the import of Chinese wares. The first style, opaque white-glazed ware, is an evident copy of Chinese wares, thought at Siraf to have been introduced around 805 (see Priestman [2011] for a recent study). It is certainly an Iraqi production, from the yellowish ware. According to Mason and Keall (1991), it was made in Basra. This has not been supported by recent work on Basra, where this ware is relatively rare. If not in Basra, then these wares should be traced to somewhere in the south of Iraq. Although called "Samarra ware," it is relatively rare at that site and was not made there, though it seems there was some local production of green and white wares. In the classic typology, the first type was decorated in cobalt blue, then with green and brown, stretching over the 9th century.

---

[3] According to Whitehouse and Williamson (1973), maritime trade was already developed under the Sasanians, but it can be suspected that the Sasanians did not develop international trade much beyond Roman activities, being mainly a land-owning family. Certainly the first major archaeological evidence comes from the end of the 8th century.

Finally lustre painting was introduced, in polychrome and monochrome forms, with production coming to an end in the middle of the 10th century—a point which coincides with the major decline of the Iraqi economy described earlier and the transfer of Far Eastern trade to the Red Sea.

Subsequent ceramic production was much more dependent on regional models. Sgraffiato decoration under splash lead glaze was introduced in the first half of the 10th century. Raqqa-style ceramics were introduced, known from Wasit and 'Ana, but made in the south of Iraq using a yellowish earthenware body in place of stonepaste. There was no production of stonepaste ceramics in Iraq.

CONCLUSION

In spite of the difficulties placed in the way of Islamic archaeology in Iraq, the political difficulties since the middle of the 20th century, and the neglect of the Islamic period by generations of Western archaeologists only interested in ancient Mesopotamia, the picture of Islamic Iraq is becoming clearer.

The Islamic period can be really divided into two: first, the great imperial period of the Caliphate, when Iraq was the metropole and the wealthiest country in the Islamic world. Then, when the great irrigation networks were abandoned, occupation shrank back to the sustainable and easily irrigable areas, very similar to other lands studied in this volume. That was a vast change compared to other regions. The baton of influence was then passed to Iran and Egypt. There was no recovery of the great Abbasid period because there could not be. The medieval state was too decentralized, based on the *iqta'* system, to generate the level of revenues necessary for relaunching a great irrigation system.

The other point about Iraq is that it is relatively easy to recover whole archaeological landscapes there, as at Samarra, because the movement of the rivers meant that the same land areas were rarely occupied at different periods, though of course medieval occupation was located more in the same regions as today. The mobility of occupation in Iraq is quite striking. It was only in the north—Mosul and the Jazira—that occupation areas were stable. But the number of Islamic period excavations and surface studies in the north is still very small, especially only in the past fifteen years in the Kurdistan Regional Government area.

REFERENCES

Adams, R. M. 1965. *Land Behind Baghdad* (Chicago: University of Chicago Press).
Adams, R. M. & Nissen, H. J. 1972. *The Uruk Countryside, the Natural Setting of Urban Societies* (Chicago: Chicago University Press).
Adams, R. M. 1981. *Heartland of Cities: Surveys of Ancient Settlement and Land Use on the Central Floodplain of the Euphrates* (Chicago: Chicago University Press).
Al-'Azzawi, A. 1994. *al-Basra, khilal al-tanqib wal-siyana lisana 1980–1985* (Sharja).

Antun, T. 2016. *The Architectural Form of the Mosque in the Central Arab Lands, from the Hijra to the End of the Umayyad Period, 1/622–133/750*. BAR international series 2790 (Oxford: Oxbow).

Al-Baladhuri, A. 1866. *Kitab Futuh al-Buldan*, edited by M. J. de Goeje (Leiden: Brill).

Creswell, K. A. C. 1940. *Early Muslim Architecture*, 1st ed., vol. II (Oxford: Clarendon Press).

Creswell, K. A. C. 1969. *Early Muslim Architecture*, 2nd ed., vol. 1 in two parts (Oxford: Clarendon Press).

Djait, H. 1986. *al-Kufa: Naissance de la ville islamique* (Paris: G. P. Maisonneuve et Larose).

Finster, B., and Schmidt, J. 1976. *Sasanidische und frühislamische Ruinen im Iraq*. Baghdader Mitteilungen, 8 (Berlin: Mann).

Finster, B., and Schmidt, J. 2005. "The Origin of 'Desert Castles': Qasr Bani Muqatil, near Karbala, Iraq," *Antiquity*, 79, 339–349.

Gasche, H., and Tanret, M. 1998. *Changing Watercourses in Babylonia, Towards a Reconstruction of the Environment in Lower Mesopotamia*, vol. I (Ghent & Chicago: University of Ghent & Oriental Institute).

Al-Hamadhani, A. (Ibn al-Faqih). 1987. "Kitab al-Buldan," in F. Sezgin (ed.), *Collection of Geographical Works by Ibn al-Faqih, Ibn Fadlan, Abu Dulaf al-Khazraji* (Frankfurt: Johann Wolfgang Goethe Universität), 1–347.

Huff, D. 1969–1970. "Zur Rekonstruktion des Turmes von Firuzabad," *Istanbuler Mitteilungen*, 19/20, 319–338.

Ibn Miskawayh, A. b. M. 1871. "*Tajarib al-Umam wataàqub al-himam*," in M. J. de Goeje (ed.), Pars sexta operis *Tadjaribo 'l-Omami, auctore Ibn Maskowaih*, Leiden.

(Eng. tr.) Amedroz, H. F. & Margoliouth, D. S. 1920. *The Experiences of the Nations: The Eclipse of the Abbasid Caliphate*, 7 vols, London.

Johns, J. 1999. "The 'House of the Prophet' and the Concept of the Mosque," in J. Johns (ed.), *Bayt al-Maqdis. Jerusalem and early Islam*. Oxford Studies in Islamic Art, vol. 9, part 2 (Oxford: Oxford University Press), 59–112.

Kennedy, H. N. 2011. "The Feeding of the Five Hundred Thousand: Cities and Agriculture in Early Islamic Mesopotamia," *Iraq*, 73, 177–199.

Lassner, J. 1970a. *The Topography of Baghdad in the Early Middle Ages* (Detroit: Wayne State University Press).

Mason, R., and Keall, E. J. 1991. "The 'Abbāsid Glazed Wares of Sīrāf and the Baṣra Connection: Petrographic Analysis," *Iran*, 29, 51–66.

Northedge, A. 2005. *The Historical Topography of Samarra, Samarra Studies* I (British School of Archaeology in Iraq/Oxbow Books).

Northedge, A. 2007. "Iraq al-Arabi: Iraq's Greatest Region in the Pre-Modern Period," in R. Visser and G. Stansfield (eds.), *An Iraq of Its Regions: The Cornerstones of a Federal Democracy* (London and New York: Hurst & Co., and Columbia University Press), 151–166.

Northedge, A. 2017. "The Foundation of Three Cities: Hira, Kufa and Najaf," in S. Mervin, R. Gleave, and G. Chatelard (eds.), *Najaf Portrait of a Holy City* (Paris/Reading: UNESCO/Ithaca Press), 3–18.

Northedge, A., Bamber, A., and Roaf, M. 1988. *Excavations at Ana*. Iraq Archaeological Reports 1 (Warminster: Aris and Philips).

Northedge, A., and Kennet, D. 1994. "The Samarra Horizon," in E. Grube (ed.), *Cobalt and Lustre, the First Centuries of Islamic Pottery*. The Nasser D. Khalili Collection of Islamic Art, vol. IX (London: The Nour Foundation), 21–35.

Northedge, A., and Kennet, D. 2015. *Archaeological Atlas of Samarra, Samarra Studies* II (British Institute for Studies of Iraq/Oxbow Books).

Nützel, W. 1982. "The End of the South Mesopotamian Civilization Caused by the Bursting of the Dykes of the Euphrates and Tigris in 629 AD," *Sumer*, 37, 1.2, 144–148.

Popovic, A. 1976. *La révolte des esclaves en Iraq au IIIe/IXe siècle* (Paris: Geuthner).

Priestman, S. M. 2011. "Opaque Glazed Wares: The Definition, Dating and Distribution of a Key Ceramic Export in the Abbasid Period," *Iran*, 49, 89–113.

Rousset, M-O. 1992. *L'archéologie islamique en Iraq: bilan et perspectives* (Damascus: Institut français de Damas).

Sarre, F., and Herzfeld, E. 1911. *Archäologische Reise im Euphrat- und Tigris-Gebiet*, 4 vols. (Berlin).

Sousa, A. 1963. *Faydanat Baghdad*, 3 vols. (Baghdad: Matba'at al-Adib).

Al-Ṭabari, M. 1879–1901. *Ta'rikh al-Rusul wal-Muluk*, edited by M. J. de Goeje et al. (Leiden).

Whitehouse, D., and Williamson, A. 1973. "Sasanian Maritime Trade," *Iran*, 11, 29–49.

Al-Ya'qubi, A. 1982. *Kitab al-Buldan*, edited by M. J. de Goeje, BGA 7 (Leiden); Fr. Trans. 1937 by G. Wiet, *Les Pays* (Cairo: Institut français d'archéologie orientale).

FURTHER READING

Adams, R. M. 1970. "Tell Abu Sarifa: A Sassanian-Islamic Ceramic Sequence from Southern Iraq," *Ars Orientalis*, 8, 87–119.

Bell, G. 1914. *Palace and Mosque at Ukhaidir: A Study in Early Mohanmadan Architecture* (Oxford: Oxford University Press).

Bennison, A. K., and Gascoigne, A. L. (eds.) 2007. *Cities in the Pre-Modern Islamic World: The Impact of Religion, State and Society* (London: Routledge).

Crone, P. 1980. *Slaves on Horses: The Evolution of the Islamic Polity* (Cambridge: Cambridge University Press).

Denoix, S. 2008. "Founded Cities of the Arab World from the Seventh to the Eleventh Centuries," in S. K. Jayyusi, R. Holod, A. Petruccioli, and A. Raymond (eds.), *The City in the Islamic World* (Leiden: Brill), 115–139.

Lassner, J. 1970b. "The Caliph's Personal Domain: The City Plan of Baghdad Re-Examined," in A. Hourani and S. M. Stern (eds.), *The Islamic City* (Oxford: Bruno Cassirer), 103–118.

Mahdi, A. M. 1969. *al-Ukhaydir* (Baghdad: Mudīrīyat al-Āthār al-'Āmmah).

Mustafa, M. A. 1956. "Taqrīr awwalī 'an al-tanqīb fī al-Kūfa lil-mawsim al-thālith," *Sumer*, 12, 2–32 (ar. sect.); Eng. trans. 1963 by C. Kessler, *Sumer*, 19, 36–65.

Northedge, A. 1994. "Archaeology and New Urban Settlement in Early Islamic Syria and Iraq," in G. R. D. King and A. Cameron (eds.), *Studies in Late Antiquity and Early Islam II, Settlement Patterns in the Byzantine and Early Islamic Near East* (Princeton: Princeton University Press), 231–265.

Northedge, A. 2008. "Umayyad and Abbasid Urban Fortifications in the Near East," in L. Korn, E. Orthmann, and F. Schwarz (eds.), *Die Grenzen der Welt, Arabica et Iranica ad honorem Heinz Gaube* (Wiesbaden: Reichert), 39–64.

Roaf, M. 1996. *Cultural Atlas of Mesopotamia and the Ancient Near East* (New York: Facts on File).

CHAPTER 2.4

EGYPT

ALISON L. GASCOIGNE

Introduction: The Lands of Egypt

The regional importance of Egypt past and present cannot be overstated. Its significance stems in great part from the country's particular geographical circumstances: forming a bridge between Africa and Asia, supported by the River Nile and other natural resources, and with access to two major maritime zones, the Mediterranean, and the Red Sea and Indian Ocean. This strategic location has created a diverse, populous, well-connected, and generally well-supplied country, capable of high levels of innovation and influence at all levels of society. Although such characteristics are clearly acknowledged in studies of Egypt's Pharaonic past, they are sometimes less conspicuous in considerations of the later phases of its history. This chapter cannot hope to provide the exhaustive account that the archaeology, history, and culture of medieval and early modern Egypt deserves, but it aims to highlight selected trends and developments that will illustrate Egypt's significance from the 7th century to the Ottoman era and beyond.

The geography of Egypt is fundamental to the country's development and prosperity. Africa's only major northward-flowing river, the Nile, provides water and fertile silt for agriculture; its annual flood cycle was completely curtailed by the construction of the Aswan High Dam only in the 1960s, creating opportunities for the rapid expansion of settlements onto ground previously inundated between July and September and causing a fundamental dislocation in historical occupation and agricultural practices. Egypt has traditionally been divided into regions defined by their relationship to the Nile: Upper and Middle Egypt, along the Nile Valley, and Lower Egypt, located in the Nile Delta, with the country's medieval capital city of al-Fustat, later Cairo, strategically located at the Delta's apex. Prior to the construction of multiple barrages during the 19th century, the landscapes of the Valley, and especially the Delta, were highly seasonal in terms of the ways in which they could be used and navigated. Complex systems of basin irrigation retained floodwaters, rendering overland travel challenging during parts of the year. Networks of canals, including many that functioned only during the flood season, facilitated movement of goods and people, although the seasonality of the canal systems did not mesh straightforwardly with that of the Mediterranean and Indian Ocean maritime spheres (Cooper 2014). It is thus not possible to understand many aspects of social and economic activities in pre-modern Egypt without an explicit awareness of the nature of the country's complex waterways and their development and use throughout the medieval and early modern eras.

In addition to the productive agricultural zones of the Nile Valley and Delta, and in fact covering more than 90% of the modern state of Egypt, are large arid areas. To the east of the Nile, these deserts tend to be rocky and mountainous, containing many resources including stone, metals, and precious minerals. To the west, the deserts are in places more sandy and contain a number of important agricultural oases along routes into the African interior, as well as upland plateaus such as the Gilf Kebir. We should not think of Egypt's desert areas as unoccupied space since it is clear that parts of them were periodically exploited not only for resource extraction, but also on a more long-term basis by nomadic groups, often with connections to the settled populations of the Nile Valley and Delta (Power 2012a).

HISTORICAL OVERVIEW: THE STATE OF THE FIELD

Recent research has altered our understanding of the nature of the Arab conquests of Egypt in fundamental ways. Alfred Butler's important 1902 (1978) study of these events focused exclusively on a single invasion route through Sinai and into the Delta, and his account of the conquests remained fixed in scholarly interpretations for more than a century. Studies by Philip Booth (2013) and Tim Power (2012b: 96–97), however, have since shown that invasions of Egypt in 639–641 took place both from north and south, with a second force probably crossing the Red Sea into Middle and Upper Egypt. It speaks to the inadequacy of ideas around the peripherality and/or atypicality of Egypt, which arguably underlie an element of scholarly non-engagement, that such striking misunderstandings have persisted within the literature for so long despite numerous syntheses of the events of the mid-7th century appearing in the intervening years (Donner 1981; Kaegi 1992).

Egypt was quickly incorporated into a complex Islamic polity as a province of some importance, not least for the supply of grain to the Hijaz; to secure this, early improvements to infrastructure included the redigging of the Nile–Red Sea Canal within the first half-century of Muslim rule (Sheehan 2010: 85–86; Cooper 2014: 95–99). Our understanding of the structure of the early Islamic state in Egypt and the nature of its governance is supported by the existence of surviving archives and finds of papyri from desert-edge sites in Middle Egypt and the Fayyum Oasis. These sources provide insights into the nature of social relations between ruler and ruled during the key transitional period of Umayyad and early Abbasid rule, and their study by scholars such as Petra Sijpesteijn addresses fundamental questions of continuity and innovation with a focus on grassroots experiences (Sijpesteijn 2013). From an archaeological perspective, the first centuries of Muslim rule saw the foundation and/or growth of a number of important cities, including al-Fustat, Tinnis, and Aswan (see later discussion). Such settlements formed part of the increasingly complex urban networks of the Islamic world, with the appearance of a style of housing in al-Fustat perhaps under the Tulunid dynasty with close parallels to Iraqi sites, in particular Samarra. The significance of the transference of architectural forms such as the so-called Samarra-*bayt* has been underanalyzed and explained in nebulous, diffusionist terms with Egypt as the passive recipient of "influence" or "fashion" from further east; scrutiny of the social and domestic developments that underpinned changes to architectural form has only recently placed human agency at the center of this debate (Harrison 2014) and further such studies, socially embedded and explicitly theorized, are overdue.

The historically overclose relationship between Islamic archaeology and art history is one factor behind the lingering tendency to date archaeological sequences and material artifacts with primary reference to historical frameworks. This has resulted in the dominance of particular periods in the scholarly literature over others. As an example, George Scanlon and colleagues produced a typology of al-Fustat houses dated to the Tulunid and Fatimid eras, with no construction assigned to the intervening century comprising the second period of Abbasid control and the rule of the Ikhshidid dynasty (Ostrasz 1977). Art-historical and, to a lesser extent, architectural and archaeological studies, have foregrounded the Fatimid period, and the existence of funding streams and institutions with particular interest in this period of Egypt's history, often linked to Ismaili Shiism, has impacted upon the reception of the period and the conservation of its monuments (Warner 2005: 46). The survival of the Old Cairo Ben Ezra Synagogue Geniza documents is a powerful aid to social historians and archaeologists concerned with the Fatimid era and later (the majority date from the 10th to 13th centuries). This fascinating range of documents provides a wealth of detail on daily life, economic activities, interactions, and attitudes among the Jewish community and those connected to it (Goitein 1967–1988). Physical remains of the period include standing mosques, churches, and mausolea (e.g., in Cairo, Minya, Luxor, Esna, Edfu, Aswan: Creswell 1952–1959; Bloom 2013) in addition to archaeological resources including excavated areas of housing and settlement (e.g., al-Fustat/Old Cairo, Aswan and Raya, Sinai), burial evidence (e.g., Kom al-Dikka, Alexandria: Prominska 1972; Istabl ʿAntar, Cairo: Gayraud 1998), monastic complexes (e.g., those in the Wadi al-Natrun and Sohag investigated by the Yale Monastic Archaeology Project), industrial activities (e.g., Old Cairo/al-Fustat: Sheehan 2010), and fortifications (e.g., Cairo, Aswan). The archaeological evidence in particular provides an emphasis on continuity from earlier phases that qualifies the challenges posed by the nature of Fatimid studies and its particular evidence base. The sources available to scholars of Fatimid Egypt are thus more diverse than for earlier periods, though not always unproblematic.

The fortification of certain coastal cities as a result of the Crusades has left archaeological traces in some cases (e.g., Tinnis: Gascoigne et al. 2020) but not in others (e.g., Dumyat/Damietta), reflecting the different levels of investigation and preservation of these sites. It is particularly unfortunate that Egypt's later medieval archaeology—that of the Ayyubid, Mamluk, and especially Ottoman periods—remains poorly investigated, and this must be a priority for future work. Fortifications have received some attention, including the remarkable Ayyubid fort of Sadr, or Qalʿat al-Gindi, with its infrastructure (mill, cisterns, stores, bath), housing, mosque, and material culture (Mouton et al. 2010). A shorter synthetic study of Mamluk fortifications restricted to the Nile Delta and Sinai has been undertaken, building on large-scale excavations in the north-east corner of Cairo's Fatimid and Ayyubid medieval city walls, which revealed activity from the end of the 10th century to the present day (Pradines 2016; Pradines et al. 2009). Substantial excavations of particular significance for later medieval and Ottoman archaeology in Egypt took place in the last third of the 20th century at Qasr Ibrim in Lower Nubia, an ecclesiastical center and fortified site that housed an Ottoman garrison from the 16th to early 19th century, now precariously located on an island in Lake Nasser and much damaged. High levels of organic preservation resulted in the retrieval of diverse and important assemblages of textiles, leatherwork, wood, plant remains, documents, and much more (Adams 1996; Veldmeijer 2012; see also Adams 2010). In addition to fortified sites, the maritime sphere has seen some later medieval archaeology. At the Red Sea port of Qusayr, the late Ayyubid-Mamluk port and an Ottoman fortification have been investigated (Peacock and Blue 2006–2011; Le Quesne 2007), while Japanese archaeologists have excavated a port of 14th- to 20th-century date at al-Kilani in Sinai (Kawatoko 2005: 853–855). Also of interest is the mid-18th-century Sadana Island shipwreck, with a cargo including Chinese export porcelain and decorated water jars (Ward 2000). Finally, recent excavations in and around Old Cairo's historic churches have focused on (often truncated and confused) stratigraphy through the medieval period right up to the 21st century (Sheehan 2010: 97–142). Much of the work just alluded to remains incompletely published and poorly accessible.

Clearly, for the present chapter, a selective approach must be taken. To that end, the focus of what follows will fall on urban sites, starting in Cairo, where much of the important existing archaeological work has been undertaken, and then considering areas more distant from the capital. Before examining cities in detail, though, the state of rural and environmental approaches within Egyptian Islamic archaeology will be briefly considered, as will artifactual evidence relating to domestic activity, trade and production, and funerary practices.

The Countryside, Agriculture, and Diet: Rural and Environmental Approaches

The neglect of rural archaeology within Egypt is to some extent inevitable due to an almost complete lack of archaeological evidence. Beyond some of the small, remote monastic and semi-nomadic sites alluded to earlier, which are hardly typical of rural subsistence activity, we know very little about the material traces of Egypt's medieval countryside. This is due in large part to the intensive nature of agricultural practices in the Nile Valley and Delta, which have largely overwritten earlier manifestations of rural life; an exploratory study of persistent landscape features such as dyke- and basin-banks and roads might provide new perspectives but is yet to be realized. To investigate the countryside, at present we cannot thus supplement important historical studies such as Rapoport's work on the Fayyum (Rapoport 2018) with archaeological data of any depth.

Environmental evidence can of course support our understanding of agricultural practices for the production of food and textile crops. Such approaches have been well established within the suite of archaeological techniques for many years, but archaeobotanical and zooarchaeological studies are not yet practiced as standard on all projects within Egypt. Restrictions on the export of archaeological material are implicated in this situation but cannot explain it entirely. The good conditions for organic preservation on many Egyptian sites provide particular incentives for rectifying this, and a handful of existing studies have shown the value of these approaches. Of particular note are the extensive archaeobotanical analyses, including ancient DNA studies, undertaken by Alan Clapham, Peter Rowley-Conwy, and others at Qasr Ibrim (Clapham and Rowley-Conwy 2009), the preliminary publications of which indicate the importance of crops and strains of African (as opposed to eastern/Indian) origin (e.g., cotton) in the diversification of cultivated plants in Egypt through late antiquity and into the Islamic period. Archaeobotanical and archaeofaunal studies are likewise ongoing in Aswan, as part of the excavations of the Swiss Institute; at Shaykh ʿAbd al-Qurna, Luxor, where a Polish team is investigating strata of the 6th to early 8th centuries; and at Dayr al-Naqlun, Fayyum, as part of the Polish excavation of an 11th- to 14th-century monastic cemetery.[1] Smaller scale studies of botanical remains by El Dorry at monastic sites in the Wadi al-Natrun and Aswan allow insights into kitchen garden agriculture and foodways at these institutions (El Dorry 2015). Beyond this, a substantial study of plant remains from Qusayr al-Qadim informs us about traded foodstuffs, while the publication of the

---

[1] I am grateful to Katerzyna Danys for this information.

faunal material from the same site—unsurprisingly dominated by sheep/goat and fish, along with studies of (plant and) animal remains from the Ottoman fort of Qusayr and a very brief note on animal (fish, pig, sheep/goat) remains from the Monastery of John the Little in the Wadi al-Natrun—are the only current zooarchaeological publications related to medieval Egypt of which I am aware (van der Veen 2011; Hamilton-Dyer 2011; Le Quesne 2007; Brooks Hedstrom et al. 2010: 224–225). Clearly much more remains to be done before we will be able to write a narrative of Islamic Egypt from this perspective.

Daily Life, Trade, and Production: The Story from Artifacts

Small finds from excavations are a neglected resource in the creation of narratives about domestic practices, trade, and manufacturing in medieval and early modern Egypt, and although such themes can be addressed to some extent with reference to pottery, there is likewise much more that remains be done with ceramics. The most commonly found archaeological artifacts from Islamic-era sites in Egypt comprise objects of pottery, glass, and stone in addition to small metal items, and, on sites with good organic preservation, wood, bone, and sometimes even fiber, basketry, textile, and papyrus and paper documents. Studies of material from excavations take the form of reports and catalogues; although not numerous, the best of these include a strong discursive and analytical element, while more basic publications describe the material with less attempt to place it into socioeconomic, or even archaeological, context. Approaches from archaeological science have been largely restricted to museum collections outside Egypt due to restrictions on the export of samples, but, in the past few years, it has become easier to apply some techniques of scientific analysis (e.g., x-ray fluorescence [XRF], petrology) in the field, and it is important that archaeologists working in the country continue to drive this agenda forward in order to allow the incorporation of Egypt into debates around materials from which it is currently largely excluded. This section considers the resources available to archaeologists focusing on portable objects and the state of associated research into social and economic practices in Egypt, excluding studies taking an art-historical perspective. It provides examples to illustrate the themes of daily life and domestic activities; trade, buying, and selling; manufacturing and industry; and funerary practices.

The archaeology of household activity can be approached in a number of ways, the most important of these being through examination of houses themselves and their contents. It is well established through the documents of the Old Cairo Geniza that textiles formed a crucial component of home contents, comprising furnishings such as throws, curtains, cushions, and mattresses, which facilitated the repurposing of domestic spaces as circumstances required. Unfortunately, these are not commonly preserved despite the survival of fragmentary domestic textiles from later medieval and early modern Egypt (e.g., from Qusayr al-Qadim: Handley 2011: 321; Qasr Ibrim: Adams 1996; 2010; these collections also include clothing fragments). Furnishings of wood and bone are evidenced by the survival of small fragments such as turned legs or inlay pieces, again well represented in the corpora of finds from Qasr Ibrim and Qusayr (and from Istabl ʿAntar: Rodziewicz 2012), as are other domestic ephemera such as brushes, basketry, pot covers, cordage, and more. Objects such as pottery and stone vessels allow some understanding of domestic practices around the storage and preparation of food and of approaches to cuisine, both food prepared in the home and that brought in from cookshops (e.g., Gascoigne 2013; Milwright 1999: 505), even though such studies have not yet gone much beyond the anecdotal (Figure 2.4.1). The ceramic assemblage of medieval Egypt is notably different from that of Greater Syria, in that it substantially lacks handmade wares. Objects that can be connected with the presence of children are rarely identified, with the exception of so-called Coptic dolls, which appeared in Egypt during early Islamic times and have been interpreted as toys connected with preparing girls for the biological and sexual aspects of their future lives (Rodziewicz 2012: 10).

As just noted, prepared meals were often bought in markets for consumption at home; many other domestic needs were likewise met by means of market purchases. Most such items would have been perishable consumables, and we must look to other

FIGURE 2.4.1 Example of a type of mass-produced and poor-quality bowl excavated from the area of the Hanging Church in Old Cairo; these vessels are very common in late medieval strata and may have been associated with the purchase of food from cookshops.

Courtesy of A. L. Gascoigne (2005; vessel no. HC283).

sources of evidence to understand local trade, in particular, coins and glass weights form a related category of objects facilitating such economic activity. Small glass weights are commonly found on sites of approximately 8th- to 11th-century date in Egypt and are variable in terms of color; many are stamped with rulers' names and/or other information. The relative importance of local, regional, and long-distance trade can be addressed by means of ceramic studies, but although a few large assemblages have been quantified (e.g., Old Cairo), publication of these has not yet been completed. That long-distance trade was commonplace is clearly evidenced by the archaeology of some of Egypt's medieval ports—Qusayr al-Qadim, for example, apparently acted as a re-bagging site for goods transported in sacks (Handley and Regourd 2009)—as well as by finds of imported objects including Chinese porcelain from many medieval sites.

In addition to objects imported through trade were those made within Egypt. Ceramic manufacture was widespread, with important centers at al-Fustat and around Aswan. Excavations in Old Cairo and al-Fustat evidence almost exclusively glazed-ware production, with multiple small-scale installations making polychrome-glazed, incised, and lustred vessels of the 10th–12th centuries and underglaze-painted wares of the 13th–15th centuries; production of ceramics continued in the area until very recently (Sheehan 2010). In Aswan, the dominant local products were unglazed wares including jars, cooking pots, jugs, bowls, lamps, and more, but also sphero-conical vessels (pers. obs.). The high quality of the kaolinitic clay of the Aswan area was recognized by medieval authors, as now: it is still transported to Cairo to be used by potters there (Milwright 1999: 506; pers. obs.). In the 19th century, glossy red-slipped ceramic vessels including clay pipes and water jars were mass-produced in Middle Egypt, in particular in Asyut, where wares related to the Tophane potteries of Istanbul were made; as in al-Fustat, this industry was organized as multiple small-scale producers (Bavay 2010).

The final sphere in which we consider artifactual evidence is burial archaeology. Funerary practices of Islamic-era Egypt are not well documented because few cemeteries of the period have been excavated. Exceptions include the multiphase cemetery at Kom al-Dikka in Alexandria; high-status Abbasid and Fatimid mausolea at Istabl 'Antar, al-Fustat; burials from the monastic complex at Dayr al-Naqlun; and a disturbed late 14th- to mid-15th-century cemetery at Qusayr al-Qadim (all discussed earlier; see in addition Macklin 2011). Finds from within burials at these sites comprise textiles and shrouding, including an important collection of inscribed, high-status textiles from Istabl 'Antar (Sokoly 2017). The Islamic distaste for the inclusion of artifacts within burials seems to have been generally observed, but fruit and flowers were placed within some graves: at Dayr al-Naqlun, foodstuffs (apple, peach, almond, grapes) were knotted into one deceased's sleeve, and a burial with dates, hazelnuts, and flowers within the shrouding was found at Qusayr al-Qadim (Zieliński 2012; Macklin 2011: 237–238). Broken objects, including pottery, lamps, glass weights, and gaming pieces, have been found in the deposits around burials (Kulicka 2008). While some of these will reflect disposal of general refuse, others will represent activities around mourning and commemoration of the deceased. Unpacking these categories is challenging, but objects such as glass bracelets seem to have been deliberately broken in mourning rituals and were found in some concentration in the cemetery area of Qusayr al-Qadim (Peacock 2011: 72–75).

Urbanism: Al-Fustat/Cairo

In light of the limitations of the preceding sources of evidence, we now turn to Egypt's medieval cities. The archaeology of Islamic Egypt has been—and continues to be—dominated by evidence from the Cairo area. Of particular note are the large-scale investigations of the city of al-Fustat that started in the 1960s and continued into the 1980s under the direction of George Scanlon and Władysław Kubiak (Kubiak 1987; Kubiak and Scanlon 1989; see also Gayraud 1998; Pradines et al. 2009; Warner 2005). The evidence from al-Fustat, in the form of house remains, streets, public and domestic drainage systems, industrial areas, and associated finds, underpins our knowledge of the development of Egypt under Muslim rule in a fundamental way. Additionally, al-Fustat is the subject of diverse historical sources, arguably the most important of which is the Old Cairo Geniza archive, mentioned earlier, which includes many documents of relevance to urban life and the structure of the city. We must accept, however, that al-Fustat was an exceptional settlement in Egyptian terms from the time of its foundation in 642 CE: although it incorporated important preexisting structures from the Roman fortress and governmental center of Babylon, a large proportion of its area was constructed on previously unoccupied terrain, and its planning and growth were specific to the particular circumstances of its genesis (Sheehan 2010: 79–96; Sheehan and Gascoigne in press; Kubiak 1987).

Al-Fustat is an important example of an early Islamic *miṣr* (pl. *amṣār*: a garrison town in which salaries were paid and taxes collected) and one for which a significant depth of spatial data is available. Early Islamic urban foundations including the *amṣār* have provided a basis for attempts to distinguish the characteristics of novel forms of urbanism in the period after the Arab conquests: the creation of new and rapidly growing settlements by means of the introduction of particular urban forms into conquered territories and the assimilation into these towns of preexisting urban concepts and ideals as a result of their occupation by factions of the "indigenous" population. Many studies of Islamic urbanism place greater weight on written descriptions than on topographic evidence, reflecting in many (but not all) cases a paucity of archaeological data. The inevitably schematic, aspatial results are emphasized by published visual representations of such cities.[2] Examples in Iraq include Baghdad (e.g., Kennedy 2004: Map 2) and Basra (Al-Sayyid 1991: 52–53); an obvious exception is Samarra (Northedge 2005). Al-Fustat/Cairo itself has formed the basis for several historically rooted studies from the late 19th century onward (Ravaisse 1887–1890; Casanova 1919; Kubiak 1987; Denoix 1992). Denoix's study does attempt some integration of historical and archaeological data, with limited

---

[2] I am grateful to Matthew Harrison for instructive discussion of this phenomenon.

success (Denoix 1992: 61). Archaeologists are equally not immune from generalizing tendencies: Whitcomb's new-style urban paradigms identify a preconceived, imposed model within Islamic cities, including examples that are both new foundations and those with continuity of occupation, but his argument remains inevitably speculative, and the nature of the developments he proposes represents a top-down approach that was perhaps more heavy-handed than the "process . . . of enablement" that is Kennedy's interpretation of acts of foundation (Whitcomb 2007, 2015; Kennedy 2010: 62). The centrality of the archaeological remains of al-Fustat to these debates places Egypt at the forefront of revisionist approaches.

Urbanism: Provincial Cities

Given the focus of the preceding debate on the *amṣār* and the dominance of al-Fustat/Cairo in the evidence for Egypt, it is clear that questions exist regarding the relationship of Egypt's provincial cities with the new capital. Most of these settlements existed prior to the Arab conquest, housing largely Christian populations. It is the aim of this section to outline in brief the state of our knowledge of the provincial urban centers of Islamic Egypt, with some consideration of how their configuration might relate to the situation during late antiquity and the extent to which they exhibited commonalities with al-Fustat. Did the size of urban areas and/or the proportion of the population living in them increase overall in early Islamic times? The foundation of settlements such as al-Fustat and their rapid growth and increasing economic importance led to the association of cities of considerable size with the new Muslim ruling elite. But how far did such urbanization stretch, and when might it have developed? Was it restricted to the new capital, did it filter to centers of administrative importance, or can it be seen throughout Egypt? It is clear that al-Fustat developed rapidly into a large center, but its growth was paralleled by a reduction in the size of the inhabited area of Alexandria. Alexandria's medieval city walls were 7,897 meters in circumference, enclosing approximately 300 hectares, a considerably smaller area than the approximately 1,000 hectares encircled by the classical enceinte and thus presumably protecting a smaller population; this process of contraction was, however, already under way during late antiquity, with some areas and features of the city abandoned or in ruin (Behrens-Abouseif 1998: 102; Haas 1997: 337–351). The reduction in size of Alexandria is thus by no means attributable to the transfer of population to the new capital at al-Fustat. Haas characterizes Alexandria as going "from the cosmopolitan queen of the eastern Mediterranean to a neglected provincial backwater" (Haas 1997: 339); however, Cooper has argued that the decline of Alexandria after the Arab conquest has been overstated. The town retained much of its urban status and strategic and economic importance, and it saw a considerable resurgence from the mid-9th century, with the return of political autonomy to Egypt (Cooper 2014: 201–203; contra Haas 1997: 343–349).

The role of Alexandria within post-conquest Egypt was as one of several fortified and garrisoned frontier towns (*ribāṭāt, thughūr*) along the Mediterranean coast, the significance of which related to defense as well as to maritime trade and its associated revenue. In addition to Alexandria, we find in particular Rashid (Rosetta), Tinnis, Dumyat, and al-Farama (Pelusium) (Cooper 2014: 195–227). Of these, Rashid was a settlement of minimal size and importance prior to Ottoman times. However, the other three sites existed in the medieval era as sizeable and populous cities. Al-Farama and Tinnis grew from existing important late antique urban centers and were endowed with infrastructure including walls under the Abbasids and Tulunids, among others; they continued in use until the mid-11th and early 13th centuries, respectively (Gascoigne et al. 2020; Lev 1999). Dumyat was less prominent than Tinnis and al-Farama in early Islamic times but survived to become the primary coastal settlement of the eastern Delta from the late 12th century. Unlike Tinnis and al-Farama, however, the location of the archaeological site of late antique and early medieval Dumyat—north of the late medieval to modern city—is uninvestigated and largely over-built. With the exception of Tinnis, then, the medieval phases of these cities remain eclipsed within scholarly literature by their classical precursors (Alexandria, al-Farama) or largely inaccessible beneath modern settlement (Dumyat, Rashid). The nature and extent of their urban plan is thus obscure.

The site of Tinnis, in Lake Manzala, has been subject to recent investigation by myself and John Cooper, and this has revealed significant aspects of the physical organization of the settlement. Although no excavation has been undertaken to clarify the chronology of the urban plan, remains cleared by archaeologists ʿAbbas al-Shinawy, al-Sayyid al-ʿAgamy ʿArafa, and Tariq Ibrahim Husseiny between 1979 and 2010 are largely early Islamic-era in date, and pottery recovered from boreholes was likewise largely from this period. Although already an important settlement during late antiquity, the archaeological remains extant on the island may thus more closely reflect the early Islamic shape of the town; at any rate Tinnis apparently increased considerably in size and prosperity in early medieval times, with changes reflecting, at least in part, new urban imperatives.

As revealed by magnetometry and the analysis of satellite imagery, the southern and central parts of Tinnis had a street grid with some rectilinear characteristics, in contrast to that uncovered during excavation at al-Fustat. Two waterways pierced the city walls, allowing access into the core of the town by boat; where the south canal crosses the fired-brick enceinte, traces remain of a large "water gate," with a land gate (one of many) a short distance to the west (Figure 2.4.2). Streets ran up to the south canal and continued on the opposite bank; traces remain of a possible connecting bridge. Houses appear to have had relatively small footprints and thick walls, indicating probable multiple stories. This is at variance with the courtyard houses preserved archaeologically at al-Fustat, although multistoried houses are described in the Geniza archive (Goitein 1967–1988, vol. 4), and the housing stock of al-Fustat was clearly more varied than has been previously acknowledged (Harrison 2015). Meanwhile, Tinnis's early medieval water supply system was complex and apparently covered all or much of the site (Gascoigne 2007).

FIGURE 2.4.2 The south "water gate" of Tinnis, looking west.

Courtesy of A. L. Gascoigne (2009).

The city was thus furnished with a semi-organized plan, and many aspects of the town's infrastructure must have been centrally maintained.

Close to the center of Tinnis's intramural area are traces of massive industrial (metal-working) complexes, with abundant surface slag and strong magnetic anomalies. The siting of these features within the urban space is of note; urban models often place such activities on the periphery of settlements due to their polluting tendencies. This latter configuration is described for sites in Central Asia, Iran, Iraq, and Greater Syria (Fedorov-Davydov 1983: 396–397; Milwright 2010: 146–147; Heidemann 2006: 47). At al-Fustat, archaeological evidence has revealed extensive industrial activity in the form of pottery and lime kilns and tanneries, following the semi-abandonment of parts of the city at the end of the 11th century; similar, broadly contemporary activity along the riverbank is evidenced by kilns and industrial debris within and around the round riverside towers of the fort of Babylon (Sheehan 2010: 83, 103–104) (Figure 2.4.3). These areas lay downwind of, and peripheral to, the new city of al-Qahira to the north, but, within the towers at least, the kilns were close to large residential and religious complexes within the walls of the former Roman fort, and activity here was apparently of some duration. The industrial works recorded at Tinnis are not far from the head of the south canal, and access to water may be a significant factor in their placement. What

FIGURE 2.4.3 Pottery kiln located inside the southern Roman riverside tower of the fortress of Babylon in Old Cairo, excavated by Old Cairo Archaeology.

Courtesy of Peter Sheehan (2008).

may have been in the extramural quarters of Tinnis, along the banks of the island, is not known as the site has subsided and its edges are now submerged. The central location of Tinnis's industrial complexes is a useful reminder that local specificities—especially in a site so peculiarly located as is Tinnis—may overturn general models.

Ports on the Red Sea, though by no means well documented, are arguably less overshadowed in the archaeological literature by their classical antecedents than are those of the Mediterranean. The important Roman settlements of Myos Hormos (Qusayr al-Qadim) and Berenike went out of use in the early 3rd and 5th/6th centuries, respectively (Peacock and Blue 2006–2011; Sidebotham 2011). Continuity can be seen at al-Qulzum (Clysma/Suez), where excavation in the 1930s indicated "extensive settlement . . . in the Ptolemaic and Roman eras—particularly the late Roman" (Cooper 2014: 237), with evidence also indicating Islamic-era occupation, continuing to the mid-12th century. The post-conquest town was not investigated in detail, however, and the site is now built over (Cooper 2014; Power 2012b: 31–32, 103, 109–112). At the late 8th- to 11th-century site of Raya in Sinai, a rectilinear fort overlooked a residential area with houses of coral blocks and mudbrick, where pre-Islamic finds also indicate some level of continuity, but the domestic quarters are not yet published in enough detail to illustrate the extent and nature of the settlement (Kawatoko 2004: 4–5, pl. 10; 2005: 851–853).

After the conquest, there are indications of a caliphal policy of deliberate establishment of coastal sites on the Red Sea (Cooper 2014: 229–246; Power 2012b: 97). Ports were founded (or reoccupied) anew: 'Aydhab (recently suggested to be two separate places, a defensive town of approximately 7.5 hectares in area and its satellite harbor about 20 kilometers to the south, c. 9th–14th centuries; Peacock and Peacock 2008; Power 2012b: 158); Qusayr al-Qadim (approximately 10 hectares; 12th to early 16th centuries; Whitcomb and Johnson 1979; Whitcomb 1982; Peacock and Blue 2006–2011); and al-Tur (approximately 400 × 200 meters, 14th–20th centuries; Kawatoko 2005: 853–855). Each of these settlements no doubt housed transient mobile traders, sailors, and pilgrims, with smaller permanent populations connected to trade and/or governance. Located in a contested border zone, 'Aydhab has been investigated most recently by means of satellite imagery, and its footprint on the ground is surprisingly light given its importance as a trading center and hajj port: "most sources indicate it was not an especially large settlement, and it may have been fairly basic" (Peacock and Peacock 2008: 4). Peacock and Peacock estimate a population in the region of 500 and identify an irregular, unplanned layout with narrow twisting streets but broadly following two different orientations at the eastern and western ends, perhaps of chronological significance (Peacock and Peacock 2008: 12–13). The considerable size of the cemeteries relative to the town was noted by an early visitor from the Egyptian Survey Department, George Murray (Cooper 2014: 238). At al-Tur, the earliest phase (14th–16th centuries) yielded evidence for public buildings overbuilt by private housing in later times (Kawatoko 2005: 853). The transition from ports with significant infrastructure under the Romans to those with more ephemeral facilities (though clearly still fit for purpose) is evidenced at Qusayr al-Qadim, where, due to siltation, sailors were making use of much reduced harbor infrastructure in its later phases (Blue 2007). The evidence may thus imply a trend away from centrally organized port structures and layouts toward more "self-organization."

The Red Sea sites clearly do not supply compelling evidence for an increase in urbanization along this coast under Islamic rule in terms of the extent of structural remains, the engineered facilities, or the apparent size of population; but, arguably, neither do they demonstrate the opposite. The data, although patchy and limited in depth, offer no support for any significant decrease in the extent of Red Sea urbanization, and the changes to maritime infrastructure are likely to reflect an altered understanding of what a port ought to offer, rather than decline and impoverishment.

One factor common to many of the towns of the Mediterranean and Red Sea coasts was the difficulties inherent in supplying their needs, especially of fresh water, but also of food, building materials, etc. Alexandria and al-Farama lay on unreliable waterways that needed constant maintenance, and, during the final phases of activity at al-Farama, drinking water had to be transported to the site by boat from Tinnis (Cooper 2014: 213). At Tinnis itself, fresh water was only available during the Nile flood season and had to be stored in cisterns to support the population during the remainder of the year (Gascoigne 2007). 'Aydhab relied on wells and cisterns for water storage, while the means by which Qusayr was watered remain unclear. The inherent insecurity of these sites underlines the discomfort of living in them, and the efforts taken to supply them indicate their economic and strategic significance.

Important urban centers were also located on Egypt's inland frontiers, most notably at Aswan on the First Cataract of the Nile. Aswan has in recent years been subject to an extensive program of archaeological investigation, led in the field by Wolfgang Müller, which has revealed major new insights into the size, development, and main features of the town from Pharaonic through medieval and into modern times (Figure 2.4.4). Late antique Aswan was a town of only some 12–13 hectares, with a population estimated by Müller to be 1,000–2,000. The early Islamic settlement was considerably larger and more populous, being furnished with new enclosure walls and a large complex possibly in Fatimid times, and with housing spreading over the Roman cemetery to the north (Müller 2014; the large complex is in Area 32, by the Coptic cathedral at the southern end of the town). The increased importance of early Islamic Aswan is attributed to its frontier location, as a garrison town, and its role in the hajj and cross-border trade, rather than to its size alone (Björnesjö 2013). Aswan enjoyed a period of particular prosperity from Umayyad times until the 11th century, due in part to gold mining and slave trading within Nubia, and tombstones from the town's important cemeteries record the presence of traders and craftsmen among the Muslim population (Björnesjö 2013: 10–11; Speiser 2013). The rarity of references to Aswan in Ayyubid and Mamluk written sources noted by Björnesjö is of interest in light of continued activity indicated by archaeological

FIGURE 2.4.4 View east across early Islamic houses in Area 84 of the Swiss-Egyptian joint mission at Syene/Aswan project, directed by C. von Pilgrim and Nasr Salama (see http://www. swissinst.ch/html/forschung_neu.html).

Courtesy of the Swiss Institute for Architectural and Archaeological Research on Ancient Egypt in Cairo (2014).

evidence from these periods, including pottery and coins, uncovered during the Swiss excavations in some areas (pers. obs.).

In contrast to the situation at the First Cataract, which formed an acknowledged physical barrier, even if not always an unproblematic political boundary, the concept of a clear frontier in the Western Desert remains nebulous, and few archaeological remains of earlier medieval date are known from the oases in this region. There was dense settlement of the Western Oases during late antiquity, and sites such as al-Qasr (Dakhla) or Shali (Siwa) indicate significant urbanization in later medieval times, with Ayyubid and Mamluk remains (Vivian 2008: 176–177, 304, 326–327).

Although the available archaeological evidence does not reflect it, the majority of Egypt's medieval urban centers lay in the interior, in the Nile Delta and Valley. These include both towns apparently broadly Coptic in character and those with evidence for a Muslim presence. The former category includes Tebtynis (c. 1800 BC–12th century CE), the medieval town of which covered about half the area of the Roman one, and the small provincial town of Jeme (c. 1150 BC–c. CE 800) (Rousset and Marchand 1999, 2000; Rousset, Marchand, and Foy 2001; Hölscher 1954). For the latter, the important town of al-Bahnasa (Oxyrhynchus) has seen a number of excavations, often flawed in execution and brief and/or imperfect in publication, with only a single archaeological study focusing on the substantial Islamic-era remains, including important architectural complexes from the 10th–16th centuries, a hoard of 200 Fatimid dinars, and a late antique to early Islamic potters' zone (Fehérvári et al. 2006). Also in Middle Egypt, the large and important late Roman cities at Zawyat al-Sultan, Ashmunayn, and Antinoöpolis appear to have gone out of use during the first centuries of Islamic rule, and the historic tendency to interpret this development as an indication of the declining size and importance of urbanism, often associated uncritically with the Arab conquest, has only recently been explicitly challenged (Kemp 2005). We should note the absence of balancing data from nearby cities such as Minya, among others, the modern buildings of which prevent access to presumably once-extensive medieval strata. Only historic buildings such as the Jami' al-Lamati, considered to be Fatimid in origin, remain to indicate the importance of this settlement under early Islamic rule (Garcin 1977). Other modern cities, including Qus, Asyut, and many more, must overlie important and inaccessible medieval archaeology. Elsewhere, interpretations of medieval urban decline and abandonment may in fact represent taphonomic processes, as is the case at Edfu (Gascoigne 2005).

CONCLUSION

This consideration of urbanization in Egypt under Islamic rule remains, inevitably, preliminary. Considerably more field investigation is needed in Egypt, especially in the inland areas of the Nile Valley and Delta. One theme that does emerge, though, is the impact of state policy, as opposed to organic factors, on the size and prosperity of urban centers, particularly those at the frontiers. Examples include the survival of Dumyat as opposed to Tinnis (see preceding discussion), the changing use of the various Red Sea ports through time (Cooper 2014: 246–251), and the movement of administrative and military status from Aswan to Qus from the mid-11th century (Björnesjö 2013: 11). Such changing politico-military priorities affected the continued prosperity and even survival of settlements at the frontier. Maintaining borders was and is a key priority of state and provincial administrations, and it would thus be interesting to know whether this situation held true for towns of the interior, where our data do not as yet allow us to go.

A second emerging theme of relevance to our understanding of Egypt's medieval cities concerns their traditional scholarly treatment: study of such sites often falls into the heuristic trap whereby medieval specificities are marginalized by "the teleological and the retrospective approaches" that frame the medieval world in terms of its ancient ancestry and/or modern descendants (Goodson et al. 2010: 4–5). This can be seen most clearly—as discussed earlier—in the configuration of Middle Egypt, where archaeologically and visually striking urban centers were succeeded in early Islamic times by obscure and poorly documented ones, and also with the scholarly reception of Mediterranean ports with phases of classical and early modern date. It is clear that Egypt's medieval and early modern archaeology deserves the much closer attention that it is increasingly receiving.

REFERENCES

Adams, W. Y. 1996. *Qasr Ibrîm: The Late Medieval Period* (London: Egypt Exploration Society).

Adams, W. Y. 2010. *Qasr Ibrim: The Earlier Medieval Period* (London: Egypt Exploration Society).

Al-Sayyid, N. 1991. *Cities and Caliphs: On the Genesis of Arab Muslim urbanism* (Westport, CT: Greenwood Press).

Bavay, L. 2010. "Fumer comme un Turc: Les pipes ottomanes provenant de la TT 29 à Cheikh Abd el-Gourna," in E. Warmenbol and V. Angenot (eds.), *Thèbes aux 101 portes: Mélanges à la mémoire de Roland Tefni*. Monumenta Aegyptiaca 12 (Turnhout: Brepols), 25–46.

Behrens-Abouseif, D. 1998. "Notes sur l'architecture musulmane d'Alexandrie," *Alexandrie Medieval*, 1, 101–114.

Björnesjö, S. 2013. "The History of Aswan and Its Cemetery in the Middle Ages," in D. Raue, S. J. Seidlmayer and P. Speiser (eds.), *The First Cataract of the Nile: One Region—Diverse Perspectives*. Sonderschrift des Deutschen Archäologischen Instituts Kairo 36 (Berlin: De Gruyter), 9–13.

Bloom, J. 2013. *The Minaret* (Edinburgh: Edinburgh University Press).

Blue, L. K. 2007. "Locating the Harbour: Myos Hormos/Quseir al-Qadim: A Roman and Islamic Port on the Red Sea Coast of Egypt," *International Journal of Nautical Archaeology*, 36, 2, 265–281.

Booth, P. 2013. "The Muslim Conquest of Egypt Reconsidered," in C. Zuckerman (ed.), *Constructing the Seventh Century* (Paris: Association des Amis du Centre d'Histoire et Civilisation de Byzance), 639–670.

Brooks Hedstrom, D., Davis, S. J., Herbich, T., Ikram, S., McCormack, D., Nenna, M.- D., and Pyke, G. 2010. "New Archaeology at Ancient Scetis: Surveys and Initial Excavations at the

Monastery of St. John the Little in Wādī al-Naṭrūn (Yale Monastic Archaeology Project)," *Dumbarton Oaks Papers*, 64, 217–227.

Butler, A. J. 1902 (1978). *The Arab Conquest of Egypt and the Last Thirty Years of Roman Dominion*, edited by P. Fraser (Oxford: Clarendon Press).

Casanova, P. 1919. *Essai de reconstruction topographique de la ville d'Al Foustât ou Misr*. Mémoires publiés par les membres de la Mission archéologique française au Caire 35 (Cairo: Institut français d'archéologie orientale).

Clapham, A. J., and Rowley-Conwy, P. A. 2009. "The Archaeobotany of Cotton (Gossypium sp. L) in Egypt and Nubia with Special Reference to Qasr Ibrim, Egyptian Nubia," in E. Weiss and A. S. Fairburn (eds.), *From Foragers to Farmers: Papers in Honour of Gordon Hillman* (Oxford: Oxbow Books), 244–253.

Cooper, J. P. 2014. *The Medieval Nile: Route, Navigation, and Landscape in Islamic Egypt* (Cairo: American University in Cairo Press).

Creswell, K. A. C. 1952–1959. *The Muslim Architecture of Egypt*. 2 vols. (Oxford: Clarendon Press).

Denoix, S. 1992. *Decrire Le Caire. Fustat Misr d'apres Ibn Duqmaq et Maqrizi* (Cairo: Institut français d'archéologie orientale).

Donner, F. M. 1981. *The Early Islamic Conquests* (Princeton: Princeton University Press).

El Dorry, M.-A. 2015. "Monks and Plants: Understanding Foodways and Agricultural Practices in an Egyptian Monastic Settlement," in M. Hawel (ed.), *Work in Progress, Work on Progress: Doktorand_innen-Jahrbuch 2015 der Rosa-Luxemburg-Stiftung* (Hamburg: VSA Verlag), 218–227.

Fedorov-Davydov, G. A. 1983. "Archaeological research in Central Asia of the Muslim period," *World Archaeology*, 14, 3, 393–405.

Fehérvári, G., Yousuf, A., Baker, P. L., Bivar, A. D. H., Bloom, J. M., Challands, A. et al. 2006. *Bahnasā (Oxyrhynchus): Final Report of the Excavations (1985–87)* (Kuwait: Dār al-Āthār al-Islāmiyya/Kuwait Foundation for the Advancement of Sciences).

Garcin, J.-C. 1977. "La mosquée Al-Lamaṭī à Minyā," *Annales islamologiques*, 13, 101–112.

Gascoigne, A. L. 2005. "Dislocation and Continuity in Early Islamic Provincial Urban Centres: The Example of Tell Edfu," *Mitteilungen des Deutschen Archäologischen Instituts Abteilung Kairo*, 61, 153–189.

Gascoigne, A. L. 2007. "The Water Supply of Tinnīs: Public Amenities and Private Investments," in A. K. Bennison and A. L. Gascoigne (eds.), *Cities in the Pre-Modern Islamic World: The Urban Impact of State, Society and Religion*. SOAS/Routledge Curzon Studies on the Middle East Series 6 (London: Routledge), 161–176.

Gascoigne, A. L. 2013. "Cooking Pots and Choices in the Medieval Middle East," in J. Bintliff and M. Caroscio (eds.), *Pottery and Social Dynamics in the Mediterranean and Beyond in Medieval and Post-Medieval Times* (Oxford: Archaeopress/BAR), 1–10.

Gascoigne, A. L., ʿArafa, A. A., Cooper, J. P., Fenwick, H., Harrison, M. J., al-Ḥusaynī, T. I. et al. 2020. *The Island City of Tinnīs: A Postmortem* (Cairo: Institut français d'archéologie orientale).

Gayraud, R.- P. 1998. "Fostat: évolution d'une capitale arabe du VIIe au XIIe siècle d'après les fouilles d'Istabl ʿAntar," in R.-P. Gayraud (ed.), *Colloque international d'archéologie islamique* (Cairo: Institut français d'archéologie orientale), 435–460.

Goitein, S. D. 1967–1988. *A Mediterranean Society: The Jewish Communities of the Arab World as Portrayed in the Documents of the Cairo Geniza*. 5 vols. (Berkeley: University of California Press).

Goodson, C., Lester, A. E., and Symes, C. 2010. "Introduction," in C. Goodson, A. E. Lester and C. Symes (eds.), *Cities, Texts and Social Networks, 400–1500* (Farnham: Ashgate), 1–17.

Haas, C. 1997. *Alexandria in Late Antiquity: Topography and Social Conflict* (Baltimore: Johns Hopkins University Press).

Hamilton-Dyer, S. 2011. "Faunal Remains," in D. P. S. Peacock and L. K. Blue (eds.), *Myos Hormos—Quseir al-Qadim: Roman and Islamic Ports on the Red Sea, Vol. 2: Finds from the Excavations 1999–2003* (Oxford: Oxbow Books/Archaeopress), 245–288.

Handley, F. J. L. 2011. "Textiles: A Preliminary Report," in D. P. S. Peacock and L. K. Blue (eds.), *Myos Hormos—Quseir al-Qadim: Roman and Islamic Ports on the Red Sea, Vol. 2: Finds from the Excavations 1999–2003* (Oxford: Oxbow Books/Archaeopress), 321–333.

Handley, F. J. L., and Regourd, A. 2009. "Textiles with Writing from Quseir al-Qadīm: Finds from the Southampton Excavations 1999–2003," in L. K. Blue, J. P. Cooper, R. Thomas, and J. Whitewright (eds.), *Connected Hinterlands: Proceedings of Red Sea Project IV held at the University of Southampton September 2008* (Oxford: BAR/Archaeopress), 141–153.

Harrison, M. J. 2014. "The Houses of Fusṭāṭ: Beyond Importation and Influence," in R. A. Stucky (ed.), *Proceedings of the 9th International Congress on the Archaeology of the Ancient Near East, 9–13 June 2014, Basel, Vol. 2* (Wiesbaden: Harrassowitz), 383–396.

Harrison, M. J. 2015. *Fusṭāṭ Reconsidered: Urban Housing and Domestic Life in a Medieval Islamic City* (Unpublished PhD diss., University of Southampton).

Heidemann, S. 2006. "The History of the Industrial and Commercial Area of ʿAbbāsid Al-Raqqa, Called Al-Raqqa Al-Muḥtariqa," *Bulletin of the School of Oriental and African Studies*, 69, 1, 33–52.

Hölscher, U. 1954. *The Excavation of Medinet Habu 5: Post-Ramessid Remains* (Chicago: University of Chicago Press).

Kaegi, W. E. 1992. *Byzantium and the Early Islamic Conquests* (Cambridge: Cambridge University Press).

Kawatoko, M. (ed.) 2004. *Archaeological Survey of the Rāya/al-Ṭūr Area on the Sinai Peninsula, Egypt* (Tokyo: Committee for Islamic Archaeology in Egypt, Middle Eastern Culture Center in Japan).

Kawatoko, M. 2005. "Multi-Disciplinary Approaches to the Islamic Period in Egypt and the Red Sea Coast," *Antiquity*, 79, 844–857.

Kemp, B. J. 2005. "Settlement and Landscape in the Amarna Area in the Late Roman Period," in J. Faiers, S. Clackson, B. Kemp, G. Pyke, and R. Reece (eds.), *Late Roman Pottery at Amarna and Related Studies*. EES Excavation Memoir 72 (London: Egypt Exploration Society), 11–56.

Kennedy, H. 2004. *The Court of the Caliphs* (London: Weidenfeld and Nicolson).

Kennedy, H. 2010. "How to Found an Islamic City," in C. Goodson, A. E. Lester, and C. Symes (eds.), *Cities, Texts and Social Networks, 400–1500* (Farnham: Ashgate), 45–63.

Kubiak, W. 1987. *Al-Fustat: its Foundation and Early Urban Development* (Warsaw: Warsaw University Press).

Kubiak, W., and Scanlon, G. T. 1989. *Fustat Expedition Final Report vol. 2: Fustat-C*. American Research Center in Egypt Reports 11 (Winona Lake: Eisenbrauns).

Kulicka, E. 2008. "The Islamic Graveyard on Kom el-Dikka in Alexandria. Excavation Season 2007/2008," *Polish Archaeology in the Mediterranean*, 20, 52–55.

Le Quesne, C. 2007. *An Ottoman and Napoleonic Fortress on the Red Sea Coast of Egypt* (Cairo: American University in Cairo Press).

Lev, Y. 1999. "Tinnīs: An Industrial Mediaeval Town," in M. Barrucand (ed.), *L'Égypte Fatimide: son art et son histoire* (Paris: Presses de l'Université de Paris-Sorbonne), 83–96.

Macklin, A. 2011. "The Muslim Necropolis," in D. P. S. Peacock and L. K. Blue (eds.), *Myos Hormos—Quseir al-Qadim: Roman and Islamic Ports on the Red Sea, Vol. 2: Finds from the Excavations 1999–2003* (Oxford: Oxbow Books/Archaeopress), 235–244.

Milwright, M. 1999. "Pottery in the Written Sources of the Ayyubid-Mamluk Period (567–923/1171–1517)," *Bulletin of the School of Oriental and African Studies,* 62, 3, 504–518.

Milwright, M. 2010. *An Introduction to Islamic Archaeology* (Edinburgh: Edinburgh University Press).

Mouton, J.- M., Guilhot, J.- O., Piaton, C., and Racinet, P. 2010. *Ṣadr: une forteresse de Saladin au Sinaï*. Mémoires de l'Académie des inscriptions et belles lettres 43 (Paris: De Boccard).

Müller, W. 2014. "Syene in the First Millennium AD," in E. R. O'Connell (ed.), *Egypt in the First Millennium AD: Perspectives from New Fieldwork* (Leuven: Peeters), 59–69.

Northedge, A. 2005. *The Historical Topography of Samarra* (London: British School of Archaeology in Iraq).

Ostrasz, A. 1977. "The Archaeological Material for the Study of the Domestic Architecture at Fustat," *Africana Bulletin,* 26, 57–86.

Peacock, D. P. S. 2011. "Glass," in D. P. S. Peacock and L. K. Blue (eds.), *Myos Hormos—Quseir al-Qadim: Roman and Islamic Ports on the Red Sea, Vol. 2: Finds from the Excavations 1999–2003* (Oxford: Oxbow Books/Archaeopress), 57–78.

Peacock, D. P. S., and Blue, L. K. (eds.) 2006–2011. *Myos Hormos—Quseir al-Qadim: Roman and Islamic ports on the Red Sea* (Oxford: Oxbow Books/Archaeopress).

Peacock, D. P. S., and Peacock, A. 2008. "The Enigma of ʿAydhab: A Medieval Islamic Port on the Red Sea coast," *International Journal of Nautical Archaeology,* 37, 1, 32–48.

Power, T. 2012a. "The Material Culture and Economic Rationale of Saracen Settlement in the Eastern Desert of Egypt," in A. Borrut, M. Debié, A. Papaconstantinou, D. Pieri, and J.-P. Sodini (eds.), *Le Proche-Orient de Justinien aux Abbassides: Peuplement et dynamiques spatiales. Actes du colloque 'Continuités de l'occupation entre les périodes byzantine et abbasside au Proche-Orient, VIIe-IXe siècles', Paris, 18–20 octobre 2007* (Turnhout: Brepols), 331–344.

Power, T. 2012b. *The Red Sea from Byzantium to the Caliphate, AD 500–1000* (Cairo and New York: American University in Cairo Press).

Pradines, S. 2016. "The Mamluk Fortifications of Egypt," *Mamluk Studies Review,* 19, 25–78.

Pradines, S., Laville, D., Matkowski, M., Monchamp, J., O'Hora, N., Sulayman, M., and Zurrud, T. 2009. "Excavations of the Archaeological Triangle: 10 Years of Archaeological Excavations in Fatimid Cairo (2000 to 2009)," *Mishkah,* 4, 177–219.

Prominska, E. 1972. *Investigations on the Population of Muslim Alexandria* (Warsaw: PWN-Editions Scientifiques de Pologne).

Rapoport, Y. 2018. *Rural Economy and Tribal Society in Islamic Egypt: A Study of al-Nābulusī's 'Villages of the Fayyum'* (Turnhout: Brepols).

Ravaisse, P. 1887–1890. *Essai sur l'histoire et sur la topographie du Caire d'après Makrîzî* (Paris: E. Leroux).

Rodziewicz, E. 2012. *Fustat 1: Bone Carvings from Fustat-Istabl ʿAntar* (Cairo: Institut français d'archéologie orientale).

Rousset, M.-O., and Marchand, S. 1999. "Tebtynis 1998, travaux dans le secteur nord," *Annales Islamologiques,* 33, 185–262.

Rousset, M.-O., and Marchand, S. 2000. "Secteur nord de Tebtynis. Mission de 1999," *Annales Islamologiques,* 34, 387–436.

Rousset, M.-O., Marchand, S., and Foy, D. 2001. "Secteur nord de Tebtynis (Fayyoum). Mission de 2000," *Annales Islamologiques,* 35, 409–489.

Sheehan, P. 2010. *Babylon in Egypt: The Archaeology of Old Cairo and the Origins of the City* (Cairo: American University in Cairo Press).

Sheehan, P., and Gascoigne, A. L. In press. "Babylon/Qaṣr al-Shamʿ: Continuity and Change at the Heart of the New Metropolis of Fusṭāṭ," in J. de Jong, S. Denoix, P. M. Sijpesteijn, and J. Bruning (eds.), *Incorporating Egypt from Constantinople to Baghdad* (in press).

Sidebotham, S. E. 2011. *Berenike and the Ancient Maritime Spice Route* (Los Angeles: University of California Press).

Sijpesteijn, P. 2013. *Shaping a Muslim State: The World of a Mid-Eighth-Century Muslim Official* (Oxford: Oxford University Press).

Sokoly, J. 2017. "Textiles and Identity," in F. B. Flood and G. Necipoğlu (eds.), *A Companion to Islamic Art and Architecture* (Hoboken, NJ: John Wiley and Sons), 275–299.

Speiser, P. 2013. "Umayyad, Tulunid, and Fatimid Tombs at Aswan," in D. Raue, S. J. Seidlmayer, and P. Speiser (eds.), *The First Cataract of the Nile: One Region—Diverse Perspectives.* Sonderschrift des Deutschen Archäologischen Instituts Kairo 36 (Berlin: De Gruyter), 211–222.

Van der Veen, M. 2011. *Consumption, Trade and Innovation: Exploring the Botanical Remains from the Roman and Islamic Ports at Quseir al-Qadim, Egypt* (Frankfurt: Africa Magna Verlag).

Veldmeijer, A. J. 2012. *Leatherwork from Qasr Ibrim (Egypt) Part 1: Footwear from the Ottoman Period* (Leiden: Sidestone Press).

Vivian, C. 2008. *The Western Desert of Egypt* (Cairo and New York: American University in Cairo Press).

Ward, C. 2000. "The Sadana Island Shipwreck: A Mideighteenth-Century Treasure Trove," in U. Baram and L. Carroll (eds.), *A Historical Archaeology of the Ottoman Empire: Breaking New Ground* (New York: Kluwer Academic/Plenum Publishers), 186–202.

Warner, N. J. 2005. *The Monuments of Historic Cairo: A Map and Descriptive Catalogue* (Cairo: American University of Cairo Press).

Whitcomb, D. 1982. *Quseir al-Qadim 1980* (Malibu, CA: Undena).

Whitcomb, D. 2007. "An Urban Structure for the Early Islamic City: An Archaeological Hypothesis," in A. K. Bennison and A. L. Gascoigne (eds.), *Cities in the Pre-Modern Islamic World: the Urban Impact of State, Society and Religion.* SOAS/RoutledgeCurzon Studies on the Middle East Series 6 (London: Routledge), 15–26.

Whitcomb, D. 2015. "Fustat to Cairo: An Essay on 'Old Cairo,'" in T. Vorderstrasse and T. Treptow (eds.), *A Cosmopolitan City: Muslims, Christians, and Jews in Old Cairo* (Chicago: Oriental Institute), 93–98.

Whitcomb, D., and Johnson, J. 1979. *Quseir al-Qadim 1978* (Cairo: American Research Center in Egypt Press).

Zieliński, J. 2012. "Appendix. Naqlun 2008: Archaeobotanical Studies," in W. Godlewski (ed.), *Naqlun (Nekloni) excavations in 2008–2009.* Polish Archaeology in the Mediterranean 21 (Warsaw: University of Warsaw Press), 210–211.

PERSIA

ROCCO RANTE

INTRODUCTION

THE archaeology of the Islamic periods in Iran, in comparison with that of the Ancient, Classical, and Late Antique Near Eastern world, is underdeveloped. The regrettable practice of past generations of removing the upper (later historical) levels of settlements in order to reach lower levels of greater interest to the archaeologists of the time has become a thing of the past. In recent decades, interest in the Islamic era and fruitful collaborations between foreign and Iranian specialists have generated new scholarly work, breathing new life into the discipline. This chapter reviews the contributions of the work from these decades.

The urban form and the ways it developed under Islam is a major theme of this chapter, reflecting the priorities of field research in Iran in recent years. A particular focus is given to urban water systems and material culture as they reveal important dimensions of daily life and the evolution of practices during the Islamic centuries.

Geography and Environment

Persia, which in this chapter includes Iran, northwest Afghanistan, and Turkmenistan, is bounded by the central Iranian deserts to the southeast, the Elborz and Zagros mountain ranges to the north and west, and the Hindu Kush to the east (Figure 2.5.1). Important urban centers flanking these mountain ranges include Hamadhān, Iṣfahān, and Iṣṭakhr, located to the east of the Zagros range; Rayy, Dāmghān, and Nīshāpūr, located to the south of the Elborz range; and Herāt and Balkh, in the northwestern region of the Hindu

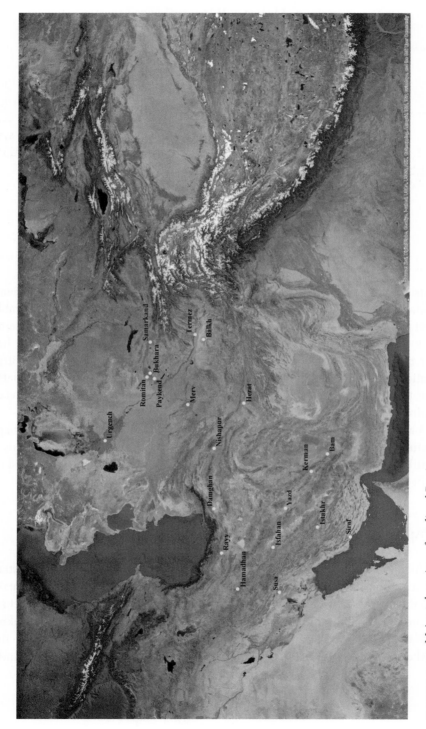

FIGURE 2.5.1 Major urban sites of medieval Persia.

Kush. Other groups of historically key cities are distributed southwest of the foothills of the Zagros, with Susa among the most important, to the south of and within the Iranian deserts; in Yazd and Kermān; and as urban ports, of which Sīrāf is the best known.

In general annual rainfall was insufficient to meet the needs of the urban centers. Rivers thus mostly assured their supply of water. A great number of Persian cities were served by water through underground water canals, or *qanāt* (Adle 2006). These cities generally were situated not very far from the mountain slopes where the *qanāt* originated and from where they were supplied with water through these underground canals and by wells. From the Iron Age, but especially from the Achaemenid period, this system of water transportation was the basis of the development of Iranian urbanization, from Azerbaijan (or probably Armenian) to the Afghan lands.

The lands of modern Iran are composed of a massive highland plateau that formed over a hard Precambrian basement. Secondary and tertiary sediments have developed on top of this, forming the landscape of the plateau. To the north, it is traversed mostly west-east by the mountainous range of Alborz, which presents double overflows to the north and south. This mountain range includes the more recent volcanic mountain of Demavand (ca. 5,600 meters), located at the northeastern part of Tehran, the capital of the country. Eastward, the mountains of Khorāsān represent the more eastern natural limit of the present-day Iranian frontier. The western and southern part is traversed by the Zagros Mountain range, from the Turkish frontier to Bandar Abbas. After reaching a maximum height of about 4,500 meters in central Iran, in the region of Isfahan the mountain range descends into the basin of Fars and rises again in the area south of Kerman. These high mountain ranges enclose two large central deserts: the Dasht-e Kavir and the Dasht-e Lut. The region as a whole is highly susceptible to earthquakes and volcanic activity, the result of the collision of the Arabian and Iranian plates that created the Zagros Mountains.

Ecology and Climate

Iran can be divided into five different ecological zones: the Caspian lowlands; the Alborz system and mountain ranges of Khorāsān; the Persian plateau (including Fars); the Zagros system (which includes the Jibāl), with the Makrān mountain ranges; and the lowlands along the Persian Gulf. These different ecosystems produce climatic regionalisms. The region as a whole lies between the continental, anticyclonic air masses of Central Asia and Siberia in the north; the Mediterranean wind regime in the center, with westerly winds and wandering depressions bringing rain and snow, especially in winter; and tropical and subtropical, even monsoonal, influences in the southern and southeastern parts of the country (Ehlers 1997). The ecological setting well represents the climatic situation of Persia. In fact, the Alborz, Khorāsān, and Zagros ranges and northwestern Persia receive considerable surplus precipitation. These regions are humid for a large part of the year, and even for the whole year for the Caspian area. The remaining portions of Persia—therefore the majority of the territory—are characterized by low annual rainfall, strong winds, and high temperatures, which together create the conditions for high evaporation and extreme aridity. Globally, precipitation decreases from north to south and from west to east, except where relief of the land disturbs this trend (Ganji 1968: 233–234, fig. 79). Intensive agricultural exploitation of some of these "marginal" zones has had a negative impact on the local environment, destroying limited vegetation cover and contributing to deforestation through soil erosion and the exhaustion of limited water resources.

HISTORIOGRAPHY

The French took the lead in archaeological fieldwork in Iran before World War II. French missions were generally the only archaeological presence in the country, having been established there since 1884 (Chevalier 2009). Interest in the antiquities of Persia has a much deeper history, however. European travelers to Persia in the 18th century described in their vivid accounts a landscape of ancient monuments and inscriptions, stimulating the interest in this civilization. In early 19th century E. Flandin (1843–1854 and 1851–1854), P. Coste (1843–1854 and 1851–1854), and R. Ker Porter (1821–1822) published architectural drawings of the monuments, as well as plans of cities, which remain invaluable resources today for archaeologists. Formal archaeological fieldwork began with excavations led by M. Dieulafoy from 1884 to 1886, J. de Morgan between 1897 and 1912, and R. de Mecquenem from 1912 to 1939. It was not only French archaeologists who were attracted to the region in this period: A. Stein led surveys and excavations in Seistan and E. Herzfeld in the region of what is today western Iran (see Miles 1940). In the 1930s R. Ghirshman launched numerous excavations in the region of Tepe Giyan, Tepe Sialk, and Susa.[1]

The postwar years witnessed an explosion of archaeological research, which focused not only on the Neolithic, Chalcolithic, Bronze, and Iron Ages, in which the Italian Mission at Seistan was most active (Tosi 1983),[2] but also on the era of Late Antiquity: the Parthian and Sasanian, and especially the Median and Achaemenid periods.[3] The primary interest of most of these missions was the pre-Islamic eras. The work of E. Schmidt is one exception. During his excavations in Rayy (1935–1936) and Tepe Hissar (1937), the German-American archaeologist systematically recorded an entire stratigraphic sequence to modern times. This is remarkable as the Islamic levels were customarily removed without properly recording them, as was the case in many countries of the day. The material culture of these strata was, moreover, rarely analyzed. Notable in this respect are the excavations in the 1930s of Nīshāpūr by the American archaeologist C. Wilkinson; unfortunately, outside of his catalogue of Abbasid-era glazed wares (Wilkinson 1973), the finds have not to this day been fully processed or studied.

---

[1] For a general bibliography of Ghirshman, see *Bio-bibliographies de 134 savants (1979)*, Acta Iranica, 4th series 1 (Leiden), 188–201.

[2] Recently Iranian archaeologists have been active in this region. Concerning the activity of Iranian archaeologists, see *Ghozāreshhāy, pānzdahamyn ghardhamā-y sālāneh bāstān shenāsy Irān 1395/2017.*

[3] For a more comprehensive survey of the archaeology of pre-Islamic Persia, see Potts (2013).

It was only well after World War II that the Islamic era became a focus of archaeological research. Among the most important projects in this regard from the 1970s were the Italian Archaeological Mission in the Masjid-e Jum'a of Isfahan (launched by the architect E. Galdieri [1972–1973] and archaeologist U. Scerrato [2001]); C. Adle's work (2015) in Zuzan, Rayy, and Qumes; D. Whitcomb's expedition to Istakhr; D. Whitehouse's excavations at Siraf (2009); and R. Holod's (1978; Holod et al. 2008) projects in central Iran (Isfahan, Rayy, Yazd, and Siraf). More recent fieldwork includes M. Y. Kiani's excavations of the city of Gurgan and its hinterland (1985); H. Chubak's excavation of Alamut (2009), beyond the Alborz Mountain; and K. R. Labbāf's fieldwork in the Khorāsān (1995–2002), which have identified numerous new sites (including Shadyakh in the region of Nīshāpūr).

PERIODIZATION AND POLITICAL HISTORY

Archaeologists in Iran have generally adopted a political (dynastic) periodization, in spite of the marked continuity in material culture during periods of dynastic transition. For example, the Islamic conquest in Persia did not generate a sudden and radical cultural change. The key moment of the "Islamic cultural conquest" of Iran should be situated in the second half of the 8th century, when the center of political and cultural life moved eastward to the Khorāsān. Excavations in the Khorāsān and at Rayy and Gurgan have produced material culture that for the first time exhibits what one generally associates with Islamic society, such as glazed pottery. Similarly, although the division of the Abbasid Empire into successor states is an important historical moment, the material culture of Persia changed little in that period and expresses only regional variants. The two most important political entities of Iran of that time, the Buyids and the Tahirids-Samanids, demonstrate a clear Persian character.

Real innovations in the art and architecture of Persia came only with the Seljuk conquests. This, however, primarily reflects elite production; the material culture of daily life in most sectors of Persian society demonstrates continuity. The Mongol invasions, similarly, brought change, but the degree to which it was destructive differs regionally. The *shahrestān* of Rayy unquestionably suffered destruction; in other cases (such as Rayy and Varamin), the political center simply moved to other towns.

SETTLEMENTS

Urban

In Persia and Central Asia the urban pattern was largely established by the time of the Islamic conquest. Ancient settlements were reoccupied—even if the dynamics of occupation were different from city to city—and modified. Documenting the structure and function of pre-Islamic settlements is, therefore, fundamental to understanding what changes did occur as a result of the conquest. The process of change—whether through state initiative, migration and conversion, or reorientation of social networks and economy—left traces in the urban form.

Apart from a very small number of cities newly established after the Islamic conquests, most urban centers of the medieval and post-medieval eras were pre-Islamic establishments. Nonetheless, as Kennedy (2008: 104) reminds us, "continuity of site did not mean continuity of urban topography." The walled extents of these cities, though, have never remained unchanged but have been restored and reconstituted while generally respecting their original spatial organization. With few exceptions, nearly all of the urban settlements built by Sasanids (and their precursors) are quadrangular in shape, a characteristic also shared by the Roman Oriental provinces (Pigulevskaya 1963: 127).

Two patterns of occupation can be observed in Persian cities. The first involves the occupation of the original (pre-Islamic) fortified nucleus and its maintenance as the political and administrative center. These cities subsequently grew beyond their ancient limits, generating suburbs, or *rabad*s. Hamadhān and Rayy belong to this group, as do Herāt (Franke 2015) and Balkh (see Le Berre and Schlumberger 1964; de la Vaissière 2010) (Figure 2.5.2), though for other reasons. The early Islamic occupation of Nīshāpūr also began from its ancient nucleus, but it was rapidly supplanted by the new Islamic city of Shādyākh, which was founded, as military headquarters, approximately 2 kilometers westward of the old one. Although a primordial Islamic occupation has been noted in Jayy, Iṣfahān shows another example of the constitution of a new Islamic city. For Jayy, it is difficult to determine the details of its urban topography beyond its quadrangular form and the remains of a "citadel" in its southwestern corner. Iṣfahān, on the other hand, was created from the merging of several villages; only in the 10th century, or slightly earlier, did an urban plan with a citadel and *shahrestān* (lower city) develop. Nevertheless, it is not yet possible to describe the urban topography and settlement of the early Islamic center, dating to the end of the 8th century, which was situated close to the Friday Mosque, more than 2 kilometers distant from the 10th century citadel.

The mound of Iṣṭakhr is an Islamic city founded within an ancient larger fortress; it rapidly lost its role as political and administrative center of the region to Shiraz, approximately 50 kilometers southwest, a place that was probably already settled at the time. Iṣṭakhr's importance lies in its strategic situation, its urban organization determined by local topography. Here the political and religious districts were located in the southern part of the mound, and the larger city expanded to the east and west.

The urban development of Gurgān[4] is quite similar to that of Iṣṭakhr: shahr-e Gurgān, about 50 kilometers northeast of ancient Astarābād, replaced that city as the political center of the region, leading to the rapid abandonment of Astarābād. A pre-Islamic establishment (Gyselen 1989: 50; Bivar 2002: 153), Shahr-e Gurgān consists of a fortified

---

[4] For more information about the global region and especially about the Great Well of Gurgān, see Sauer et al. (2013).

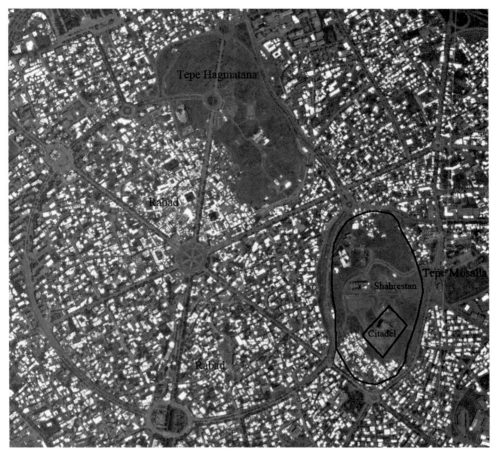

HAMADHAN

0   500 m

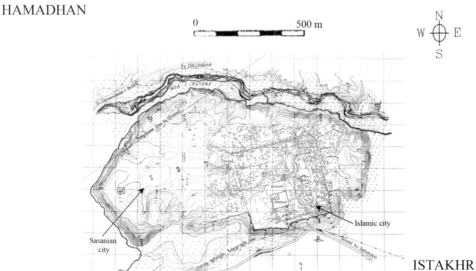

ISTAKHR

FIGURE 2.5.2 Urban topography of Hamadhān (8th–10th CE), Iranian Jibāl (Google Earth, rectified by Rante [2014]. Urban topography of Isṭakhr (8th–10th CE), Fars (Schmidt 1939; Whitcomb 1976).

city with a citadel and *shahrestān* on the right bank of the Gurgān River and a *rabad* on the bank opposite (Bosworth 2002: 153–154), a clear example of the separation of new Islamic quarters from older neighborhoods (Kiani 1985: figs. 1–3).

In Khorāsān, and particularly in its western part (which includes Nīshāpūr and Merv), urban topography developed more or less homogenously, with some localized differences in settlement dynamics and chronology. Here new cities were established between the 8th and 9th centuries; they were later surrounded by ramparts. They were conceived in an open space, in which a well-delimited portion was certainly assigned to administrative or political structures. The constitution of the *rabad* (suburb), eventually encircled by ramparts, finally completed the topography in the early Islamic period.

Zuzan presents a different case due to its smaller size and its shorter period of occupation. Nevertheless, its extensive *qanāt* system, first developed under the Parthians, documents the city's physical expansion at least until the 11th–12th centuries. The present state of research does not allow us to describe the topographical expansion inside and outside the ramparts through time. Bam, in the southern Khorāsān, presents a similar urban form in terms of scale of the Citadel and the walled city, the geometrical shape of the walled area, and the large and complex organization of *qanāts*, also constructed by the Parthians (C. Adle, see earlier discussion).

The Islamic-era development of Herāt and Balkh, the other major cities of the region, altered little of the older foundations. Cities developed above all within their ancient ramparts and later outside them in large open suburbs.[5] The same dynamic can sometime be observed in Transoxiana, as in Bukhara, in which the medieval city remained within its ancient walled space.

Kennedy's perceptive theory of *decastellamento* of Persian cities (Kennedy 2008: 103) merits a more precise definition. The move from the "small, fortified site to the larger, open position" is a dynamic which could be found in several cities in the Iranian territories. Nonetheless, it is not always possible to identify it, as is the case for Hamadhān and Rayy, or in Paykend,[6] in Central Asia. The occupation of such urban places after the Islamic conquests, while maintaining the ancient fortified portions of the city, required new open spaces to integrate communities coming from the countryside (Bulliet 2009: 8–9) as well as from the Middle East (Rante 2015a and 2015c); as many as several tens of thousands of souls might need to be resettled (see Bulliet 2009: 8; Rante 2015c). These new areas of settlement were well organized and planned and were frequently surrounded by ramparts, a feature which depended on the strategic situation of the city and the political stability of the region. The supply of water was of paramount concern in the physical development of all cities, newly established and occupied (Rante 2018). With population growth, settlement shifted outside the urban walled limits and closer to sources of water.

---

[5] Concerning Balkh and its urban development in the first century after the Islamic conquest, it should be added that the suburbs were occupied well before Islam (see de la Vaissière 2010: 517–533).

[6] Concerning this specific topic, see Rante (2018). Concerning the city of Paykend, see Semenov et al. (1988) and Rante (2013).

These developments contrast with the establishment and growth of western Islamic foundations—such as Kūfa, Baṣra, and Fusṭāṭ—where the need to settle the army determined urban structure. In the Levant, the urban form was, in part, dictated by tribal structures; land belonged to those tribal groups that first "laid stake" to them by building tents. These pieces of land (*ḥiṭṭa*) constituted administrative units, which would correspond to an equivalent division of the military (Monneret de Villard 1966: 96–97).

Main Cities of Jibāl

In the western mountainous regions of the Persian lands, usually called Jibāl, cities continued to be occupied for millennia and were located at the intersection between the Zagros and Elborz ranges, as well as along their foothills. In spite of its strategic location in western Iran, Hamadhān (Figure 2.5.1) has not been a focus of study in Islamic archaeology. Located at the point where the Zagros and Elborz Mountains meet, Hamadhān has always been a political crossroads between Mesopotamia, eastern Iran, and southern Iran. The climate is characterized by cold winters and mild summers, and the land is irrigated by waters originating from the Alvand Mountain and an extensive network of *qanāt*. It was the capital of the Median Empire (7th–6th centuries BCE)[7] and then a seasonal residence during the Parthian period, before gradually losing its importance. Past scholarship centered on the etymology of the name (ancient Ecbatana)[8] and on Herodotus's account about the famous round city (Brown 1997: 80–81). In 19th century, several visitors went to Hamadhān to collect antiquities or start archaeological excavations (Chevalier 1989: 244–253), until fortunate discoveries in 1950s revealed Median and Achaemenid material. Recently, the Iranian archaeological missions directed by M. Sarraf (2013), then by M. Azarnoush (2005), brought to light a part of the ancient city on Tell Hagmatana.

The city's topography is dominated by three hills: Tell Hagmatana, the Median citadel also reoccupied by the Parthians and Sasanians; Mosallā, on which stone and brick vestiges of a rectangular citadel have been discovered and dated to the Parthian period; and Sang-e Shīr (Figure 2.5.2). Herodotus (I, 98) described the Median "royal complex" (most probably corresponding to the citadel) built on a hill and encircled by seven rings of ramparts.[9] In the Parthian period the city seems to have been located on the Mosallā hill, which would have consisted of a rectangular space probably equipped with a citadel (or maybe the citadel remained that of Tell Hagmatana). Arabic sources provided some descriptions of the city. Ibn Hawqal (Le Strange 1930: 194; Ibn Hawqal 1964: 353–354) described Hamadhān as a fine large city, over a league square, surrounded by a rampart and an extensive suburb, probably toward the west, most probably referring to the Parthian city Mosallā hill, which developed further over the course of the Islamic periods. The city wall had four gates. According to its modern contemporary urban features, the city seems to have been expanded toward the west. A miniature map of the 16th century,

---

[7] See Dandamayev and Medvedskaya (2006).
[8] See, among others, Kent (1950: 183, 212), Frye (1986: 105), and Weissbach (1903).
[9] See the Neo-Assyrian representation of a Median city in Gunter (1982: 103–112, pls. II–Iva).

realized by Nasuh b. Karagöz b. Abdullah el-Bosnavī (commonly known as Matrakçı Nasuh), represents the city with a square citadel and *shahrestān* united by a rampart, located at the foot of the mountain range (Alvand range), and provided with water through two canals coming from the mountain, of which one seems to traverse the city while the other passes it on one side.[10]

The urban development of Hamadhān seems to be very close to that of Rayy, a city that is at present better known. Here, from the Parthian era to the Islamic occupation, the nucleus of the city approximately occupied the same surface as that of Mosallā hill, and the areas previously occupied, such as Tell Hagmatana in Hamadhān or Bibi Zubayda in Rayy, later became suburbs. In the early Islamic period Hamadhān had a citadel and a *shahrestān* at the southern and northern part of Mosallā hill, respectively, surrounded by ramparts. The suburb probably extended over the ancient Tell Hagmatana as well as the western part of the site, which is today covered by the modern city. Small streams descend from the Alvand range, south of the city, toward the north and northeast. The geomorphology of the territory and its water supply probably dictated the layout of the city.

Rayy (Figure 2.5.3) today's Shāh ʿAbd al-ʿAzīm (Shāhr-e Ray), was located on the Iranian Plateau, more precisely at the foot of the Elborz (or Alborz) mountain range which passes just to the south of the Caspian Sea (Rante 2015a).[11] To the north of the site rise the southern slopes of the Elborz range and Iran's modern-day capital Tehran. To the south extends the desert plateau that corresponds to the most westerly branch of the Dasht Kawīr, the Great Desert of Iran. The location of the ancient and medieval settlements of Rayy was thus ideal for control of east–west as well as north–south communication and trade. The site is situated in a zone where major watercourses are few. It is located on the interfluve between two great watercourses: the larger one, Karaj to the west, which supplies the town of Karaj itself, and that of Jājerud (Valles, Gholami, and Lambert 1990) to the east, which supplies the town of Warāmīn. Probably already during the period of the foundation of the fortified city the water which arrived in Rayy through smaller basins and *qanāt* came from that of Jājerud. The *qanāt*, which are likely Parthian constructions, significantly expanded the available water supply and, therefore, the potential for demographic and economic growth.

Excavations have revealed that the fortified city consisted of a citadel and a *shahrestān*, which represents the oldest part of the site (Iron Age I–II). The citadel was constructed on the summit of a rocky hill (Kuh-e Sorsore) of an almost triangular profile, and a longer ridge extends eastward where it joins the Bībī Shahrbānū mountain range. The base of the hill was encircled by an artificial canal still visible today, which most probably was used for drain water. The defensive walls surrounding the citadel follow the whole profile of the hill, also extending toward the east where they join more medieval walls. Today, nothing remains of this defensive complex as a result of modern agricultural

---

[10] See Matrakci (2000).
[11] Called Ragā under the Sasanians, the name of the town was changed to al-Rayy in the first Arab sources.

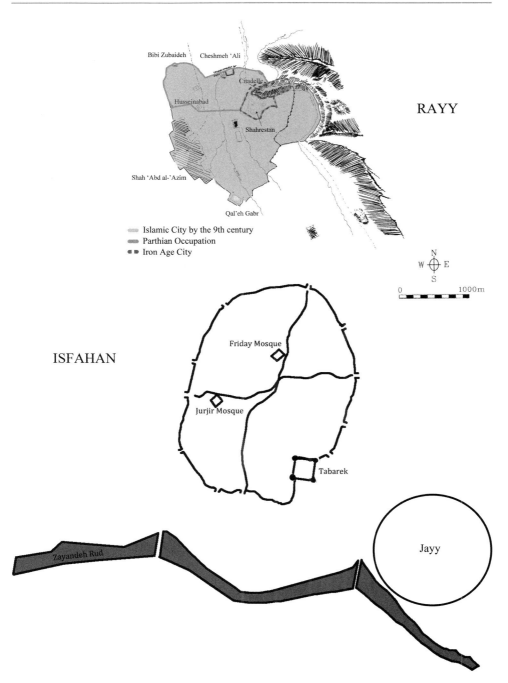

FIGURE 2.5.3 Urban topography of Rayy (9th–10th CE), Iranian Jibāl (Rante 2014). Urban topography of Iṣfahān (10th CE), Iranian Jibāl (Golombek 1974, completed by Rante 2014).

development. The citadel is composed of two lower parts that lie opposite one another: the north and south terraces. Here was located the political and royal center, at least from the Parthian period, of which some stone constructions belonging to the Islamic period still remain.

The *shahrestān*, or "inner city," is situated at the foot of the citadel in the south/southwestern section. A large square tower forms a corner at its southeastern extremity. From there a section of the rampart on the eastern side of the *shahrestān*, which has today completely disappeared, probably provided one of the gates to the town. Another entrance, still visible today, has been recently found at the southeastern part of the rampart (Rante 2015a: figs. 36–37). This last gate is an ancient one and was closed in the early Islamic period. Today the historic inner city is almost totally obscured by the modern town, whereas during the 1930s nonurbanized and nonindustrialized spaces still survived. Outside the *shahrestān*, the suburb of the city was certainly inhabited before the arrival of Islam. Unfortunately, because of the extensive modern development, it has been difficult to do archaeological investigations of the area. Schmidt's excavations, however, brought to light portions of the medieval "outer city," therefore outside the fortified urban nucleus. The morphology of Islamic suburbs (*rabad*s) is different for each. The suburbs of Rayy, likely already from the ʿAbbāsid period, were protected by walls (Rante 2015a: fig. 29). Adle's excavations (1979 and 1990) suggest that the walls constructed in the period of the extension of the town are approximately datable to the end of the 8th–10th centuries. These were revisited through recent excavations (Rante 2015a), which showed the important city planning performed by al-Mahdī, and can now be dated to the end of the 8th–9th centuries with 10th-century reconstructions. The southern part of this medieval rampart also includes the Sasanian fortress Qalʿeh Gabr, which was to become one of the several gates of the city. Today, these walls have completely disappeared. The reasons for the construction of this rampart are above all social and economic and consequently demographic. With the arrival of al-Mahdī as governor—before becoming Caliph and with the intention of making Rayy once again the capital of northern Persia—the city experienced rapid growth. Arab communities were already being transferred to Rayy from the end of the 7th century, probably initially living in suburbs around the fortified city. With al-Mahdī, these suburbs were enclosed by a rampart, testifying to the will to protect Rayy's population and economy.

Iṣfahān, known in the Sasanian period as "Aspahān" (Marquart 1901: 27–30), is located east of the Zagros range, at an altitude of approximately 1,500 meters (Figure 2.5.2). Surrounded by deserts and arid areas of the Central Iranian Plateau, the city took its water supply from the Zāyandeh Rūd, a river which flows in the middle of the modern city. Two large towns in its vicinity appear in contemporary written sources: Jayy and Yahūdiyya (Golombek 1974; see also Gaube 2008: 163–165). No consistent archaeological traces are today known of these ancient urban occupations, except the structures found during the excavations in the Friday Mosque of Iṣfahān (Galdieri 1972; Scerrato 2001), in Yahūdiyya, and a few ruins close to the Zāyandeh Rūd in the eastern part of the city where the round fortified city of Jayy was constructed. It was during the Islamic period that Jayy assumed a unique and homogenous urban form. By the end of the 8th century, corresponding to the construction of the Friday Mosque in Yahūdiyya (772), where the center of activity was transferred at least from 746 according to the numismatic data (Gaube 2008: 165), several villages located between the former center and Jayy were incorporated into a single settlement. Jayy—which originally served more royal and military functions than to house a "civilian" population—was rapidly abandoned (Golombek 1974: 23–24; Gaube 2008: 164). In similar fashion, Yahūdiyya absorbed Khūshinān. From its foundation, Iṣfahān remained without a rampart for several decades. It seems to have been around the 10th century (but probably even earlier) that the city was enclosed by a strong rampart (Golombek 1974), and in this period Muqaddasī identified 12 gates. Iṣfahān was not only a very large city for the 10th century (see Golombek 1974: fig. 3; Brignoli 2009), but was also probably the largest city of Jibāl, as related by Ibn Hawqal and Muqaddasī (Le Strange 1930: 203).[12]

Unlike the cities discussed earlier, in which the Islamic urban center grew around the fortified nucleus of the pre-Islamic, Iṣfahān included a square citadel at the southeastern edge, oriented toward the Zāyandeh Rūd (the main water supply), from the end of the 8th century. The urban center of Islamic Iṣfahān was, therefore, deliberately planned as a unit separate from the earlier settlement. Why the urban planners rejected the old round settlement and the nearby water supply of Zāyandeh Rūd to build anew barely a few kilometers to the north will be discussed later.

Fars Region: The Case of Iṣṭakhr

Excavated sites in southern and southwestern Persia with well-preserved occupational levels of the late Sasanian and early Islamic periods are few. It is clear, however, that the Marvdasht plain has been, since Achaemenid times, amenable to large-scale settlement. Here, the site of Iṣṭakhr, even if less known archaeologically, presents for the first time a sequence of occupation for the region.

Iṣṭakhr is located in the valley of the Polvār River where it opens into the Marvdasht plain. The mound is embedded between the Kūh-e Rahmat and the cliffs of Naqsh-e Rustam. The Polvār River surrounds the mound at its northern, western, and eastern sides. Considering the topography of this region, where mountain ranges are dense in the eastern and northern part and the Marvdasht plain lies in the south and eastern parts, Iṣṭakhr is strategically located and well placed for access to water on the plain. Its privileged defensive situation aside, confirmed by the strong and massive defensive system of which the ancient city is constituted (Herzfeld 1941: 276; Schmidt 1939: 107), Iṣṭakhr was probably the key site generating economic growth on the Marvdasht plain, at least between the end of the Sasanian period and the first centuries of Islam. The numerous surveys carried out by Sumner (1972) provided an overall urban framework concerning the development of settlements in conjunction with the irrigation systems for the Kur and Pulvār Rivers (Whitcomb 1979: 368). The great development of Iṣṭakhr occurred under the Sasanians. It seems, in fact, that at that time Iṣṭakhr controlled a

---

[12] On the basis of the author's calculations, and in comparison with P. Coste's plans, it should have been about 750 hectares.

major canal head for the Marvdasht district, confirming its strategic position for the economy of the region. This was to later guarantee, during the first century of Islam, a considerable expansion of the irrigation systems (Sumner 1972: 248) and thus of agricultural production, assuring the economic development of the city between the 9th and 10th centuries. These factors have contributed de facto to the urban development of the city in the early Islamic period. According to the map published by Schmidt (1939: fig. 74), the mound should cover an area of approximately 70 hectares. The mound rises on its western and eastern sides. The central zone presents a depression of the ground. In the western sector, land rises to approximately 10 meters from the level of the plain to the west and 8 meters to the northeast. In the eastern sector, the land rises approximately 12 meters from the level of the plain level to the east and to about 10–11 meters to the west. It seems thus that the eastern half of the mound is more or less 2 meters higher than the western one. According to the previous topographical studies (Herzfeld 1941; Schmidt 1939, 1940; Whitcomb 1979; Fontana et al. 2012[13]), these two areas are well distinguishable with an Islamic city to the east (Schmidt 1939, Whitcomb 1979: 363–366) and a Sasanian city to the west (Schmidt 1939: 135), the natural topography of the land separating them from one another. The latter, even if not yet well identified, could have developed in the western half of the mound and have been divided in a higher part to the west and a lower one toward the northeast, at least according to the topography. It may, however, be possible that this Sasanian occupation also expanded beyond the limits suggested by Whitcomb (1979: 364): according to Schmidt (1939: 111), the Islamic layers on the eastern area of the mound, the Islamic city, "may be superimposed on a preceding settlements, while other sections may rest on a deposit of any one of the preceding historic epochs."

The foundational strata of the Islamic city lay, in some spots, directly on virgin soil; the occupation of Iṣṭakhr, was more extensive and more compact than the preceding town (Schmidt 1939: 109).[14] All these elements suggest that the Islamic-era site extended over the whole mound, with the earliest settlement in the eastern zone. This city was, according to Whitcomb (1979: 364), square in layout, measuring approximately 16 hectares. Nevertheless, in my opinion, the Islamic city could have also developed beyond Whitcomb's square outline, generating a city of irregular perimeter including the preceding Sasanian ramparts (Schmidt 1939: 107); the southern part was occupied by political, administrative, and religious quarters, and the northern and eastern parts set aside for regular housing. The shift of the political center of the region to Shiraz, which likely happened before the Islamic conquest (Whitcomb 1985: 221–222), deprived Iṣṭakhr of the economic resources to develop a *rabad* outside the ramparts, even if Schmidt

---

[13] The topographical study of this publication unfortunately gives only general information about the numerous activities realized or to be realized, but nothing is detailed concerning the preliminary results of their investigations.

[14] The German-American archaeologist defines them as "sporadic remnants of the Islamic occupation," which I consider in any case as elements of occupation of the ground. Moreover, as for the mudbrick construction, temporary habitations are hard to recognize.

assumes that it existed (1939: 107). Inevitably suburbs existed, but they were probably within the city ramparts.

Some Main Cities in Khorāsān (Iran)

"Khorāsān"—a toponym that appears in the 6th century (for the origins of Khorāsān, see Rante 2015b)—includes Iranian Khorāsān, the westernmost part of Afghanistan to the Murghāb River, and the southern part of Turkmenistān to the Gorgān Wall, the latter recently dated to the 6th century (Sauer et al. 2013). Within this embryonic "Khorāsānian" space were the major urban centers of Nīshāpūr, Merv,[15] and Herāt,[16] as well as the smaller cities of Abiverd, Sarakhs, and Zuzan (Figure 2.5.4).

Nīshāpūr was founded at the end of the 4th century. The original city was, by today's standards, of medium size: 17.6 hectares. Its fortified nucleus included an approximately square citadel (3.5 hectares in size) and a quadrangular *shahrestān* (approximately 14.1 hectares) (Rante and Collinet 2013; Rante 2015b and 2015c). The ancient city was supplied with water through *qanāt*s, which traversed the citadel and *shahrestān* underground (Fouache et al. 2011: 99–119). The orientation of the city respected the spatial organization of water canals and *qanāt*, with the citadel placed along the mountain slope. As in many other cases, such as Bam or Rayy, and to my eyes also Iṣfahān, the citadel relied mostly on primary water sources as they entered the city—whether it was the mountain foothills, open canals, rivers, or brooks—arguably to guarantee a supply of "clean" (i.e., less polluted) water.

Although Arabic communities very soon settled around this ancient nucleus (Bulliet 1976: 73, 77–89), as was the case in Rayy (Rante 2015a), it was only with the arrival of the Ṭāhirid dynasty that other areas were likewise urbanized. 'Abd Allāh b. Ṭāhir became governor of Khorāsān in 829–30 and established his headquarters in Shādyākh, a little over 2 kilometers west of the ancient city. The new settlement, originally put to use as a military camp, rapidly assumed the features of an urban political center enclosed by a strong rampart, as the last Iranian excavations directed by R. K. Labbāf and A. Mokarramifar have shown (Rante and Collinet 2013: 6–7, fig. 6). Both urban entities, the fortified city and Shādyākh, respectively represented the eastern and western limits of Nīshāpūr until at least the Mongol invasion and its gradual depopulation. In this context, while the citadel of Rayy maintained the same royal and defensive functions (Rante 2015a), that of Nīshāpūr lost it and was largely occupied by ʿulamāʾ (Bulliet 1972: 20), inevitably modifying the urban organization. Its defensive function seems to have continued in a limited way: excavations have provided evidence of the abandonment of the original rampart of the Qohandez and the construction of a second rampart at the beginning of Period IIIa, in the second half of the 8th–11th centuries (Rante and Collinet 2013: fig. 12). The citadel of Nīshāpūr lost its strictly military function and had gradually fallen into disuse by the time of the Mongol invasion.

---

[15] Concerning Merv, see Usmanova (1992), Herrmann et al. (1993), Herrmann (1999), Kennedy (1999), and Williams (2007).

[16] See Franke (2015, 2016, 2107).

FIGURE 2.5.4 Urban topography of Nīshāpūr (8th–10th CE), Khorāsān (Bulliet 1976, completed by Rante 2014). Urban topography of Zuzan (8th–14th CE), Khorāsān (Adle 2001).

The Saffārid Yaʿqūb b. al-Lay_t_ controlled Nīshāpūr for only a few years, probably not before 896. However, he ordered important building in the town, including the construction of a *dār al-imāra*, tentatively located by Bulliet west/southwest of the large crossroads (Bulliet 1976: 75), as well as the mosque south of the ancient nucleus, showing a probable return of official buildings to the oldest part of the town. Under the Sāmānids the city, and in fact the entire region, grew considerably. The semi-independent states that evolved in this period were politically stable, creating the conditions for economic and demographic growth. Under the Seljūqs, the ancient nucleus and Shādyākh developed further. While strong ramparts protected Rayy and Iṣfahān during their demographical and urban expansion, Nīshāpūr extended its surface settlement without any defensive protection.

The establishment of Shādyākh is intimately tied to the urban history of Nīshāpūr. Wilkinson (1986: fig. 1) drew a plan of the vestiges of this city, most probably of rectangular form, of which the southwestern side measures 1,250 meters, producing a city plan of approximately 156 hectares. The southeastern side was also partially drawn, showing a 90-degree corner. The new city was traversed by a canal coming from the Mirābād River. Already at the time of its foundation at the beginning of the 9th century, Shādyākh was enclosed by a rampart, which has been partially excavated by the Iranian archaeologist R. K. Labbāf and published in several reports located at the ICAR archives in Tehran (Labbāf 1995–2002). Shādyākh, also oriented southwest with the citadel facing the city's water resources, is a perfect example of a new city built by a new dynasty. Recent excavations have brought to light an economic and socially solid city since its foundation. It is tempting here to think about a Tāhirid emulation of Sultān Kala of Merv.

According to the recent studies (Rante 2015b: 22), the Zuzan area could have marked the southern *limes* of the early embryonic Khorāsān ("Khorāsān proper") of the 6th century. This area is an arid one, and the absence of prehistorical or proto-historical human traces at the present state of research suggest that scarce water resources worked against large-scale settlement, although only systematic geo-archaeological investigations can deliver further solid information about this region.[17] Recent fieldwork in this region by C. Adle has identified previously unknown sites around Zuzan, Tepe Siyah, and Byasabad which have been dated at least to the Parthian period, testifying to settlement in the Zuzan region made possible by the introduction of *qanāts* (Adle 2002: 470). The ancient city of Zuzan appears to have been occupied during the Sasanian period, as demonstrated by the discovery of the commonplace mudbrick called *gabri* (zoroastrienne) under the main *eyvān* of the Mosque (Adle 1996: 324). Moreover, an ancient tradition linked Zuzan to the identification of a Fire Temple.[18] It seems, however, that the city acquired importance only after the Islamic occupation.

The city of Zuzan includes a high, circular citadel of an area of about 2,500 square meters, which is included in a quadrangular walled *shahrestān* covering an area of

[17]   The Franco-Iranian Archaeological Mission in Khorasan (MAFIK) is conducting a large geo-archaeological program on the whole Khorasan region.
[18]   See Adle (1996: 324 n. 21).

30 hectares. Human traces are also observable around the higher mound, especially to the south and to the west, testifying to the existence of suburbs, in some places walled, as is visible to the south. The ancient site is located in a plain and is framed by an important water course coming from the north, flowing just 3 kilometers east from it, northwest/ southeast, and by a water course to the south, flowing from the western mountains. Still today, many long *qanāts* traversing the plain are visible. As for Shādyākh, the *shahrestān* is crossed in its center by a small water course, which was likely the main water resource of the city. Today, as most probably in the past, agricultural lands are located in the southern part of the city.

The nature of the site in the early Islamic period remains mostly unknown. Zuzan was governed by local potentates with the title of *ra'īs*, sufficiently independent and sometimes powerful enough to lead rebellions (Adle 2002: 470). Traces of columns in the earliest mosque have been dated to the 9th century by Adle (2015: 104). The Franco-Iranian archaeologist also identified the second and the last third phases of the monument, respectively dated to the end of the 11th century/12th century (Phase 2) and the 13th century (Phase 3). The repeated expansion of the mosque since the 9th century testifies to demographic growth and the growing political importance of the place. The third mosque was never completed because of the death of the governor in 1218 and the Mongol invasion in 1220. On October 21, 1336, an earthquake destroyed the city and its mosque once more (Ambraseys and Melville 1982: 44–45, fig. 3.7). A later bout of cholera put a definitive end to the city (Adle 2002: 470–471). Old traditions tell us that this arid and depopulated region was repopulated in the 18th century through the deportation of Arab communities from the southwestern part of Iran (Adle 2002: 471).

The historical evolution of Zuzan, as well as its topographical evolution, is incompletely known. Nonetheless, thanks to Adle's discoveries, it is possible to envisage its urban evolution. It is most probable that the earliest settlement of Zuzan was located in the area around the circular tepe, also called Tepe Boland. Its relatively small area, approximately 2,500 square meters, would suggest that this place was used as a royal place; if so, the city was completed by the northeastern part of the *shahrestān*, situated at the foot of the citadel. Because of its aridity, the whole area was transformed thanks to the digging of *qanāts*, which guaranteed for centuries to come an adequate supply of water, in addition to the northeastern water course.

Rural

The rural sphere is an underdeveloped area of research in the archaeology of Islamic Persia as previous missions concentrated their efforts on the most important urban centers, such as Isfahan, Nīshāpūr, Rayy, and Siraf. The fieldwork that has been done suggests a typology of rural settlement that is in part related to uniquely regional ecological and topographical conditions.

The most common form of rural settlement is the clustered village, in which some hundreds or several thousands of people lived. Clustered villages are generally located in two types of landscapes: in the mountainous regions, where they are usually built on the lower slopes near irrigated valleys or on cliffs; or on the alluvial fans of arid piedmonts, where they are located at the outlets of *qanāts* or along canals, with their main streets often parallel to the watercourses. Intensively cultivated gardens, often encircled by mud walls, stand outside these villages and beyond them larger open fields of annual crops. Sometimes the buildings are clustered around a central open market, also with a mosque or shops. However, private and public services were not included. There is insufficient archaeological data to draw a classification of habitations. The houses were generally constructed from mudbrick, with additional use of stone in mountainous places, and these included a courtyard, completely enclosed by the four walls or partially enclosed and covered by a roof. We do not know yet whether these roofs were constructed with wood or were flat or domed.

Specific rural agglomerations with a defensive character are typically found in areas which were more exposed to invasions and in politically insecure zones. The most developed was the fortified village, or farmstead, called a *qalʿa*. In Iran the *qalʿa*s are mostly located on the plains and in broad valleys. The same buildings are identifiable along the ancient caravan routes, developing into caravanserais. Kleiss (1996–2001) has further demonstrated that caravanserais could have served multiple functions as both caravan stops and farmsteads.

Forms of nomadic or semi-nomadic settlements are also observable in different areas of Iran since ancient times. They were located on the fertile plains, rather than in mountainous zones. Gardens were not usual in these settlements. Tents or huts may have built around these settlements. During the medieval period, this trend probably developed because of the increase of the semi-nomadic population in Iran.

Finally, the humid climate of the Caspian lands generated another typology of rural settlement, mostly present in Gilan and Mazandaran. It has been studied especially in an ethnographical context (Bromberger 1986), and archaeological evidence is rare. It could be possible, however, that the same form existed already in Antiquity and the medieval-Islamic period.

Iranian scholars today, as an extension of their interest in the landscapes of ancient Persia, have begun to actively study rural settlements and the hinterlands of urban sites. The excavations of Jiroft by H. Chubak, who also currently direct since several years the mission of Alamut, have exposed a village dated between the 7th and 15th centuries. The village has a 6,000 square meter congregational mosque of the earliest Iranian architectural typology and is surrounded by pottery workshops, houses, and cemeteries. The site has, moreover, produced blue lustre ware, indicating the extent to which rural communities had direct and intense contact with urban markets and production centers. A. H. Said's excavations of Kaleh Sang—an 8th-century site on a river island—has revealed a *hammām* with frescoed walls. Although considered an important city since the Sasanian period, this site belongs to a genre of settlements located in the rural periphery of larger urban centers.

Archaeological surveys in the Province of Kerman, directed by A. Hashmadar, have documented a series of isolated stone buildings, both fortified and unwalled, dated by associated ceramics from the early Islamic to Seljuq-Mongol times. Once again, the fine quality of this ceramic, in contrast with the apparently "isolated" buildings beyond the urban center of Kerman, confirms the intense contacts between these entities and offers further information about daily life in these rural areas.

MATERIAL CULTURE AND DAILY LIFE

The best evidence of ceramic production comes from Siraf, where kilns of the 10th century have been discovered (Whitehouse 2009: fig. 38). A comparative study of the material coming from this quarter and that found in other domestic areas of Siraf is much needed to understand the different traditions of production and consumption as well as importation. Although a port, Siraf as a city reveals important patterns of daily life in the Islamic period. Protected by strong ramparts along the western and eastern sides, the city was supplied by water mostly from the northern mountains. Along the western coast, the potters' quarters were located *intra muros*, but far enough from the city core to avoid any air pollution. This location likely facilitated transport of pottery from workshops to markets. A watercourse divided this western side from the core of the city, eastward, where the residential quarters, commemorative places, the Great Mosque, and the bazaar were located.

The study of industrial production at Nīshāpūr has long been hampered by the methods of excavation and incomplete publication. Fortunately, recent archaeological research and publication have provided a clearer and more detailed picture of local ceramic production and its evolution from the Sasanian period to the Mongol invasion (Rante and Collinet 2013; Collinet 2015: 125–140). Moreover, intensive surveys in this region by Iranian archaeologists are revealing a wide range of locally produced ceramics (Laleh et al. 2015: 115–124).

As noted at Rayy and Nīshāpūr, production of both common objects for daily use and fine pottery seems to have increased exponentially during the Islamic periods. It is a marked shift in production and consumption from the pre-Islamic era, in which coarse or medium-coarse wares dominated urban assemblages. Mass production of high-quality glass is also a departure from production/consumption patterns of the Sasanian period, when glass seems to have produced mainly for elite patrons (see Kröger 1995).

CONCLUSION

While considerable progress has been made in the archaeology of the Islamic periods in Iran since the 2000s, the archaeological study of earlier civilizations remains a priority. The strong legacy of these earlier cultures is imprinted on urban forms and material culture for quite some time after the Islamic conquest. The unique "Islamic" character of settlement and material culture appears, as in many other countries of the Middle East, only in the 8th and 9th centuries. Future research in Iran should systematically explore this important period of political and cultural transition from the Islamic conquest to the 'Abbāsid period, significantly expand efforts to map and excavate rural sites, and expand research to investigate such topics as diet, land use, and urban and rural industry that are well developed areas of scholarship in other countries.

REFERENCES

Adle, C. 1996. "Archéologie et arts du monde iranien, de l'Inde musulmane et du Caucase d'après quelques recherches récentes de terrain, 1984–1995," *Comptes rendus des séances de l'Académie des Inscriptions et Belles-Lettres* (Paris), 315–376.

Adle, C. 2002. "Zawzan," *The Encylopaedia of Islam* (3rd ed.) (Leiden: Brill), 470–471.

Adle, C. 2006. "Qanats of Bam: An Archaeological Perspective," in N. Honari, A. Salamat, J. Sutton, and J. Taniguchi (eds.), *Qanats of Bam* (Tehran: UNESCO), 33–85.

Adle, C. 2015. "Trois mosques du début de l'ère islamique au Grand Khorasan: Bastam, Noh-Gonbadan/Haji-Piyadah de Balkh et Zuzan d'après des investigations archéologiques," in R. Rante (ed.), *The Greater Khorasan* (Berlin: de Gruyter), 89–114.

Ambraseys, N. N., and Melville, P. C. 1982. *A History of Persian Earthquakes* (Cambridge: Cambridge University Press).

Azarnoush, M. 2005. *Ghozāresh Kāvushā-y Layeh shenākhtī tepeh Heghmatāneh* (Hamadān), 21–61.

Bivar, A. D. H. 2002. "Gorgān: v. Pre-Islamic History," *Encyclopaedia Iranica*, 11/2, 151–153.

Bosworth, C. E. 2002. "Gorgān: History from the Rise of Islam to the Beginning of the Ṣafavīd Period," *Encyclopaedia Iranica*, 11/2, 153–154.

Brignoli, J.-D. 2009. *Les palais royaux Ṣafavīdes (1501–1722): architecture et pouvoir* (PhD thesis, Aix en Provence).

Bromberger, C. 1986. *Habitat, architecture et société rurale dans la plaine du Gilân, Iran septentionale* (Paris: UNESCO).

Brown, S. C. 1997. "Ecbatana," *Encyclopaedia Iranica*, 8/1, 80–84.

Bulliet, R. W. 1972. *The Patricians of Nīshāpūr: A Study in Medieval Islamic Social History* (Cambridge, MA: Harvard University Press).

Bulliet, R. W. 1976. "Medieval Nīshāpūr: A Topographic and Demographic Reconstruction," *Studia Iranica*, 5, 67–89.

Bulliet, R. W. 2009. *Cotton, Climate and Camels in Early Islamic Iran. A Moment on World History* (New York: Columbia University Press).

Chevalier, N. 1989. "Hamadan 1913. Une mission oubliée," *Iranica Antiqua*, 24, 245–253.

Chevalier, N. 2009. *Chronique des premières missions archéologiques françaises à Suse: d'après les photographies et mémoires de l'architecte Maurice Pillet* (Tehran-Paris: Institut Français de recherche en Iran/Musée du Louvre).

Chubak, H. 2009. "Alamut- Part II," *Mīrās-i Millī* [National Heritage], 3, 120–125.

Collinet, A. 2015. "Nouvelles recherches sur la céramique de Nishapur: la prospection du shahrestan," in R. Rante (ed.), *The Greater Khorasan* (Berlin: de Gruyter), 125–140.

Dandamayev, M., and Medvedskaya, I. 2006. "Media," *Encyclopaedia Iranica*, accessed at http://www.iranicaonline.org/articles/media.

de la Vaissière, É. 2010. "De Bactres à Balkh, par le Nowbahar," *Journal asiatique*, 298, 2, 517–533.

Ehlers, E. 1997. "Ecology," *Encyclopaedia Iranica*, 8/1, 84–88.

Fontana, M. V., Mireskandari, S. M., Rugiadi, M., Asadi, A., Jaia, A. M., Blanco, A., and Colliva, L. 2012. "Estakhr Project: First Preliminary Report of the Joint Mission of the Iranian Center for Archaeological Research," *Vicino Oriente*, 16, 167–180.

Fouache, E., Cosandey, Cl., Wormser, P., Kervran, M., and Labbaf Khaniki, R. A. 2011. "The River of Nīshāpūr," *Studia Iranica*, 40, 1, 99–119.

Franke, U. 2015. "Ancient Herat Revisited. New Data from Recent Archaeological Fieldwork," in R. Rante (ed.), *The Greater Khorasan* (Berlin: de Gruyter), 63–88.

Franke, U. and Müller-Wiener, M. 2016. Herat Through Time (Berlin: Staatliche Museen).

Franke, U. and Urban, T. 2017. Excavations and Explorations in Herat City (Berlin: Staatliche Museen).

Frye, R. N. 1986. "Hamadhān," *The Encylopaedia of Islam* (2nd ed.) (Leiden: Brill), III, 105–106.

Galdieri, E. 1972. *Isfahan: Masjid-i Juma: Photographs and Preliminary Report* (Rome: Istituto italiano per il medio ed estremo oriente (IsMEO)).

Ganji, M. H. 1968. "Climate," in W. B. Fisher (ed.), *The Cambridge History of Iran*, vol. 1 (Cambridge: Cambridge University Press), 212–249.

Gaube, H. 2008. "Iranian Cities," in S. K. Jayyusi, R. Holod, A. Petruccioli, and A. Raymond (eds.), in *The City in the Islamic World*, 1 (Leiden-Boston: Brill), 159–180.

Golombek, L. 1974. "Urban Patterns in pre-Ṣafavīd Isfahan: Part I, Studies on Isfahan," *Iranian Studies*, 7, 18–44.

Gunter, A. 1982. "Representations of Urartian and Western Iranian Fortress Architecture in the Assyrian Reliefs," *Iran*, 20, 103–112.

Gyselen, R. 1989. *La géographie administrative de l'Empire sassanide* (Leuven: Peeters).

Herrmann, G. 1999. *Monuments of Merv: Traditional Buildings of the Karakum* (London: Society of Antiquaries).

Herrmann, G., Masson, V. M., and Kurbansakhatov, K. 1993. "The International Merv Project. Preliminary Report on the First Season (1992)," *Iran*, 31, 39–62.

Herzfeld, E. 1941. *Iran in the Ancient Near East. Archaeological Studies Presented in the Lowell Lectures at Boston* (London: Oxford University Press).

Holod, R., Jayyusi, S., Petruccioli, A., and Raymond, A. (eds.) 2008. *The City in the Islamic World* (Leiden: Brill).

Ibn Hawqal, Abū al-Qasīm. 1964. *Kitab Sūrat al-Arḍ*, in J. H. Kramers and G. Wiet (eds.), *Configuration de la terre, II* (Paris: Maisonneuve & Larose), 349–364.

Kennedy, H. 1999. "Medieval Merv. An Historical Overview," in G. Herrmann (ed.), *Monuments of Merv: Traditional Buildings of the Karakum* (London: Society of Antiquaries), 27–44.

Kennedy, H. 2008. "Inherited Cities," in S. K. Jayyusi, R. Holod, A. Petruccioli, and A. Raymond (eds.), *The City in the Islamic World*, 1 (Leiden-Boston: Brill), 93–113.

Kent, R. G. 1950. *Old Persian: Grammar, Text, Lexicon* (New Haven, CT: American Oriental Society).

Kiani, M.-Y. 1985. *The Islamic City of Gurgān*. Archäologische Mitteilungen aus Iran. Ergänzungsbände, 11 (Berlin: Reimer).

Kleiss, W. 1996–2001. *Karavanenbauten von Iran*, 6 vols. (Berlin: Reimer).

Kröger, J. 1995. *Nishapur: Glass of the Early Islamic Period* (New York: Metropolitan Museum of Art).

Labbāf, R. Kh. 1995–2002. *Nīshāpūr Excavation*. Unpublished Reports (Tehran).

Laleh, H., Mokarramifar, A., and Lorzadeh, Z. 2015. "Le paysage urbain de Nishapur," in R. Rante (ed.), *The Greater Khorasan* (Berlin: de Gruyter), 115–124.

Le Berre, M., and Schlumberger, D. 1964. "Observations sur les remparts de Bactres," in B. Dagens, M. Le Berre, and D. Schlumberger (eds.), *Mémoires de la Délégation archéologique française en Afghanistan,* 19 (Paris: Klincksieck), 65–103.

Le Strange, G. 1930. *The Lands of the Eastern Caliphate* (Cambridge: Cambridge University Press).

Marquart, J. 1901. *Eranshahr, nach der Geographie des Ps. Moses Xorenac'i* (Berlin: Weidmann).

Matrakci, N. 2000. *Chronicle of stages of campaign of Iraq and Persia* (Tehran: Cultural Heritage Organization).

Miles, G. C. 1940. "The Writings of Ernst Herzfeld," *Ars Islamica,* 7, 82–92.

Monneret de Villard, U. 1966. *Introduzione allo studio dell'archeologia islamica* (Venezia-Roma: Istituto per la Collaborazione Culturale).

Pigulevskaya, N. 1963. *Les villes de l'Etat iranien aux époques parthe et sassanide* (Paris-La Haye: Mouton).

Potts, D. T. (ed.) 2013. *The Oxford Handbook of Ancient Iran.* (Oxford: Oxford University Press).

Rante, R. 2013. "Les fouilles de Paykend : nouveaux elements," in J. Bendezu-Sarmiento (ed.), *Archéologie française en Asie centrale. Nouvelles recherches et enjeux socioculturels* (Paris: IFEAC/DAFA/de Boccard), 219–240.

Rante, R. 2015a. *Rayy: From Its Origins to the Mongol Invasion. An Archaeological and Historiographical Study* (Leiden: Brill).

Rante, R. 2015b. "'Khorasan Proper' and 'Greater Khorasan' within a politico-cultural framework," in R. Rante (ed.), *The Greater Khorasan* (Berlin: de Gruyter), 9–25.

Rante, R. 2015c. "Nīshāpūr vi. Archeology," *Encyclopaedia Iranica,* online edition, accessed October 16, 2018, at http://www.iranicaonline.org/articles/nishapur-06-archeology.

Rante, R. 2018. "Iranian Cities: Settlements and Water Management from Antiquity to the Islamic Period," in D. Durand-Guedy, R. Mottahedeh, and J. Paul (eds.), *Cities of Medieval Iran,* special issue of *Eurasian Studies* 16, 39–76.

Rante, R., and Collinet, A. 2013. *Nīshāpūr Revisited: Stratigraphy and Ceramics of the Qohandez* (Oxford: Oxbow).

Sarraf, M. 2013. *Hegmataneh* (Tehran: ICHHTO).

Sauer, E. W., Omrani Rekavandi, H., Wilkinson, T. J., and Nokandeh, J. 2013. *Persia's Imperial Power in Late Antiquity: The Great Wall of Gorgān and the Frontier Landscapes of Sasanian Iran* (Oxford: Oxbow).

Scerrato, U. 2001. "Ricerche archeologiche nella Moschea del Venerdi di Isfahan della Missione archeologica italiana in Iran dell'IsMEO (1972–1978)," in *Antica Persia, I Tesori del Museo Nazionale di Tehran e la ricerca italiana in Iran,* Catalogo e Esposizione, Museo di Arte Orientale di Roma, 29 Maggio-22 Luglio 2001 (Rome: Edizioni di Luca), 37–43.

Schmidt, E. F. 1939. *The Treasury of Persepolis and Other Discoveries in the Homeland of the Achaemenians* (Chicago: University of Chicago Press).

Schmidt, E. F. 1940. *Flights over Ancient Cities of Iran* (Chicago: The Oriental Institute of Chicago Press).

Semenov, G. L., Mukhamedjanov, A. R., Mirzaakhmedov, D. K., and Adilov, Sh. T. 1988. *Gorodishe Paykend* (Tashkent: FAN Uzbekskoi CCP).

Sumner, W. M. 1972. *Cultural Development in the Kur River Basin, Iran: An Archaeological Analysis of Settlement Patterns* (PhD diss., University of Pennsylvania).

Tosi, M. 1983. *Prehistoric Sistan 1.* Reports and Memoirs, 19, 1 (Rome: isMEO).

Usmanova, Z. I. 1992. "New Material on Ancient Merv," *Iran,* 30, 55–64.

Valles, V., Gholami, M., and Lambert, R. 1990. "Chimie des eaux et alimentation du bassin versant du Djajerud (Iran)," *Hydrologie Continentale* 5, 1, 61–69.

Weissbach, F. 1903. "Ekbatana," in *Pauly-Wissowa Encyclopaedia*, 5, cols. 2155–2158.

Whitcomb, D. 1979. "The City of Istakhr and the Marvdasht Plain," in Deutsches Archäologisches Institut/Abteilung Teheran (ed.), *Akten des VII. Internationalen Kongresses für Iranische Kunst und Archäologie München, 7.–10. September 1976.* Archäologische Mitteilungen aus Iran Ergänzungsband 6 (München: Reimer), 363–370.

Whitcomb, D. 1985. *Before the Roses and the Nightingales: Excavation at Qasr-i Abū Nasr, Old Shiraz* (New York: Metropolitan Museum of Art).

Whitehouse, D. 2009. *Siraf. History, Topography and Environment* (Oxford: Oxbow).

Wilkinson, C. K. 1973. Nishapur: *Pottery of the Early Islamic Period* (New York: Metropolitan Museum of Art).

Wilkinson, C. K. 1986. *Nīshāpūr. Some Early Islamic Buildings and Their Decoration* (New York: Metropolitan Museum of Art).

Williams, T. 2007. "The city of Sultan Kala, Merv, Turkmenistan. Communities, neighbourhoods and urban planning from the eighth to the thirteenth century," in A. K Bennison and A. L. Gascoigne (eds.), *Cities in the Pre-Modern Islamic World. The Urban impact of religion, state and society* (London and New York: Routledge), 42–62.

FURTHER READING

Adle, C. 1979. "Constructions funéraires à Rey circa X^e–XIIe siècles," in Deutsches Archäologisches Institut/Abteilung Teheran (ed.), *Akten des VII. Internationalen Kongresses für Iranische Kunst und Archäologie München, 7.–10. September 1976.* Archäologische Mitteilungen aus Iran Ergänzungsband 6 (München: Reimer), 511–515.

Adle, C. 1990. "Notes sur les première et seconde campagnes archéologiques à Rey, Automne-hiver 1354–1355/1976–77," in F. Vallat (ed.), *Contribution à l'histoire de l'Iran, Mélanges offerts à Jean Perrot* (Paris: Editions Recherche sur les civilisations), 295–307.

Allan, J. W. 1982. *Nishapur: Metalwork of the Early Islamic Period* (New York: Metropolitan Museum of Art).

Bivar, A. D. H. 1969. *The Sasanian Dynasty.* Catalogue of the western Asiatic seals in the British Museum, Stamp seals 2 (London: British Museum).

Bosworth, C. E. 1975. "The Early Ghaznavids," in R. Frye (ed.), *The Cambridge History of Iran*, vol. 4 (Cambridge: Cambridge University Press), 162–197.

Brown, T. B. 1951. *Excavations in Azerbaijan, 1948* (London: Murray).

Bulliet, R. W. 1979. *Conversion to Islam in the Medieval Period* (Cambridge: Harvard University Press).

Callieri, P., and Chaverdi, A. A. 2017. *Persepolis West (Fars, Iran): Report on the Field Work Carried Out by the Iranian-Italian Joint Archaeological Mission in 2008–2009* (London: British Archaeological Reports Series).

de Mecquenem, R., Amiet, P. 1980. "Les fouilleurs de Suse," *Iranica Antiqua*, 15, 1–48.

de Morgan, J. 1905. *Histoire et travaux de la Délégation en Perse du Ministère de l'Instruction publique, 1897–1905* (Paris: Leroux).

de Phlanol, X. 1968. "Geography of Settlement," in W. B. Fisher (ed.), *The Cambridge History of Iran*, vol. 1 (Cambridge: Cambridge University Press), 418–432.

Dieulafoy, J. H. 1887. *La Perse, la Chaldée et la Susiane 1881–1882* (Paris: Hachette).

Dieulafoy, J. H. 1888. *À Suse. Journal des fouilles, 1884–1886* (Paris: Hachette).

Durand-Guédy, D. 2010. *Iranian Elites and Turkish Rulers. A History of Isfahan in the Seljuq Period* (New York-London: Routledge).

Ehlers, E. 1984. "Agriculture," *Encyclopaedia Iranica*, 1/6, 613–623.

Flandin, E., and Coste, P. 1843–1854 and 1851–1854. *Voyage en Perse de MM. Eugène Flandin, peintre, et Pascal Coste, architecte* (Paris: Gide et J. Baudry).

Förster, H. 1974. "Magmentypen und Erzlagerstätten im Iran," *Geologische Rundschau*, 63, 276–292.

Francfort, H.-P. 2005. "La civilisation de l'Oxus et les Indo-Iraniens et Indo-Aryens en Asie Centrale," in G. Fussman, J. Kellens, H.-P. Francfort, and X. Tremblay (eds.), *Aryas, Aryens et Iraniens en Asie Centrale* (Paris: Collège de France, publications de l'Institut de civilisation indienne, fasc. 72), 253–328.

Frye R. N. 1975. "The Sāmānids," in R. Frye (ed.), *The Cambridge History of Iran*, vol. 4 (Cambridge: Cambridge University Press), 136–161.

Fussman, G., Kellens, J., Francfort, H.-P., and Tremblay, X. 2005. *Aryas, Aryens et Iraniens en Asie Centrale* (Paris: Collège de France, publications de l'Institut de civilisation indienne, fasc. 72).

Galdieri, E. 1973. *Isfahan: Masjid-i Juma: The Al-I Buyid Period* (Rome: Istituto italiano per il medio ed estremo oriente [IsMEO]).

Gaube, H. 1977. "Innenstadt und Vorstadt. Kontinuität und Wandel im Stadtbild von Herat zwischen dem 10. und dem 15. Jahrhundert," in G. Schweizer (ed.), *Beiträge zur Geographie orientalischer Städte und Märkte* (Wiesbaden: Reichert), 213–240.

Ghirshman, R. 1935. *Fouilles de Tépé Giyan, près de Néhavend, 1931–1932* (Paris: Geuthner).

Ghirshman, R. 1938. *Fouilles de Sialk, près de Kashan, 1933, 1934, 1937* (Paris: Geuthner).

Ghozāreshhāy, pānzdahamyn ghardhamā-y sālāneh bāstān shenāsy Irān 1395/2017 (Tehran: ICAR-RICHT-ICHHTO).

Golombek, L., and Holod, R. 1978. "The Isfahan City Project: A Preliminary Report," *Archäologische Mitteilungen aus Iran*, 6, 578–590.

Herodotus. *Storie*. Vol. I (I–IV), translated and notes by L. Annibaletto, *Le storie de Erodoto* [2000] (Milan: Mondadori).

Herzfeld, E. 1935. *Archaeological History of Iran* (London: Oxford University Press).

Hinz, W. 2003. *Measures and Weights in the Islamic World*. Translated by M. I. Marcinkowski, with Foreword by C. E. Bosworth (Kuala Lumpur: National Islamic University).

Ker Porter, R. 1821–1822. *Travels in Persia* (London: Longman, Hurst, Rees, Orme and Brown).

Krumsiek, K. 1976. "Zur Bewegung der Iranisch-Afghanischen Platte (Paläomagnetische Ergebnisse)," *Geologische Rundschau*, 65, 909–929.

Madelung, W. 1975. "Minor Dynasties of Northern Iran," in R. Frye (ed.), *The Cambridge History of Iran*, vol. 4 (Cambridge: Cambridge University Press), 198–249.

Melikian-Chirvani, A. S. 1989. "Buddhism, in Islamic Time," *Encyclopaedia Iranica*, 4/5, 496–499.

Miles, G. 1938. *The Numismatic History of Rayy* (New York: American Numismatic Society).

Nasrallah, N. 2010. *Annals of the Caliphs' Kitchens. Ibn Sayyar al-Warraq's Tenth-Century Baghdadi Cookbook* (Leiden-Boston: Routledge).

Pabot, H. 1967. *Pasture Development and Range Improvement Through Botanical and Ecological Studies. Report to the Government of Iran* (FAO 2311) (Rome: FAO).

Rante, R. 2011. "Some Zoomorphic Iranian Tombs," in Y. Shindo (ed.), *Introduction to Islamic Archaeology and Art, Egypt/Iran/Southeast Asia* (Tokyo: Waseda University), 11–18.

Schmidt, E. F. 1935. "The Persian Expedition, 1934," *Bulletin of the Museum of Fine Arts of Boston*, 33, 55–59.

Schmidt, E. F. 1936. "The Excavation on the Citadel Hill," *The University Museum of Pennsylvania Bulletin* (Philadelphia), 1–2, 79–87, 133–135.

Schmidt, E. F. 1937. *Excavations at Tepe Hissar, Damghan: With an Additional Chapter on the Sasanian Building at Tepe Hissar* (Philadelphia: University of Pennsylvania Press).

Schmitt, R. 1993. "Cooking. In Ancient Iran," in *Encyclopaedia Iranica* 6/3, 246–252.

Spuler, B. 1952. *Iran in früh-islamischer Zeit* (Wiesbaden: Steiner).

Stein, A. 1928. *Innermost Asia: Detailed Report of Explorations in Central Asia, Kansu and Eastern Iran* (Oxford: Clarendon Press).

Szuppe, M. 2004. "Herāt," *Encyclopaedia Iranica*, 12/2, 206–211.

Tor, D. G. 2010. "Sanjar, Ahmad b. Malekshāh," in *Encyclopaedia Iranica*, online edition, accessed October 16, 2018, at http://www.iranicaonline.org/articles/sanjar.

van den Berghe, L. 1979. *Bibliographie analytique de l'archéologie de l'Iran ancien* (Leiden: Brill).

Yarshater, E. 2004a. "Iranian History: Iran in the Islamic Period," *Encyclopaedia Iranica* 13/3, 225–227.

Yarshater, E. 2004b. "Iranian History: The Safavids," *Encyclopaedia Iranica* 13/3, 234–238.

CHAPTER 2.6

···

MEDIEVAL TURKEY

···

SCOTT REDFORD

INTRODUCTION

THE recently published book entitled *The Archaeology of Byzantine Anatolia from the End of Late Antiquity until the Coming of the Turks* (Niewöhner 2017) contains essays on selected excavations at Byzantine sites or Classical sites with Byzantine remains and topical essays. This book raises three key issues for the Islamic archaeologist who studies medieval Turkey: issues concerning history, geography, and the nation state. The first issue, the relationship between archaeology and history, is replete with tensions. All historical archaeologists have to grapple with the traditional use of archaeology as a handmaiden of history. The archaeology of medieval Turkey should go beyond illustrating popular narratives of cultural history pulled from the textual record, such as accounts of the violence and chaos that followed the collapse of Byzantine rule, a historical event that constitutes the chronological end point of the book. The second issue relates to geographical and cultural hegemony. Geographically, the book limits its coverage to the Anatolian plateau and Turkey's western coast, the heartland of Byzantine power in the eastern half of the Empire. While the Byzantines ruled much further to the east, northeast, and southeast than the Anatolian plateau, the geographic, ethnic, linguistic, and religious map there was different, and the rule of shorter duration. What do the marginal areas, encompassing a good one-third of today's Turkey, tell us about this period? Are the stories they tell different from the "central" lands? The third issue concerns nation and ethnicity in the modern sense. Ending with "the coming of the Turks," this book, no doubt unwittingly, accepts a modern Turkish version of the history of the territories of today's Republic of Turkey. In nationalist Turkish historical narratives, the Byzantines preceded the Seljuks, and then came the Ottomans, with the latter and the last of these dynasties ethnically Turkish. While no doubt many ethnic Turks speaking Turkic languages were involved in the conquest, rule, and settlement of Anatolia in the

11th century and the setting up of states there from the 12th century onward, when medieval Islamic sources use the work "Turk" it is in relation to Türkmen nomads. Moreover, Arabic and Persian served as the written languages of the Islamic states established here. In a medieval context, what do ethnonyms like "Turk" and "Turkish" mean? The use of the phrase "the coming of the Turks" jibes with ethno-nationalist scenarios of a complex and ill-understood set of cultural, economic, ethnic, and religious transformations in the 11–14th centuries that characterize the history of the lands that comprise today's Republic of Turkey.

This complex issue—the demographic, economic, social, linguistic, and religious transformation of the lands of today's Turkey, following the collapse and only partial recrudescence of Byzantine rule and the establishment of Turco-Islamic states in lands formerly governed by the Byzantines—is the major one confronting all those who study this period, archaeologists or not. Most relevant to the not-so-neat switch from Byzantine, Greek, and Christian to Seljuk, Turkish, and Muslim are the *processes* of demographic, linguistic, religious, economic, and other transformations that took place beginning in the 11th century. These processes can be best studied archaeologically, only partially due to the nature and small number of written sources. Archaeology, with its rootedness in place, can provide insights into these ill-understood processes of transformation. Did local conditions (geographic, economic) affect the adaptation of Muslims to areas that had historically been non-Muslim? If so, it is the archaeologist's task to offer detailed case studies that, together with other kinds of written evidence, some of it archaeologically derived (coins, inscriptions, and graffiti), can be used to record and analyze change over time.

As important as it was, the rise and spread of Turco-Islamic rule in the lands of today's Turkey is not the only issue worthy of investigation at this time and in this place. The coastal lands bordering the Mediterranean, Aegean, and Black Seas were bound up in pan-Mediterranean transformations relating to the rise of the Italian merchant republics and the exponential growth of maritime commerce in the age of the Crusades. Southeastern Turkey is historically part of northern Mesopotamia (the Jazira in Arabic) and northern Syria, a region where the impact of the Crusades, the rise of the Kingdom of Armenian Cilicia, and differences in geography, economy, religion, and ethnicity made for different regional dynamics. And northeastern Turkey is geographically part of the South Caucasus, where, in the medieval period, the major Christian power until the early 13th century was the Kingdom of Georgia. In addition, a Byzantine successor state, the Empire of Trebizond, ruled the eastern Black Sea littoral. How do regional dynamics like these impact the local histories that archaeology can tell?

The habit of identifying the territories of today's Republic of Turkey (at least the 97% of them that are in Asia) with a geographical entity known as "Anatolia" (or "Anadolu" in Turkish) has, unfortunately, become widespread in both popular and scholarly literature. Be that as it may, for the purposes of this chapter, the region of "Anatolia" is confined to the Aegean coastal regions and the central plateau, as did Niewöhner in his book. In addition to this challenge of geographical nomenclature, there is a chronological one. In the calling of the period of the 11–14th centuries "medieval," this chapter will be using a term with some negative connotations. Given that this area was only recently conquered and settled by Muslims and that it shared much material culture with neighboring Christian states like the Kingdom of Armenian Cilicia, the Kingdom of Georgia, the Empire of Trebizond, the County of Antioch, and the Byzantine Empire itself, it does not make sense to call it "Middle Islamic." Historically this period has also been called "pre-Ottoman" (Cahen 1968) or even, perhaps tongue-in-cheek, "Ottoman prehistory" (Lindner 2005). The adjective "medieval" has the advantage of not being teleological in respect to another "coming": the rise and spread of the Ottoman state. The Turkish language equivalent of the word medieval, *ortaçağ*, has taken root in Turkish-language scholarship in the past two decades, partially, no doubt, as a way to avoid or bridge ethnic, religious, or dynastic labels.

The period covered by this essay starts with the collapse of rule in the eastern half of the Byzantine rule, the establishment of Turco-Islamic states in former Byzantine territories (the Seljuks, Danishmendids, Artuqids, Mengucukids, Saltukids, and others), Mongol hegemony beginning in the mid-13th century, and, after the decline of both the Seljuk and Byzantine states, the establishment of other Turco-Islamic polities here, but also in western Anatolia, which was conquered from the Byzantines beginning in the late 13th and early 14th centuries. The Ottomans were one of these polities. The Ayyubids, based in Syria and Egypt, ruled much of what is now southeastern Turkey in the first half of the 13th century.

HISTORIOGRAPHY

Archaeology in Turkey in the Late Ottoman Period

In the 19th century, part of becoming modern meant possessing an encyclopedic museum encompassing works representing the various civilizations. The Ottoman Empire, unlike its western European contemporaries, was an empire without colonies. Ottomans charged with setting up an Ottoman Imperial Museum concentrated on collecting and excavating with the purpose of display throughout their empire. Objects for display were obtained by means of excavations undertaken by the Museum itself; by means of letters to provincial governors, asking them to send historical objects to the capital; by confiscation from smugglers; and by means of the *partage* system, in which the Imperial Museums received the majority of finds from European excavations at sites within its domains. *Partage* laws were in force for only part of this period.

The collections were extensive and eclectic, and while they did include Islamic artifacts, the main aims of collecting and excavating for the Ottoman Imperial Museum mirrored the concerns of European and American museums at the time: the treasures of the ancient Near East and the Greco-Roman world. As for Islamic sites, efforts included an expedition to Raqqa, in today's Syria, in the first decade of the 20th century, to recover fine glazed medieval Islamic ceramics that had been finding their way from Raqqa to the art market in Western Europe as the result of looting (Yoltar-Yıldırım 2013). Other Islamic artifacts to enter the Museum's possession by way of archaeological excavation came from German excavations at the Abbasid palace city of Samarra in Iraq in 1911–1913, an excavation largely conducted under the supervision of Ernst Herzfeld (Çakır Phillip 2011).

Islamic Archaeology in the Turkish Republic

In the early decades of the Turkish Republic (founded 1923), a new state ideology moved away from late Ottoman imperial ideals of plurality toward a desire to connect the new nation state, called Türkiye, to the lands it now governed and to the Turks as a people. The Turkish Republic developed an interest in the relationship of this nation state to the past of the land it ruled. The most dramatic example of the shift to Anatolia was the moving of the capital from Istanbul to Ankara, closer to its geographical center. It was at this time that the word "Anadolu" or "Anatolia" became identified with the borders of the Turkish Republic. Despite a new secular, Westernizing ideology, Islamic objects, cities, and buildings were not neglected. However, they were considered Turkish first and foremost. In Istanbul in the late 19th and early 20th centuries, display-worthy objects removed from historic Islamic buildings were transported to part of the Süleymaniye complex in the city, which was renamed the Museum of Turkish and Islamic Art in 1926 (Eldem 2016). Keeping its name, it moved to its current location in 1983. In the newly established capital of Ankara, the Ethnography Museum, founded in 1930, displays Islamic art, some of it taken from Islamic institutions closed by the new state.

Archaeology gained importance partially through the interest in it on the part of Mustafa Kemal Atatürk, founder of the Turkish Republic, who aimed to link the Turkish people, language, and culture to the past of the territories of the new nation state in complex and often paradoxical ways (Redford and Ergin 2010). During this period, what we would today call Islamic archaeology developed in an atmosphere where the ethnic (Turkish) and the religious (Sunni Islamic) were largely conflated and intersected with a secular state ideology (Redford 2007).

Oktay Aslanapa was a key figure at the beginning of Islamic archaeology in Turkey. Aslanapa, one of the small numbers of Turks sent by their government to study in Germany and Austria before and during World War II, returned to Turkey in 1943. Aslanapa's whole career was spent at Istanbul University, where he held the chair of Turkish and Islamic Art. After being appointed Professor in 1960, he began excavating at various sites around Turkey (Altun 1996: 16–22, for a list of his publications).

While Islamic-period levels had of course been excavated at other sites, Aslanapa's short campaigns at places like Diyarbakır citadel, where he uncovered part of an Artuqid palace (Aslanapa 1962); Kayseri, where he investigated the Seljuk suburban palace of Keykubadiye (Aslanapa 1964); and elsewhere, constituted the first Turkish-led investigations of "Turkish" archaeological sites. However, in the domain of archaeology, Aslanapa's name is primarily linked with the excavation of Ottoman kilns in the city of

İznik, excavations which continue today, still under the auspices of Istanbul University (Figure 2.6.1). Be this as it may, the main body of Aslanapa's scholarly output was not archaeological; rather, he published extensively on all manner of Ottoman architecture, carpets, and other art historical subjects.

Aslanapa's career highlights a disciplinary curiosity of the Turkish higher educational system. In Turkish universities, after the Classical period, archaeology ceases to be the discipline with which the study of the past is taught. The history of the Byzantine, Seljuk, and Ottoman eras is studied in history departments, and its material culture not in archaeology, but in art history departments. Consequentially, for the Byzantine and Islamic periods, teachers and students who undertake excavations at sites featuring those periods teach and study in art history departments. This structuring of Turkish higher education is likely one of the reasons that post-Classical archaeology largely concerns sites with elite architecture, especially palaces, and is interested in objects, especially ceramics and tiles, more than stratigraphy and other contextual matters dear to archaeological practice elsewhere.

Another pioneer of Turco-Islamic art history and archaeology in Turkey was the German art historian Katharina Otto-Dorn. In the 1930s, her study of the Ottoman

FIGURE 2.6.1 İznik, Turkey, Aerial Photograph of the Site of the İznik Tile Kiln Excavations in 2016. Courtesy of Excavation Director Assistant Professor Belgin Demirsar Arlı. Turkish Ministry of Culture and Tourism Iznik Tile Kiln Excavations. Used with permission.

buildings at İznik led her to discover extensive scatters of Ottoman ceramics there, leading both to a lifelong interest in Islamic tiles and ceramics in Turkey but also indirectly to Aslanapa's İznik kiln excavations in the 1960s (Otto-Dorn 1941). Otto-Dorn became the first professor of Turkish and Islamic art at Ankara University, where she taught from 1954 to 1967. From the point of view of Islamic archaeology, her most signal contribution was the excavation, along with museum director Mehmet Önder, of the 13th-century Seljuk palace of Kubadabad in 1965 and 1966 (Otto-Dorn and Önder 1966, 1969). It was Turkish students of Professor Otto-Dorn who carried on the tradition of Islamic-period excavations in later decades. One, Rüçhan Arık, still directs excavations at Kubadabad palace (Arık 2000). Her spouse, Oluş Arık, another Otto-Dorn student, excavated the Seljuk palace in the citadel of Alanya, as well as undertaking excavations at the Artuqid and Ayyubid city of Hasan Keyf in southeastern Turkey in the 1990s (Arık 2004). They and their students continue to develop their teacher's interests in ceramics and tiles (Arık and Arık 2008).

Otto-Dorn was a transitional figure, bridging the gap between the large German projects and excavations of the late 19th and early 20th centuries and the rise of Turkish academic archaeology following the founding of the Republic of Turkey. As we have seen, her decade of teaching in Ankara gave rise to a new generation of Turkish art historians who excavated (and in one case continues to excavate) Islamic-period sites around Turkey. Otto-Dorn's own interest in Turkey was based on time she spent as a researcher at the German Archaeological Institute branch in Istanbul in the 1930s.

In addition to Otto-Dorn's work on İznik, in the 1930s, German scholarship produced a work important for Islamic archaeology in Turkey. This was the publication of Islamic-period material from excavations at one of the large Aegean regional Classical sites where German archaeologists had established themselves: Miletos (Wulzinger 1935). This final report was one of the first of its kind, giving careful coverage to periods postdating the Classical era, an era in which most Western archaeologists had concentrated their efforts. A young Austrian historian worked on the Islamic coins from Miletos as part of this excavation project, stoking his interest in the period of the formation of the Ottoman Empire. The career of this young scholar, Paul Wittek, constitutes a good example of another interesting part of this period: disciplinary fluidity. Although Wittek did not use archaeological evidence in his later historical works on the early Ottoman Empire, he did employ epigraphic skills honed, no doubt, by reading the legends on 14th-century coins of the local Menteşeoğulları dynasty found at Miletos in order to decipher building inscriptions, thereby informing his ground-breaking studies of the early Ottoman Empire.

All of the Turkish excavations were based at universities, but with chronic underfunding, they relied on financial support, as well as legal permission, from a Department of Antiquities (with an ever-changing name) tied first to the Turkish Ministry of Education and later the Ministry of Culture, or Culture and Tourism, the budget of which was also modest. While Turkish students and scholars certainly worked on the better-funded foreign missions, stand-alone Turkish excavations often did not possess the resources to support extended study of archaeological materials, let alone specialist scientific analyses. In recent years, Turkish museums have themselves become more active than ever in archaeology, especially of a salvage nature.

Today, the directing role of the Department of Antiquities in archaeology in Turkey is emblematized by the convening of an annual meeting of all field archaeologists with active projects in Turkey, followed by a publication of preliminary reports of that season's activities issued by the Ministry of Culture and Tourism. This practice began in 1979 and continues to this day.[1]

THE RURAL LANDSCAPE

Salvage Archaeology in the Valleys of the Tigris and Euphrates Rivers

As Turkey developed economically in the 1960s, so did the need for another kind of archaeology: salvage archaeology in the face of large projects designed to promote economic growth. While both Turkish and non-Turkish excavations continued at large important urban sites, plans were being drawn up for a series of dams on the two major rivers of Turkey: the Euphrates and the Tigris and their tributaries. Both of these rivers rise and flow through the east and southeast of the country, areas underdeveloped in relation to the rest of the country.

The first of the dam projects was on the upper Euphrates (the terms "upper" and "lower" used in this chapter refer to the location of rivers within the boundaries of Turkey), where the Keban Dam was going to be built. Between 1968 and 1974, salvage excavations, coordinated by Middle East Technical University in Ankara, took place in the valleys of the Euphrates and its affluent, the Murat Suyu, in areas scheduled to be flooded by the waters of this dam. Since then, the same university has continued its role in surveying sites in the reservoir areas of other dams on the Euphrates, Tigris, and their tributaries.[2]

---

[1] With the exception of the first volume of the *Kazı Sonuçları Toplantısı* series, the publications, beginning with Volume 2, 1980, have been scanned and put online (http://www.kulturvarliklari.gov.tr/TR,44760/kazi-sonuclari-toplantilari.html, consulted August 1, 2017). References to publications of Islamic period sites mentioned in the text and footnotes in this chapter are limited to those *not* in this publication series.

In addition, another annual symposium covers excavations (many of them salvage) undertaken by Turkish museums (http://www.kulturvarliklari.gov.tr/TR,44763/muze-calismalari-ve-kurtarma-kazilari-sempozyumu-yayinl-.html). The online publication is available beginning for the year 1990 (site consulted August 1, 2017).

[2] In 1995, these efforts were centralized under a newly created Center of Research and Assessment of Historical Environment (TAÇDAM) at Middle East Technical University. See http://www.tacdam.metu.edu.tr/publications for a list of archaeological survey publications relating to the Keban and other dam sites (site accessed August 15, 2017).

The Keban rescue excavations began a new chapter in Islamic archaeology (as indeed in other periods of archaeology) in Turkey. After the Keban Dam came the Atatürk and Birecik dams on the lower Euphrates in the 1970s and 1980s, followed by dams still being constructed on the Tigris below Hasan Keyf and on the Ilısu River, a tributary of the Tigris, and others. All of these were and are preceded by surveys and rescue excavations.

As a result of these excavations and their publications, we possess large amounts of information about literally marginal, largely riparian areas of rural southeastern Turkey. One the first observable features of this rural landscape is that settlement mounds (*höyük* in Turkish) in these river valleys were often reoccupied in the medieval period, usually beginning in the 13th century, after having been uninhabited for centuries, in some cases millennia.

In the Keban Dam region, Dutch-American and British excavations at the mound sites of Korucutepe (van Loon 1975–1980), Aşvan Kale, and the hilltop fort site of Taşkun Kale provided information different from those for other Islamic-period sites, as listed earlier. The buildings were not built of stone or baked brick, but mudbrick on a stone socle, and many of them were fortified in the medieval period. Excavations at Taşkun Kale, which was occupied for a short period in the late 13th–early 14th centuries, yielded an almost complete site plan (Figure 2.6.2), one which gives us the best idea of the architectural organization of many of these fortified hill or mound-top settlements (Redford 1998: 68–76).

The Aşvan Project of the British Institute of Archaeology at Ankara is of particular interest because it was the first in Turkey to engage with environmental archaeology, with an interest in change over time at the site and an extensive program of sampling and analysis of archaeozoological and archaeobotanical material from all levels there, as well as geomorphological, ethnoarcheological, and other surveys: an ambitious project whose publication has only now been coming to completion (Mitchell 1980; McNicoll 1983; Nesbitt, Bates, Hillman, and Mitchell 2017, with all following references to the 2017 publication). At medieval Aşvan and Taşkun Kale, archaeobotanical analysis of flotation samples found evidence for the consumption of barley, wheat, grapes, hackberries (101), some lentils, and chickpeas. Barley and wheat seem to have been of equal importance (112), with deposits of both of these found in a burned state proximate to ovens (*tandır*), leading to the postulation that they were being used to make porridge (101). As was the case at Gritille (see later discussion), bitter vetch seems to have been grown to serve as fodder (116). Irrigated crops included cotton (131).

The Aşvan and Taşkun excavations make explicit a problem raised at the beginning of this chapter in relation to Byzantine archeology. At least some, perhaps all of the inhabitants of these two sites, and, as far as this author knows, *almost all* other medieval sites excavated as part of these dam salvage excavations, were Christian. And yet coinage, ceramics, and other objects show that they participated in the material culture of the medieval Islamic world to the extent that, at Aşvan, for instance, potters produced glazed ceramics following the latest "Islamic" decorative styles, including pseudo-epigraphic and figural designs (Redford 2016: 257). Rather than recoiling in the face of Turco-Islamic

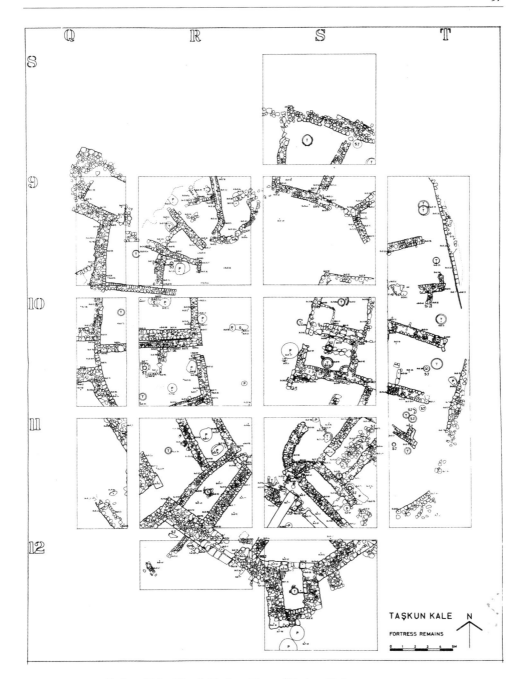

FIGURE 2.6.2 Taşkun Kale, Elazığ, Turkey. Plan of Taşkun Kale.

Anthony McNicoll, with a contribution by Roland Fletcher, *Taşkun Kale: Keban Rescue Excavations, Eastern Anatolia* (Oxford: BAR 1983) (British Institute of Archaeology at Ankara Monograph 6), Plan 1. British Institute at Ankara. Used with permission.

conquest and settlement, at least by the 13th century, rural communities such as these were thriving.

Evidence for the production of glazed ceramics at Aşvan raises another important topic: decentralization. Production of glazed earthenware vessels (mainly bowls) proliferated in the 12th–14th centuries (Allan 1974) and included rural inland sites like Aşvan. In southeastern Turkey, which was closer to the artificial paste-bodied ceramic industry in northern Syria, there was production of calcareous clay and other light-bodied ceramics that existed on a spectrum with artificial paste-bodied wares (Redford and Blackman 1997; Blackman and Redford 1994), but in general, villages, towns, and cities produced monochrome and polychrome glaze and incised glazed (sgraffito) earthenware ceramics. On the coasts of the Cilician Plain (today's Çukurova in Adana, İçel, and Hatay provinces), beginning in the 13th century, tricolor sgraffito earthenware began to be produced at rural as well as urban sites, for local consumption as well as trade by land and by sea (Blackman and Redford 2005; Redford 2004; Redford 2012a). This was a local ware that was promoted at many sites, most on the coast, linking it to the boom in maritime commerce occurring at the time. The widespread production of glazed wares, especially bowls, must have supplemented, if not partially replaced, the use of wooden vessels, which do not survive in the archaeological record but are mentioned in sources (Redford 2015: 250–251). As a result of the widespread production of glazed earthenware vessels, even small rural sites had glazed pottery. With the potential for individual portions, was there a change in eating habits and diet? And what was the intersection between glazed bowls and vessels in wood (as just mentioned), leather, and metal? As far as we can tell, even though Islamicate decoration found its way onto certain vessels, there is very little ethnic or religious component to the rise and spread of the production, distribution, and use of glazed earthenware ceramics in 13th-century Turkey: it follows similar developments elsewhere in the eastern Mediterranean and Aegean.

The widespread collection of objects made in iron from these rural sites reminds us of the mineral wealth of much of Turkey. The sheer quantity of nails may indicate that more wood was used in the construction of the mudbrick dwellings of these rural settlements than can be seen in examples of 20th-century mudbrick buildings in Turkey.

To repeat a point made earlier in this chapter, archaeology as a discipline is situated to examine all sorts of questions *not* capable of being answered by historical sources, and the impact of Islamic rule on the rural populations is one of them. To a great extent, while the recovery of small bronze crosses, some of them pectorals, and a diet that included pork give us a certain amount of evidence concerning the religion of some if not all of the inhabitants of these rural sites, we are largely ignorant of their ethnicity. Perhaps these factors deter the affixing of the label "Byzantine" to them just as much as "Islamic." Certainly, the term "Islamicate" proposed by the historian Marshall Hodgson half a century ago is apposite, although the term has not seen wide acceptance in archaeological circles. When we talk about the religion of these inhabitants, we have to wonder about the orthodoxy of their beliefs, for none of the moundtop sites excavated contained a church despite evidence of Christian belief. Only at Taşkun was a ruined church, located considerably outside the walled fort, investigated. Were there places of worship at these sites, or do the restricted means and time frame of salvage archaeology, combined with an interest in sampling multiple periods at large mounded sites, mean that extramural settlements at the base of these mounds, which may have housed churches (or mosques), are not recovered? Only in Cappadocia, with its rock-cut remains, do we have good evidence for medieval rural settlements with churches and monasteries.

As the result of the publications of excavations at Aşvan and Taşkun, the sites of Samsat (Özgüç 2009; Öney 1994; Bulut 2000), Gritille (Redford 1998), and Tille (Moore 1993) in the Karababa basin of the Atatürk dam; the site of Horum Höyük (Marro, Tibet, and Ergeç 1998; Vroom 2009) and Zeytinli Bahçe (Alvaro, Balossi, and Vroom 2004), in the Birecik dam catchment basin; and others, we have information about what life was like in these Euphrates river valley settlements in the medieval period, at exactly the time that "the Turks were coming." With the exception of Taşkun Kale, all of these sites were multiperiod settlement mounds, with the medieval remains crowning the top. At Gritille and at Tille, enlightened excavation directors permitted extensive excavation in medieval levels. At Gritille, this was combined with archaeobotanical and archaeozoological analysis. This analysis revealed the difficulty of mapping cultural change onto a chronological (and stratigraphic) horizon of only a couple of centuries. At Gritille, the data showed more continuity than change: continued reliance on pigs as a source of meat, of sheep and goat more for milk and wool, and cattle for milk and tillage more than meat. The main crops were durum wheat and, to a lesser extent barley and lentils. There was some evidence of irrigated crops: cotton and millet. The region around Gritille had been at the edges of the Franco-Armenian County of Edessa. The end of that polity in the mid-12th century brought Islamic rule to the region and greater prosperity to its Christian inhabitants.

At Tille, the entire fortified mound-top medieval settlement was excavated, giving an unparalleled picture of the origins, development, and abandonment of a Christian provincial petty ruler's household in this border region, complete with stables, fortifications, a residence, cistern, and a bathhouse (Figure 2.6.3). By contrast to the rough and ready robber baron's lair at Tille, at Samsat (Goell 1974; Redford 1995; Redford 1994), and at Tilbeşar (Rousset 2016: 225) provincial governors' palaces have been uncovered. The higher quality of ceramics and glass found there may indicate ways in which more luxurious goods traveled; Samsat itself seemed to have had its own glazed ceramic industry.

In histories of medieval Anatolia, northern Mesopotamia, northern Syria, and the southern Caucasus (the territories of the present-day Republic of Turkey), these areas are quite literally marginal to the discussions of the big historical questions of the period—the Islamification and Turkification that took place during these centuries—but are so imperfectly understood.[3] Even though much of the data was published

---

[3] Part of this marginality consists in the labeling of medieval Turkey as "Seljuk." Certainly the Seljuks were the largest of the Turco-Islamic dynasties of medieval Turkey, but perhaps as significant as their importance was their location on the Anatolian plateau, centered around their capital at Konya.

FIGURE 2.6.3 Tille, Adıyaman, Turkey. General View of British Institute at Ankara Tille Medieval Excavations, 1981, showing paved street, bathhouse, and foundations of other structures.

Courtesy of Stuart Blaylock. Used with permission.

decades ago and readily available, no archaeologist has attempted to synthesize the archaeological and historical data from southeastern Turkey, save Eger's work on the Abbasid period (Eger 2015), an era that pales in comparison to the later medieval periods in quantity of archaeological data. These sites give plenty of evidence of death, destruction, and abandonment, but the stories are largely regional and do not fit easily into master narratives of conquest, conversion, and cultural change either in Anatolia, the Jazira, or North Syria. The settlements are rural while objects, especially ceramics, point to participation in long-distance trade networks. The initial layout of many of these sites also points to the involvement of some sort of governmental organization: otherwise it is hard to explain the layout of whole sites with fortification walls, albeit simple ones made of mudbrick on a stone socle (Figure 2.6.2).

Lying as they do between the Anatolian plateau, northern Syria, and northern Mesopotamia, medieval mound-top settlements in the Euphrates and Tigris river valleys seem largely to have been abandoned in the aftermath of the Crusades when conflict between the Mamluks, who conquered the remaining Crusader states and later the Kingdom of Armenian Cilicia, and the Mongols, who defeated the Seljuks and occupied eastern Turkey, pushed the frontier zone further north and concentrated settlement around massive stone-built castles, either repaired or newly built, like that at Eski Kahta

(Dörner and Goell 1963). But the study of things Mamluk is largely confined to the Arab world, and these castles and other architectural evidence of a Mamluk presence in these regions have not received much scholarly attention, let alone excavation.

Rural Settlement in the Hatay (Antioch Region) and the Çukurova (Cilician Plain), South Central Turkey

While there are fewer rivers in the Hatay and Çukurova regions and less dam building, there is intensive agriculture as well as industrial development. In these regions of south central Turkey, there is a mixture of salvage and non-salvage archaeology, without the demands of tourism placed on coastal sites in southern and western Turkey.

Asa Eger, mentioned earlier, started his archaeological work in Turkey as part of the University of Chicago Amuq Regional Survey (1995–2005), where he served as the Islamic period specialist for this multiperiod survey of the plain around Antakya, classical Antioch (Eger 2011). Subsequently, he began work on the 9th- to 12th-century way station of Hisn al-Tinat, which he excavated as part of the Kinet Project (Eger 2010).

Excavation of the nearby site of Kinet Höyük, near the coast of the Bay of Iskenderun in northern Hatay province, was a salvage project due to encroachment of petrochemical facilities. I served as director of medieval excavations. At Kinet, the last phase of medieval habitation occurred in the late 13th–early 14th centuries, after this region had been conquered by the Mamluks. Despite the burning of the site during its conquest, it was resettled, and the production of tricolor incised earthenware vessels there continued until the site was again burned and abandoned in the early 14th century. At Kinet, then, there seems to be a correlation between the historically recorded invasions of an area and burned phases there (Redford, Ikram, Parr, and Beach 2001).

In this region, the great castles—built or rebuilt by the Armenians before or during the Kingdom of Armenian Cilicia, a great foe of the Mamluks—have been documented but, as the example of Kinet demonstrates, there is a universe of mudbrick architecture that needs to be added to any study of settlement (and fortification) in the medieval Cilician plain. Edwards's study of the stone castles built under in the 12–13th centuries by the Armenian baronies as well as the Kingdom of Armenian Cilicia posits the principle of *intervisibility* as key to understanding their location and function (Edwards 1987). Edwards also argues that these castles constituted the main settlements, without substantial urbanism. Current Italian excavations at the port city of Misis seem to indicate otherwise (D'Agata 2017: 9–11).

Like other regions east and southeast of the Anatolian plateau, this region looked in different directions. Connected by passes through the Taurus Mountains to the central plateau, it also connected through the Amanos Mountains to Antioch and northern Syria. Its Mediterranean coastline lay opposite Cyprus, a major Frankish and Italian center at this time. And alliance of the ruling powers in the Çukurova, the Armenian Kingdom of Cilicia, and the Franco-Norman Principality of Antioch with the Mongols made this area a focus of attention (albeit in different ways) to the Italian merchant republics, who traded and set up factories here in the 13th century, and the Mamluks who raided, subjected, and ultimately conquered the region in the later 14th century. Medieval period archaeology here displays evidence both of far-flung connections and conflict.

Rural Settlement on the Central Anatolian Plateau

Archaeological evidence for rural settlement is also found on the Anatolian plateau. As the central Anatolian plateau was used for herding and other animal husbandry (like raising equids) as much as if not more than agriculture before the influx of Türkmen nomads beginning in the 11th century, it is not surprising that texts tell us that this area became one of the centers for nomadic power in medieval Anatolia and later. This said, it is notable that the admittedly insufficient archaeological evidence does not document a decline in agricultural settlement due to nomadic intrusion or otherwise. Quite the opposite, the citadel mound at the Bronze Age and Iron Age site of Gordion, west of Ankara, was reoccupied for the first time since the Roman era in the 13th–early 14th centuries. In the mound-top village settlement at Gordion, metallurgy was practiced in addition to agriculture and animal husbandry. Agriculture consisted of both dry-farmed crops (wheat, barley, and lentil), grown for subsistence, and irrigated crops (rice, cotton, and millet) grown for export and likely watered by the nearby Sakarya River (Marston 2010: 401–410). This kind of new settlement of rural areas of the central Anatolian plateau in the 13th century proves not to be an isolated instance. Although we await the final publication, the Konya Plain Regional Survey documented widespread resettlement of the plain south of Konya during this period (Baird 2001). To my knowledge, only Pamela Armstrong has suggested a correspondence between the medieval ceramic record in Turkey (in this case in southwest Turkey at the site of Xanthos) and another component of the medieval landscape: the presence of nomadic Turkic populations (Armstrong 1988).

In addition to agricultural settlements, there was another kind of rural settlement in medieval Anatolia, principally on the Anatolian plateau. During a period of about a century, from the very end of the 12th century to the third quarter of the 13th, the Seljuk sultanate built dozens, perhaps hundreds, of caravanserais centering on their capital of Konya and connecting it through another central Anatolian city, Kayseri, north to the Black Sea and also west and south to the Mediterranean and the port cities of Antalya and Alanya (Erdmann 1961; Erdmann and Erdmann 1976). In addition to serving as way stations, these caravanserais served as settlement vectors for rural settlement (Redford forthcoming) as they needed people to staff the caravanserais and provide services for travelers.

Recent work with satellite imagery on part of the central trunk road running through Cappadocia has brought new information to an old question: the relationship of this new network to older ones (Turchetto 2015). Unfortunately, in recent years, the mania for restoration in Turkey has reached the countryside, and many caravanserais have been or are being rebuilt. To do so, they must be cleared of the debris of the centuries. The few publications resulting from these excavations reveal that, as might be expected, they concentrate on obtaining a plan of the original building, not digging stratigraphically and very rarely publishing finds (Bozer 2007). To my knowledge, there has been no excavation *around* a caravanserai to ascertain the kind of settlement that arose there and at what time, if at all, although a survey in the 1990s did propose that houses and water channels around the Ağzıkara Han caravanserai in Cappadocia were contemporaneous with it (Asatekin, Brackman, and Deruyter 1996). These caravanserai networks demonstrate one way in which prosperity came to the lands of today's Turkey; with its better integration into pan-Asian and pan-Mediterranean land and sea routes.

SELJUK PALACES AND SUBURBAN GARDENS

In addition to citadel palaces in the major cities of their realm, in the early to mid-13th-century Seljuk sultans and their emirs built suburban garden complexes in or just outside the irrigated zones around these same cities. The Seljuk hunting palace of Kubadabad mentioned earlier (Arık 2000) was not one of these. However, despite its isolated rural location on the shores of Lake Beyşehir west of Konya, Kubadabad bears resemblances to these garden complexes, while the larger palace there resembles a small caravanserai in layout.

The first of the Seljuk suburban garden complexes to be excavated was Keykubadiye, outside Kayseri in central Turkey (Oral 1953; Aslanapa 1964). In the 1990s, I surveyed Seljuk suburban garden complexes around Alanya and Gazipaşa on Turkey's southern coast (Redford 2000a and 2000b). This study linked these high-cultural phenomena of caravanserais and garden complexes built for the sultan and members of his court to concepts of a prosperous landscape reflecting the justice of the sultan. Whether these sultans were atypical remains to be proved, but the (admittedly spotty) archaeological data do point to an upsurge of rural settlement as well in the 13th century.

URBAN LANDSCAPES

The first century of Seljuk rule in Anatolia was plagued by instability. The prosperity that began in the late 12th century and continued until the mid-13th, and which led to more rural settlement, caravanserais, and suburban garden complexes, saw its counterpart in cities. As might be expected, like rural settlements, the cities were centers of glazed earthenware production. We have evidence for this from salvage excavations in the city of Sivas, for instance (Fındık 2011). Here, finds of heavily incised tricolor earthenware vessels, mainly bowls, help define an inland production the diameters of whose bowls are larger than those of the commercial export ceramics of the coastal regions.

Differences in diet may have made for these larger bowls, but ease of transport (stacking in baskets) may equally have affected bowl size.

One of the archaeological challenges in studying medieval Anatolia is differentiating the material culture of the Seljuks (or other Turco-Islamic dynasties ruling in the former eastern lands of the Byzantine Empire) from that of the Byzantines or other cultures present in these lands before the conquests of the 11th century or those of their neighbors. It is difficult to spot cultural change in the ceramic record. To give just one example, a kind of glazed earthenware bowl bearing sgraffito and champlevé figural imagery derived from the representation of young male court attendants at Islamic courts seems to date from *after* the collapse of Seljuk rule in the late 13th century (Redford 2012b).

While inscriptions on Seljuk buildings document an influx of craftsmen from Syria and the eastern Islamic world to medieval Turkey, especially in the 13th century, there were also architects with Greek and Armenian names like Kaluyan, Sebastos, and Kaluk working for the Seljuks at the same time. Mute, but more widespread, testimonials are found in the reuse of stone from Roman, Hellenistic, and other buildings both in rural buildings like caravanserais, but also in cities (Redford 1993). The practice of spoliation is a prominent feature of all post-Roman societies around the Mediterranean, including Byzantium. Consequently, the Turco-Islamic dynasties of medieval Turkey fell heir to Byzantine towns and cities, many of whose buildings were built with reused material, thus making them hard to date. One of the most prominent features of these towns and cities was their fortifications: city and citadel walls. In two studies of the city and citadel walls of the port towns of Antalya and Sinop, I and my colleagues Burhan Varkıvanç and James Crow have proposed that fortifications usually called Seljuk because they bear Seljuk inscriptions are actually Byzantine (Redford 2008; Redford 2014). The study of Antalya also contributed to the debunking of the well-known description of Antalya in the 14th-century travel narrative of Ibn Battuta (Ibn Battuta 1969: 124–125) that describes the city as divided into walled quarters according to religion.

In 1953, Seton Lloyd surveyed the standing monuments of the southern port city of Alanya (Lloyd and Rice 1958), attributing much of the 5 kilometers of fortification there to the Seljuk sultan who conquered it in 1221. Recent research links much of this rebuilding to the Byzantine reinvestment of the site in the 12th century (Redford 2015: 550–552). These test cases are indicative of two things—not only the importance of previous monuments, like city walls, in shaping urban space, but also the importance of comprehending the meteoric rise of the Seljuk sultanate in the period of the late 12th to mid-13th centuries. In Turkey, there is a thriving scholarly production addressing medieval urbanism, with an aim to finding and analyzing changes to the urban fabric as the result of the rise of Turco-Islamic states there. One early example of this literature available in English is by architectural historian Gönül Tankut, completed in 1970, but only published in a bilingual edition in the past decade (Tankut 2007). It is hoped that further excavations and study of standing Byzantine structures, especially but not only city and citadel walls, will lead to an integration of urban space and fabric as inherited, altered, and developed by Islamic builders and patrons into the study of urbanism in medieval Turkey.

URBAN SITES IN EASTERN AND SOUTHEASTERN TURKEY

It is not just archaeological sites—mounds—that are threatened by economic development (dams, factories, roads, and the like) in the east and southeast of Turkey. Mention was made earlier of Oluş Arık's excavations at the important medieval Islamic city of Hasan Keyf (historic Hisn Kayfa) on the Tigris River, soon to be flooded. Hasan Keyf exemplifies the complexities lying under the "master narrative" for the history of medieval Turkey discussed at the beginning of this chapter. Almost all of the considerable body of ruined and standing medieval Islamic architecture here belongs to two dynasties, the Artuqids and the Ayyubids, who are important in this region and elsewhere, but not in central Turkey. The salvage excavations of Arık, followed by those of Uluçam, have concentrated on ruined monumental architecture: especially mosques, but also commercial architecture (Figure 2.6.4). In addition to excavation and publication, the

FIGURE 2.6.4 Hasankeyf, Batman, Turkey. General view showing Şab area excavations in 2006, also showing excavated antique citadel entrance, Ottoman shops, mosque, and the citadel rock with the minaret of the Rizk mosque in the middle distance. Excavations directed by Professor Abdüsselam Uluçam, Batman University.

Courtesy of Ilse Sturkenboom. Used with permission.

"solution" to the problem of submerging under water a city that has monumental Islamic architecture (mosques, tombs, minarets, a bridge, and fortifications) has been to lift and relocate them: minarets and a tomb tower, for example, are being transported to a barren hillside overlooking the dam reservoir site where the new town of Hasan Keyf is being constructed.[4]

Other sites in the region, ones with tourism potential, are being excavated and restored at the same time and therefore experiencing the same tension between sound archaeological practice and tourism experienced more acutely in the large Classical sites of western Turkey. The medieval city of Ani, on the border between Turkey and Armenia and recently named a UNESCO world heritage site is an example of this. Ani was founded by an Armenian dynasty in the 10th century and was subsequently ruled by the Byzantines, the Great Seljuks, a local Islamic dynasty (the Shaddadids), Georgian vassals (the Zakhare), and the Mongols. As a consequence, it had a multilingual, multiethnic, and multiconfessional population. In and of itself this is nothing unusual for the medieval period in this region, as we have seen. But Ani has fortifications and other standing buildings with inscriptions both in Islamic as well as Christian languages and standing churches as well as mosques. As such, the cultural tug of war over Ani is more obvious and more strenuous than elsewhere.

The medieval city of Harran, like Ani, has tourism potential, is largely uninhabited, and has massive standing architecture, most notably a citadel and a congregational mosque. However, as it lies south of the city of Urfa near the Syrian border, its medieval history is more like that of Hasan Keyf than that of Ani in that Harran was ruled by the Ayyubids among other dynasties based in Greater Syria. In the 1950s, a British project directed by Seton Lloyd started architectural survey and excavation at the site. As part of this team, D. S. Rice, the founder of Islamic archaeology in Britain, worked mainly on the citadel and the mosque (Rice 1952) before his untimely death. In the 1980s and 1990s, Nurettin Yardımcı conducted excavations and survey at and around the site (Yardımci 2004), where excavation and restoration continue today.

Another city in southeastern Turkey, Telbeşar, is threatened by a dam on the Sacır Suyu, a tributary of the Euphrates, and it has been excavated by a French team. The medieval component of this vast site comprises a fortified Crusader and Ayyubid citadel housing a palace. The lower town has also been excavated, including city gates, streets, and houses. Survey and excavation, although partial, give us one of the best plans of a medieval settlement in Turkey (Figure 2.6.5) (Rousset 2016). Unusually, the lower town was divided into two by a wall. Archaeozoological analysis led excavators to think that this separation was likely not based on religion but perhaps class, as pork consumption was at similar levels in both quarters, while young cattle and game were consumed in the north quarter and not in the south (Berthon and Mashkour 2008: 41).

---

[4] Beginning in 2003, Abdüsselam Uluçam assumed directorship of excavations at Hasan Keyf. In addition to annual reports in *KST* (see note 2), see http://www.hasankeyfkazıları.org.tr (website consulted August 10, 2017).

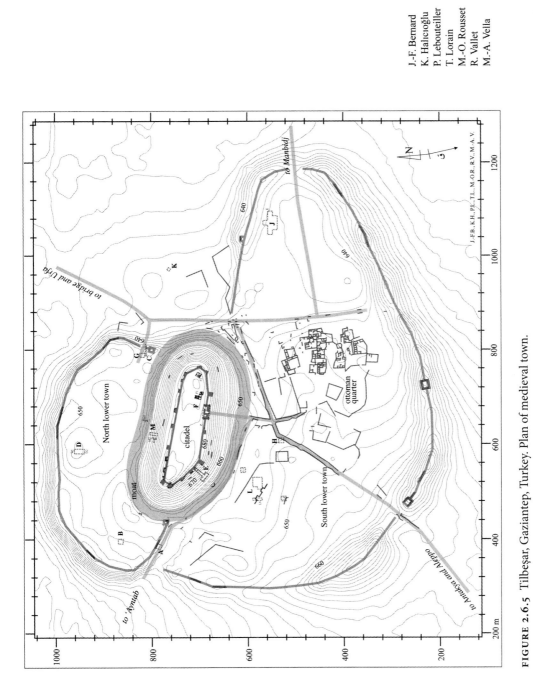

FIGURE 2.6.5 Tilbeşar, Gaziantep, Turkey. Plan of medieval town.

From Rousset, M.-O. 2016. "La forteresse médiévale de Tilbeshar (Tell Bashir, Turbessel)," in B. Perello and A. Tenu (eds.), *Parcours d'Orient. Recueil de textes offert à Christine Kepinski* (Oxford: Archaeopress), Plan 1. Used with permission.

All of these cities have great potential for urban archaeology. They are largely abandoned, and so, together with the monumental medieval architecture that stands in isolation in Anatolian cities like Kayseri, Sivas, and Konya, it has been and will be possible to study their urban development as well as a whole spectrum of urban architecture and spaces.

NAUTICAL ARCHAEOLOGY AND CONCLUSION

The bay of Serçe Limanı off the coast of southwest Turkey gave its name to an 11th-century shipwreck excavated by the Institute of Nautical Archaeology in the late 1970s. In his preface to the first monumental volume of the publication of this wreck, George Bass recounted the difficulty he had in finding scholars trained in medieval Islamic and Byzantine civilizations to help him and his students analyze the finds from this fascinating merchantman, which was likely returning to the Byzantine capital after a trip to Egypt and the Syro-Palestinian coast (Bass, xii, in Bass, Matthews, Steffy, and van Doorninck 2004). Does the Serçe Limanı wreck qualify for a place in a work on Islamic archaeology? Like many of the archaeological sites discussed in this chapter, the answer can be "yes and no," depending on how one defines Islamic archaeology. Excavators found a cargo of glass cullet from Fatimid Syria and Fatimid ceramics, metalwork, and coins. But Byzantine artifacts were also found, and the boat itself was likely Byzantine. I choose to end this essay with this shipwreck because it symbolizes one of the difficulties of disentangling the cultures that coexisted in and near states ruled by Muslims and with large Muslim populations. The Serçe Limanı wreck shows the interdependence of two eastern Mediterranean states, one Islamic, one Christian. The riverine excavations along the Tigris and Euphrates largely concern Christians living under Islamic rule, while the city of Ani displays a bewildering mixture of cultures, religions, sects, and ethnicities. However, one reason to choose the Serçe Limanı shipwreck as a means to problematize the "Islamic" part of "Islamic archaeology" is that it was a small ship on a humdrum voyage, representing a constant kind of interaction. It also lived and died *before* the "coming of the Turks" to Anatolia later the same century, thereby ridding Anatolia of the moniker of "frontier" or "border society."

The brief survey provided in this chapter does not provide any archaeological proof of violent change at the beginning of Islamic rule in Turkey. With the exception of sites in the south and southeast of Turkey, whose history was bound up with the Crusader states, Cyprus, northern Syria, and northern Mesopotamia in this period, it has little to say about the 12th century. But all regions of Turkey, and all manner of sites, rural and urban, display signs of prosperity in the 13th century, a prosperity that continues beyond the fall of the Seljuk dynasty. Indeed, it is hard to identify elements of dynastic material culture (aside from coins, of course). Differences seem to be more those related to distribution, and those based on distances from the coast and from bigger urban centers.

REFERENCES

Allan, J. 1974. "Incised Wares of Iran and Anatolia in the 11th and 12th Centuries," *Keramos*, 64, 15–22.

Altun, A. 1996. "Prof. Dr. Oktay Aslanapa ve Türk Sanatı Araştırmalarına Katkıları," in S. Mülayim, Z. Sönmez, and A. Altun (eds.), *Aslanapa Armağanı* (Ankara: Bağlam Yayıncılık), 11–22.

Alvaro, C., Balossi, F., and Vroom, J. 2004. "Zeytinli Bahçe. A Medieval Fortified Settlement," *Anatolia Antiqua*, 12, 191–213.

Arık, M. O. 2004. *Hasankeyf. Üç Dünya'nın Buluştuğu Kent* (Istanbul: İş Bankası).

Arık, R. 2000. *Kubad Abad: Selçuklu Saray ve Çinileri* (Istanbul: İş Bankası).

Arık, R., and Arık, M. O. 2008. *Tiles: Treasures of Anatolian Soil: Tiles of the Seljuk and Beylik Periods* (Istanbul: Kale Group Cultural Publications).

Armstrong, P. 1988. "Nomadic Seljuks in 'Byzantine' Lycia New Evidence," in S. Lampakis (ed.), *Η βυζαντινή Μικρά Ασία (6ος-12ος αιώνας)* (Athens: Ινστιτούτο Βυζαντινών Ερευνών), 321–338.

Asatekin, G., Brackman, P., and Deruyter, M. 1996. *Along Ancient Trade Routes: Seljuk Caravanserais and Landscapes in Central Anatolia* (Rekem-Lanaken, Belgium: Landscape Foundation).

Aslanapa, O. 1962. "Erster Bericht über die Ausgrabung des Palastes von Diyarbakır," *Istanbuler Mitteilungen*, 12, 115–128.

Aslanapa, O. 1964. "Kayseri'de Keykubadiye Köşkleri Kazısı," *Türk Arkeoloji Dergisi*, 13, 19–22.

Baird, D. 2001. "Settlement and Landscape in the Konya Plain, South Central Turkey, from the Epipalaeolithic to the Medieval Period," in H. Karpuz, A. Baş, and R. Duran (eds.), *Uluslararası Çatalhöyük'ten Günümüze Çumra Kongresi* (Çumra: Çumra Belediyesi), 269–276.

Baram, U., and Carroll, L. (eds.) 2000. *A Historical Archaeology of the Ottoman Empire. Breaking New Ground* (New York: Kluwer Academic/Plenum Publishers).

Bass, G., Matthews, S., Steffy, J. R., and van Doorninck. F. 2004. *Serçe Limanı. An Eleventh-Century Shipwreck. Volume I. The Ship and Its Anchorage, Crew, and Passengers* (College Station: Texas A&M University Press).

Berthon, R., and Mashkour, M. 2008. "Animal Remains from Tilbeşar Excavations, Southeast Anatolia, Turkey," *Anatolia Antiqua*, 16, 23–51.

Blackman, M. J., and Redford, S. 1994. "Glazed Calcareous Clay Ceramics from Gritille, Turkey," *Muqarnas*, 11, 31–34.

Blackman, M. J., and Redford, S. 2005. "Neutron Activation Analysis of Medieval Ceramics from Kinet, Turkey, Especially Port Saint Symeon Ware," *Ancient Near Eastern Studies*, 42, 83–180.

Bozer, R. 2007. "Eğirdir Han," in H. Acun (ed.), *Anadolu Selçuklu Dönemi Kervansarayları* (Ankara: T. C. Kültür ve Turizm Bakanlığı Yayınları), 237–253.

Bulut, L. 2000. *Samsat Ortaçağ Seramikleri (Sıraltı ve Lüsterler)* (İzmir: Ege Üniversitesi Edebiyat Fakültesi Yayınları).

Cahen, C. 1968. *Pre-Ottoman Turkey. A General Survey of the Material and Spiritual Culture and History c. 1071-1330* (London: Sidgwick and Jackson).

Çakır Phillip, F. 2011. "Ernst Herzfeld and the Excavations at Samarra," in Z. Bahrani, Z. Çelik, and E. Eldem (eds.), *Scramble for the Past. A Story of Archaeology in the Ottoman Empire, 1753-1914* (Istanbul: SALT), 383–397.

D'Agata, A. L. 2017. "Economia e istituzioni a Misis in Cilicia piana dall'età dell Ferro ai Mamelucchi: nodi teorici ed evidenza archeologica," *Arkeoloji ve Sanat*, 154, 1–11.

Dörner, F., and Goell, T. 1963. *Arsameia am Nymphaios* (Berlin: Gebr. Mann).

Edwards, R. 1987. *Armenian Fortifications of Cilicia* (Washington, DC: Dumbarton Oaks.

Eldem, E. 2016. "The Genesis of the Museum of Turkish and Islamic Arts," in M. Farhad and S. Rettig, *The Art of the Qur'an: Treasures from the Museum of Turkish and Islamic Arts* (Washington, DC: Arthur M. Sackler Gallery), 119–139.

Eger, A. A. 2010. "Hisn al-Tinat on the Islamic-Byzantine Frontier: Synthesis and the 2005–2008 Survey and Excavation on the Cilician Plain (Turkey)," *BASOR*, 357, 49–76.

Eger, A. A. 2011 "The Swamps of Home: Marsh Formation and Settlement in the Early Medieval Near East," *JNES*, 70, 55–79.

Eger, A. A. 2015. *The Islamic-Byzantine Frontier* (London: I. B. Tauris).

Erdmann, K. 1961. *Das anatolische Karavansaray des 13. Jahrhunderts, Vol. 1* (Berlin: Gebr. Mann).

Erdmann, K., and Erdmann, H. 1976. *Das anatolische Karavansaray des 13. Jahrhunderts, Vol. 2.* (Berlin: Gebr. Mann).

Fındık, N. Ö. 2011. "Ortaçağ Sivas'ında Sırlı Seramik," *Anadolu ve Çevresinde Ortaçağ*, 5, 185–220.

Goell, G. 1974. "Samosata Archeological Excavations, Turkey, 1967," in P. Oehser (ed.), *National Geographic Society Research Reports 1967* (Washington, DC: National Geographic Society), 83–109.

Ibn Battuta 1969. *Rihla*, H.A.R. Gibb, trans., *Ibn Battuta Travels in Asia and Africa 1325–1354* (New York: Augustus M. Kelley) [London, 1929].

Lindner, R. 2005. *Explorations in Ottoman Prehistory* (Ann Arbor: University of Michigan Press).

Lloyd, S., and Storm Rice, D. 1958. *Alanya ('Ala'iyya)* (London: British Institute of Archaeology).

Marro, C., Tibet, A., and Ergeç, R. 1998. "Fouilles de sauvetage de Horum Höyük (province de Gaziantep): deuxième rapport préliminaire," *Anatolia Antiqua*, 6, 349–378.

Marston, J. 2010. *Evaluating Risk, Sustainability, and Decision Making in Agricultural and Land-Use Strategies at Ancient Gordion* (Unpublished PhD diss., University of California, Los Angeles).

McNicoll, A. 1983. *Taşkun Kale. Keban Rescue Excavations Eastern Turkey* (Oxford: British Archaeological Reports).

Mitchell, S. 1980. *Aşvan Kale. Keban Rescue Excavations, Eastern Anatolia.* (Oxford: British Archaeological Reports).

Moore, J. 1993. *Tille Höyük 1. The Medieval Period* (Ankara: BIAA).

Nesbitt, M., Bates, J., Hillman, G., and Mitchell, S. 2017. *The Archaeobotany of Aşvan: Environment & Cultivation in Eastern Anatolia from the Chalcolithic to the Medieval Period* (London: BIAA).

Niewöhner, P. (ed.) 2017. *The Archaeology of Byzantine Anatolia From the End of Late Antiquity until the Coming of the Turks* (Oxford: Oxford University Press).

Öney, G. 1994. "Pottery from the Samosata Excavations (1978–81)," in R. Hillenbrand (ed.), *The Art of the Saljuqs in Iran and Anatolia* (Costa Mesa, CA: Mazda Publishers), 286–294.

Oral, M. Z. 1953. "Kayseri'de Kubadiye Sarayları," *Belleten*, 17, 501–517.

Otto-Dorn, K. 1941. *Das islamische İznik* (Berlin: DAI).

Otto-Dorn, K., and Önder, M. 1966. "Bericht über die Grabung in Kobadabad 1965," *Archäologischer Anzeiger*, 2, 170–183.

Otto-Dorn, K., and Önder, M. 1969. "Bericht über die Grabung in Kobadabad 1966," *Archäologischer Anzeiger*, 4, 438–506.

Özgüç, N. 2009. *Samsat, Sümeysat, Samosata, Kumaha, Hahha, Hahhum* (Ankara: Türk Tarih Kurumu), 5–28.

Redford, S. 1993. "The Seljuks of Rum and the Antique" *Muqarnas*, 10, 148–156.

Redford, S. 1994. "Ayyubid Glass from Samsat, Turkey," *Journal of Glass Studies*, 36, 81–91.

Redford, S. 1995. "Medieval Ceramics from Samsat, Turkey," *Archéologie Islamique*, 5, 55–70.

Redford, S. 1998. *The Archaeology of the Frontier in the Medieval Near East: Excavations at Gritille, Turkey* (Philadelphia: University Museum).

Redford, S. 2000a. *Landscape and the State in Medieval Anatolia: Seljuk Gardens and Pavilions of Alanya, Turkey* (Oxford: Archaeopress).

Redford, S. 2000b. "Just Landscape in Medieval Anatolia," *Studies in the History of Gardens and Designed Landscapes*, 20, 313–324.

Redford, S. 2004. "On *Saqis* and Ceramics: Systems of Representation in the Northeast Mediterranean," in D. Weiss and L. Mahoney (eds.), *France and the Holy Land: Frankish Culture at the End of the Crusades* (Baltimore: Johns Hopkins University Press), 282–312.

Redford, S. 2007. "'What Have You Done for Anatolia Today?' Islamic Archaeology in the Early Years of the Turkish Republic," *Muqarnas*, 24, 243–252.

Redford, S. 2012a. "Trade and Economy in Antioch and Cilicia in the 12th–13th Centuries," in C. Morrisson (ed.), *Trade and Markets in Byzantium* (Washington, DC: Dumbarton Oaks), 295–307.

Redford, S. 2012b. "Portable Palaces: On the Circulation of Objects and Ideas about Architecture in Medieval Anatolia and Northern Mesopotamia," *Medieval Encounters*, 18, 382–412.

Redford, S. 2014. *Legends of Authority: The 1215 Seljuk Inscriptions of Sinop Citadel, Turkey* (İstanbul: Koç University Press).

Redford, S. 2015. "Medieval Arsenals in Anatolia: Sinop and Alanya," in S. Ladstätter, F. Pirson, and T. Schmidts (eds.), *Harbors and Harbor Cities in the Eastern Mediterranean from Antiquity to Byzantium. Recent Discoveries and New Approaches (Byzas 19)* (Istanbul: Ege Yayınları), 543–552.

Redford, S. 2016. "Ceramics and Society in Medieval Anatolia" in J. Vroom (ed.), *Medieval and Post-Medieval Ceramics in the Eastern Mediterranean* (Turnhout, Belgium: Brepols), 249–260.

Redford, S. forthcoming. "Caravanserais, Roads, and Routes in Seljuk Anatolia," in L. Vandeput, D. Baird, K. Görkay, J. Haldon, M. Massa, and S. Mitchell (eds.), *Pathways of Communication: Routes and Roads in Anatolia from Prehistory to the Seljuk Period* (Cambridge: Cambridge University Press).

Redford, S., and Blackman, M. J. 1997. "Luster and Fritware Production and Distribution in Medieval Syria," *Journal of Field Archeology*, 24, 233–247.

Redford, S., and Ergin, N. (eds.) 2010. *Perceptions of the Past in the Turkish Republic: Classical and Byzantine Periods* (Leuven: Peeters).

Redford, S., Ikram, S., Parr, E., and Beach, T. 2001. "Excavations at Medieval Kinet, Turkey: A Preliminary Report," *Journal of Ancient Near Eastern Studies*, 38, 59–139.

Redford, S., and Leiser, G. 2008. *Victory Inscribed: The Seljuk Fetihname on the Citadel Walls of Antalya, Turkey* (Istanbul: AKMED).

Rice, D. S. 1952. "Medieval Ḥarrān: Studies on Its Topography and Monuments I," *Anatolian Studies*, 2, 36–84.

Rousset, M.-O. 2016. "La forteresse médiévale de Tilbeshar (Tell Bashir, Turbessel)," in B. Perello and A. Tenu (eds.), *Parcours d'Orient. Recueil de textes offert à Christine Kepinski* (Oxford: Archaeopress), 219–228.

Tankut, G. 2007. *The Seljuk City/Selçuklu Kenti* (Ankara: Middle East Technical University).

Turchetto, J. 2015. "Cappadocia from Above. L'utilizzo di immagini satellitari Corona e di Google Earth per l'individuazione di antichi tracciati stradali," in R. Brancato, G. Busacca, and M. Massimino (eds.), *Archeologi in Progress: Il cantiere dell'archeologia di domani. Atti del Covegno Catania, 23–26 maggio 2013* (Bologna: BraDypUS Editore), 399–407.

van Loon, M. (ed.) 1975–1980. *Korucutepe. Final Report on the Excavations of the Universities of Chicago, California (Los Angeles) and Amsterdam in the Keban Reservoir, Eastern Anatolia 1968–1970* 3 vols. (Amsterdam: North Holland Publishing Company).

Vorderstrasse, T., and Roodenberg, J. (eds.) 2009. *Archaeology of the Countryside in Medieval Anatolia* (Leiden: NINO).

Vroom, J. 2009. "Medieval Ceramics and the Archaeology of Consumption in Eastern Anatolia," in T. Vorderstrasse and J. Roodenberg (eds.), *Archaeology of the Countryside in Medieval Anatolia* (Leiden: NINO), 235–258.

Wulzinger, K. (ed.) 1935. *Das islamische Milet* (Berlin: de Gruyter).

Yardımcı, N. 2004. *Harran Ovası Yüzey Araştırması* 2 vols. (Istanbul: Arkeoloji ve Sanat Yayınları).

Yoltar-Yıldırım, A. 2013. "Raqqa: The Forgotten Excavation of an Islamic Site in Syria by the Ottoman Imperial Museum in the Early Twentieth Century," *Muqarnas*, 30, 73–93.

CHAPTER 2.7

OTTOMAN ANATOLIA

FILIZ YENIŞEHIRLIOĞLU*

WHY AN ARCHAEOLOGY OF OTTOMAN ANATOLIA?

THE Ottoman Empire between 1299 and 1923 covered an extensive territory around the Mediterranean and included the Balkans, Middle East, North Africa, and Anatolia. Today, almost forty nation states cover the area that was once the Ottoman Empire at different periods of history (Yenişehirlioğlu 1989). This geographical and political history has challenged the development of an Ottoman archaeology for many reasons, not the least of which are the diversity of local languages and the character of a historical memory that has not prioritized research on this period (Yenişehirlioğlu 1999). Ottoman archaeology as its own field is a relatively new area of research among scholars of both post-Ottoman nation states and that of Europe and the United States. Even though there have been occasional excavations of the Ottoman period in most of the countries of the Middle East and the Balkans—mainly salvage projects conducted in support of urban development—it has been quite difficult to follow the results of this fieldwork.[1] The published results of these and scientific excavations appear in a dizzying range of languages and in venues of limited distribution. The first international publication covering an overall approach on the subject was *A Historical Archaeology of the Ottoman Empire* (Baram and Caroll 2000). The chapters in that book mainly focus on how Ottoman archaeology can offer new insights and information on the economic and social history of different regions and provinces of the Ottoman Empire. It is a pioneering work, bringing together both theoretical and

* https://orcid.org/0000-0002-5924-8735

[1] This does not exclude the fact that there is also specific archaeological research on the Ottoman period. Publications on archaeological excavations or publications on historical archaeology that merge the results of historical research with historical archaeology also exist. See the Further Reading list at the end of this chapter for selective works since it is not the aim of this chapter to compare the Ottoman archaeology in Anatolia with research and findings from other regions of the Ottoman historical geography.

methodological approaches on how to evaluate the Ottoman-period archaeologically beyond basic archaeological field reports.

The historiography of Ottoman archaeology in Anatolia, while it shares many characteristics with other provinces of the empire, differs from them in significant ways. During the late Ottoman Period (mid-19th century), archaeology as a scientific discipline was well established at the capital, Istanbul, by Osman Hamdi Bey (1842–1910). An archaeologist and painter, he and his colleagues mainly excavated classical and Islamic sites in the Middle East, such Tyre and Sidon in Lebanon, and Raqqa in Syria. The first Royal Archaeological Museum of the Empire (Müze-i Hümayun), established in Istanbul in 1869, was constructed with the purpose of housing these findings as well as objects brought from other various sites in Anatolia (Cezar 1971). Relevant conservation and preservation regulations for the protection of cultural heritage were also implemented during this period in 1874. It was later revised by Osman Hamdi Bey in 1883 (Çal 2005). Archaeological research in Anatolia as a province of the Ottoman Empire was carried out by European archaeologists and covered mainly the Greek and Roman sites (Bahrani et al. 2011). The Palace ordered that examples of material culture from the Middle Ages be sent to the Palace. These objects consequently formed the core of the later Turkish and Islamic Museum in Istanbul (Yenişehirlioğlu 2011). However, neither the archaeology of the Middle Ages nor that of the pre-Modern and Modern periods were considered to be ancient or valuable enough to be excavated. This was also true for archaeology in general at the end of the 19th and the beginning of the 20th centuries, and Ottoman archaeology followed then the trends of world archaeology (Özdoğan 2008).

After the dissolution of the Ottoman Empire following World War I, the Republic of Turkey was founded in 1923 in Anatolia and Eastern Thrace. The strong bureaucratic structure of the previous administrative system was transferred to the new state, and excavations, museums, and cultural heritage protection were placed under the authority of the new Ministry of Education. The archaeology of Anatolia became an important cultural and ideological issue, both to prove the presence of Turks in Anatolia since antiquity and also to integrate the presence of the new state into the existing cultural norms of global cultural history. Archaeological excavations of classical sites that had started during the Ottoman period continued, and new excavation fields were opened (Arık 1950), followed by the rapid formation of new archaeological museums through the 1950s (Katoğlu 2009).

During this frenetic activity of the Early Republican period, archaeological research focused on the ancient and classical periods. The lack of studies on the archaeology of the Ottoman period is the result of two factors. First, the Ottoman period was still relatively recent, and the lifestyles and customs of everyday life were often still persistent. A traditional Ottoman house was not an example of cultural heritage but was just a "home." Traditional arts and crafts continued to be produced and disseminated, and the artisans were just people in the neighborhood. The wedding chest of every young girl was full with her grandmothers' and mothers' embroideries as well as copper utensils for the kitchen. Therefore, what was there to be researched when so much of Ottoman material culture and its physical environment continued to form the social and cultural units of everyday life?

Second, the ideology of every newly founded state is to reject its past. This was relevant in different ways in every post-Ottoman nation state, and Turkey was no exception (Yenişehirlioğlu 1999). The foundation of the Turkish Republic was the result of the modernization of the Ottoman Empire, and, as such, modernity had to refuse the past in order to establish its own social and cultural norms. This ideological rejection was supported by the idea of finding cultural and historical roots with a Turkic past as a nation-state, rather than focusing on the multiethnic, multireligious, and multilinguistic heritage of Ottoman rule. Therefore it was not until the 1950s that research on the Ottoman period in Anatolia began in earnest, a full decade after fieldwork began on Seljuk-period sites (Yenişehirlioğlu 2000a). The first excavations of a Seljuk site were launched in the 1940s under the supervision of the Turkish Historical Society founded in 1931 (see Chapter 2.6). The Seljuks, a Turkish tribe originating from Central Asia, formed the link between the Central Asian Turkic world and Anatolia. This ideology based on "turkishness" created a static historiography that identifies the Ottomans as the continuation of the Seljuks. Following this Aristotelian logic makes the Seljuks Ottoman and their social and cultural institutions similar and identical (Gündüz Küskü 2014). Archaeological interest in the Ottoman period, for its own sake, was slow to develop and under very different impulses.

THE ART HISTORICAL FOUNDATIONS OF OTTOMAN ARCHAEOLOGY

Supported by the ideological waves of the Early Republican period and following the archaeological traditions of the late Ottoman Period, the first generation of archaeologists in Turkey came from well-educated and cultured family backgrounds and attended European universities in the early days of the Republic. Their approach to archaeology was multitextual, and they were well integrated into the intellectual life of European archaeological *milieus*. However, they were not specialized in Ottoman archaeology and were interested mainly in the ancient, pre-classical, and classical periods of the Near East. This initial interest in archaeology and excavations started the formation of archaeology departments (Archaeological Institute of Istanbul University in 1934) with their curriculum based on Near-Eastern and Classical archaeology in newly founded Turkish universities.

The excavations led by these scholars, as well as those by European scientists, discarded the archaeological layers of the Middle Ages and Modern periods. Their students were thus educated with the understanding that archaeology was concerned with only the periods up until the late Roman period or roughly 5th century CE (the term "Byzantine" was not used). Even today many excavations label finds later than the Roman period as "Byzantine" or "Islamic" without any specific dating. The term "Islamic" often refers to either Seljuk or Ottoman, while the detailed identification of Umayyad, Abbasid, Arab–Islamic Dynasties, and Turkish Beylicat period occupation in Anatolia is lacking.

The emergence of Ottoman archaeology in today's Turkey owes more to the subsequent establishment of art history departments in local universities. Unlike archaeology, art history did not exist as a discipline during the Ottoman period. The founders of this discipline in Turkish universities were mainly German and Austrian art historians (fleeing the Nazi regime), whom Mustafa Kemal Atatürk, the founder of the Turkish Republic, invited to work in Turkey. Katharina Otto-Dorn from Ankara University was the first to start the Seljuk period excavations that continue in the palace of Kubadabad near Beysehir in central Anatolia (Aslanapa 1993). Art historians, rather than archaeologists, volunteered to excavate the Middle and Modern periods of Anatolia. Another art historian, Professor Oktay Aslanapa, from Istanbul University, started the first considerable excavation of the Ottoman period in İznik. Thus the artificial division of time imposed by archaeologists led to the superficial division of which periods were excavated. Ironically, the archaeologists began to criticize the excavations undertaken by art historians as lacking proper archaeological methods and claimed that the art historians were simply just "digging." Some methodological mistakes could have happened at the beginning, but at least the findings were well documented and preserved in museums rather than being discarded and thrown away, as was the practice of the archaeologists. Archaeologists continue to disregard the importance of Ottoman archaeology in their curriculums. On the other hand, these practices culminated in the newly established chair of Turkish-Islamic archaeology within the department of History of Art at one of the new state universities (University of Katip Çelebi in İzmir) in Turkey.

The division between these two archaeologies of Anatolia—the ancient and the postclassical (Seljuk and Ottoman)—continues today. Since 1980, the Turkish Ministry of Culture and Tourism has organized annually an international symposium, where the engaged scientific community reports on recent archaeological excavations, surveys, and research in museums and archaeometric examinations. These reports are published yearly. Middle Age and Modern period investigations are also included in these symposiums. However, since the number of these latter projects has increased, those art historians working on the Middle Ages and the Modern period have formed a separate group by organizing a yearly symposium which includes not only archaeological excavation and survey results but also art historical themes as well. These annual meetings have been ongoing since 1997 under the direction of an art history department of a different university each year and are consequently published (Biçer 2009).

THE PIONEERS OF SCIENTIFIC EXCAVATIONS

Ottoman archaeology in Anatolia emerged with the chance identification of Ottoman remains from pre-Ottoman excavations or from urban construction sites. These findings are mainly Ottoman ceramics, which were the primary Ottoman objects of interest excavated both at indiscriminate and at scientific excavations. Rich collections of Ottoman ceramics in European museums and private collections, and the desires of antique deal-ers, may have been influential in the great amount of interest in these types of finds.

Excavation in Miletus, a classical port city in Western Anatolia, is a good example for the first group. Excavations in the 1930s by Karl Wulzinger, Carl Watzinger, and Friedrich Sarre led to the recovery of a considerable quantity of Ottoman-period ceramic sherds and kiln residues on the site. This led Sarre to classify these sherds as "Miletus ware" (Figure 2.7.1). Thinking that these ceramics were produced in Miletus and exported from the same port, the term "Miletus ware" has become a well-established classification that is still used within the literature for simplicity. Later research and excavations have demonstrated that "Miletus ware" is a generic term for the first stage of Ottoman ceramic production.

An earlier example of indiscriminate findings was in Istanbul during the Ottoman period, during the construction of the Post and Telegram Office in Istanbul at the begin-ning of the 20th century, where ceramic sherds were found while digging the founda-tions. This time associating the sherds with textual material, Armenag Bey and Migeon Sakissian classified them as the "Golden Horn" type of Ottoman ceramics, a term that is still used much like the previous "Miletus ware," for simplicity. Later research has showed that these ceramics were produced in İznik, and no production center at the Golden Horn has yet been found to substantiate such a claim (Yenişehirlioğlu 1994).

FIGURE 2.7.1 İznik Ceramics: Miletus Ware (İznik 1 type) from the Roman Theater Excavations in İznik.

Courtesy of Nurşen Özkul Fındık.

In this regard, one should also mention the underwater findings that are not systematically and scientifically taken into consideration. Findings from a shipwreck near Istanbul revealed 18th-century Kütahya coffee cups that are conserved at the Turkish and Islamic Art Museum in Istanbul.[2] There exists no scientific underwater archaeological research on Ottoman shipwrecks in Anatolia.

The first scientific archaeology of Ottoman Anatolia started with the excavations of Ottoman İznik ceramic kilns by Oktay Aslanapa between 1963 and 1969, followed by a second excavation period that resumed in 1981 and continues to produce the discovery of kilns, ceramic sherds, kiln material, and workshops (Aslanapa 1965) (Figure 2.7.2). Ottoman ceramics of İznik production were highly appreciated by the European market, and İznik tiles decorated the walls of Ottoman monuments mainly in Istanbul. These excavations, changing the previous dating and origins of Ottoman ceramic production, defined a well-established chronology of İznik ceramic production that forms a reference point for Ottoman ceramic and tile art in general.

FIGURE 2.7.2 Excavation of the Potters' Quarter in İznik.

Courtesy of Nurşen Özkul Fındık.

---

[2] This is for the present the only example we know. The relation between the cargo and the origin of the shipwreck has not been studied.

This systematic excavation indicates to a certain extent the orientation that Ottoman archaeology would take in Anatolia and the relevant problems that would follow. One could thus confirm that Ottoman archaeology started as both an urban archaeology and as an archaeology of production. Rural archaeology of Ottoman Anatolia does not exist practically as an archaeological field of study. No rural inventory has been made of Ottoman Anatolia; deserted villages have not been a subject of research, though one unique study has surveyed some nomadic camps (Cribb 1991). Thus botanical archaeology has also not been an area of research. In certain excavations of pre-Ottoman rural areas, like in Pisidia/Tekke in southern Anatolia and also central Anatolia, the grains from the Ottoman levels have been analyzed and also compared with the Ottoman archives of the period, as reported by Mark Nesbitt and Thurstan Robinson during a conference of the Skilliter Centre for Ottoman Studies, Newnham College, Cambridge University.[3] This brings us to our later discussion that the presence of detailed historical archives might be one of the reasons why there is no interest in Ottoman rural archaeology. Since one can follow economic trends in agriculture and trade through Ottoman documentary sources, such as the tax registers (*defters*) and foundation deeds (*waqf* documents), which continue to be a target of research and publication by Turkish historians, there seems to be no interest to discover archaeologically the rural landscape of Ottoman Anatolia that still exists untouched in certain areas. Unlike archaeological research on Turkey, one can find more detailed analyses in other post-Ottoman nation states (for Cyprus, see Given and Hadjianastasis 2010; for Greece, see Davies and Davis 2007 and Davis et al. 2005); there is much new work, in the same vein, for the Arab provinces in Syria, Transjordan and Palestine (see Chapters 2.1 and 2.2).

Historical research concerning the pre-Ottoman period in post-Ottoman nation states has increased in the past decades. The inevitable relation of contemporary economic life in those countries to their pre-Ottoman past has been generally studied in urban settings relative to trade but rarely in rural areas relative to cultivation and village settlements. This kind of study needs a more multidisciplinary approach to the subject where historical, anthropological, geographical, archaeological, and ethnographical studies contribute to scientific research. New themes in archaeological research, on the other hand, such as gender, landscape, and community studies introduced innovative ways of analyzing these sets of data.

ETHNOGRAPHY AS OTTOMAN ARCHAEOLOGY

Ethnography, on the other hand, has played an important determinate role in establishing Ottoman archaeology in modern Turkey. Ethnographic methods follow three forms: an art historical study of the minor arts (a development of antiquarian collection), the study

---

[3] The conference took place in the Skilliter Centre for Ottoman Studies, Newnham College, Cambridge University (http://skilliter.newn.cam.ac.uk/?cat=3&paged=2). Unfortunately, its proceedings have not been published.

of religion and religious minorities, and scholarship drawing from modern cultural heritage management. In the first case, collectors of Ottoman art are mainly interested in objects and Ottoman material culture that they can find in the market. These objects are also in private hands and thus rather easy to acquire. Therefore, collectors of Ottoman art do not feel the necessity to follow archaeological excavations since it is much easier to find untouched, valuable pieces in daily life. The law on cultural heritage preservation considers the objects of material culture from the 19th and 20th centuries as "ethnographic," which encourages their circulation in the market, making them more available for the collectors than are archaeological findings. Nonetheless, such collections filled modern museums and have made the minor arts of the later Ottoman period available for study.

The study of religion has primarily focused on burial practices and human remains. However, it is difficult to apply these methods to later historical periods. Cemeteries both in urban and rural areas continue to be reused. Consequently, the archaeologically interesting example of religion for the Ottoman period relies heavily on understanding how the body was laid to rest. No objects are found beside the coffin. This is generally a similar situation for the study of the non-Muslim religions and their members, especially in urban areas. However an interesting new study comes from Myra excavations in Demre, famous for its church dedicated to Saint Nikolaus. The population of Demre during the Ottoman period was mainly Greek Orthodox. A number of tombs were found around this church built during the Byzantine period but renovated during the Ottoman period. Decorated circular silver plaques were found during the excavations in these tombs, and the study showed that they were part of jewelry worn by Greek women (Fındık 2015). In order to find the origins of this jewelry type, the author made a comparative study with the same type of objects found in Kastellorizo in Greece (Meis Island), off the coast of Kaş in Southern Turkey. Populations moved back and forth from the Mediterranean and Aegean islands to mainland Anatolia. Thus, comparative research between neighboring geographies helps understanding objects found in archaeological excavation.

Archaeology of religion in itself is an area of investigation of religious beliefs and ceremony. However, in the case of a multiethnic society, as in the case of the Ottoman Empire, it can reveal community identities and lifestyles. The forced exchange of populations applied in Turkey and Greece between Muslims and Orthodox in 1923 should be more carefully investigated concerning any archaeological research in their respective settlements (Yenişehirlioğlu 2005b).

Archaeology of religion in a country that continues to have the same traditions of religious culture is difficult. Yet one can find additional information in architectural research of vernacular buildings and the use of space. The houses of Christians or crypto-Christians have different details in Anatolia. For example a small niche in the house to put the statue of the Virgin Mary or Christ, the symbolism of the Dove as architectural ornamentation or on wood or plaster, hidden underground small chapels, or a cellar to produce wine. These features are more common in urban areas and have not survived in the rural ones. No systematic excavation has been conducted to research such variations.

After the foundation of the Turkish Republic, ethnographical studies were encouraged over anthropological ones. Scholars from Hungary who were already familiar with the concept and the search of a Turkic character reoriented the ethnographical research in Turkey (Turan 1999–2002). Compilations of music, language, material culture, and oral traditions were documented in rural areas among the Muslim population of Turkey. Thus, modern concepts of cultural heritage were introduced through ethnography as areas of study, drawing a more scientific interest on preservation, conservation, and documentation of such areas.

URBAN ARCHAEOLOGY

The continued occupation of Ottoman settlements into modern times, and the strati-graphic problems this produced, constitutes a primary challenge for Ottoman archaeol-ogy. This has several reasons. Anatolian cities were formed mainly by wooden houses that facilitated the spread of fires. The clearing of the destruction formed by these fires and the reconstruction of neighborhoods on older ones resulted in the loss of former layers. It is therefore quite difficult, for example, to research domestic architecture archaeologically in a city if the houses have not been constructed in stone, like those in Aleppo. On the other hand, the modernization of urban texture in the 19th century formed the construction of new streets and brought new sanitary requirements that altered completely the urban layout. Last but not least is the challenge of protecting archaeological sites during ongoing urbanization. Urban structures limit this research, and the high price of appropriation for public use makes archaeological research com-plicated and problematic.

Large-scale urban projects could constitute the means to follow archaeological find-ings as they are uncovered. If they are carefully recorded, they could add considerably to the urban archaeology of an Ottoman city. This is being done in the Balkans. The ongo-ing salvage excavation at Temeșmar (Timișoara), Romania, for example, has revealed important patterns in the ways the Ottoman conquests have transformed the urban form (see English-language survey of this project in Gaspar 2019). Such archaeological excavations in Romania have paved the way for the organization of an International Conference on Ottoman archaeology in Romania in October 2017[4].

Different types of local excavations have been carried out in Istanbul since the early 20th century, revealing a variety of glazed and unglazed pottery from the Roman, Byzantine, and Ottoman periods.[5] The construction of a natural gas system in Istanbul between 1990 and 2000 was an important chance to follow and record findings in that

[4] https://networks.h-net.org/node/11419/discussions/470274/symposium-ottoman-archaeology-romania-challenges-realities-8

[5] The cleaning of the land walls during their restoration by the Greater Municipality of İstanbul around 2000 (unpublished), the excavations started in 1968 at the Kalenderhane Camii (Church of Saint Theotokos Kyriotissa, unpublished), and those of Saraçhane (Hayes 1992) are some of these local excavations. In other cities, ongoing fieldwork in the ancient Agora of İzmir is documenting the continuity of industrial and commercial activity in the area during the Ottoman period (Gök 2015).

part of the city. The archaeological museum in Istanbul collected artifacts discovered during this work, but museum pieces alone do not explain the aspects of everyday life in a city. Had these finds been studied using statistical methods, a comparison of Ottoman material culture between the different quarters of the city could have been facilitated, resulting in a better understanding of the consumption habits among rich, poor, or middle-class neighborhoods. Unfortunately, this chance was lost. The recent excavations for the construction of the subway and the tunnel under the Bosporus (Marmaray) also revealed important material that needs to be assessed scientifically, and the huge amount of findings will necessitate a long period of research.

LANDSCAPE ARCHAEOLOGY

The study of rural areas, agricultural fields and regional surveys belong to the realm of landscape archaeology. This field is underdeveloped for Ottoman Anatolia due to the many historical and historiographical reasons discussed earlier. The only site which has been subjected to the methods of landscape archaeology is the Gallipoli battlefield from World War I (Aslan et al. 2008). The Great War between the Ottoman Empire and Germany on one side and the Allied Forces (British, French) on the opposite side had a major impact on the landscape of Anatolia. The participation of the Anzacs coming from Australia and New Zealand as part of the British Empire and the ferocious battle they had with the Ottoman troops on the Gallipoli Peninsula left innumerable material culture remains ranging from bullets to uniforms and more. All these objects are gathered and exhibited in local and private village museum collections. The vast areas of defense by both armies are noted on military plans and memoirs, and military archives form a huge aspect of the documentation that can be used for the reconstruction of this site in terms of landscape archaeology. Some trenches are still left in their original places. With the use of new technologies, this site is open for further research and reconstruction.

ARCHAEOLOGY OF PRODUCTION AND INDUSTRIAL ARCHAEOLOGY

The excavations in İznik, launched by Oktay Aslanapa, of a ceramic production center have been the only projects for many years where a large area of potters' quarters of the Ottoman period has been unearthed. These findings were enriched by the excavations at the Roman theater in İznik by Bedri Yalman who discovered yet again ceramic kilns at the cavea of the amphitheater (Özkul 2001) where there are still kilns to be excavated. The amount of material excavated in İznik is huge and the findings are preserved at the

İznik Museum whose permanent exhibition does not provide ample background on this world-renowned product. Publications also are scarce compared to the amount of findings, with the exception of a publication concerning the İznik kilns in 2001. However, no publication has been comprehensively compiled to discuss the excavations. The annual excavation reports on the site delivered each year at the Annual Conference of the Ministry of Culture do not provide enough information about all of the ongoing the research at the site.

Another ceramic production center subjected to excavation was the Tekfur Palace Ottoman kilns in Istanbul (Figure 2.7.3). Established in the 18th century within the walls of the 14th-century Byzantine palace, the kilns produced tiles similar to those of İznik, decorating the walls of mosques and palaces mainly in Istanbul (Figure 2.7.4). It was discovered for the first time that common wares were also produced in these kilns (Yenişehirlioğlu 2003). The archaeometric analysis of the paste used in this production proved to originate from the Golden Horn, as suggested in both European and Ottoman travelers accounts.

The survey of the "potters' quarter" in Eyüp, outside the land walls of Istanbul and not far from the Tekfur Palace, revealed the presence of three pottery workshops from the 19th century. Documented for the first time was the "coarse local pottery of Ottoman

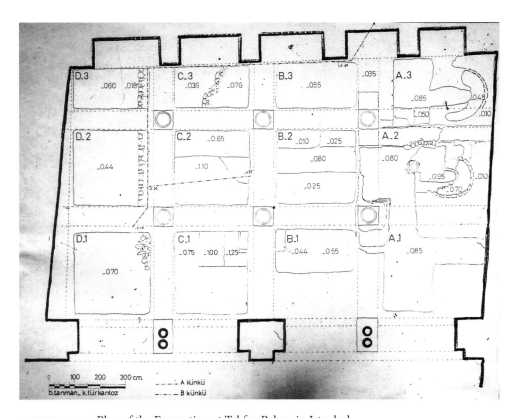

FIGURE 2.7.3 Plan of the Excavation at Tekfur Palace in Istanbul.

FIGURE 2.7.4   Tekfur Palace: 18th-century tile and ceramic kiln.

Istanbul," which was produced by the potters of this neighborhood since the 15th century (Yenişehirlioğlu 1999).

The excavations and the surveys undertaken at Demirköy in Thrace, not far from Istanbul (Danısman et al. 2007), represent industrial archaeology of the Ottoman period. A fortified residential area, foundry workshops, underground vaulted canals to bring in water to the foundry, iron furnaces, and heaps of slag and charcoal were found (Figure 2.7.5). The Samakocuk iron foundry, according to archival documents, cast cannon balls for the Ottoman artillery in the 18th and 19th centuries. The findings were supported by archaeometallurgical analysis and historical documents. Popular historiography wants to relate the site to the period of Sultan Mehmet II, as the location where his famous iron balls were cast before the capture of Istanbul.

THE ARCHAEOLOGY OF MONUMENTS

The archaeology of the Ottoman period in Anatolia in many ways continues to be a study of standing monuments. The restoration of monuments by the General Directorate of Waqfs in Turkey has entailed a series of archaeological research on mosques, medreses, and mausoleums of the Ottoman era. Generally, the surroundings

FIGURE 2.7.5   A: Demirköy (Samakocuk) Foundary Excavation, Kırıkkale; to see the site, visit http://www.kirklarelienvanteri.gov.tr/anitlar.php?id=56. B: Demirköy (Samakocuk) Foundary Excavation, Kırıkkale; to see the excavation area, visit http://www.trakyagezi.com/demirkoy-fatih-dokumhanesi/.

Courtesy of Dr. Nurcan Yazıcı Metin.

of a building are excavated to see if there were other architectural structures around; later, additional parts are reevaluated, and the original plan of the building and its surroundings are determined. This process is quite popular in Ottoman archaeology these days. Since urban archaeology is challenged by modern development and rural archaeology has yet to come of its own, it is easier to deal with single monuments both scientifically and financially. The same is true for the landscape organization of cemeteries that are considered to be in the field of Ottoman archaeology. Redressing the tombstone, cleaning the site, and studying the associated material culture finds are all considered to be aspects of Ottoman archaeology.

Palaces

Topkapı Palace in Istanbul was the long-time dwelling and administrative center of the Ottoman sultans from the 15th to the 20th century. However, the model for the architectural development of the palace is still discussed by scholars. The origin of the plan, where independent kiosks and rooms are built around a courtyard, is reminiscent of the Edirne Palace built before the Topkapı Palace; many still question if its layout comes from the hierarchical organization of tents during royal campaigns. On the other hand, constant change and renovations to these spaces makes the architectural history of the Topkapı Palace difficult to follow and establish precise documentation. Archival material should be matched by random archaeological excavations and ornamental history of the buildings and rooms.

The architectural layout and general appearance of the earliest Ottoman palaces in Yenişehir and Bursa (the first Ottoman capital) are unknown. They have not been conserved to the present day, and there are no written documents or travelers' accounts explaining their layout.

Edirne Palace was constructed under Sultan Murat II before the capture of Istanbul and continued to be used until the 20th century. It was a second palace for the sultans when they were on military campaigns to Europe and when they wanted to be away from Istanbul. Edirne Palace has unfortunately not survived due to the Ottoman-Russian wars and World War I. Some buildings belonging to the palace have survived, and several short excavation campaigns have been conducted on the site. An archaeological investigation of the structure has started recently and promises to reveal more about this important Ottoman palace and its architectural history, as well as other small objects that might be found (Özer et al. 2016) (Figure 2.7.6).

Castles and Fortresses

Descriptions of the early years of the Ottoman Beylicat period, mainly the 14th century, are scarce in written historical texts and archival documentation. Therefore, Ottoman archaeology becomes more important as a source of information for these years. Thus,

FIGURE 2.7.6   Edirne Palace excavations; see http://www.bigazete.com.tr/2016/8/edirne-sarayi-kazilari-suruyor-h23465.html.

excavations at Karacahisar have begun to search for the first Ottoman settlement that was taken from the Byzantines and where the Ottomans constructed their first monuments (Parman et al. 2006) (Figure 2.7.7). Excavations have not yet revealed an Ottoman settlement of the early period on the site but work is ongoing. Similarly, the Ottoman settlement in Bilecik was also an early period town that later was abandoned when the settlement moved farther down the valley (Altunsapan and Deveci 2002). Excavations, however, showed that the site was inhabited until the 19th century. Thus the hopes of finding an early urban settlement plan were lost.

On the other hand, cultural management issues have become an important scientific topic during the past decades in Turkey and have been influential in the research of sites and monuments. Unlike the urban texture of cities and settlements, castles and fortresses, even though preserved within a cityscape, have survived as isolated places less affected by modern urban growth. In this respect the Seddülbahir Fortress (Çanakkale)—an Ottoman fortress near Gallipoli on the Dardanelle constructed in the 15th century, enlarged in the 17th century, and reused during World War I—has been the focus of a cultural heritage management project after some excavation has been conducted.(Aslan et al. 2008).

Most of the fortresses in Anatolian towns have pre-Ottoman phases. Therefore, even though the upper layers may have been used during the Ottoman period, they do not represent pure Ottoman sites on their own. The recent excavation of Harput Fortress (Elazığ) is an example of a current project of this kind in Turkey. (Figure 2.7.8).

FIGURE 2.7.7 Karacahisar, Eskişehir.

Courtesy of Erol Altınsapan.

FIGURE 2.7.8 Harput Fortress, Elazığ: Ottoman
Soldier Uniform Button 19th-century; see http://
www.sondakika23.com/Hbr-4303-Kazi-
calismalarinda-cikanlar-sasirtiyor.html.

Courtesy of İsmail Aytaç.

The Future

The archaeology of Ottoman Anatolia is a relatively new story, one that has started quite recently. It has its methodological and practical problems that need to be solved, and it needs both financial and educational support in order to develop. Recent urban development plans will encourage research on Ottoman archaeology, and new interdisciplinary curriculums should be developed together with other areas of the social sciences; together, these can bring new insights into the social and economic history of Anatolia.

Excavations focused on the Ottoman period are not common, and the places that can be excavated are limited, as are the objects that can be found in these excavations. To compare and establish patterns of trade, settlement, and gender it will be necessary to gather and synthesize data from various sites. Both indiscriminate and systematic excavations need to be evaluated according to the space code of the findings. This is an issue that, according to the type of excavations done and the status of the area, site, or building itself, has not been taken much into consideration. Not only the sustainability of the buildings through centuries but also their constant history of reuse makes it difficult to reconstruct space and function through the centuries. For example, when a double *hammam* (one side for men and one side for women) is excavated, it is rarely considered which part was used by women and which part by men according to the remains of material culture found during excavations. Such site-specific reports do not exist. The foundation of Art History departments in numerous Anatolian cities has been instrumental in the formation of local centers of research. Those working in these departments are developing archaeological excavations and survey projects of the Middle and Pre-modern period of Anatolia. As these increase in the near future, they will enable a more detailed and refined understanding of the findings. The formation of datasets from these studies will contribute not only to art historical research but also to research focusing on different areas of history. Archaeometric analyses will complete these findings. Landscape and community archaeology, as well as gender studies, also should be taken into consideration, thus leading to a closer cooperation between social sciences and humanities.

References

Altunsapan, E., and Deveci, A. 2002. "Bilecik Orhangazi İmareti ve Osmanlı Dönemi Bilecik Kenti 2001 yılı Sondaj ve Kazı çalışmaları," in M. Denktaş, Y. Özbek, and A. S. Arslan (eds.), *VI. Ortaçağ ve Türk Dönemi Kazı Sonuçları ve Sanat Tarihi Sempozyumu, Bildiriler, 08–10 Nisan 2002, Kayseri* (Kayseri: Erciyes Üniversitesi), 41–54.

Arık, O. M. 2000. "Türk Kültürüne Yönelik Arkeolojik Çalışmalar ve Sorunları," in O. Aslanapa and E. İhsanoğlu (eds.), *Emin Bilgiç Hatıra Kitabı* (Istanbul: İSAR), 149–168.

Aslan, C., Thys-Şenocak, L., and Çelik, R. N. 2008. "Gelibolu Yarımadası Tarihsel Savaş Alanı Arkeolojisi Araştırmaları: Seddülbahir Kalesi (Research of the Historical and Battlefield Archaeology of the Gallipoli Peninsula: the Ottoman Fortress at Seddulbahir)," *TÜBA-AR*, 11, 105–120.

Aslanapa, O. 1965. *Anadolu'da Türk Çini ve Seramik Sanatı* (Ankara: Türk Kültürünü Araştırma Enstitüsü).

Aslanapa, O. 1993. *Türkiye'de Avusturyalı Sanat Tarihçleri ve Sanatkarlar: Österreichische Kunsthistoriker und Künstler in der Türkei* (Istanbul: Eren Yayıncılık).

Aslanapa, O., Yetkin, Ş., and Altun, A. 1989. *İznik Çini Fırınları Kazısı* (Istanbul: Arkeoloji ve Sanat Yayınları).

Bahrani, Z., Çelik, Z., and Eldem, E. (eds.) 2011. *Scramble for the Past: A Story of Archaeology in the Ottoman Empire, 1753–1914* (Istanbul: SALT).

Baram, U., and Carroll, L. (eds.) 2000. *A Historical Archaeology of the Ottoman Empire: Breaking New Ground* (New York: Kluwer Academic/Plenum Publishers).

Biçer, Z. 2009. "Anadolu Türk Dönemi Kazıları ve Sonuçları Sempozyumları," *Türkiye Araştırmaları Lieteratür Dergisi*, 7, 14, 629–641.

Çal, H. 2005. "Osmanlı'dan Cumhuriyete Eski Eserler Kanunları," in E. S. Yalçın (ed.), *60. Yılında İlim ve Fikir Adamı Prof. Dr. Kazım Yaşar Kopraman'a Armağan* (Ankara: Berikan Yayınları), 234–270.

Cezar, M. 1971. *Sanatta Batı'ya Açılış ve Osman Hamdi Bey* (Istanbul: İşbankası kültür).

Cribb, R. 1991. *Nomads in Archaeology* (Cambridge: Cambridge University Press).

Danışman, G., Gerritsen, F., Kaçar, M., Özbal, H., Özbal, R., Tanyeli, G., Yalçın, Ü., and Yılmaz, Z. 2007. "Demirköy- Samakocuk Iron Foundry: An Industrial Archaeology Project at an Ottoman Metal Work-Shop Complex in Thrace," *TÜBA-AR*, 10, 91–111.

Davies, S., and Davis, J. L. (eds.) 2007. *Between Venice and Istanbul. Colonial Landscape in Early Modern Greece.* Hesperia Supplement 50 (Athens: American School of Classical Studies).

Davis, J. L., Bennett, J., and Zarinebaf, F. 2005. *A Historical and Economic Geography of Ottoman Greece.* Hesperia Supplement 34 (Athens: American School of Classical Studies).

Fındık, E. F. 2015. "Myra/Demre, Aziz Nikolaos Kilisesi Rum Mezarlığından *Boucla* ve *Gounca Örnekleri*," Adalya, 18, 303–324.

Gaşpar, A. 2019. "Sgraffito Pottery in the Ottoman Timişoara. 'Palanca Mare' Suburb: ICAM Excavation Point (2015 Campaign)," *Journal of Islamic Archaeology*, 6, 1, 1–18.

Given, M., and Hadjianastasis, M. 2010. "Landholding and Landscape in Ottoman Cyprus," *Byzantine and Modern Greek Studies*, 34, 1, 38–60.

Gök, S. 2015. *Smyrna (İzmir) Agorası'nda Osmanlı İzleri. Kütahya Seramikleri (2007–2014 Kazı Dönemi).* İzmir: İzmir Büyükşehir Belediyesi Kent Kitaplığı (Izmir Metropolitan Municipal City Library).

Gündüz Küskü, S. 2014. *Osmanlı Beyliği Mimarisinde Anadolu Selçuklu Geleneği* (Ankara: TTK).

Hayes, J. 1992. *Excavations at Saraçhane in Istanbul, 2. The Pottery* (Princeton: Dumbarton Oaks).

Katoğlu, M. 2009. *Şematizmden yaratıcılığa: Cumhuriyet Türkiyesi'nde yüksek sanat (ve kültür) hayatının kamu hizmeti olarak kurumlaşması* (Istanbul: Kırmızı Yayınları).

Özdoğan, M. 2008. *Türk Arkeolojisinin Sorunları ve Koruma Politikaları* (Istanbul: Arkeoloji ve Sanat Yayınları).

Özer, M., Dündar, M., Uçar, H., Ayhan, G., and Güner, Y. 2016. "Edirne Sarayı (Saray-I Cedîd-İ Âmire) Kazısı 2014 Yılı Çalışmaları," in M. Özer (ed.), *37. Uluslararası Kazı, Araştırma ve Arkeometri Sempozyumu, Erzurum, Türkiye, 11–15 Mayıs 2015, vol. 3* (Ankara: İsmail Aygül Ofset), 595–622.

Özkul, N. 2001. *İznik Roma Tiyatrosu Kazı Buluntuları (1980–1995) Arasındaki Osmanlı Seramikleri* (Ankara: Kültür Bakanlığı Yayınları).

Parman, E., Canan, P., and Muradiye, B. 2006. "Eskişehir (Merkez Karacaşehir Köyü) Karacahisar Kalesi 2005 Yılı Kazı Çalışmaları," *28. Kazı Sonuçları Toplantısı*, 2, 1–12.

Turan, Ş. 1999–2002. *Türk Devrim Tarihi*, 5 vols. (Ankara: Bilgi Yayınevi).

Yenişehirlioğlu, F. 1989. *Ottoman Architectural Works Outside of Turkey* (Ankara: Turkish Ministry of Foreign Affairs).

Yenişehirlioğlu, F. 1994. "Haliç İşi," *Dünden Bugüne Istanbul Ansiklopedisi*, vol. 4 (Istanbul: Tarih Vakfı).

Yenişehirlioğlu, F. 1999. "Decontextualising and Recontextualising Ottoman Cultural Heritage in Post-Ottoman Nation States," in M. Korzay, N. Burçoğlu, Ş.Yarcan, and D. Unalan (eds.), *Heritage, Multi-Culturalism and Tourism 1* (Istanbul: Bogaziçi University Press), 119–142.

Yenişehirlioğlu, F. 2000a. "Eyüp Çömlekçiler Mahallesi Araştırmaları," in *Tarihi Kültürü ve Sanatıyla III:Eyüp Sultan Sempozyumu, Tebliğle, 28–30 Mayıs 1999* (Istanbul: Eyüp Belediyesi), 42–51.

Yenişehirlioğlu, F. 2003. "Tekfur Sarayı Çini Fırınları Kazısı (1995–2001)," in *24. Kazı Sonuçları Toplantısı vol. 1* (Ankara: T. C. Kültür ve Turizm Bakanlığı, Anıtlar ve Müzeler Genel Müdürlüğü), 329–344.

Yenişehirlioğlu, F. 2005b. "Common Cultural Heritage," in S. Güvenç (ed.), *Common Cultural Heritage, The Foundation of Lausanne Treaty Emigrants* (Istanbul), 24–28.

Yenişehirlioğlu, F. 2011. "Osmanlı Döneminde Koleksiyon Oluşumu: 19 Yüzyıl Sonu 20.Yüzyıl Başı Müze Envanter Defterlerinden Öğrendiklerimiz," in C. Eren, B. İşler, N. Peker, and G. Sağır (eds.), *Anadolu Kültürlerinde Süreklilik ve Değişim* (Ankara), 603–613.

Altun, A. 2006. "Türk-İslam Dönemi Kazıları," in N. Başgelen and E. Akurgal (eds.), *Toprağın altındaki geçmiş: arkeoloji: sorunlar, öneriler, kazılar* (Istanbul: Arkeoloji ve Sanat Yayınları), 119–124.

FURTHER READING

Arık, R. O. 1950. *Les fouilles archéologiques en Turquie* (Ankara: Milli Eğitim Basım Evi).

Esin, U. 1999. "Türkiye Cumhuriyeti'nin 75. Yılında Atatürk Düşüncesinde Ulusal Kimliğin Oluşturulma Sürecinde Arkeoloji'nin Yeri: Dünü, Bugünü," in Z. Rona (ed.), *Bilanço 1923–1998. Türkiye Cumhuriyeti'nin 75. Yılına Toplu Bakış I* (Istanbul: Tarih Vakfı Yayınları), 277–288.

Gerelyes, I., and Kovács, G. (eds.) 2003. *Archaeology of the Ottoman Period in Hungary* (Budapest: Hungarian National Museum).

Koşay, H., Orgun, M., Bayram, S., and Tan, E. 2013. *Osmanlı İmparatorluğu ve Türkiye Cumhuriyeti Çağlarında Türk Kazı Tarihi* I-V (Ankara: Türk Tarih Kurumu).

Petersen, A. 2017. "'Under the Yoke': The Archaeology of the Ottoman Period in Bulgaria," *Journal of Islamic Archaeology*, 4, 1, 23–48.

Vorderstrasse, T. 2014. "The Archaeology of the Ottoman Empire and Its Aftermath in the Middle East," *Near Eastern Archaeology*, 4, 292–297.

Yenişehirlioğlu, F. 2000b. "The Republican Ethic and the Family Album: Collecting and Art Historical Research in Turkey, 1923–1950," in S. Vernoit (ed.), *Discovering Islamic Art: Collections and Collectors* (London: I. B. Taurus), 182–193.

Yenişehirlioğlu, F. 2004. "Archaeology in Istanbul and the Excavations at Tekfur Palace," in S. Atasoy (ed.), *Byzantine and Ottoman Istanbul in the 15th century* (Istanbul: University of Istanbul), n. p.

Yenişehirlioğlu, F. 2005a. "L'archéologie historique de l'Empire ottoman. Bilan et perspective," *Turcica*, 37, 245–267.

CHAPTER 2.8

··

ARABIA AND THE GULF

··

ANDREW PETERSEN

It is surprising that Arabia's central place within Muslim religion and culture has not also made it the primary focus for archaeologists specializing in the Islamic period. There are a number of reasons why this has not been the case, and these may be conveniently summarized as the inaccessibility of much of the region prior to the 20th century and the sensitivity of the subject in more recent times. This subject is discussed in more detail in the "Religion" section at the end of this chapter, although for the present it should be remembered that Islamic archaeology in the region is still at a very early stage of development.

HISTORIOGRAPHY

Arabia has of course been known to the wider Mediterranean world since time immemorial because of its proximity to the ancient civilizations of Egypt, Mesopotamia, and the Levant. However, with the possible exception of south Arabia, or Arabia Felix, the region itself was outside the main centers of civilization and functioned variously as a buffer between warring states (e.g., Egypt and Persia) or as a transitional zone between different civilizations. The first European scientific exploration of Arabia did not occur until the 18th century, when the Danish king Fredrick V commissioned an expedition to Arabia (1761–1767) in order to provide more information on the geographical and cultural context of the Bible (Folsach et al. 1996). The expedition was explicitly not a colonial enterprise but instead had the purpose of making "as many discoveries for science as is possible." It is also significant that the team members were expected to have a positive attitude toward Islam and the Arabs, thus Article IX of the instructions to the participants stated "All members of the company shall show the greatest courtesy to the inhabitants of Arabia. They are not to raise any objections toward their religion." Although the expedition did not make any specific discoveries in relation to the archaeology of Islam, the expedition surveyor, Carsten Niebuhr, produced the first detailed maps of Arabia, which formed the basis for much of the 19th-century exploration of the peninsula.

During the 19th century increasing numbers of Europeans made exploratory journeys through Arabia, making observations during their travels relevant to archaeology and Arab Muslim culture. One of the most significant early travelers was the Swiss explorer Johan Ludwig Burckhardt (1784–1817) who not only (re)discovered Petra but also made important records of Mecca, Medina, and other places of interest for Islamic archaeology. Other important 19th-century explorers included Sir Richard Burton, who gave detailed accounts of Mecca, and Charles Doughty, who made detailed records of antiquities, the most prominent of which was the Nabatean city of Medain Saleh. By the beginning of the 20th century, improved transport links and expanding colonial power meant that the interior of Arabia was increasingly an area of interest. Two archaeologists of particular note were T. E. Lawrence and Gertrude Bell, both of whom made journeys deep into Arabia. However, while Lawrence had actually worked as an archaeologist at Carchemesh on the Euphrates and made an archaeological expedition to the Negev, his presence in Arabia was purely connected with the Great Arab Revolt; thus his accounts of Arabia contain very little of archaeological interest. As a woman, Gertrude Bell's journeys into Arabia were exceptional. Her journey to visit the emir of Hail was unprecedented, both because she was kept a prisoner there and because of her maps, photographs, and descriptions of a then very remote part of Arabia. However Gertrude Bell's most important contribution to the Islamic archaeology of Arabia is her publication of the desert palace of al-Ukhaidhir (Bell 1914). Although this building is today in southwestern Iraq, in cultural and geographical terms it belongs more to a northern Arabian tradition than to a Mesopotamian one. Gertrude Bell's interest in and experience of Arabia certainly surpassed that of her near contemporary K. A. C. Creswell who famously dismissed Arabia with the assertion that Arabia had no architecture before the rise of Islam (King 1993). Unlike Gertrude Bell, Creswell had no first-hand experience of Arabia; though he traveled extensively throughout the Middle East to investigate sites, he saw no reason to explore any in Arabia. The prominent position of Creswell within the development of Islamic archaeology has meant that Arabia was virtually excluded from general studies of the subject, and it is only since the 1990s that the importance of the region has begun to be recognized.

Rapid urbanization and rising living standards in Arabia have led to an increasing number of archaeological projects and investigations. The main focus of activity has been in the Arabian Gulf, where archaeology has been valued both as a means of building national identities and as a potential means of developing tourism (Petersen 2016). The first archaeological excavations in the Gulf were carried out by Aarhus University in Denmark during the 1950s on the island of Bahrain. The excavations were a collaboration between Geoffrey Bibby and P. V. Glob, who soon expanded their interests beyond Bahrain. Although the initial excavations were primarily concerned with prehistory and identifying the Dilmun civilization, the scientific methodologies combined with the expanding survey work in Saudi Arabia and the United Arab Emirates meant that large numbers of Islamic-period sites were identified and recorded. From the 1970s onward, archaeology was increasingly recognized as a national asset. Thus, in 1973, Beatrice de Cardi was commissioned to carry out an archaeological survey of Qatar that identified hundreds of sites and documented significant growth in settlement during the 18th and 19th centuries (de Cardi 1978). Elsewhere in the Gulf, John Hansman's pioneering work (Hansman 1985) at Julfar formed the prelude to several decades of work in Ras al-Khaimah, while French expeditions to Oman, Qatar, and Bahrain have led to important investigations of early Islamic sites.

Since the beginning of the 21st century there have been many new initiatives by antiquities and tourism departments within the Arabian Peninsula. For example, in 2002, the Saudi Commission for Tourism and Antiquities began a collaborative project with the French government research agency (Center National de la Recherche Scientifique [CNRS]) to investigate the archaeology of al-Hejr (Medain Saleh) as part of its bid to have the remains listed as a UNESCO World Heritage site. The partnership is significant because it is the first time that the Saudi government has worked in partnership with a foreign archaeological team since the 1970s. Although the project was only concerned with pre-Islamic antiquities, the fact that it is mentioned in the Quran (7:74–77) has considerable significance for Muslims and also potential ethical problems for archaeology (for more discussion of this issue see the later section "Religion"). In addition to excavations the Saudi state also sponsored a major traveling exhibition—Roads of Arabia—featuring both pre-Islamic and Islamic-era antiquities. Elsewhere in Arabia there have been many projects focusing on Islamic period sites. For example, the international excavations at Failaka in Kuwait have revealed a large early Islamic period site, al-Qusur, complete with two churches (see "Religion: Christian"). On the island of Bahrain the excavations at the early Islamic capital of Bilad al-Qadim, led by Tim Insoll, have revealed extensive remains from the 8th century CE onward (Insoll et al. 2016). More recently Qatar launched a major initiative to investigate a range of Islamic sites, including the large, late 18th to early 20th century city of Zubarah. In addition a number of related 18th- to 19th-century sites in the north of Qatar have been investigated, indicating a wealthy and cosmopolitan culture in an otherwise hyperarid and sparsely populated peninsula (Petersen et al. 2016).

ENVIRONMENT

In geological terms, Arabia is a relatively well-defined area in the form of the Arabian Plate, a tectonic plate wedged between the Indian and African tectonic plates. The separation from neighboring continents is visible in the form of the seas which define it on three sides. The northern limits of Arabia are more difficult to determine and, at its minimal extent, could be described by a line running from Aqaba in the west to Basra in the east or at its maximum extent by a line running from Damascus to Baghdad. In terms of physical elevation and relief the western edge of the peninsula bordering the Red Sea is dominated by the Hijaz Mountains rising to elevations of more than 2,000 meters. In

Yemen in the south-west there are mountains which reach more than 3,000 meters, and in Oman in the south-east of the peninsula there are mountains of similar height. However, away from these areas, much of the topography of Arabia is relatively low, level plateau dipping down toward sea level on the eastern coasts of the Arabian Gulf. The nonmountainous areas of Arabia can be divided into three main geographical zones: sand deserts (al-Nafud, al-Dahana, and Rub al-Khali), desert plateaus (e.g., Najd), and coastal plains.

While there is considerable diversity in the topography of Arabia, the region as a whole can be characterized as hyperarid, with almost all areas receiving less than 200 millimeters of rainfall per year and many areas having rainfall of less than 100 millimeters per year. The vegetation reflects this arid climate with few natural forests, occasional perennial areas of grassland, and some areas virtually devoid of vegetation. Similarly the natural fauna of Arabia is fairly restricted and dominated by species able to survive on restricted water supplies. It should, however, be pointed out that, prior to the 20th century, there may have been richer natural vegetation supporting more diverse wildlife. The advent of motorized transport together with powered drilling equipment enabled the establishment of wells in remote places which could supply herders whose flocks of sheep and goats were able to degrade the extant vegetation (for a description of this process, see Thalen 1979).

CHRONOLOGY

Unlike most of the pre-Islamic Middle East, much of the Arabian Peninsula was outside the direct control of the ancient empires that dominated the region. Some areas, such as the north and east of Arabia, were under the control of client states, while Yemen in the south-west was home to an indigenous civilization. However, much of the interior of Arabia remained a tribal area with no centralized authority or ruling dynasty. In the years immediately prior to the rise of Islam much of eastern and southern Arabia was ruled by local kingdoms controlled by the Sasanian rulers of Iran while the north-west of Arabia, roughly contiguous with modern Jordan, was controlled by the Ghassanids, who owed allegiance to the Byzantines. Central Arabia was the home of a number of large tribes, including the Mecca-based Quraysh.

The revelation of the Quran and Muhammad's preaching gradually brought unity of purpose to the tribes which, instead of pursuing internal disputes, were encouraged to embark on a war of conversion whereby the whole peninsula would accept monotheism and peace (Islam). The subsequent expansion of Islam outside Arabia is well known, although the internal history of Arabia is less well documented. Although Arabia remained the spiritual home of Islam during the rule of the Umayyads and Abbasids, by the 10th century much of Arabia was again outside major political blocks and would not regain its political importance until the 20th century. While some areas such as Yemen and Oman were able to develop as independent and relatively stable political entities, the rest of Arabia was either outside state control or dominated by one or more of the medieval Muslim dynasties, such as the Ayyubids or Mamluks.

From the late 15th century onward Europeans started to establish a presence in Arabia in the form of Portuguese fortified posts along the coast. The virtual blockade of the Red Sea meant that the lucrative Indian trade switched to the Persian/Arabian Gulf. This situation indirectly led to the Ottoman conquest of Arabia in the 16th century with the occupation of the Hijaz, Yemen, and the al-Hasa region of eastern Arabia. During the 17th and 18th centuries control of Arabia was a struggle between the Ottoman, Saffavid Persian, and European empires. Within this complex matrix a new force developed in the form of Ibn Saud who, through an alliance with the fundamentalist preacher Abd al-Wahab, established the first Saudi state with its capital at Dhira in central Arabia. While the first Saudi state was defeated by the Ottomans in the early 1800s, the Saudi's reemerged at the end of the 19th century and, by the early 20th century, were able to establish the Kingdom of Saudi Arabia, ruling over most of the peninsula. The only areas to resist Saudi domination were the relatively well-defined states of Yemen and Oman, while parts of the Gulf Coast remained independent under British protection.

Settlement Types

Pre-modern human settlement in Arabia can for convenience be divided into three types: urban, rural, and nomadic. Within some of the historical literature there is a perceived contrast or opposition between settled urban populations and nomadic populations. However recent work in archaeology and anthropology has demonstrated that these forms of settlement are on a continuum and in constant flux. This process is famously described by the 14th-century North African historian Ibn Khaldun, who noted how successful nomadic groups became urban only to return to nomadism once they had become too soft to defend their towns and agriculture.

Urban

Surprisingly little attention has been paid to the archaeology of Islamic cities in Arabia considering their potential relevance to the development of Muslim civilization. One of the few archaeologists to tackle this subject is Donald Whitcomb, as part of his investigations into the origins of the early Islamic city of Aqaba (Whitcomb 1996). The following discussion builds on Whitcomb's work to provide regional summaries of the archaeological evidence for urbanism.

West Arabia (The Hijaz)

In northern Saudi Arabia, the remains of al-Mabiyat (referred to as al-Qurh in the Arabic sources), near al-Ula, are visible on the Hajj road between Damascus and

Medina. Although the settlement has pre-Islamic origins, it appears to have developed into a town during the Umayyad period (see Figure 2.8.1). The town site comprises some rectangular planned enclosures interpreted as a fortified residence and an irregularly shaped settlement of 64 hectares enclosed by a city wall and ditch (Gilmore et al. 1985; Talhi et al. 1986). Dense clusters of primarily domestic buildings separated by open expanses may reflect the tribal urban layout described by Jamel Akbar in relation to the early Islamic garrison towns (Akbar 1990).

Unfortunately the two most important towns in the Hijaz—Mecca and Medina—remain unavailable for archaeological investigation. Although a number of studies based on analysis of historical sources have produced ideas of how they might have appeared in the early Islamic period. Geoffrey King has suggested that Yathrib (pre-Islamic Medina) may simply have been an agglomeration of fortified tribal units each protected by a tower with no definable town center (King 1994). Similarly, Jeddah, the port of Mecca, has not been investigated. It appears to have been founded during the early Islamic period by the caliph Uthman in 647 as an alternative to the pre-Islamic port of al-Shu'ayba (Hawting 1984). Early photographs taken in 1938, before massive modern development, show that Jeddah was a densely built settlement contained within large walls enclosing a roughly oval-shaped area. This area, now known as al-Balad, still

FIGURE 2.8.1 Abandoned mud brick houses in the al-Ain/Buraimi oasis adjacent to one of the early Islamic *qanats* and near to al-Khandaq fort.

survives within the fabric of the modern city and is divided into four quarters, possibly reflecting the land allocations of the 7th century. The old city contains a number of historic buildings which date to the Ottoman or medieval period, including the Uthman ibn Affan mosque. Most of the fabric of this ancient mosque dates to the 13th century although it does contain the remains of an early *mihrab* discovered during restoration work which may date to the Umayyad period (8th century).

Central Arabia (Najd)

The region contains two of the most important sites for investigating Arabian urbanism. The first of these is the site of Qiryat al-Fau located to 500 kilometers to the south-west of Mecca. The settlement covers an area of more than 207 hectares and includes domestic architecture, streets, and a central market place as well as a temple and tombs. The town was founded by the Kinda, a possibly Bedouin tribal group, originally from South Arabia (Bukharin 2009). The site was inhabited from the 3rd century BC up to the 5th century CE and possibly into the Islamic period (al-Ansary 1982). The importance of the city is that it represents an early example of indigenous Bedouin urbanism which may well have had parallels in pre-Islamic Mecca and Yathrib (Medina). The other important site in central Arabia is the 8th-century site of al-Rabadha located on the Hajj route (Darb Zubayda) between Mecca and Baghdad (al-Rashid 1986). The town comprises a number of large semi-fortified structures and areas of intensive domestic settlement separated by large open areas. The entire settlement covers an area of more than 1 square kilometer and includes evidence of manufacturing of glass, steatite, and metalwork. Although the site was settled in the 7th century the main phases of occupation date to the Abbasid period, spanning the 8th and 9th centuries, with evidence of intense activity clustering around the palatial compounds. Whitcomb convincingly suggests that this pattern may reflect a dispersed settlement pattern similar to that suggested by King (King 1994) for pre-Islamic Medina (Yathrib).

South Arabia (Yemen)

The pre-Islamic culture of South Arabia is well known through its inscriptions, statues, and archaeological sites, the most significant of which is Shabwa the pre-Islamic capital of the Hadhrumaut (Bretton 1991). Occupation at Shabwa has been demonstrated from the 4th century BC to the 6th century CE. Numerous houses were identified comprising multistory complexes built on mudbrick platforms with a superstructure of wooden beams. High-rise houses of this type are well known from the nearby city of Shibam (dating to the 16th century CE) and indicate a strong continuity of urban design and architecture from the pre-Islamic period.

Another pre-Islamic urban site where direct continuity to the Islamic period can be demonstrated is the town of Qana on the coast east of Aden (Sedov 1992). Analysis of the excavated material by Whitcomb has shown that it continued to be occupied well into the 8th century (Whitcomb 1996). The later period remains are mostly on lower ground around the pre-Islamic citadel and may be divided into two clusters based on the orientation of the buildings. The differing orientations of each cluster may be significant and may represent a change in population.

Zabid is probably the best known archaeological investigation of a South Arabian Islamic town. The city is located on the Tihama plain on the Red Sea coast of Yemen and was surveyed and excavated by Edward Keall of the Royal Ontario Museum in Toronto (Keall 1983). Although the area of the city was certainly occupied in the pre-Islamic period both the archaeology and the historical sources indicate that it did not develop as a significant town until the 9th century, when it was apparently founded by the Abbasid governor of Yemen, Ibn Ziyad. The plan of the city was supposedly circular, like Baghdad's, although no trace of this early city has so far been found in excavations, with the majority of the remains dating to the medieval period (12th–16th centuries) or later. Nevertheless a circular outline of the city is still visible in the modern topography of the town. Excavations within the fort reinforce the prominent position that Yemen held within the Ottoman Empire during the 16th century both as a maritime frontier against Portuguese influence and also to protect the lucrative coffee trade (see the later section "Food, Diet, and Consumption").

The other city which is likely to contain significant information about the transition to the Islamic period is Sana'a, although this has unfortunately not been the subject of archaeological excavations. However, a detailed architectural and topographic survey of the existing medieval and Ottoman town published by Serjeant and Lewcock in 1983 does give some interesting clues about the city's urban development. Prior to the arrival of Islam Serjeant argues that San'a was a protected area (*hijra*) similar to pre-Islamic Mecca.

Eastern Arabia

There is a considerable evidence for urban settlement in the region prior to the advent of Islam with sites like Muweilah in the emirate of Sharjah (UAE) demonstrating indigenous adaptation to the extremes of the Arabian environment (Magee 2007). Kennet (2005) has argued that there was a decline in urban settlement prior to the arrival of Islam in the 7th century. The only major urban center known to have survived into the Islamic period is the port of Sohar on the Battinah coast of Oman, which was a thriving seaport under both the Sasanians and the Arabs of the early Islamic period. Although considerable archaeological work has taken place around Sohar, work within the modern town has been limited and has not permitted a reconstruction of the early Islamic city (Kerveran 1983). The al-Ain/Buraimi oasis, which is linked to Sohar via the Wadi Jizi, may also have been an urban settlement, and early Islamic ceramics have been found in excavations and surveys associated with a *qanat* system (Petersen 2009). Other examples of early Islamic settlements where the plan of the settlement is visible are at Jumeirah in Dubai (Baramki 1975) and Murwab in Qatar (Guerin and al-Naimi 2009), although it is doubtful whether either of these should be considered an urban settlement (Figure 2.8.1).

Rural Settlement

Archaeologists have paid relatively little attention to the rural environment in Arabia based on a perception that all settled life was to be found in cities, with the areas outside reserved for nomads. This polarized outlook is based on the idea that rural settlements are not viable in the face of continuous Bedouin raids. While it is true that nomadic occupation of an area may inhibit the development of permanent rural settlements this is not always the case, especially where the rural populations belong to the same families or tribal groups as the nomads. Certainly archaeological and ethnographic observation from all parts of Arabia has demonstrated rural settlement in all but the most extreme desert environments.

Some areas are particularly rich and have dense networks of rural settlements, for example in the highlands of Yemen, the Batinah coast of Oman, or the date plantations of the al-Hasa Oasis in Saudi Arabia. In such areas the ecological opportunities for agriculture (plant cultivation or livestock rearing) are so significant that complex systems are developed to ensure that productive capacity of the area is maximized. For example, in Yemen there are highly developed terracing systems, some of which date back to the Bronze Age. The terracing has a number of functions which include stabilization of sediments, efficient water distribution, and optimization of available space. It has been argued that such systems promote population growth. As more terraces are built, larger populations can be supported, which are then capable of bringing more areas into cultivation (Wilkinson 2003: 190). Oman also has terraced agriculture, particularly on the slopes of Jabal Akhdar, some of which can also be dated to the Bronze Age; however, the most notable feature of the region is the development of oasis agriculture through the use of the *falaj* system. While the origins of the *falaj* system are a matter of debate they were certainly well established in Oman by the time of the early Islamic conquest (7th century), and the system seems to have been extended at this time. The main advantage of the *falaj* system is that it utilizes water resources from mountainous areas and transports them to more open and flat areas via subterranean tunnels that minimize water loss through evaporation.

Unlike the *falaj*-dependent oases of eastern Arabia, the oasis of al-Hasa is a natural oasis dependent on a vast underground reservoir of fossil water. As the largest oasis in Arabia the al-Hasa region supports a number of towns and numerous villages and smaller settlements. The area today contains numerous date palm plantations, with an estimated 30 million date palms. It is possible that the oasis was larger in the early Islamic period before sand encroachment on the eastern and northern edges of the oasis. For example, the famous 7th-century village of Juwatha disappeared underneath sand dunes only to be rediscovered in the 1970s (Hidore and Albokhair 1982: 350). Similarly excavations in the vicinity of al-Uqayr and al-Qatif revealed several villages dating from the 10th to the 12th centuries which were later covered with sand (Cornwall 1946: 42). On the basis of these excavations it has been estimated that the cultivated area around Qatif was three times larger in the first millennium CE than it was in the middle of the 20th century.

In addition to these well-known agricultural areas there were rural settlements throughout much of Arabia during the Islamic period. For example in Qatar and Bahrain there were many villages which were dependant on pearl diving. While some of these settlements developed into large cities, such as Zubarah, many others remained as villages occupied by particular family groups. These settlements usually comprise a number of features including a fort and one or more mosques, as well as fish traps built into the shallow intertidal waters. At the other extreme, far from the coast, in the Najd region of Arabia there were a series of oasis towns and villages dating back to prehistoric times. For example, the al-Kharj oasis has revealed a long history of settlement with towns and villages inhabited from the 5th to the 18th centuries (Schiettecatte et al. 2013).

Nomadic Life

Nomadism is one of the best know aspects of Arabian culture; however, very little archaeological research has been carried out into its material traces. There are of course obvious reasons for this, mostly because of the ephemeral nature of many nomadic settlements and also because of the limited range of possessions. There is also the fact that nomadic people have not traditionally been involved in defining the objectives of archaeological research (Figure 2.8.2).

One of the few projects directly addressing the archaeology of nomadic occupation in Arabia is the "Crowded Desert Project" focusing on an area of open desert in North-West

FIGURE 2.8.2 An 18th-century Ottoman fort of Mudawwara in a nomadic area of southern Jordan.

Qatar (Carvajal Lopez et al. 2016). The project considers archaeological remains from all periods over an area of 25 square kilometers which has historically been associated with nomadic occupation. More than 600 features were mapped, including campsites, Islamic and pre-Islamic cemeteries, and mosques of different sizes. Among other findings the project has demonstrated the remarkable adaptability of nomad groups in terms of housing materials, mobility, and location.

FOOD, DIET, AND CONSUMPTION

There is a considerable continuity in the traditional diet across Arabia although there are also significant regional variations. The nomadic diet is based around the consumption of animal products from sheep, goats, and camels as well as a number of plant products, most famously dates. It is probable that chicken was common as a source of protein in sedentary contexts such as towns, villages, and forts as they were not readily compatible with nomadic or semi-nomadic lifestyles (cf. Uerpmann 2017: 5). Wild mammals such as gazelle and hare were also eaten although the available evidence indicates that these formed a small proportion of the overall diet. In addition there is ethnographic and archaeological evidence for the consumption of reptiles such as lizards and turtles. Given that much of the permanent settlement in Arabia is around the coast, it is not surprising that fish formed a major proportion of the diet in most of the excavated sites (see, e.g., Beech 1998, 2003, 2004; Desse and Desse-Berset 2000; Russ and Petersen 2013). There is even evidence for dried fish being consumed by the Bedouin away from the coast. In addition to traditional food sources, both tobacco and coffee were used as stimulants from the 16th century onward.

While publication of faunal data in relation to Islamic period sites in the Middle East in general is relatively rare it is even more unusual from an Arabian context. However, a number of interesting studies can provide some insight into food consumption in pre-modern Arabia. For example the study of the faunal remains from a medieval (13th–14th century) fort of Luluyyah in Sharjah provides a rare snapshot of consumption patterns prior to the arrival of European and Turkish influences in the 16th century (Uerpmann 2017). The finds from the site confirm the dominance of sheep and goat, which together make up more than 50 percent of the faunal remains and account for nearly half of the meat eaten by the inhabitants. In addition chicken remains were identified, which the researchers regarded as compatible with the sedentary lifestyle of the inhabitants of the fort but were probably unsuitable for nomadic or semi-nomadic lifestyles. A similar picture is presented by the faunal remains recovered from the medieval fort at Aqaba in North-West Arabia, where again sheep and goat made up the bulk of the animal products consumed although there were also significant evidence of chicken consumption (51 percent of the bird bones recovered). In addition significant quantities of camel bone were identified, which comprised 25 percent of the edible mammal remains from the Mamluk (1260–1516 CE) period contexts (De Cupere et al. 2017). This pattern is repeated in the faunal remains recovered in recent excavations at

Bilad al-Qadim in Bahrain, where sheep and goat make up the largest proportion and chicken bones are also present in significant numbers (Insoll et al. 2016).

Although archaeobotanical sampling (flotation) has now become common in the region there is still a dearth of published material relating to sites of the Islamic period. However the published data do reveal a wide range of cultivated plants, including cereals. Thus barley and wheat were identified at Kush in Ras al-Khaimah UAE (Kennet 1997: 297), Bilad al-Qadim in Bahrain (Insoll 2005: 253–257), and Qalhat in Oman (Dabrowski et al. 2015). Other crops identified at these sites include lentils, sorghum, dates, olives, and grapes. Dates deserve special consideration because of their economic and cultural importance within Arabia. The entire date palm can be utilized including the leaves for thatch roofing material and the wood for structural timber (although less suitable than most other forms of wood) or as fuel. Date palm plantations form ecosystems which provide shelter for other crops as well as fruit trees. It is interesting that date stones within archaeological contexts are relatively rare, perhaps indicating that the stones were used for other purposes such as fuel for fires or, when soaked, as animal feed. Other indications of the presence of the use of dates as a dietary resource are the *madbassas* date presses which are used both to produce date syrup, *dibs*, and as a means of storing harvested dates (Petersen 2011).

Stimulants

In addition to nutritional plants a number of stimulants are traditionally consumed in Arabia including tobacco, coffee, and *qat*. Tobacco was introduced to Europe from the New World in the 16th century and became prevalent in the Ottoman Empire from the end of the 17th century, when a ban on tobacco was lifted. By the 18th century smoking tobacco in clay pipes was commonplace in the Ottoman Empire, and the habit is often associated with military sites (Simpson 2012: 195–197). In the late 18th century the Wahhabis of the First Saudi State banned smoking in territories under their control (Grehan 2006: 1367). As the primary material evidence for tobacco smoking is clay pipes, the presence or absence of pipes in archaeological contexts can be an interesting means of assessing the degree of Wahhabi influence in a particular area.

While tobacco was certainly a new introduction of the 16th century, coffee also seems to have become popular around the same time. The origins of coffee consumption are obscure although the coffee plant is indigenous to the highlands of Ethiopia and Eritrea. Historical accounts indicate that is was first brought to Yemen in the early 15th century, where it was both cultivated and consumed (Hattox 1985). The early archaeological evidence for coffee consumption includes a single carbonized coffee bean from Kush in Ras al-Khaimah which may date to as early as the 12th century. Other archaeological evidence includes 16th-century coffee cups excavated at the Ottoman Fort of Zabid in Yemen (Keall 2001). Coffee rapidly developed as an internationally sought-after commodity, leading to the growth of Mocha as the principal place of export. The presence of coffee cups on so many post-medieval archaeological sites in Arabia and a strong association with tobacco pipes suggests new lifestyles were developing within the region (cf. Grehan 2006).

Another stimulant associated with the region is the plant *qat*, which was chewed rather than smoked or drunk. It was known as a popular recreational drug among Muslim Arabs as early as the mid-14th century (Kennedy 1987: 60–78). The drug gradually increased in popularity and is now a major part of the economy in Yemen. The archaeological evidence for this stimulant has not so far been investigated although aspects which could be researched include places and means of cultivation, influence on architecture (e.g., through social gatherings), social and economic factors, and its relationship to coffee and tobacco.

TRADE

Arabia is famed for its trading links from the incense routes of antiquity to pearls and oil in the 19th and 20th centuries. Historically the trade can be divided into two main types: maritime commerce and overland trade routes. Maritime trade can be further subdivided into local exchanges within the Red Sea and the Persian Gulf and longer distance connections across the Indian Ocean. Similarly overland trade can be divided into local trade and long-distance trans-Arabian caravans.

Maritime Trade

The Indian Ocean

Indian Ocean trade can be traced through excavations at three sites in Oman: Sohar, Ras al-Hadd, and Qalhat. Together these three sites span a period of nearly 1,000 years of long-distance oceanic trade with India, the Far East, and Eastern Africa. Unfortunately the excavations of the Sasanian and early Islamic port of Sohar have been limited although enough has been revealed to confirm historical records of this being one of the major ports for trade with China (Cleveland 1959; Wilkinson and Costa 1987). Further east at Ras al-Hadd, the easternmost tip of Arabia, there are extensive remains of a maritime trading post which flourished between the 8th and 12th centuries. Ceramics at the site indicate trade with China and the Far East (Celadon), Iran (hatched sgraffiato wares), India (Gujarati water jars), and East Africa (Tana River ceramics with incised decoration). Between Ras al-Hadd and Sohar are the deserted remains of Qalhat, which flourished between the 13th and 16th centuries (Rougelle 2010). Ceramics retrieved from the site included wares from China (Longquan Celadon, blue on white porcelain, brownware jars), Thailand (SiSatchanalai stoneware), Vietnam, and Iran (Khunj, blue-speckled and turquoise wares). It also appears that both glazed and unglazed ceramics were produced in Qalhat itself from the 13th century onward (Rougelle et al. 2014). In addition to ceramics finds, evidence for the mechanism of trade include the remains of more than twenty-five anchors from within the site itself and retrieved from the sea (Vosmer et al. 1999).

The Red Sea

Trade within the Red Sea region can be investigated through the archaeological excavations at Aqaba in Jordan, Zabid in Yemen, and the Sadana Island shipwreck in the northern Red Sea. Remains of the early Islamic city of Ayla (medieval and modern Aqaba) were discovered by Donald Whitcomb in the 1980s and included a rectangular fortified structure which was the nucleus of the site. Evidence of trade included Chinese porcelain (Qingbai and Sung incised wares) and stone (chlorite schist) vessels from southern Arabia, as well as alkaline-glazed blue-green storage jars indicating contact with Iraq and the Persian Gulf. It should be pointed out that Chinese ceramics only appear in any quantity during the 10th and 11th centuries. Most of the evidence for trade relates to Africa, including Aksumite coins from Ethiopia to a hoard of Fatimid coins from Sijilmasa in southern Morocco. Not surprisingly the bulk of the trade represented at Ayla is related to Egypt, represented in the form of ceramics such as Coptic lead glazed ware from Alexandria, lustre ware, and carved ivory plaques.

Although Zabid is located more than twenty kilometers from the sea, it owes it historical significance to its trading connections (Keall 1983, 2001). During the medieval period it was served by a number of ports including al-Fazah and al-Ghlafiqa. Although the city was founded in the 9th century, the greatest period of prosperity appears to have been during the rule of the Rasulid Emirs (1229–1454), when it functioned as their capital. Excavations within the city have revealed trading connections with China, Egypt, and Iraq.

The third site representing the later phases of Red Sea trade is the Sadana Island shipwreck on the northwest coast of The Red Sea. The shipwreck is dated to the mid-18th century and more than 3,000 items were recovered, including 540 Chinese export-quality porcelain tea bowls, tobacco smoking pipes, earthenware water pipes, jewelry, and kitchen utensils as well as a range of organic materials including spices (coriander, cardamom, nutmeg, and pepper), aromatic resin, coffee beans, and coconut husks. The excavators came to the conclusion that the tea bowls were not imported directly from China but were transhipped in one of the other ports active during the Ottoman period, possibly Jeddah or Mocha (Ward 2000).

The Gulf

Trade within the Gulf has shifted between the Arabian and the Iranian littoral, and, during the early Islamic period, was dominated by the Iranian port of Siraf, which was excavated during the 1960s and 1970s. There is little evidence for a major port on the Arabian Gulf Coast during this time although the site of Kush in Ras al-Khaimah appears to have had some importance between the 5th and 12th centuries. Finds from the early Islamic period included ceramics from Iran, Mesopotamia, and India, and the excavator has suggested that it be identified with the site of Julfar mentioned in early Islamic sources (Kennet 2005). A similar picture is presented by the site of Bilad al-Qadim, which appears to have been the principal settlement on the island of Bahrain during the 11th–13th centuries. Recent excavations have confirmed that this was a site with connections to Mesopotamia, Iran, and

China although it does not seem to have been a major port. Thus the excavator concluded "The overall picture . . . is of a settlement supplied through local manufacture of pottery, and imported materials are comparatively rare" (Insoll et al. 2016: 240). The first evidence for a major port from the Islamic period comes from the site of al-Mathaf (medieval Julfar), adjacent to the modern town of Ras al-Khaimah. The major occupation of the site dates from the 14th to the 16th centuries, when there was an increase in glazed and imported Far Eastern ceramics. However this growth seems mostly connected with Julfar's position as a dependency of the Iranian port city of Hormuz.

The arrival of the Portuguese as a military and mercantile presence in the late 15th century added a new dimension to the economic geography of the Gulf. The Portuguese and later other European powers such as the Dutch and the British were keen to establish the Gulf both as a trading area in its own right and as a conduit for trade between India and Europe. This encouraged the development of indigenous trading settlements on the Arabian Gulf Coast, which developed the trade in pearls harvested from a series of pearl banks in the vicinity of Bahrain, Qatar, and the United Arab Emirates (Carter 2005). One example of this process is the site of Ruwayda in northern Qatar. The site started as a small, probably Portuguese fort in the 16th century and developed into a large settlement, 2.5 kilometers long, with three mosques, a series of warehouses, and a palatial residence. The finds from the site indicate a high standard of living with trading connections to Bahrain, Iran, Julfar (UAE), Oman, India, and China (Petersen et al. 2016). Although this was by no means a major port site it was one of a string of such settlements on the Arabian side of the Gulf in the 18th century testifying to the importance of the pearl trade as a result of growing European interest in the area (Carter 2005) (Figure 2.8.3).

FIGURE 2.8.3 Aerial view of Ruwayda in northern Qatar. The earliest enclosure on the right may be a Portuguese fort while the larger enclosure dates to the 18th century.

Overland Trade

Overland trade in the form of camel caravans forms a central part of Arabian culture from the incense routes of the Nabatean to the Hajj routes of the Islamic era. Trade also has a central place within Islamic discourse both because of Muhammad's roles as a merchant trading in Syria and because of the status of pre-Islamic Mecca as a trading city. While the central thesis of Patricia Crone's book, *Meccan Trade and the Rise of Islam* (Crone 1987), has not been generally accepted, it has drawn attention to the role of over-land trade in the development of the early Islamic state. Items traded overland included textiles (specifically silks), leather (possibly parchment), incense and perfumes (myrrh, *kundur, luban*), animals, and either wine or raisins (cf. Serjeant 1990). In addition to these long-distance trade items it is known that foodstuffs including grains such as wheat and barley would have been traded shorter distances—at least from ports to inland settlements such as Mecca and Yathrib (Medina). In terms of archaeology this has yet to be investigated in detail, although the establishment of Mecca as an annual pilgrimage destination meant that the majority of overland trade routes became pil-grimage routes which, over time, were enhanced with various facilities (see the section "Religion"). It is certainly the case that the participants in the annual Hajj were often able to pay for their journey or even make a profit by carrying out trade both along the routes to Mecca and also within the holy city itself.

One of the major commodities that were traded up until the 20th century was slaves. At the height of the slave trade in the 19th century an estimated 800,000 slaves were brought from Africa to the Gulf (Hopper 2015: 39). While slaves are frequently referred to in the historical literature, the archaeological evidence for this trade is often difficult to interpret. It is known that there were slave markets in Doha (Qatar), al-Ain (UAE), Riyadh (Saudi Arabia), and many other cities in Arabia into the 20th century. Consular reports indicate that many of the forts that are found in the region were used to house slaves while in transit, and it is probable that many of the large walled enclosures found in traditional settlements were used as collection points. Certainly the economies of desert settlements such as the al-Ain/Buraimi oasis were heavily dependent on slaves both as a traded commodity and also for intensive work in the agriculture of the date palm plantations (Hopper 2015: 51–79). The conversion of the Ben Jelmood House in Doha into a slavery museum suggests a growing readiness to accept and investigate this aspect of Arabia's past.

INDUSTRY

There is historical evidence for a wide range of manufacturing occupations in pre- and early Islamic Arabia, including textile production, leatherworking, pharmacy, per-fumery and winemaking (Serjeant 1990). However the archaeological evidence for these activities is very limited. The two main industries which are well represented in the archaeological record are mining and pottery production. Historical accounts of mining during the early Islamic period have recently been supplemented by archaeological surveys of mining and smelting sites (Heck 1999). For example, investigation of the al-Baha mining site in western Arabia indicates that three metals (gold, copper, and silver) were being mined and processed between 630 and 1100 CE (al-Zahrani 2014). In addition to producing metal ingots a range of objects were produced, including gold coins minted at Mecca. In Eastern Arabia, from a later period, there is evidence for sulfur mining at Jabla Dhana. The main period of use seems to be the 17th–18th centuries. The mines, which are not mentioned in historical sources, were probably used to supply either the Ottoman or Safavid forces with material for gunpowder (King 2003).

Yemen has a long tradition of ceramic production from the pre-Islamic period up to the present day. Archaeological evidence of medieval production has been demonstrated both on the coastal plain in the vicinity of Zabid (Mason and Keall 1988) and also in the Yemeni highlands (Mahoney 2016). A collection of traditional 20th-century Yemeni pottery in the British Museum demonstrates the continuity of ceramic traditions in south Arabia (Posey 1994). Evidence for ceramic production has been found at a number of sites in Arabia, most notably Julfar, Bahla, and Qalhat. Julfar pottery started being produced in the 14th century and continued in production until the 20th century. The ware is unglazed and has a characteristic dark orange or gray fabric sometimes decorated with red painted marks. Although it is generally hand-shaped there are a few examples that are wheel-made. Production occurred at a number of sites in the vicinity of Julfar, with several kilns identified at each site (Mitsuishi and Kennet 2013). It has been found at many sites throughout the Gulf and even as far away as Kilwa in Tanzania. At Bahla in Oman, pottery production has continued into the 21st century using traditional methods and kilns. Late medieval and early Bahla pottery is wheel-made, of higher quality than the Julfar cooking wares, and is often confused with Khunj pottery from Iran. The ruins of Qalhat, also in Oman, are one of the few sites in Arabia where ceramic kilns have been excavated. It appears that the kilns produced both glazed and unglazed pottery vessels as well as well as ceramic tiles used in the congregational mosque (Rougelle et al. 2014).

RELIGION

The archaeology of religion within Arabia is both rich and problematic. Certainly the region's position as the geographical center of the Muslim world and its connections with the origins of Islam mean that archaeology has the potential to provide some useful insights into the development of this world religion. However there are also considerable sensitivities around the use of archaeology, especially when it is used to investigate either the origins of Islam or various sects and branches of the religion.

Islam

The central focus of all Muslims is the Kaaba complex at the center of the Haram in Mecca. There have been many studies of the building based on historical descriptions and travelers accounts but no detailed archaeological study of either the building itself or its immediate vicinity (for a recent discussion of this building, see O'Meara 2018). The same applies to the Mosque of the Prophet in Medina, where there have also been extensive renovations in recent times which could have provided opportunities for archaeological investigations. This reflects a reluctance on the part of the Saudi state to allow archaeological research to call into question the historicity of their view of the formation of the Muslim religion. The Saudis are also wary of any attempt to make the graves of early Muslims into places of veneration. Ever since the formation of the First Saudi state in the 18th century there has been unease about marked graves and in particular those that were established as shrines. Thus, during the Saudi/Wahabi conquest of the al-Hasa province in eastern Arabia, shrines were destroyed and sacred trees were uprooted. With the conquest of Mecca by the Saudis in 1804, the mausoleums covering the graves of early Muslims in al-Mu'alla were destroyed (Willis 2017: 362). Later, in 1926, the Saudi forces targeted the Baqi' cemetery in Medina, where they destroyed all the mausoleums, including those marking the graves of Muhammad's first wife 'Aisha and his daughter Fatima. Eldon Rutter, who visited the cemetery soon after the event, described "a wilderness of ruined building material and tombstones- not ruined by casual hand, but raked away from their places and ground small" (Rutter 1928, vol. 2: 256–257). Within this context it is worth taking note of the recent French-Saudi archaeological investigations of al-Hejr (Medain Saleh), which potentially provides a challenge to traditional Muslim narratives of the site that associate it with the Thamudic people rather than the Nabateans (see the section "Historiography").

However, away from the holy cities themselves, there has been an interest in investigating aspects of Muslim religious life. One of the first systematic archaeological projects in Saudi Arabia was the investigation of the Darb Zubayda, the 8th-century pilgrimage route between Mecca and Baghdad (al-Rashid 1986). Later research also targeted the Syrian and Egyptian routes, as well as the routes from Yemen (al-Thenayian 1999–2000). Related projects include the investigation of the town of al-Rabadha (al-Ansary 1982), which formed part of the Darb Zubayda. There have also been archaeological surveys of mosques throughout the country in advance of restoration works.

Outside Saudi Arabia there has been more scope for the archaeology of the Muslim religion both in terms of surviving monuments and also in the outlook of the authorities. For example, in Oman there are large numbers of shrines and ancient mosques which have been documented and in some cases excavated. In Yemen there have been studies of madrasas as well as mosques and shrines. Yemen also has examples of cubical mosques which may relate to pre-Islamic temples and share architectural roots with the Kaaba in Mecca (Finster 1991). There have also been some interesting ethno-archaeological studies on Muslim pilgrimage, including documentation of visits to the shrine of Nabi Hud (McCorriston 2011).

Other Religions

The religious significance of Arabia within Islam cannot be overestimated. The importance of Arabia to Muslims is constantly reinforced from the annual pilgrimages to Mecca and Medina to the sacred status of Arabic in the Quran. However the overwhelming importance of Islam in the region has tended to obscure the fact that there have always been other religions present within Arabia. Islamic history makes it clear that both Jews and Christians as well as pagans were present in Arabia during pre-Islamic and early Islamic times. Although many of the Jewish and Christian families will have converted, there is growing archaeological evidence that churches continued to function during the early Islamic period (Carter 2008). The best publicized example is the monastery on Sir Bani Yas island in the United Arab Emirates, which flourished between 600 and 750 CE. During the period of the Himyarite rule in Yemen (115 BC–520 CE), there was a sizeable Jewish community, and in 380 Judaism was adopted as the official religion (Tobi 2013). After the fall of the Himyarite Kindom in 520, Judaism retained a presence until the mid-20th century, when the creation of Israel led many of them to relocate. Although the size of the Jewish community in Yemen is now negligible, Jewish houses and synagogues are still recognizable in San'a (Rathjens 1957). Jews were also present in Oman during the early Islamic period, and a 19th-century Jewish cemetery in Sohar has been preserved even though there is no longer a Jewish indigenous presence in the country.

More surprising than Jewish or Christian remains is the discovery of a possible Indian quarter during archaeological excavations in the Oman port city of Balid. The remains include a warehouse, a cemetery, and a trapezoidal structure which has tentatively been identified as a Hindu temple (Newton and Zarins 2014).

CONCLUSION

The archaeology of the Islamic period in Arabia is still in its early state; however, increasing attention to heritage and culture in the region indicates that it will continue to develop. One of the challenges is the temptation for states to present single-strand narratives of the past, eschewing more complex and ultimately more interesting interpretations of sites. Questions of particular interest for the future include the following: How can an understanding of ancient irrigation systems be used for sustainable agriculture? Why is there so little evidence for medieval (1000–1500) occupation outside a few urban centers. And, how can slavery be investigated through archaeological methods?

References

Akbar, J. 1990. "Khatta and the Territorial Structure of Early Muslim Towns," *Muqarnas*, 6, 22–32.

al-Ansary, A. R. 1982. "Qaryat al-Fau: A Portrait of Pre- Islamic Civilization in Saudi Arabia," *Bulletin of the School of Oriental and African Studies*, 47, 2, 344.

al-Rashid, S. A. 1986. *al-Rabadhah: a portrait of early Islamic civilization in Saudi Arabia* (Riyadh: King Saud University).

al-Thenayian, M. A. R. 1999–2000. *An Archaeological Study of the Yemeni Highland Pilgrim Route Between Sana and Mecca* (Riyadh: Deputy Ministry of Antiquities and Museums).

al-Zahrani, A. A. A. 2014. *Mining in al-Baha Region, South-Western Saudi Arabia in Islamic Era: The Archaeology of Asham* (Unpublished PhD diss., University of York).

Baramki, D. C. 1975. "An Ancient Caravan Station in Dubai," *Illustrated London News* (29 March 1975), 66.

Beech, M. 1998. "Comments on Two Vertebrate Samples from Early Islamic Jazirat al Hulaylah (5th–9th c. AD) and Early Islamic Julfar (mid 14th to 16. c. AD), United Arab Emirates," *Bulletin of Archaeology*, 24, 197–203.

Beech, M. 2003. "The Development of Fishing in the UAE: A Zooarchaeological Perspective," in D. Potts, H. Naboodah, and P. Hellyer (eds.), *Archaeology of the United Arab Emirates. Proceedings of the First International Conference on the Archaeology of the UAE* (London: Trident Press), 290–308.

Beech, M. 2004. *In the Land of the Ichthyophagi: Modelling Fish Exploitation in the Arabian Gulf and Gulf of Omanfrom the 5th Millennium BC to the Late Islamic Period*. BAR International Series 1217 (Oxford: Archaeopress).

Bell, G. 1914. *Palace and Mosque at Ukhaidir: A Study in Early Mohanmadan Architecture* (Oxford: Oxford University Press).

Bretton, J.-F. 1991. "Shabwa et les capitals sud-Arabiques," *Syria*, 68, 419–431.

Bukharin, M. D. 2009. "Toward the Earliest History of Kinda," *Arabian Archaeology and Epigraphy*, 20, 64–80.

Carter, R. 2005. "The History and Prehistory of Pearling in the Persian Gulf," *Journal of the Economic and Social History of the Orient*, 48, 2, 139–209.

Carter, R. 2008. "Christianity in the Gulf During the First Centuries of Islam," *Arabian Archaeology and Epigraphy*, 2018–2019, 71–108.

Carvajal Lopez, J. C., Morabito, L., Carter, R., Fletcher, R., and al-Naimi, F. A. 2016. "The Crowded Desert: A Multi-Phase Archaeological Survey in the North-west of Qatar," *Proceedings of the Seminar for Arabian Studies*, 46, 45–62.

Cleveland, R. 1959. "Preliminary Report on Archaeological Soundings at Sohar (Oman)," *BASOR*, 153, 11–19.

Cornwall, P. B. 1946. "Ancient Arabia: Explorations in Hasa, 1940–1941," *The Geographical Journal*, 107, 1, 28–50.

Crone, P. 1987. *Meccan Trade and the Rise of Islam* (Princeton: Princeton University Press).

Dabrowski, V., Ros, J., Tengberg, M., and Rougelle, A. 2015. "De l'origine de l'utilisation des resources végétales en Oman medieval: première etude archaéobotanique á Qalhât," *Routes de l'Orient Revue d'archéologie de l'Orient Ancien*, 2, 1–13.

de Cardi, B. 1978. *Qatar Archaeological Report: Excavations 1973* (Doha: Qatar National Museums).

De Cupere, B., Ervynk, A., Udrescu, M., Van Neer, W., and Wouters, W. 2017. "Faunal Analysis of the Castle of Aqaba (Jordan): Preliminary Results," in M. Mashkour and M. Beech (eds.), *Archaeozoology of the Near East* (Oxford: Oxbow), 443–471.

Desse, J., and Desse-Berset, N. 2000. "Julfar (Ras al Khaimah, Emirats Arabes Unis),ville por-tuaire du golfe arabo-persique (VIIIe–XVIIe siecles); exploitation des mammiferes et des poissons," in M. Mashkour, A. M. Choyke, H. Buitenhuis, and F. Poplin (eds.), *Archaeozoology of the Near East IVB: Proceedings of the Sixth International Symposium on the Archaeozoology of Southwestern Asia and Adjacent Areas* (Gronigen: ARC—Publicatie 32), 79–93.

Finster, B. 1991. "Cubical Yemeni Mosques," *Proceedings of the Seminar for Arabian Studies: Oxford 24-26 July 1990*, 21, 49–68.

Folsach, K. V., Lundbæk, T., and Mortensen, P. (eds.) 1996. *The Arabian Journey: Danish Connections with the Islamic World over a Thousand Years* (Moesgård: Forhistorisk Museum).

Gilmore, M., Ibrahim, M. Mursi, G., and al-Talhi, A. 1985. "A Preliminary Report on the First Season of Excavations at al-Mabiyat, an Early Islamic Site in the Northern Hijaz," *ATLAL*, 9, 109–125 and Plates 97–116.

Grehan, J. 2006. "Smoking and 'Early Modern' Sociability: The Great Tobacco Debate in the Ottoman Middle East (Seventeenth to Eighteenth Centuries)," *American Historical Review*, December 2006, 1352–1377.

Guerin, A., and al-Naimi, F. 2009. "Territory and Settlement Patterns During the Abbasid Period (Ninth Century AD): The Village of Murwab (Qatar)," *Proceedings of the Seminar for Arabian Studies*, 39,181–196.

Hansman, J. 1985. *Julfar: an Arabic Port: Its Settlement and Far Eastern Ceramic Trade from the 14th to the 18th Centuries* (London: Royal Asiatic Society/Routledge).

Hattox, R. 1985. *Coffee and Coffee Houses: The Origins of a Social Beverage in the Medieval Near East* (Seattle and London: University of Washington Press).

Hawting G. R. 1984. "The Origin of Jedda and the Problem of al-Shuʿayba," *Arabica*, November 1984, 318–326 and T. 31, Fasc. 3.

Heck, G. W. 1999. "Gold Mining in Arabia and the Rise of the Islamic State," *Journal of the Economic and Social History of the Orient*, 42, 3, 364–395.

Hidore, J. J., and Albokhair, Y. 1982. "Sand Encroachment in Al-Hasa Oasis, Saudi Arabia," *Geographical Review*, 72, 3 (July 1982), 350–356.

Hopper, M. S. 2015. *Slaves of One Master. Globalization and Slavery in Arabia in the Age of Empire* (New Haven and London: Yale University Press).

Insoll, T. 2005. *The Land of Enki in the Islamic Period Pearls Palms and Religious Identity in Bahrain* (London: Routledge).

Insoll, T., Almahari, S., MacLean, R., Priestman, S., al-Meeraj, M., and Overton, N. J. 2016. "Bilad al-Qadim Revisited: Recent Archaeological Research at the Al-Khamis Mosque, Ain Abu Zaydanand Abu Anbra, Bahrain," *Arabian Archaeology and Epigraphy*, 27, 215–242.

Keall, E. J. 1983. "The Dynamics of Zabid and Its Hinterland: The Survey of a Town on the Tihamah plain of North Yemen," *World Archaeology*, 14, 3, 378–392.

Keall, E. J. 2001. "The Evolution of the First Coffee Cups in Yemen," in M. Tuchscherer (ed.), *Le commerce du café avant l'ère des plantations coloniales: espaces, réseaux, sociétés (XVe–XIXe siècle)*. Cahier des annales islamologiques 20. CIRAD-CP-CAFE, IREMAM (Le Caire: IFAO), 35–50.

Kennedy, J. G. 1987. *The Flower of Paradise; The Institutionalized Use of the Drug Qat in North Yemen* (Dordecht, Netherlands: Springer).

Kennet, D. 1997. "Kush. A Late Sasanian Early Islamic Tell in Ras al-Khaimah UAE," *Arabian Archaeology and Epigraphy*, 8, 284–302.

Kennet, D. 2005. "On the Eve of Islam: Archaeological Evidence from Eastern Arabia," *Antiquity*, 79, 303, 107–118.

Kerveran, M., Soubeyran, M., and Vialatte de Pemille, A. 1983. "Suhari Houses," *The Journal of Oman Studies*, 307–316

King, G. R. D. 1993. "Creswell's Appreciation of Arabian Architecture," *Muqarnas*, 8, 94–102.

King, G. R. D. 1994. "Settlement in Western and Central Arabia and the Gulf in the 6th–8th Centuries AD," in G. R. D. King and A. Cameron (eds.), *The Byzantine and Early Islamic Near East, Vol. II: Land Use and Settlement Patterns* (New York: Darwin Press), 181–212.

King, G. R. D. 2003. *Sulphur, Camels and Gunpowder: The Sulphur Mines at Jebel Dhanna, Abu Dhabi, United Arab Emirates: An Archaeological Site of the Late Islamic Period* (Abu Dhabi: Abu Dhabi Islands Archaeological Survey).

McCorriston, J. 2011. *Pilgrimage and Household in the Ancient Near East* (Cambridge: Cambridge University Press).

Magee, P. 2007. "Beyond the Desert and the Sown: Settlement Intensification in Late Prehistoric Southeastern Arabia," *Bulletin of the American Schools of Oriental Research*, 347, 83–105.

Mahoney, D. 2016. "Ceramic Production in the Yemeni Central Highlands During the Islamic Period," in S. McPhillips and P. Wordsworth (eds.), *Landscapes of the Islamic World: Archaeology, History, and Ethnography* (Philadelphia: University of Pennsylvania Press), 129–142.

Mason, R., and Keall, E. 1988. "Provenance of Local Ceramic Industry and the Characterization of Imports: Petrography of Pottery from Medieval Yemen," *Antiquity*, 62, 452–463.

Mitsuishi, G., and Kennet, D. 2013. "Kiln Sites of the Fourteenth–Twentieth-Century Julfar Ware Pottery Industry in Ras al-Khaimah, UAE," *Proceedings of the Seminar for Arabian Studies*, 43, 225–238.

Newton, L., and Zarins, J. 2014. "A Possible Indian Quarter at al-Baleed in the Fourteenth to Seventeenth Centuries AD?," *Proceedings of the Seminar for Arabian Studies*, 44, 257–276.

O'Meara, S. 2018. *The Kaaba: Orientations in the Place of Islam* (Edinburgh: Edinburgh University Press).

Petersen, A. D. 2009. "Islamic Urbanism in Eastern Arabia: The Case of the al-'Ayn- al-Buraymi Oasis," *Proceedings of the Seminar for Arabian Studies*, 39, 307–320.

Petersen, A. D. 2011. "Research on an Islamic Period Settlement at Ras 'Ushayriq in Northern Qatar and Some Observations on the Occurrence of Date Presses," *Proceedings of the Seminar for Arabian Studies*, 41, 245–256.

Petersen, A. D. 2016. "Building the Past: Archaeology and National Development in the Gulf," in P. Erskine-Loftus, V. Hightower, and M. al-Mulla (eds.), *Representing the Nation: Museums in the Gulf* (London: Routledge), 95–108.

Petersen, A. D., al-Naimi, F. A., Grey, T., Edwards, I., Hill, A., Russ, H., and Williams, D. 2016. "Ruwayda: An Historic Urban Settlement in North Qatar," *Post-Medieval Archaeology*, 50, 2, 321–349.

Posey, S. 1994. *Yemeni Pottery* (London: British Museum Publications).

Rathjens, C. 1957. *Jewish Domestic Architecture in San'a, Yemen: With an Appendix on Seventeenth Century Documents Relating to Jewish Houses in San'a*. Oriental notes and studies (Jerusalem: Oriental Society).

Rougelle, A. 2010. "The Qalhat Project: New Research at the Medieval Harbour Site of Qalhat, Oman (2008)," *Proceedings of the Seminar for Arabian Studies*, 43, 303–320.

Rougelle, A., Renel, H., Simsek, G., and Colomban, P. 2014. "Medieval Ceramic Production at Qalhat, Oman, a Multidisciplinary Approach," *Proceedings of the Seminar for Arabian Studies*, 43, 299–316.

Russ, H., and Petersen, A. D. 2013. "Fish and Fishing During the Late Islamic Period at Rubayqa, Northern Qatar: Preliminary Results," *Proceedings of the Seminar for Arabian Studies*, 43, 277–283.

Rutter, E. 1928. *The Holy Cities of Arabia*. Vols.1 and 2 (London: Putnam).

Schiettecatte, J., al-Ghazzai, A., Charlroux, G., Crassard, R., Hilbert, Y., Monchot, H. Mouton, M., and Simeon, P. 2013. "The Oasis of al-Kharj Through Time: The First Results of Archaeological Fieldwork in the Province of Riyadh (Saudi Arabia)," *Proceedings of the Seminar for Arabian Studies*, 43, 285–308.

Sedov A. V. 1992. "New Archaeological and Epigraphic Material from Qana (South Arabia)," *Arabian Archaeology and Epigraphy*, 3, 64–80.

Serjeant, R. B. 1990. "Meccan Trade and the Islam: Misconceptions and Flawed Polemics," *Journal of the American Oriental Society*, 110, 3 (July—September 1990), 472–486.

Serjeant, R. B., and Lewcock, R. (eds.) 1983. *Ṣanā', an Arabian Islamic City* (London: World of Islam Festival Trust and Scorpion Books).

Simpson, St. J. 2012. "Finds from Qal'at 'Unaiza and Other Ottoman Forts on the Darb al-Hajj," in A. Petersen (ed.), *The Medieval and Ottoman Hajj Route in Jordan; an Archaeological and Historical Study* (Oxford: Oxbow).

Talhi, D., Ibrahim, M., Mursi, J., and Askubi, K. 1986. "Excavations at Mabiyat, Second Season 1404–1405/1984–1985," *ATLAL*, 10, 58–63 and Plates 65–72.

Thalen, D. C. P. 1979. *Ecology and Utilization of Desert Shrub Rangelands in Iraq* (The Hague: Dr. W. Junk bv Publishers).

Tobi, Y. 2013. "The Jews of Yemen in Light of the Excavation of the Jewish Synagogue in Qanī'," *Proceedings of the Seminar for Arabian Studies*, 43, 1–8.

Uerpmann, M. 2017. "Faunal Remains from the Islamic Fort at Luluyyah (Sharjah, UAE)," *Arabian Archaeology and Epigraphy*, 28, 2–10.

Vosmer, T., Agius, D., Baker, P., and Cave, S. 1999. *Oman Maritime Heritage Project Filed Report 1998 (Western Australian Maritime Museum Report No. 144)* (Perth: Western Australian Maritime Museum).

Ward, C. 2000. "The Sadana Island Shipwreck a Mid-eighteenth Century Treasure Trove," in U. Baram and L. Carrol (eds.), *A Historical Archaeology of the Ottoman Empire: Breaking New Ground* (Plenum, New York: Kluwer Academic), 186–202.

Whitcomb, D. 1996. "Urbanism in Arabia," *Arabian Archaeology and Epigraphy*, 7, 38–51.

Wilkinson, T. J. 2003. *Archaeological Landscapes of the Near East* (Tucson: Arizona University Press).

Wilkinson, T. J., and Costa, P. M. 1987. "The Hinterland of Sohar Archaeological Surveys and Excavations Within the Region of an Omani Seafaring City," *Journal of Oman Studies*, 9, 9–144.

Willis, J. 2017. "Governing the Living and the Dead, Mecca and the Emergence of the Saudi Biopolitical State," *American Historical Review*, April 2017, 346–370.

FURTHER READING

Kennet, D., Deadman, W. M., and al-Jahwari, N. S. 2016. "The Rustaq-Batinah Archaeological Survey," *Proceedings of the Seminar for Arabian Studies*, 46, 155–168.

Schmidt, K. 2012. *Das umayyadische "Wüstenschloss" und die Siedlung am Gabal Says. Band I: Architektur*. Damaszener Forschungen (Darmstadt: von Zabern).

OTTOMAN EUROPE

IBOLYA GERELYES, ATHANASIOS VIONIS, VESNA
BIKIĆ, NICULINA DINU, AND SVITLANA BILIAIEVA

INTRODUCTION

THE Exalted Ottoman State, namely the Ottoman Empire, acquired extensive territories in South-Eastern and Central Europe. Some became Ottoman vassal states (e.g., Wallachia, Moldavia, the Crimean Khanate) while others were under direct Ottoman rule (e.g., Bulgaria, Greece, Serbia). Hungary's position was unique in that, following the Battle of Mohács in 1526, the middle part of it came under direct Ottoman rule while the eastern one (Transylvania; today, along with Wallachia and Moldavia, part of Romania) became a vassal state of the Porte.

There were differences between the various territories—as attested by the archaeological record also—depending on whether they were frontier regions or parts of the interior and on whether the populations of the countries or regions in question were predominantly Muslim or Christian at the time of conquest.

Despite these factors and geographical and economic dissimilarities, in each territory of Ottoman Europe uniformity and sameness are detectable in the archaeological record, in changes to townscapes (including the introduction of Ottoman buildings), and in the design and construction of fortifications.

Ottoman soldiers dwelt in fortifications and Ottoman civilians in towns first and foremost. In these places similar or identical changes characteristic of the entire region are to be found.

In the towns, the different religious and ethnic groups lived in separate *mahalles* formed in proximity to their respective places of worship: namely, Friday mosques, Christian churches, and synagogues. Buildings associated with Islam and a Muslim way of life made their appearance on territories where none had stood before. But since in the various territories the so-called imperial style did not gain ground at the same rate, the architectural legacy was not completely uniform. A significant number of Muslim buildings reflected local building traditions (e.g., some Friday mosques had pitched roofs, not domes).

Similar tendencies regarding the fate of the Ottoman architectural legacy may be observed in Bulgaria, Serbia, and in the Ottoman-occupied parts of Hungary. Of the once very numerous Ottoman buildings, only a few now remain. Belgrade and Sofia have just one functioning Ottoman Friday mosque each. In places where there were no longer Muslim inhabitants after the period of Ottoman rule, Friday mosques were in some cases converted (or converted back) to Christian churches. In Buda, for example, the remains of an Ottoman Friday mosque are incorporated in the Capuchin Church we see today. Many Ottoman buildings were used for secular purposes.

Considering the diversity of the Empire's inhabitants, researching the lands under Ottoman rule belongs only partly to the field of Islamic archaeology. However, in the context of the Ottoman Empire as a whole, it is clear that analysis of the archaeological legacy of the non-Muslim subjects of the Empire has its place in Ottoman archaeological research and, therefore, constitutes a part of Islamic archaeology.

The written sources lend background and credibility to archaeological research and to investigations of historical monuments. An abundance of written sources relating to the period is available to researchers. A fruitful approach is to use Ottoman and West European sources together and to compare the results with the findings of archaeology. In this sense, archaeological research into the Ottoman period in Europe represents a branch of historical archaeology.

The archaeology of the Ottoman Empire counts as a young branch of European scholarship, one which has come to the fore only in the past decades. It therefore lacks the tradition enjoyed by research into earlier eras (e.g., the Roman Empire period). In many countries, Ottoman culture has been seen as alien, and research into it has been overshadowed. All this explains why the Ottoman period in Europe may appear as a Dark Age.

With regard to periodization, in the different territories conquest by the Ottomans is seen as marking the end of the medieval state, and therefore of the Middle Ages, along with the beginning of a new era.

In what follows, archaeological research on the European territories of the one-time Ottoman Empire is discussed in five short sections. These aim to identify differences and similarities between countries formerly independent but now joined in a unit. Each section contains a short historical summary and an account of the research, as well as details concerning surviving architectural legacy, settlement structure, and material culture.

THE ARCHAEOLOGY OF OTTOMAN GREECE

A popular view of the Ottoman period in the Eastern Mediterranean, after the conquest of Constantinople by the Ottoman Turks in 1453, is of a long era of continuous oppression of the Orthodox Christian populations, one characterized by negative effects on economy, daily life, and population densities. However, the study of the archaeology of this long historical period in Greece has seen a noteworthy development over the past

20 years in terms of archaeological excavation, conservation projects, surface surveys, and the publication of travelers' accounts and textual data from the Ottoman imperial archives (see Kiel 1999; Sigalos 2004; Zarinebaf et al. 2005; Davies and Davis 2007; Brouskari 2008; Vionis 2012, 2016; Bintliff 2014; Sariyannis 2014; Kolovos 2015). This is changing our understanding of the complex and rich social and economic history of the period.

The rise of field archaeology and the undertaking of intensive surface surveys by foreign schools of archaeology in the 1980s and 1990s essentially gave birth to the archaeological exploration of the period. The study of settlement patterning and layout of deserted and still inhabited villages aimed at the understanding and interpretation of the spatial arrangement of material culture and lifestyles in rural areas. Such a study was initiated in central Greece by the Durham-Cambridge Boeotia Project (Bintliff 1995, 1997, 1999; Kiel 1997) in the 1980s and later on by its successor, the Ancient Cities of Boeotia Project (Vionis 2006, 2008; Bintliff 2012: 436–477) through the examination of remaining surface traces of houses, surface ceramics, Ottoman village archival registers, and old maps.

The period of Pax Ottomanica during the second half of the 15th and most of the 16th centuries saw a tremendous demographic recovery and significant economic growth. This is attested by the surviving Ottoman *tahrir defterleri* (tax registers) for central Greece and several Aegean islands of the late 15th, 16th, and 17th centuries, with settlement mushrooming in the countryside and the rapid development of urban centers (Kiel 1997, 1999, 2007; Kolovos 2017). This development and recovery at all levels seems to have lasted until the 1580s, when the Golden Age reached its end and the Ottoman Empire entered a period of political, military, and social crisis, leading to inflation and fiscal exploitation of the peasantry, which was gradually weakened (Kiel 1997: 331; Bintliff 2012: 448–450). Consequently, many of the prospering villages originating in the 15th and 16th centuries were reduced in size while others were broken up into a number of small *çiftliks* (serf estates or commercial farms) with the rise of tax-farming during the 17th century (İnalcık 1972, 1991; Vionis 2016: 355). The 18th century seems to have been a period of slight economic and demographic recovery, as attested in tax registers, which record *çiftliks* grown to large estates with considerable numbers of inhabitants (Kiel 1997: 337–339; Bintliff 2012: 448).

Towns on the Greek peninsula expanded throughout the early period of Ottoman domination. They developed in quarters or different neighborhoods (*mahalle*) according to religious or ethnic affiliation and were centered around important mosques, churches, or synagogues; religious schools (*medrese*); bathhouses (*hamam*); and open or covered markets (*bedestan*) (Faroqhi 1997; Bintliff 2014). The depiction of the upper bazaar of Athens by Edward Dodwell in the early 19th century is a characteristic example. The gradual investment of towns in much of central and northern Greece in the textile industry during the 18th and early 19th centuries led to the accumulation of capital in the hands of a rising Greek urban elite, which found means of expressing its wealth through the construction of churches and elaborate timber-framed storeyed housing (Figure 2.9.1) (Kiel 1990; Kizis 1994; Sigalos 2004).

FIGURE 2.9.1 Timber-framed, storeyed houses at the village of Portaria, Pelion, by Edward Dodwell, 1819. https://commons.wikimedia.org/wiki/File:Dodwell_Portaria.jpg

Hamlets and *ciftliks* of the Ottoman period in mainland Greece were established around a large tower-house (*konak*), the residence of the great holder/lord (*Derebey*). *Ciftliks* spread throughout central Greece and developed as a means of investing in agriculture and irrigation works and controlling grain production for the markets of Western Europe. Harmena and Ginossati (two archaeologically explored sites in Boeotia), for example, were *ciftliks* with the typical Balkan layout. They preserve the ruins of a *konak* with a number of dispersed humble single-storey long-houses stretching below it (Vionis 2016: 361). The tradition of the long house in mainland Greece dates back to the late Middle Ages; it comprises a "peasant" house-type, built of stone or mud-brick, that survived throughout the Ottoman and early modern periods and provided a single room and undivided space for housing humans and stock under the same roof (Stedman 1996; Sigalos 2004; Vionis 2016).

Aegean island communities, on the other hand, maintained the established layout of the medieval town forms to a large degree. For example, Chora, the main town of the Cycladic island of Naxos, developed during the Ottoman period immediately outside its large late medieval defended center. Chora expanded through time, while newcomers, older inhabitants, and different groups formed different neighborhoods (Greeks in "Bourgo" and "Agora," Jews in "Evriaki," refugees from Asia Minor and Crete in "Nio Chorio") (Kouroupaki et al. 1988). Apart from the need to house newcomers and their commercial activities in an economically developing society from the 18th century onward, Chora's layout reflects the need of different populations to group themselves according to different religious beliefs, languages, and ethnic backgrounds (Vionis 2003: 201).

Pottery assemblages from Ottoman-period surveyed and excavated sites in Greece include a variety of shapes such as large storage vessels, cooking pots, medium-sized transport/storage jars, and small serving jugs (*ibrik* type). Decorated tableware consists mainly of plain glazed jugs and large painted dishes with broad everted rims. Pottery produced locally during the Ottoman period is noted to have lost the refinement of shape and decoration that characterized ceramics of the medieval era. With the exception of the more sophisticated tin-glazed imported wares from Italy (*maiolica* from Faenza, Deruta, and Montelupo) and Turkey (*İznik* ware), or their local imitations in Greece (*pseudo-maiolica* ware from Athens), the greater part of post-medieval local glazed pottery is rather thickly potted with carelessly broad *sgraffito* or painted designs (see Aslanapa et al. 1989; Hayes 1992; Korre-Zographou 1995; Poole 1997; Vroom 2003; Vionis 2012, 2016; MacKay 2015). What is more important, however, is the increased availability of glazed wares against unglazed/domestic wares at urban and rural sites during the Ottoman period.

The study of table pottery, social habits, and domestic daily life in a bottom-up approach in the Ottoman provinces has increased (Faroqhi 1986; Anastasopoulos 2012; Vionis 2012; Sariyannis 2014). Interestingly, one can identify two distinct trends of daily and dining habits in Ottoman Greece through the examination of material culture, textual, and visual sources. The first has to do with an "Eastern" lifestyle of the Greek elite and the peasantry, dining at a low table, sitting on the floor, and eating from a large communal copper tray, as narrated by Edward Clarke (1812/1816) and Edward Dodwell (1819) on the occasion of their visits to Levadeia in Boeotia and Crisso in Phocis. The second perspective has to do with a "Western" trend, identified in Ottoman-dominated areas with a stronger Western presence, such as Crete, the Ionian Islands, and the Cyclades. The material culture record and pictorial evidence (religious icons depicting meals) illustrate individual cutlery utensils, plates, glass wine jugs, and drinking glasses, with diners seated on carved stools or even chairs and armchairs around a table with a high top, suggesting separation of household activities and dedicated space for dining (Vionis 2012: 315–320).

Slavic Regions (Balkan Peninsula)

The Balkan Peninsula takes its name from the Balkan Mountains in its east. The term "Balkans" came into use with the arrival of the Ottomans and is perhaps derived from the Turkish word *balkanlik*, meaning "thickly wooded mountains" or "rugged area." The peninsula stretches from the Sava and the Danube rivers in the north to Greece and the Peloponnese in the south; it is bounded on three sides by seas—the Ionian and Mediterranean seas to the west and south, the Aegean Sea to the southeast, and the Black Sea to the northeast. This hilly and wooded area is intersected by the valleys of the

Morava, Nišava, Vardar, and Maritsa rivers—the main communication routes—and their tributaries. In Ottoman times, too, the Balkan Peninsula was rich in ore, particularly silver, as well as in cattle, leather, wool, wood, rock, and different foods.

The northern parts of the Balkans are characterized by a Middle European climate and the southern parts by a Mediterranean one, providing a favorable environment for a variety of crops and cattle breeds. Contributing to the foodstuffs already found there, the Ottomans brought bulgur, tarhana, and rice—the most important ingredients in their cuisine. The main vegetables were cabbage and onion; also grown were lentils, beans, vetch (*burçak*), spinach, carrots, beets, and courgettes (Zirojević 2005). Fish of different sorts were widely consumed. In addition to vineyards, there were orchards for fruits of different kinds. Fruit was used both fresh and dried; served with honey, it was a special treat.

The Ottoman conquest of the Balkans took more than a century. During the first phase, Bulgaria, between 1393 and 1396, Macedonia, and Thessaly were occupied, between 1393 and 1396. Then, after the fall of Constantinople in 1453, the medieval states of Serbia and Bosnia were swiftly conquered, in 1459 and 1463, respectively. In Hungarian hands by then, Belgrade was besieged unsuccessfully by the Ottomans in 1440 and 1456; it was only on August 29, 1521, that their troops finally captured the town. By the early 16th century, the Ottoman Empire was already the leading power in the Balkans. It lost territory in Hungary and Croatia under the terms of the Peace of Karlowitz in 1699, but continued to hold most of the Balkans until well into the second half of the 19th century. At the Congress of Berlin in 1878, Serbia, Montenegro, and Romania were granted full independence; Bulgaria remained part of the Ottoman Empire but was given autonomy within it. For their part, Macedonia, Kosovo, and the Sanjak of Novi Pazar remained under the direct Ottoman rule until the Balkan Wars of 1912–1913, while Bosnia and Herzegovina became part of Austria–Hungary.

The conquest represented a great political, social, and cultural turning point for the Slavic peoples of the Balkans. The Ottomans embraced many of the institutions they encountered there, integrating the local *pronoia* system with their own *timar* version of it, retaining mining legislation in its entirety, and preserving military organization. The legal status of the Orthodox Church was clarified, and, in the case of Christians, the application of Sharia law was rather flexible. All this helped the inhabitants conform with the new order and helped the conquerors strengthen their authority.

Although there were local differences, the Balkans under the Ottomans formed an entity clearly definable in geographical, social, and cultural terms. Similar patterns of cultural change can be identified throughout the peninsula during the long period of Ottoman rule, which must owe something to geographical similarities, as well as to the linguistic and social developments observable in the archaeological record. Regrettably, in the Balkan countries, archaeological research on this era may be described as meager, especially given its potential. The reasons for this should be sought primarily in a reluctance to study the region's Ottoman past. Furthermore, very few monuments outlived the end of Ottoman rule. For example, of the more than 200 mosques that once stood in Belgrade, just one still exists; and of the more than seventy that used to exist in Sofia, likewise only a single example survives.

Archaeological excavations conducted at multiple sites have yielded important data regarding the "Ottomanization" of the Balkans. Especially noteworthy are the digs conducted at the major administrative, military, and economic centers of Sofia, Skopje (Mitrevski 2007), and Belgrade (Popović and Bikić 2004; Bikić 2007) (Figure 2.9.2), as well as at the mining town of Novo Brdo (Jovanović et al. 2004), where investigations were performed in 2015 as part of a UNESCO-funded preservation and presentation project. But no less important are the excavations at Stari Bar, as everyday life there was in many ways similar to that in the Balkan hinterlands (Guštin et al. 2008; Gelichi 2006, 2008). Such archaeological fieldwork, complemented by text-based research, is shedding light on ways the Ottoman conquest transformed settlements and is delineating the basic contours of daily life in religiously and culturally heterogeneous communities.

In spite of sporadic colonization from Anatolia, the Slavic population remained predominant in Balkan villages and towns. Regrettably, there are almost no archaeological traces of villages from this period. Written sources infer that medieval settlement organization did not undergo significant changes. Depending on the climate, modest houses had porches. The inner space was organized around the fireplace—more rarely a tiled stove—in the middle of the room or against a partition wall (Redžid 1983: 87;

FIGURE 2.9.2 Belgrade in the mid-19th century. Color lithograph by Johann Georg Friedrich Poppel. 1845–1850.

Courtesy of Belgrade City Museum.

Marjanović-Vujović 1973). There were few towns established in the Balkans in the Ottoman era, and most were small. Pre-Ottoman towns—Belgrade, Smederevo, Niš, Sofia, Rudnik, Plovdiv, Edrine, Prizren, Novo Brdo, Priština, Trepča—continued to develop. Their inhabitants were of different races, ethnicities, and confessions; together with Muslims and Orthodox and Catholic Christians of diverse origins, there were Jews and Gypsies as well. The process of transformation from a fortified medieval to a Balkan town started immediately after the Ottoman conquest. Churches were turned into mosques, and caravanserais were constructed, along with multifunctional buildings combining the functions of *imaret* and *zawiye* (Popović 2006; Mitrevski 2007: 30–32; Boykov 2010, 2011). Around these new landmarks clustered *mahala*s—neighbor-hoods—inhabited by people of the same religious or ethnic background, or by members of the same guild (*esnaf*) (Šabanović 1970: 13–14). Preexisting buildings continued to be used and new ones were constructed from wood or from post and petrail (Popović and Bikić 2004: 109–130). Homes were equipped with traditional Ottoman household objects, such as İznik pottery (Bikić 2007).

Muslim and Christian *mahala*s outside the fortified areas were not different from one another. The agents of Islamization were, first and foremost, converts who contin-ued to live in their houses. This led to the gradual adoption of Ottoman culture by Slavic societies; it is therefore very hard to judge the ethnic affiliation of particular households by archaeological means. In time, the spatial organization of dwellings began to follow Ottoman fashions: the ground floor featured a kitchen and storeroom while the upper level consisted of spaces for male socialization (*selamlik*) and for family life (*haremlik*), with a central hall and reception room (Bušatlić 2011: 122–127). In Belgrade, a major distribution center for various commodities, ground floors were most often occupied by stockrooms and shops (Marjanović-Vujović 1973). More recently, research has shifted its focus to the study of daily life through analyses of archaeological contexts and categories of archaeological finds with broader social implications, such as pottery (Bikić 2017; Pletnov 2004) and clay pipes (Stančeva and Nikolova 1989; Asparuhov 1993; Todorov 2010; Bekić 2010; Gačić 2011; Bikić 2012). Ongoing archaeological and archaeometric investigations into technological and stylistic features of pottery point to inclusion of local Balkan Christians—Serbs, Bulgarians, and Greeks—in the production process.

The material culture of everyday life reflects the cultural hybridity that resulted from the incorporation of these territories into the Ottoman Empire. The distinctive culture of the Balkans emerged from the admixture of persisting traditions and a visual manifesta-tion of the culture of the conquerors. A recent discovery was the burial of a young woman in the village of Bubanj near Niš who was dressed in Serbian embroidered clothes, with rich jewelry reflecting Ottoman-era designs. The local population was not entirely unfa-miliar with this new, eclectic, cultural model—although it was different in its political and social discourse—as it drew on Byzantine and Mediterranean templates. Albeit modified, it very much resembled the heritage revived in the work of the local 16th- and 17th-century Balkan artisans employed by the Ottomans (Karamehmedović 1980: 69–79; Ivanić 1995; Gajić 2014; Bikić 2017: 213–215).

HUNGARIAN TERRITORIES

Scholarly interest in the material evidence of Ottoman rule in Hungary, in surviving buildings primarily, began in the mid-19th century. In 1868, the Archaeological Committee of the Hungarian Academy of Sciences declared its support for investigation of such buildings in the long term also and for the publication of findings obtained.

After capturing Belgrade (in 1521), seizing the southern Hungarian border castles (between 1521 and 1524), and prevailing at the Battle of Mohács under Sultan Süleyman the Magnificent (in 1526), the Ottomans were well placed to take Buda and its surrounding region. Yet the creation of the Budin Eyalet and its addition to the Ottoman Empire occurred only in 1541. Concluded in 1568, the Peace of Adrianople confirmed the status quo as it then was: namely, that the Kingdom of Hungary was already split into three parts. The middle section was joined to the Ottoman Empire; it would remain so right up until the Peace of Karlowitz (1699), which marked the Ottomans' withdrawal from Hungary.

Having earlier belonged to the Kingdom of Hungary, Transylvania was, during the period 1541–1690, a vassal state of the Ottoman Empire whose culture exerted direct influence on it. This was shown by the use there of Ottoman luxury products, chiefly at the Gyulafehérvár princely court. But apart from İznik wall tiles (Behrens-Abouseif 2005) and other high-quality ceramic products, no evidence of these artifacts has yet emerged in the archaeological record for Transylvania.

On Hungarian territory, Ottoman conquest was not accompanied by large-scale Muslim immigration. At no point did the Muslim inhabitants number more than 50,000–80,000 individuals, a group roughly one-tenth of the size of the Hungarian population present (800,000–850,000 persons) (Dávid 1998). Muslims from Anatolia did not move to villages in the Ottoman-controlled Hungarian areas. Mass Islamization did not occur. Even so, the southern part of the conquered region experienced significant ethnic change with the appearance there of groups of Balkan origin. This affected the local population: a general migration northward by the residents of the Hungarian-inhabited villages can be detected.

Since Hungarian territory formed part of the Ottoman Empire's frontier, the Ottomans created a network of border castles there for defense purposes (Hegyi 2000). Transformation of Hungarian towns into Ottoman towns took place only in those settlements where Muslims dwelt; Muslim inhabitants and non-Muslim inhabitants lived in separate neighborhoods (town quarters).

In those castles that were turned into military-administrative centers and in the towns linked to them, construction work was directed mostly toward the strengthening of defenses and the carrying out of military tasks (Fekete 1976). Only in the more protected settlements of the interior can we speak of more significant civilian-type building work, about the appearance of Friday mosques with domes, bathhouses, dervish cloisters, and mausoleums of holy men. The best examples of such transformations are the town of Pécs (in southwestern Hungary) and two suburbs along the Danube waterfront beneath the well-fortified and well-defended castle of Buda (Gerelyes 2013; Sudár 2014).

Aside from the (relatively few) standing Ottoman-era buildings known today, even at the end of the 19th century a significant number of structures from the Ottoman time, or substantial parts of them, lived on, having been incorporated into buildings put up in the 18th and 19th centuries. Thus hidden, many of these structures may have survived the 20th century and may live on today.

One-time Friday mosques and mosques can be sought in Christian churches (Gerő 2003). If a larger section of a mosque wall was incorporated into a Christian church following the departure of the Ottomans, then discrepancies with the axis of the new building—namely, its divergence from the west–east axis prescribed for Christian churches—may indicate that earlier on a Muslim place of worship stood on the site.

Conversion of mosques into Christian churches is indicated by those church buildings that feature Ottoman architectural elements in larger stretches of wall. Examples are ogee-arched window frames, *mihrab* niches, and stalactite-decorated corners. Features such as these survive from the Toygun Pasha Friday Mosque in Buda, the Ghazi Kassim Pasha Friday Mosque in Pécs, the "Mosque on Augustine Square" also in Pécs, and the Ali Pasha Friday Mosque in Szigetvár (in southwestern Hungary) (Ayverdi 1977; Molnár 1973).

The Malkoch Bey Friday Mosque in Siklós, the Özicheli Haji Ibrahim Friday Mosque in Esztergom, and a significant part of the Sultana Valide Bathhouse in Eger all survived on account of incorporation into 18th-century residential buildings. A noteworthy example of incorporation is the utilization in the 19th century of the bottom part of the southeast tower of an Ottoman gunpowder mill in Buda as a bathing pool for the Lukács Bathhouse, which operates today.

Partly because of rules regarding orientation and partly because of ground-plan layouts connected to specific function, from among the types of building found in Muslim cultures mosques, mausoleums, and bathhouses can be identified with near certainty. The identification of madrasas, inns, caravanserais, and market halls is a more difficult issue, especially when the edifice in question was erected on earlier Christian foundations or when an earlier building still standing in the Ottoman period was put to a new purpose.

Technical solutions characteristic of Ottoman architecture can be pointed out in some of the Ottoman buildings to be found in Hungary. The presence of these solutions—for example, such unequivocally Ottoman architectural elements as stalactite vaulting or ogee-arched door and window apertures—can determine the origins of a structure.

Dressed-stone walling on either side of a middle part consisting of crushed stone (rubble) was a characteristically Ottoman way of building. The whole wall was bound together by mortar containing brick dust. In the case of bathhouses, we observe rows of stone alternating with rows of bricks in a regular way.

Likewise characteristic was the use of dressed stones from Christian buildings which had been knocked down. The use of framework consisting of timber beams in brick-work and masonry is observable in military and civilian architecture alike.

Ottoman-era additions to earlier Hungarian castles are easily identifiable on the basis of building techniques used and ground plans followed. Towers and bastions with circular and polygonal ground plans are characteristic of Ottoman architecture. Old-type and new-type Italian bastions, kinds designed by Italian and Austrian military engineers, cannot be found in Ottoman architecture. Village-like residential areas formed by the garrison of a captured castle or a newly built palisaded fort were distinctive types of settlement in Ottoman Hungary.

The disintegration of the late medieval village system in Hungary and the attendant transformation of the country's settlement network can be dated to the Ottoman period. From the late 15th century already, inhabitants of the southern Hungarian counties began to migrate northward. However, on the Great Hungarian Plain one can speak only of temporary changes up to 1593; indeed, the economy of the villages there continued to be characterized by flourishing animal husbandry and large-scale exports of beef cattle westward. On the other hand, the so-called Thirteen Years' War, which broke out in 1593, brought significant destruction on the villages of the Great Plain. Large-scale internal migration took place at this time: people moved into the market towns and larger villages.

Villages and market towns in medieval Hungary belong to two types as regards their structure: those consisting of clumps of houses with gardens and those in which the houses and gardens were arranged in rows along a street or streets. This second type seems to have been more common. Its survival into Ottoman times is proved by aerial photography and by traditional archaeological research (Miklós and Vízi 2003) (Figure 2.9.3).

FIGURE 2.9.3 Aerial photograph showing, above the bend in the road, the one-time settlement of Ete (in the Sárköz district in today's Tolna County). A Hungarian-inhabited market town dating from the Middle Ages, it was abandoned around 1620 by its residents, who moved to the nearby village of Decs.

Courtesy of Zsuzsa Miklós (1996).

Within settlements, there are significant differences between the number of plots as indicated by archaeology and aerial photography and the number of *hanes* (i.e., the tax-paying family units found in the Ottoman tax registers), which is typically higher. This can be explained by the circumstance that, on some plots, two or even three houses were built as the population of the settlement increased. The archaeological data rule out the theory that dwelling houses accommodated more than one family.

Internal migration, along with the abandonment and the falling into ruin of settlements, as well as their repopulation later, can be easily followed using archaeological methods. A row of burned houses does not necessarily indicate the destruction and abandonment of a village, although some such rows can be linked to the campaign of 1526. Archaeology tells us that, as a result of abandonment of villages in the late 16th century, some plots remained uninhabited for a long time, the houses there slowly collapsed, and the wells became contaminated with the bodies of rodents and birds. In the case of the Great Hungarian Plain, it can be shown that the inhabitants of some settlements abandoned in the late 16th century established a new village just a few kilometers away. Continuity of population is proved by the continuous use of the original village cemeteries right up to and into the 18th century (Pálóczi Horváth 1993, 2003).

Archeobotanical examination of closed assemblages (e.g., the filling found in wells) helps us define settlement settings, their one-time plant cover, and the fruits and vegetables consumed in the settlement. From the point of view of the eating habits and nutrition of the inhabitants, it is instructive to compare the ratios of foods grown and foods collected from the wild. The findings of archaeobotanical investigations accord with the levy featuring in the Ottoman tax registers (i.e., with the tax paid in a given area on the basis of crops raised).

In the absence of relevant research hitherto, the South Slav component in the makeup of villages cannot be demonstrated precisely. The appearance of cemeteries exhibiting burial rites differing from the earlier ones and the discovery in burials of finds pointing to the Balkan territories mirror the ethnic changes already mentioned; namely, the northward movement of Balkan populations into Hungarian-inhabited territories. As shown later, the appearance of population groups from the Balkans is attested by the occurrence in the archaeological record of artifacts of kinds associated with them.

Ceramic artifacts of distinctive and novel kinds make their appearance in Hungary with the beginning of the Ottoman occupation in the mid-16th century: footed bowls, spouted jugs, storage vessels, and stove elements with thick walls. They were skillfully made from red clay on a foot-driven potter's wheel and coated with a monochrome lead glaze. Such material is unknown among finds from the medieval period (i.e., from before the Ottoman occupation era) and among those from the post-Ottoman period (i.e., the late 17th century onward).

It seems that neither the Hungarians forming a bloc on the Great Plain nor the residents of the Hungarian-inhabited villages in Transdanubia used the latest Ottoman wares mentioned earlier. By and large, medieval Hungarian craft traditions lived on in these areas during our period. Ceramic finds from this time belong to so-called Central European types (Bikić 2003).

One group of finds consists of unglazed pots made on a hand-turned wheel. This type of ware counted as old-fashioned in Hungary in the 16th and 17th centuries since use of the foot-driven potter's wheel had become general in the country by the first half of the 16th century. The origins of this earlier type of ware are clearly indicated by its close resemblance to archaeological and ethnographical material from the Balkans. Pots of this type do not occur in the Hungarian-inhabited villages of Transdanubia and the Great Hungarian Plain under Ottoman sway. Moreover, they are completely unknown in the Hungarian territories outside the Ottoman areas. Their occurrence is characteristic of the southern Transdanubia region, primarily of the smaller palisaded forts. As suppliers of the garrisons, the adjacent villages and countryside helped determine the artifacts at fortifications in Ottoman hands. In this way, ceramic material from castles and other such sites in the southern strip of Ottoman Hungary—in this case, the appearance of coarse ware made on a hand-turned wheel—directly mirrors the ethnic changes that took place in those parts (Gerelyes 2009).

The spread of Ottoman Balkan metal artifacts—Balkan drinking cups, rings imitative of Ottoman seal rings, disk-shaped ear-pendants, and head-dresses featuring sheet-metal pendants—overlaps with that of ceramic ware made on a hand-driven wheel. When the places where all such finds have been made are marked on a map, the same ethnic border as the one delineated by the data in the tax registers can be seen (Gerelyes 2017). These artifact types are unknown among the finds from the Hungarian-inhabited villages and market towns.

ROMANIAN LANDS

Situated at two major commercial crossroads linking Europe with Asia, the Romanian Lands benefited early on from Oriental products and later from Ottoman ones (included were metalwork; celadon, porcelain, and other ceramic artifacts; textiles; and leather goods). Ottoman material culture that impacted on Romanian customs (as regards diet, tableware, coffee drinking, and tobacco use) is evidenced less by the archaeological record than by travelers' writings and other documents, especially for the period 1600–1900.

During the Ottoman era, some Romanian-inhabited areas were under direct Ottoman administration while others were parts of autonomous state formations. In the 15th century, the Dobruja region was integrated into the Sanjak of Silistra, and one by one the Wallachian fortresses along the Danube (e.g., Giurgiu, Turnu) were occupied by the Ottomans. Around 1540, the fortress of Brăila, too, was captured, cutting the Danube route to the Black Sea, and parts of Transylvania, too, were brought under Ottoman rule in the newly created Eyalet of Temeşvar. Archaeological finds from this time have been studied mostly as manifestations of general medieval culture, meaning that some artifacts belonging to Ottoman culture (including Ottoman Balkan culture) have not yet been identified as such. Sgraffito wares are too often, and incorrectly, attributed to

Byzantine production. Furthermore, the links between the regions to the north and south of the Danube, where there are many analogies in regard to jewelry and glazed pottery, have not been fully investigated. Romanian medieval archaeology has largely concerned itself with finds of local provenance; imports are rarely studied.

The 1950s witnessed the first archaeological investigations of the Ottoman centers of power in Moldavia and Wallachia, corroborating the words of Paul of Aleppo regarding new construction work at the courts of Vasile Lupu, prince of Moldavia (r. 1634–1653), at Suceava and Jassy (Iași) (Nestor et al. 1957; Andronic and Neamțu, 1964; Andronic et al. 1967). Turning to Wallachia, archaeological investigations of such palatial structures are few in number and are largely unpublished. In the first capital, Târgoviște (Constantinescu 2009), investigations have concentrated more on architecture than on analysis of small finds. In Bucharest, the second capital of Wallachia, the urban growth of the 19th and 20th centuries led to extensive construction that destroyed earlier levels. The same problems are observable in older cities in which medieval and pre-modern layers were cut through or cleared away during the urban expansion efforts of the 19th century.

If in the period from the 1950s to the 1970s medieval archaeology in Romania focused mostly on the earlier centuries (formation of states, the chronology of towns and villages), today salvage excavations are uncovering the details of urban and regional history that had been barely studied at all. Although Dobruja was the first territory occupied by the Ottoman armies, the archaeology of the Ottoman era there has not been a priority in the way that the archaeology of the classical and Byzantine periods has. This region has, however, benefitted from monographs dealing with the administrative arrangements, demography, and economic life of fortresses and other settlements (Gemil 2008; Maxim 2012; Popescu 2013). Since 1990, research on Ottoman Dobruja has significantly increased our understanding of period fortresses, pottery, jewelry, and tobacco pipes (Stănică et al. 2016). The same is true for the Danubian *kazas* (juridical districts), Giurgiu, Turnu, and Brăila, with some published data on discoveries or history (Dinu 2010). The main problems of archaeological research are ignorance and confusion regarding the chronology of finds, with some being dated too early and others too late.

At Timișoara, in the west of the country, new research has been able to show a glimpse of daily life there during the Ottoman era by means of artifacts produced locally and in the region, as well as products imported from Asia (Drașovean et al. 2007; Kopeczny and Dincă 2012; Tănase and Dinu 2015). Major changes in the archaeological record are observable in the Banat and all other territories under the Eyalet of Temeşvar from the early 18th century onward and in the Bukovina region from 1774 onward. In Moldavia and Wallachia, such changes begin in the late 18th century, but were not complete: the boyars preserved some vestiges of Ottoman attire until the mid-19th century; in society more widely, the tradition of taking coffee and using tobacco persisted despite changes in the vessels used.

With regard to the Ottoman era, many questions still remain about the nature of border cities, Danubian territories (*kazas*), and the Dobruja region. These places figure prominently in accounts written by foreign travelers but are still relatively unknown archaeologically. The study of their workshops, crafts, dwelling houses, household items, everyday pottery, jewelry, and luxury ceramic wares could reveal much about daily life in town and country settings (Figure 2.9.4).

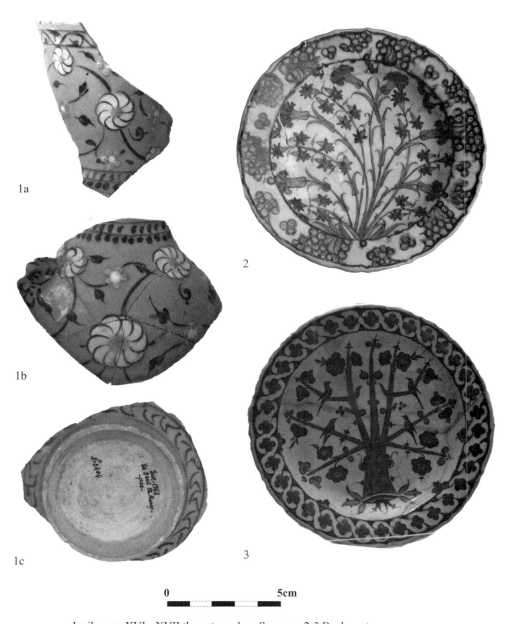

1a

1b

1c

2

3

0 ▬▬▬▬ 5cm

Iznik ware XVI - XVII th century: 1a-c Suceava, 2-3 Bucharest

FIGURE 2.9.4 İznik ware, 16th–17th centuries. 1a–c. Suceava, 2–3. Bucharest

Courtesy of Niculina Dinu (2007–2008).

NORTHERN BLACK SEA REGION

The northern region of Ottoman Europe was vast: it ran from Hungary in the west to Iran in the east, stretching across Wallachia and Moldavia, the Black Sea steppes of Ukraine, and the Caucasus Mountains all the way to the Caspian Sea (Ostapchuk and Biliaieva 2009: 137). Reaching 250,000–300,000 square kilometers in extent, these territories featured more than thirty fortresses, dozens of cities, and hundreds of settlements and nomads' camps. Ottoman sway in this region continued for more than 300 years.

The Ottomans quickly adapted to the landscapes and climates of these territories: forest-steppe in Podolia and Bukovina, steppe in the northern Black Sea and Sea of Azov areas, and the various different regions of Crimea. The assertion of Ottoman power occurred in conditions other than those found elsewhere in Europe because earlier this area was a part of the Muslim Golden Horde. The Crimean Khanate was a successor state and enjoyed unique relations with Istanbul (Ostapchuk and Biliaieva 2009: 137). It featured fortresses and cities in traditional Islamic style (e.g., the capital Bahkchysarai). In the rest of the territory, a system of provinces and an Islamic mode of life were introduced. The infrastructure of settlements included mosques, madrasas, and bathhouses. Some mosques were outstanding monuments artistically, such as the Juma-Jami Mosque (designed by Mimar Sinan) in Eupatoria (Crimea) and the Small Mosque in Ismail (school of Mimar Sinan); both survive to this day. The Ottomans repaired and rebuilt the fortresses but were late with modernization work. Ottoman administrators and garrison soldiers lived in fortresses. Various posts in the provincial administration were occupied by Tatars. Workers, especially those in construction, were often from Moldavia, an Ottoman vassal state.

During the period 1960–1990, the first data on Ottoman material culture in the region were yielded by archaeological excavations conducted not only in Crimea (Ukraine), but also at the fortresses of Azak/Azov (on the Lower Don, Russia), Khotyn (in Bukovina, Ukraine), and Kamianets-Podilskyi (in Podolia, Ukraine). These excavations were continued subsequently (Volkov 2006: 473–497; Gusach 2006: 127–141; Mysko 2009: 63–68; Nechytailo and Gorbanenko 2017: 65–75). Ottoman archaeology as a particular specialization in the Ukraine dates only from the early 1990s. Large-scale excavations at Ismail, Bilhorod-Dnistrovskyi (Akkerman), Ochakiv, and Kinburn—as well as at the above-mentioned monuments—have facilitated the study of this northern region. From 1999 to 2000, major historical, architectural, and archaeological surveys of more than 100 monuments in Crimea were conducted, revealing the degree to which Ottoman annexation impacted the urban fabric.

The cities contained narrow streets with numerous dwelling houses, markets, shops, and artisans' workshops. Male inhabitants ranged from esteemed merchants to slaves. Artisans included blacksmiths, jewelers, potters, weavers, tailors, bakers, and many fishermen. Economic life was dominated by the trade in foodstuffs, especially grain, supplied by rural, agricultural areas and exported by water to Istanbul and other cities of the Ottoman Empire. Cattle were bred by nomads on the steppes of the Nogay Horde. Large slave markets operated in Caffa, Izmail, and Kiliya; at these, captives from the steppes were traded. Most inhabitants were Tatars; the rest were Moldavians, Ukrainians, Bulgarians, Greeks, Armenians, and Jews.

As a complex of fortress, city, and port, for example, Bilhorod-Dnistrovskyi (Akkerman) had great significance (Şlapac 2001: 51–61). The Ottomans adapted its— Moldavian-built—fortress (Figure 2.9.5); this featured four courtyards and thirty-four towers. They carried out repairs to its fabric, built bastions, and created Islamic infrastructure, constructing the Great Mosque, the foundations and the minaret of which survive. The ruins of other mosques and a mausoleum, too, have been found. A small bathhouse was built in the Lower Yard and there was a larger one not far from the fortress (Biliaieva 2012: 214–216; Ersoy 2012: 338–348). The city had mosques and Christian churches of different denominations.

Ochakiv became a provincial center in 1593. On the site of its old fortress, a three-part new one was constructed in which a mosque, a pasha's palace, and administrative buildings could be found. In the city, a mosque survives, albeit rebuilt as a Christian church. In Khotyn, the Ottomans built a mosque in the New Fortress, and in Kamianets-Podilskyi they converted the Catholic cathedral into a mosque, constructing a minaret, mihrab, and minbar there.

FIGURE 2.9.5 View of Akkerman Fortress

Products from prestigious production centers in the Ottoman Empire were imported into the fortresses and cities of the northern Black Sea region. This is evidenced by precisely datable artifacts belonging to all categories of İznik and Kütahya ceramic wares, and also by tobacco pipes and jewelry. Local craftsmen produced everyday items typical of Ottoman material culture. There were other imports also, including Ukrainian pottery and glass, Moldavian pottery, and some types of Moldavian jewelry. The influence of Ottoman culture in Ukrainian territories promoted cultural integration, thus contributing to Eurasian civilization.

REFERENCES

Anastasopoulos, A. 2012. "Introduction," in A. Anastasopoulos (ed.), *Political Initiatives "From the Bottom Up" in the Ottoman Empire. Halcyon Days in Crete VII*. Symposium Held in Rethymno, 9–11 January 2009 (Rethymno: Crete University Press), 1–12.

Andronic, A., and Neamţu, E. 1964. "Cercetări arheologice pe teritoriul oraşului Iaşi în anii 1956–1960," *Arheologia Moldovei*, 2–3, 414–434.

Andronic, A., Neamţu, E., and Dinu, M. 1967. "Săpăturile arheologice de la Curtea Domnească din Iaşi," *Arheologia Moldovei*, 5, 169–270.

Aslanapa, O., Yetkin, Ş., and Altun, A. 1989. *The Iznik Tile Kiln Excavations: The Second Round (1981–1988)* (Istanbul: Historical Research Foundation).

Asparuhov, M. 1993. "Колекция лули от калето в Никопол," *Известия на музеите в северозападна България*, 21, 47–69.

Ayverdi, E. H. 1977. *Avrupa'da Osmanlı Mimârî Eserleri. I/1–2. Romanya, Macaristan* (İstanbul: İstanbul Fetih Cemiyeti).

Behrens-Abouseif, D. 2005. "From Sárospatak to Cairo: the Odyssey of a Design," in I. Gerelyes (ed.), *Turkish Flowers. Studies on Ottoman Art in Hungary* (Budapest: Hungarian National Museum), 51–54.

Bekić, L. 2010. "A Brief Introduction to Clay Pipe Finds in Croatia with Special Attention to Local Pipes Found at Fort Čanjevo in the Kalnik Hills," *Journal of the Académie Internationale de la Pipe*, 3, 1–7.

Bikić, V. 2003. *Gradska keramika Beograda (16–17.vek)—Belgrade Ceramics in the 16th–17th century*. Archaeological Institute Monographs No. 39 (Beograd: Arheološki Institut).

Bikić, V. 2007. "The Early Turkish Stratum on the Belgrade Fortress," *Byzas*, 7, 515–522.

Bikić, V. 2012. "Tobacco Pipes from the Belgrade Fortress: Context and Chronology," *Journal of the Académie Internationale de la Pipe*, 5, 1–8.

Bikić, V. 2017. "Ottoman Glazed Pottery Standardisation: The Belgrade Fortress Evidence for Production Trends," in S. Bocharov, V. François, and A. Sitdikov (eds.), *Glazed Pottery of the Mediterranean and the Black Sea Region, 10th–18th Centuries, Volume 2* (Kazan & Kishinev: Stratum), 207–216.

Biliaieva, S. 2012. *Slov'anski ta turkski svity v Ukraini (z istorii vzaemin u 13–18 st.)* (Kyiv: University "Ukraine").

Bintliff, J. L. 1995. "The Two Transitions: Current Research on the Origins of the Traditional Village in Central Greece," in J. L. Bintliff and H. Hamerow (eds.), *Europe Between Late Antiquity and the Middle Ages. Recent Archaeological and Historical Research in Western and Southern Europe*. BAR International Series 617 (Oxford: Archaeopress), 111–130.

Bintliff, J. L. 1997. "The Archaeological Investigation of Deserted Medieval and Post-medieval Villages in Greece," in G. de Boe and F. Verhaeghe (eds.), *Rural Settlements in Medieval Europe. Papers of the "Medieval Europe Brugge 1997" Conference, Volume 6* (Brugge: Archaelogical Institute for the Heritage), 21–34.

Bintliff, J. L. 1999. "The Ottoman Era in the Context of Long-Term Settlement History. A Case-Study: The Archaeological Survey of the Valley of the Muses, Boeotia, Greece," *Arab Historical Review for Ottoman Studies*, 19–20, 203–229.

Bintliff, J. L. 2012. *The Complete Archaeology of Greece. From Hunter-Gatherers to the 20th Century AD* (Oxford: Wiley-Blackwell).

Bintliff, J. L. 2014. "The Archaeology of Ottoman and Early Modern Greece," in J. L. Bintliff (ed.), *Recent Developments in the Long-Term Archaeology of Greece*. Pharos Supplement, *Journal of the Netherlands Institute at Athens* 20.1 (Leuven: Peeters), 347–369.

Boykov, G. 2010. "Balkan City or Ottoman City? A Study on the Models of Urban Development in Ottoman Upper Thrace, from the Fifteenth to the Seventeenth Century," in H. Eren and S. Ünay (eds.), *Proceedings of the Third International Congress on the Islamic Civilisation in the Balkans*, 1–5 November 2006, Bucharest, Romania (Istanbul: IRCICA), 69–85.

Boykov, G. 2011. "Reshaping Urban Space in the Ottoman Balkans: A Study on the Architectural Development of Edirne, Plovdiv, and Skopje (14th–15th centuries)," in M. Hartmuth (ed.), *Centres and Peripheries in Ottoman Architecture: Rediscovering a Balkan Heritage. Proceedings of the International Conference Centres and Peripheries in Ottoman Architecture: Rediscovering a Balkan Heritage*, 22–24 April 2010, Sarajevo, Bosnia and Herzegovina (Sarajevo: Cultural Heritage Without Borders), 32–45.

Brouskari, E. (ed.) 2008. *Ottoman Architecture in Greece* (Athens: Ministry of Culture).

Bušatlić, L. 2011. "The Transformation of the Oriental-Type Urban House in Post-Ottoman Bosnia and Herzegovina," in M. Hartmuth (ed.), *Centres and Peripheries in Ottoman Architecture: Rediscovering a Balkan Heritage* (Sarajevo: Cultural Heritage Without Borders), 122–135

Clarke, E. D. 1812/1816. *Travels in Various Countries of Europe, Asia and Africa* (London: T. Cadell & W. Davies).

Constantinescu, N. 2009. *Târgoviște, reședință voievodală (1400–1700). Cercetări arheologice, 1961–1986* (Târgoviște: Ed. Cetatea de Scaun).

Dávid, G. 1998. "Demographische Veränderungen in Ungarn zur Zeit der Türkenherrschaft," *Acta Historica*, 34, 79–87.

Davies, S., and Davis, J. L. (eds.) 2007. *Between Venice and Istanbul: Colonial Landscapes in Early Modern Greece*. Hesperia Supplement 40 (Princeton, NJ: The American School of Classical Studies at Athens).

Dinu, N. 2010. *Ceramica otomană din Dobrogea, Țara Românească și Moldova în secolele XIV–XVIII* (Unpublished PhD diss., University of Iași).

Dodwell, E. 1819. *A Classical and Topographical Tour through Greece, During the Years 1801, 1805 and 1806* (London: Rodwell & Martin).

Drașovean, F., Feneșan, C., Flutur, A., Szentmiklosi, A., El Susi, G., Kopeczny, Z., M-Kiss, H., Șeptilici, R., and Dinu, N. 2007. *Timișoara în amurgul evului mediu. Rezultatele cercetărilor arheologice peventive din centrul istoric* (Timișoara: Ed. Mirton).

Ersoy, B. 2012. "Akkerman Kalesi, Osmanli hamami," in *Ege Universite Arkeoloji kazilari* (İzmir: Ege Üniversitesi), 338–348.

Faroqhi, S. 1986. "Political Initiatives 'from the Bottom up' in the 16th- and 17th- Century Ottoman Empire: Some Evidence for Their Existence," in H. G. Majer (ed.), *Osmanistische*

Studien zur Wirtschafts- und Sozialgeschichte. In Memoriam Vančo Boškov (Wiesbaden: Harrassowitz), 24–33.

Faroqhi, S. 1997. "Social Life in Cities," in H. İnalcık (ed.), *An Economic and Social History of the Ottoman Empire* 1: *1300–1600* (Cambridge: Cambridge University Press), 576–608.

Fekete, L. 1976. *Buda and Pest under Turkish Rule. Studia Turco-Hungarica III* (Budapest: Eötvös Loránd University).

Gačić, D. 2011. *Луле из музејских збирки Србије—Каталог изложбе/The Pipes from Museum Collections of Serbia—Exhibition Catalogue* (Нови Сад/Novi Sad: City Museum of Novi Sad).

Gajić, M. 2014. *Srebrne čaše poznog srednjeg veka u Srbiji* (Beograd: Muzej primenjene umetnosti).

Gelichi, S. 2006. *The Archaeology of an Abandoned Town. The 2005 Project in Stari Bar* (Firenze: All'insegna del Giglio).

Gelichi, S. 2008. *A Town Through the Ages. The 2006–2007 Archaeological Project in Stari Bar* (Firenze: All'insegna del Giglio).

Gemil, T. 2008. *Românii și otomanii în secolele XIV–XVI* (2nd ed.). (Constanța: Ed. Ovidius University Press).

Gerelyes, I. 2009. "Garrisons and the Local Population in Ottoman Hungary: The Testimony of the Archaeological Finds," in A. C. S. Peacock (ed.), *Frontiers of the Ottoman World.* Proceedings of the British Academy 156 (New York: Oxford University Press), 385–401.

Gerelyes, I. 2013. "Ottoman Mosques and Cemeteries in the Hungarian Territories," in N. Mehler (ed.), *Historical Archaeology in Central Europe.* Society for Historical Archaeology Special Publication 10. (Rockville, MD: Society for Historical Archaeology), 185–201.

Gerelyes, I. 2017. "Ottoman-Balkan Jewellery in Ottoman Hungary: Typology and Spread," in P. Fodor and P. Ács (eds.), *Identity and Culture in Ottoman Hungary.* Studien zur Sprache und Kultur der Turkvölker Band 24 (Berlin: Klaus Schwarz Verlag), 239–254.

Gerő, G. 2003. "The History of Ottoman-Turkish Archaeological Research in Hungary," in I. Gerelyes and G. Kovács (eds.), *Archaeology of the Ottoman Period in Hungary* (Budapest: Hungarian National Museum), 17–22.

Gusach, I. 2006. "Arkheologicheskie issledovaniya na teritorii turetskoy kreposti Azak," *Istoriko-arkheologicheskie issledovaniya na Nizhnem Donu*, 21, 127–141.

Guštin, M., Bikić, V., and Mileusnić, Z. 2008. *Ottoman Times: The Story of Stari Bar, Montenegro* (Koper: Založba Annales).

Hayes, J. W. 1992. *Excavations at Saraçhane in Istanbul, 2: The Pottery* (Princeton, NJ: Princeton University Press).

Hegyi, K. 2000. "The Ottoman Network of Fortresses in Hungary," in G. Dávid and P. Fodor (eds.), *Ottomans, Hungarians, and Habsburgs in Central Europe. The Military Confines in the Era of Ottoman Conquest* (Leiden, Boston, and Köln: Brill), 163–193.

İnalcık, H. 1972. "The Ottoman Decline and Its Effects upon the Reaya," in H. Birnbaum and S. Vryonis (eds.), *Aspects of the Balkans, Continuity and Change,* Contributions to the International Balkan Conference held at UCLA, Oct. 23–28, 1969 (The Hague and Paris: Mouton), 338–354.

İnalcık, H. 1991. "The Emergence of Big Farms, Çiftliks: State, Landlords and Tenants," in *H.* Keyder and F. Tabak (eds.), *Landholding and Commercial Agriculture in the Middle East* (Albany: State University of New York), 17–34.

Ivanić, B. 1995. *Nakit iz zbirke Narodnog muzeja od 15. do početka 19. veka: katalog zbirke Umetnost pod turskom vlašću* (Beograd: Narodni muzej u Beogradu).

Jovanović, V., Ćirković, S., Zečević, E., Ivanišević, V., and Radić, V. 2004. *Novo Brdo* (Belgrade: Institute of the Protection of Cultural Monuments of the Republic of Serbia).

Karamehmedović, M. A. 1980. *Umjetnička obrada metala* (Sarajevo: Veselin Masleša).

Kiel, M. 1990. "Byzantine Architecture and Painting in Central Greece, 1460–1570. Its Demographic and Economic Basis According to the Ottoman Census and Taxation Registers for Central Greece Preserved in Istanbul and Ankara," *Byzantinische Forschungen*, 16, 429–446.

Kiel, M. 1997. "The Rise and Decline of Turkish Boeotia, 15th–19th Century: Remarks on the Settlement Pattern, Demography and Agricultural Production According to Unpublished Ottoman-Turkish Census- and Taxation-Records," in J. L. Bintliff (ed.), *Recent Developments in the History and Archaeology of Central Greece. Proceedings of the 6th International Boeotian Conference*. BAR International Series 666 (Oxford: Archaeopress), 315–358.

Kiel, M. 1999. "The Ottoman Imperial Registers. Central Greece and Northern Bulgaria in the 15th–19th Century: The Demographic Development of Two Areas Compared," in J. L. Bintliff and K. Sbonias (eds.), *Reconstructing Past Population Trends in Mediterranean Europe (3000 BC–AD 1800)* (Oxford: Oxbow Books), 195–218.

Kiel, M. 2007. "The Smaller Aegean Islands in the 16th–18th Centuries According to Ottoman Administrative Documents," in S. Davies and J. L. Davis (eds.), *Between Venice and Istanbul: Colonial Landscapes in Early Modern Greece*. Hesperia Supplement 40 (Princeton, NJ: The American School of Classical Studies at Athens), 35–54.

Kizis, G. 1994. *Πηλιορείτικη Οικοδομία* (Athens: Πολιτιστικό Ίδρυμα Ομίλου Πειραιώς).

Kolovos, E. (ed.) 2015. *Ottoman Rural Societies and Economies. Halcyon Days in Crete VIII. A Symposium Held in Rethymno, 13–15 January 2012* (Rethymno: Crete University Press).

Kolovos, E. 2017. *Όπου ήν κήπος. Η Μεσογειακή Νησιωτική Οικονομία της Άνδρου Σύμφωνα με το Οθωμανικό Κτηματολόγιο του 1670* (Heraklion: Crete University Press & Kaireios Library).

Kopeczny, Z., and Dincă, R. 2012. "Tobacco Clay Pipes Discovered in the Historical Center of Timişoara," *Ziridava* (Cluj-Napoca), 26, 1, 167–190.

Korre-Zographou, K. 1995. *Τα Κεραμικά του Ελληνικού Χώρου* (Athens: Melissa).

Kouroupaki, K., Savvari, E., Stathaki-Spiliopoulou, M., and Tsamtsouri, V. 1988. "Νάξος," in D. Philippides (ed.), *Ελληνική Παραδοσιακή Αρχιτεκτονική 2: Κυκλάδες* (Athens: Melissa), 79–110.

MacKay, C. 2015. "Three Late Medieval Kilns from the Athenian Agora," in K. F. Daly and L. A. Riccardi (eds.), *Cities Called Athens. Studies Honoring John McK. Camp II* (Lewisburg, PA: Bucknell University Press), 273–288.

Marjanović-Vujović, G. 1973. "Kuća iz druge polovine XVII veka otkopana u utvrđenom podgrađu Beogradskog grada: Donjem gradu," *Godišnjak grada Beograda*, 20, 201–226.

Maxim, M. 2012. *O istorie a relaţiilor româno-otomane cu documente noi din arhivele turceşti, volume I: perioada clasică (1400–1600)* (Brăila: Ed. Istros a Muzeului Brăilei).

Miklós, Z., and Vízi, M. 2003. "Ete—egy elpusztult középkori mezőváros a Sárközben. With summary: Ete—ein verwüsteter mittelalterlicher Marktflecken in der Landschaft Sárköz," *Móra Ferenc Múzeum Évkönyve—Studia Archaeologica* (Szeged), 9, 399–406.

Mitrevski, D. 2007. *Skopje Fortress—Archaeological Excavations 2007 and Exhibition* (Skopje: Museum of the City of Skopje).

Molnár, J. 1973. *Macaristan'da Türk Anıtları* (Ankara: TTK Yayınları).

Mysko, Y. 2009. "Keramika z rozkopok na teritorii Khotynskoi fortetsi," *Novi doslidzhennya kozatskoy doby v Ukraini*, 18.

Nechytailo, P., and Gorbanenk, S. 2017. "Midnyi posud tar rys z Kam'antsya Podilskogo," *Arkheologiya*, 2, 65–75.

Nestor, I., Diaconu, G., Matei, M. D., Martinovici, T. Constantinescu, N., and Olteanu, Ş. 1957. "Şantierul arheologic Suceava. Raport preliminar asupra săpăturilor din Campania anului 1955," *Materiale şi Cercetări Arheologice*, 5, 239–264.

Ostapcuk, V., and Biliaieva, S. 2009. "The Ottoman Black Sea Frontier at Akkerman Fortress," in A. C. S. Peacock (ed.), *The Frontiers of the Ottoman World*. Proceedings of the British Academy 156 (Oxford: Oxford University Press), 138–170.

Pálóczi Horváth, A. 1993. "Komplex településtörténeti kutatások a Nagykunságban," in I. Horn (ed.), *Perlekedő évszázadok. Tanulmányok Für Lajos 60. Születésnapjára* (Budapest: ELTE Középkori és Kora-újkori Magyar Történelmi Tanszék), 41–80.

Pálóczi Horváth, A. 2003. "The Survival of Szentkirály in the Ottoman Era," in I. Gerelyes and G. Kovács (eds.), *Archaeology of the Ottoman Period in Hungary* (Budapest: Hungarian National Museum), 201–206.

Pletnov, V. 2004. *Bitovata keramika văv Varna XV–XVIII vek* (Varna: Slavena).

Poole, J. E. 1997. *Italian Maiolica* (Cambridge: Cambridge University Press).

Popescu A. 2013. *Integrarea imperială otomană a teritoriilor din sud-estul Europei. Sangeacul Silistra (sec. XV–XVI)* (Bucureşti: Academia Română).

Popović, M. 2006. *Beogradska tvrđava (drugo dopunjeno izdanje)* (Beograd: Arheološki institut i JP "Beogradska tvrđava").

Popović, M., and Bikić, V. 2004. *Комплекс средњовековне Митрополије у Београду—истраживања у Доњем граду Београдске тврђаве. With Summary: The Complex of the Metropolitan Church in Belgrade—Excavation of the Lower Town of the Belgrade Fortress*. Посебна издања, књига/Monograph Series, No. 41 (Београд: Археолошки институт/ Belgrade: Archaeological Institute).

Redžid, H. 1983. *Studije o islamskoj arhitektonskoj baštini* (Sarajevo: Veselin Masleša).

Šabanović, H. 1970. "Urbani razvitak Beograda od 1521. do 1688," *Godišnjak grada Beograda*, 17, 9–42.

Sariyannis, M. 2014. "Time, Work and Pleasure: A Preliminary Approach to Leisure in Ottoman Mentality," in M. Sariyannis (ed.), *New Trends in Ottoman Studies*. Papers Presented at the 20th CIEPO Symposium, Rethymno, 27 June—1 July 2012 (Rethymno: University of Crete), 797–811.

Sigalos, E. 2004. *Housing in Medieval and Post-Medieval Greece*. BAR International Series 1291 (Oxford: Archaeopress).

Şlapac, M. 2001. *Belgorod-Dnestrovs'kaia krepost': Issledovanie srednevekovogo oboronnogo zodchestva* (Chişinău: Editura ARC).

Stančeva, M., and Nikolova, T. 1989. "Нови проучвания върху глинените лули от Сердика," in T. Gerasimov (ed.), *Сердика, Археологически материали и проучвания*, 2, (Sofia: n. p.), 133–141.

Stănică, A, Custurea, G., Stănică, D., and Plopeanu, E. (eds.). 2016. *Dobrogea. Coordonate istorice şi arheologice* (Iaşi, Studis).

Stedman, N. 1996. "Land-use and Settlement in Post-medieval Central Greece: An Interim Discussion," in P. Lock and G. D. R. Sanders (eds.), *The Archaeology of Medieval Greece* (Oxford: Oxbow Books), 179–192.

Sudár, B. 2014. *Dzsámik és mecsetek a hódolt Magyarországon*. Magyar Történelmi Emlékek. Adattárak (Budapest: MTA Bölcsészettudományi Kutatóközpont Történettudományi Intézet).

Tănase, D., and Dinu, N. 2015. "Faianță și porțelan din Epoca Otomană descoperite în Timișoara, străzile Lucian Blaga, Enrico Caruso și Radu Negru (Campania 2014)," *Studii și Cercetări de Istorie Veche și Arheologie*, 66, 1–2, 69–96.

Todorov, V. 2010. "Характеристика на колекцията керамични лули от Силистра. With Summary: Specifics of the Collection of Clay Tobacco-Pipes from Silistra," *Studia Archaeologica Universitatis Serdicensis, Stephanos Archaeologicos in honorem Professoris Stephcae Angelova, Supplementum* 5, 813–826.

Vionis, A. K. 2003. "Much Ado About . . . a Red Cap and a Cap of Velvet: In Search of Social and Cultural Identity in Medieval and Post-medieval Insular Greece," in H. Hokwerda (ed.), *Constructions of Greek Past: Identity and Historical Consciousness from Antiquity to the Present* (Gronigen: Egbert Forsten Publishing), 193–216.

Vionis, A. K. 2006. "The Archaeology of Villages in Central Greece: Ceramics, Housing and Everyday Life in Post-medieval Boeotia," in A. Erkanal-Öktü et al. (eds.), *Studies in Honor of Hayat Erkanal: Cultural Reflections* (Istanbul: Homer Kitabevi), 784–800.

Vionis, A. K. 2008. "Current Archaeological Research on Settlement and Provincial Life in the Byzantine and Ottoman Aegean: A Case-Study from Boeotia, Greece," *Medieval Settlement Research*, 23, 28–41.

Vionis, A. K. 2012. *A Crusader, Ottoman and Early Modern Aegean Archaeology: Built Environment and Domestic Material Culture in the Medieval and Post-Medieval Cyclades, Greece, 13th–20th Centuries AD*. ASLU 22 (Leiden: University of Leiden).

Vionis, A. K. 2016. "A Boom-Bust Cycle in Ottoman Greece and the Ceramic Legacy of Two Boeotian Villages," *Journal of Greek Archaeology*, 1, 353–384.

Volkov, I. 2006. "Zakrytyj kompleks turetskogo vremeni iz Azova," *Istoriko-arkheologicheskie issledovaniya na Nizhnem Donu*, 21, 473–497.

Vroom, J. 2003. *After Antiquity. Ceramics and Society in the Aegean from the 7th to the 20th Century A.C.: A Case Study from Boeotia, Central Greece*. PhD diss., University of Leiden. ASLU 10 (Leiden: University of Leiden).

Zarinebaf, F., Bennet, J., and Davis, J. L. 2005. *A Historical and Economic Geography of Ottoman Greece: The Southern Morea in the 18th Century*. Hesperia Supplement 34 (Princeton, NJ: American School of Classical Studies at Athens).

Zirojević, O. 2005. "Jelo i piće," in A. Fotić (ed.), *Privatni život u srpskim zemljama u osvit modernog doba* (Beograd: Clio), 233–258.

FURTHER READING

Hahn, M. 1991. "A Group of 15th/16th Century Jugs from Western Crete," *Acta Hyperborea*, 3, 311–320.

SECTION III

....

THE ISLAMIC
WEST

....

CORISANDE FENWICK

THIS section turns to the Islamic West: the Iberian Peninsula, southern Italy and Sicily, and the North African littoral (Morocco, Algeria, Tunisia, Libya), a vast region that for too long has been viewed as peripheral to broader debates in Islamic archaeology. Linguistic issues are a factor, particularly for Anglophone scholars who rarely engage with literature in Arabic or even scholarship in French, Spanish, or Italian and often find it difficult to access local publications. Scholars must also grapple with the charged relationship that Europe has with its Islamic heritage, particularly in Spain, Portugal, and Sicily, as well as the legacy of European colonialism in the 19th and 20th centuries in North Africa and sub-Saharan Africa. Further challenges come from the very different trajectories of archaeological research across the region and the limited amount of dialogue between scholars working in the Islamic West and those in the so-called Central Islamic Lands.

It is often forgotten that it was in North Africa that the earliest European excavations of an Islamic site took place. The excavations at the Qal'aa of the Beni Hammad in Algeria in 1898 and those at the ruins of Madinat al-Zahara in Spain in 1910 established the palatial focus of Islamic archaeology and its emphasis on architecture and fine objects in the West and beyond. The pioneering scholarship of scholars in the first half of the 20th century, such as Georges Marçais, Henri Terrasse, Manuel Gómez Moreno, and Leopoldo Torres Balbás continues to be important references for art and architecture today. This early promise was only slowly built on, and Islamic (and European medieval) archaeology became the poor relation to Roman and prehistoric archaeology for much of the 20th century.

The past three decades, however, have seen a new generation of Islamic archaeologists emerge who have transformed the discipline and our understanding of the Islamic West. The study of Al-Andalus (Spain and Portugal) and Sicily benefited from the growing strength of European medieval archaeology, new heritage legislation, and the spread of salvage archaeology in the 1970s and 1980s. Spain, in particular, is now one of the most intensively studied regions of the Islamic world and has evidence of sufficient quantity and quality to enable a far more detailed picture of the cities, villages, and rural landscape of al-Andalus to be drawn than was possible thirty years ago. Scholarship in al-Andalus and now Sicily leads the way in the use of scientific techniques to understand diet, migration and mobility (through aDNA and isotope analysis), environmental change, and glass and ceramic manufacturing. In comparison, Islamic archaeology in the vast region that comprises North Africa is less well developed and continues to focus on the transformation of the late antique city and new Islamic foundations. North Africa was the conduit into the Sahara, another vast region where, in recent years, archaeology has transformed and complicated our understanding of the development of Saharan urbanization, trading networks, and the spread of Islam and its roots in the pre-Islamic period. In recognition of these very different research trajectories, the section is organized geographically, with dedicated chapters on Ifrīqiya and the central Maghreb, the Maghreb al-Aqsa, the Sahara, al-Andalus, and Sicily. Finally, this section also considers the intense and complex relationships between northern Europe and Scandinavia and the Islamic world which seldom feature in standard historical and archaeological accounts of medieval Europe or the early Islamic world.

IFRIQIYA AND THE CENTRAL MAGHREB

CORISANDE FENWICK

INTRODUCTION

IT is often forgotten that North Africa played a pivotal part in the development of Islamic archaeology as a discipline through the important French excavations at the Qal'a of the Beni Hammad in Algeria in the late 19th century, one of the earliest excavations at an Islamic site by European archaeologists anywhere in the Islamic world. This early promise proved short-lived. For most of the 20th century, the Islamic period has been the preserve of art historians and historians, with only a handful of small-scale excavations conducted at the spectacular palatial-cities, mosques, ribats, and fortresses of Algeria, Tunisia, and Libya. Since the 1990s, there has been a significant rise in the number of projects and amount of evidence available, as well as a new interest in revisiting old questions and models for the Islamic period. The majority of research, however, continues to focus on the "dark age" transition from Rome to Islam and the monumental architecture of the 9th–11th centuries. This chapter charts the development of Islamic archaeology and lays out the key scholarly debates in Ifriqiya and the central Maghreb, broadly understood as encompassing modern-day Tunisia, Algeria, and western coastal Libya (Figure 3.1.1).

BACKGROUND: A BRIEF HISTORY OF IFRIQIYA AND THE CENTRAL MAGHREB

Arab armies first entered Cyrenaica from Egypt in 642, but it took many decades before the Byzantine capital Carthage fell in 697/698 and Africa became Ifriqiya (Brett 1978; Kaegi 2010; Manzano Moreno 2010). North Africa did not remain part of the caliphate

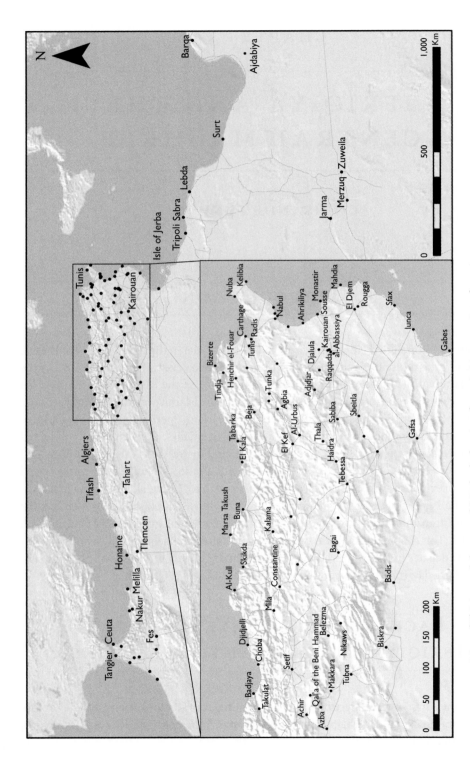

FIGURE 3.1.1 Map of Ifriqiya and the central Maghreb showing the main sites mentioned.

Courtesy of Corisande Fenwick.

for long. The Umayyads and the Abbasids never managed to establish firm control over North Africa, and the 8th century was characterized by repeated rebellions and revolts of both the local Berber populations and rival factions in the Muslim armies (Fenwick forthcoming). Caliphal rule was replaced by a series of Muslim successor states including the Rustamids (761–909) in western Algeria and the Aghlabids (800–909) in Ifriqiya itself (Talbi 1966; Anderson et al. 2017). North Africa became the seat of empires under the Shiite Fatimids (909–1171) who ruled from Tunisia before they moved their capital to Cairo in 972 (Brett 2017; Bloom 2007). The region was then ruled by their vassals, the Zirids (972–1148), a Sanhaja Berber dynasty (Idris 1962, Golvin 1957), but, within a few decades, the central Maghreb was seized by the Hammadids (1014–1152). The 11th century also saw the movement of the Banu Hilal from Egypt into the Maghreb, traditionally depicted as economically and socially devastating.

The rise of the Almohads (1120–1269) marked the first time that North Africa and al-Andalus were united under one rule (Bennison 2016). After the Almohad empire collapsed, Ifriqiya and the central Maghreb were more often under the control of a single dynasty, usually based in Tunis or in Algiers. The Hafsid dynasty (1229–1574), based in Tunis, united much of the region again though little is known archaeologically of this period (Daoulatli 1976): this was a time of great connectivity and commerce, with many Muslims from al-Andalus fleeing from the Reconquista as well as piracy against the Christian world. The Ottoman seizure of Algiers (1529), Tripoli (1551), and Tunis (1574) in the 16th century had major, if largely unexplored, implications for North Africa. Almost nothing has been written about the archaeology of the Ottoman period, though scholars have extensively studied the architecture and urbanism of North African cities in this period (Saadaoui 2001; Raymond 2002). The French conquest of Algiers in 1830, the establishment of a Tunisian Protectorate in 1881 and the Italian colony of Libya in 1911 marked the start of a complex colonial relationship with the region, within which archaeology and the Islamic past has played an important role.

ISLAMIC ARCHAEOLOGY IN NORTH AFRICA

The origins of Islamic archaeology in North Africa are inextricably entangled with the French colonial mission (Fenwick 2020: 12-25). The earliest excavations were those conducted by Paul Blanchet and General Léon de Beylié in the late 19th century at the Qal'a of the Beni Hammad in Algeria (Figure 3.1.2), the capital of the Arab-Berber Hammadid dynasty in the 11th and 12th centuries (de Beylié 1909; Marçais 1913). The excavations focused on the large-scale exposure of the mosques, palaces, and gardens and the architectural decoration and luxury items they contained, such as mosaics, stucco, metalwork, and glazed ceramics. The result was stunning catalogues of objects, inscriptions, and detailed architectural descriptions, but these provided little information on the social, economic, or political aspects of medieval life. Despite this early interest, Islamic archaeology remained a minority pursuit for many decades. France's (and later, Italy's) close ideological association

FIGURE 3.1.2 Qal'a of the Beni Hammad.

Courtesy of Corisande Fenwick.

as the successor of Rome in Africa, combined with the extraordinary number of sites with standing monumental Roman architecture, privileged the Roman period, with disastrous consequences for medieval archaeology (Lorcin 2002; Fenwick 2008). When medieval remains were encountered, they were usually destroyed without being recorded in order to reach the monumental temples, theaters, and elite housing of the early Roman period. This state of affairs continued throughout the colonial period—only a handful of small-scale excavations took place at dynastic palace-cities like al-Abbasiya (Marçais 1925) in Tunisia and Achir (Golvin 1966) and Sedrata (van Berchem 1954) in Algeria.

Islamic heritage was not entirely neglected. Orientalist interest in Islamic architecture, decoration, and the fabric of the "Islamic city" led to meticulous studies of the monuments and medinas of important cities (especially Algiers, Tunis, Tlemcen, Sousse, and Kairouan) in French-occupied territories, though not in Italian-held Libya. Detailed architectural studies of individual monuments (largely mosques, ribats, and fortifications) also took place in Algeria and Tunisia, some of which were accompanied by limited excavation (for Morocco, see Chapter 3.2). The pioneering scholarship undertaken in the first half of the 20th century by French scholars such as Georges Marçais (1876–1962), Henri Terrasse (1895–1971), Alexandre Lézine (1906–1972), Lucien Golvin (1905–2002), and others, many of whom worked in multiple North African countries, remains the essential point of reference today. This is precisely where the problem lies: in the still important work of Marçais (1954), which has not yet been supplanted as the reference manual for the Islamic art and architecture of Tunisia, Algeria, and Morocco, the focus was only on monumental architecture and elite material culture.

After Tunisia, Algeria, and Libya gained their independence, and coinciding with a burgeoning interest in medieval archaeology in Europe in the 1970s and 1980s, Islamic archaeology began to flourish. Research has continued to focus on monumental architecture and palatial centers, but very different research trajectories can be seen in the three countries. Libya, in many ways, provides the most comprehensive evidence for the early Islamic period despite being hampered by American and United Nations sanctions (1986–2004) and ongoing conflict. The pioneering work of the Libyan scholar Abdulhamid Abdussaid, who excavated medieval sites of Ajdabiya, Surt, el-Merj, and Zuwila in the 1960s and 1970s, laid the foundation for Islamic archaeology there. In the following decades, diachronic field-surveys such as the UNESCO Libyan Valleys Survey were accompanied by further major excavations at the Fatimid towns of Ajdabiya and Surt as well as the careful excavation of late phases at the coastal classical cities of Ptolemais, Leptis Magna, Sabratha, Tocra, and Berenice (see King 1989). At the time of writing, Libya has been in a state of civil war since 2011, putting much of its heritage at risk, and many of its Islamic mosques and tombs have been targeted and destroyed by Salafist militants, though this has received only limited attention from cultural heritage specialists (Brodie 2015).

In Tunisia, Islamic archaeology became a recognized department of the Tunisian Antiquities Service in 1948 under the leadership of Slimane-Mostafa Zbiss who began a systematic series of restoration works (with some excavation) in the medinas of Tunis, Monastir, Sousse, Kairouan, and Mahdia. Nonetheless, excavations remained limited in scope compared to those at Punic or Roman sites and focused on the Aghlabid foundation of Raqqada (Chabbi 1967–1968), and the later Fatimid foundations of Mahdia (Louhichi 1997) and Sabra al-Mansuriya (Zbiss 1956; Ajjabi 1985). As Patrice Cressier (2013: 119) has pointed out, it is astonishing that only three sites have been the main focus of attention for more than a hundred years—and indeed, even more remarkable that we still know so little about even these sites. Ammar Mahjoubi's (1978) excavations and analysis of the late antique and medieval layers at Henchir el-Faouar (anc. Belalis Maior) marked an important turning point in the study of the complex histories of Roman towns after the Arab conquest. At the same time, pioneering work on medieval ceramics began to establish a preliminary typology for the region (e.g., Vitelli 1981; Louhichi 1997). From then on, but particularly since the 2000s, archaeologists have examined the medieval layers of many Roman towns, as well as conducting more systematic research at sites like Sabra al-Mansuriya (Cressier and Rammah 2006) and occasionally surveying the medieval and early modern rural landscape as on Jerba (see Holod and Kahlaoui 2017).

Archaeological research has been impeded in Algeria by civil war (1991–2002) and lack of investment. Important excavations were conducted at the Almohad port of Honaine in the 1970s (Khelifa 2008) and at Sétif and Cherchel in the 1980s as part of a new wave of interest in the post-classical city (Mohamedi et al. 1991; Potter 1995). However, excavations at the Rustamid capital of Tahert are only briefly described (Cadenat 1977), and other Algerian sites, such as the so-called Idrīsid mosque at Tlemcen excavated in the 1970s, have yet to be published. New salvage excavations in the city of Algiers promise to provide important information on the medieval and Ottoman history of the city, but the number of active fieldwork projects remains low due to lack of resources and trained personnel (Khelifa 1987).

Islamic archaeology is still in its infancy in North Africa in comparison to Roman, Punic, or prehistoric archaeology, but there is an increasing desire to change this situation driven by both North African and European academics. Although there are still only a handful of national and international research projects dedicated specifically to medieval archaeology, archaeologists are now beginning to systematically include post-classical layers and sites in excavation and field survey. This has transformed our understanding of early Islamic North Africa (Fenwick 2020, for an overview), though progress is slow and remains regionally variable. Dating is the most significant challenge: in the absence of good ceramic chronologies, it is often difficult to date medieval occupation, particularly for the pivotal 8th century (Fenwick 2013: 12–14). Equally problematic, but rarely acknowledged, is the lack of attention paid by archaeologists to the 12th–19th centuries—only a handful of sites from this period have been excavated and almost none to modern standards. Our difficulties are exacerbated by the fact that the most important centers of Islamic Africa such as Kairouan, Tunis, Algiers, and Tripoli have all been occupied continuously since antiquity. Urban rescue archaeology remains rare, despite the precedent set by the UNESCO-sponsored excavations of Carthage in the 1980s. As a result, we know more about abandoned Roman towns and medieval palatial sites than those medieval or early modern towns that were continuously occupied and much more about monumental architecture than domestic dwellings, industrial complexes, or rural settlement.

CITIES

Scholarship in North Africa has focused almost exclusively on the medieval city and can be separated into two key strands divided along disciplinary lines (Fenwick 2018). The first, led primarily by classical archaeologists and inspired by Kennedy's (1985) *Polis to Madina* article, focuses on "the Fate of the Classical City": Did towns flourish after the Arab conquest, or declined in size, population and prosperity? The second, led by medieval archaeologists, might be described as the "Islamic city" debate: What were the significant monuments and public spaces of the early Islamic city?

Archaeologists have given far more attention to the first theme than the second in recent years. Scholars are in broad agreement that the 5th–6th centuries mark the point when the monuments and public spaces of the classical city were transformed into their medieval form in North Africa (Thébert and Biget 1990; Leone 2007; Pentz 2002). New fieldwork as well as the reevaluation of earlier reports is beginning to make clear, too, that the Arab conquests were not as catastrophic for North African cities as traditionally imagined. Debate centers around on how one interprets the evidence from a handful of well-excavated towns that flourished in the Roman period and were abandoned at some point in the Middle Ages (see Fenwick 2013; 2018; 2019; 2020; von Rummel 2016).

The picture that emerges is of the great degree of urban variability in the early middle ages (Fenwick 2020: 53-80). Large, fortified urban sites on major routes and ports, such as Tripoli, Sousse, Tobna, Béja, and Biskra, continued to thrive and formed the basis of the early medieval urban network. Sousse (Roman Hadrumetum), for example, continued to serve as military and regional capital under the Umayyads and Abbasids, and, in the late 8th century, a fort (*ribāṭ*) was built to guard the interior port, near or on what was presumably the Roman *forum*. The look of the town was wholly transformed in the mid-9th century by the Aghlabid emirs when Sousse became the main naval base for expeditions to Sicily through the addition of an arsenal and interior port, a Kasbah, a congregational mosque and other smaller mosques, as well as a large defensive enceinte that encircled 32 hectares and encompassed the entire city including the arsenal and interior port (Figure 3.1.3; Lézine 1956; Mahfoudh 2003; Fenwick 2018). Sousse shows us how rapidly a town could be transformed from a Roman city into a walled medieval Islamic city centered around mosque and ribat.

We don't understand the plan and layout of other towns very well, as many of them remain occupied today or have only been partially excavated. Certainly, the site of Leptis Magna (Lebda) continued to be the same size in the 9th century as in the 7th century, comprising a walled settlement of approximately 28 hectares around the port area, with some small pockets of occupation outside the walls around the market, *chalcidicum*, circus, and hunting baths (Cirelli 2001). Other towns, such as Belalis Maior, seem to have grown by the addition of extramural quarters in the 8th or 9th century to house new Muslim occupants (Fenwick 2013). The Byzantine capital Carthage is a notable exception to this pattern and is the one city which seems to have been destroyed in the aftermath of the Arab conquest. Here it is clear that the vast area inside its walls (400 hectares) was reduced to a series of small agricultural villages, perhaps centered around the Byrsa hill, which seems to have retained some semblance of urban function (Figure 3.1.4; Stevens 2016; Fenwick 2019). Carthage was not the only town to fail in the Middle Ages. Smaller towns of the northern Tunisian Tell, Numidia, and along the Tunisian coast also seem to suffer disproportionately and are abandoned or reduced to very little between the 7th and 9th century. Excavations at the small urban sites of Uchi Maius, Althiburos, and Chemtou found clear signs of abandonment between late antique layers and later medieval reoccupation during the 9th or 10th century (Gelichi and Milanese 2002; Kallala et al. 2011; Touihri 2014).

Medievalists have largely focused their attention on the new monumental architecture (mosques, ribats, and palaces) of Tunis, Kairouan, and, to a lesser degree, the palace-cities of the Aghlabid and Fatimid periods. Precise information is much less plentiful for the new foundations of Kairouan (670) and Tunis (705) than for new foundations elsewhere in the caliphate. Nonetheless, the later Arabic texts have allowed scholars to reconstruct the key points in their development (Mahfoudh 2003; Marçais 1954; Lézine 1966). Both mark an obvious break with the classical city in urban planning. Established as new Muslim cities to house the Muslim soldiers and ever-growing Muslim community, they

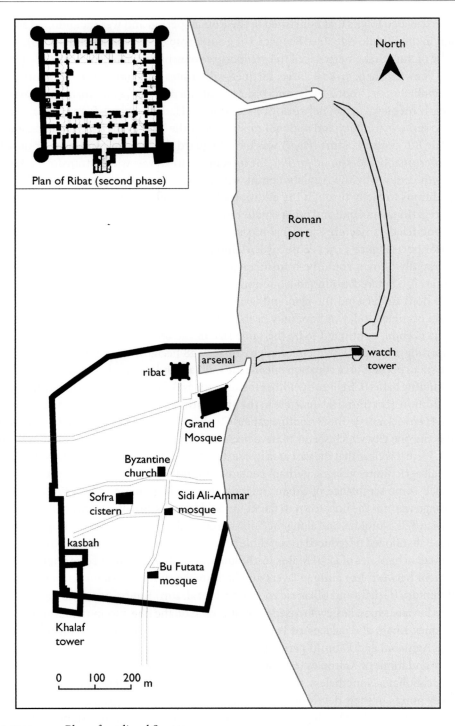

Plan of Ribat (second phase)

North

Roman
port

watch
tower

arsenal

ribat

Grand
Mosque

Byzantine
church

Sofra
cistern

Sidi Ali-Ammar
mosque

kasbah

Bu Futata
mosque

Khalaf
tower

0   100   200 m

FIGURE 3.1.3 Plan of medieval Sousse.

Courtesy of Corisande Fenwick.

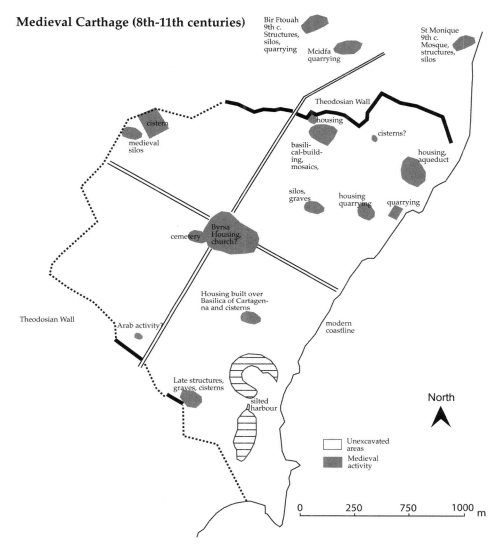

Medieval Carthage (8th-11th centuries)

Bir Ftouah
9th c.
Structures,
silos,
quarrying

Mcidfa
quarrying

St Monique
9th c.
Mosque,
structures,
silos

Theodosian Wall

housing

cisterns?

cistern

medieval
silos

basili-
cal-build-
ing,
mosaics,

housing,
aqueduct

silos,
graves

housing
quarrying

quarrying

Byrsa
Housing,
church?

cemetery

Housing built over
Basilica of Cartagen-
na and cisterns

Theodosian Wall

Arab activity?

modern
coastline

Late structures,
graves, cisterns

silted
harbour

North

☐ Unexcavated
areas

▨ Medieval
activity

0   250   750   1000 m

FIGURE 3.1.4 Plan of medieval Carthage.

Courtesy of Corisande Fenwick.

included new types of buildings including mosques and the *dar al-amara* (governor's residence) that had never been seen before in North Africa. Kairouan was laid out on an orthogonal plan (Bahri and Taamallah 2019) with a large congregational mosque and *dar al-amara* at its center and a souq. This urban model was formalized early on in the conquest of Iraq and Syria-Palestine in the 630s and 640s, and it was brought to North Africa (Akbar 1989).

After the collapse of caliphal power, the dynasties that divided up North Africa typically built their own palace-cities, often outside existing centers. For the early Middle Ages alone (700–1050), we can count at least nine Muslim capitals built and (usually) later abandoned: Tahart, al-Abbasiya, Raqqada, Achir/Bénian, Sedrata, Mahdia, Sabra al-Mansuriya, the Qal'a of the Beni Hammad, and Mansourah (Tlemcen). These short-lived settlements have all been excavated to some degree. The earliest was the Rustamid capital of Tahert (Algeria) founded in 761 to the west of the Byzantine stronghold of Tiaret. The northern part of the settlement occupies 8 hectares and was defended by a rectangular enceinte of pisé de terre. Inside, excavations revealed houses with plaster walls and roof tiles separated by narrow roads. On the southern plateau there is a large rectangular building identified by Marçais (1946) first as the early medieval kasbah, or fortress, but is more likely to be the 19th-century fortress built by the rebel Amir Abd al-Kader (Cadenat 1977). The city was destroyed by the Fatimids in 909, when the Rustamids then moved to Sedrata in the northern Sahara.

In Tunisia, the Aghlabid dynasty built new royal towns to house themselves and their retinues in the immediate vicinity of Kairouan: al-ʿAbbasiyya in 800, which was later replaced by Raqqada in 876. Marçais's limited excavations at al-'Abbasiya in the 1920s revealed only a mound of pise and mudbricks and a basin: the decorative elements are presumed to have been taken to Raqqada (Marçais 1925). Excavations there in the 1960s revealed a square fortified complex with around 109 rooms, courtyards, and annexes that is interpreted as a palace (probably the Qasr al-Sahn); a large reservoir; and a brick-making kiln (Figure 3.1.5; Chabbi 1967–1968). It was built in pisé in three successive phases and is similar in form to the Umayyad desert castles of Syria and Iraq. This is but a small fraction of Raqqada: medieval texts describe at least five royal palaces and gardens, a congregational mosque, baths, markets, and caravanserais, as well as barracks for the 10,000 enslaved Sudanese military troops with which Ibrahim II is said to have surrounded himself within the new city. These descriptions of scattered palaces, gardens, and barracks are redolent of the Abbasid palace-city Samarra in Iraq, built in 836, and would be later mirrored in Fatimid Sabra al-Mansuriya and the Qal'a of the Bani Hammad.

The Fatimids, a Shiite dynasty of caliphs who came to power, built their own new capitals. The first of these, Mahdia (al-Mahdiyya: [the city] of the Mahdi) was built on a peninsula jutting out into the Mediterranean. Easily defendable and with a harbor, access was controlled by an enormous outer wall with six towers, 10 meters in width, which was traversed by a vaulted corridor (Squifa al-Kahla) leading to the grand mosque built in around 912 but later remodeled as excavations revealed (Lézine 1965). The southern palace has been partially excavated and contains simple geometric floor mosaics which demonstrate that North African mosaic-making traditions survived well into the 10th century (Louhichi 2004). Mahdia was soon replaced by a new palace-city, Sabra al-Mansuriya, built on the outskirts of Kairouan in 947 and enclosed by a vast area of 111 hectares in an elliptical shape, in imitation of the circular city of Baghdad (Cressier and Rammah 2006). Much of the site has been destroyed by the expansion of modern Kairouan, but its basic topography is known from aerial photographs and limited excavations. The city was divided into an inner circular zone which contained at least two "palaces" and elaborate basins with pavements of *opus* sectile, mosaics, stone sculptures, and one of the most important collections of painted stucco with animal and human

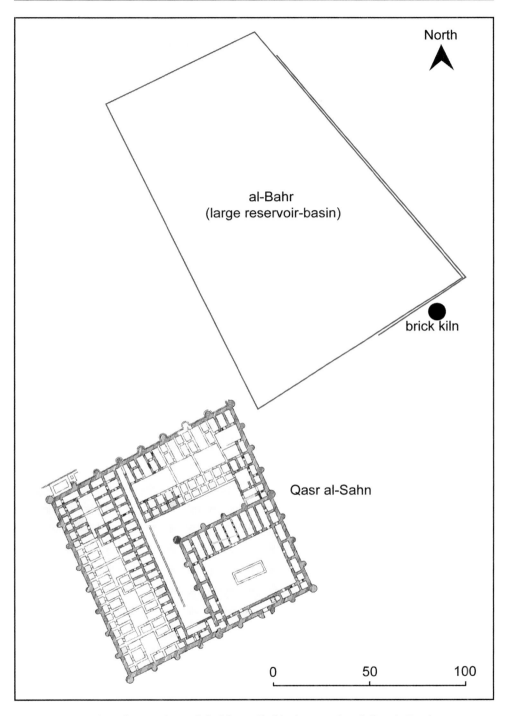

North

al-Bahr
(large reservoir-basin)

brick kiln

Qasr al-Sahn

0   50   100

FIGURE 3.1.5 Plan of Raqqada modified from Chabbi (1967–68) and Google Earth imagery.

Courtesy of Corisande Fenwick.

representations from the Maghreb before the 11th century (Barrucand and Rammah 2009). The outer zone contained residences and workshops producing glass and fine ceramics (lustre wares) and jewelry. Subsequent palace architecture, decoration, and design at the Zirid capital of Ashir (934) and the Hammadid capital of the Qal'a of the Beni Hammad (1008) owed much to the models set by the Aghlabids and Fatimids in their palace-cities outside Kairouan.

A rare glimpse into urban life beyond the palace-city comes from two sites: Sétif in Algeria and Surt in Libya. Salvage excavations at Sétif in the 1980s revealed a 10th- to 11th-century neighborhood (Mohamedi et al. 1991). The houses followed a uniform courtyard layout: an L-shaped entrance leading onto a large central courtyard surrounded by long narrow rooms which served as kitchens and sleeping/reception rooms (Figure 3.1.6). Each courtyard contained small domestic storage pits (silos) and wells and was probably also used for housing animals. This house form only appears after the Arab conquest and seems to be connected to the Arabization of society (Fentress 2013). For Fentress, this reorganization of domestic space is symbolic: the entrance protected the domestic space, and the organization of the dwelling reflects a spatial control by the paternal figure and a rigorous separation between men and women. Later a medieval rampart was constructed and a Muslim infant cemetery created just inside, possibly including a small marabout tomb. New forms of material culture speak to changing social and religious practices: filter jars were used to store water, pork was not consumed, the dead were buried on the right side with their heads to the northeast and facing Mecca. A similar pattern appears at Surt in Libya, where excavations have revealed a congregational mosque, forts, walls, and gates as well as courtyard housing, workshops, and cemeteries (Fehérvari et al. 2002). Far more is known of the urban plan, and it seems that the medieval town was surrounded by a substantial wall with two forts in the southern half, as well as an exterior fort to the northeast, and a central large courtyard mosque with a *qibla* facing south-southeast (the orientation usually used in the Maghrib) (Mouton and Racinet 2011). Our understanding of other medieval towns, newly founded or long-established centers, is extremely poor and heavily reliant on architectural studies of surviving monuments (e.g., mosques, shrines, walls, ribats) and the brief and partial summaries in the Arabic texts.

RURAL LANDSCAPES

Africa, "Rome's granary," was one of the most important agricultural producers and exporters in the Mediterranean in antiquity. Medieval Ifriqiya was equally famed for its agricultural wealth and often described as the most fertile region in the Islamic world. The region is ecologically varied and offers different possibilities for cultivation. Enough rain falls on the coast and Tell to grow grain, olives, figs, fruit trees, and vines. The more arid plains and pre-desert required floodwater or spring irrigation or the digging of wells to allow agriculture but supported pastoralism and animal husbandry. In the

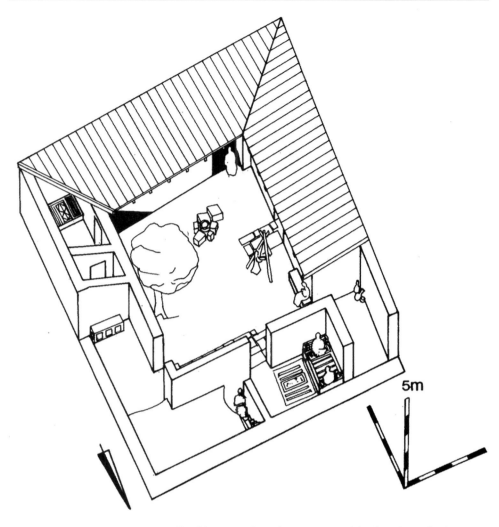

FIGURE 3.1.6 Reconstruction of building 1, 10th–11th century neighborhood, Sétif, Algeria.

Courtesy of Elizabeth Fentress.

Middle Ages, the Maghreb produced large amounts of olive oil, wine, wheat and barley, honey, saffron, dates, fruits, sesame oil, and cotton as well as producing textiles, leather, and other animal products that were exported all over the Islamic world, though this is challenging to demonstrate archaeologically (Vanacker 1973; Fenwick 2020: 81–104).

Few excavations of rural sites have taken place, and only a handful of field surveys in Tunisia and Libya have recorded the presence of medieval occupation, of which the most important are the UNESCO Libyan Valleys Survey in the 1980s, the Jerba survey in the 1990s, and the Leptis hinterland survey in the 2000s (Fenwick 2013). Although the UNESCO Libyan Valleys Survey did not systematically analyze medieval ceramics, they identified high numbers of sites in the Islamic period (Barker 1996; Sjöström 1993).

Fortified farms (*gsur*) continued to be built in the 9th century, and many Roman sites continued to be occupied. By the 11th century, the more remote and marginal wadis were abandoned for sedentary farming, and substantial medieval villages concentrated in the wettest regions of pre-desert zone in the northern Beni Ulid, Merdum, and Mansur wadi systems and the oasis at Gheriat el-Gharbia (Barker 1996: 177–178). The archaeological survey of the island of Jerba (Tunisia), as yet not fully published, recorded all phases of occupation from prehistoric periods through to the end of nominal Ottoman control in the middle of the 19th century (Holod and Kahlaoui 2017). Rural settlement boomed, where the numbers of sites had doubled by the 10th century and small farms cover the landscape, perhaps connected with the immigration of Ibadi settlers to the island.

Our best glimpse into the changing medieval and early modern countryside comes from the Italian survey in the hinterland of Leptis Magna (Lebda) conducted between 2007 and 2013 (Cirelli et al. 2012; Munzi et al. 2014). Although Leptis remained an important, if diminished, center, a significant drop in numbers of rural settlement and a decoupling of this region from broader trading circuits occurs as early as the 6th century. Between the 8th and 11th centuries, rural settlement (primarily open farms which presumably cultivated olives) increased significantly in the hinterland of the town, perhaps related to its revival by the 9th century. In the arid interior, a similar increase is seen, though the settlement pattern here is constituted of fortified villages and tower-granary structures, many newly founded. Site numbers drop again in the 12th and 13th centuries, perhaps relating to a rise in pastoralism and the abandonment of Leptis or the westward move of the Banu Hilal. A second phase of rural expansion comes in the Ottoman period, when unfortified villages and isolated houses appear (some with subterranean olive mills) alongside marabouts, and the ceramic material contains imports from Jerba and beyond.

A key, but often neglected, theme linked to that of rural settlement is that of the ecological changes and shifts in agricultural practices that occurred in the Middle Ages. The zooarchaeological evidence shows a continued reliance on sheep, goat, and cattle for milk, meat, wool, bone, and leather (Fenwick 2020: 97-99). The North African scrub landscape is ideally suited for sheep and goat herding, and it is unsurprising that they dominate the faunal assemblages in all periods. Cattle are more important for traction and meat in wetter Algeria at sites such as Cherchel and Sétif, in contrast to sites further east in Tunisia and Libya. Strikingly, there is a sharp drop in pig husbandry in the early medieval period, surely connected to the spread of Islamic dietary prohibitions. Nonetheless, at almost all sites, pig bones continue to be present in small numbers, and it seems likely that some may be wild boar, which are a common sight in the forested regions of Algeria and Tunisia today and are still hunted (and eaten).

Medieval agriculture focused on the "Mediterranean triad" of cereals, olives, and grape, supplemented by pulses (lentils, chickpeas, and beans). Olive oil was produced and exported in quantity across the Mediterranean in the Middle Ages (Jalloul 1998), though probably not on the same scale as in the Roman period. Pollen data and sediment analysis suggest that there is a decline in large-scale oleioculture in the Middle

Ages in the arid regions of southern Tunisia and Libya. In the Libyan pre-desert, for example, olive trees were intensively cultivated for olive oil in the Roman period, but by the 10th or 11th century, large-scale oleioculture had been replaced by an agricultural regime of cereal farming and pastoralism (Barker 1996: 352–357). While tree crops (grape, oil, fig, date, (sheep/goat) almond) did remain important, they appear in far smaller quantities than in the Roman period, and olive presses are absent from the medieval villages.

Andrew Watson's (1989) controversial thesis that the early Islamic period witnessed a "Green Revolution" has not been evaluated systematically in North Africa, where only limited archaeobotanical research has been conducted due to the challenges of collecting, floating, and studying samples. As yet, there is little archaeological evidence for the introduction of new crops and agricultural practices to Ifriqiya in the medieval period, and there is already evidence in late antiquity for many of Watson's "new" crops (e.g., durum wheat, sorghum, and cotton) in the irrigated Libyan Fazzan oases and pre-desert (Decker 2009). The written sources indicate that sugarcane was introduced to parts of Ifrīqiya by the 9th century (and more successfully to Sicily by the Aghlabids, where sugar molds have been found), though as yet no archaeological correlates have been uncovered. The picture is certainly more complicated, and targeted archaeobotanical and zooarchaeological work in conjunction with climatic work is urgently needed to reconstruct agricultural regimes and animal husbandry.

CERAMICS AND MATERIAL CULTURE

On the eve of the Arab conquests, North Africa was still one of the most important ceramic producers in the Mediterranean. African tablewares (African red slip ware), lamps, and amphorae were distributed across the Mediterranean. The final phases of African red slip ware production are the subject of much debate. Production at key workshop centers like Nabeul seems to continue into the early 8th century but of a lower-quality standard, with a whitish fabric and dominated by a late, simpler form of the Hayes 105 plate (Bonifay 2004: 210). Bowls such as Hayes 109 and Hayes 106 continued to be produced into the end of the 7th century, and perhaps into the 8th, based on finds in Italy and southern France (Reynolds 2016). Much more controversial and poorly understood are the 8th and 9th centuries (Cressier and Fentress 2011). Our poor knowledge of the ceramic typologies of this period certainly contributes to this haziness, but there was also a significant contraction in the level of local and long-distance trade as well as a shift toward handmade wares and local coarse wares

The introduction of glazed ceramics in the late ninth century coincides with Ifriqiya's re-emergence as a major trading hub linking sub-Saharan Africa, the Middle East and Europe (Fenwick 2020: 105-124). Scholarship has focused on three types of glazed ceramics: the yellow "Raqqada' wares of the late 9th century," metallic lustre wares of the 10th and 11th century, and Hafsid ceramics of the 14th century onward (Louhichi 2010 is the best overview). The first glazed wares appear in the late 9th century, manufactured at the Aghlabid palatial site of Raqqada (established in 876) at the same time as in Sicily and al-Andalus. The yellow wares of Raqqada (*jaune de Raqqada*)—are extremely distinctive with their mustard-yellow lead glaze and their abstract designs in green (copper) and brown (manganese). The new technique was accompanied by a new decorative repertoire of anthropomorphic and zoomorphic figures (especially birds) and the addition of specific Arabic formulas such as "al-mulk" (sovereignty) (Daoulatli 1994). These wares were widely diffused across North Africa and into sub-Saharan Africa, and their similarity with the earliest glazed wares of Palermo (*giallo di Palermo*) and those of Ifriqiya does seem to support the long-held notion that artisans originating from this part of North Africa spread new glazing techniques across Sicily (Ardizzone et al. 2015). A second variant on a white background with geometric and epigraphic decoration and no zoomorphic imagery was much more limited in quantity and diffusion, and Soundes Gragueb Chatti (2017) has recently suggested that this was a palatial production for the Aghlabid elite, inspired by Chinese Tang porcelain, and not for common use or distribution. Metallic lustre ware ceramics first appear in the 10th–11th centuries, imported from Fatimid Egypt as well as being manufactured locally. Recent excavations at the first Fatimid capital of Sabra al-Mansuriya uncovered a kiln with lustre ware wasters. Scientific analysis shows that a very different recipe (with significantly less silver) was used by the Tunisian potters to produce these ceramics (Waksman et al. 2014). Later still, under the Hafsid dynasty, Tunis became a major exporter of ceramics across the Mediterranean, especially to northern Italy, Provence, and Egypt. Ceramics are characterized by simple geometric, floral, and faunal decoration in cobalt blue and manganese brown probably produced in workshops in Tunis or its suburbs from the 14th century (Louhichi 2010).

In contrast to these luxury ceramics, almost nothing has been written about the monochrome green, brown, and yellow glazed pottery that is found widely across North Africa, though we might expect it to follow the same chronology tentatively proposed for Sicily: green glazes from the end of the 9th or beginning of the 10th followed by the introduction of less common brown and yellow monochrome glazes in the 10th–11th centuries (Ardizzone et al. 2015: 245–246). Unglazed tablewares, cooking wares, storage containers, lamps, and handmade wares which are the commonest forms are even less well understood. The rapid spread of new ceramics forms—conical bowls, platters, pitchers—in the late 9th century, may relate to changing habits in communal dining and service practices associated with Islam. The one- (or two-) handled *jarrito* with a wide cylindrical neck and flat base is a particularly characteristic form in North Africa, Spain, and Sicily and may have been used for storing yogurt or milk, a practice common in Morocco today (Reynolds 2016: 155).

While scholarship has focused on glazed ceramics, the period also saw new innovations in glass-making techniques. A radical change in glass production occurred in the Mediterranean during the late 8th and 9th centuries, when glassmakers stopped using natron from Egypt as a flux and started using plant ash instead (Henderson et al. 2004). In theory, the shift to plant ash would have allowed the emergence of primary workshops in North Africa because the raw materials no longer had to be imported, though artisans may still have imported the fine sand from Levant or glass ingots. Medieval glass workshops at Surt, Libya (10th century) and Sabra al-Mansuriya (10th–11th century) and several North African towns were known as being important production centers for different types of glass goods. Vast quantities of glass are typically found in Islamic layers at urban sites in North Africa, though they have seldom been studied and thus precise dating is challenging. Everyday items include cups and goblets, beakers, lamps, perfume flasks, and medicine bottles in similar styles to late antiquity. Some new glass forms also appear in this period, including vessels with relief-cut decoration (9th–11th century) and lustre-ware decoration (9th–11th century), probably imported from Egypt (Foy 2003). Glass was also used as window panes at palatial sites such as at Sabra al-Mansuriya and the Qal'a of the Beni Hammad.

Textiles rarely survive but were an important North African export as well as import. One of the earliest Islamic textiles was embroidered in Ifriqiya, the so-called *Marwan tiraz*, which was probably imported from Central Asia and then embroidered in a Tunisian silk workshop (dar al-tiraz), indicating that, already by this date, Abbasid-appointed governors in North Africa were receiving the most luxurious commodities from the Islamic East (Moraitou et al. 2012). In the pre-desert and Saharan regions, textiles do sometimes survive due to the arid conditions. At Ghirza in Libya, flax, cotton, and wool textiles dated to the 10th century have been recovered (Wild 1984). Most are made of a clockwise twist (Z-twist) or S2Z-plied yarns and are either undyed or decorated in multicolored bands with woven or embroidered designs. By the 10th century, textiles in the forms of carpets and embroidered cloth were one of the most important exports of Tunisia (Goitein 1967).

ARCHAEOLOGY OF RELIGION

The spread of Islam in North Africa is a contested, but understudied, topic. Archaeologists traditionally assumed that Christianity only survived precariously after the Arab conquests and that there was a large-scale and rapid conversion to Islam (see Handley 2004). Historians, in contrast, have shown that large Christian communities continued to thrive after the Arab conquests and certainly until the 11th century (Talbi 1990; Prevost 2007; Valérian 2011). The latest research suggests that, in Ifriqiya (unlike the Maghreb al-Aqsa), the spread of Islam was slow, and Christianity remained the dominant religion for several centuries (Fenwick 2020: 129-145).

Churches continued to be the major religious foci of many of the old towns, though it has proved difficult to demonstrate this archaeologically due to a tendency to date church abandonment to the Arab conquest in the 7th century. At Sbeïtla, for example, a medium-sized town which had an astonishing eight churches in use in the 7th century, including a double cathedral complex, five smaller churches, and a cemetery church, there is no evidence for a sudden destruction or abandonment of any churches after the

Arab conquest (Duval 1990). In the following centuries, some churches were repurposed for industrial or other uses, presumably reflecting a decline in the size of the Christian community over time, but at least two churches (Basilicas IV and V) continued to be used into the 10th century. Christians did not simply continue to use existing churches, but also built new ones, including at the Muslim capital of Kairouan, where funerary inscriptions attest to the existence of a substantial Christian community and church officials into the 10th century (Talbi 1990).

Mosques were not built in quantity in the 7th or 8th century outside Kairouan, Tunis (and perhaps Tripoli), where large numbers of Muslims lived (Fenwick 2013). In the old towns, mosques seem to have been initially confined to fortresses presumably for the Arab garrison troops, as in the citadels of Belalis Maior, Bagaï, and Tobna. In the 9th century, the construction of new dynastic urban foundations such as Tahart was accompanied by the construction of congregational mosques to serve their inhabitants. In the same period, congregational mosques and smaller oratories begin to be built in many of the inherited towns in Aghlabid Tunisia, coinciding with archaeological evidence for the abandonment or repurposing of churches. The great mosques of Kairouan, Tunis, Sousse (Figure 3.1.7), Sfax, and Monastir built by the Aghlabid emirs all survive today in their 9th-century form in testament to this mosque-building surge (Lézine 1966; Marçais 1954).

FIGURE 3.1.7 Great Mosque of Sousse (9th century).

Courtesy of Corisande Fenwick.

By the 11th century, most towns possessed a congregational mosque and several smaller mosques, and Islam seems to be the dominant religion, though small Jewish and Christian communities continued to thrive. The most spectacular examples of these urban mosques have been exhaustively studied by art historians (e.g., Rachid 1983), but only a handful have been excavated. The most significant are the urban mosques of Ajdabiya and Surt in Libya, both of which were rebuilt and expanded in the Fatimid period and have an octagonal minaret, similar to those found in Egypt (Blake et al. 1971; Fehérvari et al. 2002). Rural mosques, *marabout* (tombs of holy men), and the many medieval cemeteries found throughout the region have been almost entirely neglected to date, aside from studies in the Jebal Nafusa and Jerba (Prevost 2016; Holod and Kahlaoui 2017).

CONCLUSION

Islamic archaeology in North Africa is at a turning point. Despite the pivotal role that the region played in the early history of Islamic archaeology, it has suffered until recently from a lack of interest from archaeologists and the dominance of art-historical and architectural approaches. A growing community of scholars, in North Africa and Europe, using sophisticated theoretical and methodological toolkits, are turning their attention to the rich medieval heritage of Ifriqiya and beginning to transform our understanding of the medieval period. To date, however, research has primarily focused on the 7th–11th centuries and a handful of urban sites and monuments. We know far more about the transition from the late antique to Islamic city; early Islamic palaces, mosques, and ribats; and museum-quality objects than we do about trade and the economy, rural landscapes, the impact of Islam on daily life, or the introduction of new ceramic forms. Archaeological sciences need to be integrated into research projects to shed light on climate change, migration, and mobility, and on the introduction of new crops, husbandry practices, and manufacturing techniques. Later periods (up to and including the colonial period), as well as a far broader range of site types need to be examined to broaden our understanding of the Islamic world. Finally, there are a number of institutional challenges, particularly in Algeria and Libya, where conflict, security, politics, funding, and a lack of trained field archaeologists hinder archaeological research. If these challenges can be overcome, it is certain that archaeologists will play a leading role in rewriting the medieval history of Ifriqiya and the central Maghreb in coming years.

REFERENCES

Ajjabi, H. 1985. "Sabra al-Mansūriya (article in Arabic)," *Africa*, 9, 47–58.

Akbar, J. 1989. "Khaṭṭa and the Territorial Structure of Early Muslim Towns," *Muqarnas*, 6, 22–32.

Anderson, G., Fenwick, C., and Rosser-Owen, M. (eds.) 2017. *The Aghlabids and Their Neighbors: Art and Material Culture in Ninth-century North Africa* (Leiden: Brill).

Ardizzone, F., Pezzini, E., and Sacco, V. 2015. "The Role of Palermo in the Central Mediterranean: The Evolution of the Harbour and the Circulation of Ceramics (10th-11th centuries)," *Journal of Islamic Archaeology*, 2, 229–257.

Bahri, F., and Taamallah, M. 2019. "L'apport de l'archéogéographie à la restitution du plan ancien de Kairouan," in R. Bockmann, A. Leone, and P. von Rummel (eds.), *Africa—Ifriqiya. Cultures of Transition in North Africa between Late Antiquity and Early Middle Ages* (Rome: DAI), 231–244.

Barker, G. 1996. *Farming the Desert: The UNESCO Libyan Archaeological Survey* (London: The Society for Libyan Studies).

Barrucand, M., and Rammah, M. 2009. "Sabra Al-Mansuriyya and Her Neighbors During the First Half of the Eleventh Century: Investigations into Stucco Decoration," *Muqarnas*, 26, 349–376.

Bennison, A. K. 2016. *Almoravid and Almohad Empires* (Edinburgh: Edinburgh University Press).

Blake, H., Hutt, A., and Whitehouse, D. 1971. "Ajdabiyah and the Earliest Fatimid Architecture," *Libya Antiqua*, 8, 105–120.

Bloom, J. 2007. *Arts of the City Victorious. Islamic Art and Architecture in Fatimid North Africa and Egypt* (New Haven: Yale University Press).

Bonifay, M. 2004. *Etudes sur la céramique romaine tardive d'Afrique* (Oxford: Archaeopress).

Brett, M. 1978. "The Arab Conquest and the Rise of Islam in North Africa," in J. D. Fage (ed.), *Cambridge History of Africa* (Cambridge: Cambridge University Press), 490–555.

Brett, M. 2017. *Fatimid Empire* (Edinburgh: Edinburgh University Press).

Brodie, N. 2015. "Why Is No One Talking About Libya's Cultural Destruction?," *Near Eastern Archaeology*, 78, 212–217.

Cadenat, P. 1977. "Recherches à Tihert-Tagdempt 1958–1959," *Bulletin d'archéologie algerienne*, 7, 393–462.

Chabbi, M. 1967–1968. "Raqqada (résumé)," *Africa*, 2, 349–352.

Cirelli, E. 2001. "Leptis Magna in età islamica: fonti scritti e archeologiche," *Archeologia Medievale*, 28, 423–440.

Cirelli, E., Felici, F., and Munzi, M. 2012. "Insediamenti fortificati nel territorio di Leptis Magna tra III e XI secolo," in P. Galetti (ed.), *Paesaggi, Comunità, Villaggi Medievali. Atti del Convegno internazionale di studio, Bologna, 14–16 gennaio 2010* (Spoleto: Fondazione Centro Italiano di Studi sull-Alto Medioevo), 763–767.

Cressier, P. 2013. "Ville médievale au Maghreb. Recherches archéologiques," in P. Senac (ed.), *Histoire et Archéologie de l'Occident musulman (VIIe-XVe siecles), Al-Andalus, Maghreb, Sicile* (Toulouse: Maison de la Recherche), 117–140.

Cressier, P., and Fentress, E. (eds.) 2011. *La céramique maghrébine du haut moyen âge, VIIIe-Xe siècle: état des recherches, problèmes et perspectives* (Rome: École française de Rome).

Cressier, P., and Rammah, M. 2006. "Sabra al-Mansuriya. Une nouvelle approche archéologique," *Comptes-rendus des séances de l'Académie des Inscriptions et Belles-Lettres*, 150, 613–633.

Daoulatli, A. 1976. *Tunis sous les Hafside* (Doctoral thesis, Tunis: National Institute of Archeology and Art).

Daoulatli, A. 1994. "Le IXe siècle: le jaune de Raqqada," *Couleurs de Tunisie: 25 siècles de céramique* (Paris: Société Nouvelle Adam-Biro), 95–96.

de Beylié, L. 1909. *La Kalaa des Béni Hammad* (Paris: E. Leroux).

Decker, M. 2009. "Plants and Progress: Rethinking the Islamic Agricultural Revolution," *Journal of World History*, 20, 187–206.

Duval, N. 1990. "Sufetula: l'histoire d'une ville romaine de la haute-steppe à la lumière des recherches récentes," *L'Afrique dans l'Occident romain. Actes du colloque organisé par IEFR (Rome. 3–5 die. 1987)* (Rome: École française de Rome), 495–535.

Fehérvari, G., Hamdani, A., Shaghlouf, M., and Bishop, H. 2002. *Excavations at Surt (Medinat al-Sultan) Between 1977 and 1981* (London: Society for Libyan Studies).

Fentress, E. 2013. "Reconsidering Islamic housing in the Maghreb," in I. Grau Mira and S. Gutiérrez Lloret (eds.), *De la estructura domestica al espacio social. Lecturas arqueologicas del uso social del espacio* (Alicante: Universidad de Alicante), 237–244.

Fenwick, C. 2008. "Archaeology and the Search for Authenticity: Colonialist, Nationalist, and Berberist Visions of an Algerian Past," in C. Fenwick, M. Wiggins, and D. Wythe (eds.), *TRAC 2007: Proceedings of the 17th Annual Theoretical Roman Archaeology Conference* (Oxford: Oxbow), 75–88.

Fenwick, C. 2013. "From Africa to Ifrīqiya: Settlement and Society in Early Medieval North Africa (650–800)," *Al-Masāq*, 25, 9–33.

Fenwick, C. 2018. "Early Medieval Urbanism in Ifrīqiya and the Emergence of the Islamic City," in S. Panzram and L. Callegarin (eds.), *Entre civitas y madīna. El mundo de las ciudades en la península ibérica y en el norte de África (ss. IV–IX)* (Madrid: Casa de Velázquez), 283–304.

Fenwick, C. 2019. "The Fate of the Classical Cities of North Africa in the Middle Ages," in R. Bockmann, A. Leone, and P. von Rummel (eds.), *Africa—Ifrīqiya. Cultures of Transiton in North Africa Between Late Antiquity and the Early Middle Ages* (Rome: Deutsches Archäologisches Institut): 137-156.

Fenwick, C. 2020. *Early Islamic North Africa: A New Perspective* (London: Bloomsbury).

Fenwick, C. forthcoming. "The Umayyads and North Africa," in A. Marsham (ed.), *The Umayyad World* (London: Routledge).

Foy, D. 2003. "Le Verre en Tunisie: L'apport des fouilles récentes tuniso-françaises," *Journal of Glass Studies*, 59–89.

Gelichi, S., and Milanese, M. 2002. "The Transformation of the Ancient Towns in Central Tunisia during the Islamic Period: The Example of Uchi Maius," *Al-Masāq*, 14, 33–45.

`Goitein, S. D. 1967. *A Mediterranean Society: The Jewish Communities of the Arab World as Portrayed in the Documents of the Cairo Geniza* (Berkeley: University of California Press).

Golvin, L. 1957. *Le Magrib central à l'époque des Zirides* (Paris: Arts et métiers graphiques).

Golvin, L. 1966. "Le Palais de Zīrī à Achîr (Dixième Siècle JC)," *Ars Orientalis*, 47–76.

Gragueb Chatti, S. 2017. "La céramique aghlabide de la Raqqada et les productions de l'Orient islamique: parenté et filiation," in G. Anderson, C. Fenwick, and M. Rosser-Owen (eds.), *The Aghlabids and Their Neighbors: Art and Material Culture in Ninth-Century North Africa* (Leiden: Brill), 341–361.

Handley, M. 2004. "Disputing the End of African Christianity", in A. H. Merrills (ed.), *Vandals, Romans and Berbers. New Perspectives on Late Antique North Africa* (Aldershot: Ashgate), 291–310.

Henderson, J., McLoughlin, S., and McPhail, D. 2004. "Radical Changes in Islamic Glass Technology: Evidence for Conservatism and Experimentation with New Glass Recipes from Early and Middle Islamic Raqqa, Syria," *Archaeometry*, 46, 439–468.

Holod, R., and Kahlaoui, T. 2017. "Jerba of the Ninth Century: Under Aghlabid Control?," in G. Anderson, C. Fenwick, and M. Rosser-Owen (eds.), *The Aghlabids and Their Neighbors: Art and Material Culture in Ninth-Century North Africa* (Leiden: Brill), 449–469.

Idris, H. R. 1962. *La Berbérie orientale sous les Zirides, Xe-XIIe siècles* (Paris: Adrien-Maisonneuve).

Jalloul, N. 1998. "Permanences antiques et mutations médiévales: agriculture et produits du sol en Ifriqiya au haut moyen âge (ixe–xiie s.)," *Africa Romana*, 12, 485–511.

Kaegi, W. E. 2010. *Muslim Expansion and Byzantine Collapse in North Africa* (Cambridge: Cambridge University Press).

Kallala, N., Sanmartí, J., Franco, M. C. B., and Álvarez, R. 2011. *Althiburos: la fouille dans l'aire du capitole et dans la nécropole méridionale. I* (Barcelona: Universitat de Barcelona; Institut Català d'Arqueologia Clàssica).

Kennedy, H. 1985. "From Polis to Madina: Urban Change in Late Antique and Early Islamic Syria," *Past and Present*, 106, 3–27.

Khelifa, A. 1987. "Arqueología musulmana en Argelia," *Sharq al-Andalus. Estudios Árabes* 4, 203–214.

Khelifa, A. 2008. *Honaine: ancien port du royaume de Tlemcen* (Alger: Édition Dalimen).

King, G. R. D. 1989. "Islamic Archaeology in Libya 1969–1989," *Libyan Studies*, 20, 193–207.

Leone, A. 2007. *Changing Townscapes in North Africa from Late Antiquity to the Arab Conquest* (Bari: Edipuglia).

Lézine, A. 1956. *Le ribat de Sousse suivi de notes sur le ribat de Monastir* (Tunis: Imprimerie La Rapide).

Lézine, A. 1965. *Mahdiya: recherches d'archéologie islamique* (Paris: Klincksieck).

Lézine, A. 1966. *Architecture de l'Ifriqiya: recherches sur les monuments aghlabides* (Paris: Klincksieck).

Lorcin, P. M. E. 2002. "Rome and France in Africa: Recovering Colonial Algeria's Latin Past," *French Historical Studies*, 25, 295–329.

Louhichi, A. 1997. "La céramique fatimide et ziride de Mahdia d'après des fouilles de Q'sar Al-Qaïm," *Africa*, 15, 123–138.

Louhichi, A. 2004. "La mosaique de Mahdia," *Africa*, 10, 143–166.

Louhichi, A. 2010. *Céramique Islamique de Tunisie. École de Kairouan, École de Tunis* (Tunis: Éditions de l'Agence de mise en valeur).

Mahfoudh, F. 2003. *Architecture et urbanisme en Ifriqiya Médiévale* (Tunis: Centre de Publication Universitaire).

Mahjoubi, A. 1978. *Recherches d'histoire et d'archéologie à Henchir el-Faouar, Tunisie: la cité des Belalitani Maiores* (Tunis: Université de Tunis).

Manzano Moreno, E. 2010. "The Iberian Peninsula and North Africa," in C. Robinson (ed.), *The New Cambridge History of Islam* (Cambridge: Cambridge University Press), 581–621.

Marçais, G. 1913. *Les Poteries et Faiences de la Qal'a des Beni Hammad* (Constantine: Braham).

Marçais, G. 1925. "Fouilles à 'Abbâssiya," *Bulletin Archéologique*, 293–306.

Marçais, G. 1946. "Tihert-Tagdempt," *Revue Africaine*, 90, 24–57.

Marçais, G. 1954. *L'architecture musulmane d'occident: Tunisie, Algérie, Maroc, Espagne et Sicile* (Paris: Arts et métiers graphiques).

Mohamedi, A., Benmansour, A., Amamra, A. A., and Fentress, E. 1991. *Fouilles de Sétif. 1977–1984* (Alger: Agence Nationale d'Archéologie et de Protection des sites et Monuments Historiques).

Moraitou, M., Rosser-Owen, M., and Cabrera, A. 2012. "Fragments of the So-Called Marwan Tiraz," in H. C. Evans (ed.), *Byzantium and Islam: Age of Transition* (London: Yale University Press), 238–241.

Mouton, J.-M., and Racinet, P. 2011. "Surt: histoire et archéologie d'une ville médiévale libyenne," *Les nouvelles de l'archéologie*, 34–38.

Munzi, M., Felici, F., Sjostrom, I., and Zocchi, A. 2014. "La Tripolitania rurale tardoantica, medievale e ottomana alla luce delle recenti indagini archeologiche territoriali nella regione di Leptis Magna," *Archeologia medievale*, 215–246.

Pentz, P. 2002. *From Roman Proconsularis to Islamic Ifriqiyah* (Göteborg: Götesborgs Universitet).

Potter, T. W. 1995. *Towns in late antiquity: Iol Caesarea and its context* (Sheffield: Sheffield University Press).

Prevost, V. 2007. "Les dernières communautés chrétiennes autochtones d'Afrique du Nord," *Revue de l'histoire des religions*, 224, 461–483.

Prevost, V. 2016. *Les mosquées ibadites du djebel Nafusa: Architecture, histoire et religions du nort-ouest de la Libye (VIIe–XIIIe siècle)* (London: Society for Libyan Studies).

Rachid, B. 1983. *L'art religieux musulman en Algérie* (Algiers: SNED).

Raymond, A. 2002. *Arab Cities in the Ottoman Period: Cairo, Syria, and the Maghreb* (London: Routledge).

Reynolds, P. 2016. "From Vandal Africa to Arab Ifriqiya," in S. T. Stevens and J. P. Conant (eds.), *North Africa under Byzantium and Islam* (Washington DC: Dumbarton Oaks), 129–172.

Saadaoui, A. 2001. *Tunis, ville ottomane: trois siècles d'urbanisme et d'architecture* (Tunis: Centre de publication universitaire).

Sjöström, I. 1993. *Tripolitania in Transition: Late Roman to Islamic Settlement* (Aldershot: Avebury).

Stevens, S. T. 2016. "Carthage in Transition. From Late Byzantine City to Medieval Villages," in S. T. Stevens and J. P. Conant (eds.), *North Africa Under Byzantium and Islam* (Washington DC: Dumbarton Oaks), 89–104.

Talbi, M. 1966. *L'Émirat Aghlabide* (Tunis: Maisonneuve).

Talbi, M. 1990. "Le Christianisme maghrébin de la conquête musulmane à sa disparition: une tentative d'explication," in M. Gervers and R. J. Bikhazi (eds.), *Conversion and Continuity. Indigenous Christian Communities in Islamic Lands. Eight to Eighteenth Centuries* (Toronto: Pontifical Institute of Mediaeval Studies), 313–351.

Thébert, Y., and Biget, J.-L. 1990. "Afrique après la disparition de la cité classique," *L'Afrique dans l'Occident romain. Actes du colloque de Rome, 3–5 décembre 1987* (Rome: École française de Rome), 575–602.

Touihri, C. 2014. "La transition urbaine de Byzance à Islam en Ifriqiya depuis l'archéologie. Quelques notes préliminaires," in A. Nef and F. Ardizzone (eds.), *Le dinamiche dell'islamizzazione nel Mediterraneo centrale e in Sicilia: nuove proposte e scoperte recenti* (Paris: L'École Française), 131–140.

Valérian, D. 2011. "La permanence du christianisme au Maghreb: l'apport problématique des sources latines," in D. Valérian (ed.), *Islamisation et arabisation de l'Occident musulman médiéval (VIIe-XIIe siècle)* (Paris: Publications de la Sorbonne), 131–149.

Vanacker, C. 1973. "Géographie économique de l'Afrique du Nord selon les auteurs arabes du IXe siècle au milieu du XIIe siècle", *Annales. Histoire, Sciences Sociales*, 659–680.

van Berchem, M. 1954. "Sedrata. Un chapitre nouveau de l'histoire de l'art Musulman. Campagnes de 1951 et 1952," *Ars Orientalis*, 1, 157–172.

Vitelli, G. 1981. *Islamic Carthage: The Archaeological, Historical and Ceramic Evidence* (Carthage: Centre d'Etudes et de Documentation Archéologique de Carthage).

von Rummel, P. 2016. "The Transformation of Ancient Land- and Cityscapes in Early Medieval North Africa," in S. T. Stevens and J. Conant (eds.), *North Africa Under Byzantium and Islam* (Washington DC: Dumbarton Oaks), 105–118.

Waksman, Y., Capelli, C., Pradell, T., and Molera, J. 2014. "The Ways of the Lustre: Looking for the Tunisian Connection," in M. Martinón-Torres (ed.), *Craft and Science: International Perspectives on Archaeological Ceramics* (Qatar: UCL Qatar series in archaeology and cultural heritage, 1), 109–116.

Watson, A. M. 1989. *Agricultural Innovation in the Early Islamic World: The Diffusion of Crops and Farming Techniques. 700–1100* (Cambridge: Cambridge University Press).

Wild, J.-P. 1984. "Textiles from Building 32 Ghirza," in O. Brogan and D. J. Smith (eds.), *Ghirza: A Libyan Settlement in the Roman Period* (Tripoli: Libyan Antiquities Department), 291–308.

Zbiss, S.-M. 1956. "Mahdia et Sabra-mansoûriya: nouveaux documents d'art fatimide d'Occident," *Journal Asiatique*, 244, 79–93.

CHAPTER 3.2

....

THE MAGHREB AL-AQSA

....

ABDALLAH FILI

AT the start of the 8th century, the far western Maghreb became part of the *Dar al-Islam* after a rapid conquest described only fleetingly in the sources. But, in less than half a century, this region became largely independent of the eastern caliphate. The Berbers, newly Islamized, did not support the abuses perpetrated by the Umayyad governors of the region and took refuge in Kharajite and Shiite doctrines which formed the basis of new emirates, of which the most important were the Idrisids at Volubilis and then Fes (789–985), the Midrarids at Sijilmasa (757–977), the Salihids at Nakur (740–935), and the Baraghwata on the Atlantic plains (741–ca. 1060). This period of political and religious experimentation divided the Moroccan landscape until the advent of the Almohads during the first half of the 11th century. They put an end to this collection of emirates and religious doctrines and established a (Maliki) doctrinal and political unity across the Maghreb and the Iberian Peninsula (Bennison 2016). Their empire marks the pivotal role of Morocco in the cycle of autonomous Berber states of the West such as the Almohads (1147–1269), the Merinids (1269–1465), the Saadiens (1554–1636), and the Alaouites (since 1669). These political dynamics have given Morocco a very varied historical and archaeological heritage that justifies the existence of the discipline of Islamic archaeology.

And yet, from its tumultuous beginnings in colonial times until today, Islamic archaeology remains the poor relation of Moroccan archaeology. The thirteen centuries of the country's Islamic heritage do not justify its continued status as subaltern to classical archaeology, which is highly favored by funders and politicians for projects, recruitment, and training, and remains traditional in approach. Objective explanations can be found for this situation—for example, a lack of personnel and financial resources that handicaps ambitious projects—but they do not justify the lack of a vision and a strategy to overcome its shortcomings (Figure 3.2.1).

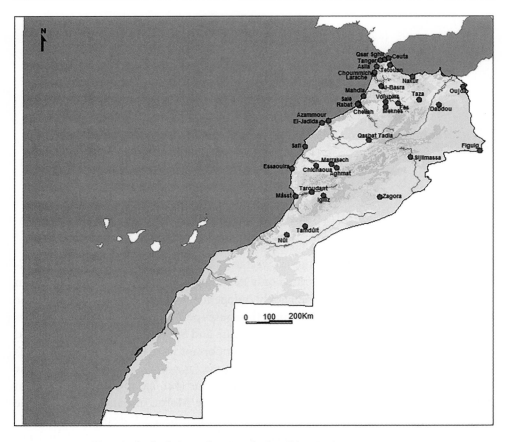

FIGURE 3.2.1 The Maghreb al-Aqsa showing the key Islamic sites.

Courtesy of Abdallah Fili and Ihssane Serrat.

HISTORIOGRAPHY AND
THE HISTORY OF RESEARCH

If we define Islamic archaeology in Morocco as the scientific analysis of remains dating back to the medieval period, the discipline was born in the late 19th century, with the arrival of the first European explorers just before direct colonization by France in 1912. It thus commenced as a colonial science, operating under the auspices and authority of the Protectorate administration. Experienced researchers including Edmond Doutté, de la Martinière, Tissot, Thouvenot, and others, many of whom had often already proved their worth in Algeria, were mobilized to map and document Morocco's heritage as part of the Scientific Mission of Morocco. They left us important descriptions of several sites and monuments of that time, as well as locating pivotal sites described in the Arabic sources such as Aghmat, Tinmal, Amergou, and Dchira (Thouvenot 1933; Doutté 1914;

Lévi-Provençal 1918). Almost no archaeological excavation, however, was conducted on any Islamic site before the 1940s. Those excavations that did occur were accidental and at sites wrongly assumed to be classical; this is the case for Dchira in the Rabat region (Terrasse 1937) or Fès al-Bali in the Fes region (Vicaire and Thouvenot 1938). On the other hand, from the 1920s, the archaeology of monuments flourished, which has heavily influenced Moroccan archaeological approaches, thanks to Henri Terrasse and Henri Basset who established a publication series on Almohad sanctuaries and fortresses in the journal *Hespéris* in 1923. The work of Evariste Levi Provençal, Robert Montagne, Djin Jacques-Meunié, and later Paul Berthier on Islamic architecture was also important in this period.

Initially, archaeological research was managed by the Department of Fine Arts and Antiquities and the Institute of Higher Moroccan Studies, both of which were created in the 1920s after the Scientific Mission of Morocco. These institutions were also responsible for teaching from 1921, although no Moroccan benefitted from training in archaeology. If the restoration of monuments was the prerogative of Fine Arts, their analysis was undertaken by the Institute of Higher Studies, both placed under the authority of Henri Terrasse in 1941. Terrasse's hand shaped Islamic archaeology in Morocco in the colonial era: he promoted the architectural approach which has analyzed most of the known medieval and early modern monuments, as well as launching several archaeological excavations, the most important of which was in Marrakech and its environs and was led by Jacques Meunié, Charles Allain, and Gaston Deverdun (Meunié et al. 1952). He was also the instigator of several large-scale studies on imperial cities, including those by Roger Le Tourneau (1947) on Fes, Gaston Deverdun (1959) on Marrakech, and Jacques Caillé (1949) on Rabat.

Islamic archaeology under the Spanish Protectorate in Northern Morocco has many points in common with French Morocco. As early as the end of the 19th century, Spanish explorers visited the same sites, such as Volubilis and Chella, as French explorers and diplomats and shared the same passion for classical archaeology and the study of monumental architecture (Gozalbes Cravioto 2005). Like the French, they also established dedicated archaeological journals, including *Tamuda*, and the "Archaeological Chronicles" of the later journal *Al-Andalus* (Cressier 2009).

After independence in 1956, the priorities of the Moroccan state were elsewhere. The absence of public demand for archaeology, coupled with the lack of Moroccan specialists, relegated archaeology to the background. Several French specialists still continued their research on the classical and prehistoric Morocco, with only Bernard Rosenberger's (1970) important work on the medieval mines. The Antiquities Service, reorganized in 1975, established an Archaeology Service whose mission was to establish a national research and training strategy and promote scientific cooperation with foreign teams. It launched two training excavations, one of which was dedicated to Islamic archaeology at the medieval site of Belyounech (1975–1978). Multidisciplinary teams, new problematics, and refined approaches gradually put an end to small-scale efforts by individuals often working alone. It is in this light that two joint programs were launched in the framework of Moroccan–French cooperation. The first was the survey of Jbala-Ghomara

(Bazzana et al. 1983–1984) launched in 1982 and dedicated to mapping the Mediterranean coastline between Tetouan and Targha; its objective was to study the evolution of the settlement hierarchy of the Targha Valley and the medieval habitat and hydraulics at the site of Taghassa. The second started in 1984 and focused on the ethnoarchaeology of firing technologies by studying potters' workshops in Morocco and their ceramic productions through a combination of survey and laboratory studies (El Hraiki 1989). In 1985, the National Institute of Archaeology and Heritage Sciences (INSAP) was created by Joudia Hassar-Benslimane and Abdelaziz Touri, marking the beginning of a new era of training and research in archaeology, and especially in Islamic archaeology. International partnerships and programs multiplied and became essential for research in medieval Moroccan archaeology, a relationship that has, however, proved to be limiting in terms of vision and strategy.

CITIES

As in the rest of North Africa (see Chapter 3.1), the urban milieu has been the focus of archaeological attention in Morocco since the colonial period. Post-independence studies continued the tradition of monumental archaeology and the focus on the imperial cities established in the colonial period through studies of the princely city of Meknes (Barrucand 1985) and Sale (Hassar-Benslimane 1992). The study of the Moroccan Islamic city through the lens of the archaeological excavation is more recent, though, in the absence of systematic rescue archaeology, excavation has largely been constrained to abandoned sites. We know very little archaeologically about the imperial cities of Fes, Marrakech, Rabat, and Meknes, which are all still living cities and do not permit excavations.

Deserted medieval cities, oddly enough, excited little interest from colonial scholars in contrast to deserted Roman cities which were the focus of extensive excavations. The American archaeologist Charles Redman was the first medieval archaeologist to have been interested in this period by beginning very successful test excavations at al-Basra and other urban sites in northern Morocco (Redman 1983–1984) before commencing extensive excavations at Ksar Seghir (Redman 1986). The creation of INSAP in the 1980s gave further impetus to archaeological research on deserted Islamic cities and the transition from classical cities, and important excavations were started at Volubilis by Aomar Akerraz, Sijilmasa by Ronald Messier, and al-Basra by Nancy Benco. Such projects remained a rarity, however, and it was not until the late 1990s that there was a dedicated effort to explore the genesis of urbanism in medieval Morocco. Combining geophysics and archaeological surveys in and around three major sites in Islamic Morocco—Nakur in the north, Aghmat in the center, and Tamdult in the south—a Moroccan-French project aimed to study the features of Moroccan urbanism, the population dynamics of the three cities, and the relationship between city and countryside (Cressier et al. 2001; Cressier 2004, 2007). Since the 2000s, a number of important

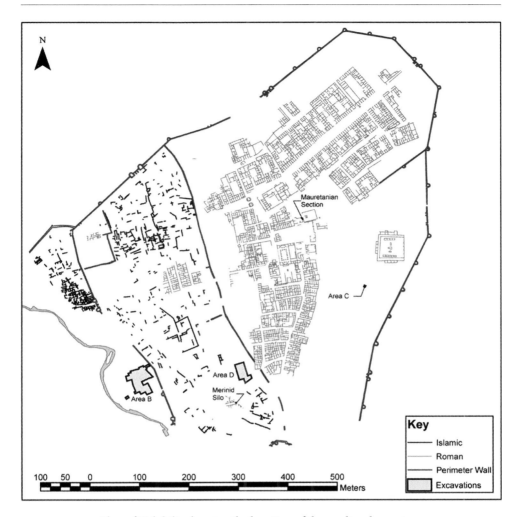

FIGURE 3.2.2 Plan of Volubilis showing the location of the medieval remains.

Courtesy of Volubilis Archaeological Project.

interdisciplinary projects on the medieval layers of Roman towns and medieval foundations have taken place, though work continues to focus on the early Islamic period at the expense of later periods.

There are two types of cities that characterize the early Islamic period: those that existed before Islam and have Roman or pre-Roman roots and those that were founded in the medieval period (see Cressier 1998, for an overview). Both remain poorly understood at present. In Morocco, research on the transition from Antiquity to the medieval period has been, until recently, the preserve of classical scholars though they were rarely interested in the medieval remains covering Roman structures. The works of Aomar Akerraz on the transition from antiquity to the Middle Ages in Volubilis (Figure 3.2.2) were exceptional for their time. He uncovered an Islamic neighborhood of the 8th–9th centuries north of the triumphal arch of Caracalla above a Roman house and a late Roman necropolis with Christian burials (Akerraz 1985, 1998). The neighborhood contained a habitat outside the 6th-century enceinte, still in use during the Islamic period, constituting perhaps a suburb outside the center of power. It contained very varied ceramic material as well as some glass crucibles attesting to the practice of glass techniques at an early period (El Hassani 2017).

Excavations in the 2000s led by Elizabeth Fentress and Hassan Limane explored other areas of the medieval city, including a zone within the walled area of the city and an extramural quarter containing the Islamic hammam of this city and a connected group of courtyard houses, which the excavators argued is connected with the arrival of Idris I at the end of the 8th century (Fentress and Limane 2011, 2019). Late antique ceramic forms persist, and it is necessary to wait until the 9th century to see progressive changes and a diversification in forms and decoration(Amorós Ruiz and Fili 2011). However, cultural change begins to be reflected in material culture. The amount of pig consumed on the site drops significantly and burial practice follows Islamic rites, while metalwork bearing Arabic inscriptions and Islamic decoration appears, such as the Volubilis seal-ring with a clear Eastern origin bearing one of the oldest Koranic inscriptions in Morocco (Fili 2014). Numismatic changes, however, are the most important at this time, and silver and bronze coins were minted at Volubilis following Islamic models (Eustache 1970–1971). Monetary production and circulation reached unprecedented levels, reflecting an intense political dynamic as seat of the Idrisid emirate but also a considerable economic activity. The research at Volubilis continues with a new ambitious project on housing and daily life at the medieval site, one led by Elizabeth Fentress, Corisande Fenwick, and Hassan Limane (2018–2022).

The contemporary Idrisid site of al-Basra (ca. 800–1100) and its hinterland in northern Morocco has also been studied in detail (Benco 2004; Ennahid 2001). Following a series of archaeological surveys carried out in al-Basra in the early 1980s, excavations took place through a number of small test trenches within the Idrisid city whose 10th-century stone enceinte with circular towers is still, in part, preserved. Production facilities for local pottery and metallurgy were located in the artisanal sector, and central courtyard houses were studied in the residential area. Unfortunately, excavation by test trench (a far too common practice) did not make it possible to fully exploit the urban and architectural study of the site. However,a detailed study of ceramics and metallurgical material was conducted and the site is one of the first medieval ceramic reference corpuses in Morocco (Benco 1987).

The town of Sijilmasa (Figure 3.2.3), the famous caravan city founded in the 8th century by the Midrarid dynasty, has been the subject of archaeological work since the 1980s but its results are poorly disseminated, with the exception of the Moroccan-American project led by Ronald Messier. The objective of this project was to understand the spatial development of the caravan city and its hinterland through excavation and analysis of the material culture. Occupation covers the 9th to the 19th century, however, the choice of test-trenching in vogue at the time has limited archaeological interpretation (Messier and Miller 2015). Excavations uncovered several levels of the

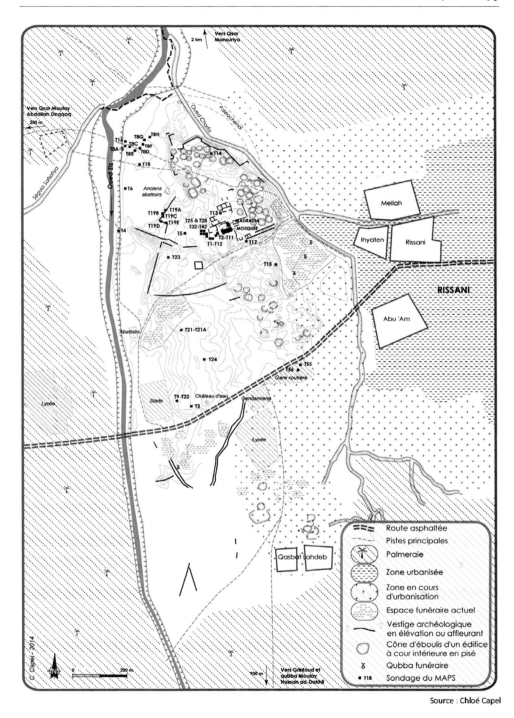

Source : Chloé Capel

FIGURE 3.2.3 Sijlmassa. Plan of the archaeological site and the sixty-three trenches excavated between 1988 and 1998.

Courtesy of Chloe Capel.

congregational mosque, established in the 11th century and enlarged and reoriented in the Almohad period (Messier 1999), as well as several residences and the defensive enceinte. The ceramics show the presence of local productions as well as ceramics imported from both North and South Sahara (Messier and Fili 2011). This material attests to the dynamics of trans-Saharan exchanges and the importance of the local economy in these exchanges (Capel and Fili 2016). A new Moroccan-French project commenced in 2012 under the direction of F.-X. Fauvelle-Aymar and L. Erbati: we await detailed publications to say more.

If the modesty of urban investment in the 8th century is surprising, Sijilmasa and Fes present a different picture by the 9th–10th centuries. Thus, in Sijlmasa, a Midrarid courtyard house reveals painted and carved decorative plaster, currently unique in Morocco, but whose oriental influence is very likely. The decoration is characterized by a deep band with geometric patterns, including a swastika and a diamond pattern enclosed in a square. An exceptional fragment is decorated with an inscribed medallion with three words from verse 286 of the second sura ("The Cow") (Messier and Fili 2011). In the same level, a fragment of wooden ceiling painted with geometric patterns was unearthed (Figure 3.2.4). Just as exceptional is the assemblage discovered in Fes under the great Qaraouiyyin mosque and dated to the 9th and 10th centuries. Rescue excavations revealed part of the foundations of the earliest Qarawiyyin mosque, founded, according to tradition, by Fatima al-Fihriyya in 857 CE and enlarged by the Umayyads of Cordoba in 958 CE (Ettahiri 2007). The plaster consists of fragments with Koranic inscriptions from Surah, II, LI, and CXII on a blue background, whose line of writing is horizontal or curved. The nature of the inscriptions suggests that the stucco comes from

FIGURE 3.2.4 Sijilmassa, decorated beam of the Midrarid period (9th-10th centuries).

Courtesy of Chloe Capel.

the walls of the Idrisid or Umayyad mosque, probably from the wall of the *qibla* that was destroyed by the Almoravids during the expansion of the mosque in 1134. The epigraphic style is archaic but very different from that of Sijilmassa. This set is added to other exceptional objects of this period, including the beam of Dawud and the so-called minbar of the Andalusians.

The study of urbanism in the 10th–16th centuries continues to be dominated by architectural studies of the imperial cities Fes, Marrakech, Rabat, and Meknes, but archaeology does provide with us a fascinating glimpse at the first Almoravid capital, Aghmat (Figure 3.2.6). Capital of a local emirate until 1057–1058, and the first Almoravid capital before the foundation of Marrakech in 1070, Aghmat was first studied within the Moroccan–French program on the origins of the Islamic city in Morocco. A more ambitious project was launched by Ronald Messier and Abdallah Fili in 2005. Funded by private means, the choice was made from the outset to focus on extensive excavation to discover the spatial organization of the city, or, more precisely, its monumental center. Few deep excavations have been conducted in Morocco to uncover the excavated remains for public display. As a result, the enhancement and restoration of the remains were placed at the center of the scientific agenda. Beginning with a focus on the monumental hammam (Fili and Messier 2015), the project then uncovered one of the palaces of the city (Figure 3.2.5; Fili et al. 2014) as well as the great mosque and its dome of ablutions (Héritier-Salama et al. 2016). These building complexes were all abandoned at the

FIGURE 3.2.5 Aghmat, the palace viewed from the north.

Courtesy of Mission Archéologique d'Aghmat.

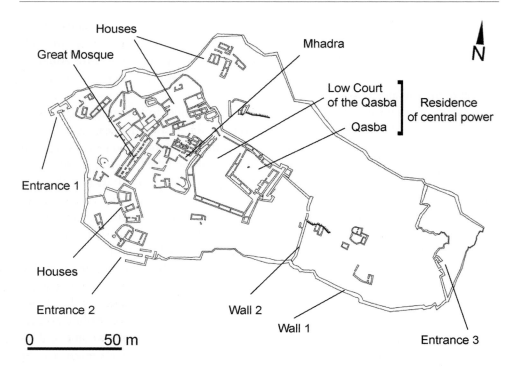

FIGURE 3.2.6 Igiliz, plan of the site showing the main buildings.

Courtesy of Mission Archéologique d'Igiliz.

end of the 14th century, with the exception of the mosque, which was reduced in size and continued to be occupied. At present, the deep soundings made in the hammam, the mosque, and the palace go back as early as the late 10th century. While the material from this period is still limited, the material of later periods is particularly rich and reveal an intense production of the luxurious ceramics in *cuerda seca* and black and white which were widely diffused in the late Middle Ages (Fili et al. 2016).

As is clear from the preceding discussion, the focus has been on major medieval foundations (al-Basra, Sijilmasa, Nakur, Aghmat) or important Roman sites (Volubilis), often the seats of medieval dynasties. Redman's (1986) pioneering work at Qsar es-Seghir shed light on at small coastal site in the Almohad and Merinid periods (ca. 1200–1458 CE) and its later transformation into a Portuguese fortification until 1550, when the town was abandoned. The central institutions of the fortified city—the mosque, hammam, and central market and a row of shops—were all excavated and were located at the center of the city, linked with wide avenues to the main gates. The houses followed the typical courtyard form but were fairly elaborate, built in brick and stone with tile (*zellij*) or wooden floors and often contained their own well and latrine. This was the earliest excavation of an Islamic site in Morocco to conduct detailed botanical, zooarchaeological, and finds analysis, though unfortunately these remain unpublished.

RURAL LANDSCAPES

Rural archaeology, which is at the heart of the problematics developed by historians and archaeologists elsewhere in the western Mediterranean since the beginning of the 1980s (see Chapters 3.4 and 3.5), has had very few adherents in Morocco. This neglect is paradoxical, as until recently, the majority of the population of Morocco lived in agro-pastoral societies. Instead, rural areas have largely been studied through colonial ethnology or sociology, although there are some exceptions. In the colonial period, one can evoke the interest in the rural fortifications of the late medieval Moroccan empires like Zagora (Meunié and Allain 1956), Tasghimout (Allain and Meunié 1951), Tigmi o Guellid (Tighjijt) (Ricard 1939), and Amergou (Lévi-Provençal 1918) or those of the Rehamna and the region of Bahrai (Allain 1954a, 1954b). However, one of the greatest works of rural archaeology remains that of Paul Berthier on Saadian sugar production and his excavation of several sugar factories in the regions of Taroudant, Essaouira, and Chichaoua (Berthier 1962, 1966, 1970). This work has not been given the recognition it deserves.

The limited work in this area has focused primarily on fortifications (Cressier 1995; Cressier and Erbati 1999; Benhima 2000; Bokbot et al. 2002). This work highlights questions about the modes of control of the landscape, the status of the occupants of these fortresses, and the role of the state and rural communities in their management. Hydraulic developments in peri-urban or rural areas has also been the focus of various work since the early 1980s (Bazzana et al. 1983–1984). Scholars have mostly focused on the agricultural hinterlands of urban agglomerations (Aghmat, Tamdult, Sijilmasa), to draw technological (Bazzana 2004) or morphological observations (González Villaescusa 2002), and, more recently, to examine the constitution of large aristocratic or princely land estates (Navarro Palazón et al. 2013). Extremely valuable, scholarly analyses on the management of these irrigated lands are still all too rare: above all, they only concern the rural world incidentally, the city and its hinterland remain at the heart of the debate (Carbonero Gamundí et al. 2002; Cressier 2006).

A major survey carried out in the Basin of Sebou (Rebuffat and Limane 2011) shows the possibilities of approaching the subject of the transition of the rural world in Romanized areas. However, the dating of sites remains challenging in the absence of tight ceramic chronologies, and renewed investment in ceramic studies is needed. The work of Mohamed Belatik (2018), recently published, on the rural territory of the Emirate of Banu Abi al-Afiya, is a good example of the possibilities of such an approach. This theme is also more complex in the regions south of the Roman *limes* (frontiers). The research undertaken in recent years in the region of Draa by Youssef Bokbot and David Mattingly (2017) and, to a lesser extent, Abdallah Fili on the region of Massa (Fili, A., 2019 "Premières découvertes antiques à Massa", *BAM24*, INSAP, Rabat, p. 63–72.), will bring new light on this issue.

A major multidisciplinary Moroccan–French project began in the early 2000s on rural settlement in the Anti-Atlas between the Middle Ages and pre-modern era. Its focus is the mountain of Igiliz of the Hargha, which served, in 1120–1130, as a refuge and place of pious retreat for the Mahdi Ibn Tumart, founder of the Almohad Empire and his followers (Van Staëvel and Fili 2006; Ettahiri et al. 2012, 2013, 2014). The site itself was an extensive and well-organized settlement occupied between the 10th and 13th centuries, surrounded by double fortification walls and dominated by a Qasba which contained reception and living rooms, domestic processing areas, and a bathroom. The rest of the site contained three mosques, the Mhadra (probably a housing area for students), and other housing. Extensive palaebotanical and zooarchaeological research at the site has shed light on farming and breeding practices, as well as the exploitation of plant resources and the history of landscapes in this mountainous area (Ruas et al. 2011).

Despite the efforts of these courageous, often pioneering, scholars, rural settlement structures and land use patterns are still very difficult to grasp, and their study remains almost absent from the agenda of archaeological research in Morocco (Benhima 2008). Aside from the study of irrigated landscapes, there is no landscape archaeology, strictly speaking, for the medieval period, and archaeoenvironmental studies are not yet systematically associated with fieldwork. The archaeology of rural settlements is rarely a focus, apart from a few isolated cases: we note in particular the exemplary excavation of the remains of the medieval reoccupation of Rirha by a team of classical scholars (Callegarin et al. 2016) and the rescue excavation of the Moulay Driss site (unpublished). On rural settlement and domestic architecture, the poverty of archaeological information is striking. Details and regional variants can only be identified for the most recent centuries, especially the colonial period. More broadly, we know nothing about the material side of the process of Islamization of the countryside, too often seen as self-evident on the basis of the texts. But scholars are becoming increasingly aware of the importance of being able to measure the rhythms of cultural change, materially rather than by text, especially in regions outside the reach of Rome, whose pre-Islamic past is still largely unknown. Despite the difficulties encountered, rural archaeology has the potential to fill the deep gaps in written sources and gradually contribute to delineating the world of the Moroccan countryside over the past two millennia. All the same, it remains a challenge: the lack of sufficient comparative materials makes the question of the dating of rural settlement a huge challenge for archaeologists in Morocco.

MEDIEVAL ARCHAEOLOGY IN MOROCCO OR ARCHAEOLOGY WITHOUT THE STUDY OF MATERIAL CULTURE

One of the most striking features of colonial Islamic archaeology in Morocco is still true today: the absence of studies of archaeological material. Even after the establishment of the Moroccan Archaeology Service, then INSAP, and the Department of Cultural Heritage, the study of the material from excavations stored in museums has not attracted much research except for sumptuous decor on wood (Cambazard-Amahan 1989), coins (El Hadri 2007), and, more recently, glass (El Hassani 2017).

There is no dispute about the importance of studying these collections, but the growing interest in Islamic ceramics across the Mediterranean during the past twenty years has had muted impact in Morocco. Since the creation of INSAP in 1986, fewer than a dozen dissertations and only two master's degrees have been awarded on medieval ceramics. It must therefore be underlined that, in Morocco, not every archaeological excavation is systematically followed by the study of the material culture, and even after a century of archaeological research, a large number of discoveries remain unstudied. The exceptions are the early Moroccan–American work at al-Basra (Benco 1987; Benco 2004), the Moroccan–British programs of Volubilis (Fentress and Limane 2019), and the Moroccan–French project at Rirha (Callegarin et al. 2016). Needless to say, this situation has negative consequences for the archaeological and historical interpretations of several research projects. The situation is worse still for other categories of material culture, and it was not until 2012 that the first study on metallic objects of a medieval Moroccan site appeared at al-Basra (Doukali 2011–2012). The first steps in the field of archaeozoology and archaeobotany are also taking place, which have become standard practice in all current fieldwork projects (Ruas et al. 2011; Ruas et al. 2016; Linstädter et al. 2012; Fuller and Pelling 2019; King 2019). By emphasizing these new approaches to field archaeology, we are beginning to reconstruct the medieval ways of life and the economic foundations of sites.

THE CHALLENGES

A number of challenges remain, however. The first of these is the dependence of medieval archaeology in Morocco on international collaborations, which offer far greater financial means than are available at a national level. These also make it possible to set up multiannual programs with more extensive analytic possibilities than national programs. The second is training. In recent years, the lack of well-trained individuals in field archaeology in Morocco poses real problems for archaeology of all periods. The recruitment of INSAP graduates into museum and heritage administration has resulted in many graduates ceasing to participate in research programs. This results in a hemorrhage at the level of middle managers who are not allowed to carry out research in the field. The older generations in INSAP are often very well trained as they were able to conduct studies up to the master's or doctoral level, but they are underexploited in their home administrations. The problem of continuing education therefore arises over the long term. For the new generations, the problem of the content of training itself arises because it is not in keeping with the new archaeological techniques. Fieldwork often lacks experienced supervisors who can train students in the field, and field schools rarely cover the study and analysis of material culture. Thus, the formation and training of new generations of field archaeologists represent a real challenge for years to come.

Moroccan university courses, often more theoretical than practical, are also held back due to the lack of qualified professors and are handicapped by the large number of students, which does not allow detailed exploration of complex issues.

The final challenge is the absence of a mature rescue archaeology. Several rescue excavations have been carried out following restorations or major development works, including those at the Lalla Hniya cemetery in Safi (1995), the Kutubiyya neighborhood in Marrakech (1995–1996) (Kafas Samir 1997), the square of the Qasba des Oudaïas in Rabat in 1999, 2003, 2006 (Erbati 2004), Qarawiyyin in 2006 (Ettahiri 2007), and al-Mazamma in 2010 (unpublished). In rural areas, the most important, but still unpublished, is that of the Moulay Driss site conducted by INSAP in collaboration with the National Society of Motorways of Morocco (SNAM), the Moroccan Association of Rock Art (AMAR, Rabat), and the National Institute of Preventive Archaeological Research (France). The most recent rescue excavation located the potters' quarter of the city of Salé and was followed in 2017 by a systematic excavation of this district, which delivered an exceptional ceramic repertoire from the 13th and 14th centuries. These interventions suffer from the lack of a clear legal framework that would allow archaeologists to intervene easily. In addition to the lack of training, there continue to be major difficulties in the management of projects, the conservation of the exposed archaeology, and the long-term storage of excavated finds. Indeed, at present, rescue excavations in Morocco are approached with the same methods as research projects; this obviously raises the problems of deadlines and the effectiveness of fieldwork.

Conclusion: Toward a New Islamic Archaeology of Morocco

The contribution of Islamic archaeology to the writing of the history of Morocco is undeniable. Where would it be without the discovery and study, as well as the protection, of the ruins of Volubilis, Nakur, and Chella from the period of the Spanish and French Protectorates to the most recent excavation and heritage activities on these sites? The objects on display in Moroccan museums alone reflect more than a century of discoveries of Islamic archaeology, from the ancient excavations to the recent discoveries at Igiliz, Volubilis, Aghmat, or Qarawiyyîn.

Today Islamic archaeology in Morocco is defined by a range of methodological approaches and practices ranging from field survey to geophysics, from extensive reconnaissance surveys with limited sondages to intensive excavation and the analysis of the territory and the landscape. These diverse approaches have resulted in hundreds of individual and joint publications that have enriched the discipline of Islamic archaeology in Morocco before and after the country's independence. A Moroccan school in this field is still far from developed, but the efforts made in training new generations of archaeologists in new techniques (e.g., field survey, ceramics, Islamic art history, archaeobotany, archaeozoology) allow us to hope that significant advances in the understanding of Moroccan archaeological sites will be made by Moroccan researchers. These new techniques could become a source of employment for graduates in archaeology if a cultural resource management unit to carry out rescue archaeology could be created—although this will require new legislative structures. It is in this area that the Moroccan university must play its role, hitherto limited, by establishing advanced training in archaeology and heritage. Growing public demand is a major factor in this development. Moroccan civil society is increasingly investing in the discovery of the Moroccan archaeological heritage and its protection and conservation. One of the major novelties is currently the development of the large open-area excavations at Igiliz, Aghmat, and Volubilis, which should allow for the gradual reconstitution of medieval villages or even of entire cities.

REFERENCES

Akerraz, A. 1985. "Note sur l'enceinte tardive de Volubilis," *BCTH*, 19, 8, 429–438.

Akerraz, A. 1998. "Recherches sur les niveaux islamique de Volubilis," in P. Cressier and M. García Arenal (eds.), *Genèse de la ville islamique en al-Andalus et au Maghreb occidental* (Madrid: Casa de Velázquez), 295–304.

Allain, C. 1954a. "Reconnaissances archéologiques dans le massif des Rehamna et la Bahira I," *Hespéris*, 40, 155–189.

Allain, C. 1954b. "Reconnaissances archéologiques dans le massif des Rehamna et la Bahira II," *Hespéris*, 41, 435–458.

Allain, C., and Meunié, J. 1951. "Recherches archéologiques au Tasghimout des Mesfeoua," *Hespéris*, 38, 381–405.

Amorós Ruiz, V., and Fili, A. 2011. "La céramique des niveaux islamiques de Volubilis (Walîla) d'après les fouilles de la mission maroco-anglaise," in P. Cressier and E. Fentress (eds.), *La céramique maghrébine au haut Moyen Age (VIIIe–Xe siècle), état des recherches, problèmes et perspectives* (Rome: École Française de Rome), 23–47.

Barrucand, M. 1985. *Urbanisme princier en islam, Meknès* et les villes royales islamiques post-médiévales (Paris: Geuthner).

Bazzana, A. 2004. "Les norias fluviales de Fès. Approche ethnoarchéologique d'une technique médiévale," in A. Bazzana and H. Bocoum (eds.), *Du Nord au Sud du Sahara: Cinquante ans d'archéologie française en Afrique de l'Ouest et au Maghreb. Bilan et perspectives* (Paris: Éditions Sépia), 331–347.

Bazzana, A., Cressier, P., Erbati, L., Montmessin, Y., and Touri, A. 1983–1984. "Première prospection d'archéologie médiévale et islamique dans le Nord du Maroc (Chefchaouen–Oued Laou–Bou Ahmed)," *Bulletin d'Archéologie Marocaine*, 15, 367–450.

Belatik, M. 2018. *Imârat Banû Abî al-'Âfiyya* (Rabat: INSAP).

Benco, N. 1987. *The early medieval pottery industry at al-Basra, Morocco* (Oxford: BAR).

Benco, N. 2004. *Anatomy of a Medieval Islamic Town: al-Basra, Morocco* (Oxford: Archaeopress).

Benhima, Y. 2000. "L'habitat fortifié au Maroc médiéval. Éléments d'un bilan et perspectives de recherche," *Archéologie islamique*, 10, 79–102.

Benhima, Y. 2008. *Safi et son territoire. Une ville dans son espace au Maroc (11e–16e siècle)* (Paris: L'Harmattan).

Bennison, A. K. 2016. *Almoravid and Almohad Empires* (Edinburgh: Edinburgh University Press).

Berthier, P. 1962. "En marge des sucreries marocaines: la maison de la plaine et la maison des oliviers à Chichaoua," *Hespéris-Tamuda*, 3, 75–77.

Berthier, P. 1966. *Les anciennes sucreries du Maroc et leurs réseaux hydrauliques. Etude archéologique et d'histoire économique* (Rabat: Imprimerie française et marocaines).

Berthier, P. 1970. "En marge des sucreries marocaines: recherches archéologiques à la zaouia bel Moqaddem (Chichaoua—Haouz de Marrakech)," *Hespéris-Tamuda*, 11, 141–169.

Bokbot, Y., Cressier, P., Delaigue, M.-C., Izquierdo Benito, R., Mabrouk, S., and Onrubia Pintado, J. 2002. "Enceintes refuges, greniers fortifiés et *qasaba*-s: fonctions, périodisation et interprétation de la fortification en milieu rural pré-saharien," in I. C. Ferreira Fernandes (ed.), *Mil Anos de Fortificações na Península Ibérica e no Magreb (500–1500), Actas do Simpósio Internacional sobre Castelos* (Lisbon: Edições Colibri), 213–227.

Caillé, J. 1949. *La ville de Rabat jusqu'au Protectorat français. Histoire et archéologie* (Paris: Publications de l'Institut des Hautes-Études marocaines).

Callegarin, L., Kbiri Alaoui, M., Ichkhakh, A., and Roux J.-C. (eds.) 2016. *Rirha: site antique et médiéval du Maroc. IV. Période médiévale islamique, IXe–XVe siècle* (Madrid: Casa de Velázquez).

Cambazard-Amahan, C. 1989. *Le décor sur bois dans l'architecture de Fès, époques almoravide, almohade et début mérinide* (Paris: Institut de recherches et d'études sur le monde arabe et musulman).

Capel, C., and Fili, A. 2016. "La fondation de Sijilmâsa: réexamen historique et découvertes archéologiques," *Hespéris-Tamuda*, 51, 39–82.

Carbonero Gamundí, M. A., Cressier, P., and Erbati, L. 2002. "Un exemple de transformation radicale et planifiée du paysage agraire au Moyen Âge: Taghssa," *Bulletin d'Archéologie Marocaine*, 19, 219–256.

Cressier, P. 1995. "La fortification islamique au Maroc: éléments de bibliographie," *Archéologie islamique*, 5, 163–196.

Cressier, P. 1998. "Urbanisation, arabisation, islamisation au Maroc du Nord: quelques remarques depuis l'archéologie," in P. Cressier, J. Aguadé, and Á. Vicente (eds.), *Peuplement et arabisation au Magreb occidental. Dialectologie et histoire* (Madrid: Casa de Velázquez), 27–39.

Cressier, P. 2004. "Du Sud au Nord du Sahara: la question de Tâmdult," in A. Bazzana and H. Bocoum (eds.), *Du Nord au Sud du Sahara. Cinquante ans d'archéologie française en Afrique de l'Ouest et au Maghreb. Bilans et perspectives* (Paris: Éditions Sépia), 275–284.

Cressier, P. 2006. "Géométrie des réseaux et marqueurs des territoires. L'image du partage de l'eau dans le paysage médiéval (Espagne et Maroc)," *Mélanges de la Casa de Velázquez*, 36, 2, 39–59.

Cressier, P. 2007. "Aghmat, une question de territoire," in P. Sénac, *Le Maghreb, al-Andalus et la Méditerranée occidentale (VIIIe–XIIIe siècle)* (Toulouse: CNRS), 81–95.

Cressier, P. 2009. "Archéologie du Maghreb islamique, archéologie d'al-Andalus, archéologie espagnole?," in M. Marín (ed.), *Al-Andalus-España, Historiografías en contraste, Siglos XVII–XXI* (Madrid: Casa de Velázquez), 131–145.

Cressier, P., and Erbati, L. 1999. "Note sur la forteresse almoravide du Tasgîmût," *Archéologie islamique*, 8–9, 55–66.

Cressier, P., Erbati, L., Acién Almansa, M., El Boudjay, A., González Villaescusa, R., and Siraj, A. 2001. "La naissance de la ville islamique au Maroc (Nakūr, Aǧmāt, Tāmdult). Résultats préliminaires de l'approche archéologique du site de Nakūr (capitale d'un émirat du haut Moyen Âge), *Actes des Premières journées nationales d'archéologie et du patrimoine*, 3, 108–119.

Deverdun, G. 1959. *Marrakech des origines à 1912* (Rabat: Éditions Frontispice).

Doukali, H. 2011–2012. *Les objets métalliques d'al-Basra* (INSAP, Rabat: Unpublished Masters thesis).

Doutté, E, 1914. *En tribu* (Paris: Geuthner).

El Hadri, M., 2007. *Les monnaies mérinides dans l'histoire monétaire du Maroc (13e–15e siècle)* (Unpublished doctoral thesis, Université Lumière Lyon 2).

El Hassani, H. 2017. *Le verre et sa production dans le Maroc antique et médiéval, essai de typologie et de chronologie* (Unpublished doctoral thesis, Université Paris-Sorbonne).

El Hraiki, R. 1989. *Recherche ethnoarchéologique sur la céramique du Maroc* (Université Paris-Sorbonne, Université Lyon 2).

Ennahid, S. 2001. *Political economy and settlement systems of medieval northern Morocco: an archaeological-historical approach* (Oxford: Archaeopress).

Erbati, L. 2004. "Deux sites urbains (IXe–XIe siècles). Casbah des Oudayas et Aghmat," in A. Bazzana and H. Bocoum (eds.), *Du Nord au Sud du Sahara. Cinquante ans d'archéologie française en Afrique de l'Ouest et au Maghreb. Bilans et perspectives* (Paris: Éditions Sépia), 285–293.

Ettahiri, A. 2007. "Vestiges archéologiques sous la mosquée Al Karawiyine," *Architecture du Maroc*, 34, 103–106.

Ettahiri, A., Fili, A., and Van Staëvel, J.-P. 2012. "Nouvelles recherches archéologiques sur la période islamique au Maroc: Fès, Aghmat et Îgîlîz," in P. Sénac (ed.), *Histoire et archéologie de l'Occident musulman (VII-XVe siècle): al-Andalus, Maghreb, Sicile* (Toulouse: CNRS), 157–181.

Ettahiri, A., Fili, A., and Van Staëvel, J.-P. 2013. "Nouvelles recherches archéologiques sur les origines de l'empire almohade au Maroc: les fouilles d'Igîlîz," *Académie des Inscriptions et Belle-Lettres, Comptes Rendus des séances*, 2 (avril-juin), 1109–1142.

Ettahiri, A., Fili, A., and Van Staëvel, J.-P. 2014. "Contribution à l'étude de l'habitat des élites en milieu rural dans le Maroc Médiéval: quelques réflexions à partir de la qasba d'Îgîlîz, berceau du mouvement almohade," in S. Gutiérrez Lloret and I. Grau Mira (eds.), *De la estructura doméstica al espacio social, lecturas arqueológicas del uso social del espacio* (Alicante: Universidad de Alicante), 265–278.

Eustache, D. 1970–1971. *Corpus des dirhams idrisites et contemporains* (Rabat: Banque du Maroc).

Fentress, E., and Limane, H. 2011. "Excavations in Medieval Settlement at Volubilis, 2000–2004," *Cuadernos de Madînat al-Zahrâ*, 7, 105–122.

Fentress, E., and Limane, H. (eds.) 2019. *Volubilis après Rome: les fouilles UCL/INSAP, 2000–2005* (Leiden: Brill).

Fili, A. 2014. "Bague-seau," in Y. Lintz, C. Délery, and B. Tuil-Lionetti (eds.), *Maroc médiéval: un empire de l'Afrique à l'Espagne* (Paris: Musée du Louvre-Hazan), 116–117.

Fili, A., Délery, C., and Messier, R. 2016. "Les céramiques à décor de cuerda seca découvertes au Hammâm d'Aghmât," *Bulletin d'Archéologie Marocaine*, 23, 283–297.

Fili, A., and Messier, R. 2015. "Le Hammam d'Aghmat (Xe–XIVe siècles)," *Hommage à Joudia Hassar-Benslimane* (Rabat: Institut National des Science de l'Archéologie et du Patrimoine 2), 345–362.

Fili, A., Messier, R., Capel, C., and Héritier-Salama, V. 2014. "Les palais mérinides dévoilés, le cas d'Aghmat," in Y. Lintz, C. Déléry, and B. Tuil-Lionetti (eds.), *Maroc médiéval: un empire de l'Afrique à l'Espagne* (Paris: Musée du Louvre-Hazan), 446–450.

Fuller, D. Q., and Pelling, R. 2019. "Plant Economy: Archaeobotanical Studies," in E. Fentress and H. Limane (eds,), *Volubilis après Rome: les fouilles UCL/INSAP, 2000–2005* (Leiden: Brill), 349–368.

González Villaescusa, R. 2002. *Las formas de los paisajes mediterráneos (Ensayos sobre las formas, funciones y epistemología parcelarias: estudios comparativos en medios mediterráneos entre la antigüedad y época moderna* (Jaén: Universidad de Jaén), 345–371.

Gozalbes, C. 2005. "Los inicios de la investigación española sobre arqueología y arte árabes en Marruecos (1860–1960)," *Boletín de la Asociacion española de orientalistas*, 41, 227.

Hassar-Benslimane, J. 1992. *Le passé de la ville de Salé dans tous ses états: histoire, archéologie, archives* (Paris: Maisonneuve et Larose).

Héritier-Salama, V., Capel, C., Fili, A., and Messier, R. 2016. "De la ville aux champs. La transformation d'Aghmat (Maroc) entre les XIVe-XVIe siècles," in C. Müller and M. Heintz (eds.), *Transitions historiques* (Paris: Éditions de Boccard), 195–208.

Kafas, S., Belatik, M., Khiara, Y., Arharbi, R. and Doudani, Z. 1997. "Fouilles de sauvetage aux abords de la Koutoubia," *Les Nouvelles Archéologiques et Patrimoniales*, 1, 15–16.

King, A. 2019. "The Faunal Remains," in E. Fentress and H. Limane (eds.), *Volubilis après Rome: les fouilles UCL/INSAP, 2000–2005* (Leiden: Brill), 369–386.

Le Tourneau, R. 1947. *Fès avant le protectorat, étude économique et sociale d'une ville de l'occident musulman* (Rabat: Editions La Porte).

Lévi-Provençal, E. 1918. "Les ruines almoravides du pays de l'Ouargha (Maroc septentrional)," *BCTH*, 194–200.

Linstädter, J., Fili, A., Mikdad, A., and Amarir, A. 2012. "Bouchih, un site almoravide sur la rive ouest de Moulouya (Rif oriental)," *Bulletin d'Archéologie Marocaine*, 22, 342–351.

Mattingly, D. J., Bokbot, Y., Sterry, M., Cuénod, A., Fenwick, C., Gatto, M. C., Ray, N., Rayne, L., Janin, K., and Lamb, A. 2017. "Long-term History in a Moroccan Oasis Zone: The Middle Draa Project 2015," *Journal of African Archaeology*, 15, 141–172.

Messier, R. 1999. "The Grand Mosque of Sijilmassa: The Evolution of a Structure from the Mosque of Ibn Abd Allah to the Restoration of Sidi Mohammed ben Abd Allah," in M. Hammam (ed.), *L'Architecture en terre en Méditerranée: histoire et perspectives. Actes du colloque international de Rabat (27–29 novembre 1996)* (Rabat: Faculté des Lettres et Sciences Humaines de l'Université Mohamed V), 287–296.

Messier, R., and Fili, A. 2011. "The Earliest Ceramics of Sijilmâsa," in P. Cressier and E. Fentress (eds.), *La céramique maghrébine du haut Moyen-Âge (VIIIe-Xe siècles). Etat des recherches, problèmes et perspectives* (Rome: Ecole française de Rome), 129–146.

Messier, R., and Miller, J. 2015. *The Last Civilized Place: Sijilmasa and Its Saharan Destiny* (Austin: University of Texas Press).

Meunié, J., and Allain, C. 1956. "La forteresse almoravide de Zagora," *Hespéris*, 43, 305–353.

Meunié, J., Terasse, H., and Deverdun, G. 1952. *Recherches archéologiques à Marrakech* (Paris: Publications de l'Institut des Hautes Etudes Marocaines).

Navarro Palazón, J., Garrido Carretero, F. L, Torres Carbonell, J. M., and Triki, H. 2013. "Agua, arquitectura y poder en una capital del Islam: la finca real del Agdal de Marrakech (ss. XII-XX)," *Arqueología de la arquitectura*, 10, 1–43.

Rebuffat, R., and Limane, H. 2011. *Carte archéologique du Maroc antique. Le bassin du Sebou 1* (Rabat: INSAP).

Redman, C. 1983–1984. "Survey and Test Excavations of Six Medieval Islamic Sites in Northern Morocco," *Bulletin d'Archéologie Marocaine, 15,* 311–350.

Redman, C. 1986. *Qsar es-Seghir: An Archaeological View of Medieval Life* (Orlando: Academic Press).

Ricard, P. 1939. "Une forteresse maghrébine de l'Anti-Atlas (XIIe siècle)," *IVe Congrès de la fédération des sociétés savantes d'Afrique du Nord* (Algiers: Société Historique Algérienne), 641–650.

Ruas, M.-P., Ros, J., Terral, J.-F., Ivorra, S., Andrianarinosy, H., Ettahiri, A., Fili, A., and Van Staëvel, J.-P. 2016. "History and Archaeology of the Emblematic Argan Tree in the Medieval Anti-Atlas Mountains (Morocco)," *Quaternary International,* 30, 114–136.

Ruas, M.-P., Tengberg, M., Ettahiri, A., Fili, A., and van Staëvel, J.-P. 2011. "Archaeological Research at the Medieval Fortified Site of Îgîlîz (Anti-Atlas, Morocco) with Particular Reference to the Exploitation of the Argan Tree," *Vegetation History Archaeobotany,* 20, 419–433.

Terrasse, H. 1937. "La céramique hispano-maghrébine du XIIe siècle d'après les fouilles du château de l'Aïn Ghaboula (Dchira)," *Hespéris,* 24, 13–23.

Thouvenot, R. 1933. "Une forteresse almohade près de Rabat Dchîra," *Hespéris,* 17, 59–88.

Van Staëvel, J.-P., and Fili, A. 2006. "Wa wasalnâ ʿalâ barakat Allâh ilâ Igîlîz: à propos de la localisation d'Igîlîz-des-Hargha, le hisn du Mahdi Ibn Tumart," *Al-Qantara,* 37, 153–194.

Vicaire, M., and Thouvenot, R. 1938. "Vestiges archéologiques dans la région de Fès El Bàli," *Hespéris,* 25, 367–376.

CHAPTER 3.3

···

THE SAHARA

···

SAM NIXON

INTRODUCTION

···

SUCH is the perceived state of Saharan Islamic archaeology that a recent article stated discouragingly: "Research on the Sahara in the early Islamic period remains a chronically under-developed field" (Mattingly et al. 2015). While currently underdeveloped, this chapter argues that Saharan Islamic archaeology is potentially a very rich field. A range of important archaeological studies have been conducted throughout the region, providing new perspectives on topics such as trans-Saharan trade, Saharan urbanism, the origins and spread of technologies, and the spread of Islam in the medieval period (Figure 3.3.1). This chapter highlights current thinking on these themes and introduces key Saharan sites to help provide further definition to the field of Saharan Islamic archaeology.

The Sahara itself is an area of approximately 3.5 million square miles, stretching from the Atlantic to the Nile. It is worth noting that the phrase "Sahara desert" is a tautology: the word Sahara (*sahra* in Arabic) means "desert." More importantly, the word "desert" does not capture the varied nature of Saharan environments. Much of the central Sahara is a highly arid landscape, defined principally by barren rocky plateaus as well as vast zones of sand dunes. While much of the region is low-lying, there are also extensive highland zones, including grasslands and oases which comprise some of the Sahara's most favorable microenvironments for habitation, such as the Ahaggar and Tibesti massifs of Algeria and Chad. At the Sahara's northern edge is the semi-desert "pre-Sahara," consisting of steppe-like scrubland and oases lying to the south of the Atlas Mountains and the coasts of southern Tunisia, Libya, and Egypt. Running along the southern edge of the Sahara is the semi-desert "Sahel" (meaning "shore" in Arabic) where the desert gradually merges with the open grasslands to the south, characterized by scrub vegetation and patchy tree coverage. These "semi-Saharan" zones are relatively rich archaeologically due to their favorable micro-environments and location on Saharan trading routes.

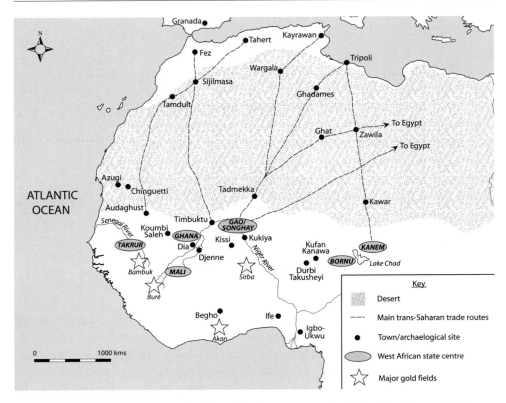

FIGURE 3.3.1 Map of principal Saharan early Islamic sites and associated trade networks.

Courtesy of Sam Nixon.

The early Islamic caliphates and North African successor-states turned their attention to the Sahara within a few decades of the conquest of North Africa. From around the 8th–9th centuries CE, traders and clerics—often associated with the Ibadi sect of Islam—established Muslim communities at existing Saharan centers, facilitating the growth of trade with West Africa and the rich resources of gold, slaves, and ivory found there (Insoll 2003; Gaiser 2010). In the 10th century, the Fatimid dynasty, based first in Tunisia, then Cairo, invested heavily in trans-Saharan routes (Devisse 1988). In the 11th century, the Almoravids, Sanhaja Berbers from Mauritania, conquered Morocco and expanded into Spain, in the process further opening up the Saharan trade routes (Bennison 2016; cf. Chapter 3.2 of this volume). This Islamic reformist movement led to an increased Islamization of significant portions of the Sahara, but also to the evolution of a strong internal dynamic to Saharan Islam. In the 11th–13th centuries, major West African empires in the western Sahara—Ghana, Mali, Songhai, and Kanem-Bornu—themselves adopted and promoted Islam within the region. Nevertheless, animist belief systems and predominantly non-Muslim lifeways were still held to by significant portions of the population through to the 19th century (Insoll 2003; Austen 2010).

Our knowledge of the medieval Sahara is informed by a slim corpus of early Arabic sources, primarily written by geographers and historians, many of whom had never visited the region (see Levtzion and Hopkins 2000). These texts do, however, provide important information about trade routes, settlements, and their Muslim communities, and some wider social and political commentary. Their emphasis on trade has driven scholarly research agendas, and much of the archaeology conducted has targeted the trading places named in the texts. Accordingly, this chapter focuses above all on medieval trans-Saharan commercial networks and their urban centers between the 8th and 15th centuries.

HISTORIOGRAPHY

The Sahara is seldom included in scholarship on Islamic art history and archaeology, which has historically focused on the Mashriq (e.g., Ettinghausen et al. 2003; Milwright 2010). In part, this is because there are only a handful of synthetic studies on the Islamic Sahara, and those that have been produced were either written some years ago and/or developed with a very focused thematic or geographical agenda (e.g., Devisse 1988; King 1989; Insoll 2006). However, it also reflects the wider neglect of Islamic Africa in modern scholarship, there being also very few treatments of North African (Boone and Benco 1999; Fenwick 2013; Fenwick 2020) and sub-Saharan Islamic archaeology (Insoll 2003).

Research has focused almost exclusively on Saharan trade and trading networks. The most extensive study hitherto is Insoll's (2006) survey of Saharan Islamic archaeology, which examined central cross-Saharan routes and the southern Saharan evidence connected to these. Beyond this, we rely on excavation monographs from a handful of Saharan sites or regional surveys, such as Mauny's (1961) corpus of medieval sites in West Africa, King's (1989) important survey of Islamic sites in Libya, and Devisse's (1988) study of West African trans-Saharan trade routes. Further useful material can be gleaned from historical studies, such as Bovill's (1933, 1968) studies on the medieval and early modern trans-Saharan networks and the work of Austen (2010), which deals primarily with modern networks.

SURVEY OF MAIN SITES

Pre-Sahara and Northern Sahara

Archaeological research in this zone has focused on the Moroccan pre-Sahara, the Saharan regions of northern Algeria, and those of northwestern Libya. Settlements such as Sijilmasa, Tamdult, Sedrata, and Ghadames played a key role as caravan stations supporting trans-Saharan trade between the Maghreb and West Africa. The story of these settlements cannot, however, be entirely reduced to their long-distance trading function; their development is associated with political and military functions, mining, and even with the movement of refugees fleeing religious persecution.

The best-known site in the Moroccan pre-Sahara is Sijilmasa, founded by the Midrarid dynasty in the 8th century (Levtzion and Hopkins 2000: 7, 22; Messier and Miller 2015; Capel 2017) and subsequently the principal center of trans-Saharan trade in the Maghreb. Sijilmasa's sprawling ruins in mud architecture extend over several kilometers. Explorations in the 1980s and 1990s included excavations of the "Great Mosque"—revealing emplacements for wooden *minbar* rails—and radiocarbon dating suggests that this post-dates the mosque referred to in early 9th-century historical records (Messier and Miller 2015: 76–77). Other important architectural evidence included the "elite residence" recorded underlying the earliest levels of the Great Mosque, featuring traces of Midrarid art in painted and carved plaster and painted wood (Messier and Miller 2015: 76–77). The wide range of material culture recorded included Islamic silver coinage (from the 11th century and later), carved stucco, oil lamps, and various items featuring Arabic inscriptions, including decorative plaster-work featuring a koranic inscription (Figure 3.3.2). The difficulty of recording intact stratigraphy, however, has hampered the development of a clear archaeological sequence (Fauvelle et al. 2014).

FIGURE 3.3.2 Vase inscribed with the word "Baraka" from Sijilmasa, Morocco, 11th century.
Courtesy of Moroccan-American Project at Sijilmasa.

While Sijilmasa was the largest medieval center in this zone, other key centers exist in the region. Tamdult, 300 kilometers further to the southwest, is described in Arabic sources as a "dependency" of Sijilmasa, consisting of a series of oasis settlements, a fort, and silver mine (Levtzion and Hopkins 2000: 22). It played an important role in the 11th century as a gathering point for the Almoravid army in its conquest of Morocco, and it continued to be occupied into the Saadian era (Rosenberger 1970). The ruins of Tamdult consist of a fortified tell surrounded by a plain with fossil irrigation terraces, industrial metallurgy zones, and outlying settlements (Figure 3.3.3). Investigations in the 1990s excavated deposits in the tell dating to the Almohad period (12th–13th centuries) (Cressier 2004). More recent work by a Moroccan/British team has revealed numerous mudbrick and *pisé* kasbah structures throughout the valley and further finds include molds for the production of coin pellets and ingots (Nixon 2018–19). Tamdult forms part of a wider regional site network, including remains from nearby Akka, including a decorated tower (Figure 3.3.4). Further afield is the fortress of Tagadirt Ougellid, where the Saadian army in the 16th century gathered prior to its journey across the Sahara to conquer Timbuktu and the wider Songhai empire. To the northeast of Tamdult, along the Draa Valley, a range of important early Islamic sites exist, including those around the town of Zagora (Mattingly et al. 2017).

FIGURE 3.3.3 The flank of the main tell at Tamdult (north face); the ruins of the fortification wall and the shrine of Sidi Shnawil are visible on top of the tell.

Courtesy of Sam Nixon.

FIGURE 3.3.4 Brick-built tower, Akka, southern Morocco.

Courtesy of Sam Nixon.

FIGURE 3.3.5 Ruins of Room A of the "palace" structure at Sedrata.

Courtesy of Max van Berchem Foundation archives.

Moving eastward into Algeria is the important regional center of Sedrata, near the town of Ouargla, itself an important late medieval center. Sedrata was founded in 909 CE by Ibadi Muslims fleeing the destruction by the Fatimids of Tahert, the capital of the Rustimid state in western Algeria (van Berchem 1960; Aillet et al. 2017). Sedrata became the effective Ibadite capital in the 10th and 11th centuries, and it played a fundamental role in trans-Saharan trade across the central Sahara, particularly to the Niger Bend. Sedrata survived until the 13th century, when its inhabitants fled to the Mzab following further persecution. The archaeological remains are well-preserved, enabling one to trace much of the town plan in its latest phase (Figure 3.3.5). Sedrata is known for its elaborate architectural decoration, namely highly ornate sculpted plaster, in abstract and vegetal designs, as well as Kufic script (Figure 3.3.6). The most significant building recorded is the "palace" structure with its towered perimeter wall: the sculpted plaster found here is at its most ornate, with tapestry-like designs and decoration paralleling such high-art forms as the Great Mosque of Cordoba (Aillet et al. 2017).

The final site to highlight is the oasis town of Ghadames, in northwestern Libya (Haarmann 1998; Mattingly and Sterry 2010). This was a significant center in antiquity (ancient Cidamus), housing a Roman garrison at various points, as well as being occupied in the Byzantine period, with evidence including stone church furniture. Islamic evidence dates back to at least the 8th century, and the town continued as an important trading hub into the Ottoman period.

FIGURE 3.3.6 Decorated plaster fragment from Sedrata.

Courtesy of Max van Berchem Foundation archives.

Central Sahara

Due to the challenges of working in the Central Sahara, very little systematic excavation or survey work has been conducted here and our knowledge of the medieval period is extremely limited. In the Libyan Fazzan, Zuwila is consistently identified as the most important medieval trading center: it became the capital of an Ibadi group in the 10th to 12th centuries. The site was occupied from the early first millennium CE (Mattingly et al. 2015; Mattingly and Sterry 2017). The standing remains of early Islamic architecture at Zuwila include *pisé* town walls; a congregational hypostyle mosque dated by radiocarbon to the 7th–9th centuries, making this one of the earliest Saharan mosques (Figure 3.3.7); and the Banu Khattab tombs, a series of domed-roof mausolea dating to the 10th–11th centuries (the latter destroyed during the Libyan civil war) (Figure 3.3.8). Several other important Islamic sites are known in the Libyan Fazzan including Jarma, which evolved from the pre-Islamic Garamantian capital and Murzuq, the regional capital in the early modern period (Mattingly 2003, 2013).

The central Sahara contains a number of important mining settlements and processing sites for salt, the crucial Saharan product traded against products from north and south. The salt mines of Teghaza in the far north of the Republic of Mali sat at the midpoint of a direct route from southern Morocco to Timbuktu and indeed explain the existence of this route (Monod 1938a, 1938b, 1940). Teghaza is recorded by various Arabic geographers who describe the salt mine and associated settlement—which also served as a caravan stop—including a seemingly fantastical but likely accurate description of houses made of salt blocks and roofed with camel skins (Levtzion and Hopkins 2000: 178, 282). The remains of a large settlement are found at Teghaza,

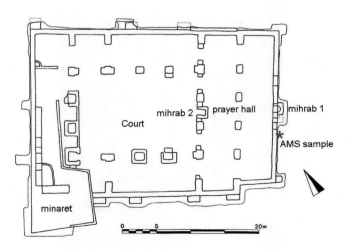

FIGURE 3.3.7 Plan of the congregational mosque of Zawila, Libya, showing position of AMS sample.

Courtesy of Mattingly et al. (2015), adapted from Abdussaid (1979).

FIGURE 3.3.8 Banu Khattab tombs, Zawila, Libya, in 1968.

Courtesy of C. Daniels, reproduced from Mattingly et al. (2015).

overlooked by a fort featuring early-modern Moroccan cannons, relics of Morocco's colonization of the mines following their conquest of Songhai in the 16th century (Monod 1938b, 1940). Limited test excavations recovered early Islamic glazed ceramics.

The central Saharan regions of Mauritania contain a number of sites associated with the important trans-Saharan route linking southern Morocco with the gold-bearing regions at the headwaters of the Niger and Senegal rivers (Figure 3.3.1). Azuggi was the base of the Almoravids following their movement northward from the Sahel in the mid-11th century (Saison 1981; Levtzion and Hopkins 2000). The site comprises a square fortress (1 hectare) within a larger site complex covering around 16 hectares, featuring rectilinear stone-built compounds with courtyards as well as Muslim cemeteries (Saison 1981). Test excavations in the early 1980s revealed an approximately 3.5-meter deep stratigraphy dated by radiocarbon to the 10th–11th centuries, correlating chronologically with the Almoravid movement, although the site might have been occupied earlier. Only limited quantities of imported glass beads and glazed ceramics have been found (Saison 1981: 72).

Among the other important, but unexcavated, Islamic sites in this region is Chinguetti. This was an important religious and scholarly center and a stopping-point for Hajj caravans by the 16th century, though it is believed to have earlier origins (Nixon 2013). Its important Islamic manuscript collections rival those of Timbuktu (Stewart and Salim 2015). The town is still occupied today, though earlier ruins in the local dry stone masonry are found in the immediate surroundings (Mauny 1955, 1961).

One of the most compelling archaeological sites of the central Sahara is the "lost caravan" of Maaden Ijafen, Mauritania, a unique instance of an "intact" trans-Saharan caravan load. Investigated in 1964 by Théodore Monod (1969), this contained 2,085 brass rod-shaped ingots (Garenne-Marot and Mille 2007), as

FIGURE 3.3.9 Cowrie shells, copper-alloy "rod" ingots, and matting fragments from the "lost caravan" of Maaden Ijafen, Mauritania.

Courtesy of Anne Haour.

well as thousands of cowrie shells spilled out from the sacks which once contained them, remnants of which were also discovered (Christie & Haour 2018; Figure 3.3.9). Radiocarbon dated to around the 12th–13th centuries, it is interpreted as a caravan load—potentially the pack of one camel—stacked up and hidden following the death or illness of the camel or camels carrying it, with a view to returning to collect it. Following test excavations, a sample of the materials was taken to l'Institut Fondamental d'Afrique Noire (IFAN) in Senegal, but the location of the site was subsequently lost, perhaps covered by shifting dunes.

Southern Sahara

Just as the northern fringes of the Sahara feature settlements which played a crucial role for trans-Saharan exchange, its southern fringes have a rich archaeological landscape of early Islamic settlements connected to trans-Saharan exchange. Among the most important of these is Tegdaoust, which can be equated with the trading town of Audaghust, described in Arabic sources of the 10th to the 14th centuries as having significant populations of North African traders and markets (Devisse 1983: 5–29). Tegdaoust was a significant urban settlement constructed primarily of stone, with a large Muslim cemetery. Excavations recorded urban deposits dating from approximately the 9th to the 14th centuries (Devisse 1983; Polet 1985; Robert-Chaleix 1989). The extensive excavations showed a well-planned urban site with a 10th-century

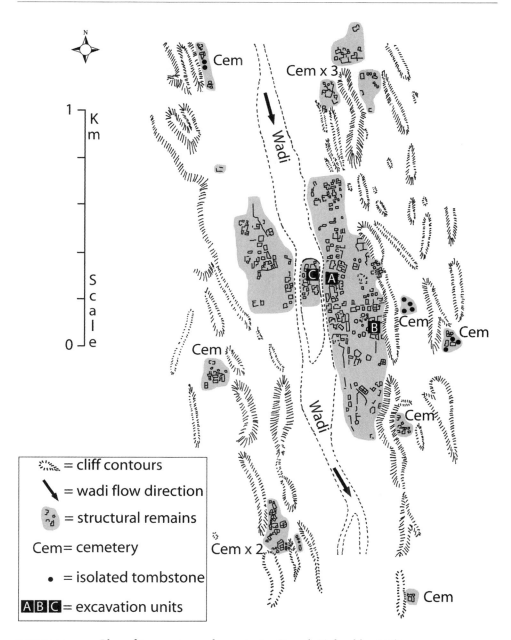

FIGURE 3.3.10 Plan of town ruins and cemeteries, Essouk-Tadmekka, Mali.

Reproduced from Nixon (2017); based on EOM aerial photos and adapted from Mauny (1961) and de Moraes Farias (2003).

mosque and a wide range of material culture. Imported goods included large quantities of glazed ceramics and glass beads—and some near-intact glass vessels—as well as tantalizing evidence of the gold trade in the form of ingots and wire and a group of Fatimid glass coin-weights (Launois and Devisse 1983; Devisse 1988).

Although Tegdaoust is often considered to be an isolated center, there are a range of settlements in the surrounding region, recorded by field survey (Robert et al. 1970: 39–67; Devisse 1983: 5–29). Finds include a cache of Almoravid dinars (Colin et al. 1983) and stone molds for producing medallions. One of these molds features Arabic writing and another features a stylised design intended to look like Arabic, the latter practically identical to a mold from Fustat (housed at the British Museum) (Ghali 1983). Other important Mauritanian sites include the undated caravan towns of Tichitt and Walata; the latter documented in Arabic texts from the 14th century (Levtzion and Hopkins 2000: 276). Likewise, we see the ruins of Ksar el Barka, seemingly of the early modern period (Naffé and Vernet 1998).

Further east, in Mali, is Essouk-Tadmekka (de Moraes Farias 2003; Nixon 2009, 2017), described by Arabic sources from the 10th–14th centuries as a significant trading town peopled by Muslim Berbers and on trade routes linking Sedrata/Ouargla with the Niger Bend at Gao (Levtzion and Hopkins 2000). The ruins (Figure 3.3.10), more than 50 hectares in extent, comprise a stone-built town, two mosques, six cemeteries, and a large open prayer ground to the north. The site is renowned for its Arabic and Tifinagh (indigenous Berber script) inscriptions found within five of the cemeteries and in the cliffs surrounding the town (de Moraes Farias 2003). The Arabic inscriptions are the earliest attested in West Africa, dated to the early 11th century CE. One inscription describes the

FIGURE 3.3.11 Arabic epigraphy in the cliffs overlooking the town ruins of Essouk-Tadmekka.

Courtesy of Sam Nixon.

town's relationship to Mecca, correlating with the meaning of Tadmekka's name in Berber, "resemblance to Mecca" (see de Moraes Farias 2017). Excavations revealed a 5-meter deep continuous architectural sequence in dry-stone walling and mud architecture dating to about 900–1400 (Nixon 2017). A rich variety of material culture was documented, with many long-distance trade goods, including a fragment of silk and a porcelain fragment from China. Evidence for crucible steel working (the first known example outside of Central Asia) and gold processing was found (Rehren and Nixon 2014, 2017; Nixon 2017), including ceramic molds, used almost certainly for producing the "unstamped" gold coinage described by Al-Bakri (Nixon et al. 2011; see illustration by Insoll Ch 4.4 this volume).

The Niger Bend contains the important trading centers of Timbuktu and Gao, which peaked under the Songhai Empire from the late 15th century. Gao is recorded in Arabic sources as early as the 9th century and continues to be occupied today (Insoll 1996, 2000; de Moraes Farias 2003; Cissé et al. 2013). The Arabic sources describe a "dual-town," with a royal town serving as the capital of the kingdom of Gao some distance from a trading center where foreign merchants were located. This division seems to be reflected in the archaeological evidence, there being both a major archaeological site below modern Gao (Gao Ancien) and the ruins of Gao-Saney, some 2 kilometers away, in a zone with no modern occupation. Like Essouk-Tadmekka, Gao-Saney has many Arabic inscriptions, dating back to the 11th century, including royal inscriptions, some on marble tombstones imported from Spain (de Moraes Farias 2003). Explorations at Gao-Saney have proved challenging due to extensive looting (Cissé et al. 2013). Nevertheless, a stratigraphic sequence, including in situ coursed mud and mudbrick architecture, has been recorded, and extensive evidence for trade goods recovered, including glass beads, vessel glass, glazed ceramics, and copper-alloys. At Gao Ancien, excavations uncovered an extensive and well-preserved building complex including the use of fired brick, mudbrick, and schist, potentially dating to the 10th–11th centuries and with a schist-pillared building hypothesized as a mosque (Insoll 1996, 2000; Cissé et al. 2013). Earlier excavations also recorded a large cache of hippopotamus ivory (Insoll 1995), as well as a gold bead and two further small fragments of gold (Insoll 2003: 105, 107, 153–155; Takezawa and Cissé 2012).

As at Gao, modern Timbuktu has obscured earlier occupation such that excavations to 5 meters depth only attained post-medieval deposits (Insoll 1998a, 2002). Nonetheless, surface finds including an 11th–12th century glazed Chinese sherd attest to the wealth of imported goods in earlier periods (Insoll 1998b). Timbuktu is first mentioned in the 14th-century Catalan Atlas (Grosjean 1978), but written sources provide limited insight into its earlier history. While certain mosques, such as Sankore and Djinguereber, are believed to have an early origin (see Nixon 2013), such is the extent of their rebuilding— a necessity due to their mud architecture needing regular repair—that we cannot determine how the current buildings relate to earlier mosque phases. Of potential significance, however, is the existence of large settlement sites such as Tombouze within 5 kilometers of Timbuktu with occupation through to the 10th century CE (Park 2010).

In the southern Saharan regions of Niger are the Kawar oasis settlements and rich salt mines (especially those at Bilma). Strategically situated at the midpoint between the Fezzan and the Kanem-Bornu states of northern Nigeria, the Kawar oases are not described in detail by Arabic geographers, though fortified settlements in this region are noted as early as the 9th century (Levtzion and Hopkins 2000: 13). Ruined settlements are found throughout the region, including the impressive mud-built fortified ruins at Djado (Lange and Berthoud 1977). While it is clear these settlements played an important role within trans-Saharan trading networks, their foundation and chronology remains open. To the west is Marendet, a trading settlement and center of early copper-working: test excavations here have recorded some of the earliest imported Islamic material culture that crossed the Sahara, including vessel glass and glass beads (Magnavita et al. 2007: 160). Likewise, Azelik-Takedda is probably the trading town and copper working site of Takedda of the Arabic sources (Bernus and Cressier 1991). The region also features the important medieval Sufi site of In Teduq (Bernus et al. 1999), as well as a range of smaller sites such as Tadeliza, Tefis, and Assodé, which shed light on religious architecture (e.g., Lhote 1973; Cressier 1989, 1992).

Trade

Trade is the dominant theme of Islamic Saharan archaeology. The early Arabic sources provide only limited commentary on Saharan trading systems and fleeting references to trade goods, particularly salt, gold, and slaves. These three commodities are generally archaeologically invisible, aside from very rare finds of gold (cf. Devisse 1983; Nixon 2017), but the archaeology of the past three decades has shown that a far more extensive range of trade goods were exchanged throughout the Sahara, including glass beads, glass vessels, glazed ceramics, and copper-alloy items, as well as rarer items such as textiles; one of the most important trade commodities but rarely recovered archaeologically. Many of the goods imported into the Sahara came from North Africa and the Mediterranean, but the recovery of Chinese porcelain and silk at Tadmekka and Timbuktu provides a tantalizing glimpse into the global scale of trade in the Islamic world (Insoll 1998b; Nixon 2017). As yet, we have a limited understanding of shifts in types and scale of commodities traded over time: the lost caravan of Maaden Ijafen (Monod 1969; Christie & Haour 2018) with its mass of copper-alloy ingots provides a fantastic archaeological snapshot into Saharan trade commodities, but we need to consider how we can explore such questions from the more piecemeal recovery of trade items.

Archaeology also provides important insights into the mechanisms of exchange. While scholars once argued that Saharan exchange operated through barter rather than money and that gold and silver were exported in their raw form to be minted into coins in North Africa, there is increasing evidence of coin-pellets or unstamped "coins" facilitating systems of commercial exchange. In addition to isolated imported Islamic coins and coin weights, coin-pellet molds have recently been identified at multiple locations within the Saharan system (Nixon et al. 2011; Nixon 2018–19).

Urbanism and Architecture

The Sahara is an ideal environment for exploring urbanism archaeologically, as the excellent preservation of those sites that were abandoned reveal town layouts and individual building forms. We have a good understanding of the latest phases of sites such as Sedrata, Essouk-Tadmekka, and Tegdaoust, but only in the very rare example of Tegdaoust has a Saharan Islamic site been excavated to reveal entire areas of the town in its earliest (9th- to 10th-century) phases (Devisse 1983; Polet 1985). Even so, the combined historical and archaeological evidence points toward an 8th–9th century evolution of Muslim urban forms in the northern Sahara (Ghadames, Sijilmasa, Tamdult) and the central Saharan Fezzan (Zawila), followed by the presence of recognizable urban Muslim centers in the southern Sahara and its fringes by the 10th century (Audaghust/Tegdaoust, Essouk-Tadmekka, Gao). The excavations at Tegdaoust reveal that a recognizable planned town form with mosque existed in the southern Sahara by the 10th century, connected with the presence of a significant Muslim trading population described in the Arabic sources (Devisse 1983), and we seem to see similar urban dynamics at Essouk-Tadmekka and Gao.

While urbanism in the Saharan world was traditionally assumed to have developed following the arrival of Muslim traders (e.g., Devisse 1988), archaeology reveals a more complex picture of Saharan urbanism predating the arrival of Islam, most strikingly demonstrated in the Garamantian cultures of the Fezzan (Mattingly 2003, 2013). Many of the key Saharan Islamic sites developed in areas with good evidence for pre-Islamic urbanism, including Sijilmasa, Ghadames, Zawila, Timbuktu, and Gao. Other sites such as Tegdaoust or Tadmekka developed in places with some form of earlier semi-permanent settlement. Tadmekka is even referred to as "Zakram" in the earliest descriptions of the town, relating to the Berber word for "town" or "built up locality," indicating the urban form was a new concept in the region (Nixon 2017). Saharan Islamic urbanism therefore appears to have evolved from earlier occupation in almost all cases rather than being plotted out on a "blank canvas."

While the focus hitherto has been on trading entrepots (e.g., Sijilmasa, Zawila, Audaghust/Tegdaoust, Essouk-Tadmekka), we need to start considering the variability of Saharan urban forms, including mining towns (Tamdult, Teghaza), "nomadic capitals" (Azugi), and smaller caravan stops. One specific question to address is the relationship between larger urban sites and internal *qasbah*, a feature at Tamdult, Zuwila, Kawar, Azugi, and Sijilmasa, but not in evidence at most West African sites. Another avenue for future research is the relationship between urban sites and the pastoral nomadic landscape surrounding many of the Saharan Islamic settlements. The contemporary and historically attested practice of nomadic pastoralists temporarily occupying Saharan towns has a correlate in urban organization, with open spaces within sites left to enable encampments to be established in and around permanent structures (Nixon 2017).

A diverse range of materials are used in Saharan architecture, relating to availability of materials and environmental conditions. Stone strongly defined the building traditions in areas with local quarries such as Tegdaoust, Essouk-Tadmekka, Azugi, Chinguetti, and

Sedrata—though this was usually combined with mud architecture, the dominant material at many Saharan sites. Important transfers of building technology and decoration have also been noted, including the very rare southern Saharan use of fired brick at Gao, a technique probably imported from North Africa (Cissé et al. 2017). At Tegdaoust we appear to see significant experimentation with different forms of mud architecture in the foundational and early levels of the site, explained by the excavators as early experimentation with North African building traditions in this southern Saharan locality (Devisse 1983).

Inevitably, the mosque has been the focus of scholarly investigation in medieval centers. We have detailed ground plans of very early Saharan mosques, including the 9th- to 10th-century mosques from Sijilmasa, Sedrata, Zuwila (possibly ca. 7th–9th century), Tegdaoust, and the possible schist mosque from Gao (see earlier description). The evidence points toward the dissemination of a hypostyle congregational mosque to major urban centers in the Sahara by the 9th–10th centuries. The minaret is recorded in the pre-Sahara at Sedrata (Aillet et al. 2017) and the central Sahara at Zuwila (Mattingly et al. 2015: 46), but not yet in the southern Sahara. Far more plentiful are mosques from the later medieval period—although almost certainly overlying earlier foundations—including a congregational pillared mosque from Essouk-Tadmekka, which is the earliest known example of the distinctive Sahelian mosque (Cressier 1992). A particular characteristic of the Sahara is evidence for open-air mosques and *musalla* (open prayer grounds), including from Tadmekka and Tegdaoust.

We have good evidence of domestic architecture, particular from the sites of Sedrata, Tegdaoust, Essouk-Tadmekka, and Azugi, where house plans are visible by survey. A particularly noteworthy feature of the southern Saharan sites of Tegdaoust and Essouk-Tadmekka is the common usage of a building form with rooms arranged around a central courtyard, far less evident in the evidence from Sedrata and the Fezzan. Parallels with the early modern and contemporary southern Sahara suggest that such large central courtyards were used for temporary tents. Individually distinctive buildings have been identified at Sijilmasa, Sedrata, and Gao, including the famous "palace" of Sedrata with its highly ornate plaster decoration (Aillet et al. 2017). Elite residences were identified at Sijilmasa based on the extensive use of paint and plaster (Messier and Miller 2015) and the use of fired brick at Gao (Cissé et al. 2013). The extensive use of red ochre for decoration at Essouk-Tadmekka (Nixon 2017) and Tegdaoust (Devisse 1983) may be a further indicator of high-status residences and is clearly the forerunner of the highly elaborate ochre and white painted decorative tradition of early modern Walata in Mauritania. Definition of "elite" buildings elsewhere in the Sahara is more difficult as such obvious markers as plaster, burnt brick, and decoration are lacking.

Technology

The origin and spread of productive technologies such as glass-making and metalworking has been a growing focus of research in recent years. Primary glass production and the production of glass beads occurred in the forest zone of Nigeria in the medieval period (Lankton et al. 2006; Babalola et al. 2017). This glass production used a specific glass recipe particular to this region, however, and the extent to which this technology was linked to imported technologies of Islamic glass production is unclear. Given the significant trade in glass beads and vessel glass across the Sahara, however, we should certainly consider some element of technology transfer, though the hypothesized production of glass beads at Tegdaoust has yet to be substantiated by technical analysis (Vanacker 1984). Evidence for glass-based technology in the Sahara—perhaps associated with a transfer of glass technologies to West Africa—is the use of crushed glass for processing gold at Essouk-Tadmekka, a gold-processing technology not documented elsewhere in the pre-modern world (Rehren and Nixon 2014).

Archaeometallurgical analysis at Saharan sites has been hugely profitable, and the detection of crucible steel production at Essouk-Tadmekka is one of the most important findings to highlight (Rehren and Nixon 2017). This is the earliest archaeological identification of this technology outside Central Asia (Akhsiket, Uzbekistan), in a form practically identical to the Islamic technology seen there. The need for steel was likely connected to the production of weapons, and the reference to the use of steel swords (*hind*) by the Almoravid army is important to highlight (Levtzion and Hopkins 2000: 164–165). The identification at this same Saharan site of ceramic molds for the production of coin blanks (Nixon et al. 2011) has since led to further identifications of this technology at the site of Tamdult in Morocco (Nixon 2018–19). This appears to relate to a wider Islamic technology of coin production which has been little discussed anywhere in the Islamic world, despite its earlier recording at an Islamic site in Pakistan (Khan 1990). This in turn relates to wider evidence for complex metal-working technologies throughout the Sahara, including smelting, smithing, and the production of ingots, ranging from, for example, the industrial quarter of Tegdaoust (Vanacker 1979) to the silver mining town of Tamdult (Nixon 2018–19).

One final area of research is the irrigation and hydrology systems which helped support life in the desert. Work in the Fezzan has provided an important illustration of the different irrigation technologies (foggara, wells, etc.) applied to maintaining agricultural systems in desert oases from antiquity to the medieval period (Mattingly 2003). There has also been some work on exploring urban hydrology, including the recent work at Sijilmasa (Soubira et al. 2015). This fundamental element of life in desert settlements, however, is still vastly underexplored.

Religion and the Spread of Islam into the Sahara

Muslim groups are first attested in the Sahara in the 9th century in the pre-Saharan towns of Sijilmasa and Ghadames and the central Saharan town of Zuwila; contemporary descriptions of southern Saharan sites do not describe Muslim groups (Levtzion and Hopkins 2000). Concrete archaeological evidence for Islam within the Sahara before the 10th century is limited to the congregational mosque at Zuwila (radiocarbon dated to the 7th–9th centuries) (Mattingly et al. 2015). By the 10th century, however, there is historical and archaeological evidence for a solid network of trading towns with Muslim communities across the Sahara, from Sijilmasa, Sedrata, and Zuwila in the north and central Sahara, to Audaghust, Tadmekka, and Gao in the south.

The adoption of Islam in the Sahara took place within a landscape of polytheistic local religions (Hachid 2000) as well as the limited presence of Christian and Jewish communities in the northern Sahara, including at Ghadames. Early Islam in the Sahara is strongly associated with Ibadi Islam and the movement of the Ibadi Rustamid capital from Tahert to Sedrata in 908; the ruins of which present significant traces of Ibadi Islam, including a mosque and cemeteries. Important early Ibadi communities were also found at Zuwila and at Essouk-Tadmekka where there is a possible Ibadi mosque and cemetery (the only one of the six cemeteries without inscriptions) (Nixon 2017). Another Kharijite sect, the Sufri, ruled Sijilmasa under the Midrarid dynasty. Sijilmasa's connections with Tegdaoust led to it also having a significant Kharijite presence (Devisse 1983), though the Shia Fatimid dynasty also invested in the western Saharan trade routes from the 10th century (Devisse 1988). In the 11th century, the Sunni (Maliki) Almoravid movement from the southern Saharan regions of Mauritania led a *jihad* throughout the western regions of the Sahara and into Morocco, strongly focused on ridding the region of Kharijite practices (Bennison 2016). Almoravid destruction of Ibadi communities appears to be discernible in the archaeology at Tegdaoust—the first town sacked by the Almoravids (Devisse 1983).

The Saharan landscape provides a range of evidence about the spaces set aside for Muslim prayer. In addition to mosques (see earlier discussion), remains of open prayer grounds (*musalla*) also provide insights into the wider landscape of prayer. At both Tegdaoust and Essouk-Tadmekka, prayer grounds are located on the perimeter of the town, likely to cater to camel caravans arriving and departing or for use for markets or festivals. Arabic epigraphy (found only at Essouk-Tadmekka and Gao) provides insights into Muslim prayer, including examples found at the entrance to Essouk-Tadmekka which instruct the viewer to recite the profession of faith twenty times before entering the town (de Moraes Farias 2017). Sufi prayer practices became important in a later phase of Saharan history, especially at the sacred complex of Tefis in Niger (Bernus et al. 1999).

Archaeology provides significant evidence for mortuary practice in the Sahara, especially cemetery organization, including from Sijilmasa, Tamdult, Sedrata, Azugi, Tegdaoust, Essouk-Tadmekka, and Gao. There is significant variability between these sites, with Azugi, Tegdaoust, and Gao each having single large cemeteries, while Tadmekka has six independent cemeteries and Tamdult three. There is also variability in the above-ground treatment of the tomb, with low rectangular plaster tomb coverings at Sedrata (Aillet et al. 2017) and inscribed headstones at Essouk-Tadmekka and Gao (de Moraes Farias 2003). Monumental tombs are rare: the Banu Khattab tombs from Zuwila are to date the only known early mausolea, though an individual elite burial at Essouk-Tadmekka was marked by a tomb enclosure with a mihrab (Nixon 2017). Very few Muslim burials have been excavated in the Sahara, certainly a result of the limited desire among existing populations to disturb Muslim burials. Early excavations of the Ibadi burials at Sedrata, however, show a distinct practice of burying the dead in small antechambers off the main burial pit, blocked off by stones, a practice considered to have pre-Islamic origins (Aillet et al. 2017: 333–334).

Further insights into Muslim lifeways come from the study of diet. While archaeobotany and zooarchaeology have seldom been employed in Saharan contexts, the evidence recovered from Jerma (Mattingly 2013) and Essouk-Tadmekka (Nixon 2017) shows the potential of such research. At Jerma, the presence of pig bones into the early modern period (if in reduced numbers) suggests that not all members of the community followed Muslim dietary laws (which forbid the consumption of pork). At Tadmekka, the recovery of wheat from circa 10th-century contexts may suggest the presence of Muslims rather than simply trade connections, as wheat consumption is described in the early Arabic sources as a marker of correct Islamic lifeways (Levtzion and Hopkins 2000: 51–52). Similarly, significant quantities of charred dog bones were recovered; of great relevance, as the consumption of dogs was identified by the Almoravids as one of the key Kharijite practices to stamp out (see Nixon 2017: 238 for references).

FUTURE DIRECTIONS

To date, Islamic archaeology in the Sahara has focused on the 8th–14th centuries and the major trading hubs described in the Arabic sources. There is clearly a need to consider the later phases of Islamic history, as well as a far broader range of site types. Much remains to be done on topics such as diet, health, agriculture, and climate or indeed of local craft and artisanal practices beyond architecture. While the Sahara did not see widespread production of the full range of commonly recognised Islamic portable arts forms—such as glazed ceramics and glass vessels—a wide range of material culture was produced in the region, and we also have some examples of local traditions of early Arabic epigraphy (de Moraes Farias 2003); the latter important evidence of local Arabic scripts long pre-dating those recorded in the Saharan manuscripts of Timbuktu and other early centers. The exploration of such new themes has great potential to extend our understanding of existing material as well as to direct new fieldwork.

The present political insecurity across much of the Sahara has led to significant destruction of Islamic cultural heritage—including tombs, shrines, and archaeological sites—and it has also made it near impossible to conduct field research in much of the region (Joy 2016; Lostal 2017). Analysis and publication of earlier excavation archives offers great potential, as illustrated by the recent publication of the archives of Sedrata (Aillet et al. 2017). There is a need for significant reflection on the very practice of Islamic archaeology in the Sahara. What value can the practice of Islamic archaeology have beyond academically-driven research agendas and results? How is Islamic archaeology as a practice viewed in the Sahara? And what specific productive steps could a "public" Islamic archaeology adopt in the region? It is clear that these questions need to be seriously considered in the coming years.

References

Aillet, C., Cressier, P., and Gilotte, S. 2017. *Sedrata* (Madrid: Casa de Velázquez).

Austen, R. 2010. *Trans-Saharan Africa in World History* (New York: Oxford University Press).

Babalola, A. B., McIntosh, S. K., Dussubieux, L., and Rehren, T. 2017. "Ile-Ife and Igbo Olokun in the History of Glass in West Africa," *Antiquity*, 91, 732–750.

Bennison, A. 2016. *The Almoravid and Almohad Empires* (Edinburgh: Edinburgh University Press).

Bernus, E., Cressier, P., Durand, A., Paris, F., and Saliege, J.-F. (eds.) 1999. *Vallée de l'Azawagh (Sahara du Niger)* (Paris: Éditions Sépia).

Bernus, S., and Cressier, P. 1991. *La Région d'in Gall—Tegidda N Tesemt (Niger)* (Niamey: Institut de Recherches en Sciences Humaines).

Boone, J., and Benco, N. 1999. "Islamic Settlement in North Africa and the Iberian Peninsula," *Annual Review of Anthropology*, 28, 51–71.

Bovill, E. 1933. *Caravans of the Old Sahara: An Introduction to the History of the western Sudan* (London: Oxford University Press).

Bovill, E. 1968 (2nd ed.). *The Golden Trade of the Moors* (London: Oxford University Press).

Capel, C. 2017. "Sijilmassa in the Footsteps of the Aghlabids: The Hypothesis of a Ninth-Century New Royal City in Tafilalt Plain (Morocco)," in G. Anderson, C. Fenwick, and M. Rosser-Owen (eds.), *The Aghlabids and Their Neighbors: Art and Material Culture in Ninth-Century North Africa* (Leiden: Brill), 531–550.

Christie, A., and Haour, A. 2018. "'The 'Lost Caravan' of Ma'den Ijafen Revisited: Re-appraising Its Cargo of Cowries, a Medieval Global Commodity," Journal of African Archaeology, 16, 2, 125–144.

Cissé, M., McIntosh, S., Dussubieux, L., Fenn, T., Gallagher, D., and Smith, A. 2013. "Excavations at Gao-Saney: New Evidence for Settlement Growth, Trade and Interaction on the Niger Bend in the First Millenium CE," *Journal of African Archaeology*, 11, 1, 9–37.

Colin, G., Babacar, A., Ghali, N., and Devisse, J. 1983. "Un ensemble épigraphie Almoravide: découverte fortuite dans le région de Tidjikja; chaton de bague découvert a Tegdaoust," in J. Devisse (ed.), *Tegdaoust III. Recherches sur Aoudaghost* (Paris: Éditions Recherche sur les Civilisations), 427–444.

Cressier, P. 1989. "La grande mosquée d'Assodé," *Journal des africanistes*, 59, 1–2, 133–162.

Cressier, P. 1992. "Archéologie de la dévotion soufi," *Journal des africanistes*, 62, 2, 69–90.

Cressier, P. 2004. "Du Sud au Nord du Sahara: la question de Tamdult (Maroc)," in A. Bazzana and H. Bocoum (eds.), *Du Nord au Sud du Sahara: Cinquante ans d'archéologie Française* (Paris: Éditions Sépia), 275–284.

de Moraes Farias, P. F. 2003. *Arabic Medieval Inscriptions from the Republic of Mali: Epigraphy, Chronicles, and Songhay-Tuãreg History* (Oxford: Oxford University Press).

de Moraes Farias, P. 2017. "Arabic and Tifinagh inscriptions," in S. Nixon (ed.). *Essouk-Tadmekka: An Early Islamic Trans-Saharan Market Town* (Leiden: Brill).

Devisse, J. (ed.) 1983. *Tegdaoust III. Recherches sur Aoudaghost* (Paris: Éditions Recherche sur les Civilisations).

Devisse, J. 1988. "Trade and Trade Routes in West Africa," in M. El Fasi (ed.), *General History of Africa, Volume 3: Africa from the Seventh to the Eleventh Century* (Berkeley: University of California Press), 367–435.

Ettinghausen, R., Grabar, O., and Jenkins-Madina, M. 2003. *Islamic Art and Architecture, 650–1250* (New Haven: Yale University Press).

Fauvelle, F.-X., Erbati, L., and Mensan, R. 2014. "Sijilmâsa: cité idéale, site insaisissable? Ou comment une ville échappe à ses fouilleurs," *Les Études et Essais du Centre Jacques Berque*, 20, 3–16.

Fenwick, C. 2013. "From Africa to Ifrīqiya: Settlement and Society in Early Medieval North Africa (650–800)," *Al-Masāq*, 25, 1, 9–33.

Fenwick, C. 2020. *Early Islamic North Africa: A New Perspective* (London: Bloomsbury).

Gaiser, A. 2010. *Muslims, Scholars, Soldiers. The Origin and Elaboration of the Ibadi Imamate Traditions* (New York: Oxford University Press).

Garenne-Marot, L., and Mille, B. 2007. "Copper-Based Metal in the Inland Niger Delta: Metal and Technology at the Time of the Empire of Mali," in S. La Niece, D. Hook, and P. Craddock (eds.), *Metals and Mines: Studies in Archaeometallurgy* (London: Archetype Publications), 159–169.

Ghali, N. 1983. "Moules à couler des médailles," in J. Devisse (ed.), *Tegdaoust III. Recherches sur Aoudaghost* (Paris: Editions Recherche sur les Civilisations), 421–426.

Grosjean, G. (ed.) 1978. *Mapamundi. The Catalan Atlas of the year 1375* (Dietikon-Zurich: Urs Graf Verlag).

Haarmann, U. 1998. "The Dead Ostrich: Life and Trade in Ghadames (Libya) in the Nineteenth Century," *Die Welt des Islams*, 38, 1, 9–94.

Hachid, M. 2000. *Les premiers Berberes: entre Mediterranee, Tassili et Nil* (Aix-en-Provence: Edisud).

Insoll, T. 1995. "A Cache of Hippopotamus Ivory at Gao, Mali; and a Hypothesis of Its Use," *Antiquity*, 69, 327–336.

Insoll. T. 1996. *Islam, Archaeology and History. Gao Region (Mali) ca. AD 900–1250* (Oxford: Tempus Reparatum).

Insoll, T. 1998a. "Archaeological Research in Timbuktu, Mali," *Antiquity*, 72, 413–417.

Insoll, T. 1998b. "A Note on a Late Eleventh-Early Twelfth Century Sherd of Southern Chinese Celadon Found at Timbuktu, the Republic of Mali, West Africa," *The Oriental Ceramic Society Newsletter*, 6, 18–19.

Insoll, T. 2000. *Urbanism, Archaeology and Trade: Further Observations on the Gao Region (Mali): The 1996 Fieldseason Results* (Oxford: BAR).

Insoll, T. 2002. "The Archaeology of Post Medieval Timbuktu," *Sahara*, 13, 7–22.

Insoll, T. 2003. *The Archaeology of Islam in sub-Saharan Africa* (Cambridge: Cambridge University Press).

Insoll, T. 2006. "Islamic Archaeology and the Sahara," in D. J. Mattingly, S. McLaren, E. Savage, Y. al-Fasatwi, and K. Gadgood (eds.), *The Libyan Desert: Natural Resources and Cultural Heritage* (London: Society for Libyan Studies), 223–238.

Joy, C. 2016. "'UNESCO Is What?' World Heritage, Militant Islam and the Search for a Common Humanity in Mali," in C. Brumann and D. Berliner (eds.), *World Heritage on the Ground: Ethnographic Perspectives* (New York: Berghahn Books), 60–77.

Khan, A. 1990. *Al-Mansurah: A Forgotten Arab Metropolis in Pakistan* (Karachi: Kifayat).

King, G. R. D. 1989. "Islamic Archaeology in Libya, 1969–1989," *Libyan Studies*, 20, 193–207.

Lange, D., and Berthoud, S. 1977. "Al-Qasaba et d'autres villes de la route centrale du Sahara," *Paideuma*, 23, 19–40.

Lankton, J., Ige, O., and Rehren, T. 2006. "Early Primary Glass Production in Southern Nigeria," *Journal of African Archaeology*, 4, 111–138.

Launois, A., and Devisse, J. 1983. "Poids de verre découverts à Tegdaoust, chronologie du site et histoire des étalons de poids en Afrique occidentale," in J. Devisse. (ed.), *Tegdaoust III. Recherches sur Aoudaghost* (Paris: Éditions Recherche sur les Civilisations), 399–419.

Levtzion, N., and Hopkins, J. (eds.) 2000. *Corpus of Early Arabic Sources for West African History* (2nd ed.) (Princeton: Markus Wiener Publishers).

Lhote, H. 1973. "Découverte des ruines de Tadeliza, ancienne résidence des sultans de l'Air," *Notes africaines*, 137, 9–16.

Lostal, M. 2017. *International Cultural Heritage Law in Armed Conflict: Case-Studies of Syria, Libya, Mali, the Invasion of Iraq, and the Buddhas of Bamiyan* (Cambridge: Cambridge University Press).

Magnavita, S., Maga, A., Magnavita, C., and Idé, O. 2007. "New Studies on Marandet (Central Niger) and Its Trade Connections: An Interim Report," *Die Zeitschrift für Archäologie Außereuropäischer Kulturen*, 2, 147–165.

Mattingly, D. (ed.) 2003. *The Archaeology of Fazzān. Volume 1, Synthesis* (London: The Society for Libyan Studies).

Mattingly, D. (ed.) 2013. *The Archaeology of Fazzaān. Volume 4, Survey and Excavations at Old Jarma (Ancient Garama) Carried Out by C. M. Daniels (1962–69) and the Fazzān Project (1997–2001)* (London: Society of Libyan Studies).

Mattingly, D. J., and Sterry, M. J. 2010. *Ghadames Archaeological Survey. Phase 1 Desk–top Report* (Unpublished consultancy report produced for the Libyan Department of Antiquities, the Ghadames Development Authority and BP).

Mattingly, D. J., and Sterry, M. J. 2017. "Zuwila and Fazzan in the Seventh to Tenth Centuries: The Emergence of a New Trading Center," in G. Anderson, C. Fenwick, and M. Rosser-Owen (eds.), *The Aghlabids and Their Neighbors: Art and Material Culture in Ninth-Century North Africa* (Leiden: Brill), 551–572.

Mattingly, D., Sterry, M., and Edwards, D. 2015. "The Origins and Development of Zuwila, Libyan Sahara: An Archaeological and Historical Overview," *Azania Archaeological Research in Africa*, 50, 1, 27–75.

Mattingly, D. J., Bokbot, Y., Sterry, M., Cuénod, A., Fenwick, C., Gatto, M. C., Ray, N., Rayne, L., Janin, K., Lamb, A. and Mugnai, N., 2017. Long-term history in a Moroccan oasis zone: The Middle Draa Project 2015. *Journal of African Archaeology*, 15, 2, 141–172.

Mauny, R. 1955. "Notes d'histoire et d'archéologie sur Azougui, Chinguetti et Ouadane," *Bulletin de l'I.F.A.N. (B)*, 17, 1, 142–162.

Mauny, R. 1961. *Tableau géographique de l'Ouest Africain au Moyen Âge d'après les sources écrites, la tradition et l'archéologie* (Dakar: IFAN).

Messier, R., and Miller, J. 2015. *The Last Civilized Place: Sijilmasa and Its Saharan Destiny* (Austin: University of Texas Press).

Milwright, M. 2010. *An Introduction to Islamic Archaeology* (Edinburgh: Edinburgh University Press).

Monod, T. 1938a. "Sur les inscriptions Arabes peintes de Ti-m-missao Sahara central," *Journal de la Société des Africanistes*, 8, 83–95.

Monod, T. 1938b. "Teghaza," *La Nature*, 3025, 289–296.

Monod, T. 1940. "Nouvelles remarques sur Teghaza (Sahara occidental)," *Bulletin de l'IFAN* 2, 248–254.

Monod, T. 1969. "Le Ma'aden Ijafen: une épave caravanière ancienne dans la Majabat al-Koubra," *Actes du 1er colloque international d'archéologie africaine, 1967* (Fort Lamy: Institut National tchadien pour les sciences humaine), 286–320.

Naffé, B., and Vernet, R. 1998. "Ksar al-Barka," *SNIM News*, 18, 30–32.

Nixon, S. 2009. "Excavating Essouk-Tadmakka (Mali): New Archaeological Investigations of Early Islamic Trans-Saharan Trade," *Azania: Archaeological Research in Africa*, 44, 2, 217–255.

Nixon, S. (ed.) 2017. *Essouk-Tadmekka: An Early Islamic Trans-Saharan Market Town* (Leiden: Brill).

Nixon, S. 2013. "'A Longing for Mecca': The Trans-Saharan Hajj and the Caravan Towns of West Africa," in V. Porter and L. Saif (eds.), *Hajj: Collected Essays* (London: British Museum Press), 65–73.

Nixon, S. 2018–19 'Investigations of the the early Islamic oases centre of Tamdult (southern Morocco).' Online report available at https://maxvanberchem.org/fr/activites-scientifiques/projets/archeologie/8-francais/176-investigation-of-the-early-islamic-oases-centre-of-tdult-southern-morocco (accessed 30th March 2020).

Nixon, S., Rehren, T., and Guerra, M.-F. 2011. "New Light on the Early Islamic West African Gold Trade: Coin Moulds from Tadmekka, Mali," *Antiquity*, 85, 1353–1368.

Park, D. 2010. "Prehistoric Timbuktu and Its Hinterland," *Antiquity*, 84, 1076–1088.

Polet, J. 1985. *Tegdaoust IV, Fouille d'un Quartier de Tegdaoust (Mauritanie Orientale): Urbanisation, architecture, utilisation de l'espace construit* (Paris: Éditions Recherche sur les Civilisations).

Rehren, T., and Nixon, S. 2014. "Refining Gold with Glass: An Early Islamic Technology at Tadmekka, Mali," *Journal of Archaeological Science*, 49, 33–41.

Rehren, T., and Nixon, S. 2017. "Crucible-steel Making and Other Metalworking Remains," in S. Nixon (ed.), *Essouk-Tadmekka: an early Islamic trans-Saharan market town* (Leiden: Brill), 188–202.

Robert, D., Robert, S., and Devisse, J. 1970. *Tegdaoust I: Recherches sur Aoudaghost* (Paris: Arts et Métiers Graphiques).

Robert-Chaleix, D. 1989. *Tegdaoust V, Une concession médiévale à Tegdaoust: implantation, évolution d'une unité d'habitation* (Paris: Éditions Recherche sur les Civilisations).

Rosenberger, B. 1970. "Tamdult: cité minière et caravanière presaharienne, IX–XIVe s.," *Hesperis Tamuda*, 11, 103–139.

Saison, B. 1981. "Azuggi: archéologie et histoire en Adrar mauritanien," *Recherche, Pédagogie, et Culture*, 9, 55, 66–74.

Soubira, T., Fauvelle-Aymar, F.-X., Erbati, E., and Mensan, R. 2015. "Sijilmāsa (Morocco): The Urbanism of a Medieval Islamic Site as Seen Through Its Hydraulic System (8th–13th Centuries AD)," *Nyame Akuma*, 84, 3–12.

Stewart, C., and Salim, S. 2015. *The Writings of Mauritania and the Western Sahara. The Arabic Literature of Africa* (Leiden: Brill).

Takezawa, S., and Cissé, M. 2012. "Discovery of the Earliest Royal Palace in Gao and Its Implications for the History of West Africa," *Cahiers d'études africaines*, 208, 813–844.

Vanacker, C. 1979. *Tegdaoust II, Fouille d'un quartier artisanal* (Paris: I.M.R.S).

Vanacker, C. 1984. "Perles de verre découvertes sur le site de Tegdaoust," *Journal des Africanistes*, 54, 31–52.

van Berchem, M. 1960. "Sedrata et les anciennes villes berbères du Sahara dans les récits des explorateurs du XIXe siècle," *Bulletin d'Institut Français d'Archéologie Orientale*, 59, 289–308.

CHAPTER 3.4

....

AL-ANDALUS

....

PATRICE CRESSIER AND SONIA GUTIÉRREZ LLORET

THE CONSTRUCTION OF AN ARCHAEOLOGY OF AL-ANDALUS

THE Arab-Berber (or Arab-Islamic from a demographic, linguistic, and religious perspective) conquest of Hispania in 711 had important consequences for the history of the western Mediterranean: the formation of an Islamic society in the Iberian Peninsula, known as al-Andalus. The term al-Andalus encompasses all those Iberian territories (modern Spain, Portugal, and initially southern France) integrated into the dar al-Islam during the Middle Ages. Its territorial limits varied and were gradually reduced between the 8th and 15th centuries, but its social implications continued until the 17th century, when the "Moriscos" (Muslims who were forced to convert to Christianity in 1502) were finally expelled (Figure 3.4.1).

This event explains the almost total rupture between the historiography of Christian Spain and that of al-Andalus. Strong ideological assumptions and the imposition of excessively dogmatic models have further handicapped the study of this region, dominated until a few decades ago by a continuist and traditional vision that viewed al-Andalus as an exotic anecdote within the history of Spain. Archaeology, however, allows us to move beyond the impasse. It reveals a different image: that of a society with a markedly *orientalized* structure that resulted from intense acculturation and left a deep imprint on its surroundings. This social and cultural transformation has been the focus of lively historiographical debates in which archaeology has been employed forcefully as a historical source in its own right. In contrast to the traditional vision of continuity, which considered Islamization as a purely cultural and superficial process, more recent research demonstrates that the implementation of this Islamic society meant widespread and profound change (Cressier and Gutiérrez Lloret 2009; Sénac 2012).

From a historiographical perspective, the archaeology of al-Andalus is younger than the traditional disciplines of prehistoric and classical archaeology. It developed only

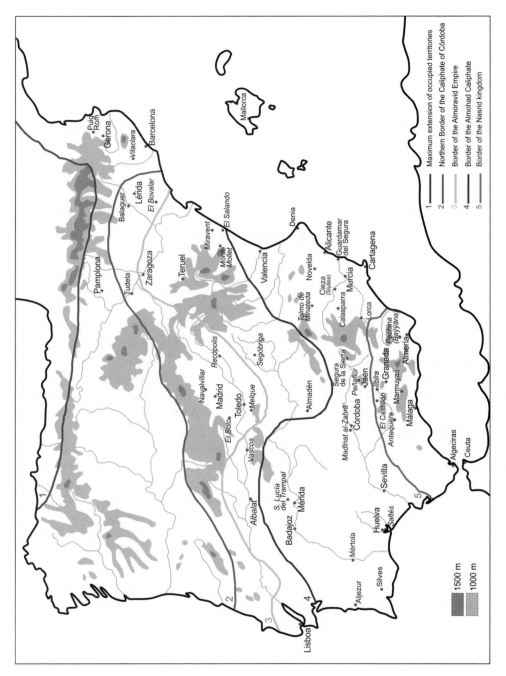

FIGURE 3.4.1 The evolution of al-Andalus (8th–15th centuries) and the principal sites mentioned.

four decades ago, but its academic recognition is even more recent. Of course, an interest in medieval Islamic remains dates back to the 19th century, but these early approaches were very different from what is now understood to be medieval archaeology. Orientalist movements influenced the creation of an exotic image of Spain in the arts of the time. The Islamic archaeology of the 20th century was characterized by different perspectives: art history, architectural restoration, and Arabism. The historiographical paradigm changed toward the end of the 1970s, strongly influenced by France and Italy. The activity of the French Casa de Velázquez was very important; Pierre Guichard's thesis on al-Andalus from a structuralist perspective was extremely influential, as was his work with André Bazzana and Patrice Cressier on fortifications and rural landscapes (Guichard 1976, Bazzana et al. 1988). Guichard's vision of al-Andalus as an Islamic and Eastern society countered the image of continuity, while the introduction of survey archaeology opened up new methodological perspectives in the study of rural settlement. Later, a Marxist Italian influence introduced a new dimension to the study of material culture, settlement, and medieval territories (Gutiérrez Lloret 2015).

New legal frameworks for heritage established in the 1980s and 1990s, and the transfer of heritage management to regional governments increased the amount of archaeological (especially medieval) excavations. Archaeological research was no longer restricted to museums, universities, and research centres, but was now also conducted by professional archaeologists (Quirós Castillo 2009; Carvajal López 2014). At the same time, there were key methodological shifts in medieval archaeology, including open area excavation, the use of the Harris Matrix, geographic information systems (GIS), archaeometry and bioarchaeology. New research focuses were also introduced (e.g., archaeology of buildings, household archaeology) which challenged the monumentalist approaches of the 19th century and the very concepts of "Islamic art," "Mozarabic," or "Mudejar." The urban and decorative programs of the Umayyad Caliphate, for example, are now explained as the original expression of a newly triumphant Islamic society, a theoretical position far removed from that of "Spanish continuity." In just a few years, an archaeology of al-Andalus that was positivist, exoticizing, and monumental was transformed into a modern archaeology that is interested in context and process, and embraces debates such as the rural landscape, social change, the exploitation of natural resources, production, and social and ideological spaces (Gutiérrez Lloret 2015).

The Urban Landscape

It is widely agreed that the city is a fiscal space which plays a central role in the administrative organization of the territory, as well as the classic locus for presenting ideology and promoting Islamic economic and social forms. Less appreciated is the contribution of archaeology to our knowledge of the cities of al-Andalus (Acién Almansa 2001; Malpica Cuello 2015). Our understanding of urban development is constrained by the continued occupation of most of the important cities. Unlike rural archaeology, which privileges the study of abandoned sites and where, therefore, it is possible to plan precise research strategies, the towns of al-Andalus are today palimpsests that have rarely been the subject of unified or coordinated excavations. Urban excavations are thus determined by problems completely unrelated to historical research, such as economic dynamics, the availability of land, and the actions of developers. Scientific advances have been greater in those cities like Córdoba, Jaén, and Cartagena where universities have been involved in research, but the involvement of museums, archaeological field schools, and town councils has also achieved excellent results in smaller cities like Mértola and Lorca.

On the other hand, the restriction of excavations to only those parts of towns (the walled centers) that are explicitly protected has resulted in the irreparable loss of fundamental evidence in town suburbs and has reinforced the image of a densely packed medina, distinct from its rural hinterland. However, the few extensive excavations carried out in peri-urban areas (around Córdoba: in the suburb of Shaqunda or western sector of al-Yanih al-Garbi-; around Jaén: Marroquíes Bajos, and in the surroundings of Valencia) have nuanced traditional models of the urban phenomenon in the Islamic West based on the classic tripartite scheme of madina-suburb-periphery, established in the middle of the past century by L. Torres Balbás (1970). In general, a sociological reading of urban topography prevails which views spatial organization as the physical translation of Muslim law (the layout of apparently irregular neighborhoods and roads) and political ideology (spaces of power: *qasaba* and *qasr*) and religion (mosques, baths, cemeteries), as well as economic activity (*suqs*, *funduqs*, craft production centers). Archaeology has clearly demonstrated that Islamic urbanism is planned and resorts, in all periods where possible, to an orthogonal arrangement in street networks and drainage system, as in the early examples of Bajjana and the suburbs of Córdoba, as well as the late ones of Pla d'Almatà (Lérida), Vascos (Toledo), Fortí de Denia, or Almohad Shaltish (Huelva) and Seville (Acién Almansa 2001).

Archaeology also provides novel answers to the key questions posed about the city: its genesis, its social character, its evolution over time (in contrast to traditional scholarship which stresses the static nature of the city), and the intervention of the state in urban processes. The issue of the static nature of Islamic urbanism has been the object of much debate and has led to the development of several different evolutionary models of the city by Torres Balbás, de Epalza, or by Navarro Palazón and Jiménez Castillo (2007). None is wholly correct, but all provide useful conceptual tools to understand the processes at play. With regard to the origins of the Islamic city on the Peninsula, arguments about the apparent continuity of Roman urbanism and the limited innovative role of Islamic urbanism are now happily overcome (Cressier and García-Arenal 1998; Valor and Gutiérrez 2014). In the Iberian Peninsula, archaeological excavations in urban centers of Roman or Visigothic origin, such as Valencia, Mérida, Córdoba (modern cities) and Recópolis, Ilbira, or El Tolmo de Minateda (abandoned cities), show that the processes of urban destructuration had already begun well before 711. These cities were not abandoned suddenly during the conquest, but were used by the conquerors to establish the new fiscal and political order before being definitively abandoned during the 8th century. They were then replaced by a new completely Islamic urbanism that met different social needs between the 9th and 11th centuries. This topographic and functional rupture is evident in new spontaneous foundations such as Bajjana and state foundations, such as Murcia and Badajoz in the 9th century or Almería and Madinat al-Zahra under the Caliphate, as well as new constructions that are built among the remains of ancient Visigothic centers of Valencia, Córdoba, and Zaragoza. Research on early Islamic urban centers (Madinat Ilbira, Tolmo of Minateda, Mérida, Jaén) shows that the city of the 8th and 9th centuries does not always respond to the canonical schemes of the "Muslim city" but was conditioned by the survival of the classical layout (Gutiérrez Lloret 1998). In the 9th–10th centuries, the gradual establishment of a territorial system based on *kuras* (administrative provinces) involved the foundation of new regional capitals and the fortification of other centres.

The process of forming this urban network had a strong and rapid demographic contribution as a consequence, particularly marked in the case of Córdoba, which was converted into the capital of al-Andalus. In this exceptional case, urban growth under the first emirs quickly overflowed the Roman walls and created large neighborhoods around the foci of religious or social Islamization (mosques or *muniyas* (agricultural estates) built by important state figures). This spectacular growth reached its peak under the caliph Abd al-Rahman III with the foundation of Madinat al-Zahra, which merged with Córdoba to create a genuine conurbation unparalleled elsewhere in the medieval West, but with antecedents in the Abbasid world and in the neighboring emirates like that of the Aghlabids of Ifriqiya, the closest to al-Andalus (Acién Almansa and Vallejo Triano 1998; Acién Almansa 2001; Cressier and Vallejo Triano 2015) (Figure 3.4.2).

THE HOUSE AND SOCIETY

Archaeology has provided more data than written sources about the material conditions of everyday life, and our knowledge of urban and rural housing is now abundant (Bazzana 1992; Orihuela 2007). While initially the bulk of information came from site-specific studies, the spread of rescue archaeology in large cities has produced important syntheses in the form of monographs for Toledo and Murcia and unpublished doctoral theses for Córdoba and Seville. The house is a good indicator of the rhythms of social Islamization. This can be seen in the appearance of the "courtyard house", a new form of domestic architecture alien to the Roman tradition (Gutiérrez Lloret 2013). The plan is that of a compact domestic unit, with specialized rooms leading off the courtyard, highly centralized and completely closed off from the outside by an oblique entrance of an eminently private character; this housing type characterizes Islamized societies throughout the Mediterranean from the middle of the 9th century. This house layout, which includes a separate bedroom, vestibule, and latrine spaces, is already present in Bajjana in the second half of the 9th century and becomes widespread from the 10th century, when it gradually incorporates a separate kitchen. The diffusion of this model is

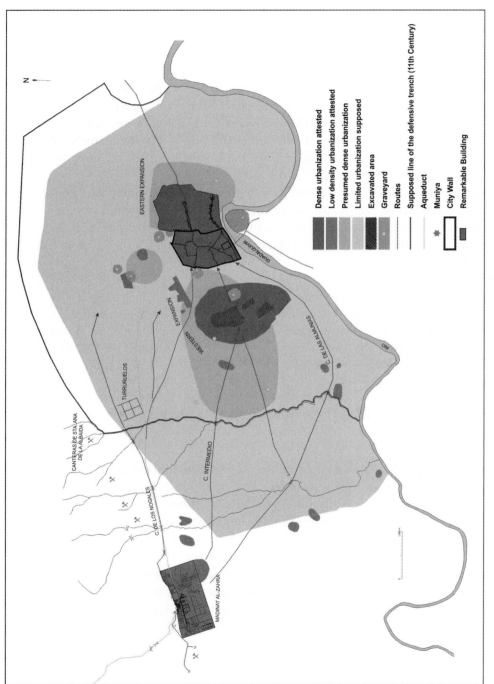

FIGURE 3.4.2 Córdoba and Madinat al-Zahra during the caliphate (10th century). The construction (936 or 940–944) of the caliphal city of Madinat al-Zahra', only 8 kilometers to the west of Córdoba, created the largest conurbation in Europe at this time. The archaeological extent is some 5,000 hectares, which included densely populated neighborhoods with orthogonal grids, mosques, cemeteries and aristocratic *muniyas*. There is no reliable estimate of the number of inhabitants, but it must have exceeded 100,000.

Courtesy of M. Acién Almansa and A. Vallejo Triano. Redrawn by V. Amorós.

slowly matched with the specialization of spaces and the increasingly frequent presence of kitchens, warehouses, and even stables, as well as the appearance in the 12th century of upper floors, galleries, and decorated porticos facing onto the courtyard rather than the exterior due to the importance of preserving privacy (and the control of women; Figure 3.4.3).

It is generally accepted that this wholly Islamic model coexists with and slowly displaces other simpler domestic patterns, formed by the association of various monocellular units around a "proto-courtyard." In certain cases, there is a gradual process of room additions which may indicate that several related families may have lived in the same domestic unit. Anthropology has often been used to identify the ethnicity of the populations concerned (as Arab or Berber immigrants), but archaeology shows that the problem is much more complex, since these simple household forms are found in both rural and urban early Visigothic and early Islamic contexts. In non-Islamized contexts, they appear in fortified enclosures (castra), such as Puig Rom in Gerona, rural villages with churches (monasteries?) such as El Bovalar in Lérida, and small open villages such as Vilaclara de Castellfollit del Boix in Barcelona and Navalvillar in Madrid, as well as in the urban centers of Recópolis, El Tolmo de Minateda, Cartagena, and Mérida. They are documented in securely Islamic contexts such as the Cordoban suburb of Shaqunda (750–811) and some rural settlements with indigenous or tribal origins: such is the case of Monte Mollet, El Salando, and Miravet (Castellón province), and Castillón de Montefrío (Granada), Marmuyas (Málaga), Alcaria Longa (Mértola-Portugal), and Peñaflor (Jaén), all dated between the 9th and 11th centuries.

From a material perspective, discussions should not focus so much on the social connotations of these models of domestic architecture, but rather on the pace of diffusion of the courtyard house within an Islamized social structure. Its distribution lessens the contrast between cities and rural settlements and produces a homogenization in the solutions adopted (urban, morphological, and constructive). This phenomenon is especially noticeable in the case of certain fortified Almohad villages (qariyas), such as Siyasa and Villa Vieja de Calasparra in Murcia, whose houses are similar to those of the urban sites of Mértola (Portugal), Saltés (Huelva), Valencia, or Murcia. In short, the appearance and the progressive spread of the model of a house complex with a central courtyard which ultimately supplants the simple dwelling (present in rural environments until much later) leads to a homogenization of domestic architecture, which in turn can be interpreted as the materialization of a total social Islamization (Gutiérrez Lloret 2012). In recent excavations, both in the metropolis of Córdoba and in small provincial cities such as Albalat (Cáceres), increasing attention is paid to the precise location of furnishings inside the house, which has illustrated that domestic and craft activities often coexisted in the same dwelling.

If the courtyard house arose as a way to control privacy (i.e., the activities of women), it is not easy to analyze this issue from archaeology alone. While one might imagine that the house is a female domain, the functional versatility of many of the areas of the house and the tenuous character of the signs left by feminine activities make it difficult to identify women or children. Generally, cooking and associated craft activities are viewed as

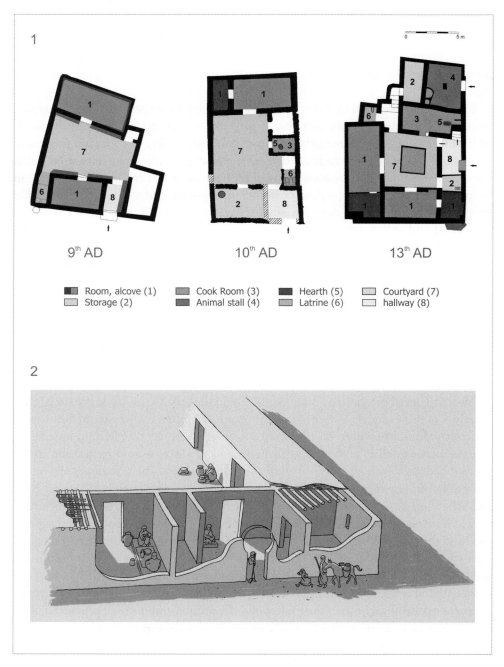

FIGURE 3.4.3 Islamic courtyard house. 1. Process of functional spatialization of the Andalusian house: Bajjana/Pechina, Córdoba, and Cieza. 2. Reconstruction of domestic social space.

Courtesy of S. Gutiérrez Lloret.

essentially feminine activities. In certain early dwellings at El Tolmo de Minateda, the hearth is associated with work benches, pantry spaces, evidence of food processing (hand mills, funnels) or artisanal tasks, most of which are attributed to the women of the family based on ethnoarchaeological observations: this is the case for weaving (spindles and whorls), baking (*tannurs*), and handmade ceramics. The presence of separate kitchens from the 10th century reinforces these assumptions. When textile and pottery craft activities leave the domestic sphere to occupy specialized urban spaces, such as workshops and potteries, the presence of women, if any, is invisible in the male-dominated production chain. Items of adornment and personal cleanliness (jewels, amulets, and cosmetics) have traditionally been considered feminine, in an anachronistic reduction that cannot be verified materially. Today we know that rings and bracelets, at least, are worn by men. On the other hand, glass bracelets which commonly have a prophylactic use in later periods, may be more typical of women and children. The only material trace of childhood outside the funerary sphere derives from the scant evidence for toys, such as miniature tableware, clearly sexed figurines female or male (the latter almost exclusively horsemen), and animals of different types.

RURAL LANDSCAPES

The archaeology of rural settlement has been dominated since the 1980s by the hypotheses formulated by P. Guichard in his book about the anthropological structure of al-Andalus (Guichard 1976). His theory, often oversimplified by its devotees, argued for a major tribal immigration (especially of North African Berbers) during the 8th and 9th centuries to the east of al-Andalus which was responsible for the early creation of peasant communities and community refuges. While historians have centered their debate on the tribal character of this new society (Acién Almansa 1995), archaeologists have focused on two issues: the characteristics of settlement networks (settlements, defensive communal constructions, and irrigation systems) and the chronology of the process (Bazzana et al. 1988).

Arabic sources use several words to designate rural settlements (*qariya, day'a, munya, harat*), with *qariya* being the most frequent, but they provide little information about their morphology. A potentially richer contribution comes from legal sources (*nawazil/* compilations of *fatwas*, or notarial forms), although these are generic and rarely refer explicitly to a specific place. Archaeology, therefore, gives materiality to the fragmentary indications of written sources. Between the 1980s and late 1990s, research in the east of the Iberian Peninsula (Sharq al-Andalus), especially in the region of Valencia and in eastern Andalusia, revealed a model in which the *qariyas*, varying in number and distance, are grouped around a simple fortification, mere hill-top, enclosure refuge, or tower (*burj*). These fortifications are rarely mentioned or described in the sources, and, when they are, they are usually designated as "*hisns*" (fortifications) a term that does not presuppose any morphology or specific function. The fragmentation of settlement in this region has been related to the social structure (tribal?) of its populations, a hypothesis that continues to generate intense debate. Castral districts or territories —fortifications (*hisn*), groups of villages (*qariya*), and systems of water exploitation— constitute the basic unit of territorial organization in mountainous areas since at least the 10th century (Bazzana et al. 1988). They were also units for production and exploitation as well as nuclei of tax collection. The link between the *hisn* and *qariya* is still a matter of discussion, although there is no doubt that this relationship is key to understanding the degree of autonomy of the peasant community with respect to state power (Eiroa Rodríguez 2012; Fernandes 2013; Fabregas and Sabaté 2015) (Figure 3.4.4).

From the Almohad period (12th–13th centuries), the number of *qariyas* with their own defensive enclosures increased, gradually acquiring features once considered exclusively urban. Archaeology must still answer many questions: When were these castral districts created —at the same time as the Arab-Berber conquest or later? Who established them— the state or the peasant communities themselves? What degree of autonomy did the *qariyas* have, and what was their relationship with the cities? And, finally, do they reflect in some way the origin of their inhabitants?

One of the most important developments in the study of rural al-Andalus is the centrality of hydraulic networks in the transformation of landscapes: catchments, ditches,

FIGURE 3.4.4 Velefique (Almería). Oblique aerial photo. The core of a castral territory. The present village is divided into three neighborhoods inherited from the three medieval *qariyas* and is dominated by the great fortress (*hisn*: H). Its lower limit corresponds to the layout of the main ditches on both sides of the ravine. The mosque (M) was situated outside the settlement.

irrigation plots, and population centers are part of the same foundational design (Cressier 2015). Hydrological resources have a greater impact on the environment and settlement because of the possibilities of practicing irrigated agriculture. Topography and the law of gravity impose a rigidity on drainage structures and limit the expansion of the irrigation systems, which allows archaeologists to reconstruct the evolution of these systems with relative ease. These principles were the basis of the so-called *hydraulic archaeology* in the 1980s that advanced the knowledge of rural Andalusian societies (Barceló et al. 1995, 1998). In the 21st century, archaeological approaches to the rural world have diversified, helped by the spread of new technologies (remote sensing and GIS) that allow the analysis of other types of landscapes such as drylands, pastures, or marshes (Kirchner 2010)

EXPLOITATION OF NATURAL RESOURCES: WATER

Hydrological resources have a greater impact on the environment and settlement because of the possibilities of practicing irrigated agriculture. The protracted debates on the Roman or Arab-Berber origin of the techniques have proved unfruitful, and it is now generally agreed that late antique knowledge of these techniques did not equate to their widespread use. Hydraulic systems are now viewed as an essential element of the colonization of new agricultural spaces and therefore as a means to analyze the development and subsequent transformations of the rural landscape. Archaeology has identified various techniques for capturing, conducting, and distributing water, the choice of which was dictated by environmental conditions as much as by the cultural and technical heritage of their constructors, some of whom were from different regions of the Middle East. It has thus proved possible to distinguish an "Andalusi hydraulics" from a 'Roman hydraulics' which privileged functional constructions for collective maintenance over monumental waterworks such as aqueducts (except in the arena of state power) (Cressier 2015).

There is an ongoing debate between scholars who argue for an early revolution in agricultural practices stemming from the standardization of irrigation and the introduction of new cultivated plant species and those who advocate a slow and progressive expansion with a smaller number of new species introduced from the East. Progress is expected with the spread of archaeobotany, which makes it possible to reconstruct when crops and plants were introduced and cultivated. Some of the earliest results have caused controversy since as yet they have not detected a significant increase of introduced botanical species that would reflect the supposed agricultural revolution introduced by the new Arab-Berber populations. Paradoxically, cities played a dynamic role in agricultural changes, not only because of the new economic demand they generated, but also because of the experimentation occurring in their hinterlands, especially in the large estates of the urban elites (*muniyas*), found in Córdoba, Granada, Jaén, Murcia, or Valencia.

Mining

For many years, historians and archaeologists ignored one of the most important elements of the Andalusian economy: mining and its associated industry, metallurgy. It was almost unanimously agreed that Roman mining was followed by a long decline only resolved in modern times. This assumption was all the more absurd since there are many written sources or archaeological findings to the contrary. As in other fields, revisions occurred in the late 1970s (Canto García and Cressier 2008). Nonetheless, there is still no "mining archeology" of al-Andalus comparable to that of other parts of Europe, but only small initiatives centered on other periods or from other disciplines which have clarified little-known aspects of the Andalusian economy (Pérez Macías and Carriazo Rubio 2010).

Important distinctions have been revealed between the mining of precious metals (gold and silver) and that of common metals (lead and especially iron), with copper occupying an intermediate position. This division is tempered by the scarcity of gold deposits, which makes al-Andalus particularly dependent on trans-Saharan traffic, and by the abundance of polymetallic deposits such as lead/silver. At one extreme, the state intervened directly to exploit the rich silver mines for suppliers of luxury crafts and especially the mints; it controlled the territory and the entire operational chain, as in the Almadén mining group (Ciudad Real province) (Grañeda Miñón 2007–2008). At the other end of the scale, seasonal peasant communities in the mining regions of the province of Teruel or in Eastern Andalusia autonomously exploited small iron deposits as a complementary activity to agriculture and animal husbandry. These differences are reflected in Islamic mining law, very different in this aspect to Roman law. All the major Roman mining zones including the Tinto River basin, Bética Mountains, and Cartagena continued to be exploited on a large scale in the Middle Ages, but this is not the case for small concessions, where discontinuities are obvious in Islamic times due, perhaps, to shifting settlement patterns or exploitation techniques.

Metallurgical workshops and artisanal forges installed in rural settlements have yet to be studied. The exploitation of non-metallic minerals (alum, etc.) is also not well understood, although they were indispensable in numerous artisanal processing activities. Among these, the extraction and transformation of salt has been privileged in recent ethnoarchaeological investigations in the salt flats of the interior (Eastern Andalusia, Aragón, Madrid) rather than those of the coast, which have been intensively exploited in the modern period.

Archaeology of Power,
Archaeology of the Palaces

The highly ornate palaces of al-Andalus—Madinat al-Zahra, the Alcazar of Seville, and the Nasrid Alhambra of Granada—have been the privileged object of study by art historians and architects since the 19th century. However, during recent years, research has been reoriented toward major historical debates on architecture as a tool of legitimization, princely ceremonial, the organization of the caliphal administration, and the waves of "orientialisation" that reached al-Andalus. Some limitations are imposed by cultural heritage and tourist management of the most famous complexes. The palaces in the time of the governors and Umayyad emirate (which would have functioned as seat of government and/or residence of the ruler) remain unknown. Four civil buildings in the archaeological area of La Morería, in Mérida, each very different from another, have been proposed as possibilities on the grounds of their monumentality and peculiar design, though this is not a decisive argument (Alba Calzado 2009). The earliest construction phase of the Alcazar of Córdoba (León Muñoz and Murillo Redondo 2009) is very difficult to reconstruct due to the significant transformations it has undergone since antiquity. In contrast, the palaces of Madinat al-Zahra (the capital founded by 'Abd al-Rahman III in 936 or 941–944) is now the most spectacular and best-known courtly ensemble of the Islamic West, thanks to the research conducted by Antonio Vallejo (Vallejo Triano 2010). He has studied and published the large audience room (the "Salón Rico"), the private apartments of the caliph and his *hajib* (chamberlain), administrative buildings, bathrooms, road and sewer systems, and gardens, as well as all their decoration. This work has identified a radical rethinking of the construction program during the course of the building works associated with the Caliph's parallel reform of state administration.

The collapse of the caliphate and the subsequent territorial division of al-Andalus multiplied the seats of power. The different dynasties competed to emulate the earlier Umayyad caliphate, displaying the signs of their identity in a collection of palaces that have not all survived. The Aljafería at Zaragoza (second half of the 11th century) is now well known although with little archaeological involvement, while the excavations of the palace of al-Ma'mun (1043–1075) in Toledo have provided limited but spectacular remains with clear eastern influence. Almería and Málaga seem to have been more faithful to Cordoban models. These examples demonstrate the double wish of the new dynasties to create their own architectural vocabulary and to adopt elements of the Umayyad legacy. In the spatial organization of the reception rooms, the tripartite basilica room was abandoned early on at the same time as the quadripartite courtyard grow in popularity. This pattern was maintained between the late 11th and mid-13th centuries, when the Almoravid and Almohad "African empires" took over (the second Taifa kingdoms were between them). Exceptional evidence is provided by the excavation of the Dar al-Sughra, Ibn Mardanish's palace in the suburb of the *madina* of Murcia, decorated with elaborate *muqarnas* and figurative paintings following Oriental models (Navarro Palazón and Jiménez Castillo 2012).

The advent of the Almohads and the unification of the two shores of the western Mediterranean resulted in the construction or transformation of many seats of power, but the largest palatial programs took place at the imperial capitals of Seville and Marrakesh. In the Alcazar of Seville, still a royal palace today, a large research project (excavations and archaeology of standing buildings) has revealed the intense building activity of the Almohads (builders of a new citadel within the city), while at the same time showing that they were less innovative in palatial architecture than in other fields (Tabales 2002). There are also interesting remains of palaces built by the Almohads or their opponents in Silves (Portugal), Jaén, or Murcia. When al-Andalus was reduced to the Nasrid kingdom of Granada (14th–15th centuries), the sophisticated palatial complexes of the Alhambra were built—today the most visited monumental site in Spain. The maintenance and restoration of the complex requires archaeological interventions such as those carried out in the Patio de los Leones, which have clarified certain functional and chronological questions but do not permit a comprehensive analysis.

Finally, there is also a peculiar type of palatial residence, the *muniyas*, agricultural estates of the urban oligarchies located on the periphery of the cities, which were perhaps temporary seats of emiral or caliphal power. The most innovative examples are found in the outlying areas of Córdoba under the emirate and the caliphate (see, e.g., al-Rumaniyya), in the Huerta of Murcia during the second taifa kingdoms (around the Castillejo of Monteagudo), and in the Vega of Granada with the Nasrids, although others are also known in Seville or Valencia. These cases allow the joint study of agricultural facilities alongside palatial buildings of varied morphology, in comparison with similar Maghrebi cases.

ARCHAEOLOGY OF RELIGION

Religious Islamization (conversion to Islam) and linguistic Arabization (adoption of the Arabic language) occurred long before social Islamization was complete, in the late 9th or even the 10th century. The spread of Islam is reflected in the appearance of a new type of religious building—the mosque—and its relationship with older buildings of worship (churches and synagogues). Surprisingly, there are no programs dedicated exclusively to the archaeology of religion (except funerary archaeology). Significant progress has been made in four fields: urban mosques, palatial mosques, rural mosques, and *ribats*. Studies of urban mosques come from art history and, to a lesser extent, the archaeology of architecture and have prioritized the great Friday mosques of Córdoba and Seville and the palatine mosques (Calvo Capilla 2014). Excavations in Córdoba have not yet given any archaeological confirmation to the theory that a church of San Vicente lay below the mosque founded by 'Abd al-Rahman I, and it cannot therefore be assumed that this was the case (Arce Sainz 2015). They have discovered its monumental latrines (*mida'*) of the 10th century. Cordoban archaeology has brought to light numerous neighborhood mosques (*masjids*) with almost standardized plans (González Gutiérrez 2012). The best-known palatial mosques (apart from those of the Nasrid Alhambra) are from the Taifa era: to that of the Aljafería, already studied, we can add that of the palace of al-Ma'mun (m. 1075) (today the convent of Santa Fe, Toledo) and that of the *qasr* of Murcia (today below the church of San Juan de Dios). Their small dimensions are similar to those of private oratory mosques, but differ from these in their luxurious ornamentation.

Rural mosques are poorly known due to the scarcity of rural archaeology, but also because of their more modest architectural forms. It is particularly striking that some of the recent discoveries in the East of al-Andalus have noncanonical features including the duplication of *mihrabs*, differentiated spaces perhaps reserved for women, and possible inhumations in the courtyard. Unlike the southern Peninsula, the absence of a minaret seems to be the rule. An exceptional mosque today is part of a farm, the Cortijo de las Mezquitas (Antequera, Málaga); it has still not been excavated (Gozalbes Cravioto 2006). The building blocks of this monumental mosque are characteristic of the Umayyad State. Its rural situation, far from the capital, cannot be easily explained, although it may perhaps be understood in the context of the "Mozarabic" rebellions of the early 10th century, insofar as it lies at the very limits of the territory controlled by 'Umar ibn Hafsun (Figure 3.4.5).

Finally, the interpretation of *ribats* (places where jihad is practiced, which can be a struggle against non-Muslims and/or a spiritual retreat) has had to be profoundly revised as a result of recent findings in Iberia. The *ribats* used to be considered buildings of "military" character, similar to the well-known Aghlabid *ribats* which are staggered along the coast of Ifriqiya (see Chapter 3.1). The discovery and excavation (1984–1992) of the *ribat* of the Dunas de Guardamar in Alicante transformed the picture, although there are still too many preconceptions about its function (Azuar Ruiz 2004). Installed at the mouth of the Segura River, on the ruins of an Orientalizing-period settlement (6th–5th century BC), the complex consists of a score of small rectangular cells, each one with a *mihrab*. They are conjoined in the shape of a mandorla around a mosque with two bays parallel to the *qibla* and without a minaret, which seems to have been originally a *musalla* (open space used for prayer). Two inscriptions give a date of the mid-10th century, although there must have been an earlier mid-9th-century phase. The complete absence of defensive elements is notable, and counters a military interpretation, while the bonding and construction techniques also rule out any intervention by the Umayyad state. The *ribat* of Guardamar should be understood as a place of spiritual retreat for a community of devotees belonging to a minority sect of Islam who exploited local natural resources and combined religious proselytizing with some commercial activity. It is not the only one of its kind: most of the *ribats* on the Atlantic coast of Morocco seem to follow this typology and function, while that of Arrifana (Aljezur, Portugal) is very similar, although somewhat later (12th–13th centuries) (Gomes and Gomes 2011).

ARCHAEOLOGY OF DEATH: CEMETERIES, POPULATIONS, BELIEFS

The spread of Islam is reflected in the adoption of new funerary rituals that became dominant across al-Andalus. In general, it is assumed that the process of Islamization reflects the dominant implantation of Islamic social norms over other contemporary

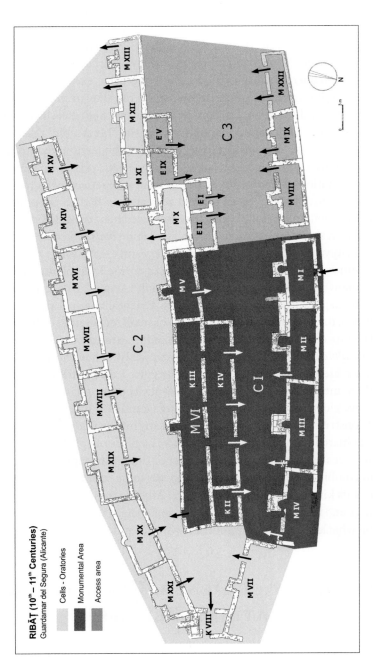

FIGURE 3.4.5 *Ribat* of the Dunas de Guardamar del Segura (Alicante). General plan of the area excavated, with indications of the different functional sectors.

Courtesy of R. Azuar Ruiz.

social forms (tribal or feudal), which reached a political expression with the Umayyad Caliphate. From this perspective, the process of Islamization transcends the phenomenon of conversion to Islam to acquire a wider social and ideological meaning. While some funerary evidence shows an early conversion in the 8th century, other material contexts (ceramics, domestic and urban spaces, epigraphy) do not support the full social Islamization of the populations until very late in the 9th century or even the 10th century (Casal García et al. 2006).

Funerary archaeology, understood as the study of funeral beliefs, practices, and customs, is a relatively recent development in al-Andalus. The modesty of Muslim tombs (often simple pits) and the lack of grave goods did not stimulate their study. The development of rescue archaeology in the old cities of al-Andalus (Murcia, Córdoba, Valencia, Granada, and Zaragoza), together with changes in excavation techniques and analysis of the corpse itself (paleopathology and bioarchaeology), have allowed us to move from the mere recognition of the graves and funerary rituals to the anthropological and historical study of the populations and their beliefs.

Al-Andalus is a privileged space to understand the rhythm, intensity, historical circumstances, and geographical conditions of the process of Islamization, which, when studied only from the documentary evidence, is difficult to generalize from. Traditional research used to begin with a priori assumptions such as the nonexistence of funerary spaces shared between confessions (e.g., Muslims and Christians) or the morphology and orientation of the burial as an indicator of religious orientation. Many of these assumptions were also based on the peculiar orientation to the south of many *qiblas* of Andalusian mosques. More recently, attempts have been made to infer chronological developments described in written records from the morphology of the grave: this cannot be confirmed as yet.

Funerary precincts containing several tomb groups have been documented at Málaga, but the few cemeteries excavated extensively suggest a relatively ordered layout, with overlapping graves in the case of urban graveyards of long use, integrated into the urban fabric by the growth of the city. In rural areas, cemeteries are often associated with the collective mosque of several farmsteads and villages (Almisserà, La Vilajoiosa-Alicante).

Excavations confirm that lying on the right lateral side, facing toward Mecca is the canonical orientation of a Muslim burial. In practice, this assumes a range of grave arrangements orientated to the southeast: from south-north (head in the south and looking east) to west-east (head in the west and looking south) and towards the *qibla*, which in al-Andalus encompasses any direction between the south and the east. The earliest usually coincide with the Christian ones in the orientation of the grave (west-east) but not in the position (right lateral position vs. supine position). Burials are always individual, except in cases related to conflicts or significant mortalities as at Tudela.

Tomb types are also variable. The majority are simple rectangular graves cut into the soil or rock, with or without a central or lateral pre-grave. The earliest graves (Pamplona, El Tosal de Manises-Alicante, El Tolmo de Minateda) almost never have a lateral pit (*lahd*), while both types co-exist at Encadenado/El Soto (Madrid) and Marroquíes

(Jaén). This formula is observed in all periods, even in the Almohad necropolis of Novelda (Alicante). Despite legal proscriptions, wooden coffins were used from the 9th to 10th century, and, in some cases, graves were completely filled with earth (Tossal de Manises in Alicante province), although hollow burial is more usual. Different types of stelae and built monuments are documented (*maqabriyas*, *qubas*, or true mausoleums, in palatial *rawdas*). Funerary epigraphy is frequent. There is no concept of grave goods, although in some cases personal objects (jewels or amulets) and objects such as lamps and ewers have been found.

Cemeteries demonstrate the early conversion of native populations, as well as the settlement of foreign populations already Islamized. In many pre-Islamic cemeteries there is a transition phase marked by the coexistence or immediate succession of Christian and Muslim rites in the same areas, keeping even the same grave orientation. This occurs in the 9th century in urban areas (Zaragoza, Segóbriga, Jaén, El Tolmo de Minateda) and in rural settings (Encadenado/Soto-Madrid). This "permeability" of funerary space illustrates a phenomenon of generational and family conversion, as the mitochondrial DNA analysis in Encadenado/El Soto: related individuals share the funerary space with their blood relatives, even after their conversion. As for the settlement of foreign Muslim populations, DNA analyses (mitochondrial and Y chromosome) has shed light on the origin of some of the people buried (Gutiérrez Lloret 2015). The latest example is that of the Plaza del Castillo in Pamplona, which is dated to the mid-8th century and contains 190 graves with individuals of both sexes and varied ages (de Miguel Ibáñez 2016; de Miguel Ibáñez et al. 2016). The many traumatic injuries in men as well as the frequency of fatal knife wounds suggest that these people were accustomed to combat: 61.8% of men were of North African origin in comparison to the significantly lower percentage (9.75%) of women. Twelve cases of dental modifications in both sexes (but especially in females) have also been documented. These practices are unknown in Roman-Visigothic Hispanic populations and are associated with an African origin on several grounds, including genetic. The presence in at least one woman with local genetic markers points to the religious conversion and cultural assimilation of the local female population. Bioarchaeological studies thus indicate that an Islamized population of foreign, probably North African, origin arrived in Pamplona in family groups in the first generation of immigrants. Similar situations have been documented in Nimes (France) and Gerona. For the first time, archaeology is able to identify the conquerors (soldiers and/or peasants) and recognize the first signs of early immigration.

Women are visible in the funerary sphere since ritual practices are applied to the whole community without discrimination. For now, the only documented exception is the concentration of perinatal and infant burials in specific areas of the necropolis. Although they are not very frequent, some cases of pregnant women have been identified, which only in cases of mature fetuses (more than 37 weeks) could account for female mortality related to pregnancy. At the moment, little can be contributed by biological markers to the issue of gender differentiation except that males undertook military activity more frequently. Female cases of deaths with violence have been documented in isolation in Jaén and Baza in Granada.

MATERIAL CULTURE: CERAMICS

Ceramics are the most abundant and significant archaeological artifact in the material record and reflect the economic, social, and cultural conditions of the period. Their study allows us to understand the technological processes and the modes of production, distribution, and consumption: they are one of the most valuable sources for reconstructing daily life in al-Andalus. Therefore, ceramics (techniques, forms, and decoration) play a central part in historiographical debates about demographic change and acculturation following the Arab-Islamic conquest. The morphological evolution of common multifunction ceramics of the late-Roman or Hispanic-Visigothic tradition (pots, jars), as well as the introduction of new forms (noria buckets, *tannur* bread ovens) in response to new cultural traditions, have been used to calculate the extent of the indigenous legacy versus the Berberization and Arabization of al-Andalus's population (Gutiérrez Lloret 2012).

During recent decades, the study of ceramics has been a key focus of European Islamic archaeology, both in Spain and Portugal as well as in Italy and France, and it has generated an enormous volume of regional publications (Catarino et al. 2012). However, the earliest scholarship was of an antiquarian nature: ceramics were part of the field of Fine Arts and limited to the glazed (so-called luxury) productions, made and used mainly in urban and palatine contexts. The key productions are the "green and manganese" typical of the Umayyad caliphate of Córdoba (10th century, but appear earlier in the Aghlabid central Mediterranean) (Cano Piedra 1996), the "cuerda seca" that becomes important in the Taifa period (11th century), and the lustre ware that appeared first in the 10th century, but flourished in the late Nasrid period until reaching the Mudejar world in the 14th and 15th centuries (García Porras 2014).

This approach was replaced by new research based on systematization and quantification during the last decades of the 20th century. This focuses on identifying and classifying productions and establishing typologies and has transformed medieval Islamic pottery into an increasingly precise chronological marker. G. Rosselló Bordoy (1991), J. Zozaya, and A. Bazzana promoted this transformation, which has made the ceramics of al-Andalus an essential referent for the entire medieval western Mediterranean. The spread of stratigraphic excavation has prompted a second shift toward contextual analysis: ceramics are now studied in relation to the other materials in occupation, abandonment, or residual contexts (Amorós Ruiz 2018). Economic and sociocultural issues are addressed: social organization of production, composition of assemblages, and consumption practices. The widespread use of archaeometry to determine the physical and chemical characteristics of pastes and glazes has revolutionized ceramic studies. Its application will allow in the future a much greater precision in the definition of ceramic workshops, the reconstruction of commercial routes and the diffusion of techniques, especially glazing (Fernández Navarro 2008; García Porras 2013).

The most spectacular progress has been made in our understanding of production processes. The Arab-Islamic conquest took place in a production context common to the rest of the late antique western Mediterranean: an environment dominated by the region-alization and crisis of Mediterranean trade, a growing tendency to self-sufficiency, and the simplification of productive processes which is far from the specialization and standardization typical of Roman ceramic production. In late antiquity, new domestic production strategies were adopted characterized by simple production and firing methods; handmade ceramics reappear with unusual vigor; the formal repertoire is greatly simplified; and patterns of distribution and consumption are purely local (Alba Calzado and Gutiérrez Lloret 2008) (Figure 3.4.6).

Conquest brought about the rapid reorganization of markets, as is evident in the spread of wheel-made ceramics, the progressive specialization of tableware, the intro-duction of a new functional series adapted to the new cultural traditions (including culi-nary and food practices), the standardization of forms and decorations, and the introduction of the first monochrome (mainly utilitarian) glazes. These were manufac-tured in urban potteries in the south-east of al-Andalus from the mid-9th century (as at Bajjana, Málaga, Córdoba, Murcia) and began to spread through various regions of al-Andalus and the western Mediterranean, as shown by shipwrecks in the south of France.

Under the caliphate, ceramics decorated in "green and manganese" appeared, possi-bly linked to the Umayyad ideological program (Cano Piedra 1996). A complex market structure developed, with production concentrated in urban workshops with a high command of technological processes (clear from the spread of glaze technology), and forms are standardized to adapt to their functions (table service, storage, transport, and lighting) (Gutiérrez Lloret 2015). The homogenization of production must be under-stood as a reflection of the homogenization and full Islamization of society that did not lessen with the political fragmentation of the Taifa Kingdoms. Dispersed production centers confirm the complexity of markets and commercial networks, a phenomenon

FIGURE 3.4.6 Transitional ceramics from Tolmo de Minateda (Albacete). Ninth-century table-ware, which includes the functional series adapted to new cultural traditions.

Courtesy of S. Gutiérrez Lloret-Tolmo de Minateda.

that archaeology has revealed for important pottery centers (Murcia, Denia, Zaragoza). This homogenizing tendency reaches its zenith with the Almoravids and Almohads, as reflected in the standardization of series and decorative techniques used for specific propagandistic reasons by the Almohads (Fernández Navarro 2008). The latest Islamic productions in Europe, those of the Nasrid Kingdom of Granada, represent the climax of a technical and ornamental mastery, as shown spectacularly in the great lustre ware vases of the Alhambra, a tradition that continued in the Mudejar and Moorish workshops of the Peninsula, especially in Valencia (García Porras 2014).

The Achievements and Outstanding Issues of Andalusian Archaeology

The archaeology of al-Andalus has made a huge qualitative leap in recent decades in the definition of its objectives and the methodologies used to achieve them. This leap is also quantitative, and it is time to ask: Have we been able to transform this evidence into historical knowledge? Have we communicated these scholarly advances to the public? In short, have we built rigorous archaeological catalogues and records and have we published them properly? The answer currently is ambiguous. Never have so many sites of the Andalusian period been excavated and documented as in the first decade of the 21st century. However, the volume of historical information has not experienced an exponential growth parallel to that of the archaeological interventions.

Progress in our knowledge of al-Andalus has not only come through archaeology but, in parallel, also through the study of textual sources, including epigraphy (and graffiti) and numismatics, two disciplines that remained excessively isolated from archaeology until recently. Archaeology has also contributed to the acquisition of increasingly precise chronological markers (above all, ceramics and absolute dating by radiocarbon) and the recent development of environmental archaeological studies, geoarchaeology, bioarchaeology, bioanthropology, and archaeometry, which have opened unsuspected possibilities. Despite all this, there are still many "dark areas." Surprising, for example, is the underdevelopment of underwater archaeology despite the spectacular results from wrecks sunk off the southern coast of France. Other thematic strands have failed to develop in the same way as landscape or agrarian archaeology and, more recently, funerary archaeology. This is the case for mining, hygiene and health, and leisure, which would deepen our understanding of economic history or *mentalities*. In the most well-studied fields (rural settlement, urbanism, artisanal productions), the accumulation of new data is accompanied by an extreme fractioning of its discoveries, and syntheses that open new research perspectives are more necessary than ever. In this way, archaeology can redefine the history of al-Andalus at the same time as underscoring that this region is the key to understanding the western Mediterranean in the Middle Ages.

References

Acién Almansa, M. 1995. "La fortificación en al-Andalus," *Archeologia Medievale. Cultura materiale. Insediamenti. Territorio*, 22, 7–36.

Acién Almansa, M. 2001. "La formación del tejido urbano en al-Andalus," in J. Passini (ed.), *La ciudad medieval: de la casa al tejido urbano* (Cuenca: Ediciones de la Universidad de Castilla-la Mancha), 11–32.

Acién Almansa, M., and Vallejo Triano, A. 1998. "Urbanismo y Estado islámico: de Corduba a Qurtuba-Madīnat al-Zahrā'," in P. Cressier and M. García-Arenal (eds.), *Genèse de la ville islamique en al-Andalus et au Maghreb occidental* (Madrid: Casa de Velázquez-CSIC), 107–136.

Alba Calzado, M. 2009. "Los edificios emirales de Morería (Mérida), una muestra de arquitectura del poder," *Anales de arqueología cordobesa*, 20, 379–420.

Alba Calzado, M., and Gutiérrez Lloret, S. 2008. "Las producciones de transición al mundo islámico: el problema de la cerámica paleoandalusí (siglos VIII y IX)," in D. Bernal and A. Ribera (eds.), *Cerámicas hispanorromanas. Un estado de la Cuestión* (Cádiz: Universidad de Cádiz), 585–613.

Amorós Ruiz, V. 2018. *Cerámica y contexto. El Tolmo de Minateda en la Alta Edad Media* (Alicante: Publicacions de la Universitat d'Alacant).

Arce Sainz, F. 2015. "La supuesta basílica de San Vicente en Córdoba: de mito histórico a obstinación historiográfica," *Al-Qanṭara*, 36, 1, 11–44.

Azuar Ruiz, R. 2004. *Fouilles de la Rábita de Guardamar I. El ribāṭ califal. Excavación e investigaciones (1984–1992)* (Madrid: Collection de la Casa de Velázquez, 85).

Barceló, M., Kirchner, H., and Navarro, C. 1995. *El agua que no duerme: fundamentos de la arqueología hidráulica andalusí*, Sierra Nevada 95 (Granada: El legado andalusí).

Barceló, M., Kirchner, H., Martí, R., and Torres, J. 1998. *The Design of Irrigation Systems in al-Andalus* (Barcelona: Universitat Autònoma de Barcelona).

Bazzana, A. 1992. *Maisons d'al-Andalus. Habitat médiéval et structures du peuplement dans l'Espagne orientale* (Madrid: Casa de Velázquez).

Bazzana, A., Cressier, P., and Guichard, P. 1988. *Les châteaux ruraux d'al-Andalus. Histoire et archéologie des ḥuṣūn du sud-est de l'Espagne* (Madrid: Casa de Velázquez).

Calvo Capilla, S. 2014. *Las mezquitas de al-Andalus*. Estudios andalusíes, 9 (Almería: Fundación Ibn Tufayl de Estudios Árabes).

Cano Piedra, C. 1996. *La cerámica verde-Manganeso de Madīnat al-Zahrā'* (Granada: El legado andalusí).

Canto García, A., and Cressier, P. 2008. *Minería y metalurgia en al-Andalus y Magreb occidental. Explotación y poblamiento* (Madrid: Casa de Velázquez).

Carvajal López, J. C. 2014. "The Archaeology of Al-Andalus: Past, Present and Future," *Medieval Archaeology*, 58, 318–339.

Casal García, M. T., León Muñoz, A., López, R., Valdivieso Ramos, A., and Soriano Castro, P. J. 2006. "Espacio y usos funerarios en la 'Qurtuba' islámica," *Anales de arqueología cordobesa*, 17, 2, 257–290.

Catarino, H., Cavaco, S., Covaneiro, J., Fernandes, I. C., Gomes, A., Gómez-Martínez, S., Gonçalves, M. J., Grangé, M., Inácio, I., Lopes, G., Santos, C., and Bugalhão, J. 2012. "La céramique islamique du Garb Al-Andalus : contextes socio-territoriaux et distribution," *Atti del IX Congresso Internazionale sulla Cerámica Medievale nel Mediterraneo (Venezia, 2009)* (Florencia), 429–441.

Cressier, P. (2015). "La maîtrise de l'eau en al-Andalus. Un marqueur d'orientalisation et une source de conflits historiographiques," in C. Richarté, R.-P. Gayraud, and J.-M. Poisson (eds.), *Héritages arabo-islamiques dans l'Europe méditerranéenne* (Paris: La Découverte), 301–314.

Cressier, P., and García-Arenal, M. (eds.) 1998. *Genèse de la ville islamique en al-Andalus et au Maghreb occidental* (Madrid: Casa de Velázquez-CSIC).

Cressier, P., and Gutiérrez Lloret, S. 2009. "Archéologie de l'Islam européen. Sept siècles de présence arabo-berbère," in J.-P. Demoule (ed.), *L'Europe. Un continent redécouvert par l'archéologie* (Paris: Gallimard), 146–157.

Cressier, P., and Vallejo Triano, A. 2015. "Madīnat al-Zahrāʾ et Ṣabra al-Manṣūriyya: Deux versions d'un même scénario," *Journal of Islamic Archaeology*, 2, 2, 139–169.

de Miguel Ibáñez, M. P. 2016. *La "maqbara" de Pamplona (s. VIII). Aportes de la osteoarqueología al conocimiento de la islamización en la Marca Superior* (Alicante: Universidad de Alicante)(http://www.cervantesvirtual.com/obra/la-maqbara-de-pamplona-s-viii-aportes-de-la-osteoarqueologia-al-conocimiento-de-la-islamizacion-en-la-marca-superior/.)

de Miguel Ibáñez, M. P, Fontecha Martínez, L., Izagirre Arribalzaga, N., and de la Rua Vaca, C. 2016. "Paleopatología, ADN y diferenciación social en la *maqbara* de Pamplona: límites y posibilidades," in J. A. Quirós Castillo (ed.), *Demografía, paleopatologías y desigualdad social en el noroeste peninsular en época medieval*. Documentos de Arqueología Medieval 10 (Bilbao: Universidad del País Vasco), 163–181.

Eiroa Rodríguez, J. A. 2012. "Past and Present of the Archaeology of the Alquerías," *Imago temporis, Medium Aevum*, 6, 49–72.

Fabregas, A., and Sabaté, F. 2015. *Power and Rural Communities in al-Andalus: Ideological and Material Representations*, TMC 15 (Turnhout: Brepols).

Fernandes, I. C. F. (ed.) 2013. *Fortificações e Território na Península Ibérica e no Magreb— Séculos VI a XVI* (Lisboa: Edições Colibri-Campo Arqueológico de Mértola).

Fernández Navarro, E. 2008. *Tradición tecnológica de la cerámica de cocina almohade-nazarí* (Granada: Grupo de Investigación THARG).

García Porras, A. (ed.) 2013. *Arqueología de la producción en época medieval* (Granada: Alhulia).

García Porras, A. 2014. "Spain and North Africa: Islamic Archaeology," in C. Smith (ed.), *Encyclopedia of Global Archaeology* (London/New York: Springer), 6955–6964.

Gomes, M. V., and Gomes, R. V. 2011. "O Ribât de Arrifana. Entre cristãos e muçulmanos no Gharb," in *Cristãos cristãos e muçulmanos na Idade Média Peninsular. Encontros e Desencontros* (Lisboa: IAP), 137–146.

González Gutiérrez, C. 2012. *Las mezquitas de barrio de* Qurṭuba. *Una aproximación arqueológica* (Córdoba: Diputación de Córdoba).

Gozalbes Cravioto, C. 2006. *El Cortijo "Las Mezquitas": una mezquita medieval en la Vega de Antequera* (Málaga: Altagrafics).

Grañeda Miñón, P. 2007–2008. "La explotación andalusí de los metales preciosos: los trabajos a bocamina," *Boletín del Museo Arqueológico Nacional*, 24–26, 141–154.

Guichard, P. 1976. *Al-Andalus. Estructura antropológica de una sociedad islámica en occidente*, Barcelona (reprinted 1995, Granada) [1977, *Structures sociales orientales et 'occidentales' dans l'Espagne musulmane* (Paris: École des Hautes Études en Sciences sociales)].

Gutiérrez Lloret, S. 1998. "From Ciuitas to Madina: Destruction and Formation of the City in South-East al-Andalus. The Archaeological Debate," in M. Marín (ed.), *The formation of al-Andalus. Part 1: History and Society.* The Formation of the Classical Islamic World, 46 (Aldershot: Ashgate Variorum), 217–264.

Gutiérrez Lloret, S. 2012. "La arqueología en la historia del temprano al-Andalus: espacios sociales, cerámica e islamización," in Ph. Sénac (ed.), *Villa 4. Histoire et Archéologie de l'Occident musulman (VIIe–XVe siècles) Al-Andalus, Maghreb, Sicile* (Toulouse: Études Médiévales Ibériques, Méridiennes), 33–66.

Gutiérrez Lloret, S. 2013. "Coming back to Grammar of the house: social meaning of Medieval households," in S. Gutiérrez and I. Grau (eds.), *De la estructura doméstica al espacio social: lecturas arqueológicas del uso social del espacio* (Alicante: Publicaciones de la Universidad de Alicante), 245–264.

Gutiérrez Lloret, S. 2015. "Early al-Andalus: an Archaeological Approach to the Process of Islamization in the Iberian Peninsula (7th to 10th centuries)," in S. Gelichi and R. Hodges (eds.), *New Directions in Early Medieval European Archaeology: Spain and Italy Compared. Essays for Riccardo Francovich* (Turnhout: Brepols), 43–86.

Kirchner, H. (ed.) 2010. *Por una arqueología agraria. Perspectivas de investigación sobre los espacios de cultivo en las sociedades medievales hispánicas.* Oxford: BAR Int. Ser. 2062.

León Muñoz, A., and Murillo Redondo, J. F. 2009. "El complejo civil tardoantiguo de Córdoba y su continuidad en el Alcázar Omeya," *Madrider Mitteilungen*, 49, 323–335.

Malpica Cuello, A. 2015. "The Emergence of the City in al-Andalus," in S. Gelichi and R. Hodges (eds.), *New Directions in Early Medieval European Archaeology: Spain and Italy Compared. Essays for Riccardo Francovich* (Turnhout: Brepols), 87–110.

Navarro Palazón, J., and Jiménez Castillo, P. 2007. *Las ciudades de Alandalús. Nuevas perspectivas* (Zaragoza: Instituto de Estudios Islámicos y del Oriente Próximo).

Navarro Palazón, J., and Jiménez Castillo, P. 2012. "La arquitectura de Ibn Mardanîsh: revisión y nuevas aportaciones," in G. M. Borrás Gualis and B. Cabañero Subiza (eds.), *La Aljafería y el Arte del Islam Occidental en el siglo XI, Actas del Seminario Internacional celebrado en Zaragoza los días 1, 2 y 3 de diciembre de 2004* (Zaragoza), 291–350.

Orihuela, A. 2007. "La casa andalusí: un recorrido a través de su evolución," *Artigrama*, 22, 299–335.

Pérez Macías, J. A., and Carriazo Rubio, J. L. 2010. *Estudios de minería medieval en Andalucía* (Huelva: Universidad de Huelva).

Quirós Castillo, J. A. 2009. "Medieval Archaeology in Spain," in R. Gilchrist and A. Reynolds (eds.), *Reflections. 50 Years of Medieval Archaeology in Britain and Beyond.* Society for Medieval Archaeology Monograph, 30 (Leeds: Maney), 173–189.

Rosselló Bordoy, G. 1991. *El nombre de las cosas en al-Andalus: una propuesta de terminología cerámica* (Palma de Mallorca: Museo de Mallorca).

Sénac, Ph. (ed.) 2012. *Villa 4. Histoire et Archéologie de l'Occident musulman (VIIe–XVe siècles). Al-Andalus, Maghreb, Sicile* (Toulouse: Études Médiévales Ibériques, Méridiennes).

Tabales, M. Á. 2002. *El Alcázar de Sevilla. Primeros estudios sobre estratigrafía y evolución constructiva* (Sevilla: Consejería de Cultura).

Torres Balbás, L. 1970. *Ciudades hispanomusulmanas*, 2 vols. (Madrid: Ministerio de Asuntos Exteriores, Instituto Hispano-Árabe de Cultura).

Vallejo Triano, A. 2010. *La ciudad califal de Madīnat al-Zahrāʾ. Arqueología de su arquitectura* (Córdoba: Almuzara).

Valor, M., and Gutiérrez, A. (eds.) 2014. *The Archaeology of Medieval Spain, 1100–1500* (Sheffield-Bristol: Equinox Publishing).

CHAPTER 3.5

......

SICILY

......

ALESSANDRA MOLINARI

History, Historiography, and the Major Debates

......

Sicily is a large and fertile island at the center of Mediterranean trading networks (Figure 3.5.1). Renewed public interest in its medieval past, a surge in research in recent years, and the richness of its archaeological and architectural heritage make it particularly fascinating for scholars of the Islamic world and beyond. Its arduous conquest from Byzantium began in 827, on the initiative of the Aghlabid emirate in Ifriqiya, continued under the Fatimid caliphate, and was only finally achieved under the Kalbid emirs (vassals of the Fatimids) in 948 (Amari 1933–1937; Metcalfe 2009; Chiarelli 2011). Under this dynasty, Sicily experienced an important period of stability and economic growth. After two decades of political crisis (ca. 1040–1060) characterized by competition between local leaders and political fragmentation, it was conquered by the Normans gradually over thirty years (1061–1091). Relations between the various autochthonous religious and cultural groups (Arab-Muslims and Greek-Christians) and the new arrivals (Normans and "Lombards," Latin-Christians) became increasingly fraught and complex during the 12th century, with key episodes of interethnic violence, with visible consequences in the archaeological record. With the fall of the Swabian dynasty in the mid-13th century, the historical and archaeological sources show that the Islamic component of the Sicily population was effectively erased.

The archaeology of Islamic Sicily has a long history but has suffered, until relatively recently, from a broader lack of interest in the Middle Ages within Italian archaeology. As early as the second half of the 19th century, Michele Amari, the great historian of the Muslims of Sicily, already showed a deep interest in the material culture of this period including inscribed objects (Amari 1971) and topography and toponymy (Amari and Dufour 1859). Nonetheless, systematic archaeological research had to wait many more years and began only in the 1970s, with the close collaboration between historians and

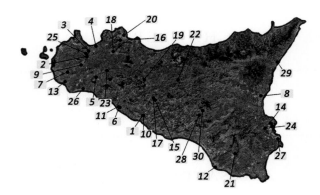

FIGURE 3.5.1 Map of Sicily with main medieval archaeological sites: 1. Agrigento; 2. Calatafimi; 3. Calathamet; 4. Calatubo; 5. Calliata; 6. Campanaio; 7. Casale Nuovo; 8. Catania; 9. Contrada Miceli; 10. Contrada Saraceno; 11. Eraclea Minoa; 12. Kaukana/Punta Secca; 13. Mazara del Vallo; 14. Megara; 15. Milena; 16. Monreale; 17. Monte Conca; 18. Monte Jato; 19. Castronovo di Sicilia; 20. Palermo; 21. Ragusa; 22. Resuttano; 23. Rocca di Entella; 24. Santa Caterina/Melilli; 25. Segesta/Caltabarbaro; 26. Selinunte; 27. Siracusa; 28. Sofiana; 29. Taormina; 30. Villa del Casale/ Piazza Armerina.

Courtesy of Google maps, by F. Giovannini.

archaeologists (for a summary of the history of research, see Molinari 2004; Arcifa et al. 2012). A partial exception is constituted by a persistent interest in so-called Arab-Norman architecture (in particular, the palaces and churches of the 12th century in Palermo) and antiquarian research on decorated "Arab-Norman" ceramics. As in the rest of Europe, it was the archaeology of abandoned villages that first stimulated the interest of scholars in the 1970s. It should be underscored, however, that research on the Islamic phases was conducted almost exclusively by medieval scholars (in the European sense), rather than by specialists of the Islamic world. While, on the one hand, this trend may have diminished the recognition of elements common to other areas of the *dar al-Islam*, on the other hand, it has favored diachronic research and the use of methodologies and approaches more common in European archaeology.

Initially, research on abandoned villages was promoted by scholars who headed the École française de Rome. The excavation of the settlement of Brucato in northeastern Sicily (Pesez 1984), although it focused primarily on the late medieval phases (13th–14th centuries), also examined part of the Islamic settlement located on the slopes of the site. The results of the 10th and 11th centuries were published systematically in the 1980s alongside with the rest of the excavation. In contrast, the excavation of Calathamet in western Sicily, an Islamic/Norman settlement, directed by J. M. Pesez immediately after that of Brucato, was published only many years later (Lesnes and Poisson 2013). A first important overview of glazed ceramics was made possible thanks to careful studies conducted in centers outside Sicily such as Pisa, where Sicilian ceramics were exported in quantity in the Middle Ages (Berti and Tongiorgi 1981; d'Angelo 1980). Even so, until very recently, investigations have focused more on the rural landscape and the Norman-Swabian phases.

In the modern cities of Sicily, while there have been emergency excavations, these were most often conducted by non-medieval specialists. On the other hand, systematic surface surveys have been particularly numerous and, despite the constraints which I will describe later, have contributed considerably to the general understanding of settlement dynamics from the late antiquity to the late Middle Ages (e.g., Johns 1985; Molinari and Neri 2004; Rizzo 2004). Rich results have come from the excavations of Monte Iato (e.g., Isler 1995), Entella (e.g., Corretti et al. 2010), and Segesta in Western Sicily (Molinari 1997). These were, in very general terms, important ancient cities with significant phases in the 10th–13th centuries.

In the past decade, the key developments have been a better knowledge of the late Byzantine phases; that is, the period immediately preceding the Islamic conquest (e.g., Rocchicella site: Arcifa and Longo 2015; Contrada Edera: Arcifa 2015, and Monte Kassar: Vassallo 2010; Carver and Molinari 2018) and a progressive refinement of the chronologies of early medieval ceramics (e.g., Arcifa and Longo 2015; Cacciaguerra 2015 ; Nef and Ardizzone 2014; Sacco 2017 and 2018). The wider availability of data coming from rescue archaeology (past and present) of a city like Palermo is producing a wealth of new data on the Islamic capital of the island and its cultural and economic role (Ardizzone et al. 2016; Sacco 2017). As we will soon see when discussing the major debates, there are still large gaps in our knowledge which stem from substantial weaknesses in research strategies to date. Nonetheless, the great progress made by historians for the Byzantine period (e.g., Prigent 2010; Nef and Prigent 2010), Islamic period (e.g., Metcalfe 2009; Nef and Ardizzone 2014) and Norman-Swabian period (Johns 2002; Metcalfe 2003; Nef 2011) and the presence of a new, dynamic generation of archaeologists (e.g., Nef and Ardizzone 2014) allow us to outline an agenda for the next decade.

Before outlining the main research themes, I would like to underscore some of the main challenges for understanding the transformations which Sicilian societies underwent or consciously implemented between the 9th and 13th centuries. The first term to clarify is that of "Islamization" and how we might recognize it in the material record (see Nef 2014 and Molinari 2016b for Sicily). The great variety of meanings that are given to this term, as well as the differences in scholarly opinion on what it is or if there is a single "ideal type" of Islamic society, suggest to me that we should limit its use to those forms of material culture closely associated with religious practice: religious buildings and funerary practices.

Sicily is a fascinating laboratory to understand the impact of changes in political and social structure on the standards and lifestyles of a population, especially those that can be read through archaeological evidence. Unfortunately, we have very unequal evidence for the different phases of the island's history, and research in areas such as bio-archaeology are starting only now. Particularly problematic is our poor understanding of the 8th and 9th centuries, especially in western Sicily. As a result, many open questions remain for the "transition" centuries, including Sicily's role within the Byzantine empire, the crisis of local aristocracies following the break between the church in Rome and Constantinople, the drop in settlement and agricultural activities, and the effects of the extremely protracted Muslim conquest, which extended from the landing in Mazara in

827 to the conquest of Messina in 976. On the other hand, there is more information for
the Norman-Swabian period (12th–13th centuries) in which there are distinct changes in
settlement patterns and in material culture.

FUNERARY PRACTICES, RELIGIOUS BUILDINGS, AND LINGUISTIC ARABIZATION

Reports of Islamic burials (lying on their side with face facing Mecca) are relatively numerous, especially in Western Sicily between the 10th–13th centuries (e.g., Palermo, Entella,
Segesta, Monte Maranfusa, Casale di Calliata: cf. Bagnera and Pezzini 2004; Bagnera 2013),
however, these have rarely been published systematically. Only at Palermo has it proved
possible to establish that some Muslim burials within the large cemetery around the port
pre-date the 10th century (Bagnera 2013). The Islamic cemetery of Segesta, however, is
securely dated between the second half of the 12th and the first half of the 13th century, a
period of rebellions by both Muslims and other locals against the Normans and Swabians.
Significantly, this cemetery overlaps chronologically with the Christian one, which, though
close, is very distinct and placed in front of a church (Molinari 1997). Currently, it is impossible therefore to identify the first generations of immigrants or converts in different parts of
the island (outside perhaps Palermo), unlike al-Andalus (Gutierrez Lloret 2016; Vigil-
Escalera 2009). The Sicily in Transition project (www.sicilyintransition.org) has commenced an extensive programme of radiocarbon (C^{14}) dating for all excavated cemeteries
between the Byzantine and Swabian periods to clarify the timing of shifts in burial practice.
It also uses ancient DNA analysis and stable isotopes of nitrogen, hydrogen, and oxygen to
understand geographical mobility (both from outside and inside the island), diet, and
health. Particularly promising is the analysis of Segesta's Muslim and Christian cemeteries,
which offers an opportunity to compare dietary practices and lifestyles of two social groups
who clearly professed different religious beliefs while living in the same settlement.

The Palermo described by Ibn Hawqal (Ibn Hawqal 2000, trans. de Simone) in the
second half of the 10th century had more than 300 mosques. However, in the old town
(al-Madina) only some walls below the Norman cathedral that may belong to the great
congregational mosque are known. Similarly, although in his rescript of 965, the caliph
al-Mu'izz (An Nuwayri, in Amari 1997–1998, II: 546) recommended that a Friday mosque
be built in each district capital in the countryside, the only certain rural mosque is the
much later mosque of Segesta (Figure 3.5.2) dug in the 1990s and dated to the 12th century, that is, during the Norman period (Molinari 1997). It is a very simple building (ca.
20 × 11 meters) of rectangular plan divided into two naves parallel to the *qibla* wall. The
mihrab niche is rectangular on the outside and elliptical on the interior. The mosque of
Segesta was built inside a settlement nucleus created by Islamized populations, who
most likely wanted to escape the Norman control. It was only in use for a few decades
and was demolished as early as the beginning of the 13th century.

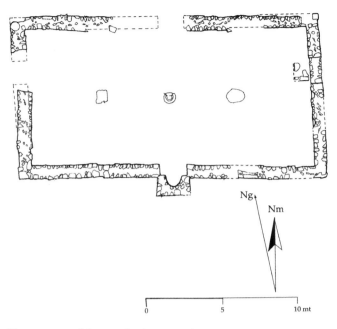

FIGURE 3.5.2 The mosque of Segesta (12th century).

Plan by A. Gottarelli.

It is extremely difficult to establish the rhythms of linguistic Arabization, which we know was never complete, for a large part of the island population still spoke Greek (and was Christian) at the time of the Norman conquest (Metcalfe 2003). Although the use of funerary or monumental epigraphy is rare in Sicily (e.g., Amari 1971; de Luca 1999; Grassi 2004), graffiti or painted lettering on everyday objects or magic amulets are known (e.g., de Luca 2003, 2004) that bear witness to the widespread use of Arabic in daily life. Of significant interest are the Aghlabid square lead seals with a central hole found around Milena and in particular on Monte Conca, in the province of Agrigento (de Luca 2003). They give the name of the issuing emir and the *hijri* date following the same protocols used in contemporary coins. These are interpreted as evidence of payment of the *jizya*, the personal tax of non-Muslims. In short, the "official language" of the Islamic state in Sicily would seem to have been exclusively in Arabic.

MATERIAL CULTURE AND EXCHANGE NETWORKS

In contrast to the sparse evidence for religious and linguistic change, the evidence of portable material culture, especially ceramics, is relatively abundant, especially for the 10th–13th centuries. Their technical and formal characteristics and spatial and temporal distribution provide valuable information on economic trends, the transformation of internal and interregional exchange networks, and different cultural and food practices as well as the introduction of new plants and agricultural techniques.

In the 7th century, even the interior of Byzantine Sicily was connected to broader Mediterranean exchange networks. African tablewares (African red slip ware) and African and eastern amphorae are widespread across the island on sites of all types. Recent analysis of distributions of typological forms across the island has identified different routes for the supply of African pottery, some directly from North Africa, while others came probably via Rome (Bonifay and Malfitana 2016). Much more controversial and poorly understood are the 8th and 9th centuries. The current state of research in both Sicily and North Africa contribute to this haziness, but there was certainly a significant contraction in the level of trade as well as a transformation of production methods toward more local ceramic forms (coarsewares and storage amphorae) (e.g., Arcifa and Longo 2015). While it cannot be ruled out that trade relations with Muslim Ifriqiya continued in some way—particularly in those areas that were directly supplied from Africa during the 7th century—the material markers that would testify to this are missing. It would seem that the break between the church of Rome, which owned large estates on the island, and the Byzantine emperor Leo III Isaurico (during the first decades of the 8th century) interrupted or severely diminished trade and exchange between Sicily and the papal seat (Ardizzone 2010; Prigent 2010). The eastern part of the island remained more connected; in particular, the capital Syracuse continued to be an important port, which had privileged relations with the Byzantine Mediterranean for the whole of the 8th century and during the 9th and 10th centuries, though with less intensity. The archaeological levels at Syracuse in this period are rich in amphorae of eastern origin (8th century) or with similar forms to those of the Byzantine world (9th) (Cacciaguerra 2015).

Located in the western part of the island that seems, to have suffered the most during the 8th century, the Aghlabid emirs' choice of Palermo as capital had important consequences for internal and international exchange networks, as well in technical and cultural changes in ceramic production. Between the end of the 9th and the beginning of the 10th century, there are a series of innovations in tablewares and cooking wares (see the various contributions on Palermo contained in Nef and Ardizzone 2014; Sacco 2017). Particularly significant is the recent attribution to Palermo workshops of yellow glazed ceramics similar to those made in Raqqada, which are considered to be the earliest glazed pottery produced in Ifriqiya (Sacco 2017). We know almost nothing about the ceramics of 8th–9th century Palermo, and therefore it is unclear whether these innovations had preparatory phases or not.

During the 10th century, a ceramic repertoire emerged similar to that of contemporary Tunisia (e.g., Gragueb Chatti 2009, Gragueb Chatti et al. 2011; Reynolds 2015), one that fits well into a shared vocabulary of forms and functions common across much of the Islamic world (Figures 3.5.3 and 3.5.4). Palermo seems to anticipate the innovations of the other Sicilian centers. Its productions were primarily (first half of the 10th

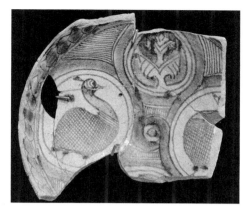

FIGURE 3.5.3 A typical glazed ceramic of Palermo (second half of 10th century).

Courtesy of Gabrieli and Scerrato (1979: 169).

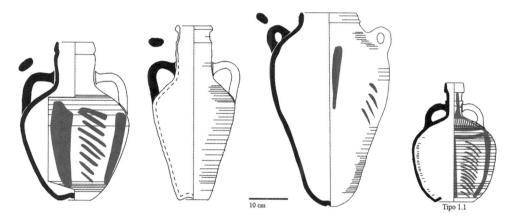

FIGURE 3.5.4 Common types of Palermo transport amphorae (10th–11th centuries)

Courtesy of V. Sacco-SicTransit Project.

century) for the urban market, but Palermitan ceramics then (second half of the
10th century) reached everywhere in the island in very high percentages. Even more
significant is the presence of Sicilian amphorae across the western Mediterranean from
North Africa to Provence (Ardizzone et al. 2016; Sacco 2018). The internal and external
exchange networks reflected in the distribution of the finewares and transport ceramics recalls to some extent the picture of the Cairo Geniza documents (Goldberg 2012).
Palermo was one of the great terminals of the Fatimid empire's commercial network,
alongside Fustat and Kairouan. One important aspect to which we will return is the
close connection between agricultural production and its commercialization: the

Sicilian amphorae would have transported goods such as olive oil, wine, salted fish, or other foodstuffs connected with the new crops (see later discussion) introduced after the Muslim conquest. Equally, and largely unattested in the written sources, the presence of Sicilian ceramics (above all amphorae) in southern Tyrrhenian Italy, Sardinia, Pisa, and Provence demonstrate that Sicily was at the center of a network of exchanges in the 10th and 11th centuries that linked different regions of the Islamic and Christian worlds.

The arrival of the Normans did not result in significant changes in the Sicilian ceramic repertoire for some time (Molinari 1994). Exchange relations with the Tyrrhenian area of the Italian peninsula, however, may have further increased during the 11th century, when Palermitan wares seem to become less dominant and are flanked by those of many other urban and rural centers. Toward the end of the 12th century, changing tastes and a relative technical decline becomes evident. With the Swabian period, this phenomenon become very diversified and pronounced (Molinari and Cassai 2006). Eastern Sicily, more profoundly changed culturally, has new productions such as proto-maiolica ware with completely new shapes, techniques, and decorations. The western island sees the continuation of locally produced ceramics, but with a significant decline in quality. Amphorae are no longer exported, and the finest ceramics now come from outside: mainly from Campania and Tunisia.

The Rural World and Agricultural Practices

To understand the transformation of Sicilian rural landscapes, we can draw on a large number of survey projects and a smaller number of systematic excavations. Our knowledge is not completely uniform in the two parts of Sicily and this is a problem, especially for those periods in which we might imagine that there were important differences in the rural history of the two zones. This is particularly true of the 8th and 9th centuries, for which information is more abundant for eastern Byzantine Sicily since the ceramics are well known. In contrast, for the 12th–13th centuries, when there were strong differences between a more decidedly Latin-Christian east and a still predominantly Muslim west, our knowledge is much richer for the Muslim areas where multiyear research projects in Monte Iato, Entella, and Segesta have provided extremely detailed data.

Some general considerations and trends can be identified (see Molinari 2016a, 2016b). In terms of the late antique landscape, the Sicilian countryside was extraordinarily vibrant until the 7th century, even in comparison with other areas of the Mediterranean. The settlement pattern appears to be progressively dominated by open villages, which received imported ceramics and seem to have a good circulation of money. The dual interest of the Byzantine state and the church of Rome is likely behind this lasting prosperity. In contrast, the 8th century produces extremely few material indicators.

However, a decrease in the number of settlements seems to occur together with a reduction in size of survived sites, especially in the west, which is not offset by new foundations. These drops seem, as we shall see, to correspond to similar drops in the pollen curve and the isotopic analyses conducted at Lake Pergusa near Enna. Systematic excavations are filling in the gaps in some cases: as in the *vicus* of Sofiana (Vaccaro et al. 2015), probably at the Villa del Casale in Piazza Armerina (Pensabene 2016; Pensabene and Sfamemi 2014, Pensabene and Barresi 2019), in Contrada Colmitella (Rizzo et al. 2012), and Casale S. Pietro in central Sicily (Carver and Molinari 2016, 2018; Carver et al. 2018). Strikingly, the abandonment of less protected open sites in favor of high sites (fortified artificially or naturally) does not seem to occur. Certainly, the Byzantine state took measures to defend the island in response to the increasingly frequent attacks from Ifriqiya, as can be seen from its administrative reorganization of Sicily as a thema (military district), the new fortifications reported in the sources, and the construction of large fortresses such as Monte Kassar (Vassallo 2010; Carver and Molinari 2018). The rural population, however, does not seem to retreat to the fortified centers. Indeed, a revolution in settlement patterns did not even occur during the 9th century in response to the long war of conquest. However, the visibility of sites with 9th-century phases continues to be very low, especially in western Sicily.

The explosion of the number and size of rural sites during the 10th century does not seem to be simply the result of our better knowledge of the ceramics of this period. Similar increases seem to be mirrored in some urban centers, above all Palermo. Existing rural sites are enlarged and new ones are established both on undefended sites and on the hilltops. The interpretation of this shift to the hilltops is controversial. In some cases, as at Entella, Calathamet, and even Monte Iato, it seems to mark the establishment or strengthening of "district capitals." The absence in these highland sites, thus far, of elite residences or fortifications of clear public initiative makes the identification of their builders challenging (Molinari 2016a). One possibility is that they are an initiative of peasant communities following pressure of the Fatimid/Kalbid state, attested in the rescript of the Caliph al-Mu'izz of 965 mentioned earlier (An Nuwayri, in Amari 1997–1998, II: 546). Revision of the typology of 11th-century ceramics should also allow us to verify whether the formation and consolidation of highland sites might stem from the fragmentation of power at the end of Kalbite rule or during the Norman conquest phase.

The 12th century is marked by the abandonment or downsizing of many unprotected sites and a marked increase in the centralized and protected sites. Sometimes abandonment seems to relate to a dramatic episode, as in the case of the Islamic village built on the Villa del Casale (Pensabene 2016; Pensabene and Barresi 2019), whose abandonment in the Norman period might hypothetically be connected to the episode of anti-Muslim violence described by Falcando. Of particular interest, then, is the appearance of private fortified residences in hilltop sites already inhabited previously or new foundations (e.g., Calathamet, Castellaccio di Campofiorito, Monte Maranfusa). This type of fortified residence is unprecedented in the Islamic period and seems to indicate the impact of a new type of elite connected with the Norman rulers: strongly militarized and with a more direct and extensive control of land and people (Molinari 2016a). The presence of these new elites seems, in some cases at least, to have triggered a series of conflicts and flights, as at Calathamet and Segesta. During the 13th century, the abandonment of open sites seems to intensify. In western Sicily, however, these abandonments are offset by the abnormal growth of hilltop sites such as those of Monte Iato, Segesta, and Entella. The Muslims rebels with their settlements in the mountains openly contested the power of the Swabian emperor, even coining their own money (D'Angelo 1995). Frederick II fought hard, sometimes even in person at places like Iato and Entella. Many Muslims were deported to Puglia, to the area of Lucera. The result of these conflicts on the archaeological record is impressive: the depopulation of the countryside and concentration of population in a few large villages, as well as a clear break in the characteristics and types of the material culture of all kinds (Molinari 2010). If we combine these material changes with the drastic reduction of the population using Arabic names and speaking Arabic described in the texts (Metcalfe 2009: 275–294), it is tempting to interpret these dramatic changes as a real "ethnic cleansing."

A key but often neglected theme closely linked to that of rural settlement is that of the "ecological" changes that must have accompanied the changes in political power, social structure and culture, agricultural and dietary practice, demographic rise and fall, and the export of rural surplus. The so-called *Green Revolution* that might have led to the cultivation of new plant species and the diffusion of new agricultural techniques in the Islamic period is a controversial topic (e.g., Watson 1983; Barbera 2007; Squatriti 2014; van der Veen 2011 and the opposing view of Decker 2009; Manzano Moreno 2018). The problems are manifold. On the one hand, we must explore whether certain plants were really new and, on the other, how widespread new plants were cultivated. Who were the promoters of these changes: the Palermitan elites or immigrant farmers? And what was the timing? Archaeology provides important evidence of the introduction of new agricultural techniques and products. In particular, *noria* pots, used to lift water from wells and often linked to irrigated agriculture (but not exclusively) appear in Palermo as early as the first half of the 10th century (e.g., Arcifa and Bagnera 2014). In the same period, molds used for the refining of sugar have also been found at Palermo (G. Battaglia and C. Mangiaracina pers. comm.). The discoveries made in some 10th- to 13th-century rubbish pits in Mazara del Vallo (excavated in 1997 but only now being studied within the Sicily in Transition project by Girolamo Fiorentino and Milena Primavera) are really telling (Primavera 2018). For example, seeds of cotton, lemon, aubergine, and watermelon (Figure 3.5.5), charred or preserved from particular conditions of storage, were detected. Even though the "agricultural revolution" needs a detailed archaeological study, it is clear that new plants and new agricultural techniques were established in Sicily from at least the 10th century, probably first in Palermo and its hinterland, but also around other strongly developed towns like Mazara del Vallo.

A second controversial topic is the impact that the Normans had on Islamic agriculture, which some scholars have depicted as destructive (see Ouerfelli 2008: 149–178, with bibliography on sugar in Sicily). Carmelo Trasselli, for example, on the grounds that sugar cane is not mentioned by al-Idrisi in his description of Sicily, decreed its end in the Norman period. Other scholars, however, note that Falcando spoke admirably of the production of sugar in Palermo at the end of the 12th century. Excavations carried

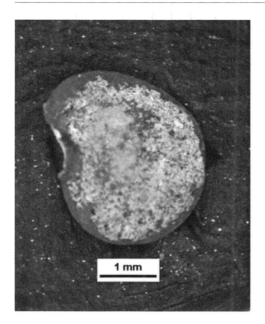
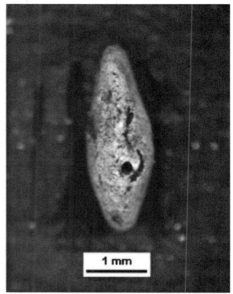

FIGURE 3.5.5 An aubergine seed found in Mazara del Vallo in an 11th-century context (research by G. Fiorentino and M. Primavera, SicTransit Project).

out in Palermo near the palace of Maredolce revealed the presence of a large sugar factory, datable to the 12th century. As we will see, however, changes in agricultural practices could have taken place in the medium term and certainly by the time of Frederick II who, in 1239, wrote to Oberto Fallamonaco in an attempt to prevent the disappearance of sugar production in Palermo.

There is no trace of the "Green Revolution" or a Norman catastrophe in the pollen and isotopic series reconstructed from the sediments of Lake Pergusa, near Enna (Sadori et al. 2016). Laura Sadori and others have identified two periods of greater humidity and intensification of agricultural activities: 450–720 and 1400–1800 CE. Between the 8th and 14th centuries, a more arid period occurred. They argue, however, that despite the greater aridity, an agricultural recovery is evident from the 12th century in the expansion of olive and cereal cultivation (including new varietals). This would seem to indicate that economic and demographic growth and new plant species that seem to be clearly legible in the archaeological record as early as the 10th century are not at all visible in the pollen series of Lake Pergusa. If the absence of the key crops (e.g., sugar cane, lemon tree, spinach, aubergine, cotton, etc) of the Green Revolution invites us to intensify investigations around, for example, Palermo and Conca d'Oro and to develop new research strategies, the expansion of olive and cereal cultivation can offer another explanation. A significant increase in the Norman and Swabian period of the so-called Mediterranean triad—cereals, olive trees, and grape vines—is not only demonstrated by the pollen evidence, but also by the written sources which explicitly describe the expansion of cerealiculture at places such as the Monreale area (Bercher et al. 1979: 536–537). An interesting interpretation of a similar phenomenon on the Iberian peninsula following the Christian conquest of al-Andalus was provided by the Catalan scholar M. Barceló (1999). He argued that the expansion of cereals, vines, and olive trees should be explained less in cultural terms and more in social terms. Products such as wheat, wine, and oil allow a more efficient extraction of peasant surplus by the new elites, as these products can be stored and stored for longer.

To answer some of these questions about the rural world, the project "The Archaeology of Regime Change. Sicily in Transition" (funded by the European Research Council: www.sicilyintransition.org) was launched in 2016 by M. O. H. Carver and the author. The research strategy combines "traditional" excavation, field survey, architectural analysis, and geophysics with a series of new analytical techniques in the field of bioarchaeology. The focus is on the area of Castronovo di Sicilia (Figure 3.5.1, n. 19 and Figures 3.5.6) in the interior of the island, halfway between Palermo and Agrigento (Carver and Molinari 2016, 2018; Carver et al. 2018). It also integrates the analysis of human and animal bones, coals, and seeds from around twenty other sites in Sicily of the Byzantine to the Swabian period. Analyses of carbon and nitrogen isotopes of the different components of the food chain will provide more sophisticated data on human and animal diet, but also on cultivation techniques (e.g., Fiorentino 2015). An additional set of analyses aims to identify the organic contents of Sicilian amphorae found on the island, as well as those discovered in shipwrecks and excavations from Tunisia to southern France. The great variety of shapes in Sicilian transport containers of the 10th–12th centuries (see Figure 3.5.4) could be linked to the transport of a variety of goods, and their considerable quantity is a clear sign of the commercial success of the island's food products. Similar analyses are planned for cooking wares whose different shapes and functions reflect changing patterns in food preparation from the Byzantine to the Swabian period, in the city as in the country.

The intensive research around Castronovo di Sicilia aims to build up a picture of changing settlement patterns, spatial use, and agricultural resources (Figures 3.5.6 and 3.5.7). In late antiquity, the site of Casale San Pietro seems to dominate; it comprises several hectares in an accessible area of the Platani River Valley, along the road that connected Palermo and Agrigento. This settlement is of a common type (similar to Sofiana) and may be considered an "agro-town." At Casale San Pietro, investigations are aimed at understanding its size, chronology, and plan. Excavations at four different points of the site, magnetometry, and surface survey indicate that, in at least some parts of the site, occupation continued without interruption from the 3rd to the 12th century. The presence of African red slip ware and amphorae until the 7th century followed by glazed pottery and amphorae of Palermitan origin from the 10th–11th centuries reveal that this site, in the interior and far from the coasts, was always connected to exchange networks within and beyond Sicily.

A few kilometers from Casale San Pietro, the mountain massif of Mount Kassar rises up to more than a thousand meters. Here the sondages, the standing remains, and surface finds tell another story. The mountain was occupied up to approximately the 5th century BC. After a long hiatus, an impressive fortress was built here with a defensive wall almost 2 kilometers long and over 3 meters wide and enclosing an area of

FIGURE 3.5.6 The territory of Castronovo with the sites investigated in the SicTransit project: 1. Mount Kassar; 2. San Luca Roman Villa; 3. San Vitale Hill; 4. Castronovo Town; 5. Ministalla; 6. Casale San Pietro.

Courtesy of G. Ciccone, SicTransit Project.

FIGURE 3.5.7 One of the trenches at Casale San Pietro (Byzantine to Norman Phase).

Courtesy of G. Ciccone/A.Meo, SicTransit Project.

approximately 90 hectares. The wall itself comprises a walkway, eleven towers, two doors, several posterns, and a rampart. Inside the walls, the space seems to contain a few buildings: a large one 30 meters in length and some houses located immediately behind the wall. This fortress contained only sparse finds, but a series of clues allow us to date its use primarily to the 8th century. Its construction is undoubtedly the result of considerable public investment, and it seems to be connected to the reorganization of the Byzantine province in response to the increase of Islamic attacks on Sicily. The fortress did not survive the Islamic conquest of this region in the mid-9th century.

The current center of Castronovo, located in an elevated position close to Mount Kassar, is in turn dominated by the hill of the Colle San Vitale on which are still visible the remains of medieval fortifications and religious buildings. Stratigraphic analysis of the masonry has identified an older nucleus, which hypothetically might date to the late Islamic period/early Norman period. The analysis of the layout of the old town of Castronovo and of the written sources related to it allow us to follow in broad terms developments from the late Islamic/Norman period up to the present day. Extremely interesting is the system of irrigated terraces and mills located immediately behind the historic center; indeed, this hydraulic system is generated by a spring (the Rabato spring) located in the oldest part of the village.

Overall, therefore, the region of Castronovo, offers extraordinary potential for the understanding of long-term dynamics, settlement hierarchies, and agricultural use of the territory (a series of paleoenvironmental analyses are planned). As far as we can tell, the construction of the fortress of Mount Kassar did not seem to affect rural settlement, which remained focused on the "agro-town" of Casale San Pietro. The settlement of Castronovo itself, however, acquired importance probably by the late Islamic period perhaps due to its considerable water resources, which allowed an extensive system of irrigated terraces. In any case, it was Castronovo that the Normans settled, and the settlement of Casale San Pietro seems to have lost importance.

THE CITIES

Urban archaeology still lacks a wider strategy in Sicily to allow us to go beyond occasional discoveries. In the past few years, however, important investigations in the historic center of Agrigento and access to the results from emergency excavations in cities such as Syracuse, Catania, Taormina, and Palermo point to some general trends (e.g., Arcifa 2016). As in the countryside, the eastern cities and the capitals Syracuse and Catania show a more complex urban profile and material culture in the late Byzantine period (7th-early 9th centuries). In contrast, Agrigento in the south and Marsala in the west show signs of crisis and economic and demographic contraction. We know almost nothing about Byzantine Palermo, although the written sources suggest that it was the most important center of northwestern Sicily, and certainly the city saw a great deal of investment from the church of Rome (until the first half of the 8th century), (Prigent

2013) particularly as the hub for its extensive rural estates. We know little about its transition into the capital of the emirate and its transformation into al-Madina (Nef 2013; Ardizzone et al. 2016). Both the written sources and archaeology show, however, that during the 10th century (especially in the latter half), Palermo became a major Mediterranean center and a "polycentric" city. To the ancient fortified nucleus of the Cassaro, the fortified citadel of Khalisa was added by the Fatimids in 937–938 to the south of the port, equipped with a mosque, the emiral residence, administrative offices, and perhaps the arsenal. The districts of Harat al-Saqaliba, Harat al-Masjid, and Harat al-jadida were distinct from each other, but not fortified. A wide range of gardens and irrigated orchards surrounded the city on its land sides. An industrial zone may be located between the area of the current railway station and Corso dei Mille. Ibn Hawqal describes it full of mosques and the most diverse markets (Ibn Hawqal, 2000, trans. de Simone 2000). As mentioned earlier, Palermitan pottery (glazed tablewares and amphorae), reach high numbers of rural sites even those far away. Seat of the emiral court and Muslim aristocracies, Palermo was an extremely important manufacturing center with close economic connections with much of the island territory, as well as serving as one of the main terminals of Fatimid trade (Goldberg 2012). Finally, it seems that some of the main innovations in ceramic techniques and forms, as well as in the cultivation of exotic plants (sugarcane) began earlier here.

CONCLUSION

Sicily was always central to broader processes of transformation in the medieval Mediterranean. Although there are still many gaps to be filled, the growing interest in medieval archaeology on the island shows great potential for a deeper understanding of socio-economic, cultural, and ecological changes connected (or not) to shifting political dynamics of this period. Certainly, the opportunities for comparing Sicilian developments with other parts of the Dar al-Islam, in particular Ifriqiya, are growing.

At the time the conquest started in 827, Aghlabid troops found an island that had been affected unevenly by the major Mediterranean transformations. Unfortunately, we know significantly less about the 9th century and the long phase of conquest and resistance. It is, however, during this period that the transformations so visible in the archaeological evidence from the 10th century began to mature. The fulcrum of the Sicilian social, economic, and cultural transformations was the great metropolis, al-Madina, Balarm (Palermo). Seat of the emiral court and Muslim aristocracy, a manufacturing center, a city rich in markets, it was a central node for exchange within the Fatimid world as well as looking toward the Christian Tyrrhenian area. The city was closely integrated into the internal networks of the island, and it seems likely that many of the changes that we see so clearly in the 10th century originated in the rural hinterland of Palermo.

Contrary to scholarly assumption, the arrival of the Normans was by no means painless, and archaeological evidence points to the need to move away from viewing Norman Sicily only from the perspective of the court and the ruling class of Palermo. The image of tolerance and peaceful coexistence between the different cultural components of the island guaranteed by the Norman rulers is much murkier when we look at the peasant world and the archaeological record. The arrival of the Normans (and with them Latin-speaking Christian immigrants) involved a gradual but profound modification of the social and natural habitat of Sicily as a result of the significant differences in the social structure and the cultural tastes of newcomers (including dietary preferences). From a mixed polyculture aimed also at supporting the industrial sector (especially textiles), there was probably a switch to a prevalence of cereals, vines, and olives. Social and cultural tensions at the end of the Norman kingdom came to a head in Swabian times. Late 13th-century Sicily is a different world to 10th-century Sicily in every way: crops, culture, language and religion, settlement models, material culture, and networks of exchange.

References

Amari, M. 1933–1937 [1854–1872]. *Storia dei Musulmani di Sicilia* (Catania: Prampolini).

Amari, M. 1971. *Le epigrafi arabiche di Sicilia: trascritte, tradotte e illustrate* (Palermo: S.F. Flaccovio).

Amari, M. (ed.). 1997–1998 [1880–1881]. *Biblioteca arabo-sicula ossia raccolta di testi arabici che toccano la geografia, la storia, la biografia e la bibliografia della Sicilia, seconda edizione riveduta da U. Rizzitano 3 vols.* (Palermo: Accademia Nazioanle di Scienze Lettere e Arti).

Amari, M., and Dufour, A. H. 1859. *Carte comparée de la Sicile moderne avec la Sicile au XIIe siècle* (Paris: Typographie de Henri Plom).

Arcifa, L. 2015. "La Sicilia bizantina agli inizi del IX secolo: nuovi dati e spunti di ricerca da Contrada Edera di Bronte (CT)," in A. Puglisi and M. Turco (eds.), *L'acqua, la roccia e l'uomo. Lago Gurrida e Sciare di Santa Venera* (Nicolosi: Parco dell'Etna), 142–155.

Arcifa, L. 2016. "Trasformazioni urbane nell'altomedioevo siciliano. Uno status quaestionis," in M. C. Parello and M. S. Rizzo (eds.), *Paesaggi urbani tardoantichi* (Bari: Edipuglia), 31–40.

Arcifa, L., and Bagnera, A. 2014. "Islamizzazione e cultura materiale a Palermo: una riconsiderazione dei contesti ceramici di Castello San Pietro," in Nef, A., and Ardizzone, F. (eds.) 2014. *Les dynamiques de l'islamisation en Méditerranée centrale et en Sicile: nouvelles propositions et découvertes récentes* (Bari-Rome: Collection de l'École Française de Rome 487 Edipuglia), 165–190.

Arcifa, L., Bagnera, A., and Nef, A. 2012. "Archeologia della Sicilia islamica: nuove proposte di riflessione," in P. Senac (ed.), Villa 4. *Histoire et archéologie de l'occident musulman, VIIe—XVe siècles* (Toulouse: Collection "Meridiennes", CNRS – Université de Toulouse-Le Mirail), 241–274.

Arcifa, L., and Longo, R. 2015. "Processi di diversificazione territoriale nella Sicilia di inizi IX secolo: il contesto di Rocchicella-Mineo (CT)," in P. Arthur and M. L. Imperiale (eds.), *Congresso Nazionale di Archeologia Medievale 7*, vol. 2 (Florence: All'Insegna del Giglio), 361–366.

Ardizzone, F. 2010. "Nuove ipotesi a partire dalla rilettura dei dati archeologici: la Sicilia occidentale," in Nef, A., and Prigent, V. (eds.), *La Sicile de Byzance à l'Islam* (Paris: De Boccard), 50–76.

Ardizzone, F., Pezzini, E., and Sacco, V. 2014. "Lo scavo della chiesa di Santa Maria degli Angeli alla Gancia (Palermo): indicatori archeologici della prima età islamica a Palermo," in Nef, A., and Ardizzone, F. (eds.). *Les dynamiques de l'islamisation en Méditerranée centrale et en Sicile: nouvelles propositions et découvertes récentes* (Rome-Bari: École Française de Rome/ Edipuglia), 197–224.

Ardizzone, F., Pezzini, E., and Sacco, V. 2016. "The Role of Palermo in the Central Mediterranean: Evolution of the Harbour and Circulation of Ceramics (10th–11th centuries)," *Journal of Islamic Archaeology*, 2, 2, 229–257.

Bagnera, A. 2013. "From a Small Town to a Capital: The Urban Evolution of Islamic Palermo (9th–mid-11th Century)," in Nef, A. (ed.), *A Companion to Medieval Palermo: The History of a Mediterranean City from 600 to 1500* (Leiden: Brill), 61–88.

Bagnera, A., and Pezzini, E. 2004. "I cimiteri di rito musulmano nella Sicilia medievale. Dati e problemi," *Mélanges de l'Ecole française de Rome. Moyen Age*, 116, 1, 231–302.

Barbera, G. 2007. "Parchi, frutteti, giardini e orti nella Conca d'oro di Palermo araba e normanna," *Italus Hortus*, 14, 4, 4–28.

Barceló Perello, M. 1999. "Saber lo que es un espacio hidraulico y lo que no es: o al-Andalus y los feudales," in A. Bazzana (ed.), *Castrum 5. Archéologie des espaces agraires méditerranéens au Moyen Âge* (Madrid-Rome: Collection de la Casa de Velázquez 55/ Collection de l'École Française de Rome 105), 277–286.

Bercher, H., Courteaux, A., and Mouton, J. 1979. "Une abbaye latine dans la société musulmane. Monreale au XIIe siècle," *Annales*, 34, 525–547.

Berti, G., and Tongiorgi, L. 1981. *I bacini ceramici medievali delle chiese di Pisa* (Roma: L'Erma di Bretschneider).

Bonifay, M., and Malfitana, D. (eds.) 2016. *La ceramica africana nella Sicilia romana* (Catania: CNR Istituto Beni Archeologici IBAM).

Cacciaguerra, G. 2015. "Cultura materiale e commerci in Sicilia fra bizantini e arabi (VIII-metà X secolo): nuovi dati sulle ceramiche fini e le anfore dai contesti altomedievali di Siracusa," in P. Arthur and M. L. Imperiale (eds.), *Congresso Nazionale di Archeologia Medievale 7*, vol. 2 (Florence: All'Insegna del Giglio,), 367–372.

Carver, M. O. H., and Molinari, A. 2016. "Sicily in Transition Research Project. Investigation at Castronovo. Results and Prospects," *FastiOnline* (www.fastionline.org/docs/FOLDER-it-2016-352.pdf).

Carver, M. O. H., and Molinari, A. 2018. "Insediamenti e cultura materiale nell'area di Castronovo di Sicilia. Secoli VI–XIII," in R. M. Carra Bonacasa and E. Vitale, "Studi in memoria di Fabiola Ardizzone. 2. Scavi, Topografia e Archeologia del paesaggio," *Quaderni Digitali di Archeologia Postclassica*, 11, 2, 29–52.

Carver, M. O. H, Molinari, A., Aniceti, V., Colangeli, F., Giannini, N., Giovannini, F., Hummler, M., Mangiaracina, C. F., Meo, A., and Orecchioni, P. 2018. "Sicily in Transition. Interim report of investigations at Castronovo di Sicilia 2016," *FastiOnline* (www.fastionline.org/docs/FOLDER-it-2018-412.pdf).

Chiarelli, L. C. 2011. *A History of Muslim Sicily* (St. Venera: Midsea Books).

Corretti, A., Michelini, C., and Vaggioli, M. A. 2010. "Frammenti di Medioevo siciliano:Entella e il suo territorio dall'altomedioevo a Federico II," in P. Pensabene (ed.), *Piazza armerina: Villa del Casale e la Sicilia tra tardoantico e medioevo* (Rome: L'Erma di Bretschneider), 147–196.

D'Angelo, F. 1980. "La ceramica nell'archeologia urbana: Palermo nel basso medioevo," in *La céramique médiévale en Mediterranée occidentale, Xe-XVe s.* (Paris: CNRS,), 175–182.

D'Angelo, F. 1995. "Le monete delle rivolte: circolazione di denari sfregiati e di Muhammad ibn Abbad," in C. A. Di Stefano and A. Cadei (eds.), *Federico II e la Sicilia dalla terra alla corona. Archeologia, architettura e arti della Sicilia in età sveva* (Palermo: Arnaldo Lombardi), 85–91.

Decker, M. 2009. "Plants and Progress: Rethinking the Islamic Agricultural Revolution," *Journal of World History*, 20, 2, 187–206.

de Luca, M. A. 1999. "L'epigrafia araba in Sicilia. Bilancio degli studi condotti nel corso dell'ultimo cinquantennio e prospettive per il Duemila," in M. I. Gulletta (ed.) *Sicilia Epigraphica* (Pisa: Scuola Normale Superiore), 197–204.

de Luca, M. A. 2003. "Reperti inediti con iscrizioni in arabo rinvenuti nel sito archeologico di Milena: i sigilli e le monete," in M. V. Fontana and B. Genito (eds.), *Studi in onore di Umberto Scerrato per il suo 75mo compleanno* (Naples: Università degli studi di Napoli L'Orientale), 231–258.

de Luca, M. A. 2004. "Talismani con iscrizioni arabe rinvenuti in Sicilia," *Mélanges de l'Ecole française de Rome. Moyen Âge*, 116, 367–388.

Fiorentino, G. 2015. "Stable isotopes in archaeobotanical research," *Vegetation History and Archaeobotany*, 24, 215–227.

Gabrieli, F., and Scerrato, U. 1979. *Gli Arabi in Italia* (Libri Scheiwiller, Milano).

Goldberg, J. L. 2012. *Trade and Institutions in the Medieval Mediterranean: The Geniza Merchants and Their Business World* (Cambridge: Cambridge University Press).

Grassi, V. 2004. "Le stele funerarie islamiche di Sicilia: provenienze e problemi aperti," *Mélanges de l'Ecole française de Rome. Moyen Âge*, 116, 1, 351–366.

Gragueb Chatti, S., Tréglia, J.-C., Capelli, C., and Waksman, Y. 2011. "Jarres et amphores de Sabra al-Mansuriya (Kairouan, Tunisie)," in P. Cressier and E. Fentress (eds.), *La céramique maghrébine du haut Moyen âge (VIIIe–Xe siècle)* (Rome: École Française de Rome), 197–220.

Gragueb Chatti, S. 2009. "Céramique commune d'époque aglabide à Raqqâda," in J. Zozaya et al. (eds.), *Actas del VIII Congreso Internacional de Ceràmica Medieval en el Mediteràneo* (Ciudad Real: A+T Ediciones), 339–354.

Gutiérrez Lloret, S. 2016. "Early al-Andalus: an Archaeological Approach to the Process of Islamization in the Iberian Peninsula (7th to 10th centuries)," in S. Gelichi and R. Hodges (eds.), *New Directions in Early Medieval European Archaeology: Spain and Italy Compared: Essays for Riccardo Francovich* (Turnhout: Brepols), 43–86.

Ibn Hawqal. *Kitab Surat al-ard*, trans. de Simone Adalgisa 2000, "Descrizione di Palermo di Ibn Hawqal," in R. La Duca (ed.), *Storia di Palermo. II. Dal tardo antico all'Islam* (Palermo: L'Epos), 116–127.

Isler, H. P. 1995. "Monte Iato," in C. A. Di Stefano and A. Cadei (eds.), *Federico II e la Sicilia dalla terra alla corona. Archeologia, architettura e arti della Sicilia in età sveva* (Palermo: Arnaldo Lombardi), 121–150.

Johns, J. 1985. "The Monreale Survey: Indigenes and Invaders in Medieval West Sicily," *Papers in Italian Archaeology*, 4, 4, 215–223.

Johns, J. 2002. *Arabic Administration in Norman Sicily: The Royal Diwan* (Cambridge: Cambridge University Press).

Lesnes, E., and Poisson, J.-M. (eds.) 2013, *Calathamet. Archéologie et histoire d'un château normand en Sicile* (Rome: École Française de Rome).

Manzano Moreno, E. 2018. "Entre faits et artefacts: interpretation historiques et donées archéologiques en al-Andalus," in L. Bourgeois, D. Alexandre-Bidon, L. Feller, P. Mane, C. Verna, and M. Wilmart (eds.), *La culture matérielle: un objet en question. Antropologie, archéologie et histoire* (Caen: Presses Universitaires de Caen), 93–11.

Metcalfe, A. 2003. *Muslims and Christians in Norman Sicily. Arabic Speakers and the End of Islam* (London: Routledge).

Metcalfe, A. 2009. *The Muslims of Medieval Italy* (Edinburgh: Edinburgh University Press).

Molinari, A. 1994. "La produzione ed il commercio in Sicilia tra il X e il XIII secolo: il contributo delle fonti archeologiche," *Archeologia Medievale*, 21, 99–120.

Molinari, A. 1997. *Segesta II. Il castello e la moschea (scavi 1989–95)* (Palermo: S.F. Flaccovio).

Molinari, A. 2004. "La Sicilia islamica: riflessioni sul passato e sul futuro della ricerca in campo archeologico," *Mélanges de l'Ecole française de Rome. Moyen Âge*, 116, 1, 19–46.

Molinari, A. 2010. "Paesaggi rurali e formazioni sociali nella Sicilia islamica, normanna e sveva (secoli X-XIII)," *Archeologia Medievale*, 37, 229–246.

Molinari, A. 2016a. "Fortified and Unfortified Settlements in Byzantine and Islamic Sicily: 6th to 11th Centuries," in H. Herold and N. J. Christie (eds.), *Fortified Settlements in Early Medieval Europe. Defended Communities of the 8th-10th centuries* (Oxford: Oxbow), 320–332.

Molinari, A. 2016b. "'Islamisation' and the Rural World: Sicily and al-Andalus. What Kind of Archaeology?," in S. Gelichi and R. Hodges (eds.), *New Directions in Early Medieval European Archaeology: Spain and Italy Compared: Essays for Riccardo Francovich* (Turnhout: Brepols), 187–220.

Molinari, A., and Cassai, D. 2006. "La Sicilia ed il Mediterraneo nel XIII secolo: importazioni ed esportazioni di ceramiche fini e da trasporto," in *Atti XXXVII Convegno Internazionale della Ceramica* (Florence: All'Insegna del Giglio), 89–112.

Molinari, A., and Neri, I. 2004. "Dall'età tardo-imperiale al XII secolo: i risultati della ricognizione eseguita nel territorio di Calatafimi," *Mélanges de l'Ecole française de Rome. Moyen Âge*, 116(1), 109–127.

Nef, A. 2011. *Conquérir et gouverner la Sicile islamique aux XIe et XIIe siècles* (Rome: École Française de Rome).

Nef, A. (ed.) 2013. *A Companion to Medieval Palermo: The History of a Mediterranean City from 600 to 1500* (Leiden: Brill).

Nef, A. 2014. "Quelques réflexions sur les conquêtes islamiques, le processus d'islamisation et implications pour l'histoire de la Sicile," in Nef, A., and Ardizzone, F. (eds.) 2014. *Les dynamiques de l'islamisation en Méditerranée centrale et en Sicile: nouvelles propositions et découvertes récentes* (Rome/ Bari: École Française de Rome /Edipuglia), 47–58.

Nef, A., and Ardizzone, F. (eds.) 2014. *Les dynamiques de l'islamisation en Méditerranée centrale et en Sicile: nouvelles propositions et découvertes récentes* (Rome/ Bari: École Française de Rome /Edipuglia).

Nef, A., and Prigent, V. (eds.) 2010. *La Sicile de Byzance à l'Islam* (De Boccard, Paris).

Ouerfelli, M. 2008. *Le sucre: production, commercialisation et usages dans la Méditerranée médiévale* (Leiden: Brill).

Pensabene, P. 2016. "Il contributo degli scavi 2004–2014 alla storia della Villa del Casale di Piazza Armerina tra IV e XII secolo," in C. Giuffrida and M. Cassia (eds.), *Silenziose rivoluzioni la Sicilia dalla tarda antichita al primo medioevo* (Catania: Edizioni del Prisma), 223–271.

Pensabene, P., and Sfamemi, C. (eds.). 2014. *La villa restaurata e i nuovi studi sull'edilizia residenziale tardoantica* (Bari: Edipuglia).

Pensabene, P., and Barresi, P. (eds.). 2019. *Piazza Armerina. Villa del Casale. Scavi e studi nel decennio 2004-2014* (Rome: L'Erma di Bretschneider).

Pesez, J.-M. (ed.) 1984. *Brucato. Histoire et archéologie d'un habitat médiéval en Sicile* (Rome: École Française de Rome).

Prigent, V. 2010, "La Sicile byzantine, entre papes et empereurs (6eme - 8eme siècle)," in D. Engels (ed.), *Zwischen Ideal und Wirklichkeit: Herrschaft auf Sizilien von der Antike bis zum Spätmittelalter* (Stuttgart: Franz Steiner Verlag), 201–230.

Prigent, V. 2013. "Palermo in the Eastern Roman Empire," in Nef, A. (ed.), *A Companion to Medieval Palermo: The History of a Mediterranean City from 600 to 1500* (Leiden: Brill), 11–38.

Primavera, M. 2018. "Introduzione di nuove piante e innovazioni agronomiche nella Sicilia medievale: il contributo dell'archeobotanica alla rivoluzione agricola araba di Andrew Watson", *Archeologia Medievale*, 45, 439–444.

Reynolds, P. 2015. "From Vandal Africa to Arab Ifriqiya Tracing Ceramic and Economic Trends Through the Fifth to the Eleventh Centuries," in J. P. Conant and S. T. Stevens (eds.), *North Africa Under Byzantium and Early Islam* (Washington DC, Dumbarton Oaks), 129–172.

Rizzo, M. S. 2004. *L'insediamento medievale nella Valle dei Platani* (Rome: L'Erma di Bretschneider).

Rizzo, M. S., Danile, L., Romano, D., Scibona, M., and Zambito, L. 2012. "Il villaggio di Colmitella (Racalmuto, AG): primi dati dallo scavo archeologico di un insediamento rurale di età altomedievale e medievale," in F. Redi and A. Forgione (eds.), *VI Congresso Nazionale di Archeologia Medievale* (Florence: All'Insegna del Giglio), 419–424.

Sadori, L., Giraudi, C., Masi, A., Magny, M., Ortu, E., Zanchetta, G., and Izdebski A. 2016. "Climate, Environment and Society in Southern Italy During the last 2000 Years. A Review of the Environmental, Historical and Archaeological Evidence," *Quaternary Science Reviews*, 136, 173–188.

Sacco, V. 2017. "Le ceramiche invetriate di età islamica a Palermo: nuovi dati dale sequenze del quartiere della Kalsa," *Archeologia Medievale*, 44, 337–366.

Sacco, V. 2018. "Produzione e circolazione delle anfore palermitane tra la fine del IX e il XII Secolo." *Archeologia Medievale*, 45, 175–91.

Squatriti P. 2014. "Of Seeds, Seasons, and Seas: Andrew Watson's Medieval Agrarian Revolution Forty Years Later," *The Journal of Economic History*, 74, 4, 1205–1220.

Vaccaro, E., La Torre, G., Capelli, C., Ghisleni, M., Lazzeri, G., MacKinnon, M., Mercuri, A. M., Pecci, A., Rattighieri, E., Ricchi, S., Rizzo, E., and Sfacteria, M. 2015. "La produzione di ceramica a Philosophiana (Sicilia centrale) nella media età bizantina: metodi di indagine ed implicazioni economiche," *Archeologia Medievale*, 42, 53–91.

Vassallo, S. 2010. "Il territorio di Castronovo di Sicilia in età bizantina e le fortificazioni del Kassar, in M. Congiu, S. Modeo, and M. Arnone (eds.), *La Sicilia bizantina: storia, città e territorio: atti del VI convegno di studi* (Caltanissetta: Sciascia), 259–276.

van der Veen, M. 2011. *Consumption, Trade and Innovation. Exploring the Botanical Remains from the Roman and Islamic Ports at Quseir al-Qadim, Egypt.* Journal of African Archaeological Monograph Series, 6 (Frankfurt am Main: Africa Magna Verlag).

Vigil-Escalera Guirado, A. 2009. "Sepulturas, huertos y radiocarbono (siglos VIII–XIII d. C.): El proceso de islamización en el medio rural del centro peninsular y otras cuestiones," *Studia historica. Historia medieval*, 27, 97–118.

Watson, A. M. 1983. *Agricultural Innovation in the Early Islamic World: The Diffusion of Crops and Farming Techniques, 700–1100* (Cambridge: Cambridge University Press).

CONTACTS BETWEEN THE ISLAMIC WORLD AND NORTHERN EUROPE IN THE PRE-MONGOL PERIOD

MAREK JANKOWIAK

NORTHERN Europe and the Islamic world, although separated by the wide belt of the steppe, were in contact from the 7th to 13th centuries. The intensity of these contacts varied over time, but vast quantities of coins, silverware, beads, and other objects of Islamic provenance were imported to Scandinavia and the Slavic lands at their peak in the 9th and 10th centuries (Figure 3.6.1). Trade seems to have been the primary reason behind the inflow of large quantities of objects of Islamic origin, especially coins, to northern Europe. It is an open debate what they were exchanged for: furs, for instance, were certainly sought after in the Islamic world (Howard-Johnston forthcoming), but the main areas of their production in northern Scandinavia and the Kama Basin do not coincide with the distribution of the finds of dirhams (Kovalev 2000–2001). Muslim sources—such as the account of Ibn Fadlan who travelled to Bulgar on the Volga in 922—emphasize the significance of slave trade, but modern research has so far focused on the numismatic material rather than the mechanisms and implications of this long-distance trade system spanning much of western Eurasia.

No comprehensive survey of finds of Islamic objects from this entire period and area exists. Important studies are, however, available, for Sweden—in the first place the exemplary survey of Jansson (1988) and the older study by Arne (1914), complemented by more recent overviews by Duczko (1998) and Mikkelsen (2008)—and Russia, where "Oriental" metal objects have been studied by Darkevich (1976) and pottery by Koval (2010). Finds of Sasanian and Islamic coins are the subject of a number of articles by Thomas Noonan and Roman Kovalev. This chapter places their findings in a broader historical and geographical context, with special attention to dirhams, the most widely distributed category of finds. Its main focus is on finds related to the period of intensive trade between the Islamic world and Scandinavia and the Slavic lands in the 9th and 10th centuries, but attention will be also given to earlier and later periods, until the Mongol invasion in mid-13th century that transformed the geopolitics of northern and eastern Europe. In terms of geography, most finds come from an area that broadly coincides with the zones of Scandinavian and Slavic settlement around the Baltic Sea and in Rus, and extends eastward to the Ural Mountains.

Such a survey raises methodological problems. The distribution of known dirham hoards, for instance, does not directly reflect their circulation in the medieval period, but rather the patterns of hoarding and recovery during and after the Viking Age as well as the intensity of modern agriculture and development which has been responsible for many of the discoveries of the past two centuries. The unusually high numbers of finds on the Baltic island of Gotland and in the Kama Basin, for instance, may reflect a special regime of hoarding or locally significant reasons for non-recovery of hoards rather than the prominence of these regions within trading systems. In both cases, the absence of written sources makes interpretation dependant on social contexts reconstructed from the archaeological material.

Historical Background

Apart from the so far unsuccessful attempts to find evidence for religious interest in Islam in the north, the impact of contacts with the Islamic world on the peoples of northern Europe has rarely been discussed. And yet trade between the Islamic world and the north in the 9th and 10th centuries coincided with a deep transformation of the political landscape in northern Europe. Its final outcome, the emergence of state structures which, by the year 1000, controlled the major part of the region, is likely to have been influenced by the importation and availability of vast quantities of Islamic coins that came to constitute a convenient marker of status and repository of wealth for northern societies.

The political organization of the Slavic lands at the beginning of the 9th century, when the first dirhams were imported to Rus, is unclear: the "tribes", usually thought to have been its basic unit, appear to have been unstable, and much of the region was probably sparsely populated. In the traditional view, the "tribes" gradually consolidated into larger political units that, under the influence of Western and Byzantine models of kingship, morphed at the end of the 10th century into such states as Rus, Poland, or Bohemia (Berend et al. 2013: 52–137). This perspective, however, does not sufficiently take into account the dynamic social and political changes reflected in the proliferation of fortified centers in the course of the 9th and 10th centuries and in the dramatic changes in settlement patterns and the depopulation of vast swathes of the Slavic lands. In the absence of earlier significant trade networks, it appears that Islamic silver, often found in the vicinity of the emerging political centers, provided the local elites with sufficient wealth to invest in military followings, which in turn enabled them to control, concentrate, and possibly enslave the surrounding populations. The adoption of Christianity by the leaders of such followings—Czech dukes at the end of the 9th century, Olga of Kiev in 946 or 957, Mieszko of Poland in 966, and Vladimir of Rus in 988—legitimized the newly formed polities and defined the map of central and eastern Europe for the centuries to come. The process was less dynamic in those parts of Scandinavia directly exposed to the inflow of the dirhams: silver encouraged the consolidation of power in the central Swedish region of Uppland, but broad access to it seems rather to have prevented the emergence of elites in other regions, for instance in Gotland.

Trade with the Islamic world depended also on the situation on the Pontic and Caspian steppe. Security and political unity provided by nomadic "empires" were not, however, prerequisites to trade across the steppe: the two most detailed accounts, of Ahmad ibn Fadlan (in 922) and Abu Hamid al-Gharnati (in the mid-12th century), show intensive short- and long-distance trade in the context of political fragmentation.

BEFORE ISLAM

Contacts between the forest zone in northern Europe and the Near East and Central Asia predate the emergence of Islam. In the late Sasanian period (4th–6th centuries), Sassanian, Byzantine, and Sogdian silverware found its way to the basin of the river Kama in the eastern part of European Russia. Around one hundred fifty vessels from some seventy findspots were known before the advent of metal detectors (Figure 3.6.1). These have primarily been studied from an art historical perspective (e.g., Cruikshank Dodd 1961; Marshak 1986, 2017; Trever and Lukonin 1987; see also Smirnov 1909) rather than for their archaeological or historical context. Vessels of different provenances are frequently found within the same hoards, which makes it likely that they were imported together to the forest zone. Property marks on the vessels in middle Persian, Sogdian, and Khorezmian suggest that they journeyed through Central Asia, whereas a cluster of finds around and to the south of the modern town of Ufa, roughly midway between Khorezm and the Kama Basin, signposts the crossing of the steppe. Silverware is absent from the area of the future Volga Bulgaria on the Lower Kama: its emergence as a major trade hub between the Near East, Central Asia, and the North therefore dates to a later time (cf. Morozov 1996).

A group of finds from Bartym (Perm Krai, Russia) sheds some light on the mechanisms of the importation of the silverware (Goldina et al. 2013). Seven Byzantine, Sasanian, and Khorezmian silver vessels were found in seven separate finds in two clusters. One of the vessels, a Byzantine bowl, contained 272 little circulated hexagrams of

Heraclius dated to 615–625; another Byzantine dish belonged at some point, according to a Sogdian inscription, to "the lord of Bukhara Dazoy"; whereas three Khorezmian bowls are inscribed with dates in the second half of the 7th century. Taken together, this material suggests importation from Central Asia in the course of the 7th century, which is consistent with the chronology of the settlement of the Nevolino culture in which they were found. The same site yielded numerous beads which—especially those made of carnelian—are likely to have been imported from Sasanian Iran. It is tempting to relate these finds with the fur trade, but the precise context of their appearance in the Kama Basin, as well as the role played by the Turkic or Khazar Khaganates, the dominant powers on the Eurasian steppe, in facilitating the exchanges remain unclear (Noonan 1982 (with a confusion between the Turks and the Khazars); de la Vaissière 2000). Given that the majority of Byzantine vessels date from before 630 CE, they may have constituted Persian loot or perhaps Byzantine diplomatic gifts for the Turks during the "last great war of antiquity"; that is, the last conflict between Byzantium and Persia (602–628).

Apart from the exceptional find of Byzantine hexagrams from Bartym, few coins accompanied the silver vessels to the basin of the Kama: a recent survey mentions finds of several Sogdian and a dozen Khorezmian pre-Islamic coins (Naymark 2015). Such coins, unknown from the Baltic area, must have been imported before the beginning of the inflow of dirhams to northern Europe in the early 9th century. By contrast, the approximately 200 Sasanian silver coins known from the Kama Basin (Morozov 1996: 150) were probably brought together with the dirhams: a dozen of hoards shows that contacts between the Kama Basin and the Islamic world continued into the 9th and 10th centuries.

The Islamic conquest of Central Asia in the first half of the 8th century and the disorders accompanying the "Abbasid revolution" probably disrupted the communications with the steppe and the forest zones further to the north. They seem to have been reestablished in the early Abbasid era, judging from the large numbers of Sogdian silverware dated to the second half of the 8th century or the first half of the 9th century and found in the Kama Basin, in similar locations as the earlier silverplate.

TRADE IN THE 9TH AND 10TH CENTURIES

The situation in the Kama Basin—abundant silverware and few coins—contrasts with that further to the west, in Rus and in the Baltic area, where hundreds of thousands of Islamic and Sasanian coins, but very few other objects of near Eastern or Central Asian provenance, have been found (Figure 3.6.1). Although the dirham hoards of northern and eastern Europe contain many Sasanian, Umayyad, and early Abbasid coins, there is no indication that their importation began before about 800 CE. The presence of these early coins rather reflects the monetary stock in circulation in the Caliphate in the early 9th century.

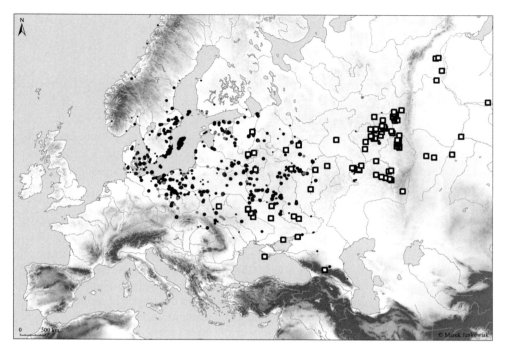

FIGURE 3.6.1 Finds of silverware of near eastern and central Asian provenance (7th-13th centuries, squares) and of dirham hoards (9th–10th centuries, circles) in northern Europe. Gray circles represent hoards of unknown size.

Contacts between the Scandinavians and the Islamic world were initially mediated by the Khazars, who controlled the steppe between the Black and the Caspian Seas from the second half of the 7th century. Glass beads, probably of Islamic origin, were imported to the northern periphery of the Khazar Khaganate in the 8th century (Callmer 2000: 59–73). Their appearance may indicate the extension to that area of Khazar commercial or tributary networks supplying the Islamic world in furs. It is likely that furs were initially the main commodity supplied by the Scandinavians, but the presence of Saqaliba (i.e., Slavic) slaves in the Islamic world from the early 9th century indicates that captives quickly became an important object of trade (Mishin 2002 on the Saqaliba in the Islamic world; Ayalon 1999: 349–352, on the term "Saqaliba").

Arab geographers of the 9th and 10th centuries confirm this impression: they describe the trade between the Scandinavians and the Muslims as exchanges of slaves and furs against dirhams and beads. Ibn Rustah, who wrote around 900 CE, is perhaps the most explicit:

> The Rus... raid the Saqaliba, sailing in their ships until they come upon them, take them captive and sell them in Khazaria and in Bulgar. They have no cultivated fields and they live by pillaging the land of the Saqaliba.... They earn their living by trading in sable, grey squirrel and other furs. They sell them for silver coins which they

set in belts and wear round their waists.... they treat their slaves well and dress them suitably, because for them they are an article of trade.

(Ibn Rustah, in Lunde and Stone 2012: 126)

The central role of the markets of Bulgar on the Volga in the 10th century is confirmed by the famous account of Ahmad ibn Fadlan who, in 922, visited Bulgar on a diplomatic mission from the Abbasid court. His report, rich in ethnographic observations on the steppe nomads, the Volga Bulgars, and the Rus, offers a unique insight into the mechanisms of trade and is consistent with the information provided by such geographers as al-Mas'udi or Ibn Hawqal. Ibn Fadlan witnessed the arrival of a group of Rus warrior-merchants with "beautiful slave girls for sale":

I saw the Rus, who had come for trade and camped by the river Itil [modern Volga].... With them, there are beautiful slave girls, for sale to the merchants.... As soon as their boats arrive at this port, each of them disembarks... and prostrates himself before the great idol, saying to it: "Oh my lord, I have come from a far country and I have with me such and such number of young slave girls, and such and such a number of sable skins... I would like you to do the favour of sending me a merchant who has large quantities of dinars and dirhams and who will buy everything that I want and not argue with me over my price."

(Ibn Fadlan, in Lunde and Stone 2012: 45–48; on this account, see Shepard and Treadwell forthcoming).

Ibn Fadlan also mentions the role of beads in this trade. Even if we do not need to take at face value his remark that one necklace of beads symbolized the wealth of 10,000 dirhams, his account emphasizes the important role that Islamic objects played in displaying status in Scandinavian society.

The quantity of dirham finds from northern Europe makes it possible to reconstruct in some detail the chronology and geography of the trade between the Scandinavians and the Islamic world (Jankowiak 2020). The inflow of dirhams to the North falls broadly into two periods, circa 800–875 and circa 900–980. They are separated by a period of lower activity in the last quarter of the 9th century.

In the first phase, dirhams, mostly minted in Iraq and northern Iran, flowed northward via Khazaria. A particularly high number of hoards with *termini post quem* (or *tpq*; i.e., dates of their latest coins, equivalent to the earliest possible date of their concealment) in the 860s and early 870s indicates intensive trading in this period. It was interrupted around 875, probably because of a lower demand for slaves from the Abbasid court and the collapse of the Scandinavian settlement in Rus (Zuckerman 2000). Dirhams are virtually absent from Rus in the following quarter-century, but finds from Sweden and Poland indicate that Baltic Scandinavians were able to maintain contacts with Khazaria by roundabout routes by-passing Rus. The hoard from Bertby (Åland Islands, *tpq* 890) shows that such contacts could be direct: it is the only known Baltic hoard with long series of die-identical coins, all of which seem to belong to Khazar imitative coinage (coins listed in Granberg 1966: 50–122; die analysis in Rispling et al.

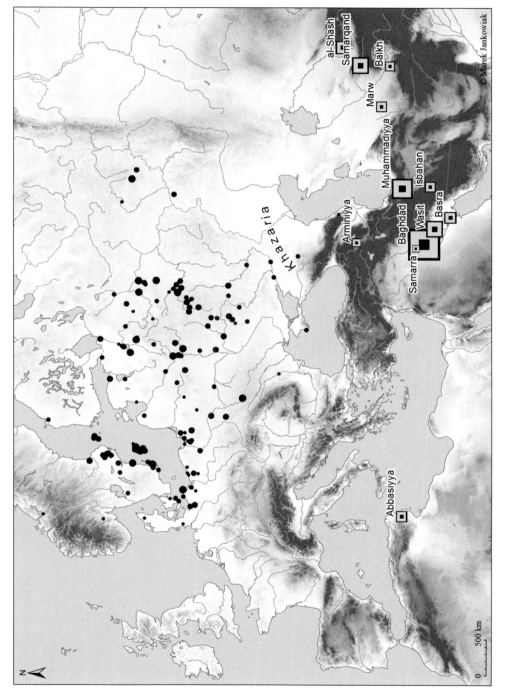

FIGURE 3.6.2 Trade in the 9th century. Circles represent hoards of dirhams and squares the main Islamic mints represented in the North.

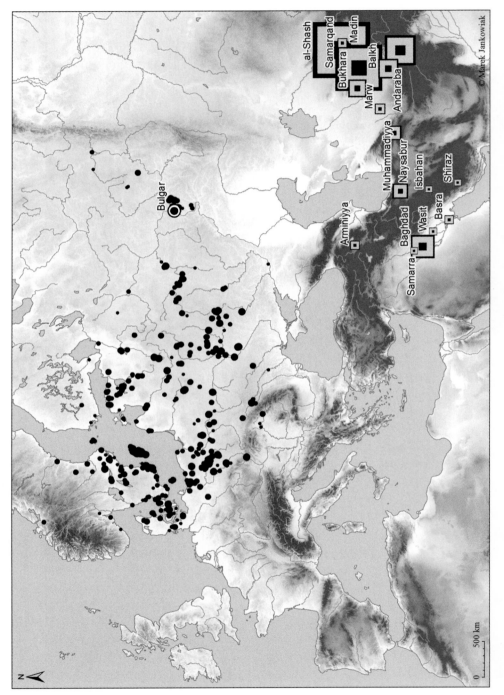

FIGURE 3.6.3 Trade in the 10th century. Circles represent hoards of dirhams and squares the main Islamic mints represented in the North.

forthcoming). Interestingly, this is also one of the rare northern hoards found in a vessel of Islamic origin or at least inspiration (see later discussion).

Trade was reinvigorated after the Samanid emir Isma'il b. Ahmad had started a mass production of dirhams in such Central Asian mints as Samarqand and al-Shash (modern Tashkent) in 893. Contacts with the North were initially still mediated by the Khazars, but around 910 a major reorientation took place with the emergence of the market of Bulgar on the Volga. Conveniently situated at the confluence of the Volga and the Kama, it replaced the markets of Khazaria as the main meeting point of Scandinavian and Muslim merchants, probably as a result of a massacre of the Rus by Muslim mercenaries of the Khazars, known from a description by al-Mas'udi (Lunde and Stone 2012: 144–146). Exchanges culminated between 920 and 950, when, judging from the distribution of the hoards, most of Scandinavia and the Slavic lands had access to dirhams. The decline began in the 950s, perhaps because of the deterioration of Samanid coinage. The inflow of dirhams to Sweden ceased about 955, but Rus and Poland had access to Islamic coins for another quarter of a century. The quantities of dirhams reaching eastern Europe after approximately 980 were very small, and the latest coins date from 1013, after which date trade between Scandinavia and Rus came to a complete halt. Its demise seems to have been caused, among other factors, by the lower availability of silver in Central Asia (the "silver crisis"; see, e.g., Noonan 1987–1991) and the disintegration of the Samanid emirate around the year 1000.

While dirhams found in northern Europe were minted almost without exception in the Near East and Central Asia, written sources attest to the existence of a lively system of trade between the western part of the Islamic world and northern Europe. Saqaliba slaves were present in large numbers in Muslim Spain, where slave soldiers of Slavic origins were one of the main pillars of Umayyad rule in the 10th century (Meouak 2004). It is likely that they were mostly brought from Prague, where an active slave market is attested in the 10th century (Třeštík 2001). The precise mechanisms of this trade remain unclear, however, as virtually no Spanish coins or objects of Andalusian provenance were found in northern Europe. A possible reason for this is that trade between central Europe and al-Andalus was mediated by merchants of other origins, no doubt mostly by Jewish trading communities frequently mentioned in the sources (Jankowiak forthcoming).

Dirham Hoards

More than 1,500 hoards containing approximately 350–400,000 dirhams are known from northern Europe and Rus (Kovalev and Kaelin 2007; Jankowiak 2020). This represents only a fraction of the original inflow, which can consequently be estimated at millions, if not tens of millions, of coins. These high figures of silver coins contrast with an almost total absence of copper or gold coins, of which only several dozens of specimens are known (Noonan 1974). Thanks to their sheer quantity and our ability to precisely date them (as opposed to western European or Byzantine coins), dirhams provide a uniquely detailed insight into the chronology, geography, and mechanisms of the trade between Muslim and Scandinavian merchants. Elemental and isotopic analysis also allows us to identify precious metals from the Islamic world that were used to create local coins or objects (e.g., Merkel 2016).

The abundance of dirham finds from northern Europe is, however, a mixed blessing because of the difficulty of publishing and processing such vast material. The most recent comprehensive catalogue of dirham hoards is—as in the case of the silverware—more than one century old (Markov 1910). A new catalogue has been compiled by Thomas Noonan, but his death in 2001 delayed its publication. In the meantime, the main sources for the study of dirham hoards are the articles of Noonan (listed in Kovalev 2001) and Roman Kovalev (e.g., Kovalev and Kaelin 2007), several recent listings of hoards (Brather 1995–1996; Adamczyk 2014; Kuleshov and Gomzin 2017), and comprehensive catalogues available for some countries (Bogucki et al. 2013–17 for Poland; Leimus 2007 for Estonia). Less detailed summaries exist for Norway (Skaare 1976), Denmark (Skovmand 1942; von Heijne 2004), Finland (Talvio 2002), and Belarus (Riabtsevich 2006–2008). The material from the two countries with the highest number of finds is particularly difficult to access: only around a quarter of Swedish material has been published (Malmer et al. 1975–2010), whereas finds from Russia, especially those discovered in the past half-century, are scattered in a variety of publications (for earlier finds, see Kropotkin 1971).

Dirham hoards are primarily found around the Baltic Sea and along the rivers of Russia, Ukraine, and Belarus (Figure 3.6.1). The most prominent cluster is located on the island of Gotland, where more than 500 Viking Age finds of silver have been recorded, of which around 350 contained dirhams (Gruszczyński 2019). Many dirham finds come also from other Baltic islands—Öland, Bornholm (an example of a successful cooperation with metal detectorists; see Ingvardson and Nielsen 2015), Saaremaa, and the Åland Islands—as well as from the southern coast of the Baltic (Polish and German Pomerania). It may seem surprising that, despite the political significance of mainland Sweden, Denmark, and Kievan Rus in this period, fewer hoards come from these areas. One reason may be that the centralized states that formed in the second half of the 10th century were able to bring the hoarded wealth back into circulation, whereas the lack of central control favored the accumulation, deposition, and non-retrieval of hoards. The exception is Greater Poland, where the cataclysmic collapse of the first Polish state in the 1030s and the dispersal of its elites prevented the recovery of buried wealth. In Rus, the most prominent clusters of hoards are found along the Oka river, in the watersheds between the major river systems in the areas of Kursk and Gnezdovo, in northern Rus (the region of Novgorod and Staraia Ladoga), and in Volga Bulgaria. From this core zone of dirham hoarding, Islamic coins and metal were redistributed further to the west—to Norway, the southern coasts of the North Sea, and the British Isles—where they survive in small numbers, but where their trace can be detected in locally produced silver ornaments and coins (Merkel 2016: 91–114).

The hoards are found in a variety of archaeological contexts. Due to the density of finds, evidence from Gotland is of particular importance: it seems—although this is debated—that hoards were mostly concealed within farmsteads, and that relatively few come from marginal areas such as moors (Östergren 1989; essays in Gruszczyński et al. 2020). In Greater Poland, many hoards were found within several hundred meters from fortified sites (Andrałojć et al. 2011), which perhaps points to a connection with the dwellings of the elite. It is, however, not uncommon to find hoards near by rivers, which signals the role of waterways in the circulation of dirhams. Most hoards for which we have information on their containers were stored in recipients usually made of clay, more rarely of metal or organic material.

The sheer scale of hoarding in the North raises the question of why were dirhams in such demand from the Scandinavians and Slavs. The extent to which they played a monetary role in the North is debated, and there is much regional variation (Metcalf 1997; Graham-Campbell and Williams 2007; Graham-Campbell et al. 2011; Kershaw and Williams 2019). Whether fragmentation can be taken to be a sign of monetary circulation is similarly controversial (Hårdh 1996; Jankowiak 2019). Dirhams were used as pendants and ornaments or were melted down and reshaped into other objects such as ingots or jewelry (Audy 2018). The variety of uses of Islamic silver in northern Europe is illustrated by one of the largest known hoards of the Viking Age, found in 1999 in Spillings (Gotland, *tpq* 870). Three deposits buried close to each other contained in total 67 kilogram of silver and 20 kilogram of bronze; the silver part included over 14,000 dirhams weighing 17 kilogram, almost 500 bangles and bracelets, 25 finger rings, 80 bars, and large quantities of other fragmented silver objects (Östergren 2009). The presence of the original dirhams, their fragments, their Khazar imitations, and of various whole and fragmented locally produced silver objects shows silver in its roles as a depository of value, means of exchange, and instrument of display that it assumed in the North.

OTHER FINDS

It is striking that, despite its intensity, trade between the Scandinavians and the Islamic world did not result in a more diverse range of goods imported to the North. In comparison with the dirhams, other objects of Islamic origin are remarkably rare.

Beads are the second most commonly found objects in the northern hoards (Callmer 1977, 1997; for a sample from a Scandinavian trading-place, see Resi 2011). Many, especially those made of rock-crystal, carnelian, and millefiori and green glass, are likely to be of Islamic origin, but their precise provenance remains speculative. A bead from Wolin, for instance, despite an ornament reminiscent of Arabic script, is likely to have been produced in northern Europe (Kokora 2016). Middle Eastern origin (e.g., Persian Gulf or Red Sea) is more secure for beads made of cowrie shells, but apart from a group of burials in Gotland they are rare. The shells themselves are almost absent from the material dated to the Viking Age (Jansson 1988: 589–592 and 635–636).

Textiles are another candidate for large-scale importation from the Islamic world. Byzantine or Islamic textiles are often mentioned in written sources, but archaeological remains are difficult to provenance. This regards in the first place, silk which could have been imported from Byzantium, the Near East, or Central Asia (there is little evidence for contacts with China in the Viking Age). The most abundant finds in Scandinavia come from Birka and the boat burial of Oseberg (Norway) dated to about 840 (Jansson 1988: 593–539; Vedeler 2014). Scraps of silk textiles are relatively common also elsewhere, from Dublin (Wallace 2016: 272–276) to Bohemia (Profantová 2009: 591), but how many of them are of Islamic or Byzantine origin is not known. Finds of unworked threads (Dublin, see Wallace 2016: 272) or even of cocoons of silkworms (Poznań, see Moldenhawer 1960) suggest that some silk textiles may have been produced locally of imported raw material. The provenance of other potentially imported textiles such as fine woolen fabrics or fabrics with gold or silver threads is even less certain.

Other objects of Islamic provenance are found only very rarely in the area of dirham hoarding. Finger rings with stones (or only the stones) engraved in Arabic have been found in Birka in Sweden, Timerevo and Staraia Ladoga in Rus, and Tankeevka in Volga Bulgaria; the inclusion of precious stones or of glass suggests an Islamic provenance also for two other rings from Birka and a lost silver ring with an emerald from Kashira (Moscow oblast': Darkevich 1976, no. 92; Jansson 1988: 578–579 and 632; Duczko 1998: 111; Kirpichnikov 2009: 342–343; Wärmländer et al. 2015). Bronze vessels are known from various contexts from Sweden and Rus. Bottle-shaped jugs have been found in rich burials in Klinta (Öland: Petersson 1958) and Aska (Östergötland: Arne 1932). Bottles from Bertby (Åland Islands: Arne 1932: 101–102), Fölhagen (Gotland: Arne 1932: 103), and Tatarskii Tolkysh (Volga Bulgaria: Darkevich 1976, no. 91a) contained hoards of dirhams with *tpq*s of 890, 971, and 984 CE respectively. The bottle from a 10th-century grave in Tuna (Uppland) was cut into halves and made into a cooking vessel (Odencrants 1934). A bronze jar was found during excavations of a medieval residential neighborhood in Novgorod (Darkevich 1976, no. 96); another jar, from the region of Velikie Luki (Pskov oblast'), has the unique form of a female head—which may, however, point toward a non-Islamic (e.g., Byzantine) provenance (Darkevich 1976, no. 97). A bronze bucket comes from the 10th- and 11th-century Liadinskii burial ground (Tambov oblast': Darkevich 1976, no. 93). A richly ornamented bronze dish is known from Toropets (Tver oblast': Darkevich 1976, no. 98); several fragments are known from Fånö (Uppland, Jansson 1988: 646).

Other bronze objects are extremely rare. Bronze or silver belt strappings and copper weights that occasionally carry Arabic or pseudo-Arabic inscriptions (e.g., Darkevich 1976, nos. 94 and 104; Jansson 1988: 607–614) should probably not be seen as imports; they are more likely to have been inspired by Islamic prototypes and produced in the steppe or in the North. Such inspirations may have been transmitted by Muslim craftsmen, as perhaps suggested by the find of a mould for belt strappings from Kiev inscribed "turk" in Arabic (Ivakin 2000: 236, fig. 8). Similarly, the balances used by Scandinavian merchants are thought to replicate Islamic models (see, e.g., Kilger 2008: 298–321). The Islamic origin of a lamp in the shape of a female head found in Gnezdovo is suggested by a small inlaid turquoise (Darkevich 1976, no. 99). A possible fragment of another lamp was found with three pairs of tongs and an incense burner in Åbyn (Gästrikland). The incense burner—a square object with a dome, resting on four animal legs with hoofs, with a long protruding handle—is thought to be of Khorasanian origin and has been tentatively dated to the 9th century (Ådahl 1990). Finally, a small figurine of Buddha, 8.4 centimeters high, was found in Helgö (Uppland), a major trading post in the early Viking Age. How it arrived in Helgö from the Swat Valley in Pakistan, where it is thought to have been produced in the 6th century, is unknown (Gyllensvärd 2004).

With the exception of the Helgö Buddha, the Islamic provenance of these objects is indicated by Kufic inscriptions, the presence of precious stones, and typological similarities. The bottles from Klinta and Tatarskii Tolkysh, as well as from Aska and Bertby, and the dishes from Toropets and Fånö form pairs of very similar objects. It is likely that most of them came from Central Asia in the 9th and 10th centuries. Some may, however, have been produced in the intermediary zone between the Islamic world and the northern forests: the ornaments on the jars from Aska and Bertby, for instance, can be interpreted as garbled Arabic inscriptions (Arne 1932: 74–75 and 102); in conjunction with the high number of dirham imitations of probably Khazar origin contained in the vessel from Bertby this raises the possibility that the vessels themselves were also manufactured in Khazaria.

The near-total absence of silver vessels in the dirham hoarding area strongly contrasts with their numbers in the Kama Basin. Only small fragments are known from Swedish hacksilver hoards; their late dates—none is earlier than the second half of the 10th century (Jansson 1988: 646–647)—suggest that they were imported from Rus to Scandinavia together with other cut silver objects after the importation of the dirhams had declined. The absence of complete silver vessels may indicate a selection bias of the Scandinavians, who seem to have been interested primarily in standardized silver objects (i.e., dirhams). The hoard from Iagoshur (*tpq* 842) in the Kama Basin, found in a silver Sogdian jug, as well as finds of Islamic silverplate from the same area—and as far north as the Arctic Circle (Iarkov and Pertsev 2018)—show, however, that vessels were still exported from Central Asia in the 9th and 10th centuries.

Finds of Islamic pottery from the Viking Age are very rare. Three very similar glazed cups come from Hemse (Gotland), Sigulda (Latvia), and the region of Suzdal' (Russia); their shapes echo those of silver cups found in the Kama Basin and attributed to Sogdian workshops of the 8th and 9th centuries (Arne 1938; Ģinters 1937; cf. Darkevich 1976, tab. 16–17). A fragment of an unglazed jar of a possibly Caucasian provenance was found in a burial in Gnezdovo (Koval 2010: 139–140). Among the glazed sherds recovered from the excavations in Novgorod, only three came from layers dated to the 10th century and nine from those of the 11th century; such finds are equally rare in the rest of Rus (Koval 2006, 2010: 186–187). No white glazed dishes characteristic for the Samanid urban centers are known from northern Europe.

Finds of glassware of possible Islamic origin are similarly rare. Among the few finds, the cylindrical translucent and partly painted glass cup from grave 542 in Birka stands out as probably the only fully preserved glass vessel; on the basis of analogies it has been attributed a Near Eastern provenance. Fragments of six glass vessels, at least two of them of Islamic origin, have been recovered from tomb 14 at Barkarby (Uppland; Lamm 1941); other possible fragments turned up in a grave from Halla (Gotland; Thunmark-Nylen 2006: 356).

Finally, traces of animals and plants native to the areas within the Islamic world have been recorded in northern Europe. Bones of camels are frequently found in Volga Bulgaria; some examples are also known from Rus, including Kiev (Kropotkin 1973). A gift of a camel by the Polish duke Mieszko I to the German king Otto III in 986 is mentioned in the chronicles (Thietmar 2001: 156). Walnuts were found in the boat burial of Oseberg (Norway), in Hedeby, and in Dublin (Winroth 2012: 78; Wallace 2016: 200 and 365); spices, such as the ones listed by Ibrahim b. Ya'qub in his report from Mainz—"pepper, ginger, cloves, nard, costus and galingale" (Lunde and Stone 2012: 163)—were also imported from the Islamic world.

Trade between northern Europe and the Islamic world in the 9th and 10th centuries was certainly more complex than a simple exchange of dirhams for slaves. But not significantly more complex. The few objects of Islamic provenance other than dirhams and beads found in Scandinavia and Rus look more like souvenirs than objects of trade. Despite the large volume of exchanges, Scandinavian–Islamic trade was rather limited in scope—or at least this is the picture that emerges from its material remains. This provisional image of northern European–Islamic interactions in the pre-Mongol period is likely to evolve in the future. Provenance studies of coins, glass beads and textiles—which are still at their beginnings (Merkel 2016; Neri et al. 2018)—will no doubt modify it in significant ways and will pose, yet again, the problem of the integration of these new data with the information provided by written sources.

FROM THE 11TH CENTURY TO THE MONGOLS

The end of the dirham trade around the year 1000 did not spell the end of the contacts between northern Europe and the Islamic world. Without the overarching framework of the Scandinavian slave trade, however, the picture becomes more complex. Indirect contacts mediated by Byzantium, the Caucasian kingdoms, and Volga Bulgaria probably played a greater role in the importation of Islamic objects to Rus and the Baltic area than, for instance, pilgrimage and crusades to Palestine. This variety of contacts is reflected in the diversity of finds from Rus: from silver and bronze vessels (Darkevich 1976), to silk (Fekhner 1982) and glazed pottery of Egyptian, Syrian, and Iranian origin (Koval 2006, 2010). Glass and glazed pottery reached also Sweden and the Baltic, albeit in small quantities (Roslund 2011). Various exotica—such as the North African monkey found at Riurikovo Gorodishche and dated by radiocarbon to the late 12th century (Brisbane et al. 2007)—accompanied these flows.

The precise mechanisms of their importation are often unclear: it is difficult, for instance, to explain the abundant finds of cowrie shells, probably imported from the Persian Gulf, in Latvia, Estonia, Ingria, and the Finno-Ugric settlement areas on the Upper and Middle Volga. They were particularly popular in Latvia, where they are found in most female burials from the 12th and 13th centuries, but very few specimens are known from Rus or Scandinavia (Mugurevich 1965: 54–59; Johansson 1995). What remains, however, beyond doubt is the role of Muslim trading communities on the steppe. The vivid description of Abu Hamid al-Gharnati (Lunde and Stone 2012: 61–92), who toured Volga Bulgaria, the Pontic steppe, and Hungary in the mid-12th century, attests to a lively trade in furs, honey, slaves, swords, mammoth tusks, and other wares conducted by Muslim merchants. Their communities, according to al-Gharnati mostly of Maghribi origin, may have looked like the Muslim settlement excavated in Hajdúböszörmény in Hungary (Antalóczy 1980). This state of affairs was upset by the Mongol invasions, which mark a watershed in long-distance connections between northern Europe and the Islamic world.

REFERENCES

Ådahl, K. 1990. "An Early Islamic Incense Burner of Bronze in a Swedish Collection," in Gh. Gnoli and A. Panaino (eds.), *Proceedings of the First European Conference of Iranian Studies* (Rome: Instituto Italiano per il Medio ed Estremo Oriente), vol. 2, 333–345.

Adamczyk, D. 2014. *Silber und Macht. Fernhandel, Tribute und die piastische Herrschaftsbildung in nordosteuropäischer Perspektive (800–1100)* (Wiesbaden: Harrassowitz).

Andrałojć, M., Andrałojć, M., Silska, P., and Szyngiera, P. 2011. *Odkrycia skarbów wczesnośredniowiecznych z terenu Wielkopolski. Kontekst archeologiczny znalezisk* (Poznań: Wydawnictwo Poznańskie).

Antalóczy I. 1980. "A nyíri izmaeliták központja, Böszörmény falu régészeti leletei I," *Hajdúsági Múzeum Évkönyve*, 4, 131–170.

Arne, T. J. 1914. *La Suède et l'Orient* (Uppsala: K.W. Appelbergs Boktryckerei).

Arne, T. J. 1932. "Ein bemerkenswerter Fund in Östergötland," *Acta Archaeologica*, 3, 67–112.

Arne, T. J. 1938. "En sino-iransk kopp," *Fornvännen*, 33, 107–113.

Audy, F. 2018. *Suspended Value: Using Coins as Pendants in Viking-Age Scandinavia (c. AD 800–1140)*, Stockholm Studies in Archaeology 74 (Stockholm: Stockholm Universitet).

Ayalon, D. 1999. *Eunuchs, Caliphs and Sultans: A Study in Power Relationships* (Jerusalem: Magnes Press, Hebrew University).

Berend, N., Urbańczyk, P., and Wiszewski, P. 2013. *Central Europe in the High Middle Ages: Bohemia, Hungary and Poland c.900-c.1300* (Cambridge: Cambridge University Press).

Bogucki, M., Ilisch, P., and Suchodolski, S. (eds.) 2013–17. *Frühmittelalterliche Münzfunde aus Polen. Inventar*, 5 vols. (Warszawa: Institut für Archäologie und Ethnologie der Polnischen Akademie der Wissenschaften).

Brather, S. 1995–1996. "Frühmittelalterliche Dirham-Schatzfunde in Europa. Probleme ihrer wirtschaftsgeschichtlichen Interpretation aus archäologischer Perspektive," *Zeitschrift für Archäologie des Mittelalters*, 23/24, 73–153.

Brisbane, M., Hambleton, E., Maltby, M., and Nosov, E. 2007. "A Monkey's Tale: The Skull of a Macaque Found at Ryurik Gorodishche During Excavations in 2003," *Medieval Archaeology*, 51, 185–191.

Callmer, J. 1977. *Trade Beads and Bead Trade in Scandinavia, ca. 800–1000 A.D.* (Bonn: Habelt).

Callmer, J. 1997. "Beads and Bead Production in Scandinavia and the Baltic Region c. AD 600–1100: A General Outline," in U. von Freeden and A. Wieczorek (eds.), *Perlen. Archäologie, Techniken, Analysen* (Bonn: Habelt), 197–201.

Callmer, J. 2000. "From West to East: The Penetration of Scandinavians into Eastern Europe ca. 500–900," in M. Kazanski, A. Nercessian, and C. Zuckerman (eds.), *Les centres proto-urbains russes entre Scandinavie, Byzance et Orient* (Paris: Lethielleux), 45–94.

Cruikshank Dodd, E. 1961. *Byzantine Silver Stamps* (Washington, DC: Dumbarton Oaks Research Library and Collection).

Darkevich, V. P. 1976. *Khudozhestvennyi metall Vostoka VIII–XIII vv.: proizvedeniia vostochnoi torevtiki na territorii Evropeiskoi chasti SSSR i Zaural'ia* (Moskva: Izdatel'stvo "Nauka").

de la Vaissière, E. 2000. "Les marchands d'Asie centrale dans l'empire khazar," in M. Kazanski, A. Nercessian, and C. Zuckerman (eds.), *Les centres proto-urbains russes entre Scandinavie, Byzance et Orient* (Paris: Lethielleux), 367–378.

Duczko, W. 1998. "Viking Age Scandinavia and Islam: An Archaeologist's View," in E. Piltz (ed.), *Byzantium and Islam in Scandinavia* (Jonsered: P. Åströms Förlag), 107–115.

Fekhner, M. V. 1982. "Shelkovye tkani v srednevekovoi vostochnoi Evrope," *Sovetskaia arkheologiia*, 2, 57–70.

Ģinters, V. 1937. "Siguldas kapukalna ķīniešu trauciņš," *Senatne un māksla*, I, 41–45.

Goldina, R. D., Pastushenko, I. Ju., and Chernykh, E. M. 2013. "The Nevolino Culture in the Context of the 7th-Century East-West Trade: The Finds from Bartym," in C. Zuckerman (ed.), *Constructing the Seventh Century*. Travaux et mémoires, 17 (Paris: Association des amis du Centre d'Histoire et Civilisation de Byzance), 865–930.

Graham-Campbell, J., and Williams, G. (eds.) 2007. *Silver Economy in the Viking Age* (Walnut Creek, CA: Left Coast Press).

Graham-Campbell, J., Sindbæk, S., and Williams, G. (eds.) 2011. *Silver Economies, Monetisation and Society in Scandinavia, AD 800–1100* (Aarhus: Aarhus University Press).

Granberg, B. 1966. *Förteckning över kufiska myntfynd i Finland* (Helsinki: Societas Orientalis Fennica).

Gruszczyński, J. 2019. *Viking Silver, Hoards and Containers: The Archaeological and Historical Context of Viking-Age Silver Coin Deposits in the Baltic c. 800–1050* (London: Routledge).

J. Gruszczyński, M. Jankowiak, and J. Shepard (eds.) 2020. *Viking-Age Trade: Silver, Slaves and Gotland* (London: Routledge).

Gyllensvärd B. 2004. "The Buddha Found at Helgö," in *Excavations at Helgö XVI. Exotic and Sacral Finds from Helgö* (Stockholm: Kungl. Vitterhets historie och antikvitets akademien), 11–27.

Hårdh, B. 1996. *Silver in the Viking Age: A Regional-Economic Study* (Stockholm: Almquist & Wiksell International).

von Heijne, C. 2004. *Särpräglat: Vikingatida och tidigmedeltida myntfynd från Danmark, Skåne, Blekinge och Halland (ca 800–1130)*, Stockholm Studies in Archaeology, 31 (Stockholm: Stockholm Universitet).

Howard-Johnston, J. 2020. "The Fur Trade in the Early Middle Ages," in J. Gruszczyński, M. Jankowiak, and J. Shepard (eds.), *Viking-Age Trade: Silver, Slaves and Gotland* (London: Routledge).

Iarkov, A. P., and Pertsev, N. V. 2018. "Islamskii import na velikom mekhovom puti," *Vestnik Severnogo (Arkticheskogo) Federal'nogo Universiteta. Gumanitarnye i sotsial'nye nauki*, 1, 25–32.

Ingvardson, G., and Sonne Nielsen, F. O. 2015. "100 Viking Age Hoards of Bornholm: Status, Challenges and Perspectives," in L. Larsson, F. Ekengren, B. Helgesson and B. Söderberg (eds.), *Small Things: Wide Horizons. Studies in Honour of Birgitta Hårdh* (Oxford: Archaeopress), 27–34.

Ivakin, G. 2000. "Kiev aux VIIIe-Xe siècles," in M. Kazanski, A. Nercessian, and C. Zuckerman (eds.), *Les centres proto-urbains russes entre Scandinavie, Byzance et Orient* (Paris: Lethielleux), 225–239.

Jansson, I. 1988. "Wikingerzeitlicher orientalischer Import in Skandinavien," *Bericht der Römisch-Germanischen Kommission*, 69, 562–647.

Jankowiak, M. 2019. "Silver Fragmentation: Reinterpreting the Evidence of the Hoards," in J. Kershaw and G. Williams (eds.), *Silver, Butter, Cloth: Monetary and Social Economies in the Viking Age* (Oxford: Oxford University Press), 15–31.

Jankowiak, M. 2020. "Flows of Dirhams and Rhythms of the Slave Trade Between the Islamic World and North-eastern Europe," in J. Gruszczyński, M. Jankowiak, and J. Shepard (eds.), *Viking-Age Trade: Silver, Slaves and Gotland* (London: Routledge).

Jankowiak, M. forthcoming. "Infrastructures and organisation of the early Islamic slave trade with northern Europe", in H. Kennedy and F. Bessard (eds.), *The Early Islamic Economy: Economic integration and social change in the Islamic world system (800–1000)* (Oxford: Oxford University Press).

Johansson, B. M. 1995. "Sub-Fossil Cowry Shells in Northern Europe: Traces of Eastern and Western Contacts with the Orient," in A.-M. Robertsson, T. Hackens, S. Hicks, J. Risberg, and A. Åkerlund (eds.), *Landscapes and Life: Studies in Honour of Urve Miller*. PACT, 50 (Strasbourg: Council of Europe), 347–352.

Kershaw, J., and G. Williams (eds.) 2019. *Silver, Butter, Cloth: Monetary and Social Economies in the Viking Age* (Oxford: Oxford University Press).

Kilger, C. 2008. "Wholeness and Holiness: Counting, Weighing and Valuing Silver in the Early Viking Period," in D. Skre (ed.), *Means of Exchange. Dealing with Silver in the Viking Age* (Aarhus: Aarhus University Press), 253–325.

Kirpichnikov, A. N. 2009. "Istoricheskoe nasledie Staroi Ladogi," in N. A. Makarov, *Arkheologicheskie otkrytiia 1991–2004 gg. Evropeiskaia Rossiia* (Moscow: Institut arkheologii RAN), 333–348.

Kokora, K. 2016. "Paciorek ze szkła ołowiowo-krzemowego znaleziony w Wolinie," *Archeologia Polski*, 61, 171–190.

Koval, V. Y. 2006. "Eastern Pottery from the Excavations at Novgorod," in C. Orton (ed.), *The Pottery from Medieval Novgorod and Its Region* (London: UCL Press), 161–192.

Koval, V. Y. 2010. *Keramika Vostoka na Rusi IX-XVII veka* (Moscow: Nauka).

Kovalev, R. K. 2000–2001. "The Infrastructure of the Northern Part of the "Fur Road" between the Middle Volga and the East During the Middle Ages," *Archivum Eurasiae medii aevi*, 11, 25–64.

Kovalev, R. K. 2001. "Bibliography of Thomas S. Noonan," *Russian History*, 28, 7–28.

Kovalev, R. K., and Kaelin, A. C. 2007. "Circulation of Arab silver in medieval Afro-Eurasia: preliminary observations," *History Compass*, 5, 560–580.

Kropotkin, V. V. 1971. "Novye nakhodki sasanidskikh i kuficheskikh monet v Vostochnoi Evrope," *Numizmatika i epigrafika*, 9, 76–97.

Kropotkin, V. V. 1973. "Karavannye puti v Vostochnoi Evrope," in *Kavkaz i Vostochnaia Evropa v drevnosti* (Moscow: Nauka), 226–230.

Kuleshov, V. S., and Gomzin, A. A. 2017. "Osteuropäische Hortfunde kufischer Münzen," in N. A. Makarov (ed.), *Die Rus im 9.–10. Jahrhundert: ein archäologisches Panorama* (Mainz: Wachholtz, Murmann Publishers), 395–401.

Lamm, C. 1941. *Oriental Glass of Mediaeval Date Found in Sweden and the Early History of Lustre-Painting* (Stockholm: Wahlström & Widstrand).

Leimus, I. 2007. *Sylloge of Islamic Coins. Estonian Public Collections* (Tallinn: Eesti Ajaloomuuseum).

Lunde, P., and Stone, C. 2012. *Ibn Fadlān and the Land of Darkness: Arab Travellers in the Far North* (London: Penguin).

Malmer, B., Jonsson, K., and Lagerqvist, L. O. (eds.) 1975–2010. *Corpus nummorum saeculorum IX-XI qui in Suecia reperti sunt*, 9 vols. (Stockholm: Almqvist & Wiksell International).

Markov, A. K. 1910. *Topografiia kladov vostochnykh monet, sasanidskikh i kuficheskikh* (St. Petersburg: Tipografiia Imperatorskoi Akademii Nauk).

Marshak, B. 1986. *Silberschätze des Orients: Metallkunst des 3.–13. Jahrhunderts und ihre Kontinuität* (Leipzig: E.A. Seemann).

Marshak, B. I. 2017. *Istoriia vostochnoi torevtiki III-XIII vv. i problemy kul'turnoi preemstvennosti* (St. Petersburg: Akademiia issledovaniia kul'tury).

Meouak, M. 2004. *Ṣaqaliba, eunuques et esclaves à la conquête du pouvoir: géographie et histoire des élites politiques "marginales" dans l'Espagne umayyade* (Helsinki: Academia Scientiarum Fennica).

Merkel, S. 2016. *Silver and the Silver Economy at Hedeby* (Bochum: VML Verlag Marie Leidorf).

Metcalf, D. M. 1997. "Viking-Age Numismatics 3: What Happened to Islamic Dirhams After Their Arrival in the Northern Lands?," *The Numismatic Chronicle*, 157, 295–335.

Mikkelsen, E. 2008. "The Vikings and Islam," in S. Brink and N. Price (eds), *The Viking World* (London: Routledge), 543–549.

Mishin, D. E. 2002. *Sakaliba (slaviane) v islamskom mire v rannee srednevekov'e* (Moscow: IV RAN "Kraft+").

Moldenhawer, K. 1960. "Jedwabnictwo w Polsce i innych krajach we wczesnym średniowieczu," *Archeologia Polski*, 5, 111–116.

Morozov, V. I. 1996. "Puti proniknoveniia sasanidskikh monet i khudozhestvennykh izdelii v Povolzh'e i Prikam'e," in D. A. Stashenkov (ed.), *Kul'tury evraziiskikh stepei vtoroi poloviny I tysiacheletiia n.e.* (Samara: Samarskii oblastnoi istoriko-kraevedcheskii muzei im. P.V. Alabina), 148–164.

Mugurevich, E. 1965. *Vostochnaia Latviia i sosednie zemli v X–XIII vv* (Riga: Zinatne).

Naymark, A. 2015. "Zamechaniia o vostochnoevropeiskikh nakhodkakh sogdiiskikh i khorezmskikh monet VI–IX vekov," in *Epokha vikingov v Vostochnoi Evrope v pamiatnikakh numizmatiki VIII–XI vv.* (St. Petersburg: Staroladozhskiy Historical-Architectural and Archaeological Museum-Reserve), 28–33.

Neri, E., Gratuze, B., and Schibille, N. 2018. "The Trade of Glass Beads in Early Medieval Illyricum: Towards an Islamic Monopoly," *Archaeological and Anthropological Sciences*, January 2018. https://doi.org/10.1007/s12520-017-0583-5.

Noonan, T. S. 1974. "Medieval Islamic Copper Coins from European Russia and Surrounding Regions: The Use of the Fals in Early Islamic Trade with Eastern Europe," *Journal of the American Oriental Society*, 94, 448–453.

Noonan, T. S. 1982. "Russia, the Near East, and the Steppe in the Early Medieval Period: An Examination of the Sasanian and Byzantine Finds from the Kama-Urals Area," *Archivum Eurasiae medii aevi*, 2, 269–302.

Noonan, T. S. 1987–1991. "The Onset of the Silver Crisis in Central Asia," *Archivum Eurasiae medii aevi*, 7, 221–248.

Odencrants, R. 1934. "Ett vikingatidsfynd med orientaliskt bronskärl," *Fornvännen*, 29, 144–152.

Östergren, M. 1989. *Mellan stengrund och stenhus: Gotlands vikingatida silverskatter som boplatsindikation* (Stockholm: Stockholm Univ., Phil. Diss).

Östergren, M. 2009. "Spillings: The Largest Viking Age Silver Hoard in the World," in A.-M. Pettersson (ed.), *The Spillings Hoard: Gotland's Role in Viking Age World Trade* (Visby: Gotlands Museum), 11–40.

Petersson, K. G. 1958. "Ett gravfynd från Klinta, Köpings sn, Öland," *Tor*, 4, 134–150.

Profantová, N. 2009. "Byzantine Coins from the 9th–10th Century from the Czech Republic," in M. Wołoszyn (ed.), *Byzantine Coins in Central Europe Between 5th and 10th Century* (Kraków: Polish Academy of Arts and Sciences), 581–598.

Resi, H. G. 2011. "Gemstones: Cornelian, Rock Crystal, Amethyst, Fluorspar and Garnet," in D. Skre (ed.), *Things from the Town: Artefacts and Inhabitants in Viking-Age Kaupang* (Oslo: Aarhus University Press), 143–166.

Riabtsevich V. 2006–2008. "Monetnye depozity zapadnykh zemel' Drevnei Rusi (materialy)," *Światowit*, 7 (48) B, 107–137.

Rispling G., Jankowiak, M., and Treadwell, L. forthcoming. *Catalogue of Dirham Imitations from Northern European Viking-Age Finds.*

Roslund, M. 2011. "Muslimskt Medelhav vid Mälaren. Spår av islamisk handel i det förmoderna Sverige," in A. Andrén (ed.), *Förmodern globalitet: Essäer om rörelse, möten och fjärran ting under 10 000 år* (Lund: Nordic Academic Press), 159–177.

Shepard, J., and Treadwell, W. L. (eds.) forthcoming. *Muslims on the Volga in the Viking Age: Diplomacy and Islam in the world of Ibn Fadlan* (London: I.B. Tauris).

Skaare, K. 1976. *Coins and Coinage in Viking Age Norway* (Oslo: Universitetsforlaget).

Skovmand, R. 1942. "De danske skattefund fra vikingetiden og den ældste middelalder indtil omkring 1150," *Aarbøger for nordisk oldkyndighed og historie*, 1942, 1–275 and I–XIV.

Smirnov, I. I. 1909. *Atlas drevnei serebrianoi i zolotoi posudy vostochnago proiskhozhdeniia naidennoi preimushchestvenno v predelakh Rossiiskoi Imperii* (St. Petersburg: Arkheologicheskaia kommissiia).

Talvio, T. 2002. *Coins and Coin Finds in Finland, AD 800–1200* (Helsinki: Suomen muinaismuistoyhdistys).

Thietmar 2001. *Ottonian Germany: The Chronicon of Thietmar of Merseburg*, trans. D.A. Warner (Manchester: Manchester University Press).

Thunmark-Nylén, L. 2006. *Die Wikingerzeit Gotlands*. vol. III: *Text* (Stockholm: Kungl. Vitterhets Historie och Antikvitets Akademien).

Třeštík, D. 2001. " 'Eine große Stadt der Slawen namens Prag' (Staaten und Sklaven in Mitteleuropa im 10. Jahrhundert)," in P. Sommer (ed.), *Boleslav II. Der tschechische Staat um das Jahr 1000. Colloquia mediaevalia Pragensia 2* (Praha: Centrum medievistických studií), 93–138.

Trever, K. V., and Lukonin, V. G. 1987. *Sasanidskoe serebro: sobranie Gosudarstvennogo Ermitaza; chudozestvennaja kultura Irana III-VIII vekov* (Moscow: Iskusstvo).

Vedeler, M. 2014. *Silk for the Vikings* (Oxford: Oxbow).

Wallace, P. 2016. *Viking Dublin: The Wood Quay Excavations* (Sallins: Irish Academic Press).

Wärmländer, S., Wåhlander, L., Saage, R., Rezakhani, K., and Hamid Hassan, S. 2015. "Analysis and Interpretation of a Unique Arabic Finger Ring from the Viking Age Town of Birka, Sweden," *Scanning*, 37, 2, 131–137.

Winroth, A. 2012. *The Conversion of Scandinavia: Vikings, Merchants, and Missionaries in the Remaking of Northern Europe* (New Haven: Yale University Press).

Zuckerman, C. 2000. "Deux étapes de la formation de l'ancien état russe," in M. Kazanski, A. Nercessian, and C. Zuckerman (eds.), *Les centres proto-urbains russes entre Scandinavie, Byzance et Orient* (Paris: Lethielleux), 95–120.

SECTION IV

SUB-SAHARAN AFRICA

TIMOTHY INSOLL

I⟨T⟩ is unnecessary to repeat or summarize the content of the chapters that follow in this section, but it is worthwhile highlighting some of the research themes that are emerging. First, the importance of archaeology is repeatedly emphasized where historical records are sparse and problematic. Second, the necessity of using a multidisciplinary approach where archaeological research has been limited is clear. It is also apparent that the amount of research completed on Islamic archaeology varies considerably across sub-Saharan Africa from areas that are very well investigated, such as the Eastern African coast, even if the explicit focus there has not always been upon Islam itself; to areas that are comparatively well-investigated, notably the Western Sahel; to those only partially investigated such as the Nilotic Sudan or the Central Sudan and Sahel; to others that have until recently been almost wholly uninvestigated such as Ethiopia and, to a lesser extent, elsewhere in the Horn of Africa. Geographical shifts in research can also be seen necessitated by political circumstances, with the cessation of research in large parts of the Horn of Africa and in the western and central Sahel regions.

A move away from focusing on mapping the presence of Islam to exploring the practice of Islam is also apparent in research. This is significant in thinking about how Islam was indigenized across sub-Saharan Africa and is an area that is particularly amenable to being evaluated archaeologically through, for example, the analysis of dietary remains (West Africa) and, where permissible, burials (Western Sahel and Ethiopia), tombs (Eastern African coast, Nilotic Sudan), or funerary epigraphy (Western Sahel). The themes of syncretism between Islam and indigenous African religions are also increasingly being considered (Western Sahel) or continuity from the pre-Islamic through Islamic periods (Nilotic Sudan). Similarly, how the Islamic past can become the focus of legend, as manifest by the Harla in Ethiopia or Shirazi on the Eastern African coast, is also a subject that is being explored. As well, the interrelationship and impact of Islam between and upon indigenous African systems of authority is being explored from an archaeological perspective (West Africa and Central Sudan and Sahel).

The phasing and patterns of Islamization are also receiving attention through exploring the patterns manifest by archaeological data in the Nilotic Sudan, Ethiopia, and the Western Sahel, for example. In some areas there has been an emphasis in research placed on investigating sectarian affiliation, whether at a broader level, such as that of Sunni or Shi'i (Eastern African Coast) or Ibadi (Western Sahel), or in a more focused form to evaluate if particular Sunni schools of law (*Madhhab*) prevailed from a certain period in particular areas, such as Shafi'i (Eastern African Coast) or Maliki (West Africa). In other areas, the importance of specific aspects of Muslim practice have been the focus of research, as with the prominence given to the archaeology and material culture of Sufism in the Nilotic Sudan, as evident through the exploration of the *khalwa* (religious school) or the importance ascribed Saints (*Awliya*) in the that region.

Commerce and other contacts with the world outside Africa are also being extensively explored archaeologically, from Ottoman contacts with the Nilotic Sudan; or between India, the Gulf, and the Eastern African Coast; or between Al-Andalus and some parts of the Western Sahel; or that of Yemeni contacts with parts of Ethiopia. This is evidence also highlighting the importance of trade as an agent of Islamic conversion and Islamization in, for instance, Ethiopia, the Western Sahel, and on the Eastern African Coast, with inter-African connections emerging as a theme of particular significance. However, this is also accompanied by the important realization that the presence of trade goods from the Islamic world or from Muslim-controlled trade networks is not necessarily indicative of conversion to Islam.

It is also obvious that many gaps in our knowledge of the archaeology of Islam in sub-Saharan Africa remain. There is a general lack of information on rural Islam, as focus has been primarily on urban centers sometimes mentioned in historical sources, usually in Arabic, and sites with more tangible material remains. There is also a severe regional imbalance in understanding, where the relevant archaeology of the Central Sudan and Sahel remains largely unknown, and Islamic archaeology in Ethiopia and the Nilotic Sudan has been seriously neglected while pre-Islamic states and civilizations such as Aksum, Meroe, or Kerma have been extensively investigated.

CHAPTER 4.1

···

EASTERN AFRICAN COAST

···

STEPHANIE WYNNE-JONES
AND JEFFREY FLEISHER

INTRODUCTION

THE archaeology of the eastern African coast over the past 1,500 years is by default the
archaeology of Islam. This region has a long-standing community of believers and a
deep history of entanglement with ideas, objects, and people from Islamic societies
around the Indian Ocean rim (Horton 1987a; Insoll 2003; LaViolette 2008;
Pouwels 1987). The current inhabitants of what is often called the "Swahili Coast" are
today practicing Muslims, living in Somalia, Kenya, Tanzania, Mozambique, and the
Comoros Islands (Horton and Middleton 2000; Wynne-Jones 2016); they trace their
religious roots back hundreds of years, to the first centuries of Islam. Archaeology has
shown they are right to do so, with evidence for Muslim populations from as early as the
8th century CE and an unbroken tradition along the coast since that time.

Yet the study of Islamic society on the eastern African coast is complicated, not
least by a lack of direct research aimed at understanding Islam. In addition, there is
only a very sparse historical record written by outsiders and visitors to the region
whose accounts are decidedly partial (Sutton 2018). This means that evidence for
Islamic life in the deeper Swahili past relies heavily on the testimony of archaeology
and the material record: the potential for an "Islamic archaeology" is immense
(although see Pouwels 1987 for a detailed consideration of east African Islam from a
historical perspective). Nevertheless, only a few scholars have attempted to engage
directly with Islam, primarily focusing on the timing and mode of conversion and
the particular sect of Islam that might be identified. This has been important—even

transformative—work, positioning the eastern African coast firmly within the dar al-Islam from earliest times and dismissing any suggestion that Islam might have been practiced exclusively by immigrant settlers from the Arab world. In this chapter we therefore review briefly this explicitly Islam-focused research and what it has contributed to our knowledge of the coastal past. We then move on to consider how a broader archaeology of Islam might be drawn from more mundane archaeologies of the coast through the objects and practices of daily life among the majority population.

CONVERSION AND PRESENCE

Histories of East African Islam

The presence of Muslims on the eastern African coast can be traced in historical sources from the 10th century onward. These glimpses come via a series of travel accounts and geographies written by Arab visitors since at this time there was no written historical tradition in eastern Africa (Freeman-Grenville 1962). The ways that outsiders refer to coastal populations are varied and opaque, and their accounts are colored by their prejudices against African peoples (compare Insoll 1994 on a similar phenomenon in western Africa). Yet, by 916 CE, al-Masudi writes of a Muslim community at a town called Qanbalu, generally thought to refer to the site of Ras Mkumbuu on Pemba, or to Pemba Island itself (Kirkman 1959). These Muslims were singled out but were definitely identified as part of the "Zanj" population he describes elsewhere. Otherwise his account is mostly restricted to detail on the trade goods and activities of coastal communities who supplied the markets of Oman, China, and India with materials such as ivory, ambergris, and leopard skins. Al-Masudi's account therefore sets up a picture that is reflected across the archaeology of east African Islam; it contains only very slight direct information on Islamic adherence but abundant evidence for the integration of the coast into Indian Ocean networks dominated by Islamic traders from which we might infer knowledge and practice of Islam.

Further detail on east African Muslims does not appear until the 14th century and the account of Ibn Battuta, who describes Muslim towns along the coast at 1331 (Freeman-Grenville 1962: 27–32). Although it is possible that Ibn Battuta did not actually travel to East Africa (Fauvelle-Aymar and Hirsch 2003), he relays stories about Mogadishu, Mombasa, and Kilwa Kisiwani, each of them towns at which a Muslim ruler and majority population were to be found. At the time of his visit, all of these communities were practicing Sunni. Ibn Battuta's account is the richest description of life in Swahili towns prior to the 15th century and describes interactions with notable leaders there. As well as testifying to the presence of Sunni populations at these coastal towns, he provides information on aspects of life that illustrate the role of Islam.

Yet it is from the 16th century, when the Portuguese arrived on the eastern coast of Africa, that the richest historical information pertains (Prestholdt 1998; Vernet 2005). Portuguese chroniclers were responsible for transcribing the indigenous *Kilwa Chronicle* at that time, as well as recording their own observations of coastal society. The *Kilwa Chronicle* found in the Portuguese sources is the earliest source for the "Shirazi" traditions, which are found in indigenous histories from towns along the coast; many other chronicles were documented in the 19th and early 20th centuries, when much of the eastern African coast was under the colonial authority of Germany and then Great Britain (Spear 1984; Pawlowicz and LaViolette 2013). These traditions relate that the towns of the Swahili coast were founded by Persian merchant princes from Shiraz, who sailed along the coast founding seven towns. They probably relate to long-standing connections between the eastern African coast and greater Islamic world and, in particular, to first-millennium connections with merchants from the Persian Gulf (Pouwels 1984). The chronicles might perhaps have some relevance to the movement of Islam to eastern Africa, and thus reflect stories about how Islam and Islamic practice came to be prominent on the coast through interaction with foreign merchants and religious leaders (Pouwels 1984, 1987; Horton and Middleton 2000). The complexity of the Shirazi parts of these chronicles should caution any scholar against seeking to apply them as historical accounts (Saad 1979). For example, the *Kilwa Chronicle* claims that Persian refugees were met by a Muslim already on the island and that a mosque had already been constructed. At the very least, these stories indicate complex and varied local experiences with Islam and foreign travelers (Allen 1993).

Hadrami immigration and links to Yemen developed apace in the 18th century, contributing to the growth and dominance of Shafi'i teachings on the coast, with a powerful center at the Riyadha in Lamu (Bang 2003, 2014). This growth was also understood as a reconnection of family ties in Yemen and Oman, suggesting earlier migrations and existing Shafi'i connections, yet, before the 18th century, they are poorly documented and difficult to see. The 18th and 19th centuries witnessed the expansion of a textual tradition that encompassed the eastern African coast, involving the circulation of Islamic texts, so this phase is better documented. Omani colonialism of the late 17th century onward brought Ibadi Islam to the coast, but this stayed largely with Omani populations and new converts (Martin 1971, 1975; Horton 2013); it became a point of distinction between the newer arrivals and older Shirazi groups who remained Sunni (Prins 1961; Middleton 1992; Glassman 1995).

Identifying Islam Through Archaeology

Most explicitly "Islamic" archaeology on the eastern African coast has focused on locating a Muslim population and identifying the sect to which they might have belonged (see summary in Insoll 2003). The latter is often a proxy for understanding the timing and direction of conversion of African populations by linking to known Shi'ite or Sunni centers in the Persian Gulf and Hadramawt.

For the earliest excavators, whose work comprises the majority of the archaeology done on the coast, Swahili towns were in themselves evidence for Islam. The eastern African coast is dotted with a series of towns known collectively as "stonetowns," but actually built of coral and lime (Figure 4.1.1). The most prominent of these today are Lamu, Zanzibar Old Town, and Mombasa, all of which were important during the 18th and 19th centuries due to Omani colonial settlement. These towns are also the heirs to a much longer tradition of Swahili stonetowns that began in the 11th century, themselves often built on the foundations of first-millennium settlements without stone architecture (LaViolette and Wynne-Jones 2018). This urban tradition is also an Islamic tradition. The standing remains of these past towns evoke parallels with Islamic towns elsewhere around the Indian Ocean and Red Sea; they contain mosques, stone houses, and tombs; and the artifactual record demonstrates a long-standing connection with Islamic trade networks through quantities of imported ceramics, glass, and beads (Horton and Middleton 2000; Wynne-Jones 2016). The presence of Muslims was assumed by the first archaeologists in this region. Indeed, they interpreted these ruins as relating to immigrant traders settling on the coast (Kirkman 1964; Chittick 1975).

Early excavations at Gede (Kirkman 1954) and Kilwa Kisiwani (Chittick 1974) thus set the scene for an Islamic archaeology that sought to trace the chronology and origins of Muslim urbanism on the coast. These works set the agenda for interpreting coastal towns as the ruins of immigrant settlements, but also established some of the priorities for coastal archaeology that continued for many years. Excavations explored the foundations and occupation of the major stone buildings, which at Kilwa included the Great Mosque (Figure 4.1.2) as well as the palace of Husuni Kubwa. Here the *Kilwa Chronicle* provided a guide to the history of the site, and much effort went into reconciling the archaeology of this African settlement with the chronology and the list of rulers found in the *Chronicle* (Chittick 1965; Freeman-Grenville 1957).

At both sites, excavation recovered evidence for a long-standing urban occupation with Indian Ocean connections from at least the 11th century. What distinguished Kilwa from Gede was stratigraphic evidence of occupation extending back to at least the 9th century CE. Chittick carried out two extremely large-scale excavations at Kilwa. Excavations at the Great Mosque served to detail several phases of construction and destruction, including an early prayer hall of the 11th century and a large domed extension during the 14th century. At Husuni Kubwa, excavations recovered a palace structure with associated audience courts and spaces probably constructed for the storage of trade goods and perhaps the conduct of trade.

More recently, one of the most consistent scholarly contributors to the archaeology of Islam on the eastern African coast has been Mark Horton. His research at Shanga transformed the landscape of coastal archaeology conceptually and methodologically (Horton 1987b, 1996). In effect he developed a new Islamic archaeology, exploring the chronology and development of Islamic practice as a component of urban life in context, rather than assuming the population were Islamic by default (Horton 1991). Although his starting assumptions were quite different from his predecessors, his objectives at Shanga mirrored those of other stonetown excavations and the

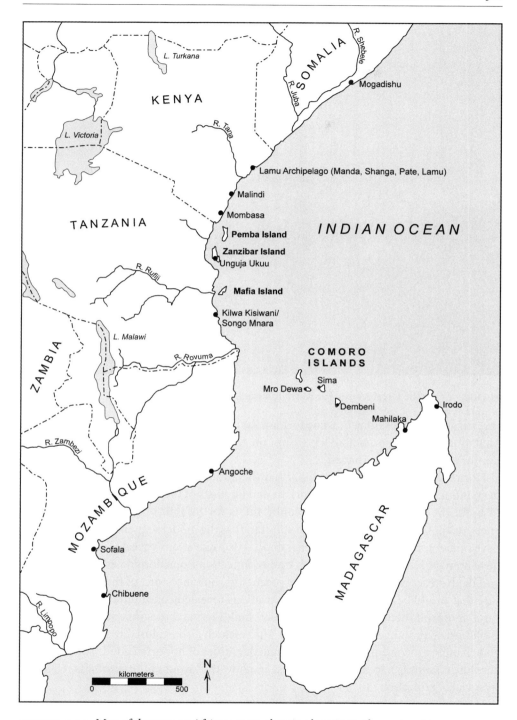

FIGURE 4.1.1 Map of the eastern African coast, showing locations of prominent towns.

FIGURE 4.1.2 The Great Mosque at Kilwa Kisiwani.

investigation of the Friday mosque formed the core of the work. Yet this was accompanied by a broader approach to life within the town and the investigation of less grand houses as well as public spaces.

Horton began with an assumption that the Swahili had indigenous roots—he had been influenced by research by historians and linguists of the time who were beginning to build the argument against a colonial thesis for Swahili origins (e.g., Nurse and Spear 1984; Allen 1993). This research still stands as the model sequence by which urban development along the coast is understood. His excavations revealed the indigenous development of a coastal village with trade connections, one dominated by early wattle and daub structures that were not just precursors, but ancestors, of the stone architecture that would be constructed later. Excavations revealed continuities in the architectural footprint between earlier and later buildings and documented the gradual evolution of an indigenous architecture. The research also explored the town's ongoing and changing involvement in trade through quantities of imported goods (calculated in absolute quantities), local craft practices, and how the layout of the town was related to its social organization.

Horton's excavations in and below the Friday mosque at Shanga likewise changed our understanding of the history of coastal Islam. Beneath the standing ruins of the 14th-century Friday mosque, Horton documented a series of earlier mosques dating back to the mid-8th century CE, giving evidence for the presence of Muslims in the earliest coastal communities. This mosque is discussed in more detail later.

Sectarian Distinctions

A range of sources, including historical documents and features of mosque architecture, have been used to explore possible sectarian distinctions among early east African Islamic communities, including Shi'a, Ibadi, and Sunni/Shafi'i. Horton has offered a number of arguments about the earliest Islamic communities in east Africa and their sectarian distinctions. During the late first and early second millennium, he identifies architectural features that might indicate Ibadi communities. These may be linked to the first Imamate situated in Oman (750–790 CE; Horton 2013; Horton and Middleton 2000: 64–7). Ibadis, Horton (2017: 255) argues, built modest mosques with "shallow mihrabs, lacking minarets and minbars" that resonated with their "austere egalitarian ethos." Such *mihrabs*, which are set into a double-thickness *qibla* wall (rather than extending to the exterior) can be found in mosques at Ras Mkumbuu and Chwaka on Pemba during the 11th century and at a contemporary mosque on Sanje ya Kati near Kilwa. A final example is on a side aisle constructed at Tumbatu mosque in the 13th century, possibly—argues Horton—to cater to Ibadi refugees fleeing Kilwa.

Other evidence might suggest the presence of Shi'a communities on the coast during this period. The *Kilwa* and other coastal *Chronicles* describe the earliest settlers as Muslims fleeing the Middle East, and Horton (2017: 255) has argued that such refugees might be "Shi'a groups living in the Yemen from the late eighth century onwards who were periodically oppressed by the Abbasid caliphate." The Shirazi traditions themselves might be a "cultural idea" (Horton 2017: 262) related to Shi'a Islam that was adopted by coastal towns: the town of Shiraz, in the Persian Gulf, was significant during the late 10th and early 11th centuries, under the control of the Shi'a Buyids, the period during which Shirazi-style mosques were built at a number of settlements along the coast. The development of different mosque styles, especially in the shape and embellishment of the *mihrab*, may also provide clues to sectarian differences. In the 11th and early 12th centuries, there were two *mihrab* styles on the coast (Horton 2004: 81): a plain style with few decorations and a more elaborate one that included inscriptions, carved coral, and inset ceramics. The former might be related to Sunni-Shafi'i groups while the latter associate with Shi'a.

By the 14th century, however, most coastal communities were Sunni/Shafi'i, based on the observations of Ibn Battuta (Freeman Grenville 1962: 27–32). Horton argues that this sectarian transformation along the coast was "probably the result of missionary activity, and the movement of noble or sharifian families from Arabia from the twelfth century onwards" (Horton 2017: 256; see also Martin 1975). However, as Horton notes, the "success of Sunni Islam may have disguised the much more heterodox situation in earlier centuries," hints of which can only be found in archaeological remains.

From Islamic Presence
to Islamic Practice

The archaeology of Islam in east Africa is thus understood primarily through particular assemblages of architecture, features, and artifacts, featuring mosques, burials, and locally minted coinage. Each of these sources has provided evidence about the origins and emergence of Islam on the coast and has allowed archaeologists to chart the growth of Islamic communities. This section discusses each of these data classes and how they have been used to mark the origins and presence of Islamic communities. However, going forward, the archaeology of Islam in east Africa will need to move beyond its emphasis on origins, documenting the centrality of Islam by focusing on the grandest mosques, and simple tracing of foreign influences in coastal materials and practices. There is an effort in some research in Islamic archaeology to reiterate and trace the way that Swahili towns and their Islamic practices were part of the larger Islamic world and then to use these connections to explain how Islam must have been practiced or experienced on the coast itself. While there is no doubt that the former is true, researchers must frame east African Islam within the larger regional and Indian Ocean world of which it was a part. However, there needs to be greater research attention paid to the way that Islam and Islamic practice structured daily life on the coast to begin to reveal unique and complicated Islamic Swahili pasts; this will not be accomplished by excavating the Friday mosque alone or reporting on only imported goods.

Mosques

The most informative line of inquiry for understanding the emergence of Islam and Islamic practice in eastern Africa has been the archaeology that has documented the architecture of east Africa's mosques. As discussed, this is partly because of the history of research here, which has meant that the mosque has often been the best-excavated part of the site. Mosques are also the most unequivocal evidence for a Muslim population and aspects of Islamic practice.

Mosques in east Africa are part of a distinctive and coherent architectural tradition. Although aspects of them *evoke* architecture in the Arabian Peninsula, they are not directly comparable with structures elsewhere and instead should be seen as a regional tradition (Garlake 1966; Horton 1991). The regional aspects of this tradition are reinforced by its great diversity, part of it chronological, part functional. What we understand about the development of Islamic practice comes primarily from the development of mosques and mosque architecture: the sizes of mosques are often regarded as proxies for the size of the Islamic community, and both the permanence of the building materials and the style of the mosque have been interpreted as indicating local adherence to Islam as well as the influences from particular Islamic regions outside of Africa.

The evolution of the Friday mosque at Shanga is crucial to this interpretation. Mark Horton's excavations there in the 1980s revealed a stratified sequence of mosques at the center of the settlement, including nine re-buildings from 780–1000 (Figure 4.1.3). The first phases, from 780–920, included small mosques of wattle and daub (Buildings A-E), with close-set rammed posts and mud walls. A small *mihrab* is evident by 850. After this mosque, Building F, Horton documents a period of transformation, in which the mosque is rebuilt first as a wooden structure (Building G), with large posts, and then from coral (Building H), at approximately 920. Building H was built with porites, a form of coral mined from coastal reefs. This mosque was in use for less than 100 years, and was then replaced by a larger porites structure at approximately 1000. Horton refers to this as the first "Friday mosque" at Shanga, arguing that it was a "building large enough to accommodate the majority of the male adult population" of the settlement and thus that it indicates majority conversion. This mosque forms the basis for the Friday mosque that endured at Shanga until 1425 when the site was ultimately abandoned. On multiple occasions during these 400 years, the structure was enlarged and embellished to accommodate an ever-expanding town population and new architectural styles. At approximately 1050 there was a dramatic destruction episode at Shanga in which buildings of porites were destroyed and robbed of their materials. The mosque itself remained intact. Over the following 200 years, the site was rebuilt (Horton calls it an "urban renewal"), with the mosque expanding in size. At first, houses and other structures continued to be built of wattle and daub, but after 1250, houses were rebuilt with coral rag, a rubbly limestone quarried on land from the remains of ancient coral reefs.

This sequence is interesting for many reasons. Of course it is fascinating because we see evidence for Islam being practiced as early as 780 on the eastern African coast, only 150 years after the death of Prophet Muhammad. We also see the development of the mosque in lock-step with the process of urban evolution, yet it becomes comparatively more prominent as time goes on. At the start, the central position of the 8th-century mosque in the settlement testifies to its importance, but it was only large enough to accommodate a small group of devotees. Horton (1996; Horton and Middleton 2000) has therefore developed a model of Islamic conversion revolving around a small initial group of (foreign?) Muslims and a gradual conversion of the wider population. The mosque also shared the central space with several other structures, including large structures interpreted as "clan houses," or at least as communal spaces, as well as kiosks and less permanent structures. The clan structures were also constructed in porites coral, but by the period of urban renewal these were dismantled and the central space was more thoroughly Islamized, as home not only to the Friday mosque but to Islamic burials and tombs.

For a long time, the early mosque at Shanga remained the only pre-1000 mosque known on the coast. There are now several possible contenders. Geophysical survey at Unguja Ukuu on Zanzibar (Fitton and Wynne-Jones 2017) and at Tumbe, Pemba (Fitton 2017) has shown large structures at both sites that, in scale and orientation, may have been early mosques. At Ras Mkumbuu on Pemba Island, Horton has found evidence for an (undated) wattle and daub structure beneath an early stone mosque, itself

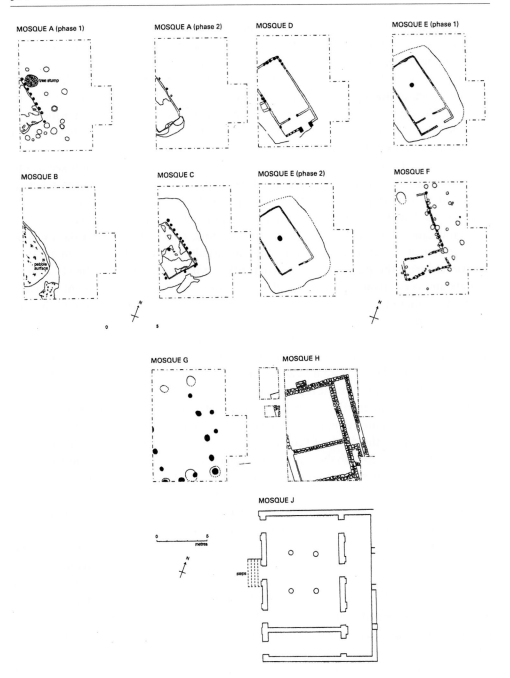

FIGURE 4.1.3 Mosque sequence at Shanga.

dated to the early 10th century. The role of these earlyites earthen mosques and the identity of the worshippers are still quite unclear. They may have served visitors to the region, a small population of local Muslims, or both. Horton suggested that the early presence of Muslims at Shanga led to a population of local converts and that it was these east African Muslims who then spread down the coast founding "Shirazi" mosques, leading to the emergence of a series of 10th- and 11th-century porites mosques. The possible early mosques on Zanzibar and Pemba might make this less tenable, suggesting instead equivalent processes at multiple locations.

What is more easily discerned in the archaeology of mosques is the widespread conversion represented by the establishment of Friday mosques built of porites at settlements along the coast in the 11th century. At this time, coral-built mosques in the "Shirazi" style are seen from Lamu to the Comoros, presumably reflecting the existence of an Islamic community. Key features of these mosques include a rectangular prayer hall; a floor laid on raised, white sand deposits; four columns/pilasters along the side walls; three doorways on the east, west, and south sides with external steps; and a deeply recessed and decorated *mihrab*. An excellent and perhaps quintessential example of this style of mosque can be seen at the site of Kizimkazi at the southern tip of Zanzibar (Figure 4.1.4). This mosque can be dated by a Kufic inscription on the *mihrab*, marking its construction date as 500 AH (1107 CE). Later (regional) additions to the coastal mosque tradition include the domed style that may have been developed at Kilwa in the 14th century—similar mosque elements can be found farther north, apparently influenced by developments at Kilwa. The Friday mosque at Chwaka on Pemba is a good additional example.

There is also ample evidence that links mosques, Islamic practice, and local power. For example, the *Kilwa Chronicle* documents how the 14th-century Sultan and wealthy merchants debated over who would renovate the Friday mosque and thus gain prominence locally (Sutton 1998, 2018). Similarly, Fleisher (2010) has also argued that embellishments of imported pottery within the Great Mosque at Chwaka represent the active efforts of a leader to reiterate local power and authority. Evidence for feasting has been found in spatial association with the mosque at 15th-century Vumba Kuu, Kenya (Wynne-Jones 2010). Additionally, grand mosques were often found adjacent to grand houses, creating a spatial linkage between political economic power and religious authority. The entrance to the Great Mosque at Kilwa Kisiwani faced what Chittick called the Great House, a large palace structure; a similar situation exists at Songo Mnara, where the Friday mosque (which was not the original, central mosque) has steps that face directly onto those of one of the largest houses (Wynne-Jones and Fleisher 2016). Thus, powerful Swahili residents built a clear spatial link between their houses and the Friday mosque, structures that were probably built with elite sponsorship. In this way, local townspeople would enact, through their daily movements associated with Islamic prayer, the structures of authority in the town.

A final example of how archaeology can begin to explore the social life of Islam more fully in Swahili towns comes from our research at Songo Mnara. Most excavations of mosques have focused on the largest, most elaborate mosques within towns, even

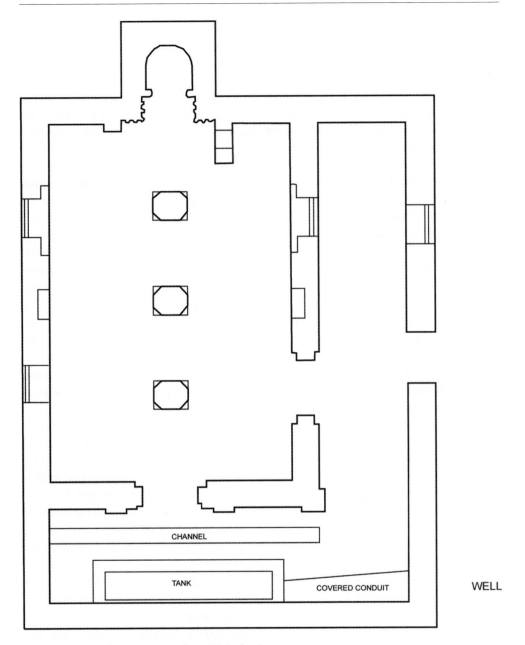

FIGURE 4.1.4 Shirazi mosque from Kizimkazi.

Courtesy of Garlake (1966), reproduced with permission.

though most large towns contained two or more mosques. Previous work at Songo Mnara continued this trend, with excavations by Chittick (1960) at the Friday mosque and then a reinvestigation of that same mosque more recently (Pradines and Blanchard 2005). However, this is just one of six mosques within the town, and our investigations of these additional mosques have allowed us (with Mark Horton) to explore connections between their positioning, use, and life in the town. We argue (Horton et al. 2017: 184) that "the relationship is a complex one that needs to take into account ritual practices, emerging social complexity, gender roles, and the evolving urban landscape." This includes insights into how mosques were positioned to make statements about Islamic adherence (four of the mosques line the western edge of the site, providing a visual landscape that greets approaching visitors, see also Pollard 2008), as well as understandings of the linkages between mosques, burials, and ongoing forms of memorialization. Key here is placing mosques within the broader urban context (Horton et al. 2017: 184): "[t]oo often mosques have been seen as isolated buildings; here we believe that understanding their chronological and spatial context within the urban framework is central in not only interpreting their architecture but also in placing Islamic practice with its wider social landscape."

Burials

Burials offer another important archaeological dataset for Islamic practice. To date, there have been very few excavations of burials on the east African coast due to sensitivities among current residents. Some burials have been excavated during larger projects on a town, when encountered in the course of other excavations, such as at Shanga, Kilwa Kisiwani, and Ras Mkumbuu. In all cases, burials followed standard Muslim practice, with the body aligned east–west and the face turned north toward Mecca. Based on the positions of the bodies, most appear to have been wrapped tightly in cloth, buried without ornaments or items, and placed in a partially flexed position. At Mtambwe Mkuu, twenty burials were found perpendicular to the standard arrangement, suggesting again the possibility of a Shi'ite presence here (Horton and Middleton 2000).

More recently, some projects have directly targeted burials through excavation. At Mtwapa, on the Kenya coast, Raaum et al. (2018) have excavated a number of graves from the 15th century in order to extract aDNA. The results are still not fully published, so little can be said about burial practice. The DNA evidence suggests more complex population dynamics than the standard Arab versus African debate has implied, with a range of mitochondrial DNA from populations in Arabia and also in the deeper interior of Africa.

At Songo Mnara, a limited program of burial excavation complemented a larger project of excavating tombs and memorials around the spaces of a 15th-century town in the Kilwa archipelago. The burials were, as expected, aligned according to standard Muslim practice with faces toward Mecca. They were tightly bound in shrouds before interment, evidenced by the positioning of the limbs upon excavation.

Perhaps more interesting than the burials themselves, though, were the grave markers at Songo Mnara. Both built tombs and simple graves (with head and foot stones) were excavated. Many had been used more than once, particularly the stone-built tombs, which had often been reopened for the interment of another body. Several children accompanied adults in the tombs. The memorials built above the graves were shown to have been constructed sometime after the burial, and the original location had often been partly forgotten or obscured, meaning that the tombs cut across limbs, marking the location of bodies only approximately. A wide range of offerings on the tombs suggested a long-term process of memorialization at these sites. One grave (marked with just a simple head and footstone), had more than 5,000 quartz pebbles laid across the ground surface above it, probably left as individual offerings over many years. Other tombs had coins, pottery, incense, and phytolith remains indicating palm fronds laid at either end. All of these suggested an important role for graves within Swahili society here. Some of the tombs are still remembered as the graves of sharifs, and offerings are still made today (Fleisher and Wynne-Jones 2012).

Coins

Another indirect line of evidence for Islam and Islamic practice in east Africa are locally minted coins. These bear witness to the presence of Muslim rulers in the towns in which they are found. The earliest coins were found at Shanga, where 8th- to 9th-century silver coins bear legends demonstrating the existence of a Muslim elite/ruler at that early date. On one side, the coins offer praise for particular rulers, while on the reverse they offer praise for Allah: "Muhammad / trusts in Allah"; "The kingdom is Allah's / and in Him trusts Abd Allah."

Unfortunately, there are no other sites that are known to have minted coins before 1000 CE. After that, the most prolific mint was at Kilwa Kisiwani, where many thousands of copper coins were struck from the 11th century onward. These were used by Chittick (1973) as a way of reconciling the archaeology with the *Kilwa Chronicle*, but this was hampered by the fact that coins seem to have very long periods of circulation. Coins that contained the names of 11th- or 12th-century rulers were in active circulation until the 15th century, making them less useful as a guide to relative dating. Archaeological finds of Kilwa coins did, however, confirm the existence of several of the rulers named in the *Kilwa Chronicle*, including the founder of the "Shirazi" dynasty at Kilwa, Ali bin al-Hasan, and the most famous ruler of the "Mahdali" dynasty, al-Hasan ibn Sulaiman. They confirmed their faith in Islam, knowledge of Arabic script, and also their awareness of the coinage systems used in the Islamic world. They did not, however, follow caliphal conventions or weight standards (Wynne-Jones and Fleisher 2012; Perkins 2013).

Horton and Middleton (2000: 56–61) have argued that an analysis of locally minted silver and copper coins offers a way to reconstruct the emergence and spread of African Muslims along the coastal corridor. Based on the first-millennium silver coins found at Shanga and a remarkable coin hoard of more than 2,000 coins found at Mtwambwe Mkuu on Pemba Island (Horton et al. 1986), they argue that these coins can be ordered chronologically through the names of the rulers listed on them. The Mtwambwe Hoard provides coins that bridge the early silver issues from Shanga and the copper coins found in the Kilwa archipelago. The names on these coins can be linked to rulers at Kilwa, but also those on Pemba, Zanzibar, and Mafia. Horton and Middleton (2000: 57) thus argue that there was a "familial relationship between rulers/minters" on these islands "suggesting that a closely related dynasty may have lived on these islands from c. 1000–1150." The names on these coins, they argue further, indicate Shi'ite associations in that they come from the Old Testament; a phrase on an early Kilwa issue, "trusts in the Lieutenant of God," also provides support for the idea that the earliest African Muslims were Shi'a.

This reconstruction offers a counternarrative to the colonial foundation of Swahili towns by Muslims from abroad. In this new model, Islam begins to be practiced by local communities during the first millennium CE on the northern Swahili coast from which a local, African Muslim dynasty is built. It was this dynasty that was able to influence settlements farther south, "founding mosques, introducing coinage...[and] convert[ing] non-Muslims or displac[ing] Muslims of other sects" (Horton and Middleton 2000: 61). This would fit with the connection between rulers named on these coins and the town of Shiraz, which, in the 11th century, was under Buyid control. Thus, the stories of Shirazi migrations may represent the movement of African Muslims and their distinctive form of Islam down the eastern African coast during the early second millennium CE.

CONCLUSION

As presented here, the eastern African Swahili coast is an Islamic society of long standing, with traditions of Islamic practice that extend back to the century after the death of Prophet Muhammad. Archaeological research offers clear evidence of the importance of Islam in Swahili towns and villages from the earliest centuries; this includes evidence of the central positioning of mosques in towns, the role of Arabic script in references to Islam on coins, and the importance of Muslim graves and memorialization in the life of the towns.

Despite these important insights into the history of Islam on the coast, it is still difficult to understand the details of Islamic practice, including the sects that dominated on the coast at various times and places and the way Islam shaped the daily life of town residents. What prevents these types of interpretations are the nature of archaeological research and evidence, a lack of historical sources that bear witness to such features/activities, and the colonial archaeological legacy in which "foreign" elements were prioritized over local ones. The current shift in research emphasis in many projects from documenting the *presence* of Islam to the *practice* of Islam in towns and villages has begun to expose the complexity of Islam along the coast during its many centuries of development and practice. New perspectives on Islam and the ways that it shaped daily life, as well as the nature of any syncretic adaptations, are sure to follow.

REFERENCES

Allen, J. de V. 1993. *Swahili Origins: Swahili Culture and the Shungwaya Phenomenon* (London: James Currey).

Bang, A. K. 2003. *Sufis and Scholars of the Sea: Family Networks in East Africa: 1860–1925* (London: Routledge).

Bang, A. K. 2014. *Islamic Sufi Networks in the Western Indian Ocean (c.1880–1940): Ripples of Reform* (Leiden: Brill).

Chittick, H. N. 1960. *Annual Report of the Department of Antiquities* (Dar es Salaam: Government Printer).

Chittick, H. N. 1965. "The 'Shirazi' colonization of East Africa," *Journal of African History*, 6, 3, 275–294.

Chittick, H. N. 1973. "On the Chronology and Coinage of the Sultan of Kilwa," *Numismatic Chronicle*, 13, 192–200.

Chittick, H. N. 1974. *Kilwa: An Islamic Trading City on the East African Coast* (Nairobi and London: British Institute in Eastern Africa).

Chittick, H. N. 1975. "The Peopling of the East African Coast," in H. N. Chittick and R. I. Rotberg (eds.), *East Africa and the Orient: Cultural Syntheses in Pre-Colonial Times* (New York/London: Africana Publishing Company).

Fauvelle-Aymar, F.-X., and Hirsch, B. 2003. "Voyage aux frontières du monde : topologie, narration et jeux de miroir dans la Rihla de Ibn Battûta," *Afrique & Histoire*, 1, 75–122.

Fitton, T., and Wynne-Jones, S. 2017. "Understanding the Layout of Early Coastal Settlement at Unguja Ukuu, Zanzibar," *Antiquity*, 91, 359, 1268–1284.

Fitton, T. 2017. *Pushing the Boat Out: A study of spatial organisation and harbour spaces in the early Swahili ports of the Zanzibar Archipelago, 550–1100 CE*. PhD thesis, University of York.

Fleisher, J. 2010. "Rituals of Consumption and the Politics of Feasting on the Eastern African Coast, AD 700–1500," *Journal of World Prehistory*, 23, 4, 195–217.

Fleisher, J. B., and Wynne-Jones, S. 2012. "Finding Meaning in Ancient Swahili Spatial Practices," *African Archaeological Review*, 29, 171–207.

Freeman-Grenville, G. S. P. 1957. "Coinage in East Africa Before Portuguese Times," *Numismatic Chronicle*, 17, 151–179.

Freeman-Grenville, G. S. P. 1962. *The East African Coast. Select Documents from the First to the Earlier Nineteenth Centuries* (London: Clarendon Press).

Garlake, P. S. 1966. *The Early Islamic Architecture of the East African Coast* (London: British Institute in Eastern Africa & Oxford University Press).

Glassman, J. 1995. *Feasts and Riot: Revelry, Rebellion, and Popular Consciousness on the Swahili Coast 1856–1888* (London: James Currey).

Horton, M. C. 1987a. "The Swahili Corridor," *Scientific American*, 257 (Sep), 86–93.

Horton, M. C. 1987b. "Early Muslim Trading Settlements on the East African Coast: New Evidence from Shanga," *Antiquaries Journal*, 67, 290–322.

Horton, M. C. 1991. "Primitive Islam and Architecture in East Africa," *Muqarnas*, 8, 103–116.

Horton, M. C. 1996. *Shanga: The Archaeology of a Muslim Trading Community on the Coast of East Africa* (Nairobi: British Institute in Eastern Africa).

Horton, M. C. 2004. "Islam, Archaeology and Swahili Identity," in D. Whitcomb (ed.), *Changing Social Identity with the Spread of Islam: Archaeological Perspectives* (Chicago: Oriental Institute Seminar no. 1), 67–88.

Horton, M. C. 2013. "Ibadis in East Africa: Archaeological and Historical Evidence," in M. Hoffmann-Ruf, A. al-Salimi and H. Gaube (eds.), *Oman and Overseas* (Tübingen: OLMS), 93–106.

Horton, M. C. 2017. "Early Islam on the East African Coast," in F. B. Flood and G. Necipoğlu (eds.), *A Companion to Islamic Art and Architecture* (Hoboken: John Wiley & Sons), 250–273.

Horton, M. C., Fleisher, J., and Wynne-Jones, S. 2017. "The Mosques of Songo Mnara in Their Urban Landscape" *Journal of Islamic Archaeology*, 4, 2, 163–188.

Horton, M. C., and Middleton, J. 2000. *The Swahili: The Social Landscape of a Mercantile Society* (Oxford: Blackwell).

Horton, M. C., Oddy, W. A., and Brown, H. 1986. "The Mtambwe Hoard," *Azania*, 21, 115–123.

Insoll, T. 1994. "The External Creation of the Western Sahel's Past: The Use and Abuse of the Arabic Sources," *Archaeological Review from Cambridge*, 13, 39–49.

Insoll, T. 2003. *The Archaeology of Islam in Sub-Saharan Africa* (Cambridge: Cambridge University Press).

Kirkman, J. 1964. *Men and Monuments on the East African Coast* (London: Lutterworth).

Kirkman, J. S. 1954. *The Arab City of Gedi: Excavations at the Great Mosque, Architecture and Finds* (London: Oxford University Press).

Kirkman, J. S. 1959. "Excavations at Ras Mkumbuu on the Island of Pemba," *Tanganyika Notes and Records*, 53, 161–178.

LaViolette, A. 2008. "Swahili Cosmopolitanism in Africa and the Indian Ocean World, A. D. 600–1500," *Archaeologies: Journal of the World Archaeological Congress*, 1, 24–49.

LaViolette, A., and Wynne-Jones, S. 2018. "The Swahili World," in S. Wynne-Jones and A. LaViolette (eds.), *The Swahili World* (London: Routledge), 1–14.

Martin, B. G. 1971. "Notes on Some Members of the Learned Classes of Zanzibar and East Africa in the Nineteenth Century," *African Historical Studies*, 4, 3, 525–545.

Martin, B. G. 1975. "Arab Migrations to East Africa in Medieval Times," *International Journal of African Historical Studies*, 7, 3, 367–390.

Middleton, J. 1992. *The World of the Swahili: An African Mercantile Civilization* (New Haven: Yale University Press).

Nurse, D., and Spear, T. 1985. *The Swahili: Reconstructing the History and Language of an African Society AD 800–1500* (Philadelphia: University of Pennsylvania Press).

Pawlowicz, M., and LaViolette, A. 2013. "Swahili Historical Chronicles from an Archaeological Perspective: Bridging History, Archaeology, Coast, and Hinterland in Southern Tanzania," in P. Schmidt and S. A. Mrozowski (eds.), *The Death of Prehistory* (Oxford: Oxford University Press), 117–140.

Perkins, M. J. 2013. *The Coins of the Swahili Coast c. 800–1500* (Unpublished PhD thesis, University of Bristol).

Pollard, E. 2008. "The maritime landscape of Kilwa Kisiwani and its region, Tanzania, 11th to 15th century AD," *Journal of Anthropological Archaeology*, 27, 265–280.

Pouwels, R. L. 1984. "Oral Historiography and the Shirazi of the East African Coast," *History in Africa*, 11, 237–267.

Pouwels, R. L. 1987. *Horn and Crescent. Cultural Change and Traditional Islam on the East African Coast, 800–1900* (Cambridge: Cambridge University Press).

Pradines, S., and Blanchard, P. 2005. "Kilwa al-Mulûk. Premier bilan des travaux de conservation-restauration et des fouilles archéologiques dans la baie de Kilwa, Tanzanie," *Annales Islamologiques*, 39, 25–80.

Prestholdt, J. 1998. *As Artistry Permits and Custom May Ordain: The Social Fabric of Material Consumption in the Swahili World, Circa 1450 to 1600* (Evanston: Northwestern University).

Prins, A. H. J. 1961. *The Swahili-speaking peoples of Zanzibar and the East African Coast: Arabs, Shirazi and Swahili* (London: International African Institute).

Raaum, R., Williams, S., Kusimba, C., Monge, J., Morris, A., and Mohamed, M. 2018. "Decoding the Genetic Ancestry of the Swahili," in S. Wynne-Jones and A. LaViolette (eds.), *The Swahili World* (London: Routledge), 81–102.

Saad, E. 1979. "Kilwa Dynastic Historiography: A Critical Study," *History in Africa*, 6, 177–207.

Spear, T. 1984. "The Shirazi in Swahili Traditions, Culture, and History," *History in Africa*, 11, 291–305.

Sutton, J. E. G. 1998. "Kilwa: A History of the Ancient Swahili Town with a Guide to the Monuments of Kilwa Kisiwani and Adjacent Islands," *Azania*, 33, 113–169.

Sutton, J. E. G. 2018. "The East African Coast: Researching Its History and Archaeology," in S. Wynne-Jones and A. LaViolette (eds.), *The Swahili World* (London: Routledge), 53–66.

Vernet, T. 2005. *Les cités-etats Swahili de l'archipel de Lamu, 1585–1810: Dynamiques endogenes, dynamiques exogenes.* (Unpublished PhD diss., Centre de recherches africaines, Université Paris I Panthéon, Sorbonne.)

Wynne-Jones, S. 2010. "Remembering and Reworking the Swahili Diwanate: The Role of Objects and Places at Vumba Kuu," *International Journal of African Historical Studies*, 43, 3, 407–427.

Wynne-Jones, S. 2016. *A Material Culture: Consumption and Materiality on the Precolonial east African Coast* (Oxford: Oxford University Press).

Wynne-Jones, S., and Fleisher, J. 2016. "The Multiple Territories of Swahili Urban Landscapes," *World Archaeology*, 48, 3, 349–362.

Wynne-Jones, S., and Fleisher, J. B. 2012. "Coins in Context: Local Economy, Value and Practice on the East African Swahili Coast," *Cambridge Archaeological Journal*, 22, 1, 19–36.

CHAPTER 4.2

....

THE NILOTIC SUDAN

....

INTISAR SOGHAYROUN EL ZEIN

INTRODUCTION

THE vast area of the Sudan, covering about 1,886,068 square kilometers (Figure 4.2.1), is characterized by its great linguistic, ethnic, and geographic diversity. Given its large territory, it has always been subject to human migration from different directions and not from only the north and east, as assumed by earlier historians (Hassan 1963: 2). Islamic culture thus entered the Sudan from different directions at different times, and this is well illustrated by the art and architecture that developed there under Islam. Another factor that influenced material culture is that Sudanese Islam bore two faces: the orthodox and the ecstatic (Sufi). Each brought a distinctive set of institutions. The first was embodied in the mosque, while the second emphasized the *khalwa* (schools to teach Quran and related science in addition to Arabic and mathematics), in which the teacher is a holy man (*sheikh, fagir*) who possesses *baraka* (blessings) received through ascetic practices and spiritual exercises. Sufism brought to Sudan the orders (*tariqa*) which dictated a new form of social organization. Consequently, popular Islam can be seen as a harmonious blending of old cultures and many non-Islamic traits that were sealed in the context of a new religion flexible enough to accommodate local beliefs. Contemporary Sudanese Muslim identity is formed, in part, from many popular non-Islamic practices, which are particularly visible at cemeteries.

The process of Islamization of the Sudan was a gradual one, beginning in the first century of Islam (7th century CE) and culminating in the rise of the Tunjur (14th century CE) and then the Keira (16th century CE) Sultanates in the west and the Fung Kingdom in the center (16th century CE) of the country. A combined reading of literary and archaeological evidence suggests that the process of Islamization in the Sudan took place in three phases (Soghayroun El Zein 2004: 12–19). Direct archaeological evidence for the first phase (20–680 AH/640–1300 CE) comes in the form of the tombstones from Lower Nubia, the eastern desert, and the Red Sea coast (Soghayroun El Zein 2004: 15). The settlement remains in Derheib and Khor Nubt in the eastern desert and the port of

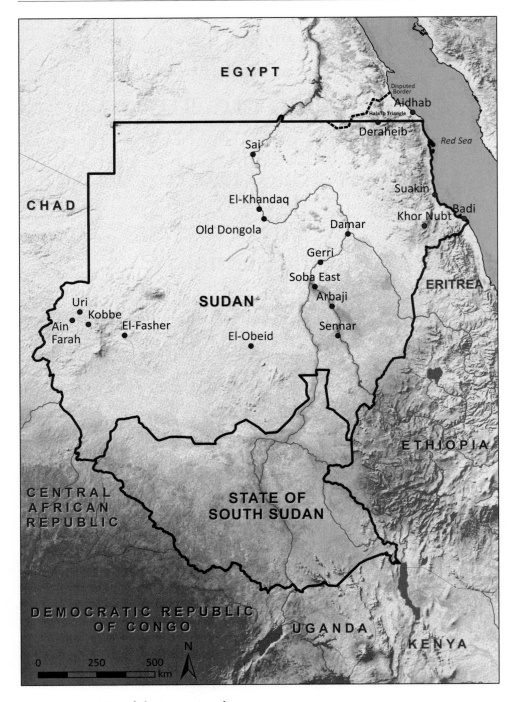

FIGURE 4.2.1 Map of places mentioned.

Badi' are among the areas that have been investigated archaeologically (Sadr et al. 1994). To the west and in Darfur, a few settlements have been the focus of archaeological study, such as Uri and Ain Farah. Phase II occupation (680–920 AH/1300–1500 CE) is best illustrated by the archaeological remains at Arbaji, Old Dongola, 'Aidhab, and 'Ain Fara. In Phase III (920–1480 AH/1500–1800 CE), the Sudan was dominated by three powers: the Funj in the middle Nile Valley, the Keira in western Sudan, and the Ottoman troops in northern Sudan and Suakin on the Red Sea coast. The archaeological evidence for this period ranges from secular to religious, funerary, and military remains, as discussed later.

It is clear from both literary and archaeological evidence that Islam has had a presence in Sudan since the first century of the Muslim era (cf. Insoll 2003). Islamization was the result of a nonorganized, peaceful process in the Nile Valley, and in the Sahel and deserts through the assimilation of Arab and Beja nomads. It took time for the new religion to be absorbed and spread. Thus, in Phase I evidence for the existence of a Muslim community is limited in comparison to Phase III. Phase II has, by comparison, received little attention and is generally regarded as a dark period; the period, on the contrary, witnessed the start of the reformation process encouraged by the rise of the powerful states of Fung and the Fur and should be a rich one for archaeological investigations.

Muslims first entered the eastern Sudan in the Abbasid period (8th century CE), when Arabs occupied wide areas in their exploitation of the gold and emerald mines of the eastern desert. With the treaty imposed on the Beja in 831, the area was opened to greater migration from Aswan in southern Egypt across the Beja lands in the eastern desert and down to the land between Badi' and Massawa (Hassan 1967: 117). The limited archaeological fieldwork in the eastern desert has focused on mining sites and has not contributed in a significant way to our understanding of the advent of Islam in the region. The picture is completely different when we turn to the Red Sea ports. The earliest Islamic archaeological remains in northeastern Sudan—the sites of Badi' and Aidhab—are found on the shores of the Red Sea and date to the mid-8th century (Kawatoko 1993: 214). Such settlements consist of a central area of coral walls and houses, cisterns, and cemeteries. 'Aidhab prospered primarily because of trade and pilgrimage (hajj); its proximity to gold mines was of secondary importance.

Suakin is the third and latest port of Sudan whose remains include mosques, *qubbas* (domed tombs), *zawiyas* (special prayer place), houses, caravanserais, and public buildings such as *muhafazas* (governor's residences) and customs buildings. It best exemplifies what was once the Red Sea building traditions, echoing the style of the early simple mosques of Mecca and Medina; such traditions have long ago disappeared from Jeddah and Massawa. The domestic buildings belong to two major phases: the "Red Sea style" produced until the early 19th century, and the "Egyptian style" of the second half of the 19th century (Greenlaw 1976: 76).

The distinctly local style of the architecture at such sites contrasts with those in Egypt, for example, in the same periods. The localisms in Sudanese material culture have much to do with its political history. Most of its land was never under the direct rule of the Islamic Caliphate except for a few places: namely, the banks of the Nile north of the Third Cataract to the frontiers with Egypt since 1583 (Ottoman domain); the Beja land, which stretches from Aswan eastward across the desert to the Red Sea littoral, from the 9th century (subjugated by Abbasid troops); and Suakin on the Red Sea from 1517 (Ottoman domain). Thus, the formal features normally associated with Islamic art and architecture are largely missing from the Sudan. Religious architecture presents an important case in point. In Sudan, it is the *khalwa*, rather than the mosque, and the sheikhs which are the center of communal religious practice. Domed tombs (the burial places of sheikhs) and shrines, therefore, occupy a privileged position in Sudanese religious belief and socio-economic life.

Few archaeological excavations focused on the Islamic era have been conducted in the Sudan; nevertheless, survey and recording of the sites continues and interest in the field is growing. Fortunately, there is a large body of contemporary texts that, if read together and critically, can enrich our knowledge of local societies of the day. They include accounts of medieval historians and geographers; official documentation (land grants, correspondence related to local disputes) issued by rulers or provincial authorities of the Funj, Fur, and Tagali; orally transmitted history (*nisba*—genealogy—documents and hagiographies), many of which were later written down; and accounts by European travelers, beginning with David Reubeni's early travels of the early 16th century to studies by contemporary historians of the 20th century.

For the purpose of this chapter the Islamic archaeological evidence will be discussed under five main headings so as to consider all socio-economic factors that have shaped people's faith.

PLACES OF PRAYER

The Mosque

Variable information on historical mosques exists. According to the *tabaqat* (biographical dictionaries) of the 19th century, the town of Sennar's market place (*suq*) was located in front of the mosque (O'Fahey 1994: 245). This has been supported by other literary evidence, including photos taken in the early 20th century and drawings by travelers in the 19th century. According to contemporary texts, the sons of Jabir were renowned as mosque builders in the Shaiqiya area. Recent investigation of the sons of Jabir revealed remains of one of their mosques in the territory of the Dufar mekdom.

Among the numerous remains of mosques attributed to Phase II are those of the mosque of Arabnarti in the northern state, which is not far from Old Dongola; here, literary evidence has also alluded to the existence of a mosque left by the first Muslim troops who entered the area (651–652 CE). The main archaeological evidence is an inscribed stone inserted in the hall of the first story of the royal palace in Old Dongola, a *mihrab* carved out of the eastern wall, and a few steps of a *minbar* (Figure 4.2.2). Other literary evidence describes the mosque of Damer (Bruce 1804), at Kutranj on the eastern bank of the Blue Nile, about 58 kilometers south of Khartoum.

FIGURE 4.2.2 Old Dongola: the inscribed foundation stone inserted in the eastern wall next to the *Minbar*

Courtesy of Intisar Soghayroun El Zein.

From the Red Sea ports and the eastern desert, the Aidhab Friday mosque was described by the Persian traveler Nasr-i-Khusraw in 1050. The mosque 96 kilometers from Sinkat is at Khor Nubt (Oman et al 1998: 33) and measures about 11 × 4 meters, built of dry stone slabs with an entrance to the south and a protruding *mihrab*. At Suakin the mosques can be compared to 16th-century Red Sea ports style rather than to the rest of the Sudan (Greenlaw 1976). Their architecture is a simple courtyard type: a *sahn* (open courtyard) surrounded by *riwaqs* (porticoes) with *minbar* and *mihrab*. There are three entrances to facilitate access from many directions. Within the *sahn* there is an ablution fountain; at the *qibla riwaq* there is a *kursi* (table for book-reading) for Quran recitation and approached by a flight of steps. All are built of coral stone with minarets attached to the building. The idea of attaching a *khalwa* to a mosque seems to be dominant in Suakin, as in the Hanafi and Shafi'i mosques.

To the west, remains of religious architecture come mainly from Darfur. At the site of 'Ain Farah many mosques were found but only two were surveyed (Arkell 1946; Paul 1954; Yunis 1979). The first one is 17 × 17 meters with L-shaped columns, built of burnt brick and plastered with mud. The literary evidence refers to Sultan Tairab in Darfur who is said to have built ninety-nine mosques. The other mosque is that of Umm al-Sultan, smaller in size (3.7 × 3.3 meters), with protruding carved *mihrab* on the eastern wall and dated to the 14th century. Paul (1954: 11) also described the Uri Mosque as 38.5 meters square, built of stone with forty-eight columns that runs around the *sahn* and three entrances to the south, north, and east. It was attributed to the 12th century.

Musa (1986: 217) mentioned another mosque at the site of Bora: Jebel Marra. It was 21 meters square with walls standing to about 2 meters high and almost 2 meters wide, built of stone slabs. It, too, was dated to sometime after the 12th century. Two mosques can be dated to the Keira sultanate. The largest and finest of the two is at Shoba, about 900 meters north-east of the palace; it has been attributed to Sultan Tairab and dated to 1760. It measures about 38.4 × 29.4 meters and had forty-seven round brick columns. The other is the Turra Mosque and is attributed to Sultan Ahmed Bakr (1682–1722). Thought to have been built originally of stone, it was rebuilt by Sultan Ali Dinar in 1910 using mudbrick and stone buttressing. In a recent visit to two sites north of al-Fashir, I studied two mosques of fired brick, with protruding *mihrab* niches and piers to support the roof. In one of them a celebrated sheikh was buried next to the *minbar* area (Figure 4.2.3). The mosque of al-Obaid in Kordofan dates to the 19th century, but there are other areas in Kordofan, such as the Nuba Mountains, that remain uninvestigated.

Churches Converted into Mosques

At Qasr Ibrim the stone-built cathedral was turned into a mosque early in the Ottoman period (1580–1700) by cutting a *mihrab* into the east wall and erecting a *minbar* alongside it (Alexander 2000: 50). Celebi, during his visit in 1672, reported that there were

FIGURE 4.2.3 North of al-Fashir, Darfur. The interior of Jadeed al Sail mosque built by Sultan Tayrab according to local informants.

Courtesy of Intisar Soghayroun El Zein.

seven mosques at Old Dongola as well as several churches converted to mosques. Other examples of churches converted into mosques are those of the Fifth Cataract region, namely on Mugrat Island and at al-Kab, Artul, and al-Koro. The Artul church conversion is a rectangular building with two doorways, each approached by steps at the south-east wall and north-west wall; no attempt was made to create a *mihrab* or *qibla* niche. At al-Koro, the apse has been transformed into a *mihrab* with mud walling (Crawford 1961: 33). The Artul mosque has four piers supporting the roof, with the minaret approached by a flight of steps.

Other Places of Prayer

These include the *zawiya*, which in Sudan is a private, local place for the five canonical daily prayers and is frequently established by a pious man for prayers and social duties. To serve these purposes, it has a simple *mihrab* and is often attached to a house or group of buildings. In Egyptian Nubia the *zawiya* is a mosque affiliated with a certain religious order (Adams 1987).

The *Eid* prayer, on the other hand, is held in a large open space, usually near cemeteries. Known as a *musalla,* it is defined by erecting a *minbar* of three or four steps from which the *imam* delivers his speech. Other simple prayer places are simple open spaces delimited by a line of stones and with a *mihrab* protrusion (much like the "desert mosques" of Transjordan and Palestine). These open mosques are a widespread phenomenon but are notoriously difficult to date.

EDUCATION, LITERACY, AND SOCIAL FORMATION

Formal literary education was provided by the institution of the *khalwa*. The word is derived from an Arabic root indicating "seclusion in the wild," much like Christian monks. The idea is that religious teachers sought to be alone in pursuit of mystics' meditation. They would isolate themselves in a cell-like room, a cave, or even inside a baobab tree. Then, as Quran teaching and all literary education became associated with the *fekki* (sheikh) who practiced seclusion and asceticism in various ways, the word *khalwa* came to mean the Quran School (and a room for guests). Most of the *khalwas* during the Funj and the Turko-Egyptian periods belonged to individuals or family groups that separated themselves from the moral struggle of tribal and intertribal life.

As time went on, the prestige of the *khalwa* was such that even the most powerful chieftains paid homage to the *khalwa fekki*. This may partly explain why the Mahdi succeeded in a comparatively short time against apparently far greater odds. This may also partly explain why movements like the Khirigeen (The Graduates' General Congress) of the early 20th century found it necessary to seek the patronage of the powerful sects of the Khatmiyya and the Ansar before any effective negotiation could be started (El-Tayib 2017: 59; Abu Hassabu 1985: 112–113). They continue to be specialists in conflict resolution, as indicated by the recent intervention of certain famous sheikhs who served to alleviate tensions between factions or mediated to convince people in Kordofan and Darfur to disarm.

There are other important roles played by the *khalwa*. These include the establishment of villages and towns. Usually the sheikh chooses an uninhabited area where basic needs are available. Here he erects a mosque, a *khalwa* for guests, student's rooms for learning, and quarters for himself. Over time the area is populated and then named after its founder (e.g., Wad al-Fadni, Wad Medani, al-Kabashi, and al-Sheikh al-Tayyib; see Soghayroun El Zein 2004: 96). Likewise the village of Debbat al Fugara, as its name suggests, was founded by holy men. It lies about 8 kilometers east of the modern town of Debba in the Northern State; it appears in the accounts of Cailliaud, Hoskins, and Belfonds as "Debbat Doleeb" (Crawford 1951: 38). The last holy man associated with the village was Sheikh Doleeb Nasi and his descendants, the remains of whose bulbous domed tombs are extant but have been in ruins since the 1820s according to Waddington and Hanbury (1822: 339).

Similarly, Al Qoz (or Goz al-Sheikh Soghayroun), which lies about 18 kilometers south of Shendi, has a *mesid* (a Sufi center of learning) which includes a mosque, a *khalw*a, and a cemetery that has been in use for the past 400 years and lies about 3 kilometers south of the village. Historical records refer to the migration of the family led by the famous Fatima bint Jabir and her son Soghayroun from the Fourth Cataract region in the 16th century. For towns, ad-Damer is a good example, which, according to oral history was founded around the 15th century. Bruce passed the town in 1772 and left a description of its buildings and economy. According to Bruce, and then Burckhardt (Bruce 1804: vi, 451, Burckhardt 1987: 266), it housed many Quran schools and students from Kordofan. Its mosque has already been described. The economy depended on agriculture and trade. Ad-Damer sat at the center of four trade routes: one going east to Suakin; one west to Kordofan; one south to Shendi, Khartoum, and Sennar; and the fourth across the Butana to Gadaref in eastern Sudan.

Trade was secure because of the existence of the *mesid* in the town. People believed that the presence of holy men protected their trade and their weekly markets, a belief that continues today. The original site was at Darru south of ad-Damer, a place associated with the holy man Hajj Eisa Ibn Gindeel Ibn 'Arman (c. 1450–1500), who established the *mesid*. The settlement later moved to Ad-Damer when Hamad ibn 'Abdel Allah erected a *mesid* around 1600, attracting the settlement of numerous tribes. In 1821, during the second Turkiyya (period of Turko-Egyptian rule), the *mesid* was destroyed, and its residents migrated from Damer, establishing new *mesid*s in Gadaref, Kassla, and Erkoweit (Figure 4.2.4). The town was revived with the Mahdiyya in 1885, and until

FIGURE 4.2.4 Erkweet, Eastern Sudan. A collection of wooden tablets (*Loah*) for learning the Quran in khalwat al Majadheeb.

Courtesy of Intisar Soghayroun El Zein.

today it attracts students from different parts of the Sudan. The modern town sprawls in different directions, with the *mesid* in the center.

Life in the *mesid* depends on a subsistence economy and is based on self-sufficiency. Land was given to the sheikhs by the sultans of Darfur and the kings of Sennar, and these were cultivated by students for their own support. In their spare time students also produced traditional objects, like wooden beds (pl., *anagreeb*; sing., *angaraib*), pottery, and head caps (*taqiya*). From the nearby woodlands they brought fuel and prepared their wooden writing tablets (*loah*). The best students copied the Quran and other religious books. Attached to each *khalwa*, and an integral part of it, is the *tekiya*: the place where food is prepared in a *khalwa* or a *mesid*. It is a Turkish term: a "tekky" is a residence of sufi sheikhs, where they live together and perform their religious duties.

THE AWLIYA (SAINTS)

Vernacular literature abounds in the stories of saints. Also, it contains much of the fundamental teaching of Islam, including the standard sufi biography of the Prophet Muhammed and many narratives from the traditions. McHugh (1994) summarized five qualities of the *fekki* in Sudan: generosity, detachment, scrupulousness, piety, and asceticism (*zuhd*). They were the necessary characteristics making the *faki* a stranger to the world and spiritually aware. The *fekki* played many roles: rainmaker, protector, mediator, and healer. On the latter function, McHugh tells us that "in Nilotic Sudan, as in Hausa, Muslim holy men had to compete with traditional specialists, and the healing faculty was perhaps the one most demanded of Sudanese holy men on a daily basis. Physical, mental, and neurological illnesses alike were regarded as evidence of possession by evil spirit or influence of the evil eye" (McHugh 1994: 65–66). Knowledge of herbs and roots were part of the *fekki*'s medical experience. His healing abilities did not end with his death; the earth around his tomb was believed to have curative properties, like Ahmed wad al-Tiraifi of the Arakiyyin, who is reported to have cured ninety-nine maladies. Thus the *fekki* contributed directly to the survival of the community: they looked after the welfare of their followers.

Evidence for literacy in the *khalwas* is supplied by the wealth of written documents uncovered from different parts of Nilotic Sudan. It includes copies of Qurans produced in these centers, administrative and legal documents related to land tenure, genealogical documents, and inscribed tombstones, which are discussed in detail later (Figure 4.2.5).

CEMETERIES AND IDENTITY

Muslim burial architecture in Sudan takes one of five different forms. Burials range from ordinary low oval mounds (*mastaba*s) and roofed or roofless square or rectangular rooms, to domed tombs and tomb towers. Regardless of the architectural form, all maintain a

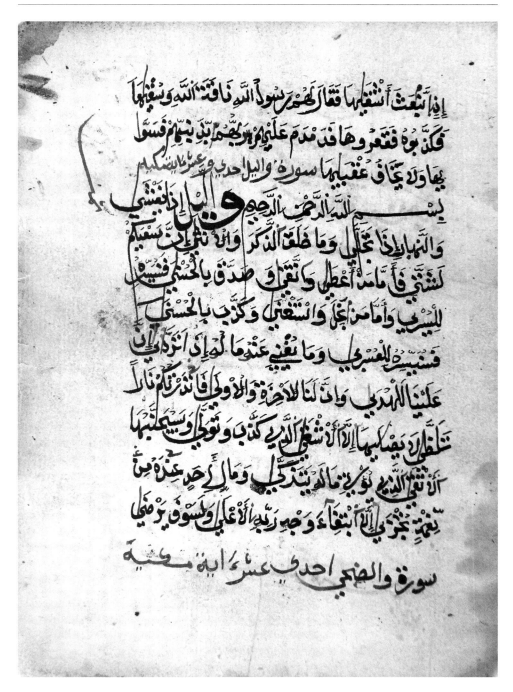

FIGURE 4.2.5 Khandaq, Northern State. A page from hand written Quran.

Courtesy of Intisar Soghayroun El Zein.

north–south orientation of the body. The deeper part of the pit is narrower to receive the body, laid on its right side, with the head facing east. Generally, the only difference in the burials is in the shroud, which consists of three pieces for women and two for men. There is no gender segregation in the graveyard except for a limited area that extends from al Khandaq to Wad Nimeiri (Northern State); here female graves—whether of adults, children, or newborns—were marked with three tombstones.

The archaeological study of cemeteries in the Sudan was long neglected, but this is now changing as their potential for answering many questions about pre-modern Muslim societies becomes appreciated. The size of and building materials used for the superstructure, for example, can provide information about the status of the deceased. Moreover, the potential for a mapping of cemeteries to locate *khalwas* mentioned in texts, for which no remains exist, cannot be underestimated. Such burial structures have recently been identified at el-Kurru, Old Dongola, el-Khandaq, Sahaba, and Hameed. According to local informants, there were once mosques and *khalwas* in the neighborhood before the area was repurposed as a burial ground.

The Qubba

More than any other burial structure, it has been the domed tomb that has historically attracted the attention of travelers and researchers, whether isolated or within a cemetery. The *qubba* is the most visible architectural manifestation of Islam in the Sudan, dotting the landscape of the Funj and Ottoman domains. *Qubbas* here take the form of beehive or conical structures, a square substructure with a dome above it, or three or more superimposed circles or squares. Most of the *qubbas* have *mihrabs*, and decoration is rare (Soghayroun El Zein 1987) (Figure 4.2.6). Unlike many other architectural forms, the Sudanese *qubba* did change in form over time and reflects different regional traditions, revealing ways in which Kushite, Meroitic, Christian, and Islamic cultures merged in the development of a uniquely Sudanese form of Islamic architecture.

The most commonplace and simple tombs, however, were built of mud or stone, with or without roof, or take the form of a ring of roughly piled stones. Famous sheikhs were generally buried in roofless rooms (s. *baniya* or *haram*; i.e., sanctuary), equipped with *mihrabs* and, sometimes, decorated entrances. At the edge of some cemeteries are located complexes of square and rectangular structures equipped with *mihrabs*. Of equal social importance to *qubbas* is the *bayan*: a flag made of a pole and piece of cloth, located next to a pile of stones or grave-like structure. The *bayan* commemorates a place where a saint is reputed to have gone into retreat, where he performed a miracle, or where he revealed himself in a dream.

Practices at Cemeteries

They are many practices around and inside *qubbas* and other lesser shrines. People will come looking for *baraka* (blessing) or healing and with other demands. As mentioned earlier, the sheikh, alive or dead, is believed to have the power of intercession and can act

FIGURE 4.2.6 Abu Raga, Northern State, north of the Third Cataract. A sheikh's *Qubba*.

Courtesy of Intisar Soghayroun El Zein.

on the person's behalf. In some cases, people would scrub the tombstone to use its powder for healing and *baraka*. Many other grave-linked practices are not part of orthodox
Islam and leave an archaeological trace. Pots were often placed on one or both sides of
the grave, for example, and were filled with water the moment the deceased was interred;
such jars were left in place. According to Cavendish (1966: 152), who observed the practice in 1964 (in Magaffil in the Omodiya and Sheikhship of Saras, Lower Nubia), the
local people placed an open bowl at the head of the grave with a tin can or another vessel
for dipping. This water was then poured over the white pebbles covering the grave, in a
form of libation, while the pourer recited verses from the Quran. During surveys carried
out in northern Sudan, the author documented various types of pots on graves; some of
them were decorated, which could be a rich area of future ceramic study.

In another practice, the grave itself was covered with pebbles, and two large palm
fronds were stuck into the ground at either end (Burckhardt 1987: 35). This practice
extended from Nubia further south along the Nile up to Atbara and ad-Damer. In the
19th century, Burckhardt (1987 269–270) gave an account of the procedure.

> [A]t a house where people celebrating the memory of some relative lately deceased,
> a basket full of white pebbles was brought over which the Quran was read. These
> pebbles were destined to be strewed over the tomb of the deceased in the manner
> which I had often observed in the tombs freshly made. Upon my enquiries concern-
> ing the custom which I confess have never seen practiced in any Mohammedan
> countries, the Feky answered that it was a mere meritorious action, that there was
> no absolute necessity for it, but it was thought that the soul of deceased when here-

after visiting the tomb, might be glad to find these pebbles in order to use them as beads in addressing its prayers to the creator. At other places prayers on the pebbles are said at the home of the deceased on the seventh day after the death. Then after two or three days the pebbles are taken and spread over the grave. These customs have not yet been reported from other parts of the Muslim world. It is not as common in Egyptian Nubia as in the Sudan.

In an alternative burial practice, *durra* (sorghum) plants could also be grown at the head of the grave. According to some people, there should be something wet near the grave (Cavendish 1966: 152). Again, a sorghum cone could be put as an offering inside a sheikh's *qubba*.

The burial grounds of sheikhs are regarded as holy and safe places to store objects of personal value. This is a widespread phenomenon in the Nile Valley and is encountered in eastern Sudan as well. For this reason, infants and newborn children were usually buried either next to a *qubba*, or a sheikh's grave.

Tombstones

These are the earliest Muslim remains so far recognized in the Sudan. The earliest are dated to the period between the 3rd and 5th centuries of the Hijra (the 9th–11th centuries of the Christian calendar). Tombstones have been found at Badi', Khor Nubt, and Deraheib in eastern Sudan, and were reported from Meinarti, Tafa, and Kalabsha in lower Nubia (Soghayroun El Zein 2004: 15). Carvings include decorative elements like zigzag designs or stars, verses from the Quran, Sufi poems, or supplications and prayers. In addition to alluding to the degree of literacy in the population, they are also good indicators of the form of Islam that prevailed in certain areas. The inclusion of Sufi poems suggests an ascetic trend in the community; the appearance of Quranic verses and supplications indicates a Sunni orientation. Tombstones are venerated by some people to the extent that they rub the stone and get the powder to be used as *baraka* and for medicinal purposes (Figure 4.2.7).

THE ARCHAEOLOGY OF TRADE

Medieval Arab historians and geographers frequently refer to Sudan's trade routes. Among the long-distance routes mentioned by the 15th-century Egyptian historian al-Maqrizi, one follows the Nile from Abu Hamad to ad-Debba, which was shortened by the Bayuda desert or eastern route of Abu Hamad–Korsko, which had been in use since the Meroitic period (al-Maqrizi in Musád 1972: 357). Trade caravans linked different parts of the region and extended from Cobbe in the west to Suakin on the Red Sea coast, and from Shendi and Berber in the north to Sennar in the south. Major caravan routes

FIGURE 4.2.7 Hafeer Mashou, Dongola region, inscribed tombstone.

Courtesy of Intisar Soghayroun El Zein.

had also penetrated deep beyond the Sudan, as far as Egypt and Ethiopia, south to the kingdom of Kulla and west to Bornu and Hausaland (El-Bushra 1971: 65). The caravan route to Suakin had opened the country to Arabia, India, and the Far East. Darb al Arba'in is the most well-known; it crossed the desert from Cobbe in Darfur to Asyut in Egypt. Other internal routes are the Meheila route, the Abu Hamad-Korsko route, the Shendi-Berber route, and the Berber-Suakin route. The latter has recently been investigated archaeologically and will be discussed in the later pilgrimage section.

Trade in Sudan took the form of local exchange, market exchange, and royal exchange (Spaulding 1984: 27). Royal exchange (foreign trade) or long-distance trade was sponsored by the head of the state: gold, ivory, and slaves were exchanged for foreign goods imported from abroad. Foreign merchants took the lead in this business, trading across international borders (Spaulding 1984).

The Funj and Fur Kingdoms were dependent on international trade, thus proximity to major trade routes was an important factor for their development. The Sudanese traders were Muslim. The fact that the early market towns were found on the crossing points of caravan routes shows their importance to long-distance trade. The Islamic kingdoms of the Funj and the Fur/Keira became interested in Kordofan for trade in slave, gold, and, gum Arabic in the 17th and 18th centuries. The items were exchanged in the urban markets of al-Obeid, Bara, Umm Ruwaba, and al-Rahad, which were all towns established by migrants from the Nile Valley. Articles from Kordofan included gum, hides, senna leaves, ivory, rhino horns, cattle, tamarinds, ostrich eggs, ostrich feathers, gold rings, grains, water-bags for oxen, salt, tobacco, sesame, wooden dishes, and slaves (Burckhardt 1987: 309; Pallme 1844: 280; Petheric 1861: 304–305).

Articles from Darfur and Sennar included camels, gum, ivory, gold, water skins, feathers, natron, tamarinds, sesame, rhino horns, slaves, whips, and alum. Ostrich eggs and feathers were among the commodities that had a considerable value. Salt, according to Burckhardt, was the second most important product in the Fifth Cataract region, and it was monopolized by the king of Shendi. Sennar traders bought this salt and sold it to the Ethiopians. Salt was distributed throughout the Sudan; the Fur of the mountains traded it along Wadi Azum as part of the local and regional economy. Indigo was one of the cornerstones of the Turkish colonial economy after 1830s, together with sugarcane and cotton. It was the monopoly of the government, and indigo factories were established at Berber, al-Matamma, 'Aliab, Thamaniyat, Marawi, Hafir, Khandaq, and Old and New Dongola to extract the dye. The remains of these factories are still standing at different sites, in varying degrees of preservation. Those in best condition can be found at Berber and Saqadi, while the one at Mettama is threatened by water seepage affecting its foundations.

Archaeological evidence for imports takes the form of textiles, metals, silver dollars, hardware, beads, semi-precious materials, firearms, and military supplies while scents, medical herbs, and spices are known mainly from literary evidence. A trader could be a wholesale merchant, a long-distance caravan merchant, or a *khabir* (literally an "expert," used to mean a caravan guide). He was the one who specialized in relatively few commodities or could finance and organize trade through agents and partners. Such traders or shopkeepers who were operating outside their area of origin were from northern

Sudan, mainly Danagla, Ja'aliyyin, and Shaygiyya (Haaland 1984: 274) and known in western and southern Sudan as the *Jallaba* (sing. *Jallabi*). About 200 names of *Jallaba* who appeared in Cairo during the 18th century or who were connected in a legal or familial way with local merchants have been preserved in court (*mahkma*) texts in Cairo. They either carry place names or tribal or racial names, like al-Dongolawi, al-Mahasi, al-Khandaqawi, and other areas like Sennar and Darfur (Walz 1978: 74).

The slow migration of the Dongolese to major trading centers of the Sudan can be dated to the late 17th century. Scarcity of land in northern Sudan and periods of political instability on the Nile, particularly in the 18th century, had led to an intermittent diaspora of *Ja'aliyyin*, *Danagla*, and others away from the river. The migrants came as *fugara* or holy men, and as *jallaba*, or traveling merchants. Their commercial skills, experience of urban life, and religious prestige led them to open up trade and trade routes and to establish towns west of the Nile (Soghayroun El Zein 2010: 103). Their network reached present-day Chad (Walz 1978: 74).

As mentioned earlier, there were some traders who specialized in particular commodities, like 'Abd Allah Bey Hamza from al-Khandaq, who traded in gum Arabic and ostrich feathers. Surviving documents show that a full load of these items was brought by Kababish nomads for his benefit in al-Khandaq. Both items originated in Kordofan and were then carried on camels to the Nile through Wadi al-Malik to Ed-Debba or through the branch of Wadi Howar to al-Khandaq. From any of these sites they would be transported by boat to Hafir, offloaded, and uploaded on camels again, joining the forty road caravans to Egypt.

To consider trade in Nilotic Sudan, certain points should be emphasized. The first is that the prime agents of Islamization during the time of the Christian kingdoms (Makkouria 6th–14th centuries, Alwa 6th–early 16th centuries) were Muslim traders from Egypt and the Arabian Peninsula. Arab nomads entered the country looking for good pastures and trade in gold, emeralds, and slaves. During that period, they penetrated as far south as Soba, the capital of the Alwa Kingdom. Al-Aswani, who is quoted in al-Maqrizi, mentions the existence of *ribat* (lodging houses) of Muslim traders in Soba, which have not yet been investigated archaeologically (al-Maqrizi 1906: 311–312).

Archaeologically, there are many towns and villages that were established because of trade. The arrival of Muslim traders resulted in the introduction of a new legal code to regulate trade and respect for contracts (Manger 1984: 13). Arabic had been the language of trade since the time of the Christian kingdoms. Traders working in areas far away from home felt the need to live in close community with each other. Traders thus created small trading societies along their routes, and they were active in founding new towns. The early traders who dominated these societies were from Egypt and Arabia, and they were engaged in foreign trade. However, in the 17th and 18th centuries a group of Sudanese traders became active in international trade, particularly during the Funj period. Dawood ibn Abd al-Jaleel, a trader from Hijaz, to cite one example, was associated with Sheikh Taj al-Deen al-Buhari, who was known as the builder of Arbaji, an important commercial center during the Funj kingdom, and its mosque (McHugh 1994: 38; Soghayroun El Zein 2004: 46). Conquest could also be linked with trade as many of the traded items were obtained by raiding in the frontier areas to the south of the states. This penetration could be followed by military conquest and thus the subjugation of these areas into the states (Soghayroun El Zein 2010).

The means of transaction have been referred to in literary sources and ranged from bartering in kind as well as coins and other monetary systems (Arkell 1961: 191; Burckhardt. 1987: 289). Foreign coins, such as the Austrian Maria Theresa coins and the al-Majeedi of the Ottomans, have been found in the ruins of Sennar and other commercial towns, like Arbaji and Qerri (Soghayroun El Zein 2004: 83). With the general commercialization of the economy in the 18th and 19th centuries, new currencies were introduced; taxes came to be paid in cash, and a relationship of debt developed among producers, lenders, and consumers.

Towns and Villages Developed Along Trade Routes

Several small towns developed from villages to service stations, where camels could rest for some time, commodities were exchanged, customs dues were collected, and caravan guides recruited. Cobbe in Darfur was famous as the terminus point for the Darb al-Arba'in and destroyed during the Mahdiyya period in the late 19th century; it has, however, never been archaeologically investigated. Other sites, like 'Ain Farah and Shoba, have received preliminary surveys (Reed 1994: 13). Old Dongola and al Khandaq are two important river ports on the Nile for the al-Debba-Mashu route. Other sites on important trade routes include Sennar (the political and commercial capital of the kingdom of Sennar, Arbaji, Gerri, Shendi and al Mettama), al-Damer, Berber, Badi and Aidhab, and Suakin on the Red Sea coast (Soghayroun El Zein 2009, 2010) (Figure 4.2.8). Forts were erected or reused at the origin of wadis, at some points along the route, or at discharge points, as at Kuban, a fort situated at the mouth of Wadi Gabgaba on the right side of the Nile and connected with mining activities in the eastern desert.

THE ARCHAEOLOGY OF PILGRIMAGE (HAJJ)

There are also many routes that were once used by pilgrims crossing the Nilotic Sudan. These routes have created temporary and permanent halts for the pilgrims. The pilgrims would travel from West Africa until they reached western Sudan; from here people would follow the famous Darb al-Arba'in trade route to Assiut, and from there to Jeddah by the way of the port of Qusair (Egypt). This route was usually taken by those who could afford to join the trade caravans. The second important route was by way of Sennar, which was taken mainly by people coming from inside Sudan, from Darfur and Kordofan.

A recent survey of the Berber–Suakin route by M. S. Bashir (2017: 204–210) was based on two main sources of information about the targeted area. The first consists of military

FIGURE 4.2.8 al Khandaq, Northern State, remains of the river port town.

Courtesy of Intisar Soghayroun El Zein.

notes and reports dating to the Anglo-Egyptian period describing sites on the route. The second is a poem by Sheikh Ibrahim al-Farash who, in his account of his journey to Mecca, describes the resting places located along the pilgrim's caravan route from Berber to Suakin. Both sources described almost exactly the same route, and a number of wadi names, wells, and mountains are mentioned in both descriptions.

Bashir's survey recorded a total of forty sites which are more or less situated near the halting points mentioned by the sources. Pilgrims' caravans started, according to oral history testimonies, from what is called locally the "pilgrims' city" in the old town of Berber (el-Mikhayrif). Here pilgrims hired guides and obtained supplies for the trip across the Eastern Desert. The city contains buildings of mudbrick and *jalous* (building material made of mud and animal dung) currently standing to about 1 meter high. The passage toward Heritili seems to be one of the main routes through the Red Sea hills, and the tracks used by donkeys or camels are well-preserved.

CONCLUSION

It is clear that continuity outweighs discontinuity in assessing the archaeology of Islam in the Nilotic Sudan. The emphasis on the sheikh is a continuation of the role of the priest in Christianity and before that in the Kushite period (c. 900 BC–350 CE) as a mediator between people and God, as healer and protector. The practice of burning incense using almost the same shape of burners since the Napatan period of around 800 BC and up to the present in *Khalwi* and *qibbab* (plural of *qubba*) is another vivid material example of this continuity. The broken burners were usually left inside the *qubba* as part of the sanctity of the place (Figure 4.2.9). Other indicators of continuity are the placing of objects outside the grave pit with grain and/or water; spreading pebbles, especially white ones, on top of the grave, a practice that can be traced back to the Kerma period of about 2500 BC; and the spinning and weaving of local cloth, which can be traced back to the Meroitic period (350 BC–350 CE) and continued in the same area in and around Shendi during the Islamic period.

The primary changes brought by Islam were the introduction of the Arabic language as the language of the Quran, the Arabization of some of the Nubian tribes who migrated to central Sudan, and the influx of some Arab tribes (e.g., the Juhaina, Kenana, and Kawahla [Hassan 1967: 143]). Other changes that accompanied Islam included the shift from the maternal to paternal systems in kingship; all Shari'a laws concerning land tenure, commercial transactions, marriage, and family issues; and the change in house plan, where a clear segregation of the male reception area (or *daiwan*) is visible. A further change is the abundance of religious buildings in the Islamic period compared to Christianity before it, where only the church represented religion in Sudan.

FIGURE 4.2.9 Simit Island, Third Cataract region, inside a *Qubba* showing remains of incense burners.

Courtesy of Intisar Soghayroun El Zein.

Much research on the archaeology of Islam in the Nilotic Sudan remains to be done, but this chapter has indicated aspects of the rich material that exist and, in many instances, await detailed investigation.

REFERENCES

Abu Hassabu, A. A. M. 1985. *Factional Conflict in the Sudanese Nationalist Movement 1918–1948.* Graduate College Publications, no. 12 (Khartoum: University of Khartoum Press).

Adams, W. Y. 1987. "Islamic Archaeology in Nubia: An Introductory Survey," in T. Hägg (ed.), *Nubian Culture Past and Present: Main Papers Presented at the 6th International Conference for Nubian Studies in Uppsala, 11–August* (Stockholm: Almquist & Wiksell International), 327–361.

Alexander, J. A. 2000. "The Archaeology and History of the Ottoman Frontier in the Middle Nile Valley," *Adumatu, 1*: 47–61.

Al-Maqrizi. 1906. Kitāb al-Khiṭaṭ al-Maqrīzīyah. Cairo: Al-Nil Press.

Arkell, A. J. 1946. "Darfur Antiquities 111: The Round Town of Uri," *SNR, 27,* 186–202.

Arkell, A. J. 1961. *A History of the Sudan from the Earliest Times to 1821* (London: University of London, Athlone Press).

Bashir, M. 2017. "Archaeological Survey Along the Berber: Suakin Caravan Route: Preliminary Report," *Sudan & Nubia,* 21, 204–210.

Bruce, J. 1804. *Travels to Discover the Source of the Nile* (Edinburgh: A. Constable).

Burckhardt, J. l. 1987. *Travels in Nubia* (London: Reprint Services).

Cavendish, M. W. 1966. "The Custom of Placing Pebbles on Nubian Graves," *Sudan Notes and Records,* 47, 151–156.

Crawford, O. G. S. 1951. *The Funj Kingdom of Sennar* (Gloucester: John Bellows).

Crawford, O. G. S. 1961. *Castles and Churches in the Middle Nile Valley.* Sudan Antiquities occasional papers no. 2 (Khartoum: Sudan Commissioner for Archaeology).

El-Bushra, S. 1971. "Towns in Sudan in the Late 18th and Early 19th Centuries," *Sudan Notes and Records,* LII, 63–70.

El-Tayib, A. 2017. *Changing Customs of the Sudan* (Khartoum).

Greenlaw, J. P. 1976. *The Coral Buildings of Suakin* (London: Oriel Press).

Haaland, G. 1984. "The Jallaba Trading System," in Manger. L. (ed.). *Trade and Traders in the Sudan.* Bergen Occasional Papers in Social Anthropology (Bergen: University of Bergen), 269–284.

Hassan, Y. F. 1963. "The Penetration of Islam in the Eastern Sudan," *Sudan Notes and Records,* 44, 1–8.

Hassan, Y. F. 1967. *The Arabs and the Sudan* (Edinburgh: Edinburgh University Press).

Insoll, T. 2003. *The Archaeology of Islam in Sub-Saharan Africa* (Cambridge: Cambridge University Press).

Kapteijns, L. 1989. "The Historiography of the Northern Sudan from 1500 to the Establishment of British Colonial Rule: A Critical Overview," *IJAHS,* 22, 251–266.

Kawatoko, M. 1993. "Preliminary Survey of 'Aidhab and Badi' Sites," *Kush,* 16, 203–224.

Manger, L. 1984. *Trade and Traders in the Sudan,* Occasional Papers in Social Anthropology 32 (Bergen: University of Bergen).

McHugh, N. 1994. *The Holy Men of the Blue Nile: The Making of an Arab-Islamic Community in the Nilotic Sudan 1500–1850* (Evanston, IL: Northwestern University Press).

Musa, I. 1986. *The Archaeology of Central Darfur in the 1st Millennium AD*, BAR S258 (Oxford: British Archaeological Reports).

Mus'ad, M. 1972 (in Arabic) *Al-Maktaba al-'Arabiya Al-Sudaniya,* Cairo: Cairo University publication.

O'Fahey, R. S. 1994. *Arabic Literature of Africa, vol. I: The Writings of Eastern Sudanic Africa to c. 1900.* (Leiden: Brill).

Oman, G., Grassi, V., and Trombetta, A. (eds.) 1998. *The Book of Khor Nubt: Epigraphic Evidence of an Islamic-Arabic Settlement in Nubia (Sudan) in the III-IV Centuries A.H./X-XI A.D.* (Naples: Istituto universitario orientale).

Pallme, I. 1844. *Travels in Kordofan* (London: J. Madden and Co.).

Paul, A. 1954. *A History of the Beja Tribes in Sudan* (Cambridge: Cambridge University Press).

Petheric, J. 1861. *Egypt, Sudan and Central Africa* (London: William Blackwood).

Reed, G. 1994. "Archaeological Remains in the Kebkabiya Area of Northern Darfur," *SARS Newsletter 7.*

Sadr, K., Castiglioni, A., and Castiglioni, A. 1994. "Preliminary Results of CeRDO's Research in the Nubian Desert," *Nyame Akuma*, 41, 66–68.

Soghayroun El Zein, I. 1987. The Islamic Domed Tombs of Central Sudan. (Unpublished MA thesis, the American University in Cairo, Egypt.)

Soghayroun El Zein, I. 2004. *Islamic Archaeology in the Sudan,* BAR S1289, Cambridge Monographs in African Archaeology (Oxford: Archaeopress).

Soghayroun El Zein, I. 2009 "The Dialogue Between the Nile and Its Hinterlands: Al-Khandaq-A Desert Terminal and River Port," *Water Culture and Identity,* NBRP, 79–108 (Bergen: University of Bergen).

Soghayroun El Zein, I. 2010. *Trade and Wadi System(s) Muslim in Sudan* (Kampala, Uganda: Fountain Publishers).

Spaulding, J. 1984. "The Management of Exchange in Sennar," in L. Manger (ed.), *Trade & Traders in Sudan* (Bergen: University of Bergen), 25–48.

Waddington, G., and Hanbury, B. 1822. *Journal of a Visit to Some Parts of Ethiopia* (London: John Murray).

Walz, T. 1978. *Trade between Egypt and Bilad As-Sudan.1700–1820.* Cairo: Institut français d'archéologie orientale du Caire.

Yunis, K. 1979. *The Site of Ain Farah and Its Cultural Significance* (Unpublished BA Honors diss., University of Khartoum, Department of Archaeology).

CHAPTER 4.3

··

ETHIOPIA AND THE
HORN OF AFRICA

··

TIMOTHY INSOLL

INTRODUCTION

THIS chapter assesses the Islamic archaeology of the Horn of Africa through considering research completed, alphabetically, by country through Djibouti, Eritrea, Ethiopia, Somalia, and Somaliland (Figure 4.3.1), providing a survey of the main sites that have been investigated. Relevant research themes that have emerged, rural and urban landscapes, Islamization, trade, diet, and epigraphy, will be considered within these country surveys as the data are currently insufficient to place these within specific subsections. Moreover, although Islamic archaeology is the focus, it is necessary to stress two further points. First, that Islamic archaeology forms part of African Iron Age archaeology and thus fits into the preexisting archaeological context. Second, that because Muslims might be present from a certain point in time, this does not imply that everyone was Muslim and a uniform suite of Islamic material culture appeared. On the contrary, the archaeology frequently reflects a continuing mosaic of different beliefs—Islamic, African indigenous religions, and in Ethiopia, also Christianity or Judaism—as well as of dynamic historical and social processes.

Islamic archaeology in Ethiopia and the Horn of Africa has been variably investigated. In Somalia, until conflict precluded all research, archaeological focus was primarily on the Indian Ocean coast as a component of the Swahili world (e.g., Chittick 1976, 1982; Sanseverino 1983), and, in Somaliland, virtually no relevant archaeological research was completed until recently (e.g., Fauvelle-Aymar et al. 2011; González-Ruibal et al. 2015, 2017; Mire 2015a). Eritrea is also now effectively closed to archaeological research but previously

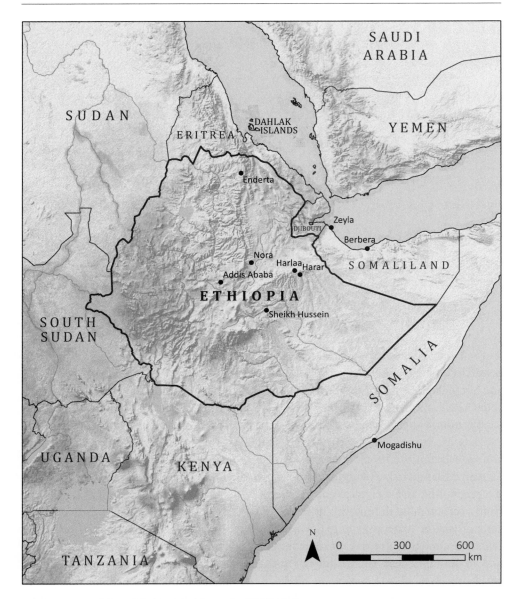

FIGURE 4.3.1 Map of the region (drawn by N. Khalaf).

the emphasis of Islamic archaeological investigation was on the Red Sea coast and Dahlak Islands (e.g., Tedeschi 1969; Oman 1974; Insoll 2001). In Djibouti, no dedicated research focusing on the Islamic period has been completed (X. Gutherz pers. comm. December 18, 2017), though some relevant material has been found (e.g., Grau 1976, 1981; Gutherz 2013: 31–32). In Ethiopia, Islamic archaeology is an area that is underexplored in comparison to, for example, the archaeology of the late Classical Kingdom of Aksum (e.g., Munro-Hay 1991; Phillipson 2000, 2004; Finneran 2007) or the architecture and archaeology of Ethiopian Orthodox Christianity (e.g., Finneran 2009, 2012; Phillipson 2009; Bosc-Tiessé et al. 2014), though this is beginning to be redressed (Fauvelle-Aymar and Hirsch 2010, 2011; Insoll 2017a, 2017b).

Djibouti

The strategic geographical position of Djibouti suggests that there is likely to be archaeological material of relevance for exploring Islamic trade networks, ports, and the connections between coastal centers with inland trade centers, as well as Islamization via nomad populations into, for example, the Danakil region of Ethiopia. Unfortunately, Islamic archaeology remains to be explored. Survey of the north coast between Obock and Doumeira recorded material of interest. At Ras Siyan, the discovery of Chinese pottery of unspecified types with approximately 200 kilograms of amphora sherds has been reported along with a cistern with a capacity of 150 cubic meters at Oued Aeygou (Labrousse 1978: 76). The interest of the investigators appears to have been in Ptolemaic navigation, but it is likely that many of the sites described are Islamic.

An interior site also of potential importance is Handoga, 10 kilometers west of Dikhil. Gutherz (2013: 31) refers to the "*enigme*" (enigma) of Handoga and describes the site as formed of several groups of round or oval stone huts. These were built of square blocks of basalt set in mud mortar with walls of 70–80 centimeters thick. This has similarities with the stone architecture of Islamic settlements in eastern Ethiopia and Somaliland described later. The location of Handoga seems to have been important and at the crossroads of several caravan routes, such as to Lake Abbe on the Djibouti-Ethiopia border, as well as Zeyla (Grau 1976: 5). Two radiocarbon dates of the 14th–15th and 16th centuries (all dates are CE unless otherwise specified) were obtained from the site, and two Arab coins of 11th- and 13th-century date and otherwise undescribed were recovered (Gutherz 2013: 31–32). Other imported materials reported include a blue-black glass bead with white decoration, a fragment of a blue glass bracelet, and part of a glass flask neck (Grau 1976: 8). Iron and copper slag and other metallurgical debris suggest that good quality metalworking was a significant activity at Handoga (Gutherz 2013: 31–32). Multiple hearths were found inside some of the huts, with twelve recorded in hut H1C alone (Grau 1981: 56). A hexagonal structure with a possible *mihrab* salient might have been a mosque, with a further two definite mosques recorded 2 kilometers north-west of Handoga. One was an outline mosque formed of a row of stone slabs and the other built of square stone blocks like the huts at Handoga (Grau 1976: 16).

ERITREA

Eritrea was critical in the early Islamic period as a staging point for relations between the formative Muslim community and the kingdom of Aksum. Building on extensive pre-Islamic connections across the Red Sea (e.g., Munro-Hay 1991; Phillipson 1998; Finneran 2007), historical records suggest close relations were maintained between the early Muslim community and Ethiopia (Kifleyesus 2006: 48). A group of the Prophet Muhammad's followers fleeing persecution in Mecca in 615 and who found asylum in the kingdom of Aksum (Lapidus 1988: 25; Kapteijns 2000: 228) provides probably the most famous example of this. Hadith also record that an Ethiopian, Bilal ibn Rabah, was appointed as the first Muezzin by the Prophet Muhammad, and the Prophet's lance, according to tradition, was given by an Ethiopian ruler to a companion of the Prophet and, in turn, to the Prophet himself (Miles 1952: 164–165; Munro-Hay 1991: 93–94; Power 2012: 95).

The Dahlak Islands

The Dahlak Islands were a likely stopping point during travel across the Red Sea from the Arabian to the African coasts, and vice versa. These have been the focus of survey by epigraphers and archaeologists (Oman 1976; Insoll 2001). The Dahlaks were one of the earliest Muslim centers of settlement in the region. "Abyssinian" pirates were recorded as having attacked Jeddah in 702–703 (Tedeschi 1969: 52), and, as a reaction to this, the islands were occupied in the early 8th century by Muslim naval forces. The islands then variously served as a place of exile and a major trade center, particularly Dahlak Kebir, the largest of the 220 or so islands that comprise the group (Insoll 2003: 51). Unfortunately, direct epigraphic correlation of this earliest Islamic period is lacking as the comparatively well-studied corpus of more than 200 basalt Arabic funerary inscriptions, relief carved in both Kufic and Nashkhi scripts, recorded from the Dahlaks date from between 911 and 1539 (Bassat 1893; Wiet 1951; Oman 1974, 1976; Schneider 1983) (Figure 4.3.2). Although they might not confirm the earliest Islamic period, they do provide interesting information. Bivar (1986: 387), for example, makes the relevant suggestion that the gravestones potentially indicate high death rates from malaria and dysentery, as a result of the drinking water being entirely obtained from cisterns in the dry season. He also indicates how the names commemorated indicate varied origins as with al-Fāriqī from Mayyāfāriqīn in Anatolia, al-Aghmātī from the Maghreb, and al-Sīrāfī presumably from Siraf in Iran.

The earliest Islamic archaeological chronology of the Dahlak Islands also remains unknown pending excavation, though survey has found the remains of an extensive settlement as well as *qubbas* (domed tombs) built from dressed coral and cisterns for water storage, cut from coral, roofed and supported by columns, and internally plastered (Insoll 2001). The numbers of cisterns on Dahlak Kebir and their clustering here and at

FIGURE 4.3.2 Muslim tombstone made by reusing a grinding stone, Dahlak Kebir, Eritrea.

Courtesy of T. Insoll.

Massawa and Kutto on the Eritrean coast indicate that the slave trade might have been significant (Puglisi 1969: 45; Insoll 2003: 54). Scatters of trade items of types widely found on the East African Indian Ocean and Red Sea coasts were also recorded on Dahlak Kebir (Insoll 2001, 2003). These include monochrome glass beads, fragments of multicolored chevron-decorated glass bracelets, and sherds of Chinese celadon (green glazed wares), blue and white porcelain, white porcelain, and Islamic sgraffiato wares of 9th- to 12th-century date and of Mesopotamian or Iranian provenance (cf. Insoll 2001). Trade was the probable primary agent of Islamization in the Dahlak Islands and on the neighboring African Red Sea coast (Insoll 2003, 2017a; Power 2012).

Mainland

On the coast itself and in interior Eritrea, Islamic archaeological research has been even more minimal. One of the most thoroughly investigated sites is the Aksumite port of Adulis south of Massawa. This does not appear to have been extensively used, if it was used at all, in the Islamic period. No relevant ceramics were reported from the extensive survey completed at the site (Peacock 2007). Only a few post-Aksumite sherds were recorded in the ceramics assemblage from previous excavations at Adulis (Zazzaro 2016: 82). These comprised four fragments of a gray-black jar and a single, thin, white-glazed base fragment described as not earlier than the 9th century in date and comparable to material from Athar in Yemen and Siraf in Iran (Zazzaro 2016: 92, 98). However, material remnants of later Ottoman influence exist on the coast and have been partially inventoried. The first sustained Ottoman contact with the Red Sea coast of Eritrea occurred in 1557, when a contingent of troops was disembarked at Massawa (Tedeschi 1969: 71). Ottoman occupation of parts of the region was to continue for some three centuries subsequently, and Massawa has several monuments attesting this, including the mosque and tomb of Sheikh Hammali founded in the 16th century (Cresti 1994). Other Ottoman sites further inland await investigation, as at Debarwa, 30 kilometers south of the Eritrean capital, Asmara, where a fort was established from the mid- to late 16th century and that was an important point on the coastal-interior trade routes (Pankhurst 1985: 68–69).

Ethiopia

Islamic archaeology in Ethiopia has been neglected (Insoll 2003, 2017b) with few notable exceptions (e.g., Fauvelle-Aymar and Hirsch 2010, 2011), a reflection perhaps of the secondary status ascribed Ethiopian Islam more widely (Ahmed 1992: 15–16). As a correlate, reviews of Islam in Ethiopia tend to lack a material dimension (e.g., Trimingham 1952; Kapteijns 2000; Kaplan 2004; Loimeier 2013). Islamic history in Ethiopia witnessed the apogee of various states and sultanates commencing with Shawā or Shoa in 896, which was absorbed by Ifat in 1280–1285 according to Huntingford (1955: 230) or 1295 according to Kapteijns (2000: 228). Ifat, one of seven Islamic sultanates recorded by al-ʾUmari in the first half of the 14th century (Hiskett 1994: 139), in turn, was weakened by internal political rivalries and conflict with the Ethiopian Christian state and gave way to the sultanate of Adal in 1420, a state which was to become the power-base of Imam Ahmad Gragn in his jihads against Christian Ethiopia until his death in 1543 (Kapteijns 2000: 229). Contemporary Islam in Ethiopia is diverse (Desplat and Østebø 2013: 11), and this is based on these deep historical roots that merit enhanced archaeological exploration.

The coastal sites of Somaliland and Eritrea through which Muslims would have transited into northern and eastern Ethiopia are considered in their respective sections. Trade, allied with proselytization, spread Islam into these parts of the Ethiopian interior (Insoll 2003: 58). Fauvelle-Aymar and Hirsch (2010: 47, 2011: 19–21) have suggested that this was through two axes, initially from the 9th to 10th centuries via the Dahlak Islands and Massawa to Shoa and, second, from the 13th century via Zeyla and Berbera to Harar and onto the southern lakes region (see also Insoll 2003: 58–59). To these should probably be added a third little-understood route connecting southeastern Ethiopia to the coast of Somalia (see later section).

Northern Route

Epigraphic survey has been completed in some areas that would have been connected with the northern Islamization/trade route, attesting the presence of Muslim communities. In the Quiha area of Tigray several basalt stelae engraved with Arabic inscriptions have been recorded dating from the 11th to 12th century (Schneider 1967). The gravestones from Enderta in Tigray have been described by Cerulli (2013: 128) as connected with families descended from "two Arab personalities," Hafs al-Yamani and 'Umar al-Yamani, merchants "who had settled there to collect and send Ethiopian merchandise to Dahlak and Massawa." Schneider (1967: 117) indicates that five gravestones allow genealogical reconstruction to these, presumably, Yemeni ancestors.

Evidence for mercantile contacts with the Muslim World has been found at sites in the Region. A fragment of white cloth with an embroidered red silk inscription bearing the name of the Abbasid Caliph al-Mu'tamid (891/278) was found in a storeroom in the Dabra Dāmmo monastery in Tigray. Coin finds in the surroundings of the monastery included Umayyad and Abbasid issues dating from between 78 and 331 AH (Mordini 1957: 75–77). This material is important in indicating economic and other relations between Muslims and Christians rather than "the existence of mutually incompatible blocs of Islam and Christianity" (Insoll 2003: 59). Similarly, from near the village of Ketetiya in South Wollo, an illicitly excavated hoard included a bronze incense burner of about 11 centimeters in diameter. This was decorated with inlaid silver geometric designs and, based on parallels with comparable objects, is likely of 13th-century date and of Ayyubid origin, possibly from northern Syria (Fauvelle-Aymar et al. 2010: 262–264).

A significant concentration of sites has also been recorded in northeastern Shoa, at the heart of the former sultanate of Ifat, around the town of Shoa-Robit (Insoll 2003: 69; Fauvelle-Aymar et al. 2006a). Tilahun (1990) describes settlements at Asberi, Rasa, Gozie, and Weissiso-Nora, and attributes them (1990: 314) to a period of "strong Islamic influence" between 896 and 1415. Of these, the latter site referred to by the shortened name of Nora has been partially excavated. The importance of this work lies in part in the fact that Nora was the first Islamic site in Ethiopia where excavation *"excède le cadre de simples repérages et sondages"* (Fauvelle-Aymar et al. 2009–2010: 58). Covering an area of approximately 15 hectares and on a defensible rocky spur, the town appears to have been spatially organized around the main mosque (Fauvele-Aymar et al. 2006b) (Figure 4.3.3). Excavation in this mosque provided a radiocarbon date of cal. CE 1165–1298 (Fauvelle-Aymar and Hirsch 2010: 36). The house walls were built of mud mortar and stone slabs shaped on their internal and external faces and approximately 60 centimeters thick (personal observation). An associated cemetery was also recorded (Fauvelle-Aymar et al. 2006a: 154–155). As in Tigray, Arabic inscribed gravestones also attest a Muslim past in Shoa. Schneider (1970) describes two from near Bishoftu and another from near Wonji; all are of some age, but undated.

FIGURE 4.3.3 A. Exterior of the mosque. B. interior of the mosque at Nora.

Courtesy of T. Insoll.

Southern Route: Harar

The southern Islamization/trade route has also been the focus of recent archaeological investigation centered on the city of Harar and the nearby abandoned settlement of Harlaa (Insoll et al. 2014, 2016; Insoll 2017b). Harar connected the eastern Ethiopian highlands, arid lowlands, and the Gulf of Aden (cf. Wilding 1980; Braukämper 2004). Harar was also a center of Islamic learning. As such, it was sometimes colloquially referred to as the "Timbuktu" of Ethiopia because of this status, and Harar was, and is, a major center of Muslim pilgrimage. It was also a locus of proselytization and a nucleus of Islamization from an unconfirmed date, perhaps from the 12th century and the migration of Muslim Argobba into the region (Braukämper 2004: 108–109), or, more likely later, as suggested by the currently available archaeological data discussed in upcoming paragraphs.

The importance of Harar is indicated by its size and is reflected in the listing of the Old City as a UNESCO World Heritage Site. The old city wall of Harar, the *djugel*, contains within it approximately 2,000 houses, 82 mosques, and more than 100 saints' tombs and shrines, the result of significant urban development over many centuries. Shrine-based ritual practices are an especially important element of Islamic ritual in Harar (cf. Foucher 1994), making it a focal point of sanctity.

Harar has significant historical depth, however the origins of Harar are obscured by conflicting traditions. These range from it being founded by Arabs from the Hadramaut

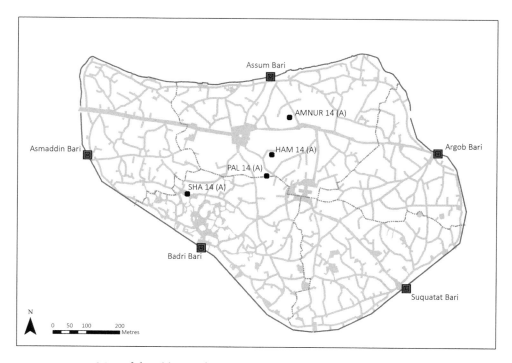

FIGURE 4.3.4 Map of the old city of Harar indicating the locations of the excavations (drawn by N. Khalaf).

in the late 7th century (Azaïs and Chambard 1931: 3), to being established by local people in the 10th century (Hecht 1987: 2), or even that it was a later foundation in the 16th century (Pankhurst 1985: 49), perhaps following the transference of the capital of the Sultanate of Adal from Dakar, possibly to be identified with Chenāhasan near Jigjiga (Huntingford 1955: 230) to Harar in 1521, as described by Braukämper (2004: 31). An alternative hypothesis, one distinguished in Harari local traditions, is that the city had dual foundation dates (Fauvelle-Aymar and Hirsch 2011: 23): the first described as occurring about the 10th century, and the second during the reign of Amir Nur (1552–1568) (Fauvelle-Aymar and Hirsch 2011). Each theory holds different implications, not just for the foundations of the city, but also for understanding the chronology of Islamic conversion and form of Islamization processes throughout the region and their links with trade networks for which Harar was also a hub.

Four test excavations have been completed in the city: in Hamburti, the Amir Nur shrine, Shagnila Toya, and at a palace site (Figure 4.3.4). Hamburti is believed locally to be the core area of early settlement in Harar; the explorer Richard Burton (1894: 40) described Gay Hamburti as "the historic rock upon which Saint Nur held converse with the prophet Khizr." Within local tradition Hamburti is referred to as the "navel" of Harar, suggesting it is a significant location in the foundation history of the city. Excavation in a domestic compound provided only modern material (Insoll 2017b). In contrast, excavation of an area of a small disused cemetery adjacent to the shrine of Amir Nur (d. 1567) did provide information on the settlement history of Harar. Amir Nur, the "patron saint" of Harar, and Shaikh Abadir (possibly early 13th century) are the two most revered saints in the city (Trimingham 1952: 249), and their shrines are among the most important Muslim sites of saintly veneration in Harar. It was during the reign of Amir Nur (1551–1568) that tradition records the Harar city wall was built and the city divided into five quarters (Ahmed 1990: 321) A sequence of Muslim burials, left undisturbed, was recorded, and an accelerator mass spectrometry (AMS) date of cal. CE 1648–1865 obtained (Insoll 2017b).

The third area excavated was in the former blacksmith quarter of Shagnila or Shagni Toya (Ahmed 1990: 325). All the features recorded—three postholes, one large and two smaller pits, and a channel—were potentially linked with iron smelting, representing a furnace base, tuyere channel, and associated shelter (Insoll 2017b). The courtyard outside the former palace of one of the Amirs of Harar was the location of the fourth excavation. Which Amir the palace belonged to is uncertain, possibly Amir Yusuf (1747–1756) or Amir Abdelshakur Yusuf (1783–1794) (cf. Hecht 1982: 60; Chiari 2015: 111). Features associated with occupation (shelters or enclosures represented by postholes), waste disposal (pit), and drainage (channel) were recorded. These were potentially for servants, guards, or visitors to the Amir (Insoll 2017b). An AMS date of cal. CE 1431–1476 was obtained from the pit fill.

Granted that excavation in Harar has thus far been limited, two preliminary observations emerge. First, evidence for participation in international trade is minimal, comprising a sherd of white glazed pottery and a single green glass flask neck from the Palace site and a sherd of blue and white ware from the undated iron-working site. Both the glass and the glazed sherds appear to be Middle Eastern products, with the blue and white glazed sherd possibly of Syrian origin, though this is not certain (R. Bridgman pers. comm. August 3, 2016). This absence of trade goods is surprising considering the role of Harar in trade networks. Second, although this could change pending further archaeological research, it currently appears that Harar is a comparatively late, possibly 16th-century foundation.

It is also important to recognize that Harar was not isolated but was part of a wider network of settlements, some Islamized, whose chronology is only now being reconstructed (Insoll 2017a). An example of such a site is Ganda Harla, 12.5 kilometers southeast of Harar. It is an extensive stone-built settlement bounded to the north by a defensive wall built of large stone blocks (Insoll et al. 2014: 104). Test excavation inside a building of uncertain function provided a radiocarbon date of cal. CE 1466–1645, which is not incompatible with the occupation sequence at Harar, to which it was potentially connected. Ganda Harla is representative of a widespread phenomenon of stone-built towns across the region studding the Danakil and Ogaden desert plains and the Harar and Arusi/Arsi highlands (Wilding 1980: 379) and spreading into Somalia and Somaliland (see later discussion). Wilding (1980: 379) describes the shared characteristics of these sites as built on defended hilltops, usually near a water supply and good grazing; set at approximately 1,800–2,000 meters above sea level, usually covering an area of less than 1,000 square meters; and with heavy stone ashlars used for defensive walling.

An association between these sites and the name "Harla" recurs in eastern Ethiopia (cf. Huntingford 1955: 233; Wilding 1980; Chekroun et al. 2011). "Harla" "Harlaa," or "Harala," refers to a people and first occurs historically as "Xarla" in the 13th-century *Universal Geography* of Ibn Saʿīd. The "Harla" are then mentioned twice in the 14th-century record of the wars of Amda Seyon (Chekroun et al. 2011: 75). They also appear in the *Futuh al Habasha* (e.g., Stenhouse 2003: 69, 76), the narrative of the jihads of Ahmad Gragn against the Christian kingdom of Ethiopia and chronicled up to 1535 by the Yemeni, Shihāb al-Dīn (Ahmed 1992: 23). "Harla" then lost its historical connection and assumed a legendary status. The name became associated with giants who were credited with building the stone towns, partly as it was believed the large stone blocks used to build features such as the wall at Ganda Harla could only have been manipulated by people of giant stature. "Harla" was also applied to funerary monuments and thus became linked with a range of sites whose origins were ascribed by the current Oromo inhabitants of much of the region to this ancient people who were there before the Oromo arrived in the latter part of the 16th century (Joussaume and Joussaume 1972: 22; Chekroun et al. 2011: 79). The extent to which the stone towns were Islamized is unclear as the category of sites linked with the "Harla" encompasses significant chronological and presumably religious and social diversity.

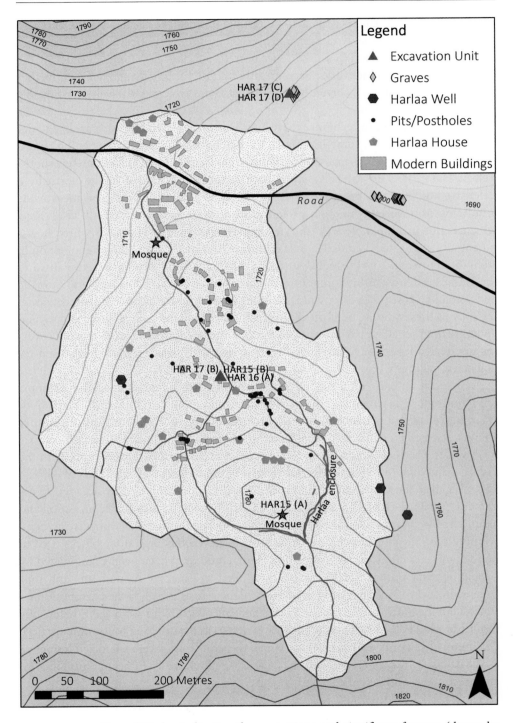

FIGURE 4.3.5 Plan of Harlaa indicating the excavations and significant features (drawn by N. Khalaf).

FIGURE 4.3.6 The burial complex partially excavated at Harlaa.

Courtesy of T. Insoll.

Southern Route: Harlaa

One stone town that was ultimately Islamized is Harlaa, about 40 kilometers north-west of Harar. This is also a site that has provided significant evidence for participation in Muslim-dominated long-distance trade networks (Insoll et al. 2016). Three areas of the site have been excavated to date: tombs and burials in an extensive cemetery, a mosque, and a series of jewelers' workshops in the settlement area (Insoll et al.2017) (Figure 4.3.5).

The presence of Muslims was attested by burials, three of which, because they were threatened by erosion, were excavated. Based on the absence of grave goods, their position in the grave (lying on their sides, heads at the northeast, faces slightly toward the northwest; i.e., toward the *qibla*, which is almost directly to north), and orientation (northeast to southwest) the burials were identified as Muslim (cf. Insoll 1999: 170–173). All three are of children aged between 2.5 and 6 years old when they died (L. Evis pers. comm. December 18, 2017). One was a simple inhumation lacking any remains of a tomb structure; the other two were a double burial, one above the other, each covered with stone slabs and placed within the same rectangular enclosure made of coralline limestone slabs laid on edge in a stone building constructed from partially shaped massive stone boulders (Insoll et al. 2017) (Figure 4.3.6). Three AMS dates were obtained from the burials spanning the period between the mid-12th and mid-15th centuries.

These burials lacked gravestones. Six engraved Arabic stelae (Schneider 1969; Insoll et al. 2016) have been recorded at Harlaa, including two recently (Insoll et al. 2016: 25–26). Four of these are undated, one has a date of 657 AH (1259–1260 CE) (Bauden 2011: 296) and another the partial date of 44x (Schneider 1969: 340), calculated as 1048–1057 CE by Chekroun et al. (2011: 79). These add to the corpus from the eastern highlands, which includes fourteen other gravestones recorded by Azaïs and Chambard (1931), with two from Heissa, seven from Lafto, three from Tchélenko, and two from Bâté (Ravaisse 1931: 283). Based on palaeographic characteristics, the Kufic-inscribed tombstones from Bâté are dated to approximately 1000 CE (Huntingford 1955: 232), and two others from Lafto have actual dates of 1267–1268/666 and 1276/675 (Ravaisse 1931: 288, 290). If the Bâté dates are correct, this would make the presence of Muslims much earlier than usually assumed in the eastern highlands. Like the Enderta tombstones, these probably indicate mercantile activity and former trade routes (Huntingford 1955: 230).

A further indicator of Islamization in Harlaa was provided by a ruined stone mosque measuring approximately 970 centimeters length by 700 centimeters in width. Excavations indicated that the *mihrab* was built of blocks of trimmed corraline limestone, and the walls were constructed from larger, less well-shaped blocks of basalt and limestone. A posthole suggested that the roof had been supported by wooden pillars (Insoll et al. 2016: 27). The selective use of corraline limestone in the *mihrab* is potentially indicative of inter-African contacts and/or architectural influences. In the Kilwa region in southern Tanzania, in the 11th–12th centuries, blocks of marine coral were used in construction, as in the first large mosque at Kilwa Kiswani (Pradines and Blanchard 2016: 14). Similarly, in the "Mosque with Two Mihrabs" at Zeyla, the first (undated) phase of the prayer hall was built with blocks of corralline limestone (Fauvelle-Aymar et al. 2011: 46). Garlake (1966: 11) describes how there was "complete mastery of working corraline limestone" on the East African coast. The use of squared coral blocks appears to have been "abandoned early" and is not evident, for example, in the Husuni Kubwa building at Kilwa at the end of the 13th century (Garlake 1966: 17). An AMS date of cal. CE 1155–1255 was obtained from the floor of the Harlaa mosque which agrees with Garlake's architectural chronology. The interpretation of inter-African connections is potentially strengthened by the similarities in the floor of the Harlaa mosque made of white lime mortar and gravel (Insoll et al. 2016: 27) and those of the East African coast constructed similarly from lime mortar and plaster (Garlake 1966: 11). Two niches were also found in the walls of the Harlaa mosque, one in the *mihrab* and a larger one adjacent to the *mihrab*. These, according to local informants, served respectively to store the Qur'an and for the Imam to sit in while delivering a sermon.

Insights into the participation of some of the population in Harlaa in trade, both Muslim-dominated Indian Ocean and Red Sea networks and regional commerce, has been recovered from the third area excavated. An occupation chronology based on ten AMS radiocarbon dates from the settlement area spanning the period between the late

5th to early 7th and late 13th to early 15th centuries has been reconstructed (Insoll et al. 2017). This is significant in including both pre-Islamic and Islamic phases, though the latter are as yet little understood. The structural complex uncovered appears to be a sequence of craft workshops used over three phases and likely associated with jewelry production. The workshop interpretation is based on features such as hearths, an upright stone anvil with a cup mark on its top surface that was possibly used as a working platform, quantities of charcoal, and metallurgical debris including slag, mold fragments, furnace brick, and a tuyere fragment. The later phase structures were particularly well built, with two large parallel stone walls of approximately 60–70 centimeters in width, and associated schist slab floors were uncovered.

The occupants of the Harlaa workshops imported and processed a range of commodities and luxury items. These included Chinese ceramics; celadon; white ware, possibly Qingbai; Islamic ceramics, black-on-yellow or "mustard" wares of likely Yemeni provenance (cf. Bridgman 2009: 136–137); and as yet unidentified green, black, and brown glazed wares. Examples of material reworking and modification were provided by some of the celadon sherds that had been shaped into small discs, perhaps to be sewn onto jewelry in the form of cabuchons, or as ring bezels. Shell working was undertaken on a significant scale. Cowry shells were being processed in large numbers on site. They were

FIGURE 4.3.7 Selection of glass and stone beads from Harlaa.

Courtesy of T. Insoll.

being split in half but also had their backs removed, with a combined total of 611 cowry backs recovered from two seasons (2016–2017) of excavation alone. Numerous glass vessel and bracelet fragments were also recorded. One bracelet fragment has raised polychrome glass drop decoration and is broadly comparable to glass bracelets from Zeyla site Z1 (cf. González-Ruibal et al. 2015: 13, 17), suggesting possible connections.

The bead assemblage was particularly diverse both in the materials and forms represented, including glass, carnelian, rock crystal, coral, and banded agate (Figure 4.3.7). Hardstone (carnelian and rock crystal) working took place on site. For example, nineteen clear quartz beads that were drilled but not polished were recovered from one context, and an agate that had split while being drilled was found with another agate and two quartz pebbles, one polished into an oval bead form. Bead drilling was further indicated by beads that had been abandoned because their holes did not meet, and both drilled and undrilled coral stems were found. A fragment of animal bone marked on one surface by five holes of different diameters also appears to have served as a protective hand guard during use of a bow drill (J. Kenoyer pers. comm. July 5, 2017). Glass beads seem also to have been made in the workshop complex, in particular red glass beads. Red glass rods, visually matching the red glass beads and potentially raw materials, were recovered, as were a red glass bead waster.

The origins of much this material are as yet unknown, but could include, besides the Chinese ceramics, Egypt and the Near East for the glass vessels and some of the glass beads and glass bracelets; the Red Sea for the coral and some of the shell, such as the *Olividae* sea shells; elsewhere in East Africa for the rock crystal (cf. Horton et al. 2017); western India for some of the carnelian beads (cf. Insoll et al. 2004); Yemen for some of the glazed pottery, such as the so-called mustard wares, and some of the glass bracelets; and the Maldives for the *Cypraea moneta* cowry shells (cf. Hogendorn and Johnson 1986). Further insight into trade connections and the potential areas of the Islamic world the inhabitants of Harlaa were indirectly connected with was provided by unstratified finds made by villagers during farming activities at the site (Insoll et al. 2016). This included three complete silver coins, ten clipped silver coins, and two bronze coins which preliminary reading indicates were mostly Ayyubid issues of the 12th–13th centuries (V. S. Curtis pers. comm. September 15, 2015). A bronze T'ang dynasty (618–907) Chinese coin was also recorded with the inscription "Kaiyuan tonbao," meaning, "circulating treasure of the new beginning" (Wilson and Flecker 2010: 38). These coins were issued from 621, but remained in circulation for a considerable time afterward (H. Wang pers. comm. September 15, 2015; cf. Cribb and Potts 1996: 109, 112).

The material from Harlaa was not exclusively consumed at the site but was likely fed into regional trade networks. Suggestions of where these consumers were can be made. Some 40 kilometers southwest of Harlaa, at Sourré-Kabanawa in the Tchercher Mountains, is a group of circular chambered stone tombs. Two of these were carbon (C^{14}) dated to cal. CE 980–1180 (monument 1) and cal. CE 770–950 and cal. CE 930–1080 (monument 3) (Joussaume 1980: 102). This chronology is comparable to Harlaa, which could have been the source of some of the grave goods recovered, including thirty-five

Cypraea annulus cowry shells, some with their backs removed; forty *Oliva ericea linne* shells and three copper bracelets from monument 3; or large numbers of small blue, green, red, and yellow glass beads, as well as copper beads and bracelets from monument 1 (cf. Joussaume 1980: plates XII–XIV). The contents of some of the Tchercher tombs might also explain the presence of clipped silver coins at Harlaa. These could have been melted down to produce silver jewelry. Although earlier in date than the Ayyubid issues recorded so far, a spiral silver ring was found in a stone pile tumulus (1) at Sourré-Kabanawa C^{14} dated to cal. CE 730–940. A silver ring also was recovered from another circular chambered tomb at Raré, dated to cal. CE 1370–1440 (Joussaume 1980: 102, Fig. 113, Pl XI) and thus much closer in date to the Ayyubid coins.

Ceramic similarities also exist between Harlaa and the Tchercher Mountains sites. At Molé (Dobba), one of a group of settlement sites with Harla characteristics, such as being surrounded by walls built of large stone blocks (cf. Azaïs and Chambard 1931; Joussaume and Joussaume 1972) and which were C^{14} dated to the 8th–11th centuries (Joussaume 1980: 102), there are local ceramic parallels in, for instance, the use of finger impressions to produce decorative bands (e.g., Joussaume and Joussaume 1972: fig. 10 [1]), or the presence of identical forms of pinched handles pierced horizontally with a hole, perhaps for suspension with a cord (e.g., Joussaume and Joussaume 1972: fig. 12 [2]). There are no reliable indications that these Tchercher settlements were Islamized, and trade goods such as imported glazed ceramics are not reported. These local ceramics could represent trade items themselves and/or the contents they once held or similarities in ceramic traditions because the populations, Muslim and non-Muslim were, at least in part, the same.

Overall, it is apparent that Islam was established in some urban contexts in eastern highland Ethiopia by at least the mid-12th century, but this was far from universal, and Islamization appears to have been linked with trade directed to the Red Sea and leading into Indian Ocean networks. It can be suggested that this was directly connected with the revival of Red Sea trade in the late 10th century following the rise of the Fatimid dynasty in Egypt (Kapteijns 2000: 228). The first date of Islamization, or at least the presence of Muslims at Harlaa, excluding the reconstructed date on the Arabic engraved gravestone discussed earlier and instead based on the radiocarbon dates from the mosque and the Muslim burials, can be placed at, potentially, the mid-12th century. The composition of these early Muslim communities is unknown but likely was of both local and foreign elements. The concept of "entanglement" (Hodder 2012: 6), in which things are connected and flow into other things (Insoll 2015: 6), would appear appropriate to begin to explain the nature of the connections which existed, encompassing religious, social, and technical connections. The possibility that Swahili and other African origin communities were present at Harlaa, based on the architectural parallels and presence of materials such as rock crystal, is intriguing and suggestive of inter-African Muslim contacts. The transfer of ideas, besides religious ones (Islam), seems to have been equally significant. Alongside possible architectural influences from the Red Sea and/or East African coast, the evidence for the production of apparently heat-altered carnelian beads, rock crystal beads, and monochrome glass beads would also all seem to indicate transfer of bead-making technologies from, potentially, Gujarat in India (cf. Kenoyer, Vidale, and Bhan 1991; Roux 2000; Francis 2002; Insoll et al. 2004) and, possibly Egypt and/or the East African Coast (cf. Francis 2002; Horton et al. 2017). Whether this also involved the transfer of craftspeople is not known.

Based on the currently available C[14] dates, Harlaa appears to have been abandoned by the early 15th century. This was perhaps due to increasing Islamization in the Tchercher and Harar areas further up in the highlands, and thus the defensible location that Harlaa provided was deemed no longer deemed unnecessary. What happened to the "Harla" is also unclear. It might be that the Harla are the ancestors of the Harari, as suggested by Braukämper (2004: 107). To assess this, more archaeological work is required in Harar to explore the generic similarities so far identified between aspects of the ceramics assemblages from Harar and Harlaa, and further C[14] dates are required from Harar to compare with the more comprehensive sequence from Harlaa (Insoll 2017b). Turning from archaeology to legend to explain the demise of the Harla, a common theme that emerges is that "Allah punished the Harla as a result of their arrogance and extravagant behaviour *in their material prosperity*" (Anonymous 2015: 27). The emphasis has been added as the material prosperity at, for example, Harlaa, is undeniable, though the divine punishment is unproved.

Nomads

Harlaa was located midway between the lowlands and the eastern highlands where Harar is situated. In the lowlands, nomad populations would have been significant (Insoll 2003: 73–76). The archaeology of Muslim nomad groups—Afar, Oromo, Somali—in Ethiopia remains to be explored. A sultanate, Aussa, was established in the single fertile area in Afar territory on the Awash River in the 16th century (Thesiger 1998). Afar stone outline mosques have been recorded, with a large stone for the *mihrab* (Jacob 1997: 186). But Afar Islam, as Lewis (1994: 172) noted, "has not yet acquired anything like as strong a hold over the nomadic population of Dankalia as it has among the Somali." This would appear to be supported by the construction until recently of varied forms of funerary monuments by the Afar. In the interior of Afar territory, stone cairns; *waidella*; or *das*, stone circles of various configurations were used. These had a burial in the center, a single entrance, and a line of upright stones indicating the deceased man's victims (cf. Thesiger 1935: 10–11, 1998: 123; Nesbitt 1934: 77, 210–212), and they reflect the persistence of a "cult of the dead" (Lewis 1994: 172).

In other areas where Muslim influence was stronger, as on the Red Sea coast (Lewis 1994: 171), Afar funerary monuments were more orthodox, with head and foot-stones used (Thesiger 1935). The archaeology and material culture of the Oromo, partly nomadic, partly sedentary, partly Muslim, partly Christian, and partly followers of indigenous religion (cf. Bartels 1990), also remains largely unexplored, though they constitute 34% of the population of Ethiopia (https://www.cia.gov/library/publications/the-world-factbook/geos/et.html). Historically, the spread of Islam among the Oromo was a slow process, and though exposed to the religion certainly from the 15th century, "the pastoral Oromo on the whole retained their traditional religion" largely until the 19th century (Hassen 1994: 150).

South and South-East Ethiopia

An exception to the lack of study of Muslim (and other) Oromo material culture is provided by Henze's (2005) survey of funerary monuments in Arsi and Bale. This indicated that "no truly ancient Oromo burial sites are known" (Henze 2005: 178). Stone slabs were sometimes cut with short Arabic inscriptions, but with Oromo not Muslim names, and square tombs with domes reflected Muslim practice. Increasing Salafist influence was leading to the diminution of elaborate tombs and grave visiting (Henze 2005: 191).

Traditions of past peoples probably similar to the Harla are also manifest in southeast Ethiopia where "Sharalla" could be a corruption of "Harla" or "Harala" (Østebø 2012: 47). Stone built settlements are found, as at Oda Roba in Bale. Bale is also the site of the Sheikh Hussein shrine, which is a significant pilgrimage center. Sheikh Hussein is credited with bringing Islam to Bale, possibly in the 12th century, and traditions state that his grave became the subject of pilgrimage soon after his death (Østebø 2012: 52). Although not an archaeological site it is again representative of shrine-based ritual practices and would merit archaeological investigation to assess the chronology of foundation and use. Other Islamic sites and inscriptions reported from Bale include the Zuktum mosque in Dirre Sheikh Hussein and the ruined Balla mosque 2–3 kilometers south, both of which, according to local sources, are of 11th-century date (Østebø 2012: 52). The Balla mosque clearly belongs to the same architectural tradition as the Harlaa and Nora mosques, being built of similar regular stone blocks (cf. Østebø 2012: illustration 2). Four inscribed undated Muslim tombstones were also recorded at Munessa, south of Addis Ababa near Lake Zuwai (Ravaisse 1931: 283).

The Ogaden and Arusi/Arsi highlands stone towns reported by Wilding (1980: 379) also await investigation. These are particularly significant for they seem to archaeologically attest a further trade and Islamization route from eastern Ethiopia direct to the coast of Somalia at Mogadishu and Merca (Wilding 1980: 380), and they would also explain the existence of the Bale Sharalla/Harla sites as part of this chain of settlements.

Somalia

Within Somalia relevant archaeological research has been limited, concentrated on the coastal strip and key towns such as Mogadishu (e.g., Chittick 1982), and wholly absent for the past two decades because of ongoing conflict. This is unfortunate, for among the Somali Islam of the Shafi'i school was already established by the 11th century (Lewis 1986, 1994: 140).

Coastal Sites

North of Mogadishu, to the border with Somaliland, little information on Islamic archaeology exists. South of Mogadishu, rare sherds of ceramics, including 14th-century celadon and 15th-century monochrome Islamic ware, otherwise undescribed, were collected during survey of a coastal site at Abai Dakhan (Chittick 1976: 126). A stone architectural tradition akin to the Swahili one previously described (and see Chapter 4.1, this volume) and utilizing coral as a building material also occurs in southern Somalia. Numerous stone monuments have been recorded, including a pillar tomb 5 meters in height at Ras Kiambone, a site where sherds of celadon ascribed a 15th- to 16th-century date along with Islamic monochrome and manganese purple wares were collected (Sanseverino 1983: 156). A further group of pillar tombs are known at Hanassa, including one with a rounded pillar that had recesses for three ceramic bowls (Sanseverino 1983: 159), presumably missing, but this is not stated. Various remains also exist at Bur Gavo or Bur Gao, the best harbor in this area of Somalia (Chittick 1969; Sanseverino 1983) and, as such, likely used by Muslim maritime traders involved in Indian Ocean trade. A pillar tomb and domed "place of prayer," along with the ubiquitous celadon sherds and fragments of Islamic monochrome wares were reported from site Bur Gao 1 by Sanseverino (1983: 163). This site was defended by a plastered coral rubble and lime plaster wall of 2.5 meters in height enclosing an area of approximately 7 hectares (Chittick 1969: 126–127). Similar town walls enclosed the settlements of Ras Kiambone and Myaandi (Sanseverino 1983: 155, 161).

Mogadishu

The origins of Mogadishu have also been variously investigated (e.g., Chittick 1982; Jama 1990; Broberg 1995) without agreement on the date of the foundation of the city (cf. Insoll 2003: 61–62). Chittick (1982), who appears to have halted his excavations near the congregational mosque in Hamar Weyne, part of the old town, for safety reasons before reaching the base of the archaeological deposits (Jama 1990: 108), suggests that Mogadishu was founded in the late 12th century and peaked in the 13th–14th centuries. This interpretation was based on the presence of likely Iranian-origin Sgraffiato of 12th-century date, black-on-yellow pottery of 14th-century date, and tomb and mosque inscriptions of 13th- to 14th-century date. However, it is possible that the city is earlier, perhaps 10th century, perhaps earlier if reports of gravestones, now missing and dated to CE 720 and 752 (Jama 1990: 107; Abdi 1992: 122) are correct (Insoll 2003: 62). Unfortunately, this awaits correlation pending the resumption of archaeological research in Somalia whose role as a stop-over for vessels trading up and down the East African coast would have been vital right from the origins of this segment of the Indian Ocean trade network (cf. Hamdun and King 1994: 16–21; Hourani 1995: 80).

Participation in trade, both local and long distance, would also appear to be indicated by several thousand copper, silver, and billon coins "collected" primarily in the vicinity of Mogadishu (Insoll 2003: 65). These predominantly date from approximately 1300–1700 and include issues of twenty-one local rulers, as well as a T'ang and several Song (960–1279) dynasty coins, and issues of the sultans of Kilwa (Freeman-Grenville 1963: 187–199). Some of the local issues were also exported from Somalia with a copper coin of Sultan Ali ibn Yusuf dating from the 15th or 16th century recovered from Julfar in Ras al-Khaimah in the United Arab Emirates (Lowick 1985: 5).

SOMALILAND

In contrast, the relative stability enjoyed in the autonomous region of Somaliland has meant that archaeological research, including on Islamic sites and material, has expanded in the past decade, both on the coast and in the interior (e.g., Fauvelle-Aymar et al. 2011; Mire 2015a, 2015b; González-Ruibal et al. 2015, 2017). This is allowing exploration of, for example, the archaeology of trade routes and contacts, Islamization, syncretism, and local Islamic practice.

Coastal Trade Centers

As already described, trade routes were directed inland from the coast. Examples of key coastal trade centers in Somaliland that also functioned as significant nodes for Islamization were Zeyla and Berbera on the Gulf of Aden. Yaqut mentions Zeyla as early as 891–892 (Pankhurst 1985: 54), and Lewis (1994: 140) suggests that this northern area of the coast was influenced by Muslims "very soon after the Hejira." Substantial settlement remains have been recorded in and around the town and on the neighboring island of Saad Din (Curle 1937; Fauvelle-Aymar et al. 2011; González-Ruibal et al. 2017). Curle (1937: 316) collected sherds of "Arab" glazed pottery and glass and Chinese celadon and blue and white wares. Blue and white Iranian frit wares of 14th- to 17th-century date and quantities of green glass of earlier 9th- to 12th-century date was also collected from the same dumps in the harbor area by González-Ruibal et al. (2017: 140), who suggest that Zeyla was particularly important between the 14th and 16th centuries. The Qiblatayn mosque or so-called mosque "*avec deux mihrab*" (Fauvelle-Aymar et al. 2011: 46) in the town has also been excavated. The name of the mosque reflects the belief that it was aligned both to Mecca and Jerusalem, thereby reflecting the prayer orientation of the earliest Muslims and was, according to oral tradition, one of the earliest mosques in sub-Saharan Africa (Mire 2015a: 129). Another excavation of a former path passing the Qiblatayn mosque yielded Yemeni "mustard" or black-on-yellow wares of 13th- to mid-14th–century date (Fauvelle-Aymar et al. 2011: 49).

Other coastal sites have been investigated by González-Ruibal et al. (2017). At Berbera, 19th-century architecture, the "product of Egyptian occupation after 1870" (González-Ruibal et al. 2017: 142) was recorded. At Bandar Abbas, 10 kilometers east of Berbera, significant quantities of imported materials were recovered including glass and carnelian beads, perforated *Cypraea annulus* cowry shells, a sherd of Gujerati red-slipped ware, and sherds of monochrome, hatched, and polychrome sgraffiato, likely of Iranian provenance and of 11th- to 12th-century date. The overall interpretation proposed (González-Ruibal et al. 2017: 144) was that this was a rare example of a foreign settlement, specifically Persian, and possibly Sirafi. While at Bulhar, the material from the Ottoman period (16th to mid-19th century), including shisha pipes, monochrome glass cobalt-blue bracelets with pressed decoration, and fragments of large stone-glazed bowls, begins to fill a chronological gap.

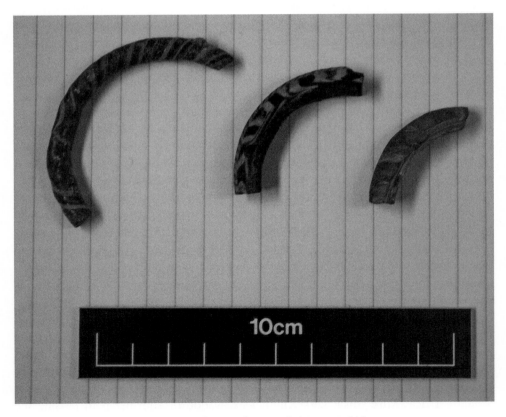

FIGURE 4.3.8 Imported glass bracelets in the British Museum (Afr. 1935.0709.106, 0709.94, 0709.97) collected by Curle in Somaliland.

Courtesy of T. Insoll.

Inland Stone Towns, Shrines, and Tombs

Mire (2015a: 129) reports forty ruined towns from Somaliland with the distribution confirming "ancient trade routes" and concentrations between Sheikh, Hargeysa, and Burao and around Boorama. Although the term "towns" is misleading in covering a range of sites in terms of "size, monumentality and occupation" (González-Ruibal et al. 2017: 153), it is still useful to employ until settlement variation is better understood. The abandoned stone towns linking the coast with the interior were initially surveyed by Curle (1937). The similarities with the stone towns already described are striking, with the principal towns of Amud, Abasa, Gogesa, and Au Bare situated at more than 1,000 meters and each with a mosque or mosques and more than 200 stone-built houses. These ranged from single-room to multiroom courtyard forms and had walls between 60 and 90 centimeters thick, built of stone blocks set with termite earth mortar (Curle 1937: 316–318), thus resembling structures already described for Harlaa, Nora, and Handoga. Imported Chinese ceramics including the ubiquitous celadons were found, with trade also manifest by imported blue, yellow, and white glass beads; multicolored glass bracelet fragments; and carnelian beads. Daily life was represented by camel, sheep, and goat bones; grinding stones; coffee beans; steatite vessel fragments; soft stone spindle whorls; and locally made black and brown burnished pottery (Curle 1937: 321–324) (Figure 4.3.8). Some of the latter share similarities with pottery from Harar, and Curle (1937: 321) refers to the "ribbed neck of a black jar" from Amud as similar to a honey jar seen from Harar. Other similarities exist in the brown burnished wares and carinated forms present in both areas (Insoll 2017b).

A more specialized trading center, a caravanserai or fort, has also been recorded at Qalcadda, 85 kilometers from Berbera on a main route into the interior. This, it is suggested, was linked with the Sultanate of Adal and is "a manifestation of the control of long distance trade by the state" (González-Ruibal et al. 2017: 152). Saints shrines are also significant in parts of Somaliland. The shrine of Aw-Barkhadle located in a medieval ruined town is described by Mire (2015b: 101) as having been a focus of pilgrimage since the 12th century. The shrine forms part of a sacred landscape also comprising hilltops, tombs, and phallic grave stones that function within fertility rituals and are the result of complex syncretic processes drawing on both pre-Islamic and Islamic elements (Mire 2015b).

As in parts of Ethiopia and Somalia, nomadic groups were key agents in early Islamization. At Iskudar, a name meaning "mixing," "aggregation," or "combination," in the Golis Mountains, what appears to have been a pre-Islamic nomad ritual center has been identified where the dead were buried and associated rituals such as feasting were completed (González-Ruibal et al. 2017: 165). Feasting was attested by faunal remains, particularly sheep/goat, many with butchery and cut marks, and linked with burial cairns. Of particular interest are the two AMS dates obtained of the mid-12th to mid-14th centuries from contexts associated with faunal remains. These are comparable to an AMS date of cal. CE 1275–1385 from a burial mound excavated at

Sofi, near Ganda Harla (Insoll et al. 2016: 30) indicating that Islamization was far from complete at this date among both nomad (Iskudar), and sedentary (Sofi) populations.

CONCLUSION

The Islamic archaeology of Ethiopia and the Horn of Africa is both rich and complex, but in most areas the study of this material is still in its infancy. The earliest Muslim contacts with the region appear to have taken place at or around the Hejira. Archaeological evidence for this is so far lacking, but different routes subsequently served as conduits for trade and Islamization from the 9th to 10th centuries in the north and the 12th to 13th centuries in the south, with a third Mogadishu-focused route as yet little understood. Recent research in eastern Ethiopia and Somaliland is significantly increasing knowledge of relevant material culture, trade contacts, and the chronology of Islamization. In some areas, a shift is also occurring, with less emphasis on cataloguing material, potsherds, or mosque forms, for instance, and more of a focus on social processes, new forms of identities, and impacts on lifeways linked with Islamization, as manifest through diet or changes in uses or relationships with architectural space and landscapes (cf. Insoll 2017a). In other areas, there is still an urgent requirement for mapping of data, basic survey, and chronological reconstruction.

Future research should focus on better understanding inter-African connections where, currently, there is an emphasis on long-distance international trade as it is tangibly represented by imported beads, glazed ceramics, and glass wares, usually of known provenance. Inter-African connections, to Nubia and the Sudanese Nile, the Swahili coast and Madagascar, or to southwest Ethiopia, are hinted at and need exploring, refuting, or confirming. The development of particular aspects of Islamic material culture and practice in the region and the focus on shrines or the incorporation of pre-Islamic ritual centers merit enhanced investigation from an archaeological perspective. Finally, besides exploring origins of towns or Islamization there is also a need to assess the collapse of the stone towns and the networks that sustained them, as well as the disappearance of the "Harla," for this all appears to link to the momentous changes that occurred in the 16th century related to jihad and Portuguese, Ottoman, and Oromo expansion (González-Ruibal et al. 2017: 168). Doing so will further permit the embedding of the Islamic archaeology of Ethiopia and the Horn of Africa within the wider context of both regional and world history.

REFERENCES

Abdi, M. 1992. *Histoire des Croyances en Somalie* (Paris: Diffusion des Belles Lettres).

Ahmed, A. M. 1990. "A Survey of the Harar Djugel (Wall) and Its Gates," *Journal of Ethiopian Studies*, 23, 321–334.

Ahmed, H. 1992. "The Historiography of Islam in Ethiopia," *Journal of Islamic Studies*, 3, 15–46.

Anonymous. 2015. *History of Harar and the Hararis* (Harar: Harari People Regional State Culture, Heritage, and Tourism Bureau).

Azaïs, R. P., and Chambard, R. 1931. *Cinq années de recherches archéologiques en Ethiopie* (Paris: Paul Geuthner).

Bartels, L. 1990. *Oromo Religion* (Berlin: Dietrich Reimer Verlag).

Bassat, R. 1893. "Les Inscriptions de l'Ile de Dahlak," *Journal Asiatique*, 9, 77–111.

Bauden, F. 2011. "Inscriptions Arabes d'Éthiopie," *Annales Islamologiques*, 45, 285–306.

Bivar, A. D. H. 1986. "Review of, Schneider, M. Stèles Funéraires Musulmanes des Îles Dahlak," *Bulletin of the School of Oriental and African Studies*, 49, 387.

Bosc-Tiessé, C., Derat, M-L., Bruxelles, L., Fauvelle, F-X., Gleize, Y., and Mensan, R. 2014. "The Lalibela Rock Hewn Site and Its Landscape (Ethiopia): An Archaeological Analysis," *Journal of African Archaeology*, 12, 141–164.

Braukämper, U. 2004. *Islamic History and Culture in Southern Ethiopia* (Münster: Lit Verlag).

Bridgman, R. 2009. "From the Tihamah Plain to Thailand and Beyond: Preliminary Analysis of Selected Ceramics from Quseir al-Qadim," in L. Blue, J. Cooper, R. Thomas, and J. Whitewright (eds.), *Connected Hinterlands*. BAR S2052 (Oxford: Archaeopress), 133–140.

Broberg, A. 1995. "New Aspects of the Medieval Towns of Benadir in Southern Somalia," in K. Ådahl and B. Sahlstrom (eds.), *Islamic Art and Culture in Sub-Saharan Africa* (Uppsala: Acta Universitatis), 111–122.

Burton, R. F. 1894 (1987). *First Footsteps in East Africa or, An Exploration of Harar Volume 2* (New York: Dover Publications).

Cerulli, E. (Weber, E. M. trans.). 2013. *Islam Yesterday and Today* (Addis Ababa: Mukhtar A. Allam).

Chekroun, A., Fauvelle-Aymar, F-X., Hirsch, B., Ayenachew, D., Zeleke, H., Onezime, O., and Shewangizaw, A. 2011. "Les Harla: Archéologie de Mémoire des Géants d'Ethiopie," in F-X. Fauvelle-Aymar and B. Hirsch (eds.), *Espaces Musulmans de la Corne de l'Afrique au Moyen Âge* (Paris: De Boccard), 75–102.

Chiari, G. P. 2015. *A Comprehensive Guide to Harar and Surroundings* (Addis Ababa: Arada Books).

Chittick, N. 1969. "An Archaeological Reconnaissance of the Southern Somali Coast," *Azania*, 4, 115–130.

Chittick, N. 1976. "An Archaeological Reconnaissance in the Horn: The British-Somali Expedition 1975," *Azania*, 11, 117–133.

Chittick, N. 1982. "Medieval Mogadishu," *Paideuma*, 28, 45–62.

Cresti, F. 1994. "La Mosquée de Sayh Hammali," in C. Lepage (ed.), *Etudes Ethiopiennes*, vol. 1 (Paris: Société Française pour les Etudes Ethiopiennes), 303–315.

Cribb, J., and Potts, D. 1996. "Chinese Coin Finds from Arabia and the Arabian Gulf," *Arabian Archaeology and Epigraphy*, 7, 108–118.

Curle, A. T. 1937. "The Ruined Towns of Somaliland," *Antiquity*, 11, 315–327.

Desplat, P., and Østebø, T. 2013. "Muslims in Ethiopia: The Christian Legacy, Identity Politics, and Islamic Reformism," in P. Desplat and T. Østebø (eds.), *Muslim Ethiopia* (Basingstoke: Palgrave Macmillan), 1–21.

Fauvelle-Aymar, F-X., Hirsch, B., Bruxelles, L., Mesfin, C., Chekroun, A., and Ayenatchew, D. 2006a. "Reconnaissance de Trois Villes Musulmanes de l'Époque Médiévale dans l'Ifat," *Annales d'Éthiopie*, 22, 133–175.

Fauvelle-Aymar, F-X., Bruxelles, L., Chekroun, A., Mensan, R., Onézime, O., Wubete, A., Ayenatchew, A., Zeleke, H., Hirsch, B., and Mohamed, A. 2006b. "A Topographic Survey and Some Soundings at Nora, an Ancient Muslim Town of Ethiopia," *Journal of Ethiopian Studies*, 39, 1–11.

Fauvelle-Aymar, F-X., and Hirsch, B. 2010. "Muslim Historical Spaces in Ethiopia and the Horn of Africa: A Reassessment," *Northeast African Studies*, 11, 25–53.

Fauvelle-Aymar, F-X., Poissonnier, B., Letricot, A., and Tesfaye, H. 2010. "Découvertes Archéologiques aux Environs de Dessié (Éthiopie)," *Annales d'Éthiopie*, 25, 261–268.

Fauvelle-Aymar, F-X., and Hirsch, B. 2011. "En Guide d'Introduction. Sur les Traces de l'Islam Ancien en Ethiopie et dans la Corne de l'Afrique," in F-X. Fauvelle-Aymar and B. Hirsch (eds.), *Espaces Musulmans de la Corne de l'Afrique au Moyen Âge* (Paris: De Boccard), 11–26.

Fauvelle-Aymar, F-X., Hirsch, B., Bernard, R., and Champagne, F. 2011. "Le Port de Zeyla et son Arrière-pays au Moyen Âge" in F-X. Fauvelle-Aymar and B. Hirsch (eds.), *Espaces Musulmans de la Corne de l'Afrique au Moyen Âge* (Paris: De Boccard), 27–74.

Fauvelle-Aymar, F-X., Hirsch, B., Ménard, C., Mensan, R., and Pradines, S. 2009–2010. "Archéologie et Histoire de l'Islam dans la Corne de l'Afrique: État des Recherches," *Civiltà del Mediterraneo*, 16–17, 29–58.

Finneran, N. 2007. *The Archaeology of Ethiopia* (Abingdon: Routledge).

Finneran, N. 2009. "Built by Angels? Towards a Buildings Archaeology Context for the Rock-Hewn Medieval Churches of Ethiopia," *World Archaeology*, 41, 415–429.

Finneran, N. 2012. "Lalibela in Its Landscape: Archaeological Survey at Lalibela, Lasta, Ethiopia, April to May 2009," *Azania*, 47, 81–98.

Foucher, E. 1994. "The Cult of Muslim Saints in Harar: Religious Dimension," in B. Zewde, R. Pankhurst, and T. Beyene (eds.), *Proceedings of the Eleventh International Conference of Ethiopian Studies, Volume 2* (Addis Ababa: Institute of Ethiopian Studies), 71–83.

Francis, P. 2002. *Asia's Maritime Bead Trade. 300 B.C. to the Present* (Honolulu: University of Hawai'i Press).

Freeman-Grenville, G. S. P. 1963. "Coins from Mogadishu, c.1300 to c.1700," *Numismatic Chronicle*, 3, 179–200.

Garlake, P. 1966. *The Early Islamic Architecture of the East African Coast* (London: Oxford University Press).

González-Ruibal, A., de Torres, J., and Fernández, M. A. F. 2015. *Report on an Archaeological Trip to Somaliland. June 2015* (Madrid: Consejo Superior de Investigaciones Científicas).

González-Ruibal, A., de Torres, J., Franco, M. A., Ali, M. A., Shabelle, A. M., Barrio, C. M., and Aideed, K. A. 2017. "Exploring Long Distance Trade in Somaliland (AD 1000–1900): Preliminary Results from the 2015–2016 Field Seasons," *Azania*, 52, 135–172.

Grau, R. 1976. "La Site de Handoga: Fouilles Archéologiques," *Pount*, 16, 4–22.

Grau, R. 1981. "Handoga: Site d'Habitat de Pasteurs Nomades?," *Archéologia*, 159, 55–59.

Gutherz, X. 2013. "L'Archéologie à Djibouti," in A. S. Chiré (ed.), *Djibouti Contemporain* (Paris: Karthala), 15–40.

Hamdun, S., and King, N. 1994. *Ibn Battuta in Black Africa* (Princeton: Markus Wiener).

Hassen, M. 1994. *The Oromo of Ethiopia. A History 1570–1860* (Trenton: The Red Sea Press).

Hecht, E-D. 1982. "The City of Harar and the Traditional Harar House," *Journal of Ethiopian Studies*, 15, 56–78.

Hecht, E-D. 1987. "Harar and Lamu: A Comparison of Two East African Muslim Societies," *Transafrican Journal of History*, 16, 1–23.

Henze, P. B. 2005. "Arsi Oromo Tomb Art: Its Evolution and Current Status," *Annales d'Éthiopie*, 21, 177–192.

Hiskett, M. 1994. *The Course of Islam in Africa* (Edinburgh: Edinburgh University Press).

Hodder, I. 2012. *Entangled. An Archaeology of the Relationships between Humans and Things* (Oxford: Wiley-Blackwell).

Hogendorn, J., and Johnson, M. 1986. *The Shell Money of the Slave Trade* (Cambridge: Cambridge University Press).

Horton, M., Boivin, N., Crowther, A., Gaskell, B., Radimilahy, C., and Wright, H. 2017. "East Africa as a Source for Fatimid Rock Crystal Workshops from Kenya to Madagascar," in A. Hilgner, S. Greiff and D. Quast (eds.), *Gemstones in the First Millennium AD* (Mainz: RGZM Verlag), 103–118.

Hourani, G. F. 1995. *Arab Seafaring* (Princeton: Princeton University Press).

Huntingford, G. W. B. 1955. "Arabic Inscriptions in Southern Ethiopia," *Antiquity*, 29, 230–3.

Insoll, T. 1999. *The Archaeology of Islam* (Oxford: Blackwell).

Insoll, T. 2001. "Dahlak Kebir, Eritrea. From Aksumite to Ottoman," *Adumatu*, 3, 39–50.

Insoll, T. 2003. *The Archaeology of Islam in sub-Saharan Africa* (Cambridge: Cambridge University Press).

Insoll, T. 2015. *Material Explorations in African Archaeology* (Oxford: Oxford University Press).

Insoll, T. 2017a. "The Archaeology of Islamisation in Sub-Saharan Africa: A Comparative Study," in A. Peacock (ed.), *Islamisation: Comparative Perspectives from History* (Edinburgh: Edinburgh University Press), 244–273.

Insoll, T. 2017b. "First Footsteps in the Archaeology of Harar," *Journal of Islamic Archaeology*, 4, 189–215.

Insoll, T., Khalaf, N., MacLean, R., and Zerihun, D. 2017. "Archaeological Survey and Excavations, Harlaa, Dire Dawa, Ethiopia January-February 2017. A Preliminary Fieldwork Report," *Nyame Akuma*, 87, 32–38.

Insoll, T., MacLean, R., and Engda, B. 2016. "Archaeological Survey and Test Excavations, Harlaa, Dire Dawa, and Sofi, Harari Regional State, Ethiopia. A Preliminary Fieldwork Report," *Nyame Akuma*, 85, 23–32.

Insoll, T., Polya, D., Bhan, K., Irving, D., and Jarvis, K. 2004. "Towards an Understanding of the Carnelian Bead Trade from Western India to sub-Saharan Africa: The Application of UV-LA-ICP-MS to Carnelian from Gujarat, India, and West Africa," *Journal of Archaeological Science*, 31, 1161–1173.

Insoll, T., Tesfaye, H., and Mahmoud, M. S. 2014. "Archaeological Survey and Test Excavations, Harari Regional State, Ethiopia, July-August 2014. A Preliminary Fieldwork Report," *Nyame Akuma*, 82, 100–109.

Jacob, P. 1997. "La Communauté Afar et l'Islam," in K. Fukui, E. Kurimoto and M. Shigeta (eds.), *Ethiopia in Broader Perspective: Papers of the Thirteenth International Conference of Ethiopian Studies. Vol. III* (Kyoto: Shokado Book Sellers), 175–188.

Jama, A. D. 1990. "Urban Origins on the Southern Somali Coast with Special Reference to Mogadishu, AD 1000–1600," in P. Sinclair (ed.), *Urban Origins in East Africa* (Stockholm: Central Board of Arts), 106–108.

Joussaume, H., and Joussaume, R. 1972. "Anciennes Villes dans le Tchercher," *Annales d'Éthiopie*, 9, 21–44.

Joussaume, R. 1980. *Le Mégalithisme en Ethiopie. Monuments Funéraires Protohistoriques du Harar* (Paris: Museum Nationale d'Histoire Naturelle).

Kaplan, S. 2004. "Themes and Methods in the Study of Conversion in Ethiopia: A Review Essay," *Journal of Religion in Africa*, 34, 373–392.

Kapteijns, L. 2000. "Ethiopia and the Horn of Africa," in N. Levtzion and R. L. Pouwels (eds.), *The History of Islam in Africa* (Oxford: James Currey), 227–250.

Kenoyer, J. M., Vidale, M., and Bhan, K. K. 1991. "Contemporary Stone Beadmaking in Khambhat, India: Patterns of Craft Specialization, and Organisation of Production reflected in the Archaeological Record," *World Archaeology*, 23, 44–63.

Kifleyesus, A. 2006. *Tradition and Transformation: The Argobba of Ethiopia* (Wiesbaden: Harrassowitz Verlag).

Labrousse, H. 1978. "Enquêtes et Découvertes d'Obock à Doumeira," *Annales d'Ethiopie*, 11, 75–82.

Lapidus, I. M. 1988. *A History of Islamic Societies* (Cambridge: Cambridge University Press).

Lewis, I. M. 1986. "Islam in Somalia," in K. S. Loughran (ed.), *Somalia in Word and Image* (Bloomington: Indiana University Press), 139–142.

Lewis, I. M. 1994. *Peoples of the Horn of Africa* (repr.) (Asmara: Red Sea Press).

Loimeier, R. 2013. *Muslim Societies in Africa* (Bloomington: Indiana University Press).

Lowick, N. 1985. "Islamic Coins and Weights from Julfar," in J. Hansman (ed.), *Julfar, an Arabian Port* (London: Royal Asiatic Society), 1–9.

Miles, G. C. 1952. "Mihrab and Anazah: A Study in Early Islamic Iconography," in G. C. Miles (ed.), *Archaeologica Orientalia in Memoriam Ernst Herzfeld* (New York: J. J. Augustin), 156–171.

Mire, S. 2015a. "Mapping the Archaeology of Somaliland: Religion, Art, Script, Time, Urbanism, Trade and Empire," *African Archaeological Review*, 32, 111–136.

Mire, S. 2015b. "*Wagar*, Fertility and Phallic Stelae: Cushitic Sky-God Belief and the Site of Saint Aw-Barkhadle, Somaliland," *African Archaeological Review*, 32, 93–109.

Mordini, A. 1957. "Un Tissu Musulman du Moyen Âge provenant du Couvent de Dabra Dāmmo," *Annales d'Ethiopie*, 2, 75–77.

Munro-Hay, S. 1991. *Aksum: An African Civilization of Late Antiquity* (Edinburgh: Edinburgh University Press).

Nesbitt, L. M. 1934. *Desert and Forest* (London: Jonathan Cape).

Oman, G. 1974. "The Islamic Necropolis of Dahlak Kebir in the Red Sea. Report on a Preliminary Survey Carried out in April 1972," *East and West*, 24, 249–295.

Oman, G. 1976. *Necropoli Islamica di Dahlak Kebir* (Naples: Istituto Universitario Orientale).

Østebø, T. 2012. *Localising Salafism. Religious Change Among Oromo Muslims in Bale, Ethiopia* (Leiden: Brill).

Pankhurst, R. 1985. *History of Ethiopian Towns from the Middle Ages to the Early Nineteenth Century* (Wiesbaden: Franz Steiner Verlag).

Peacock, D. 2007. "Pottery from the Survey," in D. Peacock, D and L. Blue (eds.), *The Ancient Red Sea Port of Adulis, Eritrea* (Oxford: Oxbow), 79–108.

Phillipson, D. 1998. *Ancient Ethiopia* (London: British Museum).

Phillipson, D. 2000. *Archaeology at Aksum 1992–1997* (London: Society of Antiquaries).

Phillipson, D. 2004. "The Aksumite Roots of Medieval Ethiopia," *Azania*, 29, 77–89.

Phillipson, D. 2009. *Ancient Churches of Ethiopia* (New Haven: Yale University Press).

Power, T. 2012. *The Red Sea from Byzantium to the Caliphate. AD 500–1000* (Cairo: The American University in Cairo Press).

Pradines, S., and Blanchard, P. 2016. "Songo Mnara. Étude Architecturale d'une Ville Swahilie Médiévale," *Taarifa*, 5, 9–33.

Puglisi, G. 1969. "Alcuni vestige dell'Isola di Dahlac Chebir e la leggènda dei Furs," *Proceedings of the Third International Conference of Ethiopian Studies* (Addis Ababa: Institute of Ethiopian Studies), 35–47.

Ravaisse, P. 1931. "Appendice 1: Stèles et Inscriptions Arabes du Harar," in R. P. Azaïs and R. Chambard, *Cinq années de recherches archéologiques en Ethiopie* (Paris: Paul Geuthner), 283–309.

Roux, V. (ed.) 2000. *Cornaline de l'Inde* (Paris: Éditions de la Maison des Sciences de l'Homme).

Sanseverino, H. 1983. "Archaeological Remains on the Southern Somali Coast," *Azania*, 18, 151–164.

Schneider, M. 1967. "Stèles Funéraires arabes de Quiha," *Annales d'Ethiopie*, 7, 107–118.

Schneider, M. 1969. "Stèles Funéraires de la Région de Harar et Dahlak (Éthiopie)," *Revue des Études Islamiques*, 37, 339–343.

Schneider, M. 1970. "Stèles Funéraires Musulmanes de la Province du Choa," *Annales d'Ethiopie*, 8, 73–78.

Schneider, M. 1983. *Stèles Funéraires Musulmanes des Îles Dahlak* (Cairo: Institut Français d'Archéologie Orientale).

Stenhouse, P. (trans.) 2003. *Futuh al-Habasa* (Hollywood [CA]: Tsehai).

Tedeschi, S. 1969. "Note Storiche Sulle Isole Dahlak," *Proceedings of the Third International Conference of Ethiopian Studies* (Addis Ababa: Institute of Ethiopian Studies), 49–74.

Thesiger, W. 1935. "The Awash River and the Aussa Sultanate," *The Geographical Journal*, 85, 1–23.

Thesiger, W. 1998. *The Danakil Diary* (London: Flamingo).

Tilahun, C. 1990. "Traces of Islamic Material Culture in Northeastern Shoa," *Journal of Ethiopian Studies*, 23, 303–320.

Trimingham, J. S. 1952. *Islam in Ethiopia* (London: Oxford University Press).

Wiet, G. 1951. "Roitelets de Dahlak," *Bulletin d'Institut de l'Egypte*, 34, 89–95.

Wilding, R. 1980. "The Desert Trade of Eastern Ethiopia," in R. E. Leakey and B. A. Ogot (eds.), *Proceedings of the 8th Panafrican Congress* (Nairobi: Louis Leakey Institute), 379–380.

Wilson, J. K., and Flecker, M. 2010. "Dating the Belitung Shipwreck," in R. Krahl, J. Guy, J. K. Wilson, and J. Raby (eds.), *Shipwrecked. Tang Treasures and Monsoon Winds* (Washington: Smithsonian Institution), 35–43.

Zazzaro, C. 2016. "Considérations sur le materiel archéologique de Bet-Khalifa," in F. Anfray and C. Zazzaro, *Recherches Archéologiques à Adoulis (Érythrée)* (Toulouse: Presses Universitaires du Midi), 79–103.

CHAPTER 4.4

....

WEST AFRICA

....

TIMOTHY INSOLL

INTRODUCTION

WEST Africa is a vast region that is bounded by the Atlantic Ocean in the west and south, the Sahara Desert in the north, and the River Niger in the east (Figure 4.4.1). North Africa and the Sahara are considered in Chapters 3.1 and 3.3 and the area east of the Niger, encompassing the central Sudan and Sahel, is considered in Chapter 4.5. It is imperative that the Islamic archaeology of West Africa is considered in conjunction with these three chapters as they are contiguous and a certain degree of overlap must exist in discussing their archaeology.

Significant environmental diversity exists in West Africa, with four main zones running longitudinally starting with the true desert in the north, followed by, moving south, the semi-desert Sahel, the grassland and wooded savannahs, and the forest zone. The Sahara is sparsely populated, primarily with transhumant pastoralists, with permanent occupation and limited agriculture concentrated only in a few locations, though it was the conduit for Islamization via trans-Saharan trade routes. The Sahel, the location of the northernmost trade centers that were hubs for early Islamic conversion, is a transitional zone and has more plentiful rainfall and diverse flora dominated by annual grasses with varying tree cover based on rainfall subzone (Le Houerou 1980: 42; Insoll 1996: 2–3) (Figure 4.4.2). Agriculture is more widely found and pastoralism is practiced (Grove 1978 409; Le Houerou 1980: 42). Further south, tree cover gradually increases, through the grassland savannahs with their low tree and shrub vegetation that merge into savannah parkland and then wooded or Guinea savannah with its predominant *Brachystegia-Julbernardia* tree cover (Adams 1999: 196–199). Finally, in the far south, though there are gaps in coverage, is the tropical rainforest zone where various types of forest are found including wet and dry evergreen, and moist and dry semi-deciduous (Martin 1991: 60–62). Agriculture dominates in the savannah and rainforest zones (Martin 1991; Adams 1999: 207–208).

The chronology of Muslim contacts with the peoples of West Africa can also be broadly considered as a north-to-south progression, with the earliest occurring where Muslim traders from North Africa met their West African counterparts in desert edge settlements such as Essouk-Tadmekka, Gao, Koumbi Saleh, and Tegdaoust (Figure 4.4.1). This is a process that began in the mid-8th century CE (all dates are CE unless otherwise specified) and continued over many centuries as foreign merchants were replaced by indigenous converts as agents of Islamization across the region (Insoll 2003). The importance of archaeology for reconstructing these processes is paramount. Relevant written historical sources are variable in their quality, quantity, and coverage. Externally derived Arabic sources, predominantly written in north African cities such as Marrakesh, Kairouan, or Cairo, can be problematic. Compiled primarily between the 9th and 14th centuries, they partially record the history of the states and cities of the Sahel and of trans-Saharan trade (cf. Levtzion and Hopkins 2000). Although of use in the insights they provide, they are often derivative (Trimingham 1962: 2) and colored by the worldviews of their authors. These were literate men living in a different cultural milieu and writing about but not necessarily directly observing practices that could seem anathema to them (Insoll 1994).

Alternatively, local chronicles such as the *Ta'rīkh al-fattāsh* (Houdas and Delafosse 1913), written by "members of the Ka'ti family" in the mid-1650s (Hunwick 2003: 2), and the *Ta'rīkh al-Sūdān,* written by 'Abd al-Sa'dī (es-Sa'dī 1900) at approximately the same time (ibid; Hunwick 1999, 2003), provide an alternative, internally generated source of historical material. These two chronicles are written in Arabic though other local historical sources can be written in indigenous languages such as Songhai or Wolof using the Arabic script (Hunwick 2003: 6). Certain locations such as, most famously, Timbuktu in Mali have exceptional local manuscript collections (cf. Hunwick and Boye 2008), and early Arabic literary traditions also existed in centers such as Djenne and Arawān, also in Mali (Hunwick 2003: 149). Elsewhere, written sources are lacking, though oral traditions can exist, providing a second body of internal historical material. A notable example of this is *Sundiata, An Epic of Old Mali* (Niane 1986) which records the conflicts between Sumanguru, the evil magician-king and Sundiata Keita, the progenitor of the Malian dynasty in the mid-13th century. These can be useful for exploring aspects of indigenous religion, or syncretism, for example, but also contain mythic elements and have to be carefully sifted and used accordingly.

The Islamic archaeological database in West Africa is better than that for some other regions of sub-Saharan Africa (cf. Insoll 2003); Ethiopia and the Horn of Africa (Chapter 4.2), or the Central Sudan and Sahel (Chapter 4.5), for instance. This allows a more detailed consideration of themes such as local Islamic practice, syncretism, diet,

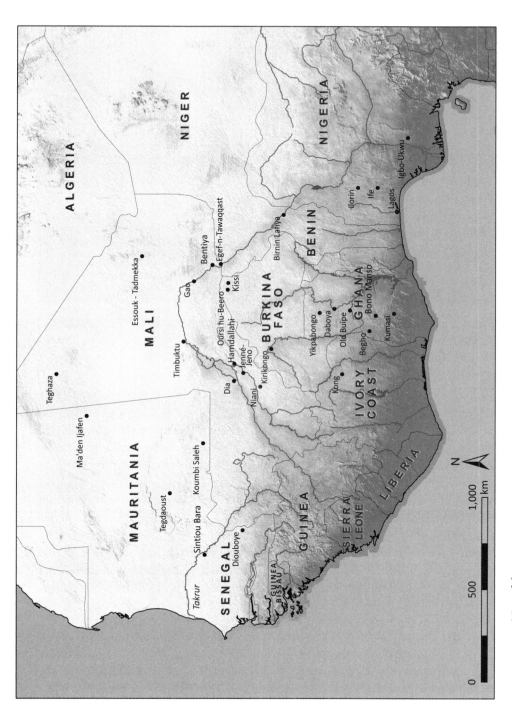

FIGURE 4.4.1 Map of the region.

Courtesy of N. Khalaf.

FIGURE 4.4.2 Sahel environment at the River Niger near Gao, Mali.

Courtesy of T. Insoll.

epigraphy, or trade and its relationship with Islamization, rather than, because of the paucity of relevant research, focusing upon solely mapping the presence of Islam archaeologically. Thus, these themes are considered, where possible, in the chronological approach to the material that is employed in this chapter. A chronological structure is preferable to a geographical or thematic framework because of the extent and complexity of the evidence (cf. Insoll 2003).

Archaeology has also revealed that the polities of West Africa, such as the Sahelian states of Ghana, Mali, and Songhai, were indigenous foundations rather than colonies established by Muslim Arab or Berber traders from North Africa, as was previously thought (e.g., Mauny 1961). This is significant in considering Islamic archaeology, as Muslims were not agents of "civilization" as was once presumed when the region was viewed through the lens of what has been described as the "Arab stimulus paradigm" (McIntosh and McIntosh 1988: 146). It is now recognized that urbanism and social complexity, for example, were developed locally (MacDonald 2011: 72), as was trade in an interregional context (Cissé et al. 2013: 37; MacDonald 2013: 836). It was to these trade patterns that long-distance trans-Saharan commerce was attached, although it, too, might have had pre-Islamic origins, as is increasingly being attested archaeologically (Magnavita 2008, 2017; MacDonald 2011, 2013; Nixon 2017a; Mattingly 2017). Hence Islam was adopted in a context of indigenously developed social complexity.

EARLY MUSLIM CONTACTS
(8TH–10TH CENTURIES)

Archaeological evidence for the presence of Muslims in the Western Sahel between the 8th and 10th centuries is rare, but for trans-Saharan trade is increasing (cf. Cissé 2017; Nixon 2017a). According to the Arabic historical sources, the first Muslim contacts with the western Sahel were those of Ibadi merchants (Lewicki 1971) from the Imamate of Tahert (Algeria), who made contact with either the Empire of Ghana or Gao, from the late 8th century. Ibadi sources also refer to trade with Tadmekka, likely in the first half of the 9th century (Lewicki 1971: 117). At Gao, archaeological evidence such as trade goods specifically from Ibadi areas has not been found, though these might have been perishable materials, as these would have formed a significant component of this trade but generally are missing archaeologically (Insoll 1996: 62–63; Mattingly and Cole 2017: 224–225). Although an Ibadi affiliation might be lacking, increasing quantities of artifacts sourced from trans-Saharan trade and dating from before 1000 CE have been found in Gao, notably glass beads from Gao-Saney and Gao Ancien (cf. Cissé 2017: 110, 117).

The first direct evidence for the presence of Muslims, however—inscribed tombstones from the site of Gao-Saney (discussed later)—is also later: early 12th-century in date, though it appears that, based on historical sources (e.g., al-Muhallabī, c. 975–985), by the late 10th century the ruler of Gao was a Muslim (Levtzion and Hopkins 2000: 168, 174), albeit not a very profound one, and that conversions among the population of the city proceeded rapidly in the 11th and 12th centuries (Insoll 1996, 2003: 235). It is a possibility that remnant Ibadi architectural influences (cf. Schacht 1954; Roche 1970; Prevost 2016) can be found in aspects of the mosque form (staircase minaret, *mihrab*) of the Western Sahel such as the mosque and tomb of Askia Muhammad at Gao (Figure 4.4.3), but this is difficult to prove and reflects also indigenous choices, materials, and a multiplicity of influences (Insoll 1996: 55–56). It is also possible, but as yet unproved, that the "Pillar House" in Gao Ancien, built around 900, was a mosque, as Cissé (2017: 113) suggests.

Essouk-Tadmekka

The evidence from Essouk-Tadmekka, whose name was recorded by al-Bakrī as meaning "the Mecca-like" (Levtzion and Hopkins 2000: 85), is earlier than at Gao, with the occupation sequence dating from the mid-first millennium CE to around 1400 (Nixon 2009: 217). Trans-Saharan trade was in operation here before the end of the 10th century, as attested by, for example, Islamic vessel glass found, with forty-three fragments from unit Ek-B dated to about the 10th–11th centuries (Nixon et al. 2017: 152). Grains of wheat (*Triticum aestivum* and *T. durum*) were also recovered

FIGURE 4.4.3 The mosque and tomb of Askia Muhammad at Gao, Mali.

Courtesy of T. Insoll.

from levels dated to about 900 (Fuller et al. 2017: 247), which Nixon (2009: 251) suggests is of great significance as possibly attesting commerce in staple cereals, but with wheat also of potential importance "to an Islamic diet" and as a luxury foodstuff. Likewise, the four grains of wheat radiocarbon dated to between 779 and 1157 found at Dia-Shoma and Dia-Mara in the Inland Niger Delta area of Mali (Murray 2005: 399) were also ascribed an exotic origin, perhaps sourced via Awdaghust (Tegdaoust) or Sijilmasa (Bedaux et al. 2005: 449).

Three fragments of ceramic coin molds dated initially to approximately 850–950 (Nixon et al. 2011: 1357–1358), and subsequently to "ca. 10th-12th centuries AD" (Nixon and Rehren 2017: 174) were also recovered from Essouk (Figure 4.4.4). The cups on one of these molds contained microscopic traces of gold, and it was suggested as probably used to make unstamped gold coin blanks for use by Muslim trans-Saharan merchants "in a standardized, exchangeable form" (Nixon and Rehren 2017: 186). The likelihood is that at least some of the population at Tadmekka were Muslim although unequivocal evidence for this period is lacking. Whether they were Ibadi is also unknown, but Nixon (2009: 247) indicates that Ibadi groups were "significantly composed of Saharan Berbers" and that the Ibadi leader Abu Yazid was born at Essouk in the late 9th century of a trader and a slave (cf. Levtzion and Hopkins 2000: 154). Essouk was also connected to Ibadi centers such as Sedrata, the Ibadi medieval center of Wargla or Wārğāla in Algeria, and Djérid in Tunisia (Aillet 2017: 79). Moreover, as de Moraes Farias (2003: cxlv) has described, the absence of definitive evidence for the presence of Muslims, such

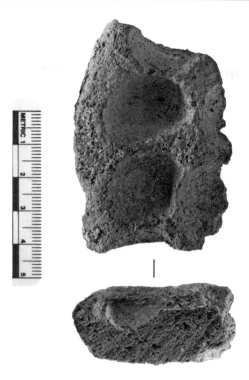

FIGURE 4.4.4 The coin molds from Essouk-Tadmekka, Mali.

Courtesy of S. Nixon.

as funerary inscriptions, might be due to the very fact that they were Ibadi "who did not engrave epitaphs." All this suggests that, in the formative period of Islamization, an Ibadi linkage is not improbable.

Tegdaoust and Koumbi Saleh

West of Gao, further archaeological evidence for the early Islamic operation of trans-Saharan trade has been found at the sites of Tegdaoust and Koumbi Saleh in Mauritania. These appear to have been linked with the Empire of Ghana, situated in southern Mauritania and northern Mali, and whose origins can probably be placed in the mid-first millennium CE (MacDonald 2013: 838). Carbon (C[14]) dates from Koumbi Saleh indicate it was occupied from the 5th to 6th centuries and is one of a number of urban sites besides Koumbi Saleh that grew at the same time: Tegdaoust, Gao, Dia, Sintiou Bara (van Doosselaere 2014: 245). Koumbi Saleh has been identified with the traders' town, mentioned in the Arabic historical sources, that was attached to the capital of the Empire of Ghana (Berthier 1997). Here, evidence for early Muslim contacts, before circa 900, is absent (Berthier 1997), though interregional trade is well-represented in this period by imported pottery from the Inland Niger Delta area of Mali, supplementing two local ceramic traditions (van Doosselaere 2014: 246). In contrast, the earliest evidence for trade contacts with the Muslim world found at Tegdaoust dates from the 9th century and consists of Ifriqiyan glazed pottery and semi-precious stones, otherwise undescribed (Robert 1970a; Vanacker 1979; Robert-Chaleix 1989).

Whether Koumbi Saleh was in fact the traders' town attached to the capital of Ghana is unproved pending identification of the latter, and it is likely that it represents a trade center without any especial political significance (cf. MacDonald 2013: 838). However, the phenomena of dual towns with one at least partly Islamized and the other non-Muslim is a recurrent phenomenon in West Africa in the first stages of Islamization (Insoll 1996, 2000). At Gao twin settlements also existed (Insoll 1996, 1997). Initially, the separation at the sites of Gao Ancien, the mercantile center and probable site of the rulers' settlement, and Gao-Saney, a manufacturing center and possible original settlement of the Arab and Berber traders, was probably due to religious differences. Recent excavations at Gao-Saney have indicated that the 6 meters of deposits date from between about 700 and 1100, and at Gao Ancien occupation has been "tentatively" dated to the mid-first millennium (Cissé 2017: 106, 110). The persistence of dual settlements after Islam had spread to the inhabitants of Gao Ancien in the late 11th to 12th centuries may have been attributable to security considerations, in particular the desirability of keeping nomads at a distance from Gao Ancien (Insoll 1996: 48).

11TH TO 14TH CENTURIES

Essouk/Tadmekka

Archaeology indicates that conversions to Islam increased after the 10th century. Direct evidence for Islamization is increasingly found in the form of mosques and Muslim burials. Essouk/Tadmekka, for example, has provided abundant epigraphic evidence (de Moraes Farias 1990, 2003). The inscriptions cover the period between around 1013–1014 CE and 1387. One of the inscriptions confirms the identification of the site as ancient Tadmekka (de Moraes Farias 2003: cxxxiv); others provide important information on Islamization, indicating that local Berber speakers were engraving the *shahada* (cf. inscription number 105 (de Moraes Farias 2003: 89) or recording the Muslim names of the engravers of inscriptions, as on inscription number 110 signed by Muhammad, son of Sulayman in 547 AH (1152 CE) (de Moraes Farias 2003: 91).

This information on Islamization, however, transcends the recording of Muslim names. Essouk/Tadmekka was a settlement connected with Sahelian Berber/Tuareg nomads, and de Moraes Farias (2003: cxx) has described how part of the process of Islamization was the "investment of Islamic meanings into spatial landmarks." This, he argues (de Moraes Farias 2003: cxx), was achieved through Muslim converts familiarizing themselves with new markers of directionality centered on the *qibla* and via engraving dates on stone. The latter producing "materialisations of axial time computed according to the Islamic calendar." These processes had occurred by not later than the 11th century, and de Moraes Farias (2003: cxx) convincingly indicates how Islamization of the landscape was facilitated by the predisposition of nomad pastoralist life to exist in a "constant state of orientation" centered on knowledge of routes, pastures, and wells. With reorientation to Islamic directionality and time, cardinal points and perceptions of auspicious or inauspicious directions "would come to be defined by reference to the position of the person at prayer and the corpse in the tomb" (de Moraes Farias 2003: cxx).

Trade also expanded at Essouk-Tadmekka during the 11th-13th centuries, indicating increased participation in trans-Saharan networks. Thirty sherds of glazed pottery were found in various contexts dated to between the 10th and 13th centuries, with the majority from the 10th-11th centuries (Nixon and MacDonald 2017). These included Maghrebi wares of uncertain provenance and a rim sherd of Chinese Qingbai porcelain of about 11th-13th centuries date (Nixon and MacDonald 2017: 123–124). In addition, 385 beads were also found (Lankton et al. 2017: 162), a comparatively small number compared to other sites in the region, but with a concentration in unit Ek-A in levels dated to the 11th–12th centuries. A further exciting and unique find was a fragment of silk Damas textile, likely from China, and from a 14th-century context (Nixon 2017b: 220). Also archaeologically attested was the route south to Gao, materially manifest, for example, by cord-wrapped stick decorated pottery of likely Gao provenance (Nixon and MacDonald 2017: 145).

Gao

At Gao, rapprochement between Muslims and non-Muslims appears to have gradually occurred, the twin settlements disappeared, and Gao-Saney ceased to be occupied around 1100 (Cissé et al. 2013: 19). This process was accelerated by conversion to Islam among the local population (Insoll 2003). Excavations in Gao Ancien uncovered a central citadel with elaborate mud and fired-brick buildings occupied in the 12th to 13th centuries (Insoll 1996, 2000). Stone buildings dating from the 10th century were also occupied and abandoned prior to the brick buildings (Takezawa and Cissé 2012: 831; Cissé 2017: 112). Parts of what appears to be a mosque and a house belonging to a rich merchant have been recorded (Insoll 1996), as well as an elite or royal residence (Cissé et al. 2013: 14). A third quarter neighboring Gao Ancien, Gadei, had buildings of a more traditional style, in mud; rather than using rectilinear plans, roundhouses were built, one of which was uncovered (Insoll 2000). The contents of this house included a large wooden bead from a set of prayer beads or Muslim "rosary" and the remains of what appears to have been the copper casing from a Muslim amulet cover (Insoll 2000). These suggest that some Muslims might have been present or that aspects of Islamic material culture were being adopted without, necessarily, conversion to Islam occurring.

The faunal remains recorded indicate the fact that not all the population of Gadei was Muslim. Ten identified faunal elements (bones) from dogs, interpreted as food refuse based on their association with other food remains (Stangroome 2000: 56) were present in levels dated to between the early/mid-11th and late 16th centuries (i.e., certainly after Islam was the dominant religion in Gao) (Insoll 2003: 239). In contrast only two identifiable dog faunal elements were recorded in the evidently more Islamized quarter of Gao Ancien (Hutton MacDonald and MacDonald 1996: 125–126; Barrett-Jolley 2000). It is not known if these constituted food refuse. In other respects, the faunal assemblages from Gadei and Gao Ancien were broadly comparable (Insoll 2003: 24), with both wild and domesticated species present (cf. Hutton MacDonald and Macdonald 1996; Barrett-Jolley 2000; Stangroome 2000).

The botanical remains recovered were not indicators of Islamization in the same way as animal species for they were not subject to dietary prohibition (cf. Insoll 1999a: 99–100) but were nonetheless informative. For example, a stone of *Phoenix dactylifera*, the date palm, recovered from Gadei, exceeded the fruit length of the native wild *P. reclinata*. This indicated either growth of dates in the region after the spread of *P. dactylifera* south of the Sahara with trans-Saharan trade or the import of dates via the same networks (Fuller 2000: 30). Similarly, one complete and several partial cotton seeds (*Gossypium* sp.) and a small charred fragment of wool or hair cloth from Gadei (Fuller 2000: 32–35) attests the possession and likely wearing of fabrics. Cotton weaving is generally regarded as having diffused from East to West Africa during the Islamic period (Watson 1983 cited in Fuller 2000: 33). Hence, indirectly, these plant remains and textile fragments provide further evidence for participation in trade networks connected to the wider Muslim world.

Inferences on connections with the Islamic world can also be drawn from the imported materials recovered. A large assemblage of glazed pottery and glass was recovered from Gao Ancien dating primarily from the 11th to 12th centuries (Insoll 1996: 63–66). This included green-, brown-, and yellow-glazed ceramics of Ifriqiyan (Tunisian) origin and others such as brown-glazed and *Cuerda Seca* wares from elsewhere in North Africa and Spain (the latter discussed later), along with fragments of glass from the same areas (Insoll 1996: 65–67, 1998b). More than a thousand glass beads were also recovered (Insoll 1996, 2000), the majority of colored glass (Figure 4.4.5), produced in vast quantities in the Middle East. Renewed excavation in Gao Ancien added a further 10,000 glass beads, and another 900 came from Gao-Saney (Cissé 2017: 117; Dussubieux 2017: 420) indicating the large quantities imported. Chemical analysis of forty-seven glass beads from Gao-Saney showed a source in the Middle East, likely to be east of the Euphrates River (Cissé et al. 2013: 29), based on the soda plant ash glass composition (Cissé 2017: 110; Dussubieux 2017: 421). Semi-precious carnelian beads have also been found in Gao Ancien (Insoll 1996).

Compositional analysis indicated that some of these are likely to be of Indian origin, probably from the coast of Gujarat in western India. Others are of West African provenance (Insoll et al. 2004). These beads were then traded onward from Gao throughout West Africa (Insoll and Shaw 1997) as discussed later.

Muslim Spain appears to have been the most active trading partner of Gao, particularly during the period of Almoravid rule, an emirate aptly described by de Moraes

FIGURE 4.4.5 Examples of stone, glass, and ceramic beads from the 1993 excavations in Gao Ancien, Mali.

Courtesy of T. Insoll.

Farias (2003: cxxv) as "Afro-European" and whose character is considered further later. Ivory was a possible export to Al-Andalus. A cache of more than fifty hippopotamus tusks was uncovered in a pit underneath a fired-brick building in Gao Ancien and radiocarbon dated to the mid-9th century (Insoll 1995). It appears that these represent a consignment of ivory that was awaiting shipment to the workshops of North Africa and for some reason was never sent (Insoll 1995). A substantial ivory trade between West and North Africa existed but is little mentioned in the Arabic sources, possibly because the use of feathers, horns, hoofs, or tusks derived from animals which were not ritually slaughtered was frowned upon by orthodox Muslims (Levtzion and Hopkins 2000: 55). Large quantities of ivory were certainly used in the workshops of the Maghreb, Islamic Spain, and Egypt, with those of Islamic Spain famed for the inlaid and carved caskets and ivory-encrusted mosque furniture which were produced in cities such as Madīnat al-Zahrā in the 10th century and in other centers during subsequent Almoravid, Almohad, and Nasrid rule (e.g., Dodds 1992: 264–269).

Sherds of lustre-ware recovered from Gao Ancien have also been found to be identical to 12th-century material recovered from excavations in Málaga (Gómez Moreno 1940), and architectural parallels are discernible between the fired-brick structures of Gao Ancien and those in the *alcazaba* in Almería (Insoll personal observation). Moreover, analysis of a small gold bead from Gadei indicated specific Almoravid connections, though with North Africa rather than with Spain. Activation analysis and laser ablation inductively coupled plasma mass spectrometry showed that the composition of the Gadei gold precisely matched gold Almoravid dinars minted at Sijilmasa in Morocco, indicating West African ore was used, in all probability sourced via Gao (Guerra 2000: 153–154).

Other Sites

South of Gao, an Islamic "frontier" appears to have existed (Insoll 2004: 100). Sites such as Egef-N-Tawaqqast and Bentiya (Kukiya), where Arabic funerary inscriptions dated to the 13th-15th centuries have been recorded (cf. de Moraes Farias 1990: 105–106; Arazi 1999: 38–39), indicate that Islamization extended to this point, but evidence for Islam dating from before the 15th century is seemingly lacking further south on the River Niger and adjacent areas in Mali and northern Niger. For example, at the site of Birnin Lafiya, a settlement mound in the Dendi region of northern Benin on the edge of the Songhai empire and the Hausa kingdoms, no evidence for the presence of Muslims was found in a sequence dated to between the 4th and 13th centuries CE (Haour et al. 2016). Similarly, at Kissi in northeast Burkina Faso, in the hinterland of the eastern Niger Bend, no evidence for Islamization was found in the settlement areas and cemeteries excavated and dated to between approximately the 2nd and 13th centuries (Magnavita 2015: 173).

The absence of evidence for the presence of Muslims, however, does not imply that this eastern arc of the River Niger was an isolated area. On the contrary, archaeology is indicating that it was connected to long-distance networks directed north to centers, for instance Gao, which it appears to have supplied with commodities such as ivory, gold, and possibly slaves, but also south into the forest zone. At Kissi, 100 kilometers west of the Niger, significant evidence for northern long-distance contacts was recovered from burials including cowry shells and approximately 4,500 stone, iron, and glass beads. Of these, some of the "more standardized" carnelian (Magnavita 2003: 130) and other agate beads could have been obtained via trans-Saharan trade, as were the glass beads, of which at least seventy predate the 8th century and thus Muslim-controlled trade networks (Magnavita 2003: 129–134; Magnavita 2017: 394–395). Also found were fragments of camel dromedary wool textiles preserved through mineralization that occurred via the association between the textiles and copper, copper alloy, and iron objects. The textiles, it was tentatively concluded, were made by people "who originally inhabited the Sahara or its fringes" and also had contacts with North Africa and the western Sahel (Magnavita 2008: 252). From Birnin Lafiya, 2 kilometers west of the Niger, marine shells indicate long-distance contacts as well, though overall, "there is a lack of significant evidence for external trade goods" (Haour et al. 2016: 706).

Rare imported trade items were also present at Oursi hu-Beero in northeast Burkina Faso. Here the remains of a house complex destroyed by fire dated to the 11th–12th centuries were investigated. Three *Cypraea moneta* cowries were found in the excavations, all pierced at the back for stringing or sewing (Petit and von Czerniewicz 2011: 110). Another site in western Burkina Faso, Kirikongo on the Mouhoun Bend, also provided rare imported materials. Eleven cowry shells were found, either *C. moneta* or *C. annulus*, three from structures, possibly ritual ancestor houses, that had burned down and dated to between 1260/1300 and 1450, and eight from infant and child burials dated slightly earlier to between 1100–1260 and 1300 (Dueppen 2012: 183, 267). Dueppen (2012: 271) is likely right in stating that this does not "necessarily imply that Kirikongo participated actively in super-regional trade networks," but instead that they were "obtained locally through down-the-line exchange." This was probably also the source of supply at Oursi hu-Beero.

Cowry shells, particularly *C. moneta* imported from the Maldive islands in the Indian Ocean via the markets of North Africa (Lovejoy 1985: 669), recur as exotic objects in West African archaeological contexts (Insoll 2003: 249). Unique archaeological testimony to the cowry shell trade that could have supplied places as diverse as Kissi, Oursi, or Yikpabongo, discussed later, was found at the Ijafen dunes in Mauritania. Dating from the 12th century, several thousand cowries that had once been in sacks, along with 2,085 bars of brass, had been buried for safe-keeping by a caravan crossing the Sahara to the western Sahel (Monod 1969) but, for reasons unknown, had never been recovered.

Imported trade items might be rare at Birnin Lafaya or Oursi, but in contrast, much further south at the forest site of Igbo-Ukwu in southeastern Nigeria vast quantities of glass beads were recorded in this indigenous religious ritual complex dated to between the 8th and 11th centuries (Shaw 1970, 1977). From the burial chamber at Igbo-Richard, one of the three site components, 102,294 beads were recovered, with a further 63,458 beads from Igbo-Isaiah, a ritual regalia store. The majority of these, 137,000, were imported monochrome glass beads with certain color preferences also discernible, as represented by the 30,000 light blue glass beads found at Igbo-Richard and the fact that 25 percent of the beads from Igbo-Isaiah, approximately 15,800 in number, were of yellow glass, indicating a preference for this color though blue glass once again dominated the Igbo-Isaiah assemblage with 27,000 beads found (Insoll 2015: 35–36). It is likely that many of these beads were obtained via trans-Saharan trade and reached Igbo-Ukwu by the eastern Niger bend route, potentially through Gao, with ivory possibly a commodity sent north in return (Insoll and Shaw 1997). The results of bead glass chemical analyses indicate that another source of the Igbo-Ukwu beads was through the "Indian Ocean trading sphere," as attested by the mineral soda glass beads found (Dussubieux 2017: 428).

Awareness of trans-Saharan trade also existed in non-Muslim contexts some 1,500 kilometers to the west, at Yikpabongo in Koma Land in northwest Ghana (the modern nation, not the ancient empire). Small numbers of cowry shells of the *C. moneta* and *C. annulus* species and occasional glass beads have been recovered from earth mounds (Anquandah 1998; Insoll et al. 2013). The mounds also yielded large assemblages of clay figurines. Cowry shells were modeled on some of these, decorating calabash hats or depicted as a bodily ornament or on a horse bridle (Anquandah 1998: 160), as well as "stamped decoration" on some of the pottery (Anquandah 1998: 78). A figurine of a bearded man riding either a horse or camel also indicates, if the latter, "awareness of lands north of the region where camels are used" (Insoll et al. 2013: 10) (Figure 4.4.6). The overall chronological sequence of these mounds has been dated by radiocarbon and thermoluminescence to between the 6th and 12th centuries (Kankpeyeng et al 2013: 480), with possible continuity through to the 14th century (Insoll et al. 2013: 9). Trans-Saharan trade cannot be seen as causative for Koma Land culture, as was once thought (Anquandah 1987; cf. Kankpeyeng et al. 2013: 485), but it may have been a factor in its demise. Slave raiding from the north to feed the markets of Gao and Timbuktu could have been one reason for the depopulation that occurred, with others being disease, migration, or changing environment (Insoll et al. 2012: 28).

These examples from non-Muslim contexts are included because, although they are not "Islamic archaeology," they are indicative of the potentially far-reaching impact of trans-Saharan trade in West Africa.

FIGURE 4.4.6 Clay rider and horse or camel figurine, Yikpabongo, Ghana, height 31 centimeters.

Courtesy of Manchester Museum, the University of Manchester/University of Ghana.

Archaeology, Islamization Patterns, and the Empire of Ghana

Information on Islamization patterns can also be reconstructed, in part, from the archaeological evidence (Insoll 1996, 2004, 2017a). Frequently, initial converts to Islam were among the ruling class, sometimes for reasons of prestige or for facilitating trade or administration through the use of Muslim officials and, importantly, via the use of Arabic writing in previously preliterate societies (Levtzion 1979: 214; Hunwick 1985a). Funerary inscriptions provide important data on these processes. Evidence for the presence of Muslims at Gao-Saney includes various inscribed Muslim tombstones, five of which would appear, from the marble they are made of and the style of epigraphy used, to have been imported ready-carved from the vicinity of Almería in Muslim Spain in the early 12th century (Sauvaget 1950; Vire 1958; de Moraes Farias 1990, 2003); that is, again indicative of flourishing Gao–Almoravid connections. It is likely that rulers such as those at Gao, in converting to Islam, seemingly, as Levtzion (2000: 66) has stressed, "adopted a middle position" between Islam and indigenous religion, patronizing Muslim religious specialists and indigenous shrines and their custodians," a pattern evident elsewhere in West Africa as well (e.g., Bravmann 1974).

Inscribed tombstones were not confined to Gao-Saney. Gao Ancien was also ringed with Muslim cemeteries, and the inscriptions recovered from these have provided additional information on Islamization processes within the region between the early 12th and 14th centuries. For example, in the Gorongobo cemetery, the oldest dated inscription (1130 CE) found in situ in Gao was recorded demonstrating the practice of Islamic funerary rites at this date (de Moraes Farias 2003: 65–66). Another gravestone from Gorongobo dated to 1210 was inscribed with the female Songhai name of either Buwy or Waybiya, dependent on the reading (de Moraes Farias 2000: 157). This suggests that Islam was becoming established among the local population of the town, beyond the circle of rulers. From the ruling classes, religious conversion gradually percolated down through society. Islam reached the townspeople, the merchants' local partners in trade, the nomads who accompanied the caravans criss-crossing the Sahara, and then the bulk of the population of the Western Sahel, the sedentary agriculturalists—Bamana, Songhai, Senufo, Dogon, Mossi, Mande, etc.—in a gradual and long drawn out process which in some contexts is still incomplete (e.g., Skinner 1964; Bravmann 1974; Glaze 1981; Stoller 1992; Levtzion 2000; Colleyn 2009). This was a process that had to yield to the need to incorporate or substitute indigenous religious beliefs and ritual practices tied to, for example, the ancestors and the land (e.g., Bravmann 1974; Zahan 1974; Glaze 1981; Rouch 1989; Insoll 1996; Levtzion 2000).

However, the processes of Islamization are far from firmly established (Insoll 2017a). The question of when and how the conversion of the ruler and people to Islam took place in the Empire of Ghana, for instance, has been the subject of some controversy. External factors have been invoked for, on the strength of the writings of Arab historians, it was thought that conversion was forced and attributable to the Almoravids, who have already been introduced and who were a reforming puritanical movement which drew its support from the Sanhaja nomads of the Western Sahara (Levtzion 1985: 138) and was ultimately to provide a dynasty which ruled parts of the Iberian Peninsula and North Africa in the late 11th to early 12th centuries (Lomax 1978: 68–90). It was believed that zealous hordes of Almoravid desert warriors, supported by soldiers from the Muslim kingdom of Takrur in Senegal, destroyed the "pagan" empire of Ghana and forcibly converted the inhabitants to Islam in 1076–1077 (cf. Trimingham 1962; Bovill 1968).

A re-evaluation of both the Arabic and local sources and the archaeological evidence (on the assumption that the identification of Koumbi Saleh with the merchant town is correct) showed this account of events to be erroneous (Conrad and Fisher 1982, 1983): in particular, no evidence for the destruction thesis emerged from the archaeological record. A large stone mosque was excavated at Koumbi Saleh, measuring 46 meters east–west by 23 meters north–south; a succession of *mihrabs* revealed that it was rebuilt three times between the 10th and 15th centuries (Berthier 1997). From this it must follow that conversion was likely a more gradual process, commencing in the late 10th to early 11th centuries and continuing thereafter. At Tegdaoust evidence for more gradual Islamization was also recorded. A necropolis aligned north–south over about 700 meters contained graves with differently oriented skeletal remains ranging from those who were buried north–south with the face to the east to others facing south with heads to the west (Robert 1970b: 65). This was interpreted by the excavators as indicating different phases of Islamization. Trade goods sourced from trans-Saharan networks at both Koumbi Saleh and Tegdaoust also attest more peaceful contacts. From Tegdaoust ceramics of Ifriqiyan, Maghreb, and Al-Andalusian provenance were recovered, as well as glass fragments said to resemble material from Fustat in Egypt (Vanacker 1979: 166–168; 1983: 522).

Similar materials were recovered from Koumbi Saleh, including blue, yellow, and green glass trade beads and five sherds of what seem to be lustre-decorated ceramics (Berthier 1997: 92). The 11th century also witnessed a realignment in the regional pottery sources that supplemented local production at Koumbi Saleh. The imports from the Inland Niger Delta are replaced with ones from the Upper Niger, and there are also shifts in the locally produced ceramic traditions that van Doosselaere (2014: 270–271) suggests might be linked with the impact of the Almoravids and, over a longer time scale, the expansion of the Empire of Mali (see later discussion). Tooth apatite and bone from three skulls recovered from the so-called Columns Tomb (Capel et al. 2015: 65) at Koumbi Saleh have also been dated to the same period. Whether the burials are Muslim is debatable (cf. Capel et al. 2015: 73–74), but the chronology again indicates the significance of events in the 11th century across the region. Although the Almoravid conversion hypothesis might be flawed, it is evident that their impact in the Western Sahel was felt. At Essouk/Tadmakka, occupation contracts from the mid-11th century, possibly as a correlate of Almoravid influence with an accompanying growth in evidence for trans-Saharan trade at Gao (Nixon 2009: 249). Certainly, at Gao, they seem to have been significant trading partners, as previously described.

To what extent there was uniformity of Muslim belief and practice in this period is also unclear. The variation in Islamic interpretations and practice that undoubtedly existed is difficult to assess archaeologically but is hinted at in the historical sources. In Takrur on the River Senegal, for example, the nature of Islam has been described by Levtzion (1973: 183) as more "zealous," with Takruris "carrying the propagation of Islam among neighbours and waging the holy war against infidels" (Levtzion 1973: 184). However, although material indicating involvement in trans-Saharan trade dating from after the late first millennium CE, such as copper objects partly made from imported copper alloys and cowry shells, is found in what was part of the Takrur polity in the Middle Senegal Valley (MSV) (Keech McIntosh and McIntosh 2016), direct evidence for Islam is lacking (Insoll 2003: 225). The distribution of the imported material also seems to be quite restricted. These materials are largely absent in the mound sites excavated by Keech McIntosh and McIntosh (2016), with the exception of what appears to be a recent glass bead, some copper objects made in part with imported alloys, and possibly a cylindrical carnelian bead (McIntosh 2016: 183–185; Fenn and Killick 2016: 296). At the site of Sintiou-Bara greater quantities of imported artifacts were found: 7,500 small brass rings ranging in size between 11 and 12 millimeters in diameter and 6–8 millimeters in depth, a silver and brass pendant, and some fragmentary *C. moneta* cowry shells, for example (cf. Thilmans and Ravise 1980: 22, 43, 49).

Sintiou-Bara might have been supplied from Tegdaoust. "Tegdaoust-style" cordoned pottery with red or dark-purple to black burnished finish is found in some of the western MSV sites, where it appears between 750 and 850/900 CE (Keech McIntosh and McIntosh 2016: 413). It has also been suggested that the shared similarities in some of the copper items recovered from Sintiou-Bara, such as small bells and possible horse trappings, are also indicative of a Tegdaoust–MSV trading circuit (Garenne-Marot 1993 cited in Keech McIntosh and McIntosh 2016: 415). These networks, likely also supplemented from Koumbi Saleh, were probably also the source of the limited imported materials found at Dioubaye in Senegal, in the area of medieval Bambuk, one of the sources of West African gold. Five glass beads along with four carnelian beads, a cowry, and a piece of copper wire dated to the 13th century (Gokee 2016: 264) were recovered and would seem to indicate the trickle-down effect of this trade.

The Empire of Mali

By the late 12th to early 13th century, Ghana disappeared, to be replaced by the Empire of Mali. Why it did remains unclear pending the outcome of further archaeological investigations. However, various causes have to be considered: a deterioration in the environment making life more precarious in the marginal Sahel; dynastic infighting, unquestionably a recurring problem of the subsequent Mali and Songhai empires; or a shift in trade patterns (see, e.g., Togola 1996). The origins of Mali are also uncertain (MacDonald 2013: 840), but, in contrast to Ghana, its center was situated away from the Sahel, in the savannah, precipitating conversions to Islam outside of the Sahelian zone.

Archaeology has been utilized in an attempt to locate the capital of Mali, with excavations undertaken within the Republic of Guinea at the site of Niani. Here the remains of various structures were uncovered: several round houses and, possibly, the *mihrab* of a mosque and an audience chamber. An attempt to match the archaeological finds with the historical description of the capital of Mali provided by the Moroccan traveler Ibn Battuta in the mid-14th century (Filipowiak 1978, 1979) has proved fruitless. No imported material, other than a few beads of 19th-century date was recovered, and there is an absence of recognizable Muslim graves at the site. Moreover, there appears to be a gap in the occupation sequence between the 13th and 16th centuries (Fauvelle-Aymar 2012: 247–248; MacDonald 2013: 840). Niani may have been an Islamized settlement, but it was not associated with the Empire of Mali in its 14th-century heyday.

A site that was likely associated with the Empire of Mali as well as Ghana for parts of its long occupation sequence (in total 800 BC to 1900 CE) was Dia (Bedaux et al. 2005: 29), mentioned earlier. Formed of various components including cemeteries and three flat mounds, Dia, Dia-Mara, and Dia-Shoma, the burial evidence is particularly intriguing. Nine types of burial, largely defined by the position of the corpse, were recorded, with a tenth composed of Muslim burials, dated to between 500 and 1200 (Bedaux et al. 2005: 149, 155). The excavators suggest that Ibadi Islam may have been influential at Dia, located as it was away from the sphere of Maliki orthodoxy (Bedaux et al. 2005: 172). This is unproved, but indicators of long-distance commerce are found: wheat, as already described, and also cotton appears in large quantities around 1000–1600 (Murray 2005: 399). Likely locally produced, as also indicated by the spindle whorls found, the cotton could also signify increasing consumption of cloth influenced by Muslim merchants (Murray 2005: 399), if not Islamization itself. Imports were comparatively rare: some glass beads and four cowries, as well as two jasper and four carnelian beads which might be from the region rather than sourced from trans-Saharan trade (Schmidt 2005: 265, 277–281).

The high point of Mali was without doubt the period of rule of Mansā Mūsā (1312–1337). Mansā Mūsā extended the empire in all directions: north to the important salt mines in the Sahara, west to Takrur on the River Senegal, and east, encompassing Gao, as far as the frontiers of Hausaland (Levtzion 1973). He is also credited with building several of the great monuments of the Western Sahel: a palace, the Madadougou in Timbuktu (as yet undiscovered); the Djinguereber mosque, also in Timbuktu; and a mosque in Gao, for example. Excavation was recently completed in the Djinguereber, and a piece of wood from the earliest floor in the mosque was radiocarbon dated to the mid-14th century. This is significant as it seems to support the tradition that the mosque was established by Mansā Mūsā (Poissonnier in press). The plan of the earliest phase of the mosque appears to have been rectangular with a series of bays parallel to the *qibla* wall facing Mecca. A second phase of mosque construction was dated to the late 15th to early 16th centuries, and a third phase saw the mosque enlarged, probably in the latter part of the 16th century, when it became the "Djinguereber," the "Great Mosque" in Songhai (Poissonnier in press). Yet perhaps the most enduring historical memorial to Mansā Mūsā's memory is the fabled pilgrimage he made to Mecca in and after 1324, as a statement of his Muslim identity, and accompanied by a vast number of retainers and huge quantities of gold (Bovill 1968).

Mali remained a powerful empire until about 1400, then faced incursions by nomadic Tuareg and a revolt by Gao, and its effective political power was finished by the mid-15th century (Levtzion 1985).

15TH–18TH CENTURIES

The Empire of Songhai

With the evolution of the third of the medieval Sahelian empires, Songhai, the progress of Islamization was varied, as reflected in historical reactions to its rulers. The origins of Songhai can be placed in what is best termed the "proto-Songhai" kingdom (Insoll 1996), which had existed since at least the 10th century around Gao, as previously described, and which had subsequently been subsumed with the Empire of Mali (Hunwick 1985a). In 1373, Gao recovered its independence from Mali and the era of Songhai expansion began. The first of the great Songhai rulers, comparable in his achievements to Mansā Mūsā, was Sonni Alī, who assumed power in about 1464 and expanded the Songhai domains (Hunwick 1985a, 1985b). Sonni Alī, however, is castigated in the *Ta'rīkh al-Sūdān* (es-Saʿdī 1900) for not being a good Muslim. On his death, in 1493, he was succeeded by the first of a new line of rulers, the Askiyās. In contrast, the assumption of power by Askiyā Muhammad signaled a new era of Islamic revival in Gao. Muslim scholarship flourished, and Askiyā Muhammad went on Hajj to fulfill his religious duty but also to "establish firmly" his image "as a Muslim ruler" (Hunwick 1985a: 342). Intriguingly, though his tomb stands in Gao, no archaeological deposits dated to the period of the Songhai Empire have yet been found, possibly as the nexus of settlement shifted to areas as yet uninvestigated.

The paramount center of Muslim scholarship in West Africa during the Songhai Empire was Timbuktu. Alongside the city of Harar in Ethiopia (Chapter 4.2), it was the preeminent center for Islamic learning in sub-Saharan Africa (Insoll 2003: 254). Islamic texts were copied and sciences studied there, notably at the Sankore mosque complex, a building still standing today. Although rebuilt, it was originally founded some time during the period when the Empire of Mali controlled the city between 1325 and 1433. Built of mudbrick and Timbuktu stone (a type of hard clay or limestone), it was the abode of the most prominent scholars (Mauny 1952; Insoll 1999b). Students were taught the Qur'an, *hadith*, and Islamic law and sciences, and they traveled to other great centers of Muslim learning such as Cairo and Mecca, from which scholars were likewise received. Many private libraries were also established within the city, the noted scholar Ahmad Bābā being reputed to have had 1,600 volumes at the time of the Moroccan conquest of Timbuktu in 1591 (Saad 1983: 79).

The history of Timbuktu is fairly well established, but archaeological research has been minimal. Besides the Sankore and Djinguereber, one other mosque dating from the medieval period still stands (Insoll 1999b). This is the Sīdī Yahyā, founded around 1440 (Mauny 1952: 901–911). Archaeological survey in Timbuktu recorded imported trade goods such as a possible sherd of southern Chinese celadon dated to the late 11th to early 12th centuries (Insoll 1998) and a multicolored glass bracelet fragment similar to material dated to the 14th century at sites on the Red Sea coast of Egypt (Whitcomb 1983: 106–107). The latter has parallels with bracelets from the salt-mining site of Teghaza in the Malian Sahara (Monod 1975: 717), through which the trade caravans probably passed on leaving Timbuktu. Comparable artifacts were not found in excavations completed adjacent to the Sankore mosque, with only material dating from the late 18th century onward being recovered (Insoll 2002). This included 306 tobacco pipe fragments that were locally produced and little influenced by either Ottoman or North African products (Insoll 2002: 16) (Figure 4.4.7). Earlier occupation levels comparable to those that have been investigated on the outskirts of the city, either pre-Islamic (cf. Post Park 2010), or comparable to those in the Djinguereber mosque, described earlier, probably remain to be excavated in Timbuktu, deeply buried under layers of sand deposited during the sandstorms that periodically occur (Insoll 1998).

Archaeologically, correlation might be lacking for the "golden age" of Timbuktu, but historically this is recorded as happening during the era of the Songhai Askiyā dynasty. The population of the city during the late 16th century has been estimated at 75,000, with 7,500 of this total being students (Saad 1983: 90). Trade supported this population,

FIGURE 4.4.7 Tobacco pipes from the 1998 excavations in Timbuktu.

Courtesy of T. Insoll.

and Timbuktu was linked through commerce and intellectual life to Djenne further south on the River Niger. From Djenne, Sudanic gold and foodstuffs were sent north to Timbuktu in exchange for commodities such as salt and finished items such as cloth. Djenne was the Islamized successor of an earlier settlement, Jenné-Jeno, abandoned about 1400, possibly because it was considered too tainted by non-Muslim practices (McIntosh and McIntosh 1980; McIntosh 1995).

The millennia-plus of indigenous power in the West African Sahel and savannah represented by Ghana, Mali, and Songhai was effectively terminated by the defeat of Songhai at the battle of Tondibi in 1591, ironically by an army from another Muslim state, Morocco, who were equipped with firearms (Hunwick 1985b: 364).

The Mande

Possibly from the 14th century, certainly from the 15th to 16th centuries, the Mande ventured south from Djenne and other centers on the Middle Niger (Insoll 2003: 333). Spurred by trade (i.e., the gold of the forest) rather than missionary zeal, they nonetheless established a presence in the northern fringes of the rainforest leading to the introduction of Islam to the region (cf. Wilks 2000). In so doing they created an archaeological legacy at sites such as Begho, Daboya, Bono Manso, and Old Buipe in northern and central Ghana (Insoll 2003: 337).

One of the most important centers was Begho, located at the junction between the savannah and the forest (Posnansky 2015: 96). Composed of some 1,500 mounds, probably the remains of collapsed compounds, occupation at Begho has been dated to between the 13th and 18th centuries (Posnansky 1973, 1987). The settlement flourished between the 15th/16th and 18th centuries, when contacts with the Middle Niger were apparently intensified (Stahl 1994: 86). The Mande occupied the Kramo quarter where a Muslim presence has been suggested on the basis of, for example, burials that were placed north–south on their backs, as opposed to those in the Dwinfour and Brong quarters where they were flexed, on their sides, and had no consistent orientation (Posnansky 1987: 19). Imported materials appear to have been rare at Begho, with a sherd of 17th-century Chinese blue and white pottery and an unspecified number of "multi-coloured beads," as well as brass, described later, referred to (Posnansky 2015: 108). The gold trade with which the Mande were so closely connected might also be represented at Begho by ceramic discs made from pot sherds described as "consistent with the Islamic system of weights" (Posnansky 2015: 107). Alternatively, these could be the stoppers for gourds or horn containers, themselves perished, as has been recorded at Koma Land in northern Ghana (cf. Insoll et al. 2013: 21).

Industrial remains were attested at Begho, with dye pits for textiles found in the Kramo quarter. A brass foundry was also found in the Dwinfour quarter, where objects such as rings and bracelets were produced (Posnansky 2015: 106–107). This is significant as brass is an indicator of trans-Saharan links because it was a metal not produced in sub-Saharan Africa until the 19th century (Craddock 1985), with earlier Islamic trade brass differentiated by a lower zinc content (5–20 percent) than later European trade brass (20–30 percent) (Fenn and Killick 2016: 285). Various imported brass vessels sourced from trans-Saharan trade have also been recorded in this region of central Ghana, including six bowls of Mamluk origin dating from the mid-14th to mid-15th centuries that formed part of non-Muslim village shrines in the Asante and Bono regions of Ghana (Silverman 1982, 1983).

Research has also recently been completed at Old Buipe, another town with Mande associations (Figure 4.4.8). Linked with the kingdom of Gonja that emerged in the mid-16th century, it progressively replaced Begho as an important market town, and its origins have been dated to the 15th century (Genequand and Apoh 2017: 140, 158). A focus of archaeological investigation has been the western or central architectural complex, which measures approximately 175 × 185 meters. Excavation revealed the walls of adjoining rooms, with the width of the walls and the amount of fill in the rooms suggesting that there had been an upper storey to the building that had been occupied, based on the C^{14} dates, in the 17th or 18th centuries. From pre-19th century contexts, locally made ceramics were recovered along with glass beads, otherwise undescribed, but of 16th–18th century date (Genequand and Apoh 2017: 151–154). Of particular interest in considering Islamization, and perhaps suggesting that the Mande were confined to one area in Old Buipe, is the spatial reconstruction which suggests that, for the 16th to 18th centuries, the mosque was not centrally placed in the town but was instead on the northwestern outskirts (Genequand and Apoh 2017: 159).

Traders from Borno and Hausaland also operated in the same area, with Salaga, again in Gonja, an important commercial center for trade to Hausaland particularly in the 19th century (Shinnie 1981: 68; Genequand and Apoh 2017: 140, 158). Mande trade centers were also established from the 16th century along the caravan trails in what is now Burkina Faso, where the Mande were known as Yarse by the Mossi (Levtzion 1968: 165), but these settlements await archaeological investigation. Similarly, in northern Ivory Coast, the Mande settlements have not been archaeologically explored. Here the Mande were known as Dyula, and Kong was a particularly important trade settlement and center of Islamic learning with five mosques in the latter part of the 19th century (Binger 1892).

The Rainforest

The southern suppliers of gold to the Mande Muslim merchants in trade centers such as Begho were the Akan (Insoll 2003: 343), a confederation of rainforest peoples including the Asante, Brong, and Baule (Garrard 1988: 1). The Asante state and its capital Kumasi have been the focus of archaeological research (cf. Shinnie and Shinnie 1995), but little evidence for northern contacts was found. This is perhaps unsurprising as the impact of Islam in Asante was minimal, though there was a Muslim community at Kumasi of traders—Mande, Hausa, Dagomba—and holy men, apparently "from as far away as the Maghreb, Egypt, and Baghdad" (Bravmann and Silverman 1987: 94). Asante Muslim

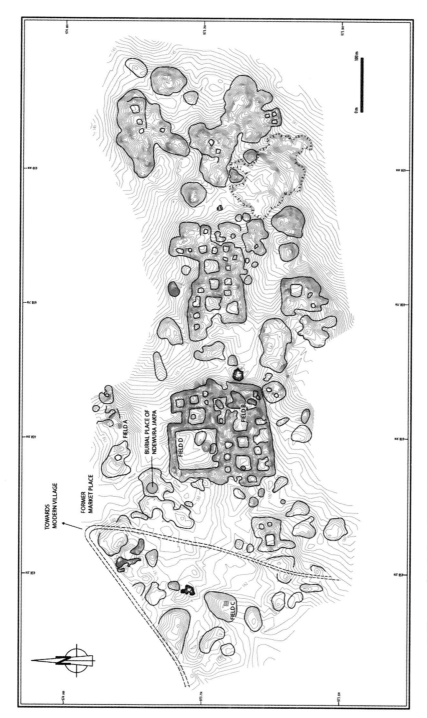

FIGURE 4.4.8 Topographical plan of Old Buipe

Survey and drawing Sylvain Dumont, Sophie Reynard, and Denis Genequand; courtesy of D. Genequand.

conversion might have been nonexistent and indigenous religious belief remained intact, but Asante material culture was influenced by Islam in the domain of magical protection (Insoll 2003: 345). Within Asante amulets were in demand at all levels of society (Owusu-Ansah 1983), with records of various rulers utilizing elements of Muslim-derived ritual and practices which they thought might benefit them, as with the Asantehene Osei Bonsu who was seen wearing a white cloth covered in Arabic writing in 1820, or Asantehene Kofi Kakari who had sandals with the soles covered in Islamic magical squares and Arabic writing later in the 19th century (Bravmann and Silverman 1987: 94, 99).

By the 17th century, and possibly as early as the 15th to 16th centuries, contacts between Muslims from Hausaland and Borno and another major ethno-linguistic group of the rainforest, the Yoruba of southwest Nigeria and adjacent parts of Benin, had occurred (Insoll 2003: 348–349). The result was that by the late 18th to early 19th centuries there were Muslim communities of varying sizes in many of the major Yoruba commercial centers such as Lagos, Oyo, Keu, and Badagry (Gbadamosi 1978). Islam in Yorubaland remains little investigated archaeologically (Insoll 2003). Instead, focus has been placed on indigenous religion, particularly as manifest via the spectacular shrines at Ife with their bronze, stone, and ceramic heads and figurines, potsherd pavements, and evidence for complex shrine-based ritual practices that have been dated in the so-called Classic period to between the 12th and 16th centuries (cf. Garlake 1974; Drewal and Schildkrout 2010; Insoll 2017b). Elsewhere in the forest zone of West Africa archaeological research on Muslim communities in, for example, Guinea, Sierra Leone, Liberia, Ivory Coast, Togo, and Benin, is largely unexplored.

19TH CENTURY

The 19th century is characterized by Islamic reform and revival in West Africa, sometimes accompanied by jihad. The Yoruba, for instance, were the focus of a jihad launched from the city of Ilorin, which they checked at the battle of Osogbo in 1840 (Gbadamosi 1978: 12). Some of the fortified hilltop sites in northern Yoruba land investigated by Usman (2003) could be linked with the military incursions of Fulani armies from Ilorin and their Nupe allies into Igbomina territory from the 1840s. Usman (2003: 207–211) describes the use of defensive mechanisms such as walls and strategically placed rock piles to slow cavalry at sites such as Gbagedi and Aun I, with the C^{14} chronology spanning the period between the late 15th and early 20th centuries.

The roots of these reform movements can be traced to the late 18th century, and they stretched from Futa Toro (Middle Senegal Valley) and Futa Djallon (Guinea) in the west to the Hausa states in the east (cf. Robinson 2000: 133–137; Gokee 2016: 55–57) (Chapter 4.5). Hiskett (1994: 114) describes their characteristic achievement as the creation of "centralized Islamic polities forged either out of the autonomous principalities of half-hearted Muslim chiefs prone to mixing or out of the fragmented pieces of the medieval empires of the Sahel." Again, archaeological sites associated with these move-ments are largely uninvestigated.

An exception is provided by two sites associated with the Fulani caliphate of Masina in Mali (cf. Robinson 2000: 139–140). Modjodjé, near Mopti in Mali was a temporary location occupied by the Caliphate's founder, Sekou Amadou, while the capital Hamdallahi was being constructed (Mayor 1997). Built of dry-stone, the remains of a mosque, Amadou's residence, and the house of his family were recorded. Of interest is that Modjodjé was built at the foot of hills occupied by the non-Muslim Dogon. This had "*transformations matérielles*" (Mayor 1997: 57) upon the nearest Dogon village, Bona, with, for instance, the abandonment of the painted circumcision place and the use of collective tombs in favor of individual burial in cemeteries (Mayor 1997: 57) (i.e., "the progress of Islamization"; Insoll 2003: 358). Hamdallahi was also investigated. Pentagonal in shape and fortified with a wall of sun-dried brick, Hamdallahi measures 2 kilometers north–south and 1.9 kilometers east–west (Gallay et al. 1990). The congre-gational mosque and Amadou's palace were placed at the heart of the city and, between these buildings and the outer enclosing wall, were numerous shops, houses, and court-yards that would have contained tents and other nomad shelters (Gallay et al. 1990). Excavation of one of these structures uncovered a large courtyard, approximately 25 × 15 meters. The disproportionate size of the courtyard to the structures suggested that both straw huts were built and cattle were kept in the courtyard (Mayor 1997: 49, 57), thus materially affirming the Fulani pastoralist identity of Hamdallahi.

Conclusion

It is evident that the rich and complex Islamic archaeology of West Africa is impossible to separate from non-Muslim traditions. The two are intertwined because Islamic archaeology in West Africa is not exotic but part of the regional narrative of the past and, as such, has been shaped and formed by the peoples and traditions of the region. Relevant material culture from mosque architecture to the use of small exogenous items such as cowry shells or beads reflects the indigenization of Islam in West Africa and its interplay within the broader cultural context. Our archaeological understanding of the subject is also fast-changing, and, since 2003, when this author last published a review of Islamic archaeology in West Africa (Insoll 2003), research has moved on immensely. Many of the gaps in the archaeological database have been filled, partly because political circumstances in the Sahel have necessitated a shift in research south away from the Saharan edge entrepot in Mauritania, Mali, or Niger to sites in Ghana, Benin, or Senegal, for example. This is exposing how far the networks of commerce extended without nec-essarily being accompanied by Islamization.

Yet many gaps in knowledge still exist. For example, more emphasis is required on exploring the archaeology of Islamic practice in West Africa rather than charting the presence of Muslims and trade goods. Reconstructing past diet and animal and plant economies is receiving good attention at some sites (e.g., Fuller 2000; Fuller et al. 2017; Barrett-Jolley 2000; Stangroome 2000; Murray 2005; MacDonald 2017), but there is room for enhanced research at others. And the analysis of trade goods needs also to incorporate more thinking about what artifacts such as beads, cowries, glass vessels, glazed ceramics, brass rods, etc. say about past notions of taste, consumption, value, and aesthetics as well as focusing on their origins. Why, for example, does Islamic vessel glass appear to stop at Saharan and Sahelian entrepots such as Gao and Timbuktu (cf. Nixon et al. 2017: 158), whereas, as described, glass beads are much more widely distributed?

These patterns would appear, in part, to relate to past concepts of value, fashion, and aesthetics, so that items such as necklaces, waist bands, and leg ornaments were more common in contexts such as Kissi, where they enter the archaeological record through burial, as opposed to Gao, where Muslim dress might have been more prevalent and because of the organic nature of cloth fail to survive archaeologically. Equally, the prevalence of certain bead color preferences is intriguing, as at Igbo-Ukwu (Insoll 2015: 35–36) or Gao-Saney where blue, blue-green, and green glass beads constituted 90 percent of the glass bead assemblage (Cissé 2017: 110). Supply or the availability of blue colorant (copper) might account for this (Cissé 2017: 122), as again might questions of taste and personal preference, and these are issues that need exploring. Similar factors may explain the differing patterns of cowry consumption where they relate to adornment rather than currency and again may have differed based on degree of Islamization as well as fashion and taste. Various research possibilities exist to further expand our understanding of Islamic archaeology in West Africa, a dynamic region with local centers of archaeological research excellence in, for example, Ghana, Senegal, Nigeria, and Mali, that are well-suited to pursuing these research aims.

References

Adams, M. E. 1999. "Savanna Environments," in W. M. Adams, A. S. Goudie, and A. R. Orme (eds.), *The Physical Geography of Africa* (Oxford: Oxford University Press), 196–210.

Aillet, C. 2017. "Le Bassin de Ouargla: Foyer Ibadite et Carrefour du Sahara Médiéval," in C. Aillet, P. Cressier, and S. Gilotte (eds.), *Sedrata. Histoire et Archéologie d'un Carrefour du Sahara Médiéval* (Madrid: Casa de Velázquez), 25–85.

Anquandah, J. 1987. "The Stone Circle Mounds of Komaland, Northern Ghana, in West African Archaeology," *African Archaeological Review*, 5, 171–180.

Anquandah, J. 1998. *Koma-Bulsa. Its Art and Archaeology* (Rome: Istituto Italiano Per l'Africa e L'Oriente).

Arazi, N. 1999. "An Archaeological Survey in the Songhay Heartland of Mali," *Nyame Akuma*, 52, 38–39.

Barrett-Jolley, S. 2000. "The Faunal Remains from Gao Ancien," in T. Insoll (with other contributions), *Urbanism, Archaeology and Trade. Further Observations on the Gao Region (Mali)*. BAR S829 (Oxford: British Archaeological Reports), 45–55.

Bedaux, R., Polet, J., Sanogo, K., and Schmidt, A. (eds.) 2005. *Recherches Archéologiques à Dia dans le Delta Intérieur du Niger (Mali)*(Leiden: CNWA Publications).

Berthier, S. 1997. *Koumbi Saleh.* BAR S680 (Oxford: Tempus Reparatum).

Binger, C. 1892. *Du Niger au Golfe de Guinée* (Paris: Hachette).

Bravmann, R. 1974. *Islam and Tribal Art in West Africa* (Cambridge: Cambridge University Press).

Bravmann, R., and Silverman, R. 1987. "Painted Incantations: The Closeness of Allah and Kings in Nineteenth Century Asante," in E. Schildkrout (ed.), *The Golden Stool: Studies of the Asante Center and Periphery* (New York: American Museum of Natural History), 93–107.

Bovill, E. W. 1968. *The Golden Trade of the Moors* (London: Oxford University Press).

Capel, C., Zazzo, A., Polet, J., and Saliège, J-F. 2015. "The End of a Hundred-Year-Old Archaeological Riddle: First Dating of the Columns Tomb of Kumbi Saleh (Mauritania)," *Radiocarbon*, 57, 65–75.

Cissé, M. 2017. "The Trans-Saharan Trade Connection with Gao (Mali) During the First Millennium AD," in D. Mattingly, V. Leitch, C. Duckworth, A. Cuénod, M. Sterry, and F. Cole (eds.), *Trade in the Ancient Sahara and Beyond* (Cambridge: Cambridge University Press), 101–130.

Cissé, M., Keech McIntosh, S., Dussubieux, L., Fenn, T., Gallagher, D., and Chipps Smith, A. 2013. "Excavations at Gao-Saney: New Evidence for Settlement Growth, Trade, and Interaction on the Niger Bend in the First Millennium CE," *Journal of African Archaeology*, 11, 9–37.

Colleyn, J-P. 2009. *Bamana* (Milan: 5 Continents).

Conrad, D. C., and Fisher, H. 1982. "The Conquest That Never Was: Ghana and the Almoravids, 1076, Part 1: The External Arabic Sources," *History in Africa*, 9, 21–59.

Conrad, D. C., and Fisher, H. 1983. "The Conquest That Never Was: Ghana and the Almoravids, 1076, Part 1: The Local Oral Sources," *History in Africa*, 10, 53–78.

Craddock, P. 1985. "Medieval Copper Alloy Production and West African Bronze Analyses— Part 1," *Archaeometry*, 27, 17–41.

de Moraes Farias, P. F. 1990. "The Oldest Extant Writing of West Africa," *Journal des Africanistes*, 62, 65–113.

de Moraes Farias, P. F. 2000. "Appendix 2. The Inscriptions from Gorongobo," in T. Insoll (ed.), *Urbanism, Archaeology and Trade. Further Observations on the Gao Region (Mali). The 1996 Fieldseason Results.* BAR S829 (Oxford: British Archaeological Reports), 156–159.

de Moraes Farias, P. F. 2003. *Arabic Medieval Inscriptions from the Republic of Mali* (Oxford: Oxford University Press).

Dodds, J. D. (ed.) 1992. *Al-Andalus. The Art of Islamic Spain* (New York: Metropolitan Museum).

Drewal, H., and Schildkrout, E. 2010. *Kingdom of Ife: Sculptures from West Africa* (London: British Museum).

Dueppen, S. A. 2012. *Egalitarian Revolution in the Savanna* (Sheffield: Equinox).

Dussubieux, L. 2017. "Glass Beads in Trans-Saharan Trade," in D. Mattingly, V. Leitch, C. Duckworth, A. Cuénod, M. Sterry, and F. Cole (eds.), *Trade in the Ancient Sahara and Beyond* (Cambridge: Cambridge University Press), 414–432.

es-Saʿdī, A. 1900. (transl. O. Houdas). *Tarikh es-Soudan* (Paris: Ernest Leroux).

Fauvelle-Aymar, F-X. 2012. "Niani *redux*. A Final Rejection of the Identification of the Site of Niani (Republic of Guinea) with the Capital of the Kingdom of Mali," in F. X. Fauvelle-Aymar (ed.), *Palethnology of Africa, P@lethnology*, 4, 235–252.

Fenn, T., and Killick, D. 2016. "Copper Alloys," in S. K. Keech McIntosh and R. J. McIntosh (eds.), *The Search for Takrur* (New Haven, CT: Yale University Press), 281–298.

Filipowiak, W. 1978. "Results of Archaeological Research at Niani," *Nyame Akuma*, 8, 32–33.

Filipowiak, W. 1979. *Études Archéologiques sue la Capitale Médiévale du Mali* (Szczecin: Muzeum Narodowe).

Fuller, D. 2000. "The Botanical Remains," in T. Insoll (ed.), *Urbanism, Archaeology and Trade. Further Observations on the Gao Region (Mali). The 1996 Fieldseason Results*. BAR S829 (Oxford: British Archaeological Reports), 28–35.

Fuller, D., Murray, M-A., and Nixon, S. 2017. "Plant Remains," in S. Nixon (ed.), *Essouk-Tadmekka. An Early Islamic Trans-Saharan Market Town* (Leiden: Brill), 241–252.

Gallay, A., Huysecom, E., Honegger, M., and Mayor, A. 1990. *Hamdallahi* (Stuttgart: Franz Steiner).

Garlake, P. 1974. "Excavations at Obalara's Land, Ife: An Interim Report," *West African Journal of Archaeology*, 4, 111–148.

Garrard, T. F. 1988. "The Historical Background to Akan Gold-Weights," in C. Fox (ed.), *Asante Brass Casting* (Cambridge: African Studies Centre), 1–13.

Garenne-Marot, L. 1993. *Archéologie d'un Métal: Le Cuivre en Sénégambie (Afrique de l'Ouest) entre le Xe et XIV Siècle* (Unpublished PhD thesis, Paris, Université de Paris I).

Gbadamosi, T. G. O. 1978. *The Growth of Islam Among the Yoruba, 1841–1908* (London: Longman).

Genequand, D., and Apoh, W. 2017. "Old Buipe (Ghana, Northern Region): Some Observations on Islamization and Urban Development at the South-Western Margins of the *Dar al-Islam*," *Journal of Islamic Archaeology*, 4, 139–162.

Glaze, A. 1981. *Art and Death in a Senufo Village* (Bloomington: Indiana University Press).

Gokee, C. 2016. *Assembling the Village in Medieval Bambuk* (Sheffield: Equinox).

Gómez Moreno, M. 1940. "La loza dorada primitíva de Málaga," *Al-Andalus*, 5, 393–398.

Grove, A. T. 1978. "Geographical Introduction to the Sahel," *The Geographical Journal*, 144, 407–415.

Guerra, M. F. 2000. "Appendix 1. A Report on the Composition of a Gold Bead from Gao," in T. Insoll (ed.), *Urbanism, Archaeology and Trade. Further Observations on the Gao Region Mali). The 1996 Fieldseason Results*. BAR S829 (Oxford: British Archaeological Reports), 153–155.

Haour, A., Nixon, S., N'Dah, D., Magnavita, C., and Livingstone Smith, A. 2016. "The Settlement Mound at Birnin Lafiya: New Evidence from the Eastern Arc of the Niger River," *Antiquity*, 90, 695–710.

Hiskett, M. 1994. *The Course of Islam in Africa* (Edinburgh: Edinburgh University Press).

Houdas, O., and Delafosse, M. (trans.). 1913. *Tarikh El-Fettach* (Paris: Ernest Leroux).

Hunwick, J. O. 1985a. *Shari'a in Songhay: The Replies of al-Maghili to the Questions of Askia al-Ḥajj Muḥammad* (London: Oxford University Press).

Hunwick, J. O. 1985b. "Songhay, Borno and the Hausa States, 1450–1600," in J. F. A. Ajayi and M. Crowder (eds.), *History of West Africa, I* (Harlow: Longman), 323–371.

Hunwick, J. O. 1999. *Timbuktu and the Songhay Empire* (Leiden: Brill).

Hunwick, J. O. 2003. *Arabic Literature of Africa. Volume 4. The Writings of Western Sudanic Africa* (Leiden: Brill).

Hunwick, J. O., and Boye, A. J. 2008. *The Hidden Treasures of Timbuktu* (London: Thames and Hudson).

Hutton MacDonald, R., and MacDonald, K. 1996. "A Preliminary Report on the Faunal Remains Recovered from Gao Ancien and Gao-Saney (1993 Season)," in T. Insoll (ed.), *Islam, Archaeology and History. Gao Region (Mali) ca. AD 900–1250*. BAR S647 (Oxford: Tempus Reparatum), 124–126.

Insoll, T. 1994. "The External Creation of the Western Sahel's Past: The Use and Abuse of the Arabic Sources," *Archaeological Review from Cambridge*, 13, 39–49.

Insoll, T. 1995. "A Cache of Hippopotamus Ivory at Gao, Mali: and a Hypothesis of Its Use," *Antiquity*, 69, 327–336.

Insoll, T. 1996. *Islam, Archaeology and History. A Complex Relationship: The Gao Region (Mali) ca. AD 900–1250*. BAR S647 (Oxford: Tempus Reparatum).

Insoll, T. 1997. "Iron Age Gao: An Archaeological Contribution," *Journal of African History*, 38, 1–30.

Insoll, T. 1998. "Archaeological Research in Timbuktu, Mali," *Antiquity*, 72, 413–417.

Insoll, T. 1999a. *The Archaeology of Islam* (Oxford: Blackwell).

Insoll, T. 1999b. "The mud mosques of Timbuktu," in C. Scarre (ed.), *The Seventy Wonders of the Ancient World* (London: Thames and Hudson), 143–146.

Insoll, T. (with other contributions) 2000. *Urbanism, Archaeology and Trade. Further Observations on the Gao Region (Mali). The 1996 Fieldseason Results*. BAR S829 (Oxford: British Archaeological Reports).

Insoll, T. 2002. "The Archaeology of Post Medieval Timbuktu," *Sahara*, 13, 7–22.

Insoll, T. 2003. *The Archaeology of Islam in Sub-Saharan Africa* (Cambridge: Cambridge University Press).

Insoll, T. 2004. "Syncretism, Time, and Identity: Islamic Archaeology in West Africa," in D. Whitcomb (ed.), *Changing Social Identity with the Spread of Islam. Archaeological Perspectives* (Chicago: Oriental Institute), 89–101.

Insoll, T. 2015. *Material Explorations in African Archaeology* (Oxford: Oxford University Press).

Insoll, T. 2017a. "The Archaeology of Islamisation in Sub-Saharan Africa: A Comparative Study," in A. Peacock (ed.), *Islamisation: Comparative Perspectives from History* (Edinburgh: Edinburgh University Press), 244–273.

Insoll, T. 2017b. "West Africa," in T. Insoll (ed.), *Oxford Handbook of Prehistoric Figurines* (Oxford: Oxford University Press), 151–177.

Insoll, T., Kankpeyeng, B., and Nkumbaan, S. 2012. "Fragmentary Ancestors? Medicine, Bodies and Persons in a Koma Mound, Northern Ghana," in K. Rountree, C. Morris, and A. Peatfield (eds.), *Archaeology of Spiritualities* (New York: Springer), 25–45.

Insoll, T., Kankpeyeng, B., Nkumbaan, S., and Saako, M. 2013. *Fragmentary Ancestors* (Manchester: Manchester Museum).

Insoll, T., Polya, D., Bhan, K., Irving, D., and Jarvis, K. 2004. "Toward an Understanding of the Carnelian Bead Trade from Western India to sub-Saharan Africa: The Application of UV-LA-ICP-MS to Carnelian from Gujarat, India, and West Africa," *Journal of Archaeological Science*, 31, 1161–1173.

Insoll, T., and Shaw, T. 1997. "Gao and Igbo-Ukwu: Beads, Inter-regional Trade and Beyond," *African Archaeological Review*, 14, 9–23.

Kankpeyeng, B., Swanepoel, N., Insoll, T., Nkumbaan, S., Amartey, S., and Saako, M. 2013. "Insights into Past Ritual Practice at Yikpabongo, Northern Region, Ghana," *African Archaeological Review*, 30, 475–499.

Keech McIntosh, S. K., and McIntosh, R. J. 2016. "Overview and Conclusions," in S. K. Keech McIntosh and R. J. McIntosh (eds.), *The Search for Takrur* (New Haven, CT: Yale University Press), 381–426.

Lankton, J., Nixon, S., Robertshaw, P., and Dussubieux, L. 2017. "Beads," in S. Nixon (ed.). *Essouk-Tadmekka. An Early Islamic Trans-Saharan Market Town* (Leiden: Brill), 160–173.

Le Houerou, H. N. 1980. "The Rangelands of the Sahel," *Journal of Range Management*, 33, 41–46.

Levtzion, N. 1968. *Muslims and Chiefs in West Africa* (Oxford: Clarendon Press).

Levtzion, N. 1973. *Ancient Ghana and Mali* (London: Methuen).

Levtzion, N. 1979. "Patterns of Islamization," in N. Levtzion (ed.), *Conversion to Islam* (New York: Holmes and Meier), 207–216.

Levtzion, N. 1985. "The Early States of the Western Sudan to 1500," in J. F. A. Ajayi and M. Crowder (eds.), *History of West Africa*, vol. I (Harlow: Longman), 129–166.

Levtzion, N. 2000. "Islam in the Bilad al-Sudan to 1800," in N. Levtzion and R. L. Pouwels (eds.), *The History of Islam in Africa* (Oxford: James Currey), 63–91.

Levtzion, N., and Hopkins, J. F. P. 2000. *Corpus of Early Arabic Sources for West African History* (Princeton, NJ: Markus Wiener).

Lewicki, T. 1971. "The Ibadites in Arabia and Africa," *Cahiers d'Histoire Mondiale*, 13, 3–130.

Lomax, D. W. 1978. *The Reconquest of Spain* (London: Longman).

Lovejoy, P. E. 1985. "The Internal Trade of West Africa before 1800," in J. F. A. Ajayi and M. Crowder (eds.), *History of West Africa*, vol. I (Harlow: Longman), 648–690.

MacDonald, K. C. 2011. "A View from the South," in A. Dowler and E. R. Galvin (eds.), *Money, Trade and Trade Routes in Pre-Islamic North Africa* (London: British Museum Press), 72–82.

MacDonald, K. C. 2013. "Complex Societies, Urbanism, and Trade in the Western Sahel," in P. Mitchell and P. Lane (eds.), *The Oxford Handbook of African Archaeology* (Oxford: Oxford University Press), 829–844.

MacDonald, K. C. 2017. "Faunal Remains," in S. Nixon (ed.), *Essouk-Tadmekka. An Early Islamic Trans-Saharan Market Town* (Leiden: Brill), 234–252.

Magnavita, S. 2003. "The Beads of Kissi, Burkina Faso," *Journal of African Archaeology*, 1, 127–138.

Magnavita, S. 2008. "The Oldest Textiles from Sub-Saharan West Africa: Woolen Facts from Kissi, Burkina Faso," *Journal of African Archaeology*, 6, 243–257.

Magnavita, S. 2015. *1500 Jahre am Mare de Kissi* (Frankfurt: Africa Magna Verlag).

Magnavita, S. 2017. "Track and Trace. Archaeometric Approaches to the Study of Early Trans-Saharan Trade," in D. Mattingly, V. Leitch, C. Duckworth, A. Cuénod, M. Sterry, and F. Cole (eds.), *Trade in the Ancient Sahara and Beyond* (Cambridge: Cambridge University Press), 393–413.

Martin, C. 1991. *The Rainforests of West Africa* (Berlin: Birkhäuser Verlag).

Mattingly, D. 2017. "The Garamantes and the Origins of Saharan Trade," in D. Mattingly, V. Leitch, C. Duckworth, A. Cuénod, M. Sterry, and F. Cole (eds.), *Trade in the Ancient Sahara and Beyond* (Cambridge: Cambridge University Press), 1–52.

Mattingly, D., and Cole, F. 2017. "Visible and Invisible Commodities of Trade: The Significance of Organic Materials in Saharan Trade," in D. Mattingly, V. Leitch, C. Duckworth, A. Cuénod, M. Sterry, and F. Cole (eds.), *Trade in the Ancient Sahara and Beyond* (Cambridge: Cambridge University Press), 211–230.

Mauny, R. 1952. "Notes d'archéologie sur Tombouctou," *Bulletin de l'Institut Français de l'Afrique Noire (B)*, 14, 899–918.

Mauny, R. 1961. *Tableau Géographique de l'Ouest Africain au Moyen Age* (Dakar Institut Français de l'Afrique Noire).

Mayor, A. 1997. "Les Rapports entre la Diina Peule du Maasina et les Populations du Delta Intérieur du Niger, vus au travers des Traditions Historiques et des Fouilles Archéologiques," in M. de Bruijn and H. van Dijk (eds.), *Peuls et Mandingues* (Paris: Karthala), 35–60.

McIntosh, R. J. 2016. "Small Finds," in S. K. Keech McIntosh and R. J. McIntosh (eds.), *The Search for Takrur* (New Haven: Yale University Press), 175–190.

McIntosh, R. J., and McIntosh, S. K. 1988. "From *siècles obscurs* to Revolutionary Centuries on the Middle Niger," *World Archaeology,* 20, 141–165.

McIntosh, S. K. (ed.) 1995. *Excavation at Jenne-jeno, Hambarketolo, and Kaniana (Inland Niger Delta, Mali), the 1981 Season* (Los Angeles: University of California Press).

McIntosh, S. K., and McIntosh, R. J. 1980. *Prehistoric Investigations in the Region of Jenne, Mali* (Oxford: British Archaeological Reports).

Monod, T. 1969. "Le 'Ma'den Ijafen: Une Epave Caravanière Ancienne dans la Majabat al-Koubra," in *Actes du 1er Colloque International d'Archéologie Africaine, 1966, Fort Lamy* (Fort Lamy: Institut National Tchadien pour les Sciences Humaines), 286–320.

Monod, T. 1975. "À propos des bracelets de verre Sahariens," *Bulletin de l'Institut Fondamental de l'Afrique Noire (B),* 37, 702–718.

Murray, S. 2005. "Recherches Archéobotaniques," in R. Bedaux, J. Polet, K. Sanogo, and A. Schmidt (eds.). *Recherches Archéologiques à Dia dans le Delta Intérieur du Niger (Mali)* (Leiden: CNWA Publications), 386–400.

Niane, D. T. 1986. *Sundiata: An Epic of Old Mali* (Harlow: Longman).

Nixon, S. 2009. "Excavating Essouk-Tadmakka (Mali): New Archaeological Investigations of Early Islamic Trans-Saharan Trade," *Azania,* 44, 217–255.

Nixon, S. (ed.) 2017a. *Essouk-Tadmekka. An Early Islamic Trans-Saharan Market Town* (Leiden: Brill).

Nixon, S. 2017b. "Miscellaneous Material Culture," in S. Nixon (ed.), *Essouk-Tadmekka. An Early Islamic Trans-Saharan Market Town* (Leiden: Brill), 216–226.

Nixon, S., Lankton, J., and Dussubieux, L. 2017. "Glass Vessels," in S. Nixon (ed.), *Essouk-Tadmekka. An Early Islamic Trans-Saharan Market Town* (Leiden: Brill), 152–159.

Nixon, S., and MacDonald, K. 2017. "Pottery," in S. Nixon (ed.), *Essouk-Tadmekka. An Early Islamic Trans-Saharan Market Town* (Leiden: Brill), 119–151.

Nixon, S., and Rehren, T. 2017. "Gold Processing Remains," in S. Nixon (ed.), *Essouk-Tadmekka. An Early Islamic Trans-Saharan Market Town* (Leiden: Brill), 174–187.

Nixon, S., Rehren, T., and Guerra, M. F. 2011. "New Light on the Early Islamic West African Gold Trade: Coin Moulds from Tadmekka, Mali," *Antiquity,* 85, 1353–1368.

Owusu-Ansah, D. 1983. "Islamic Influence in a Forest Kingdom: The Role of Protective Amulets in Early Nineteenth Century Asante," *TransAfrican Journal of History* 12: 100–133.

Petit, L. P., and von Czerniewicz, M. 2011. "Miscellaneous Finds," in L. P. Petit, M. von Czerniewicz, and C. Pelzer (eds.), *Oursi hu-beero* (Leiden: Sidestone Press), 105–126.

Poissonnier, B. in press. "The Great Mosque in Timbuktu: Seven Centuries of Earthen Architecture," in S. Pradines (ed.), *Earthen Architecture in Muslim Cultures. Historical and Anthropological Perspectives* (Leiden: Brill), 22–36.

Posnansky, M. 1973. "The Early Development of Trade in West Africa: Some Archaeological Considerations," *Ghana Social Science Journal,* 2, 87–100.

Posnansky, M. 1987. "Prelude to Akan Civilization," in E. Schildkrout (ed.), *The Golden Stool: Studies of the Asante Center and Periphery* (New York: American Museum of Natural History), 14–22.

Posnansky, M. 2015. "Begho: Life and Times," *Journal of West African History,* 1, 95–117.

Post Park, D. 2010. "Prehistoric Timbuktu and Its Hinterland," *Antiquity,* 84, 1076–1088.

Prevost, V. 2016. *Les Mosquées Ibadites du Djebel Nafūsa* (London: Society for Libyan Studies).

Robert, D. 1970a. "Les Fouilles de Tegdaoust," *Journal of African History,* 11, 471–493.

Robert, D. 1970b. "Report on the Excavations at Tegdaoust," *West African Archaeological Newsletter,* 12, 64–68.

Robert-Chaleix, D. 1989. *Tegdaoust V* (Paris: Editions Recherche sur les Civilisations).

Robinson, D. 2000. "Revolutions in the Western Sudan," in N. Levtzion and R. L. Pouwels (eds.), *The History of Islam in Africa* (Oxford: James Currey), 131–152.

Roche, M. 1970. *Le M'zab. Architecture Ibadite en Algerie* (Paris: Arthaud).

Rouch, J. 1989. *La Religion et la Magie Songhay* (Bruxelles: Editions de l'Université de Bruxelles).

Saad, E. N. 1983. *Social History of Timbuktu. The Role of Muslim Scholars and Notables 1400–1900* (Cambridge: Cambridge University Press).

Sauvaget, J. 1950. "Les épitaphes royales de Gao," *Bulletin de l'Institut Français de l'Afrique Noire (B)*, 12, 418–440.

Schacht, J. 1954. "Sur la Diffusion des Formes d'Architecture Religeuse Musulmane à Travers le Sahara," *Travaux de l'Institut de Recherches Sahariennes*, 11, 11–27.

Schmidt, A. 2005. "Parure: Perles, Labrets, Bracelets, Pendentifs et Cauris," in R. Bedaux, J. Polet, K. Sanogo, and A. Schmidt (eds.), *Recherches Archéologiques à Dia dans le Delta Intérieur du Niger (Mali)* (Leiden: CNWA Publications), 263–281.

Shaw, T. 1970. *Igbo-Ukwu* (Evanston: Northwestern University Press).

Shaw, T. 1977. *Unearthing Igbo-Ukwu* (Ibadan: Oxford University Press).

Shinnie, P. 1981. "Archaeology in Gonja, Ghana," in Anon. (ed.), *Le Sol, La Parole et l'écrit. Mélanges en Hommage à Raymond Mauny* (Paris: Société Française d'Histoire d'Outre-Mer), 65–70.

Shinnie, P., and Shinnie, A., 1995. *Early Asante* (Calgary: University of Calgary Press).

Silverman, R. 1982. "14th-15th Century Syrio-Egyptian Brassware in Ghana," *Nyame Akuma*, 20, 13–16.

Silverman, R. 1983. "Akan Kuduo: Form and Function," in D. H. Ross and T. F. Garrard (eds.), *Akan Transformations: Problems in Ghanaian Art History* (Los Angeles: Fowler Museum of Cultural History, UCLA), 10–29.

Skinner, E. P. 1964. *The Mossi of the Upper Volta* (Stanford, CA: Stanford University Press).

Stahl, A. B. 1994. "Innovation, Diffusion, and Culture Contact: The Holocene Archaeology of Ghana," *Journal of World Prehistory*, 8, 51–112.

Stangroome, C. 2000. "The Faunal Remains from Gadei," in T. Insoll (ed., with other contributions), *Urbanism, Archaeology and Trade. Further Observations on the Gao Region (Mali)*. BAR S829 (Oxford: British Archaeological Reports), 56–61.

Stoller, P. 1992. *The Cinematic Griot. The Ethnography of Jean Rouch* (Chicago: University of Chicago Press).

Takezawa, S., and Cissé, M. 2012. "Discovery of the Earliest Royal Palace in Gao and Its Implications for the History of West Africa," *Cahiers d'Etudes Africaines*, 208, 813–844.

Thilmans. G., and Ravise, A. 1980. *Protohistoire de Sénégal. T. 2. Sintiou-Bara et les Sites du Fleuve* (Dakar: IFAN).

Togola, T. 1996. "Iron Age Occupation in the Méma Region, Mali," *African Archaeological Review*, 13, 91–110.

Trimingham, J. S. 1959. *Islam in West Africa* (Oxford: Clarendon Press).

Trimingham, J. S. 1962. *A History of Islam in West Africa* (London: Oxford University Press).

Usman, A. 2003. "The Ethnohistory and Archaeology of Warfare in Northern Yoruba," *Journal of African Archaeology*, 1, 201–214.

Vanacker, C. 1979. *Tegdaoust II* (Nouakchott: Institut Mauritanien de la Recherche Scientifique).

Vanacker, C. 1983. "Verres à Décor Géométrique à Tegdaoust," in J. Devisse (ed.), *Tegdaoust III* (Paris: Association Diffusion Pensée Français), 515–522.

van Doosselaere, B. 2014. *Le Roi et le Potier* (Frankfurt: Africa Magna Verlag).

Vire, M. M. 1958. "Notes sur trois épitaphes royales de Gao," *Bulletin de l'Institut Français de l'Afrique Noire (B),* 20, 368–376.

Watson, A. M. 1983. *Agricultural Innovation in the Early Islamic World, 700–1100* (Cambridge: Cambridge University Press).

Whitcomb, D. S. 1983. "Islamic Glass from Al-Qadim, Egypt," *Journal of Glass Studies,* 25, 101–108.

Wilks, I. 2000. "The Juula and the Expansion of Islam into the Forest". in N. Levtzion and R. L. Pouwels (eds.), *The History of Islam in Africa* (Oxford: James Currey), 93–115.

Zahan, D. 1974. *The Bambara* (Leiden: Brill).

CHAPTER 4.5

···

CENTRAL SUDAN

···

CARLOS MAGNAVITA
AND ABUBAKAR SANI SULE

INTRODUCTION

THE Central Sudan and Sahel, characterized by a mixed woodland-grassland ecosystem, comprises the region between the River Niger and the surroundings of Lake Chad south of the Sahara Desert and north of the tropical rainforest. Compared to the remaining, western portions of West Africa (see Chapter 4.4), our current knowledge of the Islamic archaeology of that region is exceptionally sparse. About 15 years ago, Insoll (2003: 265) already described it as "one of the last great blank archaeological areas of sub-Saharan Africa for the archaeology of Islam" and this has not substantially changed since then. Two major and related factors account for this situation. First, there has been since the 1970s a consensual West Africa-wide archaeological research agenda that (not unjustifiably) has mainly privileged the investigation of African non-Islamic cultures and societies. Second, most archaeologists previously working in the Central Sudan and Sahel region tacitly regarded their methods as virtually pointless for the Islamic period, as historians were already making enormous progress by furnishing deep and comprehensive insights into chronology and the processes that shaped local societies since the Arab conquest of North Africa. While the latter view is obviously flawed because the historical sources have inherent limitations, the fact is that a series of important details on the historical paths once tread by the human groups and polities in the region still remain throughout unknown, vague, or at least dubious. While those deficits also pertain to the past 500 years, they mainly concern the period following the initial contact of sub-Saharan Africans with the Islamic world between 700 and 1500 CE. In fact, and as will be seen later, this is the time from which we yet have the least archaeological evidence for the impact of Islamic religion and culture in the region.

Strange though it may appear for most readers, there is hitherto nothing like a discipline of "Islamic archaeology" in West African scholarship (see Nixon 2014: 7721). On the one hand, this situation can be attributed to the main focus of archaeological investigations in the region. On the other, it mainly relates to the fact that the material manifestations of Islam in West Africa have been usually treated as constituents of indigenous cultural sequences. In fact, and as stressed by Insoll (2003: 2), the archaeology of Islam in sub-Saharan Africa can be considered an inherent part of the archaeology of sub-Saharan peoples and cultures. Particularly in the Central Sudan and Sahel, archaeological research focusing on Islamic cultural elements (e.g., architecture) has been rarely conducted (but see Bernus and Cressier 1991 for the western Aïr region). Yet, in the past few years, a number of small-scale field investigations have been showing the great potential of the theme. Drawing upon those as well as earlier relevant work and analysis, we provide here an updated view of what is currently known on the archaeology of Islam in the region.

From a temporal and geographical viewpoint, the archaeology of Islam in the Central Sudan and Sahel is intrinsically linked with the emergence and development of two of the most powerful polities (or group of polities) in the region: the Kanem-Borno Empire[1] around Lake Chad and the Hausa city-states to the west (Figure 4.5.1). As the earliest and most prominent of their kind, they were pivotal in the diffusion of the new religion and associated cultural elements in their respective spheres of influence and beyond. Due to that role, we primarily give attention to discussing evidence in one way or another related to those polities. Considering the enormous gaps presently extant in the research of material remains related to Kanem-Borno and Hausaland, we still have to draw strongly on the historical evidence for grasping the chronological context and the initial impact of contacts with the Islamic world in the region. For each of the polities and areas considered, we follow a chronological thread subdivided into three phases. First of all, and as the archaeology of the Islamic period forms a continuum with the foregoing time, we turn our attention to discuss the local pre-Islamic background in relation to the early stages of state formation, with a particular emphasis on sociopolitical organization. Second, and in view of the paucity of relevant archaeological evidence, we consider the available historical information on and interpretations of events and places related to the introduction and early development of Islam in the region. The latter will eventually serve to generate some few hypotheses on the kind of archaeological materials and contexts expected to be unearthed by future and highly needed field

---

[1] The name Kanem-Borno is a geographical concept commonly used by historians to designate this Central Sudanic polity. It refers explicitly to the two regions bordering Lake Chad in which the kingdom had its successive political and administrative centers: Kanem, east of the lake, between the 8th and 14th centuries, and Borno, west of the lake, between the 15th and 19th centuries.

FIGURE 4.5.1 The Central Sudan and Sahel region between the Niger River and Lake Chad showing the location of archaeological sites mentioned.

research projects in the region. Third and last, we discuss the better known archaeological evidence from the past 500 years, highlighting the material manifestations linked to Islamic religion and culture both in Kanem-Borno and Hausaland. Eventually, we throw a glance at those material remains hinting at the coexistence or blending of foreign (Islamic) and local (traditional) cultural elements/behaviors.

KANEM-BORNO

Though recognized both as one of the most powerful states and the longest-living Islamic monarchy from sub-Saharan Africa, Kanem-Borno (8th-19th c. CE) is presently by far better known through written and oral historical sources than through the archaeological remains it left behind. All through the past 150 years, historians' critical analysis of external and internal documents have not only generated a comprehensive chronology of relevant historical events; they also have provided insights into a vast range of details that were used for developing hypotheses on the origins and the early and later character of the state and its overall organization (for comprehensive views on Kanem-Borno's history, cf. Urvoy 1949; Trimingham 1962: 110–126; Smith 1976; Fisher 1977; Lavers 1980; Zeltner 1980; Barkindo 1985, 1992; Gronenborn 2001; Dewière 2017). In the following sections, historical information and some interpretations thereof are mainly used as a basic temporal framework for grasping and discussing the sociopolitical and economic contexts within which known (and yet unknown) archaeological remains and sites are possibly embedded. In fact, and as will become clear, there appears to exist a fairly close correlation between the sociopolitical organization of the state, the socioeconomic background of the aristocracy, and the archaeological vestiges to be found in the region. In this sense, historical information is employed in three ways: first and if no archaeological fieldwork has been ever conducted, as a guide to infer on the kind of archaeological remains to be expected on ground; second, as a rough orientation regarding dating and the identification of known but yet not examined archaeological remains; third, as a complementary source of information on archaeological sites that were already preliminarily investigated.

The Elusive Archaeology of the pre-Islamic Period (8th-11th Centuries)

As in parts of West Africa (the Senegal and Niger valleys), the existence of political elites can be regarded as have been essential in facilitating the introduction and later dissemination of Islamic religion and culture around Lake Chad. Today, there is little doubt that the rise of urbanism, sociopolitical complexity (hierarchical or heterarchical), and state-like organizations have a strong backdrop in social and economic processes taking placing locally over hundreds of years prior to the arrival of Islam in sub-Saharan Africa (McIntosh 1999; Connah 2016). While this appears to have been also the case in the Lake Chad region, we still only have a patchy archaeological understanding of how and when those processes came about (cf. Connah 1981; Gronenborn 1998; Holl 2002; Magnavita et al. 2009; MacEachern 2012). This state of affairs applies in particular to Kanem-Borno.

Archaeologically, the roots and early development of Kanem-Borno are yet completely unknown. The overall paucity of field research in Kanem (i.e., the region east and northeast of Lake Chad where this Central Sudanic state first emerged and was centered) implies that even the most basic archaeological data are still missing. In this sense, we are throughout unfamiliar both with the date and nature of human settling in the area and the material culture, specifically pottery, used locally prior to and following the foundation of the state in the 8th century CE. However, based on historical evidence, researchers have traced a scenario that possibly accounts for Kanem-Borno's emergence and early development. Though there are fundamental disagreements in a number of details such as the identity and ethnical origins of members of the early ruling elite (Urvoy 1949: 23–25; Fisher 1977: 288–289; Lange 1977: 113–114, 156–158; Zeltner 1980: 30–38; Hallam 1987: 33–34; Barkindo 1985: 230–231), historians have nevertheless concurred that Kanem-Borno beginnings are most likely a result of interactions between nomadic pastoralists and settled agriculturalists living in the Sahara–Sahel borderland (Barkindo 1985: 228). According to that scenario, a group of especially influential pastoral nomadic people began to hold sway over different sedentary peasant and other pastoral groups in the region, gradually leading to the formation of a multiethnic polity. A major characteristic of the early ruling elite itself was that it was also ethnically relatively diverse, especially in view of intertribal (alliance) marriages (Lange 1977: 66–68; Lavers 1980: 190; Lange and Barkindo 1988: 217). For a number of reasons related to local ecology and the sociopolitical structure predominant among pastoral nomadic peoples, it seems indeed very likely that, from its beginnings, the Kanem-Borno state consisted of and was governed by a loose confederacy of clans of heterogeneous origins with a dominant clan providing the ruler (Cohen 1970: 187). In this regard, it has been plausibly suggested that Kanem-Borno was far from being a highly centralized political entity in its early centuries: at least internally, the power of the ruler or king (*Mai*) was not absolute but a matter of negotiation with a supreme council (*Nokena*) of elders or representatives from various clans (Cohen 1970: 187–188). At this early stage, the ruler himself seems to have chiefly played the role of a sacred king who symbolized the unity of the state by maintaining social cohesion through his semi-divine status (Al-Muhallabi in Cuoq 1975: 78–79). As will be seen, this is indeed a recurrent theme in the history of Kanem-Borno, even centuries after the introduction of Islam. It is significant to note that the described dichotomy between political and ritual power closely approaches the kind of sociopolitical organization that A. Southall (1988) has named a *segmentary state*. Though there are voices that reasonably alert us to the uncritical use of such a comprehensive label for describing miscellaneous societies and polities (cf. Robertshaw 2010), others indeed see exactly this kind of negotiated power-sharing as a model of early African sociopolitical organization (cf. McIntosh 1999: 15–16).

If correct, the preceding described scenario has major and fundamental implications for archaeology. The economic background of the ruling elite as members of nomadic pastoralist clans alludes to a kind of court life of which mobility and the lack of permanent housing were essential components. The existence of such a highly mobile lifeway is in fact indirectly supported by Kanem-Borno's royal chronicle, the *Girgam* or *Diwan* (cf. Lange 1977). That source reveals that none of the places at which the first semi-divine kings died or were buried (late 8th to mid-11th c.) equals each other (cf. Lange 1977: 66–68). This indeed rather hints at the existence of "mobile capitals" that were located where the king temporarily stayed (Holl 2000: 62). In this sense, various authors have quite figuratively described those royal capitals as "Versailles de tentes" (Urvoy 1949: 27) or "tent-cities" (Hull 1976: 7) in allusion to the kind of lightweight constructions expected to have been used. There is no need to stress that the elusive nature of such royal camps poses great problems for archaeological research, as the mere task of locating them in the sand dune landscape of Kanem is by itself a colossal and unpromising challenge.

Apart from the elusive royal capitals, external Arabic sources on pre-Islamic Kanem-Borno point to the existence of at least a place of some importance in the region: Manan. According to geographical data provided by Ibn Said al-Magribi from first-hand information by Ibn Fatima in the 13th century (Levtzion and Hopkins 1981: 188), Manan was once most likely located to the north or northeast of Lake Chad (cf. Lange 1980: 175; Gronenbron 2001: 104). While Al-Idrisi in the 12th and Yaqut in the 13th century, drawing on a 10th-century source, described Manan as a relatively small thatch or clay settlement with only little industry and commerce (Levtzion and Hopkins 1981: 114, 171), Ibn Said clearly acknowledged it as once being the state's official pre-Islamic royal capital (cf. Levtzion and Hopkins 1981: 188). To judge from the historical accounts, the place does appear to have had neither urban character nor ever functioned as a significant commercial center. Archaeologically, however, its material remains may be comparatively easier to identify than those of the "mobile capitals" described earlier. The fact is that the general paucity of systematic archaeological research in the region has so far precluded verifying the actual existence, location, size, and nature of this and any other pre-Islamic sites in Kanem. As will be seen, while the visibility of archaeological remains related to Kanem-Borno considerably improves in the early Islamic period, the paucity of targeted field research continues to pose major problems for a full understanding of the archaeology of Islam in the region.

The Archaeology of the Early Islamic Period in Kanem (Mid-11th–14th Centuries)

From a historical viewpoint, the second half of the 11th century is of particular interest for scholars of Kanem-Borno. That time paves the way for very gradual transformations both in the ideological foundations and the sociopolitical organization of the state. As several authors convincingly suggested (Zeltner 1980: 40–45; Lange 1993: 265), the prime mover of those long-term changes appears to have been the growing influence of Islam on the court during the course of the 11th century. Political forces that sympathized with Islam and concomitantly opposed the ruling elite are thought to have perpetrated a coup d'état and founded a new dynastic line that replaced the old one (cf. Lange 1977: 68). Though the royal chronicle of Kanem-Borno furnishes evidence that the last two rulers (ca. 1067–1074 CE) of the former dynasty (Banu Duku) were Muslim converts (Lange 1977: 98; Lange and Barkindo 1988: 223), that same source attributes the introduction of Islam to Hummay (ca. 1068–1080 AD), the first king of the Banu Sayf or Banu Hummay (Lange 1977: 68). Be that as it may, the fact is that the introduction and adoption of Islam as state religion in the second half of the 11th century brought about an opening of Kanem-Borno toward the Islamic world with all its economic, social, and political consequences.

A major event inherently linked both to the dynastic change and the acceptance of Islam was the shift of the official state capital from Manan to a new place located to the southeast, named Njimi or Cimi, in the late 11th or early 12th century (cf. Ibn-Said in Levtzion and Hopkins 1981: 188). That historical event is highly significant as it is very probably associated with the very first introduction into the Central Sudan and Sahel of a new architectural element and building technology then well known in the Islamic world and beyond: fired bricks (cf. Urvoy 1949: 29). That innovation is of great archaeological relevance as it exponentially increases the visibility of settlement sites and structures linked to both Kanem-Borno and to later Islamized polities of the region (e.g., Bagirmi, Wadai). In fact, the main archaeological remains that can be presently truthfully linked to both the archaeology of Kanem-Borno and the archaeology of Islam in the region are the ruins of fired-brick constructions.

Today, a large part of our current knowledge of the archaeology of Kanem is limited to sites featuring fired-brick structures (Lebeuf 1962). Just as in the case of sites with similar constructions from the area west of Lake Chad (see later discussion), they are very probably either related to the Kanem-Borno ruling elite or to elite groups in some way connected to the former. This is indicated by both oral traditions (Seidensticker 1981; Lebeuf 1972) and the exclusive use of fired bricks in high-status constructions such as palaces, mosques, elite houses, and mausoleums west of the lake (Bivar and Shinnie 1962; Connah 1981; Seidensticker 1981). Altogether, some twelve of such localities are yet known in Kanem and the nearby Bahr-el-Ghazal. Except for a putative and yet undated mosque named Eri (Figure 4.5.2), they all consist of the ruins of fired-brick enclosures that once encompassed a number of minor and now collapsed constructions made with fired bricks or other materials (Bivar and Shinnie 1962; Lebeuf 1962). The most comprehensive description yet available on some of those places is provided by A. Gonzemai (2002), who produced sketch plans of structural remains visible on the surface. According to him, the enclosures largely vary in shape and size (round, rectangular, trapezoidal, zig-zag), ranging from less than approximately 20 x 20 meters to more than 670 × 620 meters. Some of them appear to display structural peculiarities like pathways and corridors, being in part internally quite complex.

FIGURE 4.5.2 A collapsed fired-brick wall from the putative mosque of Eri, Chad.

Courtesy of Carlos Magnavita.

It is not improbable that the enclosures themselves are merely the yet visible part of formerly larger settlements that mainly consisted of less durable domestic constructions made of clay or wood thatch. None of Kanem's fired-brick sites has been yet test-excavated or confidently dated. In fact, one of the most pressing research questions regards the time and historical context in which each of them was constructed and used. While some may date to the period when the power in Kanem was seized by a possible kindred group (Bulala) that opposed the Kanem-Borno ruling clan (Magumi) in the late 14th to early 16th centuries, others may be earlier in date (12th–14th c.) and thus definitely related to the Empire. Historically and archaeologically, the most important and potentially oldest of those sites is the one conceivably related to the ruins of Njimi or Cimi, Kanem-Borno's first Islamic capital (Figure 4.5.3). From an etymological and geographical viewpoint (Zeltner 1980: 23; Lange 1987: 159), the fired-brick ruins of Tié, approximately 1 kilometer north-northwest of the small village Tié Kalaté 1 (ca. 6 kilometers northwest of Tié Isiri 1), are presently the best match for Njimi. According to Gonzemai (2002: 46–48), those structural remains ("la citadelle") extend over an area of approximately 600 × 300 meters and consist of an asymmetrical rectangular enclosure featuring various access points and a complex interior space. While he makes no mention of a structure resembling a mosque, he refers to the remains of a large fired-brick construction as

FIGURE 4.5.3 Left: The largest debris mound from Tié near Tié Kalaté 1, Chad. Littered with fired brick fragments, the mound indicates the location of the main, now collapsed building of the site. Right: Fired brick from Tié showing a smooth surface coating. It possibly originates from one of the major buildings (i.e., the palace, the mosque) that once stood in the interior of the fired-brick enclosure.

Courtesy of Carlos Magnavita.

being the "palais royal." This appears to be the same structure that Bivar and Shinnie (1962: 8), who visited the site in 1959, call "the mosque." If the identification of the place with Njimi is correct, it is indeed here that we may expect to find the earliest mosque ever built in the Central Sudan and Sahel region. According to a historical document translated by Palmer (1936: 19–20), "the plastered mosque" (probably in fired brick) was erected there by Sultan Salmama, who, according to Lange (1977: 70), reigned between 1182 and 1210 CE.

Bivar and Shinnie (1962: 8–9) themselves rejected the identification of the Tié ruins with historical Njimi on grounds of the small site area. In fact, they give the extent of the spot covered with fired bricks as having been approximately 243 × 218 meters, substantially smaller than the figure provided by Gonzemai (2002: 46–48). A short visit of the site by one of us (C. M.) in March 2017 revealed that the dimensions provided by Bivar and Shinnie (1962) suit best the reality. While the area with visible remains may only represent a small portion of a larger settlement, it is improbable that we will ever find something similar to an exceptionally large urban center in Kanem. Apart from environmental and carrying-capacity constraints, the inexistence of such a large place is probably reminiscent of a sociopolitical organization with a low degree of centralization and a still highly mobile court life. In this respect and despite knowledge about Islamic centralized statecraft and palatial life, it appears that conservative forces within the state kept acting centrifugally against any attempt toward political centralization and religious reforms up to at least the 14th century (cf. Trimingham 1962: 117–118; Cohen 1970: 188; Lange 1993: 265–269). In addition, Kanem-Borno Muslim rulers still appear to have been to such an extent en route that only five of twenty monarchs are known to have been buried at Njimi between the late 11th and the late 14th centuries (cf. Lange 1977: 68–76).[2] In fact, it is not before the late 15th century that Kanem-Borno would have an urban capital and commercial center founded that actually deserved those labels (see later discussion). The construction of that place not only reflects a major change toward political centralization as well as reduced royal mobility; for the first time, there also appears to have emerged something like an urban Islam with some historically and archaeologically visible facets.

The Archaeology of Islam in Borno (15th–19th Centuries)

Though historical hints imply the possible establishment of elite settlements west of Lake Chad (Borno) perhaps as early as the mid-13th century (Lange 1993: 271–272), known archaeological vestiges linked to the state date thus far only from the late 15th century onward[3]. The earliest and most important of those places is the new capital Birni Gazargamo (ca. 1472–1810 CE), an approximately 340-hectare urban settlement encompassed by a circular moat-and-ditch complex built near the confluence of two major rivers (cf. Bivar and Shinnie 1962: 2–4; Connah 1981: 227–228). The construction of that place is emblematic for two of a number of key changes that are in part connected to the policy of strongly tying Kanem-Borno with the contemporaneous Islamic world.

From a sociopolitical viewpoint, the ruins of Birni Gazargamo no doubt materialize the long-awaited shift in the organization of the state toward a more centralized administration and simultaneous consolidation of the Mai's power, a condition that is in line with Islamic monarchies elsewhere. To a large extent, that change was primarily achieved by supplanting the hereditary titleholders of the traditional supreme council of elders (Nokena) through a system in which title and power were vested by distinct individuals (cf. Schulze 1910: 4; Urvoy 1949: 40; Trimingham 1962: 125–126). In addition to that, most of the nominal titleholders were now pledged to reside in the capital, thus staying under direct supervision of the Mai. The archaeological correlates of this new power structure are visible through the central location of the large (ca. 4 hectare) fired-brick palace complex which is surrounded at some distance by at least seven minor fired-brick enclosures (cf. Bivar and Shinnie 1962: fig. 1; Connah 1981: 229). A major side effect of the newly implanted political system was an increased level of stability and security that allowed a permanent use of the capital for more than 300 years. In this

---

[2] To a growing extent, the high mobility of Banu Sayf rulers between the late 11th and 14th centuries has possibly much more to do with practical factors related to state politics and economy than with a romantic attitude toward a pastoral nomadic way of life. On the one hand, the frequent absence of the rulers from the capital may be related to the wish of escaping the political control exerted by the Nokena. On the other, the ubiquitous royal mobility can be explained in terms of the enormous territorial and commercial expansion that the state witnessed in the period (cf. Urvoy 1949: 44, 48).

[3] The only potential exception is a single radiocarbon date from the site of Garumele (Haour 2008: Table 1). While the analysis of the charcoal sample provided an age estimation in the late 13th to late 14th centuries, that isolate date is currently problematic as glass beads from the same archaeological context and other radiocarbon dates point to a much later formation of cultural deposits (cf. Magnavita and Magnavita 2017: 173).

respect, it is all but surprising that, for the first time in the history of Kanem-Borno, twelve of nineteen rulers who reigned between 1470 and 1810 not only lived but also died in one place: Birni Gazargamo (cf. Lange 1977: 79–82).

Alongside changes in political affairs, the historical record suggests that there was, in the late 15th and 16th centuries, an increased preoccupation of literate men in the capital with the observance of the religious and legal premises of Islam by members of the Kanem-Borno royal house and other nobles (Trimingham 1962: 122–123). Indirectly, this could be seen as indicating that Islam was still poorly widespread among the remaining population of the capital at that time. Yet this notion is contested by a number of historical documents dating from the end of the 16th century. In this sense, two sources, respectively dated to the late-16th and mid-17th centuries, point to the existence of at least four (Friday) mosques in Birni Gazargamo (cf. Palmer 1936: 33–35; Lange 1987: 72), which in turn implies a quite vivid practice of the religion by its citizens. Several historians indeed regard the capital as a major center of Arabic-Islamic scholarship in the Central Sudan from the 16th and 17th centuries on (Hunwick 1997: 210–211; Levtzion and Pouwels 2000: 81–82). This notion is largely supported by evidence of royal policy directed to sustain the development of both Islam and state sovereignty even in rural regions far from the city. In this respect, we are acquainted with kingly instructions for the construction of scholarly settlements (*mallamati*) at Belbelec (Kalumfardo) and Gaskeru (Hunwick 1997: 211; Fisher 1975: 111–112), respectively, in the mid- to late 17th and early 18th centuries (Lavers 1971: 48). The main buildings of those places, including mosques, are said to have been built by craftsmen and fired bricks provided by the Mai personally (cf. Lavers 1971: 48).

In stark contrast to those accounts, the mid–19th-century explorer Heinrich Barth (1858, vol. 4: 23–24) considered the "very small dimensions" of the central Friday mosque he saw in Birni Gazargamo as evidence that *Salat* was mainly practiced by members of the court and that there was nothing like a medrasse in the capital. In his opinion, the lack of such an institution was a clear indication that Islamic learning in Birni Gazargamo was confined to the private realm. Barth's statement has long caused great surprise, particularly because there is at least an eyewitness report on the existence of such a facility at the main mosque of Birni Gazargamo (von Seetzen, in Lavers 1971: 43). Archaeologically, the building referred to by Barth as the central mosque mostly likely corresponds to the ruins of a 79 × 36 meter fired-brick construction located west of the palace complex and now level with the ground (cf. Lange 1987: 116; Gronenborn 2001: fig. 6.3). The apparent contradictions between the historical sources and Barth's perception of Islam in the former capital can be perhaps straightforwardly explained by archaeological reasoning. In this sense, while the historical accounts were recorded at a time when most buildings in Birni Gazargamo had been well discernible and easily identifiable, Barth was only able to see fragments of a thoroughly ruined city. In fact, the alleged central mosque near the palace complex may be the only of the capital's Friday mosques that were once built with fired bricks. This is a circumstance that may explain the "invisibility" of the other mosques as well as of building annexes that may have housed Islamic schools or colleges.

As elsewhere, lack of research and problems of visibility are a large concern in grasping the archaeology of Kanem-Borno and Islam around Lake Chad. This state of affairs is tellingly illustrated by the results of a recent pilot study that involved a geophysical survey (gradiometry) of the ruins of the central palace complex at Birni Gazargamo (Magnavita 2011). Until then, the best ground plan of that structure was produced in 1959 by a pace-and-compass survey of wall remains visible on the surface (Bivar and Shinnie 1962: fig. 1). While the gradiometry plot confirms the accuracy of the former plan, it also reveals that a number of important buried features remained thus far undiscovered (Figure 4.5.4). Two of the most important are a nearly semi-circular fired-brick wall segment attached to the northeast end of a large room at the southern part of the complex and an approximately 20 × 20 meter square structure to the southeast. The first feature clearly allows identifying the southern room with an approximately 85 × 60 meter palace mosque, while the second can be easily recognized as the foundations of a massive fired-brick minaret. Not only in view of its large size (if compared to that of the putative central mosque) does the palace mosque bear evidence of the great importance of Islam within the court; an even more amazing sign of this refers to the planning and construction of the entire palace complex because the walls of the remaining rooms or courtyards were all oriented according to those of the palace mosque (Figure 4.5.4).

Outside the capital, the only mosque yet known archaeologically comes from Garu Kime, a Kanem-Borno elite site located about 150 kilometers southeast of Gazargamo (Magnavita et al. 2009). Probably constructed in the 17th or 18th century, the site's main structures comprise a fired-brick enclosure and a neighboring fired-brick building. The latter can be easily identified as a mosque both through the existence of a *mihrab* and the northeastern orientation of the *qibla*. Just as in the case of the palace complex of Gazargamo, an important detail is that the secular structure (enclosure) nearby was likewise erected with a view to comply with the orientation of the mosque.

In view of the role played by Islam in the capital, it is nevertheless likely that most, if not all, remaining elite sites are associated with single or various mosques. Archaeologically, we presently know of only two such instances, but, historically, we are acquainted with the existence of mosques at Gambaru, Belbelec, and Gaskeru (Barth 1858, vol. 2: 225–226; Lavers 1971: 48). Also, Garumele, the second largest urban center of Kanem-Borno and now confidently dated to the late 16th or early 17th century (Magnavita and Magnavita 2017), must have featured a number of mosques, even if none has been yet located on the ground. In addition to those, four other post–16th-century fired-brick elite sites are known west of Lake Chad, but their ruins remain archaeologically thus far unexplored. While no Kanem-Borno mosque has been ever investigated archaeologically, the few geophysical surveys and test-excavations conducted at elite secular structures have revealed a remarkable architectural trend. It relates to the construction of fired-brick round huts amid the large rectangular fired-brick enclosures typical of Kanem-Borno palatial structures (Hambolu 1996; Magnavita et al. 2009; Magnavita and Magnavita 2017). This detail clearly points to a merging of traditional sub-Saharan Africa structural design with foreign (Islamic) architectural elements. Just as with architecture, historical evidence demonstrates the survival of rudiments of the pre-Islamic institution

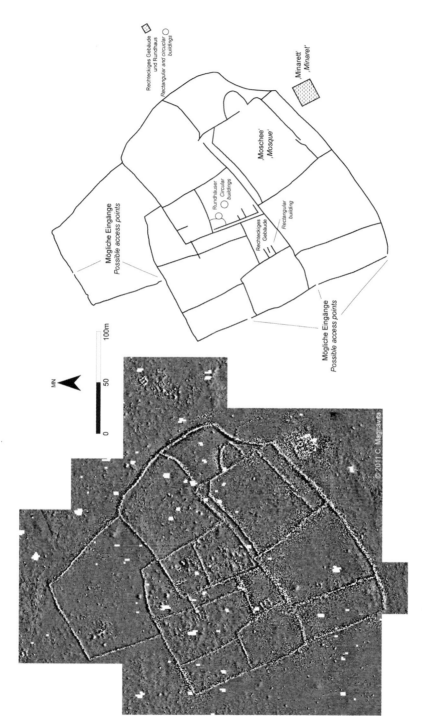

FIGURE 4.5.4 Geophysical plan of the fired-brick palace complex of Birni Gazargamo and interpretation thereof.

Courtesy of Magnavita (2011: fig. 5).

of divine kingship, such as monarch seclusion, up to the 19th century (Smith 1976: 163). This indeed visibly indicates the co-existence of traditional religious notions (i.e., king-worship) and Islamic practice up to a very late time.

The previous paragraphs furnished an update of what we know about the Islamic archaeology of Kanem-Borno within the context of historical interpretations and the currently available archaeological evidence. For reasons of space, an important point not discussed refers to the expansion of Islam beyond the limits of the Empire from the 16th century on. The mechanisms accounting for that development are no doubt manifold and involve a complex interplay of long-ranging political, social, and economic interests on both institutional and individual levels. In spite of that, Kanem-Borno's perceived or actual military and cultural supremacy rank as primary factors in the spread of Islam outside its borders. In this context, permanent military pressure indirectly led to the emergence of minor, and in part tributary, states such as Bagirmi, Mandara, and the Kotoko polities from at least the 16th century on (Barkindo 1992)[4]. That process was then followed by the very gradual conversion or autoconversion of the local political elites and populations to Islam. Just as in the case of Kanem-Borno, very little to nothing is yet known about the Islamic archaeology of those "secondary states" (but see Insoll 2003), implying a vast field of research for future scholars working in the region.

HAUSALAND

The physical extent of the Hausa area is quite extensive but fairly homogenous, delimited to the east by Borno, Niger to the north, and Benin to the west and southwards by the meridian 10° N. The Hausa cultural sphere is considered widespread across most West African nations traditionally, with northern Nigeria as its core. Following a glimpse at the archaeology of Kanem-Borno, we now set out further westward to examine the nature of sociocultural development in Hausaland and outline the influence of Islam. This region, otherwise referred to as *Kasar Hausa*, encompasses a vast territory occupied by people who identify themselves as Hausa today, basically due to shared identity elements: language, dress, Islamic belief, history, and subsistence practices. Their common historical root is tied to mythologies, expressed loosely in two popular historical documents: the *Daura* and *Kano chronicles*. They allude Hausa origins to foreign strangers such as a Baghdadi prince—Bayajidda, the acclaimed legendary hero who rescued Daura by killing a snake that allowed access to well water only on certain days. Scholarly positions exist that postulate notions of origins and indeed the process of evolution of Hausa (Sutton 2010; Last 1983; Haour 2003). A mention of Afnu in the writings of the Egyptian historian al-Maqrizi in the 15th century is considered as perhaps the

---

[4] One century earlier, Hausaland to the west is similarly thought to have experienced Kanem-Borno's regional dominance (Lovejoy 1978: 185; Sutton 1979: 197–9), though this occurred in an already partially islamized social milieu with long-established state-like structures (see later discussion).

most generally acceptable first textual reference to Hausa, when one considers the use of *Afnu/Afuno* as a synonym for Hausa in earlier times (Haour 2003). From the 8th century, there was actually nothing more than tassel allusions before that time, until the first clear mention of well-conceived Hausa cultural identity was made in the 17th century. Much of what is known about the region is derived mainly from orally inspired historical sources obtained through the agencies of traders, missionaries, travelers, and colonial records alike (Palmer 1922; Bravmann 1974; Haour 2003; Sutton 2010). Despite argument and/or agreement by scholars interested in Hausa studies as to whether Hausa is an autochthonous development or not, one thing is certain: Kanem-Borno had strong impact on certain cultural developments of Kasar Hausa, as already shown in the earlier part of the chapter.

The archaeology of Kasar Hausa is mainly characterized by large-scale occupation sites surrounded by walls and most probably related to the emergence of state-like sociopolitical organizations. Other major settlement sites were predominantly placed on hilltops, with dyeing and iron-working sites as common features generally on the landscape. Thematic subjects of interest about the Hausa states were military capabilities and engagements, where the military expansionist policy of Kano, for instance, during the 11th and 12th centuries CE is noted in some historical texts. Development of complex defensive walls is thought to be a natural shield-like response to sustain the home front when the armies are on aggressive conquest at other fronts, but are also explained as structures that create avenues to toll-gate collection of taxes from traders (Okpoko 1998; Smith 1987). For Kasar Hausa wall settlements, Kano and Zaria (associated Turunku and Kufena capitals) provide examples of urban cities that have been mentioned by early travelers and geographers of the 19th century and subsequently began to receive the attention of archaeologists interested in the reconstruction of aspects of West Africa's urbanization process (Haour 2003; Effah-Gyamfi 1986). It was reported by Haour (2003) that the series of wall fortifications of Kano cover about 20 kilometers of the circumference of the enclosure, reached heights up to 9 meters, and were surrounded by a 15-meter ditch. Likewise, the circular walls of Zaria were about 6 meters high, covering 16 kilometers in the 19th century (Haour 2003). The complex walls, expected to have been built at different periods, are not well dated and rely on relative dating. Only Leka/Maleh in the Kebbi region has been archaeologically studied and gives an early 16th-century date, expressed in an important historical text as a period of autonomy for the Kebbi monarch. From the point of view of economics, some Hausa states such as Kano, Zaria, and Katsina became important western-most terminals as trans-Saharan commerce and trading connections up to the 15th century. From there we have indirect indications of collections of remnants of dye pits and large pots for the mass production of textile materials for export (Lovejoy 1974). Sources have indicated the acceptability of Hausa attire and textile products in places as far as Tripoli and other Maghreb towns in northern Africa. In Kano area, the Rano and Dala quarters were major industrial centers for the production of textiles as noted by dyeing pits, but also for the smelting of iron, as seen from the widespread heaps of slag discovered during archaeological investigations (Sieber 1992).

Another important theme in the archaeology of Kasar Hausa is the way landscape and space is utilized and socially perceived. The development of settlements and urban system became a principal defining character of Hausaland, where, for instance, a 19th-century traveler, Henry Barth, described the parkland landscape of the Hausa area: a clearly much managed, human-made landscape. A major defining moment for Hausa demography is the average congregation of large populations supported by craft specialization guilds and respective large-scale settlements surrounded by walls, evidenced as early as the 16th century by external written sources. A number of Hausa state capitals such as Kano, Bauchi, and Zaria, whose palaces were built to accommodate the ruling dynasties who would become an important factor for the Islamization of societies of northern Nigeria, later show widespread evidence of defensive walls. Iron smelting (Sutton 1976) and textile production have left great imprints in the archaeology of the region, seen through abundance of mounds of iron slag and tuyeres on one hand and groups of dye pits reflecting the specialties of the societies, with each associated with ritual practices and taboos in their different ways. Various studies on the nature and practice of African ironworking by anthropologists and ethno-archaeologists are gradually helping us to understand the social context and meanings of ritual performance around slag mounds and production systems of past settlements, which essentially do not reflect Islamic norms (Sutton 1976). Such practices have allowed us to interpret the meaning of sites' contexts and relationships to religious systems and, in some instances, the process of Islamization as it occurs in most societies in northern Nigeria.

The Archaeology of the Pre-Islamic Period Around Kasar Hausa

We are also familiar with the settlement system, as documented by other sources that render accounts of rural settings, where the economy was tied to the land. The hierarchy was hamlet- or village-based before it evolved to the city-based settlement, with large populations surrounded by walls—a development that is perhaps largely inspired by sociopolitical developments that came with elements that were initiated indirectly by the Islamization process. Research conducted in Kasar Hausa that produced materials relevant to the pre-Islamic period is enormous but unevenly unpublished. The defining character of the period is the availability of discrete sites with diverse functions and large settlements, some probably specialized, due to evidence of by-products of industrial iron working (Sule 2010). A good number of sites such as Dala hill, Samaru West, Durbi Takusheyi, Turunku, and Kagalan fit this description. A major problem in some cases is the poor dating situation, where only the character of finds is currently available as publication of the research results after nearly half a century is still forthcoming (Priddy 1970). Priddy, for instance, reported the low mound Iron Age site RS63/32 on the east side of the river Niger that yielded complete burials with rich grave goods and skulls and skeletons of varied degree of preservation, one of which was identified as a ten-year-old child who was buried with flexed leg positions, clearly indicative of pre-Islamic burial practices around 1000 CE (Priddy 1970: 28). In the 13th–16th centuries, and as evidenced by the excavated burial mounds of Durbi Takusheyi near Katsina, pre-Islamic Hausa society was highly stratified (Gronenborn et al. 2012).

Early Development of Islam and Islamic Culture in Hausaland (10th–18th Centuries CE)

As reported earlier, some findings from Kasar Hausa reflect highly stratified social configurations of the pre-Islamic customs of a mortuary elite system. In fact, oral narratives are persistent with the idea of the existence of an elitist ruling family in pre-Islamic Katsinawa (i.e., the area between Katsina and Daura). Evidence from Durbi Takusheyi in the area excavated in 1907 by Richmond Palmer in collaboration with the Emir of Katsina, and in 1992 under the coordination of Dierk Lange and a follow-up research in 2003, presents seven tumuli with contents expressive of affluence and prestige from around the 13th–14th centuries CE (Gronenborn et al. 2012). The burials displayed rich goods such as an iron rod, spiked anklets, ivory rings, and a cap with decorated cowries, as well as a bronze pin and brass anklet, an iron bangle, glass beads, an iron spoon, ivory rings, and a cowry belt. The analyzed brass anklets were made using a lost wax technique used specifically for burial goods; wear analysis indicates that they would not have been for everyday use. Though the lost wax method of brass manufacturing is popular in Benin and Ife, there are reasons to assume a local production (Gronenborn et al. 2012). Another interesting aspect of the finds are the way the occupants of the royal burials were interred, which in Tumulus 1 and 5 displayed a burial within burial chambers, seated on furniture, with indications that the bodies were wrapped in cloth (Gronenborn et al. 2012: 263–264). The archaeological evidence from Durbi Takusheyi at Tumulus T7, dated to the 15th–16th century, showed highly ostentatious, rich articles of gold (ring and bracelets, earrings, finger rings, and pendants), metal, and glass as well as carnelian beads indicative in some instances of importation.

The source for some of the grave goods, especially in Tumulus 7, reflects possibilities of continental and regional contacts with North Africa and the Middle East, as well as with Kanem-Borno and Agadez as part of the trans-Saharan trade system during pre-Islamic times. The nature of the materials conforms to the period in the second half of the 15th century when Islamic cultures gained roots in Kasar Hausa. It could be said that, from 14th century onward, the major cities of Hausaland such as Kano and Katsina became integrated into the trans-Saharan trade system, thus perhaps accounting for the nature of the finds discussed (Okpoko 1998; Gronenborn et al. 2012). However, it is interesting, considering the nature of Durbi Takusheyi, that the people of Durbi Takusheyi drew on long-distance connections with the Islamic world but that the burials examined are not consistent with Islamic ritual. On the prosperity of the *bilad al sudan*, Leo Africanus reported during his travels in the region that, by 1512, Mali was replaced as an important trading center by the newly important but dominant centers of Kano, Katsina, Zaria, and Zamfara to the west and Borno to the east (Loimeier 2013: 66). This follow assumptions along the lines of the popular thesis that the coming of Islam to Hausaland was essentially through Wangara traders and the Islamization process of Hausa rulers. On aspects of the Hausa relationship with Borno and its influence on Hausaland in the 17th century, Barth (1960: 118) mentions how the Katsina capital that housed its prince and a population of "at least a hundred thousand souls" was a direct a vassal of the Borno Mais and had to ensure the sustained payment of a tribute of one hundred slaves. There is a strong assertion (Usman 1972) that some parts of Kasar Hausa, such as Katsina, Kano, Daura, and Zazzau, all became in some way attached to Borno by diplomacy rather than through military means. This is shown by three historical sources that give hints on this state of affairs: *Raudat al-afakar*, *Tarikh arbab* (the Kano chronicle), and *Imfaq al-maisur*. The third mentioned historical source displays strong evidence for control of most Hausa states by the Borno sultans, as tributes and gifts were permanently sent to the latter until the commencement of the Sokoto Jihad, when Hausaland was finally considered finally autonomous. Consequently, it is remarkable also to acknowledge how the long cultural contacts established between peoples long exposed to Islam from North Africa during the 17th and 18th centuries with Katsina city could have inspired the commercial and political pedigree with which the subregion came to derive such importance.

Similarly, its worth noting that the conversion of King Yaji Dan Tsamiya (1349–1385) of Kano to Islam by Wangarawa clerics from Mali is considered a threshold in the Islamization process of Kano and indeed the whole of Kasar Hausa (Bravmann 1974; Stride and Ifeka 1971). He appointed the prayer Imam and other Islamic officials and decreed that every town of Kano observe five daily prayers (Palmer 1908). King Yaji also ensured the building of the first mosque at the present Madabo Mosque, near the pagan sacred Shamus tree. Sarki Muhammad Rumfa (1463–1499), however, cut down the Shamus tree and built a second mosque consisting of a mud-roofed rectangular building, and later a Central Mosque. The mosque and its location are considered sacred to date and holier than any other structure in Kano. The Kano city layout continued to witness the dominance of public facilities such as central mosque and a market closely associated with magnificent palace occupied by powerful ruler-akin to a status of the sultan of Tunis in North Africa (Last 1983).

Islamic Heritage and Archaeology in Hausaland (19th-Century Jihad Period and Beyond)

The seed that inspired a number of new and radical sociocultural developments related to Islam and Islamic culture in Kasar Hausa is seen to have been planted from the 18th century or even earlier. This can be located in the context of migrations, trade contacts, and other kinds of interrelations linked to some waves of strong Arab and Islamic influence. Islamic heritage and archaeology in the study area are still being conceptualized, but the Sokoto Jihad led by Sheik Uthman Ibn Fodio in about 1804 impacted radically on the structure of the sociopolitical system as well as on the historical development of the whole region. Much of what is known is indirect from historical sources, with data beginning to come from related monuments and sacred landscapes studies. The popular themes in Hausa studies involve the knowledge of development from architecture, centering on the achievements recorded by the popular 19th-century master-builder, Babban Gwani, whose monuments exist throughout the northern region of Nigeria (Sule 2010; Moughtin 1972).

One major character of the archaeology of this period is the emergence of monumental mosques in settlement layouts and cities. A general pattern across the region is that royal palaces were constructed in close association with Friday mosques, usually at the center of the settlements. The visible heritage of Hausaland is characterized by flamboyant monumental architectural buildings, mosques, and palaces in Kano, Katsina, Kirfin Sama, and Zaria, mostly built around the 1830's by Muhammadu Durugu, popularly known as Babban Gwani in the field of African architectural studies. This is the general situation with most of the medieval city-built palaces constructed by that architect in Bauchi, Zaria, Kafin Madaki, Birnin Gwari, and Kano. The most prominent architectural element of those buildings is the Hausa vault (*bakan gizo*) which, just like the remaining structure, is erected using the cone-shaped Hausa *tubali* or mudbrick typical of West African architecture. In this regard, three of these monuments within the Bauchi region deserve attention: Madaki of Kafin Madaki's palace, a palace/mosque on the Kirfin Sama hill, and the Babban Gwani-built palace at the center of Bauchi town. They were all built by the 19th-century master builder before he built other palaces that are all attached with famous mosques in Kano, Zaria, and Birnin Gwari from 1830–1840. The major composition of all three edifices in Bauchi region includes the existence of the main congregational worship halls and the Shari'a courts, and all are noted to have all utilized *tubali* (mud bricks) as raw materials in their construction (Dmochowski 1990).

The importance of the monuments built by Babban Gwani cannot be overstated when examining questions related to Islam in northern Nigeria. For instance, the palace of Madaki in Kafin Madaki town near Bauchi served as an outpost residence for the defense commander-in-chief of the acclaimed founder of Bauchi town, Yakubun Bauchi I, in Kafin Madaki, which is situated about 45 kilometers north of Bauchi city. It is situated strategically toward Kano, allowing Madaki, acknowledged as a fearless army commander, to be stationed to the north of Bauchi to serve as a barricade against by a former Kano power before the Jihad of 1804. The architectural splendor and historical importance of Kafin's Madaki palace led to its declaration later as one of Nigeria's first national monuments in 1956. The fairly well-studied palace/mosques constructions achieved by Babban Gwani are those found in Zaria, Bauchi, and the Kirfin Sama hilltop (Sule 2010; Moughtin 1972).

According to Moughtin's description (1972:143), the Friday mosque in Zaria city, built in 1824 by Babban Gwani, "consists of a complex of buildings which include a main hall for worship, the Shari'a Court, and ablution chambers which act as entrance lobbies the perimeter wall" (Figures 4.5.5 and 4.5.6). Mud arches inside the buildings support domed rooftops and are characteristic features of such Hausa edifices. The mihrab is situated at the easternmost portion of the mosque-*qiblah* for the Imam, and a screened area for women exists within the Shari'a court. The internal decorative systems of the mosques display complex mud relief patterns that are highly dignified and well-defined. The walls of the buildings are thick, being an average of 1.2 meters at the base, to support and stabilize the heavy roofs. The mud walls of the building are characteristically reinforced with *azara*, which is wood from the Deleb palm.

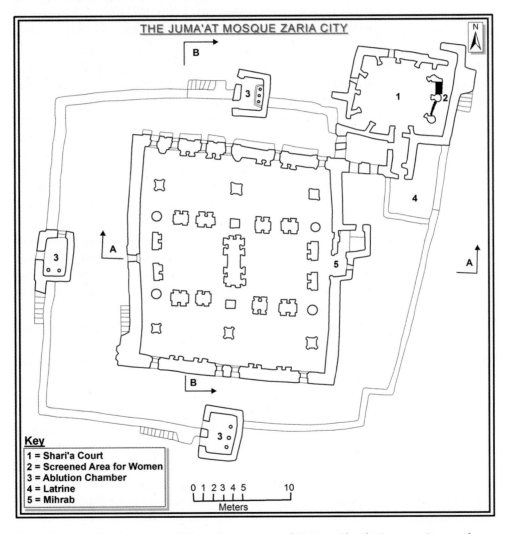

FIGURE 4.5.5 The floor plan of the Friday mosque of Zaria. 1. Shari'a Court. 2. Screened area for women. 3. Ablution chamber. 4. Latrine. 5. Mihrab

After Moughtin (1972).

FIGURE 4.5.6 Insterior of the Friday mosque, Zaria.

Courtesy of Abubakar S. Sule.

Archaeologically, little investigation is known to have taken place in Hausa cities apart from those former settlements retaining impressive "visible" features of walls in the Zaria region and the mainly unpublished works in Kano inspired by the presence of archaeologists at Ahmadu Bello University Zaria and Bayero University Kano in the decades after 1960. These limitations are due to the absence of meaningful chronological information about the settlement systems based on radiocarbon dates. Much of what is recognized of the archaeology of Kasar Hausa, excepting its mosques and palaces, is hardly sufficient to describe the Islamization process of the area. However, collaborate utilization of historical sources is likely to help current research that aims to track the influence of Islam on the sociopolitical as well as economic developments of northern Nigeria through other artifactual assemblage and sites. The defensive walls that are a major character of most of the sites studied need to be dated and considered from the point of view of the political need to organize important political structures in a common location to ease governance. It is perhaps justifiable to agree that the Islamic attitude toward centralized political structures inspired urbanism and that it is important to look at related issues, such as the construction methods of these walls and mosques.

CONCLUSION

Just as with the archaeology of the states that flourished in the region, the Islamic archaeology of the Central Sudan and Sahel is yet in its very infancy. Taken as a whole, there has been comparatively much more research on sites and material remains of pre-

Islamic societies than on those linked to people that once identified themselves as Muslims. As elsewhere in Africa and beyond, Islam was very probably first adopted and observed by the early political elites of emerging states of the region between the 11th and the late 15th centuries. Insights such as these are, however, exclusively provided by historical written and oral documents. These are indeed the major sources allowing a preliminary assessment of the time, historical setting, and consequences linked with the introduction of Islam into the region. Archaeologically, those early developments remain as yet virtually invisible due to the general paucity of targeted archaeological research in key areas and sites. This implies that contexts, structures, and finds that might furnish direct evidence of local Islamic practice prior to the 16th century are overall unknown.

Historically and archaeologically, there is much better evidence for the practice of Islam from the late 16th century on. At the western margins of Lake Chad, the foundation of Birni Gazargamo (ca. 1472), Kanem-Borno's new capital, triggered the emergence of a Central Sudanic version of urban Islam. For the late 16th and early 17th centuries, we have data hinting at the existence of both a large royal mosque and various Friday mosques for the local population. Recent preliminary studies at two of the various archaeological sites known also demonstrate that the construction of elite secular structures obeyed the orientation of mosques. This can be seen as clear evidence that earthly life was transcending and merging into the religious realm of Islam. In addition, historical accounts report on a 17th- to 18th-century royal policy directed at promoting the construction of scholarly settlements in rural areas. All this ranks as evidence that Islam began to be propagated beyond the capital at latest by this time. While the adoption of Islam by the local royal elites of Hausaland occurred later than at Lake Chad (late 14th–15th centuries), the new religion began to thrive there in an already fully developed urban environment. Just as in the case of Kanem-Borno, most Hausaland sites relevant to the theme remain, however, archaeologically unexplored. Others, such as Kano, Zaria, and Katsina, are today major modern cities so that archaeological work is only possible to a limited extent.

Against the background of the available historical evidence, the few insights currently provided by research on the archaeology of Islam in the region are truly not more than a drop in the ocean. However, while the flux of new historical documents as a major source of knowledge has long dried up, the numerous archaeological reservoirs containing fresh data on the early and late Central Sudanic states remain virtually untapped. No doubt, it is this yet poorly exploited major source that now has the potential to round off and perhaps change our current perception of the historical role of Islam in the region. Regrettably, archaeological field investigations, especially those led by Westerners, have been largely disrupted by security concerns all over large parts of West Africa since 2009. Religion-backed political extremism, ethnical conflicts, and, more recently, delinquency due to a major economic crisis fueled by falling oil prices have virtually paralyzed international archaeological research in most of the Central Sudan and Sahel. It is indeed only upon the improvement of that situation that we may expect new, fresh insights into the archaeology of Islam in the areas focused on in this chapter.

REFERENCES

Barkindo, B. 1985. "Early States of the Central Sudan: Kanem, Borno and Some of Their Neighbours to c. 1500 A.D," in J. Ajayi and M. Crowder (eds.), *History of West Africa, Volume 1* (Harlow: Longman), 225–254.

Barkindo, B. 1992. "Kanem-Borno: Its Relations with the Mediterranean Sea, Bagirmi and Other States in the Chad Basin," in B. A. Ogot (ed.), *General History of Africa, Volume 5: Africa from the Sixteenth to the Eighteenth Century* (Oxford: Heinemann), 492–514.

Barth, H. 1858. *Travels and Discoveries in North and Central Africa, 1849–1855* (London: Longman).

Barth, H. 1960. "The Seventeenth Century: The Rise of Katsena," in T. Hodgkin (ed.), *Nigerian Perspectives: An Historical Anthology* (London: Oxford University Press), 118–119.

Bernus, S., and Cressier, P. 1991. *La région d'In Gall-Tegidda N Tesem (Niger): programme archéologique d'urgence 1977–1981. Volume 4: Azelik-Takadda et l'implantation sédentaire médiévale* (Niamey: IRSH).

Bivar, A. D. H., and Shinnie, P. L. 1962. "Old Kanuri Capitals," *Journal of African History*, 3(1), 1–10.

Bravmann, R. 1974. "The Islamisation of West Africa," in R. Bravmann (ed.), *Islam and Tribal Art in West Africa* (London: Cambridge University Press), 6–14.

Cohen, R. 1970. "The kingship in Bornu," in M. Crowder and O. Ikime (eds.), *West African Chiefs. Their Changing Status Under Colonial Rule and Independence* (Ife: University of Ife Press), 187–210.

Connah, G. 1981. *Three Thousand Years in Africa. Man and His Environment in the Lake Chad Region of Nigeria* (Cambridge: Cambridge University Press).

Connah, G. 2016. *African Civilizations: An Archaeological Perspective* (Cambridge: Cambridge University Press).

Cuoq, J. M. 1975. Recueil des sources arabes concernant l'Afrique occidentale du viiie au xvie siècle : Bilad al-Sudan (Paris : Éditions du CNRS).

Dewière, R. 2017. Du Lac Tchad à la Mecque. Le Sultanat du Borno et son monde (xvie-xviie siècle) (Paris : Éditions de la Sorbonne).

Dmochowski, Z. R. 1990. *An Introduction to Nigerian Traditional Architecture (Volume 1)* (London: Ethnographica Ltd.).

Effah-Gyamfi, K. 1986. "Ancient Urban Sites in Hausaland," *West African Journal of Archaeology*, 16, 117–134.

Fisher, H. J. 1975. "The Central Sahara and Sudan," in J. D. Fage and R. Oliver (eds.), *The Cambridge History of Africa, Volume 4* (Cambridge: Cambridge University Press), 58–141.

Fisher, H. J. 1977. "The Eastern Maghrib and the Central Sudan," in J. D. Fage and R. Oliver (eds.), *The Cambridge History of Africa, Volume 3* (Cambridge: Cambridge University Press), 232–330.

Gonzemai, A. 2002. *Les briques cuites du Kanem (Tchad)* (Université de n'Djamena: Mémoire de Maîtrise).

Gronenborn, D. 1998. "Archaeological and Ethnohistorical Investigations Along the Southern Fringes of Lake Chad, 1993–1996," *African Archaeological Review*, 15(4), 225–259.

Gronenbron, D. 2001. "Kanem-Borno: A Brief Summary of the History and Archaeology of an Empire of the Central Bilad Al-Sudan," in C. R. de Corse (ed.), *West Africa During the Atlantic Slave Trade. Archaeological Perspectives* (London: Leicester University Press), 101–130.

Gronenborn, D., Adderley, P., Ameje, J., Banerjee, A., Fenn, T., Liesegang, G, Haase, C., Usman, Y., and Patscher, S. 2012. "Durbi Takusheyi: A High-Status Burial Site in the Western Central Bilad Al-Sudan," *Azania: Archaeological Research in Africa*, 47(3), 256–271.

Hallam, W. K. R. 1987. "Towards a reassessment of the early Kanem Mais," *Annals of Borno (Maiduguri)*, 4, 33–46.

Hambolu, M. O. 1996. "Recent Excavations Along the Yobe Valley," in SFB 268 (ed.), *Proceedings of the International Symposium of the SFB 268, Frankfurt/M, 13th–16th December 1995, Volume 8* (Frankfurt/M: SFB 268), 215–229.

Haour, A. 2003. *Ethnoarchaeology in the Zinder Region, Republic of Niger: The Site of Kufan Kanawa* (Oxford: Archaeopress).

Haour, A. 2008. "The Pottery Sequence from Garumele (Niger): A Former Kanem-Borno Capital?," *Journal of African Archaeology*, 6(1), 3–20.

Holl, A. F. C. 2000. *The Diwan Revisited: Literacy, State Formation and the Rise of Kanuri Domination (A.D. 1200–1600)* (London: Kegan Paul).

Holl, A. F. C. 2002. *The Land of Houlouf. Genesis of a Chadic Polity 1900 BC–AD 1800* (Ann Arbor: University of Michigan).

Hull, R. W. 1976. *African Cities and Towns Before the European Conquest* (New York: Norton).

Hunwick, J. 1997. "The Arabic Literary Tradition of Nigeria," *Research in African Literatures*, 28(3), 210–223.

Insoll, T. 2003. *The Archaeology of Islam in Sub-Saharan Africa* (Cambridge: Cambridge University Press).

Lange, D. 1977. *Le Diwan des Sultans du (Kanem-)Bornu. Chronologie et Histoire d'un royaume africain* (Wiesbaden: Franz Steiner Verlag).

Lange, D. 1980. "La région du lac tchad d'près la géographie d'Ibn Said: textes et cartes," *Annales Islamologiques*, 16, 149–181.

Lange, D. 1987. *A Sudanic Chronicle: The Borno Expeditions of Idris Alauma (1564–1576)* (Stuttgart: Franz Steiner Verlag).

Lange, D. 1993. "Ethnogenesis from Within the Chadic State: Some Thoughts on the History of Kanem-Borno," *Paideuma*, 39, 261–277.

Lange, D., and Barkindo, B. 1988. "The Chad Region as a Crossroads," in G. Mouktar (ed.), *General History of Africa (Abridged Edition), Vol. 3: Africa from the 7th to 11th Century* (London: James Currey), 216–225.

Last, M. 1983. "From Sultanate to Caliphate: Kano, 1450–1800 A.D.," in B. Barkindo (ed.), *Studies in the History of Kano* (Ibadan: Heinemann Educational Books Ltd.), 63–91.

Lavers, J. E. 1971. "A Note on Birni Gazargamu and 'Burnt Brick' Sites in the Bornu Caliphate," in A. Fagg (ed.), *Papers Presented to the 4th Meeting of West African Archaeologists, Jos 1971* (Manuscript on file, Lavers Collection, Arewa House, Kaduna).

Lavers, J. E. 1980. "Kanem and Borno to 1808," in O. Ikime (ed.), *Groundwork of Nigerian History* (Lagos: Heinemann), 187–209.

Lebeuf, A. M. D. 1962. "Enceintes de briques de la région tchadienne," in G. Mortelmans and J. Nenquin (eds.), *Actes du IV Congres Panafricain de Prehistoire et de l'Étude de Quaternaire* (Tervuren: Musée Royal de l'Afrique Centrale), 437–443.

Lebeuf, A. M. D. 1972. *Atlas pratique du Tchad* (N'Djamena: INTSH).

Levtzion, N., and Hopkins, J. F. P. 1981. *Corpus of Early Arabic Sources for West African History* (Cambridge: Cambridge University Press).

Levtzion, N., and Pouwels, R. 2000. "Islam in the Bilad al-Sudan to 1800," in N. Levtzion and R. Pouwels (eds.), *The History of Islam in Africa* (Oxford: James Currey), 63–92.

Loimeier, R. 2013. *Muslim Societies in Africa: A Historical Anthropology* (Bloomington: Indiana University Press).

Lovejoy, P. 1974. "Interregional Monetary Flows in the Precolonial Trade of Nigeria," *Journal of African History*, 15(4), 563–585.

Lovejoy, P.E. 1978. The Role of the Wangara in the economic transformation of the Central Sudan in the fifteenth and sixteenth centuries. Journal of African History 19 (2), 173–193.

MacEachern, S. 2012. "The Prehistory and Early History of the Northern Mandara Mountains and Surrounding Plains," in N. David (ed.), *Metals in Mandara Mountains Society and Culture* (Trenton: Africa World Press), 27–67.

McIntosh, S. K. (ed.) 1999. "Pathways to Complexity: An African Perspective," in S. K. McIntosh (ed.), *Beyond Chiefdoms: Pathways to Complexity in Africa* (Cambridge: Cambridge University Press), 1–30.

Magnavita, C. 2011. "Birni Gazargamo—die alte Hauptstadt Kanem-Bornos/Birni Gazargamo—the Early Capital of Kanem-Borno," in D. Gronenborn (ed.), *Gold, Sklaven, Elfenbein. Mittelalterliche Reiche im Norden Nigerias* (Mainz: RGZM), 58–61.

Magnavita, C., Adebayo, O., Höhn, A., Ishaya, D., Kahlheber, S., Linseele, V., and Ogunseyin, S. 2009. "Garu Kime: A Late Borno Fired-Brick Site at Monguno, NE Nigeria," *African Archaeological Review*, 26(3), 219–246.

Magnavita, C., and Magnavita, S. 2017. "Garumele Revisited: Retracing Vanished Fired-Brick Elite Constructions and New Data on Settlement Foundation," *African Archaeological Review*, 34(2), 155–176.

Moughtin, J. C. 1972. "The Friday Mosque, Zaria City," *Savanna: Journal of the Environmetal and Social Sciences*, 1(2), 143–163.

Nixon, S. 2014. "West Africa: Islamic Archaeology," in C. Smith (ed.), *Encyclopedia of Global Archaeology* (New York: Springer), 7720–7732.

Okpoko, A. I. 1998. "Archaeology and the Study of Early Urban Centres in Nigeria," *African Study Monographs*, 19(1), 35–54.

Palmer, H. R. 1908. "The Kano Chronicle," *The Journal of the Royal Anthropological Institute of Great Britain and Ireland*, 38, 58–98.

Palmer, H. R. 1922. "Hausa Legend and Earth Pyramids in the Western and Central Sudan," *Bulletin of the School of Oriental and African Studies*, 2(2), 225–233.

Palmer, H. R. 1936. *The Bornu Sahara and Sudan* (London: John Murray).

Priddy, A. J. 1970. "RS 63/32: An Iron Age Site near Yelwa, Sokoto Province: Preliminary Report," *The West African Archaeological Newsletter*, 12, 20–32.

Robertshaw, P. 2010. "Beyond the Segmentary State: Creative and Instrumental Power in Western Uganda," *Journal of World Prehistory*, 23(4), 255–269.

Schulze, A. 1910. *Das Sultanat Bornu mit besonderer Berücksichtigung Deutsch-Bornus* (Langensalza: Beltz).

Seidensticker, W. 1981. "Borno and the East: Notes and Hypotheses on the Technology of Burnt Bricks," in: T. C. Schadeberg and M. L. Bender (eds.), *Nilo-Saharan. Proceedings of the First Nilo-Saharan Linguistics Colloquium, Leiden, September 8–10, 1980* (Dordrecht/Cinnaminson: Foris Publications), 239–250.

Sieber, E. 1992. *Iron Age Archaeology in Kano State, Nigeria* (PhD thesis, Indiana University).

Smith, A. 1976. "The Early States of the Central Sudan," in J. Ajayi and M. Crowder (eds.), *History of West Africa, Volume 1* (London: Longman), 152–195.

Smith, A. 1987. "Some Consideration Relating to the Formation of States in Hausaland," in A. Smith (ed.), *A Little New Light: Selected Historical Writings of Abdullahi Smith* (Zaria: Abdullahi Smith Centre for Historical Research), 59–79.

Southall, A. W. 1988. "The Segmentary State in Africa and Asia," *Comparative Studies in Society and History,* 30(1), 52–82.

Stride, G. T., and Ifeka, C. 1971. *Peoples and Empires of West Africa: West Africa in History, 1000–1800* (New York: Africana Publishing Corporation).

Sule, A. 2010. "Kirfi, Bauchi: An Archaeological Investigation of the Hausa Landscape," in A. Hour and B. Rossi (eds.), *Being and Becoming Hausa* (Leiden: Brill), 165–186.

Sutton, J. 1976. "Iron-Working Around Zaria," *Zaria Archaeology Papers,* 8, 1–20.

Sutton, J. 1979. "Towards a Less Orthodox History of Hausaland," *Journal of African History* 20 (1), 179–201.

Sutton, J. 2010. "Hausa as a Process in Time and Space," in A. Haour and B. Rossi (eds.), *Being and Becoming Hausa* (Leiden: Brill), 279–298.

Trimingham, J. S. 1962. *A History of Islam in West Africa* (London: Oxford University Press).

Urvoy, Y. 1949. *Histoire de L'Empire du Bornou* (Paris: Librairie Larose).

Usman, B. 1972. "Some Aspects of the External Relations of Katsina Before 1804," *Savanna: Journal of Environmental and Social Sciences,* 1(2), 175–196.

Zeltner, J.-C. 1980. *Pages d'histoire du Kanem. Pays Tchadien* (Paris: L'Harmattan).

SECTION V

···

ASIA

···

TIMOTHY INSOLL

As with the Islamic archaeology of sub-Saharan Africa, a narrative of complexity in Asia is also evident, in its dynastic histories, monuments, trade, and cultural and social fusions. The quantity of Islamic archaeological research completed in Asia likewise varies regionally. In Central Asia, extensive archaeological fieldwork has been undertaken; until recently, however, because of language barriers and the results appearing in obscure publications, much of this research was inaccessible. In South Asia, relevant research, although having a long history stretching back to the latter 19th century, has been variable in quantity and focus, with the majority architectural rather than archaeological, and with priority given to sites associated with other religions in India and lack of funding precluding research elsewhere. In China, Islamic archaeology has been limited in scope, and in Southeast Asia, research has also been restricted in coverage and its emphasis has been primarily on trade centres, mosques, and epigraphy. Politics has also impinged on the practice of Islamic archaeology in parts of the region via the Soviet system in Central Asia and communism and the impact of the Cultural Revolution in China affecting both interpretation and practice.

Research themes again emerge. For example, archaeology is challenging the paradigm that nomadism prevailed in Central Asia and urban centers were few. Urban archaeology has expanded over the past 150 years of research with very large-scale excavations completed at numerous sites across Central Asia. The importance of maritime and land-based connections is also again apparent. From caravan routes crossing Central Asia to seaborne networks connecting the Gulf with the western coast of India, Southeast Asia, and the Muslim (and other) communities in the ports of southern China. Maritime archaeology is also growing in importance, particularly in Southeast Asia, and providing, in microcosm insights into the entangled nature of long-distance commerce. Islamization processes and influences are also becoming a focus of archaeological study, notably in Southeast Asia, where epigraphy, stylistic elements, and numismatics are providing detailed information. Opportunities also exist to explore Islamization processes in South Asia, China, and Central Asia—especially the latter, where the database is rich because of the extent of archaeological research that has been completed.

Finally, issues of preservation of Islamic archaeological heritage are also a recurring feature and raised in relation to Central Asia, China, and South Asia. Notwithstanding this, it is apparent that the potential for future archaeological research on Islamic sites, particularly in China and South Asia where neglect has been most felt, is immense.

CHAPTER 5.1

···

CENTRAL ASIA

···

PIERRE SIMÉON

INTRODUCTION

THIS vast area (more than 500,000 km²) is referred to in the sources as Mā warā' al-nahr ("land beyond the river" or Amū Daryā). The equivalent of Transoxiana, it is the great Eastern province north of K̲h̲urāsān (Figure 5.1.1). These regions were, from their conquests, among the most civilized of Dār al-Islām, able to compete with the Middle East despite their remoteness. In the collective imagination, the vast areas of steppes, oases, and deserts at the foot of high mountains are thought of as being inhabited by nomads. Yet there are more than one hundred medieval cities, including some of the largest in the Islamic world. These cities are often tripartite and develop around an old core shape with the citadel abutting the inner city (*shahrestan*) and suburb(s) (*rabad*) in different ways depending on local topography.

As in the Near East in the 9th century (all dates are CE unless otherwise specified), archaeological data often confirms a form of continuity and slow changes in material culture after conquest. The period between the 10th and 13th centuries was conducive to the development of these cities, and the primary sector was dynamic, including the extraction of many metals that came from five major mining areas (Talas, Čač-Ilaq, Farghānā, Sogdiana, and Pamir) (Simeon 2014). Men and ideas circulated from the Mediterranean to China through Central Asia. Handicrafts contributed to the economic progress and prosperity of rich oases. The commercialization of many manufactured products between the oases of Central Asia and along the major international trading networks is very visible in the remains of the archaeological material. Earthen wares painted in lustre are an unknown but significant illustration of the spread of luxury goods between Iraq and Central Asian markets (Figure 5.1.2).

These Arab-Muslim conquests are the result of the first caliph's desire to convert people to Islam (jihād) and to enlarge their territories. The regions of Central Asia and Iran were conquered at the same time as parts of Africa, from the north, in the space of one hundred years (632–732). In the 7th and 8th centuries the prosperous small

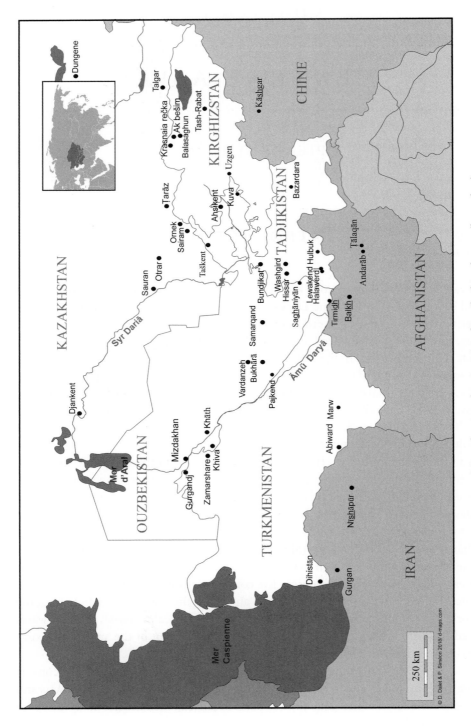

FIGURE 5.1.1 Map of region showing sites described in chapter (by author)

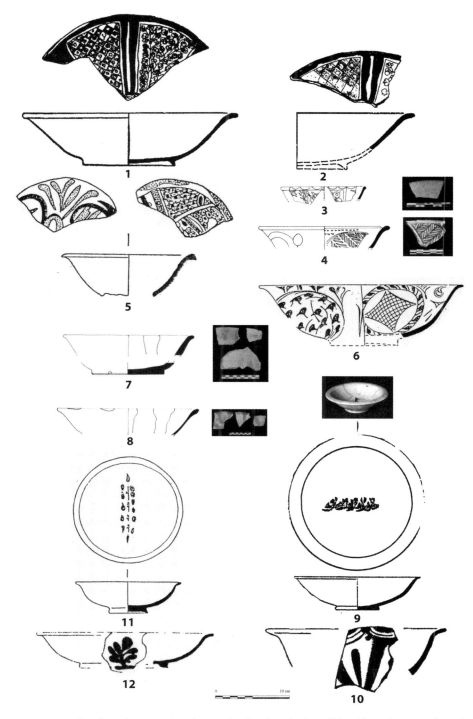

FIGURE 5.1.2 Earthern lustre-painted ceramics (1–6) and other Abbasid productions from Iraq (7–10) found in Central Asian Medieval cities: 1–2, 5, 10, 12 in Samarkand (Uzbekistan); 3–4, 6, 11 in Tashkent (Uzbekistan); 7–8 in Hulbuk (Tadjiksitan); 9 in Budrach (Uzbekistan).

Courtesy of Simeon (2018).

principalities of Central Asia were still under Chinese protection, but the conflict with the Tibetans captured the military attention of the Tangs (Beckwith 1987: 142). This was the battle over the course of the Talas River: more precisely, according to the sources, at Atlakh (mentioned by Thaʿālibī and Ibn al-Athīr), a river in the south of present-day Kazakhstan, which marks the stabilization of the border of dār al-Islām in the face of Chinese power (Barthold 1928: 236; Beckwith 1987: 139). The south of Central Asia was undergoing progressive Islamization from the Arab-Muslim conquest, the installation and the persistence of an Iranian culture through the Samanid princes (819–1005), and then the ethno-political Turkification when the Qarakhānids and Ghaznawids dynasties (9th-11th century), then the Khwārazm shāh dynasty (12th-13th century) came into power.

In the first quarter of the 13th century, the Mongol conquest of Transoxiana and Khurāsān constituted a disruption that impacted the structures of power (Aigle 2005: 119) and the networks of exchanges in an immense geographical area, which, strictly speaking, exceeded the boundaries of Central Asia. The years 1218–1220 were marked by violence and population flight and the destruction of irrigation dykes and large cities until the capture of Baghdad and the abolition of the Abbasid caliphate in 1258. The high spheres of local power were marked durably in dynastic terms, and descendants of Genghis Khan also reigned in Persia and China. From the end of the 14th century, tribal confederations (blue, white, Nogay Hordes, etc.) participated in the division of Gengiskhanid empires into various Khanats (Kazakh, Abū Saʿīd Abū al-Khaïr, etc.) who regularly demonstrated their antagonism until the 18th century and the beginnings of the Russian strategy moving toward territorial control of the Kazakh steppes.

The main settlements of Mā warāʾ al-nahr (Transoxiana) are found around large river basins, made up of about twenty small regions which overlapped in the medieval period. These regions and basins are today transnational, shared between five Federal Republics, then Soviet Republics which became independent in August 1991: Kazakhstan, Uzbekistan, Kirghizistan, Turkmenistan, and Tadjikistan. The southern territories also have strong cultural and linguistic ties with northern Iran and Afghanistan. Faced with this immense land area, the choice has been made to prioritize the presentation of regional capitals often linked with political history, and the medieval cities, their historical topography, their major buildings, and their craft activities will be discussed.

This chapter provides little data on the dense event-driven history, but it does make extensive use of both older and more recent excavation results (generally published in Russian) in order to explore both the nature of medieval cities and their surroundings. To avoid contemporary geographical breaks, we will follow the two great river basins, the first from central Amū Daryā to Khwārazm and to the edge of the desert of black sands. The second, the Syr Daryā basin, which includes the interface with the steppe. To understand the basis and extent of Russian archaeology in Central Asia, we will present the main steps from the Tsarist period (ca. 1850–1917) until the collapse of the Soviet Union (1991). A few words about the postcolonial period from 1991 to the present helps us to understand the main challenges facing our local colleagues.

CONSTRUCTION OF A FIELD OF STUDY: FROM ORIENTALISM TO RUSSIAN ARCHAEOLOGY IN CENTRAL ASIA

The Russian conquest and colonization of Central Asia took place between 1850 and 1890 under the reign of Tsar Alexander II (1855–1881), including the capture of Tashkent (1865) and Samarkand (1868). This conquest provoked Russo-British geostrategic tensions. Russia saw archaeology as one of the components of the "great game," and its administration therefore determined the possibility of conducting excavations or not (Gorshenina 2012: 8). The Tsar quickly commissioned a study program of Russian Turkestan coordinated from Moscow and St. Petersburg. It was in 1895 that the Turkish Circle of Archaeology Fellows (TKLA) was born and that the first Russian scientific missions with the Oumniakov, Viatkin, or Semënov Orientalists took place. Historical geography, epigraphy, and numismatics undergo very early important development thanks to the orientalist and archaeologist Barthold, and his thesis published in 1910 and translated into English in 1928 is still the first work of reference.

Moreover, the many Russian and European travelers, and more rarely American, brought back all types of documents including photographic archives, paper or glass plates, from archaeological sites and the large Timurid mosques of Samarkand (Bouillane Lacoste, De la Baume Pluvinel, Moser, etc.) (see also Gorshenina 2000). Some of these photographs are the only evidence of the buildings before the Russian restorations that have since taken place. In the last third of the 19th century, all research originates from Russian anthropological and ethno-linguistic studies and remains subject to political concerns: notably the search for "the origin of the Aryans" and the fascination with the paths followed by Alexander the Great. (Gorshenina 2000: 28–29). Most of the research is focused on these two questions of ancient history.

In 1919, Lenin established an Academy for the History of Material Culture (RAIMK), which replaced the Imperial Archaeology Commission. In addition, a "Heritage Safeguarding Committee" (Turkomstaris-Sredazkomstaris) was dedicated to the restoration of Islamic monuments, and, in this regard, a German mission to Uzbekistan under the direction of Kohn-Wiener took place in 1924 (Gorshenina 2003: 60). After 1917, Russia's Central Asia was divided into five closed Soviet republics, and the ensuing scientific compartmentalisation would condition research until the partial reopening of the Soviet frontiers in 1965. In this new communist state, archaeology, like other disciplines, follows Marxist doctrine, according to which all societies develop in stages to establish communism. Thus, in the Soviet tradition, the Middle Ages is subdivided into three periods: pre-feudalism (5th–11th century), feudalism (11th century to late 15th century), the disintegration of feudalism and the emergence of capitalist relations (late 15th century to first half of 17th century). In Russia and the regions of Central Asia, the prerogatives of medieval studies have been more those of economic and social structures and urbanization; indigenous civilizations have often been glorified and external contributions minimized.

The 1930s was the great period of interdisciplinary expeditions (*kompleksnoĭ ekspedicii*), integrating the geological, ethnological, and of course archaeological aspects, fruits of the new Soviet ideology, composed of scientists from Moscow and Leningrad in accordance with Marxist scientific principles (Gorshenina 2013: 27). The largest embarked on regional studies (archaeological maps) and excavations of ancient cities in Uzbekistan, southern Kazakhstan, and Turkmenistan. The number of regional expeditions was then a few dozen, and the multiplication of local researchers in the years 1930–1940 led to the foundation of the school of archaeology at the University of Tashkent by Masson, in 1940, independent from those of Moscow and Leningrad.

The achievements of archaeology in Russian colonial Turkestan are impressive, with abundant scientific publications (there are more than ten specialized periodicals), five Institutes of History, and two institutes of archaeology in Alma Aty (created in 1946) and Samarkand (created in 1970). These institutes are usually attached to an Academy of Sciences, and medieval archaeology is taught in universities. About fifty regional museums, but especially the national museums of the five capitals (Tashkent, Ashgabad, Bishkek, Dushanbe, and Alma Ata) have beautiful collections of objects from the Islamic era. After the fall of the USSR, in what some researchers call the postcolonial period, a certain institutional dispersion asserted itself; the Russian archaeologists lost their monopoly and researchers of these republics saw their finances weakened. It was at this time that Western missions, initially French, undertook excavations in Uzbekistan, in Samarkand (since 1989), then in Termez/Tirmidh (in 1993). As Gorshenina defines it, this post-Soviet archaeology is not immune to "the preference for certain prestigious historical periods" or "a massive reconstruction of heritage for tourism and commercial purposes" (Gorshenina 2011: 31). These are contemporary issues shared well beyond Central Asia.

THE CENTER AND THE NORTH OF THE AMŪ DARYĀ BASIN

This basin is now shared between Uzbekistan, Turkmenistan, and Tajikistan. Samarkand is undoubtedly the most famous city. It has been the subject of intensive Russian excavation campaigns since the end of the 19th century. Since then further research has produced more than a hundred articles, books, and a specialized periodical (*Afrasiab*, between 1969 and 1975; on the history of archaeological research in Samarkand, see Grenet 2005: 1045–1051).

The city of Samarkand was taken in 712 by Qutayba. The 8th-century Islamic city remains close to the ancient city (Afrasiab) and occupies a surface of more than 220 hectares. A Franco-Uzbek archaeological mission (MAFOUZ) resumed work on the citadel, which sheltered the administrative and religious center of the city (Bernard et al. 1990). Hence the great mosque was on the west terrace of the citadel, described by Ibn Hawqal at the end of the 10th century, then identified in 1885 by Barthold and excavated intermittently from 1904 (Viatkin). But except for its rectangular shape (75 × 127 meters) its plan remained incomplete (Buriakov et al. 1975: 79). Numismatic data and ceramics confirm its use until the 13th century (Buriakov et al. 1975: 87, 90). The continuation of the Russian excavations of the Great Mosque uncovered a palace attributed to the last Umayyad governor of Transoxiana (740–750) close to the Sogdiana palatial tradition (Bernard et al. 1990, Grenet 2008: 13–20).

In addition, several structures of Islamic housing were excavated on the southern flank of the citadel in 1991, but without being the subject of a detailed publication (Bernard, Grenet and Isamiddinov 1992). Works were also undertaken on the lower terrace from 1989, revealing a monumental palace of 1 hectare (Dār al-Imāra) (75.5 × 65 meters) probably built on the order of Abū Muslim al-Khurāsāni. This Abbasid palace is very similar to Umayyad palace architecture and was left unfinished (Karev 2000). Over this ruined palace, at least six pavilions with an overall size of 12 ×12 meters, made up of four *iwans* opening onto a square courtyard, were covered in murals. More than 500 fragments were discovered in 2000 and 2001, many of which were anthropomorphic and depicted animals and monumental Nakhsh script. The Turkic arrow bearer, whirling dancers, the saluki dog, and the fighting birds medallion are the most impressive among a unique set of paintings from the Turkic Qarakhanid dynasty (12th–13th centuries) (Karev 2003, 2005: 50).

A Samanid palace was also excavated in the first decades of the 20th century (1911–1925) in the western part of the *shahrestan* (inner city): two halls were fully decorated with impressive large stucco panels. These floral and geometric ornaments were fully described and connected with Near Eastern and similar local comparative decorative programs (Ahrarov and Rempel 1971). Dating from the years 870–880, some of the ceramics discovered were still in use at the beginning of the 10th century and could indicate a slightly different chronology. In the second half of the 9th century Samarkand was intermittently the capital of Transoxiana until the fratricidal strife between the Sāmānid brothers Naṣr and Ismā'īl. The latter established his authority in Bukhara, where the Sāmānid family preferred to reside during the 10th century.

In the mid-11th century, Samarkand became the capital of the Qarakhānid Tamgach-Bughrā-khān Ibrāhīm (1040–1068), and the size of the southern *rabad* increased, as testified by written sources and *waqf*: this *rabad* was enclosed by a wall with four gates. In the 11th–12th centuries, the growth of the city was such that it extended to the south (Voronina 1969: 32; Buriakov and Tashodzhaev 1975). The shahrestan (inner city) (more than 170 hectares) is made up of residential neighborhoods and different types of construction, a private palace, public buildings such as the Great Mosque, and cemeteries, but also artisan areas as the city grew.

Several handicraft areas with 11th- to 12th-century potters' workshops were discovered by archaeologists in the *shahrestan*, south-east and west of the second bastion and also south at the border of the rabad, a cemetery (Buriakov and

Tashodzhaev 1975: 14–15). Overall, pre-Mongolian ceramics from the Samarkand excavations have been well documented (Shishkina 1979, 1986; Shishkina and Pavshinskaja 1992). The large market and artisanal activities were outside the *rabad* near the Kish Gate, and about ten caravanserais were located, later covered by the contemporary city (Buriakov and Tashodzhaev 1975: 19). The southern *sharestan* was densely populated on both sides of the large canal which supplied the water for the city, as the Zeravshan River is not far away, but the city is higher and had no direct access to its water. The city was supplied with water by canals coming from the southern flank of the valley (Grenet 2002). Four lines of walls help to understand medieval urban development: a first around the citadel proper, the second that surrounds the *shahrestan*, the third being an extension of the second to the south, and finally the fourth enclosing the *rabad* until shāh-i Zindah. For the latter, a dozen doors are known to exist (Kish gate south, Bukhara west, China east, etc.).

The city of Samarkand continued its development toward the south and underwent a second architectural renewal when it became the capital of the Timurid empire (1370–1500). Tamerlane and his descendants moved the city south-west of the medieval town (Bala Hissar). Several buildings are emblematic of this period, the Great Mosque of Bibi-Khanum (1398–1404) and the mausoleum of Gur-Emir for Timur and his male heirs (erected in 1404), with ribbed cupolas covered by glazed colored roof tiles, both well known and published many years ago (Pope 1965: 197). On a hill northeast of Samarkand, the remains of a circular astronomical observatory more than 48 meters in diameter was rediscovered by archaeologists (Viatkin et al. 1986). At the southern tip of the medieval city, probably abandoned at that time, more than fifteen princely mausoleums form the funeral complex of Shāh-i zindah (Nemtseva et al. 1979), and other 12th-century mausoleums were rebuilt during the 15th century (Voronina 1969: 34). The early Shaybanids maintained their seat in Samarkand in the early 16th century. More changes occurred with an independent ruler in the 17th century who decided to restore the Ulugh Begh *madrassah* and built the Sheir Dor (1619–1636) and Tillya Kari *madrassah* (1646–1647) creating the Registan square.

Along the ancient road from Samarkand to Bukhara laid the portal and front-fired brick wall with corrugations of a large building, known as Ribat-i Malik, originally interpreted as a caravanserai; excavations between 1973 and 2001 by Nemtseva show successive palaces inhabited and refurbished over a long period between the 11th and 18th centuries, perhaps for the Qarakhānid governors (Nemtseva 1983, 2009). It consists of a large courtyard with a portico and two medium-sized courtyards surrounded by long rooms and separated by a corridor. It presents several interesting features, including a bath built in the south-west courtyard and a polygonal podium (6.5 meters diameter, 1 meter from the ground) in the center of the great courtyard with its 12th-century portico, perhaps for a ceremonial yurt.

On the border of the Kizil Kum desert, more than 250 kilometers to the west of Samarkand, lies the old city of Bukhara. The city is close to the lower course of the Zeravshan River, where it divides into several branches. Well known as "the Ka'ba of the Empire" according to al-Tha 'ālibī (d. 1038), the old city, covering today an area of 450 hectares, was made up of 462 monuments from the early to the modern Islamic period and was inscribed on the World Heritage list in 1993. From the recent German project, 205 monuments are public buildings including mosques, *madrasas*, caravanserais, Khānaqā-s, *hammams*, cemeteries, and water basins (Badr et al. 2012). The oasis of Bukhara underwent intense archaeological activity from the end of the 19th century (for research history in the oasis, see Shishkin 1963). The west of the oasis in particular was surveyed in detail at the end of the 1930s (Shishkin 1940), and there were important excavations in Varakhshah. In the 1970s a Bukhara archaeological team under the supervision of Muhamedjanova carried out surveys and provided measured drawings of more than thirty sites in the oasis. Since the pre-Islamic period, a large part of the oasis was protected from attacks from nomads by an earthen wall. Investigations of this wall, especially the southwestern and northeastern parts, were the subject of an Uzbeko–American joint project (2011–2014) (Mirzaahmedov and Starck 2012; Omel'chenko and Mirzaahmedov 2015).

Since independence, archeological works in Bukhara have been mainly concerned with the early Middle Ages. Thus an Italo–Uzbek team from the Universita di Roma "Sapienza" has done a set of surveys (1997–2007) and measured drawings particularly in Vardanzeh. The subsequent Italo–Uzbek excavation program focused on Vardanzeh (Pozzi, Mirzaahmedov 2010–2018). This medium sized pre-Islamic city lost importance after the Arabo–Muslim conquest, but was still occupied (like many other cities) during the middle and late Islamic period, mainly the eastern part of the citadel and the inner city (cf. Adylov and Mirzaahmedov 2001). The quadrangular citadel (ark) (c. 3 hectares) is located on the western edge of the *sharestan* (lower town); excavations took place there at the end of the 1970s (unpublished), and cross-sections of the northern and southern ramparts were drawn up (Nekrasova 1999: 40–42). According to Narshakhī it housed the Royal Chancellery where the emirs resided, the treasury, and the prison.

Many geographers present the city and its tripartite ordinance—citadel, *shahrestan*, and suburbs or *rabad*—fed by canals, with wide stone-paved streets and a solid wall with eleven doors, protecting it from Turkish raids. The Friday mosque of Bukhara and its minaret Menār-e Kalān (Kalyan), completed in 1127 and rebuilt in brick by Qarakhānid Arslan Khan, are located to the south-east of the citadel not far from the Magoki Attari mosque, covered by twelve domes. To the west of the city there is a cemetery and the family and royal mausoleum of Ismail (governor of Bukhara between 874 and 892 and emir from 893 to 907) which is undoubtedly one of the best known buildings of Islamic architecture (Bulatov 1976). Finally, outside the town, to the south, a *namazgha* (12th century) indicates the practice of festival prayers in the open air (Kochnev 1976: 31–32).

The country was flooded in 1220 and monumental construction apparently stopped until the 14th century. Some mausoleums were built outside the Karshi city gate (Sayf al-dīn al-Bukharsī, Butan Kulikha, etc.). The 16th century was a very active building period, with new mosques and madrasahs in the city center (Mir-i Arab). More recently, one of the most architecturally impressive buildings set in the west of the old city, the Khoja Zainuddin Mosque, was investigated by an German-Austrian-Uzbek research team that created a digital map of the old Bukhara city center, conducted by Professor

Korn (Badr and Tupev 2012). Many others buildings were built at the same period in the Bukhara suburbs (Chor Bakr, Faizabad Khānaqā, etc.), under the Shaybanid dynasty (1500–1598).

The complex history of the topography of the oasis and city of Bukhara was the subject of numerous studies. From historical sources and Russian archaeological data, Belenitskiĭ, Bentovich, and Bolshakov present precise reconstructions of the city and its fortifications and water channels in the 9th–10th centuries (Belenitskiĭ, Bentovich and Bolshakov 1973: 243, pl. 94–95). They propose also a reconstruction of the square-shaped *shahrestan* divided into four quadrants whose city doors are named. The geometrical shape of the *shaherstan* is somewhat similar to that of Sultan kala city in Merv, but whether this square plan is of local or exogenous origin (Indian or Chinese) is still under debate (Gaube 2004). Possibly the change of status of Bukhara as a capital increased its growth to become one of the largest cities of Central Asia at the end of the 10th century (Belenitskiĭ, Bentovich and Bolshakov 1973: 244), and Naymark has pointed out the lack of elements concerning urban density during the 8th–10th centuries (Naymark 1999: 43). Various schemes of urban growth in the south and through the west are suggested for the 11–12th centuries (Hmelniskiĭ 1996: 25, pl. 4).

Forty kilometers south-west of Bukhara, toward the Amū Daryā, the trading city of Pajkend was also surveyed: Zimina conducted a dig in the central part of the citadel as early as 1914. Then a program of Russian–Uzbek excavation began in 1939 (the Hermitage Zarafshan Expedition) with the Institute of History of Material Culture (Russian Academy of Sciences) and the Uzbekistan Committee for Preservation of Historic and Art Heritage (Supervisor: Iakubovskiĭ and Semenov from 1981). They began with topographic surveys of the city, the rectangular citadel to the northeast (1 hectare), of the two *shahrestan* (about 20 hectares), and a *rabad* (more than 80 hectares). At a later date, excavation took place on the citadel and revealed a set of administrative buildings, a large mosque with square pillars (late 14th–early 16th), and the foundations of a minaret (Muhamedjanov, Adylov et al. 1988).

In sharestan 1, a 10th-century residential area bordered by streets number 3 and 4, more than twenty houses were excavated (in a wide trench 90 meter long by 20 meters in width). In shahrestan 2, richly decorated houses provided carved and painted panels made of clay and gypsum as well as a neighborhood mosque, of which the *mihrab* was decorated. The street lined with shops between the two *shahrestan* was excavated, highlighting the diversity of craft activities—an iron workshop, a bone carving workshop, a steatite cooking pot repair shop, a pharmacological shop dating from the late 8th century—and providing a good overview of the economic dynamism of a Transoxiana merchant city. Several large caravanserais are also clearly visible to the east of the citadel, which confirms these observations. The excavations and the ceramic and glass finds were published after each campaign in specialized volumes (МБАЭ Материалы Бухарской археологической экспедиции) from the year 2000 (i.e., sixteen volumes to date). The street network and the water supply system composed of wells and water pipes is partially known. More recently, since 2009, a French–Uzbek collaboration began involving the Louvre Museum and the LA3M laboratory in Aix en Provence. Four trenches (on the citadel, in the two *shahrestans*, and into the eastern *rabad*) were dug and some geomagnetic surveys were conducted.

The topography of the south Amū Daryā with an island, made Tirmidh (Termez) the second most important crossing point after Amul (Barthold 1928: 76). The city is 60 kilometers north-west of Balkh (Afghanistan). In Tirmidh the first excavations were conducted by Professor Denike and the expedition of the Museum of Oriental Cultures of Moscow (1926–1928). From 1993, a Franco–Uzbek archaeological mission began the study of the settlement and urbanization of the ancient city of Tirmidh (Leriche and Pidaev 2001; 2008). The study of the Islamic part of Tirmidh began later, and specialist archaeologists of the Islamic period (Kervran, Genequand) succeeded one another from 1998 to 2002, without published results.

The city is well known through medieval sources (Ibn K̲h̲urradād̲h̲bih, Kudami, Ḥawqal, Maqdissī, etc.) (Masson 1940). The fortified citadel in which the governor's palace was located was on the border of the Amū Daryā from the 9th to 10th centuries. It was a port of trade and trans-shipment point for important goods on the river Amū Daryā, but these developments were destroyed by variations in the river's course. Several excavations on the citadel have shown reconstructions in baked bricks prior to those of the Timurid period. These could correspond to the repair work undertaken in 1073–1074 by Sultan Seljukid Malik shāh (according to Ibn al-Athīr). The lower town is made up of two *rabad* of more than 35 hectares that stretch from east to west. It has three gates. The defensive wall of the city is flanked by a semicircular tower, and there is another outer wall (Leriche and Pidaev 2007: 96–114). In both *shahrestan* and in the two *rabad* prospected from 2000, few structures have been documented to date. In the *shahrestan* the habitation is dense (houses with raw brick courtyards containing many refuse pits) and described as mediocre (Leriche 2013: 156).

In the first *shahrestan* (sector AC2), halfway between the citadel and the hill of Tchinguiz Tepe, a Spanish–Uzbek team (2006–2010) also found Islamic levels; these were excavated in 2009 (Martínez Ferreras 2009). In the first *rabad*, a bath and a dovecote were excavated (unpublished); streets and squares were paved with fired bricks. The city was supplied with water by a canal and underground pipes, and traces of wells and basins supplying the different neighborhoods enabled the establishment of artisanal activities. Several potters' workshops north of the second *shahrestan* and south of the first *rabad* have been located. Metallurgical crafts seem to have been very active in the second *shahrestan* (Papachristou and Ploquin unpublished field reports). Further east, in the second *rabad*, a palace with a large square basin in the middle of a monumental courtyard of more than 200 square meters, richly decorated with stucco, was discovered by Russian archaeologists (Masson 1941) (Figure 5.1.3).

Several mosques were excavated, the first being Tchor Soutoun, which had a square plan with 10-meter long side walls, and its fired brick minaret bearing a foundation date of 423/1032. To the northwest of the second *rabad*, a large building made of mudbrick has been interpreted as a Christian monastery (Leriche and Pidaev 2007: 108). Beyond the wall, to the southwest, is an Islamic necropolis and the mausoleum of the Sufi shāfi'īt

FIGURE 5.1.3 Termez palace (Uzbekistan), northern wall of the audience hall adorned with stucco, 1928.

Courtesy of the State Hermitage Museum, St. Petersburg.

Ḥfm al-Tirmidhī (founded by Qarakhānid Abū Muzaffar Aḥmad Tigha Tegīn in the 11th century).

The apogee of the Islamic city was in the 11th–12th centuries, when it was spread out over some 500 hectares (Leriche 2013: 102). The occupation of the lower city by the riverside ended abruptly with the Mongol conquest (Leriche and Pidaev 2007: 85). Between the 13th and 18th centuries the city moved about 5 kilometers from the old town: important architectural complexes are still standing (Sultan Saodat, Kokil Dora, Kyrk Kyz) and were formerly studied by Russian architects (Denike 1939a, 1939b). The city retained a commercial and strategic importance under Tamerlane, then close to Said Tirmidh (family Khudobandazade).

The center of the Amū Daryā basin is now split between Uzbekistan and Tajikistan. In the medieval period it was located on the margins of the major capitals of Mā warā' al-nahr described previously. Present-day Tajikistan included the small regions of Wakhsh, Khuttal, Shaghāniyān, and Badakhshān, over which ruled the small, little known Turkish-Iranian dynasties of the Bānidjūrids or Muḥtādjids.

In what is now central Tadjikistan, not far west of the current capital (Dushanbe), Russian primary sources from the beginning of the 20th century mention the existence of a fortress and *madrasa* buildings which were still functioning. The site of Hissar (Shuman) is made up of a citadel with a lower terrace and a *sharestan* (total of 17 hectares). It had several defensive lines, including an external water-filled ditch and fortified gates to the south. The main and monumental door is flanked by two towers opening to a square city (*registan*), with a caravanserai and three *madrasah* (Madrasah-i Kuhna, Madrasah-i Nau, and Madrasah-i Sangin). These monuments were investigated by Bretanickij (1950). Until 1870 the upper citadel hosted the Hissar beg, a local amir.

Since these first discoveries, more than twenty sites have been studied around Hissar on some 100 hectares around the city, which is surrounded by a wall (5 kilometers in length). The city, occupied since the protohistoric era, developed extensively under the Timurids (cf. Bobomullaev 2015). Extensive archaeological work on the citadel under Atahanov's leadership between 1969 and 1986 encountered mainly archaeological levels from the 15th–18th centuries, except for traces of 11th- to 12th-century *rabad*, discovered to the south and east sides of the fortress.

Many other medieval cities are located in the foothills and the plains of southwestern Tadjikistan, like Halawerd, Lewakend, Washgird, and others. The best known is probably the city of Hulbuk. It was the capital of Khuttal, seat of the Bānidjūrid dynasty which ruled the eastern margins of Central Asia (the region of Balkh, Talaqan, Andarab, and Panjshir). The citadel sheltered the governors palace, which was reached by a forecourt up to the monumental door, from where a ramp leads to a large square whose floor is covered with baked bricks and which serves two distinct areas. To the north is a large palace composed of several houses organized around courtyards, several rooms with basins in a star arrangement, and an *iwān* with a painting of two female musicians (Simeon 2012). To the south, a palace with an axial corridor of more than 40 meters, a throne room and several rooms with indistinct functions were recorded. Complete stucco decorative panels, broken into thousands of large fragments, were discovered along a monumental corridor, and inside was a luxury throne hall, the seat of the Bānidjūrid provincial court.

Archaeological research started early in the 1950s (Belenitskiĭ and Litvinskiĭ), continuing from 1953 until the civil war in the early 1990s (Guliamova). The lower city was not investigated, but urban fabric was dense over an area of approximately 70 hectares, including two baths, mausoleums, and glass and potters' workshops. Two buildings with a single portal and a central court surrounded by rooms (caravanserais), excavated from 2008, abut the southern edge of the citadel. Even if the function of these buildings in an urban location is uncertain, they could indicate control of trade by the ruling family or facilitate protection and tax collection. They may also have accommodated a military garrison.

Shaghanyian province was to the west of the Khuttal, to which it is often associated in textual evidence. Shaghanyan/Budrac (south of the town of Denau), the capital, is known from Arabic geographers of the 10th–11th centuries (Iṣṭakhrī, Muqaddasi, Bayhaqī) as a flourishing provincial center. The Muhtajids reigned for nearly 250 years from the 9th to the 11th centuries. They are known from the written sources as vassals of the Samanid emirs and patrons of the arts, but there is little evidence on the manner of their courtly life. The material culture of the place is only superficially known, with the exception of an important bronze hoard, found accidentally in the *shahrestan*, containing more than 300 objects, thus testifying to the existence of remarkable metal-lurgical activities at the site (Iliasov and Rusanov 1988; Iliasov 1989). Some soundings were also carried out on the citadel and in the city during the 1980s (Rtveladze and Iskhakov 1979) but the lower city (140 hectares) is still largely unknown.

In the east of the Amū Daryā basin on the Chinese border (Xinjang), at the eastern-most margin of Dār al-Islām, lies the Pamir region (average altitude above 2,500 meters). Medieval occupation is also evident here in the form of fortified sites or miners' villages, related to the extraction of minerals. These mountain valleys were pros-pected relentlessly from 1969 onward to draw up an archaeological map (Bubnova 2007) in often difficult conditions (Bubnova 2007). A miner's village, inhabited seasonally, was investigated at the village of Bazardara (eighty houses and a fort), where occupation was dated by coins from 987 to 1075 (Bubnova 1963, 1993; Siméon 2014). It was probably an administrative center from where the Samanids collected the money extracted from the adjacent valleys for shipment to their capital Bukhara.

A FORCED MARCH ALONG THE AMŪ DARYĀ TOWARD THE ARAL: KHWĀRAZM

The Horezmskoĭ Archeologo-Etnograficheskoĭ Ekspedicii is one of the four major Russian interdisciplinary expeditions (architecture, ethnography, linguistics, natural sciences). It was organized around the Aral Sea, under the direction of Tolstov from 1937. They systematically explored the ancient courses of the Amū Daryā Delta using aerial photography to identify more than 300 sites from all periods of time. Surveys were carried out and confirm the protohistoric occupation of most sites. Their results were published in more than a dozen volumes between 1945 and 1963, and these confirm that the sites of the Middle Ages (cities, caravanserais, other fortified sites, etc.) were often occupied from the 9th century (Tolstov 1963, MKHAE vol.7).

The largest town of medieval Khwārazm, above the Aral Sea (Bahr al- Khwārazm) is Gurgandj/al-Jurjāniya (modern Kunya Urgench), about a hundred kilometers north of Khiva, on the major trade routes interacting with Oghuz Turks, who were very active in the area, and the Rūs further north along the Volga. It became hereafter Kāth, the capital of Khwārazm in 1231 and the seat of the native dynasty Āfrīgids, who bore the title of Khwārizm-shāh. As such, it is well described in the sources (Gardīzī, Iṣṭakhrī, Ibn Ḥawqal, Muqaddasī). Today, ruins of the buildings are visible over more than 650 hect-ares, and, for this reason, the city was placed on the UNESCO World Heritage List in 2005. The central part of the city, Tash-Kala formed a polygon of about 600 × 800 meters. Archaeological surveys were conducted as early as 1928 by the Orientalists Barthold and Iakubovskii; a lot of pre-Mongol buildings have been found, among them several preserved minarets, including the one presumed to be from al-Ma'mun (11th) attached to the Friday mosque and the minaret of Kutlug Tīmūr (11th-12th centuries)

FIGURE 5.1.4 Kunya Urgench excavations (Turkmenistan) around the Al-Ma'mūn minaret by the Tolstov team, 1958.

Courtesy of the Institute of Anthropology and Ethnography, Moscow.

(60 meters high with a diameter of 12 meters) investigated by the Tolstov team in the 1950s (Figure 5.1.4). There were also fortifications with mudbrick towers and caravanserais where only the gate was made of baked bricks.

It is quite difficult to get an idea of the urban organization in successive periods because it is the standing architecture that has been the focus of research since the 1930s (Iakubovskiĭ 1930). The detailed plans and axonometrics of about fifteen great mausoleums (12th-17th centuries), still visible today (e.g., those of Tekiš, Sultān Ali, Il-Arslān, and Ibn Haljiba or that of Najm al-Dĭn Kubrā) and surrounded by the modern town) are well published (Pugachenkova 1958, 1967; Mamedov and Muradov 1998, 2000; Muradov 2011). The city was moved a few kilometers after the Mongol invasion and a 15th- to 16th-century fortified citadel is located in the southeast. Three Timurid icehouses were also surveyed in the vicinity. The decline of the city began with Timur's campaigns against Khorezm between 1372 and 1388 and continued until the 16th century, when Khiva became the new regional capital.

Important archaeological work also took place in the city of Mizdakhan in 1928 on the initiative of Iakubovskiĭ and then intermittently from 1966 until today. On the northern edge of the fortified citadel, in the lower town (Gyaur Kala) which was densely populated in the 13th-14th century, several houses were excavated. The citadel was protected by a wall with corrugations, and excavations unearthed two monumental buildings (9th- and 12th-century) probably accommodating a regional governor. The cemetery of the city, dating from the beginning of the 10th- or 11th-century Islamic period has been studied (Hodjaniazov, Yusupov and Alii 1989). The tombs are generally of four types: rectangular pits, brick vaulted, a narrow grave in a larger burial pit, or a burial chamber (for a synthesis in Khwārazm between the 8th and 14th centuries, see Amirov 2011). The partly underground mausoleum of Mazlum Khan Sulu (12th–13th centuries) represents a rare example of this kind in the region (Kdyrniazov 1989: 25–41, 112; Yusupov 1990).

Many other medieval Khwarazmian cities (such as Zamarshahre or Kāth, the regional capital in the 10th century) deserve further research. This city, located along the main channel of the Amū Daryā, remains little known but was partly destroyed by the modern city of Biruni. The city was visited by Ibn Fadlān in 921/2, and Arabic geographers (Iṣṭakhrī, Ibn-Ḥawqal, Maqdisī, Al-Bīrūnī) described the splendid bazars and the Friday mosque overlooked by the citadel where the Afrīghids governor's palace was located. They were overthrown by the Ma'mūnid amīrs of Gurgānj in 995, long the commercial rival of Kāth (Sachau 1873). Downstream from Kāth, historical geography research on Amū Daryā found that the Kerder irrigation canal (described by Iṣṭakhrī and Maqdisî in the 10th century), which measured 150 kilometers, was not carved out along its length but used a part of the old dry beds (Iagodin 2002: 15–16).

THE MARGINS OF THE BLACK SAND DESERT (KARA KUM)

The Caspian eastern margins were almost entirely inhabited by sedentary peoples and were the lands of Oghuzz Turks opening west onto the Black Sand desert (Kara Kum). At the southern end, about fifty kilometers north of the Atrek River, a former border post (ribat-i Dihistān) became the second city in the medieval province of Gurgān. The city of Dihistān prospered under the Khwārazm Shahs (995–1231) dynasty. It covers 112 hectares *intra muros* and includes monumental buildings in the center surrounded by residential neighborhoods and a citadel to the south-east. The totality is protected by a double fortification 3.5 kilometers long, in mudbricks reinforced with towers made of baked bricks (Figure 5.1.5). In its periphery, over more than 500 hectares, vestiges of medieval farming (fields, irrigation canals) can be seen. The Russian researchers Kes, Litsina, and Kostiyushenko (1980) have highlighted the existence of complex networks diverting water from the Atrek River, dating back to the Bronze Age (3rd millennium) and still active in the Medieval period. The city is little mentioned in the texts until the violent destruction in 1221 by the Mongols of the canals supplying it with water and some of the buildings, as evidenced by the human skeletons discovered in these. Seven kilometers north of the city there is an important necropol (more than 20 hectares) with six octagonal and circular mausoleums, the *namazga* mosque and minaret, and the so-called mausoleum of Sheir Kabir that became a Sufi monastery (Khanqah) excavated by Abdulloev in 2009.

FIGURE 5.1.5 Dihistān double city wall (Turkmenistan) and new gate with a bridge, western side (1.32 kilometers long).

Courtesy of Simeon (2012).

The study of the city really began in 1947, with Masson and the Multidisciplinary Expedition in Southern Turkmenia (YUTAKE) (Figure 5.1.6). They carried out surveys and studied three monumental inscriptions in Arabic on the *pishtaq* of the Great Mosque (built between 1200 and 1220 under the Khwārazm shāh Muhammad, son of Tekesh) and on two partially preserved minarets (19 meters high and 6 meters in diameter, one of which is dated 1104/5.) In 1970, the Turkmen archaeologist Atagarryev began the first excavations *intra muros* in the city, including the Great Mosque (built during the reign of Khwārazm shāh Alp Arslan between 1200 and 1220), of a *madrassa* close by a caravanserai on the eastern edge of the city (Atagarryev 1986). Two French–Turkmenian campaigns had taken place on the site in 1996–1997 under the supervision of A. Northedge, but the mission was suspended until spring 2012 when our team resumed the work.

In the extreme southeastern part of the Kara Kum Desert at the crossing point of the Amū Daryā, the oasis of Merv currently occupies a vast area extending over more than 600 hectares and shaped by the Murghab River delta. The city of Merv al-Shāhidjān is in the south central part of the oasis, on the main east–west route to Bukhara, with the city of Samarkand to the north-west and Persia and Afghanistan to the south. Situated in Khurāsān, it was a major administrative, military, and political center from the Arab-Muslim conquest beyond the Syr Daryā River (Gibb 1970: 15–17, based on Balādhurī, Yaʿqubī, and Narshakhī). The history of city events is dense and well described (Ṭabarī, Ibn Ḥawkal, Iṣṭakhrī, Muqadassī, etc.) (see Herrmann 1999, Kennedy 1999: 27–44).

FIGURE 5.1.6 Yujno turkmenistanskoj arheologicheskoj komplex ékspedicii̇ Team in Merv, in 1963; right to left: Kasimova, Lunina, Yudinckii̇, Masson, Aliev, Gulamov.

Courtesy of YUTAKE (1972).

Under the Abbasids, Merv remained the capital of K͟hurāsān province and was then the capital of the Great Seljuk Empire (11th–13th centuries) until the Mongol sack.

From 1946, the South Turkmenistan Multi-Disciplinary Archaeological Expedition (IUTAKE) under the supervision of Masson started regular archaeological seasons. Near the center and northwestern portions of Gyaur-Kala, they excavated a Bani Makhan mosque with a large cistern and several two-stage kilns, the remains of 9th-, 10th-, to 12th-century occupation (Trenches 10, 16–19). Near the mosque, 11th-century (?) Islamic burials were encountered (Trenches 7 and 13) (Herrmann et al., 1993: 43). Russian research continued under Khodzhanyazov and Koshlenko (c. 1980s–1990s).

More recently British–Turkmen investigations (1992–2000) under Georgina Herrmann and St. John Simpson conducted topographic and geophysical surveys, evaluation trenches, and five major excavations. A surface survey, conducted in Gyaur Kala (the pre-Islamic Merv city) has demonstrated population development in continuity with late Sasanian occupation. Population is denser in the south and in the center around the Friday mosque (9th-10th centuries) along an east–west roadway. Settlement seems be concentrated between the mosque in the center and the western city gate in the 11th-12th centuries (Herrmann 1994: 59, 61, fig. 1), which is somewhat at variance with previous hypotheses (Hiebert 1992: 120–121). The medieval city of the Abbasids and

Seljuks developed on both sides of Gyaur Kala. On the east Shaim Kala, hypothetically a Seljuk military camp (not confirmed by the ceramics found), was largely destroyed under a contemporary Soviet village (Herrmann 1995: 57–59).

In the west, the new city, the so-called Sultan Kala, was probably walled by Sultan Malik shāh (1072–92), and the newly founded city could have been planned following Arab-Muslim ideology (Williams 2007: 59–60). The walls of Sultan Kala city and its citadel (the so-called Shahriyar Ark) include stairways, galleries, towers, and posterns. The corroded fortifications remain up to a height of 8 meters, with towers at regular intervals and four gates. These were of 11th- and 13th-century date (Herrmann et al. 1999, 2000). The city is nearly rectangular and encloses 400 hectares protected by walls, and it was densely occupied with a large number of houses set out on a grid system of streets. Aerial photographs suggest the city was subdivided into quarters on both sides of a central east–west axis, suggesting this is the older one and, consequently, that the city developed from there towards the north and south.

Markets and bazaars were located in the central area. Water was provided by the Razik Canal running south–north between Gyaur Kala and Sultan Kala. The canal network was expanded by narrower branches into the whole city (Williams 2007: 55). On the north-east corner lay a walled citadel (Shahriyar Ark, nearly 25 hectares), probably constructed in the 11th century. A monumental rectangular building of about twenty-seven rooms around a courtyard with two Saljuk and post-Mongol occupation levels was excavated on the citadel and interpreted as an "elite domestic structure" probably for the Merv governors (Herrmann 1996: 17–19, 1997: 22).

Next to the Friday mosque in Gyaur kala, some early Islamic archaeological remains (9th-10th centuries) indicate numerous workshops specializing in different types of alloys (copper, iron, and steel). The remains of four steel furnaces may have produced tools or weapons (sabers, knives) not found during excavations (Herrmann 1997). It indicates that Merv was a major technological center for steel although there are no local sources for ores. The western suburbs of Sultan Kala also provided data on other economic activities: large potter's workshops (10th–13th centuries), especially producing molded ceramics, were dated to the Middle Islamic period (Lunina 1962). Timurid ceramics show long-term occupation (Lunina 1969). The city was also famed for textile production in cotton and ibrîsm silk (Serjeant 1972: 87–90), but it remains extremely difficult to identify archaeological evidence of this.

One of the medieval cemeteries of the Merv oasis was investigated (Pilipko 1969), but it was mainly the large funerary mausoleums which were abundantly and carefully documented, generally by architects. For example, the mausoleum of Sultan Sanjar (d. 1157) on the east–west axis, today visible in aerial photographs, shows that it was part of a larger complex (see Mamedov 2004). Among other interesting buildings which have been identified as Seljuk on the basis of brick size and ornamental brickwork is the mausoleum of Muhammad ibn Zayd; a Kufic inscription in the dome chamber indicated it was built in 1112. Some twenty small fortified houses or palaces called *köshks/kuŝks* with rooms arranged around a courtyard are typical in Central Asian architecture, some of them with patterns of exterior walls with corrugations. Other interesting buildings include Kepter Khana (a dovecote) and a 12th-century *namazgah* in the western *rabad* (Kochnev 1976: 23–27). The remains of caravanserai have been found between the city walls of Sultan Kala and Great Kyz Kala toward the south-west. Still to be discovered are the Seljuk observatory and the dozen libraries described in the sources which attracted and led to the academic training of many scholars such as Bīrūnī, Omar Khayyam, al-Marwazī, al-Kharaqī, and al-Khazīnī.

The new and smaller Timurid fortified city, known today as Abdullah Khan Kala (more than 70 hectares) was built 2 kilometers south of Sultān Kala by Shah Rukh (1408–1447) (Obel'shenko 1963: 363). Seven building phases were seen in a comprehensive study (Brun 2003). Three Timurid mausolea at Geok Gumbaz, the Talkhattan Baba Mosque, and the extensively restored mausolea of Imām Bakr and Imām shāfi'īt in the Talkhattan cemetery, and three large ice-houses and pavilions were also built during the Timurid period (see Petersen 1997; Herrmann 1999; Mamedov 2011).

Publications related to Merv are abundant, first in Russian and published in a dozen volumes (Trudy YUTAKE) (cf. Herrmann et al 1993: 41–43), then recent research in English, with excavations, military architecture, and Islamic numismatics published in the journal *Iran* (1993–2001). A final monograph focused on monumental architecture gives a place to medieval historical sources and the development of the Islamic city (Herrmann 1999). Merv was inscribed on the UNESCO World Heritage Site list in 1999. In the recent past, Williams and Kurbanshakhatov (2001–2005) focused on road networks into the oasis in connection with long-distance trade.

THE SYR DARYĀ BASIN

This encompasses a geographical region shared by four countries: Uzbekistan, northern Tajikistan, Kyrgyzstan, and southern Kazakhstan. In the medieval period, its eastern part forms the regions of Ilaq and Farghāna (today shared between Uzbekistan, Tadjikistan, and Kyrgyzstan). These regions are the easternmost of the Islamic world, bordering Kazakhstan and China. They are traditionally inhabited by nomadic Turks since the 7th–8th centuries (Turgesh, Karluks, and others) and belatedly Islamized during the 9th–10th centuries. The archaeological map of southern Kyrgyzstan was begun by Bernshtam in the early 1940s. Toponymy and the attribution of cities, including the two Qarakhanid capitals (992–1211), Uzgend and Balasaghun, have been the subject of considerable discussion in Russian literature (Masson Goriacheva 1985).

Uzgen was the second capital of the Farghāna region, from the second half of the 11th century until the death of the last Qarakhānid in 1212. The city is built between two rivers, Yassi in the north and Kara Daryā in the south. It is the fourth largest town in Farghāna, covering 1,200–1,500 hectares. It is spread over several terraces and consists of four *shahrestan* separated by ravines and protected by an enclosure (Goriacheva 1983, plan of the city pl. 15). Five soundings were conducted on the citadel in 1885 by Vesselovskiĭ, then by Bernshtam, and finally by the Yujno Kirgizskogo team in 1953–1954.

Excavations were carried out on the citadel in the center of the city (Sharestan 3); these established three periods of occupation (between the 11th and 13th centuries), with different levels of habitat with clay pipelines and big refuse pits, dumping grounds that contained ceramics (lamps; ceramic tables so-called *dastakhan*; glazed or unglazed pottery shards with molded decorations) and glass fragments. However, few complete structures were identified. One product of regional ceramics production stands out, modeled with a glazed paint decoration (Zadneprovskiĭ 1960: 226, pl.48–49). Traces of a glassmaker's workshop have been identified but not excavated in the second *shahrestan*.

To the west, a first cemetery (Shahrestan 1) replaces the center of the city from the middle of the 12th century, which moved toward the northwest (Goriacheva 2001: 108). This Islamic cemetery has many tombstones (reusing large stones polished by the river; these are called *qayrak*). According to the study of epitaphs and *kunya*, Goriacheva and Nastich establish connections between the sheikhs of Farghāna and those of the Khurāsānian sect of Karramiyya, active in Nishapur under Maḥmūd Ghaznavī (d. 993) and his son Abū Bakr Muḥammad (d. after 1030) (Goriacheva and Nastich 1983: 190–191).

To the east there is a second cemetery (Shahrestan 4), at the northeastern end of which there are three contiguous Qarakhānid mausoleums (Figure 5.1.7). Their complex fired-brick decorations and monumental inscriptions are characteristic of funerary architecture. They were excavated by the Bernshtam team before being restored in the 1980s. The first is the one of Tughrīl Khan Husayn (Qarakhānid of the eastern branch) who died in 1152 (according to its inscription read by Iakubovskiĭ in 1947), probably built next to his father's. The third dates back to some twenty years later (first quarter of the 13th century). A hundred meters to the north of the mausoleum, a Friday mosque and a *madrassa* were demolished to build the school of the modern city. Only the mid–11th-century minaret, with a conical shaft form on a square podium, is visible today.

FIGURE 5.1.7 Reverse of Kirgizistan banknote of 50 Som. 1994 series (public domain).

Further east toward China, the caravans had to stop in the caravanserais located on the edge of the cities. In very high mountain areas, such as the Tian Shan, several caravanserais remain in present-day Kirgizistan. The best known, built in stone, is probably Tash Rabat (3,500 meters altitude) dated to the 8th–12th centuries (cf. Peregudova 1989).

To the west of Farghāna is medieval Usrūshana and its capital Bundjikat (Shahrestan, north of present-day Tajikistan). Several large buildings in two lower towns and one citadel were partially excavated by the Sharistanskogo team (Negmatov 1953; Negmatov and Hmelniskiĭ 1966). The palace of Afshin attracted most attention, being characterized by a monumental hall (230 square meters) built of mudbrick and probably with wood columns. The walls were covered with plaster and painted murals (7th–8th centuries). The most famous is one depicting a wolf nursing two babies. Nearly in the center and southern part of the site, a large temple with columns was transformed into a mosque. Apart from the potters' workshops discovered on the edge of the medieval *rabad*, north-east of the Zeravshan River bordering the city, other handicraft activities are unknown (Samoĭlik 1978).

BORDER TOWNS ON THE
BANKS OF THE STEPPE

As early as the 19th century, several imperial commissions carried out scientific expeditions to southern Kazakhstan, notably the one led by Lerkh, who prospected the medieval towns (Sauran, Djankent, etc.), and Barthold, who carried out a study mission in the valleys of Cu and Talas in 1893–1894 (Akishev 1979: 9–11). It was between 1936 and 1940 that the first excavations began in the medieval towns of Ṭarāz, Talgar, and Dungene (Akishev and Baipakov 1979: 14). Then, in 1960–1970, seventy sites were prospected, surveyed, and covered by aerial photos; more than twenty publications present the detailed surveys of the Talas, Karatau, Chu, and Semiretche regions (Ageeva and Pacevitch 1958; Kozhemiako 1959). A first synthesis of archaeological work, all periods combined, was carried out from the end of the 1970s (Akishev and Baĭpakov 1979). Subsequently, the team of the Institute of Archaeology was very active in the first decade of the new millennia on about twenty sites (Kerder, Kuĭruk Tobe, Jajik, Turkestan, Sauran, etc.) (Baĭpakov 2012: 16–17, 23–24).

More recently a joint Kazakh-Russian-German archaeological expedition has been working near the mouth of the Syr Daryā in the eatern Aral region, at Djankent (2011–2016) (Härke and Arzhantseva 2016; Arzhantseva et al. 2017). The north of the Syr Daryā Basin was subdivided into valleys; Talas, Tchou, and Illy (medieval Semiretche). Border and commercial cities like Otrar, Sairam, Ṭarāz, and about forty others developed between the 10th and the 13th centuries (Figure 5.1.8). These were connected with Turk Toghuz-Oghuz nomads, and the prosperity of the cities was accompanied by the development of irrigation (Grocev 1985: 125–127; Härke and Arzhantseva 2016: 887, 889).

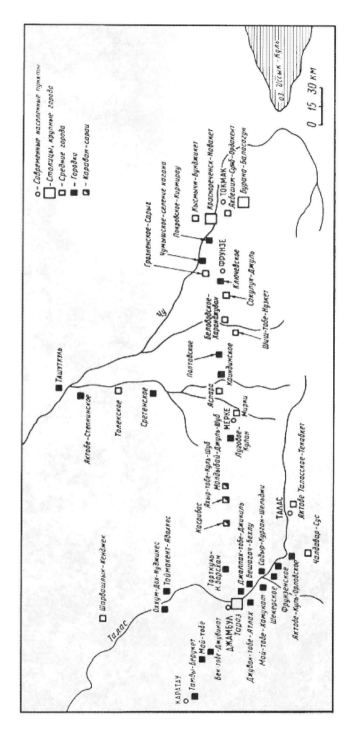

FIGURE 5.1.8 Archaeological map of South Kazakhstan medieval cities of the 9th–12th centuries investigated by the Kazakh Archaeological Institute.

Courtesy of Baipakov, Mariashev (2011).

At the confluence of the Arys and Syr Daryā Rivers, along the major arteries that follow them, the most important caravan city between the 10th and 14th centuries was Otrar (Farab). Although the Qarakhānids reigned in Otrar between 1173 and 1210, few structures of this period remain (for the medieval sources, see Akishev Baïpakov and Erzakovich 1972: 26–43). Erkasov was the first to excavate in Otrar in 1904, and systematic excavations began in 1969 and provided a first plan of the citadel (Akishev and Baïpakov 1979: 19). The citadel is located between 10 and 15 meters above the steppe, on an area of about 15 hectares. Several two- or three-room houses with courtyards (with a hearth built in the center of the room and *mastaba* along the walls) have been excavated and belong to the Middle Islamic levels (9th–13th centuries) (Akishev Baïpakov and Erzakovich 1972). The excavations in the upper city were extended in 1971–1976 to about 60,000 square meters and have revealed several densely populated neighborhoods built around narrow streets.

The housing area of the western sector extends over more than 500 × 200 meters and is dated from the 13th to 16th centuries (Akishev and Baïpakov 1979: 119, 122). In spite of the conflict between Djudshidami and Dshaghatai in the 13th–14th centuries, for the control of the middle course of the Syr Daryā River and the Otrar region, urban growth developed in the 14th century, then declined until the middle of the 18th century. Discoveries on the citadel are related to these late Islamic periods (16th–18th centuries) (Baïpakov, Akishev and Erzakovi 1981). The lower city (*rabad*) is unwalled and spread around the citadel in the 13th–14th centuries. It is still little known, despite excavations of a large bath with its hypocaust system on the southwestern side (Baïpakov, Akishev and Erzakovi 1987: 117–119, pl. 42) and also some potters' workshops on the southeastern side.

Further north in the Dzhambul region, surveys and soundings were carried out in the medieval town of Ornek in 1992 and 1993. They highlighted expanded Islamic housing that was probably semipermanent (Northedge and Rousset, 1995). To the east, above the Alatau ranges, lay the Cu region and Balasaghun city (founded in 940; Nevaket in Arabic sources, actual Burana) the second capital of the Qarakhānid kaghanat during the 11th–12th centuries, then capital of the Kara Khitaï (Western Liao) from 1130–1131. The city probably replaced Ak Beshim, located 5 kilometers north, which declined in the late 10th century according to recent Japano–Kirghiz survey (Abe 2014: 15). Balasaghun did not have a citadel, but a quadrangular wall with defensive towers surrounding the rabad (c. 2,500–3000 hectares) (Masson Goriacheva, 1985: pl. 4–5). Two large mounds in the central part of the *shahrestan* were excavated and show the existence of a 8th- or 9th–century castle (unpublished Vedutova 1984–1990). The city is well known because of the preserved minaret (11th century) over an octogonal podium; it is more than 21 meters high and was about 40 meters high initially.

This was probably a wooden mosque because various excavations have never uncovered any brick masonry (Masson Goriacheva 1985: 52). Three mausoleums were investigated, an octahedron and two cylindrical ones with portals, some of them decorated with stucco and paintings, surrounded by tombstones (*qayrak*) with Turkish or Arabic engravings (studied by Nastich 1983). A one-room mosque-mausoleum with stucco decoration was partly excavated in 1979 and then in 1984–1986. Restoration of the masonry, floors, and façades indicates several rebuilding phases. According to Masson Goriacheva (1985), the mosque and mausoleums represent a single *khānaqāh*-type worship complex, probably the original center of the 11th-century city.

In the south-west *rabad*, a large 11th- or 12th-century palace (1,550 square meters) was excavated in 1972–1974 (Masson and Goriacheva 1985: 62–63). A central courtyard reached two complexes of a dozen rooms each, and a corridor measuring 28 × 4 meters led to three rooms entirely decorated with stucco. As stated by Kolchenko "a series of other residential structures and the overall plan of Burana remain unstudied" (Kolchenko 2017: 19). In the *rabad*, at least two cemeteries were found, and a study of the Syriac inscriptions on the gravestones (in 1885) confirm the presence of an important Nestorian community. Those in Arabic were published some years later (in 1888) by the Moscow archaeological commission (Goriacheva 1983: 24).

CONCLUSION

Discussion has mainly concentrated on the pre-Mongol period until the 13th century. The archaeological data on the post-Mongol period (14th–17th centuries) are less well explored but no less numerous. In most cities, the urban center shifts, but occupation is continuous. Islamic buildings remain abundant and have often been surveyed and well-studied by Russian architects. However, the domestic structures of the Timurid and Shaybanid periods (14th–16th centuries) are not well preserved, and archaeological levels are generally less well known, but are identified by characteristic glazed ceramic objects (cf. Mirzaahmedov 1981, 1990) or by well-known coinage (Szuppe 1997; Babadjanov, Muminov, and Paul 1997).

Anyone unfamiliar with this geographical area will be struck by the intensity of research that has been conducted there for 150 years, published in the form of thousands of articles and books in Russian and supported by a strong Soviet cartographic tradition. A large number of surveys followed the course of the great rivers and their tributaries and engendered a multiplicity of studies in the field of medieval Islamic studies (textual, built or funerary architecture, historical geography and epigraphy, etc.). Islamic numismatic works are also numerous (e.g., those of Davidovich, Kochnev, Fedorov, Daudi). The whole set of data provides an unprecedented and interdisciplinary approach to medieval society and its inhabitants. As we can see, urban archaeology has undergone unparalleled development, and more than a hundred medieval medium and large cities have been identified and studied by Russian-speaking researchers.

Despite the new approaches adopted since independence, there is a lack of synthesis on, for example, domestic architecture or industrial activities (pottery, glass, metallurgy) (Figure 5.1.9). The geographical fragmentation of the region and the many people involved in research do not facilitate the sharing of work. We can only hope for a greater number of collaborations between Western archaeologists and colleagues from Central

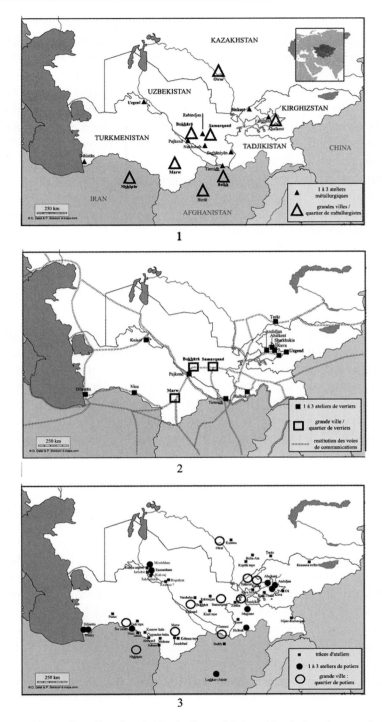

FIGURE 5.1.9 Maps of handicraft activities in Central Asian cities (9th-13th centuries) based on archaeological evidence: 1. metallurgy workshops, 2. glass workshops, 3. pottery workshops.

Courtesy of Simeon (2018).

Asia. It is also regrettable that there are no thematic or multidisciplinary summaries devoted solely to the Islamic period (except for southern Kazakhstan). The understanding of the medieval and modern architecture or material culture of several big cities such as Samarkand, Pajkend, Tirmidh, Urgenç, and Merv, based on dozens of publications spread over fifty years, is often difficult, and maps gathering together medieval sites generally are missing. We can only encourage the archaeologists in charge of these files to complete them. Moreover, preservation of the Islamic cities and archeological sites is a real challenge confronting all researchers involved in Central Asia.

REFERENCES

Abe, M. 2014. "Results of the Archaeological Project at Ak Beshim (Suyab), Kyrgyz Republic from 2011 to 2013 and a Note on the Site`s Abandonment," *Intercultural Understanding*, 4, 11–16.

Adylov, Sh. T., and Mirzaahmedov, D. K. 2001. "Iz istory Drevnego goroda Vardana I vladeniya obaviya," *Istoriya Materialnoĭ Kultury Uzbekistana*, 32, 150–157.

Ahrarov, I. K., and Rempel, L., 1971. *Reznoj ëtuk Afrasiaba*, (Tashkent: Izdatel'stvo Literatury i Iskusstva im. Gafura Guliama).

Aigle D., 2005. *Le Fârs sous la domination Mongole, politique et fiscalité (XIIIe-XVe s.)*, Studia Iranica Cahier 31, (Louvain: Peeters).

Akishev, K. A., and Baïpakov, K. M. 1979. *Voprosy arheologiĭ Kazahstana* (Alma-Ata: Nauka).

Akishev, K. A., Baïpakov, K. M., and Erzakovich, L. V. 1972. *Drevnij Otrar-Topografiya, stratigrafiya I perspectivy* (Alma-Ata: Nauka).

Amirov, Š. 2011. "Archaeological Aspects of the Early Islamic Period in Khorezm," *Archäologische Mitteilungen aus Iran und Turan*, 42, 59–66.

Atagarryev, E. 1986. *Srednevekoviĭ Dehistan* (Ashhabad: Izdatel'stvo Nauk).

Babadjanov, B., Muminov, A., and Paul, J., 1997. *Schaibanidische Grabinschriften* (Wiesbaden: Ludvig Reichter Verlag).

Badr, J., and Tupev, M. 2012. "The Khoja Zainuddin Mosque in Bukhara," *Muqarnas*, 29, 213–243.

Baïpakov, K. M., Akishev, K. A., and Erzakovi, L B., 1981. *Pozdnesrednevekovyij Otrar (XVI-XVIII vv)* (Alma ata: Izd Nauk).

Baïpakov, K. M., Akishev, K. A., and Erzakovi, L B., 1987. *Otrar v XIII-XV vekah* (Alma ata: Izdatelsstvo Nauka Kazahskoj, SSR).

Baïpakov, K. M. 2012. *Islamskaya arheologicheskaya arhitektura i arheologiya Kazahstana* (Almaty: Kazahstanskoe Arheologicheskoe obshchestvo).

Barthold, V. V. 1928 (1910). *Turkestan Down to the Mongol Invasion*, Translated from the Russian by H. A. R. Gibb (London: Oxford University Press and Luzac & Co).

Beckwith, C. I. 1987. *The Tibetan Empire in Central Asia A History of the Struggle for Great Power Among Tibetans, Turks, Arabs, and Chinese during the Early Middle Ages* (Princeton: Princeton University Press).

Belenitskiĭ, A. M., Bentovič, I. B., and Boleakov, O. G., 1973. *Srednevkovij gorod Sredneĭ Aziĭ*, (Leningrad: AN SSR Institut Arheologiĭ).

Bernard, P., Grenet, F., and Isamiddinov, M. 1990. "Fouilles de la mission franco-soviétique à l'ancienne Samarkand (Afrasiab): première campagne, 1989," *Comptes rendus des séances de l'Académie des Inscriptions et Belles-Lettres*, 134, 2, 356–380.

Bretanickij, L. S. 1950. "Architekturnye pamyatniki Gissara," *Materialy I Issledovanniya po arheologiï SSR*, 15, 199–206.

Brun, P. 2003. "Krepost steni pozdnih gorodiëe Merva", *Cultural Values*, 11.

Bubnova, M. A. 1963. "Dobicha serebro-svintsovikh rud v Shel'dzhi v IX-XIII vv," *Arkheologishekie pamiatniki Talaskoj Doliny*, ((Frunze Izdat'elstvo AN Kirg SSSR), 225–262.

Bubnova, M. A. 1993. *Drevnie rudoznatsy Pamira* (Dushanbe: Izdat'elstvo Instituti Donië).

Bubnova, M. A. 2007. *Gorno-badakhshanskaya avtonomnaya oblast, zapadniï pamir; (pamiatniki kamennogo veka –XXv)* (Dushanbe: AN respubliki Tadzhikistana).

Bulatov, M. 1976. *Mavzolej Samanidov jemchujina arhitektury Srednej Aziï* (Tashkent: Izdatel'stvo Literatury I isskustva im. Gafura Guliama).

Bulatov, M. 1986. *Observatoriya Ulugbeka v Samarkande* (Tashkent: Izdatel'stvo Istoriko-astonomicheskie Issledovaniya, XVIII).

Buriakov, Yu. F., Sadiev, M., and Fedorov, M. K. 1975. "Sobornaya mechet' Samarkanda v XI–nach. XIII vv," *Afrasiab*, 4, 77–99.

Buriakov, Yu. F., and Tashodzhaev, Sh. C. 1975. "Istoricheskaya Topografiya Samarkanda XI-nachala XIII vv," *Afrasiab*, 4, 6–22.

Bobomullaev, S. 2015. *Drevnejëaia I Drevniaia Istoriia Gissara* (Dushanbe: AN Tadjikistana Instituti Istorii Donië).

Denike, B. P. 1939a. *Arhitekturnij Ornament Srednej Aziï* (Moskva i Leningrad: Izdatel'stvo Vsesoyuznoï Akademiï Arhitektury).

Denike, B. P. 1939. "Reznaja dekorovka zdaniya raskopannoga v Termeze," in *mezhdunarodny kongres po iranskomu iskusstvu i arheologiï* (Izdatel'stvo AN SSR), 104–106.

Gaube, H. 2004. "The Origin of the Plan of Some Early Medieval Cities in Transoxiana and Eastern Iran," *Transoxiana*, 245–248.

Gibb, H. A. R. 1970 (1923). *The Arab Conquests in Central Asia* (London: James Forlong Foundation vol. III).

Goriacheva, V. D. 1983. *Srednevekovye gorodskie centry i arhitekturnye ansambli Kirgiziï. Burana, Uzgen, Safed-Bulan* (Frunze: Izdat'elstvo Institut Istoriï AN Kirgizskoï SSR, ILIM).

Goriacheva, G. 2001. "A propos de deux capitales du Khaganat Karakhanid," *Etudes Karakhanide, cahier de l'IFEAC*, 9, 91–114.

Gorshenina, S. 2000. La route de samarcande, l'asie centrale dans les objectifs des voyageurs d'autrefois (Genève: olizane eds.).

Gorshenina, S. 2003. *Explorateurs en Asie centrale: Voyageurs et aventuriers de Marco-Polo à Ella Maillart* (Genève: olizane eds.).

Gorshenina, S. 2011. "D e l'archéologie russo-soviétique en situation coloniale à l'archéologie postcoloniale en Asie centrale," in A. Galitzine-Loumpet, Sv. Gorshenina, and Cl. Rapin (éds.), *Archéologie(s) en situation coloniale: paradigmes et politiques* (vol. 1), *Nouvelles de l'archéologie*, 126, 29–33.

Gorshenina, S. 2012. *Asie centrale, L'invention des frontières et l'héritage russo-soviétique* (Paris: CNRS editions).

Gorshenina, S. 2013. "L'archéologie française dans l'Asie centrale soviétique et post-soviétique," *Cahiers de l'IFEAC*, 15, 25–40.

Grenet, F. 2002. "SAMARKAND i. History and Archeology," in *Encyclopaedia Iranica Fasc*, (New York: Columbia University), 2.

Grenet, F. 2005. "Maracanda/Samarkand, une métropole pré-mongole. Sources écrites et Archéologie," *Annales. Histoire, Sciences Sociales*, 59e année, 1043–1067.

Grenet, F. 2008. "Le palais de Nasr Ibn Sayyâr," in E. De La Vaissiere (ed.), *Islamisation de l'Asie centrale, processus locaux d'acculturation du VIIe au XIIe siècle* (Paris: Studia Iranica cahier 39), 11–28.

Grocev, V. A. 1985. *Irrigatsiia Ujnogo Kazakhstana v srednie veka*, (Alma ata: Nauka Izdat'elstvo Nauka Kazahskoj SSR).

Harke, H., and Arzhatseva, I., 2016. "Some theories, models and analogies for Dzhankent: A context for early medieval urbanization on the lower Syr-Darya," *World of Great Altai*, 2(4.2), 886–896.

Herrmann, G., and Kurbansakhatov K. 1995. "The International Merv project: Preliminary report on the third season (1994)," *Iran*, 33, 31–60

Herrmann, G., Kurbans Hakhatov, K., and Simpson St J. 1996. "The International Merv project: Preliminary report on the fourth season (1995)," *Iran*, 34, 1–22.

Herrmann, G., Kurbanshakhatov, K., and Simpson St. J. et al., 1997. "The International Merv project: Preliminary report on the fifth season," *Iran*, 35, 1–33.

Herrmann, G., 1997. "Early and Mediaeval Merv, A tale of three cities," *Proceedings of the British Academy*, 94, 1–43.

Herrmann, G. 1999. *Monuments of Merv Traditional Buildings of the Karakum* (London: The Society of Antiquaries of London No. 62).

Herrmann, G., Kurbanshakhatov K., and Simpson St. J. 1998. "The International Merv project: Preliminary report on the sixth season (1997)," *Iran*, 36, 53–75.

Herrmann, G., Kurbanshakhatov, K., and Simpson, St. J. 1999. "The International Merv Project. Preliminary Report on the Seventh Season (1998)," *Iran*, 37, 1–24.

Herrmann, G., Kurbanshakhatov, K., and Simpson, St. J. 2000. "The International Merv Project. Preliminary Report on the Eighth Season (1999)," *Iran*, 38, 1–31.

Herrmann, G., Masson, V.M., and Kurbansakhatov, K. 1993. "The International Merv Project. Preliminary Report on the First Season (1992)," *Iran*, 31, 39–62.

Hiebert, F. 1992. "The Oasis and City of Merv (Turkmenistan)," *Archéologie Islamique*, 3, 111–125.

Hmelniskiĭ, S. 1996. *Meždu Samanidami I Mongolami. Arhitectura Sredneĭ Aziĭ XI-nachala XIII, chast 1* (Berlin-Riga: Izdat'elstvo Gamajun).

Hodjaniazov, G. H., Yusupov, N. Yu., Kdyrniazov, M. Sh., Torebekov, A., Avisova, A., Saipanov, B., and Bagdasarova, N. 1989. "Arheologicheskie issledovaniya v nekropole Mizdahkan," *Vestnik Karakalpakskogo filiala Akademiĭ Nauk Uzbekskoĭ Sovetskoĭ Socialisticheskoĭ Respubliki*, 3, 65–70

Iagodin, V. N. 2002. "Contribution à la géographie historique du delta de l'Amou Darya du VIIe au XIVe siècles," *Cahiers d'Asie Centrale*, 10, 11–49.

Iakubovskiĭ, A. Y. 1930. *Razvaliny Urgencha*, Izvestiya Gosudarstvennoĭ akademiĭ istoriĭ Materialnoĭ Kultury, 6/2 (Leningrad: GAIMK).

Iiasov, Dj. Rusanov, D. V. 1988. "Klad srednevekovyh bronzovih izdelii s gorodishe Budrac," *Obshestvennye Nauki v Uzbekistane*, 1, 27–31.

Karev, Y. 2000. "Un palais islamique du VIIIe siècle à Samarkand," *Studia Iranica*, 29, 2, 273–296.

Karev, Y. 2003. "Un cycle de peintures murales d'époque Qarâkhânide (XIIème-XIIIème siècles) à la citadelle de Samarkand: le souverain et le peintre," in *Comptes rendus de l'Académie des Inscriptions et Belles-Lettres* (Paris: Académie des Inscriptions et des Belles Lettres), 1685–1731.

Karev, Y. 2005. "Qarâkhânid wall paintings in the citadel of Samarqand. First report and preliminay observations," *Muqarnas*, 22, 45–84.

Kdyrniazov, M. Š. 1989. *Materialnaia kultura gorodov Horezma v XIII-XIVv* (Nukus: Izdatel'stvo Karakalpakistan).

Kennedy, H. 1999. "Medieval Merv: An Historical Overview," in G. Herrmann (ed.), *Monuments of Merv Traditionnal Buildings of the Karakum* (London: The Society of Antiquaries of London), 26–44.

Kes, A. C., Kostyucenko, V. P., and Lisitsinag, N. 1980. *Istoriya zaseleniya I drevniee oroshenie Yugo-Zapadnoï Turkmeniï* (Moskva: Akademiya Nauk SSR, Institut geografiï, Izdatel'stvo Nauka).

Kochnev, B. D. 1976. *Srednevekovye zagorodnye kultobye sooruzheniya Sredneï Aziï* (Tashkent: Izdatel'stvo FAN Uzbekskoï SSR).

Kolchenko, V. 2017. "Medieval Towns in the Chuy Valley, Burana, Ak Beshim, Krasnaja Rechka," in B. Amambaeva and K. Yamauchi (eds.), *Protection and Research on Cultural Heritage in the Chuy Valley, the Kyrghyz Republic, Ak-Beshim and Ken-Bulun*, vol. 13 (Tokyo: Japan Center for International Cooperation in Conservation), 7–29.

Kozhemiako, P. N. 1959. *Rannesrednevekovye goroda poseleniya Chujskoï doliny* (Frunze: AN Kirgizskoï SSR).

Leriche, P., and Pidaev, ž. 2007. *Termez sur l'Oxus Cité capitale d'Asie Centrale* (Paris/Tashkent: Ifeac, Maisonneuve et Larose).

Leriche, P. 2013. "L'apport de la Mission archéologique Franco-Ouzbèke (MAFouz) de Bactrianne du Nord à l'Histoire de l'Asie centrale," *Cahiers de l'IFEAC*, 15, 135–164.

Lunina, S. B. 1962. "Goncharnoe proizvodstvo v Merve X-nachala XIII vv, Keramika antichnogo i srednevekovogo Merva," *Trudy yujno turkmenistanskoï arheologičeskoï komplex ékspediciï*, 11, 217–248.

Lunina, S. B. 1969. "Novye sbory Timuridskoï keramiki v yujnom Turkmenistane," *Obshchestvennye Nauki v Uzbekistane*, 8–9, 89–92.

Mamedov, M. 2011. *Gadymy Merw e beyik Seljuklar binagärlik zamanynyn medeniyeti. Usti yetirilen ikinji nesir* (Ashhabad: Turkmen State Publishing).

Mamedov, M., and Muradov, R. 1998. *Arhitektura Turkmenistana, kratkaya istoriya* (Moskva: Interstamo).

Mamedov, M. A. 2004. *Mavzoleï Sultana Sandjara* (Istanbul: UNDP).

Mamedov, M. A., and Muradov, R. G. 2000. *Gurgandj, arhitekturnyï putevoditel, Programma razvitya OON* (Istanbul: UNDP).

Martínez Ferreras, V. 2009. *Preliminary report of the Int. Pluridisciplinary Archaeological Expedition to Bactria*, vol. IV, unpublished.

Masson, M. 1940. "Gorodiña starogo Termeza i ih izu[1]enie," *Trudy Uzbekistanskogo filiala AN SSR*, seriia 1, vyp. 2, 5–102.

Masson, M. 1941. "Gorodishcha starogo Termeza v ih izuchenya," in *Sbornik Termezkaya arheologicheskaya kompleksnaya ékspediciya 1936 g* (Tashkent: Izdatel'stvo AN SSR), 5–122.

Masson, M. E., and Goriacheva, V. D. 1985. *Burana, Istoriya Izucheniya gorodishcha i ego arhitektunyh pamatnikov* (Frunze: Institut Istoriï Akademiya Nauk Kirgizskoï SSR, ILIM).

Mirzaahmedov, D. K. 1981. "Glazurovannaya keramika Buhary vtoroï poloviny XVII-pervoï poloviny XVIII vv," *Istoriya materialnoï kultury Uzbekistana*, 16, 96–113.

Mirzaahmedov, D. K. 1990. "Glazurovannaya keramika Tashkenta XVII v," in *Archeologisheskih raboty na vovostroykah Uzbekistana* (Tashkent: AN Uzbekistan, Izdat'eltsvo FAN), 53–65.

Mirzaahmedov, D. K., and Stark, S. 2012. "Raboty Uzbekskogo-americanskoï ékspeditsiï po izucheniyu oasisnoï steny Buhary Kampir-Devor," *Arheologicheskie Issledovanniya v Uzbekistane*, 8, 191–202.

Muhamedjanov, A. P., Adylov, Sh. T., Mirzaahmedov, D. K., and Semionov, G. L. 1988. *Gorodishche Pajkend. k probleme izucheniya srednievekovogo goroda Sredneĭ Azii* (Tashkent: Izdatel'stvo FAN Uz. SSR).

Nastich, V. N. 1983. "Arabskie i persidskie nadpisi na kaĭrakah s gorodishcha," in E. A. Davidovich (ed.), *Kirgiziya pri Karahanidah* (Frunze: Izdaťelstvo Institut Istorii AN Kirgizskoĭ SSR, ILIM), 221–234.

Naymark, A. 1999. "The Size of Samanid Bukhara: A Note on Settlement Patterns in Early Islamic Mawarannahr," in A. Petruccioli (ed.), *Bukhara: The Myth and the Architecture* (Cambridge MA: AKPIA at MIT/Harvard University), 39–60.

Negmatov, N. 1953. "Istoriko-geograficheskij ocherk Usrushany s drevneĭshih vremen po X vv," *Materialy I Issledovaniya po Arheologii SSR*, 7, 231–252.

Nekrasova, E. 1999. "La citadelle de Bukhārā," *Archéologie Islamique*, 8–9, 37–54.

Nemtseva, I. B. 1983. *Rabat-i Malik. 'Arheologicheskie issledovaniya 1973–1975, 1977 gg'in Hudozhestvennaya Kuľtura Sredneĭ Azii IX-XIIIvv* (Tashkent: Izdatel'stvo Literatury I isskustva im. Gafura Guliama), 112–148.

Nemtseva, N. B. 2009. *Rabat-i Malik, XI nacalo XVIII vv (arheologiceskie issledovaniya)* (Tashkent: Institut Français d'Etudes sur l'Asie centrale, Doc 33).

Nemtseva, N. B., Shvab, Yu. Z. 1979. *Ansambl' Shah-i Zinda, Istoriko-arhitekturnyj ocherk* (Tashkent: Izdatel'stvo Literatury I isskustva im. Gafura Guliama).

Northedge, A., and Rousset, M. O. 1995. "Ornek, étape de la "route de la soie," *Archéologie islamique*, 5, 97–121.

Obel'shenko, O. V. 1963. "Gorodishcha starogo merva Abdulla-Han kala i Baĭram-Ali-Han-kala v svete rabot Yutake 1950 g," *Trudy yujno turkmenistanskoĭ arheologičeskoĭ komplex ékspedicii*, 12, 309–349.

Omel'chenko, A. B., and Mirzaahmedov, D. K. (eds.) 2015. *Buharskiĭ oasis i ego sosedi v drevnosti i Srenevekov'e. Na osnove Materialov nauchnyh konferencii 2010 i 2011 gg. Trudy Gosudarstvennogo Érmitazha*, 75 (Sank Petersbourg: Izdatel'stvo Érmitazh).

Peregudova, S. I. A. 1989. *Tash Rabat (po materialam Arhitekturno arheologi[1]eskogo Issledovania)*, (Frunze: Akademiia Nauk Kirgizskoj SSR, Institut Istorii).

Petersen, A. D. 1997. "A Late Medieval Building in Shahriyar Ark, Sultan Kala Area 1," in G. Herrmann, K. Kurbansakhatov, St. J. Simpson et al., "The International Merv Project. Preliminary Report on the Fifth Season (1996)," *Iran*, 35, 22–26.

Pidaev, Sh. 2001. "Mosquées de quartier de l'ancienne Termez," *Archéologie Islamique*, 11, 61–74.

Pilipko, V. N. 1969. "Srenevekovoe kladbishe gorodisha Hurmuzfarra v Mervskom oazice," *Trudy yujno turkmenistanskoj arheologicheskoj komplex ékspedicii*, 14, 242–259.

Pope A. U., 1965. *Persian architecture* (London: Thames and Hudson).

Pugachenkova, G. 1958. *Puty razvitiya arkitektury yujnogo turkmenistana pory rabovladenniya i feodalisma* (Moskva: Trudy Yujnoturkmenistanskoj arheologicheskoĭ komplex ékspedicii, AN SSSR, 6).

Pugachenkova, G. 1967. *Iskusstvo Turkmenistana, ocherk c drevnejshih vremen do 1917 g* (Moskva: Izdatel'stvo Iskusstvo).

Rtveladze, E. V., and Ishakov, M. H. 1979. "Dva srednevekovykh chaganianskikh seleniya," *Istoriya materialnoĭ kultury Uzbekistana*, 15, 84–95.

Sachau, E. 1873. "Zur Geschichte und Chronologie von Khwârazm," *Sitzungsberichte der Kaiserlichen Akademie der Wissenschaften zu Wien*, 73, 471–506.

Samoĭlik, P. T. 1978. "Keramisty Usruñana," in *Po sledam drevnih kultur Taûikistana* (Dushanbe: Izdaťelstvo « Irfon »), 156–167.

Serjeant, R. B. 1972. *Islamic Textiles, Material for a History up to the Mongol Conquest* (Beirut: Librairie du Liban).

Shishkin, V. A. 1940. *Arheologi¹eskie Raboty 1937 g. v zapadnoj ‡asti Buharskogo Oasica* (Tashkent: Izdat'elstvo FAN Uzbekskoj SSSR).

Shishkin, V. A., 1963. *Varakhsha* (Moskva: Izdat'elstvo SSSR).

Shishkina, G. V. 1979. *Glazurovannaya keramika Sogda* (Tashkent: Izdat'elstvo FAN Uzbekskoj SSSR).

Shishkina, G. V. 1986. *Remeslennaja produkciya srednevekovogo Sogda, steklo keramika, vtoraya polovina VIII nachalo XIII v* (Tashkent: Izdat'elstvo FAN Uzbekskoï SSSR).

Shishkina, G. V., and Pavchinskaja, L. V. 1992. *Terres secrètes de Samarkand, Céramiques du VIIIe au XIIIe siècle, catalogue d'exposition* (Paris: Institut du Monde Arabe).

Siméon, P. 2012. "Hulbuk: An Unrecognized Site in the Shadow of the Great Capital of Central Asia, New Facts on the Material Culture of the Bānidjūrid Dynasty of Khuttal (9th–11th Century AD)," *Muqarnas*, 29, 385–421.

Siméon, P. 2014. "L'extraction minière en Asie centrale entre le VIIIe et le XIIe siècle: enjeux économiques et politiques," in S. Ferjani, A. Le Bihan, M. Onfray, and C. Trémeaud (eds.), *Matières premières et gestion des ressources, Archéo.Doct, vol.4* (Paris: Publication de la Sorbonne), 295–313.

Szuppe, M. (ed.) 1997. *L'Héritage timouride: Iran - Asie centrale - Inde, XVe-XVIIIe siècles* (Tashkent: IFEAC—Édisud).

Tolstov, S. P. 1963. "Polevye Issledovannia Horezmskoj Ekspeditsii v 1958–1961 gg," *Materialy Horezmskoj Ekspeditsii* (Moskva: Izdatel'stvo Akademiia Nauk SSSR).

Voronina, V. I. 1969. *Arhitekturnye pamiatniki Sredneï Aziï: Bukhara, Samarkand* (Leningrad: Avrora).

Williams, T. 2007. "The city of Sultan Kala, Merv, Turkmenistan: communities, neighbourhoods and urban planning from the eighth to the thirteenth century," in. Bennison, Amira K., and Gascoigne, Alison L. (eds.) *Cities in the pre-modern Islamic world: the urban impact of religion, state and society* (London: Routledge), 42–62.

Yusupov, K. 1990. "Unikalnyj pamiatnik arhitektury srednevekovogo Mizdahkana," *Arheologiya Priaral'ya*, 4, 146–158.

Zadneprovskiï, Y. A. 1960. "Arheologicheskie raboty v Yujnoï Kirgizi v 1954 godu," *Trudy Kirgizskoï arheologo-ètnograficheskoï èkspeditsiï*, 4, 214–246.

FURTHER READING

The reader is directed to all the articles related to Central Asia in the *Encyclopaedia of Islam* (2nd ed.).

Agapov, P., and Kadyrbaev, M. 1979. *Sokrovishcha drevnego Kazahstana: Drevnego Kazahstana Pamiatniki Material'noï kultury* (Alma Ata: Jalin).

Ageeva, E. I., and Pacevitch, G. I. 1958. "Iz Istoriï osedlyh poselenij I gorodov Yujnogo Kazahstana," *Trudy Instituta Istoriï, arheologii I etnografiï Akademiï Nauk Kazahskoï SSR*, 5, 3–215.

Arzhantseva, A., Härke, H., and Tazhekeev, A. A. 2017. "Between North and South: Dzhankent, Oguz and Khorezm," in N. N. Kradin and A. G. Sitdikov (eds.), *Mejdu Vostokom i Zapadom: Dvijenie Kul'tur, Tehnologiï i Imperiï* (Vladivostok: Dal'nauka), 12–16.

Avisova, A., Saipanov, B., and Bagdasarova, N. 1989. "Arheologicheskie issledovaniya v nekropole Mizdahkan," *Vestnik Karakalpakskogo filiala Akademiï Nauk Uzbekskoï Sovetskoï Socialisticheskoï Respubliki*, 3, 65–70.

Badr, J., Bruske, N., Drewello, R., and Korn, L. 2011. "A Digital Monument Archive (DMA): The Case Study of the Khoja Zainuddin Mosque in the Old City of Bukhara (Uzbekistan)," *S.AV.E Heritage, IXth International Forum*, 1–9.

Barthold, V. V. 1963–1977. *Sobranie Sochineniĭ* (Moskva: Izdatel'stvo Vostochnoĭ literatury) 9 volumes (specially volumes 1–4).

Bosworth, C. E. "CHORASMIA ii. In Islamic times," in *Encyclopaedia Iranica*, Fasc. 5, 516–517.

Bosworth, C. E., and Asimov, M. S. (eds.) 2000. *History of Civilizations of Central Asia. Volume IV. The Age of Achievement: AD 750 to the End of the Fifteenth Century* (Paris: UNESCO).

Bregel, Y. 1995. *Bibliography of Islamic Central Asia* (Bloomington: Indiana University Uralic and Altaic studies vol. 160).

Bregel, Y. 2003. *Historical Atlas of Central Asia* (Leiden-Boston: Brill).

Bulatova, V. A. 1965. "Nekropol' X-XI vv v Kuve," *Istoriya materialnoĭ kultury Uzbekistana*, 6, 139–146.

Founiau, V. (ed.) 2001. *Etudes Karakhanides, Cahiers d'Asie Centrale*, 9 (Tashkent-Aix en Provence: Édisud).

Gorshenina, S. 1999. "Premiers pas des archéologues russes et francais dans le Turkestan russe (1870–1890): méthodes de recherche et destin des collections," *Cahiers du monde russe*, 40, 3, 365–384.

Gorshenina, S. 2006. "De l'archéologie touristique à l'archéologie scientifique. L'archéologie en Asie centrale de la conquête russe du Turkestan à l'aube de l'époque soviétique: la 'non-archéologie' occidentale," in *ISIMU-6, El Redescubrimiento del Asia Central: nuevos horizontes en la historya y la arqueologya del Oriente antiguo* (Madrid: Universidad Autonoma de Madrid), 33–46.

Gorshenina, S., and Rapin, C. 2001. *De Kaboul à Samarcande, les archéologues en Asie centrale* (Paris: Gallimard La Découvertes no. 411).

Härke, H., and Arjanceva, I. 2016. "Some Theories, Models and Analogies for Dzhankent: A Context for Early Medieval Urbanization on the Lower Syr-Darya," *Mir Bolshogo Altaya*, 2(4.2), 886–896.

Hmelniskiĭ, S. 1997. *Mezhdu Samanidami I Mongolami. Arhitectura Sredneĭ Aziĭ XI-nachala XIII, chast 2* (Berlin-Riga: Izdat'elstvo Gamajun).

Iliasov, Dj. 1989. "Budrachskiy klad bronzovykh izdeliy," in *Uchenye zapiski Komissii po izucheniyu pamyatnikov tsivilizaciy drevnego i srednevekovogo Vostoka vse soyuznoy assotsiatsiĭ vostokovedov: Arkheologicheskie istochniki* (Moskva: Institut Arheologiĭ SSR), 294–305.

Kervran, M. 2001. "Fondations Qarâkhânides," in P. Leriche, Š. Pidaev, M. Gelin, and K. Abdulaev (eds.), *La Bactrianne au carrefour des routes et des civilisations de l'Asie centrale*, Actes du Colloque de Termez (1997) (Paris: Ifeac, Maisonneuve et Larose), 335–352.

McChesney, R. D. 2001. "Architecture and Narrative: The Khwaja Abu Nasr Parsa Shrine, Part I: Constructing the Complex in its Meaning, 1469–1696," *Muqarnas*, 18, 94–119.

McChesney, R. D. 2002. "Architecture and Narrative: Part II: Representing the Complex in Word and Image, 1696–1998," *Muqarnas*, 19, 78–108.

Muradov, R. 2011. *Kunya urgench gorod masterov. Vmoroe izdanie, dopolnennoe* (Ashhabad: Turkmenskaya gosudarstvennaya izdatelskaya slujba).

Mustafaev, Shch., Baĭpakov, K., Pidaev, Shch., and Hakimov, A. 2011. *Hudozhestvennaya kul'tura centralnoĭ Aziĭ I Azerbaizhana IX-XV vv*, Tom 1 Keramika, Tom 2 Steklo, Tom 3 Torevtika, Tom 4 Arhitektura (Samarkand- Tashkent: Mejdunarodnyĭ Institut Centralnoasiatskih Issledovaniĭ [MITSAI]).

Negmatov, N., and Hmelniskiĭ, S. 1966. *Srednevekovyĭ Shahristan* (Dushanbe: AN Tazhikskoĭ SSR).

O'Kane, B. 2000. "The Uzbek Architecture of Afghanistan," *Cahiers d'Asie Centrale*, 8, 130–143.

Pribytkova, A. M. 1973 (1955). *Stroitelnaya kultura Sredneĭ Aziĭ IX-XII vv* (Moskva: Izdatel'stvo Literatury po stroitel'stvy 234).

Pugachenkova, G. 1960. *Staryj Merv, putevobiteli po gorodsam i pamiatnikam* (Ashhabad: Otdel orhan pamiatnikov ministerstva kultury Turkmenskoĭ SSR).

Pugachenkova, G. A., and Rtveladze, E. V. 1987. "Archeology, Islamic Central Asia, vii," *Encyclopaedia Iranica*, vol. 2, 322–326.

Turner, M. 1999. "Investigations in Sultan Kala, Shahryar Ark: Sultan Kala Area 3. 1. Architecture, Stratigaphy and Synthesis," in G. Herrmann, K. Kurbansakhatov, St. J. Simpson et al. (eds.), "The International Merv Project. Preliminary Report on the Seventh Season (1998)," *Iran, 37*, 16–17.

SOUTH ASIA

MEHRDAD SHOKOOHY AND NATALIE H. SHOKOOHY

INTRODUCTION

IN South Asia, dominated by Buddhist and Hindu sites and monuments, the archaeology of the Muslim sites, with the exception of a few grand edifices, has never been given priority. During the British period the major sites were gradually identified, some of the better-preserved monuments restored, while ruins, if regarded as significant, were cleared of debris and rudimentary efforts were made to preserve the standing remains, with barely any significant excavation of any Muslim site. After Partition, in Pakistan, some excavations were carried out in the early Muslim sites, including ancient Daibul and al-Mansūra. In Bangladesh, the sites restored before Partition have been maintained, but lack of funds and resources limits fresh excavation or restoration. In India, while the introduction of substantial entry fees to outstanding Mughal and other sites has become a considerable source of income, many other Muslim monuments are left to dilapidate or are occupied by low-income families.

HISTORICAL BACKGROUND

Formal archaeological studies in India may be taken to have started in 1870, when the Archaeological Survey of India was established with Alexander Cunningham (1814–1893) appointed as Director, but interest in archaeology goes back much earlier. The value of the historic monuments and vast ruins was understood, and, early in the 19th century, two legislations—the Bengal Regulation of 1810 (Regulation 19, 1–3; Bengal Government 1810) and the Madras Regulation of 1817 (Regulation 7; Government of Madras 1917)—were designed to prevent vandalism, but with little effect as the East India Company had only nominal authority over the Subcontinent (Figure 5.2.1).

FIGURE 5.2.1 Map of the Indian subcontinent with the locations of the main sites discussed.

Although at the beginning there was no scholarly approach to archaeology, what attracted enlightened officials of the East India Company was the Buddhist and Hindu monuments, ancient inscriptions, and numismatics. They presented papers to the Asiatic Society of Bengal, published in the regular *Proceedings* and *Journal*. Islamic sites and monuments attracted less attention as they were everywhere to be seen and were "too recent." We come across papers regarding Muslim materials very occasionally, such as Major Colvin's report "On the Restoration of the Ancient Canals in the Delhi Territory" (Colvin 1833). Colvin, known as "the Father of Irrigation in northern India" and still remembered locally, identified the 14th-century canals excavated by Fīrūz Shah Tughluq to bring water from the Rivers Jumna and Sutlej to his newly built city of Ḥiṣār-i Fīrūza in the arid region of present Haryana, together with later canals dating from the Mughal period. The aim of restoring canals was not for their historic significance but for practical reasons as they were—and still are—a main source of irrigation. In the same volume we are enlightened with a brief "Description of a Sun Dial in the Court of Motī Masjid in the Fort of Agra" by Captain John T. Boileau (Boileau 1833). The Asiatic Society of Bengal had a particular interest in numismatics, with finds preserved in the Calcutta Museum, but their focus was mainly on ancient coins: Bactrian, Indo-Scythian, and pre-Islamic Indian. Only six years before the 1857 Mutiny, however, it published a study by E. Thomas of eight early Muslim silver coins, two of which date from 121 AH (738–739) and 162 (778–779), and the rest from the Samanids and later rulers of Khurāsān (Thomas 1851). Although at the time the archaeology of Sind and Multan was unknown, the two early Caliphate coins pointed to an Arab presence in Sind, and, over a century later, explorations of the historic Arab settlements enhanced our understanding of early Muslim architecture and urban form in South Asia (Figure 5.2.2).

Delhi was, of course, the center of Muslim power and its antiquities were described first in 1846, not in English, but in Urdu by Sayyid Ahmad Khan (1817–1898) (S. A. Khan 1854). However, the quality and characteristics of Indo-Muslim edifices were considered before this time by James Fergusson (1808–1886), a Scottish architect with a great enthusiasm for historic architecture worldwide, who plied the subcontinent between 1834 and 1845, making measured drawings of the buildings. He was later on the Committee of Architectural Antiquities of Western India set up in 1859 by Sir Bartle Frere (1815–1884), the Governor of Bombay Presidency. In 1876, Fergusson eventually published his *History of Indian and Eastern Architecture* (Fergusson 1876, Book 7: 489–609; Fergusson 1910: 186–337) which, while mainly concerned with Hindu and Buddhist antiquities, included survey plans of the then unexcavated Quwwat al-Islam mosque and the tomb attributed to Īltutmish in Delhi, Shīr Shāh's tomb at Sasaram, the Ādīna Mosque at Pandua, the Jāmiʿ mosques of Jaunpur and Ahmadabad, and the mosque called Aṛhaʾi din kā Jhoṅpṛa in Ajmer. He also produced a sketch of the 11th-century minaret at Ghazna, the upper tier of which has since fallen, making his sketch our only record of its design.

In 1861, Lord Canning, the Viceroy (1858–1862), approved a proposal by Cunningham to investigate archaeological sites and remains in North India, which, among many Buddhist and Hindu sites, included the vast area of the Delhi region occupied by the remains of several Muslim cities established in succession after the Ghurid conquest of 1191. The work laid the grounds for proper archaeological survey, but its publications without survey drawings or illustrations were discouraging, and, in 1866, the project was terminated by Lord Lawrence (Viceroy 1864–1869). Yet the necessity for an archaeological institution did not fade away, and, in 1870, the Central Government established the Archaeological Survey of India (ASI), with the fifty-seven-year-old General Cunningham as Director (Burgess 1905b: 136–140). He and his few assistants explored the antiquities of various regions, publishing their reports in twenty-three annual volumes (*ASIR*

FIGURE 5.2.2 Numismatics raised early awareness of Indo-Muslim archaeology. Two early silver Arab coins found in Multan, published in *Journal of the Asiatic Society of Bengal*, 1851. Top: *dirham* of the Umayyad Hishām b. ʿAbd al-Malik minted in Wāsiṭ in AH 121. Bottom: that of the Abbasid Mahdī minted in Madīnat al-Salām (Baghdad) in AH 162.

Cunningham Series), each supported by sketches, measured drawings, and renderings of inscriptions. The quality of the reports varies greatly. Those of Cunningham himself, while not entirely free of error, are more reliable, but those of his assistants are often unprofessional, inadequate, inaccurate, and full of statements and anecdotes gathered from local pundits and presented as historical fact. An example is the report by Archibald C. L. Carlleyle (1831–1897) on the town and fort of Bayana (Carlleyle 1878). The town was established by the Muslims in the first decade after the Ghurid conquest, and while the fort is of pre-Islamic origin, it was entirely rebuilt and remodeled by the Muslims, yet Carlleyle devotes most of his report to the pre-Islamic fictional history, inventing a name for the town: "Bāṇāsur" and another for the fort: "Santipūr" (Fleet 1885, 1886). He ignored many of the Muslim remains, designated the Jāmi' mosque of the fort as a "temple converted to mosque," and described one of the most significant early conquest mosques as a temple "considerably altered by the Muhammadans (Pathāns)." He gave an inaccurate plan of the structure and an almost comical sketch of the minaret of Dāwūd Khān in the fort. The shortcomings of this report were to the extent that Cunningham had to revisit the site and provide a fresh report correcting many of Carlleyle's slips (Cunningham 1885). With all their shortcomings, however, Cunningham and his assistants did set up the basis of systematic archaeological exploration, with a fair proportion devoted to the Muslim period. Nevertheless, their reports were regarded as unscientific and were criticized highly at the time. In 1887, Sir F. S. Growse, the founder of the Mathura archaeological museum, publicly commented "The unrevised lucubrations of General Cunningham's assistants are a tissue of trivial narrative and the crudest theories," and the *Quarterly Review* of July 1889 noted "We trust that all future Reports issued by the Archaeological Department of the Government of India will be free from the defects which mar the usefulness and impair the authority of Sir Alexander Cunningham's Series" (Burgess 1905b: 140–141) (Figure 5.2.3).

FIGURE 5.2.3 Bayana, Rajasthan, minaret of Dāwūd Khān in the Fort and its sketch by Carlleyle. An example of the inaccuracies in the early archaeological reports.

For all that, Cunningham's publications brought the extent and importance of Indian antiquities to the attention of the authorities, and, in 1873, the Duke of Argyll (1823–1900), the Secretary of State for India in London, prepared a paper signed by many of the elite of the day noting that "many of these monuments are such as, were they in Europe, would be cherished with the utmost care, and form the pride of the city, if not of the country which possessed them" and suggesting that the employment of officers to be in charge of the conservation of historical monuments be made a priority (Burgess 1905b: 144–145). The recommendations were eventually approved in 1880, resulting in the protection of a vast number of historical sites and monuments, many of which were in private hands.

Nineteenth-century India was subdivided into four major presidencies: Bengal, Madras, North-Western Provinces and Bombay, which included Gujarat and later Sind. Parallel, but independent from Cunningham's team, archaeology was being taken seriously in the Bombay Presidency, led by James Burgess (1832–1916) working mainly on his own, but in some areas assisted by a prolific archaeologist: Henry Cousens (1854–1933). Burgess first focused on Kachh (Kutch) and Kāṭhiāwāḍ (Saurashtra), and while attention was, as ever, focused on pre-Islamic material, the work included the survey of the grand Jāmiʿ of Junagadh (Burgess 1876: 144–145, pl. 25). However, the highly significant early Muslim buildings in Bhadreśvar and Junagadh—which date prior to the Muslim conquest of the region and are noted below—were missed (Burgess 1875: 11–19). Burgess's major contribution to the presentation of the Muslim period were his two monumental volumes on the antiquities of Ahmadabad, meticulously surveying almost all monuments of the sultanate of Gujarat in its capital (Burgess 1900, 1905a). His town plan of Ahmadabad is the only record of the historic town, and although many books and essays have since been written on Ahmadabad, none surpasses Burgess's work. Together with Cousens he also carried out fieldwork in northern Gujarat, including surveys of many Muslim buildings in Aṇahilvāḍā Patan (Muslim Naharwāla) such as its Jāmiʿ; the Gumaḍa, Ghazni, and Shaikh Jodh mosques; the shrine of Shaikh Farīd; and a reservoir known as Khān Sarovar (Burgess and Cousens 1903: 53–57, pls. 23–35).

Cunningham retired in 1885, and Burgess replaced him as ASI Director General the next year. His appointment only lasted for four years and, in 1889, at his own request, the post of Director General was abolished and responsibility handed to regional directors. The result was disappointing, and very little progress was made after Burgess's departure. It seems that he had been unhappy with his position. With his uncompromising attention to standing monuments, he found hardly any reliable officers to carry out exploration and survey of sites. In his own words: "It is hard to do good work without suitable tools. In Dr. Führer, however, I had one educated officer, and later, having secured the engagement of Mr. Ed. W. Smith as architectural assistant. . . . The Sharqi Architecture of Jaunpur was selected to begin with, and was completed in the second season (1887)" (Burgess 1905b: 146).

In this statement, made in 1905, Burgess was still backing Alois Anton Führer (1853–1930), a German archaeologist in the British service whose career ended in 1898 in disgrace. Führer specialized in the early Buddhist period but his excavations were considered "untrustworthy" and some of his archaeological findings "forgery" (Huxley 2004; Allen 2008/2011). In the disarray following Burgess's departure, Führer, to preserve his position, became somewhat imaginative in his later work, but whatever the arguments for or against him may have been, his excavations at Lumbini and his uncovering of the inscribed pillar of Aśoka recording the site as the birthplace of Lord Buddha has made Lumbini a world pilgrimage center while his work on Islamic Jaunpur is highly professional and commendable (Führer and Smith 1889).

In spite of Burgess's dissatisfaction as Director General, he left remarkable achievements. A New Imperial Series of the ASI was established with many publications on Muslim antiquities. Earlier in his career Burgess had founded (with his own funds) the journal *Indian Antiquary* (Temple 1922) with a supplement for inscriptions, *Epigraphia Indica*, published first in 1882, but with his new position, in 1888, it became an independent publication, a legacy which continued until 1977. Its supplements on Muslim inscriptions (*Epigraphia Indo Moslemica*, and later *Epigraphia Indica, Arabic and Persian Supplement*) are still a major tool for the specialist for establishing the dates and historical background of sites and monuments. Under his directorship Edmund Smith (d. 1901) carried out the monumental task of clearing the site and surveying the palaces and grand mosque of Fathpur Sikri, the Emperor Akbar's short-lived capital (Smith, 1894–1898). His work has inspired many later scholars who continued the study of the palaces (see Rizvi 1972; Petruccioli 1988, 1992, 2007; D. V. Sharma 2008, among many), including the discovery of the foundation of the Portuguese Jesuit chapel within the palace complex (Muhammed 1991).

Smith also carried out a survey of Akbar tomb's in Sikandra, but in Fathpur Sikri he did not extend his work to the Mughal town spread in the valley below the palaces or to the two neighboring villages Patan and Sīkrī, both containing remains of the early sultanate period. This was in accordance with the ASI policy of the time, as the amount of remains was overwhelming and attention was paid first to major sites.

With the dissolution of the central archaeological authority after 1889, the regional archaeological departments were left without appropriate direction and much of what little work was undertaken remained unpublished. It remained until 1901, when the Viceroy Lord Curzon (1859–1925), who had a special interest in archaeology, reformed the ASI as an independent department directly under his government and reestablished the post of Director General for which he appointed a young archaeologist: John Marshal (1876–1958). Curzon is said, with some justification, to have had no heart in the approach of the existing "old" archaeologists and was after new blood. Marshall was a classicist and his primary concern was Greco-Indian culture. He excavated Taxila, the Greco-Parthian town in the north of present Pakistan, and, under his direction, even earlier sites were uncovered: Mohenjo-Daro and Harappa.

It might appear superficially that the Muslim period was too recent to be of interest to Marshall. Nevertheless, after Fergusson, he was the first to write a history of the sultanate monuments in India (Marshall 1928) and, in spite of Curzon's earlier reservations, made good use of his team of archaeologists who continued with thorough and pioneering work. For example Cousens, the close colleague of Burgess, carried out a survey of

Bijapur, the ʿĀdil Shāhī capital (Cousens 1916). He also partially excavated Brahmanābād, the site of Al-Manṣūra, the Arab capital of Sind, and exposed part of a mosque (Cousens 1929: 48–59, pls. 4–9), one of the earliest specimens in the world. In the Deccan, the Niẓāms of Hyderabad emulated the organization of the ASI in their territory with a Department of Archaeology headed by Ghulam Yazdani (1885–1962) who carried out work in Wrangal (Yazdani 1916) and Mandu (Yazdani 1929). Yazdani went on to survey the town of Bidar (Yazdani 1947).

Marshall also formed an archaeological policy to govern the exploration of sites and preservation of monuments, much of which is still in force. Under his leadership the ASI produced guidelines for what should be protected and restored and what should be left to decay. The attention was given to the already better-preserved monuments and to the sites of historical importance with enough remains to be explored and protected. Another problem—a universal phenomenon of the time—was the focus of archaeology on individual monuments rather than the entire fabric of the site. The *Annual Reports of the ASI* record both the progress of explorations and the meticulous restoration works, which were carried out systematically every season. As a result, while we owe a debt to Marshall for protecting and restoring Muslim monuments that attract visitors from all over the world, a negative consequence of his policies is that we have also seen—regrettably—many ruinous sites disappearing. An example is Tughluqabad, the early 14th-century capital of Delhi. While the tomb of Ghiyāth al-dīn Tughluq—the founder of the city—and the fort were declared Protected Monuments, the entire walled town with its magnificent gates and the site of a lake, designed as an integral part of the city, were left unprotected. During the course of time and the rapid development of Delhi, the sites of the town and the lake are being built over and the stones of the massive town walls, along with those of many 14th-century structures within the town, have been carted away to build new houses.

The antiquities of Delhi suffered most from the policy of what was perceived to be "too ruinous" or "without significant historic value" and left without protection. Later the decision of the founding of New Delhi to the south—rather than the north—of Shāhjahānābād (Old Delhi) meant that, with the exception of individual buildings, the urban fabric of all sultanate sites together with their fortification walls, ruins of palaces, and other features was lost. Today we have little to go on for understanding—let alone the possibility of excavating—the early sultanate Qalʿa Rāi Pithūrā, the Khaljī capitals of Kīlūgharī and Sīrī, or the Tughluq capitals of Jahānpanāh and Fīrūzābād.

Another major policy taken under Marshall's guidance was to designate sizable protection zones around historic sites and monuments, which were often made into green space and some of which remain as parks. The zones not only prevented new development encroaching the sites, but also safeguarded the unexcavated surrounding areas for future exploration. In many cases these zones have gradually been neglected or on occasion ignored and the sites built over. An example in Delhi is the citadel of Fīrūzābād, which contains the excavated parts of Fīrūz Shāh Tughluq's palaces, the ruins of the Jāmiʿ, and its well-known minaret, the Kotla Fīrūz Shāh. The protective zone outside the citadel walls—a green space throughout the 20th century—was, in the first decade of the 21st century, designated for a commercial development around an urban square and is now built over.

Marshall's initial contract was for five years, but he remained in his post until 1928, when he relinquished his position as Director General to write a number of books and eventually retired in 1931. His retirement coincided with the rise of Gandhi's independence movement and the decline of the administration of British India. A succession of Directors General: Harold Hargreaves, Daya Ram Sahni, John F. Blakiston, and Kashinath N. Dikshit, served for short periods, while the cutting of the ASI budget in 1935 greatly reduced the effectiveness of the institution and the advent of World War II brought excavation and exploration almost to a halt. The last Director General during British India was Sir Mortimer Wheeler (1890–1976) who, between 1944 and 1947, revived the activities of the ASI; initiated a new annual, *Ancient India*; and, with Independence on the horizon, set up a number of excavations to train young Indian archaeologists. As far as the Islamic sites were concerned, however, little was achieved except routine projects of preservation and restoration. Exceptions were the detailed surveys of ʿĀdilābad, a private fortified palace of Muḥammad b. Tughluq (Waddington, 1946) and of Sulṭān Ghārī, the tomb built by Īltutmish for his son and crown prince who predeceased him (Naqvi 1947).

After Partition, the ASI remained in charge of archaeology in India, while Pakistan and subsequently Bangladesh established their own archaeological departments. In India, the ASI, with the largest budget and an inherited administration, continues its work more or less on pre-Independence lines, but the focus had shifted even more to Buddhist and particularly Hindu sites. Following Curzon's arrangement, the ASI is still not under any ministry, but directly under Central Government, and the post of Director General has on many occasions been a stepping-stone for politicians on the move to higher office. Occasionally an archaeologist has occupied the post of Director General; most have been simply administrators.

The ASI post-Independence policy restricts non-Indian experts from carrying out excavations, and while permission is often given to foreigners for exploration and survey of sites, there are still many restrictions on filming and methods of photography. Nevertheless, whatever serious but limited investigation has been carried out on Muslim sites has been mainly by non-Indian scholars (see the monumental work on Delhi by Yamamoto et al. 1967–1970; also Michell and Eaton 1991; Fussman and Sharma 1999; and the Shokoohys on northern and southern India, listed later). On the other hand, post-Independence publications on the antiquities of Muslim India are copious, mostly produced by authors who make a hasty visit to the site, take some photographs, and, with or without using the old survey drawings of the British ASI, write half-digested and often inaccurate, if not misleading, work.

The ASI continues with upkeep of the monuments and gardens of the major Muslim sites, which, with the introduction of high entrance fees for foreign visitors, provides revenue for the institution. Less well-protected and minor monuments are often left to fall apart or are occupied by local people. An example in Delhi is the tomb of Khān Jahān Tilāngānī, the first octagonal tomb built at the end of the Tughluq period and the prototype for many Sayyid, Lodī, Sūrī, and even early Mughal tombs. It was fairly well-preserved until the 1960s (Yamamoto 1967–1970, T. 76, 1: 81; 1968, 2: 136–139), but was later subdivided by several squatting households who built poorly constructed internal partitions and external extensions.

In Bangladesh, the Department of Archaeology continued to preserve what had already been designated as protected antiquities. While an Islamic republic, the severe lack of funds restricts any serious exploration and excavation of archaeological sites, of which there are many. An example is the site of Bagerhat. While the impressive Saith Gunbad and a few other mosques, as well as the tomb of Khān Jahān (dated 1459) are fairly well preserved, an area called Chilla Khāna just outside the site of the main monument is covered with archaeological debris but has not been excavated. In the same town the roofless Ḥujra Khāna and a number of ruinous mosques and shrines are dilapidating and, if not restored, will soon crumble under the monsoon rains. Khān Jahān's tomb, regarded as a shrine, while under the protection of the Department of Archaeology, is tended by its local custodians. In Sherpur, too, apart from a few Protected Monuments the historic site is neglected and shrubs and trees are growing into the walls and roofs of many structures. Bangladesh is subject to regular flooding, and in some areas the surface antiquities are washed away, but regular deposits of silt may at the same time protect features buried underground, leaving hope for future excavation.

Only in post-Independence Pakistan has serious attention been given to Muslim sites; excavations by Pakistani specialists have revealed the earliest Muslim occupations in Banbhore (the historic port of Daibul) and in Brahmanābād. Unlike the ASI, the Pakistan Department of Archaeology does not exclude foreign archaeologists from carrying out excavations, and, until recently, the Italian Institute for the Middle and Far East (IsMEO) has been particularly active in north Pakistan, revealing some of the Ghaznavid remains in Swāt. Sadly, in this area, the political unrest of recent decades has prevented both local and foreign archaeologists from continuing their work, and both in Swāt and Brahmanābād, as well as at other early sites, much remains to be uncovered.

MAJOR SITES AND THEIR REMAINS: 8TH TO EARLY 12TH CENTURY

The Arab appearance on the coasts of India goes back to pre-Islamic times and large numbers of Roman, Byzantine, and early Muslim gold coins found in India were brought via the Red Sea by the maritime traders from Syria, Iraq, and elsewhere. In South India there is a legend—not credible, but a pointer to early Muslim maritime trade—that the Jāmi' of Cranganur was founded in the eighth year of the Hijra (629–630) (Shokoohy 2003: 139–142). The present mosque, however, is unlikely to date earlier than the 17th century. Histories (al-Balādhurī 1987: 611–628; Fredunbeg 1902, 1: 81–89; Bakkarī 1938: 20–31) tell us that, at the time of the Caliph Al-Walīd, when the Muslim ships were attacked by Indian pirates, in retaliation Muḥammad b. Qāsim took an army to Sind and first took over Daibul in 93 (711–712) and within a year annexed Sind to the Caliphate.

Excavations at the site of the port of Daibul at Banbhore (Pakistan Department of Archaeology 1964; Ghafur 1966; Ashfaque 1969; F. A. Khan 1969) have uncovered the perimeter of the walled town, small parts of the palace area, and foundations of the main mosque with its inscription dated 109 (727–728), which makes the building one of the earliest known mosques in the world. The foundations reveal that the mosque had an Arab-type plan with the usual colonnade around a central courtyard, but little survives to reveal the features of the superstructure. Nevertheless, from what is left it appears that the building had stone walls and probably a light, flat roof supported by wooden columns. There is no trace of a *miḥrāb*, a significant point, leading to the question of whether early mosques had a *miḥrāb*, or if a niche indicating the *qibla* direction was a later concept. The rest of the vast site of Banbhore remains unexcavated (Figure 5.2.4).

Further north, the village of Brahmanābād is the site of al-Manṣūra (Cousens 1903–1904, 1908–1909, 1929; Farooq 1986; Hussain 1989; Rashid 1998), the Arab capital of Sind, once a sizable city which is still left practically unexcavated except for the foundations of a large mosque (described by some as the Jāmiʿ) and a smaller one, both built of brick, the main building material in Sind and Multan. The 10th-century Jāmiʿ was described by al-Muqaddasī (1906, 479) who compared it with the Jāmiʿ of ʿUmmān and mentions that it was built of stone and brick with four entrances. The excavated mosque, however, seems to have been a walled prayer hall with a single entrance to a courtyard in the eastern

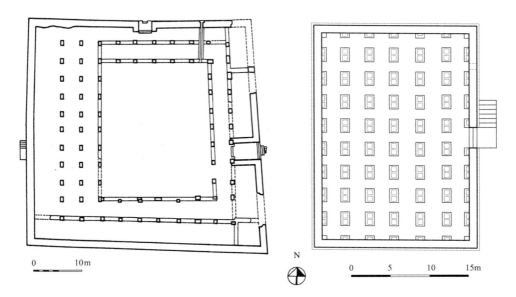

FIGURE 5.2.4 Sind, plans of early Arab mosques. Left: The Jāmiʿ of Daibul. Right: a mosque in al-Manṣūra, but unlikely to be the historic Jāmiʿ.

side. Again, the superstructure is lost, but inside the prayer hall are the foundations of massive piers that may have supported an arcaded roof, or, as some traces suggest, over each of these large piers two wooden columns probably supported a light roof.

Early in the 11th century, Multan and Swāt, to its north-east, were annexed to the Ghaznavid territory and excavations at Swāt have revealed a sizable Ghaznavid mosque, several times renovated, with stone walls and traces of wooden columns (Scerrato 1981, 1984; M. N. Khan 1985). The entire mosque was roofed, and it seems that it did not have a court-yard—at least in its final form. The fort of Nagaur is also known to have been founded at the turn of the 11th century, by Muḥammad Bāhalīm (Minhāj-i Sirāj 1984, 1: 241–242), the rebel-lious governor of Multan who eventually submitted to Bahrām Shāh in 1119. The formidable stone fort, many times repaired, remained a Muslim stronghold in the heart of the Rajput territories right up to Mughal period (Shokoohy and Shokoohy 1993: 22–24).

Multan and the nearby town of Ucch retain other remains (Cunningham 1871a: 230–241; Marshall 1928: 597–599; Brown 1981: 21–23, 32–33; Khan 1983; Hillenbrand 1992, 1994: 297, 535; Burton-Page 2008: 11, 36, 60), almost all constructed of brick and many displaying glazed tilework, a reflection of the region's association with Greater Khurāsān rather than South Asia. The oldest, the tomb of Shāh Yūsuf Gardīzī (1152), has an unusual layout and structure for the region: oblong in plan and not domed. Other tombs, such as the tombs of Shāh Bahā' al-Ḥaqq (d. 1262), Shams al-dīn Tabrīzī (d. 1276), Shādnā Shāhīd (d. 1270), and Rukn-i 'Ālam, are all built with battered walls reflecting the traditional mudbrick and pisé structures of Afghanistan. These tombs were built shortly before or during the period when Ghiyāth al-dīn Tughluq was the governor of the region, and it was he who took the style of battered walls to India, where they remained a Tughluq hallmark of the 14th century.

Muslim Maritime Trading Posts

Early Muslim geographers (Sotoodeh 1962: 66; al-Iṣṭakhrī 1961 [Arabic]: 102, 104–105; 1961 [Persian]: 147, 151; al-Muqaddasī: 1906, 477, 484, 486; Ibn Ḥauqal 1873: 227–228, 232–233) record many ports on the coasts of Gujarat with Muslim settlements, dating from the 9th and 10th centuries, including Khambāya (Cambay), Asāwul, Ṣaimūr, Sindān, and Sūbāra. Cambay remained a prominent port throughout history, but its his-toric edifices do not relate to the maritime settlers. Asāwul was later incorporated with the 15th-century Ahmadabad, and the site of Ṣaimūr, further east of Daibul, has not yet been identified. Sindān, however, may be the same as a remote village of the same name on the coast of the Gulf of Kutch (Kachh), but the site has not yet been explored. Sūbāra, on the other hand, is likely to be the same as Bhadreśvar, also recorded as Bhīswāra (Mīr Khwand 1853–1854; Khwand Mīr 1974, 2: 382–383), a port raided by Maḥmūd of Ghazna on his return from Somnath.

Bhadreśvar (Shokoohy 1988a) retains the oldest dated Muslim monuments in India. With the changes of the coastline, the site, near the far end of the Gulf of Kutch, is now about one kilometer inland, and the main mosque is half buried in sand but is partially preserved. The main mosque is a colonnaded structure with a small central courtyard and a large colonnaded portico in front of the entrance to the courtyard, a feature not seen in Banbhore and Brahmanābād or in sultanate mosques, but one appearing in virtually all those associated with maritime trade. The dated structure, however, is the Shrine of Ibrāhīm, locally attributed to one La'l Shahbāz, bearing a Kufic inscription of 554 (1160). Another small mosque near the shrine, which may be associated with it, also has a portico in front of its prayer hall. Numerous tombstones are found at the site dating from the 12th and early 13th centuries. A feature of the buildings in Bhadreśvar is that while their concept and layout conform to Muslim principles, their structure and details of ornamentation follow local traditions, a phenomenon of maritime buildings in South Asia, an example being the mosque of Abu'l-Qāsim al-Īdhajī dated 685 (1286) in Junagadh, further south of Bhadreśvar. The mosque dates thirteen years before the sultanate conquest of the region, but in Junagadh other Islamic edifices remain to be examined.

Numerous sites of Muslim maritime merchants are to be found in South India (Shokoohy 2003), in places such as Calicut, Cranganur, and Cochin on the coasts of Malabar (present Kerala) and at the site of the historic Muslim port of Qā'il, now called Kayalpatnam (the city of Kayal) in Tamil Nadu (still a Muslim town). The historic buildings of Malabar, dating from the 15th to 18th centuries, have stone walls with wooden columns and wooden tiered roofs. They do not have an enclosed courtyard, and their porch usually opens to an antechamber leading to the prayer hall, an innovation from the planning principles seen in the earlier maritime edifices. The most notable mosque in Calicut is the Mithqālpaḷḷi, built originally in the early 14th century by Nākhudā Mithqāl, a wealthy shipmaster and merchant known to Ibn Baṭṭūṭa. In 1510, it was burned by the Portuguese and was reconstructed by the Muslims in 986–987 (1578–1579). Calicut has a number of historic mosques, including the Jāmi' restored in 885 (1480–1481) and extended in about 1094 (1683).

The surviving edifices in Tamil Nadu (the historic Ma'bar of the Muslim records) are, on the other hand, built entirely of stone; and, in their planning, with a portico opening to the prayer hall or shrine, they are closer in concept to the earlier maritime traditions seen in Gujarat. In Kayalpatnam, the Jāmi' al-kabīr or Khuṭba Parriapaḷḷi bears a 19th-century copy of its original 737 (1336–1337) foundation stone. A smaller Jāmi', the Khuṭba Śirupaḷḷi, and another, the Aḥmad Nainār mosque, may be even earlier, but Kayalpatnam is rich in edifices of all periods, right up to modern times. A few stone buildings remain, imitating the wooden structures common in the past and described by Ibn Baṭṭūṭa (1987 [Arabic]: 609), now rare after the deforestation of the region. Numerous tombs and gravestones, from 806 (1404) to recent eras include genealogies of Middle Eastern settlers. The Muslim archaeology of South India is still relatively untouched (Harding 2008–2010), leaving many sites throughout Tamil Nadu and Kerala to be explored and provide a better understanding of the history and cultural traditions of the maritime settlers in India and beyond.

Delhi: Muslim Dominance,
1191 to mid-14th Century

North India was taken in 1191 by the Ghurids of Khurāsān, who, within two years, established a powerful sultanate with Delhi as their capital. Their armies penetrated as far as Bengal, but the sultanate of Bengal generally remained aloof from Delhi. Soon after the conquest, the Hindu Delhi was transformed to a Muslim city and, in the next 150 years, several other cities were built in its neighborhood: first Kīlūgharī (founded 685–688 [1286–1289]); then Sīrī (698 [1298–1299]); Tughluqābād (720 [1320–1321]); Jahānpanāh (c. 726 [1326]); and Fīrūzābad (c. 760 [1358–1359]). Early in the 20th century, when New Delhi was built south of Shāhjahānābād (Old Delhi), traces of all the earlier cities were gradually buried under the new capital, except the more distant Tughluqābād, although it, too, is now being submerged under modern development. No systematic excavations were carried out in any of these towns, and the historic urban fabric has been lost, except in Mughal Old Delhi, where the street pattern has remained unchanged, but most traditional structures are not earlier than the 19th century. Of the sultanate period, only individual buildings and some fortification walls are scattered among modern developments (Figure 5.2.5).

Sir Sayyid Ahmad Khan's 19th-century list of Delhi's monuments was followed by a comprehensive publication by the ASI in 1920 (M. Z. Hasan 1920). The sultanate monuments were again listed and some studied in detail by Tatsuro Yamamoto and his team in the 1960s (Yamamoto 1967–1970).

The architecture of the first few decades of the conquest could be crystallized into a few words: the Architecture of Dominance. It differs entirely from the architecture of the conquerors' homelands, where arcuate engineering, with its plastic quality for forming curves, arches, and domes, was already in an advanced stage. As seen in the well-known Quṭb complex (survey: Page 1926; inscriptions: Husain 1936) the early Delhi sultans chose instead to build their mosques and tombs with temple spoil. The column shafts, beams, and brackets were reassembled on a new layout, and the Hindu and Jain corbelled temple ceilings were dismantled and carefully fitted back together, topped with a cement layer to resemble Muslim domes on the exterior. The fine calligraphy of the Persian and Arabic inscriptions on the *miḥrābs*, entrances, and screen walls indicate that the early conquerors did have access to highly skilled Muslim craftsmen, but building with temple spoil, obliterating figurative carvings, was a demonstration of the new order. Architectural style, however, mellowed a generation or so later, first shown in the resurfacing and recarving of temple spoil and also often the rendering of buildings with plaster. An early example is Sulṭān Ghārī (Naqvi 1947), the tomb of Īltutmish's son, which recalls the remembered homeland. Later, with the Mongol invasion of Iran and Central Asia in 1221 causing a flood of architects, craftsmen, and artisans into India, the traditions of Middle Eastern architecture, as seen in the tomb of Sultan Balban and buildings of ʿAlā al-dīn Khaljī, replaced trabeate structural methods. In Delhi, for almost

FIGURE 5.2.5 The early 14th-century city of Tughluqabad near Delhi. Left: 1946 aerial photograph taken by the British Royal Air Force. Right: Authors' plan of the surface remains of the town and surroundings produced between 1986 and 2004, during which time the town and lake developed as suburbs of Delhi, and many ruins were obliterated by new buildings. The fort, citadel, and the tomb of Tughluq Shāh and ʿĀdilābād were saved as previously protected monuments.

half a century, the influence of ancient Indian traditions is absent, but by the 14th century the Muslim and old Indian techniques coalesced, creating a distinctive Indian architectural style, first appearing in early Tughluq buildings and reaching its maturity at the time of Fīrūz Shāh Tughluq. As for other artifacts, apart from coins, the dates of which often confirm those in the histories, lack of systematic excavation leaves us without compelling evidence. Some pottery sherds have been found, and traces of bands of turquoise glazed tiles remain in occasional 15th- and 16th-century structures, but, as a whole, the lack of good clay in north India prevented the advancement of pottery and tile making. These arts flourished only in north Pakistan, in Bengal, and to some extent in the Deccan. On the other hand, in Delhi, fine craftsmanship is displayed in the stone carving, while from the early 14th century cut stucco began to appear on structures, reaching its zenith in the 16th century.

Edifices of the early days of the conquest have survived in other regions, such as the mosque of Aṛhai din kā Jhoṅpṛa in Ajmer, the Shāhī Masjid at Bari Khatu, and the Ukhā Mandīr mosque and a prayer wall in Bayana. The prayer walls (Arabic *muṣallā*, Persian *namāzgāh*) are known in India as ʿīdgāh. The specimen in Bayana appears to be a simpler version of the 10th- to 12th-century prayer walls in Iran and Central Asia, of which only the ruins and foundations of a very few have survived (Shokoohy and Shokoohy 2006, 2020: 194–220).

The "Architecture of Dominance" did not, however, die out and, right up to the end of the 14th century, was implemented in new regions conquered by the Delhi sultanate. Examples are the Jāmiʿ of Daulatabad in the Deccan, the mosques in Dhār, the early capital of Mālwa, and numerous mosques in Gujarat's Saurashtra peninsular, mostly dating from the time of Fīrūz Shah Tughluq, himself an architect, engineer, and prolific builder who, apart from his new capital in Delhi, founded many cities such as Fatehabad and Jaunpur. His passion was expressed best, however, in Ḥiṣār-i Fīrūza, where some of its monuments and a part of its citadel, together with its royal mosque and remains of a garden pavilion, have survived as well as its extensive palace, only partly excavated, much remaining unexplored (Shokoohy and Shokoohy 1988b). Jaunpur, the seat of the 15th-century independent Sharqī sultanate, was, however, devastated by the Delhi sultan Sikandar Lodī (1489–1517), sparing only a few mosques; the modern town now covers the ruins of the old. There is, however, an outstanding bridge over the Gomti River built during the reign of the Mughal Emperor Akbar.

BENGAL (WEST BENGAL, INDIA, AND BANGLADESH)

Muslim remains in Bengal (major studies in Creighton 1817; Blochmann 1870; Cunningham 1882; Chakravarti 1909; A. A. Khan 1931; S. M. Hasan 1971; Asher 1984) demonstrate a marked difference from those of the rest of South Asia. Bengal, with its tropical climate and its isolation from Western India, had a substantial Buddhist culture with an ancient red-brick building tradition. Later Hindu temples were built of brick faced with blocks of stone. The Muslims inherited these traditions, rare elsewhere. The British ASI's interest was mainly concentrated on excavation of Buddhist and Hindu sites now mostly in Bangladesh. The ASI contribution to Muslim sites was, as usual, to clear the sites and reveal standing monuments, restoring some and preserving the ruins of selected others, but much remains to be investigated.

The oldest Muslim remains are in Tribeni (or Tribani) and are partly in ruins, but these have stone walls and piers surmounted by brick arches and domes, characteristic of many later edifices. The Muslim capital, however, was Lakhnautī, the site of which is now divided between Bangladesh and India, covering a vast area of Gaur and Ḥaḍrat Pandua. The earlier buildings, such as the Ādina Masjid (776 [1374]) and Chota Sona mosque (899–925 [1493–1519]), have again stone or stone-faced walls supporting brick arches and domes, but the Buddhist influence in the former is demonstrated in the three-lobed arch of the *miḥrāb*, where in Buddhist iconography the arch frames the head and shoulders of the Buddha. In structure and other decoration, however, the mosque follows strict Muslim traditions, and in plan the prayer hall is at the longer side of the rectangular courtyard, perhaps a reference to the Great Mosque of Damascus. In later brick buildings, liturgical requirements are observed but often expressed idiosyncratically, both in planning and structural form. Many consist of a fairly small prayer hall often covered with a single dome, with a corridor in front or running around three sides of the hall. There are corner columns, with the roof curved down toward the columns on all faces, imitating traditional domestic bamboo dwellings, as can still be seen in the peasant huts of remote villages. In about the 15th century glazed tiles were introduced in Bengal, displayed in many buildings. There is, however, a major problem in dating Bengal's sultanate edifices as, in spite of many foundation inscriptions surviving (Ravenshaw 1878; Dani 1957; Abdul Karim 1992), the inscriptions have been removed from one building to another, often more than once, and dating on stylistic grounds can be only approximate and not always reliable (Figure 5.2.6).

Other sultanate sites include Chhota Pandua in West Bengal, not far from Calcutta, where the ruinous Barī Masjid and a minaret built in exaggerated stepped tiers may date from the late 14th century, but most of the other sites are scattered in Bangladesh, in Bagerhat, Goardi, Mugapara, Sherpur, and Sonargaon (Dani 1961; Asher 1984; P. Hasan 2007). Bagerhat and its nearby site Sherpur in particular preserve a large number of Sultanate monuments, Sherpur being rich in unreported ruins still awaiting exploration, excavation, and restoration. Bengal was annexed to the Mughal Empire in 946 (1538) by Humāyūn and again in 983 (1575–1576) by Akbar; the region has numerous 16th- and 17th-century remains, including in the Bangladesh capital, Dhaka, principally a Mughal town, where the ruins of the Mughal fort and palaces attract visitors.

FIGURE 5.2.6 Gaur, the site of Lakhnautī, the Muslim capital of Bengal. Remains of unexcavated buildings of different periods can be seen in front of the Ḥājatgāh or Barā Masjid. The standing monuments are preserved and protected, but the vast site of the old capital remains unexcavated.

Mid-14th to Late 17th Century: Central and South India

The brutality and mismanagement of the Delhi sultan Muḥammad b. Tughluq (1325–1351) ended with the fragmentation of the Delhi Empire. Facing rebellions, the sultan himself had to remove his capital for a short time to Daulatabad (Mate and Pathy 1992; Qureshi 2004; Deloche 2005; Burton-Page 2008: 113–116) in the Deccan—the ancient Hindu Devagīrī, under Muslim control since 1307. The town with its well-preserved fortifications retains its already noted Jāmiʿ, a minaret, and a few other 14th- and 15th-century remains. The site has been cleared and partly excavated, providing a good example of a Hindu town converted and transformed to a Muslim layout.

Well before Muḥammad's death, independent sultanates were springing up in Maʿbar (Tamil Nadu) and the Deccan. The capital of the short-lived sultanate of Maʿbar was in Madura (Shokoohy 2003: 23–65), a major Hindu city with its magnificent Śrī Minakśi Temple, still a center of pilgrimage. The Muslim town, however, was, according to Ibn Baṭṭūṭa (1987 [Arabic]: 610), built to resemble Delhi. The old Qāḍī Tāj al-dīn Mosque, not far from the temple, may lead us to speculate how much of Muslim Madura may be under the present town, which has an entirely Hindu plan. But opposite the Hindu town and on the north bank of the Vaigai River is the enclosure containing the tombs of the two sultans—'Alā al-dīn Udaujī and Shams al-dīn 'Ādil Shāh—housed in a domed chamber surrounded by a colonnade, as well as a mosque and a few other tombs, all constructed of stone. The built-up neighborhood is now occupied by Muslims but in the past it might have been the site of the Muslim graveyard outside the town. In Tiruparangundram, where in a battle with the Vijayanagar forces the last Ma'bar sultan Sikandar Shāh fell, a mosque has been built next to his tomb under an exposed rock. Later a domed chamber was built over the rock, adjacent to the mosque. If Muslim Madura was to resemble Delhi, what is left of the mosques of the period shows that in their planning—consisting of a portico in front of the prayer hall—their style is more reminiscent of that of the Muslim trading communities, already seen in Kayalpatnam. The style of the sultans' tombs in Madura even shows links with tombs of Gujarat. What little knowledge we have on the sultanate of Ma'bar is through archaeology: a handful of coins, a few epigraphs, and the architectural remains, but much awaits exploration.

The Deccan was at first divided into two kingdoms: the Bahmanī sultanate in the north and the Hindu Kingdom of Vijayanagar, which, while employing Muslims in its army and trading with the coastal Muslim communities (who sold them, among other things, numerous horses; Varthema 1928: 50, 126), should remain outside our discussion. Nevertheless, some of their edifices incorporate Muslim traditions, such as vaults and domes (Michell and Nagaraja Rao 1990). The Bahmanīs, on the other hand, were devout Muslims, their founder 'Alā al-dīn Bahman Shāh claimed Sasanian origin, and the arches of their early buildings in their capital Gulbarga are crowned with a Sasanian style motif (Shokoohy 1994). Their structures, however, are mainly in the North Indian manner, but they abandoned the Tughluq-style battered walls. An exception is the covered Jāmi' mosque in the fort—a hybrid, displaying the planning of the mosques of the maritime communities but with a North Indian style superstructure. The fort of Gulbarga was occupied continuously, and little of the original structures remain on the surface except a bazaar street, the shops of which have been converted into houses. As usual, little systematic excavation has been carried out in the fort, the town, the royal necropolis, or any other sites of archaeological interest in the area.

Later, in 1429, the capital was taken to the newly built Bidar, where the town still retains its original street layout and many monuments. In the fort the palaces employed wood extensively, but not much is left because, when Bidar was falling to the Mughals, the buildings were set on fire intentionally to prevent the enemy using them. Nevertheless, the prevalent high quality of the tile work in the palaces and elsewhere indicates high levels of Deccani artistic achievement. The tiles have been gradually pilfered in the past few decades and presumably sold to collectors. Other major Bahmanī sites of archaeological interest include Daulatabad and its environs, as well as Raichur (Sarma 1998; Merklinger 1979), with both retaining many edifices. The site of Fīrūzābād, an unfinished town founded in 1399, has been partially surveyed (Michell and Eaton 1991: 21–64), but the remains of the palace, the Jāmi' mosque, and indeed the entire town await excavation (Figure 5.2.7).

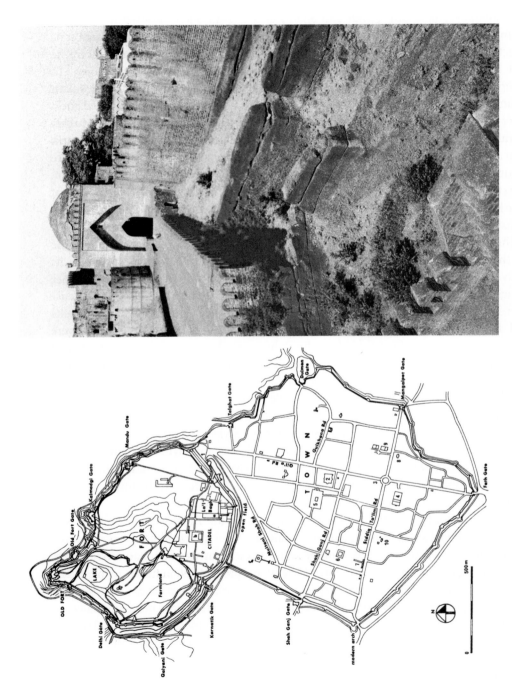

FIGURE 5.2.7 Bidar, the second Bahmani capital of the Deccan founded in 1428 on virgin ground. Left: Authors' plan of the town (after Yazdani). Most of the original urban layout is preserved including the two axial streets. Right: the formidable fort surrounded by a triple moat and its main entrance the Sharza Darwāza.

The Deccan, heavily influenced by Iranian culture, gradually became disposed to Sufi doctrines, and, by the late 15th century, the Bahmanī realm eventually disintegrated into several smaller kingdoms: the Quṭb Shāhīs in Golkonda, where the fort and a number of edifices have survived, but are not fully investigated (Sardar 2007); the Barīd Shāhīs of Bidar who replaced the Bahmanīs and have left the ruins of some palaces in the fort and numerous tombs and shrines (Yazdani 1947:13–14, 148–176); the ʿĀdil Shāhīs of Bijapur; and a number of smaller sultanates of short duration. The most significant archaeological remains are those of the ʿĀdil Shāhīs who built Bijapur as their new capital, studied by Cousins. Unlike other Muslim cities Bijapur has a roughly circular plan, approximating Hind urban planning, but Bijapur's architecture is markedly original, developed from that of the Bahmanīs. It employs new engineering practices of light walls, slim turrets, and large domed spaces, best represented in the Jāmiʿ, Sulṭān Ibrāhīm's Rauḍā, Afḍal Khān's tomb and mosque, and the Gul Gumbadh among many. Outside Bijapur stand many significant tomb chambers still awaiting investigation. In 1599, Ibrāhīm Shāh II founded near Bijapur the new, but unfinished town of Nausarpūr (Cousens 1916: 92–99), which has been neglected, but which provides ample opportunity for further exploration. The ʿĀdil-Shāhī territory went as far west as Goa, which was taken by the Portuguese in 1510, but in the nearby town of Ponda stands the Ṣafā Masjid, a curious hybrid of ʿĀdil Shāhī architectural tradition and those of the maritime settlers (Shokoohy 2003: 253–266).

15TH TO MID-16TH CENTURY: WEST INDIA

The small and short-lived sultanate of Mālwa (1392–1531), set between Gujarat and the Deccan, has left many fine edifices (archaeological reports in Cunningham 1906: 30–45; Barnes 1904; Brown 1981: 64–65; Marshall 1928: 617–625), both in their first capital Dhār and the second Mandu. Dhār, pre-Islamic in origin, was transformed to an Islamic configuration with crossing spinal streets, a fort at one corner, and a lake-sized reservoir on the lines seen in Tughluqabad. Dhār's street layout is preserved but the old town is now buried under later structures. The fort, restored in the Mughal period, contains ruins of a Mughal palace, but the major historical remains in the town are the mosque of Sultan Dilāwar Khān (808 [1405–1406]); the 15th-century Kamāl Maulā mosque and tomb; and the Lāt ki Masjid, named after a pre-Islamic iron pillar originally re-erected in front of it but pulled down by the Gujarat Sultan Bahādur. Its broken pieces are still preserved on the site. As symbols of conquest, the mosques are all built with temple spoil. Mandu (Yazdani 1929; Patil 1975), built over a natural flat top of a hill, has by contrast, an irregular perimeter, and while not much of the town is left, many palaces and other historical edifices are preserved, some in fairly good condition but many in ruins. The palaces are mainly set around lake-sized reservoirs with the Jahāz Maḥal (ship-palace) set between two of them. Most of the area within the perimeter of the walls was probably never built, but there are also remains from the time of Gujarat dominance and the Mughals. Many remains of Mandu were constructed with marble, some inlayed with other stones. The 17th-century marble architecture of Shāh Jahān is indebted to Mandu as it was his headquarters as a prince. Another major town of the sultanate was Chanderi (Cunningham 1871b: 401–412; Grade 1928; Nath 1979; Fussman and Sharma 1999) a defensive outpost founded early in the 15th century with the Katti-ghati, a gateway outside the town, carved out of solid rock, which could block entry to the territory. Chanderi is one of the best-preserved Muslim towns, with the fort, old market, and many houses and mansions still preserved but not yet fully studied. Two miles west of the town is the Kūshk Maḥal, an impressive multistoried building and probably the Sāt Manzil of histories, the residence of Maḥmūd Shāh Khaljī (1436–1469).

One of the archaeologically richest and also best-studied areas of West India is Gujarat, with numerous Islamic sites from both the pre- and post-conquest period. There is a legend in the Muslim world, unfounded but current at least since from the early 11th century, that in the very early days of Islam the pagans of Mecca smuggled the idol Manāt—whose worship was forbidden in the Qur'an (LIII, 19–25), together with the worship of *lāt* and *'uzzā*—via the maritime route to Somnath (Farrukhī Sīstānī 1335/1956: 69–71; Gardīzī 1347/1969: 190; al-Sanā'ī al-Ghaznawī, c. 1983: 512; Saʿdī 1363/1984: 374–377), providing an excuse for Maḥmūd of Ghazna's zeal (reinforced with greed) to sack the holy temple of Somnath in 1025–1026. In a vast graveyard between Veraval and Somnath the supposed graves of his soldiers are still revered by local Muslims. In the area at least two inscriptions are also preserved which refer to the maritime Muslims in the region (Hultzsch 1882; Sircar 1963; Desai 1962: 10–15, pl. 2; Shokoohy 2012: 306–310) adding to the edifices of Bhadreśvar and Junagadh the material evidence alluded to in the early Muslim geographies. Somnath, one of the holiest Hindu pilgrimage cities—and its neighboring towns, Veraval, Mangarol, and Junagadh—retain large Muslim populations who are custodians of their edifices (Burgess 1876; Cousens 1931; Shokoohy 2012: 297–335). This is not the case with the Jāmiʿ of Somnath, which is built out of temple spoil near the site of a demolished ancient temple and now serves as a museum displaying Hindu and Jain images, inflating the already uneasy Hindu–Muslim relationships in the town—a circumstance exploited by local and national politicians (Davis 2005: 92, fig. 14, 289, note 27). The Jāmiʿ is apparently later in date than other mosques, the Chaugān and Idrīs Masjids, both under Muslim custodianship and, in spite of their 14th-century origin, well preserved (Figure 5.2.8).

Gujarat was annexed to the sultanate of Delhi only in 1297—a century later than the conquest of Delhi—and one of the edifices related to the Delhi sultanate outside Somnath is the Jāmiʿ of Bharoch (c. 1297). Jalor and Sanchor, now in Rajasthan, were historically the borderland between Delhi and Gujarat territory, and the Jāmiʿ of Jalor seems to have been constructed in the early days of the conquest and completed at the time of Ghiyāth al-dīn Tughluq in 1325. Some aspects of pre-conquest Muslim traditions continue to be seen in Gujarat, and the only influence from Delhi may be in the use of temple spoil as building material and the introduction of a screen wall in front of the prayer hall, first seen in the Jāmiʿ of Cambay and later to become an important and highly decorative feature in the architecture of the Gujarat sultanate.

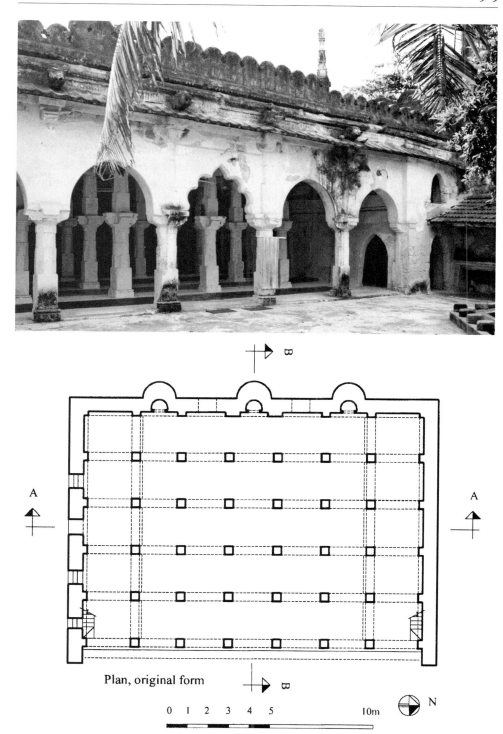

FIGURE 5.2.8 Gujarat, Somnath, the 14th-century Idrīs Masjid: plan showing the unusual upper galleries at either side of the prayer hall and a view of the prayer hall from the courtyard. Somnath, one of the holiest Hindu cities, has a sizable Muslim population, but their community and a large number of remains in the town and its environs are overlooked.

The rich architecture of this period, including mosques, shrines, step-wells, lake-size reservoirs, and even temples built with the sultans' permission were studied by Burgess and his team as noted and do not need to be repeated here. Their studies, although exhaustive, concentrated on major edifices in the main cities, such as Ahmadabad, Naharwāla (Patan), Cambay, and Champaner, and many modern publications with colorful images still rely on their survey material. The site of Champaner (Chāmpānir) (Burgess 1896: 39–44), a short-lived town founded in 1485 by Maḥmūd Bigara on a plan similar to that of Ahmadabad, is being explored and its monuments restored by the ASI. Unlike Ahmadabad, where the modern city has overpowered the old fabric, Champaner is an archaeological site and its ongoing exploration should give a deeper insight into the culture of the Gujarat sultanate.

However, Gujarat still preserves many sites and edifices that have attracted little or no attention. In the island of Diu, in spite of Portuguese dominance since the 16th century, the substantial Karao Jāmiʿ—datable to the 14th century—is one of the two main mosques still in use, and outside the town is a vast old Muslim cemetery, with shallow graves dug into solid rock but surmounted with stepped pyramidal tombstones, like those associated with the maritime settlers (Shokoohy and Shokoohy 2000a: 55–72; 2010a: 162–168). In the nearby town of Una, the Jāmiʿ, a fine specimen of the Gujarat sultanate architecture is still awaiting survey and a proper study, and there are other sites between Una and its port Dilwada still unexplored. In the Saurashtra peninsula, too, numerous sites in Junagadh are open fields for future archaeologists.

North-West India, 15th Century to the Mughal Era

To the north of Gujarat the state of Rajasthan was nominally under the dominance of Delhi but, apart from certain areas—Ajmer and the regions of Nagaur and Bayana—the rest remained in the hands of the Hindu Rajputs whose descendants made affiliations with the Mughals, some remaining influential in places such as Jodhpur, Jaipur, and Jaisalmer. Rajasthan's arid terrain, Tīmūr's attack on Delhi, and the consequent debilitated central power in Delhi during the 15th and 16th centuries contributed to the rise of autonomous—if not independent—principalities in Nagaur (Shokoohy and Shokoohy 1993) and Bayana. Shams Khān, the first independent ruler of Nagaur, was the brother of the Muẓaffar Shāh, the first Gujarat sultan, and the subsequent Khāns of Nagaur kept a close but guarded relationship with their relatives. Nagaur's architecture of this period is an amalgamation of Delhi and Gujarat styles.

Nagaur has an irregular circular fort founded in the early 12th century, and among the remains of the Delhi sultanate is the impressive 14th-century Buland Darwāza, the gate to the Khānaqāh of Ḥamīd al-dīn Chishtī. The independent Khāns, however, transformed the city to a smaller—but humbler and more modest—replica of their cousins' capital, Ahmadabad, complete with a royal square with a ceremonial gate at one end imitating the Tin Darwāza of Ahmadabad. Numerous mosques of the Khāns are scattered around the town, but in arid Nagaur it is the reservoirs and water channels in and outside the town that are of particular interest. While dilapidated, much of the old water system is still in use. Within the Nagaur territory Bari Khatu, Ladnun, and Naraina are all rich in historical remains but hardly explored archaeologically.

To the west of the region of Nagaur, Bayana's strategic position on the route from Delhi to Gwalior and the Deccan, combined with its formidable fort and natural and agricultural resources ranging from red sandstone to sugar and indigo, made it, in spite of its harsh desert environment, a prized possession of its mediaeval Hindu rulers, and it attracted the attention of the Ghurids in the very first years of the conquest. Archaeologically, it consists of three towns: Bayana on the plain, the Fort of Tahangar on the site of the ancient Hindu fortification of Viajayamandargarh, and Sikandar Lodī's unfinished garden city of Sikandra between the fort and the town. We have already noted the two substantial monuments of this period, the Jāmiʿ (now known as Ukhā Mandīr mosque) and its open prayer ground (ʿīdgāh). Other early 14th-century remains, such as the reservoir known as Jhālar Bāʾolī and an extension to the Jāmiʿ (known as Ukhā Masjid), praised by Ibn Baṭṭūṭa as "one of the finest mosques, with walls and ceilings all of stone" (Ibn Baṭṭūṭa, 1987 [Arabic]: 542–545; [tr.] 1994, 4: 774–775) set the regional style displayed in the later monuments of the autonomous Auḥadī Khāns of the 15th century and also those of Sikandar Lodi.

The architecture of Bayana (Shokoohy and Shokoohy 2000b, 2004, 2005, 2010b, 2020), isolated from Delhi, flourished independently, and diverse forms emerged. These included chatrīs (free-standing pavilions) with false domes set over flat roofs and canopies in chatrī form but with three columns on each façade and some even with a column in the center, types which never appeared elsewhere in India. The most significant architectural contribution of the Auḥadīs is the urban development in the Fort (destroyed in an earthquake in 1505 and abandoned afterwards) preserving the original street layouts, still unexplored, together with mosques, a lofty minaret dated 861 (1456–1457), the rulers' mansion, and numerous houses, leaving us with examples of 15- and 16th-century domestic dwellings rare elsewhere in India. One of the mosques, the Taletī Masjid, dating from 823 (1420), has its prayer hall protruding into the courtyard, a complete departure from the usual Indian mosque plan and first seen in the Bayana region. This formula is repeated in three other mosques of the time of Lodī dominance and was to become a characteristic of Mughal mosques.

In 910 (1504–1505) Sikandar Lodi toyed with the idea of making Bayana his new capital and began to build Sikandra, a new town to the east of the fort, but he later decided on Agra (then a village in the Bayana territory) and Sikandra was left unfinished. The town's main reservoir and the ruins of its imposing new Jāmiʿ in the Delhi style have survived. Outside the town, the gardens built by his nobles have now reverted to farmland, but the archaeological remains include reservoirs and a gateway known as Laʿl Darwāza. As a garden city Agra seems to have been designed on the prototype of Sikandra. In the region, other towns such as Didwana and Khanwa preserve numerous remains that await exploration. In Dholpur, on the borderland between the territories of Gwalior and

Bayana, the tomb of Bībī Zarrīna, Sikandar Lodī's mother (d. 922 [1516]), represents the extent of Bayana's artistic influence. The archaeological remains in Bayana, such as the multistoried step-well built in 901 (1496), a pleasure pavilion dated 940 (1533–1534), and many others indicate that the Mughal architectural style did not develop independently but had its roots engrained in the centuries-old traditions of Bayana.

With the decline of Bayana in the 16th century we enter the Mughal era, with its outstanding monuments well-preserved and well-studied. But still many sites await perusal, not just for areas to be excavated but also for the still functioning historic urban fabric of provincial towns, so far ignored by archaeologists, architects, and urban designers alike. In short, Muslim archaeological sites in the subcontinent are understudied and hardly excavated systematically. Much is left for present and future archaeologists to explore.

References

Abdul Karim 1992. *Corpus of the Arabic and Persian Inscriptions of Bengal* (Dhaka: Asiatic Society of Bangladesh).

al-Balādhurī 1987. *Futūḥ al-buldān*, A. A. al-Ṭabbāʿ (ed.) (Arabic Text) (Beirut: Muʿassisāt al-maʿārif l'il-ṭibāʿat wa al-naṣr).

al-Iṣṭakhrī 1961. *Al-masālik wa al-mamālik*, M. J. A. Al-Husaini (ed.) (Arabic Text) (Cairo: The United Arab Republic, Ministry of Culture and National Guidance, General Culture Administration).

al-Iṣṭakhrī 1961. *Masālik wa mamālik*, I. Afshar (ed.) (Persian Texts series: 9) (Tehran: Bungāh-i tarjuma wa nashr-i kitāb).

Allen, C. 2008/2011. *The Buddha and Dr. Führer: An Archaeological Scandal.* Revised 2011. (London: Haus Publishing).

al-Muqaddasī 1906. *Aḥsan al-taqāsīm fī maʿrifat al-aqālīm*, M. J. de Goeje (ed.) (Leiden: Brill).

Al-Sanāʾi al-Ghaznawī. 1329 (1950). *Ḥadīqat al-ḥaqīqa wa sharīʿat al-ṭarīqa*, M. T. Mudarris-Razavi (ed.) (Tehran).

Asher, C. B. 1984. "Inventory of key monuments," in G. Michell (ed.), *The Islamic Heritage of Bengal* (Paris: UNESCO), 37–136.

Ashfaque, S. M. 1969. "The Grand Mosque at Banbhore," *Pakistan Archaeology*, 6: 182–209, pls. 21–26.

Bakkarī, M. M. 1938. *Tārīkh-i Sindh* (Poona: Bhandarkar Oriental Research Institute).

Barnes, E. 1904. "Dhar and Mandu," *Journal of the Bombay Branch of the Royal Asiatic Society*, 21: 339–391.

Bengal Government 1810. *The Regulations and Laws Enacted by the Governor General in Council, for the Civil Government of the Whole of the Territories Under the Presidency of Fort William in Bengal*, Regulation 19: 1–3 (Calcutta).

Blochmann, H. 1870. "Notes on Places of Historical Interest in the District of Hughly," *Journal of the Asiatic Society of Bengal*, 39: 109–205.

Boileau, J. T. 1833. "Description of a Sun Dial in the Court of Motī Masjid in the Fort of Agra," *Journal of the Asiatic Society of Bengal*, 2/17: 251–252.

Brown, P. 1981. *Indian Architecture (Islamic Period)*, 1942, revised edition (Bombay: Taraporewala).

Burgess, J. 1875. *Memorandum on the Remains at Gumli, Gop, and in Kachh* (Bombay: Government Central Press).

Burgess, J. 1876. *Report on the Antiquities of Kāthiāwād and Kachh* (London: Allen).

Burgess, J. 1896. *On the Muhammadan Architecture of Bharoch, Cambay, Dholka, Champanir and Mahmudabad in Gujarat* (London: Griggs).

Burgess, J. 1900. *The Muhammadan Architecture of Ahmadabad, Part I, A. D. 1412 to 1520* (London: Griggs).

Burgess, J. 1905a. *The Muhammadan Architecture of Ahmadabad, Part II, with Muslim and Hindu Remains in the Vicinity* (London: Quartitch).

Burgess, J. 1905b. "Sketch of Archaeological Research," *Journal of the Bombay Branch of the Royal Asiatic Society*, the Centenary Memorial Volume, 1905: 131–162.

Burgess, J., and Cousens, H. 1903. *Architectural Antiquities of Northern Gujarat* (London: Quartitch).

Burton-Page, J. 2008. *Indian Islamic Architecture: Forms and Typologies, Sites and Monuments*, G. Michell (ed.) (Leiden—Boston: Brill).

Carlleyle, A. C. L. 1878. "Report of a Tour in Eastern Rajputana in 1871–2 and 1872–3," *Archaeological Survey of India* (Calcutta), 6: 40–76, pls. 4–8.

Chakravarti, M. 1909. "Notes on Gaur and Other Places in Bengal," *Journal of the Asiatic Society of Bengal*, 5: 199–235.

Colvin, J. 1833. "On the Restoration of the Ancient Canals in the Delhi Territory," *Journal of the Asiatic Society of Bengal*, 2/15: 105–127.

Cousens, H. 1903–1904. "Brahmanābād-Manṣūra in Sind," *Annual Report of the Archaeological Survey of India*, 133–144.

Cousens, H. 1908–1909. "Excavations at Brahmanābād," *Annual Report of the Archaeological Survey of India*, 79–87.

Cousens, H. 1916. *Bījāpūr and its Architectural Remains* (Bombay: Government Central Press).

Cousens, H. 1929. *The Antiquities of Sind* (Archaeological Survey of India Imperial Series, 46) (Calcutta: Government Central Publication Branch).

Cousens, H. 1931. *Somanātha and Other Mediaeval Temples in Kāthiāwāḍ* (Archaeological Survey of India Imperial Series: 45) (Calcutta: Government Central Publication Branch).

Creighton, H. 1817. *The Ruins of Gaur* (London: Black, Parbury and Allen).

Cunningham, A. 1871a. *The Ancient Geography of India* (London: Trübner).

Cunningham, A. 1871b. "Four Reports Made During the Years 1862–63–64–65 (Report of 1864–65)," *Archaeological Survey of India (Calcutta)*, 2: 401–412.

Cunningham, A. 1882. "Report on a Tour of Bihar and Bengal in 1879–80," *Archaeological Survey of India* (Calcutta), 15: 39–94.

Cunningham, A. 1885. "Report of a Tour in Eastern Rajputana in 1882–83," *Archaeological Survey of India* (Calcutta), 20: 60–88, pls. 13–18.

Cunningham, A. 1906. "Conservation of Ancient Buildings in Māndū and Dhār," *Annual Report of the Archaeological Survey of India* (report for 1903–4), 30–45.

Dani, A. H. 1957. "Bibliography of the Muslim Inscriptions of Bengal (down to A. D. 1538)," *Journal of the Asiatic Society of Pakistan*, 2, appendix (147 pp. published separately).

Dani, A. H. 1961. *Muslim Architecture of Bengal* (Dacca: Asiatic Society of Pakistan).

Davis, R. H. 2005. "Memories of Broken Idols," in I. A. Bierman (ed.), *The Experience of Islamic Art on the Margins of Islam* (Reading: Garnet), 133–168.

Deloche, J. 2005. "Etudes sur les fortifications de l'Inde. V, La forteresse de Daulatabad au Maharashtra," *Bulletin de l'Ecole Française d'Extrême Orient* (Paris), 92: 181–239.

Desai, Z. A. 1962. "Arabic Inscriptions of the Rajput Period from Gujarat," *Epigraphia Indica, Arabic and Persian Supplement* (Calcutta: Government of India Press), 1961: 12–14.

Farooq, A. A. 1986. "Excavations at Manṣūrah," *Pakistan Archaeology*, 10: 3–35.

Farrukhī Sīstānī 1335/1956. *Dīwān-i Ḥakīm Farrukhī Sīstānī*, M. Dabir-Siyaqi (ed.) (Tehran: Iqbāl).

Fergusson, J. 1876. *History of Indian and Eastern Architecture* (1st ed., in 1 vol.) (London: John Murray).

Fergusson, J. 1910. *History of Indian and Eastern Architecture*. revised edition, J. Burgess (ed. Indian Architecture) and R. P. Spiers (ed. Eastern Architecture) (in 2 vols.) (London: John Murray).

Fleet, J. F. 1885. "Sanskrit and Old-Kanarese Inscriptions, Inscription No. 151, Byānā Stone-Inscription of the Adhirāja Vijaya. – Samvat 1100," *Indian Antiquary*, 14: 8–12.

Fleet, J. F. 1886. "Sripatha, The Ancient Sanskrit Name of Byana," *Indian Antiquary*, 15: 239.

Fredunbeg, M. K. (tr.) 1902. *The Chachnama* (2 vols.) (Karachi: Commissioner's Press).

Führer, A. A., and Smith, E. W. 1889. *The Sharqi Architecture of Jaunpur* (Archaeological Survey of India, New Imperial Series, 11) (Calcutta/London: Superintendent Government Printing).

Fussman, G., and Sharma, K. L. 1999. *Chanderi 1990-1995*, Publications de l'Institut de civilisation indienne, Série 80; fasc. 68 (Paris: Diffusion de Boccard).

Gardīzī 1347 (1969). *Zain al-akhbār*, A. H. Habibi (ed.) (Tehran: Bunyād-i Farhang-i Īrān).

Ghafur, M. A. 1966. "Fourteen Kufic Inscriptions of Bhanbhore: The Site of Daibul," *Pakistan Archaeology*, 3: 65–90, pls. 25–39.

Government of Madras 1917. "Regulation VII, 1817 of the Madras Code 'for the due appropriation of the rents and produce of lands granted for the support of Mosques, Hindu Temples and Colleges or other public purposes; for the maintenance and repair of Bridges, Choultries, or Chattrams, and other public buildings; and for the custody and disposal of Escheats'" (Madras).

Grade, M. B. 1928. *Guide to Chanderi* (Gwalior: Archaeology Department).

Harding, R. 2008–2010. "Trade and Pilgrimage to South Asia Before 1000 CE, Survey in Kanyakumari District (UCL Institute of Archaeology project)," at http://www.cic.ames.cam.ac.uk/pages/harding2.html. The report is unpublished or unavailable.

Hasan, M. Z. (complier) 1920. *Monuments of Delhi, Lasting Splendour of the Great Mughals and Others*, J. A. Page et al. (eds.) (4 vols.) ASI Northern Circle (reprinted New Delhi: Aryan Books, 1997).

Hasan, P. 2007. *Sultans and Mosques: The Early Muslim Architecture of Bangladesh* (London: Tauris).

Hasan, S. M. 1971. *Mosque Architecture of Pre-Mughal Bengal* (Dacca: University Press).

Hillenbrand, R. 1992. "Turco-Iranian Elements in the Medieval Architecture of Pakistan: The Case of the Tomb of Rukn-i 'Alam at Multan," *Muqarnas*, 9: 148–174.

Hillenbrand, R. 1994. *Islamic Architecture, Form and Function* (Edinburgh: Edinburgh University Press).

Hultzsch, E. 1882. "A Grant of Arjunadèva of Gujarat Dated 1264 AD," *Indian Antiquary*, 11: 241–245.

Husain, M. M. A. 1936. "Record of All the Quranic and Non-Historical Epigraphs on the Protected Monuments in the Delhi Province," *Memoirs of the Archaeological Survey of India* (Calcutta), 47: 96–119.

Hussain, I. 1989. "Manṣūrah: The First Capital of Muslims in Sindh," *Journal of the Pakistan Historical Society*, 37/3: 293–303.

Huxley, A. 2004. "Dr. Führer's Wanderjahre: The Early Career of a Victorian Archaeologist," *Journal of the Royal Asiatic Society*, Third Series 20/4: 489–502.

Ibn Baṭṭūṭa 1958–2000. *The Travels of Ibn Baṭṭūṭa A. D. 1325–1354*, H. A. R. Gibb (tr.) (5 vols.) (London: Hakluyt Society).

Ibn Baṭṭūṭa 1987. *Tuḥfat al-nuẓẓār fī gharā'ib al-amṣār wa 'ajā'ib al-asfār*, known as *Raḥla*, T. Harb (ed.) (Arabic text) (Beirut: Dār al-kutub al-'ilmīya).

Ibn Ḥauqal 1873. *Ṣūrat al-arḍ*, M. J. de Goeje (ed.) (Leiden: Brill).

Khan, A. A. 1931. *Memoirs of Gaur and Pandua*, rev. ed. B. Stapelton (Calcutta: Bengal Secretariat Book Depot).

Khan, A. Nabi. 1983. *Multan: history and architecture* (Islamabad: Islamic University).

Khan, F. A. 1969. *Banbhore, A Preliminary Report on the Recent Archaeological Excavations at Banbhore* (3rd revised ed.) (Karachi: Department of Archaeology and Museums).

Khan, M. N. 1985. "A Ghaznavid Historical Inscription from Uḍegrām, Swāt," *East and West*, 35: 153–166.

Khan, S. A. 1854. *Āthār al-ṣanādīd*, Delhi, 1846, reprinted 1847; revised in 1852 and published with a short English introduction and title page as *Asar-oos-sunnadeed, a history of old and new rules, or governments, and of old and new buildings in the district of Delhi, complied by Syud Ahmad Khan* (Delhi: W. Demonte).

Khwand Mīr. 1974. *Ḥabīb al-Siyar*, M. Dabir-Siyaqi (ed.) (4 vols.) (Tehran: Kitāb khāna-yi Khayyām), 1333 (1954), reprinted 1353 (1975).

Marshall, J. 1928. "The Monuments of Muslim India," in W. Haig (ed.), *The Cambridge History of India* (Cambridge: Cambridge University Press), 3: 568–663, pls. 1–51.

Mate, M. S., and Pathy, T. V. (eds.) 1992, *Daulatabad: a Report on the Archaeological Investigations* (Pune: Deccan College).

Merklinger, E. S. 1979. "The Mosques of Rāičūr: A Preliminary Classification," *Kunst des Orients*, 12: 79–94.

Michell, G., and Eaton, R. 1991. *Firuzabad: Palace City of the Deccan* (Oxford: Oxford University Press).

Michell, G., and Nagaraja Rao, M. S. 1990. *Vijayanagara, Architectural Inventory of the Urban Core* (Mysore: Directorate of Archaeology & Museums, Vijayanagara Research Centre series: 5, 2 vols.).

Minhāj-i Sirāj Jauzjānī 1984. *Ṭabaqāt-i Nāṣirī*, A. H. Habibi (ed.) (2 vols.) (Tehran: Dunyā-yi kitāb).

Mīr Khwand 1853–1854. *Rauḍat al-ṣafā*, 4, no page number, but under "*dhikr-i fatḥ-i Sūmanāt*" (Tehran).

Muhammed, K. K. 1991. "Excavation of a Catholic Chapel at Fatehpur Sikri," *Indica*, 28/1: 1–11.

Naqvi, S. A. A. 1947. "Sultān Ghārī, Delhi," *Ancient India*, 3: 4–10.

Nath, R. 1979. *The Art of Chanderi: A Study of the 15th Century Monuments of Chanderi* (New Delhi: Ambika).

Page, J. A. 1926. "An Historical Memoir on the Qutb: Delhi," *Memoirs of the Archaeological Survey of India*: 22 (Calcutta: Government of India Central Publication Branch).

Pakistan Department of Archaeology 1964. Excavation at Banbhore (author not given, but under Departmental Excavations), *Pakistan Archaeology*, 1: 49–55, pls. 14–23.

Patil, D. R. 1975. *Mandu* (New Delhi: Archaeological Survey of India).

Petruccioli, A. 1988. *Fathpur Sikri: città del sole e delle acque* (Rome: Carucci).

Petruccioli, A. 1992. *Fatehpur Sikri* (Berlin: Ernst).

Petruccioli, A. 2007. *Fathpur Sikri: la capitale dell'impero Moghul, la meraviglia di Akbar* (Milan: Electra).

Qureshi, D. 2004. *Fort of Daulatabad* (Delhi: Bharataya Kala Prakashan).

Rashid, N. 1998. "Al-Manṣūrah: The Lost City," *Journal of the Pakistan Historical Society* 46/4: 61–76.

Ravenshaw, J. H. 1878. *Gaur: Its Ruins and Inscriptions* (London, Kegan Paul).

Rizvi, S. A. A. 1972. *Fatehpur Sikri* (New Delhi: Archaeological Survey of India).

Saʿdī 1363/1984. *Būstān in Kulliyāt-i Saʿdī*, M. A. Furūqī (ed.) (Tehran: Amīr Kabīr).

Sardar, M. 2007. *Golconda Through Time: A Mirror of the Evolving Deccan* (Ph.D Thesis, New York University).

Sarma, V. S. 1998. *History and Antiquities of Raichur Fort* (Delhi: Bharatiya Kala Prakashan).

Scerrato, U. 1981. "Survey of Wooden Mosques and Related Wood Carvings in the Swat Valley, Under IsMEO Activities," *East and West*, 31: 178–181, figs. 22–36.

Scerrato, U. 1984. "The Wooden Architecture of Swat and the Northern Areas of Pakistan," *East and West*, 34/4: 501–515.

Sharma, D. V. 2008. *Archaeology of Fatehpur Sikri, New Discoveries* (New Delhi: Aryan Books).

Shokoohy, M. 1988a. *Bhadreśvar, the Oldest Islamic Monuments in India* (Leiden: Brill).

Shokoohy, M. 1994. "Sasanian Emblems and Their Reemergence in the Fourteenth-Century Deccan," *Muqarnas*, 11: 65–78.

Shokoohy, M. 2003. *Muslim Architecture of South India, the Sultanate of Maʿbar and the Traditions of the Maritime Settlers on the Malabar and Coromandel Coasts (Tamil Nadu, Kerala and Goa)* (London/New York: Routledge).

Shokoohy, M. 2012. "The Legacy of Islam in Somnath," *Bulletin of the School of Oriental and African Studies*, 75/2: 297–335.

Shokoohy, M., and Shokoohy, N. H. 1987. "The Architecture of Baha al-din Tughrul in the Region of Bayana, Rajasthan," *Muqarnas*, 4: 114–132.

Shokoohy, M., and Shokoohy, N. H. 1988b. *Hiṣār-i Fīrūza, Sultanate and Early Mughal Architecture in the District of Hisar, India* (London: Monographs on Art Archaeology and Architecture).

Shokoohy, M., and Shokoohy, N. H. 1993. *Nagaur, Sultanate and Early Mughal History and Architecture of the District of Nagaur, India* (London: Royal Asiatic Society Monograph, 28).

Shokoohy, M., and Shokoohy, N. H. 2000a. "The Karao Jāmiʿ Mosque of Diu in the Light of the History of the Island," *South Asian Studies*, 16: 55–72.

Shokoohy, M., and Shokoohy, N. H. 2000b. "Domestic Dwellings in Muslim India: Mediaeval House Plans," *Bulletin of the Asia Institute*, 14: 89–110.

Shokoohy, M., and Shokoohy, N. H. 2004. "A History of Bayana – Part 1: From the Muslim Conquest to the End of the Tughluq Period," *The Medieval History Journal*, 7/2: 279–324.

Shokoohy, M., and Shokoohy, N. H. 2005. "A History of Bayana – Part 2: From the Rise of the Auḥadīs to the Early Mughal Period (Fifteenth–Seventeenth Centuries)," *The Medieval History Journal*, 8/2: 323–400.

Shokoohy, M., and Shokoohy, N. H. 2006. "The Indian ʿīdgāh and its Persian Prototype the namāzgāh or muṣallā," in P. L. Baker and B. Brend (eds.), *Sifting Sands, Reading Signs: Studies in Honour of Professor Géza Fehérvári* (London: Forge Publications, distribution SOAS), 105–119.

Shokoohy, M., and Shokoohy, N. H. 2010a. "The Island of Diu, Its Architecture and Historic Remains," *South Asian Studies*, 26: 161–190.

Shokoohy, M., and Shokoohy, N. H. 2010b. "The Mosques of Bayana, Rajasthan, and the Emergence of a Prototype for the Mosques of the Mughals," *The Medieval History Journal*, 8/2: 153–197.

Shokoohy, M., and Shokoohy, N. H., 2020. *Bayana: The Sources of Mughal Architecture* (Edinburgh: Edinburgh University Press).

Sircar, D. C. 1963. "Veraval Inscription of Chaulukya-Vaghela Arjuna, 1264 A. D.," *Epigraphia Indica* (report for 1961–2), 34/4: 141–150.

Smith, E. W. 1894–1898. *The Moghul Architecture of Fathpur-Sikri* (4 vols.) (Allahabad: Government Press).

Sotoodeh, M. (ed.) 1962. *Ḥudūd al ʿālam min al-mashriq ilʾal-maqhrib* (Tehran: University of Tehran).

Temple, R. C. 1922. "Fifty Years of 'The Indian Antiquary,'" *Indian Antiquary*, 1–16.

Thomas, E. 1851. "An Account of Eight Kúfic Silver Coins," *Journal of the Asiatic Society of Bengal*, 20/7: 537–544.

Varthema, L. di 1928. *The Itinerary of Ludovico di Varthema of Bologna from 1502 to 1508* (tr.) John Winter Jones with a discourse by R. C. Temple (London: Hakluyt Society).

Waddington, H. 1946. "'Ādilābād, a Part of the Fourth Delhi," *Ancient India*, 1: 60–76.

Yamamoto, T. et al. 1967–1970. *Delhi: Architectural Remains of the Delhi Sultanate Period* (3 vols.) (Tokyo: Institute of Oriental Culture, University of Tokyo).

Yazdani, G. 1916. "The Antiquities of Warangal," *Journal of the Hyderabad Archaeological Society*, 34–47.

Yazdani, G. 1929. *Mandu, the City of Joy* (Oxford: Oxford University Press).

Yazdani, G. 1947. *Bidar, Its History and Monuments* (Oxford: Oxford University Press).

CHINA

JACQUELINE M. ARMIJO

INTRODUCTION

WITHIN the first century of the Islamic period, Muslim traders began settling in China's major centers of international commerce: the capital city Chang'an (present day Xi'an) in central China and the port city of Canton (present day Guangzhou), along China's southeast coast. Over the centuries the number of Muslims from Central Asia and the Middle East who settled in China increased to the hundreds of thousands, eventually reaching every region of China (Figure 5.3.1).

China's Muslim population today is conservatively estimated to be more than 23 million. Of China's fifty-five officially recognized ethnic minority groups, ten are predominantly Muslim, the largest two being the Hui, who are spread throughout the country, and the Uyghur who live primarily in Xinjiang province in northwest China and who are not the focus of this chapter. The Hui are the descendants of the foreign Muslim settlers, and the Uyghur are a Turkic people who have lived in the Xinjiang region for more than a millennia (Millward 2007: 42). This chapter focuses on the Hui in the region of China historically known as the heartland, stretching as far west as present-day Yunnan, Sichuan, and Gansu provinces. Despite their long and complex history in China, the Muslims of China remain a relatively understudied field of study. The study of the archaeology of Islam in China is even more neglected.

The study of the archaeology of Islam in China is made especially challenging for several reasons. Between the 7th and 15th centuries there were two major waves of Muslim immigrants to different regions of China, and between the 18th and 19th centuries there were several periods of violent uprisings that resulted in major Muslim communities being decimated and their mosques and monuments destroyed. In the 20th century, during the Cultural Revolution (1966–1976) mosques, together with all places of religious worship in China, came under systematic attack throughout the country. Almost every mosque (estimated to be around 40,000 at that time) was damaged, and many were destroyed. During this period Muslim cemeteries were also extensively damaged.

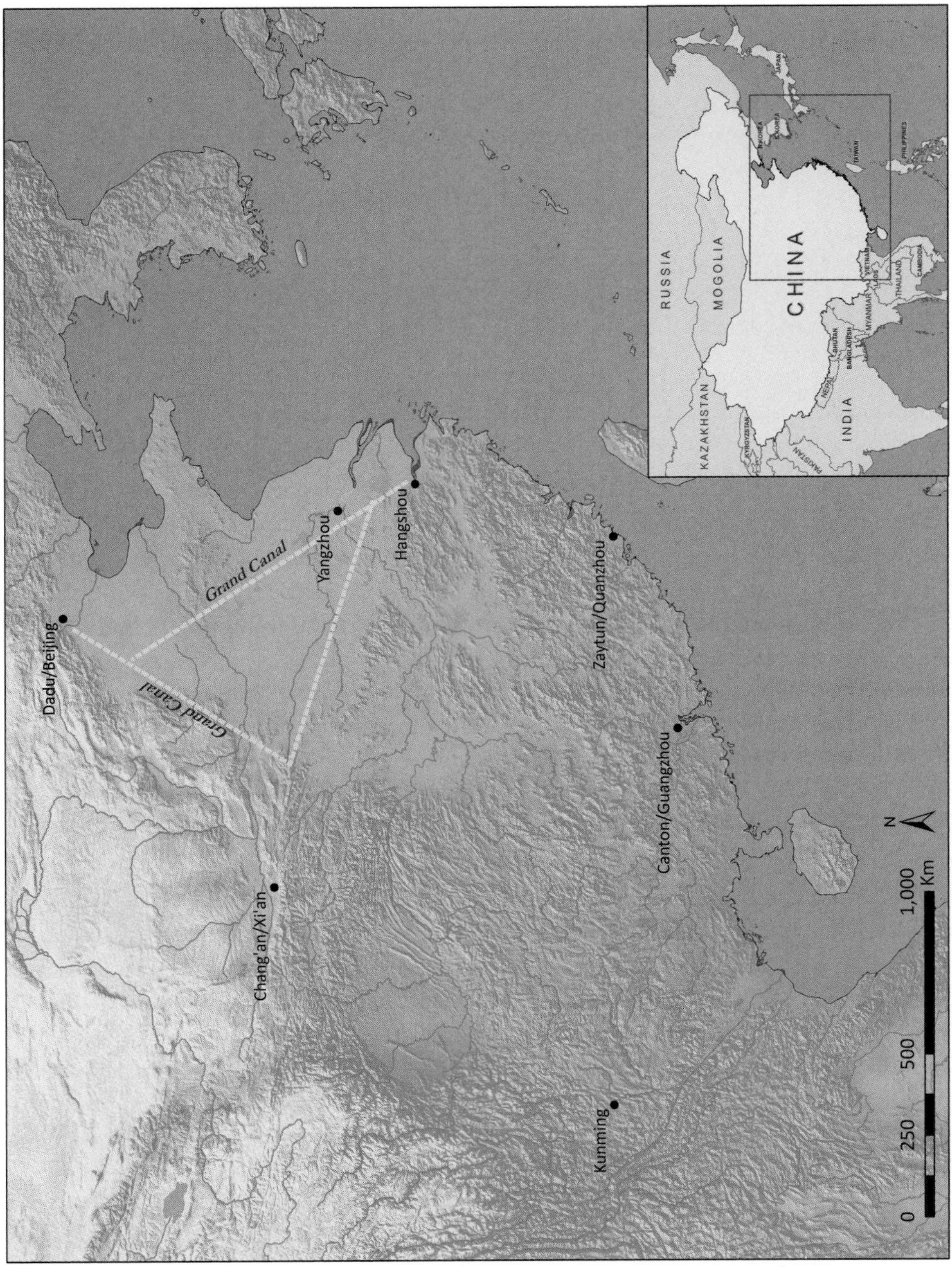

FIGURE 5.3.1 Map of the locations mentioned.

Ironically, some of the most serious damage to China's Islamic archaeological sites has occurred subsequently over the past thirty years as a result of urban Muslim neighborhoods being the "beneficiaries" of government development projects and Muslim communities across the country deciding to tear down some of their own mosques (which are traditionally strongly influenced by classical Chinese Buddhist temple architectural styles) to be replaced with mosques that are perceived as being more "authentic" by following designs more common in the Middle East (Figure 5.3.2) Some of these decisions are made by communities on their own, but in many instances foreign donors (primarily from Saudi Arabia) have expressed their disdain for what they consider to be *shirk* influence in the design and decoration of the mosques. However, there is evidence that this trend has ended, with increasing numbers of Chinese Muslim communities choosing to maintain traditional designs when renovating mosques. Interest in traditional Chinese Islamic arts and craftsmanship has been growing recently.

Although the study of the archaeology of China is one of the most developed and internationally recognized fields of study in the world (Chang 1977; Liu and Chen 2012), the study of the archaeology of Islam in China, as a field, is virtually unknown. There are no books covering the topic and no articles providing an overview of the state of the field across China. There are, however, a handful of scholars who have focused on specific examples of Islamic archaeology in China. The majority of this work is on the

FIGURE 5.3.2 The Jinbi Road Mosque in Kunming, Yunnan Province. Photo taken in late 1990s, mosque torn down in early 2000s.

Courtesy of J. Armijo.

archaeological finds found in the coastal city of Quanzhou, with the pioneering work of Wu Wenliang (1957/2005) and Chen Dasheng (1984) being the most important.

More recently two books published on historic mosques in China offer important contributions to the study of the Islamic archaeology of China. Nancy Steinhardt's *China's Early Mosques* (2016) is the first work to cover mosques throughout China, both in terms of their history and design. Another important recent work on mosques examines the history of a mosque in Hangzhou. Focusing on the history of one of the most important Persian Muslim communities in China, George Lane's *The Phoenix Mosque* (2017) provides the most in depth study of one specific mosque site in China.

This chapter begins with an overview of the history of Muslims in China that will help explain some of the reasons that the study of the Islamic archaeology of China is so challenging. The next section will highlight the limited known surviving important archaeological sources. The final section will discuss potential future developments in the field and the possible role of the Chinese government in supporting specialized study within this field as part of its massive Road and Belt Initiative seeking to link most of Asia through various trade and infrastructure projects. In addition to regularly incorporating historical Silk Road imagery and historic ties, China is highlighting the cultural ties linking it with the Middle East and using archaeological evidence from Chinese Muslim communities to document those historic links and strengthen cultural relations.

EARLIEST MUSLIM COMMUNITIES IN CHINA

During the Tang Dynasty (618–907), Chang'an developed into the largest and most cosmopolitan city in the world. With a population of more than one million, it attracted traders, as well as diplomats and envoys, from throughout Asia (Lewis 2009). It also became a city known for welcoming followers of different religions, so, in addition to having Arabs, Turks, Uighurs, Persians, Mongols, Japanese, Koreans, Sogdians, Indians, and other ethnic groups, it also had large communities of Muslims, Nestorian Christians, Jews, Mazdeans, Zoroastrians, Manicheans, and Hindus (Drake 1943).

Although historical records from the Tang Dynasty document that, between 651 and 798, there were almost three dozen official embassies from Arabia that arrived in the Chinese capital of Chang'an (Leslie 1986: 11), there is no surviving archaeological evidence that a permanent community of foreign Muslims settled in China during that time. Several mosques have steles or inscriptions claiming that the original building dated to the 7th century, but centuries of repeated rebuilding and renovations have made it difficult, if not impossible, to document those claims. In addition, no Muslim cemeteries from this period have been discovered. It appears that although there were significant groups of Muslims in China at this point, they had not yet settled long enough to form permanent communities.

During this same period increasing numbers of traders from the Persian Gulf region had been using the monsoon winds to propel their dhows as far as China, setting up temporary residences in Canton (Leslie 1986: 38–40). Once navigators had mastered the use of the monsoon winds and were familiar with the more treacherous stretches of the sea routes, it became clear that even a relatively small dhow could carry cargo more efficiently and safely than camels crossing thousands of miles/kilometers overland across challenging terrain. Dhows would leave the Gulf loaded with pearls, frankincense, and other local products, and, as they made their way across the Indian Ocean and the Straits of Malacca, they would stop at different ports along the way to pick up additional cargo before arriving in the South China Sea and putting to port in Guangzhou.

The degree to which China, as early as the 9th century, had already developed regional centers for the mass production of goods for the markets of the Gulf and the Middle East, did not become known until 1998, when a shipwrecked dhow was discovered off the coast of Indonesia. This small dhow, measuring only 60 feet in length, was heading back to the Gulf when it foundered. When the shipwreck was excavated it was found to have been carrying more than 70,000 objects, primarily pottery, but also a few luxury goods and antiques. Included among the luxury goods were four cups and three dishes made of solid gold, as well as four bowls, two platters, and exquisite wine flask made of silver. It is not known whether or not these items were intended as gifts for the royal courts of the Middle East or to facilitate safe passage and trade through the seas of South East Asia. In his study of them François Louis noted that, "Exquisitely manufactured and extremely rare, these objects figure among the most important discoveries of Tang gold and silver ever made. Even more intriguing is that this is the first such discovery made outside China" (Louis 2011: 85).

The pottery, while mass produced, also included designs meant for different Middle East markets. Analysis showed that the pottery had come from kilns in different regions of China, further indicating the degree to which the mass production of goods for foreign export had begun by the end of the 8th century. The vast majority of the ceramic ware was made up of some 55,000 painted bowls made in the kilns of Changsha in Hunan province. There were also ceramic pieces from other regions, including "green-glazed Yue tablewares from Zhejiang, large storage jars from Guangzhou, high-quality, white-glazed stonewares from Hebei and Henan, and white- and green-splashed stoneware recently confirmed as being from Gongxian" (Guy 2011: 20). The hand-sewn dhow is believed to have been built in Oman and had been heading back to the major port cities of the Gulf at that time: Siraf and Basra (Hsieh 2011: 140).

It was not until several centuries later, during the Mongol Yuan Dynasty (1271–1368), that archaeological evidence confirms the presence of large foreign Muslim communities who had settled permanently in China, built prominent mosques, and established cemeteries for their congregations. Once the Mongols had set their sights on the Chinese empire it did not take them long to conquer the entire territory. However, unlike in other regions of the world where the Mongols had formed alliances with local leaders to have them rule in their stead, in China the Mongols did not trust the Chinese to act on their behalf and instead sought out foreigners to assist in the governing of China. Tens of thousands of officials were recruited from Central and Southwestern Asia and were assigned to posts throughout the entire empire. Scientists, scholars, engineers, and other professional groups were also recruited to help develop the newly created empire. These men, who were mostly Muslim, brought with them the latest knowledge in the fields of astronomy, hydraulic and military engineering, architecture, and medicine and pharmacology. Although it is widely known that the Middle East benefitted greatly from the transfer of the papermaking skills and knowledge of gunpowder from China centuries earlier, the transfer of scientific knowledge from the Middle East and Central Asia to China is rarely noted.

In addition, hundreds of thousands of craftsmen and artisans were forcibly recruited from the regions of Central Asia and the Middle East that fell under Mongol control and sent to China to supply the imperial court with the requisite works of art and craftsmanship needed to display the wealth and grandeur of the new empire. These artisans brought with them skills and aesthetic sensibilities, many of which were gradually absorbed into Chinese artistic traditions.

Some of the contributions of these Muslim immigrants can be seen down to this day. The Mongols recruited architects and engineers to help design and build their new capital, which they called Khanbaliq and is now known as Beijing. One of the architects, Amir al-Din, oversaw the Muslim workers assigned to the massive undertaking. In the far southwest province of Yunnan, it was a Muslim from Bukhara, Sayyid 'Ajall Shams al-Din, who not only was responsible for fully incorporating this previously independent region into the Chinese state, but also undertaking a wide range of major hydraulic engineering and irrigation projects that have been in continuous use down to this day. Joseph Needham, the famous scholar of the sciences of China, was duly impressed when he visited the provincial capital Kunming in 1942 (Needham 1954: 141). For this project and other agricultural and engineering projects, Sayyid 'Ajall recruited experts from Central Asia. The descendants of these early Muslim settlers make up most of Yunnan's present-day Hui Muslim population.

Contributions to the fields of astronomy and medicine were especially significant, and, as a result, during this period a Bureau of Islamic Astro-calendric Sciences was established, as was an Office of Muslim Medicine. The former was established by Jamal al-Din, a Persian scientist who had brought with him to China a collection of Persian astronomical instruments. He had an entire observatory built to his specification in the imperial capital (Elman 2009: 66–68).

Over the following millennium, the descendants of these early settlers and those that came later evolved into an ethnic group in China that became known as the Hui (Gladney 1996). The original immigrants were mostly men who settled in different regions of China, married Chinese women, and raised their children as Muslims. Daughters were expected to marry Muslim men or men who had converted. In addition, it was a common practice for Muslim communities to adopt children that Han Chinese had abandoned during periods of famine and extreme hardship. Of China's

23 million Muslims, more than ten million are Hui, and they are spread throughout the country.

With the fall of the Mongol dynasty, Han Chinese once again took control of the empire. The Ming Dynasty (1368–1644) quickly reestablished an ethnic and cultural hierarchy that firmly placed Han Chinese at the top. By this point in time there were thousands of Muslim communities spread out all over China. Although they were allowed to maintain their religious identities, they were required to adopt Chinese names, wear Chinese clothing, and adapt to Chinese culture.

Over the next few centuries Muslim communities became so adept at adopting traditional Chinese culture and language that a concern began to develop that Muslims in China would begin to lose their religious identity. One of the most serious concerns was the loss of Arabic as a lingua franca among these communities and the resulting inability of believers to read religious texts. In response to this growing concern, a group of Chinese Muslim scholars who were extremely learned in both the Chinese Confucian Classics as well as Islamic studies set about writing a series of works in Chinese on Islamic thought. Eventually these works were compiled into a collection that became known as the *Han Kitab* (*Chinese Books*).

The project proved very effective, as the collection was used to develop curricula for Islamic schools throughout China. Chinese Muslim religious teachers traveled to different regions to establish new schools and introduce the curriculum. As certain teachers became especially popular, students from different areas would travel to study with them. These education networks overlapped with the trade networks that crisscrossed China and were often dominated by Chinese Muslims (Petersen 2017).

The Ming Dynasty was followed by the Manchu-dominated Qing Dynasty (1644–1911). By this time Chinese Muslim communities were firmly established throughout China. For a range of reasons large Muslim communities in both northwest and southwest China came into conflict with the Qing Imperial forces, and the consequences were devastating for both communities. Hundreds of thousands were killed by government forces, and hundreds of thousands more were forced to flee to neighboring regions or countries. Untold numbers of mosques and cemeteries were destroyed during this period.

During China's Civil War period (1927–1949), both the Communist Party, led by Mao Zedong, and the Nationalists, led by Chiang Kai-shek, promised China's Muslim communities religious freedom in exchange for their support. After the establishment of the People's Republic of China in 1949, the Muslims of China enjoyed a relatively peaceful period during the early years. However, in 1966, a political campaign begun by Mao to strengthen his leadership position quickly escalated and developed into the Great Proletarian Cultural Revolution, which lasted ten years, caused the death of up to two million people, and saw the widespread destruction of works of anything associated with either traditional Chinese culture or foreign culture. Muslims, their mosques, and their cemeteries were especially aggressively targeted for attack. Any artwork or work of material culture that could be linked with religion was destroyed, as was anything that had any foreign writing on it, including Arabic.

Red Guards, the students recruited to carry out house searches and the destruction of goods found to be politically suspect, were known for being brutal in their excesses. The people in whose homes these items were found were often tortured. It is difficult to describe the fear and terror caused by the excesses of these Red Guards; suffice it to say that tens if not hundreds of thousands of people committed suicide during this period. In an effort to protect themselves from the attacks of the Red Guards, throughout the country families destroyed works of art and religious items that might have been in their families for generations, if not centuries. During this period mosques throughout the country were either destroyed, defiled, or sustained serious damage. One of the most beautiful mosques in China, the Huajue Mosque in Xi'an (also known as the Great Mosque) survived relatively intact as the imam had the presence of mind to immediately repurpose the mosque as a preschool for neighborhood children. Decorated walls and wooden carvings were covered for their protection.

In the aftermath of the Cultural Revolution, Muslim communities were eventually allowed access to their mosques again, and they lost no time in repairing them. However, in most cases, very few if any of the religious objects survived. Given the overall devastation to their communities, Muslims throughout China lost no time in reviving Islamic knowledge by developing religious education projects. Shortly thereafter Chinese Muslim students were once again allowed to travel abroad to pursue more advanced religious education at centers of Islamic learning around the world (Armijo 2007).

One of the consequences of increasing numbers of students studying overseas, especially for those who studied at conservative Islamic colleges in Saudi Arabia, was their bringing back with them certain attitudes regarding traditions that had developed within Chinese Muslim communities over the centuries. When damaged mosques needed to be repaired or completely rebuilt, those who had studied overseas often pressured communities to rebuild in a style that was less Chinese and more Middle Eastern in design, as defined by Salafi interpretations as being more similar to traditional Arabian peninsula designs (Armijo 2008). After more than two decades of such renovations untold numbers of historic mosques have been stripped of their traditional Chinese Islamic designs. However, beginning in 2010, there has been a growing consciousness of the importance of not only maintaining these traditional designs, but also of training young people in these design skills.

From 2010–2012, the main mosque in Kunming, Yunnan, was renovated (Figure 5.3.3). This time the community not only decided to replicate the mosque design and structure in all its traditional Chinese temple design and decoration glory, but they even sourced the timber beams from the forests used in original construction centuries earlier. The stunning mosque, now earthquake-resistant, stands as a testament to the future and survival of traditional Chinese Islamic aesthetics. Another recent important initiative is "The Chinese House for the Arts of Islamic Arabic Calligraphy" that was established in 2009 by famed Chinese Muslim master calligraphy Ma Guangjiang (Hajji Noor Al Din) at the National Academy of Painting and Calligraphy in Henan Province. Here Chinese Muslim students are trained in the different Chinese Arabic calligraphy styles that developed over the centuries in different regions of China.

FIGURE 5.3.3 Shuncheng jie Mosque. This mosque, the main mosque for the city of Kunming, was dismantled and then completely rebuilt in 2010. The rebuilt mosque is an almost exact replica of the earlier one.

Courtesy of J. Armijo.

EXAMPLES OF MAJOR ISLAMIC ARCHAEOLOGICAL SITES IN CHINA

As mentioned earlier, Islamic archaeology is not a field of study in China, in part because the government institutions focus on earlier sites more directly related to the history of the dominant Han Chinese population. In addition, China's Muslim minority communities are spread throughout the country and lack the resources and training to carry out systematic studies about their own local histories, let alone regional or national histories.

Quanzhou, Zaytun

There is, however, one place in China where a significant collection of Islamic archaeological remains has survived. The story of how this came to be provides an important insight into the reasons for the current state of the field. Although there are numerous major cities across China that have Muslim communities who can document their continuous presence there over several centuries, ironically, it is a community that actually declined to the point of virtual extinction that has the best preserved Chinese Islamic archaeological finds. Further complicating the story is the circumstances surrounding the preservation of the remains, and their unlikely hero: Wu Wenliang (1903–1969), a high school biology teacher with an interest in archaeology. While attending Xiamen University, Wu took an archaeology course with Gustav Ecke (a visiting German professor who went on to become one of the first major historians of Chinese art and archaeology). Later, while working as a high school teacher back in his hometown of Quanzhou, he spent some twenty years "combing the surrounding countryside for interesting fragments of carved stone" (Garnaut 2006) which he stored in his backyard. However, "[a]ccording to Wu, he was able to save about 10 percent of what he knew was in Quanzhou, but much that he could not save was purchased by stonemasons who pounded the stones flat and reused them or by construction companies who paved roads with the material" (Steinhardt 2016).

Many of these gravestones (dated primarily from the late 10th to early 14th centuries) had initially been looted from cemeteries in the late 14th and early 15th centuries and used to refurbish the city walls (Pearson et al. 2002: 40). Wu kept them safe in his backyard until 1953, when he donated his collection to the recently founded People's Republic of China. In 1957, he published a book documenting some two hundred engraved stones related to the various religious communities in Quanzhou, which also included images and translations into Chinese of many of the inscriptions. A few years later he assisted in the establishment of the Quanzhou Maritime Museum, which opened in 1959, incorporating his collection. Although his collection of engraved stones was able to survive the destruction and chaos of the Cultural Revolution (1966–1976), Wu is reported to have died during this time. Over the past five decades the museum has been expanded several times and now houses what is not only the most important, but also most likely the only collection of archaeological findings related to the history of Islam in China (Figure 5.3.4).

Although in the early Islamic period the port city of Canton was the only port officially open to foreign trade in China, by 1000, Quanzhou began to eclipse Canton, and, by the end of the 13th century, it had become perhaps the greatest harbor in the world. At its height tens of thousands of foreign traders and merchants had settled in Quanzhou (Chaffee 2006). Quanzhou was first officially opened for foreign trade in 1087, during the Song Dynasty (960–1279), and the community of foreign merchants and traders began to grow and prosper. Over the next three centuries Muslims from Central Asia, Arabia, and Persia having settled and prospered in the port city, built neighborhoods and mosques, and established cemeteries. Other important foreign communities included Manichaeans, Zoroastrians, Christians, and Hindus. From various traveler's accounts, including those of Marco Polo and Ibn Battuta, these communities flourished for several centuries (Chaffee 2006).

The tombstones from this period that have survived down to this day identify Muslims from Iran, Transoxiana, Khorasan, Khwarazm, Armenia, Syria, Palestine, and

FIGURE 5.3.4 Recovered tombstones stored in the Shengyou/Al Ashab Mosque in Quanzhou, Fujian Province.

Courtesy of Orlando V. Thompson II.

Arabia (Mukai 2016: 231). There may well have been Muslims from other parts of the Islamic world who settled in Quanzhou. According to historical written records during this period there were six major mosques spread throughout the city of Quanzhou (Pearson et al. 2002: 35). Today, only the remnants of one mosque, the Shengyou Mosque ("Mosque of the Companions") also known as the Al Ashab Mosque in the Arabic and Persian sources, remains (Figure 5.3.5).

Mosques

As mentioned earlier, the 2016 publication of Nancy Steinhardt's *China's Early Mosques* represents the most comprehensive and important study to date on the mosques of China. The work covers the major mosques of different regions of China and includes their history, major renovations over time, and important historic stelae associated with each mosque. With hundreds of photographs and illustrations, the book represents an invaluable contribution to the study of mosques and their architecture in China. According to Steinhardt, of China's estimated 40,000 plus mosques, approximately thirty can be dated back to the 14th century or earlier. As an expert on

FIGURE 5.3.5 Entrance to the Shengyou/Al Ashab Mosque in Quanzhou, Fujian Province.
Courtesy of Orlando V. Thompson II.

traditional Chinese architecture, she is able to clearly identify and explain the influence of traditional Chinese Buddhist temple designs on the mosque architecture of China.

The other major work on mosques in China is *The Phoenix Mosque of Hangzhou* (2017), edited by George Lane. This work focuses on one mosque and the history of the Persian community who built it. Commonly believed to be the third oldest surviving mosque in China, the Phoenix Mosque is the only one so closely associated with the Persian immigrant community. Built by "Ala" al-Din (ʿAlāʾ-al-Din) in 1281, the mosque, though repaired and renovated numerous times over the centuries, is still used today by the local Muslim community. The mosque courtyard also houses several tombstones recovered from a Muslim cemetery that had been located nearby, but has since been destroyed. Lane's work covers the history of the mosque, the local Persian Muslim population, and their role in the history of Islam in China.

Museum Collections

Most of the limited number of fine works of Chinese Islamic art that have survived down to today did so because they were bought by collectors and taken out of China. As yet there is no known major collection of Chinese Islamic art within China. Small regional museums in Muslim communities exist in different regions of China but their collections are limited both in scope and areas represented.

Although most major international museums usually have significant Islamic art collections and Chinese art collections, it is only recently that museums have made an effort to create a separate space for works of Chinese Islamic art. Perhaps the earliest and certainly the most extensive collection is the one developed by the Islamic Arts Museum Malaysia in Kuala Lumpur. The collection includes scrolls of paintings made of objects illustrated/composed with Arabic calligraphy, as well as cloisonné, porcelain, and ceramic pieces decorated with Arabic inscriptions. Over the centuries, different communities of Muslims in China developed their own unique styles of Arabic calligraphy, which are striking in their distinctive yet familiar characteristics vis à vis the standard Arabic calligraphic styles (Ghoname 2012). Almost all of the items in this collection date to the Qing Dynasty (1644–1911).

Another of the earliest collections is the small but exquisite one developed by the David Collection in Copenhagen. Comprising only five items, the collection manages to represent most of the most important genres of Chinese Islamic art. The collection includes a celadon-glazed porcelain dish dating to the 15th in China that was later inscribed with Persian poetry, a simple tri-footed cast bronze incense burner from the early 16th century, a highly decorated gold-flecked bronze vessel with typical Chinese motif of lions and dragons, a blue-and-white porcelain *huqqa* (water pipe) made in China at the end of the 17th century, and, last but not least, an exquisite mosque lamp shaped like the glass ones found in the Middle East, but made of cloisonné, with traditional Chinese motifs in addition to Arabic calligraphy (Kadoi 2014) (Figure 5.3.6). This particular piece was loaned to the Museum of Islamic Art in Qatar for the special exhibit that accompanied its opening. The exhibit, "Beyond Boundaries: Islamic Art Across Cultures," included dozens of works of Islamic art on loan from museums around the world (Watson 2008).

Around 2015, major renovations to the Islamic art collections at both the Metropolitan Museum in New York and the British Museum in London were completed. At both museums works of Chinese Islamic art were finally highlighted and identified as such. Other museums with notable collections of Chinese Islamic art include the Topkapı Palace Museum in Istanbul; the Sheikh Safī al-Dīn Khānegāh and Shrine in Ardabil, Iran; the National Palace Museum in Taipei; the Palace Museum in Beijing; the Victoria and Albert Museum in London; the Museé Guimet in Paris; the Rijksmuseum in Amsterdam; the Aga Khan Museum in Toronto; and the Shangri La Museum of Islamic Art, Culture, and Design in Honolulu (Frankel 2018:85).

Material Culture and Burial Practices

Traditionally in China, burial sites have been one of the, if not the, most important sites for archaeological finds that included both the exquisite works of art found in

FIGURE 5.3.6 Cloisonné mosque lamp with traditional Chinese Arabic inscription. Photographed at the Museum of Islamic Art in Doha, Qatar, where it was on loan from the David Collection in Copenhagen, for the museum's inaugural exhibit "Beyond Boundaries: Islamic Art Across Cultures."

Courtesy of J. Armijo.

imperial tombs as well as items of daily use found in more simple tombs. For Chinese Islamic archaeology, however, the Muslim burial custom of only a white shroud accompanying the dead has further limited potential sources for important archaeological finds.

Although many fine works of Chinese Islamic art survived the periods of destruction in recent Chinese history, what was much less likely to survive are items made for daily use, especially ones made of wood. During extensive fieldwork in remote Muslim villages in Yunnan province in southwest China, I came across several pieces of what were undoubtedly common objects in the past but have barely survived to the present. One such item was a carved wooden box to hold a Qur'an and the other was a funerary bier. The bier, which was being stored by the side of a village mosque, was especially noteworthy as it was clearly used to transport the deceased to the cemetery (Figure 5.3.7). Unlike most biers used in the Muslim world that are open and more like stretchers, these biers are closed and shaped like coffins. Made out of sturdy wood, it was heavily decorated with engravings and Arabic calligraphy. The bier immediately brought to mind a passage from Robert Ekvall's classic study *Cultural Relations on the Kansu-Tibetan Border* (1939) that describes the vastly different burial practices of the Han Chinese with those of the Chinese Muslims and the mutual disdain they created. Born to American missionary parents in Gansu in

FIGURE 5.3.7 Funeral bier in shape of a coffin used to transport the deceased to the cemetery. Stored by the side of a Muslim village mosque in central Yunnan Province, 1998.

Courtesy of J. Armijo.

1898, Ekvall spent much of his childhood there, was fluent in Chinese, and was well-acquainted with the different local ethnic communities.

> The burial customs of the two groups differ widely. The Chinese bury their dead in coffins—costly out of all proportion to the simple scale of Chinese peasant life, for the coffin has come to be a symbol of filial piety. . . . The Moslems have fiercely resisted the use of the coffin, probably because of what they conceive to be its idolatrous connotations. Their dead are wrapped in cloths after the manner of mummies. The grave is dug straight down into the ground, and at a sufficient depth a shelf is hollowed out on one side, making in effect an artificial cave; the body is laid on this shelf. To the Chinese the Moslems are savages, who bury their dead like dogs.
>
> (Ekvall 1939: 22–23)

Clearly at least some communities of Chinese Muslims had created these impressive and sturdy biers to be able to transport their loved ones to the cemetery in a manner less likely to engender the derision of their Han Chinese neighbors. It was in fact an extraordinary example of a form of cultural accommodation. In addition, given that different Chinese Muslim communities developed different styles of Islamic Arabic calligraphy over the centuries and that these biers were clearly built to last for centuries, a close study of the inscriptions might prove to be a way to trace migrations of Chinese Muslims during periods of violent unrest. Unfortunately, extensive searches of writings on Muslims in China and correspondence with scholars of Islam in China turned up no other documented examples or even knowledge of the practice. Eventually, however, one image of a similar funerary bier was discovered in the missionary Claude Pickens's collection, discussed later.

Given the widespread destruction during the Cultural Revolution of anything that could be linked with Islam, it is no wonder that so few examples of material culture have survived.

Cai Guo-qiang Exhibit

In perhaps one of the most unusual-ever meetings of Islamic archaeology and contemporary art, Chinese artist Cai Guo-qiang, a native of Quanzhou, incorporated inscriptions from gravestones dating back to the 11th–14th centuries into one of the monumental works he created for a 2012 exhibit in Doha, Qatar (Cai et al. 2012). As a child growing up in Quanzhou he often played in the cemetery on the outskirts of the city. He remembered the unusual tombstones having strange "squiggly" designs. Decades later, when carrying out research for the Qatar exhibit, he discovered these were the graves of the Muslim traders from the Persian Gulf region who had settled in Quanzhou. To commemorate the link between these two edges of Asia across the maritime silk trading route, he had local artisans in Quanzhou carefully replicate inscriptions from the tombstones onto large boulders. The boulders were then shipped to Qatar and displayed at the entrance to his exhibit (Figure 5.3.8). Some of the calligraphic styles were traditional ones from the Middle East, whereas others reflected the evolution of Islamic calligraphy in China.

The most common epitaphs of the graves included the following:

> "Everyone will have a taste of death."
> "All enjoyments in this life are illusionary."
> "To die in a foreign land is to die a martyr."

The inscriptions had a profound effect on many of the Gulf Arab visitors, as both the reality and finality of the lives of their ancestors who had traveled so far were reified.

A Japanese scholar who has done a close study of all the surviving tombstones from along China's southeast coast argues that the "choice of exactly the same formulae [the epitaphs equating dying overseas with martyrdom] among Muslims in different port cities of China's coastal region indicates that they eventually established an

FIGURE 5.3.8 Inscribed boulders at entrance to the Mathaf: Arab Museum of Modern Art, Doha, Qatar.

Courtesy of J. Armijo.

interregional or diasporic identity of Muslim foreigners who immigrated into the region" (Mukai 2016: 255).

Photographic Collections

Because there was such extensive damage to mosques and cemeteries in the latter half of the 20th century in China, photographic collections dating from the late 19th and early 20th centuries are now an important source of visual information on the Islamic archaeology of China. Given the widespread dispersion of Christian missionaries in China during this period and their interest in all things Islamic (for reasons of more effective proselytization efforts), their photographic collections are an important source of information. The Claude Pickens Collection at Harvard University is perhaps the most important as it is both properly catalogued and readily accessible. Claude Pickens (1900–1985) was a missionary based in China from 1926–1950. During this time, he made trips to Northwest China to document the lives of Muslims there. The photographs include images of mosques, cemeteries, material culture, homes, schools, villages, and stelae. The collection is available online and can be accessed through Harvard University's main library portal. Other photographic collections at Harvard that include images related to Chinese Islamic archaeology include those of Frederick Wulsin (1891–1961), Owen Lattimore (1900–1989), and Hedda Morrison (1908–1991).

Conclusion: Role of China's Belt and Road Initiative

At this point in time, it appears that the best chance for the surviving examples of Islamic archaeology to be identified, surveyed, and preserved is for the government to make it a part of the cultural program of their massive Belt and Road investment initiative, tying all the major countries of Asia and the Middle East together through trade and infrastructure projects. China is hoping to use a range of soft power initiatives that promote cultural ties across Asia by harkening back to the historic overland Silk Road and maritime trading routes that once linked China with the countries of the Central Asia and the Middle East. Recent government-sponsored cultural initiatives have incorporated Chinese Islamic archaeological artifacts to rekindle interest in these historic links.

In 2015, as part of the Qatar-China Year of Culture events, a collection of more than one hundred works of art from five different museums in China were exhibited at Doha's Museum of Islamic Art. In addition to the expected items, such as terra cotta soldiers from the tomb of Qin Shi Huangdi and bronze vessels, there were also several items that evoked former ties, including: a classic tri-colored pottery camel from the Tang Dynasty (618–907 CE) and a blue-and-white porcelain plate adorned with Arabic calligraphy from the Ming Dynasty (1368–1644 CE). Foreign diplomats from the Middle East and other Muslim-dominant countries are also regularly invited to visit the collections of the Maritime Museum in Quanzhou.

China has already invested hundreds of millions of dollars in different cultural projects directed at the countries of the Middle East, including more than a dozen Confucius Institutes at Arab, Iranian, and Central Asian universities; thousands of scholarships for students; and an Arabic language television station (CCTV-Arabic) that broadcasts a range of programs to the region.

Given the paucity of surviving Chinese Islamic archaeological artifacts and their dispersal throughout the country, it would take a major government initiative to systematically locate, identify, and display what still exists. Given the extent to which China is depending on the Road and Belt Initiative to ensure its own economic survival, it may well just be what is needed to propel this initiative forward. One possible location of this collection would be the Hui Culture Park in Yinchuan, Ningxia. Beginning in 2010, China organized major trade fairs to promote trade with the Middle East. The biennial China–Arab expos regularly host thousands of business people, investors, and diplomats to what China hopes will become a trade hub with the Middle East as well as an international center for halal food production. As of 2016, the Hui Museum at the park was under renovation.

Another prospect for the development of one important dimension of Chinese Islamic archaeology is the growing interest in maritime archaeological research related to trade between China and the Persian Gulf region. The 1998, the Belitung shipwreck discovery documented that the trade between China and the Middle East was much more developed than earlier thought, with hundreds of thousands, if not more, ceramic pieces being custom-made in kilns in different regions in China. Both China and Qatar are currently using newly developed technology to focus on discovering shipwrecks, respectively, in the coastal regions off China (Heaver 2017) and the relatively shallow waters of the Persian Gulf.

References

Armijo, J. 2007. "Islam in China," in J. L. Esposito, J. O. Voll, and O. Bakar (eds.), *Asian Islam in the 21st Century* (Oxford: Oxford University Press), 197–228.

Armijo, J. 2008. "Muslim Education in China: Chinese *Madrasa*s and Linkages to Islamic Schools Abroad," in F. Noor, Y, Sikand, and M. van Bruinessen (eds.), *The Madrasa in Asia: Political Activism and Transnational Linkages* (Amsterdam: Amsterdam University Press), 169–187.

Cai, G. et al. 2012. *Cai Guo-Qiang: Saraab* (Milan: Skira Editore).

Chaffee, J. 2006. "Diasporic Identities in the Historical Development of the Maritime Muslim Communities of Song-Yuan China," *Journal of the Economic and Social History of the Orient*, 49, 4, 395–420.

Chang, K. C. 1977. *The Archaeology of Ancient China* (New Haven: Yale University Press).

Chen, D. 1984. *Quanzhou Yisilan-jiao shike: Islamic Inscriptions in Quanzhou* (Fuzhou: Fujian People's Publisher).

David Collection Museum. "Islam in China" collection in the David Collection Museum, Copenhagen. https://www.davidmus.dk/en/collections/islamic/cultural-history-themes/islam-in-china/art.

Drake, F. S. 1943. "Mohammedanism in the T'ang Dynasty," *Monumenta Serica*, 8, 1–40.

Ekvall, R. 1939. *Cultural Relations on the Kansu-Tibetan Border* (Chicago: University of Chicago Press).

Elman, B. 2009. *On Their Own Terms: Science in China, 1550–1900* (Cambridge: Harvard University Press).

Franke, W. 1983. "Notes on Some Ancient Chinese Mosques," in K. Sagaster and M. Weiers (eds.), *Documenta Barbarorum: Festschrift für Walther Heissig zum 70. Geburtstag* (Wiesbaden: Harrassowitz), 111–126.

Frankel, J. 2018. "Muslim Blue, Chinese White: Islamic Calligraphy on Ming Blue-and-White Porcelain," *Orientations*, 49, 2, 84–89.

Garnaut, A. 2006. "The Stones of Zayton Speak," book review in *China Heritage Quarterly*, 5, http://chinaheritagequarterly.org/scholarship.php?searchterm=005_zayton.inc&issue=005.

Ghoname, H. 2012. *Sini Calligraphy: The Preservation of Chinese Muslims' Cultural Heritage* (Masters thesis, University of Hawaii).

Gladney, D. 1996. *Muslim Chinese: Ethnic Nationalism in the People's Republic* (Cambridge: Harvard East Asian Monographs).

Guy, J. 2011. "Rare and Strange Goods: International Trade in Ninth-Century Asia," in R. Krahl (ed.), *Shipwrecked: Tang Treasures and Monsoon Winds* (Washington, DC: Smithsonian Books), 19–27.

Heaver, S. 2017. "How China Uses Shipwrecks to Weave a History of Seaborne Trade That Backs Up Its Construction of a New Maritime Silk Road," *South China Morning Post* [Hong Kong], 29 November 2017.

Hsieh, M. 2011. "The Navigational Route of the Belitung Wreck and the Late Tang Ceramic Trade," in R. Krahl (ed.), *Shipwrecked: Tang Treasures and Monsoon Winds* (Washington, DC: Smithsonian Books), 136–143.

Kadoi, Y. 2014. "From China to Denmark: A 'Mosque Lamp' in Context," *Journal of the David Collection*, 4, 202–223.

Lane, G. (ed.) 2017. *The Phoenix Mosque* (London: Gingko Library).

Leslie, D. 1986. *Islam in Traditional China: A Short History to 1800* (Belconnen: Canberra College of Advanced Education).

Lewis, M. 2009. *China's Cosmopolitan Empire: The Tang Dynasty* (Cambridge, MA: Belknap Press of Harvard University Press).

Liu, L., and Chen, X. 2012. *The Archaeology of China: From the Late Paleolithic to the Early Bronze Age* (Cambridge: Cambridge University Press).

Louis, F. 2011. "Metal Objects on the Belitung Shipwreck," in R. Krahl (ed.), *Shipwrecked: Tang Treasures and Monsoon Winds* (Washington, DC: Smithsonian Books), 84–91.

Millward, J. 2007. *Eurasian Crossroads: A History of Xinjiang* (New York: Columbia University Press).

Mukai, M. 2016. "'Muslim Diaspora' in Yuan China: A Comparative Analysis of Islamic Tombstones from the Southeast Coast," *Asian Review of World Histories*, 4, 2, 231–256.

Needham, J. 1954. *Science and Civilisation, Volume I* (Cambridge: Cambridge University Press).

Pearson, R., Li, M., and Li, G. 2002. "Quanzhou Archaeology: A Brief Review," *International Journal of Historical Archaeology*, 6, 1, 23–59.

Petersen, K. 2017. *Interpreting Islam in China: Pilgrimage, Scripture, and Language in the Han Kitab* (Oxford: Oxford University Press).

Steinhardt, N. 2016. *China's Early Mosques* (Edinburgh: Edinburgh University Press).

Watson, O. (ed.) 2008. *Beyond Boundaries: Islamic Art Across Cultures* (Doha: Museum of Islamic Art).

Wu, Y. 1957/2005. *Quanzhou zongjiao shike* (Beijing: Kexue chubanshe) [Expanded reprinting of Wu, W. 1957. *Quanzhou zongjiao shike* (*Religious Inscriptions of Quanzhou*) (Beijing: Kexue chubanshe)].

FURTHER READING

Ben-Dor, Z. 2010. "Follow the White Camel: Islam in China to 1800," in D. Morgan, and A. Reid (eds.), *The New Cambridge History of Islam, Volume 3, The Eastern Islamic World, Eleventh to Eighteenth Centuries* (Cambridge: Cambridge University Press).

Clark, H. 1995. "Muslims and Hindus in the Culture and Morphology of Quanzhou from the Tenth to the Thirteenth Century," *Journal of World History*, 6, 1, 49–74.

Krahl, R., and Guy, J. 2011. *Shipwrecked: Tang Treasures and Monsoon Winds* (Washington, DC: Smithsonian Books).

Wang, G. 2003. *The Nanhai Trade: Early Chinese Trade in the South China Sea* (Singapore: Eastern Universities Press).

CHAPTER 5.4

....

SOUTHEAST ASIA

....

ALEXANDER WAIN

INTRODUCTION

....

MODERN-DAY Southeast Asia is home to approximately 240 million Muslims, the majority of whom reside in Indonesia (the world's largest Muslim nation), Malaysia, and Brunei (Figure 5.4.1). But while Islam is widely present throughout the region, it entered the area relatively late: the earliest (verifiable) Southeast Asian Islamic kingdoms date to just the 13th century, or more than six hundred years after the rise of Islam. In spite of its comparative infancy, however, Southeast Asian Islam has witnessed the rise and fall of many noteworthy Islamic kingdoms and seen the evolution of a unique, variegated Muslim identity.

As is the case in many other parts of the Muslim world, Southeast Asia's Islamic archaeology remains largely unstudied. While the region's pre-Islamic kingdoms (notably Funan, Srivijaya, and Majapahit) have garnered considerable attention, the Islamic polities which succeeded them have inspired far fewer investigations. Melaka, for example, the region's first great Muslim empire, founded in the early 15th century, has yet to receive any serious archaeological treatment (Miksic and Geok 2017: 530–531). The east Javanese kingdom of Banten, on the other hand, Melaka's 16th-century successor, has been extensively excavated but without the results of those excavations being published in full (Dupoizat 1992). This neglect is often compounded by a perception that archaeological research is not worthwhile in Southeast Asia; the region's high humidity means organic material (including wood, the region's dominant pre-modern building material) does not survive. Moreover, the majority of Southeast Asia's early Islamic settlements were built near (or over) rivers, which have changed course over time, either destroying evidence of those settlements or rendering them hard to relocate.

Nevertheless, Southeast Asia is home to a fascinating array of Islamic artifacts, with notable studies existing in specific areas. The region's earliest surviving mosques, for example, are the subject of several important treatises, each aimed at determining the architectural origins of these distinctive, pagoda-like structures (Nasir 2004; Rasdi 2007; Njoto 2014). Several of the region's early shipwrecks have also been excavated over recent

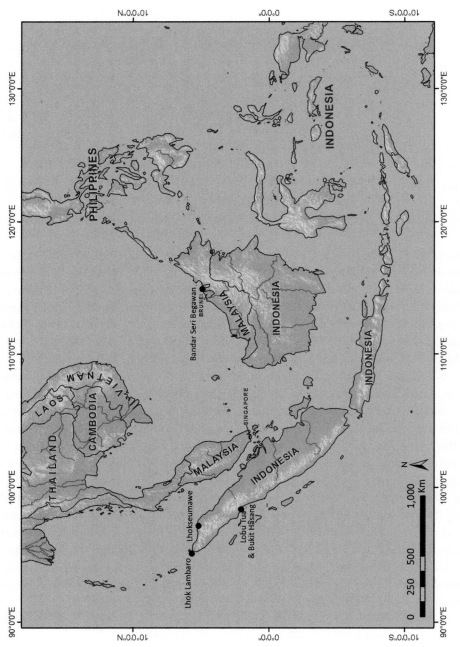

FIGURE 5.4.1 The locations of the main sites and regions.

decades, providing crucial information about the region's early trade and shipbuilding techniques that evinces early connections with the Indian Ocean and, consonant with Islamization, China (Sjostrand and Barnes 2001; Flecker 2001, 2010; Manguin 2010).

Given the broad aims and expressly Islamic focus of this chapter, however, both set within the limited space available, it would seem inappropriate to concentrate on such a narrow field as mosque architecture or on shipwrecks to which the label "Muslim" is often applied only speculatively. Rather, an exploration of known Islamic sites on which reliable archaeological data exists is evidently called for. While such sites are admittedly in short supply, four early Southeast Asian Islamic kingdoms have received the prerequisite attention, namely: Barus, Lambri, Samudera-Pasai, and Brunei. These four sites therefore constitute our focus.

Our discussion of these sites sits within a framework provided by an issue of central importance to Southeast Asian scholarship: Who was responsible for the Islamization of the region? While a desire to facilitate trade has long been accepted as the motivation behind Southeast Asia's conversion, with the earliest missionaries thereby identified as influential merchants, the origin of those missionaries remains controversial (Strathern 2017: 22–23). Since the 19th century, scholarship has favored either an Arab or an Indian origin, primarily sustaining both hypotheses with appeals to surviving textual evidence (Drewes 1968). The region's hagiographical traditions, for example, claim Southeast Asia's early missionaries were Arabs (Jones 1999; Cheah 2010), while early 16th-century Portuguese travelogues note that Indian (although not always Muslim) merchants dominated the region's commerce, perhaps suggesting they were the influential merchants who initiated Islamization (Cortesao 2005). In 1985, however, D. Lombard and C. Salmon, both scholars of Chinese civilization, challenged these perspectives. Utilizing Chinese texts that Southeast Asianists often neglect, they convincingly reassessed China's place within Southeast Asia's pre-modern trade network. Previously, Southeast Asian scholars had assumed—largely on the basis of Tomé Pires's passing remark, contained in his *Suma Oriental* (written 1513–1515), that Chinese merchants were of little account in pre-Portuguese Melaka (Cortesao 2005: 116)—that China constituted a relatively unimportant trading partner during Southeast Asia's Islamization. Between the 10th and 15th centuries, however, Lombard and Salmon were able to demonstrate intense Chinese commercial expansion. Centered on the port of Quanzhou, Fujian province, this expansion entailed extensive interaction with Southeast Asia that persisted into the early 15th century. Within that context, Lombard and Salmon also drew attention to the well-documented political and commercial dominance Muslims enjoyed in Quanzhou over the same period. Moreover, during the Yuan and early Ming Dynasties (1272–1433), evidence also emerged for substantial Chinese Muslim[1] migration from Quanzhou into Southeast Asia, just as that region began to

---

[1] Here the phrase "Chinese Muslim" refers to a Muslim of the early modern period who, of either Persian/Central Asian or Arab descent, had become resident in China. In today's parlance, they would be considered an ethnic minority. Muslims of this sort originally came to China to trade, perhaps as early as the 7th century. Initially sojourners, by the late 13th century, when this discussion begins, many were permanent settlers of long-standing diaspora communities that had begun to adopt elements of traditional Chinese culture (Benite 2005).

Islamize. Lombard and Salmon therefore argued that a connection between China and Southeast Asia's Islamization seemed probable (Lombard and Salmon 1985).

This hypothesis has since attracted the attention and, ultimately, support of several notable scholars, including R. Ptak (2001), A. Reid (2001, 2006), and G. Wade (2011, 2012). Absent from their discussions, however, has been a detailed and wide-ranging examination of Southeast Asia's early Islamic archaeology to determine whether sufficient physical evidence exists for this Chinese commercial activity and whether it bore on the region's Islamization. This chapter hopes to fill that gap. Consonant with conversion, it demonstrates that all four of the selected locations experienced a connection of some sort with China. Most notably, while the archaeological remains at Barus and Lambri suggest those locations shared their closest commercial relationships with other Southeast Asian ports, all the sites (excluding Samudera-Pasai, for which there is no systematic evidence) yielded considerable amounts of Chinese pottery, pre-modern China's principal export item. By the 15th century, these artifacts had largely eclipsed both Indian Ocean- and Southeast Asian-produced wares. Three of the sites, Lambri, Samudera-Pasai, and Brunei, also witnessed the utilization of numerous Chinese artistic motifs in association with their earliest Islamic artifacts. Most strikingly, however, Brunei provides strong evidence not only of a much earlier sultanate than previously suspected, but also of a direct connection with Quanzhou and its ruling Muslim elite.

While it shall be continually stressed that the presence of Chinese trade items and/or cultural influences do not, in themselves, establish a Chinese (Muslim or otherwise) presence at the locations considered here, the archaeology does clearly demonstrate that Southeast Asia's first Muslim kingdoms embraced Islam just as Chinese trade goods flooded that region and when Chinese cultural influences were being readily adopted by the local Muslim population. Although this does not prove Lombard and Salmon's thesis, it does sit consonant with it.

BARUS (LOBU TUA AND BUKIT HASANG)

Lobu Tua (also spelt Lobuk Tua) and Bukit Hasang are two archaeological sites located in Tapanuli Tengah (Central Tapanuli Regency), in the province of Sumatera Utara (North Sumatra), Indonesia. Situated on the west coast of Sumatra, facing out on to the Indian Ocean, they lie approximately 500 kilometers south of Banda Aceh, at the northern tip of the island. The two sites are positioned just 8 kilometers apart; while Lobu Tua is a coastal site and shows evidence of 9th- to early 12th-century occupation, Bukit Hasang is in the hinterland and was occupied from the mid-13th to 15th centuries. Given the proximity of the two sites, their similar settlement patterns, and near-consecutive periods of occupation, Bukit Hasang has been interpreted as a successor site to Lobu Tua (Miksic and Geok 2017: 402, 495).

An 11th-century Tamil-language inscription found in situ at Lobu Tua establishes the probable historical identity of the two sites. Discovered in 1873, this inscription outlines a set of dues imposed on members of the Ayyavole Tamil merchant guild when entering the *pattinam* (major port) of Barus (rendered into Tamil as Varocu), the city where the stone was erected (Sastri 1932; Subbarayalu 1998). The toponym "Barus" appears in a variety of post–2nd-century CE texts; rendered as Barussae by Claudius Ptolemy (Coedès 1910: 58, 61), Polu or Polushi by 6th-century and later Chinese texts (Ptak 1998), and Fansur by all post–9th-century Arabic travelogues (Drakard 1989; Tibbetts 1979),[2] it is always depicted as an important exporter of the fragrant resin camphor. Lobu Tua's Tamil-language inscription clearly identifies that site and (via their likely association) Bukit Hasang as the 9th- to 15th-century center of this ancient kingdom.

Precisely when Barus embraced Islam is unknown; neither of the two 19th-century Malay texts chronicling its early history, the *Asal Turunan Raja-Raja Barus* (*Origin of the Rulers of Barus*) and *Sejarah Tuangku Batu Badan* (*The History of Tuangku Batu Badan*), date conversion (Drakard 1989: 59). Melaka's court chronicle, however, the early 17th-century *Sejarah Melayu* (*Malay Annals*), claims Barus converted shortly before Samudera-Pasai—that is, during the late 13th century (Cheah 2010: 106). There is, however, no further textual or physical evidence to substantiate this claim. Rather, a survey conducted in 1978 by Indonesia's Pusat Penelitian Arkeologi Nasional (National Archaeology Research Center) examined six Muslim grave assemblages near Lobu Tua and Bukit Hasang; although only one of the recorded gravestones bore a date (1370 CE), all were found in association with 14th- to 16th-century ceramics, prompting researchers to provisionally date conversion to the 14th century (Drakard 1989: 73; Miksic and Geok 2017: 495). A subsequent 2006 survey by Universiti Sains Malaysia's Pusat Penyelidikan Arkeologi Global (Global Archaeology Research Center) confirmed this conclusion. Although later than the *Sejarah Melayu*'s estimate, this date nevertheless places Barus among the region's earliest Muslim kingdoms; while Lobu Tua likely constituted the kingdom's pre-Islamic center, Bukit Hasang may have converted within a hundred years of its mid–13th-century foundation. The archaeological remains at both sites, however, demonstrate the likely complexity of the region's Islamization: while evidence from Lobu Tua suggests the first Muslims to visit Barus were traders with connections to South India, finds at Bukit Hasang are indicative of a dramatic reorientation of trade toward the rest of Southeast Asia consonant with conversion.

As briefly mentioned, Lobu Tua is a coastal site. Located just a few hundred meters from the shoreline, it is more than 200 hectares in extent. Pusat Penelitian Arkeologi Nasional dug several test pits across the site in the 1980s, the results of which led to a further, joint French–Indonesian project between 1995 and 2000. This carried out five stages of excavation, the findings of which were published in 1998 and 2003 (Guillot 1998; Guillot et al 2003). These excavations uncovered a scattered settlement arranged around a

---

[2] Beginning with Ibn Khuradadhhib's geographical treatise, *al-Masalik wa al-mamalik* (written 846 to 886), Arabic writers also refer to a north Sumatran, camphor-producing site called Balus (Tibbetts 1979). Whether this is also a reference to Barus is disputed; although vague about its precise location, the sources agree Balus was in the Straits of Melaka, either on Sumatra's east coast or the Malay Peninsula. If this is correct, it precludes any possible association with the Barus discussed here (Drakard 1989: 61).

central enclosure, itself surrounded by earthen ramparts and ditches. Covering an area of between 7.5 and 14 hectares, 1,000 square meters of the central enclosure were excavated, revealing a densely populated area actively involved in trade: in addition to evidence of bronze manufacture and 1,000 glass beads imported from South India, the site yielded a large amount of pottery. The vast majority of the latter consisted of Southeast Asian fine paste ware, a type of red-colored earthenware found throughout the Straits of Melaka and which bears strong stylistic affinity to Indian and Sri Lankan wares. Since there is no evidence of pottery production at the site, these artifacts were likely imported from elsewhere in Southeast Asia. Sirafi (Persian Gulf) pottery from the mid-10th to early 11th centuries was also found, as well as Chinese ceramics from the mid-10th to early 12th centuries. These Chinese wares included examples of Yuezhou stoneware and Xicun ware, ceramic types also found throughout this period in Sukar, Oman, an important port at the head of the Persian Gulf (Miksic 2010: 391–392; Perret and Surachman 2012: 162–163; Miksic and Geok 2017: 402).

In addition to these finds, the aforementioned Tamil-language inscription should also be noted. Comprising twenty-six lines of text carved over three sides of a hexagonal pillar, it is dated to the month Masi, year 1010 of the Indian Śaka calendar (equivalent to February–March 1088 CE). As noted, the inscription relates to the activities of the Ayyavole trade guild, a powerful Tamil organization established in the Deccan during the 8th century CE. At its height, the Ayyavole dominated at least forty-six other merchant groups. According to the inscription, some of its members occupied a *velapuram* (seashore settlement) near Barus, from where they imposed dues on the owners, captains, and crew of trade ships (Subbarayalu 1998; Christie 1998: 257–258).

Collectively, these finds suggest that Lobu Tua sat within an Indian Ocean-orientated trade network: all the site's glass beads, in addition to a large amount of its foreign-produced pottery, originated from either South India or the Middle East. Furthermore, Lobu Tua's Southeast Asian wares are Indian influenced (although not produced at the site), while its Chinese ceramics include specific examples also found at Sukar, Oman, indicating that both localities constituted part of the same broad trade network. The site's Tamil-language inscription, moreover, testifies to the presence of an influential Indian merchant community at Barus itself, one capable of imposing its own levies on those entering the port. This suggests the connection between Barus and the Indian Ocean was direct, that merchants from the latter region visited Barus in person. In that context, it is also noteworthy that the *Asal Turunan Raja-Raja Barus* claims Barus was founded by Hindus and Chettis (Perret and Surachman 2012: 162).

Also of significance, Lobu Tua's Tamil-language inscription includes the earliest known use of the word *marakkalanayam* (ship's captain). Previously, this term has only been known from post–16th-century texts, where it specifically refers to seafaring Muslim merchants from Tamil Nadu and Kerala. Whether it also carries that meaning here is uncertain, but plausible: the inscription is a product of the Tamil cultural area, where Muslim mercantile communities existed from at least the 9th century (Subbarayalu 1998). Moreover, many members of these communities joined either the Anjuvannam or Hanjamana trade guilds, both part of the powerful Ayyavole (Perret and Surachman 2012: 164). Consequently, this inscription could tentatively evince the existence of an 11th-century Muslim presence at Barus, one closely allied to trade. If so, it has important implications for our understanding of how Islam first reached Southeast Asia.

Turning to Bukit Hasang, between 2001 and 2005, this site constituted the subject of a joint Pusat Penelitian Arkeologi Nasional and École française d'Extrême-Orient project that sought to expand existing research into the rest of the Tapanuli area. Their excavations revealed a settlement pattern similar to that of Lobu Tua—a primarily scattered site arranged around a central, densely populated and ramparted enclosure. In total, 700 square meters of Bukit Hasang have been excavated, yielding more than 43,000 ceramic sherds and 120,000 pottery sherds. Collectively, these date from the 13th to 15th centuries, firmly placing the occupation of the site within that period. Thus far, no other trade goods, such as glass beads, have been reported (Perret and Surachman 2012: 161–163).

Although the analysis of Bukit Hasang's ceramic and pottery finds remains incomplete, their composition appears to differ markedly from those at Lobu Tua. While the latter site yielded primarily Southeast Asian fine paste wares, with the majority of all remaining pottery coming from the Middle East, only 25% of finds at Bukit Hasang are Southeast Asian in origin, with the vast majority of the rest coming from China (Perret and Surachman 2012: 162–163).[3] Contemporary to Bukit Hasang's occupation, imported Chinese wares therefore eclipse all other forms of pottery at Barus. Whether this entails direct interaction between Barus and China, however, is uncertain; despite its fame as a supplier of camphor, Barus appears not to have constituted an important stopping point for Chinese ships (Ptak 1998), perhaps because the Chinese preferred to obtain this resin from Brunei (Rockhill 1915: 193–194). Consequently, the significant amount of Chinese pottery found at Bukit Hasang need not have arrived (at least entirely) aboard Chinese vessels. Rather, intermediaries were likely involved. Given no Middle Eastern trade goods have been found at the site, such intermediaries were probably not from that region. Indeed, Arabic textual references to Barus decline with the foundation of Bukit Hasang, eventually ceasing altogether by the end of the 14th century. This suggests a decline in Barus–Middle East interaction over this period (Ptak 1998: 142). Bukit Hasang's geographical position, however, overlooking the Indian Ocean, renders it highly probable that the site maintained some form of commercial interaction with India—although, unlike Lobu Tua, Bukit Hasang has thus far yielded no evidence of Indian trade goods or of Indian settlement. Indeed, shortly after the foundation of Bukit Hasang, the Tamil trade guilds (including the Ayyavole) declined in response to the disestablishment of South India's Chola dynasty, their chief patron (Perret and Surachman 2012: 171). This weakened organized Tamil commercial activity across the region. As a consequence, Bukit Hasang is unlikely to have experienced the same degree of Tamil influence seen at Lobu Tua, although influence from other regions of India remains probable.

---

[3] In addition, twenty-three Chinese coins have also been found, ten with legible inscriptions dating them to the Northern Song (eight) and Southern Song (two) periods, equivalent to the mid-10th to late 13th centuries (Miksic and Geok 2017: 495). Consequently, the majority of the legible coins pre-date the occupation of Bukit Hasang. As they do not occur in sufficient quantities to suggest use as currency, their precise significance is unclear.

Aside from Chinese pottery fragments, Southeast Asian wares alone have been found at Bukit Hasang in significant quantities. Although less prevalent than at Lobu Tua, they are more diverse; while fine paste wares predominated at Lobu Tua, Bukit Hasang has yielded a far wider array of Southeast Asian pottery types (Perret and Surachman 2012: 168–169). Although the significance of this increased variety is opaque, a greater array of pottery types plausibly suggests access to a greater variety of pottery production centers. Certainly, despite our understanding of Southeast Asian pottery production still being in its infancy, no one production center is known to have produced all the varieties found at Bukit Hasang (Miksic 2009). Conceivably, therefore, if Chinese ships did not frequent Barus in substantial numbers, and if Barus's interaction with both the Middle East and India declined contemporary to Bukit Hasang's occupation, the Chinese wares found at Bukit Hasang could have been conveyed there by Southeast Asian traders via other Southeast Asian ports. As demonstrated later, Southeast Asian ports were suffuse with Chinese ceramics over this period, rendering them eminently plausible as a source for Barus's own Chinese wares.

Significantly, these commercial developments occurred alongside Barus's Islamization: as discussed earlier, the gravestones at Lobu Tua and Bukit Hasang point toward 14th-century conversion. Consequently, if Islam arrived along the trade routes, it likely did so via other Southeast Asian ports. Indeed, Southeast Asia's first identifiable Islamic polities, the north Sumatran cities of Lambri and Samudera-Pasai (discussed later), converted shortly before Barus and are geographically situated between that kingdom and the rest of the region. Moreover, while the site of Samudera-Pasai remains lost, meaning its trade cannot be assessed accurately, Lambri has yielded examples of both Chinese and Southeast Asian wares comparable to those at Bukit Hasang. It may therefore have acted as a conduit for those trade goods—and perhaps Islamic influence, too.

Lambri (Lhok Lambaro)

Lhok Lambaro is a bay located approximately 50 kilometers east of Banda Aceh, at the northern tip of Sumatra. When E. Edwards McKinnon first surveyed the site in 1985, he uncovered evidence of a significant coastal settlement that, occupied from the late 12th to 16th centuries, has since been convincingly identified as the ancient kingdom of Lambri (or Lamuri) (McKinnon 1988).

Between 850 and 1612, Lambri appears in a plethora of Arabic, Indian, Chinese, Southeast Asian, and European texts as an important exporter of camphor (Cowan 1933; McKinnon 1988: 104). While Arabic sources provide the earliest references, by the 12th century, virtually all allusions to the kingdom come from Chinese texts. Beginning with the 1178 *Lingwai daida* of Zhou Qufei (d. 1189), Lambri is described as an important stopping point at the northwest head of Sumatra, used by Chinese ships sailing between Guangzhou and India (Hirth and Rockill 1966: 72). This function is subsequently reaffirmed by the geographer Zhao Rugua (d. 1228), in addition to the travelers Wang

Dayuan (d. 1350) (Rockhill 1915: 148–149) and Ma Huan (d. 1460) (Mills 1970: 122). Ma Huan is also the first writer to describe Lambri as Muslim: after visiting the kingdom twice with Zheng He (d. 1433/1435), once in 1414 and again in 1430, he described it as home to a thousand families, all Muslim (Mills 1970: 122–123). Since Lambri has not provided us with an account of its history, Ma Huan's observation has traditionally been accepted as a provisional date of conversion. Edwards McKinnon's findings at Lhok Lambaro, however, belie a far earlier Muslim presence.

In 1985, Edwards McKinnon surveyed the foreshore of Lhok Lambaro. Along a beach ridge between two estuaries named Kuala Pancu and Kuala Baro, both situated opposite an island called Pulau Angkasa, he found extensive evidence of settlement, including several abandoned dwellings, heaped coral, some wells, pottery sherds, glass, and rusted iron. Evidence of habitation was also evident 200 meters from the shoreline, submerged beneath the waters of the bay, at a distance of 450 meters northwest of Kuala Pancu. There, a rectangular structure was observed which local tradition identifies as the ruins of a mosque. The Dutch Orientalist C. Snouck Hurgronje also saw and described this feature in the early 20th century, when it was still above sea level (Snouck Hurgronje 1906: 82). During a later visit in 1986, Edwards McKinnon observed two further groupings of submerged structures 250–300 meters east of Kuala Pancu, where what appeared to be stone foundations were visible at low tide, the easternmost of which was rectangular and measured 50 × 30 meters. The submergence of these structures reflects the tectonically unstable nature of the site; sitting on the North Sumatran Fault, Snouck Hurgronje's testimony suggests the area has sunk by at least 2–3 meters over the past century (McKinnon 1988).

Although Edwards McKinnon was unable to conduct extensive excavations at the site, his survey recovered a number of artifacts at surface level, including pottery fragments, glass, and rusted iron. Of these, only the pottery has been studied in detail. On the beach ridge, for example, McKinnon recovered a large amount of Southeast Asian earthenware, including fine paste ware, in addition to the rim of a large, high-quality 15th-century Vietnamese blue and white basin, along with several examples of 16th-century Ming blue and white stoneware. Additional finds were also made further along the shore, several hundred meters west of Kuala Pancu, where McKinnon found 15th-century Thai Sawankhalok ware, a Pegu (Burmese) white glazed jar, more 15th-century Vietnamese wares, 16th- to 17th-century Chinese stoneware, and Southeast Asian earthenware. A Majapahit-era brick was also found at this location. In the submerged areas of the site east of Kuala Pancu, Chinese porcelain from the late 12th–17th centuries was recovered, in addition to 15th-century Sawankhalok wares (McKinnon 1988).

While the interpretation of surface-recovered pottery is necessarily problematic in the absence of detailed excavations designed to place those finds in context, the results of Edwards McKinnon's survey suggest Southeast Asian wares predominated at Lhok Lambaro overall, with Chinese ceramics constituting the principal form of imported pottery. Although apparently vanishing over the 15th century, just as Thai and Vietnamese wares began to appear, these Chinese ceramics later reemerged during the 16th century, before finally ceasing altogether in the second half of the 17th century. This is shortly after all textual references to Lambri also cease, perhaps indicating the end of the settlement.

Contrasting with the apparent abundance of Chinese, Vietnamese, and Thai ceramics, Edwards McKinnon found no evidence of either Indian or Middle Eastern pottery from any period. On that basis, Lambri's trade appears more eastward than westward looking. This conclusion must be tempered, however, by three considerations. First, elsewhere on Sumatra, including at Barus, imported glass of the sort found at Lhok Lambaro originated from either South India or the Middle East. With caution, we might therefore associate the glass artifacts at Lhok Lambaro with either or both of those regions. Second, the Southeast Asian earthenware found at Lhok Lambaro includes the same variety of red-colored fine paste ware observed at Lobu Tua; as discussed earlier, these wares are stylistically akin to South Indian and Sri Lankan examples, thereby indicating Indian influence (McKinnon 2012: 144–145). Third, at Neusu, a suburb of nearby Banda Aceh, a 12th- to 13th-century Tamil-language inscription has been recovered. While referring to the foundation of a temple, it lists various commercial regulations relating to the loss of goods, waiving of interest, and payment of royal fees (Christie 1998: 258–263). Although the inscription does not mention Lambri or provide any clear indication of who erected it, as at Lobu Tua the use of Tamil (a language not spoken locally) to espouse trade regulations suggests the existence of a South Indian merchant community in the vicinity of Lambri.

Although Edwards McKinnon's findings must necessarily constitute only a partial reconstruction, they suggest Lambri sat within a trade network extending from the Indian Ocean to Southern China. While the overall predominance of Southeast Asian wares indicates Lambri conducted the majority of its trade with other Southeast Asian ports, evidence for its international trade points toward China as its dominant partner. As at Barus, however, does this predominance indicate a direct trade link with China, or one mediated through intermediaries? To answer this question, it is pertinent to note that Chinese ceramics appear at Lhok Lambaro contemporary to Zhou Qufei's description of Lambri as a stopping point for Chinese ships traveling between China and India. Quite plausibly, therefore, these Chinese ceramics reflect a direct relationship. Certainly, if Lambri functioned as a stopping point for Chinese ships, Chinese traders, together with their merchandise, would have resided there for a part of each year; when Marco Polo (d. 1324) visited north Sumatra aboard a Chinese ship in about 1292, for example, he remained there with his crew for five months, awaiting a change in the monsoons (Cliff 2016: 239). Although this does not preclude the possibility that some of the Chinese goods recovered from Lhok Lambaro arrived via intermediaries, a significant proportion plausibly came directly from China itself.

While at Lhok Lambaro, Edwards McKinnon also examined two early assemblages of Islamic gravestones, one within the Kuala Pancu estuary itself, the other 200 meters to the east, on a headland called Ulung Batee Kapal. These gravestones are very stylistically distinctive: commonly termed *plakpling*,[4] they constitute small square towers that,

---

[4] Yatim and Nasir (1990) first applied this label to the gravestones, with Montana (1997) following suit, identifying it as a local designation. Edwards McKinnon, however, disputes this, asserting that the term *plakpling* is unknown among the locals; he feels it may be a corruption of the phrase *plang pleng*, meaning "variously decorated" (McKinnon 2012: 145). Nevertheless, because *plakpling* has become an established term within the literature, it is retained here.

tapering toward the top, are eclectically decorated on all four sides in a variety of styles. Virtually all known examples of *plakpling* are found at Lhok Lambaro[5]; made of local materials, including a soft (fossiliferous) chalky limestone found onsite, they are almost certainly of local manufacture (McKinnon 2012: 147). Significantly, they are also very early: of those which have been studied, five carry readable inscriptions, four with the dates 608 AH (1211 CE), 720 AH (1320 CE), 800 AH (1398 CE), and 804 AH (1401 CE) (Montana 1997: 90). Pottery sherds found in association with the *plakpling*, including 13th- to early 15th-century Chinese ceramics, 15th-century Sawankhalok wares, and the aforementioned local earthenware, confirm this dating. The *plakpling* therefore testify to the existence of a culturally distinct Muslim community in northwest Sumatra by the early 13th century, one self-confident enough to create its own unique Islamic funerary artifacts. Moreover, according to Montana (1997), the 608/1211 gravestone bears the name "al-Sultan Sulaiman bin Abdullah bin al-Basir." Potentially, therefore, it establishes a ruling Muslim elite in Lambri by the early 13th century, approximately eighty years before the conversion of Samudera-Pasai. If Sultan Sulaiman's father and grandfather also ruled Lambri, conversion could even date to the mid- to late 12th century (see Ricklefs 2008: 4).[6]

To date, academia has characterized the *plakpling* as evidence of Indian influence during the earliest stages of Southeast Asia's Islamization. Edwards McKinnon, for example, has likened their basic form—small square pillars tapering toward the top—to both South Indian hero stones and Indian temple gateway towers (McKinnon 2012: 145). Very little, however, upholds these comparisons. South Indian hero stones, for example, are flat, sometimes very roughly hewn rectangular stone slabs profusely decorated with human images (Kacinatan 1978). By contrast, the *plakpling* are square columns that, uniformly well-carved, carry no anthropomorphic representations of any kind. Neither do Indian temple gateway towers constitute convincing prototypes: although displaying a similar tendency to taper toward the top, these structures are stylistically and functionally quite distinct from the *plakpling* (Hardy 2007).

Nevertheless, the floral patterns adorning the upper sections of many *plakpling* are undoubtedly reminiscent of traditional Indian designs. This need not entail, however, direct Indian influence; by the early 13th century, Indian floral (and other) designs had been influencing Southeast Asian art for many centuries, including on Sumatra (Kempers 1959). A late 13th-century bilingual inscription found at Porlak Dolok, for example, near the pre-Islamic site of Padang Lawas, Sumatera Utara province, utilizes

---

[5] Outside Lhok Lambaro, only two other *plakpling* gravestones are known, one at Kampung Pango in Banda Aceh (Yatim and Nasir 1990: 36) and the other at Kampung Baru, a coastal village 93 kilometers further west, near the city of Lamno. In the latter location, a solitary *plakpling* gravestone is found on the beach; while local tradition associates it with a mid–16th-century figure called Pahlawan Syah (or Datuk Pegu), the gravestone itself is inscribed with the name Hussain and dated 790 AH (1388 CE), making it contemporary to those at Lhok Lambaro (Montana 1997: 94–95).

[6] This reading, however, is controversial: Wade (2007) has disputed it, while it sits in evident conflict with the accounts of both Marco Polo, who described Lambri as heathen in approximately 1292 (Cliff 2016: 241), and Friar Odoric of Pordenonc (d. 1331), who did the same in 1323 (cited in Miksic and Geok 2017: 497). As the gravestone disappeared in 2006, the reading cannot be checked.

numerous Indian artistic devices akin to those seen on the *plakpling* (Christie 1998: 258–263). If Sumatra had therefore been exposed to this form of Indian art prior to the production of the *plakpling*, the reoccurrence of such motifs on those latter artifacts need not mark direct Indian influence but instead the continuation of a preexisting Southeast Asian artistic tradition.

Indian-inspired designs are not, however, the only artistic designs to appear on the *plakpling*; many also carry clear indications of Chinese artistic influence, notably lotus and jasmine blossoms intertwined with eternal knot motifs (McKinnon 2012: 145). Usually found on the lower sections of the *plakpling*, these motifs occur alongside the Indian-inspired designs. They differ from them, however, by having no known precedent in Southeast Asian art (Kempers 1959). Rather, the *plakpling* mark their first known appearance, suggesting these gravestones were produced contemporary to a period of Chinese cultural influence. This conclusion would be consistent with Lambri's role as a stopping point for Chinese ships, where Chinese merchants sojourned for several months of the year and where Chinese goods, notably ceramics, were heavily distributed.

Whether the occurrence of Chinese artistic influence in association with Lambri's earliest Islamic relics belies a Chinese Muslim presence is, however, uncertain. Although Muslims played a prominent role in Chinese trade over this period, the *plakpling* may simply reflect an indigenous Muslim population's desire to imitate Chinese cultural forms recently introduced to them by trade. Equally, given that wood and not stone constituted pre-modern Southeast Asia's most-worked material during this period (Soepratno 1984), it is equally plausible that Lambri's indigenous Muslim population, lacking the expertise to work in stone, chose to employ (Muslim or non-Muslim) Chinese artisans to create the *plakpling*. These craftsmen then utilized Chinese artistic motifs as the designs most familiar to them. Lambri's first Muslims, however, evidently lived in an environment suffuse with Chinese cultural influences. These ultimately came to bear on the creation of the city's early Muslim culture.

Samudera-Pasai (Lhokseumawe)

The modern Indonesian city of Lhokseumawe, situated in Aceh province, lies approximately 200 kilometers east of Banda Aceh, on the northeast coast of Sumatra. Just outside the city, on its eastern edge, are several late 13th- to early 16th-century grave groups, most notably at Gampong Beuringen and Kuta Krueng, both situated just a few hundred meters from the shoreline. First observed by archaeologists in the early 20th century, these artifacts constitute the only known remnants of Samudera-Pasai, Southeast Asia's first prominent Muslim kingdom (Moquette 1912).

Samudera-Pasai embraced Islam during the late 13th century—the gravestone of Sultan Malik al-Saleh (Figure 5.4.2), whom the late–14th-century *Hikayat Raja Pasai* (*Chronicle of the Pasai Kings*) identifies as the kingdom's first Muslim ruler (Jones 1999), is located at Gampong Beuringen and dated Ramadan 697 AH (June/July 1297 CE). Soon

FIGURE 5.4.2 The gravestone of Malik al-Salih, dated Ramadan 1297 (Moquette 1912).

after its conversion, Samudera-Pasai became the region's foremost entrepôt, exerting considerable control over the Straits of Melaka. While the city remained prominent well into the 15th century, in 1524 Ali Mughayat Shah, the first Sultan of Aceh, attacked and destroyed it, relocating its population to Banda Aceh (Miksic and Geok 2017: 500). From that point on, Samudera-Pasai disappeared from the historical record, the precise location of its capital forgotten. Although various sites have been suggested, including Cot Astana (Moquette 1913) and the region between the rivers Jambo Aye and Krueng Pasei 20 kilometers west of Lhokseumawe (Miksic and Geok 2017: 500), no substantial trace of the city has been found save for the aforementioned gravestones.

Samudera-Pasai's gravestones first gained scholarly attention in 1912, shortly after the pacification of Aceh opened up the area of Lhokseumawe for archaeological exploration. Between 1912 and 1917, Dutch Orientalists compiled a detailed record of every early gravestone observed in the area, producing an extensive archive of photographs, inscription squeezes, and maps. The remains of this archive, including many of the original glass photographic plates, is kept at the Direktorat Perlindungan dan Pembinaan Peninggalan Sejarah dan Purbakala (Directorate for the Protection and Development of Historical and Archaeological Heritage) in Jakarta, with a partial set of photographic prints at the University Library, Leiden, under the accession Legatum Warnerianum Or. 23, 481 (Lambourn 2004: 246). This early 20th-century record remains unique and of unparalleled significance; no subsequent study of Samudera-Pasai's gravestones has attained the same level of detail. Despite this importance, although a complete list of the gravestones photographed was published in *Oudheidkundig Verslag van de Oudheidkundige Dienst in Nederlandische Indie* between 1912 and 1917, the archive has been neither published in full nor systematically studied. Rather, only a handful of photographs have ever appeared in the literature, most recently in a series of articles by E. Lambourn. The brief overview presented here draws on those published examples.

Overall, Samudera-Pasai's gravestones vary widely in form. Some of the earliest, including the well-known gravestone of Sultan Malik al-Zahir (d. 726 AH/1326 CE), son of Malik al-Saleh, constitute simple unadorned square granite columns topped with pommel-like decoration (Yatim and Nasir 1990: 14). Still others, such as that of Lalah bint al-Sultan al-Marhum al-Malik al-Zahir (d. 781 AH/1380 CE or 791 AH/1389 CE), comprise modest arched blocks of sandstone (Lambourn 2004: 212). Commencing in the early 15th century, however, Samudera-Pasai began producing a distinctive form of gravestone known locally as *batu Aceh* (Acehnese stones). Quickly replacing all earlier forms of gravestone, these artifacts were produced up until the 19th century and exported across both Sumatra and the Malay Peninsula (Lambourn 2008). Unlike other early Saumdera-Pasai gravestones, *batu Aceh* have garnered considerable scholarly attention, facilitating a discussion of them here. Like the *plakpling* of Lambri, early 15th-century examples of these artifacts evince a mixture of Indian and Chinese influences.

Beginning with those early *batu Aceh* displaying apparent Indian influence, Lambourn (2008: 267) places them at the head of the *batu Aceh* tradition, designating them Type A in her provisional typology. Grave VII at Kuta Krueng (dated 841 AH/1438 CE) typifies many examples of this Type A (Figure 5.4.3). Although unattributed, this gravestone was found amid a royal assemblage, suggesting it belonged to a member of the ruling elite (Lambourn 2004: 242). Measuring approximately 65 × 40 centimeters, it rests upon an unadorned, gently upward-curving stone base. As is characteristic of most Type A *batu Aceh*, it is undecorated save for a central panel inscription that, written in Arabic, is carved in relief, in the *naskh* script. Parallel to the top of this inscription are two pointed protrusions termed locally as *subang* (earrings) and which probably represent stylized Garuda wings. These *subang* curve upward to form "shoulders." The whole is then surmounted by a flat-topped crown with a further inscription at its center.

During the course of the 15th century, this simple form of Type A *batu Aceh* gradually became more elaborate, resulting in a highly ornate version typified by the gravestone of Malik al-Saleh. Conclusively demonstrated by Lambourn (2008) to be a late 15th-century replacement for something earlier, this artifact is made of light-colored sandstone and rests upon a wide, elaborately carved stone base. Above this base, along the lower edge of the gravestone proper, floriated geometric designs are interspersed with stylized leaf motifs that rise toward a central panel inscription. As in the preceding description, this inscription is in Arabic and carved in relief, in the *naskh* script. There are also two distinctive *subang* at its top, larger and more elaborately wrought than on Grave VII.

FIGURE 5.4.3 Grave VII at Kuta Krueng, dated 841 AH/1438 CE (Or.23, 481, photograph 59).
Courtesy of Leiden University Library, Legatum Warnerianum.

These *subang* again form "shoulders" that rise toward a crown, this time with a pointed top. Another inscription sits at the center of this crown, surrounded by elaborate geometric designs akin to those further down the monument.

Overall, both forms of Type A *batu Aceh* are suggestive of Indian influence. The geometric floriated designs and stylized leaf patterns associated with the more elaborate versions, for example, are typical of Indian art, as are Garuda wings. However, as with the Indian designs observed in association with *plakpling*, many of these motifs also occurred across pre-Islamic Southeast Asia, especially on Java. In the latter location, they frequently appeared in association with *candi* (pre-Islamic temples), as well as on later mosques and Muslim mausolea (Kempers 1959). For example, the east Javanese Muslim mausoleum, Sendang Duwur, final resting place of Sunan Sendang (d. 1585), is entered through monumental gateways bearing Garuda wings (Kerlogue 2004: 137). Significantly, therefore, Java ruled north Sumatra from 1360 to 1387; the Indian motifs observed at Samudera-Pasai may have entered the kingdom from there. If so, they represent the continuation of an earlier Southeast Asian artistic tradition, not direct contact with India during Islamization.

It should be borne in mind, however, that several early gravestones found near Lhokseumawe are from Cambay, Gujarat. At Kuta Krueng, for example, we find the gravestone of Teungku Sidi Abdullah, dated 816 AH/1414 CE. With its elegantly curved bow-shaped top, elaborate *naskh* script carved in relief, and dense geometric decoration, this artifact is typical of Cambay-produced gravestones. So, too, are Grave VI (834 AH/1430–1431 CE) at the Teungku Sareh grave group (Gampong Beuringen),

Graves II and III (undated) at the Said Syarif grave group (Gampong Mancang), and the gravestone of Na'ina Husam al-Din ibn Na'ina Amin (823 AH/1420 CE) at Kuta Krueng (Lambourn 2003). While none of these examples is stylistically equivalent to Type A *batu Aceh*, differing both in terms of form and specific decorative elements, they nevertheless demonstrate Samudera-Pasai's exposure to early 15th-century Indian funerary culture. This exposure could conceivably have informed the creation of Type A *batu Aceh*.

Turning to those *batu Aceh* suggestive of Chinese influence, Lambourn excludes these from her typology, characterizing them instead as a formative step toward the creation of Type A. They are therefore portrayed as a developmental stage predating the emergence of *batu Aceh* proper (Lambourn 2008). This conclusion, however, is problematic: the earliest Chinese-influenced *batu Aceh* actually emerge contemporary to Type A, with many more dating to the mid-15th century, long after Type A had already become well-established. Arguably, therefore, Chinese-influenced *batu Aceh* are not part of a formative tradition culminating in Type A, but a parallel one that persisted over the first half of the 15th century.

Grave XIX at Teungku Sareh constitutes an excellent example of Chinese-influenced *batu Aceh* (Figure 5.4.4). Made up of a gravestone pair, it is dated 12 Muharram 840 or 841 AH (27 July 1436/16 July 1437 CE) and attributed to Sitti Khadijah bint 'Ali bin Jamal al-Gilani. Each gravestone measures 59 × 37 centimeters and possesses the same curved

FIGURE 5.4.4 Grave XIX at Teungku Sareh, dated 12 Muharram 840 or 841 AH (27 July 1436/16 July 1437 CE) and attributed to Sitti Khadijah bint 'Ali bin Jamal al-Gilani (Or.23, 481, photograph 461).
Courtesy of Leiden University Library, Legatum Warnerianum.

shoulders and flat-topped crowns characteristic of Type A, thereby establishing them as *batu Aceh*. All Indian stylistic influences, however, including *subang*, are absent. Instead, two pairs of vertically orientated spirals carved in relief constitute Grave XIX's most prominent decorative feature. The first of these pairs occupies the crown; beginning at the very top of the gravestone, they descend parallel to the outer edge of the crown, to a point level with the shoulders. Immediately below that point, the second pair of spirals begin; small and tightly wound, they unfurl into straight lines that descend toward the gravestone's base while also dividing the surface of the headstone into three: two outer borders and a central panel. Both outer borders contain either *muhaqqaq*-style epigraphy carved in relief or a repeated geometric pattern. The central panel contains a stylized flower or star motif (possibly representative of a lantern) suspended from a rope- or vine-like design issuing from the top of the crown. Finally, the base of each gravestone bears an interlaced geometric pattern of wave-like swirls.

Numerous other *batu Aceh* are stylistically comparable to Grave XIX, including Grave VII (dated 841 AH/1437–1438 CE, name unread) at the Teungku Sidi grave group, Kuta Krueng; Grave X (dated 5 Rabi I 834 AH/21 November 1430, name unread) at the Peuet Ploh Peuet grave group, Gampong Beuringen; and Grave XVIII (dated Rabi' I 844 AH/July–August 1440 CE, name unread) at the Teungku Sareh grave group. Although we have characterized these gravestones as "Chinese influenced," their dominant spiral patterns relate to Sumatra's pre-Islamic megalithic tradition; in the Minangkabau district of Lima Puluh Kota, Sumatera Barat (West Sumatra) province, monoliths known locally as *batu tagak* feature many comparable designs (Lambourn 2004: 241). While the extent of Samudera-Pasai's interaction with Minangkabau is unknown, it seems probable this motif originated from there. Chinese influences, however, are evident throughout the rest of the decorative elements just described. For example, the geometric patterns observed in association with the borders of Grave XIX are repeated Chinese eternal knot motifs, while the swirling wave-like patterns along its base replicate a device commonly found among 13th- to 14th-century Muslim gravestones at Quanzhou, the important Chinese port. The Quanzhou-produced gravestone of an Abu Bakr ibn Husayn (dated 717 AH/1317 CE), for example, utilizes this same design, also along its base (Chen, 1984: fig. 44). Finally, the epigraphy used on the gravestones noted here are not rendered in the *naskh* script, but in *muhaqqaq*. Although by no means unique to Quanzhou, this form of script was also common there; in India, as on Type A, the *naskh* script predominated.

Reference to Quanzhou recalls an observation made by Lambourn (2004) concerning photograph Or. 23, 481 no. 478 of the Teungku Sareh grave group. This early 20th-century image captures a cenotaph to the rear of the group among numerous examples of *batu Aceh*. In shape and form, this artifact strongly resembles 14th-century Quanzhou cenotaphs, with clear Chinese-style cloud patterns along its edge. If so, Samudera-Pasai imported not just Gujarati gravestones, but also Quanzhou examples. Certainly, Quanzhou gravestones are known from elsewhere in the region, notably in Brunei (discussed later). If also present at Samudera-Pasai, they could have acted as a conduit for the Chinese motifs discussed here.

Determining whether this Chinese influence was direct is difficult in the absence of archaeology pertaining to Samudera-Pasai's main urban settlement. Nevertheless, Samudera-Pasai is known to have functioned as a stopping point for Chinese ships from Quanzhou: Marco Polo and Ibn Battuta, both of whom traveled aboard Quanzhou vessels, reportedly halted there (Cliff 2016: 239; MacKintosh-Smith 2003: 322). So, too, did Zheng He, for whom Samudera-Pasai regularly acted a launching point into the Indian Ocean. Indeed, Zheng He even invaded the polity in 1415, after becoming embroiled in a dynastic dispute there (Mills 1970: 117). Under these circumstances, a situation comparable to that at Lambri might reasonably be anticipated, in which Chinese cultural influences, possibly suffused with Islam, abounded. Moreover, the earliest examples of Chinese-influenced *batu Aceh* appear contemporary to Zheng He's final voyage (1431–1433). According to the *Ming shilu* (*Imperial Records of the Ming Dynasty*), many members of this voyage, some of them Muslims from Quanzhou, migrated to Southeast Asia; one of Zheng He's ships reputedly returned with only three of its original three hundred crew members (Reid 2001: 26). While it is impossible to know where these sailors headed, let alone whether they contributed to the *batu Aceh* tradition, Zheng He's close association with Samudera-Pasai lends credence to the possibility that some of them settled there. If so, they may have subsequently contributed to that kingdom's early Islamic culture.

Brunei (Bandar Seri Begawan)

Today, Brunei constitutes a small city state situated on the northern coast of Borneo, overlooking the South China Sea. With its capital at Bandar Seri Begawan, it is surrounded (indeed, divided in two) by the modern Malaysian state of Sarawak. Although currently one of the region's smallest sovereign nations, during the 15th and 16th centuries, Brunei ruled Borneo's entire northern coast, in addition to Sulu and southern Luzon (both now part of the Philippines). Territorially, therefore, it was one of Southeast Asia's largest kingdoms.

Chinese sources provide the earliest known references to Brunei. Although attempts have been made to link Brunei to several first millennium CE Chinese toponyms, most notably Poli (first used during the 7th century), subsequent research has refuted these attributions (Ptak 1998; Kurz 2013). Instead, the first probable Chinese reference to Brunei is the Boni of the *Taiping huanyuji* (*Universal History of the Taiping*) by Yue Shi (d. 1007), published in 978. Described as a camphor-producing country located to the southwest of China, it is said to be thirty days from Champa and forty from Srivijaya. This brief description subsequently forms the basis of all later Song accounts, including that of Zhao Rugua, with no new information emerging until Wang Dayuan. From then until the 18th century, Boni is mentioned intermittently by a range of Chinese texts, with the most detailed information appearing during the early Ming period, when two Bruneian rulers visited China in person. None of the sources, however, attains a significant degree of precision, particularly with regards to location—to the point that not all references to Boni need be to the same locality. It has been plausibly suggested that this lack of clarity belies China's comparative disinterest in Brunei (Kurz 2011). Be that as it may, these early Chinese references far exceed those from either the Middle East or India. Indeed, no Arabic or Indian text provides a clear or certain reference to Brunei prior to the 15th century (Tibbetts 1979; Vienne 2015: 31).

Scholarship remains divided over when Brunei embraced Islam. The Pusat Sejarah Brunei (The Brunei Historical Center), champion of official Brunei historiography, strongly supports 14th-century conversion; utilizing the *Silsilah Raja-Raja Brunei* (*Genealogy of the Bruneian Kings*), a supposedly late 17th- to early 18th-century text subsequently revised in 1807 (Sweeney 1965: 11, 51), they attribute conversion to Temasik and date it to 1363 (Nicholl 1989; al-Sufri 1990). Other scholars, however, utilizing early European descriptions of the region, propose a date of around 1515: while a 1514 letter from Rui de Brito Patalim, the Portuguese Captain-General of Melaka, to King Manuel I describes "Burneo" as pagan (Nicholl 1975: 4), the following year Tomé Pires (d. 1524/1540) refers to it as recently converted (Cortesao 2005: 132). As we shall see, the archaeology of Brunei refutes both these possibilities. Instead, it suggests conversion by the early 14th century and in the context of (but not necessarily resulting from) intense cultural and commercial interaction with the Muslim community at Quanzhou. In contrast to the three Sumatran locations examined earlier, Brunei bears no obvious trace of either Indian Ocean or Middle Eastern influence, at least from this early period.

Approximately 2 kilometers from the center of modern-day Bandar Seri Begawan, on the north bank of the Brunei River, sits an ancient stone-built residential structure known locally as Kota Batu (Stone Fort). Covering a modest area of 2.5 hectares, Kota Batu is one of only a handful of early Islamic Bruneian sites to have been excavated; from 1952 to 1953, archaeologist T. Harrison led a series of excavations there, which were later followed up and expanded upon in 1968 (Harrisson and Harrisson 1956; Harrisson 1958, 1970). These excavations uncovered evidence of continuous high-status occupation spanning the 10th to 17th centuries (Harrisson 1970). In all probability, the site represents Brunei's early royal compound, a structure the Italian traveler Antonio Pigafetta (d. 1534), who visited Brunei in 1521, and later Spanish sources describe as the city's principal stone-built structure (Nicholl 1975: 10, 54).

During his investigation of the site, Harrisson recovered ceramics and coinage in addition to several early Muslim gravestones. In total, the site yielded 6,230 ceramic sherds, the majority dating from the 13th to 15th centuries. They occurred in the following proportions: Chinese ceramics 66.5 percent, stoneware jars 23 percent, Vietnamese and Thai wares 3.5 percent, local earthenware 3.5 percent, and 19th century or later wares 3.5 percent (Harrisson 1970). Significantly, Harrisson also found these ceramic types in comparable proportions at Sungai Lumut, a possible 14th- to 16th-century Bruneian burial ground situated 60 kilometers west of Bandar Seri Begawan. There 6,000 sherds were recovered, 62 percent of them Chinese, 22 percent coarse stoneware jars, 13 percent Thai wares and 3 percent local earthenware (Harrisson and Shariffudin 1969). Moreover, at both sites all recovered pre–14th-century ceramics belonged to just six types of locally produced earthenware.[7] From the beginning of the 14th century, two of these types disappeared in favor of Chinese blue and white porcelain; by the early 15th century, virtually all local wares had vanished at both sites in favor of Chinese ceramics, with Thai and Vietnamese wares subsequently appearing later in the same century. Overall, these finds suggest Chinese ceramics began to permeate Bruneian markets from the beginning of the 14th century, reaching a virtual monopoly by the early 15th century. Although this dominance does not, in itself, constitute a comment on who brought those ceramics to Brunei, it demonstrates a clear Bruneian preoccupation with Chinese goods over this period. By contrast, Harrisson found no evidence of either Indian Ocean or Middle East ceramics at the site.

Turning to the coins found at Kota Batu, these ranged in date from the 10th to 16th centuries. The earliest examples were all Chinese: two from the Tang dynasty (the earliest dated 906 CE), twenty-seven from the Song, and seven from the early Ming (Miksic 2010: 395). Whether these artifacts constituted currency is uncertain; while this usage has been demonstrated elsewhere in Southeast Asia, notably at Kota Cina and Majapahit,[8] at Kota Batu Chinese coins do not occur in sufficiently large quantities to establish that practice. Their disappearance, however, does coincide with the appearance of Brunei's first locally minted Islamic coins (Brown 1970: 130–131). From the 16th century, these take the form of *pitis*, a unique type of Southeast Asian currency that, first studied by Hanitsch (1907) and found right across Brunei, remained in circulation until the mid-19th century. Significantly, they possess several stylistic features suggestive of Chinese influence.

As outlined by Gallop (2005), the majority of *pitis* bear the image of a large quadruped that, while becoming gradually more stylized over time, has been variously interpreted as a camel, bull, buffalo, tiger, ass, elephant, or cat (Hanitsch 1907; Wodak 1958; Barrett 1988: 20–34). Gallop, however, after examining the earliest known examples, has conclusively demonstrated it to be a camel design akin to those found atop the handles of Chinese Imperial Seals. Significantly, therefore, the *Ming shilu* claims the Emperor Yongle (r. 1402–1424) granted an Imperial Seal to Brunei in 1408 (Wade 2005). Although the *Ming shilu* does not describe the form of that seal, the Chinese geographer Zhang

---

[7] This is not to state that the wider Brunei region lacked exposure to imported wares prior to the 14th century. In 2002, a substantial pre-Islamic settlement was uncovered at Sungai Limau Manis, 30 kilometers inland from Kota Batu. Occupied from the 10th to mid-14th centuries, this site yielded 50,000 pottery sherds, many of them Chinese. The precise identity and function of this site remain unknown, although S. Druce has speculated that it may be a former Bruneian capital (Druce 2016: 32).

[8] Around 2,000 Tang and Song dynasty coins have been found at Sumatra's Kota Cina, the majority randomly scattered around areas of habitation, suggesting use as currency (Miksic and Geok 2017: 404). Likewise, at Trowulan-Tralaya, the site of Majapahit's capital, Chinese copper cash has also been recovered from across areas of habitation. Moreover, all surviving Majapahit-era inscriptions express monetary values in units of Chinese copper cash, whether for commercial or taxation purposes, entirely disregarding earlier Javanese forms of coinage (Wicks 1986: 59–60). There is even evidence that Majapahit cast its own examples of Chinese coins, based on Northern Song originals (Christie 1998: 169–170).

Xie (d. 1640), author of the *Dongxiyang kao* (*On the Countries in the Eastern and Western Oceans*, 1618), confirms it was surmounted with the image of an animal—although without stating which (Groeneveldt 1876: 102). Gallop notes, however, that seal designs were often standardized across nations of similar rank. Significantly, therefore, the *Ming shilu* describes the Imperial Seal sent to Siam in 1403 as being surmounted by a camel (Wade 2005). Although Siam outranked Brunei, Gallop speculates that both nations may have been entitled to the same seal since each belonged to the same region (Gallop 2005). Although this is perhaps tentative, the other decorative images found on 16th-century *pitis* reinforce the likelihood of a Chinese origin for the camel design. Thus, the camel motif is often placed on a background of swirling Chinese cloud patterns, while those *pitis* lacking camel motifs depict either a dragon's head or a bird in flight that, quite plausibly, represents a phoenix (Barrett 1988). These are also common Chinese motifs. Consequently, early *pitis* apparently constitute evidence of Chinese cultural influence in early Islamic Brunei. Moreover, since they only employ Chinese designs and were undoubtedly produced locally, Gallop further argues that they were manufactured by Chinese craftsmen living in Brunei (Gallop 2005: 278). Although this cannot be confirmed, the Spanish do testify to the existence of Chinese communities in Bruneian territory over the 17th century (Nicholl 1975).

Ultimately, however, returning to Harrisson's excavations at Kota Batu, the four Muslim gravestones he uncovered there constitute his most important discovery. This is because all of them are 15th century: while two bear legible 15th-century dates (836 AH/1432–1433 CE and 858 AH/1454 CE), the remaining two are attributable to the same period on stylistic grounds (Kalus and Guillot 2003: 261–264, 267). Consequently, these gravestones indicate that Muslims lived among Brunei's ruling elite during the first half of the 15th century, almost a century before many scholars date Brunei's conversion (Saunders 2002: 35–39). Further archaeological evidence not only supports this conclusion but also indicates the existence of a much earlier Bruneian Sultanate than previously thought, one with evident connections to China.

In 1987, a gravestone was discovered in the Brunei Museum's storeroom (Figure 5.4.5). Originally from the Dagang Cemetery 3 kilometers west of Kota Batu, it was initially described as a locally produced memorial made of granite (Haji Jibah and Haji Hassan 1987). Undated, its precise age could not be determined. It bore, however, the following inscription, identifying it as a royal gravestone belonging to a previously unknown sultan: "This tomb belongs to the late martyred Sultan, a learned and just man, a protector and conqueror. He was called Maharaja Brunei" (Chen 2000: 148). Subsequently, the gravestone was examined by Chen Dasheng. Well known for his work on South China's Muslim gravestones, Chen immediately recognized it as a Yuan-period Quanzhou Muslim memorial; its distinctive bow-shaped top, decorative bands carved in concave relief, and inscription were all typical of Quanzhou Muslim gravestones produced between 1272 and 1362. Supporting this conclusion, Chen also noticed that the gravestone was made of diabase, not granite. While diabase cannot be found in Brunei, 91 of the 111 Quanzhou gravestones studied by Chen were of this material (Chen 1984: xv). Chen therefore concluded that the Maharaja Brunei gravestone originated from

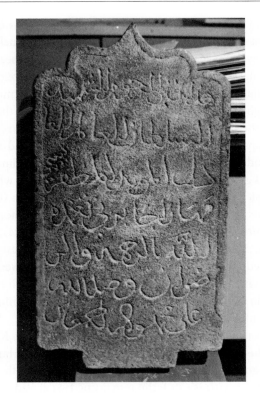

FIGURE 5.4.5 The undated gravestone of Maharaja Brunei (Kalus and Guillot 2003: Stele 23).

Quanzhou and could not be later than 1362; because of a particularly close resemblance to the Quanzhou-produced gravestone of a Fatima bint Nayna Ahmad (dated 704 AH/1304 CE), however, Chen ultimately favored an early 14th-century date (Chen 2000). Supporting this, the incised inscription on Maharaja Brunei's gravestone is executed in near identical fashion to several other inscriptions from early 14th-century Quanzhou, including that belonging to the gravestone of Abu Bakr ibn Husayn (dated 717 AH/1317 CE) (Chen, 1984: fig. 44). As well as helping to date the artifact, this final point also suggests Maharaja Brunei's gravestone was inscribed in China.

If Maharaja Brunei's gravestone is early 14th-century, it demonstrates the existence of a Bruneian Sultanate half a century before all prior estimates of Brunei's conversion. It also establishes a link between that Sultanate and Quanzhou, albeit of uncertain nature and origin. Given the highly revisionist nature of this conclusion, it is worth briefly considering what other evidence exists to support it.

Significantly, the late 16th-century Boxer Codex confirms both early conversion and a link to Quanzhou. Renowned for its seventy-five illustrations of Japanese, Chinese, Formosan, and Southeast Asian peoples, this text also contains written descriptions of various Asian kingdoms, including Brunei. When the manuscript first came to light in 1947, it was assumed to be a wholly European creation: written in Spanish and in the handwriting of Juan de Cuellar, secretary to Luis Pérez Dasmariñas, Governor of the

Philippines from 1593, its contents exhibited clear European influences, including a description of China mirroring that of Martín de Rada (Quirino 1977: 1003–1004).[9] It was quickly realized, however, that its account of Brunei differed from the rest of the text; not only did it describe Islam without condemning it (unusual for a 16th-century European source), but it recorded day-to-day information about Brunei, suggesting its author lived among the local population, something no Spaniard is known to have done. Moreover, the author knew both Tagalog and Malay, a rare skill among Spaniards. Indeed, the author frequently substitutes the Tagalog *l* for the Malay *r*, and Tagalog *r* for the Malay *d*. According to J. Carroll, this suggests the author was a Malay-speaking Tagalog whose narrative was presumably copied down by de Cuellar (Carroll 1982: 1). Given Brunei ruled the Tagalog region of Luzon until 1570, this Malay-speaking Tagalog could have accessed early indigenous accounts of Brunei's history, especially if he also lived in that kingdom for a period. As all other indigenous Bruneian histories are 19th-century, the Codex is therefore a potentially valuable source of information.

The Brunei section of the Codex claims the kingdom's first Muslim ruler was called Sultan Yusuf (Yuso). According to the text, Yusuf invaded Brunei from elsewhere in Southeast Asia, displacing the local Visayan population.[10] This supposedly occurred three hundred years before the Codex was written, or during the late 13th century—that is, roughly contemporary to Maharaja Brunei (Souza and Turley 2015: 400–401). The Codex then claims Sultan Yusuf traveled to China, where he met the Emperor and married a noble Chinese woman who was "the ruler of a city called Nantay in the kingdom of China" (Souza and Turley 2015: 402–403). According to Carroll, "Nantay" is a corruption of the Chinese *Nantaiwu*, the name of an 18-metre high tower on the southern shore of Xiamen Bay that once acted as a landmark for ships sailing to Quanzhou, just a short distance up the coast (Carroll 1982: 17). Consequently, Carroll believes Nantay is a reference to Quanzhou. If so, the Boxer Codex not only confirms Muslim rule in Brunei contemporary to Maharaja Brunei, but also a link between that early Islamic kingdom and Quanzhou.

Further establishing an early link between Brunei and Quanzhou, in 1972 a 13th-century Chinese burial marker was recovered from the Rangas Cemetery, central Bandar Seri Begawan (Franke and Ch'en 1973; Kurz 2016). Initially considered part of a large grave complex at the cemetery's center, Pg. Karim bin Pengiran Haji Osman (1993: 8) subsequently established its original location as Kota Batu, from which it had been removed in the 1930s as part of a consignment of stone intended for the construction of a shop

---

[9]   Martín de Rada (d. 1578) was an early Spanish missionary who visited China in 1575, returning to Manila the same year (Boxer 1953: lxvii, lxx, lxxvi).

[10]   The Codex claims Sultan Yusuf came from a city called "Cavin," located farther west in Southeast Asia. Carroll attempts to equate this location with Sabang, a village on Pulau Kundur, an island between Singapore and Sumatra. To sustain this conclusion he relies on three simultaneous letter substitutions common in Spanish texts: *c* for the cedilla (pronounced as an *s*), *v* for *b*, and *n* for the Malay *ng*. Putting all this together, Cavin becomes the Malay name Sabang (Carroll 1982: 17). All these substitutions, however, are provisional, problematizing Carroll's conclusion. Souza and Turley do not attempt an identification (Souza and Turley 2015: 402).

house—a fate it only avoided when purchased by an unknown individual as decoration for the grave at Rangas. When examined by W. Franke and Ch'en T'ieh-fan, the gravestone was found to bear an inscription in Chinese characters dating it to the Jing Ding period of the Song Emperor Lizong (i.e., 1260–1264) and attributing it to "Pan Yuan Master Pu of Quanzhou" (Franke and Ch'en 1973: 92–93). "Pan Yuan" is an official Song title, indicating Master Pu occupied an important official position, although what that position was is unclear. The name "Pu" in association with Quanzhou, however, recalls the powerful Muslim Pu clan. Originally from Guangzhou, this clan claimed Arab descent and, by the 12th century, had come to constitute southern China's wealthiest merchant family. By the early 13th century, they had relocated to Quanzhou under the leadership of Pu Kaizong; from 1250 to 1280, Pu Kaizong's son, Pu Shougeng, acted as Superintendent (*tiju*) of Quanzhou, in which capacity he controlled all the city's trade, including to Southeast Asia. His descendants subsequently maintained this role throughout the Yuan period (Wade 2011: 380–381, 415). Consequently, if Pan Yuan Master Pu occupied an important official position at Quanzhou, he did so during Pu Shougeng's tenure as Superintendent of the city. Conceivably, therefore, he belonged to the Muslim Pu clan. If so, his gravestone, originally located at Kota Batu, demonstrates a link between the ruling elites of Quanzhou and Brunei, recalling (but by no means confirming) the Codex's claim that Sultan Yusuf's wife also hailed from Quanzhou's ruling family.

Further supporting the existence of an early, pre-16th-century Bruneian Sultanate, in 2001 L. Kalus and C. Guillot undertook a comprehensive survey of all Brunei's pre–16th-century Islamic gravestones. In total, they found fourteen bearing pre–16th-century dates, in addition to a number of others traceable to the same period on stylistic grounds. Several of the dated examples bore names and titles indicative of a ruling Muslim elite. For example, one gravestone (dated 856 AH/1452–1453 CE) carried the name Raja Ayang bint Isma'il ibn Yusuf al-'Aziz al-Khawlani (Kalus and Guillot 2006: 139). In Malay culture, the title "Raja" is only applied to members of the royal household. Additionally, there were also the gravestones of a Tuan Amina (dated 10 Safar 883 AH/13 May 1478 CE) and Syeteria Pengiran Maharaja Dinda (dated 890 AH/1485–1486 CE, see Figure 5.4.6) (Kalus and Guillot 2003: 240, 270). While "Tuan" indicates an individual of noble (but not necessarily royal) birth, "(Syeteria) Pengiran" is applied only to those with direct blood ties to the royal family.

Arguably, however, Kalus and Guillot's most significant discovery was the gravestone of Zaynab (or possibly Sitti) bint Sultan 'Abd al-Majid ibn Yusuf ibn Muhammad Shah al-Sultan, dated 862 AH/1457–1458 CE (Kalus and Guillot 2006: 151). This artifact clearly names at least two pre-1457/1458 Bruneian sultans: Sultan 'Abd al-Majid and Muhammad Shah al-Sultan. Whether Yusuf was also a sultan is unclear as the inscription does not apply that title to him. Since Zaynab died in 1457/1458, however, her great-grandfather, Muhammad Shah al-Sultan, may have governed Brunei during the mid- to late 14th century as such a date would accord well with average reign lengths over this period. If so, he potentially relates to an event described in the Chinese sources: according to the Chinese court historian Song Lian (d. 1381), compiler of the *Yuan shi* (*Imperial Records of the Yuan Dynasty*), in 1370 the Imperial envoy Shen Zhi visited Brunei and met with a ruler called "Mahemosha" (Kurz 2011: 24–28; Pelliot 1948: 268). This is almost

FIGURE 5.4.6 Gravestone of Syeteria Pengiran Maharaja Dinda, dated 890 AH/1485–1486 CE (Kalus and Guillot 2003: Stele 21).

certainly a Chinese rendering of either Mahmud Shah or Muhammad Shah.[11] Moreover, Song Lian goes on to claim that Mahemosha, whose chief minister was a Chinese man named Wang Zongshu, sent an envoy to China called Yisimayi (Isma'il), whose arrival at the Imperial Court is recorded in the *Ming shilu*, which claims Brunei's diplomatic letter was written in a script similar to that of the Muslims (i.e., *jawi*) (Kurz 2011: 25; Wade 2005). This narrative, possibly linking to Zaynab's gravestone, reinforces the likelihood of 14th-century conversion, as suggested by the gravestone of Maharaja Brunei.[12]

---

[11] Scholars favoring 16th-century conversion have tended to dismiss this account, arguing that "Mahemosha" is the Chinese rendering of a non-Muslim title, perhaps either Sri Maharaja (Groeneveldt 1876: 110) or Maha Moksha (Nicholl 1980: 35). There is, however, very little basis for this conclusion: "Mahemosha," rendered like this or similarly, occurs frequently in the *Ming shilu*, almost always as a representation of Muhammad Shah or Mahmud Shah. Thus, Melaka's Mahmud Shah (d. 1528) is called "Mahamusha" (Wade 2005). Scholars who favor 1363 as a date of conversion associate Mahemosha with Awang Alak Betatar, the *Silsilah Raja-Raja Brunei*'s first Muslim ruler, who supposedly governed with the title Sultan Muhammad (al-Sufri 1990). The early 14th-century gravestone of Maharaja Brunei, however, makes it unlikely Mahemosha was Brunei's first Muslim ruler.

[12] This reconstruction nevertheless leaves questions unanswered. For instance, the *Ming shilu* claims Brunei's 1408 mission to the Imperial Court was accompanied by its ruler, Manarejiananai. This individual was undoubtedly non-Muslim: he ate pork and, after dying in China, was buried according to Confucian and Buddhist rites (Wade 2005). As noted by C. Brown, Yongle provided Muslims with special pork-free rations upon request and had the expertise available to bury Manarejiananai according to Islamic rites should the latter have desired it (Brown 1974: 230–231). "Manarejiananai" probably also represents a Buddhist title, such as Maharajadhiraj, Maharaja Gyana, or Maharaja Karna (Kurz 2011: 33; Nicholl 1980: 35). How this individual accords with the evidence presented here must form the subject of another paper.

Finally, the 15th-century Bruneian gravestones studied by Kalus and Guillot also share many stylistic affinities with 13th- to 14th-century Quanzhou memorials. By contrast, none demonstrates Indian influence. For example, the gravestone of Syeteria Pengiran Maharaja Dinda (Figure 5.4.6) is surmounted by a bow-shaped top akin to those at Quanzhou. Even more strikingly, both this and other examples are set upon bases carved to resemble lotus blossoms, of which near identical examples are also observable at Quanzhou (Chen 1984: fig. 50). Additionally, the faces of many Bruneian stelae bear distinctive amalgams of Chinese decorative devices, including eternal knot motifs, cloud patterns, and elaborate floral displays, all of which also appear at Quanzhou. Moreover, gravestones from both locations utilize bands carved in concave relief to both organize the surface of each head-stone and delineate individual lines of text within an inscription. Combined, these points suggest elements of Quanzhou's unique tradition of Muslim memorials continued in Brunei after its cessation in China itself. Whether this indicates Chinese settlement at Brunei, as Gallop suggested within the context of coinage, is uncertain but plausible.

Evidently, however, Brunei's early Muslim gravestones sit comfortably within the pre-ponderance of evidence assembled here indicative of Chinese cultural influence over early Islamic Brunei. Once again, whether that influence entails a direct connection with China is uncertain; Chinese influence need not indicate a Chinese presence. Nevertheless, the gravestone of Master Pu demonstrates that 13th-century Brunei hosted a senior, presumably Muslim, official from Quanzhou, a location Maharaja Brunei's memorial was evidently imported from (and plausibly inscribed at) sometime thereafter. Coupled with the Boxer Codex's narrative, these facts suggest that a direct link between Brunei and the Muslim community at Quanzhou is plausible.

Conclusion

Although the Islamic archaeology of Southeast Asia remains largely unexplored, initial excavations at various locations across the region provide us with an important—if only partial—window into the early history of this oft-neglected Muslim region. This chapter has endeavored to assemble the published results of excavations pertaining to four of the region's earliest Islamic kingdoms: Barus, Lambri, Samudera-Pasai, and Brunei. Mirroring the concerns of earlier studies, the chapter has analyzed this existing research with the intention of furthering our understanding of the context in which Southeast Asia's initial Islamization (including its conversion) took place. Focusing primarily on the late 13th to 14th centuries, we have uncovered a complex network of Muslim actors comprising individuals from the Middle East, India, China, and Southeast Asia itself.

Unusually, the first (and most westerly) of our locations, Barus, has been the subject of several in-depth archaeological investigations. At Lobu Tua, the site of pre-Islamic Barus, extensive excavations have yielded evidence indicative of a trade network orien-tated primarily toward Southeast Asia. The majority of trade goods imported from out-side the region, however, including glass beads and pottery, originated from either

South India or the Middle East, suggesting links with the Indian Ocean. Moreover, the site has yielded a Tamil-language inscription describing a South Indian settlement at Barus. This inscription also includes the word *marakkalanayam* (ship's captain); by the 16th century, this term referred exclusively to seafaring Muslim merchants from either Tamil Nadu or Kerala. Whether it does so here is speculative, but possible. If so, it provides insight into how and when the first Muslims entered the region.

At Bukit Hasang, the site of Islamic Barus, finds consonant with conversion indicate a reorientation of trade toward China. Although the analysis of Bukit Hasang's ceramics remains incomplete, initial observations indicate that the vast majority are Chinese in origin, with only a quarter originating from Southeast Asia. By contrast, very few Indian Ocean wares have been recovered. Whether the predominance of Chinese ceramics entails direct interaction with China, however, is uncertain; surviving literary evidence does not suggest Barus acted as a stopping point for Chinese ships. Rather, these Chinese ceramics may have arrived via other Southeast Asian ports; Bukit Hasang has yielded a far wider array of Southeast Asian pottery types than Lobu Tua, plausibly suggesting interaction with a broader section of Southeast Asia. If so, the kingdom could have obtained its Chinese ceramics from its Southeast Asian neighbors. This also entails that, if Islam moved around the region via the trade routes, it reached Barus from elsewhere in Southeast Asia.

Turning to Lambri, although less well-explored than Barus, finds at Lhok Lambaro indicate this early kingdom sat within a trade network stretching from the Indian Ocean to southern China. As at Barus, however, the bulk of recovered ceramics are Southeast Asian in origin, hinting at close regional ties. Nevertheless, the majority of ceramics imported from outside the region are Chinese; while these artifacts may, as at Barus, have arrived via other Southeast Asian ports, they appear contemporary to Zhou Qufei's description of Lambri as a stopping point for Chinese ships traveling between China and India. Consequently, some of them may have arrived along with Chinese traders. In addition to its ceramics, Lhok Lambaro also preserves several early Muslim gravestones. Termed *plakpling*, they were produced locally and evince both Indian and Chinese stylistic influences; while the former likely represent the continuation of a well-established pre-Islamic Southeast Asian artistic tradition, the latter have no obvious precedent in the region, rather appearing with the *plakpling*. Whether this entails direct Chinese (Muslim) involvement in the creation of the *plakpling*, however, cannot be established; these artifacts may simply reflect an indigenous Muslim population's desire to imitate Chinese cultural forms recently introduced to them by trade.

Our examination of Samudera-Pasai relied on one of the few known remnants of the kingdom: early examples of a form of gravestone known locally as *batu Aceh*. Like the *plakpling*, early surviving examples of *batu Aceh* evince a mixture of Indian and Chinese stylistic influences. Indian influence, for instance, predominates among early to late 15th-century examples of *batu Aceh*, commonly labeled Type A. These utilize several important Indian motifs, including Garuda wings. As at Lambri, however, these stylistic borrowings plausibly belie the continuation of a pre-Islamic Southeast Asian artistic tradition, not direct Indian influence. Other early 15th-century *batu Aceh*, however, demonstrate possible connections to Quanzhou: they replicate many decorative features found in association with 13th- to 14th-century Quanzhou memorials, of which at least one imported example has been found at Samudera-Pasai. Certainly, ships from Quanzhou are known to have stopped at this kingdom over the 14th and early 15th centuries. Moreover, Zheng He utilized Samudera-Pasai as a base for pushing out into the Indian Ocean; many of his crewmembers are known to have migrated to Southeast Asia. In this context, the Chinese influences observed among the *batu Aceh* may, as at Lambri, reflect a direct connection between Samudera-Pasai and China.

Turning to our final location, Brunei yielded evidence of sustained and significant Chinese influence. Chinese ceramics start to dominate at Brunei from the beginning of the 14th century onward, reaching a virtual monopoly by the early 15th century. This dominance sees the use of local pottery decline and eventually cease. By contrast, no trace of either Indian Ocean or Middle Eastern ceramics has been found. Turning to early Bruneian coinage, while Kota Batu (Brunei's ancient royal compound) has yielded a modest collection of early Chinese coins, it is uncertain whether these constituted currency. From the 16th century, however, locally produced coins termed *pitis* began to appear across Brunei, all bearing Chinese decorative motifs, including a seated camel akin to those which decorate Chinese Imperial Seals, such as the one granted Brunei in 1408. Brunei's most significant artifacts, however, are its early gravestones. These not only establish Muslim rule in Brunei by the early 14th century, far earlier than previously suspected, but also evince further connections with China. Most notably, the gravestone of Sultan Maharaja Brunei was imported from (and possibly inscribed at) Quanzhou during the early 14th century. A link with this city is further supported by the late 16th-century Boxer Codex, whose indigenously derived account of Bruneian history claims that the kingdom's first Sultan married a woman from Quanzhou's ruling elite. In that context, Brunei also preserves the mid–13th-century gravestone of a Pan Yuan Master Pu of Quanzhou. An important Chinese official, Master Pu likely hailed from the famed Muslim Pu clan of Quanzhou, which ruled that city during the late Yuan period. As his gravestone was originally housed at Kota Batu, it thereby establishes a probable link between the ruling elites of both Brunei and Quanzhou. Finally, in common with some *batu Aceh*, Brunei's early gravestones bear clear stylistic affinities to 13th- and 14th-century Quanzhou memorials. Given these combined factors, a direct link between early Islamic Brunei and China (especially the Muslim community at Quanzhou) is plausible.

Ultimately, caution is necessary when assessing the significance of the Chinese influences observed here. Their ubiquity across Southeast Asia contemporary to that region's Islamization, however, is striking. If, as is commonly supposed, Islam arrived along the trade routes, it evidently did so just as Chinese goods flooded Southeast Asian markets, creating an atmosphere suffuse with Chinese cultural influence. Although the centrality of Chinese traders to the transhipment of those goods remains uncertain, several of the examined sites reportedly acted as stopping points for Chinese vessels. Moreover, Chinese Muslims played a substantial role in Chinese trade over this period. Whether this placed them in a position to facilitate Southeast Asia's Islamization is uncertain, but a possibility worthy of further consideration in light of the evidence presented here.

REFERENCES

Al-Sufri, H. A. M. J. 1990. *Tarsilah Brunei. Sejarah Awal dan Perkembangan Islam* (Bandar Seri Begawan: Jabatan Pusat Sejarah).

Barrett, W. L. S. 1988. *Brunei and Nusantara. History in Coinage* (Bandar Seri Begawan: Pusat Sejarah Brunei).

Benite, Z. B.-D. 2005. *The Dao of Muhammad. A Cultural History of Muslims in Late Imperial China* (Cambridge: Harvard University Press).

Boxer, C. R. (ed). 1953. *South China in the Sixteenth Century. Being the Narratives of Galeote Pereira, Fr. Gaspar da Cruz, O. P., and Fr. Martín de Rada, O. E. S. A. [1550–1575]* (London: The Hakluyt Society).

Brown, C. C. 1974. "Some Ming Regulations on Provisions for Tributary Delegations," *The Brunei Museum Journal*, 3, 2, 230–231.

Brown, D. E. 1970. *Brunei. The Structure and History of a Bornean Malay Sultanate* (Bandar Seri Begawan: The Brunei Museum).

Carroll, J. S. 1982. "Berunai in the *Boxer Codex*," *Journal of the Malaysian Branch of the Royal Asiatic Society*, 55, 2, 1–25.

Cheah Boon Kheng (ed.). 2010. *Sejarah Melayu. The Malay Annals, MS Raffles no. 18 Edisi Rumi Baru*, MBRAS Reprint 17, transcr. Abdul Rahman Haji Ismail (Kuala Lumpur: The Malaysian Branch of the Royal Asiatic Society).

Chen Da-sheng 1984. *Islamic Inscriptions in Quanzhou (Zaitun)*, trans. Chen Enming (n.p.: Ningxia People's Publishing House and Fujian People's Publishing House).

Chen Da-sheng 2000. "A Brunei Sultan in the Early 14th Century: Study of an Arabic Gravestone," in V. Elisseef (ed.), *The Silk Roads. Highways of Culture and Commerce* (Oxford: Berghahn Books and UNESCO Publishing), 145–157.

Christie, J. W. 1998. "The Medieval Tamil-Language Inscriptions in Southeast Asia and China," *Journal of Southeast Asian Studies*, 29, 2, 239–268.

Cliff, N. (trans). 2016. *The Travels of Marco Polo* (London: Penguin Books).

Coedès, G. 1910. *Textes d'auteurs Grecs et Latins relatifs à l'Extrême Orient* (Paris: E. Leroux).

Cortesao, A. (trans). 2005. *The Suma Oriental of Tomé Pires. An Account of the East, from the Red Sea to China, Written in Malacca and India in 1512–1515*, 2 vols. (New Delhi: Asian Educational Services).

Cowan, H. K. J. 1933. "Lamuri—Lambri—Lawri—Ram(n)i—Lan-li—Lan-wu-li—Nan-po-li," *Bijdragen tot de Taal-, Land-en Volkenkunde*, 90, 421–424.

Drakard, J. 1989. "An Indian Ocean Port: Sources for the Earlier History of Barus," *Archipel*, 37, 53–82.

Drewes, G. W. J. 1968. "New Light on the Coming of Islam to Indonesia?" *Bijdragen tot de Taal-, Land- en Volkenkunde*, 124, 4, 433–459.

Druce, S. C. 2016. "The 'Birth' of Brunei: Early Polities of the Northwest Coast of Borneo and the Origins of Brunei, Tenth to mid-Fourteenth Centuries," in O. K. Gin (ed.), *Brunei. History, Islam, Society and Contemporary Issues* (Abingdon: Routledge), 21–44.

Dupoizat, M.-F. 1992. "Rapport préliminaire sur la céramique importée à Banten Girang," *Arts asiatiques*, 47, 1, 57–68.

Flecker, M. 2001. "A Ninth-Century AD Arab or Indian Shipwreck in Indonesia: First Evidence for Direct Trade with China," *World Archaeology*, 32, 3, 335–354.

Flecker, M. 2010. "A Ninth Century Arab Shipwreck in Indonesia," in R. Krahl, J. Guy, J. K. Wilson, and J. Raby (eds.), *Shipwrecked. Tang Treasures and Monsoon Winds* (Washington DC: Smithsonian Institution), 114–119.

Franke, W., and Ch'en T'ieh-Fan. 1973. "A Chinese Tomb Inscription of AD 1264, discovered recently in Brunei: A Preliminary Report," *The Brunei Museum Journal*, 3, 1, 91–99.

Gallop, A. T. 2005. "'Camels, Seals and the Early Tin Coinage of Brunei," *Archipel*, 70, 261–280.

Groeneveldt, W. P. 1876. "Notes on the Malay Archipelago and Malacca Compiled from Chinese Sources," *Verhandelingen van het Bataviaasch Genootschap van Kunsten en Wetenschappen*, 39, 1–144.

Guillot, C. (ed.) 1998. *Histoire de Barus, Sumatra. Le Site de Lobu Tua. I. Études et Documents* (Paris: Cahier d'Archipel 30).

Guillot, C., Dupoizat, M.-F., Perret, D., Sunaryo, U., and Surachman, H. (eds.) 2003. *Histoire de Barus, Sumatra. Le Site de Lobu Tua. II. Études archéologique et Documents* (Paris: Cahier d'Archipel 30).

Haji Jibah, N., and Haji Hassan, S. 1987. "Tomb of Maharaja of Brunei," *The Brunei Museum Journal*, 6, 3, 10–15.

Hanitsch, R. 1907. "Tin and Lead Coins from Brunei," *Journal of the Straits Branch of the Royal Asiatic Society*, 49, 111–114.

Hardy, A. 2007. *The Temple Architecture of India* (Hoboken: Wiley).

Harrisson, B. 1970. "A Classification of Archaeological Trade Ceramics from Kota Batu, Brunei," *Brunei Museum Journal*, 2, 1, 114–187.

Harrisson, B., and Shariffudin, P. M. 1969. "Sungai Lumut, a 15th Century Burial Ground," *Brunei Museum Journal*, 1, 1, 24–56.

Harrisson, T. 1958. "The Ming Gap and Kota Batu, Brunei," *Sarawak Museum Journal*, 8, 273–277.

Harrisson, T., and Harrisson, B. 1956. "Kota Batu in Brunei," *Sarawak Museum Journal*, 7, 283–319.

Hirth, F., and Rockhill, W. W. (trans) 1966. *Chau Ju-kua. His Work on the Chinese and Arab Trade in the twelfth and thirteenth Centuries, entitled* Chu-fan-chi (Amsterdam: Oriental Press).

Jones, R. (ed.) 1999. *Hikayat Raja Pasai* (Kuala Lumpur: Yayasan Karyawan dan Penerbit Fajar Bakti).

Kacinatan, N. 1978. *Hero-stones in Tamilnadu* (Madras: Arun Publications).

Kalus, L., and Guillot, C. 2003. "Les inscriptions funéraires islamiques de Brunei (Ire partie)," *Bulletin de l'Ecole Française d-Extrême-Orient*, 90–91, 229–272.

Kalus, L., and Guillot, C. 2006. "Les inscriptions funéraires islamiques de Brunei (deuxième partie)," *Bulletin de l'Ecole Française d-Extrême-Orient*, 93, 139–181.

Karim bin Pengiran Haji Osman, P. 1993. "Further Notes on a Chinese Tombstone Inscription of AD 1264," *The Brunei Museum Journal*, 8, 1–10.

Kempers, A. J. B. 1959. *Ancient Indonesian Art* (Cambridge: Harvard University Press).

Kerlogue, F. 2004. *Arts of Southeast Asia* (London: Thames and Hudson).

Kurz, J. L. 2011. "Boni in Chinese Sources: Translations of Relevant Texts from the Song to the Qing Dynasties," Working Paper Series no. 4 (Singapore: Nalanda-Sriwijaya Centre).

Kurz, J. L. 2013. "Pre-modern Chinese Sources in the National History of Brunei: The Case of Poli," *Bijdragen tot de Taal-, Land- en Volkenkunde*, 169, 213–243.

Kurz, J. L. 2016. "A Note on the Tombstone of Master Pu and the *Xishan Zazhi*," *Bijdragen tot de Taal-, Land- en Volkenkunde*, 172, 510–537.

Lambourn, E. 2003. "From Cambay to Samudera-Pasai and Gresik: The Export of Gujarati Grave Memorials to Sumatra and Java in the Fifteenth Century CE," *Indonesia and the Malay World*, 31, 90, 221–284.

Lambourn, E. 2004. "The Formation of the *batu Aceh* Tradition in Fifteenth-Century Samudera-Pasai," *Indonesia and the Malay World*, 32, 93, 211–248.

Lambourn, E. 2008. "Tombstones, Texts, and Typologies: Seeing Sources for the Early History of Islam in Southeast Asia," *Journal of the Economic and Social History of the Orient*, 51, 252–286.

Lombard, D., and Salmon, C. 1985. "Islam et Sinité," *Archipel*, 30, 1, 73–94.

Mackintosh-Smith, T. (trans) 2003. *The Travels of Ibn Battutah* (London: Picador).

Manguin, P.-Y. 2010. "New Ships for New Networks: Trends in Shipbuilding in the South China Sea in the 15th and 16th Centuries," in G. Wade, and Sun Laichen (eds.), *Southeast Asia in the Fifteenth Century. The China Factor* (Singapore and Hong Kong: NUS Press and Hong Kong University Press), 333–353.

McKinnon, E. E. 1988. "Beyond Serendib: A Note on Lambri at the Northern Tip of Sumatra," *Indonesia*, 46, 103–121.

McKinnon, E. E. 2012. "Continuity and Change in South Indian Involvement in Northern Sumatra: The Inferences of Archaeological Evidence from Kota Cina and Lamreh," in P.-Y. Manguin, A. Mani, and G. Wade (eds.), *Early Interactions between South and Southeast Asia. Reflections on Cross-Cultural Exchange* (Singapore and New Delhi: Institute of Southeast Asian Studies and Manohar), 137–160.

Miksic, J. N. 2009. "Research on Ceramic Trade, Within Southeast Asia and Between Southeast Asia and China," in J. N. Miksic (ed.), *Southeast Asian Ceramics. New Light on Old Pottery*. (Singapore: Southeast Asian Ceramic Society and Editions Didier Millet), 70–99.

Miksic, J. N. 2010. "Before and After Zheng He: Comparing Some Southeast Asian Archaeological Sites of the 14th and 15th Centuries," in G. Wade and Sun Laichen (eds.), *Southeast Asia in the Fifteenth Century. The China Factor* (Singapore and Hong Kong: NUS Press and Hong Kong University Press), 384–408.

Miksic, J. N., and Geok Yian Goh 2017. *Ancient Southeast Asia* (London: Routledge).

Mills, J. V. G. (trans) 1970. *Ying-Yai Sheng-Lan. The Overall Survey of the Ocean's Shores* (Cambridge: Cambridge University Press).

Montana, S. 1997. "Nouvelles données sur les royaumes de Lamuri et Barat," *Archipel*, 53, 85–95.

Moquette, J. P. 1912. "De Grafesteenen te Pasé en Grisee Vergeleken met Dergelijke Monumenten uit Hindoestan," *Tijdschrift voor Indische Taal-, Land- en Volkenkunde*, 54, 536–548.

Moquette, J. P. 1913. "De eerste vorsten van Samoedra-Pasé (Noord Sumatra)," *Rapporten van het Oudheidkundige Dienst*, 1913, 1–12.

Nasir, A. H. 2004. *Mosque Architecture in the Malay World*, O. S. Abdullah (trans) (Bangi: Penerbit Universiti Kebangsaan Malaysia).

Nicholl, R. (ed.) 1975. *European Sources for the History of the Sultanate of Brunei in the Sixteenth Century* (Bandar Seri Begawan: Muzium Brunei).

Nicholl, R. 1980. "Notes on Some Controversial Issues in Brunei History," *Archipel*, 19, 25–42.

Nicholl, R. 1989. "Some Problems of Brunei Chronology," *Journal of Southeast Asian Studies*, 20, 2, 175–195.

Njoto, H. 2014. "À propos des origines de la mosquée javanaise," *Bulletin de l'École française d'Extrême-Orient*, 100, 11–37.

Pelliot, P. 1948. "Le Ḥōja et le Sayyid Ḥusain de l'Histoire des Ming," *T'oung Pao*, 38, 2, 81–292.

Perret, D., and Surachman, H. 2012. "South Asia and the Tapanuli Area (North-West Sumatra): Ninth-Fifteenth Centuries CE," in P.-Y. Manguin, A. Mani, and G. Wade (eds.), *Early Interactions Between South and Southeast Asia. Reflections on Cross-Cultural Exchange* (Singapore and New Delhi: Institute of Southeast Asian Studies and Manohar), 161–175.

Ptak, R. 1998. "Possible Chinese References to the Barus Area (Tang to Ming)," in C. Guillot (ed.), *Histoire de Barus, Sumatra. Le Site de Lobu Tua*, Vol. 1: Études et Documents. (Paris: Cahier d'Archipel), 119–147.

Ptak, R. 2001. "Quanzhou: At the Northern Edge of a Southeast Asian 'Mediterranean,'" in A. Schottenhammer (ed.), *The Emporium of the World. Maritime Quanzhou, 1000–1400* (Leiden: E. J. Brill), 395–427.

Quirino, C. 1977. "Boxer Codex: A Folio of Rare Filipiniana," in A. R. Roces (ed.), *Filipino Heritage. The Making of a Nation*, Vol. 4: The Spanish Colonial Period (16th Century): The Day of the Conquistador. (Manila: Lahing Pilipino Publishing Inc.), 1003–1008.

Rasdi, M. T. M. 2007. "Mosque Architecture in Malaysia: Classification of Styles and Possible Influence," *Jurnal Alam Bina*, 9, 3, 1–37.

Reid, A. 2001. "Flows and Seepages in the Long-term Chinese Interaction with Southeast Asia," in A. Reid (ed.), *Sojourners and Settlers. Histories of Southeast Asia and the Chinese.* (Honolulu: University of Hawai'i Press), 15–49.

Reid, A. 2006. "Hybrid Identities in the Fifteenth-Century Straits of Malacca," Working Paper Series no. 67 (Singapore: Asia Research Institute, NUS).

Ricklefs, M. C. 2008. *A History of Modern Indonesia since c.1200* (4th ed.) (London: Palgrave Macmillan).

Rockhill, W. W. 1915. "Notes on the Relations and Trade of China with the Eastern Archipelago and the Coast of the Indian Ocean During the Fourteenth Century. Part II," *T'oung Pao*, 16, 1, 61–159.

Sastri, K. A. N. 1932. "A Tamil Merchant-Guild in Sumatra," *Tijdschrift voor Indische Taal-, Land- en Volkenkunde*, 72, 2, 314–327.

Saunders, G. 2002. *A History of Brunei* (2nd ed.) (London: Routledge).

Sjostrand, S., and Barnes, C. 2001. "The Turiang: A Fourteenth Century Chinese Shipwreck Upsetting Southeast Asian Ceramic History," *Journal of the Malaysian Branch of the Royal Asiatic Society*, 74, 1, 71–109.

Snouck Hurgronje, C. 1906. *The Acehnese*, 2 vols., trans. A. W. S. O'Sullivan (Leiden: Brill).

Soepratno. 1984. *Ornamen Ukir Kayu Tradisional Jawa. Ketrampilan Menggambar dan Mengukir Kayu* (Semerang: Effhar Offset Semerang).

Souza, G. B., and Turley, J. S. (eds.) 2015. *The Boxer Codex. Transcription and Translation of an Illustrated Late Sixteenth-Century Spanish Manuscript Concerning the Geography, History and Ethnography of the Pacific, South-East and East Asia* (Leiden: Brill).

Strathern, A. 2017. "Global Patterns of Ruler Conversion to Islam and the Logic of Empirical Religiosity," in A. C. S. Peacock (ed.), *Islamisation. Comparative Perspectives from History.* (Edinburgh: Edinburgh University Press), 21–55.

Subbarayalu, Y. 1998. "The Tamil Merchant-Guild Inscription at Barus. A Rediscovery," in C. Guillot (ed.), *Histoire de Barus, Sumatra. Le Site de Lobu Tua*, Vol. 1: Études et Documents (Paris: Cahier d'Archipel), 25–33.

Sweeney, P. L. A. 1965. "Silsilah Raja-Raja Berunai," *Journal of the Malaysian Branch of the Royal Asiatic Society*, 41, 2, 1–82.

Tibbetts, G. R. 1979. *A Study of the Arabic Texts Containing Material on Southeast Asia*, Oriental Translation Fund, New Series Vol. 44 (Leiden: E. J. Brill).

Vienne, M.-D. de 2015. *Brunei. From the Age of Commerce to the 21st Century* (Singapore: National University of Singapore Press).

Wade, G. (trans) 2005. *The Ming Shi-lu (Veritable Records of the Ming Dynasty). An Open Access Resource.* http://www.epress.nus.edu.sg/msl/.

Wade, G. 2007. "Quanzhou and Southeast Asian Islam in the Second Half of the 14th Century: A Moment of Change," paper presented at *Moments in the Making of Southeast Asian Islam*, Singapore, February 5–6.

Wade, G. 2011. "Early Muslim Expansion in South East Asia, Eighth to Fifteenth Centuries," in D. O. Morgan and A. Reid (eds.), *The New Cambridge History of Islam*, Vol. 3: The Eastern Islamic World Eleventh to Eighteenth Centuries (Cambridge: Cambridge University Press), 366–408.

Wade, G. 2012. "Southeast Asian Islam and Southern China in the Fourteenth Century," in G. Wade and L. Tana (eds.), *Anthony Reid and the Study of the Southeast Asian Past* (Singapore: Institute of Southeast Asian Studies), 125–145.

Wicks, R. S. 1986. "Monetary Developments in Java Between the Ninth and Sixteenth Centuries: A Numismatic Perspective," *Indonesia*, 42, 42–77.

Wodak, E. 1958. "Old Brunei Coins," *Sarawak Museum Journal*, 8, 11, 278–292.

Yatim, O. M., and Nasir, A. H. 1990. *Epigrafi Islam Terawal di Nusantara* (Kuala Lumpur: Dewan Bahasa dan Pustaka).

....

HERITAGE MANAGEMENT AND COMMUNITY DEVELOPMENT

Thematic Introduction Beyond the "Academy:"
Islamic Archaeology and Heritage Management

....

BERT DE VRIES

IRONIC ROLES OF ISLAMIC CIVILIZATIONS

THE physical remains of monumental architecture dating from the Umayyad period to the present (the "built heritage," see Chapter 6.2) have always been of interest to both academics and the general public, both in the West and in the Middle East. Local interest in these was retained because they still functioned, especially in the vital urban settings, where they are most studied. They have also captivated western scholars and visitors from the time of their "rediscovery" in the 19th century to the present, due to both romantic fascination and scholarly interest. Because such sites were always revered by local communities, visitors, and scholars, there was a sense of shared heritage that made the maintenance and preservation of standing monumental Islamic-era architecture a common goal in which local polities and religious endowments representing local communities were included. I call this popular tradition the "architecture track."

The same was not true of collapsed and buried, mostly unoccupied, archaeological sites. Unearthing and interpretation of the collapsed and buried civilizations of the Middle East by archaeologists largely excluded local inhabitants from both the research process and the assignation of heritage. Instead, local people were a source of cheap labor, useful for making local arrangements and moving dirt. Therefore, they were not crucial stakeholders in the sites being excavated. Furthermore, archaeology in the Middle East was shaped by the romantic notion that it was discovering a long-lost heritage, which occasioned the "restoration" of a previous kinship between ancient pre-Islamic civilizations and the post-Enlightenment civilization of the West. Thus Islamic era remains tended to be treated as an inconvenient overburden, a stratum of neglect and decay to be shoveled aside to reach the buried nuggets of "our" past. The modern "locals" living on this ancient landscape were treated as part of that overburden, heirs to centuries of neglect or destructive nomadic interlopers (de Vries 2013a; de Vries 2013b). I call this the behavior pattern the "archaeology track."

Historically, the architecture and archaeology tracks were interconnected documentations of Middle Eastern culture in which Islamic civilization figured in unequal measures. A good concrete example is the Princeton University Expedition to South Syria in 1905 and 1909. Its twin documentation goals were Architecture and Epigraphy, and any archaeological stratigraphy was deduced not from excavation of soil layers but from the typology of standing buildings, with absolute chronology anchored by the content and dates of inscriptions. The expedition documented Islamic buildings and Arabic texts when it came across them, but the focus was on (mostly monumental) remains of the Hellenistic to Byzantine past. Enno Littmann said, in introducing his summary of the collected corpus of 138 Arabic inscriptions:

> Outside of Bosra and the places near it no long stop was made at any real centre of Arabic civilization. Damascus was visited but not studied; Ḥamā and Ḥomṣ were seen only in passing through. Nevertheless, in some out-of-the-way places we found Arabic inscriptions and graffiti, indicating that at a certain period a sort of Arabic civilization was flourishing there.
>
> (Butler and Littmann 1905: 409)

As useful as it is, this survey was essentially a documentation of buildings, like the mosques of Bosra (Figure 6.0.1); the inception of Islamic archaeology was decades in the future.

Thus, there are two overlapping tracks leading to the current, growing view/practice that heritage preservation is to include all aspects of Islamic-period material culture and that local, largely Muslim communities have rights of participation and ownership in the recovery of and benefits from that heritage. The underlying premises making this shift possible are that (1) the material remains of the Islamic civilizations are equal in value and stature to the pre-Islamic ones, and (2) the rights of the local, living communities are on a par with those of the archaeological academy, not only for remains of the Islamic era, but also for those of the pre-Islamic ones.

BEYOND THE ACADEMY

As the chapter title implies, the business of Heritage Management means going beyond the work of the academy as traditionally understood. In the past the architecture and archaeology tracks tended to be exclusive, scholarly domains of the "academy." Publications,

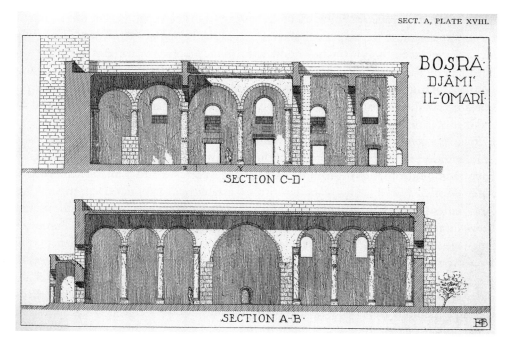

SECT. A, PLATE XVIII.

BOSRA·
DJÂMI'
IL-'OMARÎ·

SECTION C-D·

SECTION A-B·

FIGURE 6.0.1 Jami al-Omari, drawn from visits in 1905 and 1909. From Butler (1914): section A, plate XVIII.

mostly in European languages, were intended chiefly for academic colleagues engaged in scientific dialogue with each other. In the West, popularized versions of this scholarship mostly engaged an intellectually and economically elite public, though in theory these were available to anyone interested in reading the books, visiting the museums, or even joining the academy through graduate studies. Thus, the academy made a significant but limited contribution to the laying of a heritage foundation for Europe and America in which the material remains of Middle East Islamic cultures played an increasingly significant role. This is crucial and challenging in two ways. First, even as new technologies of knowledge dissemination continue to improve the popularizing outreach, the academy has difficulty penetrating or forestalling the ever-flourishing pop culture myths, perpetuated and fed by rumor and entertainment. These myths range from mistaken impressions of the destructiveness of the Islamic Conquest to the distorted identification of Islam with terrorism. And, perhaps innocently, they are perpetuated by the film industry's preference for invented stories and images purported to sell better than the academy's unvarnished "truth." Frustratingly, while archaeologists and other scholars of Islam have the critical intellectual tools to address ungrounded myths with proper knowledge, pop culture seems to prefer distortions and falsities of non-intellectual origins. (See, e.g., the fabulous palace of the sultan at Agrabah in the 1992 version of the Disney film *Aladdin*.)

Second, the recent influx of immigrants and refugees from the Islamic Middle East's conflict zones into Europe and the Americas presents a new "heritage management" challenge for the academy. The academy's challenge is to keep up its part in what is now a three-way discourse between the academy, established popular culture, and the newly arrived popular cultures from the Middle East. The academy's voice in this discourse has become especially crucial as the popular and political backlash against the increasing numbers of migrants and refugees has nurtured a populist anti-Islamic atmosphere on the streets of the United States and Europe. Therefore, the academy needs to expand its manner of articulating research results to include a level of heritage education that can mediate the conflicting pop-culture narratives of the host and immigrant populations.

In addition to their role in the West, the scholarly outputs of the Western academy have been "returning" to the Middle East itself in a complex and multifaceted process. After World War I, European authorities established national Departments of Antiquities in which local staff were trained in European archaeological methods and their libraries stocked with the works of Western archaeologists written in European languages. (In Jordan, Lancester Harding is still revered as the founder of the Department of Antiquities, and the complete set of the rare Princeton University Expedition's first-edition publications still has pride of place in its library.) Local archaeologists were trained on projects led by foreign scholars who taught the prevailing theories and methods developed in the West, and local elites received largely Western educations, whether abroad or at home, through which they absorbed the popularized versions of those outcomes mentioned earlier. This is true not only in the Middle East, but throughout the world, with the result that archeological theory and practice follow the same set of standards everywhere (e. g., the excellent archaeology textbooks written with global focus by Renfrew and Bahn 2020, which have incorporated universal standards and practices of heritage management in current editions.) In this way a discipline that was essentially Western is becoming globalized, so that, for example, someone trained in Jordanian archaeological field schools could easily transfer those skills to the study of a Mayan site in Guatemala.

A positive aspect of this situation is that local archaeologists not only share the theories and practices of this globalizing discipline of archaeology, but they also have become professional equals, increasingly staging their own locally based excavations and field schools. In some cases, like Jordan, this has brought a new spirit of collegiality and sense of common cause. As a result, local and foreign scholars are working in concert as everyone adjusts to taking up the newly pressing and growing tasks of site preservation and heritage management.

As indigenous scholars have joined the archaeological academy, the growth of material heritage awareness among Middle Eastern elites is now on a par with that in the West, but deliberate heritage awareness-raising among local, rural populations has been minimal. Instead, until recently, "locals" have continued to provide conveniently cheap labor and services without learning much about the significance of the archaeological enterprise. Here, therefore, the myths of pop culture have been allowed to evolve and flourish without much sobering correction from actual knowledge provided by the academy (e.g., "Archaeologists are digging up gold; in fact, they're stealing the gold that should rightfully go into our pockets. . . ."). A complicating factor is that this "actual" knowledge does not originate from within the culture but is the product of a foreign intellectual process now being "returned" in a form that needs "translation," not simply into Arabic, but into the more general "language" of local cultures. This knowledge gap was widened by archaeologists' predilection for pre-Islamic over Islamic material remains. Bridging this gap is the major challenge of heritage management at local levels in the Middle East itself.

In evaluating these issues, it may not be enough to see the obligation to engage in heritage management as going "beyond the academy." As we saw, the fundamental language of the academy communicates chiefly only to fellow academics but fails to communicate a real sense of heritage to popular audiences and local communities in the Middle East. If academics are serious about having a heritage management mandate, it will be necessary to alter or broaden that language to be much more inclusive by not only targeting fellow scholars as the in-group for discussion and publication, but also enfolding the members of all communities, including local ones, into the process of archaeological knowledge production. Therefore, heritage management would begin not simply with educating local communities, but also with a reeducating of the scholar-teachers to speak and write using language understandable by communities beyond the academy.

As Alisson Mickel has demonstrated, inclusion of local knowledge and expertise in the exercise of field work has been hindered by archaeologists' practice of treating locally hired participants purely as a source of physical labor, with the assumption that these "locals" have no intellectual contribution to make. In response to this, according to Mickel's research, local "hires" consider it to their economic advantage to remain silent rather than volunteer to share their own knowledge of the site (Mickel 2016). As a result, better integration of the local community into field work is not simply a matter of education and training, but also requires the establishment of a new relationship of trust by including local participants in project planning, inviting them to share their knowledge, and incorporating them in the daily consultations by "senior" staff to ensure smooth progress of the work. Deliberate application of this inclusive management style at the site of Umm al-Jimal in Jordan has resulted in an immense improvement in the quality and efficiency of the field work and has created an atmosphere of camaraderie and celebration of success in the process (Figure 6.0.2).

THE SIGNS OF RENEWAL

The inception of inclusive heritage management came through the culmination of several trends. The first of these is the maturation of Islamic archaeology. While the architecture track tended to focus on urban centers—those places in Syria avoided by the Princeton Expedition—much of the Middle East, especially the Levant, also has well-preserved Islamic-era structures scattered throughout the countryside. In Jordan, for example, the Umayyad Desert Castles, the Crusader-Mamluk castles, and the Ottoman Pilgrim route and forts have not only been much studied and preserved but have also

FIGURE 6.0.2 Umm el-Jimal master mason Awda al-Masa'eid celebrates successful replacement of ceiling molding blocks in Byzantine-Umayyad House XVIII at Umm el-Jimal, Jordan.

Courtesy of Bert de Vries (June 2014).

long been recognized as crucial elements of the country's historic and archaeological heritage (Figure 6.0.3). In this sense there always was an "Islamic archaeology" in Jordan. However, only more recently have a still relatively small number of scholars engaged in study of stratified Islamic remains and related ceramic typology. As a result, Islamic archaeology is getting established as a mature subdiscipline in the archaeological academy.

One early result of this, as exemplified by the work of Alan Walmsley among many, was the recognition that the evolution of ceramic types from Byzantine to Umayyad and Abbasid eras was interconnected and continuous. From this it followed that the dense scatter of Byzantine villages and towns continued through the Umayyad and survived into the Abbasid periods. In other words, a site like Umm al-Jimal, Jordan, famous for its Nabataean-Roman and Byzantine structures, is now also recognized for its continuation as an Umayyad town (Figure 6.0.4), possibly occupied into the Abbasid period (World Heritage Convention 2018). Taken on a larger scale, this means that the famous Umayyad Desert Castles are no longer enigmatic in their isolation, but a component of a well-populated urban-rural landscape in the Early Islamic periods.

Since then, the work of the academy has expanded with projects that specifically targeted Middle and Late Islamic sites, while archaeologists who previously concentrated on pre-Islamic eras of multiperiod sites returned to take the Islamic strata seriously this time around. In Jordan and Syria, where this happened over the past thirty years, this "new" Islamic archaeology coincided with the maturation of archival historiography

FIGURE 6.0.3 Repaired façade of Qusayr ʿAmra, Jordan, the Umayyad bath famous for its secular frescoes.

Courtesy of Bert de Vries (July 2017).

concentrating on the history of Bilād al-Shām in the Ayyubid, Mamluk, and Ottoman periods. One important case is the leading historiographic work of Adnan al-Bakhit and his students based in Jordan's universities. This provided an opportune socio-political context for the interpretation of Islamic material culture, especially for archaeologists like Bethany Walker, the co-editor of this Handbook, who personally handles stratigraphy and ceramic typology in the field, but also hand-written Arabic Mamluk and Ottoman sources in the archives (Walker 2011). As a result, Islamic archaeology is now on firmer ground for the formulation of a socio-cultural heritage than are some phases of pre-Islamic archaeology, where paucity of written sources can sometimes leave material remains in an ahistorical limbo.

Even as Islamic archaeology matured, site preservation and presentation became increasingly prevalent components of archaeological projects. UNESCO's and other organizations' push for high standards of preservation and site management have penetrated Middle East departments of antiquities and local universities, where in some cases programs in architectural preservation and tourism development exist alongside more traditional archaeology departments. Also, recently, the economic benefits of site

FIGURE 6.0.4 Mangers in a stable of Umayyad House 119, as excavated in 1993.

Courtesy of Bert de Vries (2005).

preservation and other aspects of heritage management (i.e., cultural resource management) have been increasingly recognized as having "development" value by international funding agencies. Thus, an increasing number of sites are no longer abandoned to their desolation after the digging is finished but are visually improved, with structures conserved and made accessible, explained by bilingual interpretive signs understandable to both local and foreign visitors, and provided with essential tourist services. In this way local people can no longer complain that nothing of "value" has been done after years of excavation; instead, they can see the resulting economic benefits and expect themselves to be included in the various aspects of site management now required to maintain and operate "their" site as an archaeological park (Figure 6.0.5).

HERITAGE MANAGEMENT AND THE LOCAL COMMUNITY

As described earlier, the traditional archaeological academy tended to be self-preoccupied and excluding. Today, in implementation of heritage management programs, "inclusive archaeology" and "community archaeology" are terms increasingly in

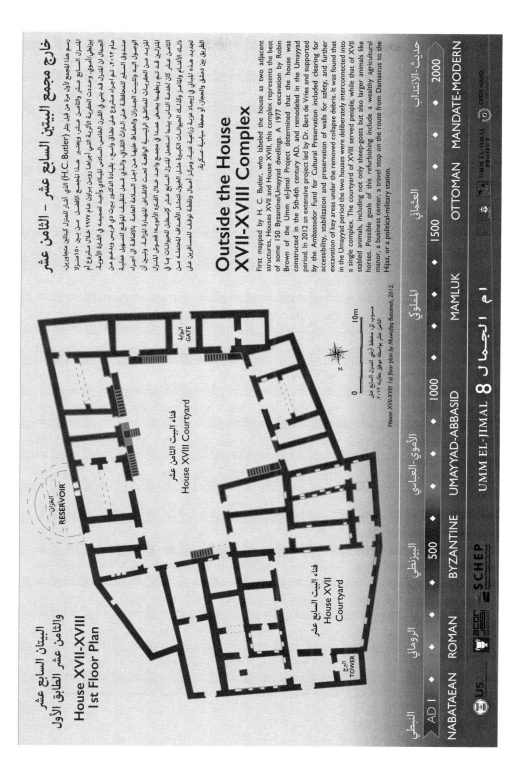

FIGURE 6.0.5 Interpretive sign introducing House XVII–XVIII, a Byzantine-Umayyad Complex at Umm al-Jimal, Jordan, produced locally from design to manufacture and installation. Courtesy of and created by the Umm el-Jimal Archaeological Project and Open Hand Studios.

vogue. This can mean that archaeologists may not simply single out those archaeological strata that represent their own or a particularly preferred people's heritage, but instead they must fairly and impartially study all strata and certainly all those considered to have heritage value by the modern local inhabitants. Inclusive archaeology in relation to site management also means that people living at archaeological sites have their own rights of access and participation in the management of those sites.

Such inclusion is not simply an act of benevolence (increased local income), but has significant added value for the process of heritage management. By realizing an income from site management and tourism services, local people will themselves appreciate the value of the site and help prevent looting. By learning to appreciate the site as a component of their own heritage, local communities can integrate the "life" of the antiquities into the life of the community in ways that will turn a "dead" site into a vibrant place where visitors are welcomed to celebrate a *shared* heritage. If done right, inclusion of the local community will not turn the site into yet another "tourist trap," but instead a welcoming place in which visitors will experience the vital energy of a living heritage with ancient remains and modern customs merged into a cultural whole (de Vries 2013a, 2013b).

Inclusive archaeology will require bridging the gap between academy and community. One starting point is education of the community. This can be done with the preparation of education manuals, training programs in site management, and other aspects of heritage management (Figure 6.0.6). An important new tool is "virtual preservation,"

FIGURE 6.0.6 Bert de Vries teaches the archaeology of Umm el-Jimal, Jordan, to a class of local community women.

Courtesy of Muaffaq Hazza (October 2014).

the open publication of digital site preservation using comprehensive visual and verbal data presented in ways understandable and relevant to all communities, ranging from the academic to the local (see, e.g., virtual Umm al-Jimal at www.ummeljimal.org.) To succeed in this, the academy's conception of archaeological field work must be expanded to include engagement with the community in ways that are akin to development work. This means expansion of field staff with specialists not only in ethnography and digital humanities, but also in community development and engagement skills, who work alongside the specialists in traditional fields like stratigraphy and ceramics. It also opens the way to project funds from development agencies that recognize components of cultural heritage as economic assets.

Abu Khafajah and Miqdadi caution that subservience to the demands of national and international development agencies could transform archaeologists from academic researchers into neo-liberal entrepreneurs (2019). Rabbat and Mulder also warn of the danger of putting the large-scale development of the Islamic built heritage (Chapter 6.2) and war-damaged urban centers (Chapter 6.4) into the hands of global neo-liberal enterprise for the creation of mass tourism without involving local communities in planning, execution and management of; i. e., a renewed form of exclusion of the "locals." Archaeologists must therefore make certain they work in partnership with the local community to enable and empower residents to be self-sufficient providers of heritage services. And they must insist that such work be informed by clear understanding of appropriate methods and standards of archaeological site research, preservation and protection. This slow, patient and informed work can be in tension with fast-paced and large-budgeted agendas of international agencies which prioritize economic achievements measured by job creation and business start-ups.

A second starting point flows from this: the academy must include the views of the community in its interpretive process. This does not just mean including trained members of the community in the interpretive process as senior field staff members. It also means study of the historic relationship between the modern community and the archaeological site through the examination of archaeological and historical sources. Most importantly, this means listening to the community and respecting its sense of the meaning of the archaeological site as a valid alternative point of view (Mickel 2016). In other words, the academy must respect and incorporate nonacademic interpretations as legitimate "voices" to be included in its publications. Such "multivocality" provides the essential ingredients for the creation of a site story in which the voice of the community counts alongside those of the academy's material, historical, and literary evidences (Hodder 2008: 196–200).

A third starting point, flowing from the second, is that the archaeological heritage must be more thoroughly contextualized in the deep literary and intellectual cultural heritage of *Islamic* civilization, ranging from early Islamic beginnings through the middle and late Islamic periods. A common observation in the ensuing chapters of this section is that heritage perspectives from the Western tradition continue to overshadow those from the Islamic tradition (Figure 6.0.7). That critique is applied to both the performance of the academy and the culture practices of the general public in the Middle

FIGURE 6.0.7 The word "overshadow" becomes literal with the appearance of "Gulf-style" high-rises in Amman's new global trade center at Abdali, seen from a mid–20th-century low-rise neighborhood of modern international-style villas.

Courtesy of Bert de Vries (October 2017)

East. A grounding of archaeological heritage in the broader Islamic culture of the historic Middle East would lead to an indigenous interpretive framework more readily understood and appreciated by local cultures. To make such integration of Islamic archaeology into its *own* broader cultural spheres effective, both the professionals in the academy and the members of local communities will need to prepare themselves deliberately in knowledge and appreciation of those broader fields of culture. For that to work, educational reform may be necessary in both the graduate schools preparing students for a career in Islamic archaeology and in the grade schools and high schools throughout the Middle East, where local students need to be taught the meaning of Islamic archaeological sites in terms of a well-grounded familiarity with the broader, indigenous, rich historic culture traditions to which they are the heirs. That would help alleviate the awkward paradox of having to see their own Islamic archaeological heritage through the lenses of Western culture, as is now still often the case.

The maturing of Islamic archaeology can be a major component in that bridging between academy and community because it is a natural foundation block in the process of heritage awareness on which an appreciation of pre-Islamic civilizations can be more easily constructed for modern Muslim communities. How all this is worked out in practice is the task of the next five chapters, which give examples and summaries of heritage management in action in the Islamic world, encompassing its relevant portions of Europe, Asia, and Africa. These range across the architecture and archaeology tracks described earlier, but each in its own setting reflects the incorporation of modern local communities in the grand venture called "heritage management."

Summary of Chapters in This Section

Chapter 6.1, by Øystein LaBianca, Elena Ronza, and Noël Harris, "Community Engagement in Site Presentation," defines and describes the practice of community archaeology in predominantly Islamic countries with the thesis that community engagement is an essential site protection strategy. The Islamic world contains many thousands of archaeological sites that have been excavated and studied; so many, that it is impossible for local and national governments to maintain and protect them from looters. In response to the needs of site maintenance and the prevention of vandalism and looting, a recent strategy is to engage communities in that project. As community engagement became more prevalent, "community archaeology" emerged as a new subdiscipline of the general field. The field engages local people as participants in site management through education and training for the care and security of sites. In the process, communities come to appreciate the archaeological remains as their own heritage and also receive economic benefits. In many cases this actually means a restoration of access to sites from which local residents had been excluded in the colonial process. In most Islamic countries, community archaeology is still in its infancy. From a general survey of the incipient practice of community archaeology in Islamic countries, the authors turn to Jordan, where they find more numerous instances of the practice both in field projects and in its enablement among local and foreign agencies. They conclude with a number of suggestions for achieving more comprehensive and sustainable community engagement practices—a list that can serve as a "how-to" manual for beginners in community archaeology. A fundamental call for change in these instructions is that archaeologists need to abandon the notion that they and their academic colleagues are the experts and that local people are there to service the application of that expertise. Instead, members of the community become partners and even managers of a broadened cultural process in which their sense of meaning deserves equal space. Even further, the archaeologist from abroad becomes a guest who needs to incorporate and observe local custom and authority as an essential component of the research agenda.

In Chapter 6.2, "Heritage in Context," Nasser Rabbat covers the role and fate of the Islamic "built heritage"; that is, the incorporation of heritage conservation and planning strategies in the context of urban planning from the early 19th century to the present in the Middle East and North Africa. While European scholars who accompanied the imperial administrations into the region were more interested in pre-Islamic architecture, the colonial authorities incorporated Islamic built heritage into their urbanization schemes as a romantic substratum in the late 19th and early 20th centuries. The nationalizing atmosphere of the later 20th century brought greater focus on the Islamic built heritage, but, with few exceptions, the European influences prevailed, even in comprehensive restoration of traditional urban neighborhoods. The trend to turn such traditional urban areas into gentrified business attractions for tourists and wealthy residents was amplified under the influence of neoliberalism and "heritage commodification" of the past several decades. After the heritage-threatening—and in several countries destructive—events following the Arab Spring, there is some promise of an "emerging inclusive discourse" through which citizens may be recruited as participants in the public management of the still surviving Islamic "built heritage."

Chapter 6.3, by Trinadad Rico, "Islamic" and "Western" Concepts of Heritage Compared," investigates more specifically whether there is a distinctive Islamic way of cultural heritage preservation vis-à-vis the Western practices that have dominated the preservation of pre-/non-Islamic heritage. The thesis of the chapter is that Islamic heritage preservation is neither allied with nor in conflict with Western principles. Rather, Islamic heritage preservation "is practiced in ways that serve agendas that are temporally and politically relevant, a role that is served by all heritage." Focus on the issue of "Islamic" versus "Western" is hindered by two distractions: Preoccupation with discussion of the destruction of non-Muslim monuments in Muslim contexts, such as the Bamiyan Buddhas, and sacralization of the terms of discourse when functioning Muslim buildings are involved. The very notion of "Islamic" heritage is complicated especially when heritage is viewed in the dynamic terms of social practice rather than the static terms governing monumental structures. To refine the issue, Rico divides the concept of heritage into three aspects: remains with specific historical origin, the mixture of tangible and intangible aspects associated with religious observance and practice, and the material culture being constantly developed in the present. These three lend themselves variously to "Islamic" versus "Western" criteria. A further complication is that the question of heritage is not treated explicitly in authoritative Islamic sources, and the usual practices are based on pre-modern maintenance processes governed by traditions of craftsmanship rather than principles of preservation. Therefore, Rico concludes that, in the absence of a general set of Islamic standards that are distinct from Western ones, it is more expedient to treat Islamic heritage preservation in accordance with the various local and temporal conditions prevalent in the Islamic world.

In Chapter 6.4 by Stephennie Mulder, "War and Recovery," the traditional notion that archaeologists operate in a neutral zone away from war is challenged. Rather, Mulder implicates archaeologists in the destruction of war. Therefore, they owe a responsibility for recovery of heritage, not only as restoration of the past but also for the integration of that past into the lives of local societies. Thus, she calls on archaeologists to become activists in response to war-caused destruction of heritage, not only in the aftermath but during its perpetration. Deliberate destruction of monuments and plunder of heritage has been endemic in warfare from the beginning of history and has been valorized in art as a macabre propaganda of victory. Only recently has the world objected and labeled the practice as "culture cleansing." Though considered a war crime since the 1954 Hague Convention, little was done to prosecute the practitioners until the practice of culture cleansing was intensified in the Islamic world's regional wars of the 21st century. When damage is from bombardment (Saudi Arabia and the United States in Yemen) or occupation (United States at Babylon), it is difficult to categorize it as "collateral" or "deliberate." However, wanton strategic destruction, such as by the Islamic State (ISIS) in and near Mosul (Assyrian antiquities and Sufi shrines), was done to propagandize punishment for proclaimed "sins" of idolatry and apostasy. Significant by-products of war are nationalist corruptions of heritage and the plunder and looting of major archaeological museums (Baghdad and Mosul). International recovery efforts, "Authorized Heritage Discourse," by international agencies and businesses, have resulted in commodified urban installations, such as downtown Beirut after the Lebanese Civil War, which are designed to attract money-laden tourists but have nothing to offer local populations recovering from protracted war trauma. Instead, Mulder recommends that war recovery projects engage local communities as major participants, not merely as installers of a prepackaged, "authorized" plan, but as participants in planning for development from the ground up. International agencies and archaeologists must consider adjusting their professional standards to make space for the local community's own perspective on meaningful war recovery of traditional residential landscapes. Thus, while professionals educate communities on the archaeological significance of local monuments, they should also be prepared to pursue non-archaeological goals, such as the incorporation of parks and other community facilities, and even the repurposing of ancient structures to suit the community's own traditional narratives of the past and discourse for the future.

The multi-authored Chapter 6.5, "Islamic Archaeologies and Narratives About the Islamic Heritage in Three Peninsulas," is a comparative essay on the nature and status of Islamic heritage. Conjoined by the co-authors' research interests, the unique historical, cultural, and political conditions of the Qatar, Iberian, and Balkan peninsulas demonstrate the regional and local diversity of "Islamic" cultural heritages. While Qatar's

Islamic past is continuous, central, and conservative in practice, those of Iberia and the Balkans are wholly or partly transitory, peripheral, and nonexistent (Iberia) to moderate (Balkans) in practice. The history of formal discourse about Islamic heritage is recent in all three places. In Qatar, that is akin to post-colonial national identity and saw its first concrete expression in the founding of a national museum in 1975. The ruling family has established world-renowned museums since then, revived Islamic architecture by sponsoring new construction, and recreated a commodified version of customary socio-economic practices. Nonetheless, the archaeology of Islamic sites has not played a significant role. Here, the Islamic past plays a major (restraining) role in national identity formation, but actual cultural practices are largely subsumed in the daily and annual cycle of religious observances. In Iberia and the Balkans, Islamic heritage is not a strong component of national identity. For example, interest in the historic role of Islam in Iberia, where the Reconquista colored reception of its Islamic past, has evolved over time. Interest in Islamic architecture and Arabic literature grew after the transitions from dictatorship to democracy in the 20th century. Museums dedicated to art and archaeology have made the material culture of Islam readily available to the public and have raised awareness of it; nonetheless, that culture is no longer a living part of contemporary society. It is a remnant of a past that is not fully claimed as one's own. In many parts of the Balkans, Islamic heritage has been suppressed in an anti-Ottoman form of local nationalisms. The notable exception is Bosnia, but there the civil war of 1992–1995 resulted in the irreversible destruction of Islamic-era monuments. The influences of Islamic heritage on popular cultural construction also vary greatly, surviving in some countries in the form of cuisine, literature, and music. State sponsorship is limited to the preservation of UNESCO-approved Ottoman-period built heritage in Albania, Bosnia, and Herzegovina. On the level of academia, the field of Islamic archaeology has limited visibility, with only the University of Sarajevo offering a program in Ottoman archaeology. Given the ambiguity of Islamic cultural heritage in the making of local nationalisms in all three areas, the authors recommend an active public outreach to improve and expand heritage education and make the resulting archaeological research accessible to the public, and to broaden the base of authority to give voice to local communities in preservation and heritage practices.

CONCLUSION: A DISTILLATION OF WHAT THESE CHAPTERS CONTRIBUTE TO GENERAL UNDERSTANDING OF "ISLAMIC HERITAGE"

As summarized earlier, the chapters of this section treat diverse aspects of Islamic heritage management, including in this a role for local communities. What follows are some generalizations that can be drawn from these chapters about the meaning of Islamic Heritage in theory and practice.

In the context of archaeology, Islamic Heritage includes the extant material remains of Islamic civilizations that have accumulated since the time of the Prophet Muhammad. These remains include the better known "built heritage" of relatively intact structures in the landscape, usually urban (the architecture track), and the "archaeological heritage" comprised of ruins and buried sites (the archaeology track). What makes this material heritage distinctly Islamic is that it represents the material remains and features of the cultures of Islamic civilization surviving—and sometimes still functioning—in the present. This heritage exists in countries that are today predominantly Muslim and in those in which Islam is part of a more remote past. In this material sense, the practice of "Islamic Heritage" is the sphere of professionals, such as archaeologists, architects, and museologists, who study, preserve, and present these remains to audiences comprised of fellow academics, tourists and visitors, and local communities. In theory these activities can—or should—follow a set professional principles and methods recognized as international standards that apply similarly to the material remains of other cultures ("Mayan Heritage" for example). Pre-Islamic remains, such as those of the Byzantine and Persian civilizations, are important formative ingredients of Islamic material cultural heritage.

However, all contributors to this section recognize that Islamic Heritage in practice is much more than the professional curation of material remains for two main reasons: (1) the nature and degree of interest in managing and celebrating Islamic Heritage varies greatly from place to place, and (2) the material remains, or "tangible" heritage, described earlier is only one component that must be considered together with other, "intangible" aspects of heritage. The first of these, regional variety, is not difficult to grasp and is well represented in the chapters of this section. Variables include, among others, government priorities, the role (if any) of Islam in modern society, and the varying nature of the material remains themselves. Internecine conflicts can and do include the destruction of the material heritage of one Islamic group by another. The authors therefore conclude that the practice of Islamic Heritage inevitably varies from region to region and country to country, and they cite numerous examples of this variety.

The second of these, the role of intangible heritage, is more complex. A significant aspect is that cultural heritage, broadly defined in this manner, is not the intellectual monopoly of academics, but also includes a conglomerate of popular traditions ranging from religious practices to local traditions, such as music, costume, and cuisine, to local stories and lore about built and archaeological heritage in familiar landscapes, folk festivals, and much more. Local traditions include stories and remembered experiences about the material heritage, both buildings and archaeological sites. Heritage management, then, should be concerned with the preservation of the immaterial, as much as the material, aspects of culture. What has been difficult for academics to accept and, therefore, implement is that local knowledge, which usually comes in the form of stories and practices that lack scientific precision, needs to be recognized as important in overall preservation strategies. In the context of Islamic archaeology, what local people know and believe about archaeological sites in their midst needs to be taken seriously alongside the more strictly archaeological information. All of this is part of the living cultural heritage that gives meaning to sites, not just as monuments to the past for scholars and tourists, but also as places that give identity and meaning to the people living there. The role of local communities is invaluable, then, not only in the sense of their role in the "community archaeology" described in this section, but also as contributors to the larger interpretive task of defining the value of buildings and things and of the meaning of sites. As a community comes to reimagine its own cultural connections, it can contribute meaningfully to both the management and celebration of the archaeological places in its midst.

On a final note, the issue of the wanton destruction of non-Islamic material culture within the Islamic world becomes more germane if seen in the context of the traditional exclusion of local populations from the archaeological heritage which was practiced by Western archaeologists in the era of colonialism and during the formation of modern nation states. One could see from this background that the destruction of archaeological remains is a form of revenge for the experience of exclusion, invasion, and occupation that still looms large in the living heritage of local people. ISIS/Da'esh propaganda could label this destruction as the rooting out of idolatry, whereas the underlying psychological reality may be a revenge for past dispossession (and a "cover" for the marketing of looted artifacts rendered "foreign" by that dispossession). Such a post-colonial approach may also be instructive in dealing with the "Western" versus "Islamic" characterization of heritage management discussed in these chapters. Even if not an operational distinction, raising the question may be occasioned by a history in which both Orientalist prejudice and anti-Western slogans have abounded. Underlying all this is a deep need for reconciliation, a making of amends, to which working for the inclusion of local people in the defining of their own Islamic Heritage could contribute immensely. I. e. community engagement in Islamic Heritage Management is a work of reconciliation and peacemaking.

References

Abu-Khafajah, Shatha and Riham Miqdadi (2019). Prejudice, military intelligence, and neo-liberalism: examining the local within archaeology and heritage practices in Jordan, *Contemporary Levant*, DOI: 10.1080/20581831.2019.1667667

Butler, H. C. 1914. Boṣrā, Part A of Southern Syria, Section A of Ancient Architecture in Syria, Division II of Publications of the Princeton University Archaeological Expedition to Syria in 1904–1905 and 1909 (Leyden: E. J. Brill).

Butler, H. C., and Littmann, E. 1905. "Preliminary Report of the Princeton University Expedition to Syria," *American Journal of Archaeology*, 9, 4 (Oct.–Dec. 1905), 389–410.

de Vries, B. 2013a. "Archaeology and Community at Umm el-Jimal," In F. al-Hmoud, ed., *Studies in the History and Archaeology of Jordan XI: Changes and Challenges* (Amman: Department of Antiquities of Jordan), 81–91.

de Vries, B. 2013b. "Archaeology and Community in Jordan and Greater Syria: Traditional Patterns and New Directions," *Near Eastern Archaeology* 76, 3, 132–140.

Hodder, I. 2008. "Multivocality and Social Archaeology," in J. Habu, C. Fawcett, and J. M Matsumaga (eds.), *Evaluating Multiple Narratives: Beyond Nationalist, Colonialist, Imperialist Archaeologies* (New York: Springer Science + Business Media, LCD), 196–200.

Mickel, A. 2016. *Why Those Who Shovel Are Silent: Local Labor, Unrecognized Expertise, and Knowledge Production in Archaeological Excavation* (PhD diss., Stanford University).

Renfrew, Colin and Paul Bahn 2020. *Archaeology: Theories, Methods and Practice* (Thames and Hudson; Eighth Edition).

Walker, B. J. 2011. *Jordan in the Late Middle Ages: Transformation of the Mamluk Frontier.* Chicago Studies on the Middle East (Chicago: Middle East Documentation Center).

World Heritage Convention 2018. "Umm el-Jimal," Tentative List. https://whc.unesco.org/en/tentativelists/6335/

FURTHER READING

Al-Sabouni, M. 2016. *The Battle for Home: The Vision of a Young Architect in Syria* (London/ New York: Thames and Hudson).

de Vries, B. 2009. "Community and Antiquities at Umm el-Jimal and Silwan: A Comparison," in E. M Meyers and C. Meyers (eds.), *Archaeology, Bible, Politics and the Media: Proceedings of the Duke University Conference, April 23–24 2009* (Winona Lake: Eisenbrauns), 161–186.

de Vries, B., and Umm el-Jimal Team. 2016. "Archaeology for the Future at Umm el-Jimal: Site Preservation, Presentation and Community Engagement," *ACOR Newsletter*, 28, 1 (Summer 2016), 1–5. http://www.blog.ummeljimal.org

CHAPTER 6.1

···

COMMUNITY ARCHAEOLOGY IN THE ISLAMIC WORLD

···

ØYSTEIN S. LABIANCA, MARIA ELENA RONZA, AND NOËL HARRIS

THE notion that local officials, school teachers, community elders, workmen, and other community members might be recruited as partners in helping to preserve, protect, interpret, and present archaeological sites is at best a nascent one in Islamic archaeology. *Community* or *public archaeology*, as such initiatives have come to be called, is also a fairly recent trend in the discipline of archaeology.[1] Community archaeology is both practical and theoretical, an activity and a methodology. It encompasses a broad range of activities and approaches toward heritage preservation, reconstruction, heritage tourism, heritage education, knowledge construction and management, and outreach (Richardson and Almansa-Sánchez 2015: 194–195).

Most archaeological projects rely to some extent on collaborative arrangements with residents living near archaeological sites; however, archaeologists from Anglophone countries working with indigenous populations were among the first to engage the local community as key partners in helping to interpret and present the archaeological record of a particular locality. In recent years, archaeologists around the globe have begun to recognize the importance of involving local communities in constructing and mediating interpretations about the past (de Vries 2013: 137; Matsuda 2016: 41; Richardson and Almansa-Sánchez 2015: 203).

[1] Charles R. McGimsey's *Public Archaeology* (1972) pioneered the term "public archaeology" "within the context of publicly funded and supported excavation and preservation of archaeological sites threatened by development works" (Richardson and Almansa-Sánchez 2015: 196). Suzie Thomas cites the United Kingdom as the location of origin for community archaeology in the 1970s. Thomas importantly notes that "the shift from 'public archaeology,' as in archaeology practiced by professionals with the public in mind . . . to archaeology that actually involved the public, or community, began to occur in the 1980s and early 1990s" (Thomas 2017: 18–19).

While community archaeology is somewhat fluid in its definition and varied in application,[2] recent projects in Islamic archaeology share an approach that considers the study of the cultural practices and material worlds of present-day inhabitants as essential to their efforts to make sense of the past uncovered by their excavations. In other words, the ethnographic study of the material correlates of contemporary cultural practices—ethnoarchaeology—is an integral part of their research agenda, playing a key role in crystallizing their vision of a community (such as at Hisban and Umm el-Jimal, de Vries 2013: 139).

Community archaeology has developed as a subspecialty in part as a result of the influence of the postcolonial critique of Orientalist approaches to archaeology (Okamura and Matsuda 2011: 8), the emergence of ethnoarchaeology as an integral part of archaeological investigation (London 2000: 2), and an increasing awareness of the potential damage and destruction of exposed architectural remains.[3] Archaeology is, by nature, a destructive undertaking (LaBianca 2017b: 8; King 2016: 60), usually producing large and unsightly holes and trenches that are unsafe for local residents and visitors, even when the excavation has been carried out with great care. Excavations also expose architectural remains to the ravages of the elements, looters, and vandalism. Modern construction projects also endanger and sometimes destroy archaeological sites (Al-Houdalieh and Tawafsha 2017: 47; Kafafi 2014: 285–286; Rawashdeh 2017: n.p.). Involving the community in interpreting, protecting, and caring for heritage sites necessitates community archaeology. Community archaeology de-colonizes excavation endeavors and involves local communities in the process of gaining back their past by contributing to its interpretation (Atalay 2012: 7, 10–11).[4] Additionally, community archaeology can address the challenges of site conservation in part by harnessing the time and skills of those living closest to the site, training them as caretakers, friends, and presenters of the archaeological heritage in their backyards. In many cases, becoming involved benefits local residents and businesses economically and socially.

The growth in the number of officially recorded archaeological sites in some regions and countries has overwhelmed the ability of national and local government agencies to monitor and care for the sites. For example, in 2015, Sada Mire published the results of a survey in Somaliland that included almost 100 new Cushitic, pre-Christian, pre-Islamic, Aksumite, and early Islamic sites. Still more sites have yet to be documented (Mire 2015:

---

[2] Thomas notes that the practice of community archaeology "is greatly affected by the social, cultural, economic and legislative settings in which it takes place." Thus, a framework that is adopted in one setting may not work in another (Thomas 2017: 16).

[3] Carmichael et al. discuss the destructive nature of archaeology and methods for ethical excavation in their chapter "Archaeological Excavation is Controlled Destruction" (Carmichael et al. 2003: 31–48). While their examples are drawn from North American archaeology, their articulation of the safety and security issues accompanying excavations are relevant.

[4] Abdelkadar Ababneh notes that while major archaeological sites in Jordan are prioritized for protection and management, secondary sites are overlooked. The values of the sites themselves are derived, he argues, from values established during the colonial period, which continue to be propagated by the scholarship of Western researchers. However, these values inadequately reflect the importance of the sites for local communities (Ababneh 2016: 42).

111). However, the Department of Archaeology in Somaliland lacks the budget and infrastructure to protect these sites (Mire 2015: 114). The situation has become more urgent due to the rapid increase in the trafficking of archaeological artifacts by private collectors in the global marketplace. Community archaeology that is informed by local perceptions of heritage and engages community members in actively preserving cultural remains is thus a promising way forward for stemming the demise and destruction of humanity's cultural heritage (Mire 2011: 78–79).

COMMUNITY ARCHAEOLOGY PROJECTS IN MENA AND OTHER PREDOMINANTLY ISLAMIC LANDS

An alternative way to gauge the impact of community archaeology on Islamic archaeology is to look for it "on the ground" in countries with predominantly Muslim populations. The following overview of projects resulted from a search of all the countries of the Middle East and North Africa (MENA) region and the following predominantly Muslim countries outside that region, including Indonesia, Pakistan, Bangladesh, Sudan, Afghanistan, Uzbekistan, Malaysia, Niger, and Somalia. MENA region countries include Algeria, Bahrain, Djibouti, Egypt, Iran, Iraq, Israel, Jordan, Kuwait, Lebanon, Libya, Malta, Morocco, Oman, Qatar, Saudi Arabia, Syria, Tunisia, United Arab Emirates, West Bank and Gaza, and Yemen. This overview should not be regarded as exhaustive in any sense, but rather as a sampling of the community archaeology projects that are happening in these countries.

Çatalhöyük Research Project, Turkey

Prior to beginning excavations at this Neolithic site (Mickel 2016: 1100), the project asked the community what individual stake they would like in the archaeological process in an effort to create a community coalition of interested parties. Additionally, the Çatalhöyük Research Project worked, through interviews and discussions, to overcome a strong community misconception that the archaeologists were not equal partners with the local community. Through these discussions with the community, a challenge was identified: the local community did not feel educated enough about archaeology to have a stake in a research partnership. To meet this challenge, the project helped produce an annual festival, archaeological lab-guide training for children and youth, a regular comic series, and a newsletter (Atalay 2012:14). These activities were an effort "to increase community knowledge about the site, and about archaeology and heritage management practices and cultural tourism strategies more broadly" (Atalay 2010: 423).

The project also began to support capacity development initiatives. A local theater-troupe was created—a community-driven creation for the community members to get involved in teaching others about the site through drama and workshops. An internship program trains community members for research, a women's craft cooperative creates archaeology-inspired designs to sell locally, and a cultural heritage board takes part in planning and management decisions (Atalay 2012: 14).[5]

The work of Allison Mickel, who has worked with both the Temple of the Winged Lions Cultural Resource Management initiative in Jordan and the Çatalhöyük Research Project, is particularly noteworthy. Mickel utilized social network analysis (SNA) to gauge the involvement of local site workers in the production of knowledge during the excavations (Mickel 2016: 1108). Mickel conducted a case study of the Çatalhöyük Research Project using this technique, examining information flow and the social structures and individuals who influence it.

Community Archaeology Project Quseir, Egypt

The Community Archaeology Project Quseir (CAPQ) stems from an archaeological project at the Roman and Mamluk site Quseir al-Qadim. CAPQ has produced extensive community archaeology research, defining seven components of community archaeology and directing interventions at Quseir. These seven components are "communication and collaboration, employment and training, public presentation, interviews and oral history, educational resources, photographic and video archive, and community controlled merchandising" (Tully 2007: 160). CAPQ has engaged in activities such as local interpretation of archaeological finds, involving the community in understanding the use of objects and subsequently incorporating these perspectives into museum displays. Additionally, CAPQ has interviewed more than 170 stakeholders about the role of the site in community identity and their relationship with other stakeholders. These interviews have provided insights into the role of history and how it has been used to construct a modern community identity. In an effort to move away from the old ideas of archaeology, CAPQ developed a curriculum to engage local children using folkloric and imaginative storytelling, a common Egyptian method of teaching history. Finally, in an effort to help the local economy, CAPQ supported the community in creating souvenirs and merchandise (Tully 2009: 71–74).

The Origins of Doha Project, Qatar

The Origins of Doha Project investigates the foundation and growth of Qatar's capital city and the lives of its inhabitants through archaeological and historical research and

---

[5] Veysel Apaydin assesses these activities and offers helpful suggestions for improving current outreach programs and developing new and relevant programs (Apaydin 2016: 839–840).

oral interviews. Urban development threatens sites within Doha itself, and project members have utilized community outreach—such as social media, online GIS, and re-photography—to raise awareness of the sites and their historical importance. As Morgan et al. (2016: 2) have noted, "These strategies address the challenges of conducting archaeological outreach amongst a rapidly changing and diverse population with widely varying perceptions of heritage."

Jericho Mafjar Project and Jericho Oasis Archaeological Park, Palestine

The first joint Palestinian–American excavation team leads the Jericho Mafjar Project (JMP) in working to preserve the Umayyad site of Khirbet al-Mafjar and reassess the previously promulgated colonial narrative (Stub 2016: 28, 32; Whitcomb and Taha 2013: 54, 60). Khirbet al-Mafjar is already an important tourist destination and school children regularly visit the site as part of their history curriculum. A new site museum, walkways and signage, and an introductory film enhance the presentation of the site (Green 2014: 86–87; Whitcomb et al. 2016: 78). A virtual reality research team has created a digital model of the Hisham Palace at Khirbet al-Mafjar in an effort to study cultural heritage sites in Palestine and gain public awareness of such sites (Ghadban et al. 2013: 119).

Khirbet al-Mafjar is also part of a larger project: the Jericho Oasis Archaeological Park (JOAP). The Park is a joint effort between Sapienza University of Rome and the Palestinian Ministry of Tourism and Antiquities – Department of Archaeology and Cultural Heritage (Nigro et al. 2015: 215). The purpose of the Park is to aid in the development of sustainable tourism and engage the community in preserving and presenting cultural heritage sites. It includes thirteen rehabilitated "archaeological, historical, cultural and natural sites," including Khirbet al-Mafjar and Tell es-Sultan, the site of ancient Jericho (Nigro et al. 2015: 216, 218). The project draws on the local population for personnel, training local students and workers to clean, restore (using local knowledge on mudbrick architecture), and maintain the sites; survey and evaluate JOAP sites; utilize computers to create signage based on information learned; and create an itinerary for and guide archaeological tours (Nigro et al. 2015: 217, 219–221).

Borobudur Temple, Indonesia

Borobudur Temple Compound is a Buddhist site from around the 8th century and has been referred to as the largest of its kind in the world. This is significant given that Indonesia is now predominantly Muslim (Wall and Black 2004: 437; Chapman 2013: 40–42). The villages around Borobudur are engaged in cultural tourism, allowing locals to benefit economically from tourist traffic and, in turn, providing visitors with the opportunity to observe traditional pottery- or tofu-making (Fatimah 2015: 569). Listed as a World Heritage, Borobudur is also the location of a World Heritage Volunteers initiative directed by the Indonesia International Work Camp of Perkumpulan Keluarga Berencana Indonesia (IIWC of PKBI). Young people, both local and international, are recruited to take part in heritage awareness and conservation activities. Volunteers clean the site and visit local schools and communities to give heritage education workshops (Moehas n.d.: n.p.).

Other Community Archaeology-Related Initiatives in Islamic Lands

To these "on the ground" evidences of community archaeology activities in the Islamic world can be added programmatic initiatives of several international organizations and professional associations.

The Abraham Path Initiative

The Abraham Path celebrates the journey of Abraham, providing travelers with a chance to experience the Middle East culturally and historically. The path is virtually accessible and, in a number of regions where the route extends, is safe for walking travelers and community-based tourism. The initiative aims to highlight the hospitality of the Middle East and to serve as a platform for experiential education (Abraham Path n.d.: n.p.).

American Schools of Oriental Research Cultural Heritage Initiatives

At present, the professional organization with the most extensive portfolio involving cultural heritage protection and preservation in the Muslim countries of the Middle East is the American Schools of Oriental Research (ASOR). The ASOR Cultural Heritage Initiatives (CHI), established in 2014, focuses on addressing the heritage crises caused by conflict in Syria, Northern Iraq, and Libya. ASOR CHI gathers data from news and social media outlets, satellite imagery, and local contacts through a vast network of heritage experts (Danti et al. 2017: 2; Danti 2015: 133–136). These data are then used for informing "the United States of America (US) Department of State (DOS) and the public, implementing emergency response projects, developing post-conflict rehabilitation plans, and producing public outreach and education initiatives educational activities" (Danti et al. 2017: 2). Results are made available to the public through the US Department of State. As part of their efforts on behalf of the hundreds of significant heritage sites that have been damaged since fighting began in 2011, they seek to engage the local community as partners "to preserve and protect cultural resources through the establishment of broad and diverse coalitions" (Danti et al. 2017: 2).

ASOR CHI has developed a methodology for cultural property protection and preservation and a workflow for analyzing CHI's large inventory of archaeological and other heritage sites and monuments that can be utilized by on-the-ground stakeholders and officials as well as by cultural heritage professionals and activists around the world (Danti et al. 2017: 4).

ASOR CHI has supported several community-based cultural heritage preservation and protection projects in Syria and northern Iraq. ASOR CHI has previously partnered with local groups in Syria including the Bosra al-Sham Antiquities Department, where ASOR CHI provided capacity building for local heritage personnel by conducting a needs assessment and then providing necessary documentation materials including computers, cameras, and a portable generator (ASOR 2016: n.p.). In another partnership, with The Day After Heritage Initiative Project (TDA), ASOR CHI provided support to volunteers from TDA to protect artifacts in the Ma'aara Museum, located in Idlib Governorate (Danti et al. 2018: 166–169).

Endangered Archaeology in the Middle East and North Africa

EAMENA utilizes satellite imagery to identify threats to archaeological sites throughout the MENA region, disseminating the data in English and Arabic through an online database (EAMENA n.d.: n.p.). Although this project is similar to ASOR CHI, the main difference is that EAMENA is concerned with a larger area, most of which includes countries that are not in open conflict (Danti et al. 2017: 3). This collaborative project among the Universities of Oxford, Leicester, and Durham gathers and analyzes the data and develops training courses in EAMENA methodologies for heritage professionals in MENA countries (Rayne et al. 2017: 2).

The Middle Eastern Geodatabase for Antiquities–Jordan

Middle Eastern Geodatabase for Antiquities (MEGA)–Jordan is the result of collaboration between the Jordanian Department of Antiquities (DoA), Getty Conservation Institute (GCI), and World Monuments Fund (WMF). MEGA–Jordan is an "open source, Web-based GIS heritage site inventory and management system" developed for heritage authorities in Jordan and Iraq (Myers and Dalgity 2012: 33–34). It can be used to record the condition of a site, disturbances, threats, individual site elements, and potential damage from development projects. MEGA–Jordan was implemented in 2011 and is being used by the World Heritage Site of Petra for a risk-mapping project (Myers and Dalgity 2012: 45–50). GCI-WMF is developing a similar database for Iraq and has released an international platform for cultural heritage inventory and management called "Arches." Arches is currently being used by ASOR CHI and EAMENA to document damaged or threatened sites (Myers et al. 2016: 218–219).

Sada Mire's Programs, Somaliland

Dr Sade Mire has worked closely with the Somaliland government, creating policies and programs to protect heritage and promote archaeological research. Mire developed the Local Education and Safeguarding Program (LESP), which aims to teach the local community and government about the importance of heritage protection and preservation. Through this program the local government has recruited community members to safeguard important archaeological sites. Specifically, LESP teaches the police to guard sites and identify stolen artifacts. Local people have aided in the development of a national inventory list of significant sites. Cultural-educational centers employ local leaders and women who produce traditional art. The skill is recorded, taught to children and youth, and the final product provides some income. A campaign to engage local communities in returning stolen antiquities has also had some success (Mire 2011: 82–88). Through TV programs, Mire has worked to educate the public about archaeology, its misuse, and its benefits, hoping to encourage the local community to take stake in their own heritage (Mire 2011: 85–86, 2015: 114). Mire advocates a knowledge-centered approach, in which locals contribute knowledge about their heritage through interviews and outreach prior to the declaration of any research assumptions (Mire 2011: 79–80).

A COMMUNITY ARCHAEOLOGY REVOLUTION IN JORDAN

Community archaeology is flourishing in Jordan, which ranks seventy-fifth—just below Egypt—in World Economic Forum's 2017 Travel & Tourism Competitiveness Report (World Economic Forum 2017: 18). There are several reasons for this: first, the country has been at peace for well over four decades, allowing tourism to emerge as one of the most important sectors of the economy. However, the tourism sector in the Middle East has struggled in the wake of the rise of the Islamic State (ISIS) and the Syrian crisis (World Economic Forum 2017: 16–17). The receptiveness and cooperative spirit of various government ministries and agencies to international collaborations in archaeological exploration and cultural resources management is another reason for the success of Jordanian community archaeology. This has resulted in a considerable number of internationally sponsored excavations and foreign aid targeting heritage-related projects and has fostered an atmosphere of openness to collaboration and experimentation (Hashemite Kingdom of Jordan General Budget Department 2018: n.p.). Credit for maintaining this atmosphere of openness must be given, first of all, to the royal family, several of whom have participated in archaeological projects in Jordan (Figure 6.1.1) and

FIGURE 6.1.1 His Majesty King Hussein (right) visited Tall Hisban in 1976 accompanied by His Majesty King Constantine of Greece (left).

Courtesy of Hisban Photo Archive, Andrews University.

who serve on the boards of various heritage-related organizations and foundations in Jordan. The government ministry most directly involved with cultural heritage management is the Department of Antiquities (DoA) under the umbrella of the Ministry of Tourism and Antiquities (MOTA). The DoA's accommodation and support of both Jordanian and international archaeological expeditions has been outstanding when compared with similar ministries and bureaucracies elsewhere in the region. Over the past two decades, they have particularly emphasized the importance of protection, preservation, and presentation of heritage sites. To this end, both MOTA and the DoA have been especially welcoming of heritage protection and presentation initiatives undertaken by various international archaeological research groups working in Jordan, which include the American Center of Oriental Research (ACOR), the British Institute in Amman (CBRL), Le Centre National de la Recherche Scientifique (CNRS), Institut français du Proche-Orient (IFPO), Istituto Superiore per la Conversazione ed il Restauro (ISCR), Istituto Superiore per la Protezione e la Ricerca Ambientale (ISPRA), and the German Protestant Institute of Archaeology (Al Adarbeh and Porter 2017: 7).

While each of these foreign research groups has contributed in various ways to advancing the work of protecting, preserving, and presenting Jordan's archaeological heritage, ACOR has played an especially important role since its establishment in 1968. For most of its history ACOR has focused its work on projects aimed at enhancing Jordan's major tourism destinations such as the Amman Citadel, the Petra Church

Project, the Temple of the Winged Lion Initiative (also in Petra), and the Madaba Archaeological Park; however, community archaeology has recently emerged as a major focus of ACOR's heritage initiatives in Jordan (Porter 2008: n.p.; USAID SCHEP n.d.: n.p.). This is partially due to programs such as Sustainable Cultural Heritage Through Engagement of Local Communities Project (SCHEP), which is funded by the US Agency for International Development. ACOR is responsible for the planning and implementation of the program in collaboration with the Department of Antiquities of Jordan.

Community-Driven Projects in Jordan

Umm el-Jimal Project (UJP), Jordan. Under the direction of Bert de Vries, this project at the Late Antique site of Umm el-Jimal has moved away from an emphasis on academic archaeological research to concentrate on site management, particularly the preservation of the site and engaging the community. This began with digital preservation with the construction of a website which documents the history, culture, and points of view of the modern community in the context of comprehensive documentation, preservation, and analysis of the archaeological site (de Vries 2013: 139, 2016: 1–2). A comprehensive program of site presentation includes the preservation of several structures, the development of a signed interpretive trail, and the creation of an Interpretive and Hospitality Center. In this process, they engaged members of the community in site management and preservation training to create a pool of local experts, with the serious and successful effort to include women (de Vries 2016: 3–4; Abu-Khafajah et al. 2015: 197). The result is the creation of "Hand-by-Hand-for-Heritage," a nonprofit corporation owned and operated by community members for carrying out various archaeological site management tasks, including excavation, conservation construction, tour guiding, and visitor hosting. The site preservation agenda has taken serious account of the community's sense of meaning and interest in the site. Examples of enhancing the community's sense of place include the creation of the West Entry Park and the provision of open space in the new Interpretive and Hospitality Center for culture celebrations and other community events. To create a specific "gift" from the antiquities to the community, the UJP Water Project entails the conservation and reactivating of the ancient runoff system for the redistribution of water for household use by the community (de Vries 2016: 2–3, 5).

Temple of the Winged Lion Cultural Resource Management (TWLCRM), Petra, Jordan. The TWLCRM initiative is aimed at stabilizing and conserving the Temple of the Winged Lion complex in Petra while inviting and empowering local communities to participate in the project. This goal is realized through the training of the local communities and by providing educational opportunities and eventual employment in site preservation and cultural resource management (Tuttle 2013: 14–22). These employment opportunities at TWLCRM are crucial for the community: more than 800 individuals were employed as of 2016. TWLCRM also involves women and youth in the archaeological restoration and documentation process (Corbett 2016: 4; Corbett and Ronza 2016: 666; Ronza 2016: 617–624; Abu-Khafajah et al. 2015: 197; Tuttle 2013: 19). Additionally, TWLCRM can boast of having a year-round presence at the site, which speaks to sustainability and increased community ownership. In 2016, TWLCRM partnered with a local nonprofit company, Sela for Vocational Training and Protection of Cultural Heritage, that managed the training component in cultural resource management. This new partnership created the necessary framework for a more sustainable future, where building local capacity is no longer conceived as the exclusive role of foreign institutions and where partnering with locals assumes new meanings and dimensions beyond high institutional collaborations (Corbett and Ronza: forthcoming; Corbett 2016: 3; Corbett and Ronza 2016: 666).

Follow the Pots (FTP), Jordan. As part of the Expedition to the Dead Sea Plain (EDSP), Follow the Pots, under the direction of Dr Morag M. Kersel and Dr Meredith S. Chesson, is engaged in work at Babadh-Dhra`, Fifa, Safi, Khirbet Khanazir, Naqa, and Numayra—all Early Bronze Age sites (Kersel and Chesson 2013: 159). Follow the Pots seeks to understand both the history and current use of pots to inform the way of life in the southern Levant during the Early Bronze Age and how that use continues into modern-day life. Importantly, FTP was founded on ideals of community archaeology, namely, involving and learning from the community. As part of learning from the community, FTP has asked the question "why does looting matter?" hypothesizing that is economically motivated (Kersel and Chesson 2011: 45–46; Kersel and Chesson 2013: 160–164). Therefore, FTP is collaborating with the community to develop ways to create "environmentally sustainable heritage tourism." Their ultimate goal is to find a sustainable solution to the problem of local looting, which is directly related to poverty, and to devise practical ways of preserving local archaeological heritage resources (Follow the Pots Project n.d.: n.p.).

Azraq Community Archaeology Program (ACAP), Jordan. The Azraq Basin in Jordan contains a number of archaeological sites ranging from prehistoric to the Islamic era. This project focuses on engaging the local community in the reconstruction, preservation, and historical interpretation of these sites. The program has achieved this engagement through a number of activities, including Ahmad Lash's project to connect oral histories with the remains of ancestral Druze homes in Azraq castle, educational programs for community schools, site visits, and other outreach events (Damick 2011: 29; Damick and Lash 2013: 143). Due to the location of the archaeological sites in Azraq, tourism is unlikely and not particularly desired by the local community. As such, ACAP has focused on making the archaeological site relevant and meaningful to the locals through "past-making." Specifically, the local community has worked with the archaeological team to map out the archaeological sites and connect them to local families, utilizing a combination of oral history and archaeological excavations. This has encouraged local engagement with the archaeological site and has "establish[ed] archaeology as part of [the] living memory of the community" (Damick and Lash 2013: 143–145).

Ghor el Safi Project, Jordan. The Gohr el Safi project is an industrial archaeology project directed by Konstantinos D. Politis and focused on the origins of the sugar industry in Jordan (Politis 2010: 1–5). The project has been promoting, helping, and supporting the implementation of numerous community activities, such as training members of the host community in the conservation of sugar pots and mosaics and making reusable brochures (Politis 2004: 262–264, 2017: 546–548). The community has also been involved in designing and implementing the construction of the Museum at the lowest place on Earth, which has created jobs within the community and has increased the flow of visitors to the area (Politis 2004: 264–268). The project has successfully engaged site stewards who have lobbied for the protection of the site and have raised awareness of its cultural heritage value through educational activities with school children. The project's long-term goals include working with local workers to restore the Islamic sugar factory so that it can be presented to the public and thus generate tourism in the area (USAID SCHEP n.d.: n.p.). In addition to community archaeological endeavors, Ghor el Safi is home to the Gohr el Safi Women Association for Social Development. The Association founded Safi Crafts, which produces eco-friendly textiles using colors from natural soil and plant dyes (Celeste 2017: n.p.).

Tall Hisban, Jordan. Andrews University-led archaeology at Tall Hisban, Jordan, has been at the forefront of the community archaeology movement in that country. Over the past two decades, the excavators of this multimillennial archaeological site have worked to turn it into a tourism destination by transforming it into an archaeological park complete with a well-signed interpretive path that includes several viewing platforms and benches overlooking certain key features. A local ironsmith made the signs and a local schoolteacher handwrote the legend in Arabic and English.

The archaeological team has also facilitated the establishment of a local nongovernmental organization, the Hisban Cultural Association, which includes leaders from the various families in the village and representatives from the Department of Antiquities, the municipality of Hisban, the Ministry of Culture, and the excavation team. The association has become a key vehicle for informing the local community about the importance of the site (LaBianca 2017b: 17; Abu-Khafajah et al. 2015: 197) (Figures 6.1.2 and 6.1.3).

Community members have provided site stewards to assist with looking after the site and keeping the excavation leadership team informed of any vandalism. Local and global site education has been facilitated by the maintenance of a dedicated website, which includes information about the site for visitors, guides, teachers, and students. A short film, *Deep Time at Tall Hisban* (available on Vimeo and YouTube), has also been produced and has received much favorable commentary in the local village and beyond.

THE CHALLENGE OF MULTIPLE PASTS AT TALL HISBAN

A key aspect of community archaeology is accepting the ethical responsibility of presenting findings to the public in a way that respects and values nonprofessional interpretations alongside professional ones (Richardson and Almansa-Sánchez 2015:

FIGURE 6.1.2 The Hisban Cultural Association was registered with the government of Jordan as a local nongovernmental organization in 2010. It has given voice to and opportunities for participation of local community members in planning for the future development of the archaeological park and a visitor center in Hisban.

Courtesy of SELA.

204).[6] One of the most challenging aspects of efforts to establish a program of community archaeology at Tall Hisban has been that the site elicits different associations and memories for different groups of people; that is to say, it has multiple pasts, each with its own constituencies and curators.[7] From the perspectives of those who live there today, it represents a link to past generations through its association with once vital burial grounds, residential caves, cisterns, herding stations, and pastures. From the perspectives of 18th- and early 19th-century travelers, the founders of the Heshbon Expedition, and many of the tourists who continue to visit the site, the place has special meaning as the leading candidate for the Heshbon remembered in thirty-seven different passages in the Hebrew Bible. From the perspective of Classics scholars, the site was an important junction town in the Roman Province of Arabia—strategically located where the *Via*

---

[6] For a specific example of conflicts in values at Umm Qais, see Ababneh (2016: 43).

[7] On the challenges of heritage discourse and the construction of an "authorized" past, see Paul Belford's 2011 article on archaeology in Telford, England. For a discussion on "instinctual" versus "authorized" heritage engagement, see the 2015 article by Abu-Khafajah et al.

FIGURE 6.1.3 The Hisban Cultural Association has requested that the Jordan Field School offer instruction in English as a second language for local school children. The demand for this among girls from the village was particularly evident in 2016.

Courtesy of Kelsey Curnutt.

Nova Triana intersects the road to Jericho and Jerusalem. To Christian pilgrims and early church history devotees, it is an important ecclesiastical center—the seat of a bishopric during Byzantine times. And to students of the history of the rise and spread of Islam, Tall Hisban is vital to understanding the processes of the Islamization of Jordan and the rural livelihoods and governance along the often-contested frontiers of successive kingdoms, caliphates, and empires, including those of the Umayyads, Abbasids, Ayyubids, Franks, Mamluks, and Ottomans (LaBianca 2017a: 3).

Given these multiple pasts, it should come as no surprise that finding a way forward for narrating and developing the site as an archaeological park has been a challenging task. Conflicts could and did arise, for example, from the fact that each of these stakeholders had their own *desired past*—ideas that animate narratives, images, and emotions about a particular past that has special value to a particular group of people. A good example is the idea that Tall Hisban was biblical Heshbon. This was a desired past of the original excavators, and it continues to be a longed-after past that has deep significance to many Israeli/Jewish and Christian visitors and pilgrims to the site. Muslim visitors have also come to see the site for this reason. At the same time, many archaeologists—and in particular many Jordanian archaeologists and heritage officials—contest this claim on the grounds that there really is no hard, empirical evidence to support it. In their view, those who would make this claim are letting their desired past override best practices of scientific archaeological interpretation. This is an example of *a contested past* for the site. And for still others, the suggestion that Tall Hisban is biblical Heshbon is simply not an option open for consideration—*a forbidden past*. These made their conviction clear when a tourism sign made and mounted by Jordanian authorities mentioning biblical Heshbon was placed along the road below the tell. The offending reference was simply stricken off the sign. Yet the biblical connection is one that members of the Jordan Tourism Board—a nongovernmental tourism promotional organization based in Amman—have recently rallied to highlight. They have found that presenting Jordan as "the land of the Bible" is essential as a business model for attracting tourists from Europe and other regions with sizable Christian populations to Jordan. In this case the Old Testament connection became part of a marketing scheme—*a propaganda past*.

What is particularly noteworthy about this conflicted situation is the extent to which it influenced efforts to narrate and account for the history of the site. It animated the search for narratives/explanations that are, in a sense, ahistorical in the sense that they are concerned more with the underlying dynamics of cultural and historical change and therefore not focused exclusively on one or another particular historical past. This quest has produced seven distinct narratives or theoretical lenses through which investigators have sought to understand and interpret the past at Tall Hisban.

First came the Food Systems lens, which focused attention on human–environment interactions and the many interrelated activities carried out throughout the ages by the local residents of Hisban in their quest for food, water, and security (LaBianca 1991: 221; LaBianca and Walker 2007: 113). Then came the Great and Little Traditions lens, which added a key political dimension to the story of adaptation to the local environment; namely, the story of the complex socio-cultural and political interactions between ordinary villagers and the elite-sponsored projects of successive imperial powers that sought to influence and control Jordan throughout the past four millennia (LaBianca 2007a). Next came the Global History lens, which focused attention on regional cultural interactions, such as those that have characterized interactions between Mediterranean and Western Asia cultures, changes over time in regional and local climate conditions, gradually intensifying webs of commerce and communication, and the devastations brought about by episodic epidemics and plagues (LaBianca 2007b: 5, 9).

To these perspectives, the Cultural Production lens added the dimension of agency, directionality, and accumulative cultural change to the multimillennial history of the region. This accumulative dimension comes into even clearer view when the Great Acceleration and Anthropocene lenses are added to the mix. These lenses make evident the degree to which the modern era is unprecedented in the extent to which humans have become the primary agents impacting the Earth's regulatory processes, ultimately threatening the prospects for humanity's survival into the future. And finally, the Community Archaeology lens was added, for even as it engaged with and gave voice to the local community, it also furnished a valuable crucible in which scholarly narratives and explanations could be tested and validated (LaBianca 2017b: 16–19, 24).

Each of these lenses brought to light different dynamic aspects of the history of Tall Hisban and vicinity, adding a certain level of complexity to investigators' efforts to account for cultural change over *la longue durée* at the site. To the extent that these narratives/explanations have been shared with the local residents of Hisban, they have been welcomed. And as they are grand narratives of sorts, their great merit is that they focus attention on our common concerns as humans—even as they also warn of the consequences for humanity of ignoring the challenges posed by the dawn, in the mid-past century, of the Anthropocene Era. These are concerns that in many ways rise above those of clashing desired pasts even as they also provide frameworks into which particular narratives of the past can be incorporated.

Thirteen Suggestions for Moving Forward with Community Archaeology

The projects summarized thus far illustrate a number of successful ways in which to conduct community archaeology. Without pretending to be exhaustive, the following are examples of actions/strategies that have been trialed with varying degrees of success as a means to move forward with a program of community archaeology:

Make capacity-building a priority. Treating local paid workers as partners in the discovery of best practices for uncovering, restoring, preserving and presenting archaeological finds empowers the community and, in particular, those individuals participating in the fieldwork. Education, whether through seminars, hands-on learning activities, workshops, or the exchange of knowledge while in the field builds understanding and respect between scientific investigators and local participants.

Invest in building local allies. Engaging the community stakeholders is vital to creating a sustainable community archaeology project (Hawkins 2004: 302). Equally as important is the inclusion of women and children in the process of restoration and representation; children who learn about their heritage at a young age grow up to be strong supporters of community endeavors to protect and maintain historical sites and take ownership of the material remains of their past.

Look for and affirm local site stewards. Local caretakers are not only allies; they are individuals who have shown a special interest in the site and in the work going on in it. Such persons hold the site and the project in high regard and report on their voluntary efforts between seasons in helping to look after the site. Such volunteers are critical to building a cadre of local partners in caring for the site, and their efforts need to be acknowledged and encouraged.

Work with local teachers and schools. Local teachers can aid in the development of curricula for use in teaching local school children about the science of archaeology, the history of the world, and the history of sites relevant to them.

Make local merchants and craftsmen your partners. Community archaeology benefits the community both culturally and economically. Supporting local vendors by purchasing equipment, supplies, and food makes allies out of local businesses.

Seek cooperation of local government agencies. The support of government agencies is crucial to successfully engaging local communities. The most successful programs have strong collaborative partnerships between various national and local agencies and institutions.

Establish a visitor welcoming area. It is important to have a welcoming area where an overview of the site, its history and interpretation, and its importance to modern communities can be shared with locals and visitors alike.

Make insertion of pathways and explanatory signage a priority. One of the most important actions a team can take to engage the local community is to invest some time and effort in developing walking paths, viewing platforms, and signage. This allows visitors and locals to explore the site independently of a guide, if necessary.

Create and maintain an attractive website. Websites and social media platforms play a key role in maintaining the engagement of the local community and project partners (Hawkins 2004: 305). Photos posted of reconstruction projects, community members at work, and heritage celebrations help to promote community archaeology and its ideals.

Hire a local agent. For projects that spend only a few weeks in the field each year (and for many projects, every other or every third year), it may make sense to hire on a part-time basis a local agent who can assist with coordination of local efforts to protect and present the site. Such an agent can also be helpful with making preparations for new field seasons and with post-season follow-up.

Organize a local association of allies (friends). By organizing a local association of allies or friends of the project, the benefits of civil society cooperation for a common good can be mobilized on behalf of the site.

Emphasize continuities from the past to the present. Connecting the modern people to the ancient past—whether by mapping ancestral homes in Azraq or demonstrating the similarities of traditional food preparation with those attested to in the archaeological record—helps communities become more than partners in an archaeological investigation: they become owners. In this way, archaeology is no longer a colonial project aimed at discovering a desired past, but a community project aimed at discovering a shared past.

Embrace the seven "multis" of community archaeology. Community archaeology is multifaceted in the following seven ways: it involves *multiyear* commitments; *multiagency* cooperation; *multidisciplinary* cooperation; *multigenerational* involvement; *multimedia* communication; *multisources* of financing; and multiple cups of tea.

Other items could certainly be added to this list of strategies. The point to emphasize here is that the process of engaging the local community is always a work in progress—*an emergent singularity* where a number of different approaches are being trialed over an extended period of time. Some approaches will show noticeable results right away, others will take more time, and some may not show any results at all, but may later be reincarnated in ways no one predicted. As stated earlier, what generates forward movement is not any one approach, but the cumulative effect of the cooperation of multiple approaches sustained over time.

Acknowledgments

Sarah Gane Burton provided research and copyediting support for this chapter.

References

Ababneh, A. 2016. "Heritage Management and Interpretation: Challenges to Heritage Site-Based Values, Reflections from the Heritage Site of Umm Qais, Jordan," *Archaeologies: Journal of the World Archaeological Congress,* 12, 1, 38–72.

Abraham Path. n.d. "Abraham Path," http://abrahampath.org.

Abu-Khafajah, S., Al Rabady, R., Rababeh, S., and al-Rahman al-Tammoni, F. 2015. "Hands-On Heritage! Establishing Soft Authority over Heritage Through Architectural Experiment: A Case Study from Jordan," *Public Archaeology,* 14, 3 (August), 191–213.

Al Adarbeh, N., and Porter, B. A. 2017. "Update of USAID SCHEP—Sustainable Cultural Heritage Through Engagement of Local Communities Project," *ASOR Newsletter* 29, 1 (Summer), 7.

Al-Houdalieh, S. H. A., and Tawafsha, S. A. 2017. "The Destruction of Archaeological Resources in the Palestinian Territories, Area C: KafrShiyān as a Case Study," *Near Eastern Archaeology,* 80, 1, 40–49.

Apaydin, V. 2016. "Effective or Not? Success or Failure? Assessing Heritage and Archaeological Education Programmes: The Case of Çatalhöyük," *International Journal of Heritage Studies,* 22, 10, 828–843.

ASOR 2016. "Migration & Restoration Work at Bosra Al Sham," http://www.asor.org/news/2016/08/bsad-summary/.

Atalay, S. 2010. "'We Don't Talk About Çatalhöyük, We Live It': Sustainable Archaeological Practice Through Community-Based Participatory Research," *World Archaeology,* 42, 418–429.

Atalay, S. 2012. *Community-Based Archaeology: Research with, by, and for Indigenous and Local Communities* (Berkeley: University of California Press).

Belford, P. 2011. "Archaeology, Community, and Identity in an English New Town," *The Historic Environment,* 2, 1 (June), 49–67.

Carmichael, D. L., Lafferty III, R. H., and Molyneaux, B. L. 2003. *Excavation* (Walnut Creek, CA: AltaMira Press).

Celeste, A. 2017. "Gohr Al Safi Women Teach People Natural Dying Techniques," *The Jordan Times,* http://jordantimes.com/news/local/ghor-al-safi-women-teach-people-natural-dying-techniques.

Chapman, W. 2013. *A Heritage of Ruins: The Ancient Sites of Southeast Asia and Their Conservation* (Honolulu: University of Hawaii Press).

Corbett, G. J. 2016. "A Temple Transformed: The TWLCRM Initiative Hits Its Stride," *ACOR Newsletter,* 28, 2 (Winter), 1–4.

Corbett, G. J., and Ronza, M. A. Forthcoming. "Making Social Engagement Sustainable: Insights from the Temple of the Winged Lions Cultural Resource Management Initiative in Petra," in S. Abu Kafajah and A. Badran (eds.), *Community Heritage in the Arab Region* (New York: Springer).

Corbett, G. J., and Ronza, M. E. 2016. "Petra: Temple of the Winged Lions," in G. J. Corbett, D. R. Keller, B. A. Porter, and C. P. Shelton, "Archaeology in Jordan, 2014 and 2015 Seasons," *American Journal of Archaeology,* 120, 4, 631–672.

Damick, A. 2011. "Landscapes of the Past: Place, Space, and the Construction of Meaning in the Azraq Community Archaeology Project," *Bulletin for the Council for British Research in the Levant,* 6, 1, 28–34.

Damick, A., and Lash A. 2013. "The Past Performative: Thinking Through the Azraq Community Archaeology Project," *Near Eastern Archaeology,* 76, 3, 142–150.

Danti, M., Branting, S., and Penacho, S. 2017. "The American Schools of Oriental Research Cultural Heritage Initiatives: Monitoring Cultural Heritage in Syria and Northern Iraq by Geospatial Imagery," *Geosciences,* 7, 4, Article 95, 1–21.

Danti, M. D. 2015. "Ground-Based Observations of Cultural Heritage Incidents in Syria and Iraq," *Near Eastern Archaeology,* 78, 3, 132–141.

Danti, M. D., Gabriel, M., Penacho, S., Raynolds, W., Cuneo, A., Kaercher, K., Ashby, D., Kristy, G., O'Connell, J., and Halabi, N. 2018. *January 2018 Monthly Appendices. ASOR Cultural Heritage Initiatives (CHI): Planning for Safeguarding Heritage Sites in Syria and Iraq* (Boston: American Schools of Oriental Research Cultural Heritage Initiatives).

de Vries, B. 2013. "Archaeology and Community in Jordan and Greater Syria: Traditional Patterns and New Directions," *Near Eastern Archaeology,* 76, 3, 132–141.

de Vries, B. 2016. "Archaeology for the Future at Umm el-Jimal: Site Preservation, Presentation, and Community Engagement," *ACOR Newsletter,* 28, 1 (Summer), 1–5.

EAMENA. n.d. "Database," http://eamena.arch.ox.ac.uk/resources/database-2/. Also see: https://eamena.arch.ox.ac.uk/

Fatimah, T. 2015. "The Impacts of Rural Tourism Initiatives on Cultural Landscape Sustainability in Borobudur Area," *Procedia Environmental Sciences,* 28, 567–577.

Follow the Pots Project. n.d. "Guiding Ideas," http://followthepotsproject.org/?page_id=135.

Ghadban, S., Hassan, R., Aboudi, O., and Khateeb, Y. 2013. "The Development of an Interactive Virtual Environment for Hisham Palace in Jericho, Palestine," *International Journal of Architectural Research,* 7, 2, 118–135.

Green, J. 2014. "Jericho Mafjar: Hisham's Palace Site and Museum Project," in G. J. Stein (ed.), *The Oriental Institute 2013–2014 Annual Report* (Chicago: University of Chicago Press), 85–87.

Hashemite Kingdom of Jordan General Budget Department 2018. "Chapter: 1802 Ministry of Tourism and Antiquities/Department of Antiquities," Law No. (1) for the Year 2018, General Budget Law for the Fiscal Year 2018. Last modified March 21, 2018, http://www.gbd.gov.jo/GBD/en/Budget/Index/general-budget-law.

Hawkins, D. E. 2004. "Sustainable Tourism Competitiveness Clusters: Application to World Heritage Sites Network Development in Indonesia," *Asia Pacific Journal of Tourism Research,* 9, 3 (September), 293–307.

Kafafi, Ze. A. 2014. "Modern Human Activities Impact on the Archaeological Heritage: An Example from the Site Jebel Abu Thawwab," in P. Bieliński, M. Gawlikowski, R. Koliński, D. Ławecka, A. Sołtysiak, and Z. Wygnańska (eds.), *Proceedings of the 8th International Congress on the Archaeology of the Ancient Near East,* 3 (Wiesbaden: Otto Harrassowitz Verlag), 283–294.

Kersel, M. M., and Chesson, M. S. 2011. "Not the Usual Suspects: New Directions in Community Archaeology," *The SAA Archaeological Record,* 11, 4, 43–46.

Kersel, M. M., and Chesson, M. S. 2013. "Tomato Season in the Ghor Es-Safi: A Lesson in Community Archaeology," *Near Eastern Archaeology,* 76, 3, 159–165.

King, T. F. 2016. *Doing Archaeology: A Cultural Resource Management Perspective* (Abingdon, UK: Routledge).

LaBianca, Ø. 2017b. "Community Archaeology at Tall Hisban" *Andrews University Seminary Studies,* 55, 1, 5–27.

LaBianca, Ø., and Walker, B. J. 2007. "Tall Hisban: Palimpsest of Great and Little Traditions of Transjordan and the Ancient Near East," in T. E. Levy, P. M. Michèle Daviau, R. W. Younker, and M. Shaer (eds.), *Crossing Jordan: North American Contributions to the Archaeology of Jordan* (London: Equinox), 111–120.

LaBianca, Ø. S. 1991. "Food Systems Research: An Overview and a Case Study from Madaba Plains, Jordan," *Food and Foodways*, 4, 3–4, 221–235.

LaBianca, Ø. S. 2007a. "Great and Little Traditions: A Framework for Studying Cultural Interaction Through the Ages in Jordan," *Studies in the History and Archaeology of Jordan*, 9, 275–289.

LaBianca, Ø. S. 2007b. "Thinking Globally and Also Locally: Anthropology, History and Archaeology in the Study of Jordan's Past," in T. E. Levy, P. M. Michèle Daviau, R. W. Younker, and M. Shaer (eds.), *Crossing Jordan: North American Contributions to the Archaeology of Jordan* (London: Equinox), 3–11.

LaBianca, Ø. S. 2017a. "Tall Hisban" Sidebar, in R. Clark, L. T. Geraty, L. G. Herr, Ø. S. LaBianca, and R. W. Younker, "The Madaba Plains Project @ 50," *ACOR Newsletter*, 29, 1 (Summer), 3.

London, G. 2000. "Ethnoarchaeology and Interpretations of the Past," *Near Eastern Archaeology* 63, 1, 2–8.

Matsuda, A. 2016. "A Consideration of Public Archaeology Theories," *Public Archaeology*, 15, 1, 40–49.

McGimsey, C. R. 1972. *Public Archaeology*. Studies in Archaeology (Cambridge, MA: Academic Press).

Mickel, A. 2016. "Tracing Teams, Texts, and Topics: Applying Social Network Analysis to Understand Archaeological Knowledge Production at Çatalhöyük," *Journal of Archaeological Method and Theory*, 4, 1095–1126.

Mire, S. 2011. "The Knowledge-Centred Approach to the Somali Cultural Emergency and Heritage Development Assistance in Somaliland," *African Archaeological Review*, 28, 71–91.

Mire, S. 2015. "Mapping the Archaeology of Somaliland: Religion, Art, Script, Time, Urbanism, Trade and Empire," *African Archaeological Review*, 32, 111–136.

Moehas, D. n.d. "WHV – Borobudur Village Project," World Heritage Volunteers. World Heritage Centre, http://press-files.anu.edu.au/downloads/press/p223681/html/ch05-daud.xhtml?referer=&page=9

Morgan, C. L., Carter, R., and Michalski, M. 2016. "The Origins of Doha Project: Online Digital Heritage Remediation and Public Outreach in a Vanishing Pearling Town in the Arabian Gulf," *Proceedings of the 20th Conference on Cultural Heritage and New Technologies 2015* (Vienna: Stadtarchäologie Wien), 1–8.

Myers, D., and Dalgity, A. 2012. "The Middle Eastern Geodatabase for Antiquities (MEGA): An Open Source GIS-Based Heritage Site Inventory and Management System," *Change Over Time*, 2, 1, 32–57.

Myers, D., Dalgity, A., and Avramides, I. 2016. "The Arches Heritage Inventory and Management System: A Platform for the Heritage Field," *Journal of Cultural Heritage Management and Sustainable Development*, 6, 2, 213–224.

Nigro, L., Ripepi, G., Hamdan, I., and Yasine, J. 2015. "The Jericho Oasis Archaeological Park: 2015 Interim Report Italian-Palestinian Cooperation for Protection and Valorization of Archaeological Heritage," *Vicino Oriente*, 19, 215–243.

Okamura, K., and Matsuda, A. 2011. "Introduction: New Perspectives in Global Public Archaeology," in K. Okamura and A. Matsuda (eds.), *New Perspectives in Global Public Archaeology* (London: Springer), 1–18.

Politis, K. 2004. "The Conservation and Heritage Management of the Sanctuary of Lot at Dayr 'Ayn 'Abāṭa," *Studies on the History and Archaeology of Jordan*, 10, 259–268.

Politis, K. 2010. "Ancient Landscapes of the Ghores-Sāfi: Surveys and Excavations 1997–2009," *ACOR Newsletter*, 22, 2 (Winter), 1–5.

Politis, K. 2017. "Ghawr As-Safi Survey, Excavation and Conservation Project 2013 and 2015," *Annual of the Department of Antiquities of Jordan*, 58, 541–549.

Porter, B. 2008. "Projects Retrospective," *ACOR*, September 2008, https://www.acorjordan. org/projects-retrospective-2/.

Rawashdeh, S. 2017. "Community Needed to Preserve Archaeological Sites," *The Jordan Times*, June 4, 2017, http://www.jordantimes.com/news/local/community-needed-preserve-archaeological-sites.

Rayne, L., Bradbury, J., Mattingly, D., Philip, G., Bewley, R., and Wilson, A. 2017. "From Above and on the Ground: Geospatial Methods for Recording Endangered Archaeology in the Middle East and North Africa," *Geosciences*, 7, 4, Article 100, 1–31.

Richardson, L.-J., and Almansa-Sánchez, J. 2015. "Do You Even Know What Public Archaeology Is? Trends, Theory, Practice, Ethics," *World Archaeology*, 47, 2, 194–211.

Ronza, M. E. 2016. "Building Awareness: The Challenge of Cultural Community Engagement in Petra: The Temple of Winged Lions Cultural Resources Management Initiative," *Studies in the History and Archaeology of Jordan*, 12, 617–624.

Stub, S. T. 2016. "Expanding the Story," *Archaeology*, 2016, November/December, 26–33.

Thomas, S. 2017. "Community Archaeology," in G. Moshenska (ed.), *Key Concepts in Public Archaeology* (London: University College London), 14–30.

Tully, G. 2007. "Community Archaeology: General Methods and Standards of Practice," *Public Archaeology*, 6, 3, 155–187.

Tully, G. 2009. "Ten Years On: The Community Archaeology Project Quseir, Egypt," *Treballs d'Arqueologia*, 15, 63–78.

Tuttle, C. A. 2013. "Preserving Petra Sustainably (One Step at a Time) The Temple of the Winged Lions Cultural Resource Management Initiative as a Step Forward," *Journal of Eastern Mediterranean Archaeology and Heritage Studies*, 1, 1, 1–23.

USAID SCHEP n.d. "Fact Sheet," http://www.usaidschep.org/contents/Objectives-Fact-Sheet-.aspx.

USAID SCHEP n.d. "Ghawr as Safi," http://usaidschep.org/Contents/Ghor-as-Safi.aspx.

Wall, G., and Black, H. 2004. "Global Heritage and Local Problems: Some Examples from Indonesia," *Current Issues in Tourism*, 7, 4–5, 436–439.

Whitcomb, D., Jennings, M., Creekmore, A., and Arce, I. 2016. "Khirbet al-Mafjar: New Excavations and Hypotheses for an Umayyad Monument," *Near Eastern Archaeology*, 79, 2, 78–87.

Whitcomb, D., and Taha, H. 2013. "Khirbat al-Mafjar and its Place in the Archaeological Heritage of Palestine," *Journal of Eastern Mediterranean Archaeology and Heritage Studies*, 1, 1, 54–65.

World Economic Forum 2017. "The Travel & Tourism Competitiveness Report 2017" (Geneva: World Economic Forum).

Further Reading

Ababneh, A., Darabseh, F. M., and Aloudat, A. S. 2016. "The Management of Natural and Cultural Heritage: A Comparative Study From Jordan," *The Historic Environment: Policy and Practice*, 7, 1, 3–24.

Beale, N. 2012. "How Community Archaeology Can Make Use of Open Data to Achieve Further Its Objectives," *World Archaeology*, 44, 4, 612–633.

Bourdieu, P. 1993. *The Field of Cultural Production: Essays on Art and Literature*, edited by Randal Johnson (Cambridge: Polity Press).

Crutzen, P. J. 2002. "Geology of Mankind," *Nature*, 415, 23.

de Vries, B. 2012."Community and Antiquities at Umm el-Jimal and Silwan: A Comparison," in E. M. Meyers and C. Meyers (eds.), *Archaeology, Bible, Politics and the Media: Proceedings of the Duke University Conference, April 23–24 2009* (Warsaw, IN: Eisenbrauns), 161–186.

#de Vries, B. 2013."Archaeology and Community at Umm el-Jimal," in *Studies in the History and Archaeology of Jordan XI: Changes and Challenges* (Amman, Jordan: Department of Antiquities of Jordan), 81–91.

Elsorady, D. A. 2012. "Heritage Conservation in Rosetta (Rashid): A Tool for Community Improvement and Development," *Cities*, 29, 379–388.

Gould, P. G. 2016. "On the Case: Method in Public and Community Archaeology," *Public Archaeology*, 15, 1 (February), 5–22.

Hodder, I. 2011. "Is a Shared Past Possible? The Ethics and Practice of Archaeology in the Twenty-First Century," in K. Okamura and A. Matsuda (eds.), *New Perspectives in Global Public Archaeology* (London: Springer), 19–28.

LaBianca, Ø. 2009. "The Poly-Centric Nature of Social Order in the Middle East: Preliminary Reflections from Anthropological Archaeology," in P. Biekkowski (ed.), *Studies on Iron Age Moab and Neighbouring Areas in Honour of Michele Daviau*. Ancient Near Eastern Studies Supplement, 29 (Leuven: Peeters), 1–5.

LaBianca, Ø. S. 1984. "Objectives, Procedures, and Findings of Ethnoarchaeological Research in the Vicinity of Hesban in Jordan," *Annual of the Department of Antiquities*, 28, 269–287.

LaBianca, Ø. S. 1990. *Sedentarization and Nomadization: Food System Cycles at Hesban and Vicinity in Transjordan* (Berrien Springs, MI: Andrews University Press).

LaBianca, Ø. S., and Arnold Scham, S. (eds.) 2006. *Connectivity in Antiquity: Globalization as a Long-Term Historical Process* (London: Equinox).

Luke, C. M., and Kersel, M. M. 2013. *United States Cultural Diplomacy and Archaeology: Soft Power, Hard Heritage*. Routledge Studies in Archaeology, 6 (New York: Routledge).

Moser, S., Glazier, D., Phillips, J. E., Nasser el Nemr, L., Saleh Mousa, M., Nasr Aiesh, R., Richardson, S., Conner, A., and Seymour, M. 2002. "Transforming Archaeology through Practice: Strategies for Collaborative Archaeology and the Community Archaeology Project at Quseir, Egypt," *World Archaeology*, 34, 2, 220–248.

Moshenska, G. 2017. "Introduction: Public Archaeology as Practice and Scholarship Where Archaeology Meets the World," in G. Moshenska (ed.), *Key Concepts in Public Archaeology* (London: University College London), 1–13.

Mubaideen, S., and Al Kurdi, N. 2017. "Heritage Conservation and Urban Development: A Supporting Management Model for the Effective Incorporation of Archaeological Sites in the Planning Process," *Journal of Cultural Heritage*, 28, 117–128.

Pardoe, C. 1990. "Sharing the Past: Aboriginal Influence on Archaeological Practice, a Case Study from New South Wales," *Aboriginal History*, 14, 2, 208–223.

Perring, D., and van der Linde, S. 2009. "The Politics and Practice of Archaeology in Conflict," *Conservation and Management of Archaeological Sites*, 11, 3–4, 197–213.

Simmons, A. H., and Najjar, M. 2013. "Joint Custody: An Archaeological Park at Neolithic Ghwair I, Jordan," *Near Eastern Archaeology*, 76, 3, 178–185.

Steffen, W., Broadgate, W., Deutsch, L., Gaffney, O., and Ludwig, C. 2015. "The Trajectory of the Anthropocene: The Great Acceleration," *The Anthropocene Review*, 2, 1, 81–98.

Tennie, C., Call, J., and Tomasello, M. 2009. "Ratcheting up the Ratchet: On the Evolution of Cumulative Culture," *Philosophical Transactions of the Royal Society of London B: Biological Sciences*, 364, 2405–2415.

Throsby, D. 2016. "Investment in Urban Heritage Conservation in Developing Countries: Concepts, Methods and Data," *City, Culture and Society*, 7, 81–86.

CHAPTER 6.2

·······································

HERITAGE IN CONTEXT

·······································

NASSER RABBAT

THE built heritage in the Middle East is in greater danger today than it has been since the mid-19th century, when archeological and historic sites were open fields for the collector, the antiquarian, and the looter. Vicious and destructive civil wars or a variation thereof in Syria, Iraq, Libya, and Yemen have destroyed entire urban districts and countless valuable buildings and artifacts and left the rest in jeopardy with hardly any governmental or communal protection. Milder forms of civil strife still simmering in Afghanistan, Pakistan, Egypt, Tunisia, Palestine, and Algeria have exposed many of their remote historical sites and provincial museums to the vagaries of lawlessness and international criminal networks specializing in looting and trafficking of historical artifacts. Some of this illegal trafficking is finding its way to the burgeoning art markets and private collections of the Arabian Gulf countries, which have developed an appetite for collecting art as alternative investment and as a sign of the worldly and urbane lifestyle adopted by their elite while their neighborhoods crumble. Egypt, finally, the cornerstone of the region, which reverted back to a military regime hoping that it could regain some security and stability, is unable to rein in what appears to be organized looting of its historic sites, including those in the heart of its capital, and the dismantling or damaging of their fragile artifacts. The Middle Eastern heritage is in peril precisely because an entire regime of nation states based on a European plan that dates back to World War I is dissolving, and there are no reassuring indications of what will replace it other than the chaos that reigns today (Dabashi 2012).

This is, of course, an unusual introduction to the topic of heritage and its preservation assigned to me by the editor of this volume. But it is not inappropriate. In fact, any discussion of heritage and its preservation is per force predicated on a sense of shared identity with a defined territory and a collective history, and this is exactly what is being challenged today in the Middle East (Appiah 2006). That facile notion of heritage that stems from a secure national identity is hard to sustain in today's Middle Eastern environment as both history and geography are being contested, reclaimed, and reconfigured by groups within or outside the borders of the nation state. Consequently, the heritage itself is being divided and reappropriated, and the unfortunate parts of it that fall under the custody of a group that does not recognize it as its own heritage, or as heritage at all, is being destroyed. This was most spectacularly demonstrated when the Taliban blew up the Buddhas of Bamiyan in Afghanistan in March 2001 as relics of paganism and thus alien heritage (Flood 2002). But more recent acts of vandalism and destruction of Pharaonic and Islamic treasures in Egypt; of mosques, churches, castles, and historic and modern statues in Iraq and Syria; the wanton massive bombardment of world heritage sites in Syria, Yemen, Libya, and Iraq; and the looting of museums across the region show that the phenomena of destruction is broader than just a collateral casualty of civil strife or swift fundamentalist reaction against allegedly forbidden art. In fact, the selectivity and thoroughness of the destruction, the indifference of a large percentage of the people whose presumed heritage is being destroyed, and the complicity of many of the political actors, including foreign governments, in these heinous acts suggest that not only the importance of preserving the heritage, but the meaning and scope of heritage itself are far from resolved in the contemporary Middle East (Shaw 2015).

The destruction of heritage in the Middle East is not a recent trend, even though its disastrous consequences have become more flagrantly apparent in the last couple of years with the crumbling of law and order in most countries of the region (Mulder 2017). The road to the current situation, however, was neither straightforward nor even predictable. It was in fact paved with good intentions, which aimed at nothing less than instituting a built heritage of the nation and worked very hard at preserving and rehabilitating as much of its landmarks as possible. That these efforts have been undermined by conspiracy, neglect, ignorance, greed, official flippancy, and recently a destructive ideological streak is in no way an indication of their insincerity. It only points to a fundamental failure at understanding the context in which the notion of heritage has been imported, implanted, and marketed in the Middle East as a buttress of a preordained national pride when the definitions of both heritage and nationalism themselves had been unstable, challenged, and ultimately rejected by several dissenting and vigorously ideological contenders to the national collective identity. Reexamining the checkered history of this process of matching heritage to national identity as it meandered through colonialism, modernization, and the botched project of nation-building would help us appreciate the political and geopolitical context of heritage definition and preservation and its political, socioeconomic, and urban repercussions, all of which had a direct impact on which historic cities were preserved or rehabilitated and which neglected, which monuments in these cities were privileged and restored and which ignored—and, the most revealing question, why.

IN THE BEGINNING WAS THE *COMITÉ*

Like nationalism, interest in the built heritage as a standing proof of national history in the modern Middle East was both inspired by European models and fueled by a mounting resistance to European colonialism. Ironically, the first concerted effort at preserving heritage in a Middle Eastern country was initiated by a Frenchman and an agent of French cultural imperialism: Auguste Mariette Pasha, who in 1858 was appointed the first "Conservator of Egyptian Monuments" by Saïd Pasha, the ruler of Egypt, only a few years after he had been accused of theft and destruction when he was digging in Egypt and brazenly sending all of his findings to the Louvre (David 1994). But as an official in the Egyptian administration, Mariette established the first Egyptian Museum in 1863 and regulated the excavations in Egypt, which had until then been more like looting expeditions led by European archeologists and adventurers who blatantly collected artifacts for their countries' museums and private collectors. His reforms, however, did not eliminate the practice that has cost Egypt countless treasures; they just legalized it through an arrangement of dividing the finds 50–50 with the Egyptian government while providing the latter with a supervisory role in the division of the artifacts. This procedure was not always effective. Many superior artifacts were still finding their ways to European institutions. The German archeologist Ludwig Borchardt, for example, tricked the Egyptian inspectors in 1912 into believing the famous bust of Nefertiti, the pride of place in the Neues Museum in Berlin, was of inferior quality. In this way, he was able keep it in the Prussian half of the finds (Breger 2005).

Understandably, attention to Egypt's Islamic culture was slower in coming for the two main parties interested in Egyptian heritage: the European explorers and the Egyptians themselves. The Egyptians were only beginning to reconstruct their national identity following the brief but challenging French occupation of 1798–1801 and the reformist project of Muhammad 'Ali Pacha (1805–48). They were only slowly discovering the importance of this built and lived-in heritage in consolidating that identity and in mooring it in their country's glorious history. The Western archeologists, scholars, and collectors, and Europe behind them, saw Ancient Egypt as a primordial stage in the West's own civilizational evolution. Their interest in its heritage thus amounted to an almost para-national pursuit, one that translated into the ardent acquisition of Egyptian artifacts and the building of special museums to display them, starting with the Département des Antiquités Égyptiennes at the Louvre Museum, founded in 1827, under the directorship of Jean-François Champollion. Islamic Egypt, on the other hand, did not enjoy the same status in the eyes of Europe. It actually belonged to another civilizational path that was historically antagonistic to Europe, and one that Europe was concurrently in the process of colonizing. Nonetheless, interest in the cultures of Islam had been part of the European scholastic tradition for centuries, and it was intensifying with the onset of the Colonial Age, which brought with it an ease of travel and safe access to regions that were formerly closed to foreigners in addition, of course, to a growing interest among the European ruling classes in understanding the cultures of the countries they were about to colonize in order to rule them better. Moreover, the fast pace of demolition or disfiguring of Islamic monuments in Cairo in particular, most of which was due to hasty expansion, alarmed those Europeans who studied them and the educated Egyptians who had begun to see them as cultural markers. Pressure from learned societies and prominent scholars was mounting to counter that downward trend, so, in December 1881, the Comité de Conservation des Monuments de l'Art Arabe was established in Cairo by Khedive Tawfiq to manage and supervise the conservation of Egypt's Islamic monuments and artifacts (El-Habashi 2001, 2003).

The Comité, which was dominated by European scholars and architects from its founding until its dissolution after the revolution of July 1952, played a major role not only in deciding which Islamic monuments to preserve and how, but also in defining the meaning of heritage and the scope and function of its conservation for generations to come. Historicist and at times antiquarian in its collective thinking, the Comité focused more on the early periods, Tulunid, Fatimid, Ayyubid, and especially Mamluk, and paid little attention to Ottoman or later monuments, which it considered to be either foreign to Egypt or derivative. Unsurprisingly, the selection of monuments to preserve was based primarily on their aesthetic value and touristic appeal, to the detriment of other considerations. Moreover, strongly adhering to a method that viewed style as developing along a steady evolutionary trajectory, the Comité restored monuments that had lost many of their distinguishing features to reflect their standing in such a strict stylistic evolution. The mosque of al-Salih Tala'i', for instance, a late Fatimid mosque built in the 1160s and totally ruined when the Comité decided to restore it, was reconstructed to stylistically look midway between the al-Aqmar mosque, a Fatimid oratory constructed in 1125, and the Madrasa of al-Salih Najm al-Din Ayyub completed in 1248, without any actual archeological or archival proof (Bierman 1995) (Figures 6.2.1, 6.2.2, and 6.2.3).

But the most significant aspect of the Comité's approach to preservation is that it had little interest in the city as a living urban whole. This was perhaps because awareness of

FIGURE 6.2.1 Façade of al-Aqmar mosque.

Courtesy of Nasser Rabbat.

FIGURE 6.2.2 Façade of the mosque of al-Salih Tala'i'.

Courtesy of Nasser Rabbat.

the larger context of heritage preservation was still in formation even in nations that had been conserving and rehabilitating historic monuments for a long time, such as France and England. It may also have been so because Cairo was seen as a socially and spatially cohesive pre-modern city at the turn of the 20th century, when the Comité was at the height of its activities. Or it could have been that the members of the Comité, who were mostly Western Orientalists, held the romantic view of their peers that contemporary Cairo was hopelessly mired in its medieval mess and saw their mission as rescuing its monuments from the disorder that engulfed them by restoring to them their original appearance, untainted by their long history of modifications and restorations or their functionality in present times. Conserving, clearing access to, and staging spectacular perspectives of the monuments as precious objects to be visited and admired by those who could appreciate them (i.e., Westerners and enlightened Westernized Orientals) was thus the Comité's top priority.

This antiquarian approach, copied by most Middle Eastern national conservation organizations that followed in the next century, resulted in museumifying and/or monumentalizing architecture as independent from its urban fabric or socioeconomic context. That some of the surrounding and sustaining urban fabric needed to be cleared and some lifestyles disrupted in the process was justified as a preservation imperative, or at least this is how many master plans produced in the middle of the 20th century presented it. An earlier example of this approach is the modernizing plan of old Cairo initiated by Khedive Isma'il (r. 1863–79) and advocated by 'Ali Pasha Mubarak in the 1880s,

FIGURE 6.2.3 Façade the Madrasa of al-Salih Najm al-Din Ayyub.

Courtesy of Sheila Blair and Jonathan Bloom.

which involved the erasure of entire areas to provide straight vehicular access to the dense urban fabric of the medieval city. Like his patron Khedive Isma'il, Mubarak, a French-educated Egyptian who was minister of Public Works, was fascinated by Hausmann's plan of Paris with its swift incisions into the old, dense fabric of the pre-modern city, which Mubarak examined first-hand when he visited Paris with his sovereign for the Exposition Universelle of 1867. The Comité resisted the plan on the grounds of its disregard of the historical monuments, which it had removed in large numbers irrespective of their historical or artistic values. Mubarak, who was an ex-officio member of the Comité, argued that the old city needed this intervention to provide it with better circulation, hygienic standards, and infrastructural services. But the plan was only half-executed as the Egyptian government fell into bankruptcy and became unable to carry out the large-scale modernizing plans initiated by the overambitious Khedive Isma'il. The plan was discarded altogether after the country was occupied by Great Britain in 1882. Vestiges of it, however, in the form of cut-through streets in the dense urban fabric of the old city of Cairo, kept on appearing in subsequent interventions right down to the end of the 20th century.

THE COLONIAL LAYER

The early debates between conservationists and modernizers occasioned by the intervention in old Cairo under Khedive Isma"' No this is a 'ayn in Arabic and is expressed with one apostrophe il intensified under colonial rule. Preoccupied with spatial control and security in the densely populated cities of the Middle East, the colonial authorities adopted planning strategies that enabled surveillance, military movement, and crowd control. They also openly held more extreme views about the civilizational difference between the West and the East ("never the twain shall meet," as Rudyard Kipling would have it), which often translated into urban separation between the colonized natives and the colonizing administrative class made up of colonial officers, settlers, and Westernized locals who were mostly non-Muslims. The old cities or medinas, however, continued to be the hubs of urban life in the colonies, and the planning strategies of colonial control had to be coupled with more practical considerations, such as vehicular access, essential infrastructure, and the provision for tourism in conjunction with the continuing efforts at monuments' preservation. The monuments to be preserved conformed to the received ideas about the cultures that produced them. Hybrid or modern, European-influenced monuments that challenged the notions of cultural separation or discontinuity with the past received hardly any attention from the colonial conservationists. Some of these monuments, like the Boujloud Gate in Fez (rebuilt by the French in 1913) (Aygen 2013) or the Jerusalem Clock Tower at the Jaffa Gate (built by the Ottomans in 1907 and demolished by the British in 1922) were actually demolished as stylistically inauthentic and alien to the traditional environment in which they stood (Chesterton 1920).

The different nature of the colonial enterprise in the various colonies of the Middle East resulted in distinct overall planning approaches. In the cities of North Africa, where France and Italy—the former occupying Morocco, Algeria, and Tunisia, the latter Libya—envisaged the settling of colonials as a means to perpetually lay claim to the land, new cities or *nouvelles villes* exclusively reserved for the colonials were planned next to the historic medinas where the native population lived. Such, for instance, was the strategy promulgated by General Hubert Lyautey, the first French Resident General in

Morocco, whose architect, Henri Prost, produced plans for Marrakesh, Fez, Meknes, Rabat, and Casablanca that mummified the historic medinas and isolated them from the *nouvelles villes* established in the late 1910s and 1920s (Radoine 2002). An extreme example of the North African dual colonial city is Le Corbusier's 1933 Plan Obus for Algiers. It proposed a gigantic viaduct connecting a business center on the docks to an undulating, oppressively massive residential zone on the hillside behind the city via a rapid motorway perched above the "Arab City" or the *Casbah* (Figure 6.2.4). Encapsulating themes of detachment, segregation, surveillance, and intentional neglect, the plan treated the Casbah more as an exotic yet despised spectacle, or as a colorful reserve for the natives to be seen from above but not to be incorporated in the new scheme (Lamprakos 1992).

In the cities of Iraq, Syria, Lebanon, and Palestine, colonized later after the dissolution of the Ottoman Empire and in a softer fashion with no European settlers (except for Palestine), the colonial authorities intervened directly in the old medinas by cutting wide, straight boulevards that connected them to the new, European-style neighborhoods developed outside for the bourgeois classes that were increasingly adopting European customs and lifestyles. This was the case in cities like Damascus, Aleppo,

FIGURE 6.2.4 Architectural model of Plan Obus

Courtesy of FLC/ADAGP, Paris/Artists Rights Society (ARS), New York 2018. Photograph by Lucien Hervé. The Getty Research Institute, Los Angeles (2002.R.41). 56638248-f905-4cca-b89f-393f5b32da4c@exchange.mit

Beirut, Baghdad, Jerusalem, Jaffa, and other smaller cities in the region, even though the migration of the bourgeoisie to the new neighborhoods dated back to the end of the Ottoman period when the reforms (*tanzimat*) adopted European modernization as a way to catch up with the West (Hanssen et al. 2002).

The first post-independence governments in the still-forming nation states of the Middle East were controlled by the bourgeois and land-owning classes. Nationalist in a romantic way, they deployed a blend of political liberalism, social conservatism, modernization, and laissez-faire economics as the framework of their state-building (Watenpaugh 2006). They maintained most of the colonial (read modern) economic, administrative, and social policies and structures in matters of zoning, hygiene, landscape, and traffic but tried to nationalize the cityscape through a few symbolic gestures like changing the streets' names that the colonial authorities Europeanized back to Arabic, removing statues of colonial figures and replacing them with national heroes, and patronizing architectural styles for public buildings that harked back to the glorious local, Arabic, or Islamic past. Colonial urban planning, however, continued to be the driving force behind the development of their cities long after the end of colonial rule. Michel Écochard, for instance, a French architect-planner who worked under colonial rule in Syria, Lebanon, and Morocco on master plans for Damascus, Beirut, and Casablanca, was hired by the post-independence governments in these three and other Middle Eastern countries (Iran, Kuwait, and Oman) to produce master plans for Saida in Lebanon (1956–1958), Beirut (1963), Damascus (1964–1968), and Tabriz, Mashhad, and Tehran in Iran (1967, 1971, and 1978, respectively) among many other postcolonial cities (Verdeil 2012). Écochard had started his career in Mandate Syria in the 1930s, working primarily as a restoration architect of all types of historic buildings (from the 18th-century Azem Palace in Damascus to the 2nd-century arched gate of Palmyra). His fascination with highlighting the importance of historical monuments might have informed his later approach to rehabilitating historic cities. A common feature in his plans for the historic cities' centers like Aleppo, Damascus, and Mashhad, is the clearing of spatial cordons around major monuments in an attempt to highlight their historic and artistic values that is reminiscent of the smaller scale interventions of the Comité de Conservation des Monuments de l'Art Arabe in Cairo more than half a century earlier.

But Écochard's was only one attitude among many toward planning the historic cities of the Middle East in this transitional period between colonialism and independence. Other approaches existed, ranging from the radically modernist to the highly historicist or fictionally historical. Frank Lloyd Wright's approach, for instance, was decidedly very romantic and unabashedly fanciful in its engagement with the notion of heritage. His plan for Greater Baghdad in 1957–1958, which comprised an opera house, museums, a zoo, and a university campus centered on an island in the middle of the river Tigris and spread on the two banks, is nothing less than a modernist Oriental fantasy (Levine 1996). Recalling the Round-city of al-Mansur, built in the 8th century, the project came complete with an assortment of naïve references to what an American raised at the end of the 19th century would have thought of the Orient through his reading of the *One Thousand and One Nights* (Figure 6.2.5). A 100-meter-tall, gilded statue of the Caliph Harun

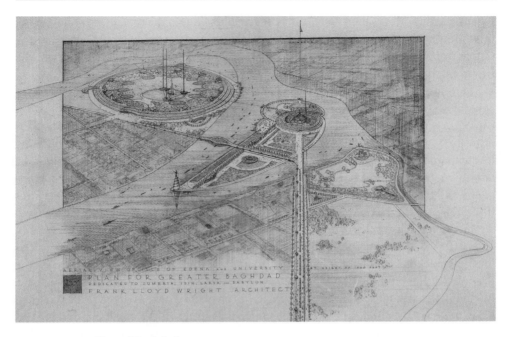

FIGURE 6.2.5 Plan of Baghdad.

al-Rashid, the alleged Caliph of the Arabian Nights, was to be mounted on a spiraling base resembling the Malwiya Minaret at the 9th-century Mosque of al-Mutawakkil in Samarra to form the northern tip of the island complex. The vertical faces were to depict camels climbing the spiraling ramp, a favorite topos of the Orient. The opera house, a domed structure ringed by an arcade and sliced by a gigantic arch, was to be decorated with scenes from the Arabian Nights, and its perforated dome wrapped around a statue of none other than Aladdin holding his lamp, in addition to two statues of Adam and Eve in the surrounding garden, symbolizing the Garden of Eden, all from the imagination of a master architect who implored local building professionals in a lecture he delivered in Baghdad to connect to "what is deep in the spirit of the place" (al-Sultany 2008).

NATIONALISM AND MODERNIZATION

The rather gentle and paternalistic form of post-independence government that continued the patterns of traditional patronage and class structure was shattered after 1948. The insertion of Israel in the heart of the Arab East caused deep fissures in an already embattled political culture, with the youth and disenfranchised provincial masses clamoring for a bigger role in the definition of their countries' national identity. A series of military coups ensued (Syria 1949, Egypt, 1952, Iraq 1957) promising deliverance on many internal and external fronts but ending up by obliterating the budding civic values inherited from their bourgeois predecessors (Owen 2002). Lacking some of the crucial components of legitimate governments, these incompetent military regimes overcompensated by an exaggerated reliance on the politics of class and identity. New, powerful concepts, such as historical identity, authenticity, and the recovery of the Arabic cultural roots, rose to the pinnacle of political and public interests (Choueiri 2000). Heritage, *turāth* in Arabic, became a byword for a protracted cultural debate between traditionalism and modernism that occupied the intelligentsia for decades to come. But the actual preservation of the built heritage remained as it was under colonial authorities, a mostly artistic pursuit aimed at conserving valuable historical monuments, though these buildings had now been endowed with new meanings as sources of national pride and signs of cultural genius that preceded the colonial disruption.

In the meantime, the military regimes adopted ambitious modernization programs, complete with land reforms, socialization of basic services, and huge urban projects that were meant to herald the new age of progress. The socialist framework was predicated on a modern working class that was defined and celebrated through grandiose, poorly conceived, and hastily implemented agricultural, industrial, educational, and infrastructural projects (Rogan 2000). This changed the face of Arab cities, which acquired new, large governmental complexes, whole new administrative and industrial districts, a variety of public housing projects, and universities, schools, and entertainment facilities. This formal architectural modernism, sometimes softened by symbolic references to history or gestures toward climate and site, apparently rested on the assumption that modernist building projects could stand in for expressions of modernity. In that, they joined other symbols of modernity, such as dress codes, appearances, behavior, and attitudes copied from the West, that did not penetrate into the society beyond the urbane, educated classes.

National modernization, alas, remained incomplete in the face of inherited or created geopolitical, historical, and social contradictions. It further suffered from corruption and autocratic mismanagement, compounded by the protracted yet irresolute conflict with Israel and the overwhelmingly interventionist Cold War politics that drowned the region in endless scheming. The startling defeat in the war of 1967 with Israel ushered the end of the grand plan of building modern states by exposing its structural, historical, and ideological contradictions (Mitchell 2000). The 1970s and 1980s saw the dismantling of the faltering socialist experiments and their gradual replacement with a statist form of crony capitalism, initiated in Egypt by Anwar al-Sadat, with the misleadingly liberal name *infitāḥ* (opening up).

The autocratic regimes, however, clung to power. Over the next two decades, they hardened into tyrannical dictatorships devoid of any political pretensions, whose sole purpose was to enrich their narrow base of supporters while their countries faced acute administrative and management problems, infrastructural exhaustion, demographic explosion, and socioeconomic inequality that affected the provinces more than it did the cities. Consequently, desperate rural migration flooded the cities in the 1980s and

1990s, which swelled at an unprecedented rate to house the bursting poor population in any available areas, which included the old urban cores (Barakat 1993). Degradation accelerated as a result, which prompted calls for a more holistic understanding of the import of the built heritage and its urban, socioeconomic, and political entanglements. The historic cities urgently needed more sensible urban management that would balance the requirements of heritage preservation, public services, and economic development. Plans were drawn and financial support was sought from national governments, international organizations, and Western donor governments that were pushing for a global custody of endangered national cultural heritage, although they were motivated less by the socioeconomic conditions of the old cities' dwellers and more by their own interests (World Bank 2001).

Sanaa, Yemen, led the way when the government established the General Organization for the Preservation of Old Sana'a in 1984 and proceeded to ask the UNESCO, the UN Development Programme (UNDP), and several Western countries for funding and technical expertise in preparing and executing a comprehensive plan for the preservation of the old city. The project lasted several years and resulted in the rehabilitation of many sections of the old city, the upgrading of its infrastructure, and the training of a new generation of conservators (Lamprakos 2015). Deemed successful, Old Sana'a was designated a UNESCO World Heritage Site in 1988, and was awarded an Aga Khan Award for Architecture in 1995. Damascus, Aleppo, Jeddah, Kuwait, Tunis, Rabat-Salé, Fez, Marrakesh, Tripoli, Cairo, Jerusalem, Hebron, and other cities followed, with new plans ratified by UNESCO and supported by international aid agencies that aimed to move from conserving individual monuments to rehabilitating the old city as a living and economically viable urban entity with an integrated architectural heritage (Hassan et al. 2008). Some of these projects were more successful than others; some were abandoned due to lack of funding or of sustained governmental commitment; and some are still ongoing.

But this is only half the story. The top-down policy directives, so characteristic of the erratic, authoritarian, and corrupt regimes, ignored the most important constituent of the old cities: their native inhabitants. Eager to exploit the newly rehabilitated districts in the old cities and to bring in tourism as a means of diversifying income in hard currency, the authorities mostly adopted those sections of the master plans that brought upmarket restaurants, chic artisanal shops, and boutique hotels to the old city without any sustained attempt to remedy the disastrous housing situation or to upgrade the rundown infrastructure, let alone address any of the severe demographic, social, and economic problems facing the inhabitants. The exceptions to this general state of affairs were the few holistic projects of conservation that treated the city as a living urban entity with an integrated architectural heritage. Examples include the now canceled revitalization of al-Darb al-Ahmar in Cairo by the Aga Khan Trust for Culture, which lasted for more than fifteen years and aimed at rehabilitating this historical district adjacent to the newly established al-Azhar Park along the Ayyubid walls of the city (Daftary et al. 2010). Also of note are the Hebron Rehabilitation Committee's revitalization project of the old city of Hebron and the revitalization of Birzeit historic center by Riwaq (Centre for

Architectural Conservation, Ramallah) in Palestine, both of which received the Aga Khan Award for Architecture, the first in 1998 and the second in 2013.

Neoliberalism and Heritage Commodification

By the end of the 20th century, a palpable neoliberal push toward more investment in tourism and entertainment shifted the interest in heritage toward further luxury projects that sometimes encompassed whole neighborhoods in the old cities, which were turned into art colonies, luxury hospitality zone, or museum and artisanal areas. Moreover, preserving the built heritage became a topic of public policy debates, scholarly conferences, TV programs, and aid packages, especially those negotiated with the UNDP, UNESCO, the USAID, the EU Directorate-General for International Cooperation and Development, and the various EU countries' cooperation organizations, as well as the Aga Khan Development Network (AKDN). It also became a lucrative profession, with an entire subsector of research groups, design firms, and construction companies, as well as touristic services focused on heritage conservation and rehabilitation (Alsayyad 2001). The region thus entered the 21st century with part of its historic cities overrestored or misrestored and turned into glitzy settings for high-end cultural activities and tourist attractions while the rest of the urban fabric still suffered from the chronic problems of poverty, overcrowding, and neglect, to which were added the new problems resulting from manipulated planning such as unequal development, targeted gentrification, and overloading of the already stretched infrastructure (Silver 2010).

Regional and global events at the end of the 20th century tightened the grip of the already potent blend of statism and crony capitalism over the Middle Eastern countries while further weakening their social fiber and the little leftover economic stability from earlier times. First was the series of strategic realignments, ruinous civil wars, invasions, and counter-invasions that befell the region from the Lebanese civil war (1975–1991) to the devastation of Iraq after the American-led invasion of 2003. The collapse of the Soviet Union in 1991 and the dissolution of its socialist model further emboldened an already rampant capitalism to extend its reach all over the globe (Gelvin 2005). The Arabian Gulf states, having lain outside the centers of Arabic culture for so long, emerged at this juncture as the new economic powerhouses of the region. Awash in oil cash and eager to diversify and secure new sources of income, they presented the perfect combination of lucrative markets and affluent partners in global capitalism.

Following the model of Dubai, the Gulf cities underwent the world's most phenomenal real estate boom in the past twenty years (Bagaeen 2007). These "utopian capitalist cities," to use Mike Davis's term, acquired super-slick high-rises and lavish shopping malls that broke all previous norms of size, form, function, and, often, economic purpose and urban vision (Davis 2006). They also almost totally razed the remnants of their traditional urban fabrics both to erase the memories of the days of poverty and to make way for new, more profitable developments. A few restored houses, sustained by nostalgia and huge infusions of capital, were left standing alone like museum pieces with no real connection to the bustling city around them (Cooke 2013).

The effects of this real estate capitalism, however, were felt more in the older and poorer cities of the region. Having become the most accessible and attractive job market for the masses of unemployed Middle Eastern and South Asian workers and the supplier of the majority of tourists visiting poorer countries, the Gulf city-states exerted tremendous influence not only on the economy, but also on the cultural and social mores of their neighboring countries. They also wielded considerable control over urban development through their real estate investment. Dubai-style developments spread into historic cities like Cairo, Damascus, Beirut, and Rabat, which accelerated their physical decay by cutting through their urban fabrics and siphoning funds away from their public services (Rowe and Sarkis 1998). But the most alarming consequence of this relentless manipulation of capital was the fading away of the civic qualities that were slowly acquired in the old cities over the past two centuries and their replacement by a market-driven commodification process, one that split the cities into two extremes. On one end, the old, poor quarters were robbed of the last vestiges of civil life and turned into run-down village-like neighborhoods living by their own informal and traditional codes. On the other end, the newly rich districts, which mushroomed on the peripheries of the cities, assumed a consumerist and globalized identity that has no local feel or sense of belonging ('Abd al-Fattah 1999; Abaza 2001; Bagaeen 2012).

WHAT NOW?

The popular revolts of the tragic "Arab Spring" that erupted in 2011 were partially a response to these dismal living conditions (Noueihed and Warren 2012). The masses of protesters aimed at nothing less than to redress the unjust political and socioeconomic perversion that had for more than half a century impressed upon them an obligation to sacrifice their civil rights and economic security for their repeatedly redefined national identity. They demanded more equitable urban and economic policies and more say in their affairs and their future. But their revolts were subverted by a combination of entrenched, corrupt regimes and militant fundamentalist movements or a struggle between the two, aided often by external actors. These revolts ultimately failed to effect any real change, except perhaps in Tunisia. Instead, we have today destructive civil wars or variations thereof raging all over the region and political instability or a return to autocratic rule in most countries. We have massive displacements of population that are not only changing the demographics of the region and its neighbors, but also upsetting the balance between the urban and the rural and overcrowding cities whose infrastructures are already crumbling under the weight of enormous populations. We have destroyed cities and villages in Syria, Yemen, Iraq, and Libya and threatened heritage everywhere, if not by violence, vengeance, and destruction, then by neglect, ignorance, and commodification. And we have a rising tide of a new and self-righteous fundamentalist thinking that rejects all principles, not only of modern life, but also of civic society (Farouk-Alli 2006).

These devastating post-2011 developments painfully exposed and magnified the glaring contradictions in the understanding of heritage and its relation to identity in the Middle East. They revealed the need to rethink the conceptual framework of heritage and to devise a long-term plan that combines political and social rehabilitation and material and urban reconstruction together with heritage preservation. This may be enabled through the formulation of a right to heritage that builds on the thinking that has evolved in the past two decades on *the right to the city*: an inclusive and egalitarian discourse that engages, in addition to the professional and technical aspects of its subject matter, a set of encompassing political, social, legal, and financial issues (Harvey 2003). These may range from decisions about governance, legal framework, and fair representation to the use of education to teach citizens about their rights and duties and to highlight the ties that bind them to their towns or cities and their country at large and, finally, to the primacy of public funding over private investment in accommodating the socio-economic needs of citizens and in providing for the welfare of the cities and historic sites and the upkeep of their infrastructure and services as well as their historic monuments. This civic framing should aim to rescue the actual built heritage from neglect, capitalist commodification, bureaucratic calcification, and, most importantly, the kind of extremist bigotry that benefitted from the chaos reigning in the region today to spread its destructive doctrine.

References

Abaza, M. 2001. "Shopping Malls, Consumer Culture and the Reshaping of Public Space in Egypt," *Theory, Culture & Society*, 18, 5, 97–122.

'Abd al-Fattah, N. 1999. "The Anarchy of Egyptian Legal System: Wearing Away the Legal and Political Modernity," in B. Dupret, M. Berger, and L. al-Zwaini (eds.), *Legal Pluralism in the Arab World* (The Hague: Kluwer Law International), 159–172.

Alsayyad, N. (ed.) 2001. *Consuming Tradition, Manufacturing Heritage: Global Norms and Urban Forms in the Age of Tourism* (London/New York: Routledge).

Appiah K. A. 2006. *Cosmopolitanism: Ethics in a World of Strangers* (New York: W.W. Norton & Company).

Aygen, Zeynep. 2013. *International Heritage and Historic Building Conservation: Saving the World's Past* (New York: Routledge).

Bagaeen, S. 2007. "Brand Dubai: The Instant City; or the Instantly Recognizable City," *International Planning Studies*, 12, 2, 173–197.

Bagaeen, S. 2012. "Gated Urban Life Versus Kinship and Social Solidarity in the Middle East," in S. Bagaeen and O. Uduku (eds.), *Gated Communities: Social Sustainability in Contemporary and Historical Gated Developments* (London: Earthscan), 15–26.

Barakat, H. I. 1993. *The Arab World: Society, Culture, and State* (Berkeley: University of California Press).

Bierman. I. A. 1995. "Urban Memory and the Preservation of Monuments," in Jere Bacharach (ed.) *The Restoration and Conservation of Islamic Monuments in Egypt* (Cairo: American University in Cairo Press), 1–10.

Breger, C. 2005 "Imperialist Fantasy and Displaced Memory: Twentieth-Century German Egyptologies" *New German Critique*, 96, 135–169.

Chesterton, G. K. 2013. *The New Jerusalem.* CreateSpace Independent Publishing Platform, The Project Gutenberg eBook, http://www.gutenberg.org/cache/epub/13468/pg13468-images.html

Choueiri, Y. M. 2000. *Arab Nationalism a History: Nation and State in the Arab World* (Oxford: Blackwell).

Cooke, M. 2013. *Tribal Modern: Branding New Nations in the Arab Gulf* (Berkeley: University of California Press).

Dabashi, H. 2012. *The Arab Spring: The End of Postcolonialism* (London/New York: Zed Books).

Daftary, F., Fernea, E. W., and Nanji, A. (eds.) 2010. *Living in Historic Cairo: Past and Present in an Islamic City* (London: Azimuth Editions).

David, E. 1994. *Mariette Pacha. 1821–1881* (Paris: Pygmalion).

Davis, M. 2006. "Fear and Money in Dubai," *New Left Review,* 41 (September–October 2006), 46–68.

El-Habashi, A. 2001. *Athar to Monuments: The Intervention of the Comite de Conservation des Monuments de l'Art Arabe* (PhD diss., University of Pennsylvania).

El-Habashi, A. 2003. "The Preservation of Egyptian Cultural Heritage Through Egyptian Eyes: The Case of the Comité de Conservation des Monuments de l'art Arabe," in J. Nasr and M. Volait (eds.), *Urbanism: Imported or Exported?* (London: Academy Press), 155–183.

Farouk-Alli, A. 2006. "The Second Coming of the Theocratic Age? Islamic Discourse After Modernity and Postmodernity," in I. Abu-Rabi (ed.), *The Blackwell Companion to Contemporary Islamic Thought* (London: Wiley-Blackwell), 285–301.

Flood, F. B. 2002. "Between Cult and Culture: Bamiyan, Islamic Iconoclasm, and the Museum," *The Art Bulletin*, 84, 4, 641–659.

Gelvin, J. 2005. *The Modern Middle East: A History* (Oxford: Oxford University Press).

Hanssen, J., Philipp, T., and Weber, S. (eds.) 2002. *The Empire in the City: Arab Provincial Capitals in the Late Ottoman Empire* (Würzburg: Ergon in Kommission).

Harvey, D. 2003. "The Right to the City," *International Journal of Urban and Regional Research*, 27, 4, 939–941.

Hassan, F. de Trafford, A. and Youssef, M. (eds.) 2008. *Cultural Heritage and Development in the Arab World* (Alexandria, Egypt : Bibliotheca Alexandrina).

Lamprakos, M. 1992. "Le Corbusier and Algiers: The Plan Obus as Colonial Urbanism," in N. AlSayyad (ed.), *Forms of Dominance on the Architecture and Urbanism of the Colonial Enterprise* (Aldershot, UK: Avebury), 183–210.

Lamprakos, M. 2015. *Building a World Heritage City: Sanaa, Yemen* (Burlington, VT: Ashgate).

Levine, N. 1996. *The Architecture of Frank Lloyd Wright* (Princeton, NJ: Princeton University Press).

Mitchell, T. (ed.) 2000. *Questions of Modernity* (Minneapolis: University of Minnesota Press).

Mulder, S. 2017. "Imagining Localities of Antiquity in Islamic Societies," *International Journal of Islamic Architecture*, 6, 2, 229–254.

Noueihed, L., and Warren, A. 2012. *The Battle for the Arab Spring: Revolution, Counter-Revolution and the Making of a New Era* (New Haven, CT: Yale University Press).

Owen, R. 2002. *State Power and Politics in the Making of the Modern Middle East* (London: Routledge).

Radoine, H. 2002. "French Territoriality and Urbanism: General Lyautey and Architect Prost in Morocco (1912–1925)," in F. Demissie (ed.), *Colonial Architecture and Urbanism in Africa: Intertwined and Contested Histories* (London: Routledge), 11–32.

Rogan, E. L. 2009. *The Arabs: A History.* (New York: Basic Books).

Rowe, P. G. and Sarkis, H. (eds.) 1998. *Projecting Beirut: Episodes in the Construction and Reconstruction of a Modern City* (Munich: Prestel).

Shaw, W. 2015. "The Concept of Heritage in Relation to World Arts: a Matrimony of Others," in Leila el-Wakil (ed.) *Patrimoine et Architecture* 21–22 (April, 2015), 106–113.

Silver, H. 2010. "Divided Cities in the Middle East," *City & Community*, 9, 4, 345–357.

Al-Sultany, Kh. 2008. *Half a Century After the Creation of the "Wright" Projects in Baghdad: Plans for the Imagined Architecture* (Escola Tècnica Superior d'Arquitectura de Barcelona: Departament de Composició Arquitectònica).

Verdeil, E. 2012. "Michel Ecochard in Lebanon and Syria (1956–1968). The Spread of Modernism, the Building of the Independent States and the Rise of Local Professionals of Planning," *Planning Perspectives*, 27, 2, 249–266.

Watenpaugh, K. D. 2006. *Being Modern in the Middle East: Revolution, Nationalism, Colonialism, and the Arab Middle Class* (Princeton, NJ: Princeton University Press).

World Bank 2001. *Cultural Heritage and Development: A Framework for Action in the Middle East and North Africa* (Washington, DC: World Bank).

FURTHER READING

Abu-Lughod, J. L, and Hay, R. 1977. *Third World Urbanization* (Chicago: Maaroufa Press).

Ajami, F. 1985. "The Crisis of Arab Bourgeoisie," *Journal of Arab Affairs*, 4, 1 (Apr 30, 1985), 1–18.

AlSayyad, N., Bierman, I. A., and Rabbat, N. O. (eds.) 2005. *Making Cairo Medieval* (Lanham, MD: Lexington Books).

Ansari, G. 1985. "Modernization in the Arabian Gulf States: A Paradigm of Cultural Change," *The Eastern Anthropologist*, 38, 3, 189–205.

Bamyeh, M. A. (ed.) 2012. *Intellectuals and Civil Society in the Middle East: Liberalism, Modernity and Political Discourse* (London: I. B. Tauris).

Basar, S., Carver, A., and Miessen, M. (eds.) 2007. *With/Without: Spatial Products, Practices & Politics in the Middle East* (Dubai: Bidoun and Moutamarat).

Betts, R. F. 1985. *Uncertain Dimensions: Western Overseas Empires in the Twentieth Century* (Minneapolis: University of Minnesota Press).

Bonine, M. E. 1997. *Population, Poverty, and Politics in Middle East Cities* (Gainesville: University Press of Florida).

Bush, R. 1999. *Economic Crisis and the Politics of Reform in Egypt* (Boulder, CO: Westview Press).

Chaichian, M. A. 2009. *Town and Country in the Middle East: Iran and Egypt in the Transition to Globalization, 1800–1970* (Lanham, MD: Lexington Books).

Elsheshtawy, Y. (ed.) 2004. *Planning the Middle East City: An Urban Kaleidoscope in a Globalizing World* (New York: Routledge).

Foley, S. 2010. *The Arab Gulf States: Beyond Oil and Islam* (Boulder, CO: Lynne Rienner Publishers).

Grandinetti, T. 2015. "The Palestinian Middle Class in Rawabi: Depoliticizing the Occupation," *Alternatives: Global, Local, Political*, 40, 1 (February 2015), 63–78.

Harrigan, J., and El-Said, H. 2009. *Economic Liberalisation, Social Capital and Islamic Welfare Provision* (Basingstoke, UK: Palgrave Macmillan).

Harvey, D. 1985. *The Urbanization of Capital: Studies in the History and Theory of Capitalist Urbanization* (Baltimore, MD: Johns Hopkins University Press).

Harvey, D. 2013. *Rebel Cities: From the Right to the City to the Urban Revolution* (London: Verso.

Hatem, M. 1985. "Conservative Patriarchal Modernization in the Arabian Gulf," *Contemporary Marxism*, 11 (Fall 1985), 96–109.

Isenstadt, S., and Rizvi, K. (eds.) 2008. *Modernism and the Middle East: Architecture and Politics in the Twentieth Century* (Seattle: University of Washington Press).

Jankowski, J. P., and Gershoni, I. (eds.) 1997. *Rethinking Nationalism in the Arab Middle East* (New York: Columbia University Press).

Khalaf, S. 2006. "The Evolution of the Gulf City Type, Oil, and Globalization," in J. W. Fox, N. Mourtada-Sabba, and M. al-Mutawa (eds.), *Globalization and the Gulf* (London: Routledge), 244–265.

Lewcock, R. B. 1986a. *The Campaign to Preserve the Old City of Sana'a*. Report Number 3 (Paris: UNESCO).

Lewcock, R. B. 1986b *The Old Walled City of Sana'a* (Paris: UNESCO).

McNeill, W. H, and Adams, R. 1978. *Human Migration: Patterns and Policies* (Bloomington: Indiana University Press).

Moore, C. H. 1974. "Authoritarian Politics in Unincorporated Society: The Case of Nasser's Egypt," *Comparative Politics*, 6, 2 (Jan. 1974), 193–218.

Moore, C. H. 1986. "Money and Power: The Dilemma of the Egyptian Infitah," *Middle East Journal*, 40, 4, 634–650.

Nafziger, J. A. R, and Nicgorski, A. M. 2009. *Cultural Heritage Issues: The Legacy of Conquest, Colonization, and Commerce* (Leiden: Martinus Nijhoff Publishers).

Oren, M. B. 2002. *Six Days of War: June 1967 and the Making of the Modern Middle East* (Oxford: Oxford University Press).

Ormos, I. 2002. "Preservation and Restoration: the Methods of Max Herz Pasha, Chief Architect of the Comité de Conservation des Monuments de l'art Arabe, 1890–1914," in J. Edwards (ed.), *Historians in Cairo. Essays in Honor of George Scanlon* (Cairo: American University in Cairo Press), 123–153.

Owen, R. 2012. *The Rise and Fall of Arab Presidents for Life* (Cambridge, MA: Harvard University Press).

Polk, W. R. 1991. *The Arab World* (2nd ed.) (Cambridge, MA: Harvard University Press).

Pratt, N. 2006. *Democracy and Authoritarianism in the Arab World* (Boulder, CO: Lynne Rienner Publisher).

Reid, D. M. 2002. *Whose Pharaohs?: Archaeology, Museums, and Egyptian National Identity from Napoleon to World War I* (Berkeley: University of California Press).

Salamé, G. (ed.) 1994. *Democracy Without Democrats?: The Renewal of Politics in the Muslim World* (London: I. B. Tauris).

Sanders, P. 2008. *Creating Medieval Cairo: Empire, Religion, and Architectural Preservation in Nineteenth-Century Egypt* (Cairo: American University in Cairo Press).

Ṣāyigh, Y, and Shlaim, A. 1997. *The Cold War and the Middle East* (Oxford: Clarendon Press).

Sergeant, R. B., and Lewcock, R. (eds.) 1983. *Sana: An Arabian Islamic City* (London: World of Islam Festival Trust).

Shechter, R. 2008. "The Cultural Economy of Development in Egypt: Economic Nationalism, Hidden Economy and the Emergence of Mass Consumer Society During Sadat's Infitah," *Middle Eastern Studies*, 44, 4, 571–583.

Shechter, R. 2009. "From Effendi to Infitāh? Consumerism and Its Malcontents in the Emergence of Egyptian Market Society," *British Journal of Middle Eastern Studies*, 36, 1, 21–35.

Sonbol, A. 2000. *The New Mamluks: Egyptian Society and Modern Feudalism* (Syracuse, NY: Syracuse University Press).

Théliol, M., and Jarrassé, D. 2008. *Le regard français sur le Patrimoine marocain: conservation, restauration et mise en valeur de l'architecture et de l'urbanisme des quatres villes impériales durant le protectorat (1912–1956)* (Thèse doctorat, Histoire de l'art contemporain, University of Bordeaux 3).

Thompson, E. 2000. *Colonial Citizens: Republican Rights, Paternal Privilege, and Gender in French Syria and Lebanon* (New York: Columbia University Press).

Wright, G. 1991. *The Politics of Design in French Colonial Urbanism* (Chicago: University of Chicago Press).

IS THERE AN "ISLAMIC" PRACTICE FOR THE PRESERVATION OF CULTURAL HERITAGE?

TRINIDAD RICO

INTRODUCTION

THE question of whether it is possible to identify a coherent, unified "Islamic" philosophy and practice of heritage preservation in Muslim contexts arises out of an important set of interests within critical heritage studies, particularly relating to the politics of representation and recognition. As part of these efforts, the enquiry into heritage practices in the context of Islam has traditionally been examined in relation to "Western" standards of preservation and has given rise to two types of assumptions: either there is a particular "Islamic" way of practicing preservation of cultural heritage, which falls in line with a "Western" Euro-centric preservation philosophy and is therefore less visible due to its assimilation into homogeneous safeguarding practices of global heritage organizations; or there is an "Islamic" way of practicing preservation, which conflicts with "Western" preservation practices and principles in visible ways that can be documented. For example, some scholars have asked why Mecca, the "heart" of Islam, is *still* not nominated to UNESCO's Organization's World Heritage List (van der Aa 2005: 5; see also Bennett 1977: 29). Although these calls may be motivated by the desire to prove that the global model for heritage preservation has limited application, I would argue that the result is, invariably, to suggest incompatibility between "Western" philosophies and practices of heritage preservation and those of the Muslim world (van der Aa 2005: 5; Pocock 1997: 267). Therefore, the absence of the most significant site for the history of the *umma* in a global heritage assemblage raises some questions—not about practices sanctioned by Islam, but about heritage and preservation studies and its commitment to the study of "non-Western" heritage preservation practices (Figures 6.3.1, 6.3.2, and 6.3.3). Heritage debates related to Islam have leaned toward the theme of unresolved conflict due precisely to an absence of a well-developed debate on heritage and Islam. For the purposes of this discussion, I refer to principles of conservation and preservation as parts of a coherent practice that is informed by a concern with the management and permissibility of change in material culture that is perceived to have some form of heritage value.

Interpretations of the motivations behind observed heritage practices, and the blanket generalizations that are subsequently drawn about the modes of engagement of Muslim communities with their heritage resources, are not new or particularly nuanced (Rico and Lababidi 2017; Rico 2014). Development projects in the holy city of Mecca, which include destruction and adaptation of places of alleged heritage value in the history of Islam, have been used by scholars to question the commitment of Muslims to their own heritage, while preservationists have also questioned why the world-famous sites of Nimrud and Ur failed to be nominated for World Heritage status by the Iraqi state (Prott 1992: 4) or how the ruins of Babylon were imaginatively reconstructed by Saddam Hussein in 1987 (Rothfield 2009) – two deeply political issues. When weaved together, these implicit accusations and documented challenges convey one message: the Muslim world is either indifferent to, adverse to, or incompatible with the preservation of heritage value as defined in contemporary global standards. These have often been used to suggest that "Islam" moderates or obstructs those global principles of

FIGURE 6.3.1 Abandoned mosque, northern Qatar, 2013.

FIGURE 6.3.2   Continuously occupied mosque, west of Al Khor in Qatar, 2015.

FIGURE 6.3.3   Restored mosque in Al Ruwais, northern Qatar, 2016.

conservation of cultural heritage that a Euro-centric preservation philosophy is built on, which are significantly modeled on strict ideas of authenticity, the significance of material integrity, and public access (cf. Smith 2006).

In part, the misrepresentation of Muslim contexts in heritage preservation debates is related to the geographic and cultural context of Islam, which overlaps significantly with the politics of heritage issues and debates across the Middle East, a region that is unfortunately analyzed primarily through the lens of conflict and destruction (e.g., Watenpaugh 2016). Disparate events such as the 2001 destruction of the Bamiyan Buddhas in Afghanistan, the aftermath of the Arab Spring in 2011, and the ongoing destruction of heritage sites across the Middle East at the time of writing have dominated critical discussions of heritage preservation practices in and of the Muslim world. This has often facilitated the stringing together of geographically and temporally isolated cases into a coherent narrative to construct a hostile regional attitude to the preservation of heritage value. When this homogeneity is examined more closely, however, none of these examples can be said to exemplify an "Islamic" philosophy or practice of preservation. Nonetheless, this handful of examples, themselves quite atypical, are used to construct a prototype for preservation concerns in Muslim contexts—a position built on a careful selection of data that, once popularized, erase the lack of diversity of voices and the epistemological traditions that built it (cf. Abu-Lughod 1987: 160, in reference to the construction of the idea of an "Islamic city").

Therefore, there is a third possibility that needs to be discussed in an examination of an "Islamic" philosophy and practice of heritage preservation in Muslim contexts in order to disrupt this unproductive dichotomy: the likelihood that heritage preservation in the context of Muslim communities is neither in alliance nor in conflict with "Western" principles of conservation, practices of preservation, or management of heritage values, but rather is practiced in ways that serve agendas that are temporally and politically relevant for the construction of national and regional narratives of identity and belonging. In this chapter, I first explore the relationship between "Islamic" and "Western" philosophies and practices of heritage preservation to demonstrate how they have arisen from a particular set of interests and debates within critical heritage studies. I then look at the question of the representation of Islamic objects, places, and practices on international heritage registers and how this has been explained by scholars. Finally, I consider attempts to codify "Islamic" preservation practices and philosophies and suggest some of the histories of heritage preservation that should be incorporated in debates about Islam, Muslims, and heritage preservation. In this chapter, I suggest that the ways in which Islamic heritage and preservation practices have been represented within critical studies of heritage has hindered a productive debate of situated practices of heritage *in* and *of* Islam in their own terms. As elsewhere in the world, heritage in and of Islam is not coherent but is shaped by contingent politically and historically situated circumstances. Therefore, a more productive engagement with these questions would involve exploring the ways in which heritage constructs are mobilized and vernacularized, rather than to assume that a homogeneous "Islamic" conservation philosophy or practice is or should be discernable.

BETWEEN THE "WEST" AND THE "NON-WEST"

Efforts to search for and understand the interrelation between an "Islamic" and a "Western" preservation practice stem from a deep-rooted assumption that principles of conservation, as they have been established and articulated in many doctrinal documents, constitute the cornerstone of heritage management and have or should have universal application (i.e., Brandi 1963). To be "Western" in heritage practice has been aligned with a privileging of concepts of authenticity and integrity put forward by the Venice Charter of 1964 (ICOMOS 1964) and operationalized through the World Heritage Convention of 1972 (UNESCO 1972). However, a counter position that defines a critical turn in heritage studies has challenged the authority of these principles and the documents that espouse them (i.e., Byrne 1991). This is based on a growing understanding of non-Western heritage contexts which has suggested that the Western model in fact damages alternative legitimate forms of heritage preservation in those contexts where integrity and authenticity may be assigned and valued independently of the material constituencies of a heritage subject (i.e., Wei and Aass 1989; Adams 1998; Byrne 2014 among others). Critical heritage scholars have therefore argued that a Euro-centric model for heritage preservation established a "patrimonial regime" of truth (Hafstein 2007: 76) which constructs and operationalizes a moral imperative to conserve and an "authorized heritage discourse" (Smith 2006) to enforce it. This privileges monumentality and grand scale, aesthetically identifiable and innate "age-value," and an accompanying expert judgment. Indicators of successful cultural stewardship in this model revolve around a desire to minimize the effects of deterioration, assuming that an adversity to decay is a universal concern. On the other hand, work on heritage practices in "non-Western" contexts demonstrated that arresting processes of decay may in fact undermine in many cases the very heritage value that conservation is claiming to preserve (Byrne 1995; Karlström 2005; Rico 2016, among others).

While debates on heritage and Islam may not explicitly align practices of cultural heritage preservation to a dominant Euro-centric or a "non-Western" tradition, it could be argued that a polarization of discussions of both heritage *in* and *of* Islam has done exactly that kind of sorting. This is because discussions that associate heritage and Islam have focused primarily on assessments of destruction, as mentioned earlier. Despite experts in Islamic law, culture, and the arts openly voicing the mischaracterization of this prototypical position (e.g., Elias 2012; UNESCO 2005; Harmanşah 2015) and the growing realization that an East–West divide in heritage historiography is also a fabrication constructed on very fragmentary data (i.e., Akagawa 2016; Harvey 2001), this rhetoric continues to shape, in essence, attitudes to a Muslim context for the work of heritage preservation. Hence, diverse preservation practices across the broad Muslim world that do not necessarily align with any kind of articulated approach can be nonetheless perceived as remaining "non-Western" or, perhaps more accurately, "anti-Western." Meanwhile, the presence of "Islamic heritage" in the strictest a historical aesthetic and chronological sense has been somewhat absent in global heritage assemblages. A relative absence of Islamic heritage in global heritage debates and assemblages such as the World Heritage List model can be explained as a result of heritage preservation principles that are better suited to curate Judeo-Christian heritage disproportionately (Labadi 2005). However, in general, the inclusion of functioning religious buildings in the realm of global heritage has been challenging, in large part, because of the complexity of incorporating any religious value into an all-encompassing secular and universal heritage value. The study of religious value in cultural heritage debates has not been easily accommodated overall (Paine 2013). As discussed in a special issue of *Material Religion* that addressed heritage and the sacred (Meyer and de Witte 2013), there are inherent obstacles in any heritage of the sacred because heritage discourses and constructs involve processes of sacralization and secularization that come into conflict with the legitimate authority of religious objects and performances. Therefore, the study and practice of heritage preservation offer uncertain grounds for the examination and support for living religions: while some scholars have advocated for a harmonious and inseparable conceptualization of sacred values and heritage management in this type of heritage resource (e.g., Karlström 2013), others have called for the exclusion of "the spirits" from heritage programs (e.g., Berliner 2013). Heritage practices in Muslim contexts, however, vary significantly in the way that heritage and sacred values are implicated on any given heritage construct, largely due to the fluidity of what is interpreted to be legitimate "Islamic" heritage subjects and practices in consideration of the fact that Islam is a living religion.

From Islamic Heritage to Muslim Heritage Practices

Rather than consider Islamic heritage as solely the product of a process of production of aesthetic, historic, and scientific value rooted in the past across the Islamic world (largely associated with the golden age of Muslim civilization), it is more fitting from the perspective of heritage and preservation studies to refer to the heritage of Muslim communities in all its temporal and social complexity because the focus of this field has shifted from a study of objects to a study of social practices, processes, and experiences. Rami Daher and Irene Maffi (2014: 8) have pointed out the many different terminologies and concepts in Muslim societies that embody in part or fully the idea of cultural heritage: the contemporary term designated across the Middle East to refer to heritage is *turāth* (inheritance), while historically, they point out that Arab travelers and geographers referred to *ʿajāʾib* (wonders). These are closely related to *athār* (ruins, material traces of the past), which has been used in association with antiquities, while *turāth shaʿbī* (oral traditions) became popular in the 1950s and 1960s as part of nationalist ideologies that privileged folklore and traditions and would constitute what today is discussed as "intangible heritage." In addition, the term *habous* and *waqf* (religious endowments) designate not heritage value but rather shared and significant societal resources to be protected and prioritized. This significant overlap of these terms over the contemporary domain of cultural heritage preservation, they argue, is managed through a careful hierarchization of religious and secular heritage (Daher and Maffi 2014: 9–10).

Traditionally, Muslim societies have relied on *waqf,* an Islamic institution supported by social and religious practices, to identify, value, and maintain resources that include historic resources. The parallels between *waqf* and legislative and moral principles of preservation are notable. As an instrument for the identification and promotion of heritage value, the system of endowments promoted (and in many places continues to actively promote) traditional building upkeep and maintenance in a way that can be seen as parallel with practices and objectives in heritage preservation today, determining specific uses of cultural resources in perpetuity and for the benefit of society (Essi 2008). But these are not necessarily in concordance with modern conservation principles and its priorities and standards, and they have very diverse spheres of influence in different cultural contexts. Scholars have discussed how the *waqf* system was weakened through its centralization under Ottoman rule and beyond. For example, *waqf* became a target during the British colonial period in the late 1800s and early 1900s for a variety of reasons, including a desire to de-privilege Ottoman authority and a perception that Ottoman heritage was "too new" at the time to be considered worthy of preservation (Sabri 2015; see Çelik 2016). The authority of the *waqf* has been further diminished as a byproduct of modernization in the past fifty years, when its assets were handed over to central governments in the process of "nationalizing" properties. This shift has left historic resources vulnerable to politicization and contestation (see discussions in Daher and Maffi 2014: 11). As an active instrument of nation-building projects across the Islamic world, cultural heritage preservation can be seen as complementing and expanding *waqf* beyond the realm of "the Islamic" as the nations of the Muslim world invest in the preservation of their historic fabric and traditions. From this perspective, the designation of an Islamic heritage could incorporate any material culture and performance that is directly associated with the sacred values and histories of Islam. This includes any heritage place or tradition that pays homage, performs, and operationalizes those values and histories in the recent past or in the present. In a parallel debate, Oleg Grabar has argued that what constitutes "Islamic art" is less related to its materiality and more related to its rightful place in a tradition (Grabar 1973). Therefore, contemporary heritage preservation debates support a shift from the study of an idealized Islam to the study of expressions of Islam in material culture that consider the contemporary expression and complex sets of realities that vary across countries and regions of the Muslim world (see discussions in Aga Khan Trust for Culture 1990).

In consideration of the broadening definition of what constitutes a concern for heritage preservation in the context of Islam, the degree to which the construction of heritage value for a broader Muslim heritage must conform to *ḥalāl* forms of consumption (i.e., regulated by religious doctrine) is debatable (Moors 2012). In large part, the problem lies in making a distinction between the idea of a study of heritage that has been sanctioned to act as "Islamic heritage" and the modes of preservation that are sensitive to Islamic values across Muslim communities through time. "Islamic heritage" in itself is hardly a monolithic construct: in fact, it could be seen as a trilogy of diverse heritage typologies—a heritage produced in a specific time in the past that is defined by experts and aesthetically oriented, a tradition that has tangible and intangible aspects as the result of religious observances and practices, and a material culture that is constantly being constructed in the present as part of a living practice worldwide which reflects on the built environment.

The first of these heritage iterations is an archetype of traditional Western heritage constructs that emphasizes monumentality, aesthetics, and connoisseurship. Academic and public debates on preservation issues for Islamic heritage weigh heavily on this type of heritage orientation, with an emphatic focus on issues of heritage at risk (see history and use of this concept in Rico 2016). This shows not simply a concern associated with the thematic dominance of conflict and iconoclasm, but also with more nuanced discussions of the marginalization of "the Islamic" in heritage assemblages that favor instead a more "universally appealing" heritage of Christianity (Addison 2003; Alsayyad 2008; Bille 2013) or a more "globally appealing" historical narrative of the region. For example, monumental sites such as al-Dariyah and Hafiz Railway (Aksoy 2017) and Madā'in Sāliḥ (Alrawaibah 2014) in the Kingdom of Saudi Arabia are successfully made to align with global preservation approaches and suggest a strong support for the use of heritage for nation-building agendas and, simultaneously, the globalizing agendas of UNESCO (Exell and Rico 2014).

The second iteration of "Islamic heritage" centers on the role and authority of continuous performance as a legitimate and continuous process of constructing heritage value. In heritage studies, this has been discussed under the concept of "living heritage" and "intangible heritage" (Miura 2005). Notions of heritage as practice have been more widely discussed as part of an appreciation of "non-Western" approaches to heritage preservation that move away from the monumental and material qualities and are instrumental for an articulation of any heritage of living religion (cf. Rico 2019). Accordingly, some scholars have argued that, while there is no defined practice for the conservation of cultural heritage in the context of Islam, conservation has a definite place in Islamic practices (see Ariffin 2013): from the most sacred form of conservation, *ḥifz al-Qurʾān* (the preservation of the Quran), which includes preservation of its proper recitation, reading, and exegesis; to *ḥifz al-ḥadīth* (the preservation of the teachings of the Prophet), which includes the preservation of the procedures for evaluating and documenting *hadiths*; to the conservation of the three holiest mosques, *al-masjid al-haram* in Mecca, *al-masjid al-nabawī* in Medinah, and *al-masjid al-aqṣā* in Jerusalem, which are practices that emphasize the continued service and function as places of prayer and pilgrimage of these sites; and, finally, to *ḥifz al-arḍ* (the protection of the natural environment). Mohammed Arkoun, in addition, argues that while cultural conservation in Muslim societies is as related to nationalist movements as it is for Western societies, the concern for conservation is not rooted in a historical methodology, but in a theological one, beginning after the death of the Prophet when his companions became the living memories of the Quranic revelation (Arkoun 1990: 25).

The third understanding of Islamic heritage for the purposes of this discussion articulates authenticity as a contemporary and ongoing cultural production without necessarily articulating any formal heritage value. This, it could be argued, is the most neglected type of discussion about processes of heritage construction, not only in the context of Muslim societies. As an analytical viewpoint that is marginalized in both traditional "Western" and alternative "non-Western" heritage debates alike, discussions of a contemporary and future heritage value raise the distinction between an "Islamic heritage" and the production of continuous "Muslim heritage(s)," that is, sets of practices that put into conversation cultural values espoused by Islam with other sets of heritage and/or cultural values. For example, this could include the production and recognition of contemporary art by Muslim artists (George 2010), the role of modern architectural developments and innovation in the modern cities of the "Islamic world" as the creation of new visual legacies (Isenstadt and Rizvi 2008), and the complex channels of expertise that are involved in the continuous construction and reconstruction of mosques (i.e., Cantone 2012; Rizvi 2015). For example, Charlotte Joy's (Joy 2012) ethnographic work on the politics of heritage management in Mali highlights the unique social practices that give significance to the mosques of Djenné, constructing authenticity through material, immaterial, and modernizing practices that come into conflict with Euro-centric heritage preservation organizations and their ideas of an authenticity rooted in the past (Joy 2012: 105–107). These ongoing discussions about the contemporary production of heritage value continue to be marginal in heritage debates across the globe, putting the study of a heritage of religion at odds with the discipline.

"Islamic" Preservation of Cultural Heritage

Regardless of which definition of "Islamic heritage" is addressed through this debate, what would constitute an intrinsically Islamic preservation philosophy? Despite the occasional regional *fatwa* dictating different attitudes to antiquities, their handling, and appropriate perception, *shariah* does not offer any explicit and consensual advice on the specifics of preservation. A rare discussion in the literature of conservation practices, however, communicates specific protocols for the handling and disposal of manuscripts and segments of Qur'anic text (Zekrgoo and Barkershli 2005), which are guidelines attached to notions of pollution in Islam. The relative absence of guidance for heritage preservation was, in fact, the subject of much of the discussion following the destruction of the Bamiyan Buddhas in Afghanistan. The Doha Conference of 'Ulamâ on Islam and Cultural Heritage that followed this incident in December 2001 drafted and proposed a Doha Statement (UNESCO 2005). On this occasion, the invited *'ulamâ* and *fuqahâ* (Islamic jurists) under the patronage of UNESCO, the Islamic Educational Scientific and Cultural Organization (ISESCO), and the Arab League Educational Cultural and Scientific Organization (ALECSO) emphasized the tradition of tolerance promoted by the Muslim religion with regards to the heritage of others, putting to rest momentarily the debates around the tolerance to *jahiliyya* (the time of ignorance, used to refer to a history that pre-dates the Prophet) in the construction and management of heritage. In accordance with the precepts of the Qur'an and with the *sunna* of the Prophet (see *ḥadīth* and other *tafṣīr* in UNESCO 2005: 9–10), the conveners unanimously condemned the destruction of pre-Islamic monuments and voiced the preferred position in Islam for the preservation and management of heritage as one of tolerance that invited further dialogue.

A closer reading of the Doha Statement (Rosen 2008) has suggested two key aspects that need to be considered to better qualify the interaction between Islamic values and heritage values. On the one hand, Rosen observed that the ability of non-Islamic heritage to be preserved and managed in line with Western preservation standards hinges on making changes to the original intent of the monument during its interpretation, in such a way that the possibility of idolatry is erased (as it has been documented for the treatment of pre-Islamic heritage in Egypt and Mesopotamia; see Feener 2017). Interestingly, this observation may stand in direct contrast to classic Euro-centric preservation philosophy, which assigns heritage value incrementally in accordance to how closely the interpreted use and form remain to an original, authentic use and intention. It is also a transformation that prevents the coexistence of multiple heritage values— specifically, sacred and secular. On the other hand, Rosen points out that the Doha Statement clarifies that preservation is deemed to be acceptable only in the event that it serves the purpose of propagating truth and eliminating falsehood (UNESCO 2005: 41). Therefore, the uses to which heritage are put throughout its life-history, but in particular in the present, become critical and need to be carefully monitored.

The instruments that support a situated discussion of "Islamic" preservation in the present are limited. The Qur'an and the *hadith* offer no direct guidance on *imitatio Muhammadi*—the practice of following the Prophet's example in every aspect of life— relating to the challenges of preservation. A Qur'anic story of the reconstruction of the Kaaba around the year 600 gives a rare glimpse into a particular approach that the Prophet used to establish an adequate legitimate authority toward the monument. The *surat* Rasul Allah, which provides an account of one of the biographies of Muhammad, narrates how Muhammad settled a Quraish quarrel about where to place the Black Stone during the Kaaba's reconstruction. The different tribes divided up the Kaaba into lots in order to accomplish the task, but when it came to the placement of the Black Stone, it was not clear who should carry it out. Muhammad's solution was to put the stone on a cloak and have the elders of all the clans raise the stone to its place; then the Prophet himself set the stone in its final place (Jeffery 1962). This example also suggests that the Kaaba has a long history of interventions as an object of spiritual, historical, and social value that is subjected to recognizable approaches to preservation supported by the *ḥadīth* (e.g. Al Sunan AlSughra, Book 24, Hadith 2900). It has also been intervened on extensively in the modern era for the purposes of maintenance of its function. These practices include the cyclical replacement of the *kiswah* (black and gold silk covering), the ritual cleaning ceremony that occurs before the start of Ramadan and Hajj, and the occasional replacement of the silver door (Al-Syed 2009)—repairs that take great care to preserve the original artisanship and the use of appropriate materials. In addition, the area around the Kaaba has gone through several phases of development and expansion, including the introduction of electricity in 1953, and further projects of expansion in 1988 and 2015 (Ja'fari 2014) in order to increase its carrying capacity—a challenge for any heritage site that lies at the center of a living religion. These changes to the historical layout of the site have invariably affected the urban, architectural, and aesthetic qualities of al-Ḥaram in response to the pressures of accommodating a growing number of pilgrims. In short, the Kaaba and the al-Ḥaram have historically endured pressures familiar to heritage discourse and preservation practice world-wide, navigating typical tensions in heritage preservation between ideas of authenticity, integrity, and authorship. It is not the fact that the Kaaba has sustained alterations and repairs that is significant for this discussion, but rather the way that these alterations and adaptations are recognizable heritage preservation approaches elsewhere. Its life-history offers an array of tangible and intangible heritage preservation approaches that involve the interaction of different forms of expertise, historical authenticity, contemporary value, and the management of performances attached to sacred values.

DISCUSSION AND CONCLUSION

The study of Islamic heritage and preservation practices is fraught with obstacles and preconceptions that have hindered a productive debate of situated practices of heritage *in* and *of* Islam in their own terms. These challenges have ranged from a moralization of time, to a moralization of territory, to a moralization of expertise and have worked against the empowerment of Muslim voices and agency in the work of heritage preservation. Fortunately, the misappropriation of ideas of *jahiliyya* in discussions of stewardship of "Islamic heritage" and "pre-Islamic heritage" alike has been significantly challenged by scholars who demonstrate the diverse and nonlinear ways in which the past and the present are made to connect and be incorporated through constructions of "Islamic heritage" assemblages (see debates in Rico 2017). In addition, a Muslim "social imaginary" (Arkoun 1973) has informed the way that Muslim cultures have visualized themselves alongside ahistorical and romanticized visions of the past (cf. Said 1978). These epistemological legacies have implications for the debates put forward in this chapter and constitute the core of a concern with heritage ethics in the context of a heritage of Muslim communities. This concern asks: What are the repercussions of seeking a uniquely "Islamic" approach to heritage preservation concerns and practices? How does this objective navigate away from false dichotomies of "East" and "West" while honoring any distinction or resistance that may emerge to a dominant Euro-centric practice?

The global cartographic distribution of cultural heritage is not a carefully curated assemblage that obeys national or regional borders or follows concepts of periodicity. These delimitations, among others, are temporally and politically constructed through specific practices of heritage valuation and preservation. In reality, heritage typologies for the expanded notion of "Islamic heritage" could be found in vastly different contexts and constructs, posing a particular challenge for any efforts to address the management of legitimate Muslim heritages in critical heritage studies (i.e., Kahera 2002; Amar 2014). Rather than examine the coherence of heritage developments in a region that is broadly defined as the Muslim world, what is and should be increasingly addressed are fully vernacularized heritage constructs and preservation debates. These are given shape in explicit temporal contexts, adapted strategically to local policies, and constructed on local values and traditions that include the realm of the sacred, rather than responding to the clear dichotomies which have been perceived to exist between "Western" and "non-Western" models of heritage practice (see discussions in Rico and Engmann 2019). The challenge in this question is to avoid constructing a preservation ethos that is essentially and uniquely "Islamic" and to consider, instead, how a further fragmentation of problematic heritage cartographies supports the study and preservation of Muslim heritages as heritages practices that construct their own ontological borders.

References

Abu-Lughod, J. L. 1987. "The Islamic City: Historic Myth, Islamic Essence, and Contemporary Relevance," *International Journal of Middle East Studies,* 19, 2, 155–176.

Adams, C. 1998. "Japan's Ise Shrine and Its Thirteen-Hundred-Year-Old Reconstruction Tradition," *Journal of Architectural Education,* 52, 1, 49–60.

Addison, E. 2003. "The Roads to Ruins: Accessing Islamic Heritage in Jordan," in U. Baram and R. Yorke (eds.), *Marketing Heritage: Archaeology and the Consumption of the Past* (Lanham, MD: Alta Mira Press), 229–247.

Aga Khan Trust for Culture 1990. "Contemporary Expressions of Islam in Buildings: The Religious and the Secular, in Expressions of Islam in Buildings," *International Seminar on Expressions of Islam in Buildings, Jakarta and Yogyakarta* (Indonesia: Aga Khan Trust for Culture).

Akagawa, N. 2016. "Rethinking the Global Heritage Discourse: Overcoming 'East' and 'West'?," *International Journal of Heritage Studies,* 22, 1, 14–25.

Aksoy, Ö. 2017. "Framing the Primordial: Islamic Heritage and Saudi Arabia," in T. Rico (ed.) *The Making of Islamic Heritage: Muslim Pasts and Heritage Presents* (London: Palgrave Macmillan), 67–89.

Alrawaibah, A. 2014. "Archaeological Site Management in the Kingdom of Saudi Arabia: Protection or Isolation?," in K. Exell and T. Rico (eds.), *Cultural Heritage in the Arabian Peninsula: Debates, Discourses and Practices* (Farnham, UK: Ashgate), 143–156.

Alsayyad, N. 2008. "From Modernism to Globalization: The Middle East Context. Modernism and the Middle East: Architecture and Politics in the Twentieth Century," in S. Isenstadt and K. Rizvi (eds.), *Modernism and the Middle East: Architecture and Politics in the Twentieth Century* (Seattle: University of Washington Press), 255–266.

Al-Syed, A. 2009. "Kaaba Gold Door Maker Passes Away," *Arab News,* 8 November 2009, http://www.arabnews.com/node/329778.

Amar, P. 2014. *The Middle East and Brazil: Perspectives on the New Global South* (Bloomington: Indiana University Press).

Ariffin, S. I. 2013. "Islamic Perspectives and Malay Notions of Heritage Conservation," in K. D. Silva and N. K. Chapagain (eds.), *Asian Heritage Management: Contexts, Concerns, and Prospects* (Abingdon, UK: Routledge), 65–86.

Arkoun, M. 1973. *Essais sur la pensée islamique* (Paris: Maisonneuve et Larose).

Arkoun, M. 1990. "The Meaning of Cultural Conservation in Muslim Societies," in A. H. Imamuddin and K. R. Longeteig (eds.), *Architecture and Urban Conservation in the Islamic World* (Geneva: The Aga Khan Trust for Culture).

Bennett, P. H. 1977. "What Is the World Heritage Convention?," *Canadian Geographical Journal*, 93, 3, 22–29.

Berliner, D. 2013. "Editorial Statement: Heritage and the Sacred: Introduction," *Material Religion: The Journal of Objects, Art and Belief*, 9, 274–280.

Bille, M. 2013. "The Samer, the Saint and the Shaman: Ordering Bedouin Heritage in Jordan," in A. Bandak and M. Bille (eds.), *Politics of Worship in the Contemporary Middle East: Sainthood in Fragile States* (Leiden: Brill), 101–126.

Brandi, C. 1963. *Teoria del restauro* (Rome: Edizioni di Storia e Letteratura. [reprint Turin: G. Einaudi, 1977]).

Byrne, D. 1991. "Western Hegemony in Archaeological Heritage Management," *History and Anthropology*, 5, 2, 269–276.

Byrne, D. 1995. "Buddhist Stupa and Thai Social Practice," *World Archaeology*, 27, 2, 266–281.

Byrne, D. 2014. *Counterheritage: Critical Perspectives on Heritage Conservation in Asia*. Routledge Studies in Heritage (London/New York: Routledge).

Cantone, C. 2012. *Making and Remaking Mosques in Senegal* (Leiden: Brill).

Çelik, Z. 2016. *About Antiquities: Politics of Archaeology in the Ottoman Empire* (Austin: University of Texas Press).

Daher, R., and Maffi, I. 2014. "Introduction," in R. Daher and I. Maffi (eds.), *The Politics and Practices of Cultural Heritage in the Middle East: Positioning the Material Past in Contemporary Societies* (London: I. B. Tauris), 1–54.

Elias, J. J. 2012. *Aisha's Cushion: Religious Art, Perception and Practice in Islam* (Cambridge: Harvard University Press).

Essi, E. 2008. "Islamic Waqf and Management of Cultural Heritage Palestine," *International Journal of Heritage Studies*, 14, 380–385.

Exell, K., and T. Rico. 2014. *Cultural Heritage in the Arabian Peninsula: Debates, Discourses and Practices* (Farnham, UK: Ashgate).

Feener, R. M. 2017. "Muslim Cultures and Pre–Islamic Pasts: Changing Perceptions of 'Heritage," in T. Rico (ed.) *The Making of Islamic Heritage: Muslim Pasts and Heritage Presents* (London: Palgrave Macmillan), 23–43.

George, K. M. 2010. *Picturing Islam: Art and Ethics in a Muslim Lifeworld* (Malden, MA: Wiley-Blackwell).

Grabar, O. 1973. *The Formation of Islamic Art* (New Haven: Yale University Press).

Hafstein, V. 2007. "Claiming Culture: Intangible Heritage Inc., Folklore, Traditional knowledge," in D. Hemme, M. Tauschek, and R. Bendix (eds.), *Prädikat "Heritage": Wertschöpfungen aus kulturellen Ressourcen* (Münster: LIT Verlag), 81–119.

Harmanşah, Ö. 2015. "ISIS, Heritage, and the Spectacles of Destruction in the Global Media," *Near Eastern Archaeology*, 78, 3, 170–177.

Harvey, D. C. 2001. "Heritage Pasts and Heritage Presents: Temporality, Meaning and the Scope of Heritage Studies," *International Journal of Heritage Studies*, 7, 4, 319–338.

ICOMOS 1964. *International Charter for the Conservation and Restoration of Monuments and Sites (The Venice Charter)*. Second International Congress of Architects and Technicians of Historic Monuments, Venice, 1964, https://www.icomos.org/charters/venice_e.pdf

Isenstadt, S., and Rizvi, K. (eds.) 2008. *Modernism and the Middle East: Architecture and Politics in the Twentieth Century* (Seattle: University of Washington Press).

Ja'fari, A. 2014. "Expansion of the Grand Mosque in Mecca. From «the Righteous Caliphs» to «the Saudi State» [توسعة الحرم المكي من الخلفاء الراشدين إلى الدولة السعودية]," *Al-Hayat*, http://www.alhayat.com/article/572287.

Jeffery, A. 1962. *A Reader on Islam: Passages from Standard Arabic Writings Illustrative of the Beliefs and Practices of Muslims* (The Hague: Mouton & Co).

Joy, C. 2012. *The Politics of Heritage Management in Mali: From UNESCO to Djenne* Walnut (Creek, CA: Left Coast Press).

Kahera, A. I. 2002. *Deconstructing the American Mosque: Space: Gender, and Aesthetics* (Austin: University of Texas Press).

Karlström, A. 2005. "Spiritual Materiality: Heritage Preservation in a Buddhist World?," *Journal of Social Archaeology*, 5, 3, 338–355.

Karlström, A. 2013. "Spirits and the Ever-Changing Heritage," *Material Religion: The Journal of Objects, Art and Belief, Special Issue: Heritage and the Sacred*, 9, 3, 395–399.

Labadi, S. 2005. "A Review of the Global Strategy for a Balanced Representative and Credible World Heritage List 1994–2004," *Conservation and Management of Archaeological Sites*, 7, 89–102.

Meyer, B., and de Witte, M. 2013. "Heritage and the Sacred: Introduction," *Material Religion: The Journal of Objects, Art and Belief, Special Issue 'Heritage and the Sacred*, 9, 3, 274–281.

Miura, K. 2005. "Conservation of a 'Living Heritage Site', a Contradiction in Terms? A Case Study of Angkor World Heritage Site," *Conservation and Management of Archaeological Sites*, 7, 1, 3–18.

Moors, A. 2012. "Popularizing Islam: Muslims and Materiality – Introduction," *Material Religion: The Journal of Objects, Art and Belief, Special Issue: Popularizing Islam: Muslims and Materiality*, 8, 3, 272–279.

Pocock, D. 1997. "Some Reflections on World Heritage," *Area*, 29, 3, 260–268.

Prott, L. V. 1992. "From Admonition to Action: UNESCO's Role in the Protection of Cultural Heritage," *Nature and Resources*, 28, 3, 4–11.

Rico, T. 2014. "Islamophobia and the Location of Heritage Debates in the Arabian Peninsula," in K. Exell and T. Rico (eds.), *Cultural Heritage in the Arabian Peninsula: Debates, Discourses and Practice* (Farnham, UK: Ashgate), 19–32.

Rico, T. 2016. *Constructing Destruction: Heritage Narratives in the Tsunami City. UCL Institute of Archaeology Critical Cultural Heritage Series* (New York/London: Routledge).

Rico, T. 2017. "The Making of 'Islamic Heritage: An overview of disciplinary interventions'," in T. Rico (ed.), *The Making of Islamic Heritage: Muslim Pasts and Heritage Presents*. Heritage Studies in the Muslim World (New York: Palgrave Pivot), 1–12.

Rico, T. 2019. "Islam, Heritage, and Preservation: An Untidy Tradition," *Material Religion: The Journal of Objects, Art and Belief*, 15, 2 (June 2019, Heritage, Islam and the Vernacular), 148–163.

Rico, T., and Lababidi, R. 2017. "Extremism in Contemporary Heritage Debates About Islam," *Future Anterior: Journal of Historic Preservation History, Theory, and Criticism*, 14, 1 (Summer 2017), 95–105.

Rico, T. and Engmann, R. 2019. "Heritage, Islam and the Vernacular," *Material Religion: The Journal of Objects, Art and Belief*, 15, 2: 141–147.

Rizvi, K. 2015. *The Transnational Mosque: Architecture and Historical Memory in the Contemporary Middle East* (Cape Hill: University of North Carolina Press).

Rosen, L. 2008. "Book Review: Proceedings of the Doha Conference of 'Ulama on Islam and Cultural Heritage. Doha, Qatar. December 30–31, 2001, p. 73 in English and Arabic each. New York: UNESCO, 2005," *International Journal of Cultural Property*, 15, 101–103.

Rothfield, L. 2009. *The Rape of Mesopotamia: Behind the Looting of the Iraq Museum* (Chicago: University of Chicago Press).

Sabri, R. 2015. "Transitions in the Ottoman Waqf's Traditional Building Upkeep and Maintenance System in Cyprus During the British Colonial Era (1878–1960) and the Emergence of Selective Architectural Conservation Practices," *International Journal of Heritage Studies*, 21, 5, 512–527.

Said, E. 1978. *Orientalism: Western Conceptions of the Orient* (London: Penguin Books).

Smith, L. 2006. *Uses of Heritage* (New York: Routledge).

UNESCO 1972. *Convention Concerning the Protection of the World Cultural and Natural Heritage* (Paris: UNESCO).

UNESCO 2005 *Proceedings of the Doha Conference of 'Ulamâ on Islam and Cultural Heritage. Doha, Qatar, 30–31 December 2001* (Doha: UNESCO).

van der Aa, B. J. M. 2005. "Preserving the Heritage of Humanity? Obtaining World Heritage Status and the Impacts of Listing. Spatial Sciences" (Unpublished PhD diss., Rijksuniversiteit Groningen).

Watenpaugh, H. 2016. "Cultural Heritage and the Arab Spring: War over Culture, Culture of War and Culture War," *International Journal of Islamic Architecture,* 5, 2 (July 2016), *Special Issue on Heritage and the Arab Spring,* 245–266.

Wei, C., and Aass, A. 1989. "Heritage Conservation: East and West," *ICOMOS Information,* 3, 3–8.

Zekrgoo, A. H., and Barkeshli, M. 2005. "Collection Management of Islamic Heritage in Accordance with the Worldview and Shari'ah of Islam," in H. Stovel, N. Stanley-Price, and R. Killick (eds.), *Conservation of Living Religious Heritage: Papers from the ICCROM 2003 Forum on Living Religious Heritage: Conserving the Sacred.* ICCROM Conservation Studies 3. (Rome: ICCROM), 94–101.

CHAPTER 6.4

··

WAR AND RECOVERY

··

STEPHENNIE MULDER

THE role of war and military activity in the history of archaeology is the tale of a paradox. Archaeologists are often seen today as saviors of the past in times of conflict; however, that recent identification obscures a more complex history. From the earliest days of modern scientific archaeology, the field has been enmeshed with the politics of war and colonial occupation. It was arguably with Napoleon's invasion of Egypt in 1789—which brought the first scientific mission of European researchers interested in the material past to the Middle East—that the modern association of archaeology with occupation and warfare was first forged. In more recent times, archaeology has been used as a means to justify conquest and occupation and as a pretext for the gathering of military intelligence, while simultaneously, war's destructive activities and the attendant interruption of archaeological exploration and research are widely decried by those in the profession. Despite this paradox—one seemingly built into the very history and practices of the profession itself—it is still common for archaeologists outside of conflict zones to enact a stance of professional detachment and scientific objectivity, arguing that a discipline concerned with the past can have little to say about present conflicts (Pollock 2016; Hamilakis 2003, 2009; al-Quntar 2013). The history of archaeology, war, and recovery in Islamic lands, which includes conflicts in the Balkans, the Middle East, Africa, and South Asia, has been central to both the creation and longevity of this paradoxical stance. This chapter aims to examine the issue of war and recovery through the lens of archaeology in Islamic regions in the period from the late 19th to the early 21st century.

WAR

In the late 19th and early 20th centuries, as the discipline of scientific archaeology developed in tandem with the colonial enterprises of Western powers, archaeologists were frequently engaged with activities related to furthering the goals of colonial occupation and military activity in the Middle East. Archaeologists—many of them foundational figures within the field like C. Leonard Woolley, T. E. Lawrence, Max von Oppenheim, and Gertrude Bell—served in military intelligence roles, particularly during the period of the breakdown of the Ottoman Empire and the creation of new nation states in the Middle East. These scholars' archaeological surveys and excavations frequently served as cover for, and facilitated, intelligence-gathering (Bernhardsson 2005; Richter 2008; Gossman 2013; Foster et al. 2005; Heine 2006; Pollock 2016). Despite these archaeologists' role in furthering military activities, they are often presented uncritically in popular culture and in the history of archaeology, and their fame—as beloved culture heroes—extends now to film and museum exhibits (Pollock 2016: 217). Furthermore, the use of archaeology to justify colonial and military occupation is still ongoing. In Israel, archaeology has been employed to justify the occupation and seizure of land (Abu el-Haj 2001: 228–34, 258–62; Greenberg 2009), and, in the aftermath of the destruction of the Bamiyan Buddhas by the Taliban in 2001 and during the 2003 US invasion of Iraq, archaeology was used in the media and by some archaeologists as a justification for military activity and occupation. By highlighting the Western, UNESCO-sanctioned notion of "universal heritage" and emphasizing the danger to a heritage ostensibly shared by all humankind, the media messaging leading up to the war utilized the protection of archaeological heritage as one additional pretext for military occupation (Pollock and Lutz 1994; Seymour 2004; Pollock and Bernbeck 2005; Pollock 2008, 2016: 217–218. These justifications rarely included the desires and needs of local populations with respect to their heritage. During the Syrian conflict, particularly during the period of the Islamic State (ISIS; Islamic State in Iraq and Syria) occupation of Palmyra and also during the battle for the Iraqi city of Raqqa—both of which are sites of Islamic archaeological significance—some archaeologists worked to draft a call for military intervention in order to protect archaeological heritage.

However, despite—or perhaps because of—this involvement, war has also been an impetus for important shifts in the historiographical and epistemological underpinnings of the field of archaeology and thus in archaeologists' and cultural heritage workers' understanding of the meaning and purpose of the field. In the late 20th and early 21st centuries, in the aftermath of conflicts in the Balkans, Africa, and the Middle East, the field of archaeology underwent an epistemic shift that has led archaeologists to adopt a newly self-reflexive viewpoint with respect to the purpose and meaning of the discipline of archaeology in wartime. In recent decades, as the field of Islamic archaeology has grown and matured, these questions have formed an insistent backdrop to fieldwork and to other forms of professional practice as conflicts have developed and worsened in many regions of the Islamic world. Within the field of archaeology, a number of broadly defined positions have emerged, revolving around questions raised by archaeologists' encounter with new challenges emerging from modern conflict situations: Are archaeologists neutral arbiters of the past, or do we also owe allegiance to living people? In wartime, should archaeologists be advocates for ancient sites, for objects, or for living human beings, or all of the above? Is archaeological expertise mainly concerned with the material remains of the past, or do archaeologists also have an obligation to use our knowledge about the past to shape the narratives of the present? And, in the face of contemporary threats such as the deliberate, ideological destruction of heritage sites by groups like the Serb and Croat armed forces, the Taliban, and ISIS, and the growing commodification of archaeological patrimony on the antiquities market, what professional and ethical standards should archaeologists adopt (Pollock 2016: 216)?

The destruction of cultural and archaeological heritage in wartime, whether inadvertent or deliberate, is not a new phenomenon. Indeed, some of the earliest records of human history speak of the razing of temples, palaces, and cities in an effort to erase the memory of a conquered ruler or group (Keeley 1997; Bahrani 2006, 2008). For as long as humans have made war, cultural sites, buildings, and objects have been used as a mechanism for the destruction of identity and memory and the erasure of peoples. Such actions were often memorialized and therefore appear in the archaeological record. The memorialization of these events in works of art and in monuments often falls into a framework whereby the representation of acts of destruction is a crucial aspect of the act of punishment itself, forming a "semiotics" of war that is as important as the making of war itself—by which the image or representation of an act of destruction forms a crucial aspect of its demoralizing power (Latour 2002: 14; Shaw 2015; Harmanşah 2015: 175). In ancient Assyria and Babylon, for example, representations of conquest and destruction of both people and heritage were viewed as actively participating in the process of that destruction (Bahrani 2008: 16), while such images were also found in the ancient Mediterranean world—one need look no further than the Arch of Titus, with its famed images of the looting and public display of religious objects from the Temple in Jerusalem, for confirmation.

While it is obvious that human lives have more value than stones, the long history of the destruction of heritage in wartime, and the valorization of that destruction in art and monuments, is perhaps itself the best evidence that the elimination of culture has always been viewed as a powerful tool of conquest and as a key strategy for eliminating the *value* humans accord to their lives. Indeed, the socially demoralizing and destabilizing effect of cultural destruction was as well-known to premodern peoples as it is to those who perpetrate more modern forms of warfare, and the taking of human lives has almost always gone hand in hand with the destruction of heritage. The eradication of cultural heritage has an effect of permanent erasure of the social meanings that define human relationships, and, in the aftermath of cultural destruction, a group will often cease to exist as a distinct entity. In taking human lives, conquerors erase the existence of people: but in destroying culture, conquerors aim to erase the memory and identity of entire *peoples*. Or—put differently—a conqueror may eliminate individual human beings, but to make an entire group cease to exist, they must also destroy culture. In recent years, the destruction of heritage has been defined by UNESCO and other organizations as a form of "cultural cleansing": the elimination of populations by eliminating the traces of their presence in the landscape, leaving them without a "home" to return to and thus multiplying their emotional and psychological trauma (Cunliffe 2012, 2014; Cunliffe et al. 2016: 2). Crucially, in denying people their past, perpetrators also deny them a future by destroying the cultural memory that human groups rely on to promote social cohesion (Bevan 2016: 12, 18; Brosché et al. 2017: 250).

Despite the long history of cultural destruction in wartime, it was not until the late 19th and early 20th centuries that international organizations began to grapple with an appropriate legal response to these acts. In the aftermath of World War II, as the concept of human rights emerged and began to be developed into an international legal framework, a consensus evolved that deliberate destruction of historic sites should be included within the nascent framework for the definition of genocide. The UN struggled with how to respond to the human and cultural cost of the war, which had leveled cities and historic monuments throughout Europe. As part of the process of drafting the Convention on the Prevention and Punishment of the Crime of Genocide, the initial proposal made by lawyer Raphael Lemkin defined the deliberate or collateral damage of cultural heritage as a war crime, viewing it as an important precursor to, and attribute of, genocide. However, the final legal convention, which went into effect in 1951, had excised the provisions on the destruction of cultural patrimony after having been overruled by member states concerned that indigenous people and former slaves might initiate legal proceedings against their own governments (Bevan 2016: 12–13). Thus, the articles on cultural crimes were struck from the initial genocide conventions, and instead, a separate legal statute, the Hague Conventions on the Protection of Cultural Property, was enacted in 1954. The Hague Conventions prohibited attacks on historic monuments and cultural heritage by occupying powers except in cases of military necessity. The Additional Protocols, adopted in 1977, eliminated the "military necessity" waiver and prohibited all attacks against historic monuments (Gerstenblith 2010, 2014). However, as Bevan has shown, despite the passage of other UN heritage-related protections—most prominently the UNESCO Convention on the Means of Prohibiting and Preventing the Illicit Import, Export and Transfer of Ownership of Cultural Property, which was enacted in 1970—the application of these statues and guidelines by means of prosecution is politically fraught and has only been carried out infrequently. Major 20th-century acts of cultural destruction, such as the bombings of Dresden, Hamburg, Hiroshima, Tokyo, Vietnam, or Cambodia, have never been brought to trial. When prosecution has occurred, as with charges brought in the International Criminal Tribunal for the former Yugoslavia with the prosecutions of former Serb and Croat army generals like Slobodan Milošević, Ratko Mladić, or Slobodan Praljak (the general who ordered the destruction of the bridge in Mostar, Bosnia-Herzegovina), perpetrators have only been charged with cultural destruction in association with other crimes (Walasek 2015; Brammertz et al. 2016). However, with the increasing recognition of the gravity of crimes of cultural cleansing, this long-standing pattern may be changing. In 2016, the first conviction for a crime against culture was handed down in the International Criminal Court. Ahmad al-Faqi al-Mahdi, a senior leader of the al-Qaeda–affiliated Ansar Eddine armed group, was convicted of intentionally directing attacks against Islamic religious buildings and historical monuments in Timbuktu, Mali, in June and July 2012. He admitted his guilt to the court and was sentenced to nine years in prison. Many observers viewed this as a landmark case establishing a precedent for future such convictions (Guardian 2016; Casaly 2016; Davis 2016).

The further development of a clear legal and governmental response to wartime destruction of heritage has become increasingly urgent in the early 21st century, as conflicts have multiplied in archaeologically-rich areas across the Islamic world. A key problem is that international heritage protections were, for the most part, developed for interactions between States parties, whereas many current conflicts are asymmetrical: between state and non-state actors. Additionally, many cultural heritage workers and archaeologists specialized in the region are not familiar with the legal frameworks protecting property, in part because of their complexity. Some researchers have attempted to directly address this issue by publishing simplified overviews (Cunliffe et al. 2016: 2–3; van der Auwera 2013). This is all the more necessary in that military engagements in archaeologically-rich areas of the Islamic world seem only to be increasing in number. In addition to Lebanon and the Balkans in the late 20th century, violent conflicts have either been ongoing or have newly emerged in regions of significance for Islamic archaeology, including Palestine, Iraq, Syria, Libya, Lebanon, Mali, Yemen, Afghanistan, and Pakistan. Other regions not engaged in active conflict have nevertheless suffered from instability or political and ideological shifts that have negatively impacted heritage: for example, in Egypt, Turkey, Saudi Arabia, and various regions of South and Southeast Asia, including India and Myanmar. In these conflicts, cultural heritage or archaeology has been frequently employed as a weapon of war or as an ideological manipulation of the past, "a form of structural violence that ranges from the deployment of archaeology in media campaigns to its use as a justification for land grabs" (Pollock 2016: 216).

Despite a number of common characteristics among incidents of wartime heritage destruction, most research has focused on specific case studies, rather than on an attempt to analyze underlying motivations across different conflict situations (Gamboni 1997; Lambourne 2001; Layton et al. 2001; Rothfield 2008, 2009; Noyes 2013; Cunliffe 2014; Cunliffe et al. 2014, 2016; Stig Sørensen and Viejo-Rose 2015). However, increasingly, scholars have attempted to conceptualize the broader motivations and contexts in which cultural destruction is likely to occur in order to develop more effective response strategies (Brosché et al. 2017). Within this framework, various types of conflicts and kinds of destruction are posited. With respect to conflicts that are likely to incur damage to heritage sites, four types can be identified: (1) conflicts between state actors, such as characterized 20th-century warfare (World Wars I and II); (2) conflicts involving state breakdown, for example civil wars like those in Iraq in 1991 and Syria after 2011, which often result in situations of asymmetrical warfare; (3) inter-communal strife, such as the relatively new phenomenon of tensions between Islamic Sunni and Shiʻa interpretive communities or in South Asia between Hindus and Muslims; and (4) forms of ideologically-motivated apocalyptic violence like that of al-Qaeda, ISIS, or the Taliban.

Within this typology of conflict, two broad categories of damage to heritage sites can also be identified: so-called *collateral damage*—whereby the destruction of cultural heritage is not the primary goal of military activity—and *intentional destruction*, in which an attack on heritage is the goal and purpose of military action. In truth, however, it is frequently difficult to distinguish between the two. It is common, for example, for military actors to claim damage is "collateral" in an attempt to avoid possible later prosecution for deliberate targeting of heritage. Such was the case in the International Tribunal for the Former Yugoslavia, when Serb and Croat generals claimed that destruction of mosques and other Bosnian heritage sites was incidental and ancillary to other military goals despite evidence of deliberate targeting. It is also common for assertions of intentionality to be either claimed or disputed as a point of political propaganda—many examples could be derived from World War I and World War II, including the German bombing of Reims cathedral or the Allied bombing of Dresden, which leveled the city's famous Frauenkirche, as well as vast swathes of the city (Rehberg and Neutzner 2015). Both events were claimed by their perpetrators as having been acts of military necessity, while the opposing side viewed the targeting of cultural sites as a deliberate action aimed at signaling power and brutality (Brosché et al. 2017: 3).

In the Islamic world, conflicts in Syria, Libya, and Yemen have provided a grim new litmus test for this fine line between ancillary and intentional destruction of heritage sites. In Syria, almost from the beginning of the conflict, the Syrian government targeted not only its own people but also their sites of heritage, frequently claiming military necessity. One early, and prominent, example was the Syrian government's shelling of the Crusader and Mamluk castle of Crac des Chevaliers in 2012. The government claimed the action was necessary because the site had been occupied by rebel groups. A similar logic has underscored the shelling of civilian areas in Aleppo and other cities in Syria by both the government and by rebel groups, as well as the government's widespread use of barrel bombs, which have had a devastating toll in terms of civilian loss of life as well as loss of heritage. The destruction of the ancient, labyrinthine *suq* in Aleppo, including the elegant, 11th-century minaret of the Umayyad mosque (a foundational monument for Islamic architecture; Figure 6.4.1) as well as dozens of other important medieval-era religious and mercantile foundations located inside the *suq*, was one outcome of the totalizing logic of military engagement employed in the conflict. The Aleppo citadel, built on an ancient tell with many standing structures dating to the Middle Islamic period, suffered significant damage from shelling. One evaluation of destruction in the city of Aleppo estimated that of 210 sites of cultural significance, twenty-two were destroyed, forty-eight severely damaged, thirty-three had sustained moderate damage, and thirty-two were possibly damaged (Cunliffe et al. 2014).

In addition to shelling, the deliberate occupation of heritage sites by military actors and their subsequent damage and looting are also outcomes of conflicts in Syria and Iraq. In Iraq, after the 2003 US occupation, the ancient sites of Babylon and Ur were occupied by Coalition forces, causing extensive damage to sensitive archaeological materials. At Babylon, the military base grew to occupy an area of 150 hectares, housing 2,000 soldiers (Curtis, 2009). The World Heritage site of Palmyra, an ancient trading city in the Syrian desert famous for its standing temples and theater, its colonnaded street, and elaborate tower and underground tombs, is also an important site of Islamic heritage. Though Palmyra is almost always framed as a site of ancient heritage, it has

FIGURE 6.4.1 The 11th-century minaret of the Umayyad Mosque in Aleppo in 2005 (destroyed 2015).

Courtesy of Stephennie Mulder.

been continuously occupied since ancient times, and many of its temples were, in fact, used as churches and mosques for centuries: indeed, much longer than they served as temples. The Temple of Bel, for example, was a temple for about 200 years but a church and a mosque for at least 1,500 years (Mulder 2017). It was during the period of the French colonial occupation of Palmyra that the site was reimagined and created as an "ancient" site by the French archaeologist Henri Seyrig. Seyrig facilitated the depopulation of the *temenos* of the Temple of Bel, which had until then been the living Islamic village of Tadmur, inhabited by the local community for hundreds of years. The temple is still surrounded by a fortification built in the Middle Islamic period, and numerous other Islamic structures survive, including an important medieval citadel on the mountain overlooking the city (Mulder 2017; Shaw 2017) (Figure 6.4.2). During the Syria conflict, the site of Palmyra was occupied first by Syrian government forces, and later by ISIS. While ISIS's destructive activities at the site were widely reported in the media, the previous occupation of the site by Syrian army forces, which lasted for more than two years between 2012 and 2015, also did considerable damage, including the construction of artillery positions, dykes, and berms, and the creation of new roads in archaeologically sensitive areas (Ali 2015). There also emerged video and photographs apparently recording looting by members of the Syrian army. The question of whether this damage should be considered ancillary or deliberate is one that is, as yet, unanswered.

FIGURE 6.4.2 View of the castle at Palmyra, built in the 13th century by al-Mujahid Shirkuh on a hill overlooking the Great Colonnade, Palmyra, Syria.

Courtesy of Stephennie Mulder.

In addition to the ostensibly "collateral" damage caused by the shelling and military occupation of archaeological sites, the patently deliberate destruction of archaeological and cultural heritage sites is also employed as a strategy of war designed to demoralize civilian populations and destroy identity and social cohesion. The most well-known example of this is the actions of ISIS, whose widely publicized acts of deliberate heritage destruction dominated Western news media coverage during their expansion across Syria and Iraq in 2014–2015. ISIS's highly mediatized spectacles of destruction appeared designed to achieve two goals: to perpetrate acts of cultural cleansing on local populations and, simultaneously, to challenge and defy Western cultural norms surrounding the "universal" value of heritage. ISIS used cultural destruction as a means of capturing media attention and to project a propagandistic message that Western and local governments were powerless to stop their advance. The visual spectacle of ISIS's filmic destruction of cultural heritage and its rapid dissemination on the internet became a recruitment tool and a potent propaganda mechanism for the group. The amplification of the group's actions by the Western media only served to further that goal (Harmanşah 2015). ISIS framed its actions as a mechanism of iconoclasm in the religious sense (by, in its members' words, following in the footsteps of the Prophet Muhammad in destroying ancient statues as an act of religious pietism). But they were also an attempt to challenge the Western heritage discourse, which they did by means of analogy: framing Western heritage veneration as a secular form of "idolatry" and their actions as destroying the objects of Western heritage "worship." It is worth emphasizing that there is little evidence for any sort of pattern of deliberate, ideologically motivated heritage destruction in Islamic history (Flood, 2016). In fact, medieval and early modern Islamic communities developed rich and complex traditions for venerating and interpreting the material traces of prior civilizations, even, in many cases, according them didactic, spiritual, or religious significance (Mulder, 2017). ISIS appeared, instead, to be following a modern precedent set by the Taliban, which carried out a similar act of mediatized cultural heritage destruction when it demolished the Bamyan Buddhas in 2001 (Flood 2002; Colwell-Chanthaphonh 2003) (Figure 6.4.3). Interestingly, in doing so, the Taliban made a similar argument about the Western heritage discourse or, as Laurajane Smith has termed it, the "Authorized Heritage Discourse" (Smith 2006: 4), with respect to the Bamiyan destruction. Initially, the Taliban leader Mullah Omar had argued that the statues should be preserved to provide tourist revenue, but later, claiming that Western aid organizations seemed more concerned about the fate of the statues than that of the Afghan people who were then experiencing famine, he decided to destroy them to bring international attention to what he perceived as misplaced values in the international community (Reddif 2004). This quite recent, apocalyptic conceptualization of heritage as both a religious and a Western cultural "idol," and of the destruction of heritage as a means of perpetrating an act of ideological warfare in an asymmetrical conflict against more militarily powerful Western enemies, is now well-established. In Mali, rebels claimed "There is no world heritage, it doesn't exist. The infidels must not get involved in our business" (Elias 2013: 157). Such statements reveal the limits of the notion of "universal" heritage and illuminate how that very framework can itself be turned into an ideological weapon (Lowenthal 1998; van der Auwera 2012).

ISIS's actions in Iraq, Syria, and Mali received worldwide attention between 2012 and 2015. This was particularly true in Iraq, with the live, social media–streamed destruction of the Mosul museum and of Nineveh, but also in Syria, with the demolition of the Temple of Bel and the murder of archaeologist Khaled al-As'ad, and in Mali, where local Islamist rebels targeted beloved Sufi mosques and shrines. It is important to remember,

FIGURE 6.4.3 A combination photo of the 180-foot-high Buddha statue in Bamian, central Afghanistan on December 18, 1997, left, and after its destruction on March 26, 2001.

Courtesy of Muzammil Pasha, Sayed Salahuddin/Reuters

however, that at the same time ISIS was also carrying out a comprehensive campaign of destruction of local sites of heritage, including tombs, shrines, and other holy places, that was clearly not targeted at a Western audience but designed to damage local identity and social cohesion. One project, Monuments of Mosul in Danger, has catalogued at least forty-seven deliberate acts of destruction of Islamic heritage sites in Mosul (Oriental Institute of the Czech Academy of Sciences 2017). Notably, in contrast to the international media attention devoted to the destruction of ancient sites, these local acts of destruction were almost entirely absent from Western media coverage. Thus, while ISIS clearly used the deliberate destruction of ancient heritage as a means of external propaganda, destruction of local heritage was an equally important strategy designed as a mechanism to exert power and control over local populations by means of cultural cleansing (Melčák and Beránek 2017). In Mali, too, though the International Criminal Court's prosecution cited the Sufi shrines' designation as world heritage sites as the compelling reason for charges against al-Mahdi, it was in fact the impact on local communities that was of primary concern for al-Mahdi himself, who, in an apology delivered during his trial, expressed remorse only for his actions' impact on local communities (Casaly 2016).

In Yemen, an asymmetrical conflict between the government, supported by Saudi Arabia, and rebel Houthi groups has also caused widespread devastation to important sites of Islamic heritage. However, there the loss may be more extreme for, unlike in Syria, where the systematic study of the Islamic material past has been established for well over a century, in Yemen the study of Islamic archaeology and heritage sites has only been under way for a few decades. The venerable Great Mosque in Sanaʻa is one of the earliest religious sites in Islam and a foundational monument of Islamic architecture, with some sections dating to the 7th century. Sanaʻa has been continuously occupied for at least 2,500 years, and the city's religious and cultural heritage is nearly unparalleled in its richness, containing 106 mosques, 12 *hammam*s (bath houses) and 6,500 houses that were built prior to the 11th century, ornamented with a unique South Arabian "gingerbread" style of architectural decoration. However, the city was only subjected to a comprehensive study in the 1980s and 1990s and was added to the World Heritage list in 2011 (Davidson and Serageldin 1995; Sergeant and Lewcock 1983). Ongoing Saudi aerial bombardment in Yemen, backed by US arms, appears targeted toward the deliberate destruction of heritage sites (Antiquities Coalition 2015; UNESCO 2015), and dozens of sites of archaeological value have been damaged or destroyed (Khalidi 2017). The invisibility of this destruction in both academic discussion and in the popular media, not to mention the urgent issue of massive endangerment to human life in Yemen, puts into sharp relief claims of the "universality" of human rights and heritage often cited by UNESCO and other international organizations. Inaction on Yemen has been sharply condemned by archaeologists and heritage workers (Khalidi 2017: 737) who point to a long-standing pattern of selective action to save heritage as representing an "archaeology of power," whereby action or inaction in the face of deliberate destruction is used as "means to obliterate, silence and negate other histories and ways of dwelling in the same space" (Meskell 1998: 5; see also Brodie 2015a). A similar argument has been made for Libya, which has a rich Islamic heritage that is similarly underexplored, including dozens of Islamic-period archaeological and heritage sites ranging from the remains of a Fatimid-era mosque in Ajdabiya to Ottoman khans and mosques (Brodie 2015b; Rayne et al. 2017).

In addition to deliberate destruction, there are other means by which archaeology and heritage is utilized as a tool to advance particular ideological or political agendas in conflict situations and sometimes even outside of direct military confrontations. These include communal, religious, and national disputes over history and land ownership. Ongoing Israeli sponsorship of archaeological projects in Israel and Palestine has been long used as a political tool and as a justification for land grabs by means of claiming ownership over sites of Biblical heritage. The area of Silwan outside of the old city of Jerusalem, for example, has become one such nexus of contestation wherein the ancient past is selectively used to dispossess current residents of their land and property. The area has been occupied since the Bronze Age, but the representation of the site is largely controlled by Israeli archaeologists and the private group El-Ad, who present only archaeological findings that exhibit links to King David and other Biblical figures. There, archaeology has been used to dispossess Palestinians of their property (Abu el-Haj 2001: 228–231; Pollock 2016: 217; see also Hassan and Hanafi 2010). In response, some Palestinians have claimed looting of Jewish archaeological sites is an act of resistance to

Israeli occupation (Abu el-Haj 2001: 231). Similarly, controversies in India between Hindu nationalists and Muslims over heritage sites often revolve around contested sites of heritage, most famously in the case of the Babri Masjid in Ayodhya. The mosque, built in Mughal times on the site of a previous Hindu temple to Rama, became the focus of Hindu nationalists who wished to rebuild the pre-Islamic Hindu temple in 1992. In December of that year, more than 200,000 Hindus assembled on the site and destroyed the mosque, leading to weeks of riots in which more than 2,000 people were killed (Hansen 1999: 185).

Another outcome of war and military conflict is that it disrupts peacetime mechanisms for preserving the integrity of archaeological sites and museums, leading to lawlessness and lack of oversight that creates an opportunity for looting and destruction. Although looting of archaeological sites is a persistent phenomenon even in peacetime, the potential for looting increases exponentially in conflict situations or in situations of political instability, both because of the breakdown of peacetime mechanisms for control, such as on-site guards, and because war increases market incentives and opportunities for unscrupulous dealers to exploit local people who may turn, in the absence of other sources of income, to subsistence looting. In the Syria conflict between 2012 and 2015, satellite-based monitoring by various groups recorded a staggering increase in looting at some sites. One analysis indicated that of Syria's 15,000 or so major archaeological sites, at least 3,000 have been looted since the war began, and some sites, such as Dura Europos, though only minimally disturbed before the war, have now been more than 70 percent looted. Although ISIS received the largest share of media attention for its highly systematized looting operations, looting occurred in areas under control of all parties in the conflict (Casana 2015: 147, 150), including under the Syrian government and rebel groups. Satellite-based monitoring programs during the Syrian conflict developed out of geospatial imaging surveys made in the aftermath of the 2003 US occupation of Iraq (Parcak 2010; Stone 2008a). Although it has been argued that such surveys provide valuable information that may not be available from ground survey alone, geospatial imaging raises important ethical issues. As dual-use technologies first developed for military surveillance, these technologies link archaeologists to work that derives from and in some cases advances military objectives, particularly because geospatial images are often taken without consent of those in adjacent living settlements on the ground. While some archaeologists have used these technologies without regard for these ethical concerns, others have responded with a more self-reflexive stance (AAAS 2015), urging caution and sensitivity when using these technologies. More generally, the question of whether archaeologists should work with the military has been a contested one. The issue was raised in the sixth World Archaeological Congress in 2008, and, by a clear majority, members voted to uphold a resolution that archaeologists should "resist any attempts by the military and governments to be co-opted in any planned military operation, for example by providing advice and expertise to the military on archaeological and cultural heritage matters. Such advice would provide cultural credibility and respectability to the military action" (Albarella 2009: 106).

Similarly, the potential for wartime looting and destruction of museum objects is also an urgent issue that was brought into sharp relief after the destruction of anthropomorphic imagery in the Kabul museum and the looting of the National Museum of Iraq in Baghdad in 2003 (Colwell-Chanthaphonh 2003; Stone 2008b; Rothfield 2009), leading some archaeologists to call for greater coordination between archaeologists and the military (Malin-Boyce and Trimble 2009: 116; see also Rush 2012, 2015). However, ISIS's deliberate, mediatized destruction of the museum in Mosul in 2015 and its attack on Western heritage "idolatry" has raised the question of whether the framework of "universal" heritage, with a history that includes ties to military activities and colonial occupation, is itself the problem (Albarella 2009; Harmanşah 2015; de Cesari 2015; Shaw 2015; Pollock 2016).

Recovery

In response to these concerns, in the early 21st century, a changing model for the nature and definition of heritage in postwar recovery is being framed within the field of archaeology and heritage management. It is marked by a strong critique of 20th-century "universalist" models of heritage in the aftermath of late–20th-century conflicts in Islamic lands, including Lebanon and the Balkans, and it is rapidly evolving in the context of the post-2003 wars in Afghanistan and Iraq, as well as more recent conflicts in Syria, Yemen, Libya, and Mali. The shift develops in the context of new theoretical understandings of how the concept of heritage is constituted, maintained, and acculturated, and it closely considers the role of archaeology in that process (Ferguson 2010). This critique illustrates the ways that global hegemonic models of heritage are not truly "global" in their conception and implementation, but in fact largely derive from Western frameworks and definitions. These "global" heritage models have sometimes been enmeshed with colonial or wartime goals, or they tend to be commodified and aim to bolster national narratives and promote tourism, one of the primary means of commodification of heritage. Turning archaeological heritage into a commodity, particularly in the aftermath of conflict, has been shown to be deeply alienating, and, as argued earlier, arguably leads to its endangerment by neglect or, worse, its active destruction in subsequent conflict situations. These concerns should be at the forefront of any recovery effort.

Two prominent examples of the commodification of heritage occurred during the recovery from a post-conflict situations in Lebanon and the Balkans. In Beirut, after the peace agreement of the Ta'if accord was finalized in 1990, a private company, Solidère, was formed to oversee reconstruction of the city center, which had been the locus of intense fighting between various factions in the civil war. Solidère was controlled by the millionaire politician Rafik Hariri, and the company was solely entrusted with the reconstruction of the downtown district, an area that had both the greatest historic significance and which had also been the scene of the fiercest fighting. Solidère was, controversially, legally entrusted with the power to expropriate land and property. Property owners were to be compensated with shares in Solidère stocks. Subsequently, throughout the 1990s, Solidère pursued an aggressive policy of razing war-damaged properties in the downtown area, creating a virtual *tabula rasa* in what had been the social and communal heart of the city. By 1993, it was estimated that some 80 percent of the downtown urban fabric had been destroyed. Only one-third of that was due to the war (Makdisi 1997: 674). This structural and spatial erasure was combined with the relocation of some 2,600 families, owners, and tenants (Larkin 2009: 5), creating a profound disruption of living historical memory within the city. Solidère's thirty-year plan (1994–2024) is highly attuned to archaeological heritage and aims to create a "layered city of memory" in which the past informs the future. However, that past is highly selective and commodified, with an aim of creating a carefully mediated experience of a cosmopolitan, tourist-friendly global city. The plan includes a "heritage trail" celebrated through the display of recent excavations of Canaanite and Roman ruins, as well as mosques, churches, Ottoman khans, and French colonial promenades. In the process, most visible remnants of the war have been erased (Nagel 2000). For the many Lebanese young people today, the downtown is a space of amnesia, distant, "out of place," and cut off from everyday life in the city (Larkin 2009).

A similar process of spatial cleansing and highly commodified reconstruction was pursued in the postwar redevelopment of some areas in the Balkans. This was particularly the case in Mostar, where that process centered on reconstruction of the highly semiotically charged Stari Most bridge (Figure 6.4.4). The Stari Most, built in 1566–1567 when Bosnia-Herzegovina was part of the Ottoman Empire (Pašić 2004: 5; Riedlmayer 2002: 103), had, over time, become a potent symbol linking heterogeneous Orthodox, Catholic, and Muslim communities on either side of the river Neretva, and its destruction in 1993 by Croat forces was viewed as an act that symbolized the traumatic fracturing of the social and religious fabric of the former Yugoslavia during the conflict (Greer 2010). In postwar Mostar, instead of a privatized, neoliberal redevelopment scheme like that in Beirut, the reconstruction of the bridge was carried out by a coalition of international actors including UNESCO, the Turkish Government, and the World Bank, alongside local and national coalitions. However, the goal of creating a space designed in large part for international tourist consumption and the marketing of a new, post-conflict message of a "unified" city was similar. The bridge, meticulously resurrected by means of a precise reconstruction from stones quarried from the original site and salvaged from the destroyed bridge itself, was completed in 2004, and inaugurated with much fanfare, the ceremony attended by hundreds of international leaders, including the Prince of Wales. In its current form, the bridge functions both as a highly scripted symbol of reunification, "internationally sanitised and romanticised in its symbolism and purpose" (Forde 2016: 477), and while it is appreciated by some Mostar residents, it has also been criticized for being a "prosthetic" that erases the traumatic experience of local people in order to project a touristically gratifying redemptive vision of unification (Bryman 2004: 2). At the same time, and somewhat incongruously, the trauma of the conflict is also commodified near the bridge through the sale of touristic memorabilia from the war, turning it into a site of "dark tourism" (Foley and Lennon 2000: 11).

FIGURE 6.4.4 The Ottoman Stari Most bridge, originally built in 1566–1567 in Mostar, Bosnia-Herzegovina. It was destroyed by Croat forces in 1993 and reconstructed in 2004. This photo was taken just prior to completion of the reconstruction.

Courtesy of Stephennie Mulder.

Considering the frequently problematic outcomes of many often well-intentioned reconstruction efforts, recent scholarship has begun to propose new ways of conceiving of heritage with the aim of developing more resilient, locally-based models of heritage management in post-conflict recovery (Amartunga and Haigh 2011). This research is based in a critique of what Laurajane Smith has famously called the "Authorized Heritage Discourse," a set of often-unexamined assumptions about the definition and meanings of heritage that promote a certain group of Western elite values as though they were universally applicable. The authorized heritage discourse, as seen in the examples just described, typically privileges "monumentality and grand scale, innate artefact/site significance tied to time depth, scientific/aesthetic expert judgement, social consensus and nation building" (Smith 2006: 11–12) and de-privileges local and non-expert understandings of heritage. Although the conception of world heritage, as promoted by UNESCO and other organizations as well as by many archaeologists, is largely positively connoted, it is viewed by some observers and—as in the case of ISIS and the Taliban, by some combatants—as "an extension of the colonial project, traveling to, knowing and mapping territories outside one's own national boundaries." Furthermore, it values notions of property ownership that may not always be relevant for local communities: "the language of the UNESCO conventions reinforces Western notions of value and rights, while the ownership and maintenance of the past is suffused with the concepts surrounding property" (Meskell 2002: 568), whereas for many local people, sites of heritage are not conceived within a framework of "ownership."

As noted at the beginning of this chapter, this critique also brings attention to the positioning of archaeologists as the ostensible "creators" of heritage and, as such, the role that heritage professionals might play in postwar recovery. To return to the questions posed earlier, are archaeologists neutral arbiters of the past, or do we also owe allegiance to living people? In wartime, should archaeologists be advocates for ancient sites, for objects, for living human beings, or all of the above? Is archaeological expertise mainly concerned with the material remains of the past, or do archaeologists also have an obligation to use our knowledge about the past to shape the narratives of the present (Pollock 2016: 216)? Many archaeologists outside of conflict zones still view themselves as neutral, empirical observers with research interests situated primarily in the past, but new paradigms invite us to imagine a different role for our profession in postwar reconstruction. Increasingly, archaeologists and other heritage workers are responding to this critique by acknowledging that they are researchers of the past who inevitably assist in shaping the present. This view, when applied to archaeological heritage, moves away from a notion of heritage as applicable primarily to monumental, site-based, and expert-curated objects and localities and away from a dichotomy between tangible and intangible heritage. Some researchers have argued that all heritage is intangible, living, and created in the *present*, and this view holds that the process of archaeological research and heritage management is constitutive (Smith 2006: 3). This critique foregrounds several intertwined proposals: that heritage is not merely a material "thing" located in the past, but a social *process*, a set of evolving values and meanings that are continually constituted and reconstituted in the present. It also argues for greater agency to be afforded to local people in the constitution and protection of their heritage. As part of this process, archaeologists examine the meanings accorded to the past by people in the present, a process that is particularly relevant in the case of postwar recovery.

If spatial cleansing and heritage commodification are major themes to avoid in recovery processes, the engagement of local communities via the recovery of war-damaged heritage sites in ways that are, first and foremost, meaningful to them should be foregrounded as worthy of archaeologists' involvement in any reconstruction effort. Such projects must be part of larger post-conflict development strategies (Calame 2005). Furthermore, these efforts must go beyond the tokenism of "soliciting community input" or "local surveys" for projects that have been largely designed and executed by international or non-local stakeholders. The UNESCO nomination process, for example, makes overtures to local people; however, it is common for its phrasing to be paternalistic, "interpolating locals and their heritage into predetermined schemes of global world heritage" (Meskell 2002: 569). What would such a vision of locally grounded post-conflict heritage recovery look like? How can archaeologists use our knowledge about the past to support local people in constituting their narratives of the past in the present? It is likely that it would entail an expansion or rejection of our present "universal" notion of heritage. It may invite us to move away from the "museumification" of heritage sites, allowing them to be used and experienced by local people in ways that do not now fit into the largely commodified and tourism-oriented vision of global heritage. It may include, for example, archaeologists' participation in the construction of novel sites of engagement like community centers, playgrounds, or parks inside or as part of heritage sites, or the rebuilding of traditional architecture by and for local people.

It may also include challenging our very notion of "authenticity" by allowing sites to decay, or allowing them to be used or transformed in ways that may alter their "traditional" historic fabric. Within the universalist heritage discourse, such approaches currently fall under the widespread framing of "heritage at risk," a framing that has recently been problematized as one that reveals the cultural biases of global heritage models (Rico 2015), particularly as not all cultures view the evidence of temporal transformation of material culture as a feature to be avoided. The implementation of the International Committee on Archaeological Heritage Management (ICAHM) charter in Thailand mandates the preservation of existing physical fabric of religious shrines (stupas), whereas Thai practice acknowledges the spiritual necessity of decay, reflected in the Buddha's final lesson on impermanence (Byrne 1995). Similarly, the preservation of the Ise Shrine in Japan mandates that it be rebuilt every twenty years, following a tradition that stretches back some thirteen hundred years (Adams 1998). Such ideas of transformative authenticity contrast with contemporary "universalist" notions of authenticity, which are rooted in the Western philosophical tradition and tend to be static and materialist in nature. However, it has recently been shown that authenticity in fact adheres to the affective relationships between people, places, and things, and not necessarily in the materiality, unaltered state, or time-depth dimensions of the objects themselves (Jones 2010; Rico 2017). Parallels can be found with some Islamic shrines in Syria, which have been continuously restored, renewed, and revived for nearly a thousand years (Mulder 2014) and which, for local people, still retain a powerful aura of an authentic connection to the deceased holy person. To be sure, there is a philosophical tension between the goal of avoidance of spatial cleansing and the expansion of our notion of authenticity to include paradigms that include contemporary use and spatial transformation over time—and it is a tension that elides easy, one-size-fits-all solutions. Australia, which has become a leader in constructing heritage in a partnership with indigenous communities, provided an innovative way forward in 1999, with the signing of the Burra Charter. The charter declares that heritage may be cared for and used by local people if deemed appropriate, or some tracts may be declared off limits except to indigenous communities (Burra Charter 1999). The charter, crafted with the direct input of Australia's indigenous peoples, reflects a different notion of heritage than the familiar one reflected in the "Authorized Heritage Discourse."

Looking beyond the Stari Most, Mostar offers another example of a site of locally based and locally constructed postwar recovery in the form of the youth cultural center Omladinski Kulturni Centar (OKC) Abrašević. The OKC Abrašević was founded by a local consortium after the war as a space on the prior frontlines of the conflict at the center of the city that aimed to provide education and skills development for young people outside of the context of school. It was initiated with the goal of serving as a space of encounter and cooperation between youth on both sides of Mostar. Like the bridge, the center rehabilitated a heritage site that had been damaged in the war—in this case, by restoring and utilizing the space of the old socialist club. However, unlike the metaphorical rehabilitation provided by the restoration of the bridge, the OKC Abrašević was instituted and developed largely by local people with the goal of providing a local social space of reconciliation. It engages "deeply into the local community in terms of cooperating with schools, fan clubs, NGO's cultural groups and so forth" and also exists as a space that is "open to everyone" (Kappler 2014: 173–174), going beyond symbolism to reinhabit a cultural site damaged in the war as a locally scripted site of community building.

In recent years, a number of projects have embraced a local or a community-centered approach to postwar recovery in Islamic lands. One method is to begin to determine the history of a distinctly "Islamic" notion of heritage, an effort that aims to illuminate and emphasize emic approaches to the past within societies influenced by Islamic civilization. Not surprisingly, considering that Islam embraces a cultural sphere that has had a global presence since medieval times and which spans more than 1,400 years, such projects have found that Islamic notions of heritage are varied, rich, and diverse. What is clear is that Islamic civilization, as both a religious tradition and as a sphere of cultural influence, developed sophisticated mechanisms for appreciation, veneration, and preservation of pre-Islamic and Islamic heritage. In many cases, these heritage preservation practices are maintained into the present (Rico 2015; Mulder 2017). These projects can educate and inform archaeologists and heritage workers both inside and outside of conflict situations and provide a framework for alternative heritage models during postconflict reconstruction. Such models have a firm grounding in historical sources that discuss the place of the material past in Islamic societies.

On the ground, other approaches have aimed to directly support and provide assistance to local people and to heritage workers during conflict situations with an eye to preparing for postwar recovery, while others are designed to understand the dynamics that drive destruction and looting in a particular area, with a goal of including local people in conversations about what is lost when casual or subsistence looting becomes a widespread cultural practice. Although the challenges and difficulties of assisting heritage workers in protecting heritage during conflict situations are often seen as insurmountable by the preservation community, there are organizations that have been able to do just that, working outside the framework of state parties that often encumber international bodies like UNESCO. One highly successful example in which heritage workers received direct support to carry out in-country archaeological protection during a conflict situation was executed by the Saving the Heritage of Syria and Iraq (SHOSI) initiative in 2014. This group, operating as a joint initiative of the Penn Heritage Center and the Smithsonian Institute, was able to provide emergency training and material support for stabilizing threatened heritage to a group of Syrian heritage workers. These workers were then able to use the training and the materials provided by SHOSI to stabilize the wall-mounted mosaics in the museum of Ma'arrat al-Nu'man (al-Quntar and Daniels 2015). When the museum was later hit by a regime barrel bomb, it caused extensive damage to the structure, but the mosaics were preserved. Similarly, ethnographic and archaeological work of the Follow the Pots Project, which engages with local communities in Jordan's Dead Sea Plain, has revealed a variety of motivations for looting and also aims to assist in partnering with local people to preserve the value of archaeological excavation of objects (Kersel 2019; Kersel and Chesson 2013a, 2013b). In Mali, Daouda Keita, chair of the department of archaeology at the University of Bamako, Mali, has initiated a community archaeology project at the destroyed tombs in Timbuktu and developed a "culture bank" concept, which provides microloans to owners of archaeological and other cultural objects in an effort to deter looting (Keita and Tessougue 2014: 66). In Libya, projects that aim to collaborate directly with the Department of Antiquities and with local communities to develop community-based solutions to monitor and assess the situation of archaeologically sensitive areas have also been initiated (Abdulkariem 2013; Nebbia et al. 2016).

Such projects show how recovery can and ideally must be initiated and sustained even during wartime, and how the solutions to even complex problems are limited only by poverty of imagination, an imagination that has too often been shaped by the limiting frameworks of the universal heritage discourse. Future recovery efforts in war-impacted areas of the Islamic world should embrace creative solutions that begin, from the ground up, with local peoples' input and needs, and the role of archaeologists in heritage restitution should be viewed as an important psychological component to healing from the trauma of war (Harrowell 2016). Such a stance will enable the building of new and more resilient responses to wartime destruction, strengthening collective memory and identity, and enabling local people to find, and create, a future in the past.

REFERENCES

AAAS 2015. "Satellite Imaging of Cultural Sites in Conflict: A Cautionary Note," American Association for the Advancement of Science, https://www.aaas.org/news/satellite-imaging-cultural-sites-conflict-cautionary-note.

Abdulkariem, A. 2013. "Involving the Local Community in the Protection of the Heritage and Archaeology of Cyrene," *Libyan Studies*, 44, 103–106.

Abu el-Haj, N. 2001. *Facts on the Ground: Archaeological Practice and Territorial Self-Fashioning in Israeli Society* (Chicago: University of Chicago Press).

Adams, C. 1998. "Japan's Ise Shrine and Its Thirteen-Hundred-Year-Old Reconstruction Tradition," *Journal of Architectural Education*, 52, 1, 49–60.

Albarella, U. 2009. "Archaeologists in Conflict: Empathising with Which Victims? A response to Malin-Boyce and Trimble," *Heritage Management*, 2, 1, 105–114.

Ali, C. 2015. "Palmyra: Heritage Adrift," Online publication, The Association for the Protection of Syrian Archaeology (APSA) and The American Schools of Oriental Research (ASOR), 1–59. http://www.asor.org/chi/reports/special-reports/Palmyra-Heritage-Adrift

al-Quntar, S. 2013. "Syrian Cultural Property in the Crossfire: Reality and Effectiveness of Protection Efforts," *Journal of Eastern Mediterranean Archaeological Heritage Studies*, 1, 4, 348–351.

al-Quntar, S., and Daniels, B. 2015. "Responses to the Destruction of Syrian Cultural Heritage: A Critical Review of Current Efforts," *International Journal of Islamic Architecture*, 5, 2, 381–397.

Amaratunga, D., and Haigh, R. 2011. *Post-disaster Reconstruction of the Built Environment: Rebuilding for Resilience* (London: Wiley Blackwell).

Antiquities Coalition, The 2015. "More than Collateral Damage: The Systematic Destruction of Yemen's Cultural Heritage in Yemen's Civil War," https://theantiquitiescoalition.org/blog-posts/more-than-collateral-damage-the-systematic-destruction-of-cultural-heritage-in-yemens-civil-war/.

Bahrani, Z. 2006. "Babylon: A Case Study in the Military Occupation of an Archaeological site," in N. Agnew and J. Bridgland (eds.), *Of the Past, for the Future: Integrating Archaeology and Conservation* (Los Angeles: The Getty Conservation Institute), 240–246.

Bahrani, Z. 2008. *Rituals of War: The Body and Violence in Mesopotamia* (New York: Zone Books).

Bernhardsson, M. T. 2005. *Reclaiming a Plundered Past: Archaeology and Nation Building in Modern Iraq* (Austin: University of Texas Press).

Bevan, R. 2016. *The Destruction of Memory: Architecture at War* (London: Reaktion Books).

Brammertz, S.; Hughes, K. C., Kipp, A.; and Tomljanovich, W. B. 2016. "Attacks against Cultural Heritage as a Weapon of War," *Journal of International Criminal Justice*, 14, 5, 1143–1174.

Brodie, N. 2015a. "Syria and Its Regional Neighbors: A Case of Cultural Property Protection Policy Failure?," *International Journal of Cultural Property*, 22, 2–3, 317–335.

Brodie, N. 2015b. "Why Is No One Talking About Libya's Cultural Destruction?," *Near Eastern Archaeology*, 78, 3, 212–217.

Brosché, J., Legnér, M., Kreutz, J., and Ijla, A. 2017. "Heritage Under Attack: Motives for Targeting Cultural Property During Armed Conflict," *International Journal of Heritage Studies*, 23, 3, 248–260.

Bryman, A. 2004. *The Disneyization of Society* (London: Sage).

Burra Charter 1999. "The Burra Charter: The Australian ICOMOS Charter for the Conservation of Cultural Places of Cultural Significance," http://icomos.org/autsralia/burra.html

Byrne, D. 1995. "Buddhist Stupa and Thai Social Practice," *World Archaeology*, 27, 266–281.

Calame, J. 2005. "Post-war Reconstruction: Concerns, Models and Approaches," *Macro Center Working Papers* Paper 20, https://docs.rwu.edu/cgi/viewcontent.cgi?article=1018&context=cmpd_working_papers.

Casaly, P. 2016. "Al Mahdi Before the ICC," *Journal of International Criminal Justice*, 14, 5, 1199–1220.

Casana, J. 2015. "Satellite Imagery-Based Analysis of Archaeological Looting in Syria," *Near Eastern Archaeology*, 78, 3, 142–152.

Colwell-Chanthaphonh, C. 2003. "Dismembering/Disremembering the Buddhas: Renderings on the Internet During the Afghan Purge of the Past," *Journal of Social Archaeology*, 3, 1, 75–98.

Cunliffe, E. 2012. *Damage to the Soul: Syria's Cultural Heritage in Conflict*. (Palo Alto, CA: Global Heritage Fund).

Cunliffe, E. 2014. "Archaeological Site Damage in the Cycle of War and Peace: A Syrian Case Study," *Journal of Eastern Mediterranean Archaeology and Heritage Studies*, 2, 3, 229–247.

Cunliffe, E., Muhesen, N., and Lostal, M. 2016. "The Destruction of Cultural Property in the Syrian Conflict: Legal Implications and Obligations," *International Journal of Cultural Property*, 23, 1, 1–31.

Cunliffe, E., Pederson, W., Fiol, M., Jellison, T., Saslow, C., Bjørgo, E., and Boccardi, G. 2014. *Satellite-Based Damage Assessment to Cultural Heritage Sites in Syria* (Geneva: UN Institute for Training and Research).

Curtis, J. 2009. "Relations Between Archaeologists and the Military in the Case of Iraq," *Papers from the Institute of Archaeology*, 19, 2–8.

Davidson, C. C., and Serageldin, I. 1995. "Conservation of Old Sana'a, Yemen," in C. C. Davidson and I. Serageldin (eds.), *Architecture Beyond Architecture: Creativity and Social Transformations in Islamic Cultures: The 1995 Aga Khan Award for Architecture* (London: Academy Editions), 40–48.

Davis, L. M. 2016. *War Spoils Culture: International Legal Instruments and the Destruction of Cultural Heritage During Armed Conflict* (Saarbrücken, Germany: LAP LAMBERT Academic Publishing).

de Cesari, C. 2015. "Post-Colonial Ruins: Archaeologies of Political Violence and IS," *Anthropology Today*, 31, 6, 22–26.

Elias, J. J. 2013. "The Taliban, Bamyian, and Revisionist Iconoclasm," in S. Boldrick, L. Brubaker, and R. Clay (eds.), *Striking Images. Iconoclasms Past and Present* (Burlington, VT: Ashgate), 145–164.

Ferguson, N. (ed.) 2010. *Post-conflict Reconstruction* (Newcastle: Cambridge Scholars Publishing).

Flood, F. B. 2002. "Between Cult and Culture: Bamiyan, Islamic Iconoclasm, and the Museum," *Art Bulletin*, 84, 4, 641–659.

Flood, F. B. 2016. "Idol-Breaking as Image-Making in the 'Islamic State,'" *Religion and Society: Advances in Research*, 7, 116–138.

Foley, M., and Lennon. J. J. 2000. *Dark Tourism: The Attraction of Death and Disaster* (London: Cengage Learning EMEA).

Forde, S. 2016. "The Bridge on the Neretva: Stari Most as a Stage of Memory in Post-Conflict Mostar, Bosnia–Herzegovina," *Cooperation and Conflict*, 51, 4, 467–483.

Foster, B. R., Foster, K. P., and Gerstenblith, P. 2005. *Iraq Beyond the Headlines: History, Archaeology, and War* (London: World Scientific Publishing Company).

Gamboni, D. 1997. *The Destruction of Art: Iconoclasm and Vandalism Since the French Revolution* (London: Reaktion Books).

Guardian, The 2016. "ICC's First Cultural Destruction Trial to Open in The Hague; War Crimes Trial of Ahmad al-Faqi al-Mahdi, Accused of Destroying Mausoleums in Timbuktu, Will Begin on Tuesday," *The Guardian* (London), February 28, 2016, https://www.theguard-ian.com/law/2016/feb/28/iccs-first-cultural-destruction-trial-to-open-in-the-hague.

Gerstenblith, P. 2010. "The Obligations Contained in International Treaties of Armed Forces to Protect Cultural Heritage in Times of Armed Conflict," in L. W. Rush (ed.), *Archaeology, Cultural Property, and the Military* (Woodbridge, UK: Boydell Press), 4–14.

Gerstenblith, P. 2014. "Beyond the 1954 Hague Convention," in R. Albro, and B. Ivey (eds.), *Cultural Awareness in the Military: Developments and Implications for Future Humanitarian Cooperation* (New York: Palgrave Macmillan), 83–98.

Gossman, L. 2013. *The Passion of Max von Oppenheim: Archaeology and Intrigue in the Middle East from Wilhelm II to Hitler* (Cambridge: Open Book Publishers).

Greenberg, R. 2009. "Towards an Inclusive Archaeology in Jerusalem: The Case of Silwan/the City of David," *Public Archaeology*, 8, 1, 35–50.

Greer, P. 2010. "Bridge-Building in Mostar: From Fragmented Stumbling Blocks to Overarching Narrative Solutions," in N. Ferguson (ed.), *Post-Conflict Reconstruction* (Newcastle: Cambridge Scholars Publishing), 119–132.

Hamilakis, Y. 2003. "Iraq, Stewardship, and the 'Record': An Ethical Crisis for Archaeology," *Public Archaeology*, 3, 2, 104–111.

Hamilakis, Y. 2009. "The 'War on Terror' and the Military-Archaeology Complex: Iraq, Ethics, and Neo-Colonialism," *Archaeology, Journal of the World Archaeology Congress*, 5, 1, 39–65.

Hansen, T. B. 1999. *The Saffron Wave: Democracy and Hindu Nationalism in Modern India* (Princeton, NJ: Princeton University Press).

Harmanşah, Ö. 2015. "ISIS, Heritage, and the Spectacles of Destruction in the Global Media," *Near Eastern Archaeology*, 78, 3, 170–177.

Harrowell, E. 2016. "Critical Review: Looking for the Future in the Rubble of Palmyra: Destruction, Reconstruction and Identity," *Geoforum*, 69 (February 2016), 81–83.

Hassan, I. S., and Hanafi, S. 2010. "(In)Security and Reconstruction in Post-Conflict Nahr Al-Barid Refugee Camp," *J. Palestine Stud.*, XL, 1, 27–48.

Heine, P. 2006. "Die 'Nachrichtenstelle für den Orient' und die deutsche Öffentlichkeit," *Spektrum Iran*, 19, 2, 8–13.

Jones, S. 2010. "Negotiating Authentic Objects and Authentic Selves: Beyond the Deconstruction of Authenticity," *Journal of Material Culture*, 15, 2, 181–203.

Kappler, S. 2014. *Local Agency and Peacebuilding: EU and International Engagement in Bosnia-Herzegovina, Cyprus and South Africa (Re-Thinking Peace and Conflict Studies)* (Basingstoke: Palgrave Macmillan).

Keeley, L. H. 1997. *War Before Civilization: The Myth of the Peaceful Savage* (New York: Oxford University Press).

Keita, D., and Tessougue, M. M. 2014. "Contraintes et défis du developpement durable du tourisme au pays Dogon," *Etudes Maliennes*, 81, 52–73.

Kersel, M. M. 2019. "Itinerant Objects. The Legal Lives of Levantine Artifacts," in Y. Assur-Landau, E. Cline, and Y. M. Rowan (eds), *The Social Archaeology of the Levant: From Prehistory to the Present* (Cambridge: Cambridge U.niversity Press).

Kersel, M. M., and Chesson, M. S. 2013a. "Tomato Season in the Ghor es-Safi: A Lesson in Community Archaeology," *Near Eastern Archaeology*, 76, 3, 158–164.

Kersel, M. M., and Chesson, M. S. 2013b. "Looting Matters. Early Bronze Age Cemeteries of Jordan's Southeast Dead Sea Plain in the Past and Present," in S. Tarlow and L. Nilsson Stutz (eds.), *The Oxford Handbook of the Archaeology of Death and Burial* (Oxford: Oxford University Press), 677–694.

Khalidi, L. 2017. "The Destruction of Yemen and Its Cultural Heritage," *International Journal of Middle East Studies*, 49, 4, 735–738.

Lambourne, N. 2001. *War Damage in Western Europe: The Destruction of Historic Monuments During the Second World War* (Edinburgh: Edinburgh University Press).

Larkin, C. 2009. "Reconstructing and Deconstructing Beirut: Space, Memory and Lebanese Youth," *Conflict in Cities and the Contested State: Divided Cities/Contested States* Working Paper 8, http://www.conflictincities.org/PDFs/WorkingPaper8_21.5.09.pdf.

Latour, B. 2002. "What Is Iconoclash? Or Is There a World Beyond the Image Wars?," in B. Latour and P. Weibel (eds.), *Iconoclash: Image Wars in Science, Religion and Art* (Cambridge MA: MIT Press), 14–37.

Layton, R., Stone, P. G., and Thomas, J. (eds.) 2001. *Destruction and Conservation of Cultural Property* (London: Routledge).

Lowenthal, D. 1998. "Fabricating Heritage," *History and Memory*, 10, 1, 5–24.

Makdisi, S. 1997. "Laying Claim to Beirut: Reconstruction, Urban Narrative and Spatial Identity in the Age of Solidere," *Critical Inquiry*, 23, 674.

Malin-Boyce, S., and Trimble, M. K. 2009. "Archaeology in Zones of Armed Conflict," *Heritage Management*, 2, 1, 115–116.

Melčák, M., and Beránek, O. 2017. "ISIS's Destruction of Mosul's Historical Monuments: Between Media Spectacle and Religious Doctrine," *International Journal of Islamic Architecture*, 6, 2, 389–418.

Meskell, L. 1998. "Archaeology Matters," in L. Meskell (ed.), *Archaeology Under Fire: Nationalism, Politics and Heritage in the Eastern Mediterranean and Middle East* (London: Routledge), 1–12.

Meskell, L. 2002. "Negative Heritage and Past Mastering in Archaeology," *Anthropological Quarterly*, 75, 3, 557–574.

Mulder, S. 2014. *The Shrines of the ʿAlids in Medieval Syria: Sunnis, Shiʿis and the Architecture of Coexistence* (Edinburgh: Edinburgh University Press).

Mulder, S. 2017. "Imagining Localities of Antiquity in Islamic Societies," Special Issue, *International Journal of Islamic Architecture*, 6, 2, 229–256.

Nagel, C. 2000. "Ethnic Conflict and Urban Redevelopment in Downtown Beirut," *Growth and Change*, 31, 211–234.

Nebbia, M., Leone, A., Bockmann, R., Hddad, M., Abdouli, H., Masoud, A. M., Elkendi, N. M., Hamoud, H. M., Adam, S. S., and Khatab, M. N. 2016. "Developing a Collaborative Strategy to Manage and Preserve Cultural Heritage During the Libyan Conflict. The Case of the Gebel Nafusa" *Journal of Archaeological Method and Theory*, 23, 971–988.

Noyes, J. 2013. *The Politics of Iconoclasm. Religion, Violence and the Culture of Image Breaking in Christianity and Islam* (London: I. B. Tauris).

Oriental Institute of the Czech Academy of Sciences 2017. Monuments of Mosul in Danger, http://www.vedakolemnas.cz/miranda2/m2/sys/galerie-download/VKN_73WEB.pdf?0.5285864602818287.

Parcak, S. 2010. "Protecting Global Heritage from Space in Times of War," in L. Rush (ed.), *Archaeology, Cultural Property and the Military* (Newcastle, UK: International Centre for Cultural Heritage Studies), 167–176.

Pašić, A. 2004. "Conservation and Revitalisation of Historic Mostar, Aga Khan Historic Cities Programme," http://archnet.org/system/publications/contents/3480/original/DPC1419.pdf?1384775278.

Pollock, S. 2008. "Archaeology as a Means for Peace or a Source of Violence? An Introduction," in M. T. Starzmann, S. Pollock, and R. Bernbeck (eds.), Special Issue: Imperial Inspections: Archaeology, War and Violence. *Journal of the World Archaeological Congress*, 4, 3, 356–367.

Pollock, S. 2016. "Archaeology and Contemporary Warfare," *Annual Review of Anthropology*, 45, 215–231.

Pollock, S., and Bernbeck, R. (eds.) 2005. *Archaeologies of the Middle East: Critical Perspectives* (Malden, MA: Blackwell).

Pollock, S., and Lutz, C. 1994. "Archaeology Deployed for the Gulf War," *Critical Anthropology*, 14, 3, 263–284.

Rayne, L., Sheldrick, N., and Nikolaus, J. 2017. "Endangered Archaeology in Libya: Recording Damage and Destruction," *Libyan Studies*, 48, 23–49.

Reddif 2004. "The Rediff Interview/Mullah Omar" April 12, 2004, http://www.rediff.com/news/2004/apr/12inter.htm.

Rehberg, K.-S and Neutzner, M. (2015). "The Dresden Frauenkirche as a Contested Symbol: The Architecture of Remembrance after War," in M. L. Stig Sørensen and D. Viejo-Rose (eds.), *War and Cultural Heritage: Biographies of Place* (Cambridge: Cambridge University Press), 98–127.

Richter, T. 2008. "Espionage and Near Eastern Archaeology: A Historiographical Survey," *Public Archaeology*, 7, 4, 212–240.

Rico, T. 2015. "Heritage at Risk: The Authority and Autonomy of a Dominant Preservationist Framework," in K. Lafrenz Samuels and T. Rico (eds.), *Heritage Keywords: Rhetoric and Redescription in Cultural Heritage* (Boulder: University of Colorado Press).

Rico, T. 2017. *The Making of Islamic Heritage: Muslim Pasts and Heritage Presents* (Singapore: Palgrave McMillan).

Riedlmayer, A. 2002. "From the Ashes: The Past and Future of Bosnia's Cultural Heritage," in M. Shatzmiller (ed.), *Islam and Bosnia: Conflict Resolution and Foreign Policy in Multi-Ethnic States* (London: McGill-Queen's Press), 99–103.

Rothfield, L. 2008. *Antiquities Under Siege: Cultural Heritage Protection After the Iraq War* (Lanham: Altamira Press).

Rothfield, L. 2009. *The Rape of Mesopotamia: Behind the Looting of the Iraq Museum* (Chicago: University of Chicago Press).

Rush, L. 2012. *Archaeology, Cultural Property, and the Military* (Suffolk: Boydell Press).

Rush, L. 2015. "Partnership Versus Guns: Military Advocacy of Peaceful Approaches for Cultural Property Protection," in A. González-Ruibal and G. Moshenska (eds.), *Ethics and the Archaeology of Violence* (New York/London: Springer), 181–197.

Sergeant, R. B., and Lewcock, R. (eds.) 1983. *Sana: An Arabian Islamic City* (London: World of Islam Festival Trust).

Seymour, M. 2004. "Ancient Mesopotamia and Modern Iraq in the British Press, 1980–2003," *Current Anthropology*, 45, 3, 351–368.

Shaw, W. M. K. 2015. "Destroy Your Idols," *X-Tra Online*, 18, 1, http://x-traonline.org/article/destroy-your-idols/.

Shaw, W. M. K. 2017. "In Situ: The Contraindications of World Heritage," *International Journal of Islamic Architecture*, 6, 2, 339–366.

Smith, L. 2006. *Uses of Heritage* (New York: Routledge).

Stig Sørensen, M. L., and Viejo-Rose, D. 2015. *War and Cultural Heritage: Biographies of Place* (Cambridge: Cambridge University Press).

Stone, E. 2008a. "Patterns of Looting in Southern Iraq," *Antiquity*, 82, 125–138.

Stone, P. G. 2008b. *The Destruction of Cultural Heritage in Iraq* (Suffolk, UK: Boydell Press).

UNESCO 2015. "Emergency Action Plan for the Safeguarding of Yemen's Cultural Heritage Announced," https://en.unesco.org/news/emergency-action-plan-safeguarding-yemen-s-cultural-heritage-announced.

van der Auwera, S. 2012. "Contemporary Conflict, Nationalism, and the Destruction of Cultural Property During Armed Conflict: A Theoretical Framework," *Journal of Conflict Archaeology*, 7, 1, 49–65.

van der Auwera, S. 2013. "International Law and the Protection of Cultural Property in the Event of Armed Conflict: Actual Problems and Challenges," *Journal of Arts Management, Law & Society*, 43, 4, 175–190.

Walasek, H. 2015. *Bosnia and the Destruction of Cultural Heritage* (London: Routledge).

CHAPTER 6.5

···

ISLAMIC HERITAGE IN THREE PENINSULAS

Qatar, Iberia, and the Balkans

···

JOSÉ C. CARVAJAL LÓPEZ, JELENA ŽIVKOVIĆ,
ALKINDI ALJAWABRA, AND RIM LABABIDI

THE qualification of "Islamic" for heritage is problematic. Given the close relationship between the field of heritage and that of archaeology, it is useful to consider the definition of Islamic heritage in the light of the recent debate about Islamic archaeology. An ongoing debate in the field of Islamic archaeology is over definition: What are the common characteristics across regions? Although the history of Islamic archaeology starts at some point between the 19th and 20th centuries (Milwright 2010: 11–20; Rogers 1974; Vernoit 1997), there was not a concern with a formal definition of common and distinctive program of the discipline (cf. Grabar 1971, 1976) until the ground-breaking contribution of T. Insoll (Insoll 1999), when he proposed an alternative agenda under the denomination of "Archaeology of Islam." Not entirely convinced with Insoll's suggestions, many Islamic archaeologists took on the challenge of defining a scope for the discipline. As of today, the most accepted definition is probably that which perceives the discipline as a containing field that includes a wide range of interests and approaches to research on Islamic communities of all periods (cf. Milwright 2010: 6–11). While this wide-encompassing definition could be accepted, when applied to Islamic heritage, it faces some challenges because of the local context of conformation of Islamic heritage, which can result in very different and potentially contradictory approaches within the same field.

Another controversial definition is that of "heritage." To avoid a long debate that has no space here, the analysis of heritage used in this text will be articulated along the three axes suggested by Sørensen and Carman (2012): the material component of heritage, the documented discourses about it, and the attitude that the people and communities take toward it. In this text the material component of Islamic heritage considered will be the actual history (or at least what it is factually known about it) and the formation and development of the Islamic past of the region, which is the root of every narrative about heritage. The official (political and academic) discourses about this past are the second point analyzed because of the relevance they have in shaping perceptions about Islamic heritage. And finally, the communities considered are the diverse inhabitants of the peninsulas, the people who ultimately shape and are influenced by Islamic heritage.

ONE HISTORY OF ISLAM, DIFFERENT ISLAMIC PASTS

There is a clear line of history of Islam starting with Muhammad's message in Mecca and Medina, the rise of the Islamic polity and its eventual partition, and the expansion of the Islamic creed around vast zones of the world in different periods. The three peninsulas that are the object of this study are or have been scenarios of relevant parts of the history of Islam and, at the same time, part of the histories of each regional context (Figure 6.5.1). This means that the communities living in the three peninsulas, whether Muslims or not, have their identities influenced by an inarguable past related to the history of Islam (for the sake of convenience, it will be termed "Islamic past" here), through which different narratives have been threaded.

The logical starting point is Qatar, inserted in the history of Islam almost from the beginning (Serjeant 1978: 150–151) and continuing until today. During the long period that extended from the rise of Islam in the 7th century until the collapse of Ottoman Empire at the start of the 20th century, Arabia continued to be the spiritual and ancestral core of the Islamic community, although it became a periphery with respect to the different centers of economic, cultural, and political leadership of the Islamic world. Maintaining a control over Arabia, or at least the Hijaz, was paramount for Muslim rulers, for it is the land of the holiest sites in Islam, which Muslims from all around the world visit every year to do their pilgrimage (Walker 2010). Moreover, controlling the strategic coast lines of Arabia was key to trade connections. In particular the Gulf, where Qatar is located, served in different periods as a channel of Indian Ocean trade (Carter 2012; Kennet 2004; Priestman 2013). In cultural terms, Qatar traditionally followed very closely developments in the Arabian Peninsula, particularly in the Kingdom of Saudi Arabia. Wahhabism, the most conservative doctrine of interpretation of Islam (DeLong-Bas 2004; Rundell 2014), has had great cultural and political influence there. However, Qatar was also part of the British sphere of influence in the Gulf, and this accounted for important elements of divergence in its historical trajectory with respect to that of Saudi Arabia. Qatar gained its full independence in 1971, and it underwent a period of extremely rapid development after the access of the Emir Hamad bin Khalifa (r. 1995–2013) to power (Kamrava 2013).

The Islamic past of Iberia is represented by al-Andalus. This region fell under Islamic rule during the 8th century (711–714) as a result of the last wave of expansion led by the

Iberia (Al-Andalus). Scale = 463 km   The Balkans (Rumeli). Scale = 629 km   Qatar. Scale = 126 km

FIGURE 6.5.1 Map indicating the situation of the three peninsulas considered in the text.

Umayyad dynasty (661–750). Of all the peninsulas considered in this chapter, Iberia can be considered the closest in terms of pre-Islamic cultural and social coordinates to the core Islamic areas of the Mediterranean Middle East as it shared a common Roman inheritance with them. Thus, when Arab settlers carried their culture and language to Iberia al-Andalus, they were spreading over a familiar cultural background, and al-Andalus soon became an integral part of the Dār al-Islām (Chalmeta Gendrón 2003). Cordoba, capital of a Caliphate in the 10th century, continued to be ruled by the descendants of the Umayyad dynasty after they were overthrown by the Abbasids in the Middle Eastern core of the Islamic Empire (Manzano Moreno 2010). The Caliphate was followed by a number of dynastical states that held a position of weakness with respect to the Christian states of the north of the Peninsula until the Naṣrid Sultanate of Granada was conquered by a Christian alliance in 1492 (Fierro 2011; Mediano 2011; Viguera-Molins 2011). Between 1492 and 1619, the Moriscos, descendants of the defeated Muslims who were forcefully converted to Christianity, lived in the Iberian Peninsula under rules designed to erase their cultural memory (Caro Baroja 1976). The Moriscos were expelled between 1609 and 1619, and, with their departure, the Islamic history of Iberia ended, although the mark of more than nine centuries of history remains.

A different Islamic polity appeared in the Balkans after their military conquest by the Ottoman Empire between the mid-14th and the mid-16th centuries. The Ottoman sultans legitimated their power over the Dār al-Islām by acting as protectors of the holy sites, defenders of Sunnī Islam, and victors against infidels (Faroqhi 2009; Inalcik 1973). The gradual incorporation of Christian polities in the Balkans (*Rumeli*) triggered social changes with long-lasting effects. Historically, Islamization, understood as the religious conversion of non-Muslims and the creation of a new social order, has been considered the most relevant change (Minkov 2004; Vasić 1991; Zhelyazkova 2002). The dynamics of this process varied across the region depending on specific religious, cultural, and socio-economic conditions (Antov 2016) that are important in understanding heritage policies in modern countries. In the eastern part of the Balkans, migrations of Turkic Muslims played a significant role (Kiel 2009) while in the western part the creation of Muslim communities was achieved with the conversion of Christians through the involvement of numerous agents such as the state, military, *gāzī* warriors, *devşirme* levy, and Sūfī mystics (Krstić 2011). The pace of conversion was uneven across *Rumeli*, and although some urban centers and provinces (such as Bosnia) experienced large-scale Islamization, the Balkan population overall remained predominately Christian. The process of social and cultural transformations generated by the spread of Islam ceased in the 18th century, and the warfare eventually led to Ottoman territorial decline from the 19th century onward. National uprisings in Serbia, Greece, Romania, and Bulgaria; the Balkan Wars (1912–1913); and World War I (1914–1918) put an end to Ottoman political dominance in the Balkans. However, unlike in Iberia, the presence of Islam and Muslim communities outlasted the imperial collapse. The Balkans is the only region in Europe today where indigenous Islam constitutes an important component of political and cultural life.

This brief discussion shows that divergent historical paths made the cultural manifestations of Islam distinctive within each area. Differences stem from the diverse pre-Islamic substrata on which Islam emerged and the process of transmission and adaptation of the body of knowledge that made Islamic society possible under specific historical conditions. Therefore some common cultural elements used as drivers of Islam acquired relevant contextualized meanings that contribute to shaping differential perceptions of heritage in the present. Connections to an Islamic past (as in Qatar and parts of the Balkans), as opposed to breaks with or rejection of that past (as in the case of Iberia and the largest part of the Balkans), have been important factors in regional constructions of heritage. These differences have important implications in the official discourses about the Islamic past and its heritage.

Politics of Discourses About Islamic Pasts

In this section the creation of academic and official discourses about Islamic pasts is considered. It is necessary to adopt a historical approach as changing political circumstances enable or constrain research on and investment in Islamic heritage. In the cases of Iberia and the Balkans, this approach starts from the moment at which the Islamic past ends (or is considered to end) and therefore becomes part of the historical discourse and eventually of heritage. In Qatar and in those parts of the Balkans in which Islam is present, the definition of what is Islamic heritage is less historical and more political, and it is necessary to understand it in the context of debates about the conception of the past and of heritage itself.

The consideration of discourses about Islamic pasts in Qatar and in the wider context of the Arab world reveals that they play a prominent role in the socio-cultural and political developments of the current Arab postcolonial states. The Islamic past was mobilized by the Arab Nationalist Movement, a secular movement that reached its peak under the leadership of Nasser's Egypt and that considers the peoples of the Arab world as one nation bound together by a common linguistic, cultural, religious, and historical heritage. The movement embraces the Islamic past and Islam itself as its main pillars (Valbjørn 2009) in its aim to form the state according to the European model of a nation state (Choueiri 2003). This ideology was not entirely accepted in Gulf countries as it posed a threat to the legitimacy of their rulers (Partrick 2009) and therefore a more traditional, Islamist mobilization of the Islamic past was adopted, using tribal and religious identities to reinforce rulers' domestic legitimacy (Partrick 2009; Tibi 1997).

Since the mid-20th century, postcolonial Arab states fostered a solid heritage industry to support their national and Arab identities and to legitimize themselves through the definition of a national culture (Al-Sayyad 2001; Daher and Maffi 2013: 21). This included building and enlarging museums (Watenpaugh 2004: 197), archaeological excavations (Vernoit 1997), and a very active emphasis on popular traditions (Al-Sayyad 2001). In Qatar, the first and most prominent achievement of the Emir

Khalifa bin Hamad Al-Thani (r. 1972–1995) after independence was the creation of Qatar National Museum in 1975, through which he sought to develop a "founding myth" for his nation (Crystal 1995: 162). The case of Qatar is particularly interesting considering its lack of historical monumental Islamic architecture, due to the particularities of its history and demography; its peripheral situation with respect to the traditional urban centers of the Islamic world; and the poor conditions of conservation within the country. This does not, however, forfeit a firm identification of the population with a mainstream consideration of Islamic heritage represented not only by historical monuments, but also by the reenactment of this heritage in current aesthetical, architectural, and artistic representations, as explained in the next section. It is therefore necessary to emphasize the political construction of Islamic heritage.

In general, postcolonial Arab states reproduced the same colonial discourse about heritage, one that consisted of defining the region through its classical heritage (Daher and Maffi 2013). However an effort was made to reinsert and emphasize those Islamic elements that were neglected in the colonial discourse. This is particularly important in Arab states that adopted an Islamist approach to the past, where the ideas of Islam, Islamic pasts and nation-building are inextricably linked. For example, the current Constitution of Qatar establishes that Qatar is an Arab state, that Islam is its religion, and the *Sharīʿa* the source of its laws (Constitution of Qatar 2004, article 1). Also, Wahhabism imposes a moral commitment to safeguarding religious tradition and practices in the name of returning to a purer form of Islam (a controversial point that has been repeatedly revisited in the thriving debates on the notion of construction/deconstruction of heritage in Islam) (cf. Rico and Lababidi 2017). In consequence, the past is conceived essentially as a source for learning lessons and as a guide for the future (Hodjat 1995). Hence, heritage is a resource.

Given that Islamic culture is of limited relevance in modern times in Iberia and most of the Balkans and is considered a "thing of the past," the Islamic component plays little role in current heritage discourses there. The nationalist component, however, is still relevant because in most national narratives of Iberia and the Balkans an Islamic entity is constructed as the "oppressor" against whom a struggle of the "people" (i.e., the nationals) ends in the construction of the "community" (the nation). In Iberia, for example, the case of Spain is particularly telling because official history made the Visigothic kingdom (418–711 CE) the direct ancestor of the Spanish monarchy (Barbero and Vigil Pascual 1978), thus justifying the use of the term *Reconquista* (meaning "recovery") for the process of expansion of the Christian Iberian states over the Muslim territories during the Middle Ages. After the defeat of the last Muslim states, Spain strived to "clean its record" of much of Islamic cultural traces (Caro Baroja 1976; Fuchs 2009). In the following centuries the global expansion of Spain was accompanied by the development of an imperial narrative in which the defeat of the Muslims was considered a mythical foundational period (Carvajal López 2014). Later, in the 18th century, interest in Islamic history emerged as the Islamic past was seen by scholars of the Enlightenment as a resource to overcome traditional barriers to development. The first compilation and classification of Arabic historical texts that were conserved in the Royal Library of El

Escorial took place in this century (Monroe 1970: 23–45), as well as the first description of Islamic works of art and architecture in Spain (Almagro Gorbea 2015). A similar interest, yet to a minor degree, is detected in Portugal (Mendes Drumond Braga 2010). Islamic history became part of the interest of the educated bourgeoisie and, if still down-played, started to be present in the national debate about history (Monroe 1970). For a long time, until the last quarter of the 20th century, this debate was about determining the presence of an Islamic inheritance in Iberian, and particularly Spanish, identities (cf. Castro 1954; Sánchez Albornoz 1956). The Spanish Civil War and the rise of the regimes of Franco and Salazar did not end interest in the country's Islamic past, but it hindered its study through a fierce repression of intellectuals (Baldó Lacomba 2011). The return of democracies in the late 1970s was a game-changing factor in the consideration of Islamic heritage. The promotion of alternative views of Iberian history fostered a real interest in the period of al-Andalus and its heritage on their own terms, not exclusively as elements of Spanish and Portuguese national identities (Carvajal López 2014).

In the Balkans, Islam and the notion of an Islamic past have been actively employed in the construction of modern nations. Despite being secular by constitution, the Balkan states have made abundant use of ambiguous interpretations of Islam and the Ottoman period in negotiating current social arrangements (Todorova 2009: 182). Prominent dif-ferences in discourses about Islamic pasts reflect the plurality of historical, cultural, and political realities of different areas. In predominantly Orthodox countries, such as Bulgaria, Greece, Serbia, and Romania, national identities have been constructed in opposition to Islam and the Ottoman Empire. The dominant nationalistic narrative conceives the medieval Christian polities as the political roots of the states and that their "natural" development was interrupted by the Ottoman conquest. Therefore Islam was seen as an "alien" culture imposed by the Ottomans, one that dragged the region into backwardness (Todorova 1996: 48). In order to renew the cultural connection with Christian Europe and erase traces of Islam, these states undertook a policy of clearing Ottoman-related architecture and made extensive modifications to urban spaces in the 19th century, thus symbolizing their break with the past (Costantini 2013; Karidis 2014; Pantelić 2011). New models of urbanization and architecture inspired by Europeanization became important markers of these new collective identities and gen-eral social progress. The vanishing material culture associated with Islam was seen as a historical relic of the "Ottoman yoke," the unwanted past, one with no role in a process of nation-building (Kiel 2009: 157). In the course of the 20th century, a similar animosity was shown toward the region's sizeable Muslim communities who are often regarded as "traitors" of the forefathers' faith or as victims of the Ottoman oppression; in either case, they are seen as a reminder of a foreign-dominated past (Antov 2016: 31; Hajdarpašić 2008).

On the other hand, Islam played a crucial role in the formation of the Bosnian Muslim nation (Adanir 2002). Unlike other Balkan areas, Bosnia experienced an early conver-sion of the local population shortly after the Ottoman conquest in 1463 (Filipović 1991: 246; Zhelyazkova 2002). Islamization led to profound cultural changes and to a distinc-tive identity for the growing community (Adanir 2002: 284). After the Austro-Hungarian occupation of 1878, the Habsburgs gave political support to the idea of Bosnian nationhood, but this initiative was strongly opposed by the Serbian Orthodox and the Croatian Catholic communities (Banac 1984: 360). In spite of their nominal support, the Habsburg authorities conducted urban changes in Sarajevo, replacing Ottoman monuments with buildings constructed in the Vienna Ringstrasse style, all in the name of Westernization and cultural modernization (Donia 2002). Although Bosnian Muslims gained more political rights after World War II in Yugoslavia, it was not until 1971 that they were de jure recognized as a distinctive nation (Malcolm 1994: 193–212). In that period, an essential contribution to studies of Islam in Bosnia and Yugoslavia was made by the Oriental Institute in Sarajevo, founded in 1950 (Cviko 1986; Kolaj Ristanović 2014; Zlatar 2004). Unfortunately, Bosnian material culture suffered great damage during the civil war in Yugoslavia (1992–1995), which caused irrecoverable losses to its Islamic cultural heritage (Chapman 1994).

Two main points emerge from this short survey of official discourses. The first one is that the Islamic pasts play a predominant role in shaping the nationalistic discourses of the countries under the scope of this chapter. This has an impact in the configuration of Islamic heritage depending on whether the elements that compose it fall within the category of something to be celebrated or something to be erased from the memory of the community. The second point involves the diversity within national or academic communities and the capacity of minorities to express alternative views or dissent with respect to official narratives. The diversity of narratives about Islamic heritage makes a difference not only in providing a more nuanced view of heritage: it can be often the reason why material elements of the past are conserved, as the cases in Iberia and the Balkans show. The role of the memory of communities beyond official discourses therefore requires analysis.

People and Islamic Heritage: The Sources of Cultural Construction

Today, it is widely accepted that heritage is a discursive construction (Smith 2006) of "meanings, values and material consequences" (Harvey 2008:19). In other words, heritage is the selective use of the past for contemporary purposes (Ashworth and Graham 2005), and this selective use is always as much about forgetting as remembering the past (Graham 2002). This section investigates the ideas of Islamic pasts and Islamic heritages from below by reviewing their presence in the popular and everyday life of the people.

In Qatar, as in other Islamic countries, the memory of the Islamic past is present in everyday socio-cultural and religious practices. For example, reading or recitation of Quranic verses is part of the prayer practice of Muslims five times every day (Figure 6.5.2). The Quran is full of stories and narratives, memories of Islamic pasts that

FIGURE 6.5.2 Interior of Al-Qubib Mosque in Doha city center. Islamic heritage in Qatar is part of daily life for citizens and most residents, as it is in certain places in the Balkans.

Courtesy of Alkindi Aljawabra.

are usually presented as a source for learning lessons (Hodjat 1995). Similar to this is the Friday pray sermon (*khuṭba*). Although originally conceived as a space during which issues of everyday life could be discussed under the guidance of an imam, with time it acquired a less participative character and became a speech that is delivered in the form of stories from the Islamic pasts that serve to orientate on issues of the present. The *khuṭba* can be heavily influenced or even serve as a platform for messages of the state (see the online text for the *khutba* of Dubai: Awqaf.ae. 2017). Additionally, everyday "national" dress is now perceived as a traditional and Islamic dress that represents pride in and respect for the past (Cooke 2014). Another relevant socio-cultural practice is poetry, which is an oral tradition that has wide appeal among both the public and elites. This appeal is very clear in the great success of *Million's Poet*, a TV program in the style of *American Idol*, in which participants perform their own poetry; it is broadcast from the UAE and is watched by a hundred million viewers across the Arab World (Cooke 2014; Langham and Barker 2014). Poetry is known as *dīwān al-'Arab* (the archive of the Arabs), and it has an integral connection to socio-political life and Arab cultural consciousness (see Alshaer 2013, 2016). Less classical, but also very effective ways of transmitting memories of the Islamic past are series and films, and Islamic TV channels (El-Sayed 2009; Galal 2014). In general, memories of Islamic past are present everywhere, even in the simplest forms of everyday communication and the use of the Arabic language itself.

Since the development of official policies of heritage is particularly recent in Qatar, the weight of the public perception of the past is still heavy, and heritage politics have to deal with it as a key factor. This is both an enabling and a constraining element for original discourses about heritage: enabling because it provides a counterweight to the nationalistic interest of the state to create a monolithic discourse for the past and constraining because the rigid structure of Qatari society, overwhelmingly identified with Wahhabism, is particularly reticent to the reception of anything that might be perceived as an external influence. In this context, the heritage policy in Qatar functions as an essential component in enforcing the traditional legitimacy of the ruling family and the social cohesion of the society, on one hand, and to balance the rapid process of modernization and change, on the other (Kamrava 2013).

The situation is quite different in Iberia and the Balkans. Many traditions in Iberia are impregnated with Islamic elements, from gastronomy and agriculture to vocabulary. The official Latin languages of Iberia (Portuguese, Spanish, Catalan, and Galician) emerged in close contact with the Arabic. Spanish, for example, contains 4,000 words of Arabic (Cano Aguilar 1999: 53), making it the second most influential language in Spanish after Latin (Lapesa 1981: 133). Some parts of the Iberian landscape are also characteristically reminiscent of the Islamic past. Old fortified towns and fortresses bear powerful memories (e.g., Malpica Cuello 1996) and so do many rural landscapes, with their practices of irrigation and their rich agriculture (AA.VV. 1995).

In spite of all this, most people hold ambivalent attitudes toward the region's Islamic past. Although European Orientalism was only loosely based on historical and archaeological facts, it gave value to the memory of the Islamic period of Iberia in the 18th and 19th centuries (Irving 1832). A good example is the case of the Alhambra (Figure 6.5.3), which came to be considered a national monument in 1870 (Belmonte Medina 1999: 77). A combination of the Islamic elements of Spanish identity and the Romantic orientalist spirit were highlighted by B. Infante (1885–1936) in the defense of an Andalusian particularity. Infante's intellectual work influenced artists like the composer M. de Falla (1876–1946) and the poet F. García Lorca (1898–1936) (Holt Shannon 2015: 119–157), who

FIGURE 6.5.3 The skyline of the Alhambra of Granada (Spain) is one of the most recognizable images that reflect the combination of solid materiality and romantic stamp that is characteristic of the heritage of al-Andalus in Iberia.

Courtesy of dkatana/Pixabay.

belonged to an extremely influential generation of artists in Spanish culture working to underline a tradition of liberalism and anti-clericalism in politics.

The challenge for preserving Islamic heritage in Iberia is educational. In spite of its influence in popular culture, there is a traditional lack of knowledge about Islamic heritage because of an interposed cultural distance between Islam and the Latin roots of Iberian identities. There certainly remains an inertia from past educational systems which emphasized the confrontational view of both influences (e.g., Sánchez Albornoz 1956 for Spain). Since the emergence of Iberian democracies, however, increases and improvements in archaeological and historical research have made knowledge about the Islamic past much more accessible to the public (Carvajal López 2014). This translates into lively debates about the relevance of Islamic culture in which, unfortunately, scientifically established facts do not always find a good representation (García Sanjuán 2013), but which also accounts for the interest of the public in the relevance of Islam as part of their own identity.

Since the process of Islamization in the Balkans is historically related only to the expansion of the Ottoman political entity, the terms "Islamic" and "Ottoman" heritage often appear as synonyms. However, the term "Ottoman heritage" is generally preferred in the literature because it does not invoke religious affiliation, at least nominally. In this way, the notion of heritage is detached from the contested topic of religious conversion of Christians. It also appears as more applicable to the wider scope of tangible heritage that is not necessarily related to Islamic sacred monuments (Figure 6.5.4). Beyond the academic community, contemporary societies also construct and label their Islamic

FIGURE 6.5.4 Old Mostar Bridge (Bosnia-Herzegovina), iconic image of Ottoman heritage in the Balkans, and a UNESCO World Heritage site.

Courtesy of ottarikoc/Pixabay.

heritage in different ways. This duality of terminology usually unfolds in line with Balkan polymorphic cultural identities.

In a similar fashion to Muslim communities in the Middle East, the Balkan counterparts keep a symbolic connection with the Islamic past through everyday religious rituals. At the same time, the centuries-long internal developments of religious practices, expressed mostly in vernacular languages, account for some distinguishing characteristics of local Islam (Norris 1993). One of them is a strong historical attachment to Sufism (Aščerić-Todd 2015) that has been renewed in the past three decades in Bosnia, gaining support from the youngest generations of Muslims (Vukomanović 2008). Its supporters in Bosnia mostly gather in the Ottoman-period *tekke* (Vukomanović 2008: 139) thus keeping their heritage alive.

In other areas of the Balkans where Muslim communities have a less visible presence, Islamic heritage has an ambiguous meaning. Interestingly, in this context the notion of Turks/Ottomans is considered more negative than that of Islam itself. On the one hand, a survey conducted on a representative number of participants in Serbia showed that Turks (meaning the Ottomans) are seen as the archenemy of the nation while an absolute majority characterized the Ottoman period as the era of a "long-lasting Turkish yoke" (Stojanović 2010). Modern states usually support the negative image of Islamic/ Ottoman heritage through ethnocentric educational policies (Felezeu and Cupcea 2015; Koulouri 2002). The Ottoman tangible heritage remains physically invisible in urban and rural landscapes, which contributes to a perception of the historical irrelevance of this heritage for the development of modern communities. On the other hand, the intangible heritage associated with the Ottoman past is much more recognizable in the domain of popular culture (Todorova 2009: 180). There is a shared understanding that the cultural similarities between different Balkan nations, expressed in food, music, coffee, tobacco-smoking, language, and religious syncretism, are related to the Ottomans. (Todorova 1996: 60). One example is the *sevdalinka,* a type of traditional Muslim urban music from Ottoman Bosnia that is still popular in other countries of the former Yugoslavia (Petrović 1974; 1988). People from different backgrounds in the Balkans have become familiar with Islamic heritage through the literature as well, especially in works of Yugoslav writers like Ivo Andrić (1892–1975) and Meša Selimović (1910–1982).

The common element that emerges in this revision of popular sentiment about the Islamic pasts in the three peninsulas is that it carries a potentially challenging interpretation of the present in each of the three cases. This does not mean that the interpretations of the past are at all similar. Whereas in Iberia and the Balkans the Islamic past fits into nationalistic narratives with positive and negative overtones, in Qatar the past links directly with the present and the controversy that it provokes is different. The reproduction of Western heritage practices by official agents without consideration of the divergent views of social groups produces a lack of engagement with heritage and thus contributes to the appropriation of the field of heritage by the state. This comparison between the different treatments and effects of the Islamic heritage in the three regions under analysis can be seen in greater relief when focusing on the politics of the past thirty to fifty years.

CURRENT POLITICS OF ISLAMIC HERITAGE

A review of the development of heritage politics in the three areas of comparison during the past decades can give better insight into the current and potential situation of Islamic heritage.

Heritage management in Qatar is a recent development, having emerged with the establishment of the National Museum (1975) and the first Antiquities Law (1980). Current heritage politics in Qatar are in line with heritage politics developed through the Islamic World Educational, Scientific and Cultural Organization (ISESCO), founded in 1982 and funded mainly by the Gulf States, with similar mechanisms and functions to UNESCO for the protection of Islamic heritage. More recently, the traditional lines of heritage politics of Qatar were revisited by the Emir Hamad (r. 1995–2013). While his father Khalifa (r. 1972–1995) had embraced a selective view of the past with the establishment of the first National Museum in the Old Emiri Palace, Hamad turned the civic myth into a luxurious tangible urban scene through a vibrant heritage industry. This includes the creation of world-class iconic museums, such as the Museum of Islamic Art of Doha (MIA; Figure 6.5.5) and later the creation of Qatar Museums "to develop, sustain and promote the cultural sector" (QM 2017).

FIGURE 6.5.5 The Museum of Islamic Art of Doha is an iconic example of Islamic heritage used in the branding strategy developed by Qatar.

Courtesy of Edwardstaines/Dreamstime.

The current politics of heritage in Qatar have a problematic relationship with Islamic archaeology. While written sources on Qatari history are few for the period before the 19th century, there are very important archaeological sites of the Islamic era, including Zubarah, which is featured in the World Heritage List of UNESCO (UNESCO 2017), and the exceptional site of Murwab (Guerin and al-Na'imi 2009, 2010), among others. Yet, with the exception of Zubarah, these sites do not figure in mainstream debates on the country's cultural heritage. This is partly a consequence of the term "Islamic heritage" in itself: unlike in Iberia or the Balkans, the term "Islamic" does not make reference to any specific historical period, but to religion as a facet of daily life. However, the influence of foreign perspectives has made the term "Islamic heritage" acceptable beyond the purely religious sphere when applied to particular styles of art and architecture. These are prestigious fields which Qatar can put at the service of its strategies of branding (Peterson 2006) and citizenship construction (Babar 2014). Islamic heritage is therefore highlighted as a form of national identity, with narratives that are grand and simple at the same time. The MIA is a good example: it fosters the central role of Qatar as an important center in the Islamic world and therefore places Islamic art at the service of the nationalist ideal of the state.

Outside the scope of this "Islamic heritage" for branding strategies, local and particularistic narratives of heritage are abundant and quite successful. Qatar's heritage industry includes the preservation of popular manifestations of heritage (folklore) and the reinvention of traditions. Examples of this include the reconstruction of Sūq Waqif, a traditional Qatari *sūq*; the restorations of forts, wells, and old buildings; the creation of Katara Cultural Village (where traditional forms of architecture from different parts of the Islamic world are combined in a cultural complex); compilations of oral history; the promotion of knowledge on traditional modes of life (i.e., books on pearling and the historical novels of Abdulaziz Al Mahmoud); and transforming traditional ways of living such traditional dress, falconry, and camel races into national sports, cultural artifacts, and nationalist symbols (Cooke 2014; Kamrava 2013).

In Iberia, the current politics of heritage have their start with the beginning of the democratic regimes (Constitution of Portugal 1976; Constitution of Spain 1978) and with the primary heritage laws, issued in 1985 in both countries, which were modified in later years. In both countries, the Islamic past was explicitly recognized as worthy of documentation and protection, with several places placed under the qualification of World Heritage Sites (UNESCO 2017). The inclusion of Islamic heritage among the body of cultural heritage of the country made possible its normalization and inclusion in academic and cultural debates. This has produced an unprecedented attention to the Islamic past in the heritage sector, with abundant creation of national and local museums and interpretation centers (e.g., the Archaeological Site of Madīnat al-Zahrā') or the expansion of existing ones (e.g., collections in the National Museum of Spanish-Arab Art in the Alhambra, or the National Museums of Archaeology of Spain and Portugal). The main challenge that Islamic heritage faces today is common with the concerns related to other fields: the clash between the specialists and the public. In general, academic archaeologists have shown little interest in engagement with the public, and that task has fallen on the shoulders of freelance archaeologists or managers of cultural institutions. This has produced a gap between archaeology as a product of research and archaeology for public consumption (cf. Borrego et al. 2001; Carvajal López 2014: 330–331). Another problem regarding Iberian Islamic heritage is its need to connect to communities that do not live in the peninsula today and that can claim a direct connection with the expelled minorities of the 16th and 17th centuries (González Alcantud 2012).

The countries of the modern Balkans have different heritage policies that mostly reflect their national-projected historical narratives. Importantly, in the past decade, UNESCO recognized three Ottoman-period monuments and urban areas from Albania and Bosnia-Herzegovina as World Heritage Sites (UNESCO 2017). This sets an important precedent for the different states. In Serbia, for example, only a few Ottoman-period monuments and historic areas have been recognized as part of the national cultural heritage and are protected by the law (Republički zavod za zaštitu spomenika kulture-Beograd 2017). On the contrary, in Bosnia-Herzegovina, a number of Ottoman-period monuments have been identified (Kuş et al. 2010) and protected as cultural heritage of national importance (Mulaić Handan 2010).

In the Balkans, only standing monuments have so far been declared tangible cultural heritage of the Ottoman period. Furthermore, most of these monuments are of religious relevance for Muslims in the region but not to the rest of the population. As archaeological sites and objects are absent in most academic and museum frameworks, there is a lack of social awareness about their historical value. This is not due to scarcity of material culture, however. Archaeological excavations in Belgrade have revealed a vast array of material remains essential for understanding everyday life in an Ottoman town (Bikić 2007; Marjanović-Vujović 1973; Popović and Bikić 2004). The archaeological work conducted in Greece (Bintliff 2013) and in Bulgaria (Petersen 2017) shows a wide range of possibilities for the discovery and revaluation of the Ottoman-period material culture. Unfortunately, these positive but isolated examples of academic engagement have not yet produced a change in the general picture. With the exception of the University of Sarajevo, regional universities do not offer programs in Ottoman archaeology. The remains of the Ottoman period are still often identified as "post-Byzantine," a sign of the academic interest in highlighting a continuity in the local cultural development under Ottoman rule but one not influenced by it (Todorova 1996). Archaeology, therefore, has the great potential to bring to light the cultural heritage of the Ottoman period, especially in countries where standing monuments are few (Baram and Carroll 2002).

CONCLUSION: THE CHALLENGES AND POTENTIAL OF ISLAMIC HERITAGE

This short review illustrates a variety of approaches to the definition, consideration, and investigation of Islamic heritage. This variety is not surprising because the concept of heritage itself is heavily dependent on the socio-political, legal, and material contexts in which it is developed. Following the proposal of Sørensen and Carman (2012), the approach taken in this chapter has aimed less at a definition and more at a contextual analysis of Islamic heritage, taking into account its material Islamic pasts, the official discourses about them, and the sentiments of local communities toward them.

The Islamic eras are significant components of the history of the three regions under study, but the process of their inclusion in discourses and narratives about Islamic heritage is a much more complicated issue. On the one hand, this is a result of the variety of socio-cultural practices developed in the wide historical background of Islam. In Qatar, the demographic coexistence between Bedouins and settled communities, its relative peripheral situation with respect to the great cities of the Islamic core in the Middle East, and the distant influence of the cultures of the Indian Ocean account for particular developments. Iberia was farther from the Islamic heartlands than Qatar, but its common pre-Islamic cultural background and its closest participation in economic, social, and intellectual developments of the Islamic Mediterranean made it part of the mainstream culture. As for the Balkans, their late inclusion in the Dār al-Islam and their social structure, divided into religious communities in a subordinate position to an Ottoman/Islamic elite, generated very specific conditions. Therefore it is clear that the local manifestations of Islamic culture were deeply influenced by the pre- and non-Islamic cultures which they encountered in every region. This is a question which remains for history and archaeology to clarify.

Conversely, it must be remembered that heritage is not the accumulation of the remains of the past but the reenactment of that past on the bases of its political use, and therefore it is necessary to account for the historical process of the selection of elements to be remembered or forgotten. Part of this selection reflects the degree to which there is a connection to or break with the Islamic past. When the Islamic past is considered to have an end, as in Iberia and some areas of the Balkans, Islamic heritage becomes a set of material elements created during a well-delimited period of time. However, in Qatar and in some areas of the Balkans, there is a continuum between the Islamic past and the present, and therefore the general understanding of what is Islamic heritage is essentially related to everyday socio-cultural and religious practices. Alternatively, the heritage sector of Qatar, influenced by Western management practices, has come to accept and foster the idea of a global Islamic heritage as a part of its current strategies of branding and development of national identity. A closer look at it shows, however, that there is no connection between this "Islamic heritage," which is considered to be part of the touristic resources of the country, and the material past of Qatar.

The official discourses about Islamic heritage are the second point of interest in this work. The chapter shows that the relationship between the idea of nation and the role of the Islamic past in it are a fundamental part of the discourse on Islamic heritage and therefore for understanding the degree of local support for its research, diffusion, and preservation. While in the many narratives of the Balkans the Islamic past is considered a dark period of the national histories and there is a subsequent lack of willingness to invest in its research, in Arab-Islamic countries like Qatar, Islam is a pillar of national culture.

The authoritarian character of some governments in the regions under study is another factor to take into account when considering official discourses. In authoritarian regimes, the past is a resource of justification, and scholarship in these circumstances is conservative by default, not prone to provide revisionary narratives about the past. Past Iberian and Balkan authoritarian states (like Albania or Greece) are valid examples, but it is particularly interesting to focus on the national heritage policies in many Arab authoritarian states, where colonial discourses of heritage, which contributed to the justification of regimes, were reformulated and fostered to a large extent (Daher and Maffi 2013). This in general has created a disjunction between the perceptions of heritage of the state and of the people. The opposite situation can be documented in the case of Iberia. In the 18th century, politicians and intellectuals began to perceive their Islamic past as a potential source of innovation and prestige for national identity and invested in its research. In this case, nationalism had a positive influence, fostering interest in the Islamic past of Iberia. It was crucial that this interest and subsequent research results were transmitted to the public. As a result, Islamic heritage has become part of public debate and of even wider political identities.

The last point of analysis involved the perceptions of people about Islamic heritage. In Iberia and the Balkans, Islamic pasts are a fundamental part of their national character. In both cases the narratives about them can be located between, and usually close to, two extremes: one which models the Islamic past as a period of constraint on the freedom and supposedly true national character of the people of the territory, and another one that is in general positive and places emphasis on the prosperity, cultural creativity, and connectivity that the Islamic past facilitated. The similarities end there. In Iberia, and particularly in Spain, the embracing of the Islamic past by progressive and anti-clerical political movements, on the one side, and of Romantic-Orientalist intellectuals, on the other, has helped to raise awareness and appreciation for the region's Islamic heritage. In the Balkans, conversely, nationalist politics has made a similar acceptance of this heritage difficult. However, and particularly after the Yugoslavian Civil War, the positive narratives about the Islamic past are finding support from Muslim minorities and from certain intellectual sectors that see the Ottoman past as a common heritage and, therefore, a potential resource to facilitate communication among the many peoples of the region. The situation is somewhat different in Qatar because the Islamic past links directly with the present. The particular history of Qatar and other Gulf states, marked by a traditional political system and a conservative Islamic orientation, has served to avoid excessive external influence. However, in the past decades there has been an adoption and a reproduction of the Western heritage discourse and management practices that has resulted in a broken conception of heritage in many Arab-Islamic countries, where the politics of heritage are the responsibility of state officials with essentially nationalist aims that often conflicts with local interests and priorities.

In all the regions under analysis Islamic heritage can be mobilized as a tool for social inclusion or exclusion. The communities that identify most closely with Islamic heritage are not necessarily well represented in the legal systems that are in charge of it (e.g., some Muslim minorities of the Balkans and the Shiʿite community of Qatar, which comprises 10 percent of the citizens; PRC 2009: 41). There are no similar cases in Iberia, but many distinctive communities of Muslims currently living outside the peninsula can claim a direct connection with the minorities expelled from Spain in the 17th century. They intimately identify with the Islamic heritage of Iberia, in some cases keeping material and linguistic tokens of their links with their Iberian past. Islamic heritage here is therefore linked to a claim of belonging to the past of a space to whom the community is foreign. This is not totally dissimilar to the idea of a common heritage joining people across different countries, as is the case of Islamic heritage with all the communities of Arab-Islamic countries. To return to the case of the Balkans, Muslim minorities can claim a common heritage across the borders of the different nations of the Balkans, thus lending a sense of unity to the region that is lost in current nationalist politics. There is therefore a value for Islamic heritage beyond that of mere touristic resource, a value that is common to all the groups of people linked to Islamic history in any way, and one that can be used as a resource to connect different communities across the globe. For Muslims, this value is made possible because of the solid sense of the geographical topology of Islam, centered on Mecca and understood as an interconnected network of historical and currently relevant places. This topological sense is lost in communities where Islam has not remained as a main pillar of society, as in Iberia and much of the Balkans.

Islamic heritage can be mobilized as a tool for social inclusion and for cultivating connections with communities beyond current borders. The role of Islamic archaeology, widely understood as the research on material elements of the Islamic past, should not be underestimated here. In any of the three regions under analysis it is apparent that the investment of time and resources in research produces a much-needed positive and critical vision of Islamic heritage. A positive vision of Islamic heritage is key to place the Islamic past in its right context and inform the public about its own connections with the Islamic community, as the cases of Iberia and the Balkans show. A critical view is fundamental if we are to avoid manipulations and overinterpretations of the material past. While the nature of heritage as essentially political cannot be denied, the constraints of interpretation of available evidence on the past should be always presented as a way to offer an informed debate on the past. Given the vertiginous pace of growth of Qatar and other Gulf countries, it is imperative that archaeology occupies a more relevant niche in the heritage scene.

Islamic archaeology is defined as the archaeological study of particular communities. Islamic heritage, likewise, reflects the cultural heritage of peoples, of communities. Acknowledging this has important implications. On the one hand, it requires informed communities and therefore continued investment in research on Islamic heritage, and particularly of archaeology. On the other hand, it involves increasing the body of stakeholders beyond those stipulated by current laws. Most importantly, it appropriately emphasizes what is probably the most interesting characteristic of Islamic heritage: its potential to connect different communities across time and space while at the same time celebrating these distinctive traits that make each community unique.

Acknowledgments

The participation of JCL and RL in this chapter was made possible by NPRP-Grant 7-551-6-18 from the Qatar National Research Fund. The statements and interpretations presented here are solely those of the authors.

REFERENCES

AA.VV. 1995. *La agricultura de al-Andalus* (Granada: El Legado Andalusí).

Adanir, F. 2002. "The Formation of a 'Muslim' Nation in Bosnia-Hercegovina: A Historiographic Discussion," in F. Adanir and S. Faroqhi (eds.), *The Ottomans and the Balkans: A Discussion of Historiography* (Leiden, Boston: Brill), 267–304.

Almagro Gorbea, A. 2015. "Las Antigüedades Árabes en la Real Academia de San Fernando," in A. Almagro Gorbea (ed.), *El legado de al-Ándalus. Las antigüedades árabes en los dibujos de la Academia* (Granada: Patronato de la Alhambra y el Generalife), 13–29.

Al-Sayyad, N. 2001. *Consuming Tradition, Manufacturing Heritage: Global Norms and Urban Forms in the Age of Tourism* (London/New York: Routledge).

Alshaer, A. 2013. "Poetry in the Arab Spring: A Historical Perspective," in L. Sadiki (ed.), *Routledge Handbook of the Arab Spring* (London: Routledge), 392–407.

Alshaer, A. 2016. *Poetry and Politics in the Modern Arab World* (London: C. Hurst).

Antov, N. 2016. "Emergence and Historical Development of Muslim Communities in the Ottoman Balkans: Historical and Historiographical Remarks," in T. Dragostinova and Y. Hashamova (eds.), *Beyond Mosque, Church, and State: Alternative Narratives of the Nation in the Balkans* (Budapest: Central European University Press), 31–57.

Aščerić-Todd, I. 2015. *Dervishes and Islam in Bosnia: Sufi Dimensions to the Formation of Bosnian Muslim Society* (Leiden: Brill).

Ashworth, G. J., and Graham, B. J. 2005. *Senses of Place: Senses of Time* (Farnham: Ashgate).

Awqaf.ae 2017. www.awqaf.ae.

Babar, Z. R. 2014. "The Cost of Belonging: Citizenship Construction in the State of Qatar," *Middle East Journal*, 68, 3, 403–420.

Baldó Lacomba, M. 2011. "Represión franquista del profesorado universitario," *Cuadernos Antonio de Nebrija*, 14, 1, 31–51.

Banac, I. 1984. *The National Question in Yugoslavia* (Ithaca, NY: Cornell University Press).

Baram, U., and Carroll, L. 2002. "The Future of the Ottoman past," in U. Baram and L. Carroll (eds.), *A Historical Archaeology of the Ottoman Empire: Breaking New Ground* (New York: Kluwer Academic Publishers), 3–27.

Barbero, A., and Vigil Pascual, M. 1978. *La formación del feudalismo en la Península Ibérica* (Crítica/Historia 4, Barcelona: Editorial Crítica).

Belmonte Medina, P. M. 1999. "Historia jurídica del patrimonio de la corona durante el Sexenio Revolucionario (1868–1874)," *Derecho y Opinión*, 7, 68–79.

Bikić, V. 2007. "The Early Turkish Stratum on the Belgrade Fortress," *BYZAS*, 7, 515–522.

Bintliff, J. L. 2013. "Considerations for Creating an Ottoman Archaeology in Greece," *Hesperia Supplements*, 40, 221–236.

Borrego, J. D., Fuentes, R. M., and del Moral, A. 2001. "La difusión del patrimonio islámico. consideraciones desde la actualidad," *Anales de Arqueología Cordobesa*, 12, 397–420.

Cano Aguilar, R. 1999. *El español a través de los tiempos* (Madrid: Arco/Libros).

Caro Baroja, J. 1976. *Los moriscos del Reino de Granada. Ensayo de historia social* (Madrid: Itsmo).

Carter, R. 2012. *Sea of Pearls: Seven Thousand Years of the Industry That Shaped the Gulf* (London: Arabian Publishing.)

Carvajal López, J. C. 2014. "The Archaeology of al-Andalus. Past, Present and Future," *Medieval Archaeology*, 58, 1, 318–339.

Castro, A. 1954. *La realidad histórica de España* (Mexico: Porrúa).

Chalmeta Gendrón, P. 2003. *Invasión e islamización: la sumisión de Hispania y la formación de al-Andalus*. Colección Al-Andalus/Universidad de Jaén (Jaén: Universidad de Jaén).

Chapman, J. 1994. "Destruction of a Common Heritage: The Archaeology of War in Croatia, Bosnia and Hercegovina," *Antiquity*, 68, 258, 120–126.

Choueiri, Y. M. 2003. *Modern Arab Historiography: Historical Discourse and the Nation-State* (London/New York: Routledge).

Constitution of Portugal 1976. https://www.constituteproject.org/constitution/Portugal_2005.pdf.

Constitution of Qatar 2004. http://portal.www.gov.qa/wps/wcm/connect/5a5512804665e3afa5 4fb5fd2b4ab27a/Constitution+of+Qatar+EN.pdf?MOD=AJPERES.

Constitution of Spain 1978. https://www.boe.es/legislacion/documentos/ConstitucionINGLES.pdf.

Cooke, M. 2014. *Tribal Modern: Branding New Nations in the Arab Gulf* (Berkeley: University of California Press).

Costantini, E. 2013. "Dismantling the Ottoman Heritage? The Evolution of Bucharest in the Nineteenth Century," in E. Ginio and K. Kaser (eds.), *Ottoman Legacies in the Contemporary Mediterranean* (Jerusalem: The European Forum at the Hebrew University), 231–254.

Crystal, J. 1995. *Oil and Politics in the Gulf: Rulers and Merchants in Kuwait and Qatar* (Cambridge: Cambridge University Press).

Cviko, F. 1986. "Survey of Development of Yugoslav Ottoman Studies," *Prilozi Za Orijentalnu Filologiju*, 36, 7–36.

Daher, R., and Maffi, I. 2013. "Introduction," in R. Daher and I. Maffi (eds.), *The Politics and Practices of Cultural Heritage in the Middle East: Positioning the Material Past in Contemporary Societies* (London/New York: Library of Modern Middle East Studies. I. B. Tauris Palgrave Macmillan), 1–54.

DeLong-Bas, N. 2004. *Wahhabi Islam: From Revival and Reform to Global Jihad* (Oxford: Oxford University Press).

Donia, R. J. 2002. "Fin-de-Siècle Sarajevo: The Habsburg Transformation of an Ottoman Town," *Austrian History Yearbook*, 33, 43–75.

El-Sayed, M. 2009. "Religious Islamic Satellite Channels: A Screen That Leads You to Heaven," *Reuters Institute Fellowship Paper* (Oxford: Reuters Institute for the Study of Journalism).

Faroqhi, S. 2009. *The Ottoman Empire: A Short History* (Princeton: Markus Wiener Publishers).

Felezeu, C., and Cupcea, A. 2015. *The Image of the Ottoman in the History Textbooks From Romania and Bosnia and Herzegovina in the post-Communist Period* (Istanbul: the Isis Press).

Fierro, M. 2011. "The Almohads (524–668/1130–1269) and the Ḥafṣids (627–932/1129–1526)," in M. Fierro (ed.), *The New Cambridge History of Islam. Volume 2. The Western Islamic World. Eleventh to Eighteenth Centuries* (Cambridge: Cambridge University Press), 66–105.

Filipović, N. 1991. "Islamizacija Bosne u prva dva desetljeća osmanske vlasti," *Prilozi za orijentalnu filologiju*, 41, 53–65.

Fuchs, B. 2009. *Exotic Nation. Maurophilia and the Construction of Early Modern Spain* (Philadelphia: University of Pennsylvania Press).

Galal, E. 2014. *Arab TV-Audiences: Negotiating Religion and Identity* (Frankfurt am Main, New York: PL Academic Research).

García Sanjuán, A. 2013. *La conquista islámica de la Península Ibérica y la tergiversación del pasado: del catastrofismo al negacionismo*. Estudios (Madrid: Marcial Pons Historia).

González Alcantud, J. A. 2012. "Los moriscos y su antropología. Reflexiones al hilo del cuarto centenario de la expulsión de los moriscos de España," *Gazeta de Antropología* 28, 3, article 6.

Grabar, O. 1971. "Islamic Archaeology: An Introduction," *Archaeology*, 24, 3, 196–199.

Grabar, O. 1976. "Islamic Art and Archaeology," in L. Binder (ed.), *The Study of the Middle East* (New York: John Wiley), 229–264.

Graham, B. 2002. "Heritage as Knowledge: Capital or Culture?," *Urban Studies*, 39, 5–6, 1003–1017.

Guerin, A., and al-Na'imi, F. 2009. "Territory and Settlement Patterns During the Abbasid Period (Ninth Century AD): The Village of Murwab (Qatar)," *Proceedings of the Seminar for Arabian Studies*, 39, 181–96.

Guerin, A., and al-Na'imi, F. 2010. "Preliminary Pottery Study: Murwab Horizon in Progress, Ninth Century AD, Qatar," *Proceedings of the Seminar for Arabian Studies*, 40, 17–34.

Hajdarpašić, E. 2008. "Out of the Ruins of the Ottoman Empire: Reflections on the Ottoman Legacy in South-Eastern Europe," *Middle Eastern Studies*, 44, 5, 715–734.

Harvey, D. C. 2008. "The History of Heritage," in B. Graham and P. Howard (eds.), *The Ashgate Research Companion to Heritage and Identity* (Farnham, UK: Ashgate), 19–36.

Hodjat, M. 1995. "Cultural Heritage in Iran: Policies for an Islamic Country" (PhD diss., University of York).

Holt Shannon, J. 2015. *Performing Al-Andalus: Music and Nostalgia Across the Mediterranean* (Bloomingtong: Indiana University Press).

Inalcik, H. 1973. *The Ottoman Empire: The Classical Age 1300–1600* (London: Phoenix).

Insoll, T. 1999. *The Archaeology of Islam* (London: Blackwell).

Irving, W. 1832. *The Alhambra: A Series of Tales and Sketches of the Moors and Spaniards* (Philadelphia: Carey and Lea).

Kamrava, M. 2013. *Qatar, Small State, Big Politics* (Ithaca, NY: Cornell University Press).

Karidis, D. N. 2014. *Athens from 1456 to 1920. The Town Under Ottoman Rule and the 19th-Century Capital City* (Oxford: Archaeopress).

Kennet, D. 2004. *Sasanian and Islamic Pottery from Ra's al-Khaimah: Classification, Chronology and Analysis of Trade in the Western Indian Ocean* (Oxford: Archaeopress).

Kiel, M. 2009. "The Incorporation of the Balkans into the Ottoman Empire, 1353–1453," in K. Fleet (ed.), *The Cambridge History of Turkey Volume 1 Byzantium to Turkey 1071–1453* (Cambridge: Cambridge University Press), 138–192.

Kolaj Ristanović, I. 2014. "Pregled razvoja orijentalnih studija na tlu bivše Jugoslavije 1857–1950," *Arhiv*, 1, 2, 153–168.

Koulouri, C. 2002. *Clio in the Balkans: The Politics of History Education* (Thessaloniki: Center for Democracy and Reconciliation in Southeast Europe).

Krstić, T. 2011. *Contested Conversions to Islam: Narratives of Religious Change in the Early Modern Ottoman Empire* (Stanford, CA: Stanford University Press).

Kuş, A., Şimşek, F., and Dıvarcı, İ. 2010. *Rumeli'de Osmanlı Mirası: Bosna Hersek, Kosova/ Ottoman Heritage in Rumelia: Bosnia Herzegovina, Kosovo* (Istanbul: Nildem Global Sigorta ve Reasürans Brokerliği).

Langham, E., and Barker, D. 2014. "Spectacle and Participation: A New Heritage Model from the UAE," in K. Exell and T. Rico (eds.), *Cultural Heritage in the Arabian Peninsula: Debates, Discourses and Practices* (Farnham, UK: Ashgate), 85–98.

Lapesa, R. 1981. *Historia de la lengua española* (Madrid: Gredos).

Malcolm, N. 1994. *Bosnia: A Short History* (New York: New York University Press).

Malpica Cuello, A. 1996. *Poblamiento y castillos en Granada* (Granada: Fundación Legado Andalusí).

Manzano Moreno, E. 2010. "The Iberian Peninsula and North Africa," in C. Robinson (ed.), *The New Cambridge History of Islam. Volume 1. The Formation of the Islamic World Sixth to Eleventh Centuries* (Cambridge: Cambridge University Press), 581–621.

Marjanović-Vujović, G. 1973. "Kuća iz druge polovine XVII veka otkopana u utvrđenom podgrađu Beogradskog grada - Donjem Gradu,"*Godišnjak grada Beograda,* 20, 201–228.

Mediano, F. 2011. "The Post-Almohad Dynasties in al-Andalus and the Maghrib (Seventh-Ninth/Thirteenth-Fifteenth Centuries)," in M. Fierro (ed.), *The New Cambridge History of Islam. Volume 2. The Western Islamic World. Eleventh to eighteenth centuries* (Cambridge: Cambridge University Press), 106–143.

Mendes Drumond Braga, I. M. R. 2010. "Manuscritos árabes e Arabistas em Portugal," in M. Ammadi (ed.), *Manuscritos místicos: formas y contenidos* (Casablanca: University Hassan II Aïn Chock), 49–62.

Milwright, M. 2010. *An Introduction to Islamic Archaeology* New Edinburgh Islamic surveys (Edinburgh: Edinburgh University Press).

Minkov, A. 2004. *Conversion to Islam in the Balkans: Kisve Bahasi Petitions and Ottoman Social Life 1670–1730* (Leiden/Boston: Brill).

Monroe, J. T. 1970. *Islam and the Arabs in Spanish Scholarship* (Leiden/Boston: Brill).

Mulaić Handan, M. 2010. "Izvještaj o stanju arhitektonskog i arheološkog naslijeđa, radni dokument," http://old.kons.gov.ba/main.php?mod=vijesti&extra=aktuelnost&action=view &id_vijesti=667&lang=1.

Norris, H. T. 1993. *Islam in the Balkans: Religion and Society Between Europe and the Arab World* (Columbia: University of South Carolina Press).

Pantelić, B. 2011. "Nationalism and Architecture: The Creation of a National Style in Serbian Architecture and Its Political Implications," *Journal of the Society of Architectural Historians,* 56, 1, 16–41.

Partrick, N. 2009. *Nationalism in the Gulf States.* Kuwait Programme on Development, Governance and Globalisation in the Gulf States Vol. 5 (London: London School of Economics, The Center for the Study of Global Governance), http://eprints.lse.ac. uk/55257/1/Patrick_2009.pdf

Petersen, A. 2017. "Under the Yoke: The Archaeology of the Ottoman Period in Bulgaria," *Journal of Islamic Archaeology,* 4, 1, 23–48.

Peterson, J. E. 2006. "Qatar and the World. Branding for a Micro-state," *Middle East Journal* 60, 4, 732–748.

Petrović, A. 1988. "Paradoxes of Muslim Music in Bosnia and Herzegovina,"*Asian Music,* 20, 1, 128–147.

Petrović, R. 1974. "Folk Music of Eastern Yugoslavia: A Process of Acculturation: Some Relevant Elements," *International Review of the Aesthetics and Sociology of Music,* 5, 1, 217–224.

Popović, M., and Bikić, V. 2004. *Kompleks srednjovekovne mitropolije u Beogradu* (Beograd: Arheoloski Institut).

PRC 2009. "Mapping the Global Muslim Population: A Report on the Size and Distribution of the World's Muslim Population," Pew Research Center online report http://allafrica.com/ download/resource/main/main/idatcs/00011909:cbf45d797f6515d212cec2ec5ef6fb5f.pdf.

Priestman, S. 2013. *A Quantitative Archaeological Analysis of Ceramic Exchange in the Persian Gulf and Western Indian Ocean, AD c.400–1275* (PhD diss., University of Southhampton).

QM 2017. http://www.qm.org.qa/en/area/cultural-heritage.

Republički zavod za zaštitu spomenika kulture-Beograd 2017. http://www.heritage.gov.rs/ cirilica/nepokretna_kulturna_dobra.php.

Rico, T., and Lababidi, R. 2017. "Extremism in Contemporary Cultural Heritage Debates About the Muslim World," *Future Anterior,* 14, 1, 94–105.

Rogers, J. M. 1974. *From Antiquarianism to Islamic Archaeology* (Cairo: Istituto italiano di cultura per la R. A. E).

Rundell, E. S. 2014. "Shedding New Light on the Life of Muhammad ibn Abd Al-Wahhab," in N. Mouline (ed.), *The Clerics of Islam: Religious Authority and Political Power in Saudi Arabia* (New Haven, CT: Yale University Press), 46–69.

Sánchez Albornoz, C. 1956. *España, un enigma histórico* (Buenos Aires: Editorial Sudamericana).

Serjeant, R. B. 1978. "Historical Sketch of the Gulf in the Islamic Era from the Seventh to the Eighteenth Century AD," in B. de Cardi (ed.), *Qatar Archaeological Report. Excavations 1973* (Oxford: Oxford University Press), 147–163.

Smith, L. 2006. *Uses of Heritage* (London: New York: Routledge).

Sørensen, S. M. L., and Carman, J. 2012. "Heritage Studies: An Outline," in S. M. L. Sørensen and J. Carman (eds.), *Heritage Studies: Methods and Approaches* (London: Routledge), 11–28.

Stojanović, D. 2010. "U ogledalu 'drugih'," in V. Dimitrijević (ed.), *Novosti iz prošlosti. Znanje, neznanje, upotreba i zloupotreba istorije* (Beograd: Beogradski centar za ljudska prava), 13–32.

Tibi, B. 1997. *Arab Nationalism: Between Islam and the Nation-State* (London: Macmillan).

Todorova, M. 1996. "The Ottoman Legacy in the Balkans," in C. Brown (ed.), *Imperial Legacy: The Ottoman Imprint on the Balkans and the Middle East* (New York: Columbia University Press), 45–78.

Todorova, M. 2009. *Imagining the Balkans* (Oxford: Oxford University Press).

UNESCO 2017. http://whc.unesco.org/en/list/.

Valbjørn, M. 2009. "Arab Nationalism(s) in Transformation: From Arab Interstate Societies to an Arab-Islamic World Society," in B. Buzan and A. Gonzalez-Pelaez (eds.), *International Society and the Middle East: English School Theory at the Regional Level* (London: Palgrave Macmillan UK), 140–169.

Vasić, M. 1991. "Islamizacija u jugoslovenskim zemljama," *Prilozi za orijentalnu filologiju,* 41, 425–441.

Vernoit, S. 1997. "The Rise of Islamic Archaeology," *Muqarnas,* 14, 1–10.

Viguera-Molins, M. J. 2011. "Al-Andalus and the Maghrib (from the Fifth/Eleventh Century to the Fall of the Almoravids," in M. Fierro (ed.), *The New Cambridge History of Islam. Volume 2. The Western Islamic World. Eleventh to Eighteenth Centuries* (Cambridge: Cambridge University Press), 19–47.

Vukomanović, M. 2008. *Homo viator: religija i novo doba* (Beograd: Čigoja štampa).

Walker, B. J. 2010. "The Globalizing Effect of Hajj in the Medieval and Modern Eras," in Ø. S. LaBianca and S. Arnold Scham (eds.), *Connectivity in Antiquity. Globalization as a Long-Term Historical Process* (London: Routledge), 62–74.

Watenpaugh, H. Z. 2004. "Museums and the Construction of National History in Syria and Lebanon," *The British and French Mandates in Comparative Perspective,* 1, 315–320.

Zhelyazkova, A. 2002. "Islamization in the Balkans as an Historiographical Problem: The Southeast-European Perspective," in F. Adanir and S. Faroqhi (eds.), *The Ottomans and the Balkans. A Discussion of Historiography* (Leiden/Boston: Brill), 223–267.

Zlatar, B. 2004. "The Oriental Institute in Sarajevo, 1950–2001," in M. Koller and K. Karpat (eds.), *Ottoman Bosnia: A History in Peril* (Madison: Center of Turkish Studies, University of Wisconsin), 39–43.

Index